T5-CRS-516
In the center of a sunflower
you can find 21 spirals in one direction
and 34 in the other direction.

Fibonacci sequence: 0, 1, 1, 2, 3, 5, 8, 13, 21, 34, 55, 89, 144, etc.
Each number is found by adding the two preceding numbers.
34
21

Visit *The Learning Site!*
www.harcourtschool.com

Printed in the United States of America

ISBN 13: 978-0-15-354177-3
ISBN 10: 0-15-354177-6

2 3 4 5 6 7 8 9 10 032 16 15 14 13 12 11 10 09 08

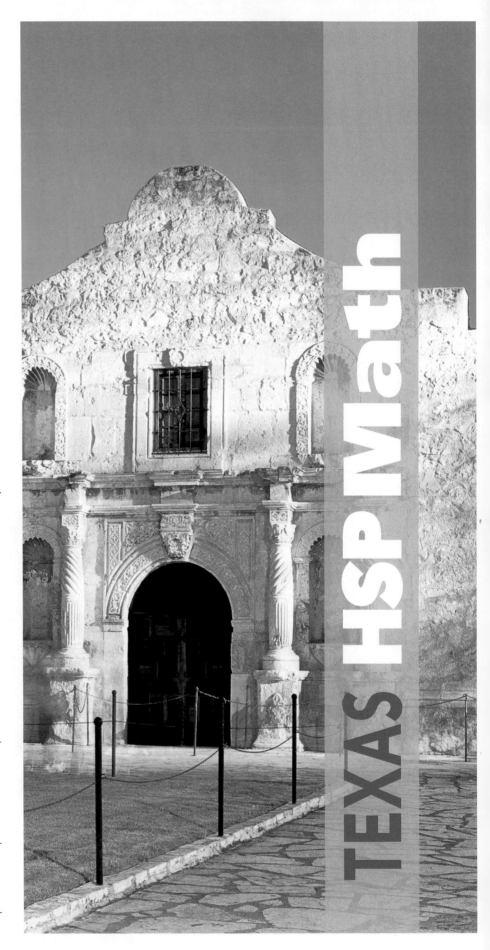

TEXAS HSP Math

Mathematics Advisor

Tom Roby
Associate Professor of Mathematics
Director, Quantitative
Learning Center
University of Connecticut
Storrs, Connecticut

Senior Authors

Evan M. Maletsky
Professor Emeritus
Montclair State University
Upper Montclair, New Jersey

Joyce McLeod
Visiting Professor, Retired
Rollins College
Winter Park, Florida

Authors

Angela G. Andrews
Assistant Professor,
Math Education
National-Louis University
Lisle, Illinois

Minerva Cordero-Epperson
Associate Professor of Mathematics
and Associate Dean of the
Honors College
The University of Texas
at Arlington
Arlington, Texas

James Epperson
Associate Professor
Department of Mathematics
The University of Texas
at Arlington
Arlington, Texas

Barbara Montalto
Mathematics Consultant
Assistant Director of
Mathematics, Retired
Texas Education Agency
Austin, Texas

Karen S. Norwood
Associate Professor of
Mathematics Education
North Carolina State University
Raleigh, North Carolina

Janet K. Scheer
Executive Director
Create-A-Vision
Foster City, California

Jennie M. Bennett
Mathematics Teacher
Houston Independent
School District
Houston, Texas

Juli K. Dixon
Associate Professor of
Mathematics Education
University of Central Florida
Orlando, Florida

Lynda Luckie
Director, K–12 Mathematics
Gwinnett County Public Schools
Suwanee, Georgia

David D. Molina
Program Director, Retired
The Charles A. Dana Center
The University of Texas at Austin

Vicki Newman
Classroom Teacher
McGaugh Elementary School
Los Alamitos Unified
School District
Seal Beach, California

Tom Roby
Associate Professor of
Mathematics
Director, Quantitative
Learning Center
University of Connecticut
Storrs, Connecticut

David G. Wright
Professor
Department of Mathematics
Brigham Young University
Provo, Utah

Program Consultants and Specialists

Russell Gersten
Director, Instructional
Research Group
Long Beach, California
Professor Emeritus of
Special Education
University of Oregon
Eugene, Oregon

Valerie Johse
Elementary Math Specialist
Office of Curriculum
& Instruction
Pearland I.S.D.
Pearland, Texas

Robin C. Scarcella
Professor and Director
Program of Academic English
and ESL
University of California, Irvine
Irvine, California

Michael DiSpezio
Writer and On-Air Host,
JASON Project
North Falmouth, Massachusetts

Tyrone Howard
Assistant Professor,
UCLA Graduate School
of Education
Information Studies
University of California
at Los Angeles
Los Angeles, California

Concepcion Molina
Southwest Educational
Development Lab
Austin, Texas

Understand Whole Numbers and Operations

Math on Location 1

1 Understand Place Value 2

Show What You Know. 3
1 Place Value Through Hundred Thousands 4
2 Hands On: Model Millions 8
3 Place Value Through Millions 10
4 Compare Whole Numbers 12
5 Order Whole Numbers. 16
6 Problem Solving Workshop
Strategy: Use Logical Reasoning 20

Extra Practice 24
Practice Game: Climb the Math Mountain 25
Chapter 1 Review/Test 26
Enrich: Numbers in Other Cultures 27
Getting Ready for the TAKS 28

2 Add and Subtract Whole Numbers 30

Show What You Know. 31
1 Algebra Relate Addition and Subtraction. 32
2 Round Whole Numbers to the Nearest
10, 100, and 1,000 34
3 Mental Math: Addition and Subtraction Patterns . . . 38
4 Mental Math: Estimate Sums and Differences 40
5 Mental Math Strategies. 44
6 Problem Solving Workshop
Skill: Estimate or Exact Answer 48
7 Add and Subtract Through 4-Digit Numbers 50
8 Subtract Across Zeros. 54
9 Choose a Method. 56

Extra Practice 60
Chapter 2 Review/Test 62
Enrich: Use Logical Reasoning 63
Getting Ready for the TAKS 64

3 Algebra: Use Addition and Subtraction 66

Show What You Know. 67
1 Addition Properties 68
2 Write and Evaluate Expressions. 70
3 Addition and Subtraction Equations. 74
4 Problem Solving Workshop
Strategy: Work Backward 78
5 Ordered Pairs in a Table 82

Extra Practice 84
Technology Connection:
Spreadsheet: Graph Ordered Pairs 85
Chapter 3 Review/Test 86
Enrich: Use Relational Thinking. 87

Unit Review/Test 88

DVD from The Futures Channel with Texas Chapter Projects and VOCABULARY POWER 1

READ Math WORKSHOP 77
WRITE Math WORKSHOP 47

GO ONLINE Technology

Harcourt Mega Math: Chapter 1, pp. 6, 18; Chapter 2, p. 36; Chapter 3, p. 76, Extra Practice: pp. 24, 60, 84
The Harcourt Learning Site: www.harcourtschool.com
Multimedia Math Glossary: www.harcourtschool.com/hspmath

The World Almanac for Kids

Languages We Speak at Home in Texas 90

Multiplication and Division Facts

Math on Location 93

4 Multiplication Facts 94

Show What You Know 95
1 Algebra Relate Addition and Multiplication 96
2 Multiply Facts Through 5 98
3 Multiply Facts Through 10 100
4 Hands On: Multiplication Table Through 12 104
5 Problem Solving Workshop
Strategy: Guess and Check 106

Extra Practice 110
Practice Game: Down and Up 111
Chapter 4 Review/Test 112
Enrich: Number Relationships 113
Getting Ready for the TAKS 114

5 Division Facts 116

Show What You Know 117
1 Algebra Relate Multiplication and Division 118
2 Divide Facts Through 5 120
3 Divide Facts Through 10 122
4 Divide Facts Through 12 126
5 Problem Solving Workshop
Skill: Choose the Operation 128
6 Factors and Multiples 130

Extra Practice 134
Practice Game: Hopscotch Facts 135
Chapter 5 Review/Test 136
Enrich: Common Factors 137
Getting Ready for the TAKS 138

6 Algebra: Patterns, Expressions, and Equations 140

Show What You Know 141
1 Patterns on the Multiplication Table 142
2 Number Patterns 144
3 Problem Solving Workshop
Strategy: Look for a Pattern 148
4 Multiplication Properties 152
5 Write and Evaluate Expressions 156
6 Find Missing Factors 160
7 Multiplication and Division Equations 162
8 Problem Solving Workshop
Strategy: Write an Equation 166
9 Ordered Pairs in a Table 170

Extra Practice 172
Technology Connections:
Calculator: Evaluate Expressions 173
Chapter 6 Review/Test 174
Enrich: Predict Patterns 175

Unit Review/Test 176

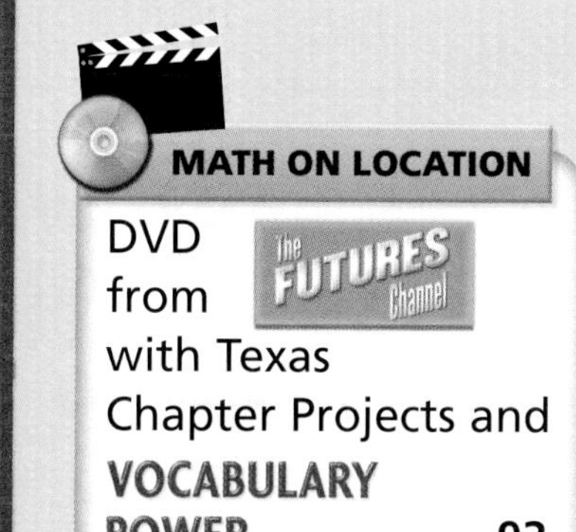

DVD from The Futures Channel with Texas Chapter Projects and VOCABULARY POWER 93

. 103

WRITE Math WORKSHOP 155

GO ONLINE Technology

Harcourt Mega Math: Chapter 4, p. 105; Chapter 5, p. 124; Chapter 6, p. 164, Extra Practice: pp. 110, 134, 172
The Harcourt Learning Site: www.harcourtschool.com
Multimedia Math Glossary: www.harcourtschool.com/hspmath

The World Almanac for Kids

Hummingbirds 178

Multiply by 1- and 2-Digit Numbers

Math on Location 181

7 Understand Multiplication 182

Show What You Know. 183
1 Mental Math: Multiplication Patterns. 184
2 Mental Math: Estimate Products 186
3 Hands On: Model 2-Digit by 1-Digit Multiplication 188
4 Record 2-Digit by 1-Digit Multiplication 190
5 Problem Solving Workshop Strategy: Draw a Diagram 194

Extra Practice 198
Technology Connections: iTools: Base-Ten Blocks. 199
Chapter 7 Review/Test 200
Enrich: Lattice Multiplication. 201
Getting Ready for the TAKS 202

8 Multiply by 1-Digit Numbers 204

Show What You Know. 205
1 Multiply 2-Digit Numbers 206
2 Multiply 3-Digit Numbers 208
3 Multiply with Zeros 210
4 Choose a Method. 212
5 Problem Solving Workshop Skill: Evaluate Reasonableness. 214

Extra Practice 216
Practice Game: Multiplication Marathon 217
Chapter 8 Review/Test 218
Enrich: Distributive Property 219
Getting Ready for the TAKS 220

9 Multiply by 2-Digit Numbers 222

Show What You Know 223
1 Mental Math: Multiplication Patterns 224
2 Multiply by Tens 226
3 Mental Math: Estimate Products 228
4 Problem Solving Workshop
Strategy: Solve a Simpler Problem 230
5 Model 2-Digit by 2-Digit Multiplication 234
6 Record 2-Digit by 2-Digit Multiplication 236
7 Practice Multiplication 240
8 Choose a Method 242
9 Problem Solving Workshop
Skill: Multistep Problems 244

Extra Practice 246
Chapter 9 Review/Test 248
Enrich: Use Multiplication Properties 249

Unit Review/Test 250

DVD from The Futures Channel with Texas Chapter Projects and VOCABULARY POWER 181

READ Math WORKSHOP 193

WRITE Math WORKSHOP 239

GO ONLINE Technology

Harcourt Mega Math: Chapter 7, p. 189; Chapter 8, p. 213; Chapter 9, p. 237, Extra Practice: pp. 198, 216, 246
The Harcourt Learning Site: www.harcourtschool.com
Multimedia Math Glossary: www.harcourtschool.com/hspmath

The World Almanac for Kids

Space Travel. . . 252

Geometry

Math on Location 255

10 One- and Two-Dimensional Geometric Figures 256

Show What You Know. 257
1 Points, Lines, and Rays. 258
2 Classify Angles 260
3 Line Relationships 262
4 Polygons. 264
5 Classify Triangles 268
6 Classify Quadrilaterals 270
7 Circles. 274
8 Problem Solving Workshop
Strategy: Use Logical Reasoning 276

Extra Practice 278
Chapter 10 Review/Test 280
Enrich: Use Visual Thinking 281
Getting Ready for the TAKS 282

11 Transformations, Symmetry, and Congruence 284

Show What You Know. 285
1 Congruent Figures 286
2 Hands On: Translations. 288
3 Rotations 290
4 Reflections 292
5 Symmetry 294
6 Problem Solving Workshop
Strategy: Act It Out 298
7 Hands On: Tessellations 302
8 Geometric Patterns 304

Extra Practice 306
Technology Connections:
iTools: Geometry 307
Chapter 11 Review/Test 308
Enrich: Tangrams 309
Getting Ready for the TAKS 310

12 **Three-Dimensional Geometric Figures** 312

Show What You Know. 313
1 Faces, Edges, and Vertices 314
2 Draw Solid Figures 318
3 Patterns for Solid Figures 320
4 Problem Solving Workshop
Strategy: Make a Model 322

Extra Practice 326
Practice Game: Build the View 327
Chapter 12 Review/Test 328
Enrich: Patterns in Prisms and Pyramids 329

Unit Review/Test 330

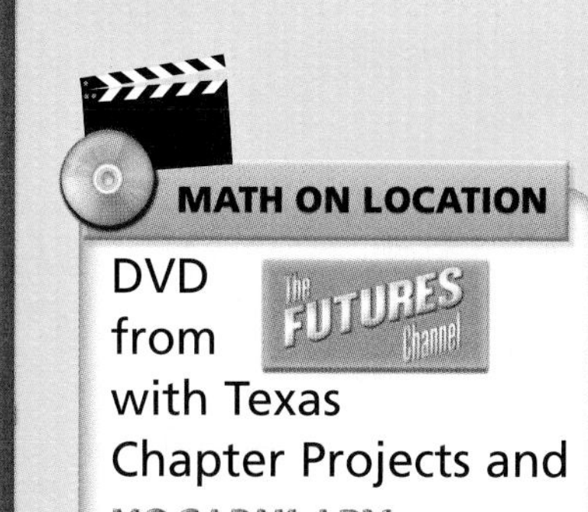

DVD from The Futures Channel with Texas Chapter Projects and VOCABULARY POWER 255

READ Math WORKSHOP 273

WRITE Math WORKSHOP 317

GO ONLINE Technology

Harcourt Mega Math:
Chapter 10, p. 266; Chapter 11, p. 296; Chapter 12, p. 315,
Extra Practice: pp. 278, 306, 326
The Harcourt Learning Site:
www.harcourtschool.com
Multimedia Math Glossary:
www.harcourtschool.com/hspmath

The World Almanac for Kids

Looking at Toys 332

Divide by 1-Digit Divisors

Math on Location 335

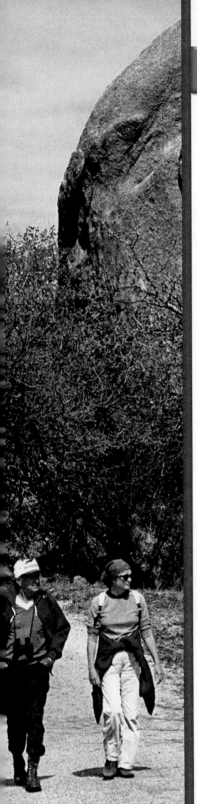

13 Understand Division 336

Show What You Know. 337
1 Hands On: Divide with Remainders 338
2 Hands On: Model 2-Digit by 1-Digit Division. . . . 340
3 Record 2-Digit by 1-Digit Division 342
4 Problem Solving Workshop
Strategy: Compare Strategies 346
5 Mental Math: Division Patterns. 348
6 Mental Math: Estimate Quotients. 350
7 Place the First Digit 352

Extra Practice 354
Practice Game: Divide All Five 355
Chapter 13 Review/Test 356
Enrich: Short Division. 357
Getting Ready for the TAKS 358

14 Practice Division 360

Show What You Know 361

1 Problem Solving Workshop
Skill: Interpret the Remainder 362

2 Divide 3-Digit Numbers 364

3 Zeros in Division 368

4 Choose a Method 372

5 Find the Average 374

Extra Practice 376

Technology Connection:
Calculator: Remainders 377

Chapter 14 Review/Test 378

Enrich: Mental Math: Multiplication and Division . . 379

Unit Review/Test 380

MATH ON LOCATION

DVD from The Futures Channel with Texas Chapter Projects and **VOCABULARY POWER** 335

READ Math WORKSHOP 345

WRITE Math WORKSHOP 367

GO ONLINE Technology

Harcourt Mega Math: Chapter 13, p. 339; Chapter 14, p. 370, Extra Practice: pp. 354, 376
The Harcourt Learning Site: www.harcourtschool.com
Multimedia Math Glossary: www.harcourtschool.com/hspmath

The World Almanac for Kids

Amazing Collectibles . . . 382

Fractions and Decimals

Math on Location 385

15 Understand Fractions and Mixed Numbers 386

Show What You Know. 387
1 Read and Write Fractions 388
2 Model Equivalent Fractions. 392
3 Problem Solving Workshop
Strategy: Compare Strategies 396
4 Hands On: Compare Fractions 398
5 Order Fractions 400
6 Read and Write Mixed Numbers 402
7 Compare and Order Mixed Numbers 406

Extra Practice 410
Technology Connection:
iTools: Fractions 411
Chapter 15 Review/Test 412
Enrich: Add and Subtract
Like Fractions 413
Getting Ready for the TAKS 414

16 Understand Decimals and Place Value 416

Show What You Know. 417
1 Relate Fractions and Decimals. 418
2 Hands On: Equivalent Decimals 422
3 Relate Mixed Numbers and Decimals 424
4 Fractions, Decimals, and Money 428
5 Hands On: Compare Decimals 432
6 Hands On: Order Decimals 434
7 Problem Solving Workshop
Skill: Draw Conclusions 436

Extra Practice 438
Practice Game: Order, Please! 439
Chapter 16 Review/Test 440
Enrich: Decimals to Thousandths 441
Getting Ready for the TAKS 442

17 Add and Subtract Decimals and Money 444

Show What You Know 445
1 Hands On: Model Addition 446
2 Hands On: Model Subtraction 448
3 Use Money 450
4 Add and Subtract Decimals and Money 454
5 Problem Solving Workshop
Strategy: Make a Table 458

Extra Practice 462
Practice Game: Decimal Train 463
Chapter 17 Review/Test 464
Enrich: Model Addition of Metric Measurements . . . 465

Unit Review/Test 466

MATH ON LOCATION

DVD from The FUTURES Channel with Texas Chapter Projects and **VOCABULARY POWER** 385

READ Math WORKSHOP 427

WRITE Math WORKSHOP 409

GO ONLINE Technology

Harcourt Mega Math: Chapter 15, pp. 399, 404; Chapter 16, p. 420; Chapter 17, pp. 447, 449, Extra Practice: pp. 410, 438, 462
The Harcourt Learning Site: www.harcourtschool.com
Multimedia Math Glossary: www.harcourtschool.com/hspmath

The World Almanac for Kids

Cool Kites 468

Time, Temperature, Data, and Combinations

Math on Location 471

18 Time and Temperature 472

Show What You Know. 473
1 Measure Time. 474
2 Elapsed Time 476
3 Problem Solving Workshop
Skill: Sequence Information. 480
4 Elapsed Time on a Calendar 482
5 Temperature: Fahrenheit. 484
6 Temperature: Celsius 486

Extra Practice 488
Technology Connections:
iTools: Measurement 489
Chapter 18 Review/Test 490
Enrich: 24-Hour Clock 491
Getting Ready for the TAKS 492

19 Collect, Display, and Interpret Data 494

Show What You Know. 495
1 Collect and Organize Data 496
2 Sort Data 500
3 Make and Interpret Pictographs 502
4 Choose a Reasonable Scale 504
5 Interpret Bar Graphs 506
6 Hands On: Make Bar and Double-Bar Graphs . . . 508
7 Problem Solving Workshop
Skill: Make Generalizations 510
8 Algebra Graph Ordered Pairs 512

Extra Practice 514
Chapter 19 Review/Test 516
Enrich: Find Median, Mode, and Range 517
Getting Ready for the TAKS 518

20 Combinations 520

Show What You Know . . . 521
1 Hands On: Model Combinations . . . 522
2 Combinations . . . 524
3 Tree Diagrams . . . 528
4 Problem Solving Workshop
Strategy: Make an Organized List . . . 532
5 More About Combinations . . . 536

Extra Practice . . . 540
Practice Game: Fashion Show . . . 541
Chapter 20 Review/Test . . . 542
Enrich: List All Possible Outcomes . . . 543

Unit Review/Test . . . 544

DVD from The Futures Channel with Texas Chapter Projects and
VOCABULARY POWER . . . 471

READ Math WORKSHOP . . . 499

WRITE Math WORKSHOP . . . 539

Technology

Harcourt Mega Math: Chapter 18, p. 478; Chapter 19, p. 507, Extra Practice: pp. 488, 514
The Harcourt Learning Site: www.harcourtschool.com
Multimedia Math Glossary: www.harcourtschool.com/hspmath

The World Almanac for Kids

Record High Temperatures 546

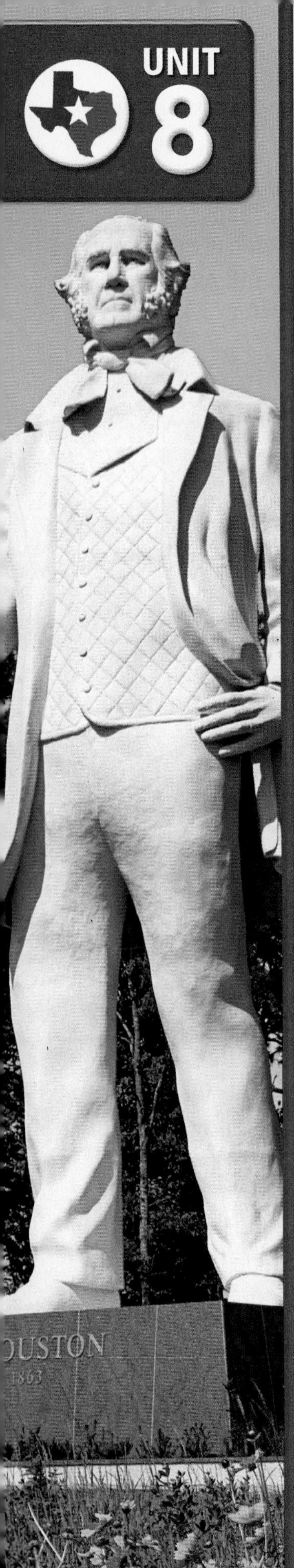

Measurement

Math on Location 549

21 Customary Measurement 550

Show What You Know. 551
1 Measure Fractional Parts 552
2 **Algebra** Change Customary Linear Units 556
3 Weight 558
4 Customary Capacity 560
5 **Algebra** Change Units 562
6 Problem Solving Workshop
Strategy: Compare Strategies 564

Extra Practice 566
Technology Connection:
Calculator: Change Customary Measures 567
Chapter 21 Review/Test 568
Enrich: Add and Subtract Customary Measurements 569
Getting Ready for the TAKS 570

22 Metric Measurement 572

Show What You Know. 573
1 Metric Length 574
2 Mass 578
3 Capacity 580
4 Problem Solving Workshop
Strategy: Make a Table 582
5 Choose the Appropriate Tool and Unit 584
6 Reasonable Estimates 588

Extra Practice 592
Practice Game: Centimeter Swim 593
Chapter 22 Review/Test 594
Enrich: Change SI(Metric) Units 595
Getting Ready for the TAKS 596

23 Perimeter and Area 598

Show What You Know 599
1 Hands On: Estimate and Measure Perimeter 600
2 Perimeter 602
3 Algebra Find Perimeter 604
4 Problem Solving Workshop
Strategy: Compare Strategies 608
5 Estimate Area 610
6 Algebra Find Area 614
7 Perimeter and Area of Complex Figures 618
8 Relate Perimeter and Area 620

Extra Practice 624
Practice Game: 3 Steps Forward, 2 Steps Back 625
Chapter 23 Review/Test 626
Enrich: Perimeter of a Circle 627
Getting Ready for the TAKS 628

24 Volume 630

Show What You Know 631
1 Estimate and Measure Volume of Prisms 632
2 Problem Solving Workshop
Skill: Too Much/Too Little Information 636
3 Compare Volume of Prisms 638
4 Relate Volume and Capacity 640

Extra Practice 642
Practice Game: Shipping Yo-Yos 643
Chapter 24 Review/Test 644
Enrich: Use a Formula 645

Unit Review/Test 646

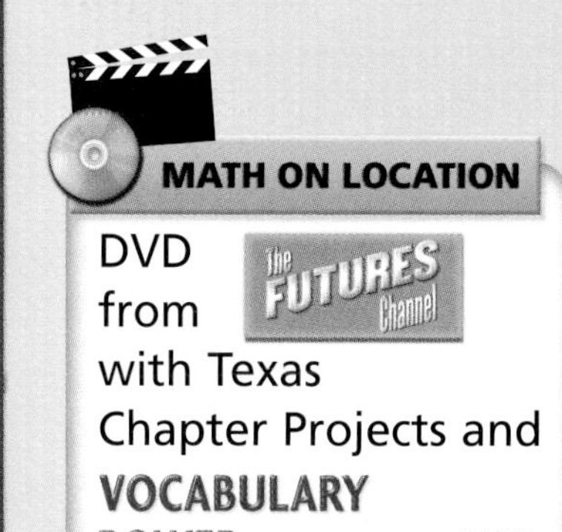

DVD from The Futures Channel with Texas Chapter Projects and VOCABULARY POWER 549

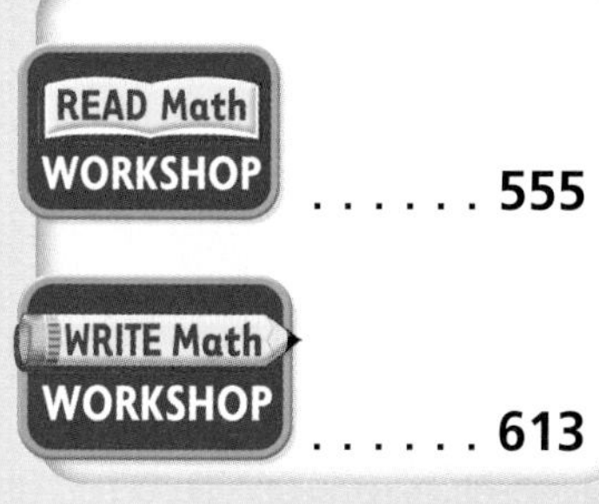

READ Math WORKSHOP 555

WRITE Math WORKSHOP 613

GO ONLINE Technology

Harcourt Mega Math: Chapter 21, p. 554; Chapter 22, p. 576; Chapter 23, p. 616; Chapter 24, p. 634, Extra Practice: pp. 566, 592, 624, 642
The Harcourt Learning Site: www.harcourtschool.com
Multimedia Math Glossary: www.harcourtschool.com/hspmath

The World Almanac for Kids

Wildlife Habitats 648

Student Handbook

Review the TEKS H2
Test-Taking Strategies H32
Basic Facts Review H40
Table of Measures H44
Texas Essential Knowledge and Skills H46
Glossary H49
Index H62

TALK, READ, and WRITE About Math

Mathematics is a language of numbers, words, and symbols.

This year you will learn ways to communicate about math as you **talk**, **read**, and **write** about what you are learning.

The table and the bar graph show the speeds of some of the fastest steel roller coasters in the United States.

Steel Roller Coasters

Roller Coaster	Park	Speed (in miles per hour)
Kingda Ka	Six Flags Great Adventure Jackson, New Jersey	128
Top Thrill Dragster	Cedar Point Sandusky, Ohio	120
Superman: The Escape	Six Flags Magic Mountain Valencia, California	100
Millennium Force	Cedar Point Sandusky, Ohio	93
Titan	Six Flags Over Texas Arlington, Texas	85
Phantom's Revenge	Kennywood West Mifflin, Pennsylvania	82

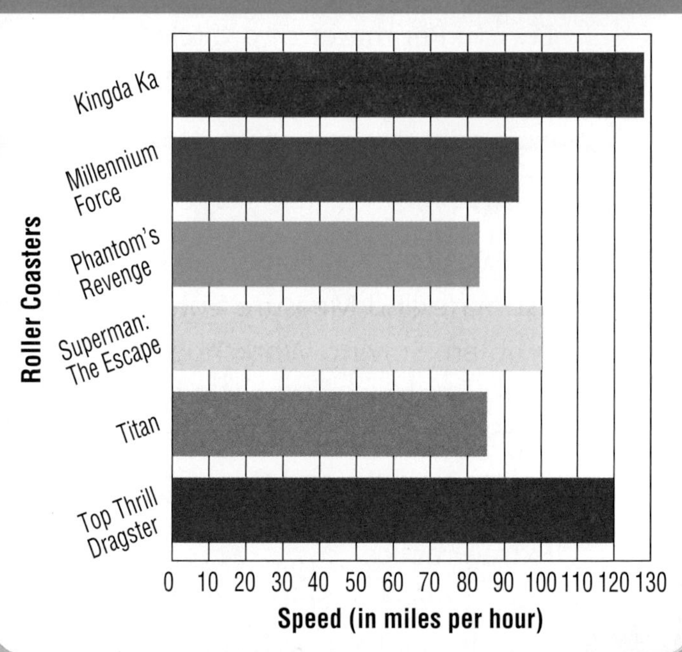

TALK Math

Talk about the table and the bar graph.

1. What information is in the table but is not in the bar graph?
2. What is the difference in the way the data are organized in the table and on the bar graph?
3. What do the numbers along the bottom of the bar graph represent?
4. Why is it important that the spaces between the numbers on the bar graph are the same size?

READ Math

Read the data in the table and on the bar graph.

4. In what city and state is the fastest roller coaster located?
5. What is the difference in speed of the Kingda Ka and Phantom's Revenge?
6. What is the difference in speed of the two roller coasters in Sandusky, Ohio?
7. Which two roller coasters have a difference in speed of 35 miles per hour?

WRITE Math

Write a problem about the bar graph.

This year you will write many problems. When you see **Pose a Problem**, you look at a problem on the page and use it to write your own problem.

In your problem you can
- change the numbers or some of the information.
- exchange the known and unknown information.
- write an open-ended problem that can have more than one correct answer.

These problems are examples of ways you can pose your own problem. Solve each problem.

Problem How much faster is the Kingda Ka than the Millennium Force?

- **Change the Numbers or Information**
  How much faster is the Millennium Force than the Titan?
- **Exchange the Known and Unknown Information**
  The speed of the Millennium Force is 93 miles per hour. Which roller coaster has a speed that is 27 miles per hour faster than the Millennium Force?
- **Make the Problem Open-Ended**
  Name a roller coaster with a speed between 90 and 125 miles per hour.

Pose a Problem Chose one of the three ways to write a new problem. Use the information in the table and on the bar graph.

UNIT

1 Understand Whole Numbers and Operations

Flowers are packaged by the dozen and prepared for shipment to flower businesses.

Flowering plants must be watered and cared for until they are shipped to customers.

Florists make arrangements by combining specific numbers of different colors.

VOCABULARY POWER

TALK Math

What math is used in **Math on Location**? How could you find if there are more red flowers or yellow flowers prepared for shipment?

READ Math

REVIEW VOCABULARY You learned the words below last year. How do these words relate to **Math on Location**?

compare to describe whether numbers are equal to, less than, or greater than each other

estimate to find an answer that is close to the exact amount

greater than (>) a symbol used to compare two numbers, with the greater number given first

less than (<) a symbol used to compare two numbers, with the lesser number given first

WRITE Math

Copy and complete the table using the word pairs shown below. Use what you know about numbers and operations.

addition, subtraction — addition, sum — odd, even
subtraction, count backward — regroup, compare
digit, place value — fact family, number sentence
subtraction, difference — sum, difference — compare, order
greater than, less than — sum, total

Same	Opposite	Go Together	Not Related
	addition subtraction		

GO ONLINE Technology
Multimedia Math Glossary link at
www.harcourtschool.com/hspmath

1 Understand Place Value

The Big Idea The position of a digit determines its value.

The King Ranch in south Texas is bigger than the state of Rhode Island. Its area is 825,000 acres. The first cattle on it were longhorns, which are still raised there.

Investigate

More cattle live in Texas than in any other state. What are some ways to compare numbers of cattle, as shown in the table?

Texas Cattle

Year	Population
1987	13,020,910
1992	13,242,832
1997	14,504,444
2002	13,978,987

GO ONLINE **Technology**
Student pages are available in the Student eBook.

Show What You Know

Check your understanding of important skills needed for success in Chapter 1.

▶ Place Value Through Thousands

Find the value of the underlined digit.

1. $8\underline{2}4$ **2.** $59\underline{1}$ **3.** $\underline{3}74$ **4.** $\underline{5},312$

5. $1,04\underline{3}$ **6.** $9,\underline{2}08$ **7.** $\underline{2},307$ **8.** $7,\underline{8}61$

▶ Read and Write Whole Numbers Through Thousands

Write each number in standard form.

9. thirty-five **10.** eight hundred four **11.** seven thousand, two hundred twenty-one

12. seventy-eight **13.** five hundred sixty-three **14.** two thousand, forty-six

15. $600 + 40 + 9$ **16.** $3,000 + 200 + 8$ **17.** $5,000 + 700 + 50 + 1$

▶ Compare Whole Numbers Through Thousands

Compare. Write <, >, or = for each ●.

18. 203 ● 230 **19.** 65 ● 56 **20.** 888 ● 881 **21.** 98 ● 103

22. 5,339 ● 5,393 **23.** 422 ● 4,222 **24.** 3,825 ● 5,283 **25.** 7,881 ● 7,881

VOCABULARY POWER

CHAPTER VOCABULARY

compare
digit
equal to (=)
expanded form
greater than (>)
less than (<)
millions
not equal to (≠)
order
period
place value
standard form
word form

WARM-UP WORDS

period Each group of three digits separated by commas in a multidigit number

standard form A way to write numbers by using digits

expanded form A way to write numbers by showing the value of each digit

word form A way to write numbers by using words

1 Place Value Through Hundred Thousands

OBJECTIVE: Model, read, write, and identify the place value of whole numbers through hundred thousands.

Quick Review

Write in standard form.

1. 6 tens 5 ones
2. 4 hundreds 2 tens
3. 8 tens 9 ones
4. 7 hundreds 7 ones
5. 5 hundreds 3 tens 1 one

Vocabulary

period

standard form

word form

expanded form

Learn

PROBLEM The cost of caring for a pet can really add up. Did you know that the average yearly cost to take care of a medium-sized dog is $1,115?

You can use base-ten blocks to show the cost.

Activity

Materials ■ base-ten blocks

Model 1,115 in more than one way.

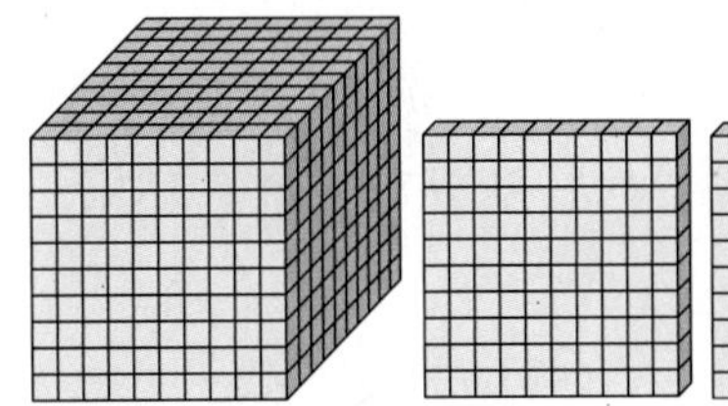

1 thousand 1 hundred 1 ten 5 ones shows 1,115.

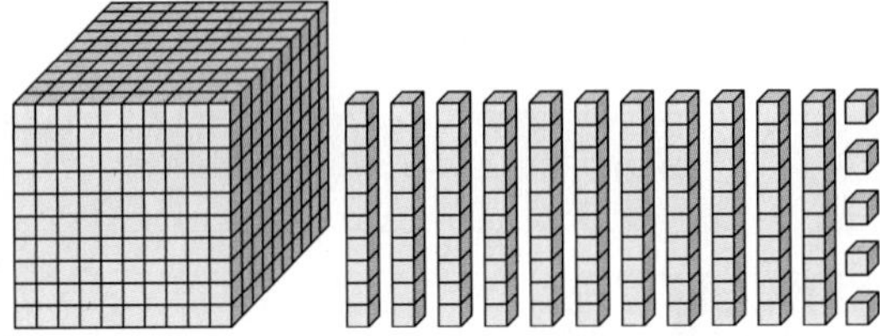

Think: 1 hundred = 10 tens

1 thousand 11 tens 5 ones shows 1,115.

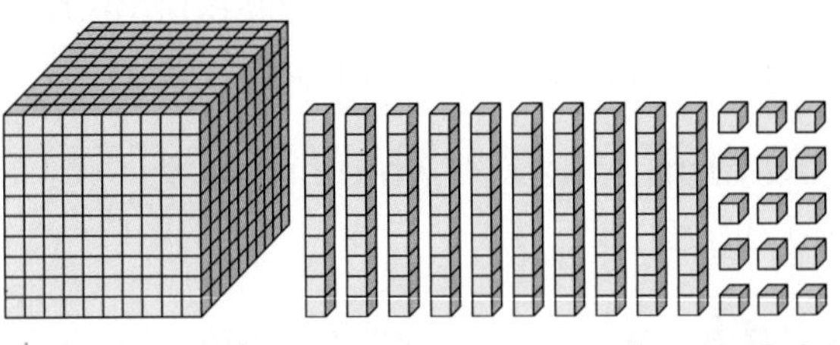

Think: 1 ten = 10 ones

1 thousand 10 tens 15 ones shows 1,115.

- Are these different ways to show 1,115 related? Explain.

TEKS 4.1A use place value to read, write, compare, and order whole numbers through 999,999,999. *also,* 4.14A, 4.14D, 4.15A, 4.15B

Understand Place Value

In 2004, the number of Labrador retrievers registered with the American Kennel Club was 146,692. What is the value of the digit 4 in 146,692?

A place-value chart can help you understand the value of each digit in a number. The value of a digit depends on its place-value position in the number.

Example Use place value to find the value of a digit.

PERIOD

THOUSANDS			ONES		
Hundreds	**Tens**	**Ones**	**Hundreds**	**Tens**	**Ones**
1	4	6,	6	9	2

1 hundred thousand	4 ten thousands	6 thousands	6 hundreds	9 tens	2 ones
$1 \times 100{,}000$	$4 \times 10{,}000$	$6 \times 1{,}000$	6×100	9×10	2×1
100,000	40,000	6,000	600	90	2

← Multiply the digit by its place value to find the value of each digit.

So, the value of the digit 4 is 40,000.

Each group of three digits separated by commas in a multidigit number is called a **period**. Commas separate the periods. Each period has ones, tens, and hundreds in it. The number 146,692 has two periods, ones and thousands.

You can use place value and period names to read 146,692 and to write 146,692 in different forms.

Standard Form: 146,692

Word Form: one hundred forty-six thousand, six hundred ninety-two

Expanded Form: 100,000 + 40,000 + 6,000 + 600 + 90 + 2

ERROR ALERT

When numbers have zeros, you do not need to write or represent the digit 0 in word form or expanded form.

More Examples

A **Standard form:** 70,186

Word Form: seventy thousand, one hundred eighty-six

Expanded Form: 70,000 + 100 + 80 + 6

B **Standard Form:** 306,409

Word Form: three hundred six thousand, four hundred nine

Expanded Form: 300,000 + 6,000 + 400 + 9

Guided Practice

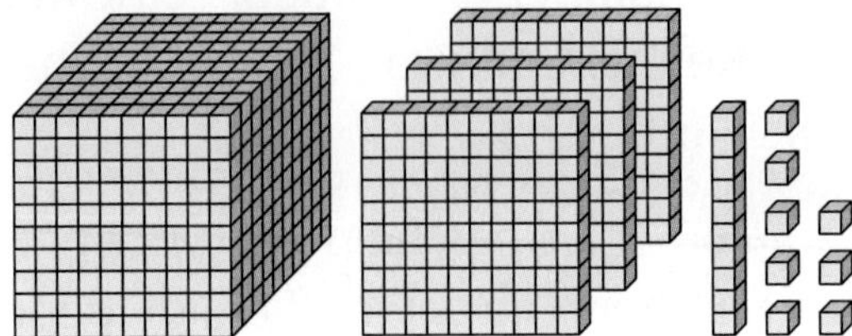

1. Name the number shown by the model. What are two other ways can you model this number?

Write each number in two other forms.

2. four hundred seven thousand, fifty-one
3. 90,000 + 6,000 + 200 + 80 + 1
4. TALK Math **Explain** how you can use the standard form of a number to write the number in word form.

Independent Practice and Problem Solving

Write each number in two other forms.

5. 70,000 + 4,000 + 50 + 6
6. five hundred thousand, two hundred six
7. 981,416
8. 80,308

Complete.

9. 340,680 = three hundred forty _?_, six hundred eighty = ■ + 40,000 + ■ + 80
10. ■ + 6,000 + 400 + 3 = 56,4■■ = fifty-six thousand, four _?_ three

Write the value of the underlined digit in each number.

11. <u>4</u>35,258
12. 36<u>8</u>,109
13. 5<u>7</u>0,217
14. 129,<u>6</u>34

USE DATA For 15–17, use the table.

15. How many poodles were registered in 2004? Write the number in two other forms.
16. Which breed had nineteen thousand, three hundred ninety-six dogs registered in 2004?
17. Represent the number of Pointers in as many different ways as you can. Use models, pictures, or numbers.
18. **FAST FACT** In 2001, an English mastiff set a world record for heaviest dog with a weight of 282 pounds. Describe two different ways that you could use base-ten blocks to show this number.

Dogs Registered by the American Kennel Club in 2004

Breed	Number Registered
Bulldogs	19,396
Pointers	512
Poodles	32,671
Pomeranians	21,269

19. **Reasoning** What number is 100 less than the greatest number you can make if you use the digits 2, 3, 4, 5, and 9 exactly once?

Technology CD ROM
Use Harcourt Mega Math, Fraction Action, *Number Line Mine*, Level A.

Extra Practice on page 24, Set A

20. **Reasoning** Les wrote a number between 700 and 900 that had one zero. What might the number be?

21. **WRITE Math** Cameron wrote this sequence of numbers: 437, 447, 457, 467. **Describe** the pattern you see.

Mixed Review and TAKS Prep

22. Find the next number in the pattern. (Grade 3 TEKS 3.6A)

4, 8, 12, 16, 20, ■

23. A toy factory makes 345 bears and 265 dolls. How many bears and dolls do they make? (Grade 3 TEKS 3.3B)

24. **TAKS Prep** What is the value of the digit 8 in 382,425? (Obj. 1)

A 80

B 800

C 8,000

D 80,000

25. **TAKS Prep** A movie theater's weekend ticket sales totaled one hundred thousand, forty-six dollars. What is this number in standard form? (Obj. 1)

F 100,046 **H** 104,006

G 100,064 **J** 140,006

Problem Solving and Reasoning

NUMBER SENSE You can name numbers in different ways.

The number of dog bones shown can be named as 1 thousand 3 hundreds 1 ten 2 ones or 500 + 500 + 100 + 100 + 100 + 10 + 2.

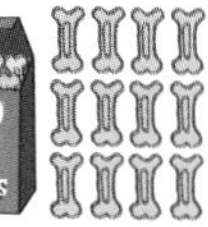

Name numbers using numbers and words.	Name numbers using numbers and operation signs.
4,100	**1,247**
4 thousands 1 hundred	1,000 + 200 + 40 + 7
41 hundreds	500 + 500 + 240 + 7
410 tens	1,250 − 3
4,100 ones	1,300 − 53

Name each number two ways using numbers and words.

1. 150 **2.** 705 **3.** 479 **4.** 862 **5.** 2,464

Name each number two ways using numbers and operation signs.

6. 308 **7.** 1,305 **8.** 2,300 **9.** 4,550 **10.** 576

LESSON 2 HANDS ON

Model Millions

OBJECTIVE: Understand the magnitude of numbers through millions.

Quick Review

Write the word form of each number.

1. 5,234 **2.** 72,806
3. 96,041 **4.** 352,629
5. 842,597

Vocabulary

millions

Investigate

Materials ■ 10-by-10 grid paper ■ crayons ■ tape

A stack of 1 million one-dollar bills is as tall as a nine-story building. One million is the next counting number after 999,999. One million is written as 1,000,000 in standard form.

A Draw a dot in each box in 1 column of the 10-by-10 grid paper. Each dot represents 1 one-dollar bill. How many one-dollar bills does this grid represent?

B Draw a dot in each box of the grid. How many one-dollar bills does one grid represent when filled?

C Tape your grid paper to other students' grid papers. Write the number of 1 one-dollar bills that are represented by the sheets of grid paper taped together.

- How many sheets of grid paper will you need to represent 1,000 one-dollar bills? 10,000 one-dollar bills? 100,000 one-dollar bills? 1,000,000 one-dollar bills?

A

C

Draw Conclusions

You can look for a pattern to find how many sheets of grid paper you will need to show 1,000,000 one-dollar bills. Copy and complete the table.

1. What pattern did you use to complete the table? Explain.
2. **Analysis** How can picturing what a model of 1 million looks like help you better understand the relative size of numbers?

Model Millions

Total Dollars	Sheets of Paper
100	1
1,000	10
10,000	100
100,000	■
1,000,000	■

TEKS 4.1A use place value to read, write, compare, and order whole numbers through 999,999,999. *also* **4.14A, 4.14D, 4.15A, 4.15B**

Connect

The period to the left of thousands is **millions**.
One million is equal to 10 hundred thousands.

You can use place value and period names to help you read numbers in millions.

In 1989, Pablo Picasso's painting, entitled *Les Noces de Pierrette*, sold for $51,671,920. Look at the amount paid for the painting in the place-value chart.

MILLIONS			THOUSANDS			ONES		
Hundreds	Tens	Ones	Hundreds	Tens	Ones	Hundreds	Tens	Ones
	5	1,	6	7	1,	9	2	0

The number 51,671,920 is read as fifty-one million, six hundred seventy-one thousand, nine hundred twenty.

TALK Math

Would the population of a large country be counted in thousands or millions? Give some examples of things that can be counted in the millions.

Practice

Solve.

1. How many hundreds are in 1,000?
2. How many hundreds are in 10,000?
3. How many thousands are in 100,000?
4. How many thousands are in 1,000,000?

Tell whether the number is large enough to be in the millions or more. Write *yes* or *no*.

5. the number of miles from Earth to the sun
6. the number of people in your class
7. the number of grains of sand on a beach
8. the number of bees living in a beehive
9. the number of students riding on a school bus
10. the number of people living in the United States

Choose the number in which the digit 7 has the greater value.

11. 7,500,000 or 75,000,000
12. 35,007,000 or 35,070,000
13. 19,070,000 or 700,000
14. 237,100,000 or 71,100,000

15. **WRITE Math** **Describe** how 10,000 sheets of 10-by-10 grid paper and 1,000 thousands blocks are related.

LESSON 3

Place Value Through Millions

OBJECTIVE: Read, write, and identify the place value of numbers through millions.

Quick Review

Write the number of hundreds in each.

1. 70,000
2. 100,000
3. 9,000
4. 300,000
5. 50,000

Learn

PROBLEM You can write the number 92,955,628 in standard form, word form, and expanded form.

Example Use place value to write and read numbers in millions.

PERIOD

MILLIONS			THOUSANDS			ONES		
Hundreds	Tens	Ones	Hundreds	Tens	Ones	Hundreds	Tens	Ones
	9	2,	9	5	5,	6	2	8

Standard Form: 92,955,628

Word Form: ninety-two million, nine hundred fifty-five thousand, six hundred twenty-eight

Expanded Form: 90,000,000 + 2,000,000 + 900,000 + 50,000 + 5,000 + 600 + 20 + 8

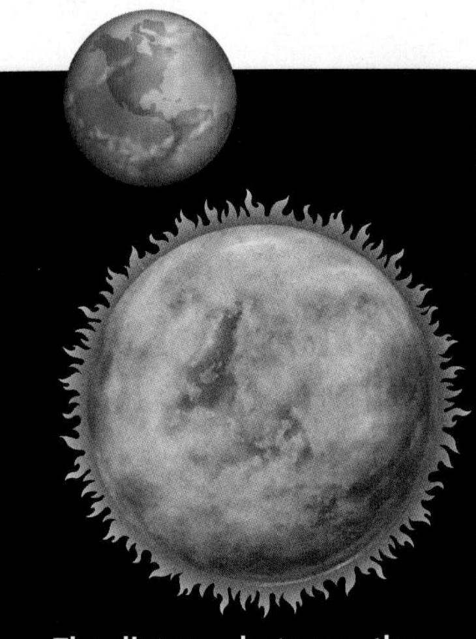

The distance between the Earth and the sun is about 92,955,628 miles.

More Examples

A **Standard Form:** 5,200,007

Word Form: five million, two hundred thousand, seven

Expanded Form: 5,000,000 + 200,000 + 7

B **Standard Form:** 860,092,170

Word Form: eight hundred sixty million, ninety-two thousand, one hundred seventy

Expanded Form: 800,000,000 + 60,000,000 + 90,000 + 2,000 + 100 + 70

- How do you find the value of the digit 4 in 45,213,073?

Math Idea
You can use place value and period names to read and write numbers in three forms.

Guided Practice

1. How can you use place value and period names to write the number 5,324,904 in word form?

Write each number in two other forms.

2. ninety million, four hundred eight thousand, seventeen
3. 365,009,058

TEKS 4.1A use place value to read, write, compare, and order whole numbers through 999,999,999. *also* **4.14A, 4.15A, 4.15B**

4. TALK Math **Explain** how you can use the expanded form of a number to write the number in standard form.

Independent Practice and Problem Solving

Write each number in two other forms.

5. forty-seven million, five hundred eight thousand

6. two hundred three million, forty thousand, six hundred nineteen

7. 60,570,020

8. 400,000,000 + 60,000 + 5,000 + 100

Use the number 63,145,973.

9. Write the name of the period that has the digits 145.

10. Write the name of the period that has the digits 63.

11. Write the digit in the millions place.

12. Write the value of the digit 6.

Find the sum. Then write the answer in standard form.

13. 4 thousands 3 hundreds 2 ones + 5 thousands 2 tens 4 ones

14. 3 ten thousands 4 hundreds 8 tens + 4 ten thousands

USE DATA For 15–16, use the Average Distance from the Sun picture.

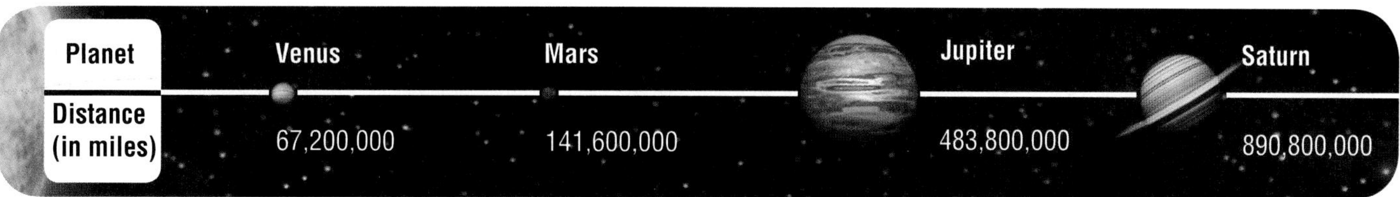

Planet
Distance (in miles)
Venus
67,200,000
Mars
141,600,000
Jupiter
483,800,000
Saturn
890,800,000

15. What is the average distance of Saturn from the sun?

16. Which planet has an average distance of four hundred eighty-three million, eight hundred thousand miles from the sun?

17. WRITE Math **Explain** how trading the position of the digit 2 and the digit 4 in 129,304,718 affects the value of the number.

Mixed Review and TAKS Prep

18. What is 100 more than 45,678? (TEKS 4.1A, p.4)

19. There are 12 inches in 1 foot. How many inches are there in 3 feet? (Grade 3 TEKS 3.11A)

20. **TAKS Prep** What is the value of the digit 7 in 78,423,106? (Obj. 1)

    A 70,000
    B 700,000
    C 7,000,000
    D 70,000,000

Extra Practice on page 24, Set B

LESSON 4 Compare Whole Numbers

OBJECTIVE: Compare numbers through millions using base-ten blocks, number lines, and place value.

Quick Review

Write the value of the digit 5.

1. 23,456,869
2. 961,408,325
3. 542,679,007
4. 72,086,050
5. 135,461,009

Vocabulary

not equal to (≠)

Learn

PROBLEM Crystal Palace Cave in Alaska is 429 feet deep. French Creek Cave in Montana is 434 feet deep. Which is deeper, Crystal Palace Cave or French Creek Cave?

Example 1 Use base-ten blocks.

To find which cave is deeper, compare 429 and 434.

Compare the values of the blocks in each place-value position from left to right. Keep comparing the blocks until the values are different.

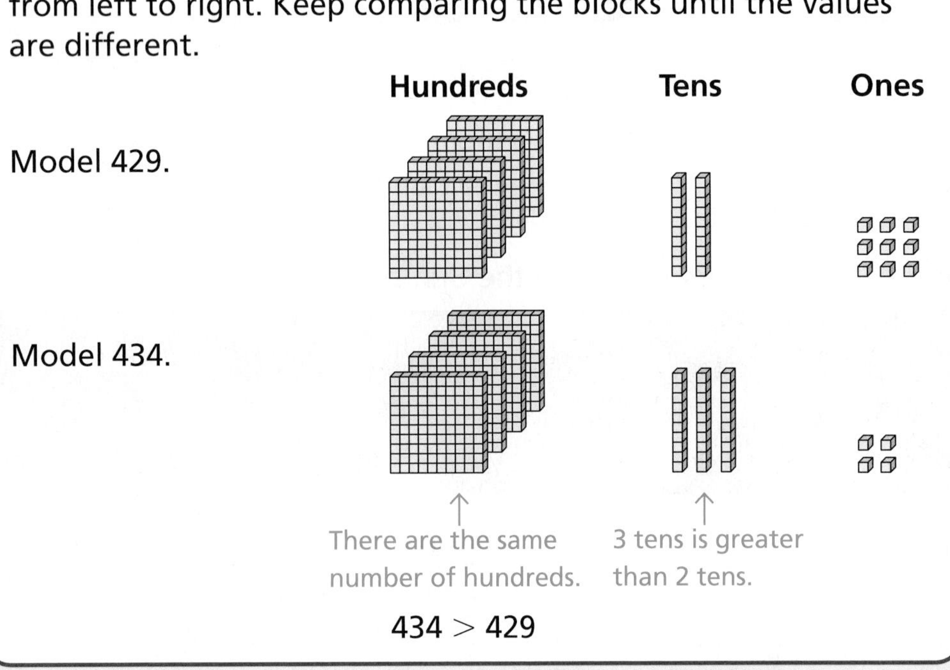

Hundreds
Tens
Ones
Model 429.
Model 434.
There are the same number of hundreds.
3 tens is greater than 2 tens.

434 > 429

So, French Creek Cave is deeper than Crystal Palace Cave.

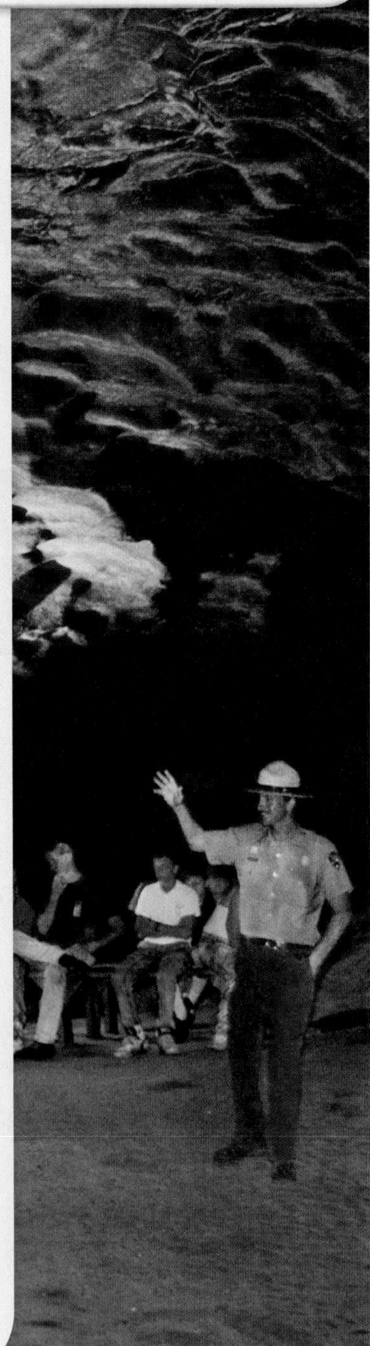

Example 2 Use a number line.

Compare 10,408 and 10,433.

10,408 ↓ 10,433 ↓

10,400 10,410 10,420 10,430 10,440 10,450

10,408 is to the left of 10,433.

So, 10,408 is less than 10,433.

10,408 < 10,433

10,433 is to the right of 10,408.

So, 10,433 is greater than 10,408.

10,433 > 10,408

TEKS 4.1A use place value to read, write, compare, and order whole numbers through 999,999,999.
also **4.14A, 4.14D, 4.15A, 4.15B**

Example 3 Use a place-value chart.

Mammoth Cave National Park in Kentucky had 1,898,822 visitors in 2002 and 1,888,126 visitors in 2004. In which year were there more visitors?

Compare 1,898,822 and 1,888,126.

MILLIONS			THOUSANDS			ONES		
Hundreds	Tens	Ones	Hundreds	Tens	Ones	Hundreds	Tens	Ones
		1,	8	9	8,	8	2	2
		1,	8	8	8,	1	2	6

Step 1

Start with the first place on the left. Compare the millions.

1,898,822
↓ 1 = 1
1,888,126

There are the same number of millions.

Step 2

Compare the hundred thousands.

1,898,822
↓ 8 = 8
1,888,126

There are the same number of hundred thousands.

Step 3

Compare the ten thousands.

1,898,822
↓ 9 > 8
1,888,126

9 ten thousands are greater than 8 ten thousands. So, 1,898,822 > 1,888,126.

Math Idea

To compare numbers, start at the left and compare the digits in each place-value position until the digits differ.

So, there were more visitors in 2002.

Example 4 Compare different numbers of digits.

Compare 21,623,785 and 103,317,256. Write <, >, or =.

21,623,785
↑ 0 < 1
103,317,256

So, 21,623,785 < 103,317,256.

Example 5 Compare to make a relationship true.

What numbers make this relationship true?

26■ ≠ 265 Think: What digits are not equal to 5?

Replace ■ with 0, 1, 2, 3, 4, 6, 7, 8, or 9.

260, 261, 262, 263, 264, 266, 267, 268, and 269 are **not equal to** 265.

So, the digits 0, 1, 2, 3, 4, 6, 7, 8, or 9 make the relationship true.

Guided Practice

1. Use the base-ten blocks to compare 324 and 332. Write the lesser number.

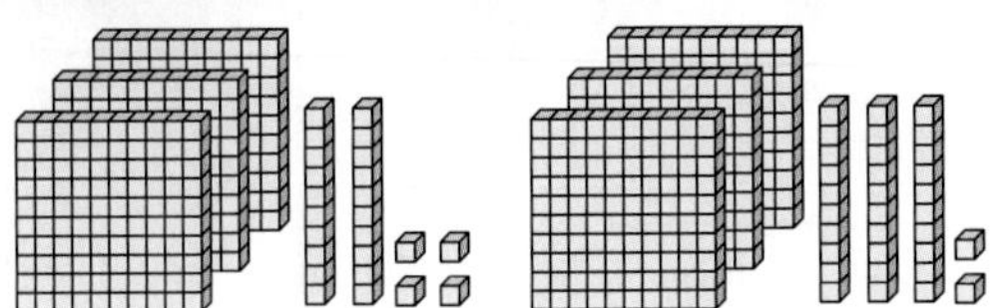

2. Use the number line to compare 5,327 and 5,341. Write the greater number.

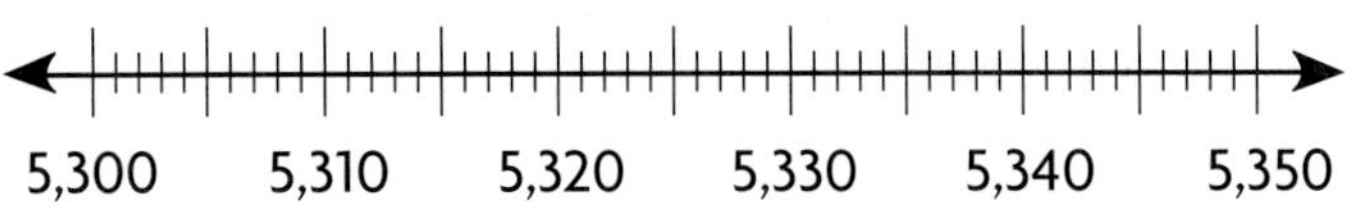

Compare. Write $<$, $>$, or $=$ for each ●.

3. 45,595 ● 45,585
4. 631,328 ● 640,009
5. 528,807,414 ● 5,699,001
6. TALK Math **Explain** how to compare 79,308 and 79,354.

Independent Practice and Problem Solving

Use the number line to compare. Write the lesser number.

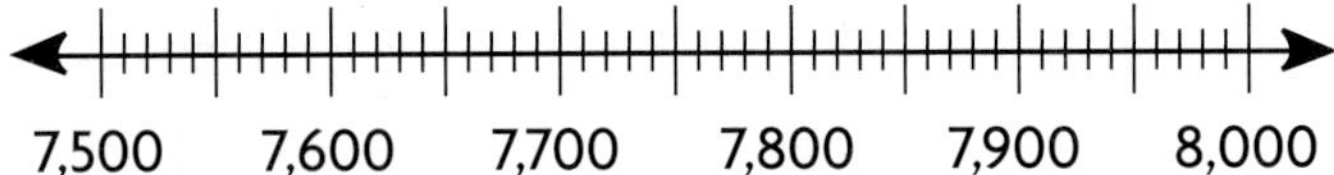

7. 7,710 or 7,680
8. 7,800 or 7,680
9. 7,584 or 7,616

Compare. Write $<$, $>$, or $=$ for each ●.

10. 2,212 ● 2,600
11. 41,190 ● 41,090
12. 63,803 ● 6,409
13. 88,304 ● 88,304
14. 5,249,116 ● 41,090
15. 439,064 ● 440,000,438
16. 8,279,314 ● 8,279,299
17. 975,408 ● 912,005,300
18. 7,512,720 ● 8,510,001

Algebra **Find all of the digits that can replace each ■.**

19. 420 $\neq$ 4■0
20. 7,486 $\neq$ 7,48■
21. 3,■15 $\neq$ 3,129

USE DATA For 22–24, use the table.

22. Which ocean trench is deeper, Tonga or Marianas?
23. Which ocean trench has a depth less than 34,000 feet?
24. **Pose a Problem** Write a problem that compares two numbers from the Deepest Ocean Trenches table.

Deepest Ocean Trenches

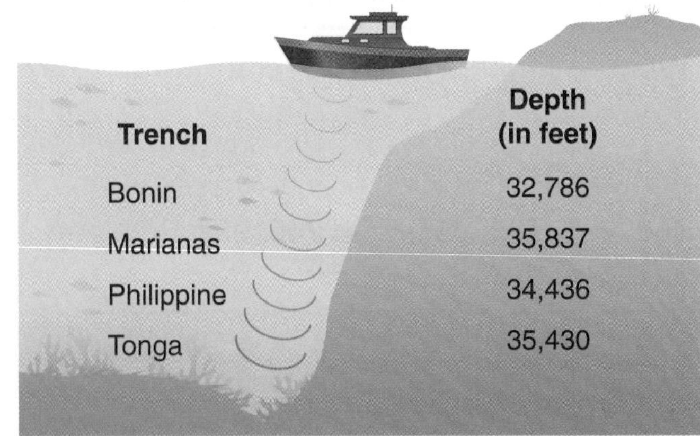

Trench	Depth (in feet)
Bonin	32,786
Marianas	35,837
Philippine	34,436
Tonga	35,430

 Extra Practice on page 24, Set C

25. WRITE Math **What's the Error?** Max said that 36,594 is less than 5,980 because 3 is less than 5. Describe Max's error and give the correct answer.

26. **Reasoning** Which is greater, the number that is 1,000 less than 16,892 or the number that is 10,000 less than 26,892. **Explain** how you know.

Mixed Review and TAKS Prep

27. Write the time. (Grade 3 TEKS 3.12B)

28. **TAKS Prep** Which number is greatest? (Obj. 1)

A 549,300

B 4,004,030

C 5,490,003

D 594,030

29. Name the customary unit you would use to measure the length of a butterfly. (Grade 3 TEKS 3.11A)

30. **TAKS Prep** Ms. Ling's class set a goal collecting 1,200 cans of food each day. After 3 days they had collected 1,225 cans, 1,050 cans, and 1,243 cans. Which total was less than their daily goal? (Obj. 1)

A 1,243 cans

B 1,225 cans

C 1,200 cans

D 1,050 cans

Problem Solving and Reasoning

VISUAL THINKING A **benchmark** is a known number of things that helps you understand the size or amount of a different number of things.

Use the benchmark to choose the best estimate for the number of bats it would take to cover the whole wall of the cave.

To cover the wall, it would take about 4 times the benchmark number.

$10 + 10 + 10 + 10$, or $4 \times 10 = 40$

The most reasonable estimate for the number of bats it would take to cover the entire wall is 40 bats.

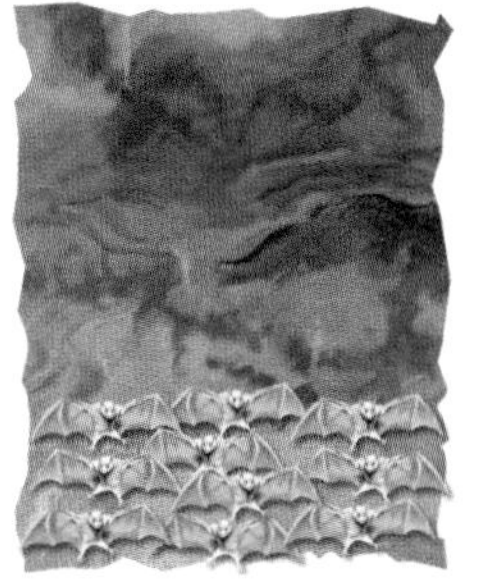
10 bats

10, 20, 30, or 40

- Will your estimate be less than, more than, or the same amount as the benchmark number? **Explain.**

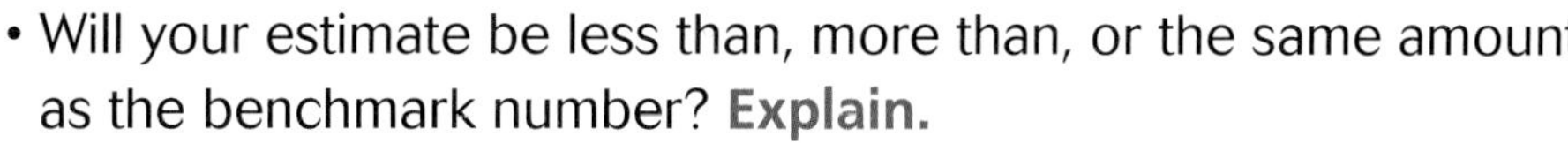

Use the benchmark to choose the best estimate for each amount.

1. 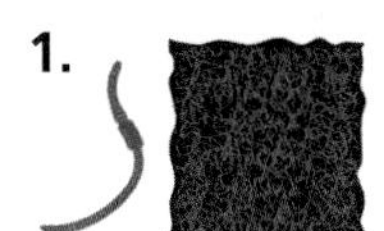
1,000 worms 500, 750, 1,000, or 1,500

2. 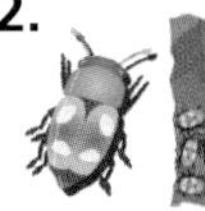 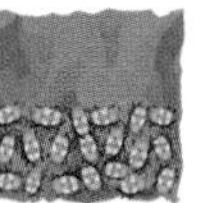
20 beetles
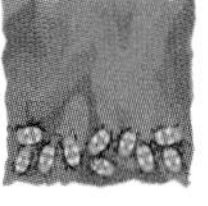
10, 20, 60 or 120

3. 
200 spiders

50, 100, 200 or 400

LESSON 5

Order Whole Numbers

OBJECTIVE: Order numbers through millions using base-ten blocks, number lines, and place value.

Quick Review

Compare. Write <, >, or = for each ●.

1. 5,322 ● 5,330
2. 32,086 ● 9,002
3. 75,461 ● 75,461
4. 284,500 ● 285,111
5. 3,284,500 ● 662,796

Learn

PROBLEM Did you know that the giant sequoia is the world's largest kind of tree? Sequoia National Park in California is home to many of the largest sequoias. Three of the largest trees in the park are 275 feet tall, 241 feet tall, and 255 feet tall. Order the heights of the trees from greatest to least.

Example 1 Use base-ten blocks.

Order 275, 241, and 255 from greatest to least.

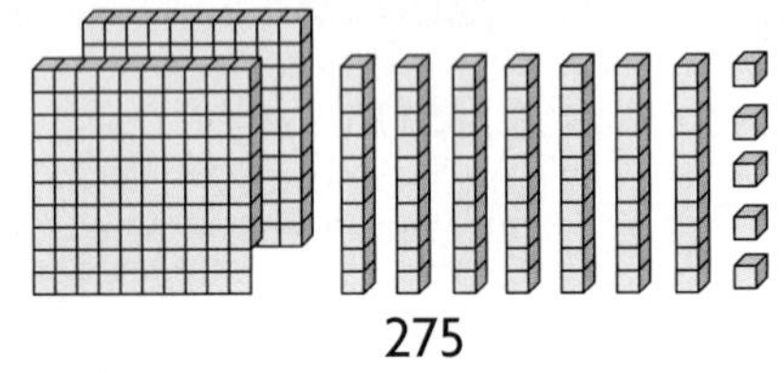

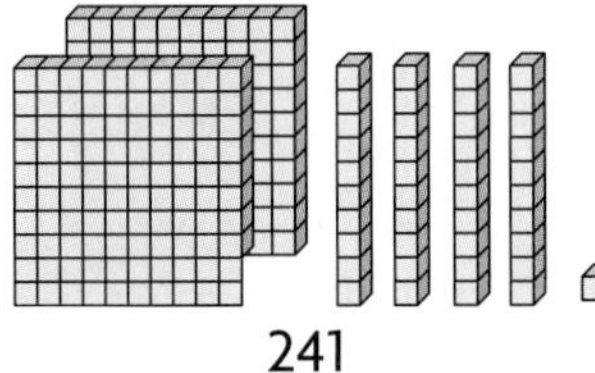

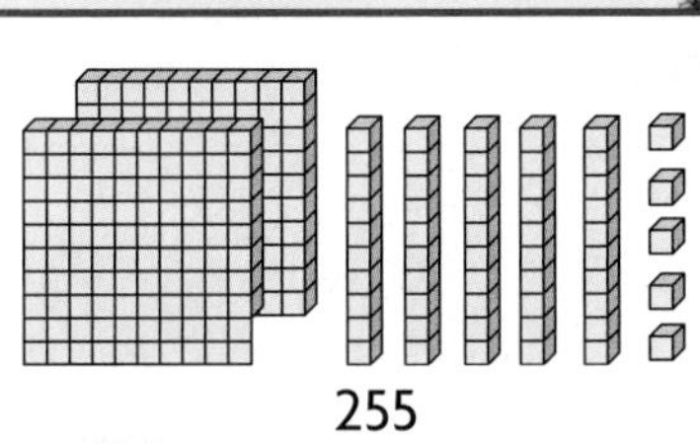

Step 1

Compare the hundreds. There are the same number of hundreds.

Step 2

Compare the tens. The model for 275 has the most tens, so it is the greatest number.

Step 3

Compare the tens in 241 and 255. The model for 255 has more tens, so it is greater than 241.

So, from the greatest to least, the numbers are 275, 255, 241.

So, the heights of the trees in order from greatest to least are 275 feet, 255 feet, and 241 feet.

Example 2 Use a number line.

Order 20,650; 21,150; and 20,890 from greatest to least.

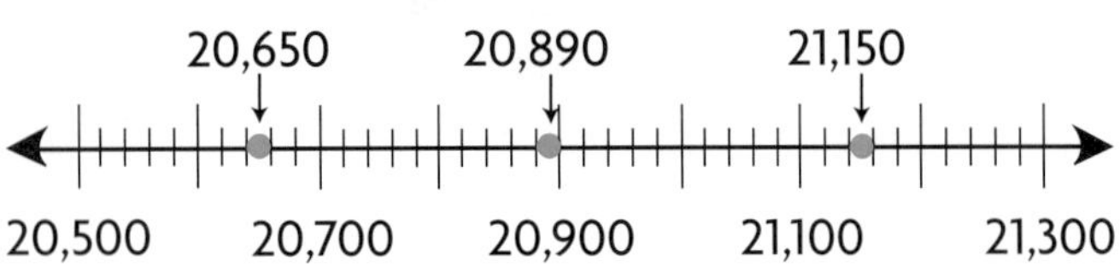

So, the numbers in order from greatest to least are 21,150; 20,890; and 20,650.

TEKS 4.1A use place value to read, write, compare, and order whole numbers through 999,999,999. *also* **4.10, 4.14A, 4.14D, 4.15A, 4.15B**

Example 3 Use place value.

The table shows the number of visitors to Sequoia National Park during three years.

You can order the number of visitors for each year by using a place-value chart.

Order 1,418,519; 1,552,258; and 1,520,835 from least to greatest.

Visitors to Sequoia National Park	
Year	**Number of Visitors**
2002	1,418,519
2003	1,552,258
2004	1,520,835

MILLIONS			THOUSANDS			ONES		
Hundreds	Tens	Ones	Hundreds	Tens	Ones	Hundreds	Tens	Ones
		1,	4	1	8,	5	1	9
		1,	5	5	2,	2	5	8
		1,	5	2	0,	8	3	5

Math Idea
When you compare and order numbers you must begin comparing at the greatest place-value position.

Step 1

Start with the first place on the left. Compare the millions.

1,418,519
↓ $1 = 1$
1,552,258
↓
1,520,835

There are the same number of millions.

Step 2

Compare the hundred thousands.

1,418,519
↓ $4 < 5$
1,552,258
↓
1,520,835

Since $4 < 5$, 1,418,519 is the least of the three numbers.

Step 3

Compare the ten thousands in the other two numbers.

1,552,258
↓ $5 > 2$
1,520,835

Since $5 > 2$, 1,552,258 is greater than 1,520,835.

$1{,}418{,}519 < 1{,}520{,}835 < 1{,}552{,}258$

So, the number of visitors in order from least to greatest are 1,418,519; 1,520,835; and 1,552,258.

- Explain how you would order 102,535,458; 105,236,030; and 120,539,078 from greatest to least.

Guided Practice

1. Use the base-ten blocks to order 1,027; 1,105; and 1,041 from least to greatest.

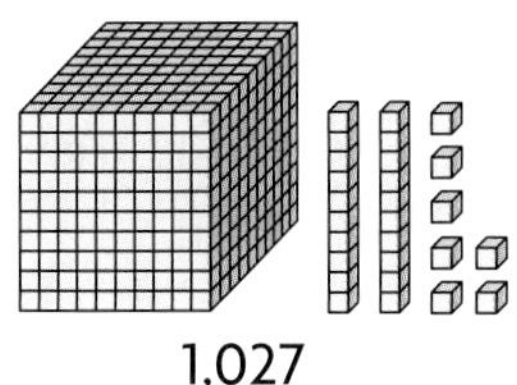
1,027

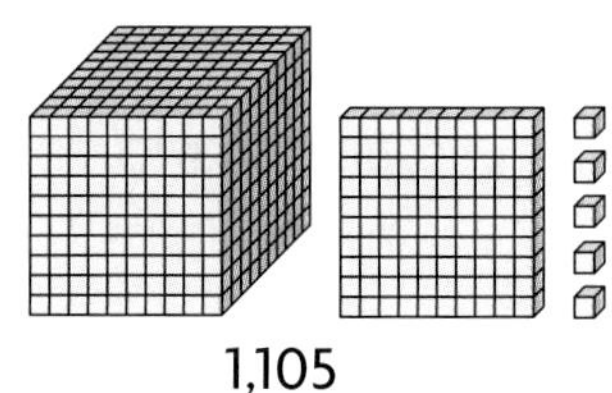
1,105

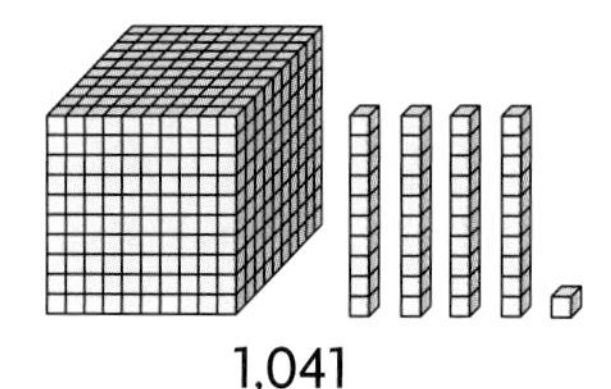
1,041

Solve.

2. Use the number line to order 4,788; 4,793; and 4,784 from least to greatest.

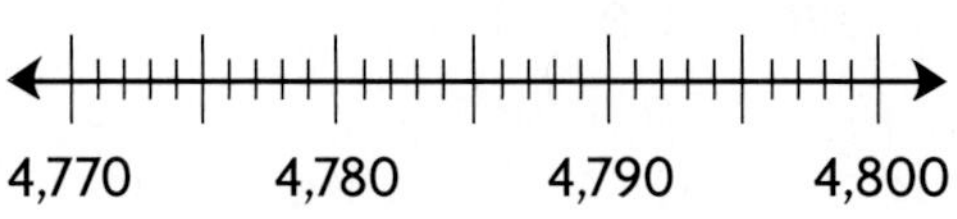

Write the numbers in order from least to greatest.

3. 55,997; 57,000; 56,038

4. 787,925; 1,056,000; 789,100

5. **TALK Math** **Explain** how knowing the number of digits in each number can help you order a set of whole numbers.

Independent Practice and Problem Solving

Write the numbers in order from greatest to least.

6. 8,523; 8,538; 8,519

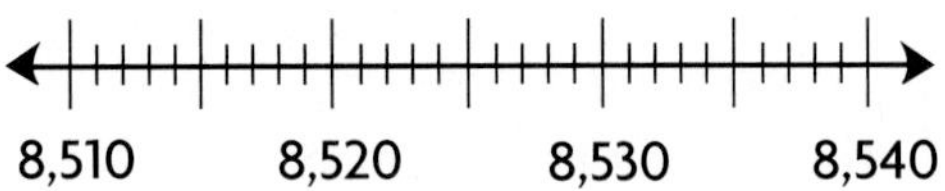

7. 43,050; 42,938; 42,951

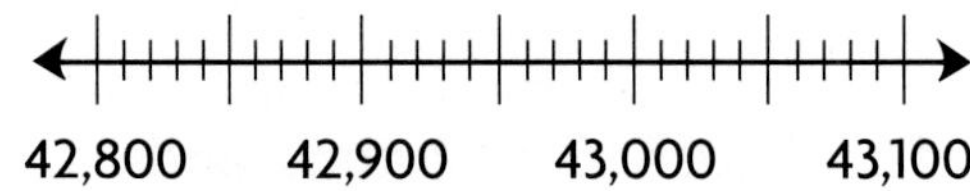

8. 623,096; 68,999; 621,960

9. 3,452,805; 3,542,805; 542,905

10. 7,122,890; 700,122,089; 70,122,098

11. 939,822; 9,398,820; 9,398,802

12. 430,000,459; 43,000,549; 403,000,456

13. 8,778; 870,780; 878,070; 807,870

Algebra **Write all of the digits that can replace each ■.**

14. 567 < 5■5 < 582

15. 3,408 < 3,■30 < 3,540

16. 52,780 > 5■,790 > 50,120

17. 4,464,545 > 4,4■3,535 > 4,443,550

USE DATA For 18–20, use the map.

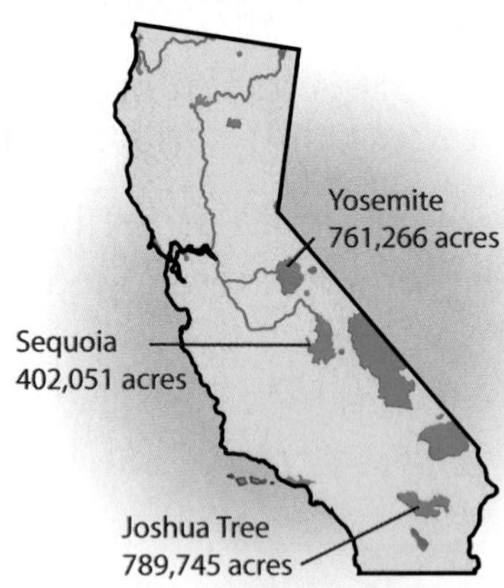

18. Name the national parks in order from least number of acres to greatest number of acres.

19. Which park has less than 500,000 acres?

20. In a comparison of the number of acres in Yosemite National Park and in Joshua Tree National Park, in which place do the digits first differ?

21. **Reasoning** A number has 4 different odd digits. The difference between the greatest digit and the least digit is 6. The number is greater than 2,000 and less than 3,160. What is the number?

22. Janine, Erik, and Mario collect rare coins. Janine has 357 coins, Erik has 361 coins, and Mario has 349 coins. Who has the most coins?

CD ROM **Technology**
Use Harcourt Mega Math, Fraction Action, *Number Line Mine,* Level B.

 Extra Practice on page 24, Set D

23. **WRITE Math** ▸ **What's the Error?** Emma ordered three numbers from least to greatest. Her work is shown at the right. Describe her error. Write the numbers in the correct order.

Emma's Work

3,258
33,438 $6 < 8$
33,246 $3 < 5$

So, from least to greatest, the numbers are 33,246; 3,258; 33,438

24. **WRITE Math** ▸ **What's the Question?** There are three numbers: 643,251; 633,512; and 633,393. The answer is 633,512.

Mixed Review and TAKS Prep

25. What is a name for a polygon with exactly 4 sides? (Grade 3 TEKS 3.8)

26. **TAKS Prep** Which shows the numbers in order from least to greatest? (Obj. 1)

A 102,397; 102,395; 102,359

B 216,001; 216,101; 216,010

C 422,956; 422,596; 422,298

D 575,029; 575,209; 575,290

27. Ellie bought a T-shirt for \$8.95. She paid with a \$10 bill. How much change did she receive? (Grade 3 TEKS 3.1C)

28. **TAKS Prep** Movie theater ticket sales for three days this week were \$4,235; \$6,478; and \$5,049. Which amount is the greatest? (Obj. 1)

Problem Solving and Reasoning

NUMBER SENSE Numbers are used in many ways.

Counting	Measuring	Locating	Labeling
There are 2,256 books.	The room is 14 feet by 12 feet.	Apartment 605 is on the sixth floor.	The number on his soccer jersey is 17.

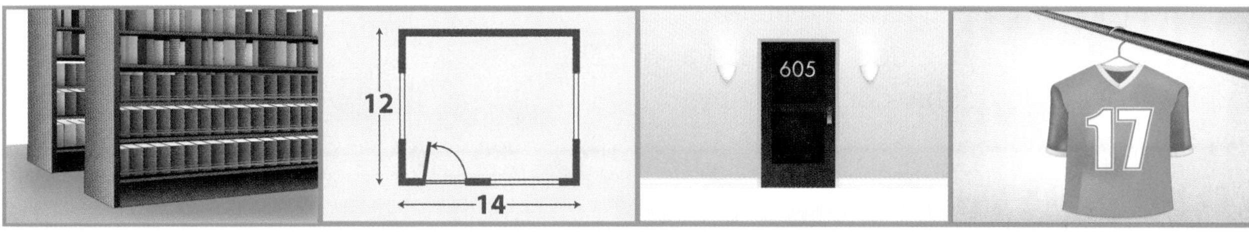

Tell which way each number is used.

1. The lake is 127 feet deep.
2. Ling lives in apartment 533.
3. Max wears the number 34 on his baseball uniform.
4. There were 101,213 fans at a football game.

LESSON 6

Problem Solving Workshop
Strategy: Use Logical Reasoning

OBJECTIVE: Solve problems by using the strategy *use logical reasoning.*

Learn the Strategy

Sometimes a problem has clues that help you find the solution. Organizing the clues can help you use logical reasoning to draw conclusions and solve the problem.

Sometimes, the clues can be organized in a list.

Kari, Nora, and June are the only runners in a race. June finishes before Nora. Kari is not last. June is not first.

In what position did each runner finish?

1st	2ND	3rd
Kari	~~Kari~~	~~Kari~~
~~Nora~~	~~Nora~~	Nora
~~June~~	June	~~June~~

Sometimes, the clues can be organized in a Venn diagram.

Ben is thinking of a number from 45 to 60. The sum of the digits is greater than 10. The product of the digits is less than 30.

What number is Ben thinking of?

Sum of Digits >10 | Product of Digits <30

Sum of Digits >10 only: 59, 58, 48, 49, 56, 57

Both: 47

Product of Digits <30 only: 53, 52, 60, 54, 51, 55, 50, 46, 45

Sometimes, the clues can be organized in a table.

Max, Anya, and Troy each have a different kind of pet. The pets are a dog, a cat, and a fish. Troy's pet does not bark or swim. Anya does not have a dog.

What pet does each person have?

	Dog	Cat	Fish
Max	Yes	No	No
Anya	No	No	Yes
Troy	No	Yes	No

TALK Math

Look at the third problem. Which boxes can be filled in using only the clue about Troy's pet? Explain.

TEKS 4.1A use place value to read, write, compare, and order whole numbers through 999,999,999. *also* **4.14B, 4.14C, 4.15A, 4.15B, 4.16B**

Use the Strategy

PROBLEM Baseball games were played on Friday, Saturday, and Sunday. The number of people who attended were 32,431; 44,462; and 44,064. The greatest number of people attended Saturday's game. Fewer than 40,000 people attended Sunday's game. How many people attended each day?

Read to Understand
Plan
Solve
Check

Read to Understand

- **Use a graphic aid to organize the clues.**
- **What information is given?**

Plan

- **What strategy can you use to solve the problem?**

  You can use logical reasoning.

Solve

- **How can you use the strategy to solve the problem?**

  Look at one clue at a time. Make a table to record the information you know, and draw conclusions.

	32,431	44,462	44,064
Friday			
Saturday			
Sunday			

  The greatest number of people went to Saturday's game. The greatest number in the problem is 44,462. So, write yes in Saturday's row for 44,462. Write no in the rest of the row for Saturday and the rest of the column for 44,462.

	32,431	44,462	44,064
Friday		No	
Saturday	No	Yes	No
Sunday		No	

  Fewer than 40,000 people went to Sunday's game. The only number that is less than 40,000 is 32,431. Write yes in Sunday's row for 32,431 and no in the rest of that row and column.

  That leaves one number for Friday, 44,064. Write yes in the table to show this.

	32,431	44,462	44,064
Friday	No	No	Yes
Saturday	No	Yes	No
Sunday	Yes	No	No

  So, 44,064 people went to Friday's game; 44,462 people went to Saturday's game; and 32,431 people went to Sunday's game.

Check

- **Look back at the problem. Do your work and your answer make sense? Explain.**

Guided Problem Solving

1. Ed, Nick, Sandra, and Ty collect baseball cards. Ed has less than 500 cards. Sandra has more than 700 cards. Nick has more cards than Sandra. How many baseball cards does each person have?

   First, make a table like the one shown to organize the information given in the problem.

   Then, use the information given in the problem to complete the table.

   Finally, use logical reasoning to answer the question.

	447	568	703	764
Ed	Yes	No	No	No
Nick	No			
Sandra	No			
Ty	No			

2. Leena, Theo, Chris, Ann, and Bob are waiting in line for hockey tickets. Leena is not first or last. Theo is behind Leena but is not last. Chris is in front of Leena. Ann is behind Bob. In what order are they standing in line?

3. **What if** a basketball team has a score that is a 2-digit number. The sum of the digits is 8. The difference between the digits is 2. The tens digit is less than the ones digit. What is the score?

Problem Solving Strategy Practice

Use logical reasoning to solve.

4. Copy and complete the magic square. Each row and column should have a sum of 12.

2	■	7
■	■	0
■	1	■

5. Look at the record crowds list. Richard forgot to write the name of the sport for each crowd. Use these clues to decide what the record crowd is for each sport.

   - Football did not have the smallest record crowd.
   - Soccer's record crowd is greater than 150,000 people.

Record Crowds at a Single Football Game, Baseball Game, and Soccer Game
199,854 people
103,985 people
92,706 people

6. WRITE Math Will, Rachel, Owen, and Kara are standing in line to enter the stadium to watch a track meet. Will is in front of Owen. Owen is last in line. Rachel is first. Kara is after Rachel. In what order are they standing in line? **Explain.**

Mixed Strategy Practice

USE DATA For 7–9, use the information about sports collectors' items shown in the art.

7. Mr. Clay, Mr. Juarez, and Ms. Michaels buy the Annika Sorenstam golf ball, the Tom Brady Super Bowl football, and the Larry Bird signed basketball. Mr. Juarez spends less than $300. Mr. Clay spends more than Ms. Michaels does. Which item does each person buy?

8. **Pose a Problem** Look back at Problem 7. Change the items that Mr. Clay wants to buy.

9. **Open-Ended** Mr. Krauss bought a Sandy Koufax baseball card for $135. He used $20-bills, $10-bills, and $5-bills to make exactly $135. The total number of bills that Mr. Krauss used is fewer than 12. What combination of bills might Mr. Krauss have used?

10. Tina saves money to buy a baseball card that costs $30. After 2 weeks, she has $10. After 3 weeks, she has $15. After 4 weeks, she has $20. How long do you think it will take her to save $30?

Choose a STRATEGY

- Draw a Diagram or Picture
- Make a Model or Act It Out
- Make an Organized List
- Look for a Pattern
- Make a Table or Graph
- Guess and Check
- Work Backward
- Solve a Simpler Problem
- Write an Equation
- Use Logical Reasoning

Babe Ruth signed baseball
Price: $38,157
Wayne Gretzky Hockey Puck
Price: $494
Mickey Mantle game bat
Price: $37,604
Annika Sorenstam golf ball
Price: $287
Larry Bird signed basketball
Price: $326
Tom Brady signed Super Bowl XXIX football
Price: $499

CHALLENGE YOURSELF

More kids than ever before are playing sports. For example, in 2005, an average of 17,500,000 kids were playing soccer, 204,000 were playing lacrosse, and 2,200,000 kids were playing baseball.

11. Mariah plays lacrosse. Compared to soccer and baseball, is she part of a group that has the most kids participating or the least?

12. George is writing down the number of kids that participate in each type of sport. He wrote down the number for football incorrectly. He knows that the number is less than the numbers for soccer and baseball, but more than the number for lacrosse. Could the number be 200,600 or 260,000? **Explain** how you know.

Extra Practice

Set A Write each number in two other forms. (pp. 4–7)

1. $700,000 + 3,000 + 600 + 4$
2. 27,683
3. seventy-six thousand, four hundred thirty-two
4. eight hundred ninety-one thousand, two hundred fifty
5. 116,508,906
6. $60,000 + 800 + 90$

Set B Use the number 827,916,401. (pp. 10–11)

1. Write the name of the period that has the digits 827.
2. Write the name of the period that has the digits 916.
3. Write the digit in the ten millions place.
4. Write the digit in the thousands place.
5. Write the value of the digit 8.
6. Write the value of the digit 9.

Set C Compare. Write <, >, or = for each ●. (pp. 12–15)

1. 1,409 ● 1,389
2. 6,794 ● 8,005
3. 56,006 ● 56,006
4. 37,106 ● 37,008
5. 10,006 ● 2,789
6. 6,807,043 ● 6,870,034
7. 4,345,119 ● 535,119
8. 88,416 ● 101,871,415
9. 2,124,156 ● 1,124,156
10. Doug's family drove 768 miles on Saturday and 524 miles on Sunday. On which day did they drive farther?
11. During the school book fair, 1,123 books were sold the first week and 1,032 books were sold the second week. During which week were fewer books sold?

Set D Write the numbers in order from least to greatest. (pp. 16–19)

1. 48,004; 48,040; 40,804
2. 30,004; 3,074; 3,704
3. 90,654; 900,645; 9,998
4. 603,086; 68,306; 68,360
5. 221,829,459; 283,000; 2,820,999
6. 5,408,517; 5,460,500; 4,558,590
7. Sales at Toy Mart for three days this week were \$2,571; \$1,897; and \$3,342. Which amount is the greatest?
8. Theater attendance for performances on Friday was 16,207 people, for Saturday was 28,771 people, and for Sunday was 16,270 people. On which day was attendance the least?

Technology
Use Harcourt Mega Math, The Number Games, *Number Line Mine,* Levels A, B.

Climb the Math Mountain

Who's Climbing

2 or 3 players

Get Your Climbing Gear!

- Number cards (0–9, three of each)
- Coins (a different kind of coin for each player)
- Paper

Start Climbing!

- Each player draws 6 horizontal lines on a sheet of paper. Each line needs to be long enough to fit a number card on it.
- Each player selects a different kind of coin and places the coin on CAMP 1. Players shuffle the number cards and place them facedown in a stack.
- The object of the game is to make the greatest number. Players take turns drawing a card and placing it on one of his or her 6 lines until each player has made a 6-digit number.
- Once a player has placed a number card on a line, it cannot be moved.
- The player with the greatest number moves his or her coin up the mountain to the next camp. If the numbers are the same, each player moves to the next camp.
- Players return the number cards to the stack, shuffle them, and repeat the steps to play another round.
- The first player to reach CAMP 7 wins.

Chapter 1 Review/Test

Check Vocabulary and Concepts

Choose the best term from the box.

VOCABULARY
expanded form
million
period

1. One _?_ is equal to 10 hundred thousands. (TEKS 4.1A, p. 9)
2. In 549,167,001 the digits 1, 6, and 7 are in the same _?_. (TEKS 4.1A, p. 5)

Check Skills

Write each number in two other forms. (TEKS 4.1A, pp. 4–7, 10–11)

3. two hundred thirty-four thousand, one hundred forty-six
4. 78,091
5. 30,000,000 + 600,000 + 8,000 + 500 + 7
6. fifty-three million, seven hundred thousand, eighty
7. 702,655
8. 1,000,000 + 40,000 + 1,000 + 30

Write the value of the underlined digit in each number. (TEKS 4.1A, pp. 4–7, 10–11)

9. $90,\underline{6}59$
10. $\underline{5}01,462$
11. $4,\underline{7}15,001$
12. $80\underline{4},183,712$
13. $\underline{3}42,500,654$

Compare. Write <, >, or = for each ●. (TEKS 4.1A, pp. 12–15)

14. 27,985 ● 28,064
15. 523,406 ● 523,406
16. 3,416,125 ● 3,408,926

Write numbers in order from least to greatest. (TEKS 4.1A, pp. 16–19)

17. 207,409; 270,210,009; 27,420
18. 7,029,400; 6,258,414; 6,285,484

Check Problem Solving

Solve. (TEKS 4.14C, pp. 20–23)

19. George is thinking of a number between 70 and 90. The sum of the digits is less than 12. The product of the digits is greater than 25. What is George's number?
20. **WRITE Math** Matt and 3 friends played an electronic game. Their scores are shown at the right. Tina had more than 10,000 points. Rosa had more points than Tina. Sam had less than 5,000 points. How many points did each friend have? **Show** a table or an organized list that supports your solution.

GO ONLINE **Technology** Use *Online Assessment.*

Enrich • Numbers in Other Cultures

Numeration Systems

Our numeration system uses Arabic numerals, or digits 0–9, and is based on groupings of ten. Some ancient cultures had numeration systems that used other numerals or symbols to represent numbers. The table below compares Arabic, Roman, and Egyptian numerals.

Arabic	0	1	2	3	4	5	6	7	8	9	10	50	100	500	1000
Roman		I	II	III	IV	V	VI	VII	VIII	IX	X	L	C	D	M
Egyptian		I	II	III	II II	III II	III III	IIII III	IIII IIII	IIIII IIII	𓎆		𓍢		𓆼

To write Roman numerals as Arabic numerals:

- Add if the values of the symbols are the same or if they decrease from left to right. A symbol cannot repeat more than 3 times.
- Subtract if a symbol's value is less than the value of the symbol to its right.

Examples

A Write CXIII in Arabic numerals.

Think: C represents 100, X represents 10, and each I represents 1.

So, CXIII is 100 + 10 + 1 + 1 + 1, or 113.

B Write MCD in Arabic numerals.

Think: M represents 1,000, C represents 100, and D represents 500.

Since C < D, CD is 500 − 100, or 400. So, MCD is 1,000 + 400, or 1,400.

To write Egyptian numerals as Arabic numerals: Find the sum of the symbols.

C Write 𓆼𓍢𓍢III in Arabic numerals.

Think: 𓆼 represents 1,000, 𓍢 represents 100, and I represents 1.

So, 𓆼𓍢𓍢III is 1,000 + 100 + 100 + 1 + 1 + 1, or 1,203.

D Write 𓆼𓆼𓎆𓎆𓎆𓎆𓎆𓎆 in Arabic numerals.

Think: 𓆼 represents 1,000, and 𓎆 represents 10.

So, 𓆼𓆼𓎆𓎆𓎆𓎆𓎆𓎆 is 1,000 + 1,000 + 10 + 10 + 10 + 10 + 10 + 10, or 2,060.

Try It

Write Roman numerals as Arabic numerals.

1. LXXXVIII **2.** CCXCV **3.** MCMXIV **4.** MMDCIX

Write Egyptian numerals as Arabic numerals.

5. 𓎆III **6.** 𓍢𓍢𓍢𓎆𓎆IIIIII **7.** 𓍢𓍢𓍢𓍢𓍢𓍢𓍢𓍢𓍢𓎆𓎆𓎆𓎆𓎆IIIIIII **8.** 𓆼𓆼𓍢𓍢𓍢𓍢𓎆𓎆𓎆𓎆𓎆𓎆𓎆

WRITE Math ▸ **Explain** the advantages in writing numbers using the Arabic numeration system compared with using the Roman and Egyptian numeration systems.

Getting Ready for the TAKS
Chapter 1

Number, Operation, and Quantitative Reasoning TAKS Obj. 1

1. In 2002, the number of cats in the United States was about seventy-six million, four hundred thirty thousand. What is this number in standard form?

   A 76,430 **C** 76,430,000

   B 76,000,430 **D** 760,430,000

Test Tip **Understand the problem.**

See item 2. Be sure you understand what the problem asks. Item 2 asks you to find a set of numbers that is in order from *greatest to least*. So, a list that is in order from least to greatest would be incorrect.

2. Which set of numbers is in order from greatest to least?

   F 736,849; 739,489; 1,725,089

   G 1,725,089; 739,489; 736,849

   H 1,725,089; 736,849; 739,489

   I 739,489; 736,849; 1,725,089

3. Which of these is the number 305,082?

   A $300,000 + 50,000 + 800 + 2$

   B $300,000 + 50,000 + 80 + 2$

   C $30,000 + 5,000 + 800 + 2$

   D $300,000 + 5,000 + 80 + 2$

4. **WRITE Math** Wendy says that 235,340 is exactly 1,000 less than 245,340. Do you agree? **Explain** how you know.

Patterns, Relationships, and Algebraic Thinking TAKS Obj. 2

5. The table below shows the number of players needed to make a certain number of volleyball teams.

Volleyball				
Number of Teams	1	2	3	4
Number of Players	6	12	18	24

   How many players would be needed to make 8 volleyball teams?

   F 6 **H** 36

   G 32 **J** 48

6. Which multiplication sentence is related to this division sentence?

   $$12 \div 4 = \blacksquare$$

   A $3 \times 12 = \blacksquare$

   B $3 \times 4 = \blacksquare$

   C $4 \times 12 = \blacksquare$

   D $4 \times 8 = \blacksquare$

7. If 2 insects have 8 legs and 4 insects have 16 legs, how many legs do 8 insects have?

   F 32 **H** 20

   G 24 **J** 16

8. **WRITE Math** **Explain** how you can find the tenth term in this number pattern.

   2, 5, 8, 11, 14, 17

Geometry and Spatial Reasoning TAKS Obj. 3

9. Which figure is a pentagon?

A 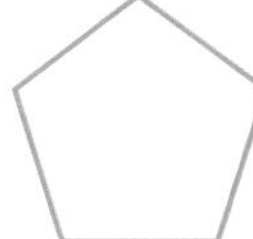

B 

C 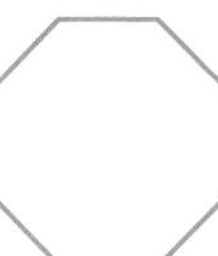

D 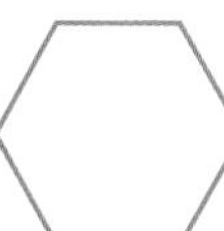

10. What number is represented by *P* on the number line?

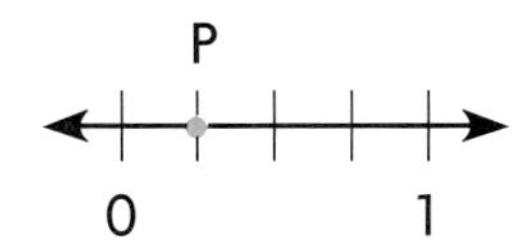

F $\frac{1}{4}$

G $\frac{2}{4}$

H $\frac{3}{4}$

J 1

11. **WRITE Math** Do these triangles appear to be congruent? **Explain** how you know.

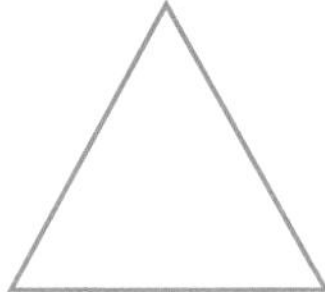 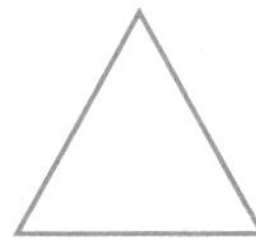

Probability and Statistics TAKS Obj. 5

12. The bar graph shows the number of books Enrique read during the past three months.

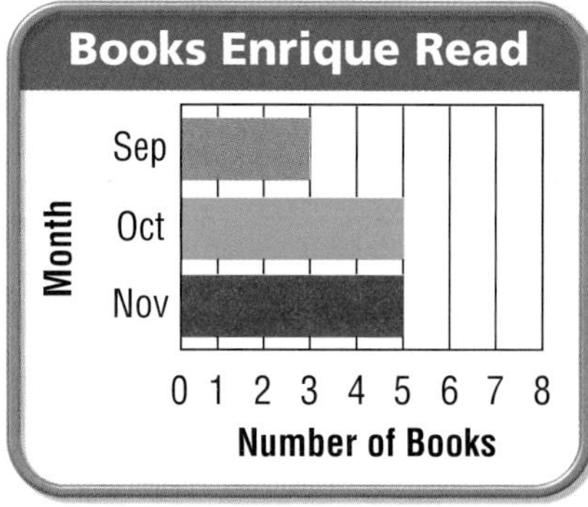

How many books did Enrique read in the three months altogether?

A 3 **B** 5 **C** 8 **D** 13

13. Look at the pictograph.

Spinner Experiment	
Red	○○○○
Yellow	○○○
Blue	○○○○○○
Key: Each ○ = 3 spins.	

How many times did the pointer stop on blue?

F 6 **G** 12 **H** 18 **J** 24

14. **WRITE Math** A bag has 3 yellow marbles, 4 red marbles, and 2 blue marbles of the same size. Which term best describes the probability of pulling a blue marble from the bag—*more likely than*, *less likely than*, or *equally likely as*? **Explain** your answer.

2 Add and Subtract Whole Numbers

The Big Idea Addition and subtraction of multi-digit numbers is based on single digit addition and subtraction facts and base ten and place value concepts.

TEXAS FAST FACT

The San Antonio River is about 180 miles long. It flows into the Guadalupe River. In San Antonio, you can take a 35-minute boat tour of 2 to 3 miles of the river.

Investigate

You can buy tickets for River Walk boat tours at 3 different ticket stations. Use the data in the table to write a daily tourist report. In your tourist report, estimate the differences to compare the numbers of tickets bought at all the stations on Monday and Tuesday.

San Antonio River Walk Boat Tour

Ticket Station	Tickets Bought on Monday	Tickets Bought on Tuesday
Historia	1,986	2,314
Clearwater	1,631	1,787
Fiesta	198	245

Technology
Student pages are available in the Student eBook.

Show What You Know

Check your understanding of important skills needed for success in Chapter 2.

Regroup Tens as Hundreds

Regroup. Write the missing numbers.

1. 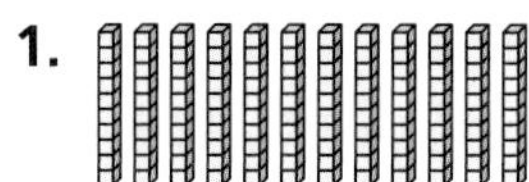

12 tens = ■ hundred ■ tens

2. 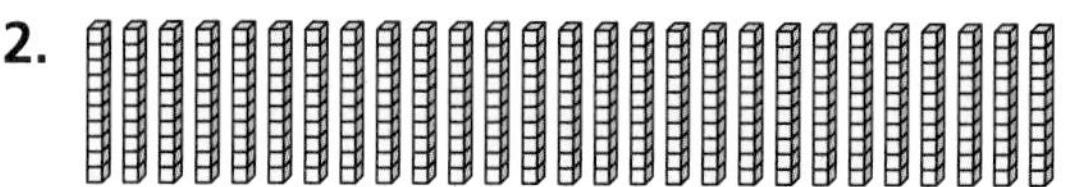

27 tens = ■ hundreds ■ tens

Regroup Hundreds as Tens

Regroup. Write the missing numbers.

3. 2 hundreds = ■ tens

4. 3 hundreds = ■ tens

5. 1 hundred 1 ten = ■ tens

Two-Digit Addition and Subtraction

Find the sum or difference.

6. 23 + 46 **7.** 67 − 35 **8.** 13 + 28 **9.** 41 − 17 **10.** 61 − 40

11. $\begin{array}{r} 29 \\ +\ 57 \\ \hline \end{array}$ **12.** $\begin{array}{r} 31 \\ +\ 49 \\ \hline \end{array}$ **13.** $\begin{array}{r} 52 \\ +\ 36 \\ \hline \end{array}$ **14.** $\begin{array}{r} 87 \\ -\ 28 \\ \hline \end{array}$ **15.** $\begin{array}{r} 73 \\ -\ 24 \\ \hline \end{array}$

VOCABULARY POWER

CHAPTER VOCABULARY

compatible numbers
difference
estimate
fact family
inverse operations
pattern
round
sum

WARM-UP WORDS

inverse operations Operations that undo each other. Addition and subtraction are inverse operations.

fact family a set of related addition and subtraction equations

round to replace a number with another number that tells about how many or how much

ALGEBRA

Relate Addition and Subtraction

OBJECTIVE: Use the inverse relationship between addition and subtraction to solve problems.

Quick Review

1. 9 + 4 = ■
2. 12 − 6 = ■
3. 7 + 8 = ■
4. 11 − 4 = ■
5. 5 + 8 = ■

Vocabulary

inverse operations

fact family

Learn

PROBLEM Justin can do 8 pull-ups in a row. His older brother Marcus can do 15 pull-ups in a row. How many more pull-ups can Marcus do than Justin?

Addition and subtraction are opposites, or **inverse operations**. One operation undoes the other. A set of related addition and subtraction sentences using the same numbers is a **fact family**.

Example Use the inverse operation and a related fact.

Subtract. 15 − 8

Think: 8 + ■ = 15

Use a fact family to solve the problem.

8 + 7 = 15, so 15 − 8 = 7.

Math Idea
You can use inverse operations and related facts to check answers to problems.

So, Marcus can do 7 more pull-ups than Justin.

- What are the facts in the fact family for 7, 8, and 15?

More Examples Find the missing number.

A Use related facts.

13 − ■ = 4

Think: 13 − 4 = ■

13 − 4 = 9, so 13 − 9 = 4.

B Use inverse operations.

■ − 5 = 6

Think: 5 + 6 = ■

5 + 6 = 11, so 11 − 5 = 6.

- What operation can you use to solve the problem ■ + 8 = 12? Explain.

Guided Practice

1. Keisha did 8 more push-ups than Tara did. Keisha did 17 push-ups. How many push-ups did Tara do? Copy and complete the related addition fact. Then use it to solve the problem.

17 − 8 = ■

8 + ■ = 17

TEKS 4.3A use addition and subtraction to solve problems involving whole numbers. *also* **4.7, 4.14A, 4.15A, 4.15B**

Write a related fact. Use it to complete the number sentence.

2. $14 - \blacksquare = 8$ 3. $5 + \blacksquare = 12$ ✓4. $\blacksquare - 9 = 6$ ✓5. $\blacksquare + 4 = 11$

6. TALK Math **Explain** why the fact family with the numbers 8 and 16 only has two number sentences instead of four.

Independent Practice and Problem Solving

Write a related fact. Use it to complete the number sentence.

7. $11 - \blacksquare = 7$ 8. $\blacksquare + 7 = 13$ 9. $8 + \blacksquare = 12$ 10. $\blacksquare + 5 = 11$

11. $\blacksquare - 9 = 8$ 12. $6 + \blacksquare = 12$ 13. $10 - \blacksquare = 7$ 14. $\blacksquare - 3 = 8$

15. $\blacksquare - 4 = 8$ 16. $3 + \blacksquare = 9$ 17. $11 - \blacksquare = 2$ 18. $\blacksquare + 4 = 13$

Write the fact family for each set of numbers.

19. 4, 7, 11 20. 5, 5, 10 21. 6, 7, 13 22. 3, 9, 12

For 23–24, use the pictograph.

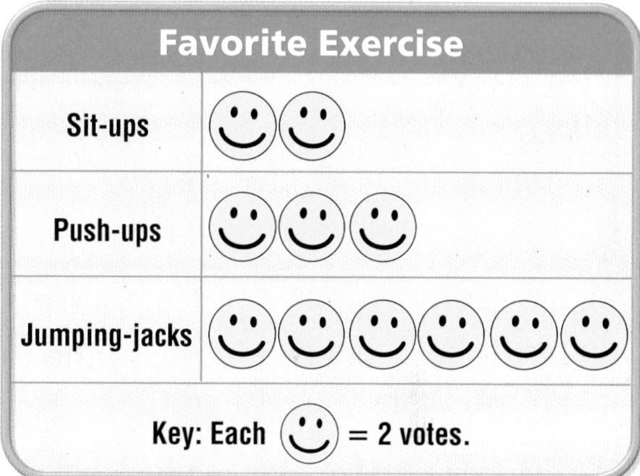

23. How many more votes did jumping-jacks get than push-ups? What related facts can you use to solve this problem?

24. If sit-ups gets 4 more votes, how many votes will sit-ups and push-ups have in all?

25. WRITE Math **What's the Error?** Jan was asked to write a related fact for $7 + 4 = 11$. She wrote $7 - 4 = 3$. **Explain** why Jan's answer is incorrect. What is the correct answer?

Mixed Review and TAKS Prep

26. A newspaper ad showed these prices: mini-van: \$30,010; truck: \$29,998; sports car: \$30,100. List the prices in order from least to most expensive. (TEKS 4.1A, p. 16)

27. Chan's website had 2,014 visitors and Lori's website had 1,987. Sheila's website had more visitors than Lori's, but fewer than Chan's. What are five possible numbers of visitors Sheila's website could have had? (TEKS 4.1A, p. 16)

28. **TAKS Prep** Which of the following sets of numbers cannot be used to make a fact family? (Obj.1)

A 8, 9, 17

B 1, 3, 5

C 7, 7, 14

D 2, 7, 9

Extra Practice on page 60, Set A

2 Round Whole Numbers to the Nearest 10, 100, and 1,000

OBJECTIVE: Round whole numbers to the nearest 10, 100, or 1,000.

Quick Review

Write the value of the underlined digit.

1. 234 (underlined: 3)
2. 1,547 (underlined: 1)
3. 25,652 (underlined: 2)
4. 356,721 (underlined: 6)
5. 1,756,432 (underlined: 4)

Vocabulary

round

Learn

PROBLEM In 2002, Texas welcomed 88,365 immigrants from around the world. A Texas newspaper stated that Texas welcomed about 80,000 immigrants. Is the newspaper's estimate reasonable?

When you **round** a number, you replace it with a number that tells about how many or about how much. Rounded numbers are often easier to compute. Round 88,365 to the nearest thousand.

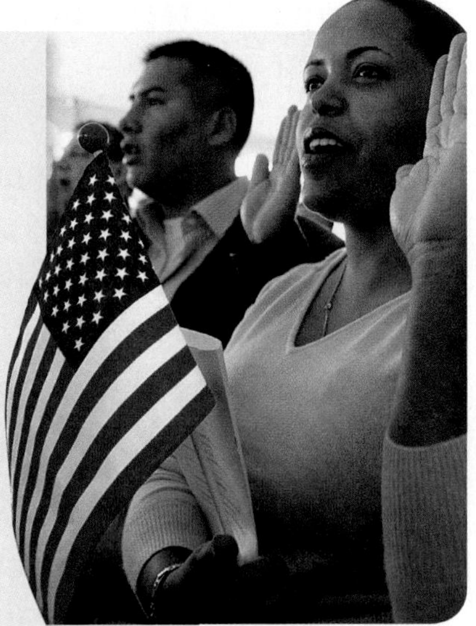

ONE WAY **Use a number line.**

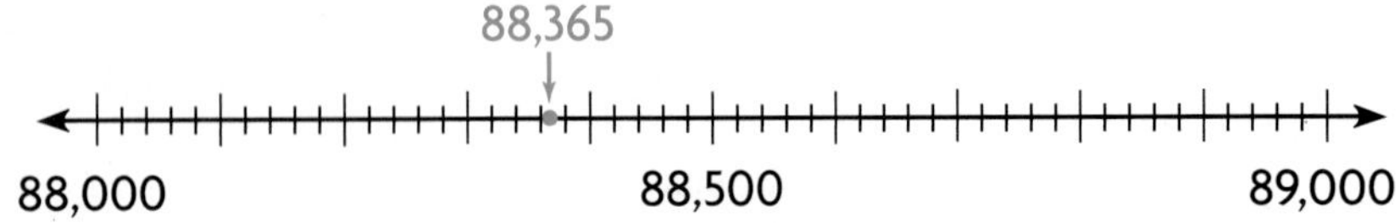

Think: 88,365 is between 88,000 and 89,000. 88,365 is closer to 88,000 than to 89,000.

So, 88,365 rounded to the nearest thousand is 88,000. 88,000 is not close to 80,000, so the newspaper's estimate is not reasonable.

ANOTHER WAY **Use place value to round numbers.**

Round 88,365 to the nearest hundred.

- Find the place to which you want to round.
- Look at the digit to the right. If the digit to the right is *less than 5*, the digit in the rounding place stays the same. If the digit to the right is *5 or greater*, the digit in the rounding place increases by 1.
- Change all the digits to the right of the rounding place to zero.

place to be rounded to – hundreds

↓

88,365

↓

88,365

The digit in the tens place is 6. Since $6 > 5$, the digit 3 increases by 1.

$88,365 \rightarrow 88,400$

So, 88,365 rounded to the nearest hundred is 88,400.

- When might you use rounded numbers instead of exact numbers? Explain.

TEKS 4.5A round whole numbers to the nearest ten, hundred, or thousand to approximate reasonable results in problem situations. *also* **4.10A, 4.14A, 4.15A, 4.15B**

Example

The table shows distances immigrants may travel to Houston, Texas, from different cities around the world. About how far do immigrants from London and Frankfurt travel to Houston?

Distances Immigrants Travel to Houston, Texas	
From	**Distance (in miles)**
Bangkok, Thailand	9,253
Frankfurt, Germany	5,245
London, England	4,860
New Delhi, India	8,366
Tel Aviv, Israel	7,079
Tokyo, Japan	6,682

Round the distances below to the nearest thousand miles.

London to Houston 4,860 → 5,000

Frankfurt to Houston 5,245 → 5,000

So, immigrants from London and Frankfurt travel about 5,000 miles to Houston.

More Examples

A Round to the nearest thousand.

45,278 is between 45,000 and 46,000.

place to be rounded to ↓

45,278

Look at the hundreds digit. Since 2 < 5, the digit 5 stays the same.

So, 45,278 rounded to the nearest thousand is 45,000.

B Round to the nearest hundred.

7,832 is between 7,800 and 7,900.

place to be rounded to ↓

7,832

Look at the tens digit. Since 3 < 5, the digit 8 stays the same.

So, 7,832 rounded to the nearest hundred is 7,800.

C Round to the nearest ten.

145,278 is between 145,270 and 145,280.

place to be rounded to ↓

145,278

Look at the ones digit. Since 8 > 5, the digit 7 increases by 1.

So, 145,278 rounded to the nearest ten is 145,280.

D Round to the nearest ten dollars.

$697 is between $690 and $700.

place to be rounded to ↓

$697

Look at the ones digit. Since 7 > 5, the digit 9 increases by 1. Regroup 10 tens as 1 hundred.

So, $697 rounded to the nearest ten dollars is $700.

- How does understanding place value help you round numbers?

ERROR ALERT

When you round a 9 to the next greater digit, remember to regroup to the next greater place value.

Guided Practice

1. In 2002, a total of 71,105 immigrants came to the United States from India. Use the number line to round this number to the nearest hundred.

71,105

71,100 71,150 71,200

Round each number to the place value of the underlined digit.

2. 4,567 3. 3,476,321 4. $234 ✓5. 3,476,321

Round each number to the nearest ten, hundred, and thousand.

6. 7,809 7. 39,365 8. 442,896 ✓9. 8,851,342

10. **TALK Math** **Describe** all the numbers that, when rounded to the nearest thousand, are 312,000.

Independent Practice and Problem Solving

Round each number to the place value of the underlined digit.

11. 3,769 12. 7,507 13. 374,156 14. 1,715,149

15. 5,645,408 16. 4,792,300 17. $921 18. $99,814

Round each number to the nearest ten, hundred, and thousand.

19. 4,683 20. 1,169 21. 26,431 22. 475,435

23. 1,943,232 24. 7,899,161 25. 3,346,561 26. 6,374,233

27. Write five numbers that round to 4,000.

28. What is the greatest whole number that rounds to 3,000? What is the least?

29. **Reasoning** Write three numbers that round to 570 when rounded to the nearest ten and to 600 when rounded to the nearest hundred.

30. **FAST FACT** In 2002, Michigan had 21,787 immigrants. Round this number to the nearest thousand and the nearest ten thousand. Which rounded number is closer to the original number?

USE DATA For 31–33, use the table.

31. Is the number of immigrants from China closer to 61,000 or 62,000?

32. Round the number of immigrants from Mexico to the nearest thousand.

33. From which country did the fewest immigrants come?

34. Euro's answer rounds to 7,000. Write three numbers that could be his exact answer.

35. **WRITE Math** **Explain** how to round 982 to the nearest hundred.

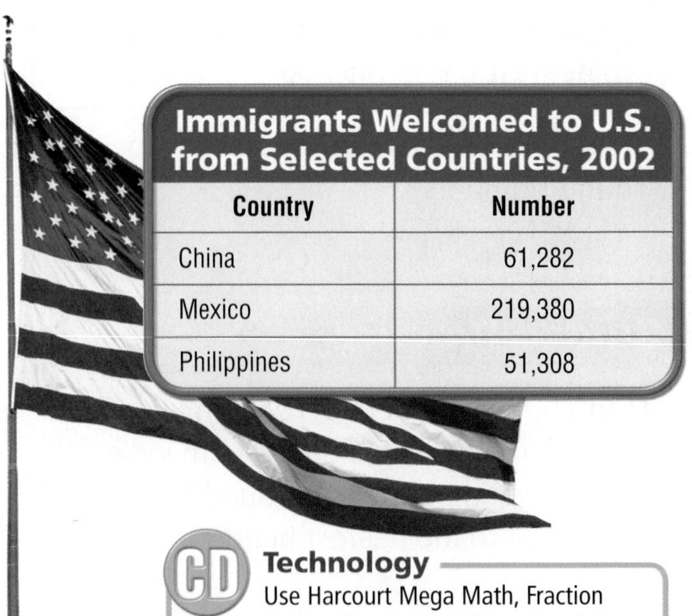

Immigrants Welcomed to U.S. from Selected Countries, 2002

Country	Number
China	61,282
Mexico	219,380
Philippines	51,308

CD ROM **Technology** Use Harcourt Mega Math, Fraction Action, *Number Line Mine*, Level C.

 Extra Practice on page 60, Set B

Mixed Review and TAKS Prep

36. Write two million, twenty thousand, two hundred ninety-seven in standard form. (TEKS 4.1A, p. 10)

37. TAKS Prep Mae's family drove about 25,000 miles last year. Which could be the exact number of miles they drove? (Obj. 1)

A 25,813 miles
B 25,502 miles
C 24,538 miles
D 24,489 miles

38. Write a related number sentence and use it to find the missing number. (TEKS 4.7, p. 32)
$15 - \blacksquare = 7$

39. TAKS Prep Jai's younger brother erased part of Jai's homework. He knows that his number rounds to 5,800. What is the missing digit? 5,■85 (Obj. 1)

Problem Solving and Reasoning

NUMBER SENSE Sometimes rounded numbers are used because you do not need to know exact amounts or quantities. At other times, the exact amounts cannot be counted or measured, or they may change often. Which numbers in the paragraph below are rounded?

The Ellis Island Immigration Museum is open between 9:30 A.M. and 5:00 P.M. Almost 2,000,000 people visit the museum each year. Many visitors take guided tours that last about 50 minutes. There are 3 floors of exhibits at the museum.
Think: Words like *almost* and *about* tell you that a number is not an exact amount.

So, the numbers 2,000,000 and 50 are rounded because they may change often.

Identify any rounded numbers. Explain why you think exact numbers are not used.

1. The museum has taped more than 1,300 interviews with immigrants who passed through Ellis Island. The oldest person interviewed was 106 years old, and the youngest was 46.
2. A ferry ride to Ellis Island costs $11.50 for adults and children 13 and older, $9.50 for seniors, and $4.50 for children 4–12. The ferry ride takes about 10 minutes. Don's mother has $60 to buy ferry tickets for 5 people.

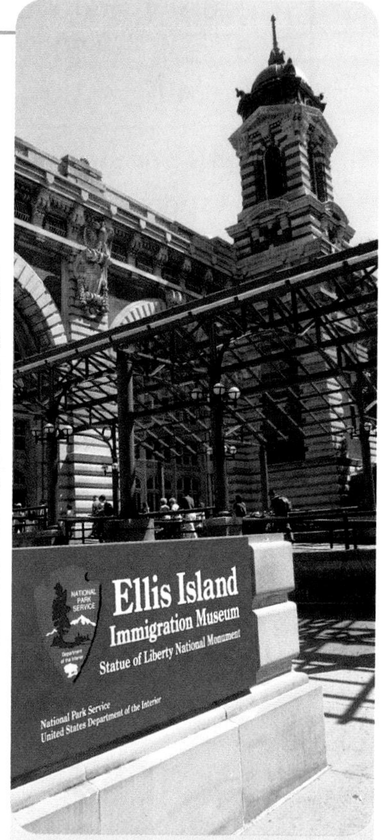

▲ Between 1892 and 1954, about 12,000,000 immigrants entered the U.S. through Ellis Island.

LESSON 3

MENTAL MATH

Addition and Subtraction Patterns

OBJECTIVE: Identify and use patterns in addition and subtraction.

Quick Review

1. 5 + 8
2. 16 − 9
3. 3 + 9
4. 12 − 6
5. 9 + 7

Learn

PROBLEM The table shows the approximate numbers of plant and animal species in the United States that are threatened, or in danger of becoming extinct. About how many plant and animal species are endangered in all?

Endangered Plant and Animal Species in the United States

Type of Species	Approximate Number
Animals	400
Plants	600

It is easy to mentally add or subtract tens, hundreds, thousands, and ten thousands if you use basic facts and a pattern.

Example Add. 600 + 400

6 + 4 = 10 — 6 ones + 4 ones = 10 ones ← basic fact

60 + 40 = 100 — 6 tens + 4 tens = 10 tens

600 + 400 = 1,000 — 6 hundreds + 4 hundreds = 10 hundreds

So, there are about 1,000 threatened or endangered plant and animal species in the United States.

- What pattern do you see in the number sentences above?

Math Idea

As the number of zeros being added increases, the number of zeros in the sum increases. The same is true when you subtract.

More Examples Use a basic fact and a pattern.

A

14 − 6 = 8 ← basic fact

140 − 60 = 80

1,400 − 600 = 800

14,000 − 6,000 = 8,000

B

5 + 5 = 10 ← basic fact

50 + 50 = 100

500 + 500 = 1,000

5,000 + 5,000 = 10,000

Guided Practice

1. Write a basic fact that can help you subtract 300 from 1,000 mentally. Use it and a pattern to solve the problem. 1,000 − 300 = ■

Use mental math to complete the pattern.

2. 5 + 8 = 13
50 + 80 = ■
500 + 800 = ■

3. 12 − 6 = ■
120 − 60 = ■
1,200 − 600 = ■

✓4. 9 + 5 = 14
■ + 50 = 140
900 + 500 = ■

✓5. ■ − 8 = 5
130 − ■ = 50
■ − 800 = 500

6. **TALK Math** **Explain** why 130,000 − 80,000 is easier to subtract than 924 − 387.

TEKS 4.3A use addition and subtraction to solve problems involving whole numbers. *also* 4.14A, 4.14C, 4.15A, 4.15B, 4.16A

Independent Practice and Problem Solving

Use mental math to complete the pattern.

7. ■ + 6 = 10
40 + ■ = 100
400 + 600 = ■
4,000 + 6,000 = ■

8. ■ − 8 = 7
150 − 80 = ■
1,500 − ■ = 700
15,000 − 8,000 = ■

9. ■ − 7 = 7
140 − ■ = 70
■ − 700 = 700
14,000 − 7,000 = ■

10. 9 + 4 = ■
90 + ■ = 130
900 + 400 = ■
■ + 4,000 = 13,000

11. ■ − 6 = 5
110 − 60 = ■
1,100 − ■ = 500
11,000 − 6,000 = ■

12. 3 + ■ = 12
30 + ■ = 120
■ + 900 = 1,200
3,000 + 9,000 = ■

Use mental math patterns to find the sum or difference.

13. 50 + 70
14. 800 + 900
15. 130 − 60
16. 1,100 − 400
17. 7,000 + 9,000
18. 60,000 + 70,000
19. 12,000 − 7,000
20. 110,000 − 80,000

USE DATA For 21–23, use the bar graph.

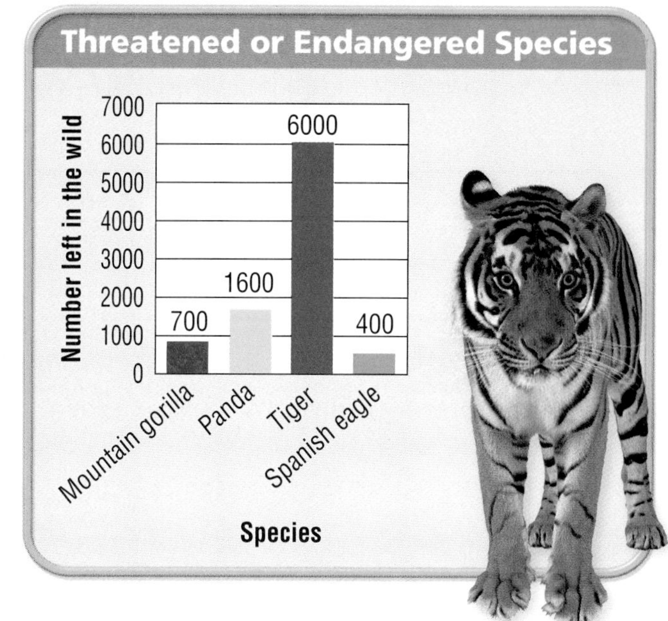

21. How many more pandas are there in the wild than mountain gorillas and Spanish eagles combined?

22. If the number of mountain gorillas increases by 50 each year, how many will there be in 3 years?

23. **Pose a Problem** Use the information in the graph to write a mental math problem. Have a classmate solve the problem.

24. WRITE Math **What's the Error?** Jason thinks the sum of 500 + 900 is 140,000. Describe Jason's mistake and find the correct sum.

Mixed Review and TAKS Prep

25. Round 3,017,920 to the nearest thousand. (TEKS 4.5A, p. 34)

26. Anna wants to put a wallpaper border around the top of her bedroom. The bedroom is 12 feet by 14 feet. How many feet of wallpaper will she need? (Grade 3 TEKS 3.11B)

27. **TAKS Prep** Which number is represented by ■? (Obj. 1)

800 + ■ = 1,500

A 7
B 70
C 700
D 7,000

Extra Practice on page 60, Set C

MENTAL MATH

Estimate Sums and Differences

OBJECTIVE: Estimate sums and differences.

Quick Review

1. 800 + 500
2. 9,000 + 3,000
3. 1,900 − 800
4. 6,000 − 2,000
5. 9,000 − 4,000

Vocabulary

estimate

compatible numbers

Learn

PROBLEM On the first two Saturdays in December, 1,149 and 1,074 people visited the El Paso Zoo. About how many people visited the zoo the first two Saturdays?

You can estimate to find about how many people. An **estimate** is a number close to an exact amount.

ONE WAY **Use rounding.**

Estimate the sum. 1,149 + 1,074

1,149	→	1,000	Round each number to the nearest thousand.
+ 1,074	→	+ 1,000	
		2,000	Then add.

So, about 2,000 people visited the zoo the first two Saturdays.

You can find a closer estimate by rounding to a lesser place.

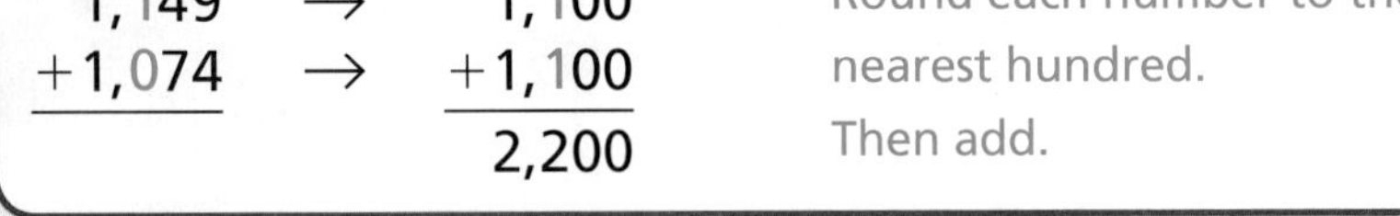

1,149	→	1,100	Round each number to the nearest hundred.
+ 1,074	→	+ 1,100	
		2,200	Then add.

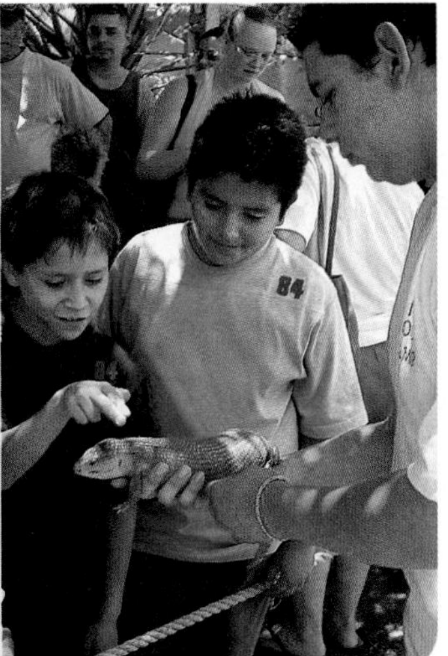

So, a closer estimate is about 2,200 people.

- Explain why rounding to a lesser place gives a closer estimate to the actual sum.

Compatible numbers are easy to compute mentally. Use properties and compatible numbers to estimate a sum.

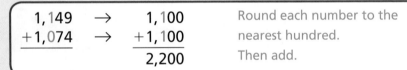

ANOTHER WAY **Use compatible numbers and properties.**

Estimate the sum. 46 + 28 + 67

46 + 28 + 67	Find compatible numbers. **Think:** 40 + 60 = 100
40 + 28 + 60	Use the Commutative Property.
28 + 40 + 60	
28 + (40 + 60)	Use the Associative Property.
28 + 100 = 128	

So, the sum is about 128.

Remember

The Commutative Property of Addition states that you can add numbers in any order and the sum remains the same. 4 + 5 = 5 + 4

The Associative Property of Addition states that you can group numbers in different ways and the sum remains the same. 4 + (6 + 2) = (4 + 6) + 2

TEKS 4.5A round whole numbers to the nearest ten, hundred, or thousand to approximate reasonable results in problem situations. *also* **4.1A, 4.3A, 4.15A, 4.15B, 4.16B**

Estimate Differences

ONE WAY **Use rounding.**

On December 3, attendance at El Paso Zoo was 1,149. On November 26, attendance was 1,008. About how many more people visited the zoo on December 3?

Estimate the difference. 1,149 − 1,008

1,149	→	1,100	Round each number to the nearest hundred.
−1,008	→	−1,000	
		100	

So, about 100 more people visited the zoo on December 3.

You can find a closer estimate by rounding to a lesser place.

1,149	→	1,150	Round each number to the nearest ten.
−1,008	→	−1,010	
		140	

So, a closer estimate is 140 more people.

ANOTHER WAY **Use compatible numbers.**

At the zoo animal art show, there were 1,142 entries by third graders and 1,583 entries by fourth graders. About how many more fourth graders entered than third graders?

Estimate. 1,583 − 1,142

1,583	→	1,500	**Think:** 1,500 − 1,000 is easy to compute mentally.
−1,142	→	−1,000	
		500	

So, about 500 more fourth graders entered than third graders.

Guided Practice

1. Estimate 3,612 + 4,225 by rounding to the nearest thousand. Then estimate the sum by rounding to the nearest hundred. Which is closer to the actual sum?

Use rounding to estimate.

2. $92 + 79$

3. $632 - 214$

4. $7{,}368 - 1{,}842$

5. $362 + 581$

6. $2{,}591 + 3{,}284$

Use compatible numbers to estimate.

7. $\begin{array}{r} 407 \\ + 681 \\ \hline \end{array}$

8. $\begin{array}{r} 1,639 \\ - 947 \\ \hline \end{array}$

9. $\begin{array}{r} 7,137 \\ + 9,205 \\ \hline \end{array}$

10. $\begin{array}{r} 2,832 \\ - 1,638 \\ \hline \end{array}$

✓11. $\begin{array}{r} 9,206 \\ - 2,358 \\ \hline \end{array}$

12. TALK Math **Explain** why you can find more than one estimate for a sum or difference.

Independent Practice and Problem Solving

Use rounding to estimate.

13. $\begin{array}{r} 7,409 \\ + 6,186 \\ \hline \end{array}$

14. $\begin{array}{r} 8,932 \\ - 5,341 \\ \hline \end{array}$

15. $\begin{array}{r} 63 \\ - 47 \\ \hline \end{array}$

16. $\begin{array}{r} 72 \\ + 49 \\ \hline \end{array}$

17. $\begin{array}{r} 2,782 \\ - 1,154 \\ \hline \end{array}$

18. $\begin{array}{r} 259 \\ + 684 \\ \hline \end{array}$

19. $\begin{array}{r} 746 \\ - 309 \\ \hline \end{array}$

20. $\begin{array}{r} 9,472 \\ - 2,612 \\ \hline \end{array}$

21. $\begin{array}{r} 592 \\ + 473 \\ \hline \end{array}$

22. $\begin{array}{r} 942 \\ - 372 \\ \hline \end{array}$

Use compatible numbers to estimate.

23. 10,732 − 8,961
24. 1,070 − 508
25. 22,579 − 16,067
26. 384 + 225 + 587
27. 282 + 25 + 51 + 172
28. 2,467 + 511 + 1,124 + 542

Adjust the estimate to make it closer to the exact sum or difference.

29. 7,395 + 4,098
Estimate: 11,000

30. 8,905 − 3,241
Estimate: 5,000

31. 25,319 − 12,946
Estimate: 12,000

For 32–35, use the table.

32. Use compatible numbers and properties to estimate the attendance at the zoo from Wednesday through Saturday.

33. About how many more people came on Friday than Thursday?

34. Estimate Sunday's attendance if 427 more people came than on Wednesday.

35. From Sunday to Tuesday, attendance was about 630 people. Estimate the attendance for the whole week.

36. WRITE Math **Explain** how a rounded sum compares to the exact sum if the addends are rounded to a lesser place value.

Zoo Attendance

Day	Number of People
Wednesday	67
Thursday	178
Friday	350
Saturday	1,149

 Extra Practice on page 60, Set D

Mixed Review and TAKS Prep

37. Weekday sales at a store totaled \$100,956 while weekend sales totaled \$101,013. Were weekday or weekend sales greater? (TEKS 4.1A, p.12)

38. TAKS Prep A weather balloon at an elevation of 7,890 meters dropped 1,624 meters to collect data. Which is the best estimate of the elevation where the weather balloon collected the data? (Obj. 1)

A 9,000 meters
B 8,000 meters
C 6,000 meters
D 5,000 meters

39. A movie was seen by 8,438 people on Friday, 8,294 people on Saturday, and 8,489 people on Sunday. On which day did the greatest number of people see the movie? (TEKS 4.1A, p.16)

40. TAKS Prep This year, students sold 943 magazine subscriptions for a fund raiser. Last year they sold 86 fewer subscriptions. About how many total subscriptions did they sell last year and this year? **Explain** your answer. (Obj. 1)

MATH POWER Problem Solving and Reasoning

NUMBER SENSE When you estimate, you get either an overestimate or an underestimate. An **overestimate** is greater than the exact answer. An **underestimate** is less than the exact answer.

There were 3,648 people at the first concert. There were 4,574 people at the second concert. About how many people attended the two concerts in all?

Examples

A Round to the greater thousand.

$$\begin{array}{r} 3,648 \\ +\ 4,574 \\ \hline \end{array} \quad \begin{array}{c} \rightarrow \\ \rightarrow \end{array} \quad \begin{array}{r} 4,000 \\ +\ 5,000 \\ \hline 9,000 \end{array}$$

Both rounded addends are greater than the original addends. So, the estimate is an overestimate.

B Round to the lesser thousand.

$$\begin{array}{r} 3,648 \\ +\ 4,574 \\ \hline \end{array} \quad \begin{array}{c} \rightarrow \\ \rightarrow \end{array} \quad \begin{array}{r} 3,000 \\ +\ 4,000 \\ \hline 7,000 \end{array}$$

Both rounded addends are less than the original addends. So, the estimate is an understimate.

So, between 7,000 and 9,000 people attended the concert.

Tell why the estimate is an overestimate or an underestimate.

1. 574 + 652
Estimate: 1,100

2. 2,904 + 5,601
Estimate: 7,000

3. 2,714 + 1,906
Estimate: 3,000

4. 5,714 + 3,822
Estimate: 10,000

LESSON 5

Mental Math Strategies

OBJECTIVE: Use mental math strategies to find sums and differences.

Quick Review

1. 20 + 50
2. 300 + 800
3. 1,300 − 400
4. 1,100 − 600
5. 7,000 + 2,000

Learn

PROBLEM The high school choir and orchestra are giving a concert. There are 56 students in the choir. There are 37 students in the orchestra. At the concert, each student has a chair on the stage. How many chairs are needed?

Sometimes you don't need paper and pencil to add or subtract. Use these strategies to help you add or subtract mentally.

ONE WAY **Use the *Break Apart* Strategy.**

A Addition

Find the sum. 56 + 37

Think: 56 = 50 + 6
37 = 30 + 7

Add the tens. 50 + 30 = 80

Add the ones. 6 + 7 = 13

Add the sums. 80 + 13 = 93

So, 93 chairs are needed.

B Subtraction

Find the difference. 76 − 42

Think: 76 = 70 + 6
42 = 40 + 2

Subtract the tens. 70 − 40 = 30

Subtract the ones. 6 − 2 = 4

Add the differences. 30 + 4 = 34

So, 76 − 42 = 34.

- Why do you think this strategy is called the break apart strategy?

More Examples

C Addition

Find the sum. 235 + 412

200 + 400 = 600
30 + 10 = 40
5 + 2 = 7
600 + 40 + 7 = 647

D Subtraction

Find the difference. 458 − 136

400 − 100 = 300
50 − 30 = 20
8 − 6 = 2
300 + 20 + 2 = 322

TEKS 4.3A use addition and subtraction to solve problems involving whole numbers. *also* 4.14A, 4.15A, 4.15B

OTHER WAYS

E Use a *Friendly Number* Strategy.

You can change one number to the nearest 10 and then adjust the other number to add or subtract mentally.

Subtraction is easier if the number you subtract is a friendly number. To get a friendly number, increase the number you subtract to the next ten. Then add the same amount to the other number to adjust the answer.

Find the difference. 56 − 38

Think: Add to 38 to make a number with 0 ones.

Add 2 to 38 to get 40.	38 + 2 = 40
Add 2 to 56 to adjust the difference.	56 + 2 = 58
Subtract.	58 − 40 = 18

So, 56 − 38 = 18.

- Why do you use the next friendly ten for 38 instead of 56?

F Use a *Swapping* Strategy.

When you add numbers, you can swap digits with the same place value. Sometimes this helps you make a friendly number.

Find the sum. 239 + 194

Think: 194 is close to the friendly number 200.

Swap the ones digits.	234 + 199
Add 1 to 199 to get 200.	199 + 1 = 200
Subtract 1 from 234 to adjust the sum.	234 − 1 = 233
Add.	200 + 233 = 433

So, 239 + 194 = 433.

- Explain how to solve the problem by swapping the digits in a different place.

Guided Practice

1. Find 68 + 56 mentally. Add 2 to 68 to make the next friendly number. Subtract 2 from 56 to adjust the sum. What is the sum?

Add or subtract mentally. Tell the strategy you used.

2. 86 − 43 3. 72 + 39 4. 62 − 29 5. 867 − 425 6. 145 + 213

7. TALK Math **Explain** how to find 478 − 215 using mental math.

Independent Practice and Problem Solving

Add or subtract mentally. Tell the strategy you used.

8. 94 − 57 **9.** 16 + 58 **10.** 95 + 36 **11.** 38 + 75 **12.** 93 − 46

13. 152 − 79 **14.** 238 + 431 **15.** 286 − 159 **16.** 723 + 142 **17.** 442 − 238

18. 758 − 426 **19.** 384 + 218 **20.** 276 + 79 **21.** 576 − 98 **22.** 726 − 314

Find the sum or difference.

23. 462 − 18 **24.** 79 − 42 **25.** 134 + 112 **26.** 27 + 335 **12.** 86 + 63

28. 656 − 429 **29.** 64 + 58 **30.** 47 − 39 **31.** 211 + 725 **32.** 137 − 19

For 33–35, use the table and mental math.

33. How many instruments make up the orchestra?

34. Use mental math to find how many more strings there are than woodwinds and brass combined.

35. Alyvia has 100 instrument stands. How many more does she need so each instrument has a stand?

36. WRITE Math **Explain** how to find 87 − 53 using the break apart and friendly number strategies. Which is easier to use?

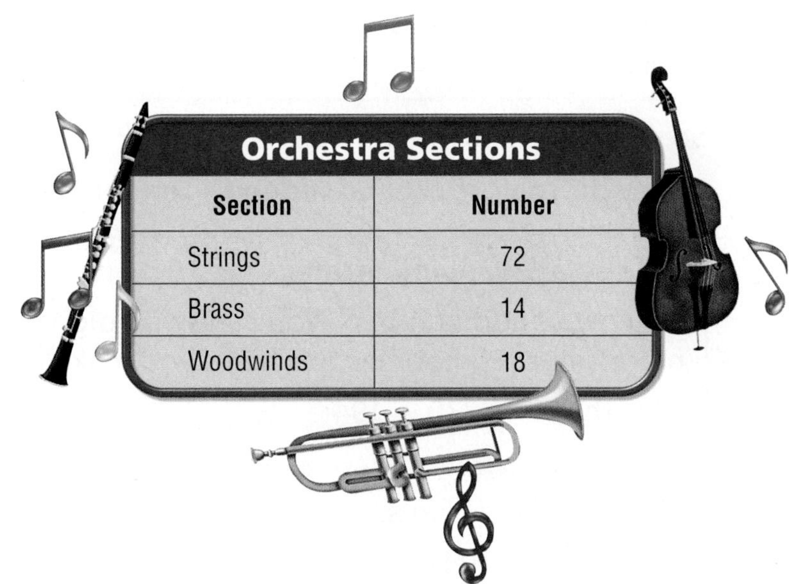

Orchestra Sections

Section	Number
Strings	72
Brass	14
Woodwinds	18

Mixed Review and TAKS Prep

37. The number of people at a concert, rounded to the nearest hundred, is 5,400. What is the actual number of people if the digit in the tens place is 8 and the digit in the ones place is 2? (TEKS 4.5A, p. 34)

38. There were 623 people at the concert on Friday. On Saturday, 287 more people attended the concert than attended on Friday. About how many people attended the concert in all? (TEKS 4.5A, p. 40)

39. **TAKS Prep** Dan wants to buy an apple that costs 48¢ and a banana that costs 45¢. He adds 2¢ to 48¢ to find the total mentally. How should he adjust the sum to find the total? (Obj. 1)

A Add 2¢ to 45¢

B Add 5¢ to 45¢

C Subtract 2¢ from 45¢

D Subtract 5¢ from 45¢

Extra Practice on page 61, Set E

Write to Explain

Writing to explain how you use mental math strategies can help you learn how to add and subtract greater numbers in your head.

Three groups of students are practicing for a dance concert. There are 19 students in the first group, 17 students in the second group, and 12 students in the third group. How many students are practicing?

Read the explanation Ryan gave for his solution.

Tips

To write an explanation:

- Your first sentence should tell what the problem is.
- Use words such as first, next, and finally to explain your steps.
- Use correct math vocabulary.
- Show your computations.
- Write a statement to summarize the answer.

I need to add 19 + 17 + 12. First, I can use the friendly number strategy to add 19 + 17. I add 1 to 19 to make 20 and subtract 1 from 17 to make 16 because I know that the sum of 20 + 16 is the same as the sum of 19 + 17. Add 20 + 16 = 36.

Next, I need to find the sum of 36 + 12. I use the break apart strategy. 36 = 30 + 6 and 12 = 10 + 2. So, I can add the tens and ones to find the sum.

I add 30 + 10 = 40, 6 + 2 = 8, and 40 + 8 = 48. The sum is 48. So, there are 48 students practicing.

Problem Solving **Write to explain how you used mental math strategies to solve.**

1. There are 18 fourth graders, 14 fifth graders, and 23 sixth graders in the choir. How many students are in the choir?

2. Would you use mental math to subtract $185 - 67$?

Problem Solving Workshop
Skill: Estimate or Exact Answer

OBJECTIVE: Solve problems by using the skill *estimate or exact answer.*

Read to Understand
Plan
Solve
Check

Use the Skill

PROBLEM The safe maximum flying weight of the plane is 1,600 pounds. The weights of some items are in the table below. Is the total weight of the plane, oil, fuel, extra equipment, baggage, and pilot less than 1,600 pounds? What is the maximum total weight the passengers can be?

Whether you need an estimate or exact answer depends on the situation.

Step 1 Find the total weight of the pilot and loaded plane.

You do not need to know the exact weight to find if it is less than 1,600 pounds. You can estimate this weight to compare to 1,600 pounds.

Round to the next ten pounds. Then add.

973 + 15 + 20 + 146 + 95 + 150
↓ ↓ ↓ ↓ ↓ ↓
980 + 20 + 20 + 150 + 100 + 150 = 1,420

1,420 pounds < 1,600 pounds

Step 2 Find how much weight is left for passengers.

Find the difference between the total weight of the loaded plane and the safe maximum flying weight. Find an exact answer.

Add to find the exact weight of the loaded plane.

973 + 15 + 20 + 146 + 95 + 150 = 1,399

Subtract the exact weight from 1,600.

1,600 − 1,399 = 201

There are 201 pounds left for passengers.

So, the total weight of the loaded plane is less than 1,600 pounds, and the maximum total weight of the passengers is 201 pounds.

Light Plane Weights

Item	Weight (in pounds)
Empty Plane	973
Oil	15
Extra Equipment	20
Fuel	146
Baggage	95
Typical Pilot/adult	150
Safe Maximum Weight	1,600

Think and Discuss

Explain whether to estimate or find an exact answer. Then solve.

a. If there were no baggage or extra equipment, what is the maximum total weight of passengers the loaded plane could hold?

b. Two bags weigh 95 pounds. If one of them weighs 47 pounds, about how much does the other bag weigh?

TEKS 4.5A round whole numbers to the nearest ten, hundred, or thousand to approximate reasonable results in problem situations. *also* **4.3A, 4.14A, 4.14C, 4.15A, 4.15B, 4.16B**

Guided Problem Solving

1. Horseshoe Falls in Australia is 502 feet high. Students measured their school and found that it was 210 feet long and 80 feet wide. Which is greater, the height of Horseshoe Falls or the distance around the outside of the school?

   First, decide if you need an estimate or an exact answer.

   Then, decide how you will compare the two numbers.

   Finally, make the comparison.

2. **What if** the students estimated that the school was about 200 feet long and about 100 feet wide? **Explain** why you should estimate or find an exact answer.

3. To be an airline pilot, you must fly a total of at least 1,500 hours. Dan flew 827 hours last year and 582 hours this year. How many more hours must he fly to be an airline pilot?

Mixed Applications

Explain whether to estimate or find an exact answer. Then solve the problem.

4. The school hallway is 190 feet long. If Carlos walks the length of the school hallway 3 times, will he have walked at least 500 feet? How far will he have walked?

5. The auditorium has 360 seats. There are 189 fourth-grade students and 170 fifth-grade students. If all the fifth-grade students sit in the auditorium, how many seats are left for fourth-grade students?

USE DATA For 6–8, use the bar graph.

6. How many degrees warmer was Meridian's highest January temperature than Greenville's?

7. The difference between the highest and lowest January temperatures at the Jackson station was 57°F. Find Jackson's lowest temperature in January.

8. In 2006, Vicksburg's highest January temperature was about 26°F warmer than normal. What was the normal temperature in Vicksburg in January?

9. WRITE Math **Explain** when you might need an exact answer and when you can estimate.

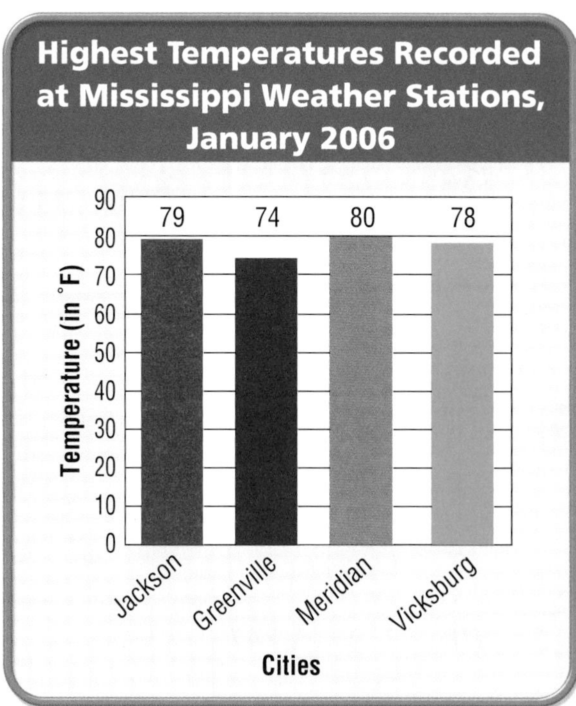

Add and Subtract Through 4-Digit Numbers

OBJECTIVE: Add and subtract to 3-digit and 4-digit numbers.

Quick Review

Tino wants to buy a skateboard that costs $46. He has $28. How much more money does he need?

Learn

PROBLEM In spring, some monarch butterflies fly 1,718 miles from their winter home in Mexico to South Dakota. They fly another 1,042 miles to reach their summer home in Ontario, Canada. How far do the butterflies fly in all?

ONE WAY **Use place value.**

Add. 1,718 + 1,042 **Estimate.** 2,000 + 1,000 = 3,000

Step 1	Step 2	Step 3	Step 4
Add the ones. Regroup 10 ones.	Add the tens.	Add the hundreds.	Add the thousands.
$\begin{array}{r} \scriptstyle 1 \\ 1{,}718 \\ +1{,}042 \\ \hline 0 \end{array}$	$\begin{array}{r} \scriptstyle 1 \\ 1{,}718 \\ +1{,}042 \\ \hline 60 \end{array}$	$\begin{array}{r} \scriptstyle 1 \\ 1{,}718 \\ +1{,}042 \\ \hline 760 \end{array}$	$\begin{array}{r} \scriptstyle 1 \\ 1{,}718 \\ +1{,}042 \\ \hline 2{,}760 \end{array}$

So, the butterflies flew 2,760 miles in all. Since 2,760 is close to the estimate of 3,000, the answer is reasonable.

ANOTHER WAY **Use column addition.**

Add. 578 + 769 **Estimate.** 600 + 800 = 1,400

Step 1 Draw lines to separate each place. Add each column.

	H	T	O
	5	7	8
+	7	6	9
	12	13	17

Step 2 Regroup 17 ones as 1 ten 7 ones. 13 tens + 1 ten = 14 tens

	H	T	O
	5	7	8
+	7	6	9
	12	13	17
	12	14	7

Step 3 Regroup 14 tens as 1 hundred 4 tens. 12 hundreds + 1 hundred = 13 hundreds

	H	T	O
	5	7	8
+	7	6	9
	12	13	17
	12	14	7
	13	4	7

Step 4 Regroup 13 hundreds as 1 thousand 3 hundreds.

	H	T	O
	5	7	8
+	7	6	9
	12	13	17
	12	14	7
	13	4	7
1	3	4	7

So, 578 + 769 = 1,347.

TEKS 4.3A use addition and subtraction to solve problems involving whole numbers. *also* **4.5A, 4.14A, 4.15A, 4.15B, 4.16B**

Subtract Through 4-Digit Numbers

In autumn, some monarch butterflies fly 3,825 kilometers from southern Canada to their winter home in central Mexico. A butterfly has flown 1,948 kilometers. How much farther is its winter home?

READ Math

Add to find a total or how many in all.
Subtract to compare how much more or how much less.

ONE WAY **Use place value.**

Subtract. 3,825 − 1,948 **Estimate.** 4,000 − 2,000 = 2,000

Step 1	Step 2	Step 3	Step 4
Subtract the ones. Regroup 2 tens 5 ones as 1 ten 15 ones.	Subtract the tens. Regroup 8 hundreds 1 ten as 7 hundreds 11 tens.	Subtract the hundreds. Regroup 3 thousands 7 hundreds as 2 thousands 17 hundreds.	Subtract the thousands.
1 15 3,825 −1,948 7	11 7 1 15 3,825 −1,948 77	17 11 2 7 1 15 3,825 −1,948 877	17 11 2 7 1 15 3,825 −1,948 1,877

So, the butterfly's winter home is 1,877 kilometers farther. Since 1,877 is close to the estimate of 2,000, the answer is reasonable.

ANOTHER WAY **Use a number line.**

You can use a number line to find 724 − 243.

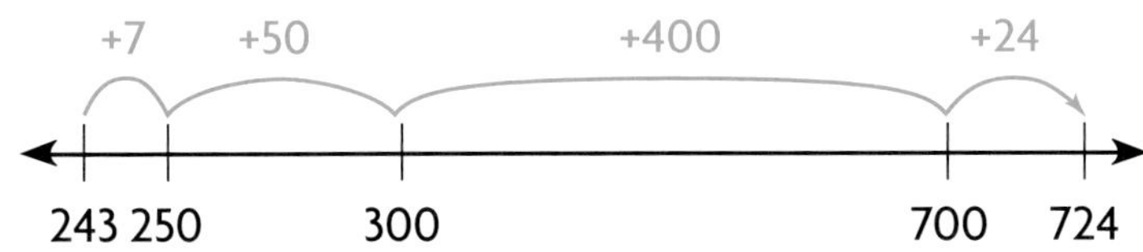

Add the numbers above the number line to find the difference between 243 and 724.

7 + 50 + 400 + 24 = 481

So, 724 − 243 = 481.

More Examples

A

7,849
−3,618
4,231

B

11
7 1 13
8,239
− 782
7,457

C

10
8 0 17
9,179
−2,183
6,996

• How can you use place value to add or subtract 4-digit numbers?

Guided Practice

1. Copy each step of the problem at the right. Then tell what is happening in each step.

Step 1: $\begin{array}{r} 7\cancel{1}^{0}\cancel{4}^{14} \\ -438 \\ \hline 6 \end{array}$ Step 2: $\begin{array}{r} \cancel{7}^{6}\cancel{1}^{0\,10}\cancel{4}^{14} \\ -438 \\ \hline 76 \end{array}$ Step 3: $\begin{array}{r} \cancel{7}^{6}\cancel{1}^{0\,10}\cancel{4}^{14} \\ -438 \\ \hline 276 \end{array}$

Estimate. Then find the sum or difference.

2. $\begin{array}{r} 309 \\ +892 \\ \hline \end{array}$ 3. $\begin{array}{r} 3,867 \\ -1,432 \\ \hline \end{array}$ 4. $\begin{array}{r} 2,608 \\ +4,193 \\ \hline \end{array}$ ✓5. $\begin{array}{r} 726 \\ +2,643 \\ \hline \end{array}$ ✓6. $\begin{array}{r} 6,983 \\ -4,275 \\ \hline \end{array}$

7. **TALK Math** **Explain** how you know which places to regroup to subtract.

Independent Practice and Problem Solving

Estimate. Then find the sum or difference.

8. $\begin{array}{r} 957 \\ +409 \\ \hline \end{array}$ 9. $\begin{array}{r} 7,345 \\ -1,213 \\ \hline \end{array}$ 10. $\begin{array}{r} 8,936 \\ +\ \ 385 \\ \hline \end{array}$ 11. $\begin{array}{r} 2,375 \\ +1,098 \\ \hline \end{array}$ 12. $\begin{array}{r} 9,133 \\ -4,217 \\ \hline \end{array}$

13. $\begin{array}{r} 536 \\ -273 \\ \hline \end{array}$ 14. $\begin{array}{r} 4,892 \\ +\ \ 708 \\ \hline \end{array}$ 15. $\begin{array}{r} 8,423 \\ -2,785 \\ \hline \end{array}$ 16. $\begin{array}{r} 7,419 \\ -\ \ 846 \\ \hline \end{array}$ 17. $\begin{array}{r} 6,045 \\ +1,742 \\ \hline \end{array}$

18. $\begin{array}{r} 918 \\ -726 \\ \hline \end{array}$ 19. $\begin{array}{r} 6,245 \\ +1,534 \\ \hline \end{array}$ 20. $\begin{array}{r} 8,329 \\ -\ \ 953 \\ \hline \end{array}$ 21. $\begin{array}{r} 7,962 \\ -2,358 \\ \hline \end{array}$ 22. $\begin{array}{r} 3,407 \\ +2,936 \\ \hline \end{array}$

Algebra Find the missing digit.

23. $\begin{array}{r} 9\blacksquare 6 \\ +\ 437 \\ \hline 1,383 \end{array}$ 24. $\begin{array}{r} 6,532 \\ -\ 4,1\blacksquare 5 \\ \hline 2,407 \end{array}$ 25. $\begin{array}{r} \blacksquare,158 \\ -\ \ 437 \\ \hline 1,721 \end{array}$ 26. $\begin{array}{r} 3,657 \\ +\ \ 2\blacksquare 4 \\ \hline 3,901 \end{array}$

USE DATA For 27–28, use the table.

27. How many more butterflies roosted on September 2 than on September 3 and 4 combined?

28. **Pose a Problem** Write a problem like problem 27 by changing the dates.

29. **Reasoning** Add an even 4-digit number and an odd 4-digit number. Is the sum odd or even? **Explain.**

30. **WRITE Math** **What's the Question?** Angelina's nature group counted 622 butterflies roosting on Monday. On Tuesday, they counted 458 butterflies. The answer is 164 butterflies.

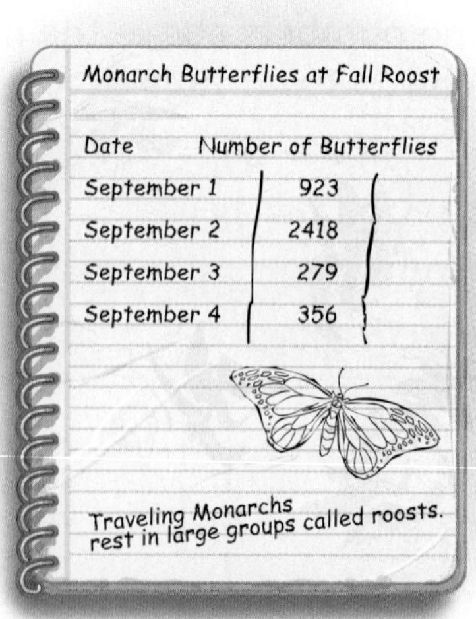
Monarch Butterflies at Fall Roost

Date	Number of Butterflies
September 1	923
September 2	2418
September 3	279
September 4	356

Traveling Monarchs rest in large groups called roosts.

Technology
CD ROM Use Harcourt Mega Math, The Number Games, *Tiny's Think Tank*, Levels B, C.

 Extra Practice on page 61, Set G

Mixed Review and TAKS Prep

31. What number makes this number sentence true? $5 + \blacksquare = 12$ (TEKS 4.7, p. 32)

32. **TAKS Prep** Greg has put 1,372 pieces of his puzzle together. He has 1,128 pieces left to finish the puzzle. How many pieces are in the puzzle? (Obj. 1)

A 244

B 256

C 2,490

D 2,500

33. When you add two odd numbers, is it certain or impossible that the sum will be odd? (Grade 3 TEKS 3.13C)

34. **TAKS Prep** Students collected 875 cans during the first month of their aluminum drive. The second month, they collected 2,155 cans. How many more cans did they collect the second month than the first month? **Explain.** (Obj. 1)

Problem Solving and Reasoning

VISUAL THINKING You can use a number line to visualize a problem and to help you solve the problem.

Driving from Green Bay, Wisconsin to Wheaton, Illinois, on major highways, you go through Milwaukee, Wisconsin and Wheeling, Illinois.

What is the distance from Wheeling to Wheaton?

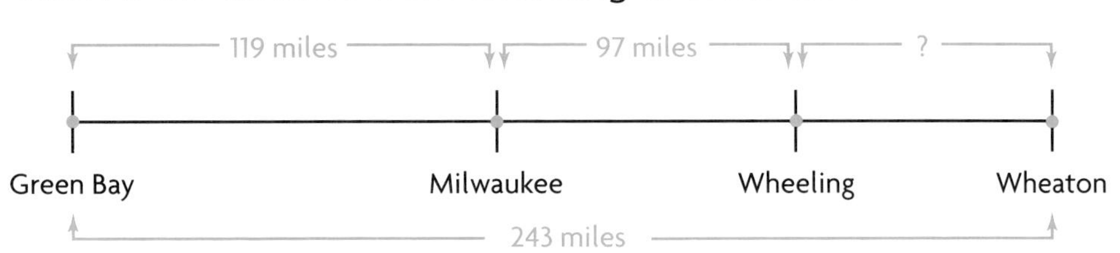

Look at the distances on the number line.

Add to find the distance from Green Bay to Wheeling. $119 + 97 = 216$

Subtract to find the distance from Wheeling to Wheaton. $243 - 216 = 27$

So, the distance from Wheeling to Wheaton is 27 miles.

Draw a number line to find the distance. Label the letters on the number line in alphabetical order.

1. *A* to *D* is 185 miles. *B* to *C* is 57 miles. *C* to *D* is 94 miles. Find A to B.

2. *A* to *D* is 278 miles. *A* to *B* is 43 miles. *C* to *D* is 129 miles. Find *B* to *C*.

Subtract Across Zeros

OBJECTIVE: Subtract whole numbers across zeros.

Quick Review

1. 7,543 − 3,924
2. 8,351 − 427
3. 6,254 − 1,683
4. 5,832 − 678
5. 3,425 − 1,789

Learn

PROBLEM A volcano is an opening in the earth's crust that erupts hot gases and melted rock called lava. Mount Popocatepetl is an active volcano in central Mexico. One eruption took place in 2005. The Aztec Indians first recorded an eruption in 1347. How many years passed between these two eruptions?

Example **Subtract.** 2,005 − 1,347 **Estimate.** 2,000 − 1,300 = 700

There are not enough ones, tens, or hundreds to subtract, so you have to regroup.

Step 1	Step 2	Step 3	Step 4
Regroup 2 thousands as 1 thousand 10 hundreds.	Regroup 10 hundreds as 9 hundreds 10 tens.	Regroup 10 tens 5 ones as 9 tens 15 ones	Subtract.
1 10 ~~2~~,~~0~~05 −1,347	9 1 ~~10~~10 ~~2~~,~~0~~~~0~~5 −1,347	9 9 1 ~~10~~~~10~~15 ~~2~~,~~0~~~~0~~~~5~~ −1,347	9 9 1 ~~10~~~~10~~15 ~~2~~,~~0~~~~0~~~~5~~ −1,347 658

So, 658 years have passed between the eruptions. Since 658 is close to the estimate 700, it is reasonable.

- In Step 1, why is it necessary to regroup 2 thousands?

ERROR ALERT

Remember that when the bottom digit is greater than the top digit, you need to regroup to subtract. Regroup from the next greater place value to the left that is not 0.

More Examples

A
```
   9
 4 10 10
 5  0  0
−1  6  4
 3  3  6
```

B
```
    11
 3, 1 10
 4, 2 0 8
−2, 4 5 2
 1, 7 5 6
```

C
```
 6 10 4 10
 7, 0 5 0
−3, 3 1 9
 3, 7 3 1
```

Guided Practice

1. Copy the problem at the right. Regroup the ones, tens, and hundreds. Then subtract. What is the difference?

$$\begin{array}{r} 200 \\ -165 \\ \hline \end{array}$$

TEKS 4.3A use addition and subtraction to solve problems involving whole numbers. *also* **4.5A, 4.14A, 4.15A, 4.15B, 4.16B**

Estimate. Then find the difference.

2. 706 − 289	**3.** 2,030 − 907	**4.** 9,000 − 6,208	**5.** 6,400 − 1,583	**6.** 3,000 − 1,076

7. TALK Math **Explain** why you need to regroup to find 5,010 − 328. What is the difference?

Independent Practice and Problem Solving

Estimate. Then find the difference.

8. 2,008 − 724	**9.** 604 − 238	**10.** 800 − 476	**11.** 7,000 − 4,369	**12.** 4,201 − 3,050

13. 720 − 519 **14.** 6,200 − 3,685 **15.** 2,060 − 1,077 **16.** 7,000 − 1,225

Choose two numbers from the box to make each difference.

3,000 3,400 3,040 274 2,074 2,704

17. 1,326 **18.** 2,766 **19.** 336 **20.** 926 **21.** 2,726

USE DATA For 22–24, use the table.

22. How many years passed between the eruptions of the Chiginagak and Veniaminof volcanoes?

23. Which two volcanoes have the greatest difference in elevation? Find the difference.

24. WRITE Math **What's the Error?** Cole said Veniaminof is 4,225 feet higher than Aniakchak. Explain Cole's mistake and describe his error. How much higher is Veniaminof?

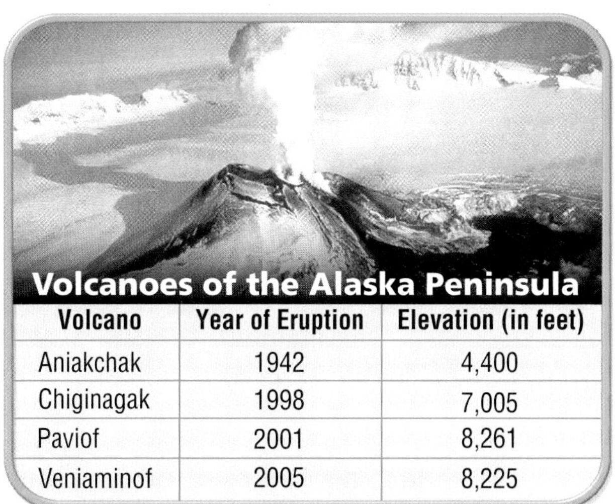

Volcanoes of the Alaska Peninsula

Volcano	Year of Eruption	Elevation (in feet)
Aniakchak	1942	4,400
Chiginagak	1998	7,005
Paviof	2001	8,261
Veniaminof	2005	8,225

Mixed Review and TAKS Prep

25. There are 2,382 students enrolled in the community soccer program. How many students are there, rounded to the nearest hundred? (TEKS 4.5A, p. 34)

26. Bo's class collected 738 pounds of paper and 589 pounds of glass. About how many pounds of paper and glass did they collect? (TEKS 4.5A, p. 40)

27. **TAKS Prep** A movie theater has 3,000 seats. There were 2,682 people at the first showing of the movie. How many empty seats were there? (Obj. 1)

A 318 **C** 1,682

B 428 **D** 5,682

Extra Practice on page 61, Set G

Lesson 9 Choose a Method

OBJECTIVE: Choose paper and pencil, a calculator, or mental math to add and subtract to 7-digit numbers.

Quick Review

1. 703 + 317
2. 820 − 416
3. 6,004 + 1,683
4. 9,000 − 3,678
5. 3,400 − 769

Learn

PROBLEM Saturn has more moons than any planet in the solar system. Two of its moons are Titan and Iapetus. Titan is 1,221,850 kilometers from Saturn. Iapetus is 2,339,450 kilometers farther from Saturn than Titan is. How far is Iapetus from Saturn?

Use paper and pencil.

Add. 1,221,850 + 2,339,450 **Estimate.** 1,000,000 + 2,000,000 = 3,000,000

Step 1

Add the ones and tens. Regroup.

```
          1
  1,221,850
 +2,339,450
         00
```

Step 2

Add the hundreds. Regroup.

```
         11
  1,221,850
 +2,339,450
        300
```

Step 3

Add the thousands. Regroup.

```
       1 11
  1,221,850
 +2,339,450
      1,300
```

Step 4

Add the ten thousands, hundred thousands, and millions.

```
       1 11
  1,221,850
 +2,339,450
  3,561,300
```

Use a calculator.

So, Iapetus is 3,561,300 kilometers from Saturn. The answer is close to the estimate of 3,000,000, so 3,561,300 is reasonable.

- Is mental math a good method for finding the sum of these numbers? Explain.

Math Idea

You can find a sum or difference by using paper and pencil, a calculator, or mental math. Choose the method that works best with the numbers in the problem.

Use mental math.

Add. 41,570 + 4,020 **Estimate.** 41,000 + 4,000 = 45,000

Step 1	Step 2	Step 3
Break apart 4,020 to add. 4,020 = 4,000 + 20	Add the thousands. 41,570 + 4,000 = 45,570	Now add the tens. 45,570 + 20 = 45,590

So, the sum is 45,590. The answer is close to the estimate of 45,000, so 45,590 is reasonable.

TEKS 4.3A use addition and subtraction to solve problems involving whole numbers. *also* **4.5A, 4.14A, 4.14D, 4.15A, 4.15B**

Subtract Greater Numbers

Saturn's diameter at its equator is 120,536 kilometers. Its diameter between the poles is 108,728 kilometers. How much greater is Saturn's diameter at the equator than between the poles?

Use paper and pencil.

Subtract. 120,536 − 108,728

Estimate. 120,000 − 110,000 = 10,000

Step 1	Subtract the ones and tens. Regroup.	120,536 − 108,728 = 08
Step 2	Subtract the hundreds. Regroup.	120,536 − 108,728 = 808
Step 3	Subtract the thousands, ten thousands, and hundred thousands.	120,536 − 108,728 = 11,808
Step 4	Add to check.	108,728 + 11,808 = 120,536

Use a calculator.

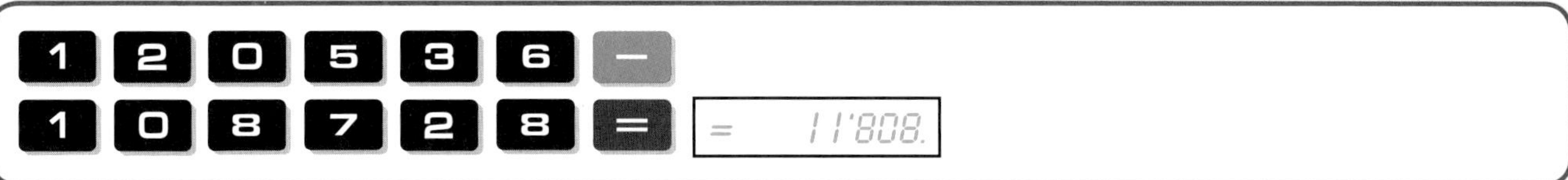

So, the diameter at the equator is 11,808 kilometers greater. The answer is close to the estimate of 10,000, so 11,808 is reasonable.

Use mental math.

Subtract. 143,000 − 9,000

Estimate. 140,000 − 10,000 = 130,000

You can use the friendly number strategy.

Add 1,000 to 9,000 to get 10,000.	9,000 + 1,000 = 10,000
Add 1,000 to 143,000 to adjust the difference.	143,000 + 1,000 = 144,000
Subtract.	144,000 − 10,000 = 134,000

So, the difference is 134,000. The answer is close to the estimate of 130,000, so 134,000 is reasonable.

- How do you decide which method to use when adding and subtracting greater numbers?

Guided Practice

1. Tell which problem would be easier to solve using mental math. Then find the sum.

   a. 241,156 + 176,812

   b. 340,100 + 204,000

Find the sum or difference. Write the method you used.

2. 342,007 + 569,305
3. 706,300 − 401,000
4. 945,322 − 461,070
5. 6,280,000 + 1,300,000

6. **TALK Math** **Explain** why mental math is a better method for finding 170,000 + 25,300 than finding 170,000 − 25,300.

Independent Practice and Problem Solving

Find the sum or difference. Write the method you used.

7. 850,540 − 200,310
8. 3,287,004 + 2,069,506
9. 3,506,721 + 4,080,000
10. 4,528,300 − 2,175,700
11. 5,302,700 + 410,000
12. 592,014 − 286,728
13. 632,004 − 12,000
14. 5,838,672 + 3,415,059

Algebra **Find the missing digit.**

15. 43■,257 + 253,019 = 692,276
16. 892,■43 − 250,742 = 642,201
17. 538,627 − 2■4,394 = 274,233
18. 2,4■7,308 + 3,896,321 = 6,313,629

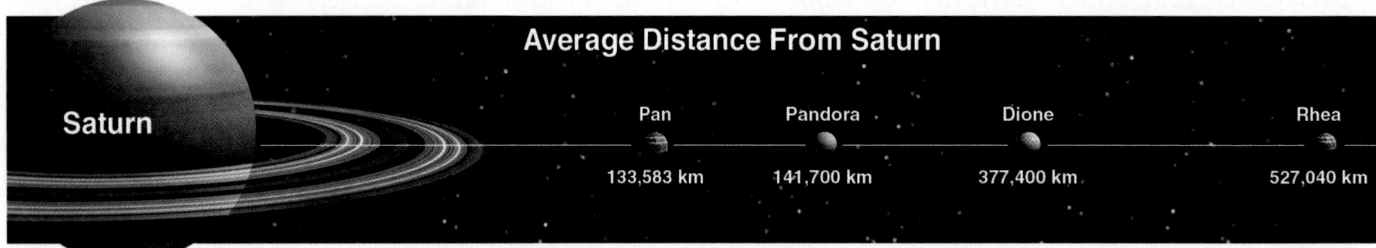

USE DATA **For 19–21, use the information in the picture.**

19. Helene orbits Saturn 243,817 kilometers farther away than Pan does. Which moon orbits Saturn at the same distance as Helene?

20. How much farther from Saturn is Rhea than Pan and Pandora combined?

21. **Pose a Problem** Write a problem like Problem 20 by changing the moons.

22. **WRITE Math** **Explain** which method to use to find how much closer Dione is to Saturn than Rhea is. Why is the method you chose the best one to use?

 Extra Practice on page 61, Set H

Mixed Review and TAKS Prep

23. Deb's and Sid's families went to Alabama. Deb's family traveled 1,757 miles and Sid's family traveled 563 miles. About how much farther did Deb's family travel? (TEKS 4.3A, p. 50)

24. Nick wants to score 5,000 points in a video game. He has scored 3,752 points. How many more points must he score to reach his goal? (TEKS 4.3A, p. 50)

25. **TAKS Prep** The United States has 9,161,923 square kilometers of land and 469,495 square kilometers of water. What is the total area of land and water in the United States? (Obj. 1)

26. **TAKS Prep** There are 135,663 kilometers of coastline that border the Pacific Ocean. There are 111,866 kilometers of coastline that border the Atlantic Ocean. How many more kilometers of coastline border the Pacific Ocean? (Obj. 1)

A 23,797 kilometers

B 24,203 kilometers

C 24,807 kilometers

D 247,529 kilometers

Problem Solving and Reasoning

"Rats live on no evil star" is a sentence palindrome.

NUMBER SENSE A palindrome is a word that reads the same forward or backward. *Mom* and *radar* are word palindromes. There are also number palindromes such as 33, 404, and 2,002.

You can use addition to make number palindromes.

Step 1	Step 2	Step 3	Step 4
Write a number. 348	Reverse the digits. 843	Add the two numbers. 348 + 843 1,191	Keep reversing and adding until you make a palindrome. 348 + 843 1,191 + 1,911 3,102 + 2,013 palindrome → 5,115

Use each number to make a number palindrome.

1. 421 **2.** 236 **3.** 48 **4.** 637 **5.** 1,384

Extra Practice

Set A Write a related fact. Use it to complete the number sentence. (pp. 32–33)

1. 14 − ■ = 8 **2.** 12 − ■ = 3 **3.** ■ + 9 = 17 **4.** 6 + ■ = 13

5. ■ − 5 = 6 **6.** ■ + 9 = 15 **7.** 8 + ■ = 16 **8.** ■ − 8 = 4

Write the fact family for each set of numbers.

9. 6, 7, 13 **10.** 8, 6, 14 **11.** 4, 5, 9 **12.** 8, 7, 15

Set B Round each number to the place value of the underlined digit. (pp. 34–37)

1. 5$\underline{6}$,479 **2.** $\underline{8}$47 **3.** 2,372,8$\underline{4}$8 **4.** 291,$\underline{6}$21

5. 4,78$\underline{5}$,421 **6.** 4$\underline{9}$8 **7.** 7,$\underline{4}$28 **8.** 2,468,$\underline{3}$57

Round each number to the nearest ten, hundred, and thousand.

9. 7,602 **10.** 92,677 **11.** 47,491 **12.** 48,725

13. 9,718 **14.** 61,499 **15.** 149,173 **16.** 2,098,511

Set C Use mental math to complete the pattern. (pp. 38–39)

1. 5 + ■ = 11
50 + 60 = ■
500 + ■ = 1,100
5,000 + 6,000 = ■
50,000 + ■ = 110,000

2. 7 + ■ = 16
70 + 90 = ■
700 + ■ = 1,600
7,000 + 9,000 = ■
70,000 + ■ = 160,000

3. 4 + ■ = 10
40 + 60 = ■
400 + ■ = 1,000
4,000 + 6,000 = ■
40,000 + ■ = 100,000

Use mental math patterns to find the sum or difference.

3. 30 + 80 **4.** 900 − 400 **5.** 1,500 − 800

6. 40,000 + 90,000 **7.** 1,700 − 800 **8.** 70,000 + 50,000

9. 50,000 + 80,000 **10.** 160,000 − 50,000 **11.** 120,000 + 60,000

Set D Use rounding to estimate. (pp. 40–43)

1. $\begin{array}{r}458\\+997\\\hline\end{array}$ **2.** $\begin{array}{r}320\\+391\\\hline\end{array}$ **3.** $\begin{array}{r}4{,}764\\-1{,}841\\\hline\end{array}$ **4.** $\begin{array}{r}925\\-647\\\hline\end{array}$

5. $\begin{array}{r}5{,}382\\+1{,}403\\\hline\end{array}$ **6.** $\begin{array}{r}7{,}931\\+4{,}899\\\hline\end{array}$ **7.** $\begin{array}{r}2{,}061\\+1{,}312\\\hline\end{array}$ **8.** $\begin{array}{r}7{,}439\\-4{,}377\\\hline\end{array}$

Set E Add or subtract mentally. Tell the strategy you used. (pp. 44–47)

1. 89 − 37 **2.** 520 + 275 **3.** 497 − 309 **4.** 752 + 244 **5.** 607 − 299

6. 614 + 345 **7.** 489 − 56 **8.** 380 + 98 **9.** 677 − 470 **10.** 393 + 427

11. Mr. Chase is ordering 249 pencils and 290 erasers. Use mental math to determine the total number of items Mr. Chase is ordering. Tell what method you used.

Set F Estimate. Then find the sum or difference. (pp. 50–53)

1. 563 + 261 **2.** 732 − 124 **3.** 6,409 + 3,188 **4.** 7,698 − 2,677

5. 2,713 − 1,950 **6.** 4,888 + 3,621 **7.** 5,377 − 2,298 **8.** 4,056 + 5,275

Set G Estimate. Then find the difference. (pp. 54–55)

1. 500 − 379 **2.** 4,036 − 2,305 **3.** 3,009 − 2,873 **4.** 6,080 − 3,592

5. 4,700 − 2,891 **6.** 5,040 − 398 **7.** 12,900 − 3,875 **8.** 20,708 − 18,969

9. Women ran in the 1,500-meter race for the first time in the summer Olympic games of 1972. How many years ago was this?

Set H Find the sum or difference. Write the method you used. (pp. 56–59)

1. 430,009 + 250,091 **2.** 675,900 − 350,500 **3.** 4,900,275 + 100,125 **4.** 3,729,638 + 4,982,114

5. 6,357,918 + 2,387,899 **6.** 4,379,692 − 3,489,753 **7.** 1,468,345 − 759,926 **8.** 6,241,255 − 2,198,042

9. According to the 1990 census, the population of Texas was about 16,986,000. In 2000, the census reported that the population of Texas had grown to about 20,862,000. About how many more people lived in Texas in 2000 than in 1990?

Technology
Use Harcourt Mega Math, The Number Games, *Tiny's Think Tank*, Levels B, C.

Chapter 2 Review/Test

Check Vocabulary and Concepts

Choose the best term from the box.

VOCABULARY
inverse operations
regroup
round

1. Addition and subtraction are opposite or ? . (TEKS 4.3A, p. 32)
2. When you ? , you find a number that is close to the exact amount. (TEKS 4.5A, p. 34)

Check Skills

Write a related fact. Use it to complete the number sentence. (TEKS 4.3A, pp. 32–33)

3. $■ - 8 = 6$
4. $9 + ■ = 14$
5. $■ + 4 = 11$
6. $12 - ■ = 6$

Round each number to the nearest ten, hundred, and thousand. (TEKS 4.5A, pp. 34–37)

7. 67,231
8. 681,392
9. 740,488
10. 9,783,904

Use mental math patterns to find the sum or difference. (TEKS 4.3A, pp. 38–39)

11. 70 + 60
12. 8,000 − 5,000
13. 30,000 − 20,000
14. 40,000 + 20,000
15. 90 − 30
16. 800 + 600
17. 150,000 − 80,000
18. 60,000 + 50,000
19. 21,000 − 7,000

Estimate by using rounding or compatible numbers. (TEKS 4.5A, pp. 40–43)

20. 349 + 348
21. 584 − 207
22. 6,799 − 3,256
23. 4,893 + 1,877

Add or subtract mentally. Tell the strategy you used. (TEKS 4.3A, pp. 44–47)

24. 81 + 49
25. 497 − 206
26. 344 − 190
27. 499 + 99

Estimate. Then find the sum or difference. (TEKS 4.3A, pp. 50–53, 54–55, 56–59)

28. 6,895 + 2,156
29. 9,084 − 3,486
30. 47,083 + 37,951
31. 60,539 − 18,574

Check Problem Solving

Solve. Explain why an exact answer or an estimate is needed. (TEKS 4.16B, pp. 48–49)

32. There are 76 students in the third grade and 92 students in the fourth grade. Rachel buys 180 cookies. Does she have enough to give each student one cookie?
33. WRITE Math Mr. Becker has $7,000. **Explain** how to use estimation to find whether he has enough to buy furniture for $2,459, a stereo for $2,359, and a TV for $2,599.

GO ONLINE **Technology** Use *Online Assessment.*

Enrich • Use Logical Reasoning

WORK UP OR DOWN

In a number pyramid, each number is found by adding the two numbers below it. In the pyramid at the right, $25 = 10 + 15$, $10 = 2 + 8$, and $15 = 8 + 7$.

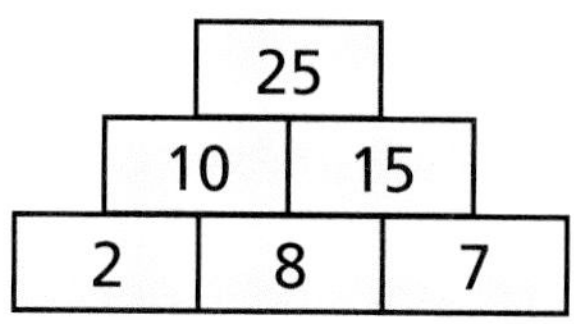

You can find missing numbers in a number pyramid by using addition and subtraction.

To find A: Think $121 + A = 238$, so $A = 238 - 121 = 117$.

To find B: Think $A + B = 247$, so $B = 247 - A = 247 - 117 = 130$.

To find C: Think $419 + 532 = C$, so $C = 951$.

1,855
904 | **C**
485 | 419 | 532
238 | 247 | 272 | 260
121 | ***A*** | ***B*** | 142 | 118

Examples

A Find the missing numbers *M* and *N*.

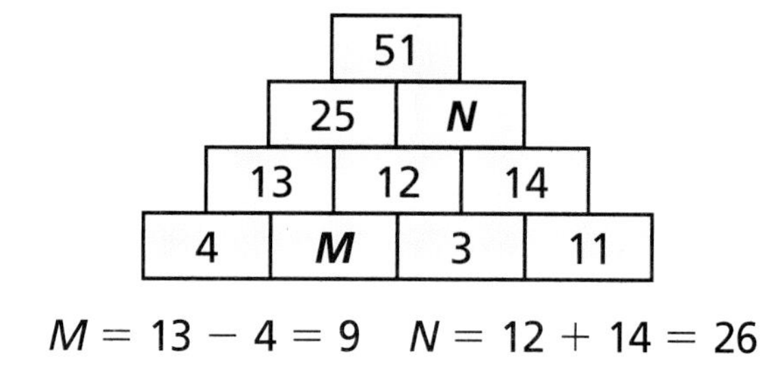

$M = 13 - 4 = 9$ $N = 12 + 14 = 26$

B Find the missing numbers *R*, *S*, and *T*.

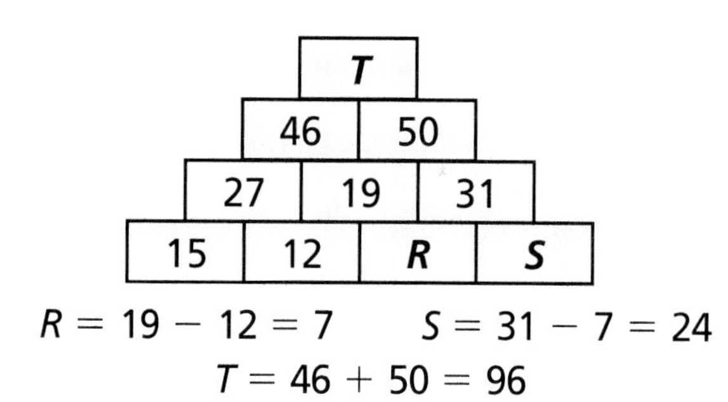

$R = 19 - 12 = 7$ $S = 31 - 7 = 24$
$T = 46 + 50 = 96$

Try It

Find the missing numbers.

1.

Z
16 | 19
11 | ***Y*** | 14
9 | 2 | 3 | ***X***

2.

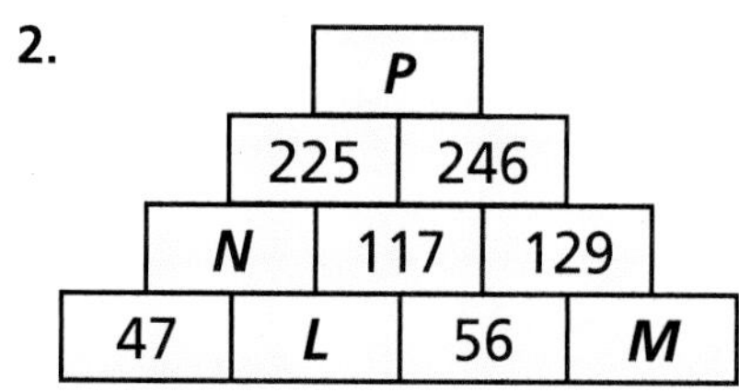

WRITE Math **Explain** how you found each missing number in problem 2.

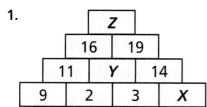

Getting Ready for the TAKS
Chapters 1–2

Number, Operation, and Quantitative Reasoning

TAKS Obj. 1

1. The first year's budget for the new zoo is $839,745. Which digit is in the ten thousands place?

   A 3 **B** 7 **C** 8 **D** 9

Look for important words.

See item 2. Look for the key words in the problem to help you decide whether to add or subtract.

2. The table below shows play attendance. How many more people attended on Friday than on Wednesday?

Play Attendance				
Day	Wed	Thu	Fri	Sat
Number	1,659	2,344	4,618	4,328

   F 2,669 **H** 5,987

   G 2,959 **J** Not here

3. Which list shows the numbers 48, 29, 37, 54, and 18 in order from least to greatest?

   A 48, 29, 37, 54, 18

   B 54, 48, 37, 29, 18

   C 18, 37, 29, 48, 54

   D 18, 29, 37, 48, 54

4. WRITE Math **Explain** how to round 3,749 to the nearest hundred.

Measurement TAKS Obj. 4

5. Which rectangle has an area of 20 square units?

   F 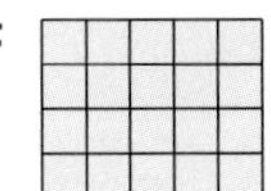

   G 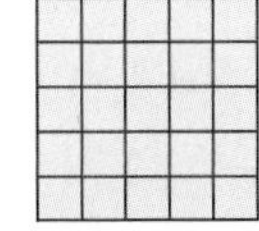

   H 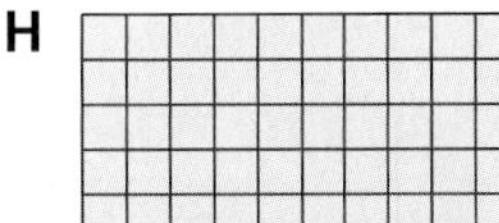

   J 

6. What temperature is shown on the thermometer?

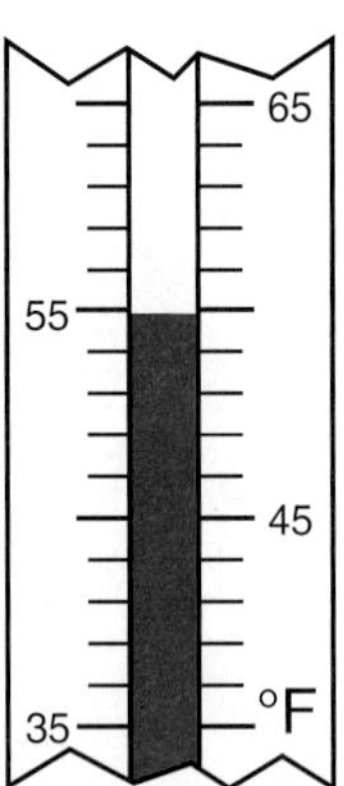

   A 65°F

   B 55°F

   C 45°F

   D 35°F

7. WRITE Math **Explain** how to read the time shown on the clock below.

Patterns, Relationships, and Algebraic Thinking TAKS Obj. 2

8. Which number sentence is **NOT** part of the fact family that includes $4 \times 5 = 20$?

   F $5 \times 4 = 20$

   G $20 \div 5 = 4$

   H $20 \div 4 = 5$

   J $5 + 4 = 9$

9. The table shows the relationship between the number of spiders and the number of legs. What is the missing number?

Spider Legs				
Spiders	1	2	3	4
Legs	8	16	■	32

   A 19

   B 20

   C 24

   D 28

10. What might the missing number be in the following pattern?

$$50, 46, 42, ■, 34$$

   F 36

   G 37

   H 38

   J 40

11. WRITE Math **Explain** how to start at 4 and count by fours to 20.

Geometry and Spatial Reasoning TAKS Obj. 3

12. Which two figures below do **NOT** appear to be similar?

   A

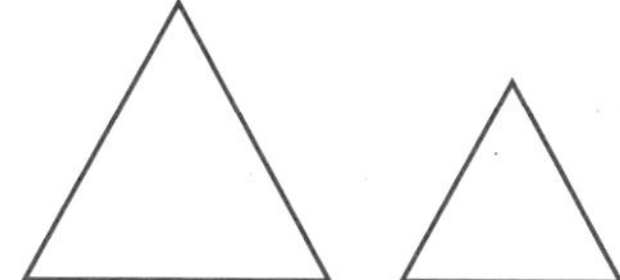

   B

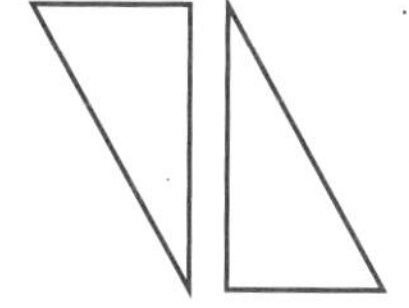

   C

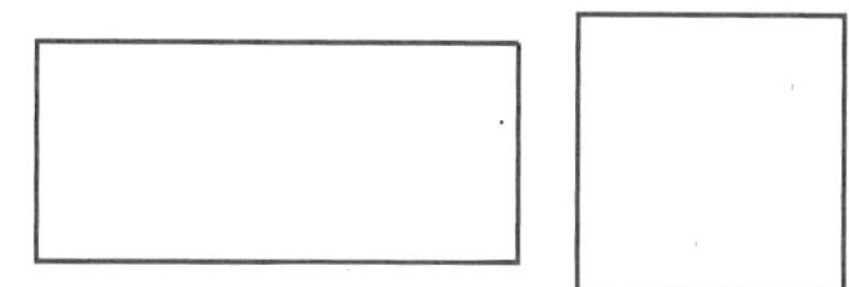

   D

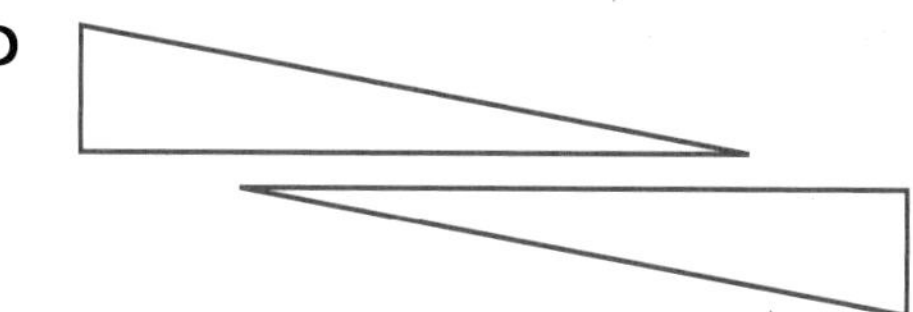

13. What is the name of the solid figure shown below?

   F Cube

   G Circle

   H Rectangular prism

   J Cylinder

14. WRITE Math **Describe** how a rectangle and a square are alike and how they are different.

3 Algebra: Use Addition and Subtraction

The Big Idea Properties and the concepts of algebra are used to evaluate expressions and solve addition and subtraction equations.

Investigate

Bowlers play 10 frames, or rounds. Each frame starts with 10 pins standing. A bowler may roll two balls in each frame to try to knock down all the pins. Suppose the first ball knocks down only some of the pins. If 4 pins are left standing, use the equation $4 + p = 10$ to find how many pins were knocked down. What addition or subtraction equations can you write to find the number of pins that could be knocked down by a first ball?

TEXAS FAST FACT

Special Olympics Texas is one of the world's largest Special Olympics programs. There are 20 sports. About 25,000 athletes with disabilities take part.

GO ONLINE **Technology**
Student pages are available in the Student eBook.

Show What You Know

Check your understanding of important skills needed for success in Chapter 3.

Addition and Subtraction

Find the sum or difference.

1. $8 + 5 = ■$ **2.** $12 + 7 = ■$ **3.** $16 - 3 = ■$

4. $12 - 9 = ■$ **5.** $9 + 8 = ■$ **6.** $15 + 7 = ■$

7. $11 - 3 = ■$ **8.** $14 + 5 = ■$ **9.** $25 - 8 = ■$

Find the Missing Number

Find the missing number.

10. $5 + ■ = 11$ **11.** $16 - ■ = 9$ **12.** $8 + ■ = 15$

13. $13 - ■ = 4$ **14.** $■ + 4 = 9$ **15.** $■ - 7 = 4$

16. $■ - 8 = 5$ **17.** $17 - ■ = 8$ **18.** $■ + 6 = 14$

19. $3 + ■ = 10$ **20.** $■ - 5 = 9$ **21.** $■ + 2 = 11$

Number Patterns

Predict the next number in the pattern.

22. 14, 21, 28, 35, ■ **23.** 6, 13, 20, 27, ■

24. 125, 225, 325, 425, ■ **25.** 88, 92, 96, 100, ■

26. 35, 30, 25, 20, ■ **27.** 253, 263, 273, 283, ■

VOCABULARY POWER

CHAPTER VOCABULARY

Associative Property
Commutative Property
equation
expression
fact family
Identity Property
inverse operations
ordered pair
parentheses
variable

WARM-UP WORDS

Commutative Property of Addition the property that states that when the order of two addends is changed, the sum is the same

Identity Property of Addition the property that states that when you add zero to any number, the sum is that number

Addition Properties

OBJECTIVE: Identify and use the properties of addition.

Quick Review

1. 90 + 30
2. 82 + 15
3. 17 + 22
4. 9 + 7
5. 45 + 13

Vocabulary

Commutative Property
Identity Property
Associative Property

Learn

PROBLEM Jared and Savon collect swirled and clear marbles. They have the same number of marbles. Jared has 38 swirled marbles and 23 clear marbles. Savon has 38 clear marbles. How many swirled marbles does Savon have?

The **Commutative Property of Addition** states that numbers can be added in any order and the sum will be the same.

Example 1 Use the Commutative Property.

Jared's marbles				Savon's marbles		
38 swirled	plus	23 clear	equals	38 clear	plus	■ swirled
↓	↓	↓	↓	↓	↓	↓
38	+	23	=	38	+	■

Since 38 + 23 = 38 + 23, then ■ = 23.

So, Savon has 23 swirled marbles.

The **Identity Property of Addition** states that when you add zero to any number, the sum is that number.

Example 2 Use the Identity Property.

If Savon has no other swirled marbles, how many swirled marbles does he have in all?

23 + 0 = 23
0 + 23 = 23

So, Savon has 23 swirled marbles in all.

The **Associative Property of Addition** states that the way addends are grouped does not change the sum.

Math Idea
Parentheses ( ) tell which operation you will do first.

Example 3 Use the Associative Property.

Matilda has 16 red, 24 yellow, and 18 blue shooter marbles. How many shooter marbles does she have in all?

16 + (24 + 18)	= (16 + 24) + 18	
16 + 42	= 40 + 18	Use the Associative Property.
58	= 58	Use mental math.

So, Matilda has 58 marbles.

TEKS 4.3A use addition and subtraction to solve problems involving whole numbers. *also* **4.14A, 4.14D, 4.15A, 4.15B, 4.16A**

Guided Practice

1. Which shows an example of the Commutative Property?

   $(13 + 17) + 22 = 13 + (17 + 22)$ $\quad$ $46 + 21 = 21 + 46$ $\quad$ $67 + 0 = 67$

Find the missing number. Name the property you used.

2. $73 + \blacksquare = 73$
3. $47 + \blacksquare = 56 + 47$
4. $\blacksquare + (31 + 18) = (24 + 31) + 18$
5. TALK Math **Explain** how to use the Commutative and Associative Properties to add $62 + 79 + 38$ mentally.

Independent Practice and Problem Solving

Find the missing number. Name the property you used.

6. $93 + 28 = 28 + \blacksquare$
7. $\blacksquare + 0 = 31$
8. $35 + (42 + \blacksquare) = (35 + 42) + 56$
9. $69 = \blacksquare + 69$
10. $59 + 85 = \blacksquare + 59$
11. $(76 + 97) + 19 = 76 + (\blacksquare + 19)$

Change the order or group the addends so that you can add mentally. Find the sum. Name the property you used.

12. $450 + 83 + 50$
13. $78 + 32 + 46$
14. $125 + 62 + 75$
15. $64 + 15 + 36 + 30$

USE DATA For 16–17, use the table.

16. Use the Associative Property to find the total number of green, red, and blue marbles that Serena has.
17. Serena has 10 fewer clay marbles than the total number of green and black marbles. How many clay marbles does she have?
18. WRITE Math **Explain** how you know which addition property to use to solve a problem.

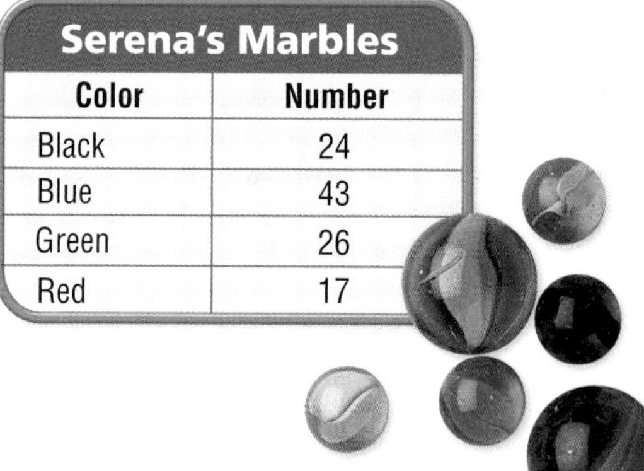

Serena's Marbles

Color	Number
Black	24
Blue	43
Green	26
Red	17

Mixed Review and TAKS Prep

19. What unit should Mary Jane use to measure the height of the classroom door? Tell why. (Grade 3 TEKS 3.11)
20. An airplane flight is 2,035 miles long. The plane makes one stop after 628 miles and a second stop after 745 miles. How many miles are left? (TEKS 4.3A, p. 50)
21. **TAKS Prep** Jameson has 28 gold coins, 27 silver coins, and 12 bronze coins. Explain how to use addition properties to find the total number of coins Jameson has. Then solve the problem. (Obj. 1)

Extra Practice on page 84, Set A

LESSON 2

Write and Evaluate Expressions

OBJECTIVE: Write and evaluate addition and subtraction expressions.

Quick Review

What is 5 more than each number?

1. 7 **2.** 10
3. 16 **4.** 23
5. 35

Vocabulary

expression
variable

Learn

PROBLEM Monica had \$15 to go to the mall. Her mom gave her \$5 more. She spent \$7 on a pair of earrings. How much money does she have left?

You can write an expression to show how much money Monica has left. An **expression** has numbers and operation signs, but does not have an equal sign.

Think: \$15 plus \$5 minus \$7

$(15 + 5) - 7$

Find the value of $(15 + 5) - 7$.

$(15 + 5) - 7$ Add \$15 and \$5.

$20 - 7$ Subtract \$7 from \$20.

\$13

So, $(15 + 5) - 7$ is 13. Monica has \$13 left.

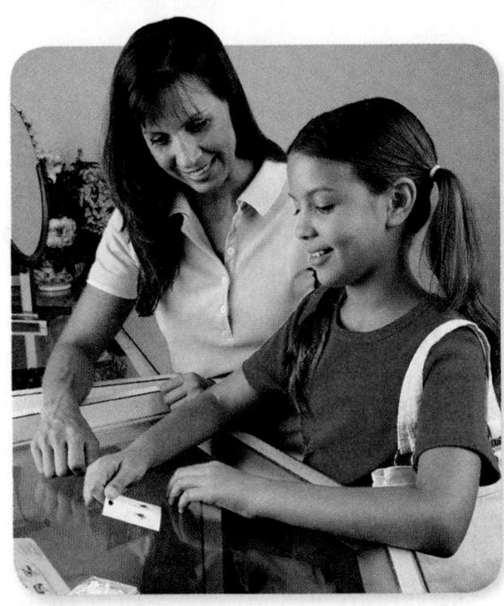

Example Find the value of the expression.

\$15 − (\$6 + \$3) Add \$6 and \$3.

\$15 − \$9 Subtract \$9 from \$15.

\$6

ERROR ALERT

Always do the operation in parentheses first, even if it comes second in the expression.

More Examples Find the value of the expression.

A $(18 - 7) + 3$

$(18 - 7) + 3$ Subtract 7 from 18.

$11 + 3$ Add 11 and 3.

14

B $18 - (7 + 3)$

$18 - (7 + 3)$ Add 7 to 3.

$18 - 10$ Subtract 10 from 18.

8

- Why do you always find the value in the parentheses first?

TEKS 4.15B relate informal language to mathematical language and symbols. *also* 4.3A, 4.14A, 4.15A

Expressions with Variables

Kyla buys a ticket to the water park. She spends $3 for lunch. What expression shows how much money she spends in all?

A **variable** is a letter or symbol that represents an unknown number. You can use a variable to show how much Kyla spends on the ticket.

price of ticket	plus	money spent for lunch
↓	↓	↓
■	+	3

So, the expression ■ + 3 shows how much money Kyla spends in all.

Suppose admission to the water park costs $8. How much money does Kyla spend in all? Find the value of ■ + 3 when ■ = 8 to find how much she spends in all.

ONE WAY **Use a model.**

Use pattern blocks to model the expression ■ + 3. Let ⬡ represent the price of the ticket and let ■ represent $1.

⬡ ■■■

■ + 3

To find the value of ■ + 3 if ■ = 8, replace ⬡ with 8 ■s. Place the ■s in one group to show the value of the expression.

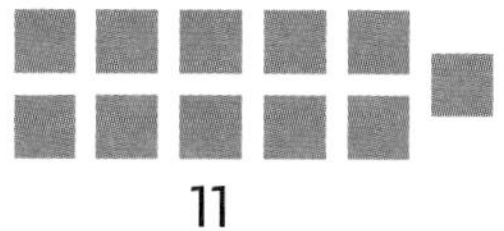

11

So, Kyla spends $11 in all.

ANOTHER WAY **Use symbols.**

Use the expression ■ + 3.

■ + 3
↓
8 + 3 — Replace ■ with 8, since the admission price is $8.
↓
11 — Add.

So, Kyla spends $11 in all.

A letter can also be used as a variable.

Examples Find the value of the expression.

A $18 - n$ if $n = 6$.

$18 - n$ — Replace n with 6.
↓
$18 - 6$ — Subtract 6 from 18.
↓
12

So, the value of the expression is 12.

B $9 + (y - 7)$ if $y = 15$.

$9 + (y - 7)$ — Replace y with 15.
↓
$9 + (15 - 7)$ — Subtract 7 from 15.
↓
$9 + 8$ — Add.
↓
17

So, the value of the expression is 17.

Guided Practice

1. There are 10 grapes in a bowl. Sara eats some of the grapes. Let g be the number of grapes she eats. Write an expression to show how many grapes are left.

Find the value of each expression.

2. $9 - (3 + 2)$
3. $10 - (8 - 5)$
4. ■ + 25 if ■ = 7
5. $13 - n$ if $n = 6$

Write an expression with a variable. Tell what the variable represents.

6. Peter hangs 3 posters on the wall. Amber hangs some more posters on the wall.
7. Alisha found some shells on the beach. She gave 4 of them to Lance.
8. TALK Math **Explain** how to find the value of the expression $12 - (5 + m)$ if $m = 3$.

Independent Practice and Problem Solving

Find the value of each expression.

9. $14 + (7 - 3)$
10. $17 - (5 + 6)$
11. ■ − 18 if ■ = 30
12. $20 - (5 - c)$ if $c = 3$
13. $(9 - 8) + 4$
14. $(6 + 9) - 2$
15. 8 − ■ if ■ = 6
16. $(33 - m) + 3$ if $m = 11$

Write an expression with a variable. Tell what the variable represents.

17. Denise had some rubber stamps. She loaned 6 rubber stamps to her teacher.
18. Jimmy has 16 model cars. He buys some more model cars.
19. Isis had 7 different collections. She started some more collections.
20. Ramiro had some money. He gave $20 to Anya.

Write words to match each expression.

21. $4 + a$
22. 15 − ■
23. $c - 6$
24. ■ − 9

USE DATA For 25–26, use the sign.

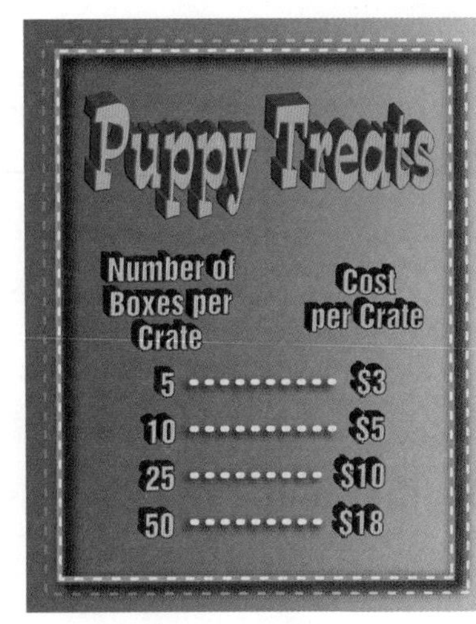

Puppy Treats
Number of Boxes per Crate
Cost per Crate
5 .... $3
10 .... $5
25 .... $10
50 .... $18

25. Keisha wants to buy 30 boxes of puppy treats for her local animal shelter. Will Keisha save more money if she buys 3 crates of 10 boxes, or 1 crate of 5 boxes and 1 crate of 25 boxes? How much will she save?
26. What is the least amount that it will cost Greg to buy 15 boxes?
27. Tyler donated 50 boxes of treats. He gave 15 boxes to shelter A and some to shelter B. Write an expression to show how many boxes Tyler donated to shelter B.

Extra Practice on page 84, Set B

28. **Reasoning** Place parentheses in the expression $16 - 7 - 4$ so the expression has a value of 13.

29. **WRITE Math** **What's the Error?** Taylor said the value of $20 - (9 + x)$ is 20 if $x = 9$. Describe how Taylor could have made the error. Find the correct value.

Mixed Review and TAKS Prep

30. A bag holds 1 red tile, 1 green tile, and 5 blue tiles of the same size. Which color tile is Tia most likely to choose if she selects a tile without looking? (Grade 3 TEKS 3.13C)

31. **TAKS Prep** There are 8 children around the table. Some of the children leave. Which expression shows the number of children still at the table? (Obj. 6)

    A $8 + c$ **B** $c - 8$ **C** $8 - c$ **D** $c + 8$

32. On different days Josh sold 35, 27, and 15 raffle tickets. Show how to use addition properties and mental math to find the total number of raffle tickets Josh sold. (TEKS 4.3A, p. 68)

33. **TAKS Prep** There are 9 pears in a basket. Singh and Allie each take 2 pears. Write an expression that shows the number of pears left in the basket. How many pears are left in the basket? (Obj. 6)

Problem Solving and Reasoning

VISUAL THINKING You can use a number line to find the value of an expression that uses whole numbers.

Use a number line to find the value of (5 + 8) − 3.

First, start at 5 and count on 8 spaces from 5.

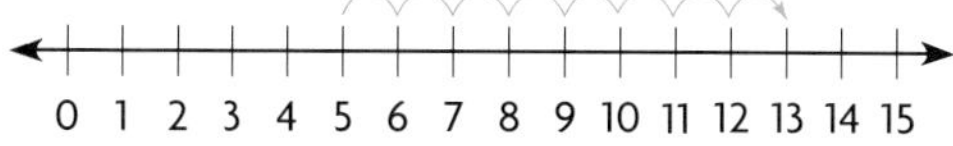

Then, count back 3 spaces. The number you end at is the value of the expression.

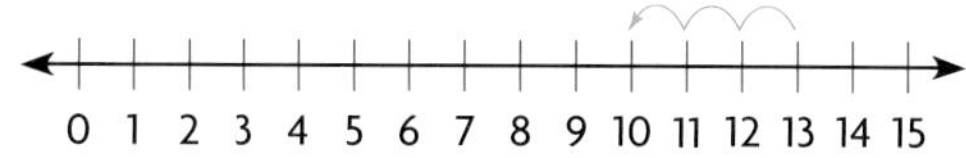

So, (5 + 8) − 3 = 10.

Use a number line to find the value of each expression.

1. $(6 + 5) - 4$
2. $(14 - 7) + 3$
3. $(13 - 4) - 5$
4. $(8 + 4) - 7$

LESSON 3

Addition and Subtraction Equations

OBJECTIVE: Write and solve addition and subtraction equations.

Quick Review

1. $17 + 6$
2. $25 - 8$
3. $56 + 24$
4. $93 - 32$
5. $73 + 29$

Vocabulary

equation

Learn

PROBLEM A service dog has completed 4 months of its 9-month training program at Canine Companions. What equation can you write to show how many months the dog has left to finish its training?

An **equation** is a number sentence stating that two amounts are equal.

Example 1 Write an addition equation.

Match the words to write an equation. Use the variable m to show the number of months left to finish his training.

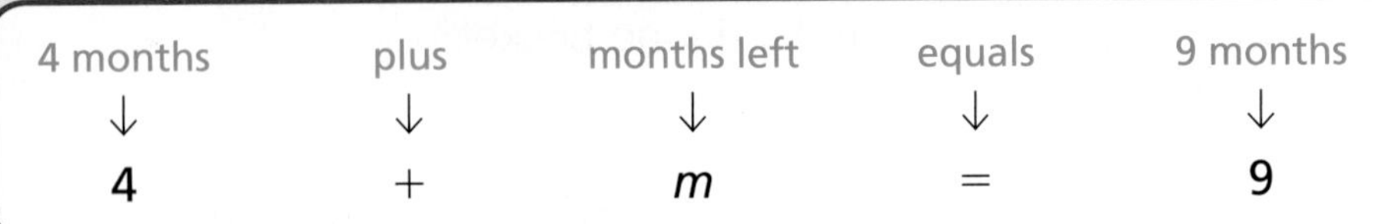

So, the equation is $4 + m = 9$.

Example 2 Write a subtraction equation.

There are 10 dog biscuits in a bowl. After the dogs eat some, there are 3 dog biscuits left.

Let b represent the number of dog biscuits eaten.

10 dog biscuits	minus	dog biscuits eaten	=	3 dog biscuits left
↓	↓	↓	↓	↓
10	−	b	=	3

- **What if** there are 12 dog biscuits in the bowl? After some more dog biscuits are put in the bowl, there are 17 dog biscuits. How would the equation change?

Example 3 Write a problem for the equation $m - 3 = 4$.

m	minus	3	=	4
↓	↓	↓	↓	↓
money Ben has	−	money Ben spends	=	money Ben has left

After spending \$3 for a dog bone, Ben has \$4 left. How much money did Ben have to start with?

TEKS 4.15B relate informal language to mathematical language and symbols. *also* 4.3A, 4.14A, 4.14C, 4.14D, 4.15A

Solve Equations

An equation is true if the values on both sides of the equal sign are equal. You solve an equation when you find the value of the variable that makes the equation true.

In the problem, to find how many months the service dog has left to finish its training, you can solve the equation $4 + m = 9$.

ONE WAY **Use the strategy guess and check.**

Materials ■ Equabeam™ balance

You can use the Equabeam balance to find the number that makes $4 + m = 9$ a true equation.

Step 1

Show 4 on the left and 9 on the right.

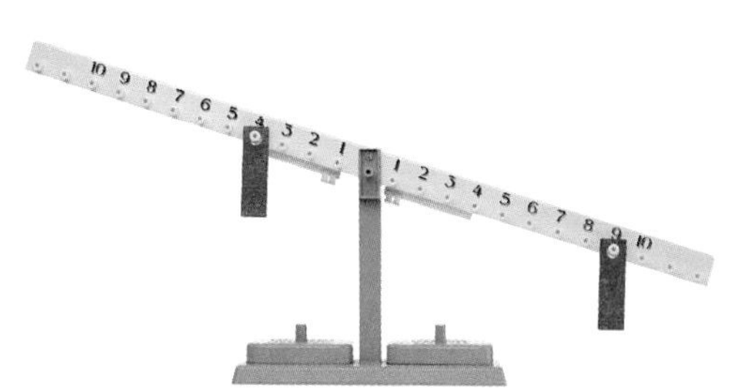

Step 2

Replace m with 4.	Place 4 on the left side.
$4 + 4 \stackrel{?}{=} 9$	$8 \neq 9$
Replace m with 5.	Place 5 on the left side.
$4 + 5 \stackrel{?}{=} 9$	$9 = 9$ ✔

So, the service dog has 5 months left to finish its training.

ANOTHER WAY **Use mental math.**

Solve.	$14 - d = 8$	**Think:** 14 minus what number equals 8?
	$d = 6$	
Check:	$14 - 6 \stackrel{?}{=} 8$	Replace d with 6.
	$8 = 8$ ✔	The equation is true.

So, the value of d is 6.

• How can you check that your equation is true?

Guided Practice

1. Which number, 8 or 9, makes the equation $n + 5 = 14$ true?

Write an equation for each. Choose a variable for the unknown. Tell what the variable represents.

2. A box has 24 pens. There are some blue pens and 8 red pens.

✓3. Emil has 18 stamps. After he uses some stamps, he has 12 stamps left.

Solve the equation.

4. $x + 9 = 17$ 5. $c - 6 = 7$ 6. $15 + \blacksquare = 21$ 7. $13 - n = 4$

8. TALK Math **Explain** how to make the equation $20 + a = 29$ true.

Independent Practice and Problem Solving

Write an equation for each. Choose the variable for the unknown. Tell what the variable represents.

9. There are 15 apples in the box. Some are green apples and 9 are red apples.

10. Andrea had some money. She spent $8 and had $4 left.

Solve the equation.

11. $4 + b = 16$ 12. $\blacksquare - 5 = 20$ 13. $m - 9 = 12$ 14. $24 - n = 21$

Write words to match the equation.

15. $m + 5 = 13$ 16. $15 - n = 4$ 17. $12 - p = 8$ 18. $y - 6 = 8$

USE DATA For 19–20, use the table.

19. How many more hearing dogs graduated than service dogs?

20. **Pose a Problem** Write and solve an equation that compares the total number of hearing dogs and service dogs that graduated. Tell what the variable represents.

Graduating Dogs

Month	Hearing	Service
February	8	2
May	5	4
November	9	4

21. **Reasoning** If $6 = m + 4$ and $c + m = 7$, find m and c.

22. WRITE Math Compare the values of n for $n + 8 = 12$ and $12 - n = 8$. **Explain** how you solved each equation.

Mixed Review and TAKS Prep

23. A magazine has 207,620 readers. Write the number in word form. (TEKS 4.1A, p. 4)

24. A display has 35 dolls in it. Some of the dolls are sold. Then 6 are returned. Write an expression for the number of dolls in the display now. (TEKS 4.3A, p. 70)

25. **TAKS Prep** Art class lasts 45 minutes. Students work 35 minutes on their projects, then clean up. Which equation can be used to find how long cleanup, c, lasts? (Obj. 6)

A $35 + c = 45$ **C** $45 + c = 35$

B $35 - c = 45$ **D** $c - 45 = 35$

Technology
Use Harcourt Mega Math, Ice Station Exploration, *Arctic Algebra*, Level S.

Extra Practice on page 84, Set C

Are We There Yet?

Cause and Effect

Levi's and Cindy's families are meeting at South Padre National Seashore for vacation. Both families live the same distance from the seashore. Levi's family drives 196 miles the first day and 223 miles the second day to reach the seashore. Cindy's family drives 195 miles the first day. How far does Cindy's family drive on the second day to reach the seashore?

Cause and effect can help you understand this problem.

Cause	Effect
The first day, Cindy's family drives fewer miles.	The second day, Cindy's family drives more miles than Levi's.

South Padre Island National Seashore has 70 miles of shoreline. Sixty-five of those miles are beaches.

Write an equation that shows the distances each family travels. Let d represent the distance Cindy's family drives on the second day.

Levi's family		Cindy's family	
first day	second day	first day	second day
↓	↓	↓	↓

$$196 + 223 = 195 + d$$

Compare the numbers in the equation to solve.

- Use mental math to make an addend on the left side of the equation the same as the one on the right side.
  Think: Since 196 is one more than 195, d has to be one more than 223 for the equation to be true.

Problem Solving **Use cause and effect to solve.**

1. Solve the problem above.
2. Hannah's and Ravi's families plan to camp together near South Padre National Seashore. They live the same distance from the campground. Hannah's family drives 142 miles on the first day and the rest of the way on the second day. Ravi's family drives 143 miles on the first day and 176 miles on the second day. How far does Hannah's family drive on the second day? Write an equation. Tell what the variable represents and then solve.

Problem Solving Workshop
Strategy: Work Backward

OBJECTIVE: Solve problems using the strategy *work backward*.

Learn the Strategy

When you work backward to solve a problem, you start with the end result and use the facts in the problem to work back to the beginning of a problem.

Work backward from a total.

There are 16 pelicans at the pier. When more pelicans fly to the pier, there are 20 pelicans. How many more pelicans fly to the pier?

When you add to find a total, you can subtract to work backward to solve.

Write an addition equation to model the problem.

$16 + p = 20$ Let p = number of pelicans that fly to the pier.

To find the value of p, work backward.

$20 - 16 = p$

Work backward from an end time.

Raymond and Charity got to the library at 3:45 P.M. It takes 20 minutes to walk to the library from Charity's house, and Raymond got to Charity's house 15 minutes before they left for the library. At what time did Raymond arrive at Charity's house?

Use a model to find the time Raymond arrived at Charity's house.

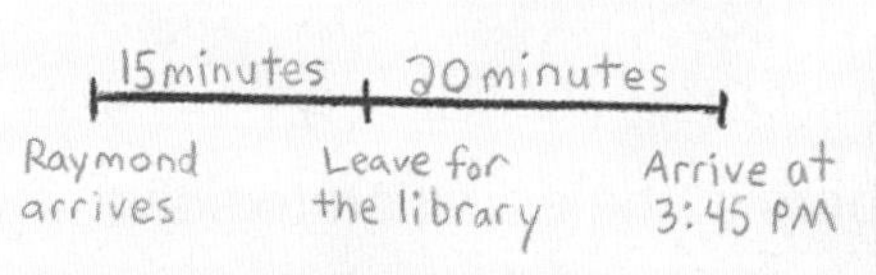

To find the time Raymond arrived at Charity's house, work backward.

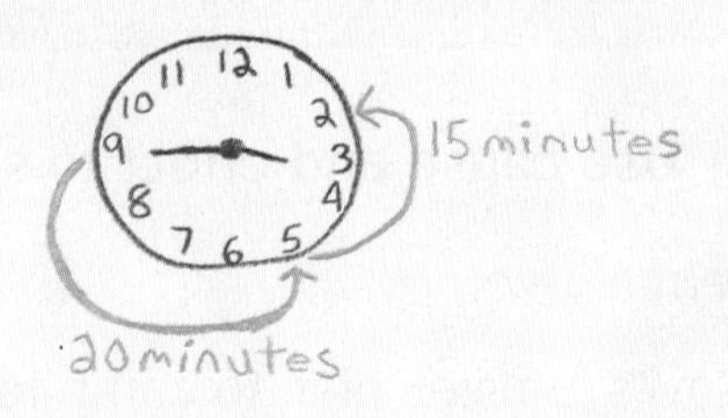

TALK Math

How can you check your answer to the first problem?

TEKS 4.15B Relate informal language to mathematical language and symbols. *also* **4.3A, 4.14A, 4.14B, 4.14C, 4.15A, 4.16B**

Use the Strategy

PROBLEM A wildlife preserve in Zimbabwe, Africa, has a habitat for lions. The rangers released 8 lions back into the wild and then received 12 lions from another preserve. Now there are 24 lions at the preserve. How many lions did the preserve have before the release?

Read to Understand

- **What information will you use?**

Plan

- **What strategy can you use to solve the problem?**

  You can write an equation with a variable. Then solve the problem by working backward.

Solve

- **How can you use the strategy to solve the problem?**

  Write an equation with a variable to model the problem.

Make sure the equation shows the sequence of events.

Think: There were some lions before the release. Eight lions were released. Then the preserve received 12 lions. Now there are 24 lions.

Choose a variable. Let *b* represent the number of lions before the release. To find the value of *b*, work backward.

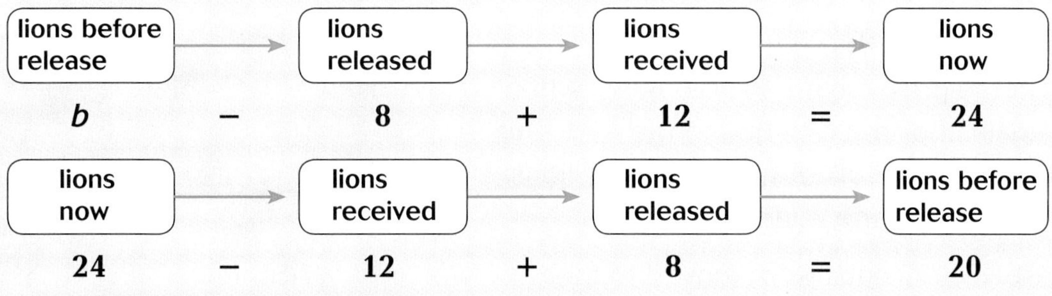

So, there were 20 lions before the release.

Check

- **What other strategies could you use to check your answer?**

Guided Problem Solving

1. There are many volunteer teams that feed the lions at Léon Preserve. Another preserve needed help, so 10 volunteer teams left. The next day, 4 new volunteer teams arrived and now Léon Preserve has 15 teams. How many teams were there originally?

First, choose a variable. Tell what the variable represents.	Let v represent the original number of volunteer teams.
Next, write an equation.	$v - 10 + 4 = 15$
Then, work backward.	$15 - 4 + 10 = v$
Finally, solve the equation.	$21 = v$

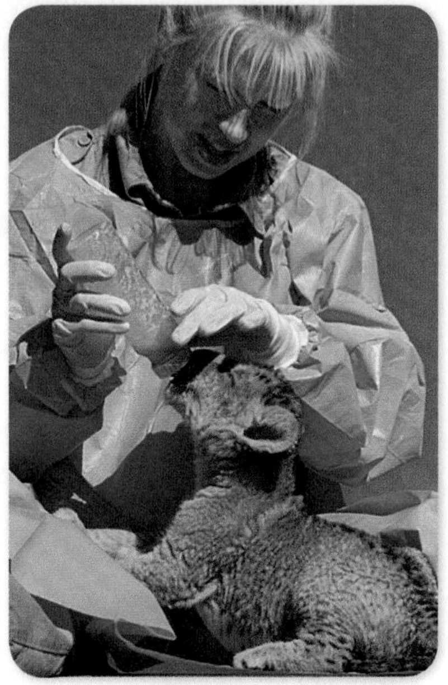

2. **What if** 5 volunteer teams left and 11 arrived? How many teams were there originally?

3. Many volunteer teams must patrol and clean the lion preserve. Twelve teams leave the preserve on patrol. Seven teams arrive to clean. There are 23 teams at the preserve now. How many volunteer teams were there originally?

Problem Solving Strategy Practice

Work backward to solve.

4. It costs $2,900 to volunteer for 4 weeks at a lion breeding project. There is an extra cost for each additional week. It costs Jeff $3,500 to volunteer for 5 weeks. How much does each additional week cost?

USE DATA For 5–6, use the table.

5. The mature lions at the preserve are injured lions. When they are healthy again, they are returned to the wild. This year, the preserve had a total of 11 injured mature lions. How many were returned to the wild?

6. WRITE Math Last week, 7 cubs were moved to the adolescent group, and 4 cubs were born. **Explain** how to find how many cubs the preserve had last week.

7. **FAST FACT** The largest recorded African lion weighed 690 pounds. The difference in weight between the largest lion and an average lion is 120 pounds. How much does an average African lion weigh?

Preserve Lion Population

Age	Number
Cubs	18
Adolescents	14
Mature	2
Older	7

Mixed Strategy Practice

8. Daily duties for each animal include grooming, walking, and feeding. If a volunteer is in charge of 7 animals, how many daily duties will the volunteer do?

USE DATA For 9–10, use the bar graph.

9. There were more volunteers for the lion project during the summer than during the spring. If 105 people volunteered in the summer, how many more volunteers were there than in the spring?
10. During a two-week stay at the wildlife preserve in the summer, there were 17 fewer volunteers than the total number for the spring. How many volunteers were there in the two-week period?
11. **Pose a Problem** Look back at Problem 7. Write a similar problem by exchanging the known and unknown information.
12. **Open-Ended** Zawati Preserve had some volunteers. Some of the volunteers went to other preserves. Zawati Preserve has 12 volunteers left. How many volunteers might have been there to begin with and how many might have left for other preserves?
13. Volunteers rescued a lion, an elephant, and a leopard from traps. They rescued the lion before the leopard. The lion was not the first animal rescued. In what order did the volunteers rescue the animals?

CHALLENGE YOURSELF

Visitors to the wildlife preserve can take a guided tour to see the animals. There were 373 visitors to the preserve in January and 388 visitors in February.

14. Each month, the preserve had 15 more visitors than the month before. How many visitors did the preserve have in June, July, and August combined?
15. During January, 151 more children than adults visited the preserve. Draw a diagram to find how many adults visited the preserve during January.

Choose a STRATEGY

- Draw a Diagram or Picture
- Make a Model or Act It Out
- Make an Organized List
- Look for a Pattern
- Make a Table or Graph
- Guess and Check
- Work Backward
- Solve a Simpler Problem
- Write an Equation
- Use Logical Reasoning

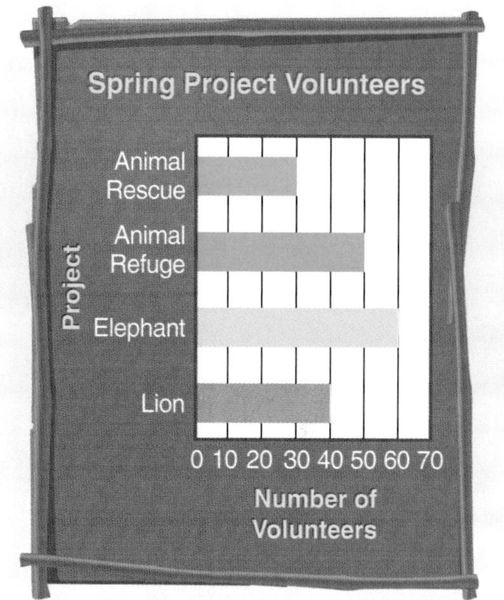

Ordered Pairs in a Table

OBJECTIVE: Describe the relationship between two sets of related data as ordered pairs in a table.

Quick Review

Add 12 to each number.

1. 6
2. 14
3. 23
4. 35
5. 60

Vocabulary

ordered pair

Learn

PROBLEM A pattern of figures is made using triangles that are 1 unit long on each side. The perimeter of the first figure is 3 units. The second figure has 2 triangles and a perimeter of 4 units. The third figure has 3 triangles and a perimeter of 5 units. Find a rule for the perimeter of a figure using the number of triangles in the figure.

Activity **Materials** ■ triangle pattern blocks

- Use pattern blocks to model the pattern.
- Make an input/output table. You can use variables to show the input and output. The input, *t*, is the number of triangles, and the output, *p*, is the perimeter.
- Look for a pattern in the table. Pattern: The output is 2 more than the input, *t*.

Input	Output
t	*p*
1	3
2	4
3	5
4	■
5	■

So, the rule is that the perimeter is 2 greater than the number of triangles.

Each input and its output in the table make up an ordered pair. An **ordered pair**, such as (1,3), is a related or matched pair of numbers always arranged the same way—the first number followed by the second number. The rule describes the relationship between the numbers.

Examples **Find a rule. Use your rule to find the next two ordered pairs.**

Input	*x*	12	15	18	21	24
Output	*y*	8	11	14	■	■

Rule: Subtract 4 from *x*.

Test your rule for each pair of numbers in the table.

$21 - 4 = 17$ $24 - 4 = 20$

So, the next two ordered pairs are (21,17) and (24,20).

Input	*b*	9	17	24	31	39
Output	*c*	16	24	31	■	■

Rule: Add 7 to *b*.

Test your rule for each pair of numbers in the table.

$31 + 7 = 38$ $39 + 7 = 46$

So, the next two ordered pairs are (31,38) and (39,46).

TEKS 4.7 The student is expected to describe the relationship between two sets of related data such as ordered pairs in a table. *also* **4.3A, 4.14A, 4.14C, 4.14D, 4.15A, 4.15B, 4.16A**

Guided Practice

1. Rule: Add 15 to *r*. What are the next two numbers in the pattern?

Input	*r*	7	9	12	16	20	23
Output	*s*	22	24	27	31	■	■

Find a rule. Use your rule to find the next two ordered pairs.

2.

Input	*a*	12	25	31	43	59
Output	*b*	20	33	39	■	■

3.

Input	*m*	62	58	47	31	24
Output	*n*	57	53	42	■	■

4. TALK Math **Explain** why it is important to test your rule with all the numbers in an input/output table.

Independent Practice and Problem Solving

Find a rule. Use your rule to find the next two ordered pairs.

5.

Input	*x*	35	42	63	75	80
Output	*y*	24	31	52	■	■

6.

Input	*w*	14	21	45	■	■
Output	*x*	34	41	65	73	92

Use the rule to make an input/output table.

7. Add 16 to the input.
8. Subtract 10 from the input.
9. Add 23 to the input.
10. Subtract 17 from the input.

USE DATA For 11–12, use the table.

11. Write a rule for the information in the Hot Lunch Accounts table.
12. Enrique's account had $21 on Monday. He has lunch each day. How much was in his account on Friday after lunch?
13. WRITE Math **What's the Question?** Mabel has $16 on Friday after spending $4 each day that week for lunch. The answer is $36.

Hot Lunch Accounts

Before	After
$16	$13
$24	$21
$29	$26
$33	$30

Mixed Review and TAKS Prep

14. Channel 2 had 78,553 viewers on Sunday. Rounded to the nearest thousand, how many viewers did they have? (TEKS 4.5A, p. 34)
15. Dan has $38. He buys a book and has $11 left. How much did the book cost? (TEKS 4.3A, p. 44)
16. **TAKS Prep** Write a rule for the table.

Input	*r*	14	23	31	39
Output	*s*	8	17	25	33

Extra Practice on page 84, Set D

Extra Practice

Set A Find the missing number. Name the property you used. (pp. 68–69)

1. $62 + 46 = 46 + ■$
2. $53 + (64 + ■) = (53 + 64) + 19$
3. $■ + 0 = 92$
4. $98 = ■ + 98$
5. $(23 + 77) + 54 = 23 + (■ + 54)$
6. $79 + 63 = 63 + ■$

Set B Find the value of each expression. (pp. 70–73)

1. $11 + (8 - 4)$
2. $24 - (7 + 9)$
3. $6 - (10 - 8)$
4. $13 + (15 - 8)$
5. $■ - 15$ if $■ = 65$
6. $25 - (9 - c)$ if $c = 4$
7. $53 + ■$ if $■ = 18$
8. $16 - (c + 4)$ if $c = 7$

Write an expression with a variable. Tell what the variable represents.

9. Nikolai had some cookies. He gave 7 cookies to his friends.
10. Donna has 12 books. She buys some more at the book fair.

Set C Write an equation for each. Choose the variable for the unknown. Tell what the variable represents. (pp. 74–77)

1. Garrett has 36 DVDs. Some are movies, and the other 9 are games.
2. Kristi spends \$4 for a sandwich. She has \$8 left.
3. Fatima has 12 pair of earrings. Four pair are gold and the rest are silver.
4. Lachlan and his father used 3 cans of paint. They had 5 cans to begin with, and they have some left.

Solve the equation.

5. $9 + n = 17$
6. $■ - 8 = 15$
7. $n - 15 = 20$
8. $30 - b = 20$
9. $k - 33 = 7$
10. $g + 19 = 25$
11. $41 + m = 59$
12. $9 + ■ = 100$

Set D Find a rule. Use your rule to find the next two ordered pairs. (pp. 82–83)

1.

Input	x	4	8	12	16	20
Output	y	16	20	24	■	■

2.

Input	x	32	47	55	■	■
Output	y	23	38	46	73	88

3.

Input	x	19	27	38	46	72
Output	y	26	34	45	■	■

4.

Input	x	71	80	85	■	■
Output	y	68	77	82	89	95

CD ROM **Technology**
Use Harcourt Mega Math, Ice Station Exploration, *Arctic Algebra,* Levels B, F, Y.

TECHNOLOGY CONNECTION

Spreadsheet: Graph Ordered Pairs (TEKS 4.14D, 4.7, 4.15A, 4.15B)

You can represent geometric patterns in tables and on graphs.

Materials ■ spreadsheet program ■ tiles

Step 1 Use square tiles to model the pattern of figures up to a figure with 10 blocks.

Step 2 Make an input/output table for the number of squares and the perimeter of each figure. Write ordered pairs for each input/output value.

Input (number of squares)	Output (perimeter in units)	Ordered Pair
1	4	(1,4)
2	6	(2,6)
3	8	(3,8)
4	10	(4,10)
5	■	■

Step 3 Enter the input/output data into a spreadsheet. To move among cells in the spreadsheet, use the arrow keys or click on the desired cell.

	A	B
1	Number of Squares	Perimeter (in units)
2	1	4
3	2	6
4	3	8
5	4	10
6	5	12
7	6	14
8	7	16

Step 4 Make a graph of the input/output data. Enter a title and labels for the graph.

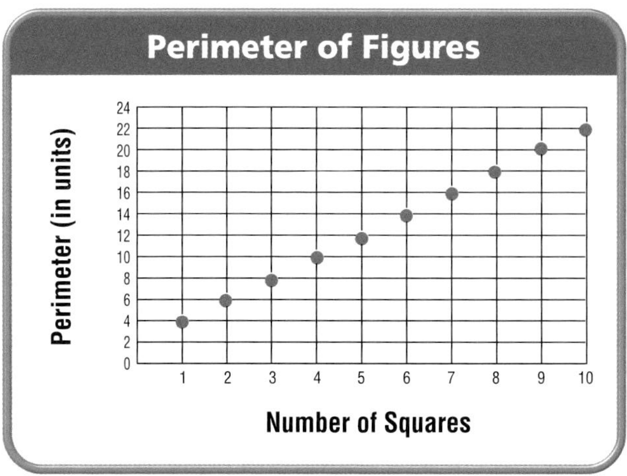

Try It

1. Which ordered pair corresponds to a figure with 10 blocks?

2. **Explore More Explain,** in units, the relationship between the number of squares and the perimeter.

Chapter 3 Review/Test

Check Vocabulary and Concepts

Choose the best term from the box.

VOCABULARY
Associative Property of Addition
Commutative Property of Addition
equation

1. An $\underline{?}$ is a number sentence stating that two amounts are equal. (TEKS 4.15B, p.74)
2. Numbers can be added in any order and the sum will be the same. This is called the $\underline{?}$. (TEKS 4.3A, p. 68)

Check Skills

Find the missing number. Name the property you used. (TEKS 4.3A, pp. 68–69)

3. $52 + 28 = 28 + ■$
4. $■ + 0 = 67$
5. $28 + (12 + ■) = (28 + 12) + 38$

Find the value of each expression. (TEKS 4.15B, pp. 70–73)

6. $16 + (9 - 5)$
7. $27 - (7 + 8)$
8. $25 + (11 - 7)$
9. $33 - (10 - 6)$
10. $■ - 12$ if $■ = 52$
11. $45 - (d + 9)$ if $d = 4$
12. $36 + (15 - y)$ if $y = 7$
13. $14 + ■$ if $■ = 25$

Solve the equation. (TEKS 4.15B, pp. 74–77)

14. $8 + d = 15$
15. $k - 7 = 35$
16. $n + 21 = 24$
17. $17 - b = 9$
18. $a + 7 = 23$
19. $8 + g = 21$
20. $m - 9 = 12$
21. $26 - w = 18$

Find a rule. Use your rule to find the next two ordered pairs. (TEKS 4.7, pp. 82–83)

22.

Input	x	23	35	49	56	71
Output	y	36	48	62	■	■

23.

Input	x	26	34	46	■	■
Output	y	11	19	31	58	77

Check Problem Solving

Solve. (TEKS 4.15B, pp. 78–81)

24. Ellie had 37 stuffed animals in her collection. Her aunt gave her some more stuffed animals to add to her collection, so now she has 43. How many stuffed animals did her aunt give her?

25. **WRITE Math** Manuel saved \$64 for a new bicycle, including the \$18 he earned mowing lawns. Write an equation. **Explain** how to work backward to find how much money Manuel had before he mowed the lawns.

Enrich • Use Relational Thinking

Baseball Cards

Mike has 27 baseball cards and buys 18 more cards. Laura has the same number of baseball cards as Mike after she buys 19 cards. How many baseball cards did Laura have before she bought 19 cards?

You can write an equation to find the number of baseball cards Laura had.

Mike's **Laura's**

27 cards + 18 cards = x cards + 19 cards

$$27 + 18 = x + 19$$

Think: The value of the left side of an equation is the same as the value of the right side.

Use relational thinking to find the value of x without computing.

$27 + 18 = x + 19$

$27 + 18 = 26 + 19$ **Think:** 19 is 1 more than 18, so x is 1 less than 27.

$x = 26$

So, Laura had 26 baseball cards before she bought 19 cards.

All Star Examples

A $12 + 9 = 10 + 8 + n$

$12 + 9 = 10 + 8 + 3$

$n = 3$

Think: 10 is 2 less than 12, and 8 is 1 less than 9.

So, n is 2 + 1, or 3.

B $75 - 36 = 75 - 35 - s$

$75 - 36 = 75 - 35 - 1$

$s = 1$

Think: 75 is equal to 75, and 35 is 1 less than 36.

So, s is 1.

Take a Swing

Use relational thinking to find the value of the variable.

1. $8 + 5 = p + 6$

2. $85 - 25 = 75 - y$

3. $449 + 862 = 450 + b$

4. $100 - 77 = s - 79$

5. $14 + 38 = 14 + 36 + x$

6. $99 - 68 = 99 - 66 - t$

7. $55 + 59 = 50 + 50 + c$

8. $432 - 167 = 432 - 67 - n$

9. $87 + 56 = 86 + 55 + p$

Ninth Inning

WRITE Math **Explain** how you used relational thinking to solve problem 7.

Unit Review/Test
Chapters 1–3

Multiple Choice

1. The table shows daily attendance at some amusement parks in 2004 and 2005.

Daily Amusement Park Attendance	
Year	**Number of Visitors**
2004	899,000
2005	917,000

How many more amusement park visitors were there in 2005 than in 2004? (TAKS Obj. 1)

A 18,000

B 19,000

C 20,000

D Not here

2. Which of the following is another way to write $90,000 + 3,000 + 600 + 40 + 3$? (TAKS Obj. 1)

F 93,643

G 93,463

H 90,643

J 90,463

3. Sherri found a grand piano that costs $29,445. To the nearest thousand, how much does the piano cost? (TAKS Obj. 1)

A $30,000

B $29,500

C $29,000

D $20,000

4. Which digit is in the millions place in 35,970,241? (TAKS Obj. 1)

F 9

G 7

H 5

J 3

5. A flight from New York to Austin costs $453 in July and $298 in October. About how much more does the flight cost in July than in October? (TAKS Obj. 1)

A $50

B $150

C $250

D $800

6. Jake had $43. He spent some on music and $3 on a magazine. Now he has $21 left. How much does he spend on music? (TAKS Obj. 1)

F $24 **H** $19

G $21 **J** $17

7. Raul's age is greater than 20 and less than 50. The ones digit is 4 more than the tens digit. Which could be Raul's age? (TAKS Obj. 1)

A 40

B 37

C 25

D 15

Technology Use *Online Assessment.*

8. Which rule describes the data in the table? (TAKS Obj. 2)

Input	x	5	7	9	11	13
Output	y	14	16	18	20	22

F Add x to y

G Add 9 to x

H Subtract 9 from x

J Subtract x from y

9. Marcos had some comic books. At Cory's Comics he bought 4 more. Now Marcos has 43 comic books in all. How many comic books did Marcos have before he went to Cory's Comics? (TAKS Obj. 1)

A 39

B 40

C 43

D 47

10. The table shows the number of cars that use Exit 8 on Trans-State Parkway on different days.

Exit 8 Traffic	
Day	**Number of Cars**
Sunday	2,451
Monday	3,612
Tuesday	3,519

How many cars in all use Exit 8 on Sunday and Monday? (TAKS Obj. 1)

F 1,161

G 5,063

H 6,062

J 6,063

11. Which digit makes the number sentence true? (TAKS Obj. 1)

$$4{,}201{,}351 > 4{,}20\blacksquare{,}351$$

A 3

B 2

C 1

D 0

Short Response

12. Find a rule. Use your rule to find the next two ordered pairs. (TAKS Obj. 2)

Input	x	21	26	32	37	50
Output	y	17	22	28	■	■

13. The first edition of the *Oxford English Dictionary* was published in 1928. The third edition was published online in 2000. How many years after the first edition was the third edition published? (TAKS Obj. 1)

14. A music group printed 20,000 postcards. They handed out 16,263. What is the best estimate of how many postcards were not handed out? (TAKS Obj. 1)

15. An online store received 8,827 orders on Monday. On Tuesday, just 1,993 orders were left to be shipped. How many orders were shipped on Monday? (TAKS Obj. 1)

Extended Response WRITE Math

16. Kathleen's computer stores 900 songs. She has 883 songs and wants to add 15 more. Will 15 more songs fit on Kathleen's computer? Do you need an exact answer or an estimate? **Explain.** (TAKS Obj. 1)

17. Alma is 9 years old. Her brother Paco is 5 years older. Make an input/output table to show their ages next year, in 3 years, in 5 years, and in 10 years. **Explain** how the data sets are related. (TAKS Obj. 2)

Texas

Problem Solving

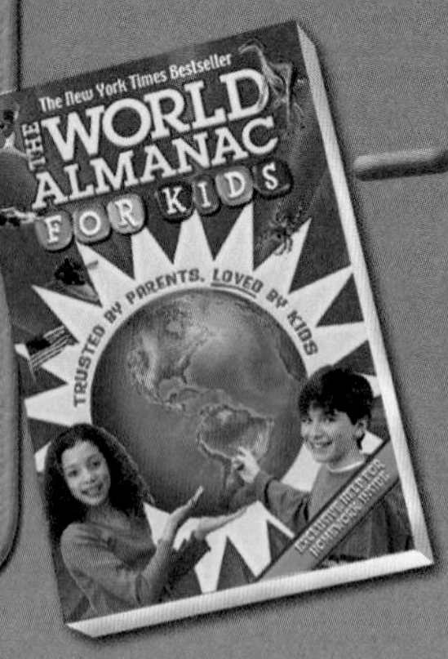

Languages We Speak

Languages at Home in Texas

No one is sure how many languages there are in the world, but there are certainly more than 4,000. Most people in Texas speak English. However, many people speak other languages, too.

Language Spoken at Home in Texas

Language	Number of Speakers Over 5 Years Old
Arabic	32,000
Chinese	103,000
English Only	13,648,000
French	58,000
Spanish	5,529,000
Vietnamese	129,000

FACT·ACTIVITY

Use the table above to answer the questions.

1. What digit will be in the thousands place if you add the number of Arabic speakers and Chinese speakers together?
2. Which language has a number of speakers with the digit 5 in the ten thousands place?
3. Do more speakers over 5 years old speak English Only or Spanish at home?
4. Order the languages from least number of speakers to greatest number of speakers.
5. Which language has the digit 3 in the greatest place-value position?
6. Write the number of Chinese speakers in word form.
7. WRITE Math **Explain** how to compare the number of French speakers to the number of Arabic speakers.

23 18 9 20 9 14 7 9 14 3 15 4 5

In 1838, the American inventor Samuel F. B. Morse developed a code for sending messages over electrical wires. His code used short pulses (dots) and long pulses (dashes) of electricity to represent letters and numbers. Morse code allows people to communicate over long distances without speaking.

Morse Code

A	B	C	D	E	F	G	H	I	J	K	L	M
.-	-...	-.-.	-..	.	..-.	--.	....	..	.---	-.-	.-..	--

N	O	P	Q	R	S	T	U	V	W	X	Y	Z
-.	---	.--.	--.-	.-.	...	-	..-	...-	.--	-..-	-.--	--..

1	2	3	4	5	6	7	8	9	0
.----	..---	...--	....-	.....	-....	--...	---..	----.	-----

ALMANAC Fact

A museum dedicated to Thomas Alva Edison is located in Beaumont, Texas. Edison invented a way for two messages to travel over a telegraph wire at the same time, instead of just one.

Telegraph operators tap a key like this to send messages in Morse code.

FACT·ACTIVITY

Use codes to answer the questions.

1. Texas is also called the Lone Star State. Write Texas' nickname in Morse code.
2. The title of this page is written in a simple number code. The chart to the right shows the code used. Use the code to find the title of this page.
3. Make up your own number code.
   - Make a different code using the same 26 letters.
   - How can you use number patterns to make a new code?
   - How can you use what you know about place value to make up a new code?
   - Write a message in your code. Do not put the solution on the page. Have a few classmates try to crack your code!

Number Code

A = 1	B = 2	C = 3	D = 4
E = 5	F = 6	G = 7	H = 8
I = 9	J = 10	K = 11	L = 12
M = 13	N = 14	O = 15	P = 16
Q = 17	R = 18	S = 19	T = 20
U = 21	V = 22	W = 23	X = 24
Y = 25	Z = 26		

UNIT

2 Multiplication and Division Facts

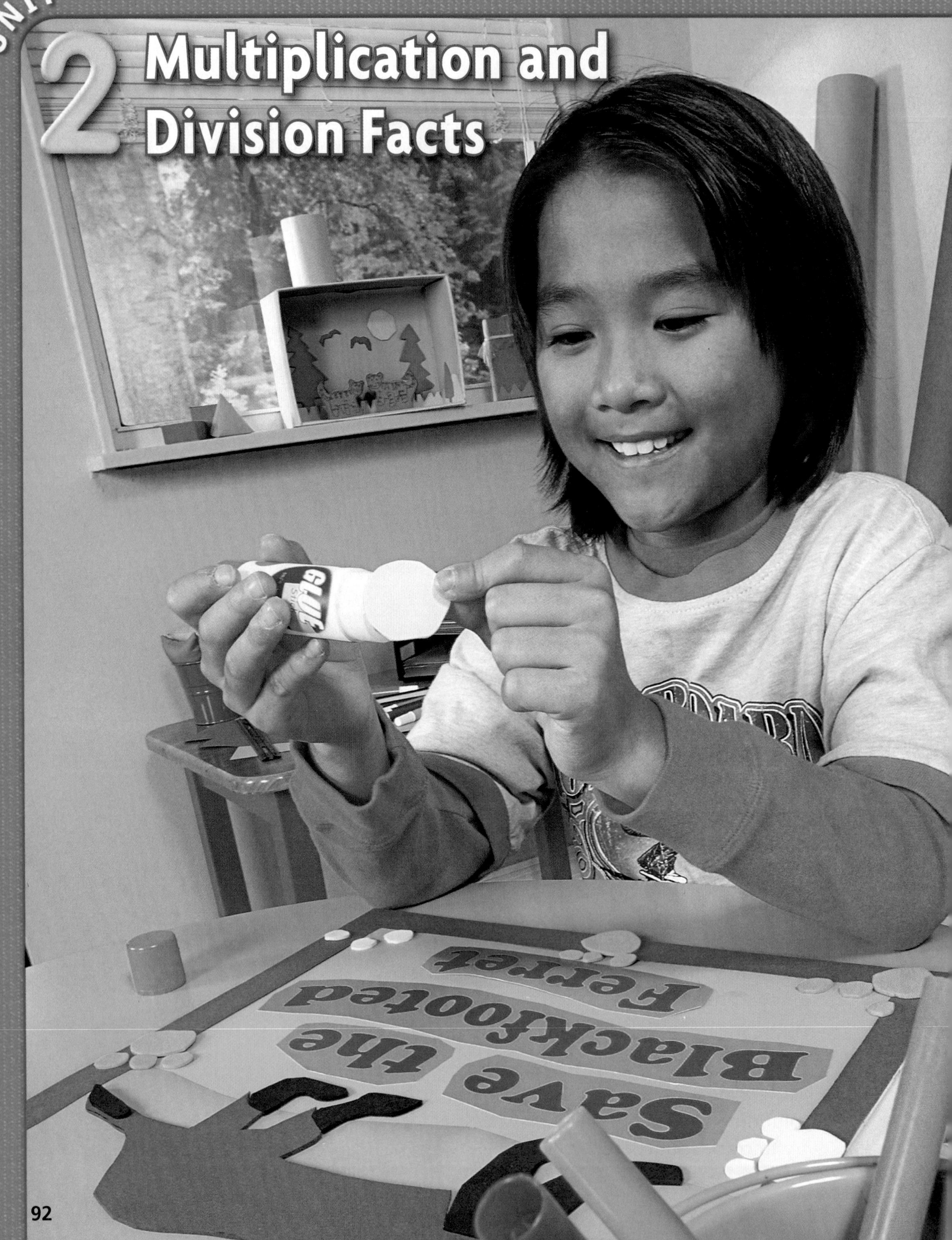

Math on Location

with **Texas Chapter Projects**

1

Many families like this baby black-footed ferret's family of 4 are protected and fed by scientists.

2

Family groups are prepared to live in divided areas in the wild by living in similar, but protected, areas.

3

Protection and preparation equal multiple strong families for a species once considered extinct.

VOCABULARY POWER

TALK Math

Look at the words below the first **Math on Location** photograph. If each family group in the protected area has the same number of ferrets as that family, how could you find the number of ferrets in 6 family groups?

READ Math

REVIEW VOCABULARY You learned the words below when you learned multiplication and division basic facts. How do these words relate to **Math on Location**?

divide to separate into equal groups; the opposite operation of multiplication

fact family a set of related multiplication and division, or addition and subtraction, number sentences

multiply when you combine equal groups, you can multiply to find how many in all; the opposite operation of division

WRITE Math

Copy and complete the Venn diagram below. Use what you know about multiplication and division facts to complete the Venn diagram.

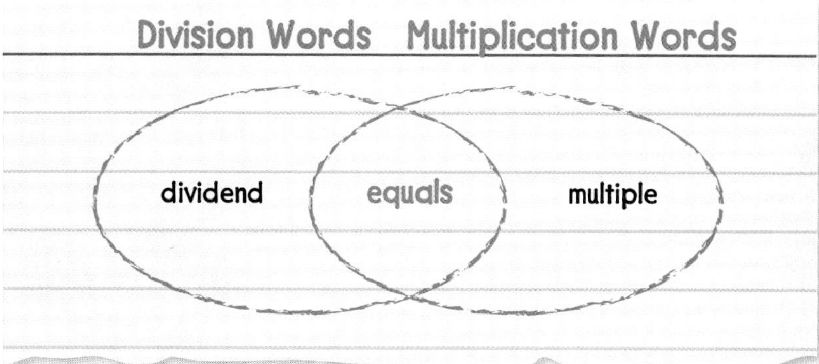

GO ONLINE **Technology**
Multimedia Math Glossary link at
www.harcourtschool.com/hspmath

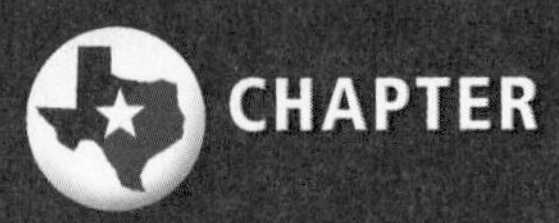

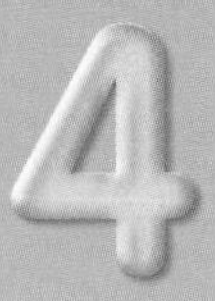

CHAPTER

4 Multiplication Facts

The Big Idea Basic fact strategies for multiplication and division are based on properties, patterns, and number relationships.

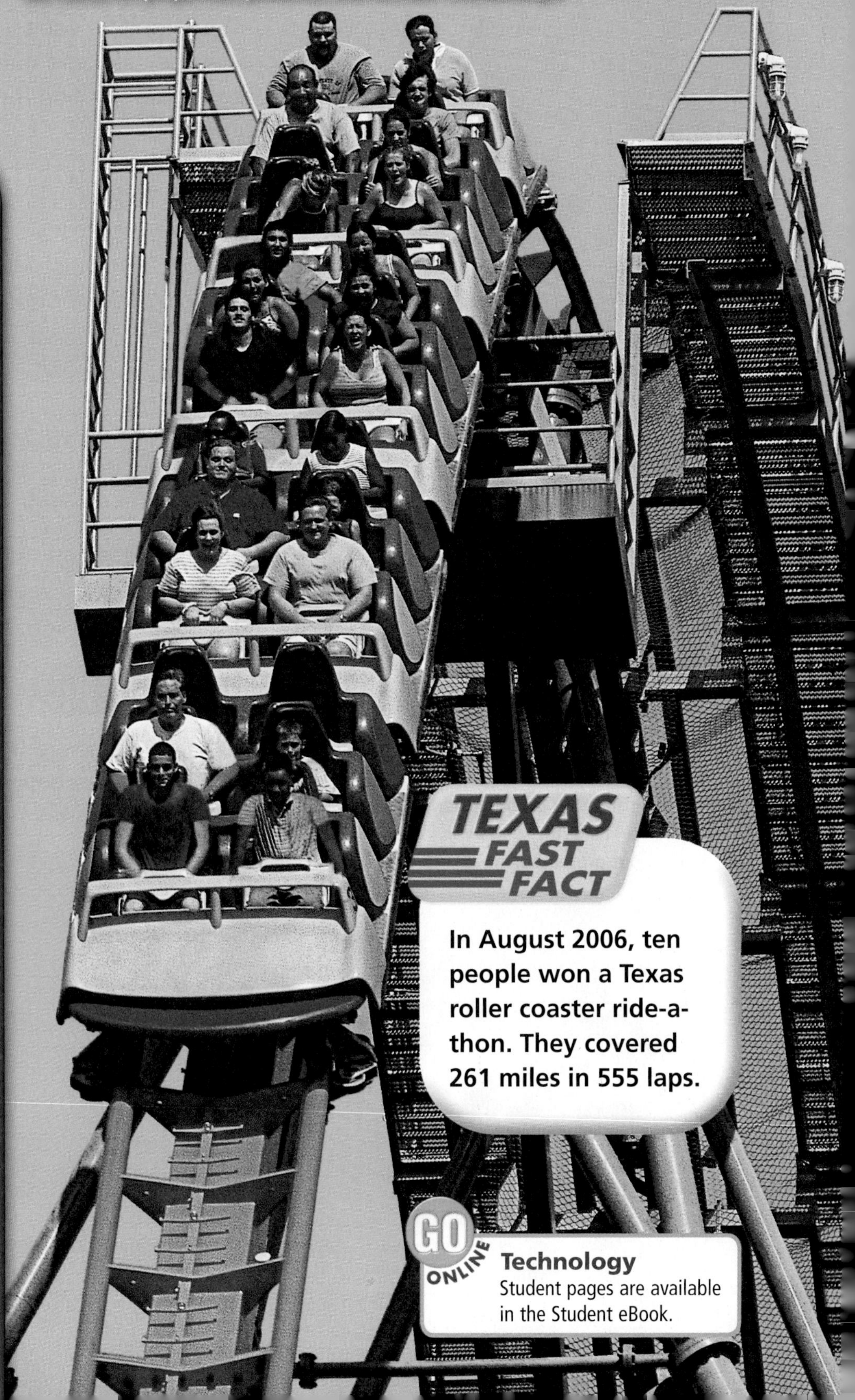

Investigate

Use the bar graph. Suppose there are at least 2 cars on each roller coaster train and each train is filled. What are the possible numbers of cars in each train? Choose a roller coaster, and draw pictures of how the train could look.

Roller Coaster Train Capacity

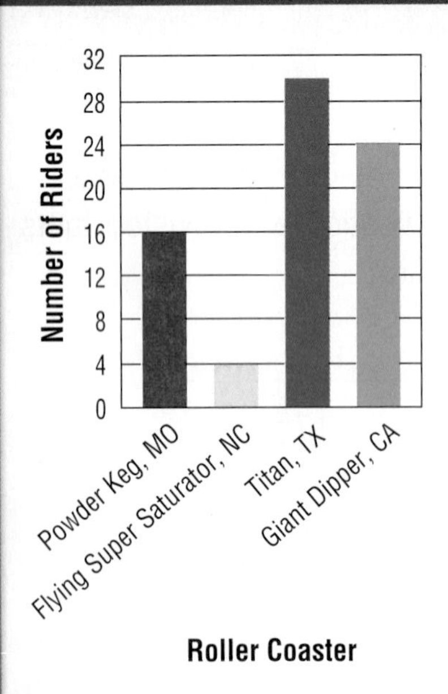

TEXAS FAST FACT

In August 2006, ten people won a Texas roller coaster ride-a-thon. They covered 261 miles in 555 laps.

GO ONLINE **Technology**
Student pages are available in the Student eBook.

Show What You Know

Check your understanding of important skills needed for success in Chapter 4.

▶ Number Patterns

Skip-count to find the missing numbers.

1. 2, 4, 6, 8, ■, ■

2. 5, 10, ■, 20, 25, ■

3. 3, 6, ■, 12, 15, ■

4. ■, 8, 12, 16, ■, 24

▶ Meaning of Multiplication

Copy and complete each number sentence.

5.

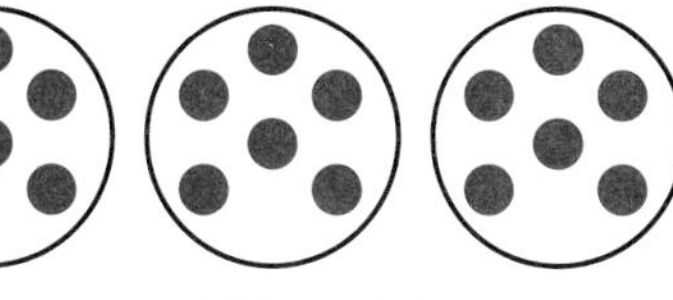

■ groups of ■ = ■

6.

■ rows of ■ = ■

7.

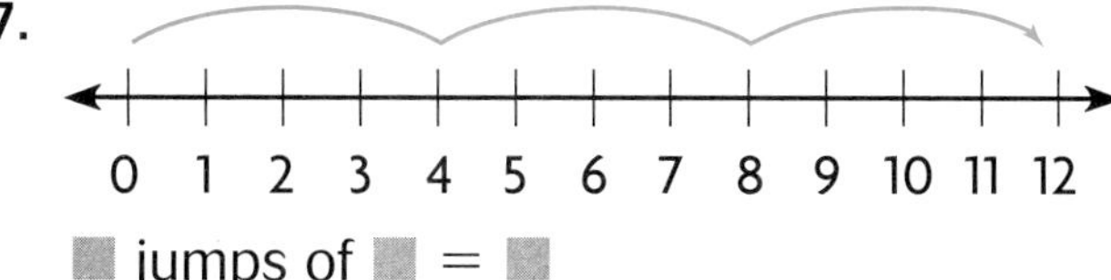

■ jumps of ■ = ■

8.

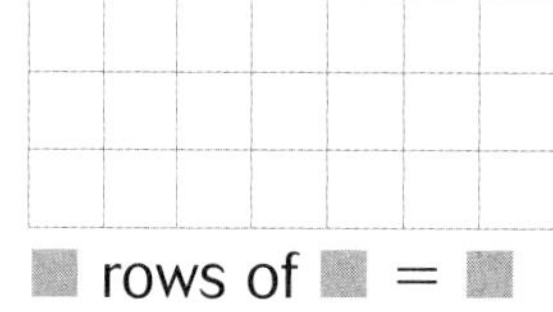

■ rows of ■ = ■

▶ Multiplication Properties

Find the product. Tell which property you used to help you.

9. 6×3

10. 0×9

11. 7×1

12. 8×2

VOCABULARY POWER

CHAPTER VOCABULARY

addition
array
factor
multiple
multiply
product
Commutative Property of Multiplication
Identity Property of Multiplication
Zero Property of Multiplication

WARM-UP WORDS

multiply when you combine equal groups, you can multiply to find how many in all; the opposite operation of division

factor a number that is multiplied by another number to find a product

product the answer to a multiplication problem

ALGEBRA

Relate Addition and Multiplication

OBJECTIVE: Relate repeated addition to multiplication.

Quick Review

1. 7 + 7
2. 3 + 3 + 3
3. 8 + 8
4. 9 + 9 + 9 + 9
5. 6 + 6 + 6

Vocabulary

multiply

Learn

You can add or multiply to find how many in all. When you **multiply**, you join equal-size groups.

PROBLEM The miniature train ride has 6 cars. Each car holds 4 people. How many people at a time can ride the train?

Example Use repeated addition and multiplication.

Draw a picture to show 6 groups of 4.

Add to find how many in all.	Multiply to find how many in all.
Write: 4 + 4 + 4 + 4 + 4 + 4 = 24	**Write:** 6 × 4 = 24, or $\begin{array}{r} 4 \\ \times 6 \\ \hline 24 \end{array}$
Read: 6 fours equal 24.	**Read:** 6 times 4 equals 24.

So, 24 people at a time can ride the train.

ERROR ALERT

Remember that the multiplication sign (×) is different from the plus sign (+). 6 × 4 means 6 groups of 4. 6 + 4 means 6 and 4 more.

More Examples Write related addition and multiplication sentences.

A Array

Think: 4 rows of 5

5 + 5 + 5 + 5 = 20
4 × 5 = 20

B Number Line

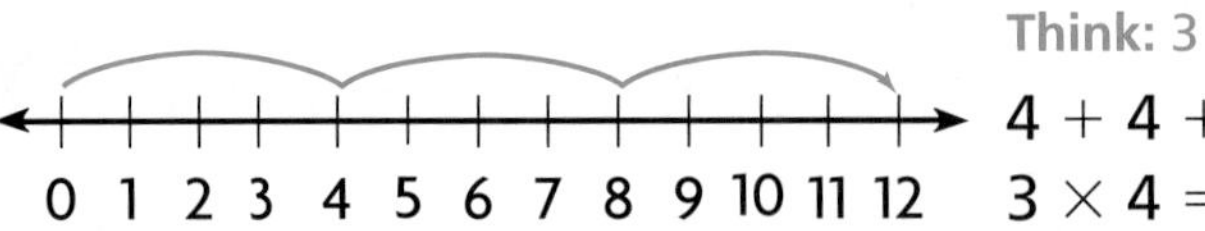

Think: 3 jumps of 4

4 + 4 + 4 = 12
3 × 4 = 12

Guided Practice

1. Copy and complete.

3 + 3 + 3 + 3 + 3 = ■
5 groups of ■ = ■
■ × ■ = ■

TEKS 4.4B represent multiplication and division situations in picture, word, and number form. *also* **4.3A, 4.4A, 4.4D, 4.6A, 4.14A, 4.15A, 4.15B**

Write related addition and multiplication sentences for each.

2. 

3. 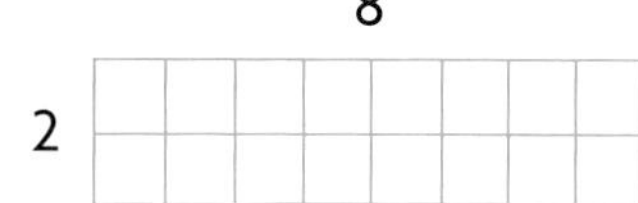

4. 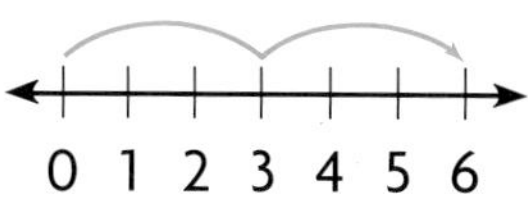

5. **TALK Math** **Explain** how you know when you can use multiplication to solve a problem.

Independent Practice and Problem Solving

Write related addition and multiplication sentences for each.

6.

7.

8.  

Write the related addition or multiplication sentence. Draw a picture that shows the sentence.

9. $5 + 5 = 10$
10. $2 + 2 + 2 + 2 + 2 = 10$
11. 8 groups of 4 equal 32.
12. $3 \times 6 = 18$
13. 4 groups of 7 equal 28.
14. $4 + 4 + 4 + 4 = 16$

Reasoning **Tell whether the number sentence is *true* or *false*. If false, explain how you know.**

15. $3 \times 7 \stackrel{?}{=} 7 + 7 + 7$
16. $6 \times 6 \stackrel{?}{=} 12 + 6$
17. $4 + 4 + 4 + 4 \stackrel{?}{=} 5 \times 4$
18. $4 \times 6 \stackrel{?}{=} 12 + 12$
19. $5 + 5 + 5 + 5 \stackrel{?}{=} 4 \times 5$
20. $3 \times 9 \stackrel{?}{=} 9 + 9$

21. Thirty-six people at a time can ride the Scrambler. Each car holds 3 people. If 8 cars are full and the rest of the cars are empty, how many more people can get on?

22. Each ride costs 3 tickets. Sara wants to ride 9 different rides. How many tickets does she need?

23. Andy says $10 \times 2 = 20$. How can he check his answer?

24. **WRITE Math** **What's the Error?** To find the product of 4×6, Tony found the sum of $4 + 4 + 4 + 4$. Describe his error, and find the correct answer.

Mixed Review and TAKS Prep

25. There were 26 people in line for a ride. After some people got on the ride, 12 people were left in line. Write and solve an equation to find how many people got on the ride. (TEKS 4.15B, p. 74)

26. Rob drew a polygon with exactly five sides. What figure did he draw? (Grade 3 TEKS 3.8)

27. **TAKS Prep** A roller coaster can hold 4 people in 1 car. How many people can 10 cars hold? (Obj. 1)

A 6
B 14
C 15
D 40

Extra Practice on page 110, Set A

LESSON

2 Multiply Facts Through 5

OBJECTIVE: Multiply facts from 0 through 5.

Quick Review

Write the multiplication expression for each.

1. 4 + 4
2. 3 + 3 + 3 + 3 + 3
3. 2 + 2 + 2
4. 5 + 5 + 5
5. 1 + 1 + 1 + 1

Vocabulary

factor product

Learn

PROBLEM A barbecue stand at the State Fair has 5 tables. There are 4 seats at each table. How many seats does the stand have?

The numbers that you multiply are called **factors**. The answer is the **product**.

Example 1 Draw equal-size groups.

Multiply. 5 × 4

MODEL	THINK	RECORD
	5 tables 4 seats at each table 20 seats in all	4 ← factor × 5 ← factor 20 ← product

So, the barbecue stand has 20 seats.

Example 2 Use a number line.

Lena waited 2 minutes in line at the stand. Paul waited 4 times as long. For how long did Paul wait?

Multiply. 4 × 2

MODEL	THINK	RECORD
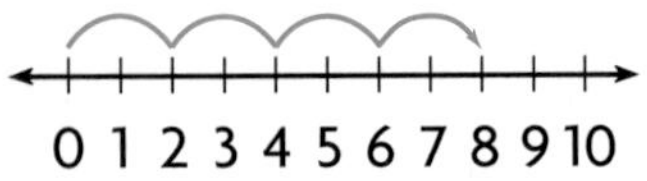	4 jumps of 2 equals 8.	4 ← factor × 2 ← factor 8 ← product

So, Paul waited 8 minutes.

Example 3 Make an array.

At the stand, pieces of pie are displayed in 3 rows with 5 pieces in each row. How many pieces of pie are there?

Multiply. 3 × 5

MODEL	THINK	RECORD
	3 rows 5 pieces of pie in each row 15 pieces of pie in all	5 ← factor × 3 ← factor 15 ← product

So, there are 15 pieces of pie.

▲ The first State Fair of Texas, in Dallas, was held in 1886.

TEKS 4.4B represent multiplication and division situations in picture, word, and number form. *also* **4.4A, 4.4C, 4.4D, 4.6A, 4.14A, 4.15A, 4.15B, 4.16A**

Guided Practice

Find the product for each model.

1. 1×2

2. 2×5

3. 3×2

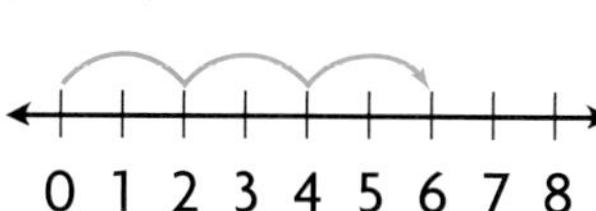

Find the product.

4. 3×3 5. 1×5 6. 7×4 7. 2×2 8. 5×2 9. 8×3

10. **TALK Math** **Explain** how to find the product of 0 and any factor and how to find the product of 1 and any factor. Give an example of each.

Independent Practice and Problem Solving

Find the product.

11. 3×4 12. 9×5 13. 1×3 14. 0×4 15. 7×5 16. 2×3

Algebra Find the value of $n \times 4$ for each value of n.

17. $n = 3$ 18. $n = 1$ 19. $n = 2$ 20. $n = 4$ 21. $n = 5$ 22. $n = 10$

USE DATA For 23–24, use the menu.

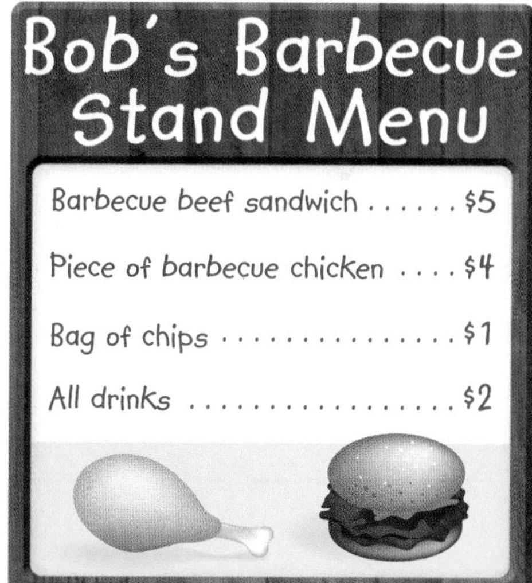

23. Ben bought 2 barbecue beef sandwiches and a drink. How much change did he get from a $20 bill?
24. How much will it cost to buy 3 pieces of barbecue chicken, 1 barbecue beef sandwich, and 4 drinks?
25. **FAST FACT** At 212 feet, the Texas Star at Fair Park is the tallest Ferris wheel in North America. Each car holds 5 to 6 people. How many people can ride in 5 cars?
26. **WRITE Math** **What's the Question?** The answer is 16.

Mixed Review and TAKS Prep

27. Out of a shipment of 1,000 light bulbs, 85 bulbs are broken. How many light bulbs are not broken? (TEKS 4.3A, p. 54)
28. Dave had some apples. He ate 5 of them. Write an expression to show how many apples Dave has left. (TEKS 4.15B, p. 70)
29. **TAKS Prep** Madison displays her miniature dolls on 4 shelves. There are 5 dolls on each shelf. How many dolls are displayed on the shelves in all? (Obj. 1)

Extra Practice on page 110, Set B

LESSON 3

Multiply Facts Through 10

OBJECTIVE: Multiply facts through 10.

Quick Review

Skip-count to find the missing number.

1. 3, 6, 9, ■, 15
2. 10, 8, 6, ■, 2
3. 4, 8, 12, ■, 20
4. 21, 18, 15, ■, 9
5. 25, 20, 15, ■, 5

Learn

Using strategies can help you learn the multiplication facts that you do not know.

PROBLEM A checkerboard has 8 squares on each side. How many squares are on a checkerboard?

To find the product of 8 and 8, you can break apart one of the factors into products you know.

HANDS ON

Activity Use the break apart strategy.

Materials ■ centimeter grid paper

Multiply. 8×8

Step 1

Draw a square array that is 8 units wide and 8 units long. Think of the area as 8×8.

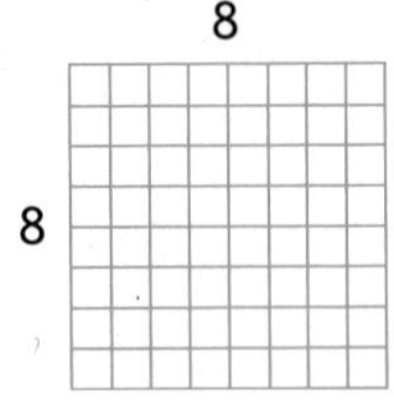

Step 2

Cut apart the array to make two smaller arrays for products you know.

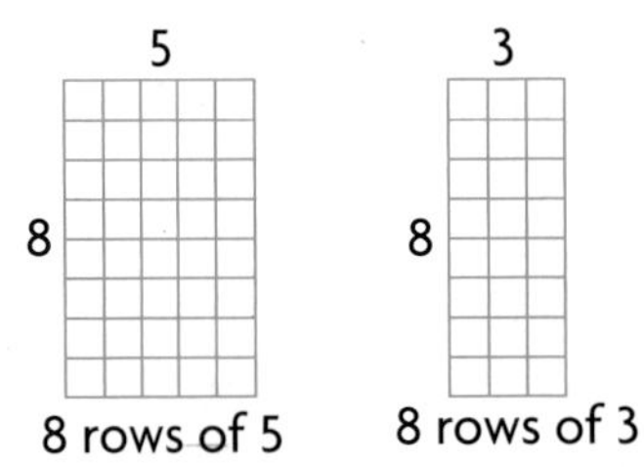

The factor 8 is now 5 plus 3.

Step 3

Find the sum of the products of the two smaller arrays.

$8 \times 5 = 40$
$8 \times 3 = 24$
$40 + 24 = 64$

So, there are 64 squares on a checkerboard.

- **What if** you cut apart the array horizontally? What other ways can you break apart the 8×8 array?
- Use grid paper and the break apart strategy to find 9×7.
- Does the break apart strategy always work? Explain.

TEKS 4.6A use patterns and relationships to develop strategies to remember basic multiplication and division facts (such as the patterns in related multiplication and division number sentences (fact families) such as $9 \times 9 = 81$ and $81 \div 9 = 9$). *also* **4.4A, 4.4B, 4.4C, 4.4D, 4.14A, 4.14C, 4.14D, 4.15A, 4.15B**

More Strategies

Use a multiplication table.

Multiply. 5×7

Find the row for the factor 5. Find the column for the factor 7.

Look down column 7. The product is found where row 5 and column 7 meet.

×	0	1	2	3	4	5	6	7	8	9	10
0	0	0	0	0	0	0	0	0	0	0	0
1	0	1	2	3	4	5	6	7	8	9	10
2	0	2	4	6	8	10	12	14	16	18	20
3	0	3	6	9	12	15	18	21	24	27	30
4	0	4	8	12	16	20	24	28	32	36	40
5	0	5	10	15	20	25	30	35	40	45	50
6	0	6	12	18	24	30	36	42	48	54	60
7	0	7	14	21	28	35	42	49	56	63	70
8	0	8	16	24	32	40	48	56	64	72	80
9	0	9	18	27	36	45	54	63	72	81	90
10	0	10	20	30	40	50	60	70	80	90	100

So, $5 \times 7 = 35$.

Math Idea

The Commutative Property of Multiplication states that you can multiply any two factors in any order and get the same product. So, if you know that $6 \times 9 = 54$, you also know that $9 \times 6 = 54$. You need to memorize only half of the facts in the multiplication table.

Use the Commutative Property.

Multiply. 3×10

Think: $10 \times 3 = 30$

So, $3 \times 10 = 30$.

Use a pattern.

Multiply. 6×7

Start at 0. Skip-count by sixes 7 times.

Think: 0, 6, 12, 18, 24, 30, 36, 42

So, $6 \times 7 = 42$.

Use doubles.

Multiply. 8×9

Think: The factor 8 is an even number. $4 + 4 = 8$

$4 \times 9 = 36$

$4 \times 9 = 36$

$36 + 36 = 72$

So, $8 \times 9 = 72$.

- Why can you use the doubles strategy to multiply 4×9 but not 5×9?

Guided Practice

1. Copy the sentences. Use the arrays to complete the sentences.

$6 \times 4 = ■$

$6 \times 5 = ■$

$6 \times 9 = ■ + ■$

So, $6 \times 9 = ■$.

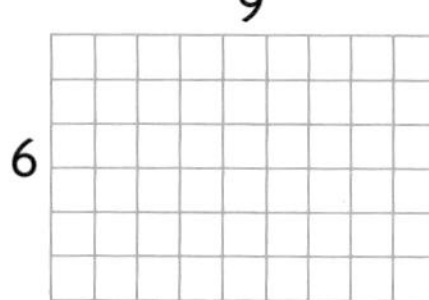

4
6

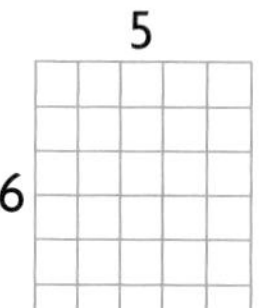

Find the product. Show the strategy you used.

2. 5×6 3. 7×9 4. 4×8 5. 2×7 6. 10×5 7. 3×9

8. TALK Math **Explain** two ways to use strategies to find 8×7.

Independent Practice and Problem Solving

Find the product. Show the strategy you used.

9. 4×10	10. 6×6	11. 8×10	12. 3×9	13. 8×8	14. 9×10
15. 0×8	16. 1×9	17. 7×6	18. 10×10	19. 2×6	20. 4×9
21. $\begin{array}{r} 3 \\ \times 7 \\ \hline \end{array}$	22. $\begin{array}{r} 10 \\ \times 6 \\ \hline \end{array}$	23. $\begin{array}{r} 7 \\ \times 7 \\ \hline \end{array}$	24. $\begin{array}{r} 4 \\ \times 7 \\ \hline \end{array}$	25. $\begin{array}{r} 9 \\ \times 9 \\ \hline \end{array}$	26. $\begin{array}{r} 10 \\ \times 8 \\ \hline \end{array}$

Algebra Find the value of the coins.

27.

Nickels	5	6	7	8	9	10
Cents	25	■	■	■	■	■

28.

Dimes	1	2	4	6	8	10
Cents	10	■	■	■	■	■

USE DATA For 29–31, use the Game 1 Results.

29. In checkers, a king is 2 checkers stacked. Tanya has 3 kings. How many single checkers does she have?

30. What is the greatest number of kings that Jamal could have?

31. Ed had the same number of checkers left at the end of each game. He ends the checkers marathon with a total of 45 checkers left. How many games did Ed play?

Game 1 Results

32. WRITE Math Find the missing numbers. Describe the relationships between the products. **Explain** why this happened.

$6 \times 2 =$ ■
$6 \times 4 =$ ■
$6 \times 8 =$ ■
$6 \times 16 =$ ■

Mixed Review and TAKS Prep

33. In a pictograph, 1 symbol equals 4 cats. How many cats do 7 symbols equal? (Grade 3 TEKS 3.13A)

34. There are 3 erasers in a package. How many erasers are in 5 packages? (TEKS 4.4C, p. 98)

35. **TAKS Prep Explain** how to use the break apart strategy to find 6×8. (Obj. 2)

 Extra Practice on page 110, Set C

Are You Game?

Reading Skill **Visualize**

A growing number of kids are having fun playing chess. Many are joining clubs, playing in tournaments, and even competing online.

Maya's chess club has 6 members. Each member will play 4 games during a tournament this weekend. How many games will the club members play altogether?

Visualizing the information given in a problem can help you understand the situation. When you visualize, you picture something in your mind.

▼ In addition to being fun, chess sharpens both thinking and social skills. The United States Chess Federation has about 100,000 members, and more than half of them are kids. More than 1,550 students from around the country competed in the 2005 National K–12/Collegiate Chess Championship held in Houston, Texas.

Make a list of models that can be used to help solve the problem, and then picture each model in your mind.

Think about which model best represents the situation.

↓

Picture the situation in your mind. Then draw a picture.

Models

groups of objects

number line

array

multiplication table

Problem Solving **Visualize to understand the problem.**

1. Solve the problem above.
2. Barney and Lauren are playing a card-matching game. Before they begin, they place 7 cards down in each of 6 rows. How many cards do they place facedown?

LESSON HANDS ON

4 Multiplication Table Through 12

OBJECTIVE: Multiply facts through 12.

Quick Review

1. 10×9
2. 8×7
3. 0×10
4. 2×8
5. 9×9

Vocabulary

multiple

Investigate

Materials ■ blank multiplication table

You can use patterns and strategies to help you complete a multiplication table for the facts of 11 and 12. Copy the table.

Remember

The Zero Property states that the product of 0 and any number is 0. The Identity Property states that the product of 1 and any number is that number.

×	0	1	2	3	4	5	6	7	8	9	10	11	12
0	0	0	0	0	0	0	0	0	0	0	0	■	■
1	0	1	2	3	4	5	6	7	8	9	10	■	■
2	0	2	4	6	8	10	12	14	16	18	20	■	■
3	0	3	6	9	12	15	18	21	24	27	30	■	■
4	0	4	8	12	16	20	24	28	32	36	40	■	■
5	0	5	10	15	20	25	30	35	40	45	50	■	■
6	0	6	12	18	24	30	36	42	48	54	60	■	■
7	0	7	14	21	28	35	42	49	56	63	70	■	■
8	0	8	16	24	32	40	48	56	64	72	80	■	■
9	0	9	18	27	36	45	54	63	72	81	90	■	■
10	0	10	20	30	40	50	60	70	80	90	100	■	■
11	■	■	■	■	■	■	■	■	■	■	■	■	■
12	■	■	■	■	■	■	■	■	■	■	■	■	■

A Use the Zero Property to complete the row and column for 0. Use the Identity Property to complete the row and column for 1.

B Use doubles to complete the row and column for 2.

C Count on to complete the rows and columns for 3 through 10.

D Use the break apart strategy to find 11×11, 11×12, and 12×12.

E Now complete the rest of the table.

Draw Conclusions

1. Compare your break apart strategy to find 12×12 with your classmates' break apart strategies. What can you conclude?
2. **Application** What strategy could you use to find the product of 20 and 5? Find the product. Describe the strategy you used.

TEKS 4.6A use patterns and relationships to develop strategies to remember basic multiplication and division facts (such as the patterns in related multiplication and division number sentences (fact families) such as $9 \times 9 = 81$ and $81 \div 9 = 9$). *also* **4.4C, 4.4D, 4.7, 4.14C, 4.14D, 4.15A, 4.15B, 4.16A**

Connect

The product of two counting numbers is called a **multiple** of each of those numbers. To find multiples of any counting number, multiply by the counting numbers 1, 2, 3, 4, and so on. You can also find the first 12 multiples of a number by looking across a row or down a column in a multiplication table.

Find the multiples of 3 shown in the multiplication table.

Look at the row or column for 3. A multiple of 3 is any product that has 3 as a factor. Do not list 0.

So, 3, 6, 9, 12, 15, 18, 21, 24, 27, 30, 33, and 36 are all multiples of 3.

- **Reasoning** Explain why all the multiples of 6 are also multiples of 3.
- Are all multiples of 5 odd numbers? Explain.

TALK Math

How do strategies and patterns help you learn multiplication facts?

Practice

Find the product. Show the strategy you used.

1. 6×11
2. 12×10
3. 11×12
4. 4×12
5. 11×4
6. 11×3
7. 12×8
8. 9×11
9. 5×11
10. 12×12
11. 6×12
12. ✓ 11×7

For 13–16, use the multiplication table.

13. What are the first 12 multiples of 7?
14. What are the first 12 multiples of 12?
15. What are the first 12 multiples of 10?
16. ✓ What are the first 12 multiples of 11?

Algebra Use the rule to find the missing numbers.

17. Multiply the input by 8.

Input	Output
2	■
4	■
8	■
■	72

18. Multiply the input by 7.

Input	Output
3	■
6	■
■	49
■	63

19. Multiply the input by 11.

Input	Output
1	■
10	■
11	■
12	■

20. Multiply the input by 12.

Input	Output
2	■
■	48
5	■
■	120

21. **WRITE Math** What could be the missing factors in ★ × ▲ = 48? Find as many factor pairs as you can. **Explain** how you found these factors.

Technology
Use Harcourt Mega Math, The Number Games, *Up, Up, and Array,* Levels A, B, C, D.

Problem Solving Workshop
Strategy: Guess and Check

OBJECTIVE: Solve problems by using the strategy *guess and check*.

Learn the Strategy

Sometimes, you can make an educated guess to solve a problem and then check your guess to see whether it fits the problem conditions. It is a good strategy to use when one condition depends on another condition.

Make a list to record your guesses.

What are three consecutive numbers whose sum is 15?

Think: The sum is less than 20, so the addends must be 1-digit numbers.

Guess 1: 2 + 3 + 4 = 9 too low
Guess 2: 3 + 4 + 5 = 12 too low
Guess 3: 4 + 5 + 6 = 15 ✓

Make a table to record your guesses.

Mary is thinking of two numbers. The sum of the numbers is 15, and the difference of the numbers is 3. What are Mary's numbers?

Guess	Check		Does It Check?
	Sum	Difference	
8 and 7	8+7=15	8−7=1	The sum is 15. The difference is 1.
10 and 5	10+5=15	10−5=5	The sum is 15. The difference is 5.
9 and 6	9+6=15	9−6=3	The sum is 15.✓ The difference is 3.✓

Draw a picture to record your guesses.

Write 2, 3, 4, and 5 in each outer circle so the sums of the numbers across and down are equal.

Guess 1: $2 + 1 + 4 = 7$ and
$3 + 1 + 5 = 9$

Guess 2: $3 + 1 + 4 = 8$ and
$2 + 1 + 5 = 8$ ✔

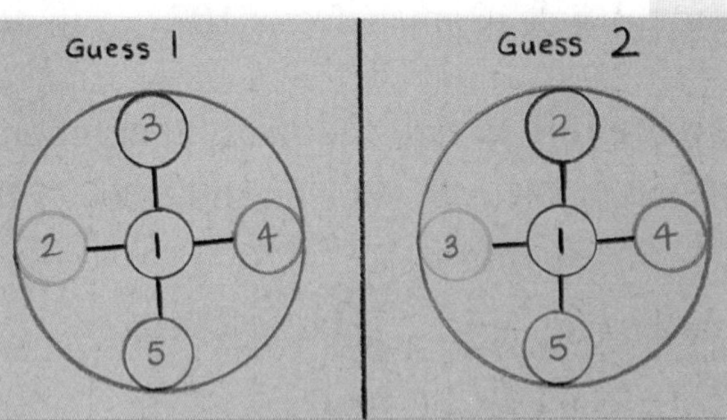

To use the strategy, make a guess, check your guess, and then revise the guess until all conditions in the problem are met.

TALK Math
How can you use the first guess to make a better guess?

TEKS 4.14C select or develop an appropriate problem-solving plan or strategy, including drawing a picture, looking for a pattern, systematic guessing and checking, acting it out, making a table, working a simpler problem, or working backwards to solve a problem. *also* **4.3A, 4.4C, 4.4D, 4.14A, 4.14B, 4.15A, 4.15B**

Use the Strategy

PROBLEM On rainy days, Raul likes to solve riddles. He found this riddle in a book about numbers.

The product of two numbers is 24. Their sum is 11. What are the numbers?

Read to Understand

- **Identify the details given.**
- **Are there details you will not use? If so, what?**

Plan

- **What strategy can you use to solve the problem?**
  You can guess and check to solve the problem.

Solve

- **How can you use the strategy to solve the problem?**
  Make a table to record your guesses.

Think: What are the factors of 24?

Use what you know about multiplication facts to make a guess. Check your guess and test another pair of factors, if needed. Guess until all the problem conditions are met.

Guess	Check		Does it Check?
	Product	Sum	
2 and 12	$2 \times 12 = 24$	$2 + 12 = 14$	The product is 24. The sum is 14.
4 and 6	$4 \times 6 = 24$	$4 + 6 = 10$	The product is 24. The sum is 10.
3 and 8	$3 \times 8 = 24$	$3 + 8 = 11$	The product is 24. ✔ The sum is 11. ✔

So, the numbers are 3 and 8.

Check

- **How do you know your answer is correct?**
- **What other strategy could you use to solve the problem?**

Guided Problem Solving

1. Erica is thinking of two numbers. The difference of the two numbers is 5. The product of the numbers is 24. What are Erica's numbers?

   First, make a table.

   Next, make a guess based on the facts.

   Then, adjust and guess again until you find the two numbers.

Guess	Check		Does it Check?
	Difference	Product	
6 and 4	$6 - 4 = 2$	$6 \times 4 = 24$	The difference is 2. The product is 24.

2. **What if** the product of the two numbers is 36? What would Erica's numbers be?

3. Marc likes to solve word scrambles and mazes. Yesterday he solved 10 word scrambles and mazes in all. He solved 2 more word scrambles than mazes. How many word scrambles did Marc solve yesterday?

Problem Solving Strategy Practice

Guess and check to solve.

4. Tina and Larry played a memory game. Tina scored twice as many points as Larry did. Together they scored 30 points. How many points did Tina score?

5. Marie bought two puzzle books. Together the books cost $17. One book costs $3 more than the other. How much did each book cost?

USE DATA For 6–8, copy and complete the puzzle.

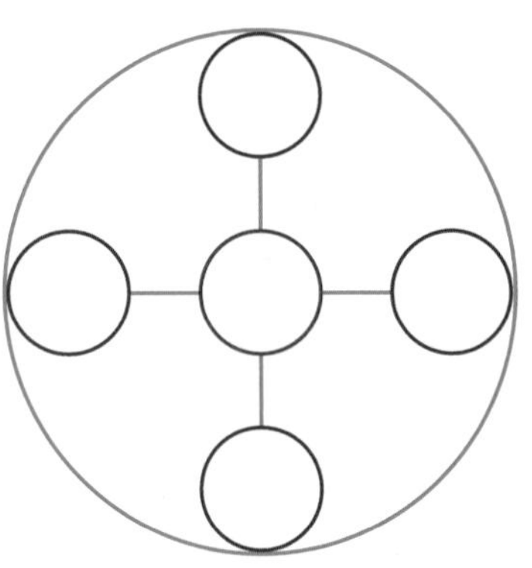

6. Write 2 in the center circle. Write 3, 4, 6, and 8 in the outer circles so that the products across and down are equal.

7. Write 3 in the center circle. Write 2, 4, 6, and 8 in the outer circles so that the sums across and down are equal.

8. Write 4 in the center circle. Write 2, 3, 6, and 9 in the outer circles so that the products across and down are equal.

9. André is thinking of a number. The number times itself is less than 150 but greater than 75. The sum of the number and itself is less than 20. What is the number?

10. WRITE Math **Sense or Nonsense** Maria says that the sum of two numbers is 6 and their product is 5. Does Maria's statement make sense? **Explain.**

Mixed Strategy Practice

USE DATA For 11–15, copy and complete the table.

	Sum	Product	Difference	Two Numbers
11.	14	48	■	■, ■
12.	11	■	5	■, ■
13.	12	35	■	■, ■
14.	■	40	6	■, ■
15.	15	■	9	■, ■

16. Jimmy designed a maze made up of triangles. If you can move only forward, and never retrace your steps, how many different ways can you walk through his maze?

17. Karen, Rex, Jan, and Tara were waiting in line for their riddle cards at the maze. Tara was behind Rex. Karen was not next to Jan. Jan was first in line. Karen was between Rex and Tara. In what order were they standing in line?

18. **Pose a Problem** Look back at Problem 9. Write a similar riddle.

19. **Open-Ended** John is thinking of two odd numbers that add up to 26. What could John's numbers be?

Choose a STRATEGY

- Draw a Diagram or Picture
- Make a Model or Act It Out
- Make an Organized List
- Look for a Pattern
- Make a Table or Graph
- Guess and Check
- Work Backward
- Solve a Simpler Problem
- Write an Equation
- Use Logical Reasoning

▼ Corn maze in Hondo, Texas

CHALLENGE YOURSELF

Ryan is working on number puzzles in a book. It takes him 2 minutes to complete a puzzle rated *Easy*, and 3 minutes to complete one rated *Hard*.

20. On Monday, Ryan worked for 25 minutes and completed a total of 11 puzzles. How many *Hard* puzzles did he complete? How many *Easy* ones?

21. On Tuesday, Ryan worked for 30 minutes and completed the same number of *Easy* puzzles as *Hard* puzzles. **Explain** how you can find how many *Easy* and how many *Hard* puzzles Ryan completed on Tuesday.

Extra Practice

Set A Write the related addition or multiplication sentence. Draw a picture that shows the sentence. (pp. 96–97)

1. $8 + 8 = 16$
2. $5 \times 4 = 20$
3. 4 groups of 6 equal 24.
4. $4 \times 3 = 12$
5. $7 + 7 + 7 + 7 + 7 = 35$
6. $9 + 9 + 9 = 27$
7. $5 + 5 + 5 + 5 + 5 = 25$
8. 5 groups of 2 equal 10.
9. $10 + 10 + 10 = 30$

Tell whether the number sentence is *true* or *false*. If false, explain how you know.

10. $7 \times 5 \stackrel{?}{=} 5 + 7$
11. $3 + 3 + 3 \stackrel{?}{=} 3 \times 3$
12. $3 \times 5 \stackrel{?}{=} 5 + 5 + 5$

Set B Find the product. (pp. 98–99)

1. 2×5
2. 1×1
3. 5×3
4. 3×4
5. 0×1
6. 9×3
7. 4×1
8. 6×2
9. 0×5
10. 3×2
11. 5×5
12. 3×0
13. 8×1
14. 7×3
15. 4×4
16. Michael jogged 2 miles each day for 4 days. How far did Michael jog in all?
17. A roller coaster at an amusement park has 5 cars. Each car can hold 4 people. How many people can ride the roller coaster on one trip?

Set C Find the product. Show the strategy you used. (pp. 100–103)

1. 5×6
2. 6×10
3. 3×9
4. 7×7
5. 3×8
6. 4×9
7. 7×9
8. 8×9
9. 6×8
10. 9×9
11. 8×8
12. 9×6
13. 2×6
14. 4×10
15. 3×7
16. $\begin{array}{r} 3 \\ \times 6 \\ \hline \end{array}$
17. $\begin{array}{r} 4 \\ \times 8 \\ \hline \end{array}$
18. $\begin{array}{r} 6 \\ \times 6 \\ \hline \end{array}$
19. $\begin{array}{r} 4 \\ \times 7 \\ \hline \end{array}$
20. $\begin{array}{r} 10 \\ \times 10 \\ \hline \end{array}$
21. There are 7 vans available to take students on a field trip to the planetarium. Each van can hold 6 students. How many students can the vans hold altogether?
22. In the library, Rachel arranged 5 shelves of books with 8 books on each shelf. How many books did Rachel arrange?

CD ROM Technology
Use Harcourt Mega Math, The Number Games, *Up, Up, and Array,* Levels A, B, C, D.

DOWN AND UP

Burrowers!
2 players

Dig In!
- Multiplication facts cards
- Multiplication table
- Number cube labeled 1 to 6
- 2 coins

START

Go back 2 spaces

Take another turn

Lose a turn

Move forward 2 spaces

Go back 2 spaces

Move forward 2 spaces

Lose a turn

Take another turn

FINISH

Burrow Down!

- Players shuffle the multiplication facts cards and place them facedown in a stack.
- Each player selects a different coin and places the coin on START.
- Players take turns drawing a card and finding the product. The other player uses a multiplication table to check the answer.
- If the answer is correct, toss the number cube and move that number of spaces. If you land on a space containing a direction, follow that direction.
- If the answer is incorrect, the player loses a turn.
- The first player to reach the FINISH line wins.

Chapter 4 Review/Test

Check Vocabulary and Concepts

Choose the best term from the box.

VOCABULARY
factor
multiple
product

1. In a multiplication problem, each of the numbers being multiplied is called a _?_. (TEKS 4.4B, p. 98)
2. The _?_ is the answer to a multiplication problem. (TEKS 4.4B, p. 98)

Check Skills

Write the related addition or multiplication sentence.
Draw a picture that shows the sentence. (TEKS 4.6A, pp. 96–97)

3. $6 + 6 + 6 + 6 + 6 + 6 = 36$
4. $4 \times 8 = 32$
5. 3 groups of 9 equal 27.
6. $2 + 2 + 2 + 2 + 2 = 10$

Find $5 \times n$ for each value of n. (TEKS 4.4C, pp. 98–99)

7. $n = 3$
8. $n = 0$
9. $n = 4$
10. $n = 2$
11. $n = 5$

Find the product. (TEKS 4.4C, pp. 98–99, 100–103)

12. 4×3
13. 6×7
14. 7×9
15. 9×5
16. 6×6
17. 8×9
18. 10×6
19. 0×4
20. 5×7
21. 4×7
22. 5×8
23. 2×9
24. 6×4
25. 8×3
26. 9×10
27. 9×4

Use the multiplication table on page 104. (TEKS 4.6A, pp. 104–105)

28. What are the first 12 multiples of 3?
29. What are the first 12 multiples of 5?
30. What are the first 12 multiples of 11?
31. What are the first 12 multiples of 12?

Check Problem Solving

Solve. (TEKS 4.14C, pp. 106–109)

32. Emma is thinking of two numbers. The sum of the two numbers is 14, and the product is 48. Find the two numbers.
33. WRITE Math Joe and Sonya played a game. Joe scored twice as many points as Sonya did. Together they scored 24 points. How many points did Sonya score? **Explain** how you know.

GO ONLINE **Technology** Use *Online Assessment.*

Enrich • Number Relationships

EVEN or Odd?

Eric is making smoothies for his family. Some family members want 2 cups of blueberries, and some want 3 cups of blueberries in their smoothies. Will Eric use an even or odd number of cups when he makes the smoothies?

Is the product even or odd when you multiply two even numbers? two odd numbers? an even number and an odd number?

A Even × Even	B Odd × Odd	C Even × Odd
$2 \times 2 = 4$	$3 \times 1 = 3$	$2 \times 1 = 2$
$2 \times 4 = 8$	$3 \times 3 = 9$	$2 \times 3 = 6$
$2 \times 6 = 12$	$3 \times 5 = 15$	$2 \times 5 = 10$

So, if Eric uses 2 cups for an even number of people, he will use an even number of cups in all. If he uses 3 cups for an odd number of people, he will use an odd number of cups in all. If he uses 2 cups for an odd number of people, he will use an even number of cups in all.

- Is the product even or odd when you multiply three even numbers?
- Is the product even or odd when you multiply three odd numbers?

Try It

Tell whether the product is *even* or *odd*.

1. 4×7 **2.** 5×9 **3.** 6×8 **4.** 9×7

5. 8×6 **6.** $8 \times 4 \times 6$ **7.** $7 \times 9 \times 5$ **8.** $4 \times 6 \times 2$

9. Is the product even or odd when you multiply 5 by an even number? an odd number? **Explain.**

10. Is the product even or odd when you multiply two even numbers and an odd number? **Explain.**

WRITE Math **Explain** how you can tell whether a product of two or more numbers will be even or odd.

Getting Ready for the TAKS
Chapters 1–4

Number, Operation, and Quantitative Reasoning TAKS Obj. 1

1. The table shows the prices of movie tickets at Second Street Cineplex.

Ticket Prices	
Type of Ticket	**Price**
Adult	$9
Student	$6
Senior	$5

Lee's family bought 2 adult tickets and 3 student tickets. How much did they spend?

A $42 **C** $33

B $36 **D** $15

Test Tip **Decide on a plan.**

See Item 2. Think about which operation would be needed to solve the problem. Then find the number sentence that shows it.

2. Each week, Philip saves $8. How much money has Philip saved after 4 weeks? Which number sentence can be used to find the total number of dollars he saved?

F $8 \div 4 = \blacksquare$

G $8 + 4 = \blacksquare$

H $8 - 4 = \blacksquare$

J $8 \times 4 = \blacksquare$

3. **WRITE Math** ▸ **Explain** how you know that 92,143 is greater than 92,047.

Patterns, Relationships, and Algebraic Thinking TAKS Obj. 2

4. Which rule describes the ordered pairs in the table?

Input	x	4	7	10	12	15
Output	y	9	12	15	17	20

A Subtract x from 7.

B Add 7 to x.

C Add 5 to x.

D Subtract x from 5.

5. What are the missing numbers in the pattern shown below?

$$2 \times 8 = 16$$
$$4 \times 8 = 32$$
$$\blacksquare \times \blacksquare = 64$$

F 4, 6 **H** 6, 8

G 6, 6 **J** 8, 8

6. **WRITE Math** ▸ Pauline has 12 flowers with the same number of petals. The table shows the numbers of petals in different numbers of flowers.

Flower Petals	
Number of Flowers	**Number of Petals**
2	22
4	44
6	66
8	88

Explain how to find the total number of petals in 12 flowers.

Geometry and Spatial Reasoning TAKS Obj. 3

7. In Washington, D.C., there is a building called the Pentagon. Which figure represents the shape of that building?

A 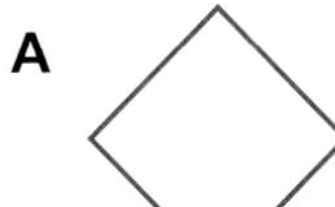

B 

C 

D 

8. Which number is represented by point *M* on the number line?

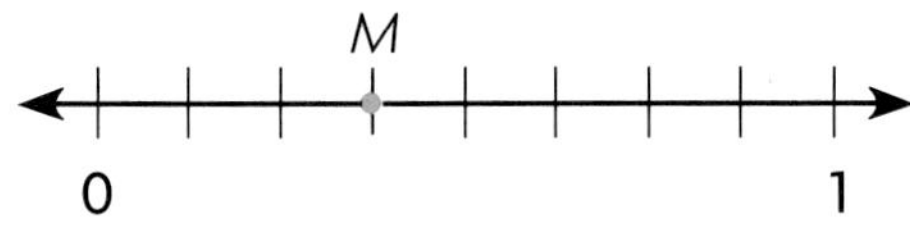

F $\frac{1}{8}$

G $\frac{2}{8}$

H $\frac{3}{8}$

J $\frac{6}{8}$

9. **WRITE Math** Which two figures appear to be congruent? **Explain** your answer.

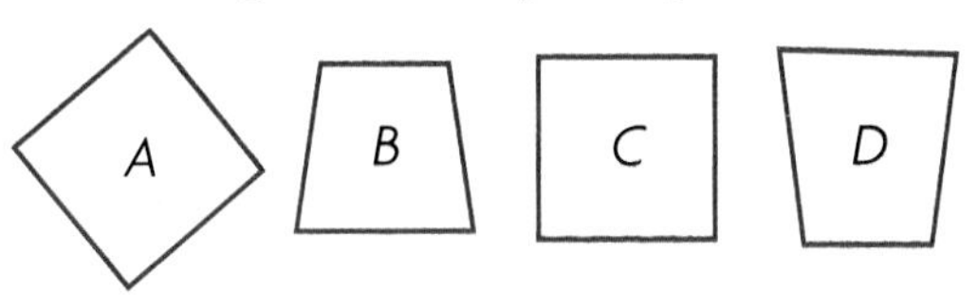

Measurement TAKS Obj. 4

10. Darren is planning to build a small patio behind his house. His plans are shown below. Each square represents 1 square foot.

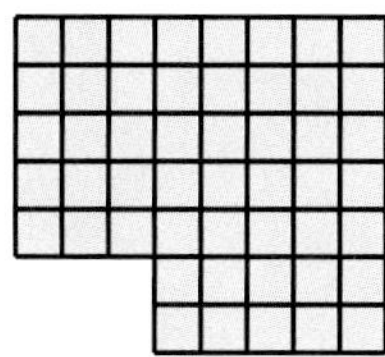

What is the area of the patio in square feet?

A 56 square feet

B 50 square feet

C 45 square feet

D 40 square feet

11. What time is shown on the clock below?

F 3:15 P.M.

G 3:20 P.M.

H 4:15 P.M.

J 4:20 P.M.

12. **WRITE Math** Each side of a square game board is 14 inches long. **Explain** how to find the perimeter of the board.

5 Division Facts

The Big Idea Basic Facts for division are based on properties, patterns, and number relationships.

TEXAS FAST FACT

The Everyones Art Car Parade—the world's largest—takes place in Houston. It began in 1988 with 40 entries. In 2006, there were more than 260 entries.

The day before the Everyones Art Car Parade, caravans of art cars visit hospitals, schools, and community centers. Suppose each caravan has a different number of art cars. Use the data shown in the table. How many different equal groups of at least 2 cars can there be in each caravan? Draw pictures to show them.

Parade Caravans

Caravan	Number of Cars
A	60
B	54
C	42
D	48
E	56

Technology
Student pages are available in the Student eBook.

Show What You Know

Check your understanding of important skills needed for success in Chapter 5.

▶ Number Patterns

Count back to find the missing numbers.

1. 40, 35, 30, 25, ■, ■, ■

2. 56, 49, 42, 35, ■, ■, ■

3. 21, ■, 15, 12, ■, ■

4. 42, 36, ■, 24, ■, ■

▶ Multiplication Facts

Find the product

5. 4×8

6. 9×6

7. 5×7

8. 12×8

9. 10×7

10. 2×11

11. 6×12

12. 8×9

▶ Meaning of Division

Answer the questions for each picture.

13. How many tiles are there in all?

14. How many equal rows are there?

15. How many tiles are in each row?

16. How many stars are there in all?

17. How many equal groups are there?

18. How many stars are in each group?

VOCABULARY POWER

CHAPTER VOCABULARY

array
dividend
divisor
fact family
factor
inverse operations
multiple
product
quotient

WARM-UP WORDS

inverse operations operations, such as multiplication and division, that undo each other

fact family a set of related multiplication and division sentences using the same numbers

dividend the number that is to be divided in a division problem

LESSON 1

ALGEBRA

Relate Multiplication and Division

OBJECTIVE: Relate multiplication to division.

Quick Review

Write an addition sentence and a multiplication sentence for the picture.

Vocabulary

inverse operations

fact family **divisor**

dividend **quotient**

Learn

PROBLEM A box of crayons holds 2 rows of 8 crayons each. How many crayons does the box hold?

Example 1 Use repeated addition.

$2 \times 8 = n$ Think: $2 \times 8 = 8 + 8$, or 16.

↓

$2 \times 8 = 16$

So, the box holds 16 crayons.

Multiplication and division by the same number are opposite operations, or **inverse operations**. One operation undoes the other.

A **fact family**, a set of related multiplication and division sentences using the same numbers, shows this relationship.

factor		factor		product	**dividend**		**divisor**		**quotient**
2	×	8	=	16	16	÷	8	=	2
8	×	2	=	16	16	÷	2	=	8

← fact family for 2, 8, 16

Example 2 Use a related multiplication sentence.

Another box holds 16 crayons. There are 2 crayons of each color. How many colors of crayons are in the box?

$16 \div 2 = n$ Think: $8 \times 2 = 16$, so $16 \div 2 = 8$.

↓

$16 \div 2 = 8$

So, the box holds 8 colors of crayons.

Guided Practice

Copy and complete the fact family.

1. $4 \times 8 = 32$ $32 \div ■ = 4$

   $8 \times ■ = 32$ $■ \div 4 = 8$

TEKS 4.6A use patterns and relationships to develop strategies to remember basic multiplication and division facts (such as the patterns in related multiplication and division number sentences (fact families) such as 9 x 9 = 81 and 81÷ 9 = 9). also **4.4B, 4.4C, 4.4D, 4.4E, 4.14A, 4.15A, 4.15B**

Write the fact family for the set of numbers.

2. 2, 5, 10
3. 3, 4, 12
4. 2, 6, 12
5. 2, 3, 6
6. 1, 3, 3
7. TALK Math **Explain** how to use a fact family to write the related multiplication and division sentences.

Independent Practice and Problem Solving

Write the fact family for the set of numbers.

8. 2, 7, 14
9. 1, 4, 4
10. 3, 5, 15
11. 3, 3, 9
12. 5, 6, 30

Find the value of the variable. Then write a related sentence.

13. $24 \div 8 = n$
14. $3 \times 10 = c$
15. $8 \div 1 = y$
16. $36 \div m = 9$
17. $7 \times a = 28$
18. $6 \times 1 = b$
19. $35 \div 5 = p$
20. $18 \div 9 = n$
21. $8 \times c = 40$
22. $y \div 3 = 7$

USE DATA For 23–24, use the pictograph.

23. **What if** the crayon factory made 8 different shades of yellow? How many symbols would represent 8 shades in the pictograph?
24. How many different shades of crayon colors does the crayon factory make?
25. **FAST FACT** The average American child will use up about 730 crayons by the age of 10, or about 6 crayons each month. About how many crayons will a child use up in 4 months?
26. WRITE Math **What's the Error?** Dale says that 2×6 is in the same fact family as $6 \div 2$. Is he right? **Explain** why or why not.

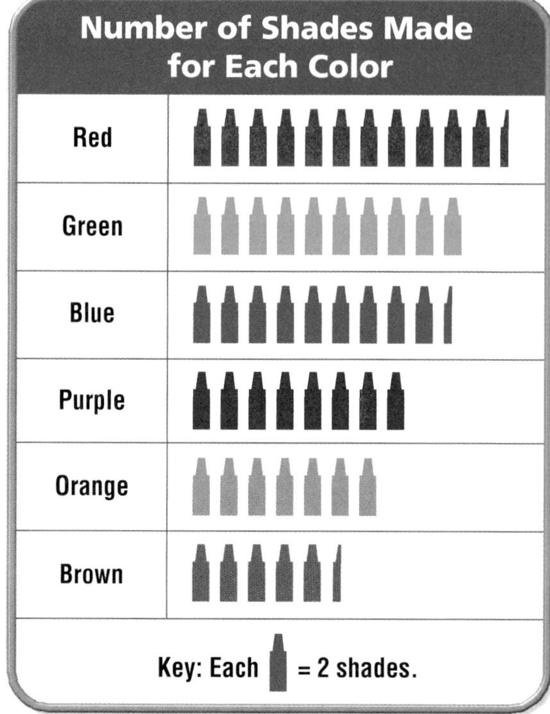

Mixed Review and TAKS Prep

27. Use the pictograph above. How many more shades of green crayons does the crayon factory make than shades of purple crayons? (Grade 3 TEKS 3.13B)
28. There are 24 crayons in a box. Randee removes some crayons. Write an expression that shows the number of crayons left in the box. (TEKS 4.15B, p. 70)
29. **TAKS Prep** Suzy colored 3 pages in a coloring book. Don colored 6 times as many pages as Suzy colored. How many pages did Don color? (Obj. 2)

   A 3
   B 6
   C 9
   D 18

Extra Practice on page 134, Set A

LESSON 2

Divide Facts Through 5

OBJECTIVE: Divide facts through 5.

Quick Review

Ben bought 6 postcards. He put an equal number of postcards on each of 3 scrapbook pages. Draw a picture to show how many postcards he put on each page.

Learn

PROBLEM The Strand covers 25 square blocks between 20th and 25th Streets. The district is 5 blocks long. How wide is it?

Example 1 Make an array.

Divide. $25 \div 5$

MODEL	THINK	RECORD
	25 blocks in all 5 blocks long 5 blocks wide	$25 \div 5 = 5$, or $5\overline{)25}$ with quotient 5 25 → dividend, 5 → divisor, 5 → quotient

So, the Strand is 5 blocks wide.

▲ The Strand National Historic District, in Galveston, Texas, has many shops, restaurants, and museums. Some of the oldest buildings date back to 1855.

Example 2 Use a number line.

In a gift shop at the Strand, José bought 15 pens. There were 3 pens in each box. How many boxes did he buy?

Divide. $15 \div 3$

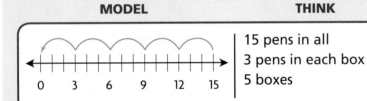

MODEL	THINK	RECORD
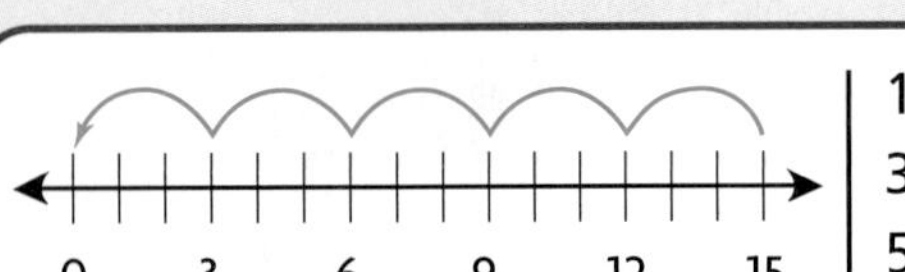	15 pens in all 3 pens in each box 5 boxes	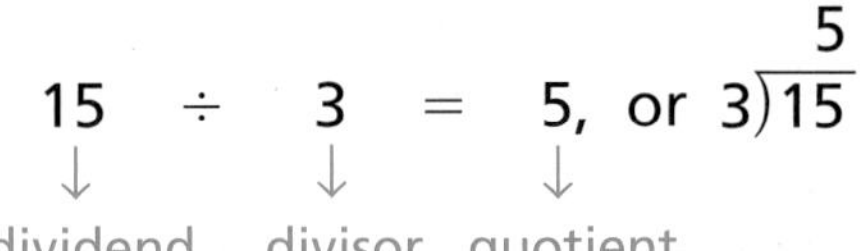 $15 \div 3 = 5$, or $3\overline{)15}$ with quotient 5 15 → dividend, 3 → divisor, 5 → quotient

So, José bought 5 boxes.

Example 3 Draw equal-size groups.

A tour guide led 12 people through the Strand. There were 4 people in each group. How many groups did the guide have?

Divide. $12 \div 4$

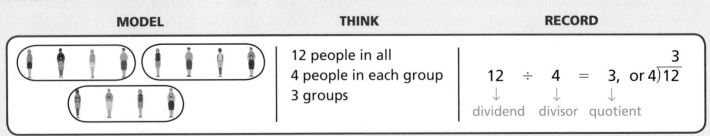

MODEL	THINK	RECORD
	12 people in all 4 people in each group 3 groups	$12 \div 4 = 3$, or $4\overline{)12}$ with quotient 3 12 → dividend, 4 → divisor, 3 → quotient

So, the tour guide had 3 groups.

TEKS 4.4B represent multiplication and division situations in picture, word, and number form; *also* 4.4C, 4.14A, 4.15A, 4.15B

Guided Practice

Make a model to find the quotient. Draw a picture of your model.

1. $16 \div 4$ **2.** $2\overline{)10}$ **3.** $8 \div 2$ **4.** $20 \div 5$ **5.** $3\overline{)9}$ **6.** $9 \div 9$

Find the quotient.

7. $10 \div 2$ **8.** $21 \div 3$ **9.** $5 \div 5$ **10.** $4\overline{)8}$ ✓**11.** $24 \div 4$ ✓**12.** $5\overline{)15}$

13. TALK Math **Explain** two different ways to model $45 \div 5$.

Independent Practice and Problem Solving

Find the quotient.

14. $18 \div 2$ **15.** $4 \div 4$ **16.** $10 \div 1$ **17.** $4\overline{)32}$ **18.** $6 \div 1$ **19.** $5\overline{)30}$

20. $3 \div 3$ **21.** $12 \div 3$ **22.** $2\overline{)12}$ **23.** $20 \div 4$ **24.** $2\overline{)6}$ **25.** $3\overline{)27}$

Algebra **Find the missing numbers.**

26. $6 \div 3 = ■$ **27.** $10 \div ■ = 2$ **28.** $18 \div 3 = ■$ **29.** $■ \div 2 = 7$

USE DATA For 30–31, use the diagram.

30. Write a multiplication sentence to find the total number of passengers on the trolley. Then write a related division sentence.

31. Eight more people get on the trolley. Then 4 groups of 2 people get on. If 4 people sit in each row, how many rows are filled on the trolley?

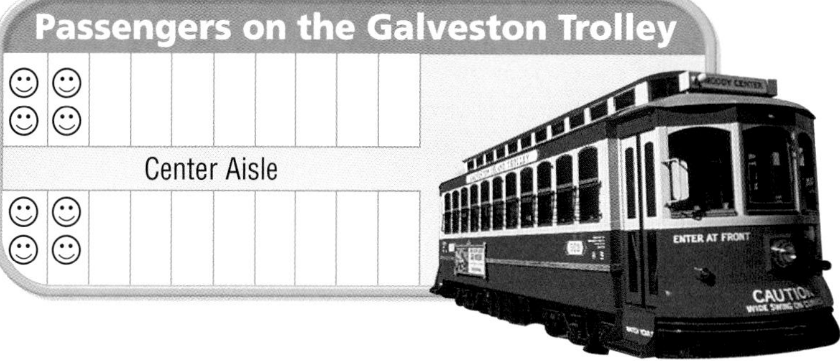

32. WRITE Math **What's the Question?** The answer to a division sentence is 2.

33. **Pose a Problem** Write a word problem that can be solved by using the number line.

0 5 10 15 20 25

Mixed Review and TAKS Prep

34. Which measurement best describes the width of a desk, 2 inches or 2 feet? (Grade 3 TEKS 3.11A)

35. Ty read 5 books each month for 3 months. How many books did he read? (TEKS 4.4C, p. 98)

36. **TAKS Prep** Sandy divided 35 packs of cards evenly among 5 friends. How many packs did each friend get? (Obj. 1)

A 5 **C** 7

B 6 **D** 8

Extra Practice on page 134, Set B

LESSON 3 Divide Facts Through 10

OBJECTIVE: Divide facts through 10.

Quick Review

Find the missing number.

1. 2 × 4 = ■
2. 12 ÷ 3 = ■
3. 4 × ■ = 16
4. 3, 6, 9, ■, 15
5. 25, 20, 15, ■, 5

Learn

PROBLEM Jane took 54 pictures at the Texas Wild! exhibit. She is reviewing the pictures on her computer. If there are 6 rows of pictures, how many columns of pictures will show up on her screen?

Activity 1 Use the break apart strategy.

Divide. 54 ÷ 6

Step 1

Draw a rectangle to show an area model of 54.

	?
6	54

Step 2

Break apart the rectangle to make two smaller parts for division facts you know.

	5	4
6	30	24

Step 3

Find the sum of the quotients of the two smaller parts.

30 ÷ 6 = 5
24 ÷ 6 = 4
5 + 4 = 9

So, Jane will have 9 columns of pictures.

▲ At the Texas Wild! exhibit of the Fort Worth Zoo, you can see the many different animals that are native to Texas.

Activity 2 Use doubles.

Materials ■ counters

Divide. 40 ÷ 8

Step 1

Think: The divisor is an even number. 8 is double 4.

Make an array with 40 counters.
Place 4 counters in each row.
There are 10 rows of 4 counters.

Step 2

Since 8 is double 4, 40 ÷ 8 will be half of 40 ÷ 4.

So, 40 ÷ 8 = 5.

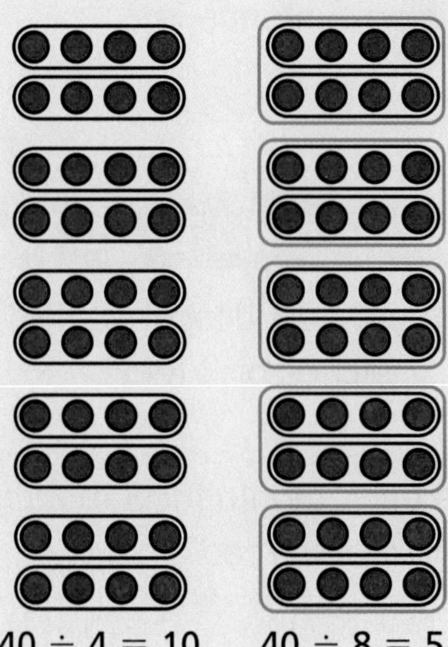

TEKS 4.6A use patterns and relationships to develop strategies to remember basic multiplication and division facts (such as the patterns in related multiplication and division number sentences (fact families) such as 9 × 9 = 81 and 81 ÷ 9 = 9). *also* **4.4A, 4.4B, 4.4C, 4.7, 4.14A, 4.14D, 4.15A, 4.15B, 4.16A**

More Strategies

Use a multiplication table.

Since division is the inverse of multiplication, you can use a multiplication table to find a quotient.

Divide. 56 ÷ 8

Think: 8 × ■ = 56

The divisor, 8, is the given factor in the related multiplication fact.
Find the row for the given factor, 8.

The dividend, 56, is the product in the multiplication table.
Look across to find the product, 56.

Look up to find the missing factor, 7.
The quotient is the missing factor, 7.

So, 56 ÷ 8 = 7.

×	0	1	2	3	4	5	6	7	8	9	10
0	0	0	0	0	0	0	0	0	0	0	0
1	0	1	2	3	4	5	6	7	8	9	10
2	0	2	4	6	8	10	12	14	16	18	20
3	0	3	6	9	12	15	18	21	24	27	30
4	0	4	8	12	16	20	24	28	32	36	40
5	0	5	10	15	20	25	30	35	40	45	50
6	0	6	12	18	24	30	36	42	48	54	60
7	0	7	14	21	28	35	42	49	56	63	70
8	0	8	16	24	32	40	48	56	64	72	80
9	0	9	18	27	36	45	54	63	72	81	90
10	0	10	20	30	40	50	60	70	80	90	100

- **Reasoning** Use the multiplication table to show that 0 ÷ 6 = 0. Then use the table to show that 6 ÷ 0 = ■ does not make sense.

Math Idea

Fact families can help you find the answers to division problems. Look at the related facts in the fact family for 5, 9, and 45.

9 × 5 = 45 45 ÷ 5 = 9
5 × 9 = 45 45 ÷ 9 = 5

Use a related multiplication fact.

Divide. 63 ÷ 9

Think: 9 × 7 = 63

So, 63 ÷ 9 = 7.

Use a pattern.

Divide. 42 ÷ 6

Count back from 42 by sixes.

Think: 42, 36, 30, 24, 18, 12, 6, 0

So, 42 ÷ 6 = 7.

Use a related division fact.

Divide. 35 ÷ 7

Think: 35 ÷ 5 = 7

So, 35 ÷ 7 = 5.

Guided Practice

1. Use the area model to copy and complete the division sentences.

40 ÷ 8 = ■
32 ÷ 8 = ■
72 ÷ 8 = ■ + ■
So, 72 ÷ 8 = ■.

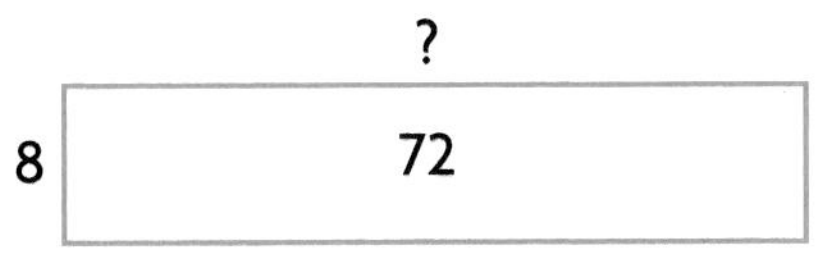

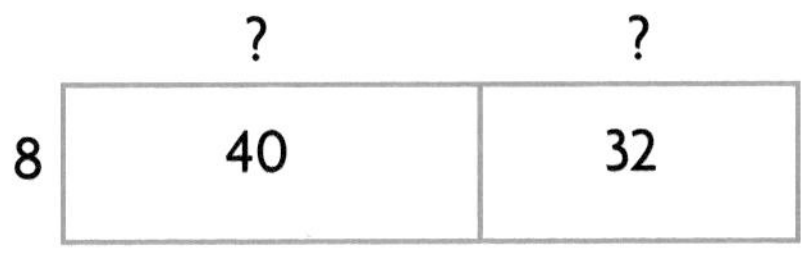

Find the quotient. Show the strategy you used.

2. $70 \div 7$
3. $12 \div 6$
4. $21 \div 7$
5. $27 \div 9$
6. $64 \div 8$

Write the related multiplication or division fact. Then find the quotient.

7. $16 \div 8$
8. $32 \div 8$
9. $60 \div 10$
10. $63 \div 7$
11. $49 \div 7$

12. TALK Math **Explain** two ways to use strategies to find $63 \div 7$.

Independent Practice and Problem Solving

Find the quotient. Show the strategy you used.

13. $18 \div 9$
14. $60 \div 6$
15. $42 \div 7$
16. $54 \div 9$
17. $30 \div 10$
18. $9\overline{)36}$
19. $7\overline{)14}$
20. $8\overline{)8}$
21. $6\overline{)0}$
22. $7\overline{)28}$

Write the related multiplication or division fact. Then find the quotient.

23. $56 \div 7$
24. $100 \div 10$
25. $48 \div 8$
26. $45 \div 9$
27. $24 \div 6$
28. $30 \div 6$
29. $24 \div 8$
30. $9 \div 9$
31. $36 \div 6$
32. $81 \div 9$

Algebra Find the missing dividend or divisor.

33. $■ \div 8 = 2 + 3$
34. $■ \div 9 = 6 + 4$
35. $48 \div ■ = 12 - 6$
36. $70 \div ■ = 16 - 9$

USE DATA For 37–39, use the Texas Horned Lizard Watch table.

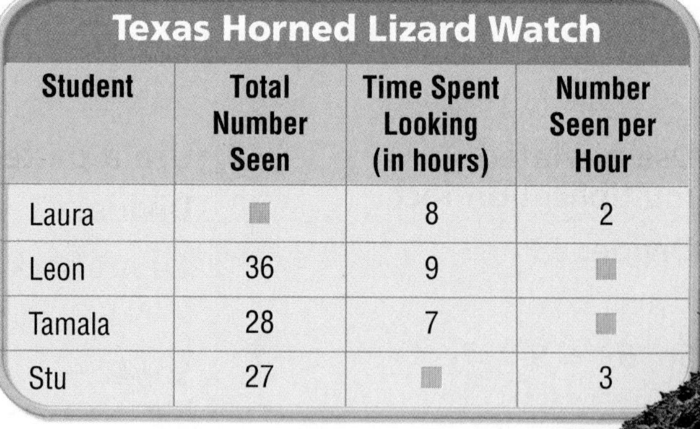

Texas Horned Lizard Watch

Student	Total Number Seen	Time Spent Looking (in hours)	Number Seen per Hour
Laura	■	8	2
Leon	36	9	■
Tamala	28	7	■
Stu	27	■	3

37. For how long did Stu look for horned lizards?
38. Who saw more horned lizards per hour—Leon or Stu?
39. Who saw more horned lizards per hour—Leon or Tamala?
40. The female horned lizard lays 13 to 45 eggs. She sits on her eggs for 1 night. Then she leaves them and never comes back. After 35 to 45 days, the eggs will hatch. About how many weeks is that?
41. WRITE Math **What's the Error?** When asked to write a pair of related division facts, Nina wrote $18 \div 9$ and $18 \div 6$. Is her answer correct? **Explain.**
42. **Reasoning** How are the dividends and quotients related in these facts?

    $16 \div 8$ and $32 \div 8$

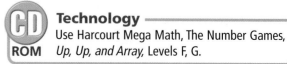

Technology
Use Harcourt Mega Math, The Number Games, *Up, Up, and Array,* Levels F, G.

Extra Practice on page 134, Set C

Mixed Review and TAKS Prep

43. Mark arranged his model cars in 6 rows of 4 cars each. What number sentence can be used to find the number of cars Mark arranged? (TEKS 4.4C, p. 100)

44. Rosa has a box of beads, all the same size. The table shows the number of beads of each color in the box.

Bead Colors			
Color	Green	Blue	Yellow
Number in Box	195	159	200

If Rosa takes 1 bead out of the box without looking, which color will she most likely get? (Grade 3 TEKS 3.13C)

45. **TAKS Prep** A school has 72 spelling bee awards hanging on a wall. If there are 9 awards in each row, how many rows are there? (Obj. 2)

A 10

B 9

C 8

D 7

46. **TAKS Prep** Use a number line to find $48 \div 6$. **Describe** the pattern you used. (Obj. 2)

Problem Solving and Reasoning

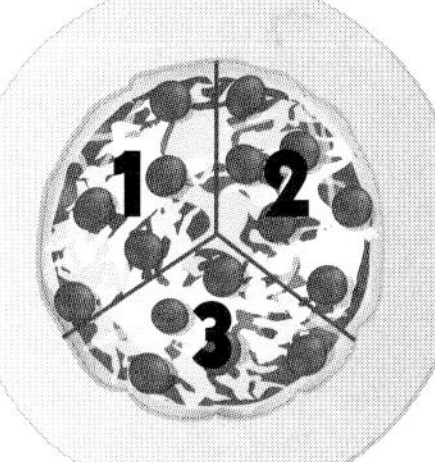

NUMBER SENSE Division and fractions both show the sharing of equal numbers of things or the making of equal-size groups.

Mavi and her 2 sisters want to share 2 small pizzas equally.

Think: Mavi and her 2 sisters = 3 people.

So, 2 pizzas must be divided into 3 equal-size groups.
This can be written as $2 \div 3$, or $\frac{2}{3}$.

Mavi

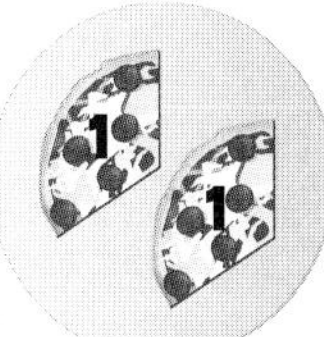

Sister 2

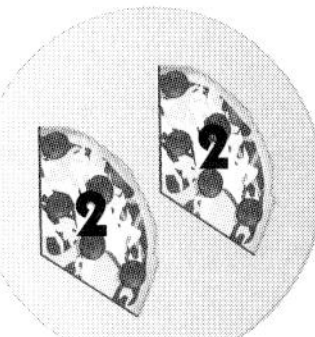

Sister 3

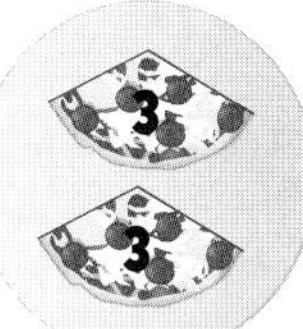

So, each sister will have 2 slices of pizza, or $\frac{2}{3}$ of a pizza.

Write the division problem as a fraction.

1. $6 \div 2$ **2.** $1 \div 4$ **3.** $1 \div 3$ **4.** $32 \div 8$ **5.** $5 \div 6$

LESSON 4

Divide Facts Through 12

OBJECTIVE: Divide facts through 12.

Quick Review

1. 11 × 12
2. 12 × 6
3. 11 × 9
4. 12 × 10
5. 11 × 11

Learn

You can use related multiplication facts to find a quotient or a missing divisor.

PROBLEM Machi is making European Union flags for a social studies project. The flag, which stands for Europe's unity and identity, has 12 stars. Machi has 144 stars. How many flags can she make?

Example 1 Find the quotient.

Divide. 144 ÷ 12 = ■

Think: 12 × ■ = 144

Find the row for the given factor, 12.
Look across to find the product, 144.
Look up to find the missing factor, 12.
12 × 12 = 144, so 144 ÷ 12 = 12.

So, Machi can make 12 flags.

×	0	1	2	3	4	5	6	7	8	9	10	11	12
0	0	0	0	0	0	0	0	0	0	0	0	0	0
1	0	1	2	3	4	5	6	7	8	9	10	11	12
2	0	2	4	6	8	10	12	14	16	18	20	22	24
3	0	3	6	9	12	15	18	21	24	27	30	33	36
4	0	4	8	12	16	20	24	28	32	36	40	44	48
5	0	5	10	15	20	25	30	35	40	45	50	55	60
6	0	6	12	18	24	30	36	42	48	54	60	66	72
7	0	7	14	21	28	35	42	49	56	63	70	77	84
8	0	8	16	24	32	40	48	56	64	72	80	88	96
9	0	9	18	27	36	45	54	63	72	81	90	99	108
10	0	10	20	30	40	50	60	70	80	90	100	110	120
11	0	11	22	33	44	55	66	77	88	99	110	121	132
12	0	12	24	36	48	60	72	84	96	108	120	132	144

Example 2 Find the missing divisor.

Divide. 132 ÷ ■ = 12

Think: ■ × 12 = 132

Find the factor, 12, in the top row.
Look down to find the product, 132.
Look left to find the missing factor, 11.
11 × 12 = 132, so 132 ÷ 11 = 12.

So, 132 ÷ 11 = 12.

- Explain how you can use multiplication to check 110 ÷ 11 = 10.

ERROR ALERT

Be sure to use the quotient and divisor as the factors and the dividend as the product in the related multiplication sentence.

Guided Practice

1. Find 72 ÷ 12. Write the fact family. Use the divisor as the factor and the dividend as the product. The quotient will be the missing factor.

Use the multiplication table to find the quotient. Write a related multiplication sentence.

2. $48 \div 12$ **3.** $110 \div 10$ **4.** $99 \div 11$ ✓**5.** $60 \div 5$ ✓**6.** $108 \div 12$

7. TALK Math **Explain** how you can use a multiplication table to show that 7×12 is related to $84 \div 12$.

Independent Practice and Problem Solving

Use the multiplication table to find the quotient. Write a related multiplication sentence.

8. $12 \div 12$ **9.** $84 \div 7$ **10.** $55 \div 5$ **11.** $120 \div 10$ **12.** $33 \div 11$

13. $24 \div 2$ **14.** $121 \div 11$ **15.** $36 \div 12$ **16.** $88 \div 11$ **17.** $132 \div 11$

Algebra Find the quotient or missing divisor.

18. $36 \div 3 =$ ■ **19.** $77 \div 7 =$ ■ **20.** $108 \div$ ■ $= 12$ **21.** $96 \div 8 =$ ■

22. $120 \div$ ■ $= 10$ **23.** $66 \div$ ■ $= 6$ **24.** $132 \div 12 =$ ■ **25.** $60 \div 5 =$ ■

26. At the sixth grade's Model United Nations, 96 countries will be represented. If 12 chairs are set up in each row, how many rows will the students need to set up so that each representative has a chair?

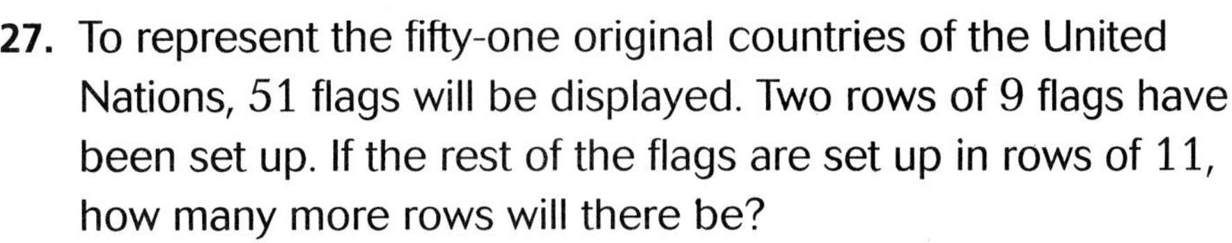

27. To represent the fifty-one original countries of the United Nations, 51 flags will be displayed. Two rows of 9 flags have been set up. If the rest of the flags are set up in rows of 11, how many more rows will there be?

28. **FAST FACT** The flag of the United States has 50 stars. The rows repeat in a pattern of 6 stars and then 5 stars. How many rows of stars are in the flag?

29. WRITE Math The quotient of $144 \div 12$ is greater than the quotient of $132 \div 12$. How much greater? **Explain** how you know without having to divide.

Mixed Review and TAKS Prep

30. Which is greater—4,564 or 4,654? (TEKS 4.1A, p. 12)

31. Mary orders 12 dozen hot dog buns for a camp cookout. How many buns will she have? (TEKS 4.4C, p. 104)

32. **TAKS Prep** Which number is missing from the number sentence? (Obj. 2)

$110 \div$ ■ $= 10$

A 9 **B** 11 **C** 10 **D** 12

Extra Practice on page 134, Set D

Problem Solving Workshop
Skill: Choose the Operation

LESSON 5

OBJECTIVE: Solve problems by using the skill *choose the operation.*

Use the Skill

PROBLEM Nancy is baking cookies to take to a party. There will be 12 people at the party. She mixes enough cookie dough for each person to have 4 cookies. Then she bakes the cookies on cookie sheets for 11 minutes. How many cookies will Nancy bake in all?

This chart will help you decide which operation you can use to solve the problem.

Add	Join groups of the same or different sizes
Subtract	Take away or compare groups
Multiply	Join equal-size groups
Divide	Separate into equal-size groups or find how many in each group

Since Nancy bakes 12 equal groups of 4 cookies, you can multiply to find how many cookies she will bake in all.

number of people		number of cookies for each person		total number of cookies
↓		↓		↓
12	×	4	=	48

So, Nancy will bake 48 cookies in all.

- What other operation could you use to solve this problem? Explain how you solved the problem.

Think and Discuss

Tell which operation you would use to solve the problem. Explain your choice. Solve the problem.

a. The Sandwich Shop served 3,275 lunches in May and served 4,250 lunches in June. How many lunches did the Shop serve in all?

b. Raul's class made $200 from this year's bake sale. Last year, the class made $178. How much more did they make this year?

c. The cafeteria served 132 pizza lunches. Each pizza was cut into 12 slices. If each student received 1 slice, how many pizzas were served?

TEKS 4.4C recall and apply multiplication facts through 12 x 12 also **4.3A, 4.4B, 4.6A, 4.14A, 4.14B, 4.14C, 4.15A, 4.15B, 4.16B**

Guided Problem Solving

Read to Understand
Plan
Solve
Check

Tell which operation you would use to solve the problem. Then solve the problem.

1. Russell made 36 ounces of trail mix to take on a hiking trip. He poured equal amounts of the trail mix into 4 bags. How many ounces of trail mix are in each bag?

   Think: What operation can you use to find how many ounces of trail mix are in each bag?

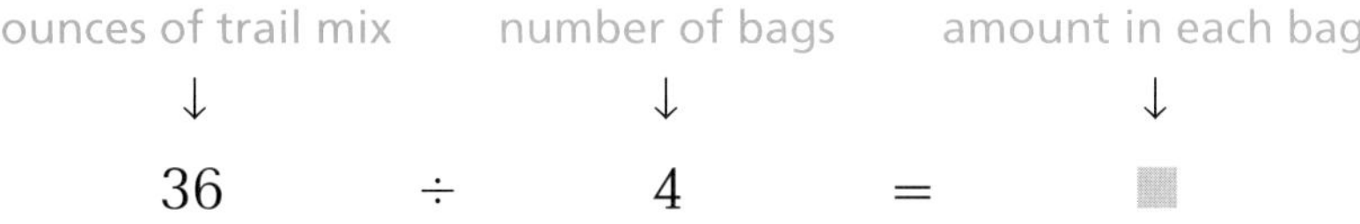

2. **What if** Russell poured equal amounts of the trail mix into 6 bags? How many ounces of trail mix would be in each bag?

3. The hiking trip is on Friday. On Thursday, the high temperature was 67°F. Russell hopes that it will be 8° warmer on Friday. What temperature is Russell hoping for?

Mixed Applications

USE DATA For 4–7, use the information in the picture.

4. Donald wants to place flower bouquets on 6 tables. How much will the flower bouquets cost in all?

5. Sonya bought 3 boxes of crackers. What number sentence can be used to find the amount of money Sonya spent on 1 box of crackers?

6. Art wants to send out 24 invitations for his party. How many boxes of cards will he need? How much will they cost?

7. Look at Mr. Hill's shopping list. What information is needed to find the total amount of money he spent at the grocery store?

8. **Pose a Problem** Write a word problem for the number sentence $48 \div 12 = n$. Then solve the problem.

9. **WRITE Math** Orange Park charges $11 per day per person. Deer Park charges $2 per hour per person. Help Lisa choose the less expensive park to hold her picnic if 12 people come to the picnic for 5 hours. **Explain** how you decided.

Mr. Hill's Shopping List

3 boxes of crackers
2 gallons of orange juice
2 loaves of bread
1 bouquet of flowers

Lesson 6 Factors and Multiples

OBJECTIVE: Find factors and multiples using arrays and number lines.

Quick Review

1. 8×4
2. 6×7
3. 2×9
4. 5×5
5. 3×10

Learn

A factor is a number multiplied by another number to find a product. Every whole number greater than 1 has at least two factors, that number and 1.

$18 = 1 \times 18$ (1 and 18: factor, factor) $\quad 7 = 7 \times 1 \quad 342 = 1 \times 342$

Many numbers can be broken into factors in different ways.

$16 = 1 \times 16 \quad 16 = 4 \times 4 \quad 16 = 2 \times 8$

Activity

Materials ■ square tiles ■ grid paper

Make arrays to show all the factors of 24.

- Use all 24 tiles to make an array. Record the array on grid paper. Write the factors shown by the array.

12
2

$2 \times 12 = 24$
Factors: 2, 12

- Make as many different arrays as you can with 24 tiles. Record the arrays on grid paper and write the factors shown.

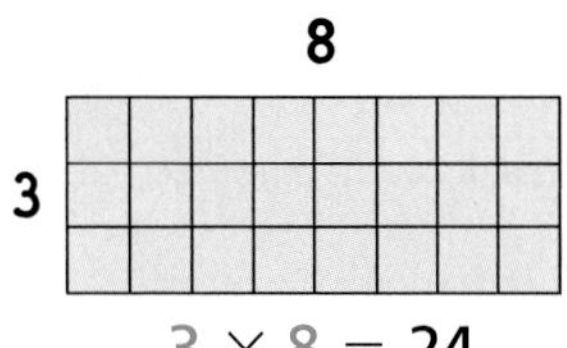

$3 \times 8 = 24$
Factors: 3, 8

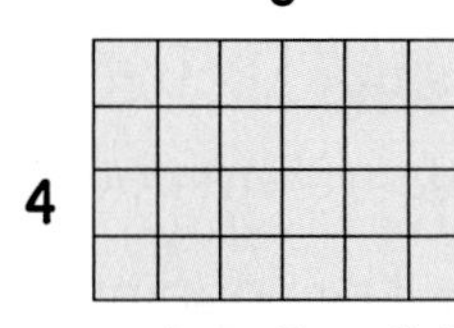

$4 \times 6 = 24$
Factors: 4, 6

$1 \times 24 = 24$
Factors: 1, 24

So, the factors of 24 are 1, 2, 3, 4, 6, 8, 12, and 24.

- Can you arrange the tiles in each array another way and show the same factors? Explain.

ERROR ALERT

Don't forget to list 1 and the number itself as factors.

TEKS 4.4A model factors and products using arrays and area models. *also* **4.4C, 4.14A, 4.14D, 4.15A, 4.15B**

Find Multiples

To find multiples of any counting number, skip-count or multiply by the counting numbers 1, 2, 3, and so on.

> **Math Idea**
> A multiple of a counting number is any product that has that number as a factor. The number of multiples a number has is endless.

PROBLEM Rachel has a new charm bracelet with 18 links. She put a charm on each link that is a multiple of 3. Which links have charms?

ONE WAY **Make a model.**

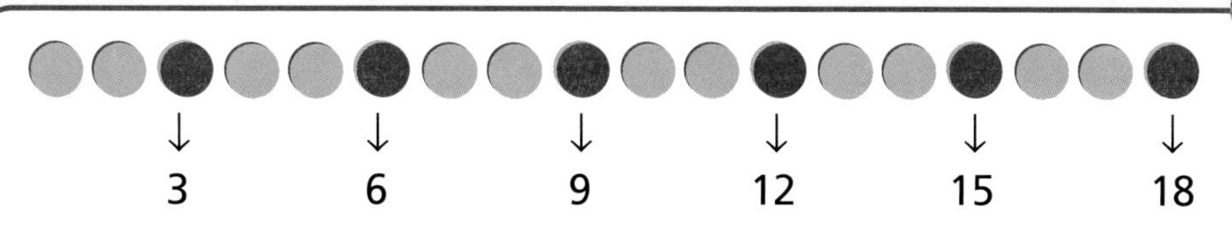

The numbers of the red counters are all multiples of 3.

So, the 3rd, 6th, 9th, 12th, 15th, and 18th links have charms.

- **What if** the bracelet had 27 links? Which other links would have charms?

ANOTHER WAY **Multiply and make a list.**

Find the first six multiples of 4.

$1 \times 4 = 4$	$2 \times 4 = 8$	$3 \times 4 = 12$	$4 \times 4 = 16$	$5 \times 4 = 20$	$6 \times 4 = 24$

So, the first six multiples of 4 are 4, 8, 12, 16, 20, and 24.

- Explain how you know that 30 is a multiple of 5.
- Can a number that is a multiple of 3 have 5 as a factor? Explain.

Guided Practice

1. Use the arrays to name the factors of 12.

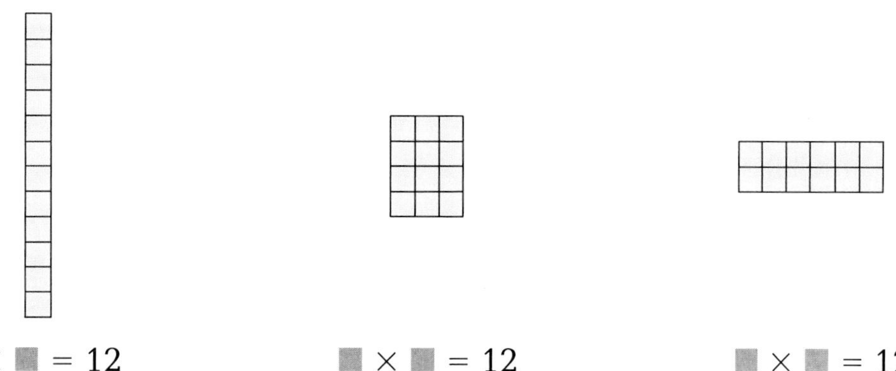

■ × ■ = 12 ■ × ■ = 12 ■ × ■ = 12

The factors of 12 are 1, ■, 3, ■, 6, and ■.

Use arrays to find all the factors of each product.

2. 20 3. 5 4. 49 5. 28 ✓6. 25

List the first ten multiples of each number.

7. 6 8. 2 9. 11 10. 4 ✓11. 8

12. TALK Math **Explain** how the numbers 3 and 12 are related. Use the words *factor* and *multiple* in your explanation.

Independent Practice and Problem Solving

Use arrays to find all the factors of each product.

13. 30 14. 42 15. 9 16. 50 17. 33

18. 64 19. 21 20. 72 21. 18 22. 17

List the first ten multiples of each number.

23. 9 24. 1 25. 7 26. 10 27. 12

28. 3 29. 8 30. 5 31. 2 32. 6

Is 6 a factor of each number? Write *yes* or *no*.

33. 6 34. 16 35. 48 36. 24 37. 18

Is 36 a multiple of each number? Write *yes* or *no*.

38. 8 39. 9 40. 6 41. 36 42. 5

Algebra Find the missing multiple.

43. 4, 8, ■, 16 44. 7, 14, 21, ■ 45. 5, ■, 15, 20 46. 9, 18, 27, ■

USE DATA For 47–48, copy and complete the Venn diagram. Then use it to solve the problems.

47. What multiples of 4 are not factors of 48?

48. What factors of 48 are also multiples of 4?

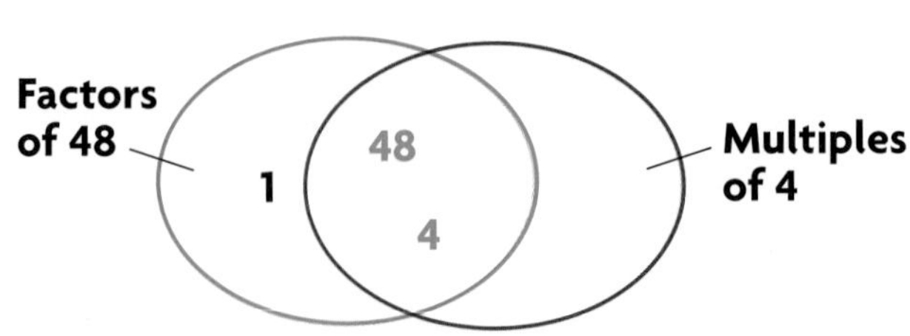

49. Kia paid $40 for two charms. The price of each charm was a multiple of $4. What are the possible prices for the charms?

50. WRITE Math **What's the Question?** The answer is 1, 2, 3, 6, 9, and 18.

 Extra Practice on page 134, Set E

Mixed Review and TAKS Prep

51. Find a rule. Use your rule to extend the pattern. (TEKS 4.7, p. 82)

Input	x	50	61	108	123	177
Output	y	47	58	105	■	■

52. In 1999, Dallas had 1,076,214 people. Houston had 1,845,967. Which city had more people? (TEKS 4.1A, p. 12)

53. TAKS Prep Ana is arranging 9 photos on a bulletin board. She wants to put the photos in equal rows. In what ways can she arrange the photos? (Obj. 1)

A Rows of 1, 3, or 6

B Rows of 1, 2, or 9

C Rows of 1, 3, or 9

D Rows of 3, 6, or 9

54. TAKS Prep What multiple of 9 is also a factor of 9? (Obj. 1)

Problem Solving and Reasoning

LOGICAL REASONING Starting June 1, an ice-cream truck visits Sasha's street every 3 days and Brad's street every 5 days. What are the first 2 days the truck visits both streets on the same day?

S	M	T	W	T	F	S
1	2	3	4	5	6	7
8	9	10	11	12	13	14
15	16	17	18	19	20	21
22	23	24	25	26	27	28
29	30	31				

The days the ice-cream truck visits both streets on the same day are common multiples of 3 and 5.

A **common multiple** is a multiple of two or more numbers. You can use a number line to find common multiples.

Example Use a number line.

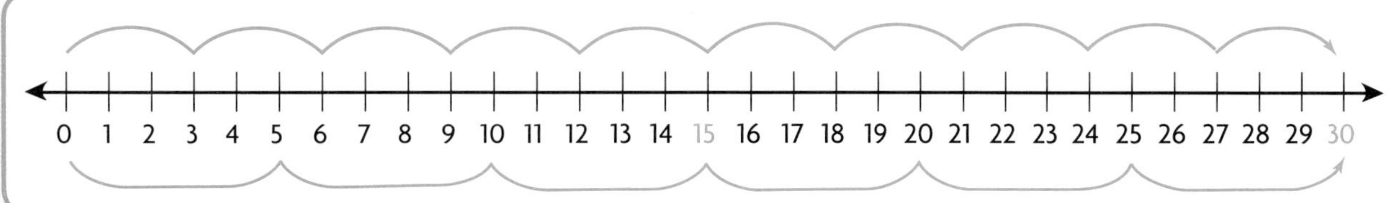

So, the first 2 days the truck visits both streets are June 15 and 30.

List the first six multiples of each. Find the common multiples.

1. 2 and 4 **2.** 9 and 12 **3.** 4 and 8 **4.** 3 and 4

5. 3 and 6 **6.** 2 and 5 **7.** 3 and 9 **8.** 5 and 10

Extra Practice

Set A **Write the fact family for the set of numbers.** (pp. 118–119)

1. 4, 5, 20 2. 3, 4, 12 3. 5, 9, 45 4. 6, 7, 42 5. 8, 9, 72

Set B **Find the quotient.** (pp. 120–121)

1. $8 \div 2$ 2. $3\overline{)18}$ 3. $21 \div 3$ 4. $5\overline{)40}$ 5. $4 \div 4$ 6. $28 \div 4$

7. A roller coaster at an amusement park can hold 32 people on each trip. Each car holds 4 people. How many cars does the roller coaster have?

Set C **Find the quotient. Show the strategy you used.** (pp. 122–125)

1. $42 \div 7$ 2. $63 \div 9$ 3. $54 \div 6$ 4. $45 \div 9$ 5. $30 \div 6$ 6. $72 \div 8$

Write the related multiplication or division fact. Then find the quotient.

7. $14 \div 2$ 8. $49 \div 7$ 9. $36 \div 9$ 10. $16 \div 8$ 11. $35 \div 5$ 12. $27 \div 9$

Set D **Use the multiplication table on page 126 to find the quotient. Write the related multiplication sentence.** (pp. 126–127)

1. $56 \div 8$ 2. $48 \div 4$ 3. $88 \div 8$ 4. $60 \div 5$ 5. $44 \div 4$

Find the quotient or missing divisor.

6. $24 \div ■ = 12$ 7. $70 \div 7 = ■$ 8. $55 \div ■ = 5$ 9. $96 \div ■ = 12$

10. Mr. Ingalls packed the same number of muffins in each of 12 boxes. He packed a total of 144 muffins. How many muffins did he pack in each box?

11. Fiona read 77 pages in her book over spring break. She read the same number of pages each day for the week. How many pages did she read each day?

Set E **Use arrays to find all the factors of each product.** (pp. 130–133)

1. 24 2. 35 3. 41 4. 56 5. 32

List the first ten multiples of each number.

6. 7 7. 11 8. 12 9. 10 10. 6

CD ROM **Technology**
Use Harcourt Mega Math, The Number Games, *Up, Up, and Array,* Levels E, F, G, H.

PRACTICE GAME

HOPSCOTCH FACTS

Hoppers!

2 teams, at least 2 players on each team

Get Set!

- Number cards (1–12, two sets)
- Two-color counters (1 for each team)

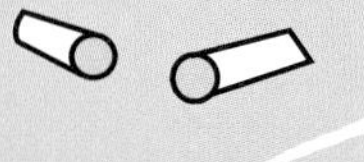

Hop!

- Players shuffle each set of number cards and place them facedown in two stacks.
- Teams take turns. A player chooses one card from each stack. A teammate uses those numbers to write a basic multiplication or division fact sentence.
- If the fact sentence is correct, the team places a counter on 1. The cards are placed in discard stacks.
- If a player makes an incorrect fact sentence on the first or second turn, that team loses a turn. If a player makes an incorrect fact sentence after his or her team has hopped past 2 on the game board, that team moves its counter back two spaces.
- On each turn, teammates trade roles.
- If all the number cards are used, players shuffle each set and place them facedown to use again.
- The first team to reach 10 wins.

Chapter 5 Review/Test

Check Vocabulary and Concepts

Choose the best term from the box.

VOCABULARY
dividend
divisor
inverse operations
quotient

1. In $36 \div 9 = 4$, 4 is the ___?___. (TEKS 4.4B, p. 118)
2. In a division problem, the number you divide by is called the ___?___. (TEKS 4.4B, p. 118)
3. Multiplication and division by the same number are opposite, or ___?___. One operation undoes the other. (TEKS 4.6A, p. 118)

Check Skills

Write the fact family for the set of numbers. (TEKS 4.6A, pp. 118–119)

4. 3, 4, 12
5. 2, 5, 10
6. 3, 9, 27
7. 4, 6, 24

Find the quotient. (TEKS 4.4B, pp. 120–121, 122–125, 126–127)

8. $18 \div 3$
9. $12\overline{)36}$
10. $28 \div 4$
11. $5\overline{)25}$
12. $30 \div 6$
13. $35 \div 7$
14. $24 \div 8$
15. $4\overline{)32}$

Write the related multiplication or division fact. Then find the quotient. (TEKS 4.6A, pp. 122–125)

16. $56 \div 7$
17. $54 \div 6$
18. $42 \div 7$
19. $60 \div 10$

Find the quotient or missing divisor. (TEKS 4.6A, pp. 126–127)

20. $40 \div 5 = ■$
21. $49 \div ■ = 7$
22. $63 \div 7 = ■$
23. $84 \div ■ = 12$
24. $54 \div ■ = 9$
25. $64 \div 8 = ■$
26. $99 \div ■ = 9$
27. $50 \div 5 = ■$

Use arrays to find all the factors of each product. (TEKS 4.4A, pp. 130–133)

28. 40
29. 48
30. 90
31. 44

Check Problem Solving

Solve. (TEKS 4.14B, pp. 128–129)

32. Max has 36 pennies. If he makes stacks of 4 pennies, how many stacks will he have?
33. WRITE Math Audrey bought a dozen rolls at the bakery. **Explain** how can she find the cost of 1 roll.

GO ONLINE **Technology** Use *Online Assessment.*

Enrich • Common Factors

The Baker's Dilemma

Mrs. Smith has 16 vanilla cookies and 24 chocolate cookies to put in bags. She wants to put the same number of cookies in each bag, but not mix the types of cookies. How many cookies could she put in each bag if she wants to use them all?

You can solve the problem by finding the common factors of 16 and 24. A **common factor** is a number that is a factor of two or more numbers.

Recipe

Make a list of factors for 16 and 24. Circle the factors the numbers have in common.

Factors of 16: 1, 2, 4, 8, 16

Factors of 24: 1, 2, 3, 4, 6, 8, 12, 24

So, Mrs. Smith could put 1, 2, 4, or 8 cookies in each bag.

Mix It

A Find the common factors of 18 and 30.

Factors of 18: 1, 2, 3, 6, 9, 18

Factors of 30: 1, 2, 3, 5, 6, 10, 15, 30

The common factors are 1, 2, 3, and 6.

B Find the common factors of 8 and 15

Factors of 8: 1, 2, 4, 8

Factors of 15: 1, 3, 5, 15

The common factor is 1.

Sample It

Write the common factors for each set of numbers.

1. 20 and 28

2. 25 and 35

3. 10 and 21

4. 14 and 28

5. 18 and 24

6. 16 and 30

7. 27 and 36

8. 28 and 32

9. Which common factor of 12 and 16 is the greatest?

10. Which common factor of 18 and 27 is the greatest?

Bake-Off

Explain how you know that any two numbers always will have at least one common factor.

Getting Ready for the TAKS
Chapters 1–5

Number, Operation, and Quantitative Reasoning TAKS Obj. 1

1. Kristin has 63 photographs from her vacation displayed on 9 pages of her album. There are the same number of photographs on each page. How many photographs are on each page?

   A 9

   B 8

   C 7

   D 6

2. The table shows the numbers of students at two schools in the same town.

Students at Local Schools	
School	**Number of Students**
Rosewood	972
Hickory	723

   Which sentence correctly compares the number of students at the schools?

   F Rosewood has 149 more students than Hickory.

   G Rosewood has 159 more students than Hickory.

   H Rosewood has 249 more students than Hickory.

   J Hickory has 259 more students than Rosewood.

3. **WRITE Math** **Explain** how to round $1,159 to the nearest hundred dollars.

Patterns, Relationships, and Algebraic Thinking TAKS Obj. 2

4. Which number sentence is a division fact related to $6 \times 12 = 72$?

   A $12 \times 6 = 72$

   B $12 \div 6 = 2$

   C $5 \times 12 = 60$

   D $72 \div 6 = 12$

Test Tip **Get the information you need.**

See item 5. Look for the relationship of each number to the number that comes after it.

5. What number is missing in the pattern below?

   21, 28, 35, ■, 49

   F 45 **H** 40

   G 42 **J** 38

6. **WRITE Math** The table shows the number of legs a number of spiders have.

Spider Legs	
Legs	**Spiders**
48	6
40	5
32	4
24	3

   Write a rule to describe the pattern in the table. **Explain** how you decided what rule to write.

Geometry and Spatial Reasoning TAKS Obj. 3

7. Which term best describes this figure?

A Square

B Rectangle

C Pentagon

D Quadrilateral

8. Aaron drew a figure with exactly 3 sides. Which figure did Aaron draw?

F Triangle

G Rectangle

H Square

J Not here

9. Which statement is true?

A All right angles are congruent.

B All rectangles are congruent.

C All squares are congruent.

D All circles are congruent.

10. WRITE Math ▸ Look at the pentagon below. Does the blue line appear to be a line of symmetry? **Explain** why or why not.

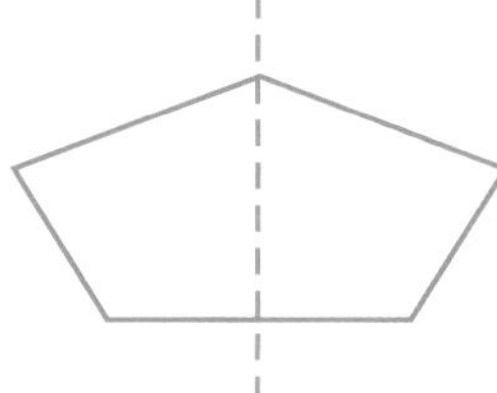

Probability and Statistics TAKS Obj. 5

11. Kate has a box of chocolates with different fillings.

Chocolate Fillings	
Filling	**Number of Chocolates**
Caramel	2
Peanut	6
Almond	2
Vanilla	4

If Kate picks one chocolate from the box without looking, which of the following statements best describes a possible outcome?

F Kate is less likely to choose peanut than caramel.

G Kate is more likely to choose peanut than almond.

H Kate is equally likely to choose almond or vanilla.

J Kate is more likely to choose vanilla than peanut.

12. WRITE Math ▸ The pictograph shows information about the top three favorite foods at Hillside School.

Students' Favorite Food	
Ice Cream	♦ ♦ ♦ ♦ ♦ ♦ ♦
Spaghetti	♦ ♦ ♦ ♦ ♦ ♦
Hamburgers	
Key: Each ♦ =12 students.	

What information is needed to complete the pictograph? **Explain** your answer.

6 Algebra: Patterns, Expressions, and Equations

The Big Idea Properties and the concepts of algebra are used to evaluate expressions and solve multiplication and division equations. Patterns can be generalized with words and symbols.

TEXAS FAST FACT

In 1900, a very large prairie dog "town" was observed in the Texas High Plains. It measured 100 miles by 250 miles. About 400,000,000 prairie dogs lived there.

Investigate

In their "towns," prairie dog families go in and out of tunnels they dig in the earth. Suppose there are 5 prairie dogs in each family. Use the table to write multiplication and division equations for the number of prairie dog families inside a tunnel, outside a tunnel, and altogether.

Prairie Dog Towns

	Prairie Dogs	
Tunnel	Inside Tunnel	Outside Tunnel
A	25	10
B	30	15
C	35	20
D	40	25

Technology
Student pages are available in the Student eBook.

Show What You Know

Check your understanding of important skills needed for success in Chapter 6.

▶ Use a Rule

Copy and complete each table.

1.

Team	2	3	4	5	6
Players	12	18	24	■	■

Rule: Multiply the number of teams by 6.

2.

Dimes	4	5	6	7	8
Pennies	40	50	■	70	■

Rule: Multiply the number of dimes by 10.

3.

Legs	12	16	20	24	28
Cows	3	4	5	■	■

Rule: Divide the number of legs by 4.

4.

Inches	12	24	36	48	60
Feet	1	2	■	4	■

Rule: Divide the number of inches by 12.

▶ Fact Families

Copy and complete each number sentence.

5. $5 \times 3 =$ ■
$15 \div$ ■ $= 3$

6. $6 \times 7 =$ ■
$42 \div$ ■ $= 7$

7. $4 \times 9 =$ ■
$36 \div$ ■ $= 9$

8. $7 \times 9 =$ ■
$63 \div$ ■ $= 9$

▶ Number Patterns

Write the next three possible numbers in each pattern.

9. 3, 6, 9, 12, ■, ■, ■

10. 42, 36, 30, 24, ■, ■, ■

11. 18, 27, 36, 45, ■, ■, ■

12. 36, 32, 28, 24, ■, ■, ■

VOCABULARY POWER

CHAPTER VOCABULARY

equation
ordered pair
expression
square number
Associative Property of Multiplication
Commutative Property of Multiplication
Distributive Property
Identity Property of Multiplication
Zero Property of Multiplication

WARM-UP WORDS

square number the product of any number and itself

Zero Property of Multiplication the property that states that the product of 0 and any number is 0

Identity Property of Multiplication the property that states that the product of 1 and any number is that number

Patterns on the Multiplication Table

OBJECTIVE: Identify patterns on the multiplication table.

Quick Review

Name the pattern unit.

1. 1, 2, 3, 1, 2, 3, 1, 2, 3
2. 2, 4, 2, 4, 2, 4, 2, 4
3. 3, 0, 7, 3, 0, 7, 3, 0, 7
4. 8, 5, 8, 5, 8, 5, 8, 5
5. 6, 5, 4, 6, 5, 4, 6, 5, 4

Vocabulary

square number

Learn

You can use a multiplication table to explore number patterns.

Activity **Materials** ■ multiplication table

- Find 4 × 4. Circle the product.
- Shade the squares for all the products above the row for 4 and to the left of the column for 4. Look at the array you shaded. What shape do you see?

A number that can be modeled with a square array is called a square number. A **square number** is a number that is the product of any number and itself.

- Continue multiplying to find the other square numbers in the table. Circle the square numbers. What do you see?
- Compare the number to the left of and above each square number. What pattern do you see?

The product of two counting numbers is a multiple of each of those numbers. To find the multiples of 4, multiply by the counting numbers 1, 2, 3, and so on. Look at the row or the column for the factor 4.

- List the multiples of 4 shown in the table. What patterns do you see?
- Look at the multiples of 1, 3, 5, 7, 9, and 11. What patterns do you see?

×	0	1	2	3	4	5	6	7	8	9	10	11	12
0	0	0	0	0	0	0	0	0	0	0	0	0	0
1	0	1	2	3	4	5	6	7	8	9	10	11	12
2	0	2	4	6	8	10	12	14	16	18	20	22	24
3	0	3	6	9	12	15	18	21	24	27	30	33	36
4	0	4	8	12	(16)	20	24	28	32	36	40	44	48
5	0	5	10	15	20	25	30	35	40	45	50	55	60
6	0	6	12	18	24	30	36	42	48	54	60	66	72
7	0	7	14	21	28	35	42	49	56	63	70	77	84
8	0	8	16	24	32	40	48	56	64	72	80	88	96
9	0	9	18	27	36	45	54	63	72	81	90	99	108
10	0	10	20	30	40	50	60	70	80	90	100	110	120
11	0	11	22	33	44	55	66	77	88	99	110	121	132
12	0	12	24	36	48	60	72	84	96	108	120	132	144

Guided Practice

1. Use the array to find the square number. ■ × ■ = ■

Find the square number.

2. 6 × 6 3. 2 × 2 4. 9 × 9 5. 1 × 1 6. 4 × 4 ✓7. 11 × 11

TEKS 4.6A use patterns and relationships to develop strategies to remember basic multiplication and division facts (such as the patterns in related multiplication and division number sentences (fact families) such as 9 × 9 = 81 and 81 ÷ 9 = 9. *also* **4.4C, 4.7, 4.14D, 4.15A, 4.15B, 4.16A**

Use the multiplication table.

8. What pattern do you see in the multiples of 5?

9. Which multiples have only even numbers?

10. TALK Math **Explain** how patterns in the multiplication table can help you remember multiplication facts.

Independent Practice and Problem Solving

Find the square number.

11. 3×3
12. 6×6
13. 8×8
14. 10×10
15. 7×7
16. 12×12

Use the multiplication table.

17. What pattern do you see in the multiples of 8?

18. What pattern do you see in the first 9 multiples of 10?

19. What pattern do you see in the ones digits of multiples of 2?

20. What pattern do you see in the multiples of 4 and multiples of 12?

Reasoning Write *true* or *false*. If the statement is false, explain why.

21. All of the multiples of 6 are multiples of 3.

22. For any multiple of 5, the ones digit is 5.

USE DATA For 23–25, use the Facts of Nine table.

Facts of Nine
$1 \times 9 = 9$
$2 \times 9 = 18$
$3 \times 9 = 27$
$4 \times 9 = 36$
$5 \times 9 = 45$
$6 \times 9 = 54$
$7 \times 9 = 63$
$8 \times 9 = 72$
$9 \times 9 = 81$
$10 \times 9 = 90$

23. How does the pattern of the tens digits in the products relate to the pattern of the factors?

24. How do the digits of each product relate to the factor 9?

25. **Explain** how you can use the patterns to find 9×9 without using the table.

26. **Reasoning** Use the rule *3 less than 2 times the number* to make a pattern. Start with 4. What is the fifth number in the pattern?

27. WRITE Math Look at the multiples of 2 and 4 in the multiplication table. **Explain** how they are alike and how they are different.

Mixed Review and TAKS Prep

28. Would you measure the length of a goldfish in inches, in feet, or in miles? (Grade 3 TEKS 3.11A)

29. Find the missing number. (TEKS 4.3A, p. 68)

$$12 + 64 = \blacksquare + 12$$

30. **TAKS Prep** The multiples of which number are double the multiples of 3? (Obj. 2)

A 2 **C** 9

B 6 **D** 12

Extra Practice on page 172, Set A

LESSON 2

Number Patterns

OBJECTIVE: Identify, describe, extend, and make patterns.

Quick Review

Find the missing number.

1. 5 × ■ = 15
2. 7 + ■ = 13
3. 12 ÷ ■ = 3
4. 50 − ■ = 40
5. 830 + ■ = 930

Learn

PROBLEM Morgan counts as he juggles three balls. He tosses the red ball on the count of 3, 6, 9, and 12. What numbers will he count for the next two tosses of the red ball?

Example 1

Find a rule. Then find the next two numbers in your pattern.

3, 6, 9, 12, ■, ■

Step 1

Think: What rule changes 3 to 6?

Try multiply by 2 because 2 × 3 = 6.

Test: 2 × 6 ≠ 9

Try add 3 because 3 + 3 = 6.

Test: 6 + 3 = 9   9 + 3 = 12

The rule add 3 works.

Step 2

Use the rule to find the next two numbers in the pattern.

+3 +3 +3 +3 +3

3, 6, 9, 12, 15, 18

So, he will count 15, 18 for the next two tosses of the red ball.

If a number pattern increases, try addition or multiplication. If it decreases, try subtraction or division.

Example 2

Find a rule. Then find the missing numbers in your pattern.

35, 31, 27, ■, 19, 15, ■

Step 1

Write a rule for the pattern.

Try subtract 4.

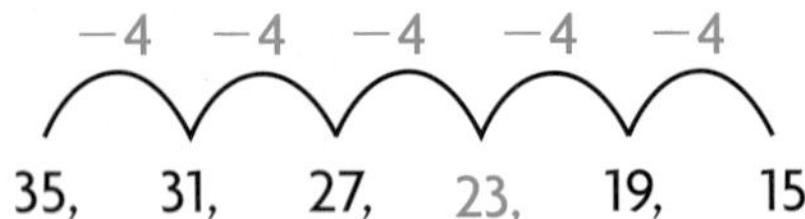

The rule subtract 4 works.

Step 2

Use the rule to find the missing numbers in your pattern.

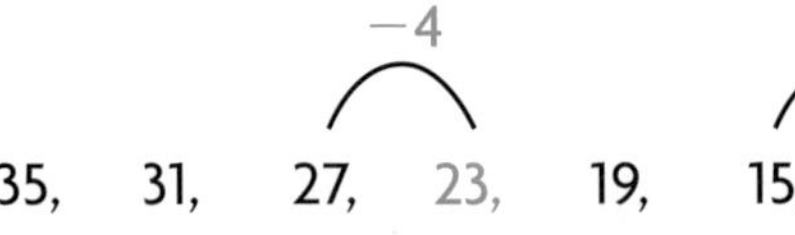

So, the missing numbers are 23 and 11.

- Look at this pattern: 1, 2, 4, ■. If the missing number is 8, what is a rule for your pattern? If the missing number is 7, what is a rule for your pattern?

TEKS 4.7 The student uses organizational structures to analyze and describe patterns and relationships. *also* 4.3A, 4.4C, 4.14A, 4.14C, 4.14D, 4.15A, 4.15B, 4.16A

Find and Make Patterns

The rules for some patterns have more than one operation. When numbers in a pattern increase **and** decrease, try two operations.

Math Idea

You can use the strategy *look for a possible pattern* to help. Compare each number with the next.

Example 3 **Use two operations.**

Find a rule. Then find the next two numbers in your pattern.

5, 1, 10, 2, 20, 4, 40, ■, ■

Step 1

Write a rule for the pattern.

Try divide by 5, multiply by 10.

÷ 5 × 10 ÷ 5 × 10 ÷ 5 × 10

5, 1, 10, 2, 20, 4, 40

The rule divide by 5, multiply by 10 works.

Step 2

Use your rule to find the missing numbers.

$40 \div 5 = 8$ $10 \times 8 = 80$

So, the next two numbers in the pattern are 8 and 80.

Example 4 **Use a calculator.**

Use the rule *add 13, multiply by 4* to make a pattern.
Start with 1. Find the next three numbers in the pattern.

Step 1

Enter the first operation. Press:     

Step 2

Enter the second operation. Press:    

Step 3

Find the second number in the pattern. Press: 

Step 4

Find the third number in the pattern. Press: 

Op1 Op2
14 X 4
1 56

Step 5

Find the fourth number in the pattern. Press: 

Op1 Op2
56 + 13
1 69

So, the next three numbers in the pattern are 14, 56, and 69.

Guided Practice

1. What are the next two numbers in the pattern?

−2 −2 −2

58, 56, 54, 52, ■, ■

Find a rule. Then find the next two numbers in your pattern.

2. 18, 28, 38, 48, ■, ■

3. 4, 7, 5, 8, 6, 9, 7, ■, ■

4. TALK Math **Explain** how to find missing numbers in a number pattern.

Independent Practice and Problem Solving

Find a rule. Then find the next two numbers in your pattern.

5. 775, 675, 575, 475, ■, ■

6. 160, 80, 40, 20, ■, ■

7. 47, 52, 51, 56, 55, 60, 59, ■, ■

8. 99, 95, 98, 94, 97, 93, 96, ■, ■

Algebra Find a rule. Then find the missing numbers in your pattern.

9. 2, 4, ■, 16, 32, 64

10. 46, 40, ■, 28, 22, ■, 10

11. ■, 130, 145, 160, 175, ■

Use the rule to make a number pattern. Write the first four numbers in the pattern.

12. Rule: Divide by 2. Start with 24.

13. Rule: Subtract 8. Start with 72.

14. Rule: Add 3, subtract 2. Start with 16.

15. Jordan is juggling 3 balls. He starts by keeping 1 ball in his hand and tossing 2 balls into the air. The diagram shows how many balls are in the air and in his hand with each toss. How many balls will be in the air and in his hand with the next toss?

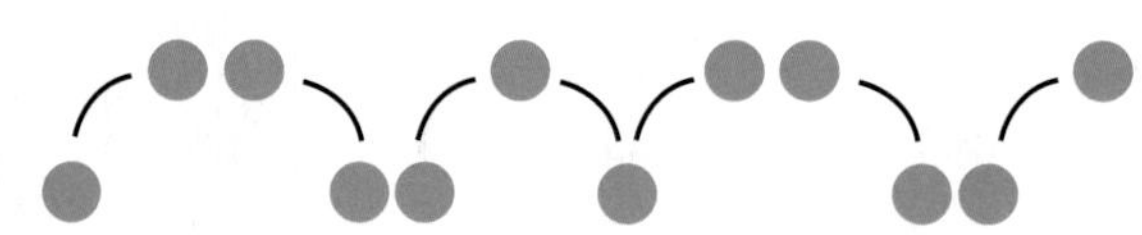

16. Carolyn counts as she juggles 4 balls. She tosses the red ball on the count of 4, 8, 12, and 16. What numbers will she count when she tosses the next two red balls?

17. **Pose a Problem** Make a number pattern. Write the first six numbers. Have a classmate write a rule for your pattern and use that rule to find the next two numbers.

18. **Reasoning** Look at the following number pattern: 2, 4, 8, ■. What is a rule for the pattern if the missing number is 14? What is a rule for the pattern if the missing number is 16?

19. WRITE Math **Explain** how you can tell by looking at a pattern that a rule for the pattern might have two operations.

Technology
CD ROM Use Harcourt Mega Math, The Number Games, *Tiny's Think Tank*, Level K.

 Extra Practice on page 172, Set B

Mixed Review and TAKS Prep

20. Sophie has 12 stickers. Write all the ways she could arrange them in equal rows. Then write all the factors of 12. (TEKS 4.4A, p. 130)

21. The table shows populations for different states. Which state in the table has the least population? (TEKS 4.1A, p. 16)

Number of People in Three States	
State	**Population**
California	33,145,121
Illinois	12,128,370
Texas	20,044,141

22. **TAKS Prep** Which of the following describes a rule for this pattern? (Obj. 2)

5, 9, 7, 11, 9, 13, 11

A Add 2.

B Multiply by 2.

C Add 4, subtract 2.

D Add 2, multiply by 2.

23. **TAKS Prep** What might be the next two numbers in this pattern? (Obj. 2)

24, 21, 18, 15, ■, ■

Problem Solving and Reasoning

ALGEBRA Fibonacci, a mathematician from Italy, discovered the following number pattern about 800 years ago.

1, 1, 2, 3, 5, 8, 13, . . .

What might the next two numbers in the pattern be?

▲ Fibonacci numbers are found by counting petals on a daisy or spirals on a pinecone.

Step 1

Write a rule for the pattern.

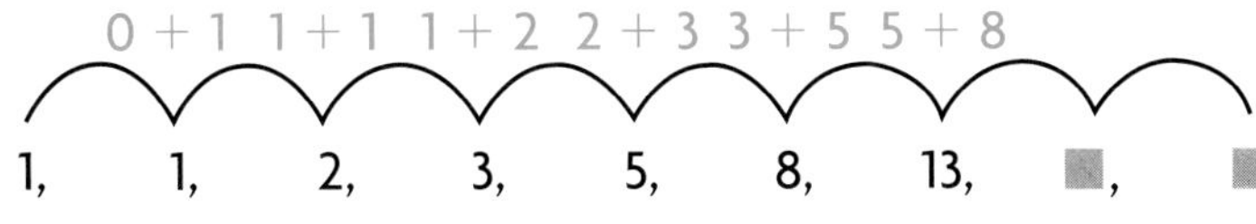

Rule: Start at 1. Find the sum of the two previous whole numbers.

Step 2

Use the rule to find the next two numbers in the pattern.

8 + 13 = 21

13 + 21 = 34

So, the next two numbers in the pattern are 21 and 34.

1. Is the number 144 in the Fibonacci pattern? **Explain** your answer.

2. Choose a number. Use it to write a pattern similar to the Fibonacci pattern.

LESSON 3

Problem Solving Workshop
Strategy: Look for a Pattern

OBJECTIVE: Solve problems by using the strategy *look for a pattern*.

Learn the Strategy

Patterns can be found everywhere in the real world. You can use math to talk about patterns in nature, architecture, music, dance, art, and language. You can use patterns to solve problems.

Geometric patterns can be based on color, size, shape, position, or number of figures.

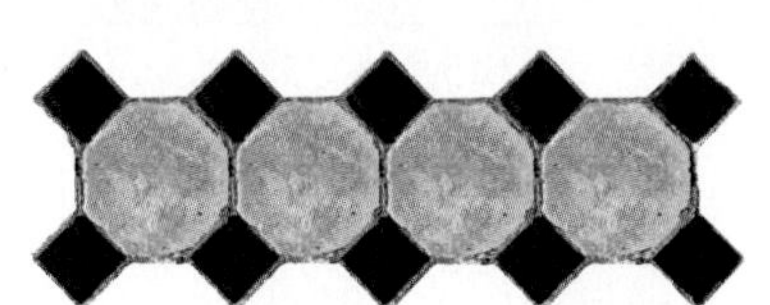

What might be the next floor tile to be put down?

The last tiles were two rhombuses. So, the next tile might be an octagon.

Pattern unit: 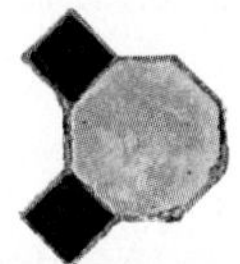

Number patterns can increase, decrease, repeat, or stop.

What is the date of the third Wednesday in May?

Rule: Start at 3. Add 7. 3, 10, 17, 24, 31

So, the third Wednesday in May is the 17th.

May						
Sun	Mon	Tue	Wed	Thu	Fri	Sat
	1	2	(3)	4	5	6
7	8	9	(10)	11	12	13
14	15	16	17	18	19	20
21	22	23	(24)	25	26	27
28	29	30	(31)			

Some visual patterns can be described using numbers.

Erin is building a model of a skyscraper with square tiles. She will build one more array for the base of the skyscraper. How many squares might be in the base if the pattern continues?

Rule: Increase the number of rows and columns of tiles by 1.

So, the base will be a 5-by-5 array, with 25 tiles.

Design	Number of Tiles
1-by-1 array	1
2-by-2 array	4
3-by-3 array	9
4-by-4 array	16

TALK Math

How can finding a rule help you predict what comes next?

TEKS 4.14C select or develop an appropriate problem-solving plan or strategy, including drawing a picture, looking for a pattern, systematic guessing and checking, acting it out, making a table, working a simpler problem, or working backwards to solve a problem. *also* **4.3A, 4.7, 4.14A, 4.14B, 4.15A, 4.15B, 4.16A, 4.16B**

Use the Strategy

PROBLEM Claire's family is putting a wall with the stair-step pattern shown in their bathroom. If they want the wall to be 5 cubes tall, how many cubes will they need?

Read to Understand

- **What information is given?**

Plan

- **What strategy can you use to solve the problem?**
  You can look for a pattern to solve the problem.

Solve

- **How can you use the strategy and graphic aids to solve the problem?**
  Write a rule for the pattern.

Design	Pattern Description	Number of Cubes
	1-cube base, 0 on top	1
	2-cube base, 1 on top	3
	3-cube base, then 2, then 1 on top	6
	4-cube base, then 3, then 2, then 1 on top	10

Rule: For each new design, the base has 1 more cube than the design before.

Use the rule to find the number of cubes in a wall that is 5 cubes tall.

So, a wall that is 5 cubes tall has 15 cubes.

Check

- **Look at the Number of Cubes column. What is a number pattern for the number of cubes in each figure?**

Guided Problem Solving

Read to Understand
Plan
Solve
Check

1. Parker is building a model of a ziggurat wall with blocks. How many blocks might he place in the next row?

   Write a rule for the pattern.

   Rule: Subtract ■ from the previous row.

   Use the rule to find the number of blocks in the next row.

   9 − ■ = ■

▲ A ziggurat is a kind of ancient temple.

2. **What if** Parker continued the pattern? Could the pattern continue without end? **Explain.**

3. The table shows the number of windows on each floor of a skyscraper. How many windows might be on the tenth floor?

Floor	1	2	3	4	5	6	7	8	9
Number of Windows	4	8	6	10	8	12	10	14	12

Problem Solving Strategy Practice

Find a pattern to solve.

4. Draw a pattern unit for the two center rings of the tree grate. The photograph shows one fourth of the tree grate. How many large trapezoids might be in the center ring of the whole grate?

5. Many brick columns use this pattern. Write a number pattern that describes the lengths of the bricks in each row.

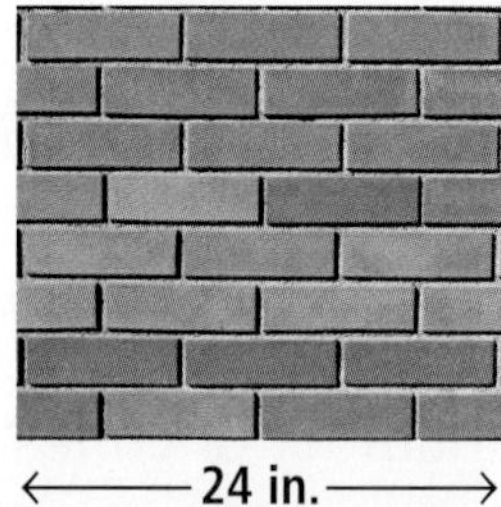

6. The mailboxes in Hannah's apartment building are in an array. Some of the numbers have fallen off the mailboxes. Look for a pattern in the rows. Look for a pattern in the columns. What might be the missing numbers?

Height: 1,483 ft
Petronas Tower
Kuala Lumpur
Malaysia

Height: 986 ft
Eiffel Tower
Paris
France

Height: 1,046 ft
Chrysler
Building
New York City

Height: 1,250 ft
Empire State
Building
New York City

Choose a STRATEGY

Draw a Diagram or Picture
Make a Model or Act It Out
Make an Organized List
Look for a Pattern
Make a Table or Graph
Guess and Check
Work Backward
Solve a Simpler Problem
Write an Equation
Use Logical Reasoning

Mixed Strategy Practice

USE DATA For 7–10, use the information in the picture.

7. Two buildings have a difference in height of 60 feet. Which are the two buildings?

8. The U.S. Bank Tower in Los Angeles is x feet taller than the Eiffel Tower. The U.S. Bank Tower is 1,018 feet tall. What is x?

9. **Pose a Problem** Look back at Problem 7. Write a similar problem by changing the difference in height.

10. **WRITE Math** One mile is 5,280 feet. Estimate to find whether all four skyscrapers put together would be about one mile high. **Explain** how you estimated.

11. **Open-Ended** Use grid paper to draw a picture of a skyscraper. Include a numerical pattern in your drawing. For example, the number of windows on each floor might increase by 3. Write a rule for your pattern.

CHALLENGE YOURSELF

The Eiffel Tower, at 986 feet tall, was the tallest building in the world when it was built in 1889 in Paris, France. It takes 50 tons of paint to cover the Eiffel Tower.

12. Before the Eiffel Tower was completed, the Washington Monument was the world's tallest building. The Washington Monument stands 555 feet tall. Is the Eiffel Tower more than or less than twice as tall as the Washington Monument? **Explain.**

13. The Eiffel Tower is painted every 7 years. If they painted the tower for the first time in 1889, in what year did they get to a total of 100 tons of paint? **Explain** how you found your answer.

Multiplication Properties

OBJECTIVE: Identify and use the properties of multiplication.

Quick Review

1. 3×1
2. 5×3
3. 2×6
4. 7×0
5. 8×2

Vocabulary

Zero Property
Identity Property
Commutative Property
Associative Property
Distributive Property

Learn

The properties of multiplication can help you find products of two or more factors.

MULTIPLICATION PROPERTIES

The **Zero Property** states that the product of 0 and any number is 0.

$3 \times 0 = 0$

The **Identity Property** states that the product of 1 and any number is that number.

$1 \times 3 = 3$

The **Commutative Property** states that you can multiply two factors in either order and get the same product.

$2 \times 3 = 6$ $\quad$ $3 \times 2 = 6$

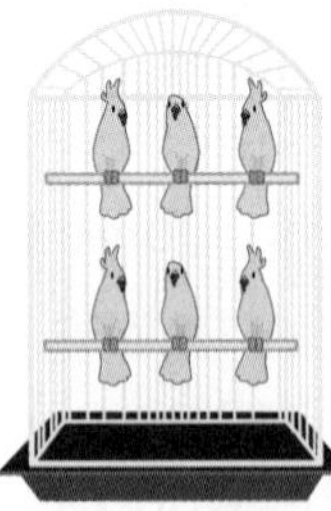

The **Associative Property** states that you can group factors in different ways and get the same product. Use parentheses ( ) to group the factors you multiply first.

$(4 \times 2) \times 3 = 24$ $\quad$ $4 \times (2 \times 3) = 24$

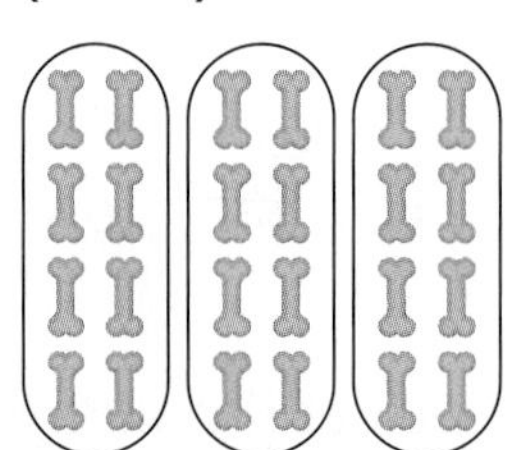

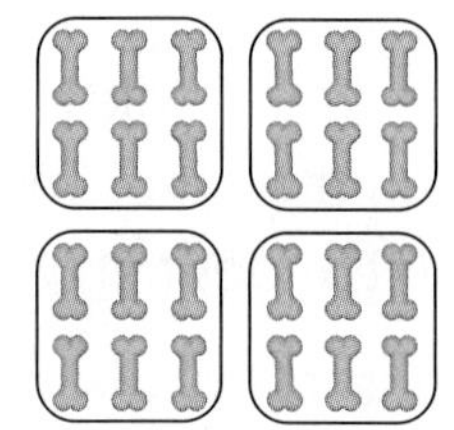

- Use counters to show two ways you can group $3 \times 2 \times 5$ to find the product. Are the products the same? Explain. Make a drawing to record your models.

Example 1 Use the properties to find the missing factor.

A $■ \times 12 = 0$
$0 \times 12 = 0$ Zero Property

So, $■ = 0$.

B $9 \times ■ = 8 \times 9$
$9 \times 8 = 8 \times 9$ Commutative Property

So, $■ = 8$.

TEKS 4.4C recall and apply multiplication facts through 12 × 12. *also* **4.4A, 4.4B, 4.6A, 4.14A, 4.14C, 4.14D, 4.15A, 4.15B, 4.16A, 4.16B**

The Distributive Property

PROBLEM At the pet store, the rabbits are in a pen that is 4 feet long by 12 feet wide. What is the area of the pen?

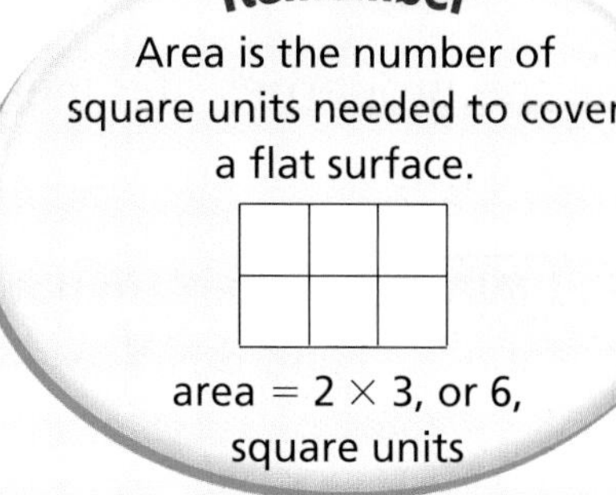

Remember
Area is the number of square units needed to cover a flat surface.
area = 2 × 3, or 6, square units

Activity Use the Distributive Property.

Materials ■ square tiles

The **Distributive Property** states that multiplying a sum by a number is the same as multiplying each addend by the number and then adding the products.

Multiply. 4×12

Step 1

Make a model to find 4×12. Use square tiles to build an array.

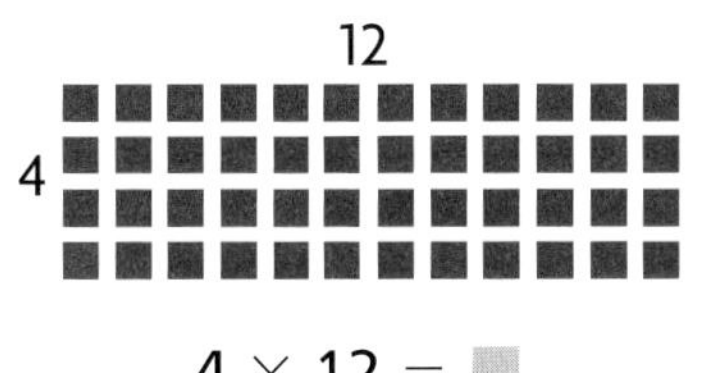

$4 \times 12 = \blacksquare$

Step 2

Break apart the array to make two smaller arrays for products you know.

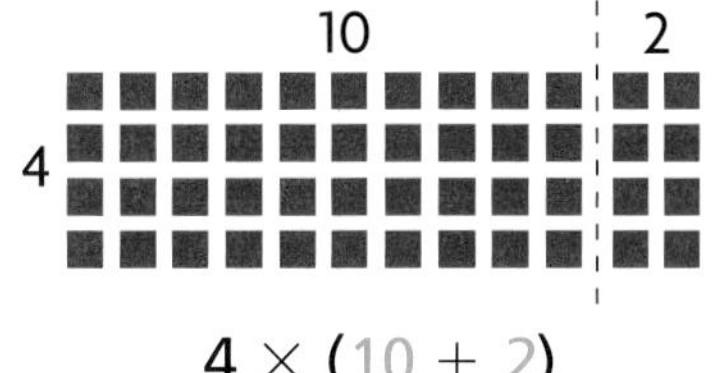

$4 \times (10 + 2)$

Step 3

Use the Distributive Property to show the sum of two products.

$(4 \times 10) + (4 \times 2)$

$\downarrow \qquad\qquad \downarrow$

$40 + 8 = 48$

So, the area of the pen is 48 square feet.

Using the properties can help you find the value of multiplication expressions.

Example 2 Use the properties and mental math.

A Find 8×12.

$8 \times 12 = 8 \times (10 + 2)$ **Think:** $12 = 10 + 2$

$= (8 \times 10) + (8 \times 2)$ Distributive Property

$= 80 + 16$

$= 96$

B Find $5 \times 5 \times 2$.

$5 \times 5 \times 2 = 5 \times (5 \times 2)$ Associative Property

$= 5 \times 10$

$= 50$

C Find $2 \times 7 \times 5$.

$2 \times 7 \times 5 = 2 \times 5 \times 7$ Commutative Property

$= (2 \times 5) \times 7$ Associative Property

$= 10 \times 7$

$= 70$

- Is $27 \times (48 - 48) = 0$ true? Explain how you can easily see this.

Guided Practice

1. Use the Associative Property to find the missing factor. $(12 \times ■) \times 4 = 12 \times (3 \times 4)$

Use the properties and mental math to find the value.

2. $1 \times 56 \times 1$
3. $24 \times 0 \times 6$
4. $8 \times 3 \times 3$
5. 7×12

6. **TALK Math** **Explain** how the Commutative Property is true for 4×8 and 8×4. Make a model or draw a picture.

Independent Practice and Problem Solving

Use the properties and mental math to find the value.

7. $9 \times 7 \times 0$
8. $2 \times 4 \times 7$
9. $8 \times 5 \times 2$
10. $6 \times 9 \times 1$

Find the missing number. Name the property you used.

11. $8 \times 6 = 6 \times ■$
12. $5 \times 12 = (5 \times 10) + (5 \times ■)$
13. $(4 \times 5) \times 2 = 4 \times (■ \times 2)$

Make a model and use the Distributive Property to find the value.

14. 5×12
15. 3×12
16. 6×12
17. 12×9

Show two ways to group by using parentheses. Find the value.

18. $3 \times 2 \times 5$
19. $8 \times 7 \times 1$
20. $7 \times 0 \times 2$
21. $2 \times 6 \times 2$

22. There are 2 tables, each with 3 tanks with 5 fish in each. There are also 3 tables, each with 2 tanks with 5 fish in each. Are the quantities the same? **Explain.**

23. There are 9 tanks with 11 tetras in each and 12 tanks with 7 mollies in each. Are there more tetras or mollies? How many more?

24. **Pose a Problem** Write a problem that can be solved using the product $(4 \times 2) \times 8$.

25. **WRITE Math** **What's the Question?** The product is 19. **Explain** how you know.

Mixed Review and TAKS Prep

26. Josh read 72 pages of a 200-page book. Then he read 39 more pages. How many pages are left to read? (TEKS 4.3A, p. 50)

27. There are 7 boxes and 42 books. Each box can hold the same number of books. How many books can fit in each box? (TEKS 4.4B, p. 122)

28. **TAKS Prep** A chef receives 2 boxes, each of which has 4 cartons of eggs. There are 12 eggs in each carton. How many eggs does the chef receive? (Obj. 1)

A 50 **C** 72

B 52 **D** 96

Extra Practice on page 172, Set C

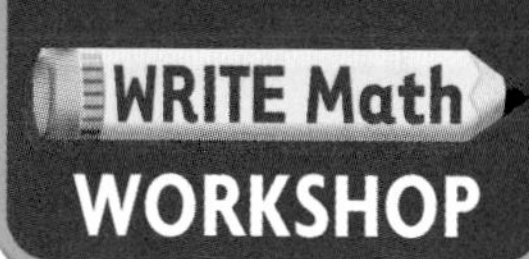

Write to Prove or Disprove

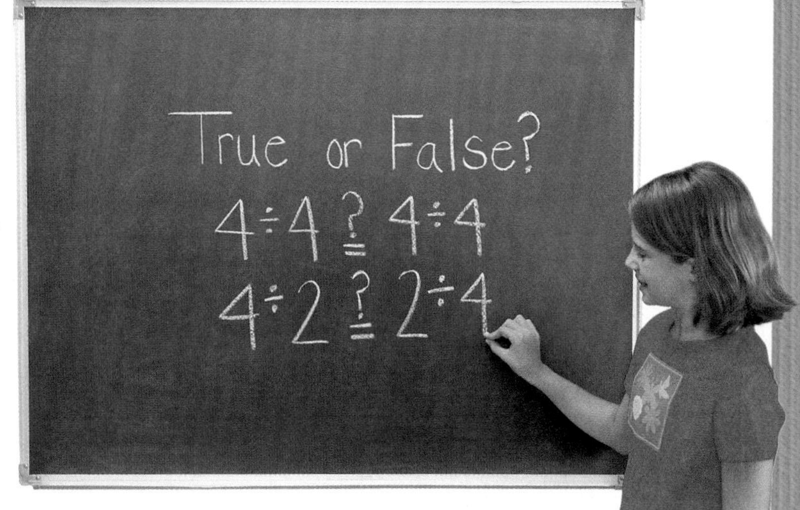

Sometimes, you must evaluate whether a number sentence or math idea is true or false. You can use what you know about operations and properties to prove or disprove whether the multiplication properties are true for division.

Sharon's group wants to know if the Commutative Property is true for division. The members of her group wrote this explanation to show what they learned.

We can try different division problems to prove or disprove that the Commutative Property works for division. We decided to try $6 \div 6$ and $6 \div 3$.

First, we asked if $6 \div 6 \stackrel{?}{=} 6 \div 6$. Both quotients equal 1. So, the number sentence is true, and the Commutative Property works for this division problem.

Next, we asked if $6 \div 3 \stackrel{?}{=} 3 \div 6$. In this example, the divisor and the dividend are different numbers. $6 \div 3 = 2$ and $3 \div 6 = \frac{3}{6}$. The quotients 2 and $\frac{3}{6}$ are not equal. So, this number sentence is false.

Finally, our group members agreed that since the second number sentence is false, division is not commutative.

Tips

To write to prove or disprove:

- Use correct math vocabulary.
- State the math idea you are proving or disproving.
- Decide on at least two examples to use to test your idea.
- Show your computations, and explain what you learned about each of your examples.
- To prove, every case needs to be tested. To disprove, only one false case is needed.
- Show your reasoning by making a conclusion about each example.
- Finally, write a conclusion that states whether you proved or disproved the math idea you were testing.

Problem Solving Write to prove or disprove each property for division.

1. Zero Property

2. Identity Property

LESSON 5

Write and Evaluate Expressions

OBJECTIVE: Write and evaluate multiplication and division expressions with variables.

Quick Review

1. 6×3
2. 4×5
3. 9×7
4. $24 \div 3$
5. $36 \div 9$

Learn

PROBLEM Diana collects stamps. She has 5 times as many stamps in her collection now as when she started the collection. Model and write an expression for the number of stamps she has now. Then find how many stamps she has now if she started with 3 stamps.

Remember

An expression is part of a number sentence that has numbers and operation signs but does not have an equal sign. A variable can stand for any number. You can use any letter as a variable.

Example 1

ONE WAY **Use a model.**

Use pattern blocks to model the expression.

Let ⬡ represent the number of stamps Diana started her collection with, and let ■ represent 1 stamp.

⬡ ⬡ ⬡ ⬡ ⬡ ← number of stamps she has now

Since she started with 3 stamps, replace each ⬡ with 3 ■s.

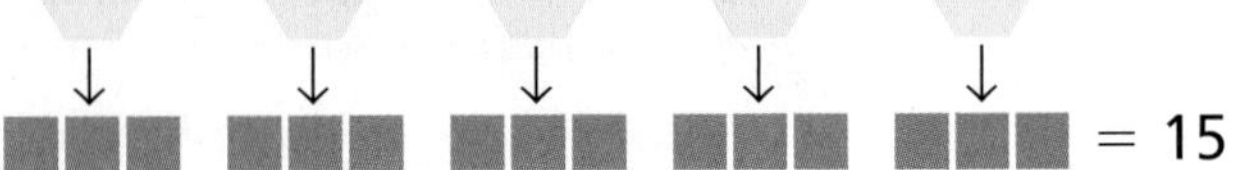

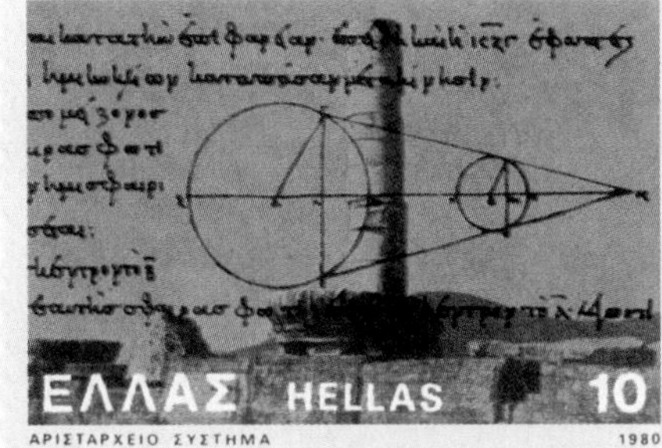

ANOTHER WAY **Use symbols.**

Write an expression with a variable.

Let n represent the number of stamps Diana started her collection with.

$5 \times n$ ← number of stamps she has now

Find the value of $5 \times n$ if $n = 3$.

$5 \times n$

↓

5×3 Replace n with 3, since she started with 3 stamps.

↓

15

So, Diana has 15 stamps in her collection now.

- How could you use the Associative Property to rewrite and then to find the value of $(d \times 4) \times 3$ if $d = 6$?

TEKS 4.15B relate informal language to mathematical language and symbols. *also* 4.4B, 4.4C, 4.14A, 4.14D, 4.15A

Example 2

Carl keeps his stamps in a stamp album. He fills a page with 24 stamps in equal rows. Model and write an expression for the number of stamps in 1 row. Then find how many stamps are in each row if he puts the stamps in 4 rows.

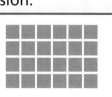

ONE WAY **Use a model.**

Use pattern blocks to model the expression.

Use 24 ■s to represent 24 stamps.

Put the ■s into 4 equal rows.

ANOTHER WAY **Use symbols.**

Write an expression with a variable.

Let r represent the number of equal rows of stamps.

$24 \div r$ ← number of stamps in each row

Find the value of $24 \div r$ if $r = 4$.

$24 \div r$
↓
$24 \div 4$ Replace r with 4 since there are 4 equal rows.
↓
6

So, Carl put 6 stamps in each row.

READ Math

These multiplication phrases have the same meaning:

- 4 groups each with n objects
- $4 \times n$
- 4 times a number, n

These division phrases have the same meaning:

- n objects separated into 6 groups
- $n \div 6$
- a number, n, divided by 6

Example 3 **Write an expression to match the words. Then find the value of the expression.**

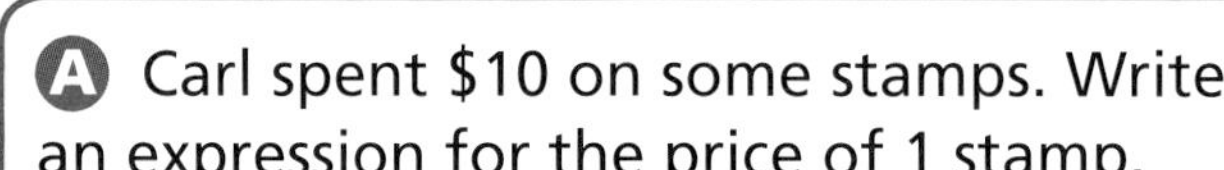

A Carl spent $10 on some stamps. Write an expression for the price of 1 stamp.

total cost ÷ among a number of stamps
↓ ↓
$10 \div s$ ← s is the number of stamps.

Suppose he bought 5 stamps.

$10 \div s$
↓
$10 \div 5$ Replace s with 5.
↓
2

So, Carl spent $2 on each stamp.

B Carl bought some $3 stamps. Write an expression for the total amount he spent.

a number of stamps × price of each stamp
↓ ↓
$s \times 3$ ← s is the number of stamps.

Suppose he bought 8 stamps.

$s \times 3$
↓
8×3 Replace s with 8.
↓
24

So, Carl spent $24 for 8 stamps.

Guided Practice

1. There are 2 boxes of crayons, with c crayons in each box. Find the total number of crayons, $2 \times c$, if $c = 8$.

Write an expression that matches the words. Tell what the expression represents.

2. 3 times a number of words, w, in a spelling list
3. a handful of keys, k, divided equally and put on 4 key chains

Find the value of the expression.

4. $2 \times p$ if $p = 9$
5. $6 \times w$ if $w = 7$
6. $40 \div m$ if $m = 5$
7. $s \div 3$ if $s = 27$

8. **TALK Math** **Explain** how to find the value of $8 \times k$ and $36 \div k$ if $k = 4$.

Independent Practice and Problem Solving

Write an expression that matches the words. Tell what the expression represents.

9. the price of some toys, t, at \$5 each
10. several pages, p, that have 10 stickers each
11. a number of books, b, divided equally and put on 6 shelves
12. 16 miniature cars divided equally into a number of display cases, c

Find the value of the expression.

13. $c \times 8$ if $c = 3$
14. $9 \times y$ if $y = 7$
15. $v \div 8$ if $v = 32$
16. $25 \div q$ if $q = 5$
17. $a \div 2$ if $a = 12$
18. $b \times 4$ if $b = 8$
19. $72 \div b$ if $b = 9$
20. $7 \times r$ if $r = 8$

Match the expression with the words.

21. $9 \div y$
22. $6 \times (y \times 3)$
23. $9 \times y$
24. $(6 \div y) + 3$

a. 6 times the product of y and 3

b. the dividend of 9 divided by y

c. 6 divided by y, and add 3

d. 9 times y

Find the value of each expression if $n = 7$. Then write $<$, $>$, or $=$.

25. $59 - 58$ ● $n \div 7$
26. 9×3 ● $42 \div n$
27. $4 \times n$ ● $26 + 4$

28. Angela buys some sheets of stamps. Each sheet has 10 stamps. Write an expression for the number of stamps she buys. How many more stamps are on 9 sheets than on 6 sheets?

29. **FAST FACT** In 1932, it cost 3¢ to mail a letter. By 2007, the price was 5 cents more than 12 times as much. How much did it cost to mail a letter in 2007?

 Extra Practice on page 172, Set D

30. **Reasoning** Use the Commutative and Associative Properties to rewrite and then to find $(5 \times n) \times 2$ if $n = 9$. **Explain** how you found your answer.

31. **WRITE Math** **What's the Error?** Blaine claims that $w \times 8$ is 16 if $w = 8$. What error might Blaine have made? Write the correct answer.

Mixed Review and TAKS Prep

32. Mabel had some apple slices. She ate 3 of them. Write an expression for the number of apple slices Mabel has left. (TEKS 4.15B, p. 70)

33. **TAKS Prep** Cody has 40 postcards. He puts the cards into equal stacks. Write an expression for the number of cards in each stack. How many postcards are in each stack if he makes 5 stacks? **Explain.** (Obj. 6)

34. Show two ways to use parentheses to group $6 \times 2 \times 3$. Find the products. (TEKS 4.4C, p. 152)

35. **TAKS Prep** Dan has 6 times as many coins as Suzie. Let s represent the number of coins Suzie has. Which expression shows the number of coins Dan has? (Obj. 6)

   A $6 + s$

   B $6 - s$

   C $6 \times s$

   D $6 \div s$

Problem Solving connects to Art

Since 1934, the United States Postal Service has sold special stamps to raise money to buy wetlands for the National Wildlife Refuge System. Each year there is an art contest. The two winning pictures are used on Federal Duck Stamps. Each Federal Duck Stamp sells for $15. In 1989, the Junior Duck Stamp program was started for students from kindergarten through high school.

Write an expression that matches the words.

1. the total of 2 stamps on each Artist Commemorative card, c

2. the price of a number of Federal Duck Stamps, s, that cost $15 each

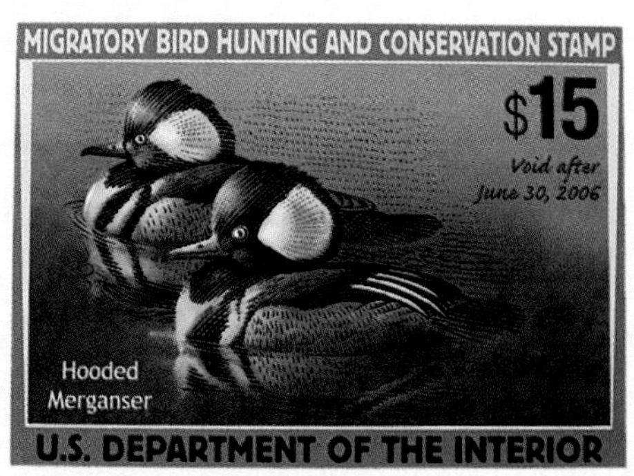

▲ A winning stamp from 2005

Each Junior Duck Stamp, s, costs $5. Find the total cost for the number of stamps.

3. $s = 8$

4. $s = 5$

5. $s = 7$

LESSON 6

Find Missing Factors

OBJECTIVE: Use multiplication and division to find missing factors.

Quick Review

Write the fact family.

1. 2, 5, 10
2. 3, 6, 18
3. 5, 7, 35
4. 6, 8, 48
5. 9, 9, 81

Learn

PROBLEM A basketball club has 10 members. How many teams of 5 players each can play at the same time?

When you know the product and one factor, you can use a model or a fact family to help you find the missing factor.

$\blacksquare \times 5 = 10$ **Think:** What number times 5 equals 10?

ONE WAY **Use a model.**

Draw 10 counters in rows of 5. Count the number of rows to find the missing factor. There are 2 rows of 5 counters.

ANOTHER WAY **Use a fact family.**

Use a related division sentence to find the missing factor.
$10 \div 5 = 2$, so $2 \times 5 = 10$. The missing factor is 2.

So, 2 teams can play at the same time.

Remember
A variable is a symbol or letter that stands for a number or numbers you don't know.

More Examples Find the missing factors.

A

$\star \times 8 = 56$
$\star = 7$

Think: What number times 8 equals 56?

Check: $7 \times 8 \stackrel{?}{=} 56$
$56 = 56$ ✔

Replace ★ with 7. The sentence is true.

The missing factor is 7.

B

$9 \times n = 45$
$n = 5$

Think: 9 times what number equals 45?

Check: $9 \times 5 \stackrel{?}{=} 45$
$45 = 45$ ✔

Replace n with 5. The sentence is true.

The missing factor is 5.

- How could you use division to solve Examples A and B?

Guided Practice

1. The first factor in a multiplication sentence is 3, and the product is 30. Use the model to find the missing factor.

$3 \times \blacksquare = 30$

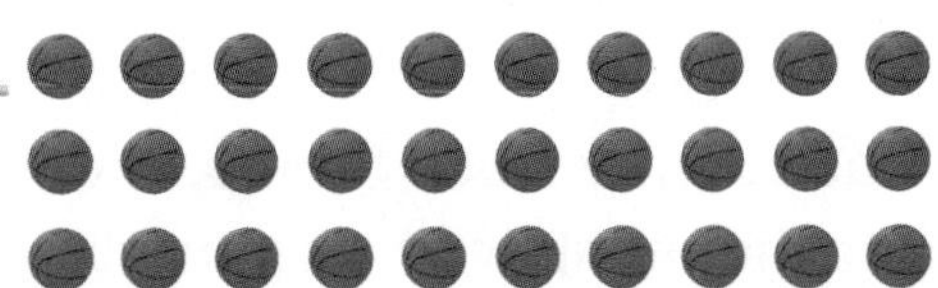

TEKS 4.6A use patterns and relationships to develop strategies to remember basic multiplication and division facts (such as the patterns in related multiplication and division number sentences (fact families) such as $9 \times 9 = 81$ and $81 \div 9 = 9$). *also* **4.4A, 4.4B, 4.4C, 4.14A, 4.15A, 4.15B**

Find the missing factor.

2. $n \times 5 = 55$
3. $6 \times$ ▼ $= 72$
4. $10 \times g = 70$
5. ■ $\times 11 = 132$
6. TALK Math **Explain** the relationship between factors and products. Use an example to show what you mean.

Independent Practice and Problem Solving

Find the missing factor.

7. ■ $\times 2 = 18$
8. $12 \times p = 12$
9. ★ $\times 9 = 72$
10. $11 \times r = 110$
11. $g \times 10 = 120$
12. $4 \times d = 32$
13. $7 \times n = 63$
14. $c \times 10 = 50$
15. ■ $\times 3 = 40 - 4$
16. $7 \times$ ■ $= 43 + 6$
17. $3 \times$ ■ $= 19 + 5$
18. ■ $\times 8 = 20 - 4$

USE DATA For 19–21, use the table.

19. Each football team has 1 coach. Three teams and their coaches are arranged for a photograph. How many people are in the photograph?
20. **Reasoning** In a game, 2 basketball teams play against each other. You want to find out how many players are on the court during a game. In a multiplication sentence, will the answer be a product or a factor?
21. **Pose a Problem** Look back at Problem 19. Write a similar problem by exchanging the known and unknown numbers.

Sports Teams

Sport	Players
Baseball	9
Basketball	5
Football	11
Ice Hockey	6
Soccer	11
Volleyball	6

22. High school basketball games last 32 minutes. There are 4 quarters in each game. Write a number sentence that can be used to find the number of minutes in each quarter.
23. WRITE Math A sports team needs to reserve a field for a game. The players collect \$88 in all to pay for the field. Each player paid \$8. **Explain** how to find how many players are on the team.

Mixed Review and TAKS Prep

24. Ken used a key of 2 to make a pictograph using the data in the table above. How many symbols should he draw to show the number of volleyball players? (Grade 3 TEKS 3.13A)
25. Mia has some toys. She gave 2 toys to her friends. Write an expression for the number of toys Mia has now. (TEKS 4.15B, p. 70)
26. **TAKS Prep** Mark buys 36 eggs. Each carton holds 12 eggs. Which number sentence can be used to find the number of egg cartons Mark buys? (Obj. 2)

   A ■ $\times 36 = 12$
   B ■ $\times 4 = 12$
   C ■ $\times 9 = 36$
   D ■ $\times 12 = 36$

Extra Practice on page 172, Set E

LESSON 7

Multiplication and Division Equations

OBJECTIVE: Write and solve multiplication and division equations.

Quick Review

1. $56 \div 8$
2. 4×9
3. $45 \div 5$
4. 6×7
5. $48 \div 8$

Learn

PROBLEM Sofie is making a number of bracelets to sell at the school craft fair. Each bracelet uses 6 beads. She has 24 beads. What equation can you write to find the number of bracelets she can make?

Remember
An equation is a number sentence that shows that two amounts are equal.

Example 1 Write multiplication equations.

A The number of bracelets times 6 beads each is 24 beads.

$b \times 6 = 24$ ← b is the number of bracelets.

So, the equation is $b \times 6 = 24$.

If the missing information changes, the equation changes.

B 4 bracelets times the number of beads is 24 beads.

$4 \times n = 24$ ← n is the number of beads.

C 4 bracelets times 6 beads each is the total number of beads.

$4 \times 6 = t$ ← t is the total number of beads.

Example 2 Write division equations.

Ethan pays $12 to make spin-art pictures. Each picture costs $4 to make. What equation can you write to find the number of pictures he can make?

A $12 divided equally among the number of pictures is $4.

$12 \div p = 4$ ← p is the number of pictures.

So, the equation is $12 \div p = 4$.
If the missing information changes, the equation changes.

B The total cost divided equally among 3 pictures is $4.

$t \div 3 = 4$ ← t is the total cost of the pictures.

C $12 divided equally among 3 pictures is the cost of each picture.

$12 \div 3 = c$ ← c is the cost for each picture.

TEKS 4.15B relate informal language to mathematical language and symbols. *also* **4.4B, 4.4C, 4.14A, 4.14C, 4.14D, 4.15A**

Solve Equations

You can solve equations by using different strategies and methods.

ONE WAY **Use the strategy *guess and check*.**

Materials ■ Equabeam™ balance

Use the Equabeam balance to solve $10 \div n = 2$.

Place a weight on 10 on the left side.

Guess how many weights you need to place on 2 on the right side to restore balance.

Check your guess. Repeat until you restore balance.

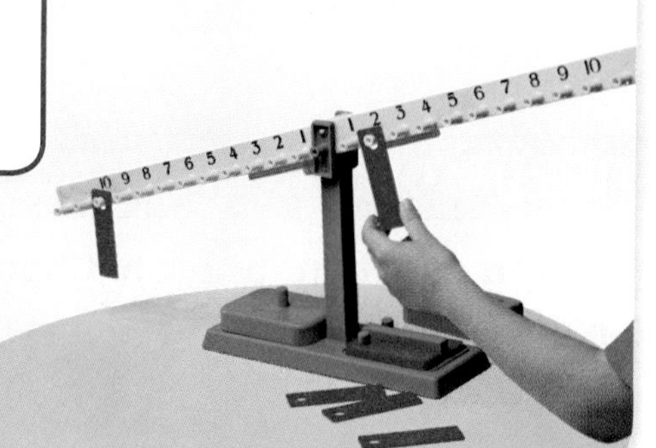

- How many weights do you need to place on 2? What is the value of n?
- Guess the value of b in $9 \times b = 18$. Check your guess. What is the value of b?

ANOTHER WAY **Use the strategy *work backward*.**

A **Solve.** $n \times 7 = 28$

$28 \div 7 = n$ — **Think:** work backward and use inverse operations.

$4 = n$

Check: $4 \times 7 \stackrel{?}{=} 28$ — Replace n with 4.

$28 = 28$ ✔ — The equation is true.

So, the value of $n = 4$.

B **Solve.** $32 \div y = 4$

$32 = 4 \times y$ — **Think:** work backward and use inverse operations.

$8 = y$

Check: $32 \div 8 \stackrel{?}{=} 4$ — Replace y with 8.

$32 = 32$ ✔ — The equation is true.

So, the value of $y = 8$.

Guided Practice

1. Choose the equation that shows the total number of clay animals, a, divided equally among 4 shelves is 8 animals each.

   a. $4 \div a = 8$ **b.** $a \div 4 = 8$ **c.** $8 \div 4 = a$

Write an equation for each. Choose the variable for the unknown. Tell what the variable represents.

2. An equal amount of money for each of 6 hand-painted hats is a total of \$30.

3. The total number of rings divided equally among 4 friends is 2 rings for each friend.

Solve the equation.

4. $3 \times n = 21$

5. $d \div 6 = 8$

6. $z \div 5 = 4$

7. $a \times 7 = 63$

8. **TALK Math** **Explain** how to use the strategy *work backward* to find n in the equation $7 \times n = 42$.

Independent Practice and Problem Solving

Write an equation for each. Choose the variable for the unknown. Tell what the variable represents.

9. Three knitted scarves at an equal cost for each is a total cost of \$27.

10. 12 potholders divided equally among a number of bags is 3 potholders each.

11. The same number of necklaces in each of 6 boxes makes a total of 42 necklaces.

12. The total number of toys divided equally among 6 shelves is 9 toys on each shelf.

Solve the equation.

13. $4 \times n = 32$	14. $c \div 7 = 7$	15. $p \times 5 = 35$	16. $k \div 3 = 9$
17. $144 \div d = 12$	18. $6 \times e = 48$	19. $99 \div n = 11$	20. $7 \times f = 63$
21. $m \div 8 = 7$	22. $54 \div n = 6$	23. $3 \times h \times 2 = 18$	24. $2 \times n \times 6 = 60$

USE DATA For 25–26, use the picture.

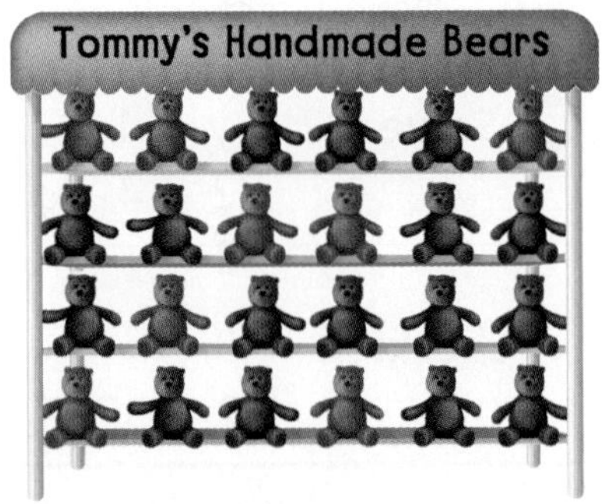

25. **What if** Tommy made 12 more teddy bears? How could he arrange them on the shelves so that each shelf has the same number of bears?

26. Tommy sells 24 bears. He sells 8 bears each hour. Write an equation to find how many hours it takes him to sell the bears. Solve the equation.

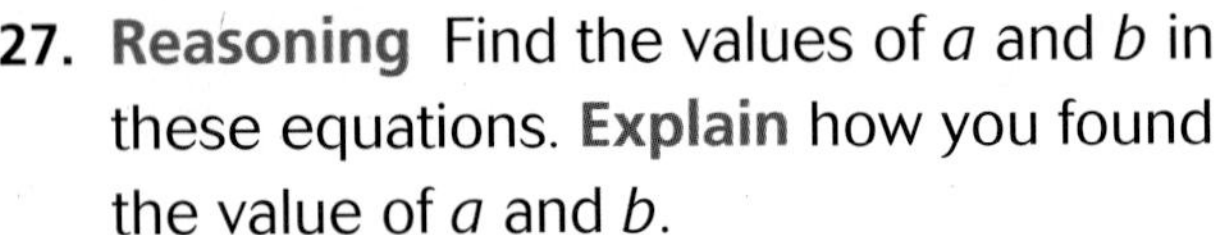

27. **Reasoning** Find the values of a and b in these equations. **Explain** how you found the value of a and b.

$$a \times 6 = 18 \text{ and } a \times b = 12$$

28. **WRITE Math** **Sense or Nonsense** Pam says that n equals any number in the equation $n \times 0 = 0$. Does Pam's statement make sense? **Explain.**

CD ROM **Technology**
Use Harcourt Mega Math, Ice Station Exploration, *Arctic Algebra*, Levels F, T.

 Extra Practice on page 172, Set F

Mixed Review and TAKS Prep

29. Maia used 4 green beads, 8 blue beads, and 12 yellow beads to make 1 necklace for the craft fair. Use these data to make a pictograph. (Grade 3 TEKS 3.13A)

30. **TAKS Prep** Some friends are at the movies. The friends pay $30 in all for admission. Each ticket costs $6. Write an equation to show how many friends are at the movies. Then solve the equation. (Obj. 6)

31. Megan has 27 buttons. Each shirt needs 3 buttons. How many shirts can she sew buttons on? (TEKS 4.4B, p. 122)

32. **TAKS Prep** In which equation does $n = 2$? (Obj. 6)

A $14 \div n = 12$ **C** $2 \div n = 4$

B $18 \div n = 9$ **D** $8 \div n = 2$

Problem Solving and Reasoning

ALGEBRA Since the scale is balanced, the weight of the purse and hat on the left side is equal to the weight of the shoes and hat on the right side. Will the scale be balanced if you take away one hat from each side?

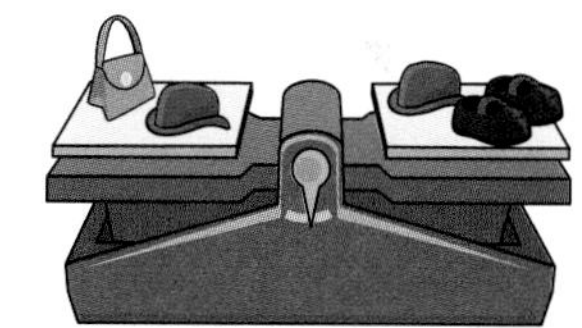

Balancing an equation is like balancing a scale. If both sides of the equation have the same value (except by 0) added, subtracted, multiplied, or divided, the equation remains true.

Write an equation for the weight of one purse.

Step 1

Take away one hat from each side.

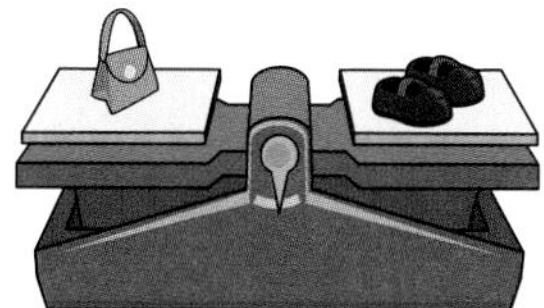

Both sides stay equal.

Step 2

Let p represent one purse.
Let s represent one shoe.

1 purse equals 2 shoes.

$p = 2 \times s$

- **What if** one shoe weighs 3 ounces? How much will one purse weigh?

Use the art of the balance scale at the right.

1. Write an equation for the balance scale. Let d represent the weight of a doll and t represent the weight of a teddy bear.
2. **What if** one doll weighs 5 pounds? How much will one bear weigh?

LESSON 8

Problem Solving Workshop
Strategy: Write an Equation

OBJECTIVE: Solve problems by using the strategy *write an equation.*

Learn the Strategy

Often, words in a problem describe relationships that can be written as an equation. You can use the equation to solve the problem. A variable in the equation represents an unknown number in the problem.

Suppose there are a total of 10 counters. Some are red, and the rest are yellow. Study the words and equations in the table below. Each equation shows how the counters are related. Let r represent the number of red counters and y represent the number of yellow counters.

Words Describing Relationships	Equation
There are a total of 10 counters. Some are yellow, and 8 are red.	$10 = y + 8$
There are 2 yellow counters. The number of yellow counters is 6 less than the number of red counters.	$r - 6 = 2$
There are 8 red counters. The number of red counters is 4 times the number of yellow counters.	$y \times 4 = 8$
There are 2 yellow counters. The number of yellow counters is one fourth the number of red counters.	$2 = r \div 4$

When writing an equation, look for words that signal whether you should add, subtract, multiply, or divide. Decide what information is unknown, and use a variable to represent the unknown number.

TALK Math

Jill buys 15 cards. Dan buys 3 cards. To show how many times as many cards Jill buys than Dan, Jill writes $3 \times c = 15$ and Dan writes $15 \div c = 3$. Is the value of c the same in both equations? Explain how the equations are alike and how they are different.

TEKS 4.14B solve problems that incorporate understanding the problem, making a plan, carrying out the plan, and evaluating the solution for reasonableness. *also* **4.3A, 4.4B, 4.4C, 4.14A, 4.14C, 4.14D, 4.15A, 4.15B, 4.16B**

Use the Strategy

PROBLEM A group of cranes is called a sedge. Each fall, whooping cranes migrate in small sedges to Aransas National Wildlife Refuge, in Texas. If 48 whooping cranes migrate to the refuge and there are the same number of cranes in each of 6 sedges, how many cranes are in each sedge?

Read to Understand
Plan
Solve
Check

▼ At nearly 5 feet tall, adult whooping cranes are the tallest birds in North America.

Read to Understand

- What are you asked to find?
- What information will you use?

Plan

- **What strategy can you use to solve the problem?**

You can write an equation to solve the problem.

Solve

- **How can you use the strategy to solve the problem?**

Visualize how the facts are related. Write an equation to show the number of cranes in each sedge. Then use mental math to solve the equation.

total number of cranes		number of cranes in each sedge		number of sedges	
↓		↓		↓	
48	÷	n	=	6	← n is the number of cranes in each sedge.
		n	=	8	**Think:** 48 divided by what number is 6?

So, there are 8 whooping cranes in each sedge.

Check

- How can you check your answer?
- What other strategy could you use to solve the problem?

Guided Problem Solving

Read to Understand
Plan
Solve
Check

1. Whooping cranes normally migrate in small sedges of fewer than 10 birds. A scientist counted 9 sedges with an equal number of cranes in each. If she counted a total of 36 cranes, how many cranes did she count in each sedge?

   First, visualize how the facts are related.

   Next, write an equation. Choose a variable for the unknown, and tell what the variable represents.

   9 sedges with a number of cranes in each is 36 cranes.

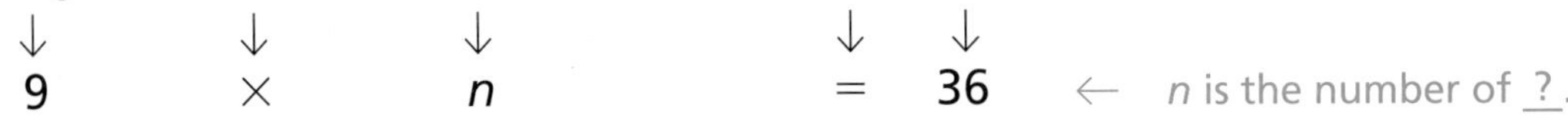

   Finally, use mental math to solve the equation.

2. **What if** the scientist counted a total of 63 whooping cranes? How many cranes did she count in each sedge?

3. A biologist first counted pairs of whooping cranes at their nesting ground. Later, when the cranes migrated, the biologist counted 54 nesting pairs of whooping cranes. That is 9 times as many as she first counted. How many pairs of whooping cranes did the biologist first count?

Problem Solving Strategy Practice

Write an equation to solve.

4. In 2005, there were a total of 477 whooping cranes. Some of the cranes live in the wild, and 136 cranes live in captive centers. How many cranes live in the wild?

USE DATA For 5–7, use the table.

5. The bird with the greatest wingspan is the wandering albatross. The albatross's wingspan is 59 inches more than the wingspan of the whooping crane. What is the wingspan of the albatross?

6. Whooping cranes have a wingspan greater than the length of most cars. How many feet long is the crane's wingspan? Think: 1 foot = 12 inches

7. **WRITE Math** How many times as great, w, is the bald eagle's wingspan compared with the Allen's hummingbird's wingspan? Write two equations you could use to solve the problem. **Explain** how you can solve each equation.

Bird Wingspans

Bird	Wingspan (in inches)
Whooping Crane	84
Snow Goose	54
Bald Eagle	80
Western Scrub-Jay	15
Allen's Hummingbird	4

Mixed Strategy Practice

8. Whooping cranes begin to migrate from Canada to Texas in the fall. They arrive at the refuge in Texas about 1 month later, where they stay about 6 months. If they migrate back to Canada in April, in what month do they begin to migrate to Texas?

9. In March 2005, there were 3 young cranes at the Patuxent Wildlife Research Center in Maryland. At the same time, there were 33 young cranes at Aransas National Wildlife Refuge. How many times as many young cranes were at Aransas than at Patuxent?

Choose a STRATEGY

- Draw a Diagram or Picture
- Make a Model or Act It Out
- Make an Organized List
- Look For a Pattern
- Make a Table or Graph
- Guess and Check
- Work Backward
- Solve a Simpler Problem
- Write an Equation
- Use Logical Reasoning

USE DATA For 10–11, use the table.

10. In 1995, the number of whooping cranes at Aransas was 6 more than twice the number of cranes in 1980. What was the crane population at Aransas in 1995?

11. From 2001 to 2004, the whooping crane population decreased by 3, increased by 11, increased by 9, and increased by 22. What was the crane population each year from 2001 to 2004?

12. **Pose a Problem** Look back at Problem 9. Write a similar problem by changing the known and unknown.

13. **Open-Ended** Thirty-six cranes are migrating to Texas. If the cranes migrate in sedges with no bird left out and there are fewer than 10 cranes in each sedge, how many cranes might there be in each sedge?

Aransas Whooping Crane Population

Year	Number
1960	33
1970	56
1980	76
1990	146
2000	177
2005	218

CHALLENGE YOURSELF

A clutch is the total number of eggs a bird lays. Whooping cranes usually lay 2 eggs per clutch, and most shorebirds lay 4 eggs per clutch.

14. The number of eggs in a mountain chickadee's clutch is 1 more than 3 times the number of eggs in a whooping crane's clutch. How many eggs are usually in a mountain chickadee's clutch?

15. A biologist counted the number of eggs in the clutches of a pelican, a duck, and a whooping crane. He counted 1 egg, 4 eggs, and 12 eggs. There were more eggs in the duck's clutch than in a pelican's clutch. The clutch with the least number of eggs is a crane's. How many eggs were in each bird's clutch?

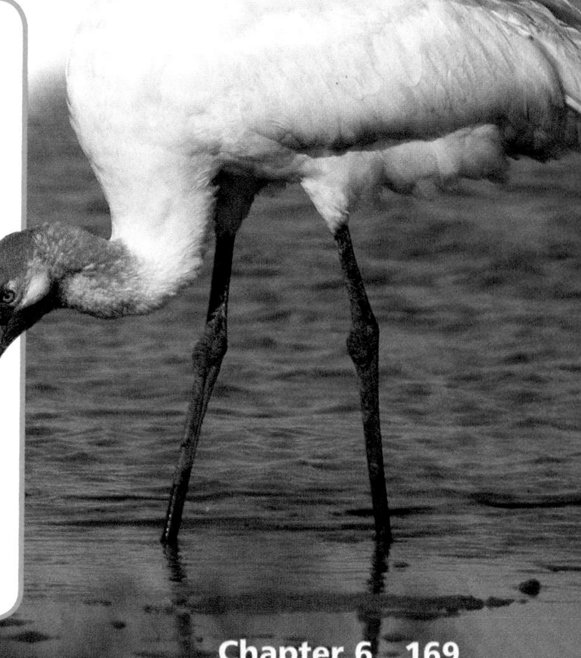

LESSON 9

Ordered Pairs in a Table

OBJECTIVE: Describe the relationship between two sets of related data shown as ordered pairs in a table.

Quick Review

1. 5×7
2. 8×6
3. $32 \div 4$
4. $63 \div 9$
5. 3×6

Learn

PROBLEM One gallon of milk equals 4 quarts of milk, 2 gallons of milk equal 8 quarts, and 3 gallons equal 12 quarts. How many quarts of milk do 4 gallons equal?

▲ One cow can produce more than 188 gallons of milk in a month.

You can use an input/output table to find a rule that relates the number of gallons to the number of quarts.

Input (in gallons)	Output (in quarts)
1	4
2	8
3	12
4	■

Look for a pattern to find the rule.

Pattern: Each output is the input multiplied by 4.

Rule: Multiply the input by 4.

← Input: 4 Output: $4 \times 4 = 16$

So, 4 gallons equal 16 quarts of milk.

You can use variables to show the input and output.

ERROR ALERT

A rule must work for each ordered pair in the table. So, you should test your rule with each ordered pair in the table.

Examples

A Find a rule for the table. Use your rule to find the next two numbers in the pattern.

Pattern: Each output, *f*, is the input, *y*, divided by 3.
Rule: Divide *y* by 3.

So, the next two numbers in the pattern are 8 and 10.

Input, *y* (in yards)	Output, *f* (in feet)
6	2
12	4
18	6
24	■
30	■

Think:

$6 \div 3 = 2$

$12 \div 3 = 4$

$18 \div 3 = 6$

← $24 \div 3 = 8$

← $30 \div 3 = 10$

B Use the rule divide *n* by 11 to find the value of *p* to complete the table.

Think: What number divided by 11 equals 8?

$88 \div 11 = 8$
$99 \div 11 = 9$

Input, *n*	22	33	55	77	■	■
Output, *p*	2	3	5	7	8	9

- **What if $y = 36$ in Example A? What is the value of *f*? Explain.**

TEKS 4.7 The student is expected to describe the relationship between two sets of related data such as ordered pairs in a table. *also* **4.4B, 4.4C, 4.6A, 4.11B, 4.14C, 4.15A, 4.15B, 4.16A**

Guided Practice

1. The rule is multiply w by 6.
   What is the next number in the pattern?

Input, *w*	4	5	6	7	8
Output, *z*	24	30	36	42	■

Find a rule. Use your rule to find the missing numbers.

2.

Input, *b*	90	70	60	50	30	20	10
Output, *c*	9	7	6	■	■	■	■

3.

Input, *r*	2	3	5	6	8	9	10
Output, *s*	18	27	45	■	■	■	■

4. **TALK Math** **Explain** how to use the table to write a rule to find the distance in miles, d, a truck travels on g gallons of gas. Use your rule to complete the table.

Input, *g*	1	2	3	4
Output, *d*	12	24	36	■

Independent Practice and Problem Solving

Find a rule. Use your rule to find the missing numbers.

5.

Input, *x*	14	28	42	56	70	77	84
Output, *y*	2	4	6	■	■	■	■

6.

Input, *d*	3	4	6	■	■	■	11
Output, *f*	15	20	30	40	45	50	55

Use the rule to make an input/output table.

7. Divide the input by 10.
8. Multiply the input by 10.
9. Multiply the input by 8.
10. Divide the input by 9.

USE DATA For 11–12, use the food pyramid for kids.

11. How many cups of milk should a kid drink in 2, 3, 4, and 5 days? Make an input/output table. Write a rule to solve.

12. **WRITE Math** **Explain** how to find a rule and use your rule to find total number of ounces of grain a kid should eat in 3 days.

For an 1,800-calorie diet, you need to eat or drink the amount shown from each group every day.

Grains	Vegetables	Fruits	Milk	Meat & Beans
6 ounces	$2\frac{1}{2}$ cups	$1\frac{1}{2}$ cups	3 cups	5 ounces

Mixed Review and TAKS Prep

13. Tim has 50 cars. He has 10 times as many cars as trucks. How many trucks does he have? (TEKS 4.4B, p. 122)

14. Kay will read 48 pages. She will read 8 pages a day. Write an equation to find how many days it will take her to read the pages. Tell what the variable represents. (TEKS 4.15B, p. 166)

15. **TAKS Prep** The table shows how many granola bars are in 3, 6, and 9 boxes. How many bars are in 12 boxes? (Obj. 2)

Boxes, *b*	Bars, *g*
3	6
6	12
9	18

Extra Practice on page 172, Set G

Extra Practice

Set A Use the multiplication table on page 142. (pp. 142–143)

1. What pattern do you see in the ones digit of the multiples of 5?
2. What pattern do you see in the multiples of 6?
3. What pattern do you see in the multiples of 3 and multiples of 9?
4. What pattern do you see in the multiples of 2 and multiples of 3?

Set B Find a rule. Then find the next two numbers in your pattern. (pp. 144–147)

1. 38, 41, 44, 47, 50, ■, ■
2. 211, 216, 221, 226, 231, ■, ■
3. 29, 36, 33, 40, 37, 44, 41, ■, ■
4. 59, 54, 56, 51, 53, 48, 50, ■, ■

Set C Use the properties and mental math to find the value. (pp. 152–155)

1. $2 \times 7 \times 5$
2. $2 \times 0 \times 31$
3. $1 \times 6 \times 7$
4. $3 \times 8 \times 2$
5. A grocery store received a shipment of 2 crates, each with 10 cases of juice boxes. There are 6 juice boxes in each case. How many juice boxes did the grocery store receive?

Set D Find the value of the expression. (pp. 156–159)

1. $d \times 9$ if $d = 6$
2. $f \div 7$ if $f = 49$
3. $6 \times n$ if $n = 8$
4. $56 \div q$ if $q = 7$
5. Allison pasted 10 pictures on each of *n* pages in her album. Write an expression to show the total number of pictures in the album.

Set E Find the missing factor. (pp. 160–161)

1. $4 \times m = 24$
2. $6 \times w = 36$
3. $c \times 9 = 72$
4. $8 \times$ ■ $= 53 + 3$

Set F Solve the equation. (pp. 162–165)

1. $3 \times n = 21$
2. $c \div 9 = 1$
3. $t \times 4 = 28$
4. $h \div 4 = 10$
5. $r \div 6 = 5$
6. $56 \div m = 7$
7. $3 \times w \times 3 = 36$
8. $3 \times n \times 4 = 24$

Set G Find a rule. Use your rule to find the missing numbers. (pp. 170–171)

1.

Input, *a*	6	12	18	24	30
Output, *b*	1	2	3	■	■

2.

Input, *m*	4	5	6	■	■
Output, *n*	32	40	48	56	64

Technology
Use Harcourt Mega Math, Ice Station Exploration, *Arctic Algebra,* Levels C, F, H, K, T.

TECHNOLOGY CONNECTION

Calculator: Evaluate Expressions (TEKS 4.14D, 4.4B, 4.4C, 4.14A, 4.15A, 4.15B)

A mail-order company sells boxes of holiday cards. The company charges $12.00 per box plus a flat shipping fee of $3.00. How much does an order of 7 boxes of holiday cards cost? 9 boxes?

You can use the TI-15 calculator to find the cost of an order. Find the value of the expression $(12 \times b) + 3$ if b is the number of boxes ordered.

Step 1 Press the following keys to prepare the calculator:

Now the calculator is programmed to first multiply by 12 and then to add 3.

Step 2
Find the value of the expression $12 \times b + 3$ if $b = 7$.

Step 3
Find the cost for an order of 9 boxes of holiday cards.

So, an order of 7 boxes of holiday cards costs $87, and an order of 9 boxes of holiday cards costs $111.

Remember

When you use the Op1 and Op2 keys, order is important.

is different from

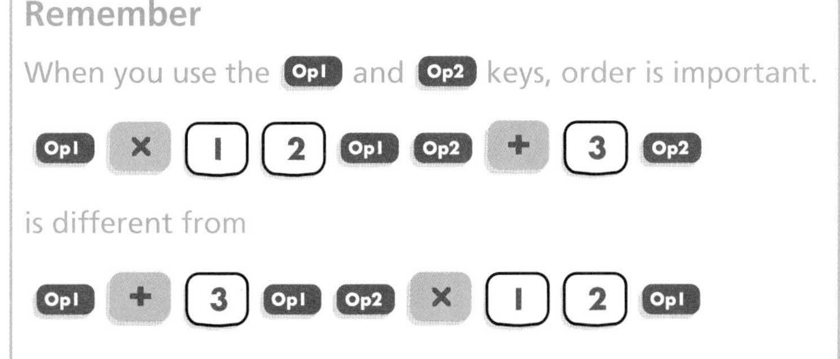

Tips

Before entering a new problem, clear the stored operations.

Try It

Use a TI-15 calculator to find the cost of each order.

1. 7 or 9 boxes of cards for $14 each plus a $5 shipping fee
2. 2 or 3 books for $23 each plus a $4 shipping fee
3. **Explore More Explain** how you would find the cost of an order of any number of the same item if shipping were included in the price.

Chapter 6 Review/Test

Check Vocabulary and Concepts

Choose the best term from the box.

VOCABULARY
Commutative Property
Identity Property
Zero Property

1. The __?__ states that when the order of two factors is changed, the product is the same. (TEKS 4.4C, p. 152)
2. The __?__ states that the product of 0 and any number is 0. (TEKS 4.4C, p. 152)

Check Skills

Find a rule. Then find the next two numbers in your pattern. (TEKS 4.7, pp. 144–147)

3. 34, 38, 42, 46, 50, ■, ■
4. 89, 84, 79, 74, 69, ■, ■

Write an expression that matches the words. Tell what the expression represents (TEKS 4.15B, pp. 156–159)

5. a number of toys, *t*, divided equally among 8 cats
6. a number of binders, *b*, that have 3 rings each

Write an equation for each. Choose the variable for the unknown. Tell what the variable represents. (TEKS 4.15B, pp. 162–165)

7. Five paperback books at an equal cost for each is a total cost of $30.
8. 32 slices of pizza divided equally among a number of friends is 4 slices each.

Solve the equation. (TEKS 4.15B, pp. 160–161, 162–165)

9. $8 \times n = 56$
10. ■ $\div 3 = 4$
11. $d \times 10 = 30$
12. ■ $\div 7 = 7 + 2$
13. ■ $\div 2 = 8$
14. $25 \div p = 10 - 5$
15. $2 \times g \times 5 = 30$
16. $5 \times n \times 3 = 15$

Find a rule. Use your rule to find the missing numbers. (TEKS 4.7, pp. 170–171)

17.

Input, *x*	20	25	30	35	40	45
Output, *y*	4	5	6	■	■	■

18.

Input, *n*	3	4	5	■	■	■
Output, *m*	27	36	45	54	63	72

Check Problem Solving

Solve. (TEKS 4.14C, pp. 148–151, 166–169)

19. Meredith has a puzzle for her classmates. When she says 5, the answer is 10. When she says 8, the answer is 16. When she says 10, the answer is 20. What is a possible pattern?
20. **WRITE Math** Sam counted 3 times as many robins this year as he did last year. This year he counted 18 robins. **Explain** how to write an equation to find the number of robins he counted last year.

GO ONLINE **Technology** Use *Online Assessment.*

Enrich • Predict Patterns

Growing, Growing, Growing

You can use diagrams, tables, and equations to predict patterns.

Each square table can seat 1 student on a side. How many students can sit at 4 tables placed end-to-end? What equation can you use to predict the number of students who can sit at any number of tables placed end-to-end?

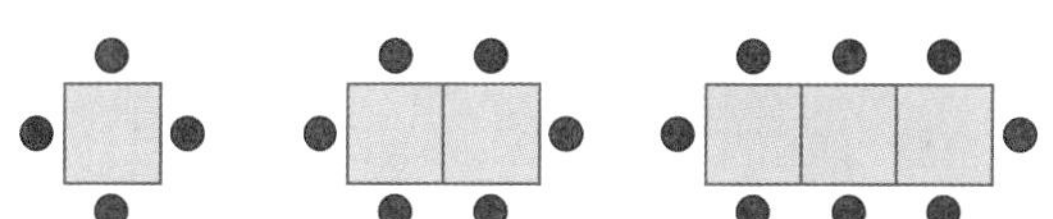

Input; tables	1	2	3	4
Output; students	4	6	8	

Complete the input/output table to predict the number of students who can sit at 4 tables placed end-to-end. Describe the pattern for the number of students who can sit at any number of tables placed end-to-end.

$(2 \times t) + 2 = s$

Rule: Each table seats 2 students plus 1 student at each end.

So, 10 students can sit at 4 tables placed end-to-end.

Try It

Copy and complete the table for the pattern. Then describe the pattern.

1.

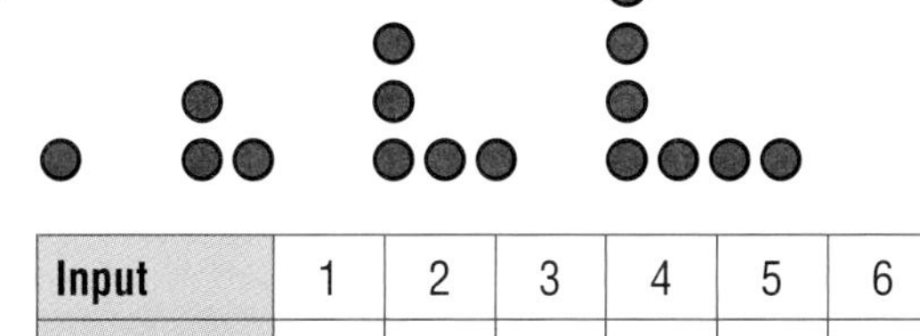

Input	1	2	3	4	5	6
Output	1	3				

2.

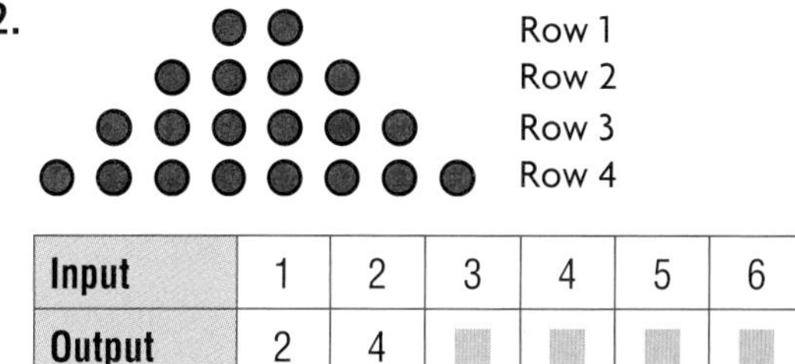

Input	1	2	3	4	5	6
Output	2	4				

3.

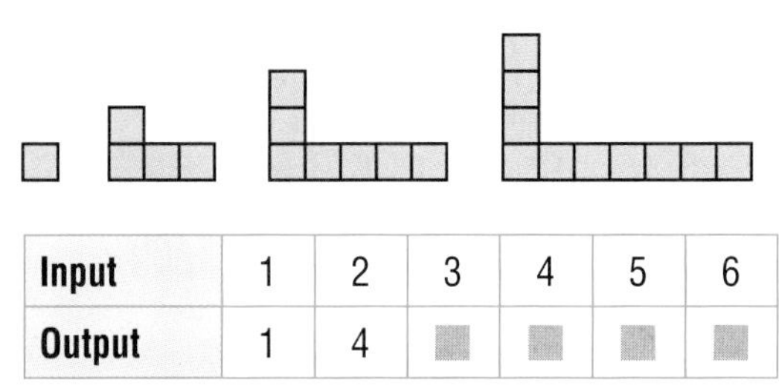

Input	1	2	3	4	5	6
Output	1	4				

4.

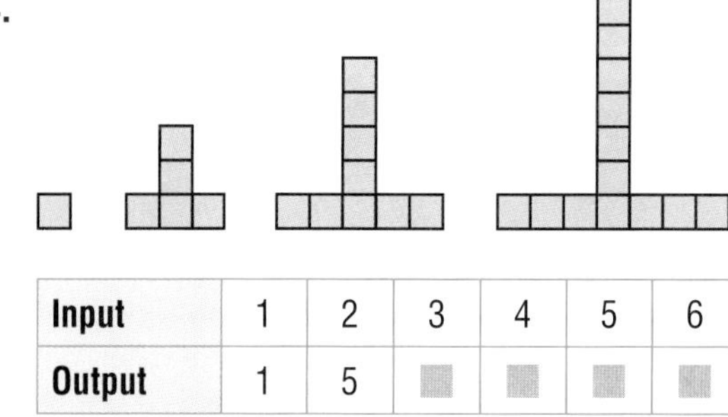

Input	1	2	3	4	5	6
Output	1	5				

WRITE Math ▸ **Explain** how you can predict the number of students who can sit at 12 tables by using the equation. $(2 \times t) + 2 = s$.

Unit Review/Test
Chapters 4–6

Multiple Choice

1. The table below shows taxi fares for trips outside the city.

Taxi Fares					
Distance (in km)	1	3	5	7	9
Fare	\$2	\$6	\$10	\$14	■

Which shows the taxi fare for a 9-kilometer trip? (TAKS Obj. 2)

A \$9

B \$15

C \$18

D \$27

2. Which pair of numbers best completes the number sentence? (TAKS Obj. 1)

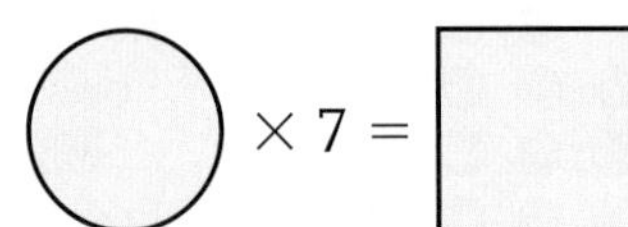

F 3 and 14

G 5 and 35

H 4 and 40

J 6 and 49

3. A hotel has 5 floors. Each floor has 4 rooms. Each room has 2 beds. Which expression does **NOT** describe the total number of beds in the hotel? (TAKS Obj. 1)

A $4 \times 2 \times 2$

B $5 \times 2 \times 4$

C $2 \times 4 \times 5$

D $4 \times 5 \times 2$

4. Manuel is buying 4 dozen lemon tarts from a bakery. The table below shows the different discounts the bakery offers.

Bulk Discount Prices		
Discount 1	**Discount 2**	**Discount 3**
\$11 per dozen	\$1 per tart	\$48 per 4 dozen

Which discount gives Manuel the best price? (TAKS Obj. 1)

F Discount 1

G Discount 2

H Discount 3

J The discounts are the same.

5. Sally baked cookies for the Chess Club bake sale. She put 11 cookies in each package. She sold 5 packages. How many cookies did Sally sell? (TAKS Obj. 1)

A 60

B 55

C 54

D 48

GO ONLINE **Technology** Use *Online Assessment.*

6. What number makes this equation true? (TAKS Obj. 2)

$$\blacksquare \times 5 = 21 + 9$$

F 3

G 5

H 6

J 10

7. Natasha is reading a book. The book is 99 pages long. How many pages must Natasha read each day to finish the book in 9 days? (TAKS Obj. 1)

A 8

B 9

C 10

D 11

8. Which number sentence is **NOT** in the same fact family as $6 \times 9 = \blacksquare$? (TAKS Obj. 2)

F $\blacksquare \div 9 = 6$

G $\blacksquare \div 6 = 9$

H $9 \times 6 = \blacksquare$

J $9 \times \blacksquare = 6$

9. Which expression best represents the arrangement of hearts shown below? (TAKS Obj. 1)

A $4 + 4 + 4 + 4$

B 4×4

C $3 + 3 + 3 + 3$

D 3×4

Short Response

10. Write an expression to show that Evelyn spent $12 on a number of toys. (TAKS Obj. 6)

11. Ben had softball practice at the same time every week for 9 weeks. He spent a total of 36 hours at practice. Write and solve an equation to find the number of hours Ben spent at softball practice each week. (TAKS Obj. 6)

12. The volleyball team is going to a restaurant for dinner. Each table at the restaurant can seat 4 people. There are 20 people on the team. How many tables are needed at the restaurant? (TAKS Obj. 1)

13. Mrs. Lin buys 11 boxes of party invitations. Each box has 12 invitations. How many invitations does Mrs. Lin buy in all? (TAKS Obj. 1)

Extended Response WRITE Math

14. There are 3 times as many girls as boys in a ballet class. There are 12 girls in the class. **Explain** how to write an equation to find the number of boys in the ballet class. (TAKS Obj. 6)

15. Reena claims that the following number sentence is true.

$$8 \times 6 = (4 \times 6) + (4 \times 6)$$

Explain how to draw an array to show whether she is correct. (TAKS Obj. 1)

16. **Explain** how to use mental math to find the product. (TAKS Obj. 1)

$$10 \times 5 \times 0$$

Texas

Problem Solving

Hummingbirds

The Hummingbird Roundup

The Texas Hummingbird Roundup keeps track of the 18 kinds of hummingbirds in the state. Volunteers help scientists by filling out surveys when they see hummingbirds in their area. On the survey, abbreviations are used to identify the hummingbirds that the volunteers observed.

Blue-throated Hummingbird (BLUH)

Hummingbird Observations

SEPTEMBER			
Week of Sep 14–20	Species	Male	Female
	RTHU	6	2
	BLUH	3	2
	GRVE	4	2
	unknown		5
Total hours observing: 3			

Green Violet-ear (GRVE)

Ruby-throated Hummingbird (RTHU)

FACT·ACTIVITY›

For 1–3, use Marissa's observations from the table above.

1. If Marissa doubles the number of hours she spends observing each week, how many total hours will she have observed at the end of the third week?
2. If Marissa sees the same number of unknown hummingbirds each week for the next 12 weeks, how many unknown hummingbirds will she see?
3. **Pose a Problem** Look back at Problem 2. Write a similar problem about female hummingbirds.

There are at least 2 species of hummingbirds in each county in Texas. Some hummingbirds have only been seen by scientists a few times throughout history!

How Many Hummingbirds?

To help make the Roundup easier, scientists divided Texas into 10 regions. Most species of hummingbirds can be found in more than one region.

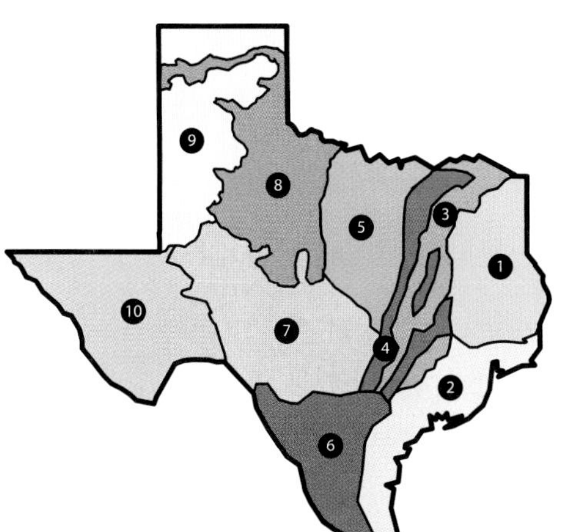

1. Piney Woods of East Texas
2. Gulf Coast Prairies and Marshes
3. Post Oak Savannah
4. Blackland Prairies
5. Cross Timbers and Prairies
6. South Texas Plains
7. Edwards Plateau
8. Rolling Plains
9. High Plains
10. West of the Pecos

FACT · ACTIVITY

Suppose you are a hummingbird observer taking part in the Hummingbird Roundup.

1. Select the region of Texas where you live. Copy and fill out the table for the number of each type of hummingbird you might see. Each Texas region has at least two different kinds of hummingbirds. Use the abbreviations for the names. You can also use the category "unknown."
2. Compare your "observations" with those of other classmates. Write multiplication and division problems about your results. Have a classmate solve the problems.

ALHU: Allen's
ANHU: Anna's
BBLH: Broad-billed
BCHU: Black-chinned
BEHU: Berylline
BLUH: Blue-throated
BTLH: Broad-tailed
BUFH: Buff-bellied
CAHU: Calliope
COHU: Costa's
GRMA: Green-breasted Mango
GRVE: Green Violet-ear
LUHU: Lucifer
MAHU: Magnificent
RTHU: Ruby-throated
RUHU: Rufous
VCHU: Violet-crowned
WEHU: White-eared

Hummingbird Observations

Month			
Week of Sep 14–20	Species	Male	Female
	unknown		
Total hours observing:			

UNIT

3 Multiply by 1- and 2-Digit Numbers

Math on Location

with **Texas Chapter Projects**

1

Meals are developed so astronauts have a balanced diet eating 4 pounds of food and 10 cups of water each day.

2

Over 200 dishes, such as these scrambled eggs, are prepared through a process called freeze-drying.

3

The packages for a menu cycle of 10 days or longer are boxed for storage in the space module.

VOCABULARY POWER

TALK Math

What math do you see in the **Math on Location** photographs? How can you find how many pounds of food and how much water the astronauts have in 30 days?

READ Math

REVIEW VOCABULARY You learned the words below when you learned about multiplication facts. How do these words relate to **Math on Location**?

factor a number that is multiplied by another number to find a product

multiple the product of two counting numbers is a multiple of each of those numbers

product the answer to a multiplication problem

WRITE Math

Copy and complete a word definition map like the one below. Use what you know about multiplication to answer the questions.

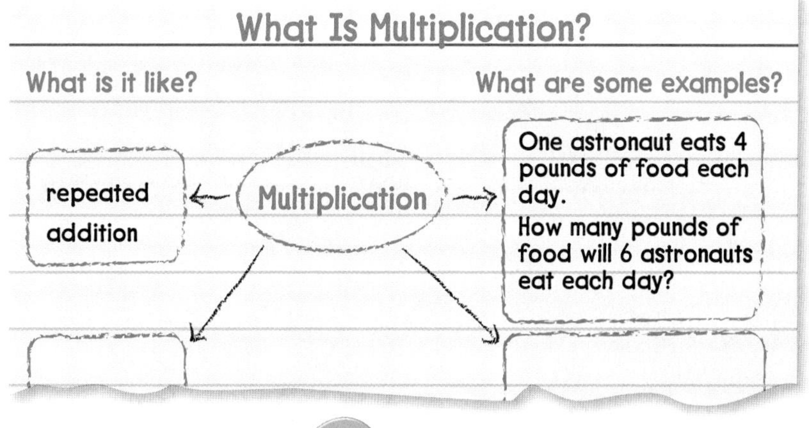

Technology
Multimedia Math Glossary link at
www.harcourtschool.com/hspmath

7 Understand Multiplication

The Big Idea Multiplication of multi-digit whole numbers is based on place value and the basic multiplication facts.

At the Cameron Park Zoo in Waco, you can see white rhinos. A white rhino's front horn is 37 to 79 inches long. The rear horn is up to 22 inches long.

Investigate

In Africa, large and small animals often live side by side. Use the data for each animal. What are some different ways you can use multiplication to compare their sizes?

Animal Heights and Weights

Type of Animal	Average Height (in inches)	Average Weight (in pounds)
African Wild Dog	30	60
Antelope	72	2,000
African Elephant	126	11,000
Giraffe	192	2,500
Gorilla	66	400
White Rhino	72	5,000

GO ONLINE **Technology** Student pages are available in the Student eBook.

Show What You Know

Check your understanding of important skills needed for success in Chapter 7.

Regroup Tens and Ones

Regroup. Write the missing numbers.

1. 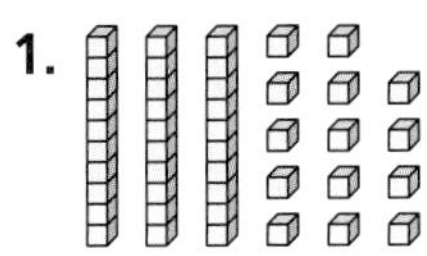

3 tens 14 ones = ▒ tens 4 ones

2.

5 tens 21 ones = ▒ tens ▒ one

3. 7 tens ▒ ones = 8 tens 3 ones

4. ▒ tens 28 ones = 6 tens 8 ones

Multiplication Facts

Find the product.

5. 6×3 **6.** 4×4 **7.** 5×9 **8.** 6×2

9. 8×7 **10.** 9×8 **11.** 7×4 **12.** 0×5

Model Multiplication

Write a multiplication sentence for each model.

13.

14.  

15. 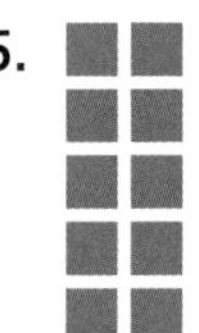

VOCABULARY POWER

CHAPTER VOCABULARY

array
compatible numbers
estimate
factor
mental math
multiple
partial product
pattern
product
regroup
round

WARM-UP WORDS

multiple the product of two counting numbers is a multiple of each of these numbers

partial product a method of multiplying in which the ones, tens, hundreds, and so on are multiplied separately and then the products are added together

compatible numbers numbers that are easy to compute mentally

LESSON 1

MENTAL MATH

Multiplication Patterns

OBJECTIVE: Use a basic fact and a pattern to multiply mentally.

Quick Review

1. 7×9
2. 3×4
3. 2×5
4. 6×6
5. 8×3

Learn

It is easy to multiply whole numbers mentally by multiples of 10, 100, and 1,000 if you know the basic facts.

PROBLEM Moe's Sun Fun rents 400 body boards each month. How many body boards do they rent in 6 months?

Example **Use mental math to multiply.** 6×400

Multplication can be thought of as repeated addition.

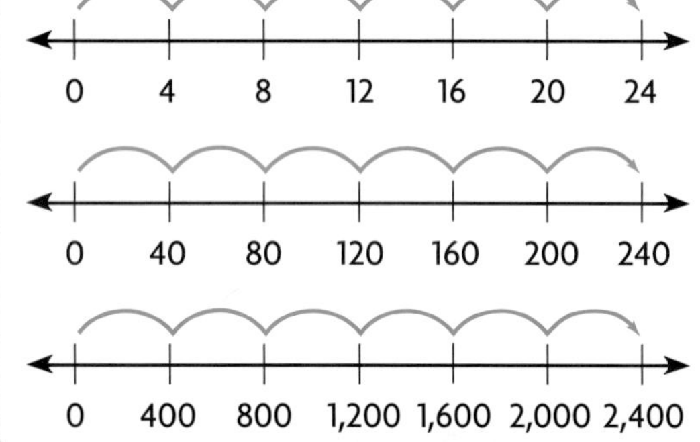

$6 \times 4 = 24$ ← basic fact

$6 \times 40 = 240$

$6 \times 400 = 2{,}400$

So, Moe's Sun Fun rents 2,400 body boards in 6 months.

- What pattern do you see in the number sentences?

More Examples

A Basic fact with a pattern

$4 \times 7 = 28$ ← basic fact

$4 \times 70 = 280$

$4 \times 700 = 2{,}800$

$4 \times 7{,}000 = 28{,}000$

B Basic fact with a zero

$8 \times 5 = 40$ ← basic fact

$8 \times 50 = 400$

$8 \times 500 = 4{,}000$

$8 \times 5{,}000 = 40{,}000$

Math Idea

As the number of zeros in a factor increases, the number of zeros in the product increases.

Guided Practice

1. What basic multiplication fact does this picture represent? Use it to find 7×30 and $7 \times 3{,}000$.

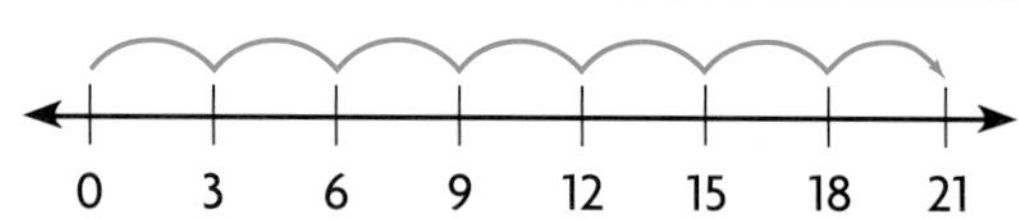

TEKS 4.6B use patterns to multiply by 10 and 100. *also* **AF 1.1; 4.4B, 4.4C, 4.14A, 4.15A, 4.15B, 4.16A**

Use mental math to complete the pattern.

2. $4 \times 8 = 32$
$4 \times 80 = ■$
$4 \times 800 = ■$

3. $6 \times 2 = 12$
$6 \times 20 = ■$
$6 \times 200 = ■$

4. $9 \times 6 = ■$
$9 \times 60 = ■$
$9 \times 600 = ■$

5. $4 \times 5 = 20$
$4 \times ■ = 200$
$4 \times 500 = ■$

6. TALK Math **Explain** how to use a basic fact and a pattern to find $9 \times 7{,}000$.

Independent Practice and Problem Solving

Use mental math to complete the pattern.

7. $3 \times 7 = 21$
$3 \times 70 = ■$
$3 \times 700 = ■$
$3 \times 7{,}000 = ■$

8. $10 \times 2 = ■$
$10 \times 20 = ■$
$10 \times 200 = ■$
$10 \times 2{,}000 = ■$

9. $3 \times 9 = 27$
$3 \times 90 = ■$
$3 \times ■ = 2{,}700$
$3 \times 9{,}000 = ■$

10. $12 \times 5 = 60$
$12 \times ■ = 600$
$12 \times 500 = ■$
$12 \times ■ = 60{,}000$

Use patterns and mental math to find the product.

11. 9×700 **12.** $6 \times 8{,}000$ **13.** 7×700 **14.** $5 \times 9{,}000$

15. 5×40 **16.** 8×900 **17.** $9 \times 9{,}000$ **18.** $4 \times 3{,}000$

Algebra Find the value of *n*.

19. $9 \times 80 = n$ **20.** $5 \times n = 3{,}000$ **21.** $7 \times n = 56{,}000$ **22.** $n \times n = 100$

USE DATA For 23–24, use the table.

23. Make an input/output table to find the cost *(c)* to rent surfboards for different numbers of days *(d)*. Write an equation to show a rule.

24. WRITE Math Gary rented snorkeling gear and swim fins for 2 weeks. Sue rented swim fins and a wetsuit for 9 days. Sue paid more than Gary. **Explain** why this happened.

Beach Rentals

Item	Per Hour	Per Day	Per Week
Surfboard	$10	$20	$85
Skimboard	$5	$18	$60
Snorkeling Gear	$5	$18	$65
Swim Fins	$3	$8	$25
Wetsuit	$5	$15	$50

Mixed Review and TAKS Prep

25. Write 150,210 in word form. (TEKS 4.1A, p. 4)

26. A piano keyboard has 88 keys. An octave is 8 keys. How many octaves does a piano keyboard have? (TEKS 4.4B, p. 160)

27. **TAKS Prep** Which number is missing from this equation? (Obj. 1)

$4 \times ■ = 12{,}000$

A 3
B 30
C 300
D 3,000

Extra Practice on page 198, Set A

LESSON 2

MENTAL MATH

Estimate Products

OBJECTIVE: Estimate products by rounding factors or using compatible numbers, and then finding the product mentally.

Quick Review

Write the basic fact shown on the number line.

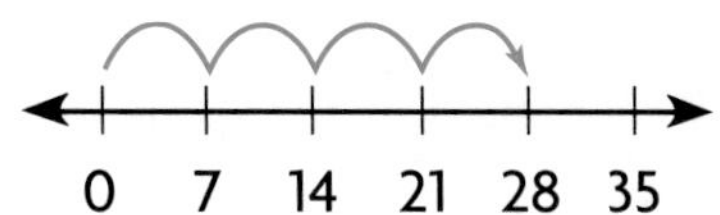

Learn

Sometimes you can solve a problem by finding an estimate.

PROBLEM An African elephant is the largest living land mammal. It uses its trunk to pick up objects that weigh up to 3 times as much as a 175-pound person. About how much weight can an African elephant pick up with its trunk?

ONE WAY **Use rounding and mental math.**

Estimate. 3×175

Step 1	Step 2
Round the greater factor to the nearest hundred. 3×175 ↓ 3×200	Use mental math. $3 \times 2 = 6$ ← basic fact $3 \times 20 = 60$ $3 \times 200 = 600$

So, an African elephant can pick up about 600 pounds with its trunk.

▲ An elephant can reach as high as 23 feet with its trunk.

ANOTHER WAY **Use compatible numbers and mental math.**

In one day, an African elephant eats 9 bags of food. Each bag weighs 57 pounds. How many pounds of food does the elephant eat?

Estimate. 9×57

Step 1	Step 2
Find compatible numbers. 9×57 ↓ 10×50	Use mental math. $10 \times 5 = 50$ ← basic fact $10 \times 50 = 500$

So, the African elephant eats about 500 pounds of food.

More Examples **Estimate the products.**

A Compatible numbers
6×129
↓
$6 \times 120 = 720$

B Nearest ten
8×45
↓
$8 \times 50 = 400$

C Nearest thousand
$5 \times 7{,}441$
↓
$5 \times 7{,}000 = 35{,}000$

- How could you use a number line to estimate 4×52?

TEKS 4.5B use strategies including rounding and compatible numbers to estimate solutions to multiplication and division problems. *also* **4.5A, 4.4D, 4.5A. 4.6B, 4.15A, 4.15B**

Guided Practice

Round the greater factor. Then use mental math to estimate the product.

1. 4×32 **2.** 7×98 **3.** 5×182 **4.** 3×415 **5.** 6×95

Estimate the product. Write the method.

6. 8×42 **7.** 2×67 **8.** 6×281 **9.** $9 \times 6{,}221$ **10.** 7×759

11. TALK Math **Explain** how you know whether an estimate of 560 is less than or greater than the exact product of 8 times 72.

Independent Practice and Problem Solving

Estimate the product. Write the method.

12. 4×37 **13.** 6×23 **14.** 5×630 **15.** $3 \times 1{,}914$

16. 9×23 **17.** 4×47 **18.** 4×978 **19.** 9×881

20. 89×3 **21.** 709×4 **22.** $2{,}509 \times 7$ **23.** $\$545 \times 8$

USE DATA For 24–26, use the graph.

24. About how many more pounds of food do 5 monkeys eat in 6 weeks than 5 wallabies?

25. Pose a Problem Use the information in the graph to write a problem. Have a classmate solve the problem.

26. WRITE Math **What's the Error?** Tracy says that 8 lemurs eat about 160 pounds of food per week. Is she correct? **Explain.**

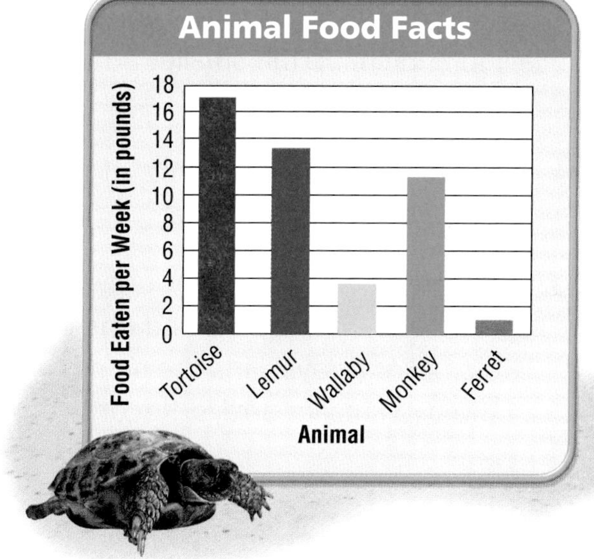

Mixed Review and TAKS Prep

27. Which is less: 6×10 or 9×7? (TEKS 4.4C, p. 100)

28. Estimate the sum of 21, 23, 37, 15, 38, and 12 by rounding each number to the nearest ten and then adding. (TEKS 4.5A, p. 40)

29. TAKS Prep Which number sentence would give the best estimate for 9×758? (Obj. 1)

A $9 \times 600 = ■$

B $9 \times 700 = ■$

C $9 \times 800 = ■$

D $9 \times 900 = ■$

Extra Practice on page 198, Set B

LESSON 3 HANDS ON

Model 2-Digit by 1-Digit Multiplication

OBJECTIVE: Model multiplication by using arrays.

Quick Review

Estimate the product.

1. 3 × 81
2. 2 × 109
3. 9 × 79
4. 5 × 55
5. 7 × 2,390

Vocabulary

partial product

Investigate

Materials ■ centimeter grid paper ■ base-ten blocks

You can break apart numbers to make them easier to multiply.

A Draw a rectangular array on grid paper to find 6 × 18.

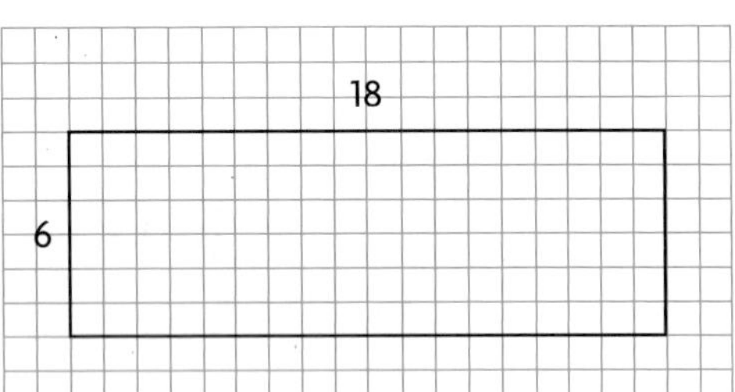

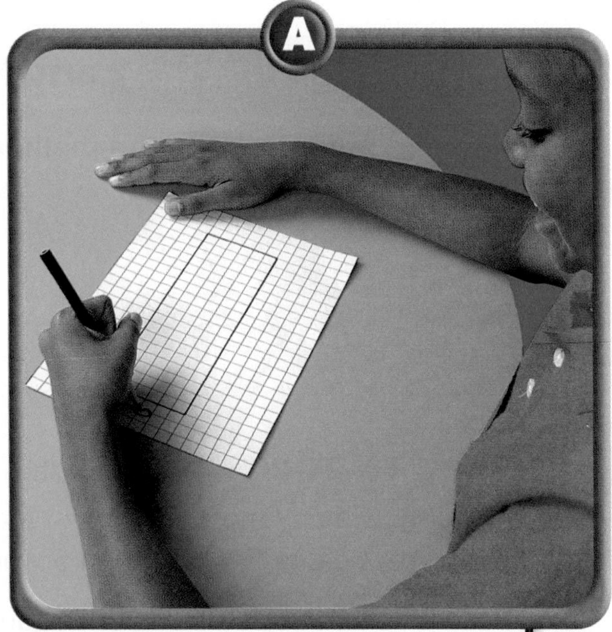

B Use the break-apart strategy to make two smaller arrays for products you know. Draw a line and shade the smaller arrays. Use two different colors.

C Find the sum of the products of the two smaller arrays. Record your answer.

D Draw the array again. Now, draw a line to break apart the array into tens and ones. Shade the two smaller arrays. Find the sum of the products of the two smaller arrays. Record your answer.

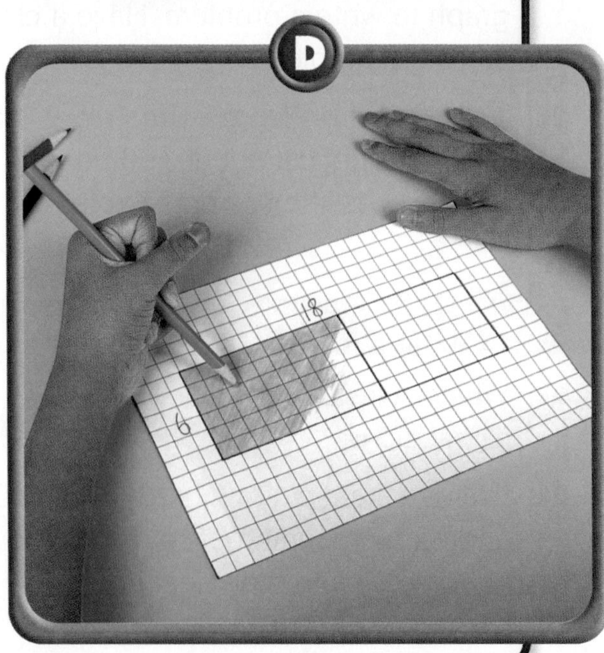

Draw Conclusions

1. Explain how you found the total number of squares in each array.
2. Compare your product with those of other classmates. What can you conclude? Explain.
3. **Evaluation** Which do you think is easier to find, the sum of 7 × 20 and 7 × 3 or the sum of 7 × 15 and 7 × 8? Explain.

TEKS 4.4A model factors and products using arrays and area models. *also* **4.1A, 4.4B, 4.4D, 4.14C, 4.14D, 4.15A, 4.15B**

Connect

You can solve the same problem by using base-ten blocks to show tens and ones.

Step 1

Make a model to find 6×18. Use tens and ones.

6 rows of 1 ten 8 ones

Step 2

Break the model into tens and ones.

$(6 \times 1 \text{ ten})$ $(6 \times 8 \text{ ones})$

↓ ↓

(6×10) (6×8)

↓ ↓

60 48

Step 3

Add the tens and the ones to find the product.

$(6 \times 10) + (6 \times 8)$

↓ ↓

60 + 48

↓

108

So, $6 \times 18 = 108$.

In Step 2, the model was broken into two parts. Each part shows a **partial product**. The partial products are 60 and 48.

TALK Math

How does breaking apart the model into tens and ones make finding the product easier?

Practice

Find the product.

1. 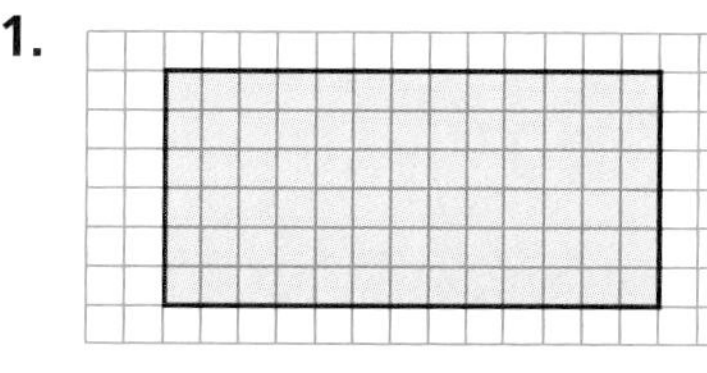

$6 \times 13 = \blacksquare$

2. 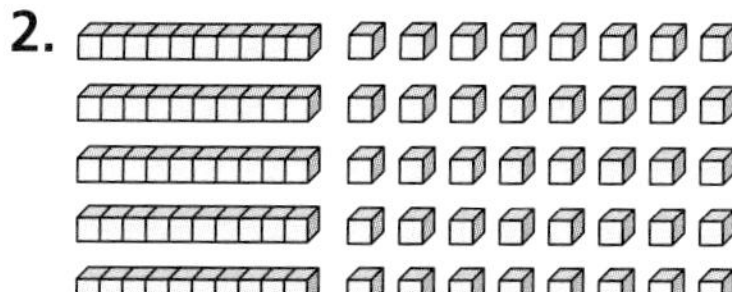

$5 \times 18 = \blacksquare$

3. 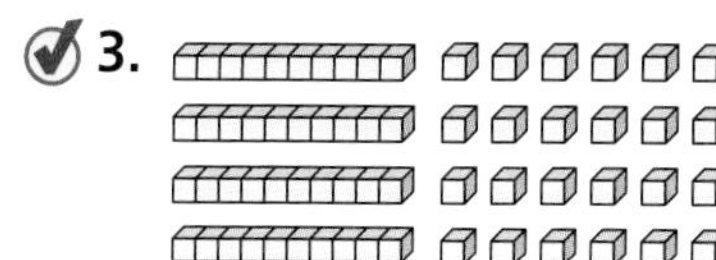

$4 \times 16 = \blacksquare$

Use grid paper or base-ten blocks to model the product. Record your answer.

4. 2×21	5. 3×17	6. 7×15	7. 9×14
8. 2×16	9. 4×19	10. 5×22	11. 9×19
12. 7×13	13. 9×21	14. 6×23	15. 8×24

16. **WRITE Math** **Explain** how modeling partial products can be used to find the products of greater numbers.

Technology
Use Harcourt Mega Math, The Number Games, *Up, Up, and Array,* Level J.

LESSON 4 Record 2-Digit by 1-Digit Multiplication

OBJECTIVE: Find products using partial products, place value, and regrouping.

Quick Review

Jim drew the model shown. Write a multiplication sentence that matches the model .

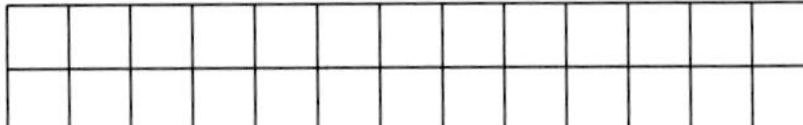

Learn

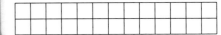

PROBLEM A roadrunner would rather run than fly. It can easily outrun a human. It can zip across the desert at speeds up to 22 feet per second. How far can a roadrunner run in 6 seconds?

ONE WAY **Use partial products.**

Multiply. 6×22 **Estimate.** $6 \times 20 = 120$

	MODEL	THINK	RECORD
Step 1	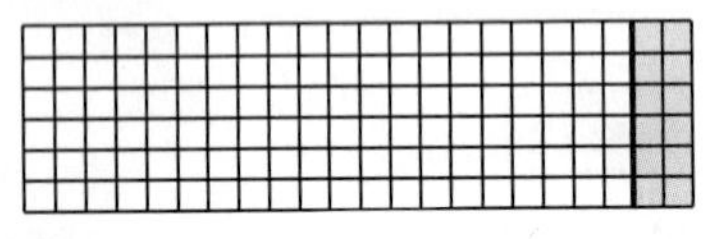	Multiply the ones.	22 × 6 12 ← 6 × 2 ones = 12 ones
Step 2	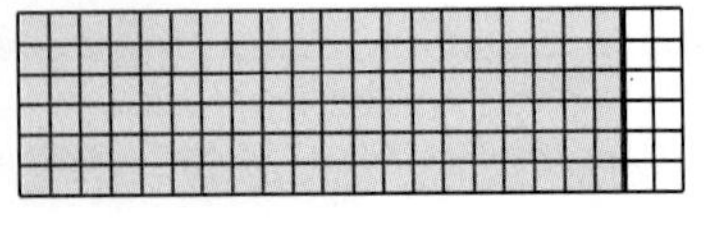	Multiply the tens.	22 × 6 12 120 ← 6 × 2 tens = 12 tens
Step 3	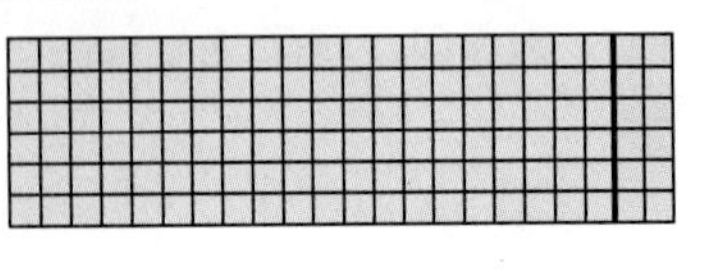	Add the partial products.	22 × 6 12 +120 132

So, the roadrunner can run 132 feet in 6 seconds. Since 132 is close to the estimate of 120, it is reasonable.

Math Idea
You can use an estimate to see whether your answer is reasonable.

- **What if** a roadrunner ran 21 feet per second for 6 seconds? Would its total distance be greater than or less than 132 feet? Explain your reasoning.

TEKS 4.4D use multiplication to solve problems (no more than two-digits times two-digits without technology). *also* **4.1A, 4.5B, 4.14A, 4.14C, 4.14D, 4.15A, 4.15B, 4.16B**

ANOTHER WAY **Use place value and regrouping.**

Example 1 Use place value without regrouping.

How far can a roadrunner run in 3 seconds?

Multiply. 3×22 **Estimate.** $3 \times 20 = 60$

	MODEL	THINK	RECORD
Step 1		Multiply the ones. 3×2 ones $= 6$ ones	22 $\times\ 3$ 6
Step 2		Multiply the tens. 3×2 tens $= 6$ tens	22 $\times\ 3$ 66

So, a roadrunner can run 66 feet in 3 seconds. Since 66 is close to the estimate of 60, it is reasonable.

READ Math

The multiplication sentence $3 \times 22 = 66$ can be expressed in different ways.

3 groups of 22 equal 66.

The product of 3 and 22 is 66.

3 times 22 equals 66.

Example 2 Use place value and regrouping.

How far can a roadrunner run in 8 seconds?

Multiply. 8×22 **Estimate.** $8 \times 20 = 160$

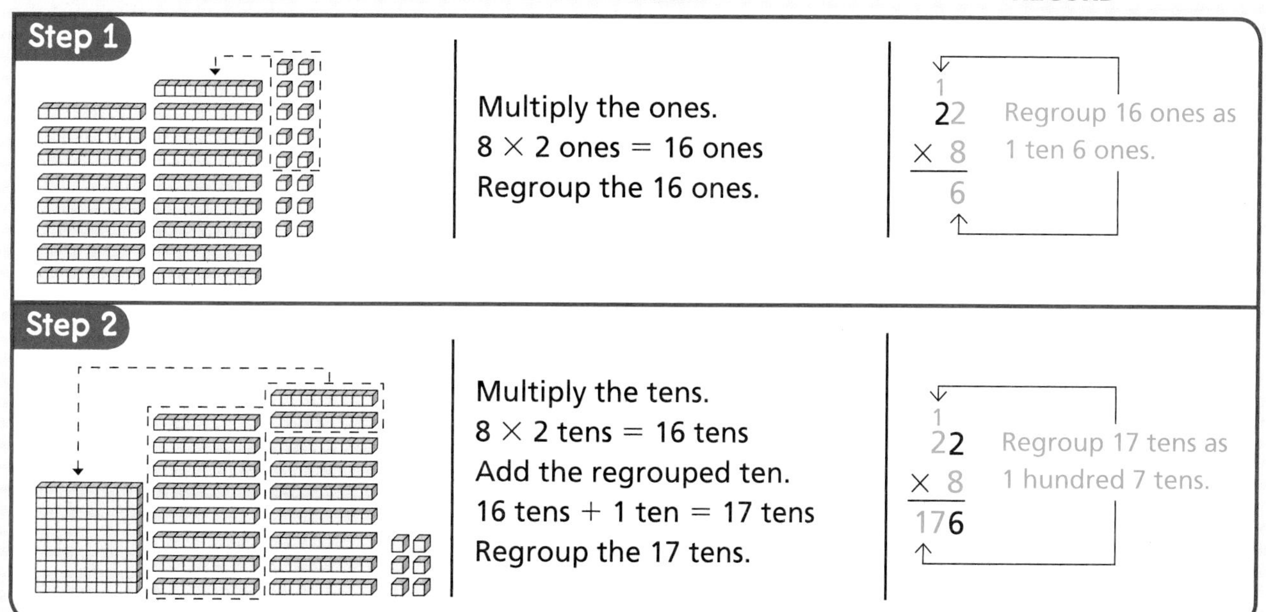

	MODEL	THINK	RECORD
Step 1		Multiply the ones. 8×2 ones $= 16$ ones Regroup the 16 ones.	$\overset{1}{2}2$ $\times\ 8$ 6 Regroup 16 ones as 1 ten 6 ones.
Step 2		Multiply the tens. 8×2 tens $= 16$ tens Add the regrouped ten. 16 tens + 1 ten = 17 tens Regroup the 17 tens.	$\overset{1}{2}2$ $\times\ 8$ 176 Regroup 17 tens as 1 hundred 7 tens.

So, a roadrunner can run 176 feet in 8 seconds. Since 176 is close to the estimate of 160, it is reasonable.

Guided Practice

1. Make the model shown. Then use your model to find and record the product.

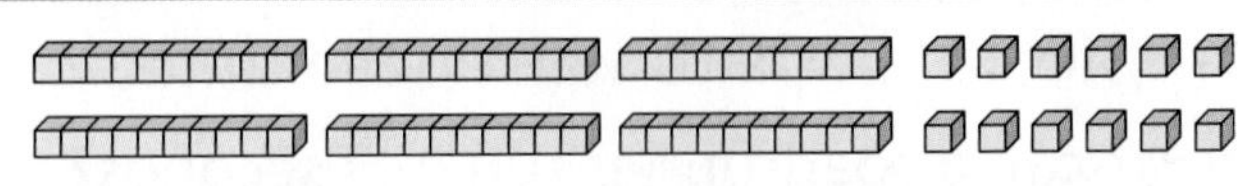

2×36

Estimate. Then record the product.

2. 42×4
3. 32×2
4. $\$63 \times 7$
5. 81×5
6. 57×4

7. **TALK Math** **Explain** how to record your work to find 4×52.

Independent Practice and Problem Solving

Estimate. Then record the product.

8. 33×2
9. $25¢ \times 3$
10. 36×8
11. 29×6
12. $\$94 \times 5$

Write each partial product. Then record the product.

13. 8×17
14. 6×42
15. 9×53
16. 3×67
17. 9×96

Algebra **Write a rule. Find the missing numbers.**

18.

Number of Pounds, p	2	3	4	5	6
Number of Ounces, o	32	48	64	■	■

19.

Number of Feet, f	1	2	3	4	5
Number of Inches, i	12	24	■	48	■

20. In one second, a blacktailed hare can run 51 feet and a cottontail hare 22 feet. How much farther can a black-tailed hare run than a cottontail hare in 7 seconds?

21. ***FAST FACT*** A black-tailed hare hops 5 to 10 feet at a time. It can reach speeds of 44 to 51 feet per second. How far can it hop in 5 seconds?

22. Antelope jackrabbits can leap 22 feet in a single jump. How far can it travel in 9 leaps?

23. **WRITE Math** 6×87 is more than 5×87. How much more? **Explain** how you know without multiplying.

Mixed Review and TAKS Prep

24. A room had 18 computers. Three were added, and then 6 were removed. Write an expression to show this situation. (TEKS 4.15B, p. 70)

25. What is the place value of the digit 5 in 234,523? (TEKS 4.1A, p. 4)

26. **TAKS Prep** Al bought a book for $25 and 3 toys for $13 each. How much change did he get back from a $100 bill? (Obj. 1)

 Extra Practice on page 198, Set C

Miles of Trails

Use Graphic Aids

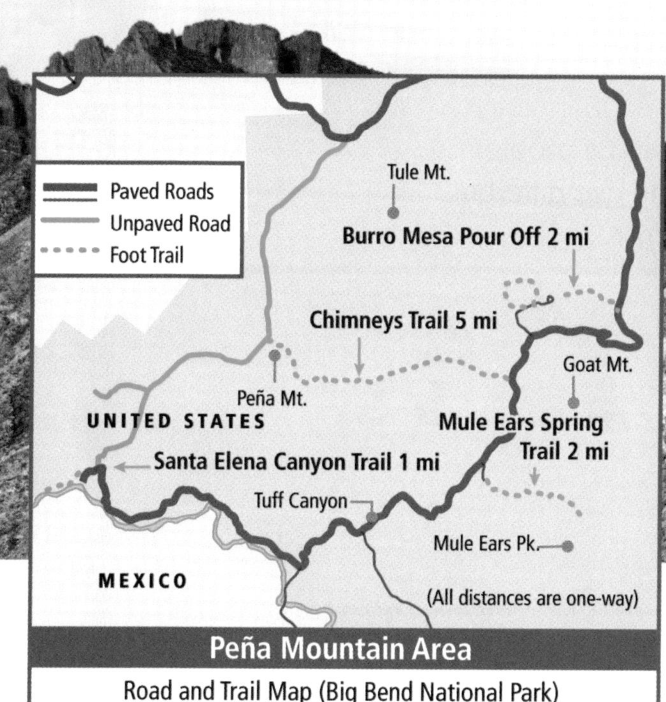

Peña Mountain Area

Road and Trail Map (Big Bend National Park)

Big Bend National Park, in West Texas, has over 150 miles of hiking trails. There are also trails for horseback riding and bicycling.

Big Bend National Park in West Texas offers a variety of activities for families. Daily exercise helps people think more clearly, sleep better, and maintain a healthy weight. The table shows the number of calories a 75-pound person might burn in 15 minutes.

Calories Burned in 15 Minutes

Activity	Calories Burned
Bicycling	88
Hiking	65
Horseback Riding	41

Problem Solving Read graphic aid. Use the information to solve the problems.

1. Jason went horseback riding for 30 minutes and went bicycling for 45 minutes. How many calories did he burn?

2. Which activity burns about twice as many calories as horseback riding?

3. On a camping trip, Jason and his parents hiked the Chimneys, Mule Ears Spring, Santa Elena Canyon, and the Burro Mesa Pour Off trails each day for 4 days. How many miles did they hike in all?

4. **WRITE Math** Jason wants to compare the heights of waterfalls in the park. Which graphic aid would you use to show the heights: a table, a picture, a bar graph, or a map? **Explain** your answer.

Problem Solving Workshop
Strategy: Draw a Diagram

OBJECTIVE: Solve problems by using the strategy *draw a diagram.*

Learn the Strategy

Drawing a diagram or picture can help you understand a problem. It also sometimes makes the solution visible. You can use different types of diagrams to show different types of problems.

A diagram can show position.

Sally threw the softball 135 feet. Arturo threw it 155 feet, and Joe threw it 140 feet.

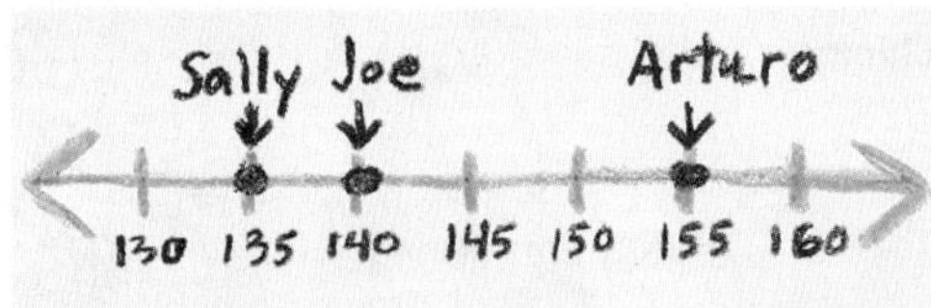

A diagram can show size.

Matt's puppy weighs 2 pounds more than twice the weight of Ann's puppy. Together the puppies weigh 26 pounds.

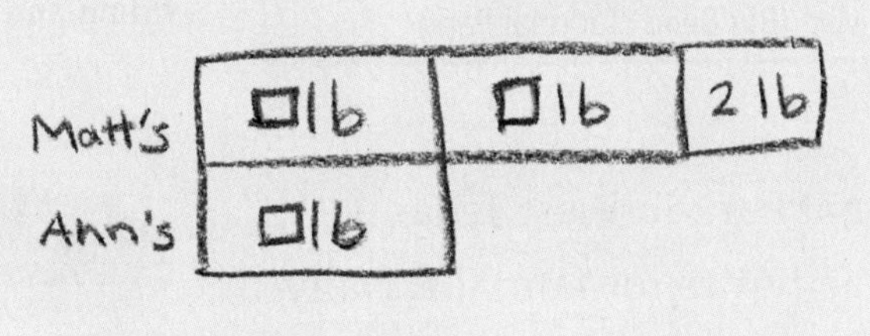

A diagram can show direction.

Noelle walked 5 blocks north and 5 blocks west. She then continued 3 blocks south to her friend's house.

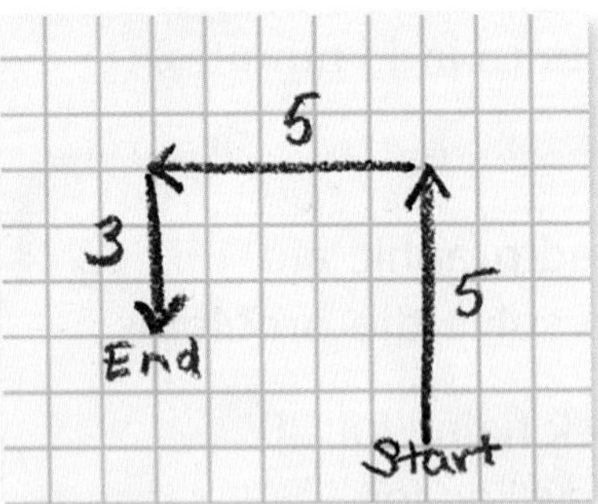

TALK Math

What are some questions that can be answered by using each of the diagrams shown above?

To draw a diagram, carefully follow the information or action given in the problem. Keep the diagram simple. Label the parts to show what they represent.

TEKS 4.14C select or develop an appropriate problem-solving plan or strategy, including drawing a picture, looking for a pattern, systematic guessing and checking, acting it out, making a table, working a simpler problem, or working backwards to solve a problem *also* **4.4A, 4.4D, 4.14A, 4.14B, 4.15A, 4.15B, 4.16B**

Use the Strategy

Read to Understand
Plan
Solve
Check

PROBLEM At the sea park, one section in the stadium has 9 rows with 32 seats in each row. In the center of each of the first 6 rows, 8 seats are in the splash zone. How many seats are not in the splash zone?

Read to Understand

- **Summarize what you are asked to find.**
- **What information will you use?**

Plan

- **What strategy can you use to solve the problem?**
  You can draw a diagram to help you solve the problem.

Solve

- **How can you use the strategy to solve the problem?**
  Draw a diagram of the section.

Draw an array that shows 9 rows of 32 seats. In the center, outline an array that shows 6 rows of 8 seats for the splash zone.

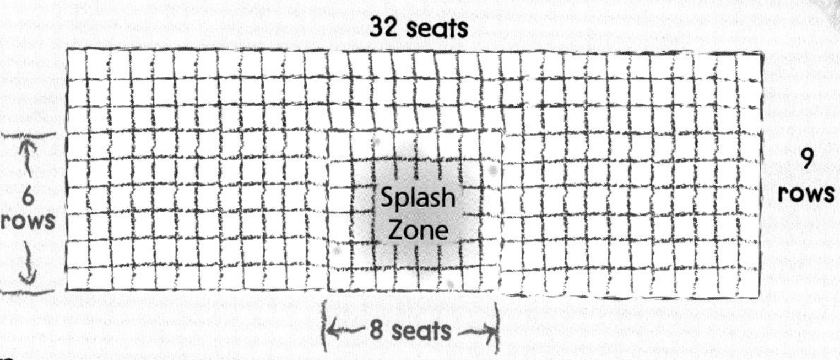

Find the total number of seats in the section.

$$\begin{array}{r} 32 \\ \times\ 9 \\ \hline 288 \end{array}$$ ← total number of seats

Find the number of seats in the splash zone.

$$\begin{array}{r} 8 \\ \times\ 6 \\ \hline 48 \end{array}$$ ← number of seats in splash zone

Then, find the number of seats **not** in the splash zone.

$$\begin{array}{r} 288 \\ -\ 48 \\ \hline 240 \end{array}$$

288 ← total number of seats
48 ← number of seats in splash zone
240 ← number of seats **not** in splash zone

So, 240 seats are not in the splash zone.

Check

- **How can you check your answer?**
- **What other ways could you solve the problem?**

Guided Problem Solving

Read to Understand
Plan
Solve
Check

1. The seats in Section A and Section B of the stadium are all taken for the last show of the day. Section A has 8 rows of 14 seats each. Section B has 6 rows of 16 seats each. How many people are seated in Sections A and B for the last show?

First, draw a diagram.

Then, find the number of seats in each section.

Finally, find the total number of seats.

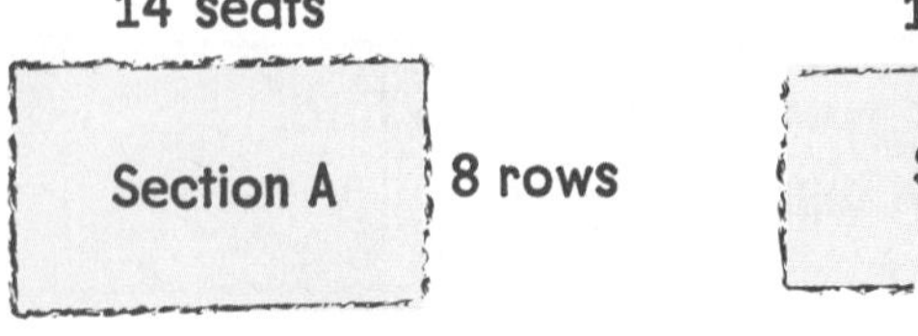

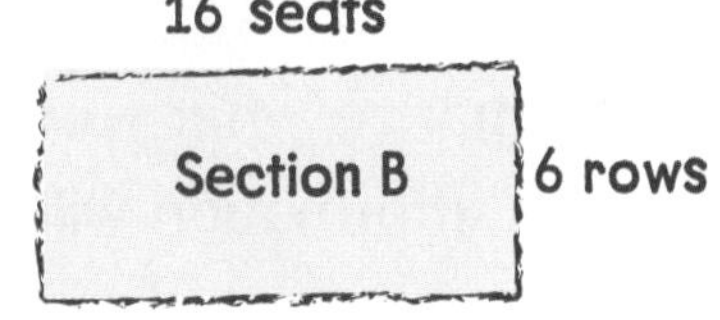

Section A: $8 \times 14 = \blacksquare$ Section B: $6 \times 16 = \blacksquare$

2. **What if** Sections A and B in Problem 1 each had 7 rows? How many people would have been seated?

3. Carol, Juan, Tami, and Brad are the first four people in line to see the Open Ocean exhibit. Carol is not first in line. Tami has at least two people ahead of her in line. Juan is third. Give the order of the four in line.

Problem Solving Strategy Practice

Draw a diagram to solve.

4. Matt, Julio, and Frank each bought a toy fish. Matt's fish is 10 inches longer than Julio's fish. Frank's fish is 2 inches longer than twice the length of Julio's fish. Julio's fish is 12 inches long. Find the length of each toy fish.

USE DATA For 5–6, use the graph.

5. Mr. Torres took his students to the dolphin show. Each row in the stadium had 11 seats. One adult sat at each end of a row, and each group of 4 students was seated between 2 adults. Mr. Torres sat in a row by himself. How many adults were there?

6. **WRITE Math** Another section of the stadium has rows of 24 seats each. Describe at least two ways Mrs. Allen's class can sit if an equal number of students sit in each row.

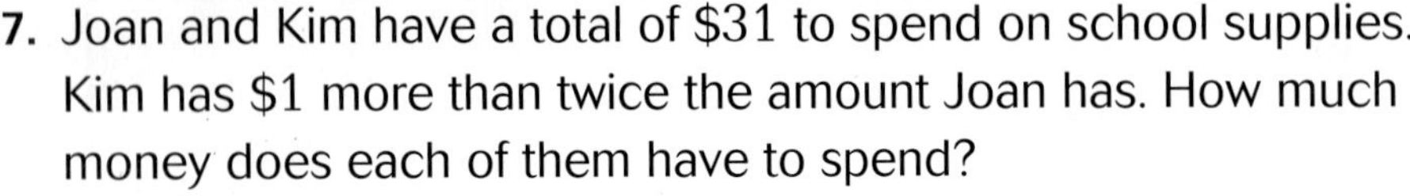

7. Joan and Kim have a total of $31 to spend on school supplies. Kim has $1 more than twice the amount Joan has. How much money does each of them have to spend?

Mixed Strategy Practice

USE SCIENCE DATA For 8–13, use the information in the picture.

8. How many Pilot whales laid end to end would it take to be longer than one Blue Whale?

9. A Gray whale is 43 feet long. List the whales shown in order from the greatest difference in length from the length of the Gray whale to the least difference in length.

10. Mr. Jeremy owns a car that is 12 feet long. How many cars like Mr. Jeremy's parked end to end would equal the length of a Bowhead whale?

11. **Pose a Problem** Look back at Problem 9. Write a similar problem by changing the type of whale and the number.

12. **Open-Ended** Write three different expressions that equal the length of the Fin whale, using one or more operations.

CHALLENGE YOURSELF

Stan researched whale populations and found that there are about 150,000 fin whales and 14,000 blue whales in the world.

13. The number of blue whales is about 2,000 more than 3 times the number of right whales. About how many right whales are there?

14. There are about 10,000 humpback and 8,000 bowhead whales in the world. **Explain** how you can find the difference between the number of fin whales and the total number of blue, humpback, and bowhead whales.

Choose a STRATEGY

- Draw a Diagram or Picture
- Make a Model or Act It Out
- Make an Organized List
- Look for a Pattern
- Make a Table or Graph
- Guess and Check
- Work Backward
- Solve a Simpler Problem
- Write an Equation
- Use Logical Reasoning

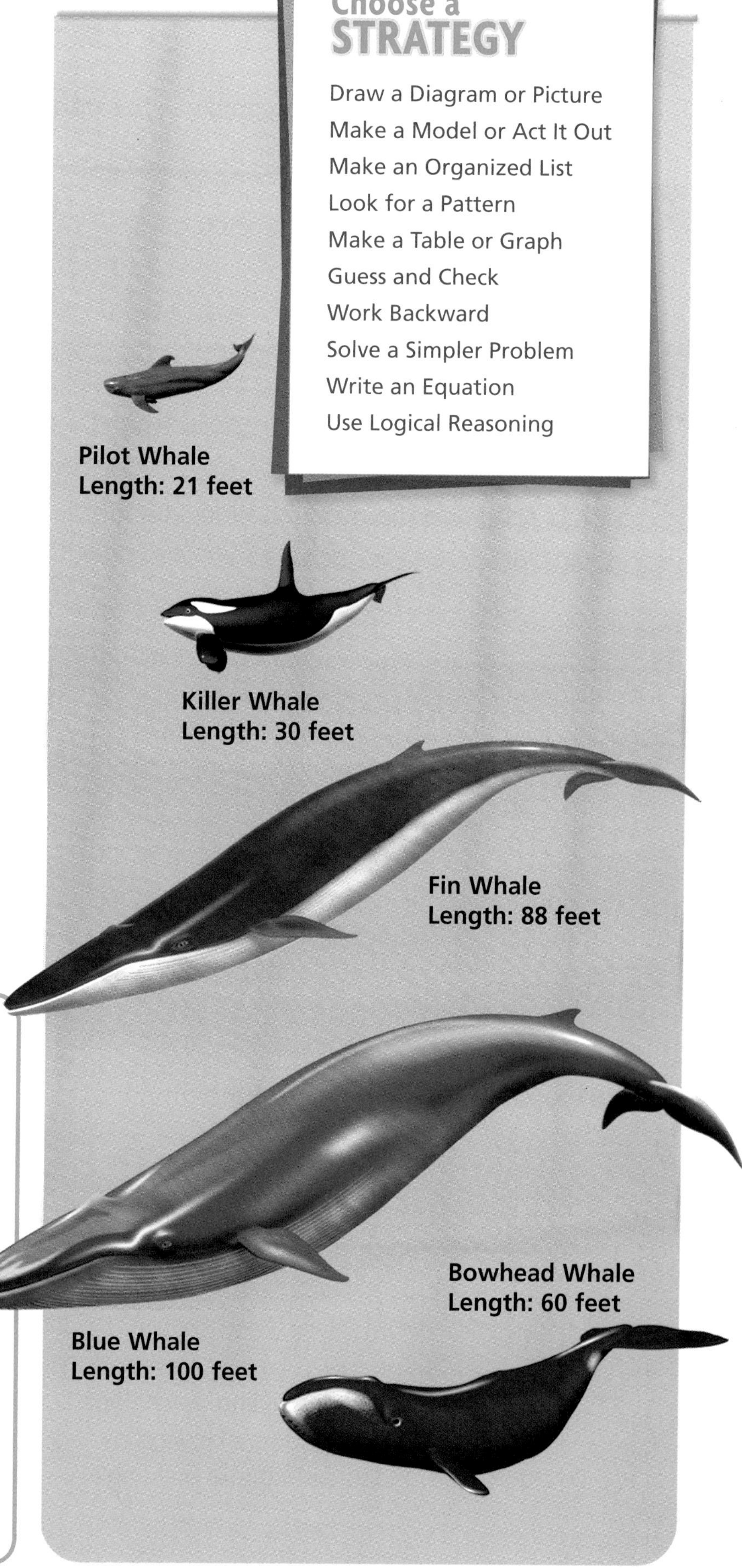

Extra Practice

Set A Use mental math to complete the pattern. (pp.184–185)

1. $6 \times 4 = 24$
   $6 \times 40 = \blacksquare$
   $6 \times 400 = \blacksquare$
   $6 \times 4{,}000 = \blacksquare$
2. $5 \times 8 = \blacksquare$
   $5 \times 80 = \blacksquare$
   $5 \times 800 = \blacksquare$
   $5 \times 8{,}000 = \blacksquare$
3. $9 \times 9 = 81$
   $9 \times \blacksquare = 810$
   $9 \times 900 = \blacksquare$
   $9 \times \blacksquare = 81{,}000$
4. $7 \times \blacksquare = 42$
   $7 \times 60 = \blacksquare$
   $7 \times \blacksquare = 4{,}200$
   $7 \times 6{,}000 = \blacksquare$
5. $8 \times 3 = \blacksquare$
   $8 \times \blacksquare = 240$
   $8 \times 300 = \blacksquare$
   $8 \times 3{,}000 = \blacksquare$
6. $4 \times 9 = \blacksquare$
   $4 \times 90 = \blacksquare$
   $4 \times \blacksquare = 3{,}600$
   $4 \times \blacksquare = 36{,}000$
7. $3 \times 7 = \blacksquare$
   $3 \times 70 = \blacksquare$
   $3 \times \blacksquare = 2{,}100$
   $3 \times \blacksquare = 21{,}000$
8. $2 \times 12 = \blacksquare$
   $2 \times \blacksquare = 240$
   $2 \times \blacksquare = 2{,}400$
   $2 \times 12{,}000 = \blacksquare$

Set B Estimate the product. Write the method. (pp.186–187)

1. 3×56
2. $8 \times \$21$
3. 2×865
4. $5 \times \$689$
5. $7 \times 4{,}133$
6. 5×32
7. 4×88
8. 6×78
9. $3 \times \$56$
10. 7×94
11. $\begin{array}{r} \$59 \\ \times\ \ 4 \\ \hline \end{array}$
12. $\begin{array}{r} 82 \\ \times\ 9 \\ \hline \end{array}$
13. $\begin{array}{r} 876 \\ \times\ \ 8 \\ \hline \end{array}$
14. $\begin{array}{r} \$5{,}236 \\ \times\ \ \ \ 6 \\ \hline \end{array}$
15. $\begin{array}{r} 3{,}462 \\ \times\ \ \ 5 \\ \hline \end{array}$
16. $\begin{array}{r} 232 \\ \times\ \ 4 \\ \hline \end{array}$
17. $\begin{array}{r} 436 \\ \times\ \ 6 \\ \hline \end{array}$
18. $\begin{array}{r} \$614 \\ \times\ \ \ 9 \\ \hline \end{array}$
19. $\begin{array}{r} 1{,}857 \\ \times\ \ \ 2 \\ \hline \end{array}$
20. $\begin{array}{r} \$7{,}746 \\ \times\ \ \ \ 7 \\ \hline \end{array}$
21. Gavin saves the tickets from all of the Houston Astros games he attends. He has attended 38 games each year for the past 4 years. Estimate the number of tickets he has saved.
22. Maria wants to save $121 out of every paycheck she receives. About how much money will she save in 6 weeks?

Set C Estimate. Then record the product. (pp.190–193)

1. 7×27
2. $6 \times \$45$
3. 7×47
4. 8×64
5. 9×36
6. $5 \times 17¢$
7. 2×31
8. $8 \times \$92$
9. $4 \times \$18$
10. 6×33
11. $9 \times \$39$
12. 6×56
13. 4×74
14. 8×52
15. $7 \times \$75$
16. $\begin{array}{r} 23 \\ \times\ 3 \\ \hline \end{array}$
17. $\begin{array}{r} 91 \\ \times\ 3 \\ \hline \end{array}$
18. $\begin{array}{r} 26 \\ \times\ 3 \\ \hline \end{array}$
19. $\begin{array}{r} \$42 \\ \times\ \ 8 \\ \hline \end{array}$
20. $\begin{array}{r} 83 \\ \times\ 9 \\ \hline \end{array}$
21. There are 9 floors in a building. Each floor on one side has 27 windows. How many windows are on that side of the building?
22. Mrs. Gomez drives a total of 74 miles each day to and from work. How many miles does she drive in 5 days?

CD ROM **Technology**
Use Harcourt Mega Math, The Number Games, *Tiny's Think Tank,* Level J.

TECHNOLOGY CONNECTION

iTools: Base-Ten Blocks (TEKS 4.14D, 4.1A, 4.4D, 4.15A, 4.15B, 4.16B)

Juan can ride his bicycle at a rate of 16 miles per hour on flat roads. How far could he ride at that same rate in 5 hours?

Step 1	Click on *Base-Ten Blocks*. Then select *Multiply* from the *Activities* menu.	
Step 2	Click on the tens block. Then click 1 time in the workspace. Next, click the ones block and click 6 times in the workspace. If you make a mistake, click on the eraser. Notice that 1×16 appears at the bottom of the workspace.	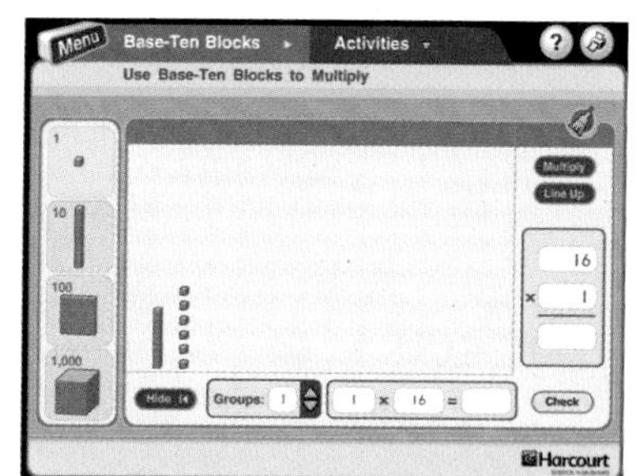
Step 3	Next, move your cursor to *Groups*, and click the up arrow until 5 appears. Each click adds a group of 16 blocks. Now the expression reads 5×16, and the workspace shows 5 groups of 16.	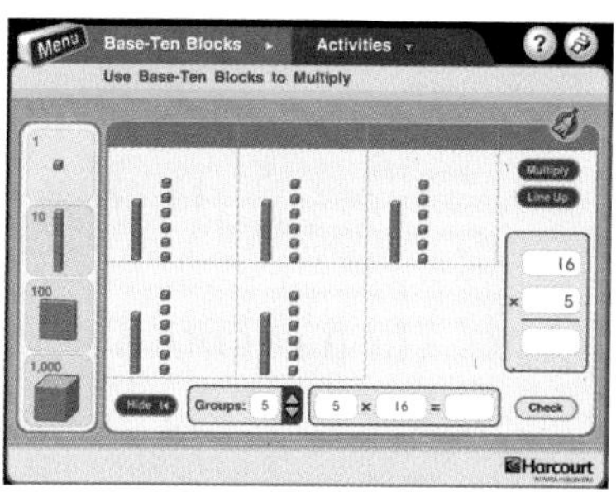
Step 4	Click on *Multiply*. Then click on *Regroup* until there are no more ones to regroup.	
Step 5	Count the blocks in the group. Type your answer. Then click on *Check* to verify your answer.	

So, Juan could ride 80 miles in 5 hours.
Click on the broom to clear the workspace.

Try It

Follow the same steps to multiply.

1. $\begin{array}{r} 34 \\ \times\ 2 \\ \hline \end{array}$
2. 9×21
3. $\begin{array}{r} 88 \\ \times\ 3 \\ \hline \end{array}$
4. 4×56
5. $\begin{array}{r} 47 \\ \times\ 6 \\ \hline \end{array}$
6. **Explore More Explain** how the *Base-Ten Blocks* show the relationship between multiplication and addition.

Technology
*i*Tools are available online or on CD-ROM.

Chapter 7 Review/Test

Check Vocabulary and Concepts

Choose the best term from the box.

VOCABULARY
estimate
multiply
partial products

1. To find the product of a 2-digit number and a 1-digit number, you can multiply the ones, multiply the tens, and add the _?_ together. **(TEKS 4.4A, p. 188)**
2. You can _?_ to find a number that is close to the exact amount. **(TEKS 4.5B, p. 186)**

Check Skills

Use mental math to complete the pattern. **(TEKS 4.6B, pp. 184–185)**

3. $2 \times 4 = 8$
   $2 \times 40 =$ ■
   $2 \times 400 =$ ■
   $2 \times 4{,}000 =$ ■
4. $3 \times 6 =$ ■
   $3 \times$ ■ $= 180$
   $3 \times 600 =$ ■
   $3 \times$ ■ $= 18{,}000$
5. $10 \times 7 =$ ■
   $10 \times 70 =$ ■
   $10 \times$ ■ $= 7{,}000$
   $10 \times 7{,}000 =$ ■
6. $8 \times 9 =$ ■
   $8 \times$ ■ $= 720$
   $8 \times 900 =$ ■
   $8 \times 9{,}000 =$ ■

Estimate the product. Write the method. **(TEKS 4.5B, pp. 186–187)**

7. 8×26
8. 9×539
9. $4 \times 1{,}562$
10. $6 \times \$722$
11. $7 \times \$654$
12. 5×324
13. 8×476
14. $3 \times 2{,}799$
15. 4×721
16. 9×562

Estimate. Then record the product. **(TEKS 4.4D, pp. 190–193)**

17. 43×6
18. 89×7
19. 57×4
20. $\$84 \times 3$
21. 93×7
22. 56×3
23. $\$76 \times 5$
24. 82×9
25. $\$37 \times 4$
26. 96×4
27. $7 \times \$36$
28. 2×46
29. $3 \times \$67$
30. 6×38
31. $4 \times \$65$

Check Problem Solving

Solve. **(TEKS 4.14C, pp. 194–197)**

32. Section A of the theater has 4 rows of 18 seats each. Kathy's class has reserved the 14 seats in the center of each of the first 3 rows. How many seats in Section A are not reserved?
33. **WRITE Math** June arranged 4 rows of 24 souvenirs each. If 12 of the souvenirs are toy whales, how many of the souvenirs are not toy whales? **Show** how her arrangement might look.

GO ONLINE **Technology** Use *Online Assessment.*

Enrich • Lattice Multiplication

LATTICE WORK

▲ The Schumacher House at the San Antonio Botanical Garden in San Antonio, Texas was built using wooden lattice work.

Lattice multiplication was introduced in Europe about 800 years ago, and is a way to multiply greater numbers. It's called *lattice* multiplication because of the lattice, or grid, on which the multiplication is recorded.

Multiply. 3×62

Step 1

Draw a 2×1 lattice. Then write 62 across the top and 3 down the right side. Write $\times$ above 3. Draw a diagonal line through each of the boxes.

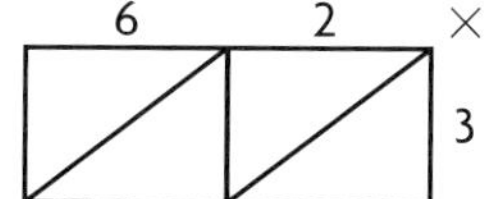

Step 2

For each box, multiply the number at the top of that column by the number at the right of the row. Write the tens digit above the diagonal and the ones digit below it. If a product has only one digit, write a zero above the diagonal.

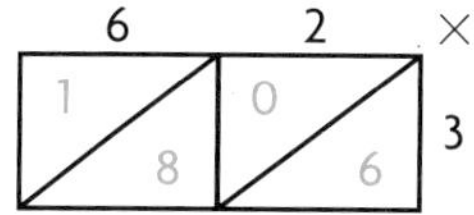

Step 3

Add along the diagonals. Start with the lower right corner. If needed, regroup to the next diagonal. Write the sums along the bottom and left side of the lattice.

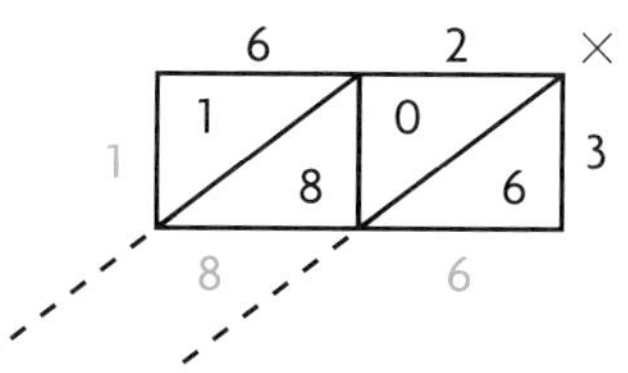

Step 4

Read the product by moving down the left side and across the bottom.

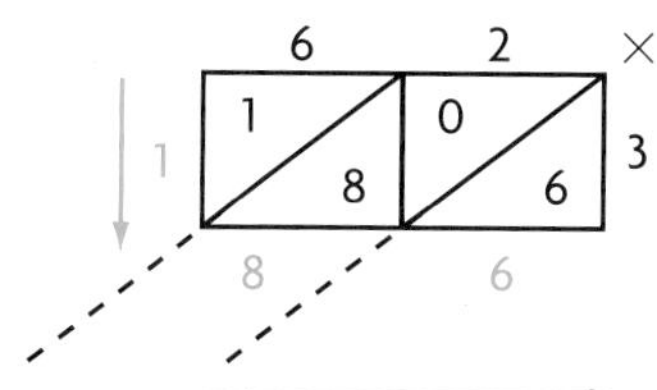

So, $3 \times 62 = 186$.

Try It

Use lattice multiplication to find the product.

1. 5×25 **2.** 6×55 **3.** 3×78 **4.** 4×99

WRITE Math **Explain** how lattice multiplication is like using partial products.

Getting Ready for the TAKS
Chapters 1–7

Number, Operation, and Quantitative Reasoning TAKS Obj. 1

1. In 2003, there were 45,033 beagles and 52,530 golden retrievers registered with the American Kennel Club. How many more golden retrievers were registered than beagles?

   A 7,497

   B 7,507

   C 17,507

   D 97,563

Eliminate choices.

See Item 2. You can eliminate choices that do not have the digit 6 in the tens place. Then start at the left, and compare the digits in each place-value position until the digits differ.

2. Maggie drew the five cards with the numbers shown below.

    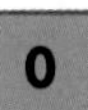

   If she uses each card only once, what is the greatest number possible with the digit 6 in the tens place?

   F 48,620

   G 82,460

   H 84,260

   J 86,420

3. WRITE Math **Explain** how to round 9,327 to the nearest thousand.

Patterns, Relationships, and Algebraic Thinking TAKS Obj. 2

4. The table below shows the cost of hot dogs at Hot Dog Haven.

Hot Dog Prices				
Number of Hot Dogs	1	2	3	4
Price	\$2	\$4	\$6	\$8

   Which expression shows how to find the cost of 14 hot dogs?

   A $14 - 2$

   B $14 + 2$

   C $14 \div 2$

   D 14×2

5. Tim sells potatoes by the bag. The table shows how many pounds are in each bag.

Potatoes				
Number of Bags	3	5	7	8
Number of Pounds	30	50	70	■

   If Tim sells 8 bags of potatoes, how many pounds of potatoes is that?

   F 10

   G 80

   H 140

   J Not here

6. WRITE Math **Explain** how you can use multiplication to find the number that makes this equation true.

$$■ \div 12 = 12$$

Geometry and Spatial Reasoning TAKS Obj. 3

7. James drew the figures below.

Which statement is true?

A They are all quadrilaterals.

B They all have the same perimeter.

C They are all have the same area.

D They all have at least 2 lines of symmetry.

8. Which of these figures is a hexagon?

F 

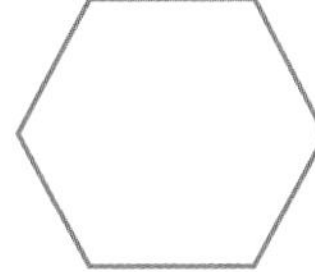

G

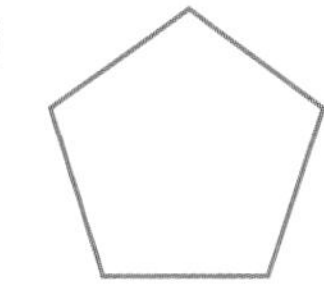

H

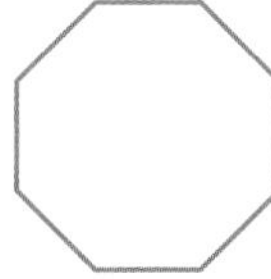

J

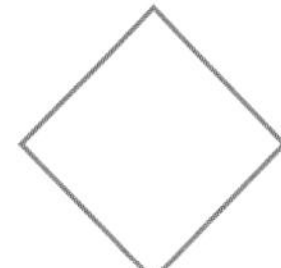

9. **WRITE Math** Karen is drawing a rectangle. She says that it has 2 right angles and 2 acute angles. Do you agree? **Explain** why or why not.

Probability and Statistics TAKS Obj. 5

10. Elena made a bar graph to show the results of her marble experiment.

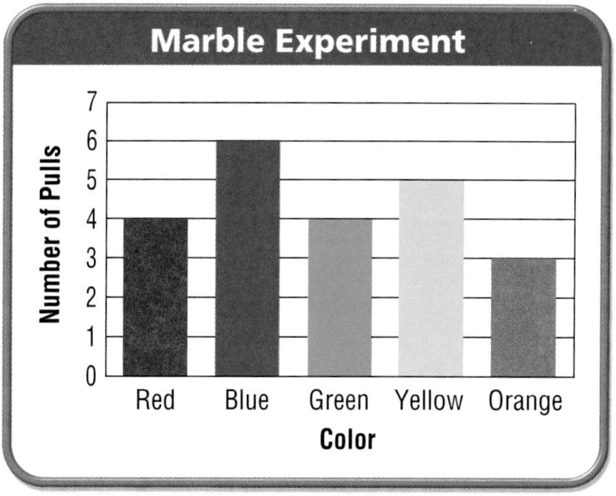

How many blue and yellow marbles did Elena pull?

A 9 **C** 11

B 10 **D** 22

11. Look at the spinner.

On which colors is the spinner equally likely to stop?

F blue and red **H** green and yellow

G red and yellow **J** blue and green

12. **WRITE Math** Pat is tossing a coin in the air. Predict how it will land. **Explain.**

8 Multiply by 1-Digit Numbers

The Big Idea Multiplication of multi-digit whole numbers is based on place value and the basic multiplication facts.

Investigate

Suppose you have 15 acres of land. You want to plant at least 2 acres of each crop shown in the bar graph. Decide how many acres of each crop you will plant. How many bushels of each crop will be produced?

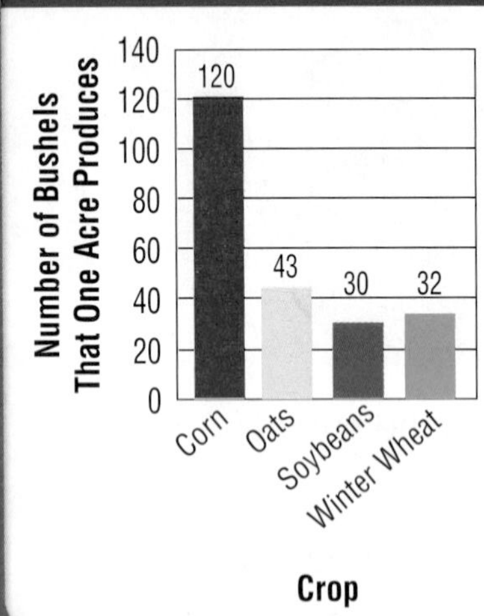

TEXAS FAST FACT

Texans eat about 70 quarts of popcorn per person every year.

GO ONLINE Technology
Student pages are available in the Student eBook.

Show What You Know

Check your understanding of important skills needed for success in Chapter 8.

▶ Model and Record Multiplication of 2-Digit by 1-Digit Numbers

Record the product.

1.

2.

3.

4.

▶ Regroup Hundreds and Tens

Regroup. Write the missing numbers.

5. 48 tens = ■ hundreds 8 tens

6. 7 hundreds 21 tens = ■ hundreds ■ tens

7. 5 hundreds ■ tens = 6 hundreds 8 tens

8. 2 hundreds ■ tens = 3 hundreds 5 tens

▶ Partial Products

Find each partial product.

11. 8×17 **12.** 5×41 **13.** 3×260 **14.** 4×35

15. 2×79 **16.** 6×47 **17.** 7×52 **18.** 9×18

VOCABULARY POWER

CHAPTER VOCABULARY

estimate
partial product
regroup

WARM-UP WORDS

partial product a method of multiplying in which the ones, tens, hundreds, and so on are multiplied separately and then the products are added together

estimate find an answer that is close to the exact amount

regroup exchange amounts of equal value to rename a number

LESSON 1

Multiply 2-Digit Numbers

OBJECTIVE: Multiply 2-digit numbers by 1-digit numbers.

Quick Review

The model represents as the sum of the two partial products shown. Write the product.

Learn

PROBLEM Three fourth-grade classes at Pine Crest Elementary are going on a field trip to the Texas Sports Hall of Fame in Waco. Each class has 24 students. How many total students are going on the field trip?

Example 1 Use place value and regrouping.

Multiply. 3×24 **Estimate.** $3 \times 20 = 60$

THINK	RECORD
Step 1 Multiply the ones. 3×4 ones $= 12$ ones Regroup the 12 ones.	$\begin{array}{r} \scriptstyle 1 \\ 24 \\ \times\ 3 \\ \hline 2 \end{array}$ Regroup 12 ones as 1 ten 2 ones.
Step 2 Multiply the tens. 3×2 tens $= 6$ tens Add the regrouped ten. 6 tens + 1 ten = 7 tens	$\begin{array}{r} \scriptstyle 1 \\ 24 \\ \times\ 3 \\ \hline 72 \end{array}$

So, 72 students are going on the field trip. Since 72 is close to the estimate of 60, it is reasonable.

▲ The Texas Sports Hall of Fame preserves Texas sports history.

More Examples

A No regrouping

$$\begin{array}{r} 61 \\ \times\ 4 \\ \hline 244 \end{array}$$

B Partial products

$$\begin{array}{rl} 53 & \\ \times\ 7 & \\ \hline 21 & \leftarrow 7 \times 3 \text{ ones} = 21 \text{ ones} \\ +350 & \leftarrow 7 \times 5 \text{ hundreds} = 35 \text{ hundreds} \\ \hline 371 & \end{array}$$

Guided Practice

1. Explain how to find 6×47 by using place value.

TEKS 4.4D use multiplication to solve problems (no more than two digits times two digits without technology).
also **4.5A, 4.5B, 4.15A, 4.15B, 4.16B**

Estimate. Then find the product.

2. $\begin{array}{r} 21 \\ \times\ 4 \\ \hline \end{array}$ **3.** $\begin{array}{r} 15 \\ \times\ 3 \\ \hline \end{array}$ **4.** $\begin{array}{r} 17 \\ \times\ 6 \\ \hline \end{array}$ ✓**5.** $\begin{array}{r} 42 \\ \times\ 3 \\ \hline \end{array}$ ✓**6.** $\begin{array}{r} 59 \\ \times\ 4 \\ \hline \end{array}$

7. **TALK Math** **Explain** the difference between multiplying using place value and multiplying using partial products.

Independent Practice and Problem Solving

Estimate. Then find the product.

8. $\begin{array}{r} 41 \\ \times\ 8 \\ \hline \end{array}$ **9.** $\begin{array}{r} 33 \\ \times\ 5 \\ \hline \end{array}$ **10.** $\begin{array}{r} 55 \\ \times\ 7 \\ \hline \end{array}$ **11.** $\begin{array}{r} 26 \\ \times\ 6 \\ \hline \end{array}$ **12.** $\begin{array}{r} 37 \\ \times\ 9 \\ \hline \end{array}$

13. 4×53 **14.** 6×28 **15.** 9×19 **16.** 5×78 **17.** 8×94

USE DATA For 18–19, use the table.

18. If the Texas Rangers win twice as many games in 2010 as they won in 2005, how many games will they win?

19. If the Seattle Mariners played the same number of games but won twice as many as the number shown, how many more wins would the team have than losses?

American League West 2005 Wild Card Standings

TEAM	WIN	LOSSES
Los Angeles Angels of Anaheim	95	67
Oakland Athletics	88	74
Texas Rangers	79	83
Seattle Mariners	69	93

20. **FAST FACT** In Game 5 of the 1999 NBA championship, Tim Duncan scored 31 points for the San Antonio Spurs. His team won the game with 16 more than twice as many points scored by Duncan. How many points did the Spurs score in all?

21. **WRITE Math** **Explain** how you could teach someone to multiply a 2-digit number by a 1-digit number using partial products.

Mixed Review and TAKS Prep

22. Estimate 7×122 by rounding to the nearest ten. (TEKS 4.5B, p. 186)

23. Tom and Rita's swim teams won 27 meets altogether. Rita's team won 3 more meets than Tom's. How many meets did each team win? (TEKS 4.14C, p. 106)

24. **TAKS Prep** Jeff bought 4 packages of balloons for a party. Each package has 36 balloons. How many balloons does Jeff have in all? (Obj. 1)

A 124 **C** 134

B 132 **D** 144

Extra Practice on page 216, Set A

LESSON 2

Multiply 3-Digit Numbers

OBJECTIVE: Multiply 3-digit numbers by 1-digit numbers.

Quick Review

1. 2×22
2. 2×15
3. 4×31
4. 3×54
5. 5×62

Learn

PROBLEM Nearly 675 gallons per minute erupt from the Clepsydra Geyser in Yellowstone National Park, in Wyoming. How many gallons of water erupt in 3 minutes?

Example **Multiply.** 3×675 **Estimate.** $3 \times 700 = 2,100$

	THINK	RECORD
Step 1	Multiply the ones. 3×5 ones = 15 ones Regroup the 15 ones.	$\begin{array}{r} {\scriptstyle 1} \\ 675 \\ \times\ \ 3 \\ \hline 5 \end{array}$ Regroup 15 ones as 1 ten 5 ones.
Step 2	Multiply the tens. 3×7 tens = 21 tens Add the regrouped ten. 21 tens + 1 ten = 22 tens Regroup the 22 tens.	$\begin{array}{r} {\scriptstyle 2\,1} \\ 675 \\ \times\ \ 3 \\ \hline 25 \end{array}$ Regroup 22 tens as 2 hundreds 2 tens.
Step 3	Multiply the hundreds. 3×6 hundreds = 18 hundreds Add the regrouped hundreds. 18 hundreds + 2 hundreds = 20 hundreds	$\begin{array}{r} {\scriptstyle 2\,1} \\ 675 \\ \times\ \ 3 \\ \hline 2,025 \end{array}$

So, nearly 2,025 gallons of water erupt in 3 minutes. Since 2,025 is close to the estimate of 2,100, it is reasonable.

More Examples

A No regrouping

$\begin{array}{r} 234 \\ \times\ \ 2 \\ \hline 468 \end{array}$

B Regrouping

$\begin{array}{r} {\scriptstyle 4\,7} \\ 359 \\ \times\ \ 8 \\ \hline 2,872 \end{array}$

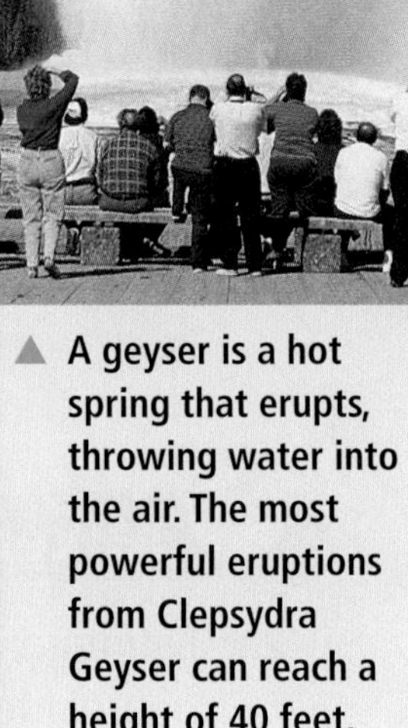

▲ A geyser is a hot spring that erupts, throwing water into the air. The most powerful eruptions from Clepsydra Geyser can reach a height of 40 feet.

Guided Practice

1. Copy each step of the problem at the right. Then tell what is happening in each step.

Step 1 $\begin{array}{r} {\scriptstyle 2} \\ 274 \\ \times\ \ 6 \\ \hline 4 \end{array}$ **Step 2** $\begin{array}{r} {\scriptstyle 4\,2} \\ 274 \\ \times\ \ 6 \\ \hline 44 \end{array}$ **Step 3** $\begin{array}{r} {\scriptstyle 4\,2} \\ 274 \\ \times\ \ 6 \\ \hline 1,644 \end{array}$

TEKS 4.4D use multiplication to solve problems (no more than two digits times two digits without technology).
also **4.5A, 4.5B, 4.14A, 4.15A, 4.15B, 4.16B**

Estimate. Then find the product.

2. 124×2
3. 183×4
4. 229×7
5. 858×6
6. 294×5

7. **TALK Math** **Explain** how many digits the product 4×861 will have.

Independent Practice and Problem Solving

Estimate. Then find the product.

8. 243×2
9. 714×3
10. 512×8
11. 445×7
12. 789×9

13. 3×827
14. 4×836
15. 6×315
16. 8×192
17. 5×286

Algebra Find the missing digits.

18. $\blacksquare \times 2\blacksquare3 = 486$
19. $9 \times \blacksquare3\blacksquare = 5{,}688$
20. $2 \times \blacksquare67 = 1{,}134$

USE DATA For 21–23, use the graph.

21. Which geyser's maximum eruption height is about 2 times as high as that of Round Geyser?

22. **What if** Steamboat is added to the graph? Its maximum eruption height is about 2 times as high as that of Old Faithful. Order the geysers from least to greatest maximum eruption height.

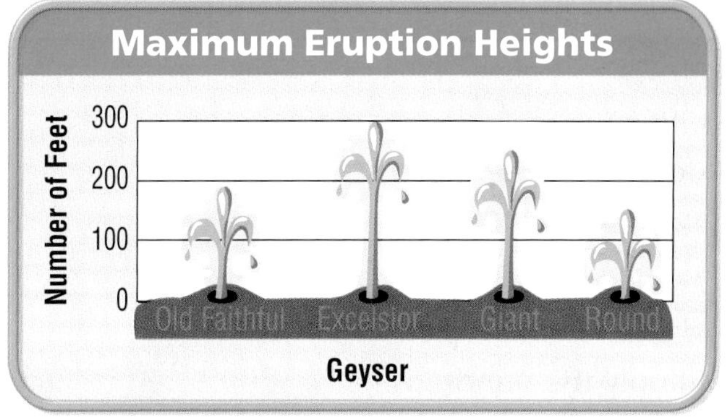

23. **Pose a Problem** Look back at Problem 21. Write a new problem by exchanging the known and the unknown information.

24. **WRITE Math** **Sense or Nonsense** Joe says the greatest possible 3-digit by 1-digit product is 111. Does Joe's statement make sense? **Explain.**

Mixed Review and TAKS Prep

25. Rachel baked 3 batches of 36 cookies. How many cookies did she bake in all? (TEKS 4.4D, p. 206)

26. Find the missing number. (TEKS 4.6A, p. 160)

$$8 \times \blacksquare = 56$$

27. **TAKS Prep** One box of nails holds 255 nails. How many nails are in 7 boxes? (Obj. 1)

A 1,530 **C** 1,785
B 1,715 **D** 2,040

Extra Practice on page 216, Set B

LESSON 3

Multiply with Zeros

OBJECTIVE: Multiply numbers with zeros by 1-digit numbers.

Quick Review

Lynn has 127 stickers. Jose has 3 times as many stickers as Lynn has. How many stickers does Jose have?

Learn

PROBLEM Marisol's family drives to visit her grandmother each summer and winter. The distance one way is 804 miles. What is the total number of miles her family drives to see her grandmother each year?

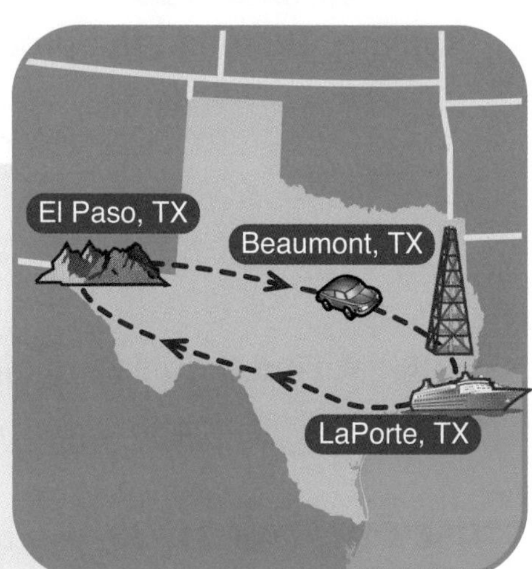

Example

Multiply. 4 × 804 **Estimate.** 4 × 800 = 3,200

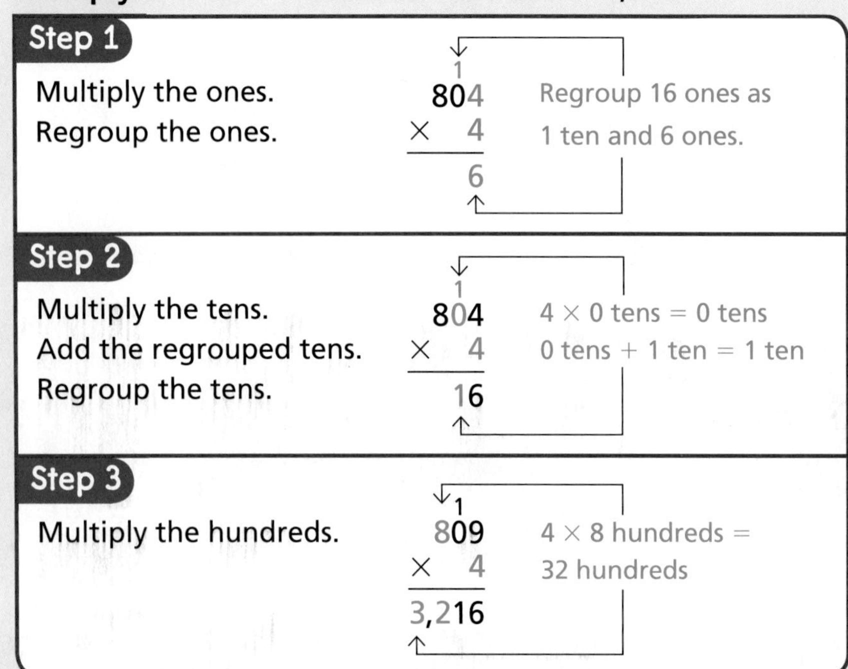

Step 1
Multiply the ones.
Regroup the ones.
1
804
× 4
6
Regroup 16 ones as
1 ten and 6 ones.
Step 2
Multiply the tens.
Add the regrouped tens.
Regroup the tens.
1
804
× 4
16
4 × 0 tens = 0 tens
0 tens + 1 ten = 1 ten
Step 3
Multiply the hundreds.
1
809
× 4
3,216
4 × 8 hundreds =
32 hundreds

ERROR ALERT

In Step 2, the 3 tens above the 0 tens have to be added after multiplying 4 by 0 tens.

So, Marisol's family drives 3,216 miles each year to visit her grandmother. Since 3,216 is close to the estimate of 3,200, it is reasonable.

More Examples

A Multiply a 2-digit number

$$\begin{array}{r} 40 \\ \times\ 9 \\ \hline 360 \end{array}$$

B Multiply money amounts

$$\begin{array}{r} \overset{2}{} \\ \$708 \\ \times\quad 3 \\ \hline \$2,124 \end{array}$$

Multiply the same way you multiply whole numbers. Write the dollar sign in the product.

TEKS 4.4D use multiplication to solve problems (no more than two digits times two digits without technology). *also* **4.14A, 4.15A, 4.15B, 4.16B**

Guided Practice

1. Copy the problem at the right. Multiply the ones, then regroup. Multiply the tens. Do you have to regroup? Then multiply the hundreds. What is the product? $\begin{array}{r} 303 \\ \times \quad 6 \\ \hline \end{array}$

Estimate. Then find the product.

2. $\begin{array}{r} 103 \\ \times \quad 6 \\ \hline \end{array}$
3. $\begin{array}{r} 720 \\ \times \quad 8 \\ \hline \end{array}$
4. $\begin{array}{r} \$309 \\ \times \quad 2 \\ \hline \end{array}$
5. $\begin{array}{r} \$406 \\ \times \quad 5 \\ \hline \end{array}$
6. $\begin{array}{r} \$608 \\ \times \quad 4 \\ \hline \end{array}$
7. TALK Math **Explain** how you can find 6×240.

Independent Practice and Problem Solving

Estimate. Then find the product.

8. 3×130
9. 7×201
10. $2 \times \$506$
11. 4×850
12. $6 \times \$402$
13. 9×704
14. $5 \times \$905$
15. 4×280
16. 3×550
17. $8 \times \$809$

USE DATA For 18–19, use the picture.

18. Marisol took the elevator from the lobby to the observation deck and back twice. What is the total number of feet she traveled?

19 A builder wants to build a skyscraper that is 100 feet less than 3 times as tall as the San Jacinto Monument. What will be the height of the skyscraper?

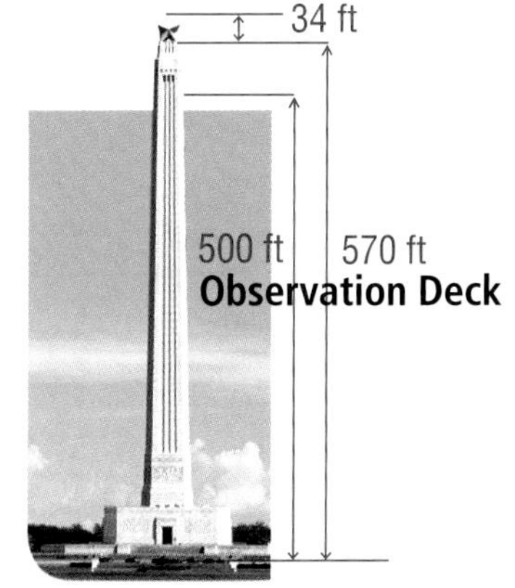

San Jacinto Monument

20. **Reasoning** Can two different multiplication problems have the same estimated product? **Explain** your thinking.

21. WRITE Math **What's the Question?** Don, Kay, and Jane each have 3 rolls of film. They can take 24 pictures with each roll. The answer is 216 pictures.

Mixed Review and TAKS Prep

22. Greg tosses a coin 5 times and gets tails each time. How likely is he to get tails if he tosses again? (Grade 3 TEKS 3.13C)

23. Kim buys 4 packs of paper. Each pack has 512 sheets. About how many sheets does she buy in all? (TEKS 4.4D, p. 208)

24. **TAKS Prep** Liz bought 2 tennis rackets for \$109 each. How much did she spend? (Obj. 1)

A \$209 **C** \$218

B \$211 **D** \$118

Extra Practice on page 216, Set C

LESSON 4

Choose a Method

OBJECTIVE: Practice multiplication by 1-digit numbers.

Quick Review

1. 7×3
2. 8×9
3. 3×57
4. 9×82
5. 6×404

Learn

PROBLEM Each year the International Space Station stores meals weighing a total of 9,072 kilograms for its crew. How many kilograms of meals will it store over 4 years?

Example Use pencil and paper.

Multiply. $4 \times 9{,}072$ **Estimate.** $4 \times 9{,}000 = 36{,}000$

Step 1

Multiply the ones.

$$\begin{array}{r} 9{,}072 \\ \times \quad 4 \\ \hline 8 \end{array}$$

Step 2

Multiply the tens.
Regroup the tens.

$$\begin{array}{r} \scriptstyle 2 \\ 9{,}072 \\ \times \quad 4 \\ \hline 88 \end{array}$$

Regroup 28 tens as 2 hundreds 8 tens.

Step 3

Multiply the hundreds.
Add the regrouped hundreds.

$$\begin{array}{r} \scriptstyle 2 \\ 9{,}072 \\ \times \quad 4 \\ \hline 288 \end{array}$$

4 x 0 hundreds = 0 hundreds
0 hundreds + 2 hundreds = 2 hundreds

Step 4

Multiply the thousands.

$$\begin{array}{r} \scriptstyle 2 \\ 9{,}072 \\ \times \quad 4 \\ \hline 36{,}288 \end{array}$$

So, 36,288 kilograms of meals will be stored over 4 years.

▲ Food flown on space missions and eaten on the International Space Station is developed at the Space Food Systems Lab at the Johnson Space Center in Houston.

In Step 3, the 2 hundreds above the 0 hundreds must be added after multiplying 4 by 0 hundreds

More Examples

A Use mental math.

$4 \times 1{,}102$

Think: Solve a simpler problem.

$4 \times 2 = 8$ and $4 \times 1{,}100 = 4{,}400$

$8 + 4{,}400 = 4{,}408$

B Use a calculator.

$8 \times 5{,}619$

1

Enter

8 X 5619 =
44952

Estimate to check. $8 \times 6{,}000 = 48{,}000$

TEKS 4.4D use multiplication to solve problems (no more than two digits times two digits without technology).
also 4.14A, 4.14C, 4.14D, 4.15A, 4.15B, 4.16B

Guided Practice

1. How can you use mental math to find $6 \times 2{,}025$?

Find the product. Write the method you used.

2. 40×3
3. 310×6
4. $2{,}647 \times 8$
5. $5{,}005 \times 5$
6. $2{,}231 \times 4$

7. **TALK Math** Explain which method would you use to multiply $2 \times 5{,}050$.

Independent Practice and Problem Solving

Find the product. Write the method you used.

8. 120×5
9. 504×4
10. $2{,}500 \times 6$
11. $5{,}005 \times 7$
12. $6{,}541 \times 9$

Algebra **Find the missing number.**

13. $7 \times 23\blacksquare = 1{,}638$
14. $\blacksquare \times 713 = 4{,}278$
15. $9 \times 622 = \blacksquare{,}598$

16. Each of the 7 members of a 7 day space shuttle flight eats 25 servings of fresh food. How many total servings of fresh food does the crew eat?

17. **WRITE Math** **What's the Error?** Keisha says that $4 \times 1{,}316$ is 4,244. Describe and correct her error.

18. **Reasoning** Gene used addition to find the product 4×365. Show how Gene found the product. **Explain** why it might be easy to make a mistake by using this method.

19. The seven crew members each eat 34 servings of rehydratable food, or food that needs water added to it, when following a 7-day shuttle menu. How many total servings would the crew eat during a 14-day mission?

Mixed Review and TAKS Prep

20. Find the missing number.

    $12 \times \blacksquare = 96$ (TEKS 4.6A, p. 126)

21. Roy estimates that 8×537 is about 5,000. What is a more reasonable estimate? (TEKS 4.5A, p. 186)

22. **TAKS Prep** What is 7×611? **Explain** how you solved the problem. (Obj. 1)

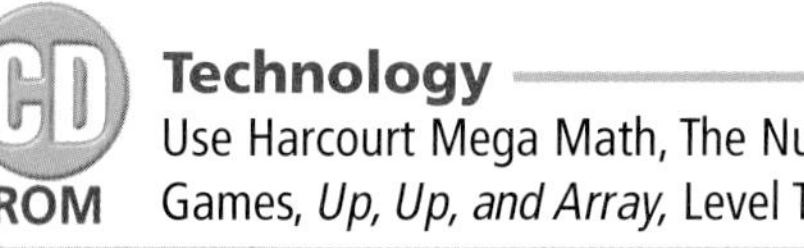

Technology
Use Harcourt Mega Math, The Number Games, *Up, Up, and Array,* Level T.

Extra Practice on page 216, Set D

OBJECTIVE: Solve problems by using the skill *evaluate reasonableness*.

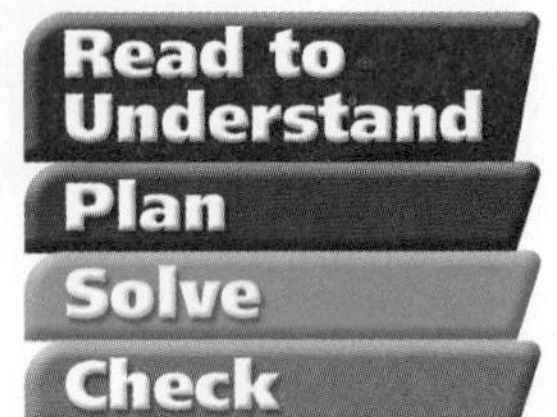

Use the Skill

PROBLEM The average person eats 160 bowls of cereal a year. How many bowls of cereal does a family of 4 eat in a year?

Start by choosing an operation. To find the answer to this question, you must multiply.

You can use basic facts to find compatible numbers to estimate 4×160.

Think: It is easy to multiply 4×200 and 4×120.

$4 \times 200 = 800$ $\qquad$ $4 \times 120 = 480$

So, the answer is between 480 and 800.

Find 4×160.

$$\begin{array}{r} \overset{2}{1}60 \\ \times \quad 4 \\ \hline 640 \end{array}$$

Now decide whether your answer is reasonable.

Since 640 is between 480 and 800, it is a reasonable answer.

So, a family of 4 eats 640 bowls of cereal a year.

- What other way could you check to see whether your answer is reasonable and makes sense?

TALK Math

How can you use estimation to evaluate the reasonableness of answers to 3-digit by 1-digit multiplication problems?

Think and Discuss

Solve the problem. Then evaluate the reasonableness of your answer. Explain.

a. Mark has 647 baseball cards. He sells 40 of them at a garage sale and gives 15 of them to a friend. How many cards does Mark have left?

b. Judi has 9 boxes of balloons. Each box has 125 balloons. How many balloons does Judi have in all?

c. Morgan's Greenhouse has plants arranged in 7 rows with 110 plants in each row. How many plants are there?

TEKS 4.16B justify why an answer is reasonable and explain the solution process. *also* **4.4D, 4.5B, 4.14A, 4.14B, 4.14C, 4.15A, 4.15B, 4.16B**

Guided Problem Solving

Solve the problem. Then evaluate the reasonableness of your answer.

1. More than 294 million people in the United States start the day with a bowl of cereal. How many bowls of cereal are eaten in the United States each week?

   First, decide which operation to use.

   Think: 7×294

   Next, solve the problem.

   Then, decide whether your answer is reasonable.

2. **What if** you were asked how many bowls of cereal people in the United States eat in 2 weeks? Would an answer of 6,174 million bowls be reasonable? Why or why not?

3. The Franklins have a breakfast budget. Each week, they spend \$5 for cereal, \$7 for bacon, \$4 for bread, \$2 for eggs, and \$3 for juice. How much will they spend on breakfast in 4 weeks?

Mixed Applications

4. Each month, the Franklins record the total amount spent on breakfast. If they spend the same amount each month, after 3 months, they've spent \$252. Use this information to make a bar graph showing each monthly total for 6 months. Explain why your graph is reasonable.

5. Paul's father is a salesman. He drove 1,235 miles the second week, 987 miles the third week, and 845 miles the fourth week. During the four-week period, he drove a total of 3,742 miles. How far did he drive the first week?

6. Matt wants to fence a square corner of the yard for his dog. One side of the square is 41 feet long. How much fencing does Matt need?

7. The average high temperature in a Mojave Desert town is 108°F. The average low is 33°F. How many degrees warmer is the high temperature than the low temperature?

8. WRITE Math A group of 6 students each gave equal amounts to purchase a gift. The change from the purchase was \$12. How much change should each student receive? **Explain.**

▲ The world's tallest thermometer is in Baker, California. Its height of 134 feet represents the highest temperature recorded (134°F) in that part of the Mojave Desert.

Extra Practice

Set A Estimate. Then find the product. (pp. 206–207)

1. $\begin{array}{r} 37 \\ \times\ 5 \\ \hline \end{array}$
2. $\begin{array}{r} 48 \\ \times\ 6 \\ \hline \end{array}$
3. $\begin{array}{r} 59 \\ \times\ 7 \\ \hline \end{array}$
4. $\begin{array}{r} 62 \\ \times\ 6 \\ \hline \end{array}$
5. $\begin{array}{r} 73 \\ \times\ 7 \\ \hline \end{array}$
6. 5×72
7. 3×41
8. 8×28
9. 9×37
10. 4×16
11. Carlos baked 7 batches of cookies for his school's bake sale. Each batch made 28 cookies. How many cookies did Carlos bake?
12. Leanne walked 5 miles every day for two weeks. How many miles did she walk?

Set B Estimate. Then find the product. (pp. 208–209)

1. $\begin{array}{r} 335 \\ \times\ \ 6 \\ \hline \end{array}$
2. $\begin{array}{r} 427 \\ \times\ \ 7 \\ \hline \end{array}$
3. $\begin{array}{r} 634 \\ \times\ \ 9 \\ \hline \end{array}$
4. $\begin{array}{r} 693 \\ \times\ \ 8 \\ \hline \end{array}$
5. $\begin{array}{r} 746 \\ \times\ \ 4 \\ \hline \end{array}$
6. 3×683
7. 6×729
8. 4×935
9. 5×826
10. 9×287
11. 7×245
12. 6×472
13. 5×774
14. 7×384
15. 8×261
16. Ms. Boyd drives a total of 247 miles to and from work each week. How far does she drive in 6 weeks?

Set C Estimate. Then find the product. (pp. 210–211)

1. 4×507
2. $3 \times \$760$
3. 5×603
4. 8×209
5. $6 \times \$490$
6. 9×380
7. 7×708
8. $4 \times \$601$
9. 6×804
10. 3×700
11. Myra has 403 stamps. Her sister Rebecca has 5 times as many stamps as Myra. How many stamps does Rebecca have?

Set D Find the product. Write the method you used. (pp. 212–213)

1. 3×405
2. $6 \times 3{,}009$
3. $5 \times 4{,}050$
4. $9 \times 3{,}057$
5. 7×902
6. $8 \times 2{,}176$
7. $4 \times 7{,}083$
8. 6×370
9. $7 \times 3{,}006$
10. $3 \times 8{,}097$
11. $5 \times 3{,}418$
12. $7 \times 3{,}481$
13. $6 \times 8{,}735$
14. $4 \times 3{,}219$
15. $8 \times 6{,}437$
16. Amir ordered 750 packages of bottled water for the season for the track team. If each case has 24 bottles, how many bottles of water does he have?
17. Emily read an average of 144 pages each week during summer break. How many pages did she read in all over 8 weeks of break?

CD ROM **Technology**
Use Harcourt Mega Math, The Number Games, *Up, Up, and Array,* Level J.

PRACTICE GAME

Multiplication Marathon

On Your Mark!

2 players

Get Set!

- Number cards (0–9, four of each)
- 2 coins

START

WATER

FINISH

GO!

- Players shuffle the number cards and place them facedown in a stack.
- Each player selects a different coin and places the coin on START.
- Players take turns drawing three number cards from the stack.
- Players use the cards to make and solve a 2-digit by 1-digit multiplication problem.
- The player with the greater product moves his or her coin one space.
- Once both players reach the WATER table, each draws four number cards and makes and solves a 3-digit by 1-digit multiplication problem.
- The first player to reach the FINISH line wins.

Chapter 8 Review/Test

Check Concepts

1. Explain how to use place value and regrouping to find the product 8×46. (TEKS 4.4D, p. 206)
2. Show how to use partial products to find the product 8×46. (TEKS 4.4D, p. 206)

Check Skills

Estimate. Then find the product. (TEKS 4.4D, pp. 206–207, 208–209, 210–211)

3. 46×5
4. 367×6
5. 564×4
6. 98×9
7. 726×8
8. 305×3
9. 62×7
10. 508×6
11. $\$74 \times 9$
12. $\$307 \times 9$

Find the product. Write the method you used. (TEKS 4.4D, pp. 212–213)

13. 58×4
14. 376×6
15. $\$208 \times 4$
16. 47×3
17. 277×8
18. $\$39 \times 7$
19. $\$508 \times 4$
20. 468×6
21. 608×3
22. 56×9
23. 380×7
24. 492×6
25. 36×7
26. $\$650 \times 4$
27. $\$509 \times 7$
28. $3 \times 3{,}004$
29. $3 \times 1{,}467$
30. $9 \times 2{,}832$
31. $4 \times 1{,}203$

Check Problem Solving

Solve. (TEKS 4.16B, pp. 214–215)

32. Jamie makes bead necklaces. She bought 6 bags of beads with 175 beads in each bag. Is it reasonable to say that Jamie bought about 1,000 beads? Why or why not?

33. WRITE Math Alex has a recipe for 3 dozen cookies. If he triples the recipe, he says he will have enough cookies for 100 people. **Explain** how Alex knows that his answer is reasonable.

GO ONLINE **Technology** Use *Online Assessment.*

Enrich • Distributive Property

Run for Fun

Each student in the Running Club plans to run for 35 minutes, 5 days a week. How many total minutes will each student run per week?

You can use mental math and the Distributive Property of Multiplication to find the product. The property states that multiplying a sum by a number is the same as multiplying each addend by the number and then adding the products.

Find 5×35.

$5 \times 35 = 5 \times (30 + 5)$ Think: $35 = 30 + 5$

$= (5 \times 30) + (5 \times 5)$ Use the Distributive Property.

$= 150 + 25$

$= 175$

So, each student will run a total of 175 minutes per week.

Warm Up

A Find 7×94.

Think: $94 = 90 + 4$

$7 \times 94 = 7 \times (90 + 4)$

$= (7 \times 90) + (7 \times 4)$

$= 630 + 28$

$= 658$

B Find 3×132.

Think: $132 = 100 + 30 + 2$

$3 \times 132 = 3 \times (100 + 30 + 2)$

$= (3 \times 100) + (3 \times 30) + (3 \times 2)$

$= 300 + 90 + 6$

$= 396$

Work Out

Use mental math and the Distributive Property to find the product.

1. 6×31 **2.** 4×92 **3.** 3×124 **4.** 5×318

5. 4×212 **6.** 5×240 **7.** $8 \times 2{,}005$ **8.** $6 \times 4{,}052$

9. Monica has dance class twice a week. Each class is 55 minutes long. How many minutes does Monica spend in class each week?

10. The Swim Club has 14 members. Each day, they swim 4 laps to warm up. How many warm-up laps do the members swim each week?

Cool Down

WRITE Math **Explain** why using the Distributive Property makes finding a product easier.

Getting Ready for the TAKS
Chapters 1–8

Number, Operation, and Quantitative Reasoning TAKS Obj. 1

Get the information you need.

See Item 1. To solve, find the price of one adult ticket. Then multiply to find the price of three tickets.

1. The Andersons are going on a whale-watching tour. A child ticket costs $\$89$ and an adult ticket costs $\$199$. If the Andersons buy 3 adult tickets, how much will they pay in all?

   A $\$267$

   B $\$288$

   C $\$497$

   D $\$597$

2. Which of these is the number 1,203,000?

   F One million, two hundred and three thousand, one hundred

   G One million, two hundred three thousand

   H One million, two hundred thousand, three hundred

   J One million, two hundred three

3. WRITE Math Elena says that the best estimate of $374 + 531$ is 800. Do you agree? **Explain.**

Patterns, Relationships, and Algebraic Thinking TAKS Obj. 2

4. Kate is baking 3 batches of cookies and 4 batches of brownies. She needs 2 sticks of butter for each batch. Which number sentence shows how many sticks of butter Kate needs?

   A $7 \times 2 = ■$

   B $7 + 2 = ■$

   C $3 \times 2 = ■$

   D $12 \times 2 = ■$

5. The table shows about how many Slovenian tolars you would receive in 2005 for different amounts of U.S. dollars.

Number of Tolars			
Dollars	1	2	3
Tolars	193	386	■

   How should you find how many tolars you would receive for 3 U.S. dollars?

   F Multiply 193 by 3.

   G Divide 386 by 2.

   H Add 193 and 193.

   J Multiply 386 by 3.

6. WRITE Math **Explain** how to use a related division sentence to solve the equation.

$$7 \times ■ = 42$$

Geometry and Spatial Reasoning

TAKS Obj. 3

7. Tiffany drew a triangle with three equal sides.

Which statement about Tiffany's triangle is true?

A It has at least one right angle.

B It has at least two right angles.

C It is an equilateral triangle.

D It is a right triangle.

8. Carl drew a cylinder. Which could be the figure that Carl drew?

F

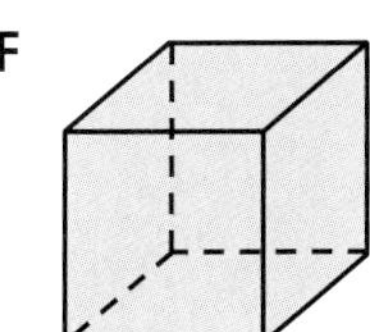

G

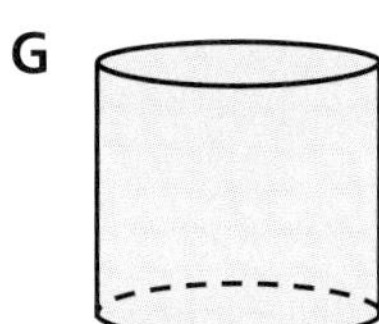

H

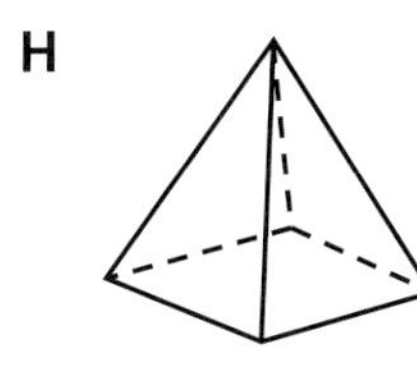

J

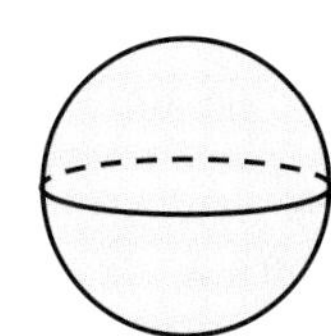

9. WRITE Math **Explain** the difference between a pentagon and a hexagon.

Measurement TAKS Obj. 4

10. David's bedroom is a square.

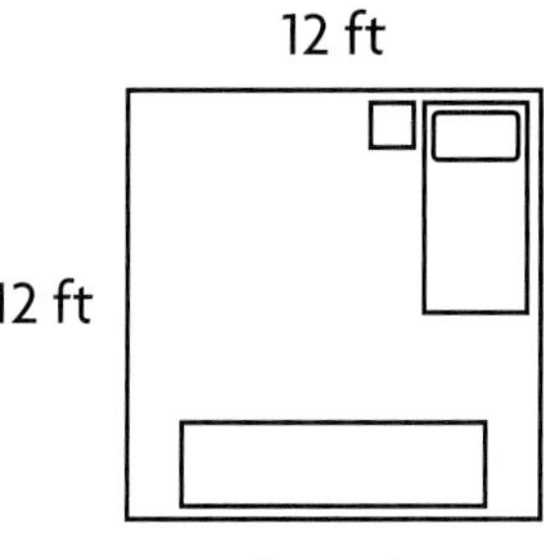

David's Bedroom

What is the perimeter of David's bedroom?

A 12 feet

B 24 feet

C 48 feet

D 144 feet

11. Mrs. Monroe left the house this morning at the time shown on the clock.

At what time did she leave her house?

F 6:07 A.M.

G 6:35 A.M.

H 7:06 A.M.

J 7:30 A.M.

12. WRITE Math Maya says she lives 2 meters from her school. Do you agree? **Explain**.

9 Multiply by 2-Digit Numbers

The Big Idea Multiplication of multi-digit whole numbers is based on place value and the basic multiplication facts.

Ellis Island, in New York Harbor, was the first stop for many European immigrants to the U.S. between 1892 and 1954. However, more than 130,000 immigrants arrived in the U.S. in Galveston.

Investigate

The sculpture in the photo is called *American Flag of Faces.* If you look at it from one angle, you see faces of immigrants. From another angle, you see a flag. As you walk, what you see changes from faces to a flag and back again. The sculpture has 13 rows and 29 columns of blocks, with 2 photos on each block. How can you break apart 13 × 29 to find the number of blocks in sculpture?

American Flag of Faces
by Pablo Delano

Height: 9 feet
Width: 16 feet $6\frac{3}{4}$ inches
Depth: 3 feet 2 inches

- The sculpture is made of clear plastic blocks. As a viewer moves, the flag appears to be waving.

Technology
Student pages are available in the Student eBook.

Show What You Know

Check your understanding of important skills needed for success in Chapter 9.

▶ Estimate Products

Estimate the product.

1. $\begin{array}{r} 14 \\ \times\ 7 \\ \hline \end{array}$
2. $\begin{array}{r} 31 \\ \times\ 6 \\ \hline \end{array}$
3. $\begin{array}{r} 45 \\ \times\ 5 \\ \hline \end{array}$
4. $\begin{array}{r} 88 \\ \times\ 3 \\ \hline \end{array}$
5. $\begin{array}{r} 604 \\ \times\ \ \ 8 \\ \hline \end{array}$
6. $\begin{array}{r} 555 \\ \times\ \ \ 3 \\ \hline \end{array}$
7. $\begin{array}{r} 119 \\ \times\ \ \ 4 \\ \hline \end{array}$
8. $\begin{array}{r} 353 \\ \times\ \ \ 9 \\ \hline \end{array}$

▶ Distributive Property

Find the product.

9\.

10\. 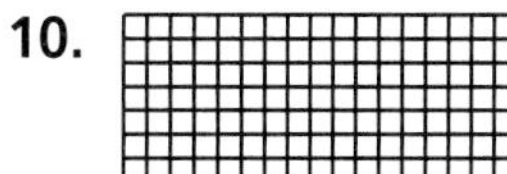

11\. 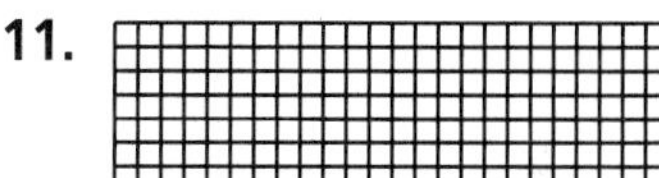

▶ Multiply 2-, 3-, and 4-Digit Numbers by 1-Digit Numbers

Estimate. Then find the product.

12. $\begin{array}{r} 29 \\ \times\ 8 \\ \hline \end{array}$
13. $\begin{array}{r} 726 \\ \times\ \ \ 4 \\ \hline \end{array}$
14. $\begin{array}{r} 87 \\ \times\ 5 \\ \hline \end{array}$
15. $\begin{array}{r} 858 \\ \times\ \ \ 3 \\ \hline \end{array}$
16. $\begin{array}{r} 317 \\ \times\ \ \ 5 \\ \hline \end{array}$
17. $\begin{array}{r} 4{,}274 \\ \times\ \ \ \ \ 7 \\ \hline \end{array}$
18. $\begin{array}{r} 506 \\ \times\ \ \ 9 \\ \hline \end{array}$
19. $\begin{array}{r} 3{,}108 \\ \times\ \ \ \ \ 6 \\ \hline \end{array}$

VOCABULARY POWER

CHAPTER VOCABULARY

addend
Distributive Property
multiple
partial product
product

WARM-UP WORDS

multiple the product of two counting numbers is a multiple of each of those numbers

Distributive Property the property that states that multiplying a sum by a number is the same as multiplying each addend by the number and then adding the products

partial product a method of multiplying in which the ones, tens, hundreds, and so on are multiplied separately and then the products are added together

MENTAL MATH
Multiplication Patterns

OBJECTIVE: Use a basic fact and a pattern to multiply mentally by multiples of 10, 100, and 1,000.

Quick Review

1. 9 × 12
2. 7 × 6
3. 8 × 11
4. 9 × 9
5. 10 × 4

Learn

PROBLEM The actual length of an adult bumblebee is about 12 millimeters long. The photo shows part of the bee under a microscope at 10 times its actual size. What would the length of the bee appear to be at a magnification of 100 times its actual size?

Example 1 **Multiply.** 12 × 100

Use what you know about 1-digit multiplication to help you multiply by 2-digit numbers. The number lines show repeated addition.

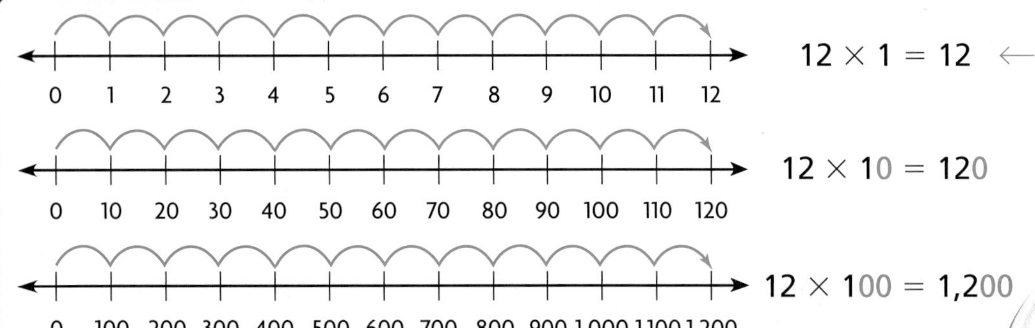

So, the bumblebee would appear to be 1,200 millimeters long.

• What pattern do you see in the number sentences?

Math Idea
The number of zeros in the factors should match the number of zeros in the product, unless the product of the basic fact has a 0.

More Examples

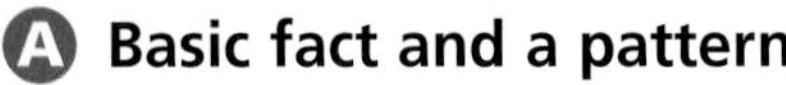

A Basic fact and a pattern

6 × 9 = 54 ← basic fact
60 × 90 = 5,400
60 × 900 = 54,000

B Basic fact with a zero and a pattern

10 × 10 = 100 ← basic fact
10 × 100 = 1,000
10 × 1,000 = 10,000

Guided Practice

1. What product does this number line show? Use it to find 12 × 20 and 12 × 200.

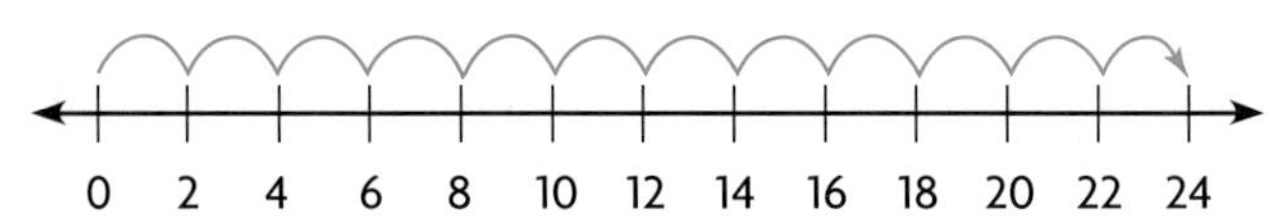

TEKS 4.6B use patterns to multiply by 10 and 100. *also* **4.4B, 4.4C, 4.4D, 4.14A, 4.15A, 4.15B, 4.16A**

Use patterns and mental math to find the product.

2. 10×400
3. 11×60
4. 12×900
5. $11 \times 1{,}000$
6. $12 \times 6{,}000$

7. TALK Math **Explain** how to find $11 \times 4{,}000$ by using basic facts and patterns.

Independent Practice and Problem Solving

Use patterns and mental math to find the product.

8. 11×50
9. 10×20
10. 12×700
11. 12×600
12. $11 \times 8{,}000$
13. $30 \times 6{,}000$
14. 40×900
15. $10 \times 5{,}000$
16. 70×80
17. $20 \times 3{,}000$

Algebra **Copy and complete the tables by using mental math.**

18. 1 roll = 50 dimes

Rolls	20	30	40	50	60
Dimes	1,000	■	■	■	■

19. 1 roll = 40 quarters

Rolls	20	30	40	50	60
Quarters	800	■	■	■	■

	×	6	70	800	9,000
20.	60	360	■	■	■
21.	70	■	4,900	■	■

	×	6	70	800	9,000
22.	80	■	■	64,000	■
23.	90	■	■	■	810,000

USE DATA For 24–25, use the table.

24. **What if** you wanted to magnify a carpenter bee 9,000 times? What would the length be?

25. If you magnified a termite 4,000 times and a wasp 3,000 times, which insect would appear longer? How much longer?

Insect Lengths

Insect	Length (in mm)
Carpenter Bee	19
Fire Ant	4
Termite	12
Wasp	15

26. **Reasoning** How can you use what you know about 1-digit multiplication patterns to multiply by a 2-digit number?

27. WRITE Math **Explain** what the product of any factor times 100 always has.

Mixed Review and TAKS Prep

28. Which is greater, 5,006,719 or 5,017,691? (TEKS 4.1A, p. 12)

29. There are 64 paper cups in a box. How many cups are in 8 boxes? (TEKS 4.4D, p. 190)

30. **TAKS Prep** How many zeros are in the product $50 \times 10{,}000$? (Obj. 1)

A 4
B 5
C 6
D 7

Extra Practice on page 246, Set A

LESSON 2

Multiply by Tens

OBJECTIVE: Multiply 2-digit numbers by multiples of ten using place value and mental math.

Quick Review

1. 0×10
2. 2×0
3. 3×10
4. 4×100
5. $5 \times 1{,}000$

Learn

PROBLEM Animation for a computer-drawn cartoon requires about 15 frames per second. How many frames would need to be drawn for a 60-second cartoon?

ONE WAY **Use place value.**

Multiply. 15×60

THINK	RECORD
Step 1 Multiply by the ones. Place a zero in the ones place.	$\begin{array}{r} 15 \\ \times\ 60 \\ \hline 0 \end{array}$ ← 0 ones × 15 = 0 ones
Step 2 Multiply by the tens.	$\begin{array}{r} 15 \\ \times\ 60 \\ \hline 900 \end{array}$ ← 6 tens × 15 = 90 tens

So, 900 frames would need to be drawn for a 60-second cartoon.

ANOTHER WAY **Use mental math.**

Multiply. 16×40

You can use halving and doubling.

Step 1	Step 2
Find half of 16 and double 40. $16 \div 2 = 8$ and $40 \times 2 = 80$	Multiply. $8 \times 80 = 640$

So, $16 \times 40 = 640$.

- What is another way that you can use halving and doubling to multiply 16×40?

Math Idea

When you multiply a whole number by a multiple of ten, the digit in the ones place of the product is always zero.

Guided Practice

1. Multiply 18×20. Tell what method you chose. What is the first step to find the product? What is the second step?

TEKS 4.6B use patterns to multiply by 10 and 100. *also* 4.4B, 4.4D, 4.4C, 4.14A, 4.15A, 4.15B, 4.16A

Choose a method. Then find the product.

2. 15×10 3. 19×20 4. 34×40 5. 78×60 6. 90×18

7. **TALK Math** **Explain** which method of multiplying 2-digit numbers by multiples of ten you prefer, and give reasons why.

Independent Practice and Problem Solving

Choose a method. Then find the product.

8. 55×70 9. 64×30 10. 49×50 11. 88×20 12. 89×60

13. 20×27 14. 50×46 15. 30×68 16. 92×90 17. 40×77

Algebra Find the missing digit.

18. $64 \times 40 = 2{,}56■$ 19. $29 \times 50 = 1{,}▲50$ 20. $3★ \times 47 = 1{,}410$

21. $●7 \times 90 = 5{,}130$ 22. $20 \times ■9 = 1{,}980$ 23. $20 \times 8▲ = 1{,}740$

USE DATA For 24–27, use the table.

Title	Date Released	Frames per Second
The Enchanted Drawing©	1900	20
Little Nemo©	1911	16
Snow White and the Seven Dwarfs©	1937	24
Pinocchio©	1940	19
The Flintstones™	1960–1966	24

Animated Productions

24. How many frames did it take to produce 50 seconds of *Pinocchio*?

25. Are there more frames in 10 seconds of *The Flintstones* or 14 seconds of *The Enchanted Drawing*?

26. Write a multiplication problem that shows the total number of frames in 30 seconds of Little Nemo.

27. **Pose a Problem** Look back at Problem 24. Write a similar problem by changing the animated production and the number.

28. **WRITE Math** **What's the Error?** Tanya says that the product of a multiple of ten and a multiple of ten will always have only one zero. Is she correct? **Explain.**

Mixed Review and TAKS Prep

29. What is the next number in the pattern? (TEKS 4.16A, p. 144)

$3, 6, 12, 24, ■$

30. If a pack of stickers costs \$3, how much will Pam pay for 14 packs of stickers? (TEKS 4.4D, p. 190)

31. **TAKS Prep** Jade jogs 10 miles a week. How far will she have jogged in a year? (Obj. 1)

A 520 miles

B 530 miles

C 600 miles

D 620 miles

Extra Practice on page 246, Set B

LESSON 3

MENTAL MATH

Estimate Products

OBJECTIVE: Estimate products by rounding factors or using compatible numbers and then finding the product mentally.

Quick Review

1. 60×20
2. 30×50
3. 90×10
4. 80×400
5. 70×600

Learn

PROBLEM If the Smith family opens the door of their refrigerator 266 times in one week, about how many times is it opened during one year?

The average number of times a refrigerator door is opened each day is 38 times.

ONE WAY **Use rounding and mental math.**

Estimate. 52×266

Step 1	Step 2
Round each factor. 52×266 ↓ ↓ 50×300 **Think:** There are 52 weeks in a year.	Use mental math. $5 \times 3 = 15$ $50 \times 30 = 1{,}500$ $50 \times 300 = 15{,}000$

So, the Smith family opens the refrigerator door about 15,000 times during one year.

- Will the actual number of times the refrigerator is opened in a year be greater than or less than 15,000? Explain.

Remember

To round a number:
- Find the place to which you want to round. Look at the digit to its right.
- If the digit is less than 5, the digit in the rounding place stays the same.
- If the digit is 5 or greater, the digit in the rounding place increases by 1.
- Change all digits to the right of the rounding place to 0.

ANOTHER WAY **Use compatible numbers and mental math.**

Compatible numbers are numbers that are easy to compute mentally.

Step 1	Step 2
52×266 ↓ ↓ 50×300 **Think:** 50×30 is easy to compute mentally.	Multiply. If $5 \times 3 = 15$ and $50 \times 30 = 1{,}500$ Then $50 \times 300 = 15{,}000$

More Examples **Estimate the products.**

A Nearest ten

$\$57 \times 83 \rightarrow \$60 \times 80 = \$4{,}800$

B Nearest hundred and nearest ten

$795 \times 26 \rightarrow 800 \times 30 = 24{,}000$

C Compatible numbers

$795 \times 26 \rightarrow 800 \times 25 = 20{,}000$

- Why are the products for rounding in Example B different from the products for compatible numbers in Example C?

TEKS 4.5B use strategies including rounding and compatible numbers to estimate solutions to multiplication and division problems. *also* **4.1A, 4.4D, 4.5A, 4.6B, 4.14A, 4.15A, 4.15B, 4.16B**

Guided Practice

1. To estimate the product 62×28 by rounding, how would you round the factors? What would the estimated product be?

Estimate the product. Choose the method.

2. 96×34
3. $\$39 \times 26$
4. 78×74
5. $\$23 \times 62$
6. 41×178

7. **TALK Math** **Explain** how you know if your estimate will be greater than or less than the exact answer when you are estimating a product.

Independent Practice and Problem Solving

Estimate the product. Choose the method.

8. 54×73
9. 34×80
10. $\$67 \times 23$
11. 56×27
12. 19×45
13. 61×318
14. 52×680
15. 26×448
16. 69×573
17. 24×393
18. 51×61
19. 28×31
20. $\$74 \times 85$
21. 55×39
22. 81×94

USE DATA For 23 and 25, use the data on page 228.

23. Len has two refrigerators in his house. How many times in a 2 week period are the refrigerator doors opened?
25. If Mel opens his refrigerator door 36 times every day, about how many times will it be opened during the month of February?
27. **Reasoning What's the Question?** I am thinking of two numbers that are multiples of ten. The answer is 2,800.
24. New refrigerators cost about \$97 per year to run. About how much will it have cost to run by the time it is 25 years old?
26. ***FAST FACT*** The average person in the United States eats about 23 quarts of ice cream each year. There are 27 students in Kay's class. About how many quarts of ice cream did Kay's class eat last year?
28. **WRITE Math** **Explain** how you can estimate 19×123 using compatible numbers.

Mixed Review and TAKS Prep

29. Name the geometric figure that has exactly 3 angles. (Grade 3 TEKS 3.8)
30. What is the product of 72 and 10? (TEKS 4.6B, p. 226)
31. **TAKS Prep** Choose the best estimate for the product 75×231. (Obj. 1)

   A 24,000
   B 21,000
   C 16,000
   D 1,600

Extra Practice on page 246, Set C

Problem Solving Workshop
Strategy: Solve a Simpler Problem

OBJECTIVE: Solve problems by using the strategy *solve a simpler problem*.

Learn the Strategy

Solving a simpler problem can help you solve more difficult problems.

Break Apart

A Factors

At the museum, an average of 89 visitors each hour view an exhibit. How many visitors will view the exhibit in a 7 hour period?

Break apart 89 into 80 + 9. Multiply each addend by 7. Then add the partial products.

$(7 \times 80) + (7 \times 9)$
$560 + 63$
623

B Addends

The baking contest at the county fair this year had 1,342 entries. Last year, there were 2,879 entries. How many entries have there been in the last two years?

Break apart the numbers by writing them in expanded form. Find the partial sums. Then add the partial sums.

$1{,}000 + 300 + 40 + 2$
$+2{,}000 + 800 + 70 + 9$
$3{,}000 + 1{,}100 + 110 + 11 = 4{,}221$

Find a pattern.

How many straws will be needed to make 5 hexagons?

Find the number of straws in the first figure. Then find the number of straws needed to construct each hexagon that follows.

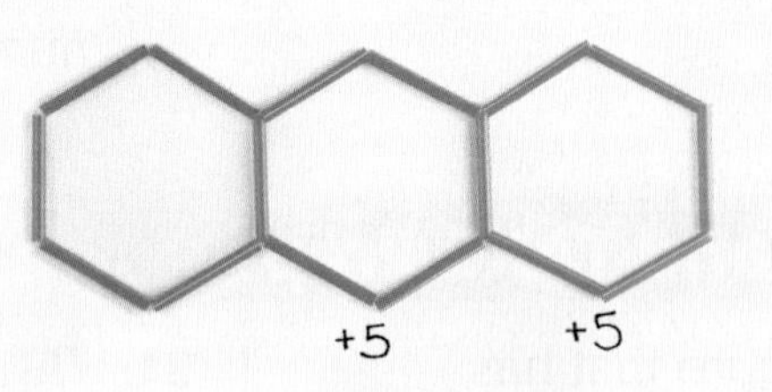

TALK Math

What was done to make each problem simpler to solve?

TEKS 4.14C select or develop an appropriate problem-solving plan or strategy, including drawing a picture, looking for a pattern, systematic guessing and checking, acting it out, making a table, working a simpler problem, or working backwards to solve a problem. *also* **4.1A, 4.4B, 4.4C, 4.4D, 4.14A, 4.14B, 4.15A, 4.15B, 4.16B**

Read to Understand
Plan
Solve
Check

Use the Strategy

PROBLEM During the month of February, people all over North America participate in the Great Backyard Bird Count. Here are results for the 2006 count of Bohemian waxwings in the Great Lakes region. Use the key. At least how many Bohemian waxwings were counted in all in locations that counted more than 15 of them?

Read to Understand

- **Use a graphic aid.**
- **What information is given in the map?**
- **What operation will you use?**

Plan

- **What strategy can you use to solve the problem?**
  You can solve a simpler problem. One of the factors is 16. So you can use the Distributive Property to break apart 16 into factors that are easier to multiply and solve simpler problems.

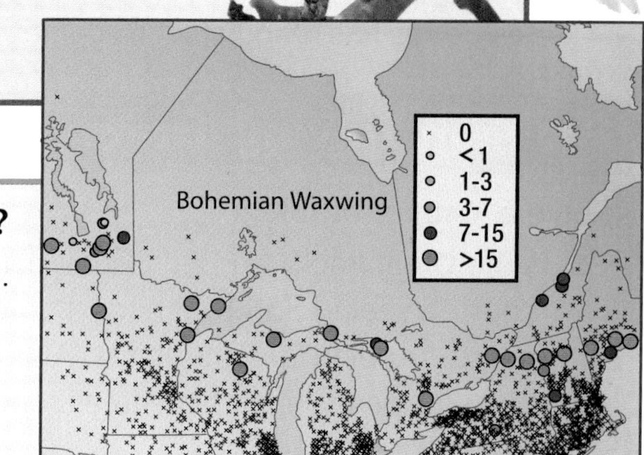

Solve

- **How can you use the strategy to solve the problem?**
  Break apart 16 as $10 + 6$. Multiply each addend by 21. Then add the partial products.

$$\begin{aligned} 16 \times 21 &= (10 + 6) \times 21 \\ &= (10 \times 21) + (6 \times 21) \\ &= 210 + 126 \\ &= 336 \end{aligned}$$

So, at least 336 Bohemian waxwings were counted in all in locations that counted more than 15 birds.

Check

- **What other ways could you solve the problem?**
- **Look back at the problem. Does the answer make sense? Explain.**

Guided Problem Solving

Read to Understand
Plan
Solve
Check

1. In the state of Michigan, 172 participants in the Great Backyard Bird Count reported seeing about 30 mallards each. About how many mallards did they report in all?

   First, think about what you are asked to find.

   Think: 30×172

   Next, break apart one factor into numbers that are easy to multiply.

   $(30 \times 100) + (30 \times 70) + (30 \times 2)$

   Then, multiply and add the partial products.

▲ Mallards are found in almost every state.

2. **What if** the participants reported seeing 50 mallards each? How would your answer be different?

3. When Maggie goes on bird watching trips, she sees at least 45 birds. She has taken 12 bird watching trips a year over the past 16 years. How many birds has Maggie seen?

Problem Solving Strategy Practice

Solve a simpler problem.

4. In the Great Backyard Bird Count, participants in New Jersey reported seeing 353,992 birds. Participants in Delaware reported seeing 274,694 birds. Altogether, how many birds did participants in the two states report seeing?

5. Participants in Texas reported seeing the greatest number of birds, 497,122. Participants in New York reported seeing 264,620 birds. How many more birds were reported in Texas than in New York?

6. Nationwide, participants reported seeing 843,635 Canada geese but only 207,324 American crows. How many more Canada geese were seen than American crows?

7. Participants in New York sent in 222 checklists for wild turkeys. The total number of wild turkeys reported was about 18 times the number of checklists. About how many wild turkeys were reported?

8. WRITE Math Participants reported seeing 156,002 northern cardinals and 337,777 American goldfinches. How many northern cardinals and American goldfinches were reported altogether? **Explain.**

Mixed Strategy Practice

9. African ostrich eggs weigh 3 pounds each. Females lay up to 60 eggs in a group nest. How much could the eggs in the nest weigh?

10. According to legend, every year swallows arrive in San Juan Capistrano, California, on March 19 and leave on October 23. How long do the birds stay in San Juan Capistrano?

USE DATA For 11–17, use the information in the picture.

11. The wandering albatross has the largest wingspan of any bird. If it flies at its maximum speed for 10 hours, how far will it fly?

12. How much farther can a mallard fly in 2 hours than a house sparrow?

13. Which bird has a maximum length 8 times as long as a house sparrow?

14. **Pose a Problem** Look back at Problem 12. Write a similar problem by changing the types of birds and the number of hours they fly.

15. **Open-Ended** Write three different expressions that equal the maximum speed of the mallard. Use one or more operations.

CHALLENGE YOURSELF

The peregrine falcon is the fastest bird in the world. It can dive at a maximum speed of 217 miles per hour.

16. Write and solve a multiplication equation and an addition equation that shows the speed of the falcon and the speed of the carrion crow.

17. A peregrine falcon is 15 inches long. How can you compare the length of a falcon and the lengths of the birds pictured?

Choose a STRATEGY

- Draw a Diagram or Picture
- Make a Model or Act It Out
- Make an Organized List
- Look for a Pattern
- Make a Table or Graph
- Guess and Check
- Work Backward
- Solve a Simpler Problem
- Write an Equation
- Use Logical Reasoning

◀ Carrion crow: maximum length is 20 inches and maximum speed is 31 miles per hour.

▲ House sparrow: maximum length is 6 inches and maximum speed is 31 miles per hour.

◀ Wandering albatross: maximum length is 48 inches and maximum speed is 34 miles per hour.

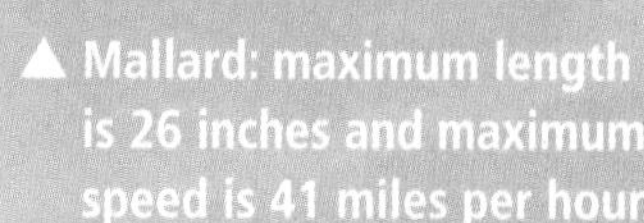

▲ Mallard: maximum length is 26 inches and maximum speed is 41 miles per hour.

LESSON 5 Model 2-Digit by 2-Digit Multiplication

OBJECTIVE: Model multiplication by using arrays.

Quick Review

Estimate the product.

1. 21×18
2. 59×28
3. 19×39
4. 27×52
5. 303×49

Learn

PROBLEM Matthew's family owns an apple orchard. The orchard has 17 rows of trees with 26 trees in each row. What is the total number of trees in the orchard?

You can make a model and break apart factors to make it easier to find the product.

HANDS ON Activity

Materials ■ grid paper ■ base-ten blocks ■ color pencils

Step 1

Outline a rectangle that is 17 units long and 26 units wide. Think of the area as 17×26.

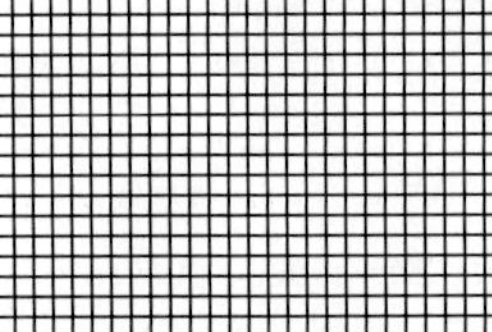

Step 2

Break apart the model into smaller arrays to show factors that are easy to multiply.

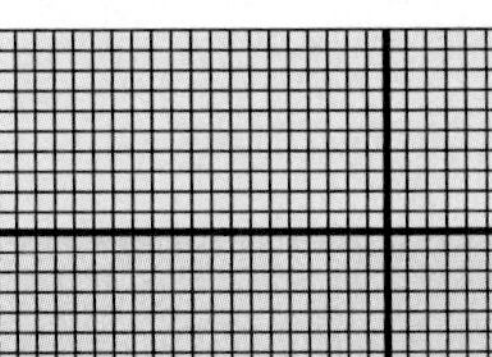

Step 3

Find the number of squares in each of the smaller arrays. Add the partial products.

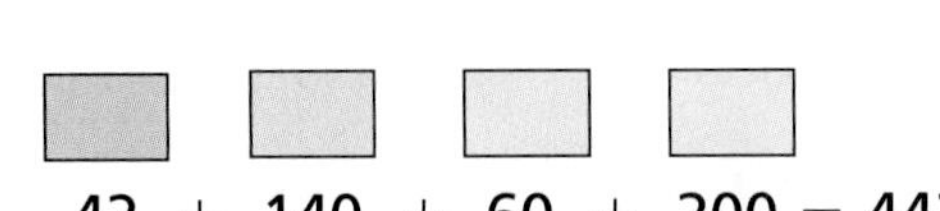

So, there are 442 trees in the orchard.

- **What if** the orchard plants 2 more rows with 26 trees in each? How many more trees would there be in the orchard?

TEKS 4.4A model factors and products using arrays and area models. *also* **4.4B, 4.4C, 4.4D, 4.14A, 4.14C, 4.15A, 4.15B**

Guided Practice

1. Copy and complete each step of the problem at the right. Then tell what is happening in each step.

Step 1
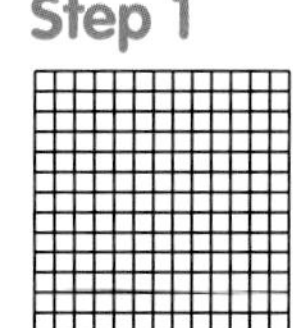
Step 2
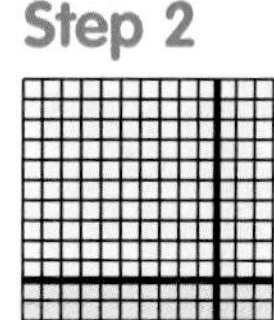
Step 3
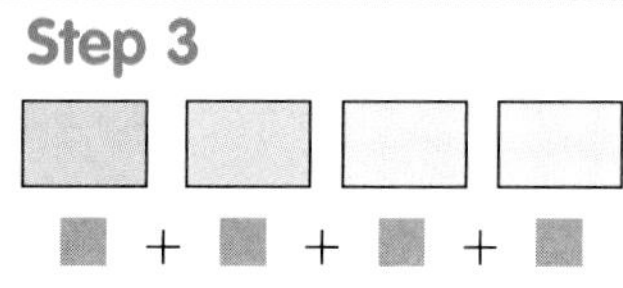

Use the model and partial products to solve.

2. 16×23

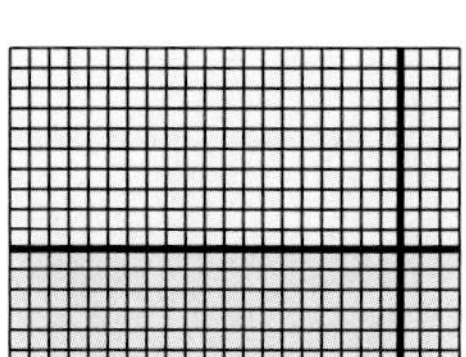

3. 19×18

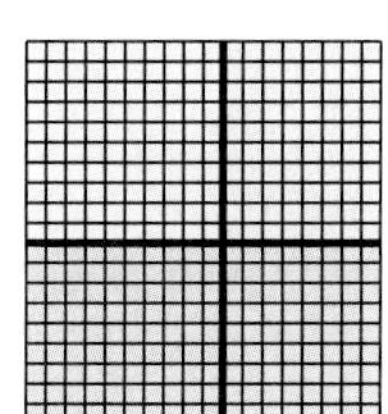

4. 17×25

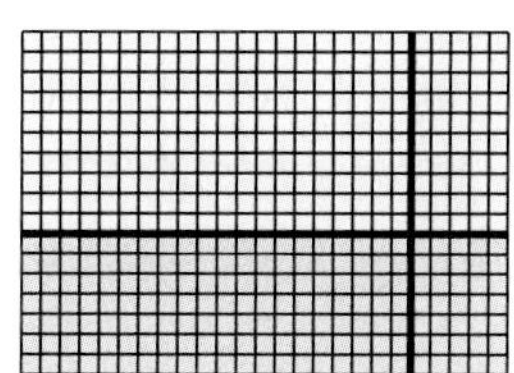

5. **TALK Math** **Explain** how breaking apart a model makes finding a product easier.

Independent Practice and Problem Solving

Use the model and partial products to solve.

6. 14×24

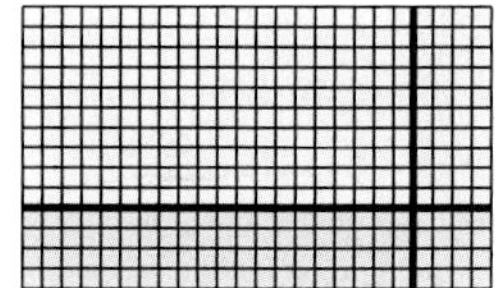

7. 17×22

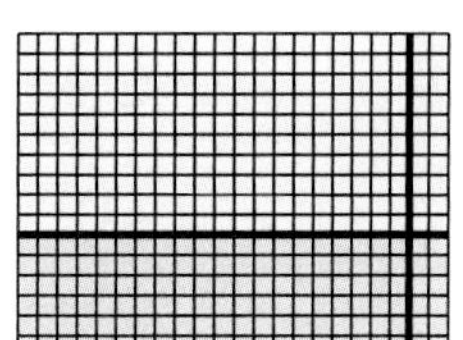

8. 16×28

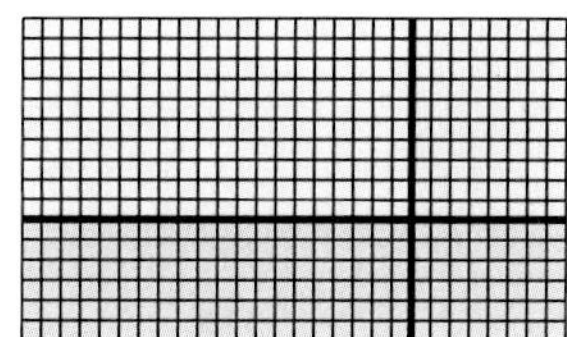

9. ***FAST FACT*** Each person in the United States eats an average of 65 fresh apples a year. How many apples do three families of 4 eat each year?

10. Apples harvested from an average tree can fill 20 bushel-sized boxes. If 1 row of Matthew's family orchard has 17 trees, how many boxes of apples can one row fill?

11. One tree uses the energy of 50 leaves to produce one apple. How many leaves does it take to produce 15 apples?

12. **WRITE Math** **Explain** how to find 37×28 by using a model.

Mixed Review and TAKS Prep

13. Name the faces of a square pyramid. (Grade 3 TEKS 3.8)

14. What is the best estimate for 27×4? (TEKS 4.5B, p. 186)

15. **TAKS Prep** What product is shown by the model? (Obj. 1)

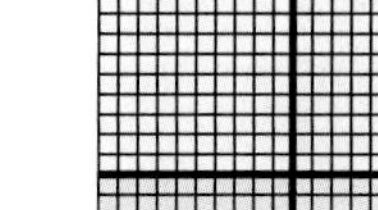

Extra Practice on page 246, Set D

LESSON 6

Record 2-Digit by 2-Digit Multiplication

OBJECTIVE: Find products by using partial products and place value.

Quick Review

1. 9 × 80
2. 2 × 67
3. 4 × 21
4. 7 × 15
5. 6 × 36

Learn

PROBLEM The amount of time it takes you to burn without sunscreen multiplied by the SPF number of your sunscreen tells you how long you can stay in the sun safely. Without sunscreen, Aaron will burn in about 15 minutes if the UV index is 8. If Aaron puts on lotion with SPF 45, how long can he stay in the sun?

▲ Sunscreen is labeled with a sun protection factor level, or SPF level. Checking the UV index, or the intensity of the sun for the day, can help you determine what level of sun protection you need.

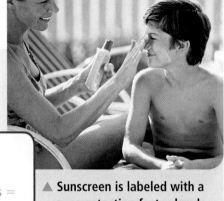

ONE WAY **Use arrays and partial products.**

Multiply. 15 × 45 **Estimate.** 20 × 40 = 800

	MODEL	THINK	RECORD
Step 1	40, 5 by 10, 5 array	Multiply the ones by the ones.	45 ×15 25 → 5 × 5 ones = 25 ones
Step 2	40, 5 by 10, 5 array	Multiply the tens by the ones.	45 ×15 25 200 → 5 × 4 tens = 20 tens
Step 3	40, 5 by 10, 5 array	Multiply the ones by the tens.	45 ×15 25 200 50 → 10 × 5 ones = 50 ones
Step 4	40, 5 by 10, 5 array	Multiply the tens by the tens. Then add the partial products.	45 ×15 25 200 50 +400 → 10 × 4 tens = 40 tens 675

So, if Aaron puts on SPF 45, he can stay in the sun for 675 minutes. Since 675 is close to the estimate of 800, it is reasonable.

ERROR ALERT

Line up partial products in the correct place-value position

TEKS 4.4D use multiplication to solve problems (no more than two digits times two digits without technology).
also **4.4A, 4.4B, 4.4C, 4.5B, 4.14A, 4.14D, 4.15A, 4.15B, 4.16B**

ANOTHER WAY

Example 1 Use place value.

Multiply. 32 × 31 **Estimate.** 30 × 30 = 900

Step 1	Step 2	Step 3
Think of 32 as 3 tens 2 ones. Multiply by 2 ones. 31 ×32 62 ← 2 × 31	Multiply by 3 tens, or 30. 31 ×32 62 930 ← 30 × 31	Add the partial products. 31 ×32 62 +930 992

So, 32 × 31 is 992. Since 992 is close to the estimate of 900, it is reasonable.

Example 2 Use place value with regrouping.

Multiply. 57 × 43 **Estimate.** 60 × 40 = 2,400

Step 1	Step 2	Step 3
Think of 57 as 5 tens 7 ones. Multiply by 7 ones. 2 43 ×57 301 ← 7 × 43	Multiply by 5 tens, or 50. 1 ~~2~~ 43 ×57 301 2150 ← 50 × 43	Add the partial products. 1 ~~2~~ 43 ×57 301 +2150 2,451

So, 57 × 43 is 2,451. Since 2,451 is close to the estimate of 2,400, it is reasonable.

Guided Practice

1. Which product will you find first when you multiply 29 × 54 by using partial products? Which product will you find next? Find the product.

Estimate. Then choose either method to find the product.

2. 15 ×17
3. 21 ×19
4. 34 ×43
5. 76 ×31
6. 89 ×47

7. **TALK Math** **Explain** how you know in which place to begin when you multiply by 2-digit numbers.

Technology
Use Harcourt Mega Math, The Number Games, *Up, Up, and Array,* Level K.

Independent Practice and Problem Solving

Estimate. Then choose either method to find the product.

8. 36×14 **9.** 63×42 **10.** $\$82 \times 29$ **11.** 71×13 **12.** 57×79

13. $\$75 \times 32$ **14.** 80×27 **15.** 55×48 **16.** $\$25 \times 25$ **17.** 41×98

18. 19×41 **19.** $\$33 \times 17$ **20.** 28×39 **21.** 52×61 **22.** $82 \times \$65$

23. 76×24 **24.** 82×97 **25.** 15×43 **26.** $45 \times \$90$ **27.** 35×53

USE DATA **For 28–30, use the bar graph.**

28. Last year, Sun Beach Parasail had 17 riders on each rainy day. How many riders in all parasailed last year on rainy days?

29. Sun Beach Parasail had 15 riders on each cold day. How many riders in all parasailed last year on cold days?

30. **Pose a Problem** Look back at problem 29. Make the problem more open-ended.

31. Last week, Sheila planted 12 rows of seedlings with 15 seedlings in each row. This week, she planted 50 more seedlings. How many seedlings did she plant in all?

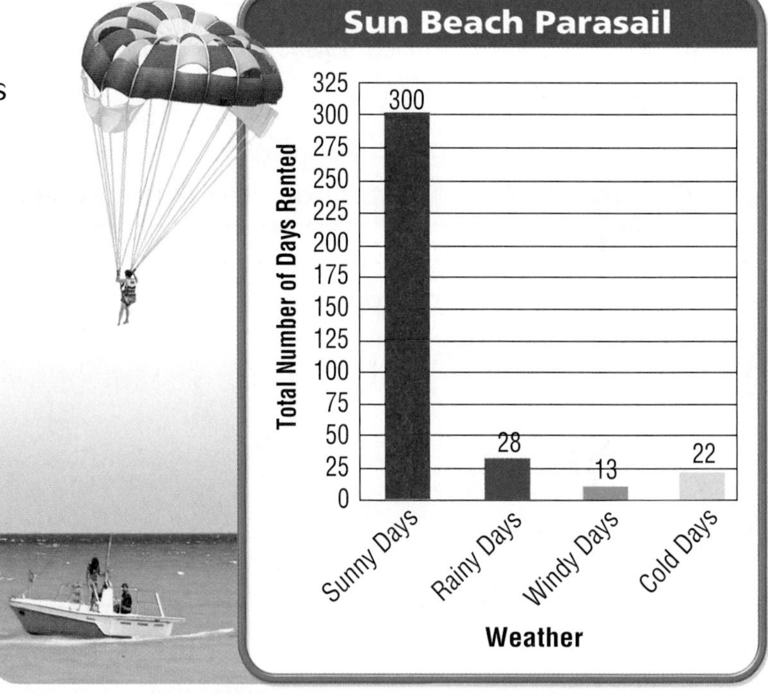

32. **Reasoning** Use the digits 1, 2, 3, and 5 to make two 2-digit numbers that will have the greatest product. Find the product.

33. **WRITE Math** Write a paragraph telling the method you like to use to multiply 2-digit numbers. **Explain** why you use this method.

Mixed Review and TAKS Prep

34. Look at the graph above. How many windy days were there? (Grade 3 TEKS 3.13B)

35. A group of 25 students each jumped rope for 30 minutes. How many minutes in all did they jump rope? (TEKS 4.6B, p. 226)

36. **TAKS Prep** Dave bought 18 shrubs to plant in his garden. Each shrub cost \$14. How much did the shrubs cost in all? (Obj. 1)

A \$182 **C** \$225

B \$222 **D** \$252

 Extra Practice on page 247, Set E

Write to Explain

WRITE Math WORKSHOP

Writing an explanation helps you describe the steps you use to solve a problem.

David knows that the distance around the Earth is divided into 24 equal time zones–one zone for each hour of the day. Each time zone measures about 1,036 miles at the equator. David uses this information to solve this problem: What is the distance around the Earth at the equator?

Read David's explanation of how he used multiplication to find the answer.

Multiply the number of time zones by the measure of each time zone to find the distance around the Earth at the equator.

$24 \times 1{,}036$

First, break apart 1,036 into $1{,}000 + 30 + 6$.

Then, multiply each addend by 24.

$(24 \times 1{,}000) + (24 \times 30) + (24 \times 6)$

$\downarrow \quad \downarrow \quad \downarrow$

$24{,}000 + 720 + 144$

Finally, find the sum of $24{,}000 + 720 + 144$. *The sum is 24,864.*

So, the distance around the Earth at the equator is about 24,864 miles.

Tips

To write an explanation:

- First, identify the question.
- Then use time-order words, such as first, next, then, and finally to explain the steps in your answer.
- Use correct math vocabulary.
- Show all necessary computations.
- State your answer in the last sentence.

Problem Solving Explain how to solve each problem.

1. One degree of longitude is about 111 kilometers wide at the equator. What is the distance between two cities along the equator that are 12 degrees of longitude apart?

2. Each time zone spans 15 degrees of longitude. At the equator, each degree of longitude spans 60 nautical miles. How many nautical miles are in a time zone at the equator?

Practice Multiplication

OBJECTIVE: Practice multiplying by 2-digit numbers.

Quick Review

1. 17×7
2. 45×0
3. 9×12
4. 8×15
5. 15×30

Learn

PROBLEM In 1914, Henry Ford streamlined the assembly line to make a Model T Ford car in 93 minutes. How many minutes did it take to make 75 Model Ts?

▲ The first production Model T Ford was assembled at the Piquette Avenue Plant in Detroit on October 1, 1908.

Example 1 Use place value.

Multiply. 75×93

THINK	RECORD
Multiply by the ones. Multiply by the tens. Add the partial products.	$\begin{array}{rl} {}^{2}\!\!\not{1} & \\ 93 & \\ \times\ 75 & \\ \hline 465 & \leftarrow 5 \times 93 \\ +\,6510 & \leftarrow 70 \times 93 \\ \hline 6{,}975 & \end{array}$

So, it took 6,975 minutes to make 75 Model T Fords.

Math Idea

Use what you know about 1-digit multiplication to multiply 2-digit numbers by 2-digit numbers.

Example 2 Different ways to multiply

You can use different ways to multiply and still get the correct answer. Both Shawn and Patty solved 67×36 correctly, but they used different ways.

Look at Shawn's paper.

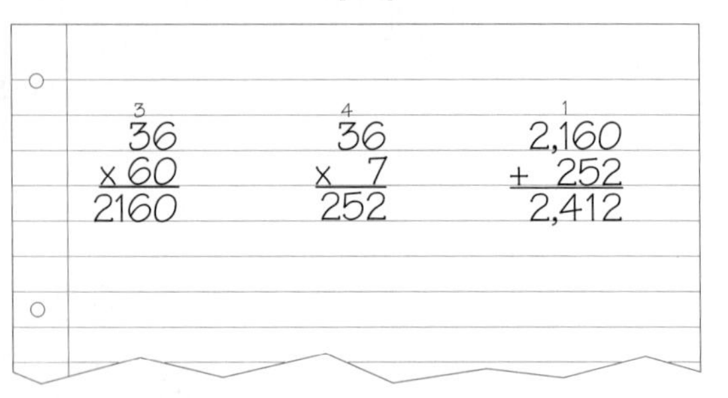

So, Shawn's answer is $67 \times 36 = 2{,}412$.

Look at Patty's paper.

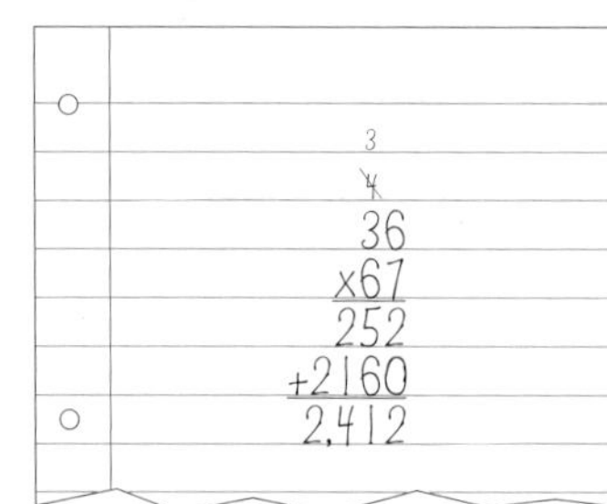

So, Patty also found $67 \times 36 = 2{,}412$.

- What method did each student use to solve the problem?

Guided Practice

1. What is the first partial product when you multiply 40×56? What numbers would you multiply next? Find the product.

TEKS 4.4D use multiplication to solve problems (no more than two digits times two digits without technology). *also* **4.1A, 4.5B, 4.14A, 4.15A, 4.15B, 4.14D, 4.16B**

Estimate. Find the product.

2. $\begin{array}{r} 68 \\ \times 53 \\ \hline \end{array}$ **3.** $\begin{array}{r} 40 \\ \times 19 \\ \hline \end{array}$ **4.** $\begin{array}{r} 58 \\ \times 76 \\ \hline \end{array}$ **✓5.** $\begin{array}{r} \$99 \\ \times\ 30 \\ \hline \end{array}$ **✓6.** $\begin{array}{r} 91 \\ \times 27 \\ \hline \end{array}$

7. TALK Math **Explain** how to find 20×48.

Independent Practice and Problem Solving

Estimate. Find the product.

8. 38×47 **9.** 92×87 **10.** 27×25 **11.** 14×80 **12.** $\$27 \times 13$

13. 34×54 **14.** 17×29 **15.** $42 \times \$36$ **16.** 62×27 **17.** 57×87

Algebra Use each factor in the box only once. Estimate the products to find the missing factors.

11	44	59	32	12	18

18. The product is between 100 and 150.

19. The product is between 700 and 800.

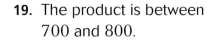

20. The product is between 1,500 and 2,000.

$\begin{array}{r} \square\square \\ \times\ \square\square \\ \hline \end{array}$

USE DATA For 21–22, use the pictures.

▲ Sports Car

▲ Monster Truck

21. The hobby shop sold 32 remote control sports cars last year. How much did the shop make from the cars?

22. Which costs more, 23 sports cars or 21 racing buggies? How much more?

23. WRITE Math **What's the Error?** Barry said that 40×29 is 440. Is he correct? **Explain.**

Mixed Review and TAKS Prep

24. The total area of Texas is 268,581 square miles. What is the area rounded to the nearest thousand? (TEKS 4.5A, p. 34)

25. A soccer team ordered 15 uniforms at \$19 each. How much did the uniforms cost in all? (TEKS 4.4D, p. 236)

26. **TAKS Prep** A restaurant ordered 15 boxes of napkins. Each box holds 29 napkins. How many napkins did the restaurant order? (Obj. 1)

A 295

B 335

C 395

D 435

Extra Practice on page 247, Set F

LESSON 8 Choose a Method

OBJECTIVE: Choose mental math, paper and pencil, or a calculator to find products.

Quick Review

1. 10 × 56
2. 75 × 85
3. 22 × $17
4. 40 × 83
5. $20 × 24

Learn

PROBLEM Alan is having a party at a ceramics studio. There will be 30 children and the cost is $12 per child. How much will Alan's party cost?

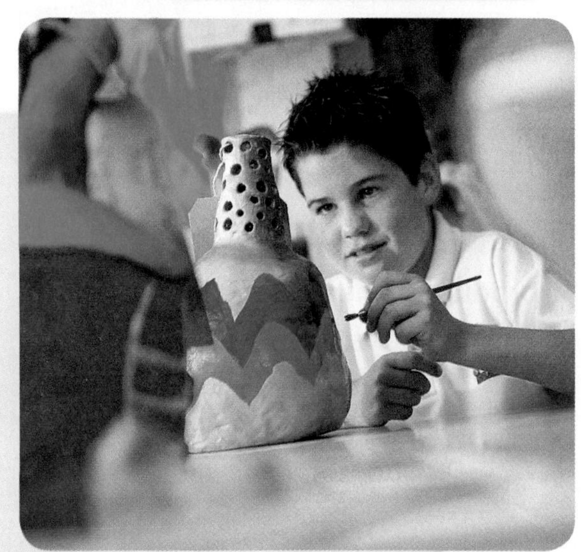

Example 1 Use mental math.

12 × 30 = ■

Think: 12 × 30 = (10 × 30) + (2 × 30)

↓ ↓

300 + 60

360

So, Alan's party will cost $360.

- Explain why using mental math is a good idea for finding this product.

More Examples

A Use paper and pencil.

55 × 44

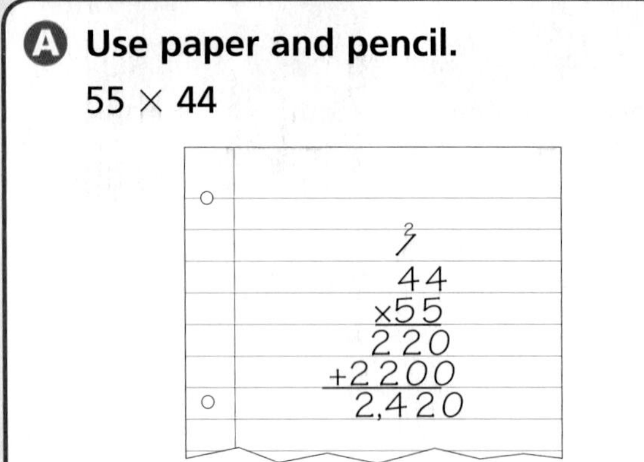

B Use a calculator.

36 × 574

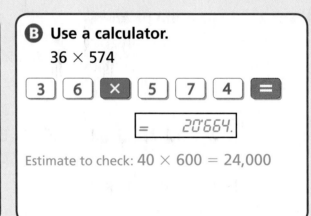

3 6 × 5 7 4 =

= 20664.

Estimate to check: 40 × 600 = 24,000

- Would you use a calculator, paper and pencil, or mental math to find the product $37 × 425? Explain your choice.

Guided Practice

1. Would you choose paper and pencil or mental math to multiply 54 × $57? **Explain** your choice.

TEKS 4.4D use multiplication to solve problems (no more than two-digits times two-digits without technology). *also* **4.5B, 4.14A, 4.15A, 4.15B, 4.14D, 4.16B**

Estimate. Then find the product. Write the method you used.

2. $\$33 \times 22$ **3.** 50×50 **4.** 55×22 ✓**5.** 80×30 ✓**6.** 333×24

7. TALK Math **Explain** why you chose the method to find the product for Problem 6.

Independent Practice and Problem Solving

Estimate. Then find the product. Write the method you used.

8. 44×20 **9.** 70×60 **10.** 547×92 **11.** 45×22 **12.** 999×36

13. 55×13 **14.** 75×21 **15.** 77×27 **16.** 67×50 **17.** $70 \times \$16$

18. 46×30 **19.** 550×20 **20.** 65×31 **21.** 246×84 **22.** 34×88

Algebra **Use a calculator to find the missing digit.**

23. $44 \times 234 = 10,\blacksquare 96$ **24.** $2\blacksquare \times 392 = 10,584$ **25.** $19 \times 5\blacksquare 0 = 9,880$

26. $51 \times 558 = 2\blacksquare,458$ **27.** $32 \times 773 = 24,73\blacksquare$ **28.** $67 \times 1\blacksquare 9 = 7,973$

29. The studio sells tiles to paint for $11 each. Seventeen of the children bought a tile to paint. Was the total spent more than or less than $186? How do you know?

30. The total cost for a weekend party at the studio is $360. On weekdays, the total cost drops to $11 per person. How much would Alan's studio party for 30 children cost on a weekday?

31. Thirteen of the children wanted to buy souvenir cups at the studio. Each cup costs 25 cents. How much will the cups cost?

32. WRITE Math **What's the Error?** Puja used mental math to multiply 80×50. She says that the product is 400. Describe and correct her error.

Mixed Review and TAKS Prep

33. What might the missing number in this pattern be? (TEKS 4.6A, p. 144)

7, 14, 21, 28, ■, 42

34. Tim ordered 37 binders for his office. Each binder cost $4. How much did the binders cost in all? (TEKS 4.4D, p. 190)

35. **TAKS Prep** What is the best method to multiply 21×60? (Obj. 1)

A Mental math

B Calculator

C Paper and pencil

D Not here

Extra Practice on page 247, Set G

Problem Solving Workshop
Skill: Multistep Problems

OBJECTIVE: Solve problems by using the skill *multistep problems.*

Use the Skill

PROBLEM The Chicago World's Fair of 1893 introduced the first Ferris wheel. It had 36 cars. Each car could carry 60 passengers. The Pacific Wheel in Santa Monica, California, can carry 6 passengers in each of its 20 cars. How many more passengers could the first Ferris wheel carry?

▲ The Ferris wheel at Chicago World's Fair was 250 feet tall.

First, find the total number of people each wheel can hold.

	number of cars ↓		capacity of each car ↓	total capacity ↓
1893 Ferris wheel	36	×	60	= 2,160
Pacific Wheel	20	×	6	= 120

Then, find out how many more the 1893 Ferris wheel could carry. Then subtract: $2{,}160 - 120 = 2{,}040$

So, the first 1893 Ferris wheel could carry 2,040 more passengers.

• Look back at the problem. Does your answer make sense? Explain how you know.

Think and Discuss

What steps would you take to solve the problem? Solve the problem.

a. Gold braid comes in 15-foot rolls and costs \$25 per foot. Silver braid comes in 31-foot rolls and costs \$12 per foot. What is the total cost of one roll of each type of braid?

b. Ms. Kimble teaches 6 music classes of 20 students each school day. In her Monday classes, 80 of the students are fourth graders. How many students are not fourth graders?

c. In one class, Mr. Thacker handed out 14 sheets of construction paper to each of the 20 students. He had 40 sheets of construction paper left over. How many sheets of construction paper did he start with?

▲ The Pacific Wheel is the world's first solar powered Ferris wheel. It is 130 feet tall.

TEKS 4.4D use multiplication to solve problems (no more than two digits times two digits without technology). *also* **4.3A, 4.14A, 4.14C, 4.15A, 4.15B, 4.16B**

Guided Problem Solving

Read to Understand
Plan
Solve
Check

1. A small Ferris wheel at a carnival makes a complete trip around in 20 seconds. Julia rode the Ferris wheel for 20 trips. Alexa rode it for 25 trips. How much longer was Alexa on the Ferris wheel?

   What steps do you need to take to solve the problem?

   First, find the amount of time each girl was on the Ferris wheel.

   Then subtract the amount of time that Julia was on the Ferris wheel from the amount of time that Alexa was on it.

   Solve the problem.

2. **What if** the Ferris wheel made a complete trip every 30 seconds? How much longer was Alexa on it than Julia was?

3. Rides at a carnival cost $2 each. There were 20 rides. A group of 22 students went on every ride once. How much money was spent to ride all of the rides?

Mixed Applications

USE DATA For 4–6, use the table.

4. Maya and Carla want to go to the carnival each night for a week. Each girl has $75. Do they have enough to attend every night?

5. The Terrell family has 4 people. How much will it cost to go to the carnival if they go on Saturday?

6. How much more will Robert spend if he goes to the carnival on Friday and Saturday than if he goes on Monday and Wednesday?

Carnival Admission

One-Night Tickets

Night	Cost
Monday through Wednesday	$12
Thursday through Friday	$15
Saturday	$20

7. Zora ran 2 laps around the gym the first week, 4 laps the second week, 8 laps the third week, and 16 laps the fourth week. If the pattern continues, how many laps will she run in the fifth week?

8. WRITE Math Chen strung paper lanterns across the patio to the kitchen and then 10 feet down the hallway. At the end of the hallway, she strung the lanterns 6 feet into her playroom. She strung a total of 24 feet of lanterns. How long was the section from the patio to the kitchen? **Explain.**

Extra Practice

Set A **Use mental math and patterns to find the product.** (pp. 224–225)

1. 10×30
2. 11×400
3. 12×200
4. 11×700
5. $11 \times 6{,}000$
6. $40 \times 5{,}000$
7. 50×60
8. $12 \times 9{,}000$
9. 10×800
10. $70 \times 3{,}000$
11. The actual length of a wasp is 15 millimeters. How long would the wasp appear to be under a microscope at a magnification of 200 times its actual size?

Set B **Choose a method. Then find the product.** (pp. 226–227)

1. 14×60
2. 28×30
3. 36×50
4. 47×80
5. 56×70
6. 77×30
7. 49×40
8. 67×30
9. 89×50
10. 38×90
11. 20×63
12. 38×80
13. 50×25
14. 54×60
15. 36×40
16. Ms. Michaels has 30 packages of construction paper. Each package has 25 sheets of paper. How many sheets of paper does she have?

Set C **Estimate the product. Choose the method.** (pp. 228–229)

1. 63×24
2. 48×57
3. 32×21
4. 59×68
5. $\$37 \times 49$
6. 32×43
7. 458×61
8. 37×297
9. 378×29
10. 201×32
11. 33×56
12. $\$687 \times 29$
13. 799×33
14. 78×67
15. 607×48
16. A drawbridge opens 19 times each week. About how many times does the drawbridge open in one year?

Set D **Use the model and partial products to solve.** (pp. 234–235)

1. 15×21

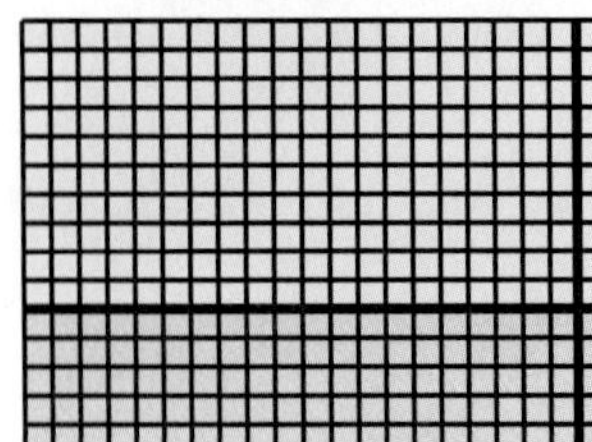

2. 14×24

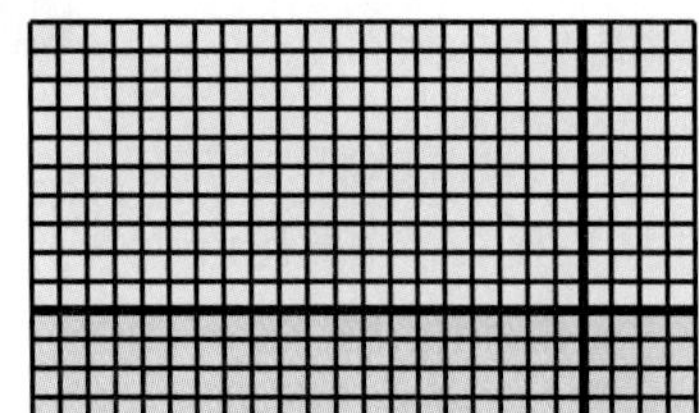

3. 18×23

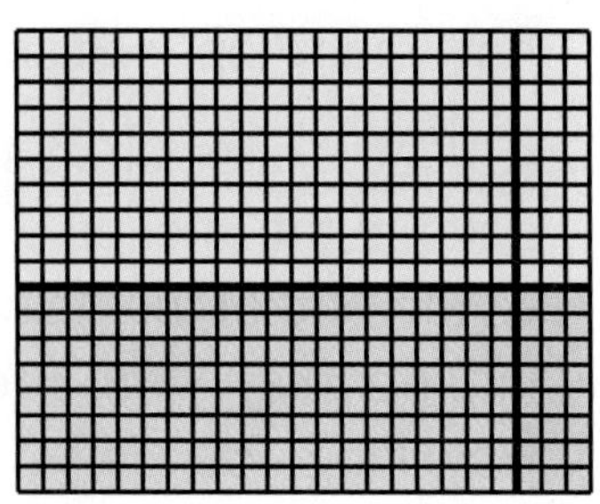

CD ROM **Technology**
Use Harcourt Mega Math, The Number Games, *Up, Up, and Array,* Levels I, K.

Set E Estimate. Then choose either method to find the product. (pp. 236–239)

1. $\begin{array}{r} 29 \\ \times\ 74 \\ \hline \end{array}$ 2. $\begin{array}{r} 43 \\ \times\ 56 \\ \hline \end{array}$ 3. $\begin{array}{r} 63 \\ \times\ 45 \\ \hline \end{array}$ 4. $\begin{array}{r} 83 \\ \times\ 17 \\ \hline \end{array}$ 5. $\begin{array}{r} 37 \\ \times\ 64 \\ \hline \end{array}$

6. $\begin{array}{r} 34 \\ \times\ 28 \\ \hline \end{array}$ 7. $\begin{array}{r} 73 \\ \times\ 35 \\ \hline \end{array}$ 8. $\begin{array}{r} 88 \\ \times\ 32 \\ \hline \end{array}$ 9. $\begin{array}{r} 49 \\ \times\ 51 \\ \hline \end{array}$ 10. $\begin{array}{r} 57 \\ \times\ 27 \\ \hline \end{array}$

11. $78 × 54 12. 26 × 59 13. $66 × 17 14. 13 × 28 15. 94 × 41

16. Each page of a photo album holds 15 pictures. If there are 45 pages, how many pictures will the photo album hold?

Set F Estimate. Find the product. (pp. 240–241)

1. $\begin{array}{r} 53 \\ \times\ 44 \\ \hline \end{array}$ 2. $\begin{array}{r} 32 \\ \times\ 56 \\ \hline \end{array}$ 3. $\begin{array}{r} 31 \\ \times\ 35 \\ \hline \end{array}$ 4. $\begin{array}{r} \$37 \\ \times\ 62 \\ \hline \end{array}$ 5. $\begin{array}{r} 57 \\ \times\ 84 \\ \hline \end{array}$

6. $\begin{array}{r} 43 \\ \times\ 73 \\ \hline \end{array}$ 7. $\begin{array}{r} 21 \\ \times\ 14 \\ \hline \end{array}$ 8. $\begin{array}{r} \$29 \\ \times\ 56 \\ \hline \end{array}$ 9. $\begin{array}{r} 57 \\ \times\ 83 \\ \hline \end{array}$ 10. $\begin{array}{r} 88 \\ \times\ 25 \\ \hline \end{array}$

11. $56 × 47 12. 13 × 89 13. 21 × 18 14. $54 × 32 15. 29 × 34

16. The library lends an average of 44 books a day. How many books are checked out in 16 hours?

Set G Estimate. Then find the product. Write the method you used. (pp. 242–243)

1. $\begin{array}{r} 50 \\ \times\ 34 \\ \hline \end{array}$ 2. $\begin{array}{r} 95 \\ \times\ 67 \\ \hline \end{array}$ 3. $\begin{array}{r} 42 \\ \times\ 80 \\ \hline \end{array}$ 4. $\begin{array}{r} 14 \\ \times\ 26 \\ \hline \end{array}$ 5. $\begin{array}{r} 899 \\ \times\ 42 \\ \hline \end{array}$

6. $\begin{array}{r} 832 \\ \times\ 58 \\ \hline \end{array}$ 7. $\begin{array}{r} 6{,}492 \\ \times\ 15 \\ \hline \end{array}$ 8. $\begin{array}{r} 2{,}881 \\ \times\ 23 \\ \hline \end{array}$ 9. $\begin{array}{r} 4{,}261 \\ \times\ 51 \\ \hline \end{array}$ 10. $\begin{array}{r} \$5{,}698 \\ \times\ 33 \\ \hline \end{array}$

11. 941 × 72 12. 1,975 × 17 13. 814 × 29 14. 658 × 46 15. 3,219 × 52

16. A soccer uniform costs $19. The team has 16 members. How much will be spent for the team's uniforms?

Chapter 9 Review/Test

Check Concepts

1. Explain how to use mental math to find 12×50. (TEKS 4.6B, pp. 224–225)
2. What is the pattern when multiplying a number by a multiple of ten? Give an example of the pattern. (TEKS 4.6B, pp. 226–227)
3. Explain how to find 8×37 by breaking apart a factor. (TEKS 4.4D, pp. 230–231)

Check Skills

Estimate the product. Choose the method. (TEKS 4.5B, pp. 228–229)

4. 36×47
5. 58×34
6. $\$76 \times 38$
7. 92×24
8. 42×73
9. 405×28
10. 624×36
11. 18×763
12. $\$64 \times 26$
13. 509×49

Estimate. Find the product. (TEKS 4.4D, pp. 226–227, 234–235, 236–239, 240–241)

14. 44×60
15. 62×70
16. 57×80
17. 36×50
18. 92×35
19. $\$37 \times 81$
20. 63×48
21. $\$241 \times 25$
22. 73×49
23. 508×27
24. 58×39
25. 87×44
26. $\$567 \times 35$
27. 607×46
28. $\$289 \times 28$

Check Problem Solving

Solve. (TEKS 4.14C, pp. 230–231, 244–245)

29. Allison's parents put $175 each month into her college fund account. How much do they put in the account during 1 year?
30. George buys 20 dozen eggs for the Community Pancake Breakfast. How many eggs does he buy?
31. Sandy sold 35 adult tickets and 48 child tickets for the breakfast. An adult ticket costs $6 and a child ticket costs $3. How much did Sandy collect for the tickets?
32. Each level of a parking garage holds 110 cars. There are 5 garages with 6 levels in each garage. How many cars can be parked in all the garages?
33. **WRITE Math** **List** the steps needed to find 46×63.

GO ONLINE **Technology** Use *Online Assessment.*

Enrich • Use Multiplication Properties

TAKE A SEAT

There are 6 sections of seats in Bianca's school auditorium. Each section has 15 groups of seats. Each group has 50 seats. How many seats are there in the auditorium?

Stage

You can use the Commutative and Associative Properties of Multiplication to make partial products that end in 0.

The Commutative Property of Multiplication states the order in which you multiply does not change the product. The Associative Property of Multiplication states the way in which you group the factors does not change the product.

Multiply. $6 \times 15 \times 50$

$6 \times 15 \times 50 = 6 \times 50 \times 15$ ← Commutative Property

$= 300 \times 15$

$= 4{,}500$

So, the auditorium has 4,500 seats.

Opening Act

Use mental math to find the value.

A Associative Property

$(14 \times 25) \times 8 = 14 \times (25 \times 8)$

$= 14 \times 200$

$= 2{,}800$

B Commutative Property

$3 \times 37 \times 10 = 3 \times 10 \times 37$

$= 30 \times 37$

$= 1{,}110$

Perform

Use mental math to find the value.

1. $3 \times 11 \times 30$
2. $5 \times (20 \times 35)$
3. $6 \times 32 \times 50$
4. $8 \times (25 \times 60)$
5. $(90 \times 4) \times 25$
6. $10 \times 12 \times 7$
7. $5 \times 40 \times 18$
8. $(21 \times 7) \times 80$
9. There are 13 members on the swim team. Each member swims 20 laps at practice. If they practice 5 days a week, how many laps does the team swim each week?
10. An apartment building has 8 floors. Each apartment has 12 windows, and there are 10 apartments on a floor. How many windows are there in the building?

Encore!

WRITE Math **Explain** how using the properties make it easier to multiply 3 factors mentally.

Unit Review/Test
Chapters 7–9

Multiple Choice

1. The diagram shows a section of seats in the school gymnasium.

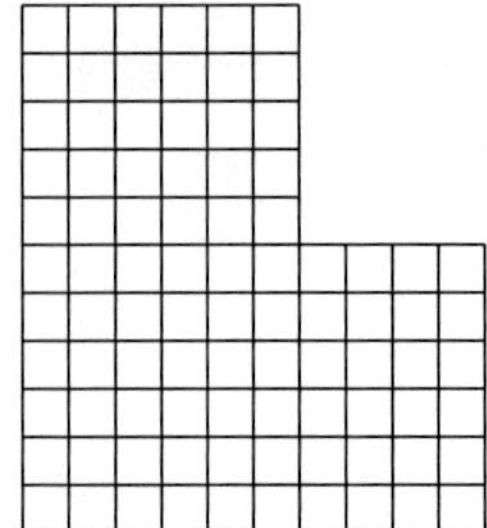

Which of the following situations is represented by the diagram? (TAKS Obj. 1)

A A section with 5 rows of 6 seats and a section with 6 rows of 10 seats

B A section with 6 rows of 5 seats and a section with 6 rows of 10 seats

C A section with 6 rows of 5 seats and a section with 5 rows of 10 seats

D A section with 5 rows of 6 seats and a section with 5 rows of 10 seats

2. Sue buys 21 packages of hamburger buns for the school picnic. Each package has 8 buns. What is the best estimate of the number of buns Sue buys? (TAKS Obj. 1)

F 160 **H** 200

G 180 **J** 240

3. Taylor's family sold 2,000 toy cars this year at the flea market. They charged \$4 for each car. How much money did they receive? (TAKS Obj. 1)

A \$800 **C** \$80,000

B \$8,000 **D** \$800,000

4. Monte watched 5 history videos for his history project. Each video was 75 minutes long. Which number sentence shows how to find the total number of minutes Monte spent watching the videos? (TAKS Obj. 1)

F $75 - 5 = \blacksquare$

G $5 + 75 = \blacksquare$

H $5 \div 75 = \blacksquare$

J $75 \times 5 = \blacksquare$

5. Which pair of numbers best completes the equation? (TAKS Obj. 1)

$\bigcirc \times 400 = \square$

A 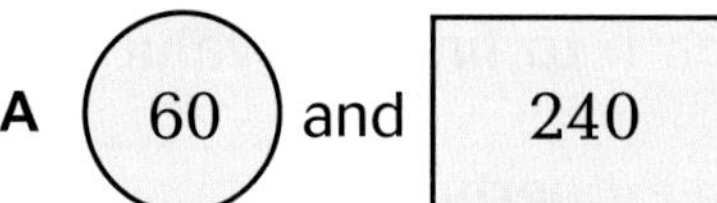 60 and 240

B 60 and 2,400

C 6 and 2,400

D 6 and 24,000

6. There are 54 cases of yo-yos in a warehouse. Each case contains 24 yo-yos. Which is the best estimate for the number of yo-yos in the warehouse? (TAKS Obj. 1)

F 10,000 **H** 100

G 1,000 **J** 10

GO ONLINE Technology Use *Online Assessment.*

7. This week, the box office sold 179 tickets at $18 each for the puppet show. How much money did the box office collect? (TAKS Obj. 1)

A $197

B $1,422

C $3,222

D $3,422

8. Lily's Laundromat has 20 washing machines. Each machine can wash about 50 loads of laundry each week. About how many loads of laundry can be washed each week at Lily's? (TAKS Obj. 1)

F 100

G 1,000

H 10,000

J 100,000

9. Mr. Sanders bought 2 holly bushes and 3 spider plants for his landscape business.

Jackson's Nursery Plant Sale	
Plant	**Price**
Azalea	$49
Holly	$69
Spider	$35

Which expression can be used to find the total amount he spent? (TAKS Obj. 1)

A $(69 \times 3) \times (35 \times 2)$

B $(69 \times 2) \times (35 \times 3)$

C $(69 \times 3) + (35 \times 2)$

D $(69 \times 2) + (35 \times 3)$

Short Response

10. There are 24 baseballs in each case. How many baseballs are there in 9 cases? (TAKS Obj. 1)

11. One section of bleachers in a school gymnasium has 17 rows. Each row can seat 42 people. What is a good estimate of the number of people that can sit in that section? (TAKS Obj. 1)

12. Last year, Rosewood Middle School bought 15 new desks for every classroom. There are 23 classrooms. How many new desks did the school buy in all? (TAKS Obj. 1)

Extended Response WRITE Math

13. Mr. Valdez earns $17 an hour. Yesterday he worked 8 hours. Did Mr. Valdez earn more than or less than $200? **Explain** how you can tell without calculating an exact answer. (TAKS Obj. 1)

14. The problem below shows part of the product 4×58. What two digits are missing? **Explain** how to find them. (TAKS Obj. 1)

$$\begin{array}{r} 58 \\ \times\ 4 \\ \hline \blacksquare\blacksquare 2 \end{array}$$

15. Use each of the digits 3, 5, 7, and 9 once to make a three-digit factor and a one-digit factor that will give the greatest product possible. **Explain** how you found your answer. (TAKS Obj. 1)

Texas

Problem Solving

Space Travel

Texas and Space

On July 20, 1969, at 4:17 P.M., *Apollo 11's* lunar module *Eagle* landed on the moon. Neil Armstrong communicated the good news to the Johnson Space Center in Houston, Texas by saying, "The *Eagle* has landed." Neil Armstrong became the first person to walk on the moon.

Millions heard about the lunar exploration from reporter Walter Cronkite, who was on the air for 27 hours reporting the events. A lunar rock is on display at the University of Texas.

Neil Armstrong

lunar rock

Walter Cronkite

The Apollo lunar module was about 21 feet tall and 14 feet wide.

FACT·ACTIVITY

Use the data on this page to answer the questions.

1. The *Apollo 11* astronauts collected about 49 pounds of soil and rock samples. About how many ounces was this?
   Think: 1 pound = 16 ounces
2. On July 16, 1969 at 9:32 A.M., *Apollo 11* launched into space. About how many hours passed from the launch to landing on the moon?
3. WRITE Math **Explain** how you would find the Apollo Lunar Module's height and width in inches.

Suit Up for Space

The Apollo space suits were each one piece. Each member of the 3-person crew had 3 suits: a flight suit, a training suit, and a backup suit. The 2 backup astronauts had 2 suits each: a flight suit and a training suit.

Today's shuttle space suits are made in parts. The parts, such as a space helmet, can be made in different sizes.

Space helmets must provide oxygen for breathing, protection from extreme temperatures, and a visor to reflect harmful rays from the sun. Space helmets can include a slot for fruit and cereal snacks and adjustable blinders to block out the sun.

ALMANAC Fact

Every summer, the Johnson Space Center sponsors day camps for children ages 4 to 14. These kids get to learn how to communicate by satellites, design a robot, and explore actual space suits used by astronauts!

FACT • ACTIVITY

Use the information about Apollo space suits.

1. How many space suits were needed for one Apollo flight?
2. How many would have been needed for 12 Apollo flights?

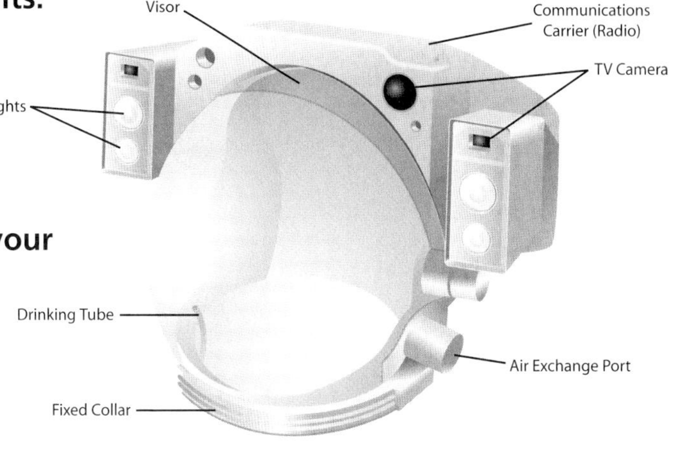

Use the diagram. Design, draw, and label your own space helmet for a mission to Mars.

- Will your helmet have visors and lights? How many of each?
- How many parts will be needed in all?
- Choose the number of astronauts to join you. What is the total number of helmet parts needed?
- Describe some extra items you would include in your own space helmet. How many parts will your helmet have? How many will you and your crew need in all?
- If 4 missions like yours can be sent at the same time, what is the total number of helmet parts needed?

UNIT 4 Geometry

Math on Location

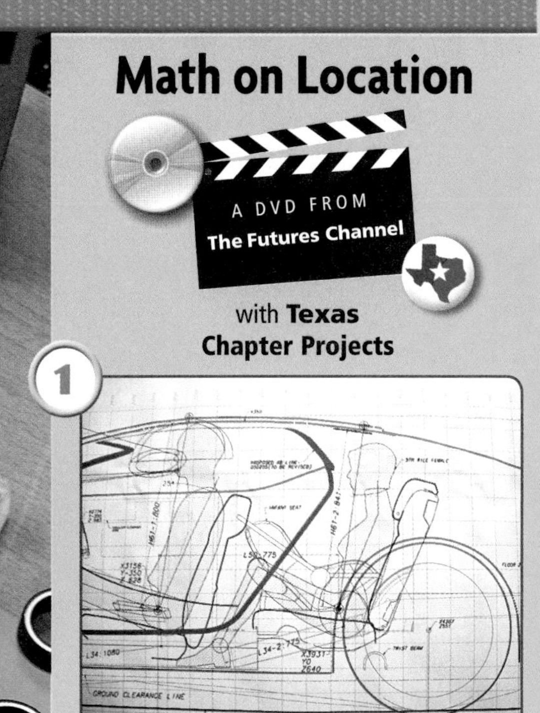

with **Texas Chapter Projects**

1

Designers and engineers use points, lines, angles, and plane figures in concept drawings.

2

The drawing is made into a 3-dimensional clay model to test its resistance to air.

3

A top-view drawing shows the symmetry in the car's design.

VOCABULARY POWER

TALK Math

What math do you see in the **Math on Location** photographs? What geometric words can you use to talk about car designs?

READ Math

REVIEW VOCABULARY You learned the words below when you learned about geometry. How do these words relate to **Math on Location**?

angle a figure formed by two rays or line segments that share an endpoint

circle a closed figure made up of points that are the same distance from the center

polygon a closed plane figure with straight sides that are line segments

WRITE Math

Copy and complete the degrees of meaning grid below for geometric figures. Use what you know about geometry to complete the grid.

General	Less General	Specific	More Specific
polygon			
solid figure			

Technology
Multimedia Math Glossary link at **www.harcourtschool.com/hspmath**

10 One- and Two-Dimensional Geometric Figures

The Big Idea Points, lines, planes, and their classifications and relationships are the building blocks of geometry.

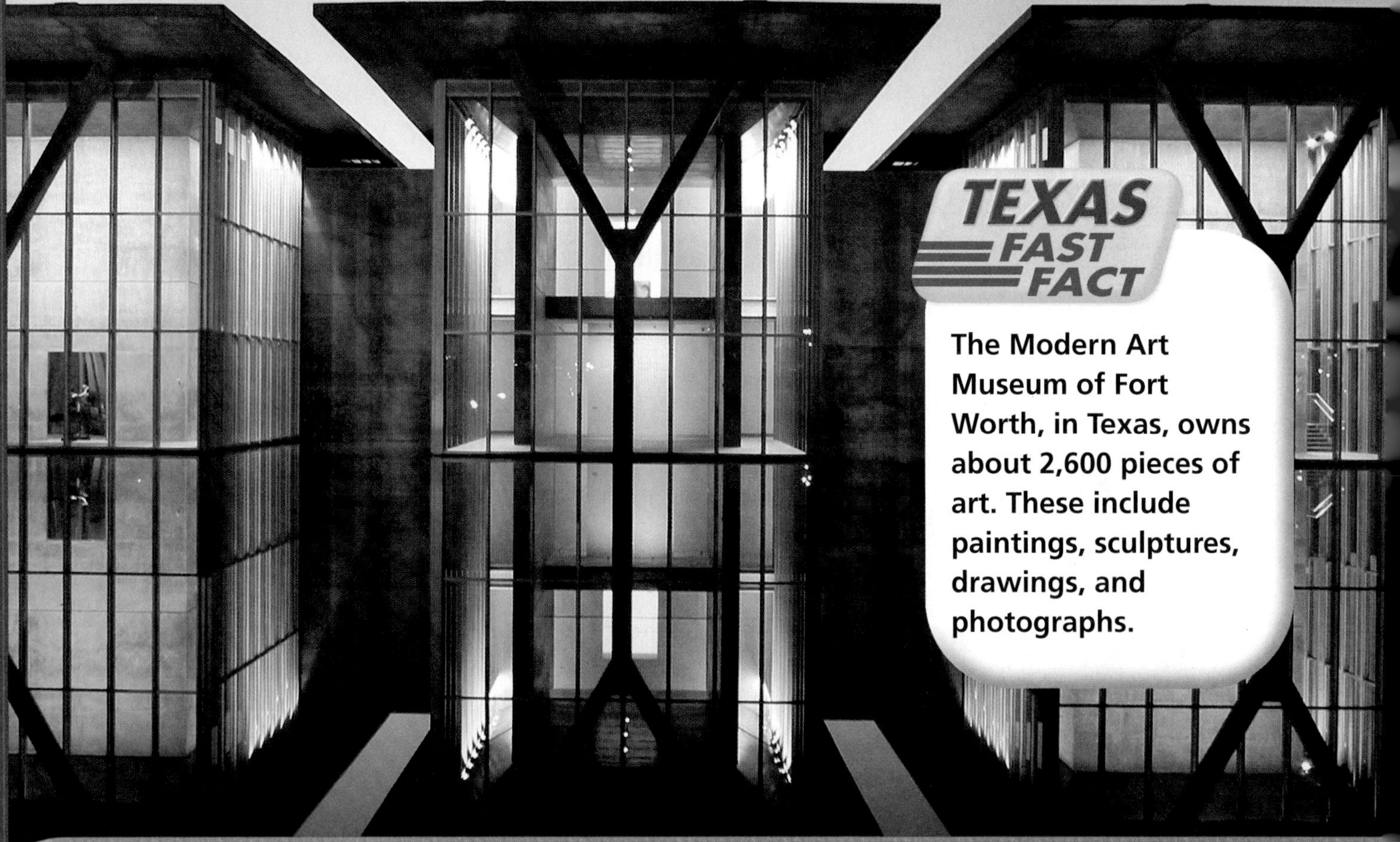

TEXAS FAST FACT

The Modern Art Museum of Fort Worth, in Texas, owns about 2,600 pieces of art. These include paintings, sculptures, drawings, and photographs.

Investigate

Homage to Victory Boogie Woogie No. 2, by Leon Polk Smith, hangs in the Modern Art Museum of Fort Worth. What geometric figures do you see in the painting? Draw a picture by combining two or more of those figures.

GO ONLINE **Technology**
Student pages are available in the Student eBook.

Show What You Know

Check your understanding of important skills needed for success in Chapter 10.

▶ Identify Geometric Figures

Write the name of each figure.

1.

2.

3.

4.

5.

6.

7.

8.

▶ Types of Lines

Describe the lines. Write *parallel* or *intersecting*.

9.

10.

11.

12.

▶ Sides and Angles

Write the number of sides and angles in each figure.

13. 

14. 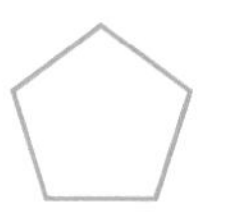

15. 

16. 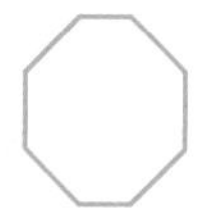

17. 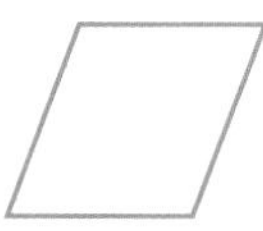

18. 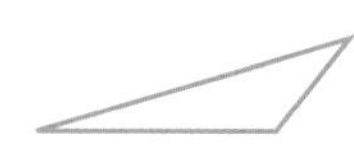

19. 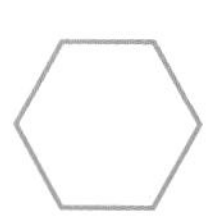

20. 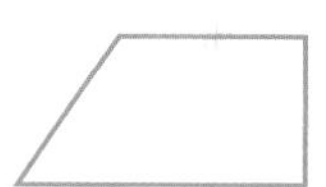

VOCABULARY POWER

CHAPTER VOCABULARY

center
circle
decagon
degree (°)
dimension
endpoint
intersecting lines
obtuse triangle
one-dimensional
parallel lines
perpendicular lines
plane
radius
regular polygon

WARM-UP WORDS

plane a flat surface that continues without end in all directions

endpoint the points at either end of a line segment or the starting point of a ray

dimension is a measurement along a straight line of length, width, or height of a figure

LESSON 1 Points, Lines, and Rays

OBJECTIVE: Identify, describe, and draw points, lines, line segments, rays, and planes.

Quick Review

Draw a line segment.

Vocabulary

point, line, line segment, endpoint, ray, dimension, plane, one-dimensional, two-dimensional

Learn

The vocabulary of geometry helps describe plane and solid figures you see both in nature and in the things people make. You can use the following geometric ideas and terms to describe the world around you.

TERM AND DEFINITION	DRAW IT	READ IT	WRITE IT	EXAMPLE
A **point** names an exact location in space.	A •	point *A*	point *A*	
A **line segment** is part of a line. It has two **endpoints**, the points at either end of the line segment, and all of the points between them.	D •———• E	line segment *DE* or line segment *ED*	$\overline{DE}$ or $\overline{ED}$	
A **line** is a straight path of points that continues without end in both directions with no endpoints.	←B———C→	line *BC* or line *CB*	$\overleftrightarrow{BC}$ or $\overleftrightarrow{CB}$	
A **ray** is part of a line that has one endpoint and continues without end in one direction.	F •———G→	ray *FG*	$\overrightarrow{FG}$	EXIT
A **plane** is a flat surface that continues without end in all directions.	K M L	plane *KLM*	plane *KLM*	

A plane is named by at least three points that are in the plane and do not form a straight line.

Dimension is a measurement along a straight line of length, width, or height of a figure. **One-dimensional** is a measure in only one direction, such as length. **Two-dimensional** is a measure in two directions, such as length and width. A rectangle is an example of a two-dimensional figure. Its dimensions are length and width.

TEKS 4.8 The student identifies and describes attributes of geometric figures using formal geometric language. *also* 4.14A, 4.15A, 4.15B

Guided Practice

1. Name the figure at the right. Think: It has 2 endpoints. A ●———● B

Name a geometric term that best represents the object.

2. tip of a tack
3. train track rail
4. flagpole
5. laser beam

6. TALK Math **Explain** how lines, line segments, and rays are alike and different.

Independent Practice and Problem Solving

Name the geometric term that best represents the object.

7. one way arrow
8. tip of a marker
9. parking lot
10. edge of a desk

Name an everyday object that represents the term.

11. line
12. line segment
13. ray
14. plane

Draw and label an example of each.

15. line XY
16. point H
17. ray MN
18. plane PQR

USE DATA For 19–20, use the photo.

19. What geometric term describes where 2 walls and a floor meet?
20. What features on the building show line segments?
21. **Reasoning** Draw four points. What is the greatest number of line segments you can draw by connecting the points?
22. Write all the names for this ray. R S T
23. WRITE Math **Explain** how you know which path is the shortest distance between point C and point D.

a. C D b. C D

Mixed Review and TAKS Prep

24. Use a basic fact and a pattern to find 12×700. (TEKS 4.6A, p. 224)
25. Jake bought a bowling ball on sale for \$56.79. To the nearest ten dollars, how much did it cost? (TEKS 4.5A, p. 34)
26. **TAKS Prep** Which geometric term best describes the yellow line in the photograph above? (Obj. 3)

A Plane
B Line segment
C Line
D Ray

Extra Practice on page 278, Set A

LESSON 2

Classify Angles

OBJECTIVE: Identify and describe right, acute and obtuse angles.

Quick Review

Write the name of each figure.

1. •
2. ⟶
3. ⟷
4. •—•
5.

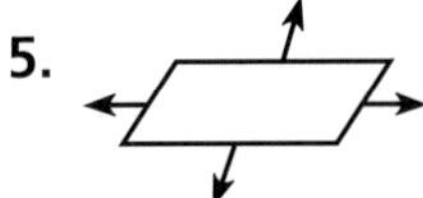

Vocabulary

angle
vertex
degree (°)
acute angle
right angle
obtuse angle

Learn

Two rays or line segments with the same endpoint form an **angle**. The shared endpoint is called a **vertex**.

DRAW IT	READ IT	WRITE IT
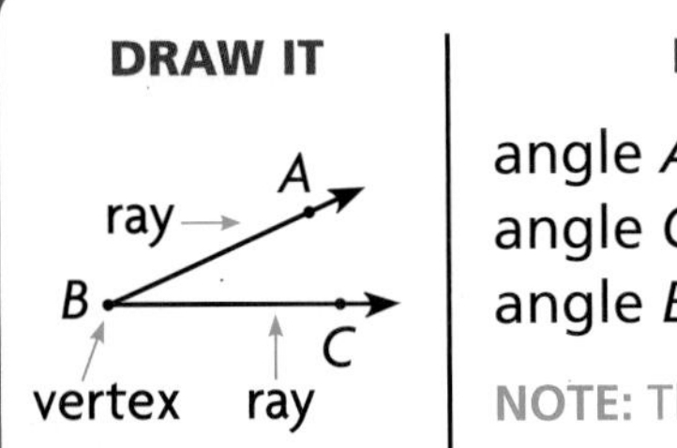	angle *ABC* angle *CBA* angle *B*	$\angle ABC$ $\angle CBA$ $\angle B$

NOTE: The vertex is always the middle letter or the single letter that names the angle.

PROBLEM In the Martian Matrix exhibit, angles are formed where the steel supports meet. The angle marked in yellow has the same measure as $\angle ABC$ above. Classify $\angle ABC$.

▲ The Martian Matrix Playscape at NASA's Johnson Space Center help students explore space station living.

Example Classify angles by comparing.

The unit used for measuring angles is a **degree (°)**.

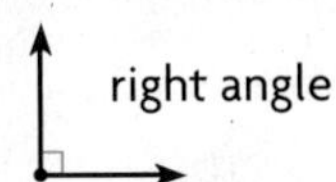	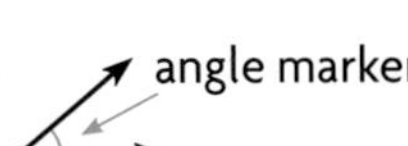	
right angle	angle marker	angle marker
A **right angle** measures 90°. The square marker shows a right angle forms a square corner.	An **acute angle** is an angle with a measure less than a right angle.	An **obtuse angle** is an angle with a measure greater than a right angle and less than a straight line.

So, the angle in the photo is an acute angle.

Activity Make a right angle.

Make a right angle by using a sheet of paper like this. Fold the paper twice evenly to make what appears to be a right angle.

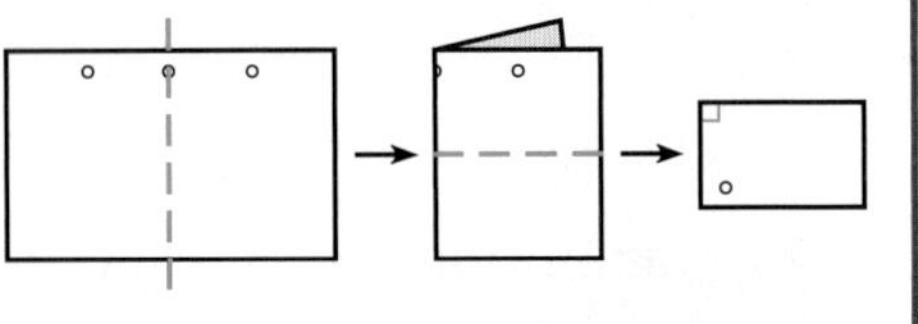

- Use the right angle to classify these angles as right, acute, or obtuse.

a.  **b.**  **c.** 

TEKS 4.8A identify and describe right, acute, and obtuse angles. *also* **4.14A, 4.14D, 4.15A, 4.15B, 4.16A, 4.16B**

Guided Practice

1. Classify the angle as acute, right, or obtuse.
   Think: Compare the angle to a right angle.

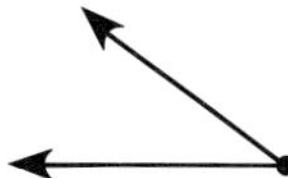

Classify each angle as *acute, right,* or *obtuse.*

2. 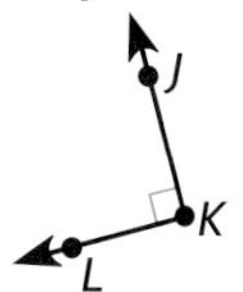

3. 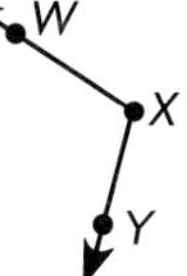

4. 

5. 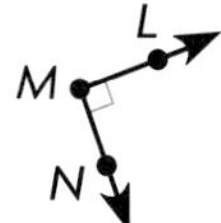

6. **TALK Math** Describe the number and types of angles found in the letter **X**.

Independent Practice and Problem Solving

Classify each angle as *acute, right,* or *obtuse.*

7.

8.

9. 

10. 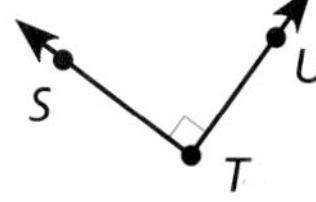

Draw and label an example of each.

11. right angle *ABC*
12. obtuse angle *DEF*
13. acute angle *MNO*
14. right angle *JKL*

For 15–16, use the picture of the bridge.

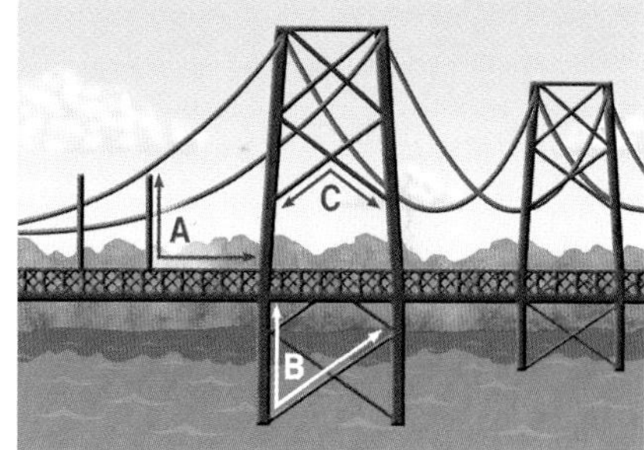

15. What type of angle does Angle *B* appear to be?
16. Which angle appears to be an obtuse angle?
17. **WRITE Math** **What's the Error?** Quan says there is only 1 right angle in the letter **F**. What error is he making? Correct his error.
18. Identify and name an obtuse angle, a right angle, and an acute angle in the Figure *X*.

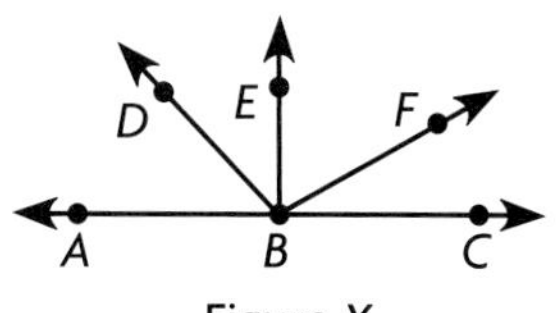

Figure *X*

Mixed Review and TAKS Prep

19. Tell the time as shown on the digital clock two different ways. (Grade 3 TEKS 3.1B)

20. **Explain** how a line and a ray are different. (TEKS 4.8 p. 258)

21. **TAKS Prep** At what time do the hands of a clock represent a right angle? (Obj. 3)
    A 12:30
    B 3:00
    C 3:15
    D 6:00

Extra Practice on page 278, Set B

LESSON 3

Line Relationships

OBJECTIVE: Identify, describe, and draw intersecting, parallel, and perpendicular lines

Quick Review

What is the name for the angle that forms a square corner?

Vocabulary

intersecting lines

parallel lines

perpendicular lines

Learn

PROBLEM Participants march in the Independence Day parade in Montclair, New Jersey. Use the terms below to identify an example of each type of line on the parade route map.

TERM AND DEFINITION	DRAW IT	READ IT	WRITE IT
Lines that cross each other at exactly one point are **intersecting lines**. They form four angles.	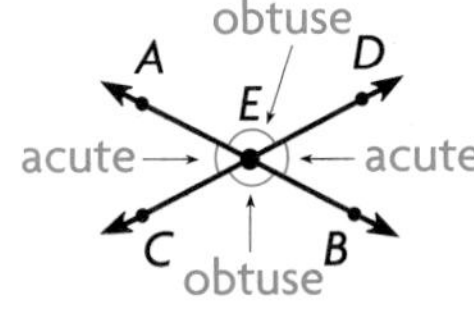	Line *AB* intersects line *CD* at point *E*.	$\overleftrightarrow{AB}$ intersects $\overleftrightarrow{CD}$ at point E.
Lines in the same plane that never intersect and are always the same distance apart are **parallel lines**.	H J F G	Line *FG* is parallel to line *HJ*.	$\overleftrightarrow{FG} \parallel \overleftrightarrow{HJ}$ The symbol $\parallel$ means "is parallel to."
Lines that intersect to form four right angles are **perpendicular lines**.	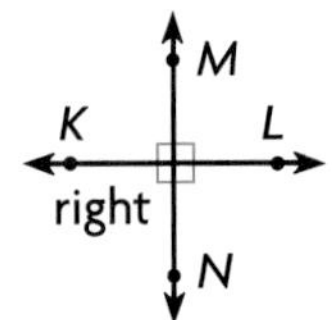	Line *KL* is perpendicular to line *MN*.	$\overleftrightarrow{KL} \perp \overleftrightarrow{MN}$ The symbol $\perp$ means "is perpendicular to."

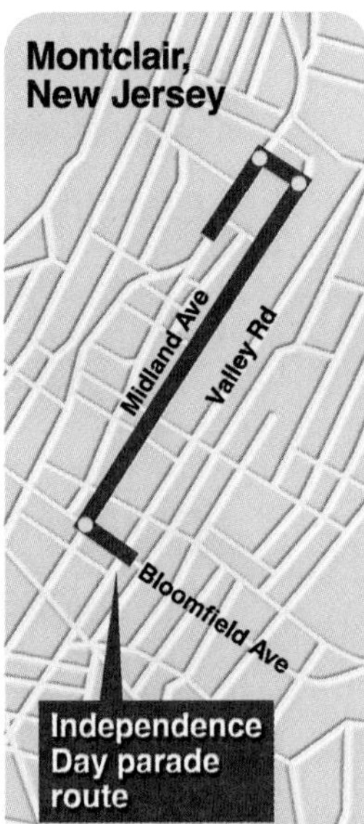

▲ The red line shows the Independence Day parade route.

• What term identifies the relationship between Midland Avenue and Valley Road?

Activity **Materials** ■ paper ■ straightedge

Fold paper to make intersecting, parallel, and perpendicular lines.

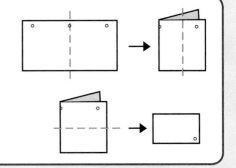

- As shown in the diagram at the right, fold the paper in half twice so that the vertical edges meet. Which term best identifies the three crease lines after you unfold the paper?
- Now fold the paper in half the other way. When you open the paper, describe how the crease lines appear? Which terms best identify the crease lines?

- Use grid paper to draw a pair of parallel lines, a pair of intersecting lines, and a pair of perpendicular lines.

TEKS 4.8B identify and describe parallel and intersecting (including perpendicular) lines using concrete objects and pictorial models. *also* **4.14A, 4.14D, 4.15A, 4.15B, 4.16A**

Guided Practice

1. How do you know if two lines are parallel? How do you know if two lines are perpendicular?

Name any line relationships you see in each figure. Write *intersecting, parallel,* or *perpendicular.*

2. 

3. 

✓4. 

✓5. 

6. **TALK Math** How does the symbol ∥ help you remember its meaning?

Independent Practice and Problem Solving

Name any line relationships you see in each figure. Write *intersecting, parallel,* or *perpendicular.*

7. 

8. 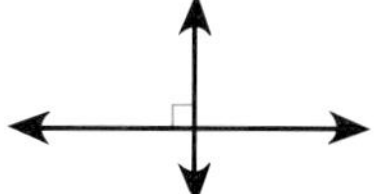

9. 

10. 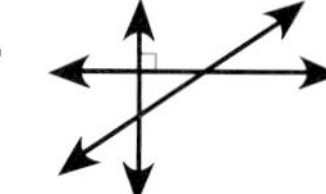

USE DATA For 11–13, use the map.

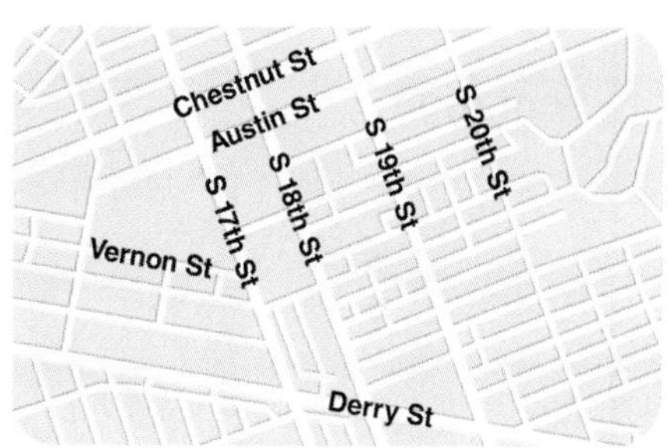

11. Name a street that appears to be parallel to S 17th Street.
12. Name a street that appears to be parallel to Vernon Street and intersects S 17th Street. Classify the angle.
13. What street intersects both S 17th Street and S 19th Street and appears to be perpendicular to them? Classify the angles.
14. **WRITE Math** **What's the Error?** Trina says that all intersecting lines are perpendicular lines. Explain her error.

Mixed Review and TAKS Prep

15. A bag has 8 green and 6 red marbles all the same size. Are you more likely, less likely, or equally likely to draw a red marble than a green marble from the bag? (Grade 3 TEKS 3.13C)
16. What geometric term describes an edge of a photograph? (TEKS 4.8, p. 258)
17. **TAKS Prep** Which best describes perpendicular lines? (Obj. 3)
    - **A** They never meet.
    - **B** They form four right angles.
    - **C** They form one acute angle.
    - **D** They form one obtuse angle.

Extra Practice on page 278, Set C

LESSON

4 Polygons

OBJECTIVE: Identify, classify, and describe polygons and determine whether polygons are regular or not regular.

Quick Review

Write the number of sides each figure has.

1. 

2.

3.

4.

5.

Vocabulary

polygon **hexagon**
triangle **octagon**
quadrilateral **decagon**
pentagon **regular polygon**

Learn

A **polygon** is a closed plane figure formed by three or more straight sides that are line segments which intersect at the endpoints. Polygons are named by the number of sides or number of angles they have.

PROBLEM Name the polygons you see in this painting by artist Paul Klee.

Polygon	Example	Sides and Angles
triangle		3 sides 3 angles
quadrilateral		4 sides 4 angles
pentagon		5 sides 5 angles
hexagon		6 sides 6 angles
octagon		8 sides 8 angles
decagon		10 sides 10 angles

▲ Paul Klee, a Swiss painter who lived from 1879 to 1940, is considered one of the most original painters of modern art.

So, you can see triangles, quadrilaterals, a pentagon, and a hexagon in the painting.

- Can a polygon have a different number of sides than angles?
- Do any of the figures with curved paths in Klee's painting form polygons? Explain your answer.
- **What if** you cut a hexagon into 2 polygons? What 2 polygons could be formed?

TEKS 4.8C use essential attributes to define two- and three-dimensional geometric figures. *also* **4.14A, 4.14D, 4.15A, 4.15B, 4.16A**

Example **Decide if each figure is a polygon.**

Polygon	Not a Polygon	Not a Polygon	Not a Polygon
		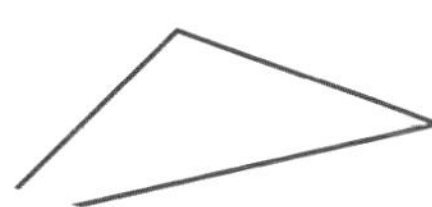	
Closed plane figure with 5 sides and 5 angles So, it is a polygon.	Sides intersect, but not at the endpoints. So, it is not a polygon.	Line segments do not connect. So, it is not a polygon.	A curved path is not a line segment. So, it is not a polygon.

- How can you tell what kind of polygon a figure is?
- Find an example of a polygon in the classroom. Describe the polygon.

A **regular polygon** has all sides equal in length and all angles equal in measure.

Regular Polygons

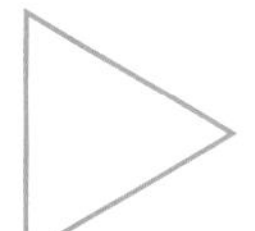
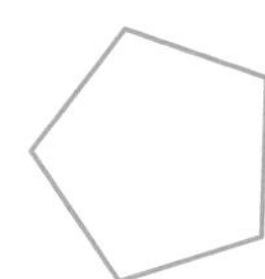
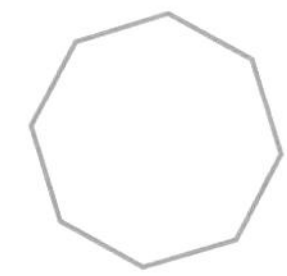

All sides have equal length.
All angles have equal measure.

Not Regular Polygons

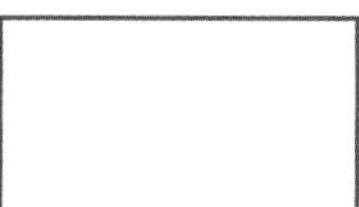
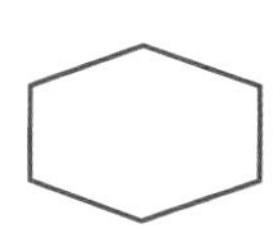
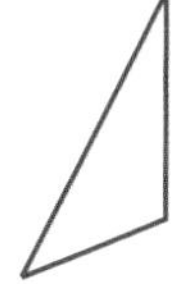

Not all the sides have equal length.
Not all the angles have equal measure.

- **What if** the quadrilateral had all sides equal? Would it be regular?
- **What if** the hexagon had all sides equal? Would it be regular?

Activity

Materials ■ dot paper ■ ruler

Draw a regular quadrilateral.

Step 1 Mark four points that are all the same distance apart.

Step 2 Connect the four points to form a regular quadrilateral.

Draw a quadrilateral that is not regular.

Step 1 Mark four points that are not the same distance apart.

Step 2 Connect the four points to form a quadrilateral that is not regular.

- How are the two quadrilaterals alike? How are they different?

Guided Practice

1. Does the figure have straight sides? Is it a closed figure? Is the figure a polygon?

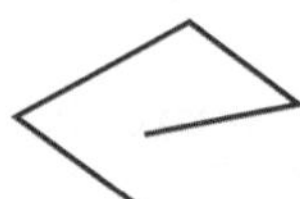

Name the polygon. Tell whether it appears to be *regular* or *not regular*.

2.

3.

4.

5. 

6. TALK Math **Explain** how you would draw a regular polygon with five sides and five angles on dot paper.

Independent Practice and Problem Solving

Name the polygon. Tell if it appears to be *regular* or *not regular*.

7. 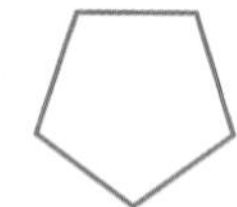

8. 

9. 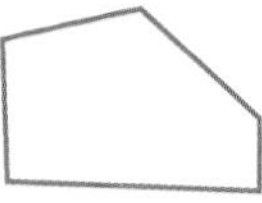

10. 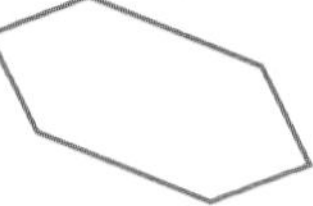

Tell if each figure is a polygon. Write *yes* or *no*. Explain.

11. 

12. 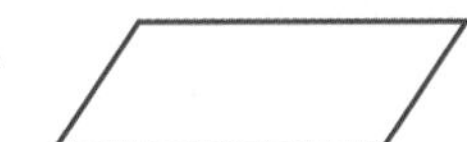

13. 

14. 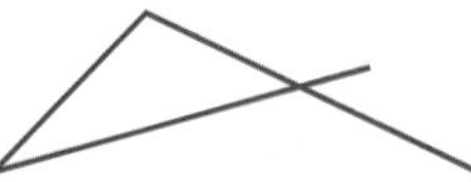

Use dot paper to draw each polygon.

15. a triangle that is not regular
16. a pentagon that is not regular
17. a hexagon that is not regular
18. a regular quadrilateral

19. Choose the figure that does not belong. **Explain.**

A

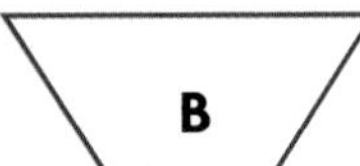

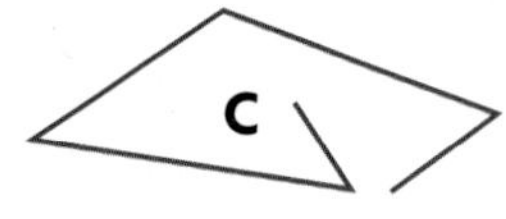

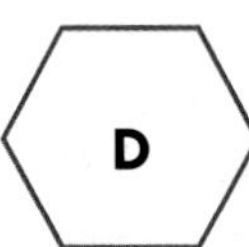

USE DATA For 20–21, use the painting.

20. **Reasoning** Is the brown figure in the center of Picasso's painting a polygon? **Explain** your thinking.

21. What polygons do you see in the painting?

22. WRITE Math **What's the Question?** Samir drew a picture with 2 triangles, 3 quadrilaterals, and 4 pentagons. The answer is 38.

▲ **Pablo Picasso's *Mandolin and Guitar***

Technology
Use Harcourt Mega Math, Ice Station Exploration, *Polar Planes,* Level D.

 Extra Practice on page 278, Set D

Mixed Review and TAKS Prep

23. Enrico bought a barbecue grill for $139 and a vacuum cleaner for $229. To the nearest hundred dollars, about how much did Enrico spend? (TEKS 4.5A, p. 40)

24. **TAKS Prep** Which of these polygons has more than five sides? (Obj. 3)

A Triangle

B Pentagon

C Octagon

D Rectangle

25. Classify the angle below. Write *acute*, *obtuse*, or *right* to describe the angle. (TEKS 4.8A, p. 260)

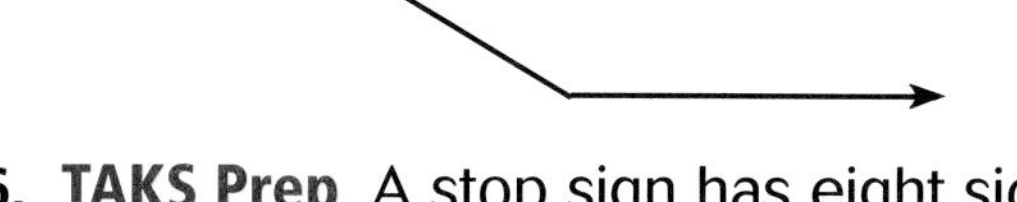

26. **TAKS Prep** A stop sign has eight sides of equal length and eight angles of equal measure. What is a good description for this figure? (Obj. 3)

Problem Solving connects to Art

Geometry

Architecture is the art and science of designing and building structures. Architects want to build structures that are pleasing to the eye. Architect I. M. Pei faced challenges when he designed the award winning East Wing of the National Gallery of Art on land shaped like a triangle.

Mr. Pei moved to the United States from Shanghai, China, to study architecture when he was 18. His designs won the Pritzker Prize in 1983. Mr. Pei works in the abstract form with stone, concrete, glass, and steel.

▲ I. M. Pei

1. Name the polygons you see in the aerial view of the East and West wings of the National Gallery.

2. How many sides does the polygon at the front of the photograph of the East Wing have?

▶ An aerial view of the East and West Wings

▶ The National Gallery of Art is located in Washington, D.C. This is a view of the East Wing.

LESSON 5

Classify Triangles

OBJECTIVE: Classify triangles by the lengths of their sides and the measures of their angles.

Quick Review

Draw a regular polygon.

Vocabulary

equilateral triangle
isosceles triangle
scalene triangle
right triangle
acute triangle
obtuse triangle

Learn

PROBLEM Objects shaped like triangles are often found in nature. One example is the leaf of a cottonwood tree. What type of triangle does this cottonwood leaf appear to be?

▲ The leaf of a cottonwood tree appears to be shaped like a triangle.

Example Classify triangles.

Classify by the lengths of their sides.

An **equilateral triangle** has 3 equal sides.

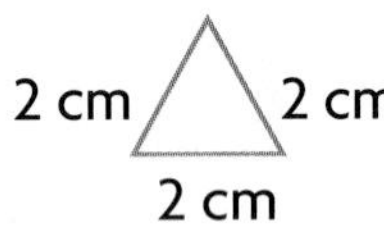

An **isosceles triangle** has 2 equal sides.

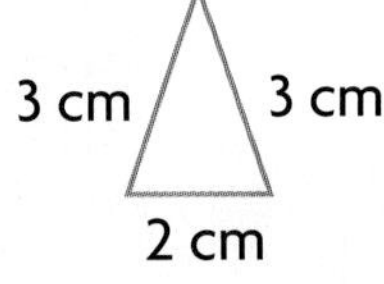

A **scalene triangle** has no equal sides.

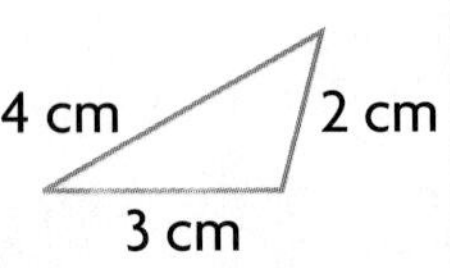

Classify by the measures of their angles.

A **right triangle** has 1 right angle.

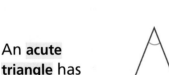

An **acute triangle** has 3 acute angles.

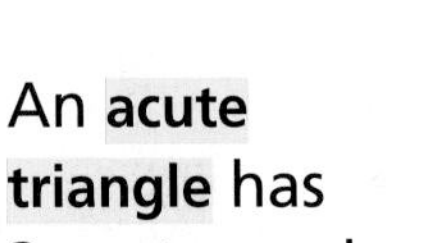

An **obtuse triangle** has 1 obtuse angle.

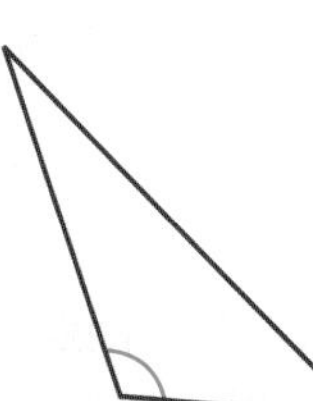

So, the cottonwood leaf appears to look like an equilateral triangle and an acute triangle. You may use the corner of a piece of paper to check.

- Is the equilateral triangle above also a regular triangle?
- Which of the two sides of a right triangle are perpendicular?

Math Idea
An equilateral triangle has 3 equal angles. An isosceles triangle has 2 equal angles. A scalene triangle has no equal angles.

Guided Practice

1. How many sides of the triangle are equal? What types of angles does the triangle have?

8 cm
10 cm
6 cm

TEKS 4.8C use essential attributes to define two-and three dimensional geometric figures. *also* **4.8A, 4.8B, 4.14A, 4.14D, 4.15A, 4.15B**

Classify each triangle. Write *isosceles, scalene,* or *equilateral.* Then write *right, acute,* or *obtuse*.

2. 3 in., 5 in., 4 in.

3. 9 ft, 6 ft, 7 ft

4. 9 yd, 9 yd, 9 yd

5. TALK Math **Explain** the difference between a right, an acute, and an obtuse triangle.

Independent Practice and Problem Solving

Classify each triangle. Write *isosceles, scalene,* or *equilateral*. Then write *right, acute,* or *obtuse*.

6. 10 ft, 10 ft, 17 ft

7. 5 in., 13 in., 12 in.

8. 3 in., 3 in., 3 in.

Classify each triangle by the lengths of its sides.

9. 4 in., 4 in., 4 in.

10. 30 cm, 40 cm, 50 cm

11. 3 ft, 7 ft, 7 ft

Measure the sides of each triangle using a centimeter ruler. Then classify.

12. 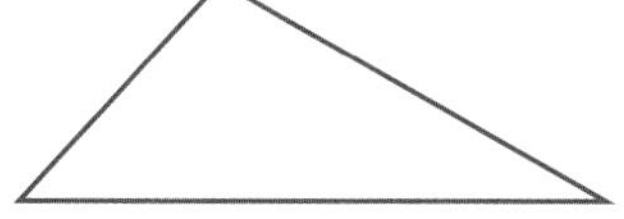

13. 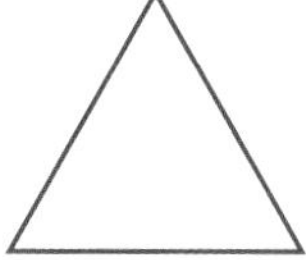

14. 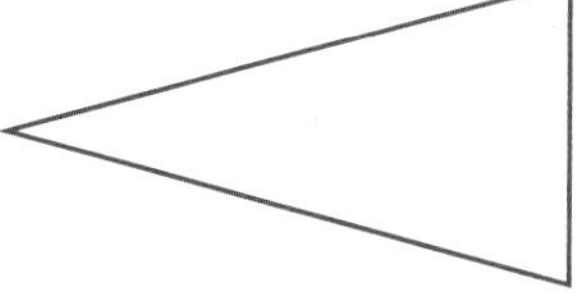

USE DATA For 15, use the photograph.

15. **FAST FACT** The American crocodile's head appears to be shaped like a triangle. Classify the shape of the head by the lengths of its sides. Write *isosceles*, *scalene*, or *equilateral*.

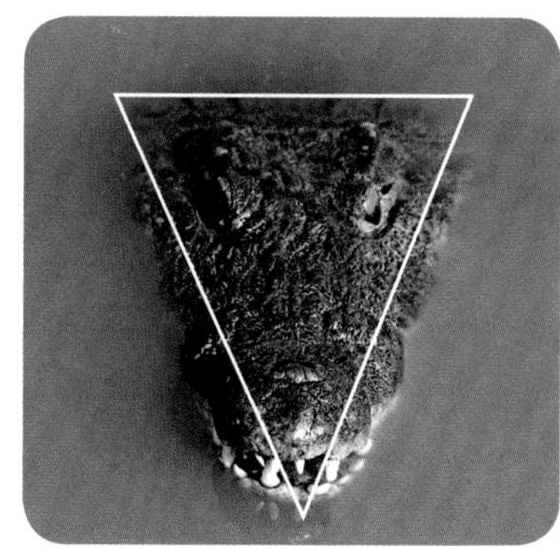

16. Draw 2 equilateral triangles that share a side. What polygon is formed? Is it a regular polygon?

17. WRITE Math **Explain** how a triangle can be isosceles and obtuse.

Mixed Review and TAKS Prep

18. Find the missing factor. (TEKS 4.4C, p. 160)

$\blacksquare \times 3 = 18$

19. What is the name of the polygon that has exactly 8 sides? (TEKS 4.8C, p. 264)

20. **TAKS Prep** Which kind of triangle has 3 equal sides? (Obj. 3)

A Square
B Scalene
C Right
D Equilateral

Extra Practice on page 279, Set E

LESSON 6

Classify Quadrilaterals

OBJECTIVE: Identify and classify quadrilaterals.

Quick Review

Draw a quadrilateral.

Vocabulary

parallelogram

rhombus

trapezoid

Learn

Architects use quadrilaterals when designing buildings. A quadrilateral is a polygon with 4 sides and 4 angles. There are many kinds of quadrilaterals. They can be classified by their features.

HANDS ON

Activity

Materials ■ geoboard ■ rubber bands ■ dot paper

Copy each quadrilateral on a geoboard. Use dot paper to record your work.

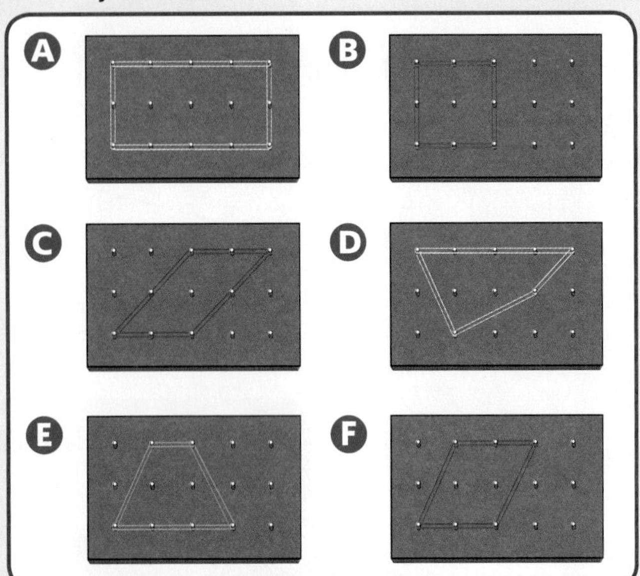

▲ PPG Place in downtown Pittsburgh, Pennsylvania has at least two special types of quadrilaterals.

- Which quadrilaterals shown above have 2 pairs of parallel sides? Which of these do you see in the photo?
- Which quadrilaterals shown above have 4 right angles? Which of these do you see in the photo?
- Which quadrilaterals shown above have 2 pairs of opposite sides that are equal? Which of these do you see in the photo?
- Which quadrilateral shown above has only 1 pair of parallel sides? Do you see this quadrilateral in the photo?
- Draw and extend line segments of quadrilateral B to make lines. Identify and describe any line relationships you see.

TEKS 4.8C use essential attributes to define two- and three-dimensional geometric figures. *also* **4.8A, 4.8B, 4.14A, 4.14D, 4.15A, 4.15B, 4.16A**

Special Quadrilaterals

There are five special types of quadrilaterals: **parallelogram**, square, rectangle, **rhombus**, and **trapezoid**. Each has different features, and some can be classified in more than one way. Use the diagram to help you identify each type of quadrilateral.

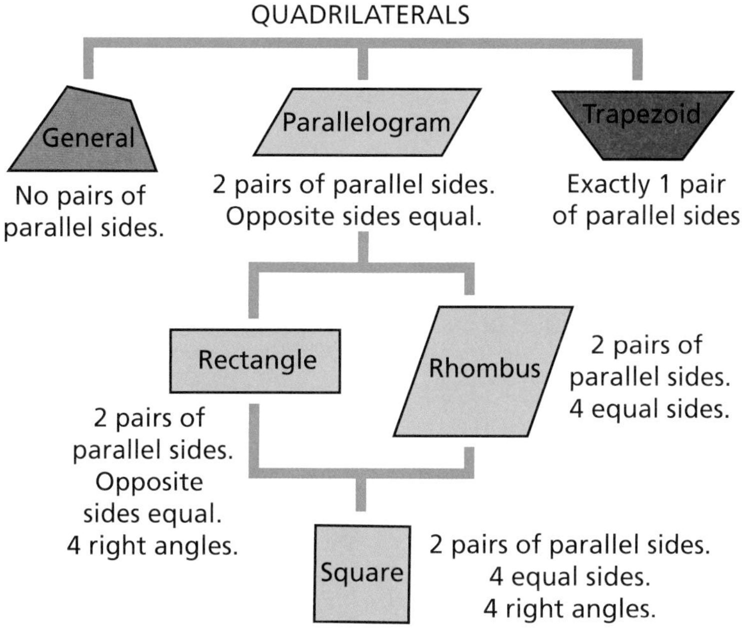

▲ ***Geometrico*** **by Mario Carreno**

- Which quadrilaterals are parallelograms? not parallelograms?
- Is a square a rhombus? a rectangle? Explain.

Guided Practice

1. Which are rectangles? Which is a trapezoid? Which are parallelograms?

A B C

Classify each figure in as many of the following ways as possible. Write *quadrilateral, parallelogram, rhombus, rectangle, square*, or *trapezoid*.

2. 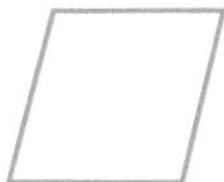

3. 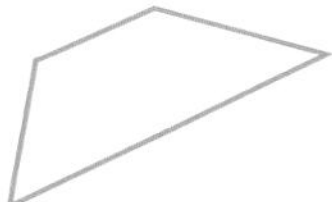

4. 

5. 

Draw an example of each quadrilateral.

6. It has 2 pairs of equal and parallel sides.

7. It has 4 right angles.

8. It has no parallel sides.

9. TALK Math **Explain** how quadrilaterals that are parallelograms are different from quadrilaterals that are not parallelograms.

Independent Practice and Problem Solving

Classify each figure in as many of the following ways as possible. Write *quadrilateral, parallelogram, rhombus, rectangle, square,* or *trapezoid.*

10. 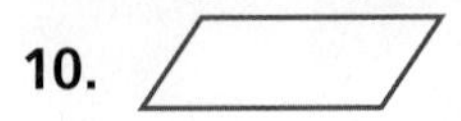

11.

12.

13.

Draw an example of each quadrilateral.

14. It has 1 pair of parallel sides.

15. It has 4 equal sides.

16. It has 2 pairs of parallel sides.

USE DATA For 17–18, use the photograph.

17. What are the different ways to classify the quadrilateral shown on the side of the building?

18. **Pose a Problem** Write a problem using the photograph and solve it.

19. **Reasoning** Is a square also a parallelogram? **Explain.**

20. Draw three equilateral triangles. Arrange them so they form one quadrilateral. What type of quadrilateral do they form?

For 21–24, write the letters of the figures that answer the questions.

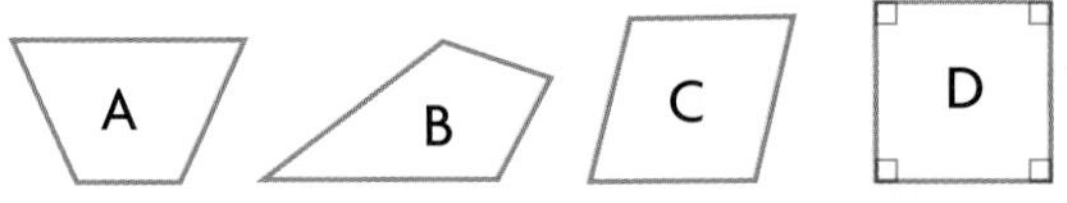

21. Which are parallelograms?

22. Which are rectangles?

23. Which are quadrilaterals?

24. **WRITE Math** **Explain** how a quadrilateral can be classified in more than one way. Give an example.

Mixed Review and TAKS Prep

25. Which line is perpendicular to $\overleftrightarrow{AB}$? (TEKS 4.8B, p. 262)

26. Is a book about 8 inches wide or 8 feet wide? (Grade 3 TEKS 3.11)

27. **TAKS Prep** Which is the best description of the figures? (Obj. 3)

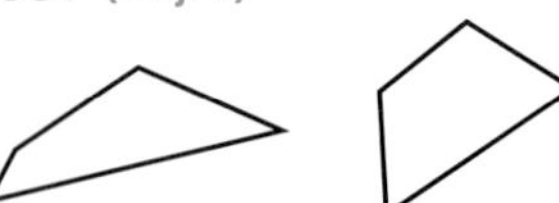

A Quadrilaterals

B Parallelograms

C Trapezoids

D Rectangles

 Extra Practice on page 279, Set F

Building Models

Classify and categorize

▲ The Fountain Place skyscraper in Dallas, Texas, has a ten-sided exterior of vertical and angled walls.

Students made a cardboard model of the Fountain Place skyscraper. They cut out rectangles and trapezoids to make the sides of the building as outlined in the photo at the right. Then, they used triangles to complete the frame of the building. How many types of quadrilaterals did the students need to make their model?

Using the reading strategy *classify and categorize* can help you organize and understand information in math problems. Use the table to *classify and categorize* the plane figures.

Quadrilaterals			Not Quadrilaterals
No parallel sides	1 pair of parallel sides	2 pairs of parallel sides	
General			

Problem Solving Classify and Categorize to understand the problem.

1. Solve the problem above.
2. Look at the drawing to the right. A student decided to cut out two separate figures and then combine them to make the entire side of the building. How could he cut the figures?

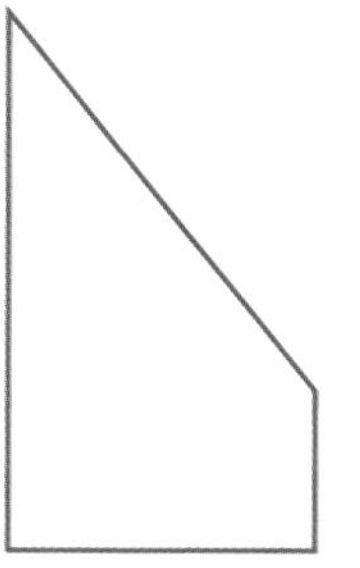

Circles

OBJECTIVE: Identify, draw, and label parts of a circle.

Quick Review

1. 2×11
2. $14 \div 2$
3. 15×2
4. $10 \div 2$
5. $26 \div 2$

Vocabulary

circle **radius** **diameter**
center **compass**

Learn

PROBLEM A hurricane is a large tropical cyclone with winds that spin around the storm's "eye". The spinning winds of a hurricane form a shape that appears to look like a circle. Around what geometric point do the winds spin?

Example Identify parts of a circle.

A **circle** is a closed figure made up of points that are the same distance from the center. A circle can be named by its center, which is labeled with a capital letter.

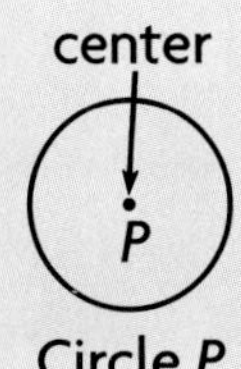

Circle P

A tropical cyclone is called a hurricane if winds are greater than 74 miles per hour.

Other parts of a circle:

A **diameter** is a line segment that passes through the center of a circle and has endpoints on the circle.

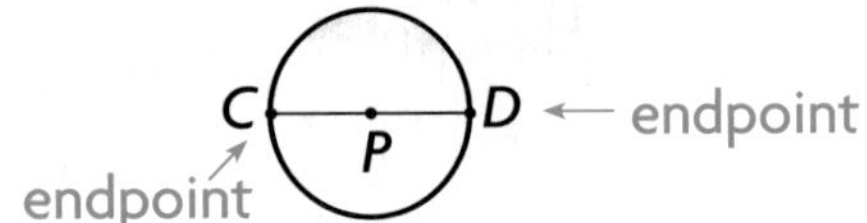

diameter: $\overline{CD}$

A **radius** is a line segment with one endpoint at the center of the circle and the other endpoint on the circle.

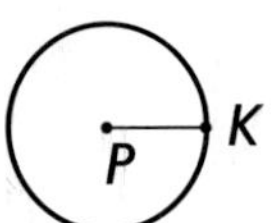

radius: $\overline{PK}$

The radius of a circle is half the length of the diameter.

So, the winds spin around the geometric point called the center, or eye, of the hurricane.

A **compass** is a tool used to construct circles.

Activity Materials ■ compass ■ ruler

Step 1

Draw a point to be the center of the circle. Label it with the letter P.

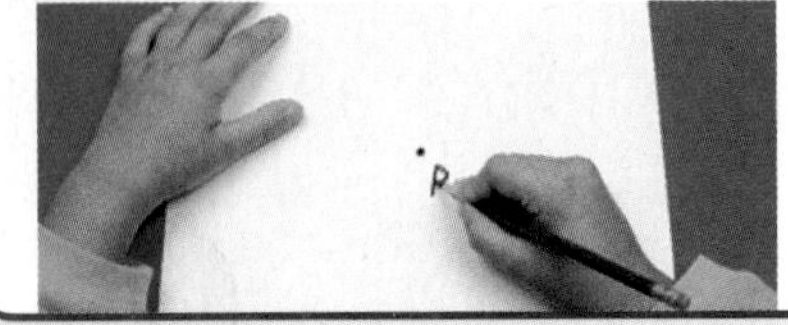

Step 2

Set the compass to the length of the radius you want.

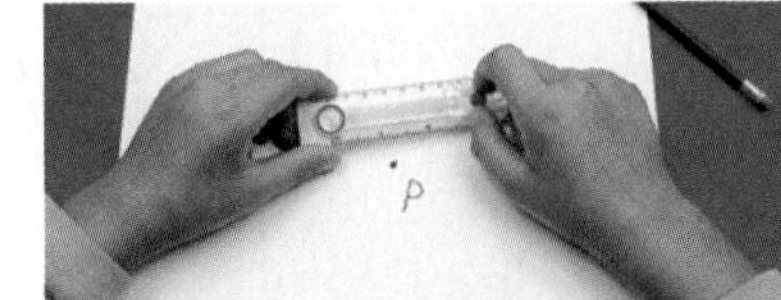

Step 3

Hold the compass point at point P, and move the compass to make the circle.

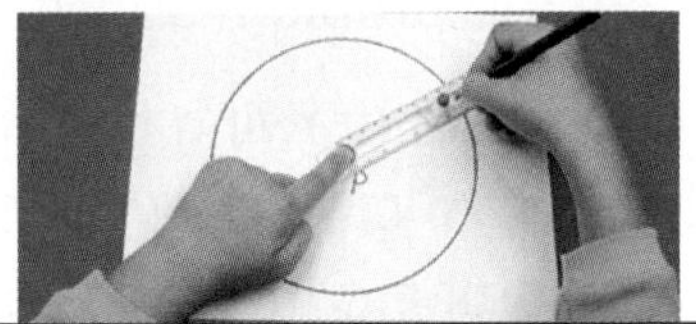

TEKS 4.8C use essential attributes to define two- and three-dimensional geometric figures. *also* **4.11A, 4.14A, 4.14D, 4.15A, 4.15B**

Guided Practice

1. A circle has a diameter of 12 inches. How would you find the length of the radius?

Construct circle *J* with a 5-centimeter radius. Label each of the following.

2. radius: $\overline{JA}$
3. radius: $\overline{JD}$
4. diameter: $\overline{BC}$

5. TALK Math **Describe** The relationship between the radius and the diameter.

Independent Practice and Problem Solving

Construct circle *L* with a 2-inch radius. Label each of the following.

6. radius: $\overline{LN}$
7. diameter: $\overline{MO}$
8. diameter: $\overline{QR}$

For 9–12, use the drawing of circle *Z* and a centimeter ruler. Copy and complete the table.

	Name	Part of Circle	Length in cm
9.	$\overline{ZY}$	?	■
10.	$\overline{ZW}$	?	■

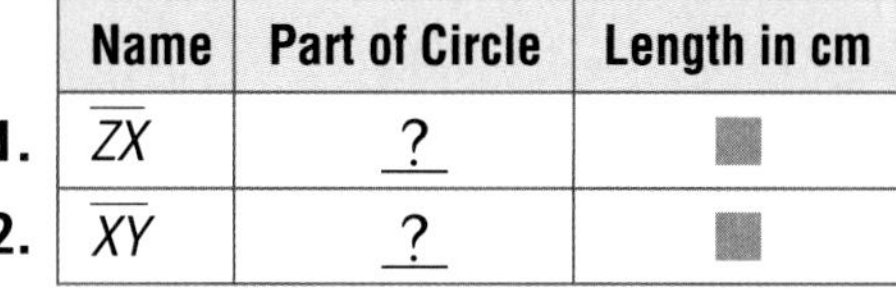

	Name	Part of Circle	Length in cm
11.	$\overline{ZX}$	?	■
12.	$\overline{XY}$	?	■

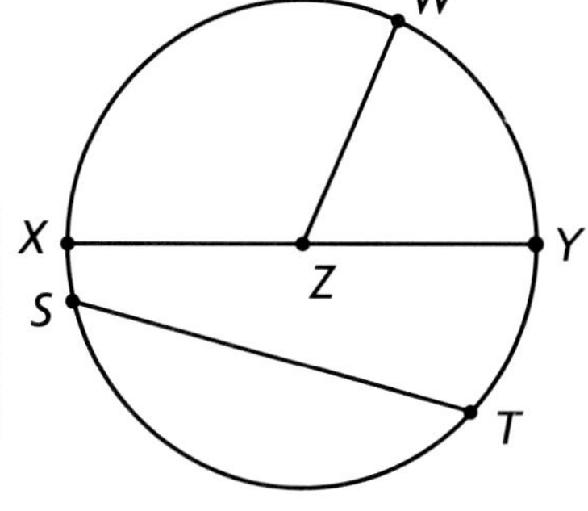

USE DATA For 13–15, use the diagram.

13. **FAST FACT** The strength of a hurricane is measured by its size and by the force of its winds. What is the radius of Hurricane A in miles?
14. What is the diameter of Hurricane B in miles?
15. How much greater is the diameter of Hurricane B than the diameter of Hurricane A?
16. WRITE Math **Explain** why a circle can have more than one radius.

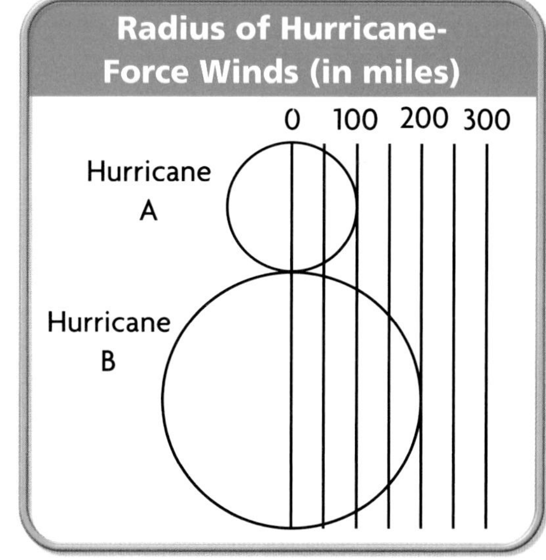

Mixed Review and TAKS Prep

17. Make a bar graph that compares the length of the hurricanes in the figure above. (Grade 3 TEKS 3.13A)
18. The sides of a triangle are 8 cm, 6 cm, and 8 cm. Is the triangle isosceles, scalene, or equilateral? (TEKS 4.8, p. 268)
19. **TAKS Prep** What is the length of the radius of a circle with a diameter of 22 inches? (Obj. 3)

A 11 inches
B 12 inches
C 22 inches
D 44 inches

Extra Practice on page 279, Set G

Problem Solving Workshop
Strategy: Use Logical Reasoning

OBJECTIVE: Solve problems by using the strategy *use logical reasoning.*

Vocabulary
Venn diagram

Use the Strategy

PROBLEM Jack's parents have five swimming pool diagrams shaped like plane figures. They ask Jack to sort the diagrams into two piles according to whether or not each pool has a right angle. How can the figures be sorted?

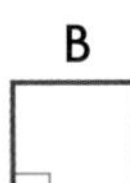

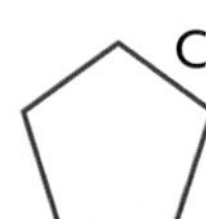

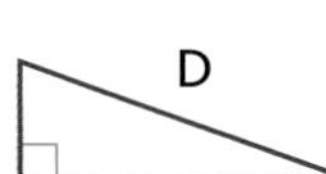

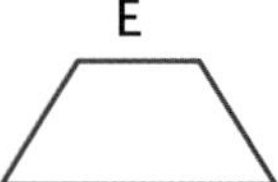

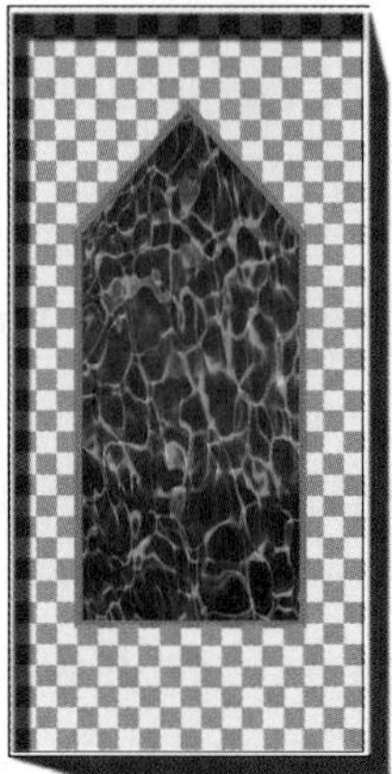
Pentagon Swimming Pool Design

Read to Understand

- **Classify and categorize the plane figures.**
- **What information is given?**

Plan

- **What strategy can you use to solve the problem?**
  You can use logical reasoning.

Solve

- **How will you solve the problem?**
  Use logical reasoning.
  Make a Venn diagram with 2 overlapping ovals. **Venn diagrams** show relationships among sets of things. Label one oval *With Right Angle* and the other oval *Without Right Angle*. Write the letter of the figure in a Venn diagram. In the area where the two ovals intersect, write the letter of the figure that fits both categories.

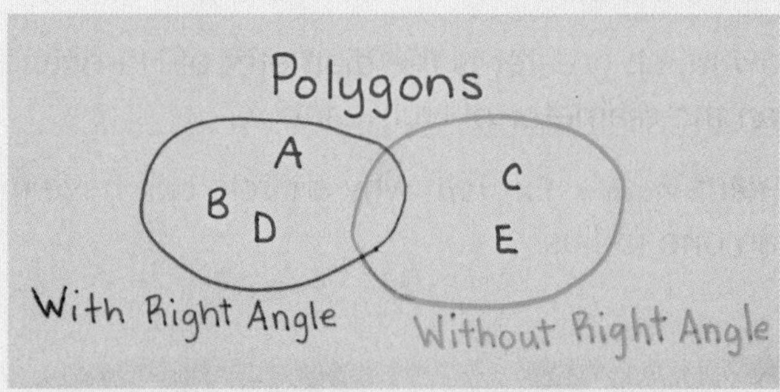

So, Jack sorted swimming pool diagrams C and E into the *Without Right Angle* pile and diagrams A, B, and D into the *With Right Angle* pile.

Check

- **How do you know your answer is correct?**

TEKS 4.14C select or develop an appropriate problem-solving strategy, including drawing a picture, looking for a pattern, systematic guessing and checking, acting it out, making a table, working a simpler problem, or working backwards to solve a problem. *also* **4.8A, 4.8C, 14.4A, 4.14B, 4.15A, 4.15B, 4.16A**

Guided Problem Solving

1. Which of the swimming pool diagrams below have at least one set of parallel sides and at least one acute angle?

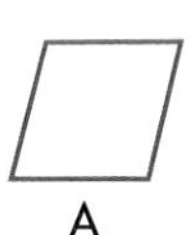
A

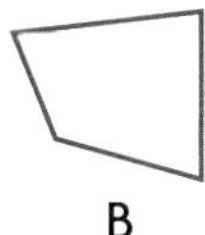
B

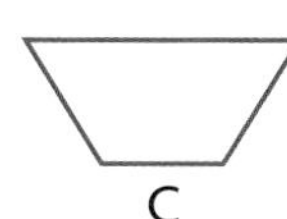
C

D

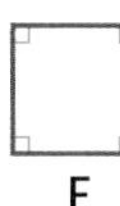
E

First, choose a strategy.

Next, draw and label a Venn diagram with overlapping ovals. Label one oval "At Least 1 Set of Parallel Sides" and the other oval "At Least 1 Acute Angle".

Then, use the diagram to classify and categorize the figures to help you organize and understand the information.

2. **What if** you were asked to find the swimming pool diagrams that had at least two sets of parallel sides and at least one obtuse angle? What would your answer be?

3. George wants to design a swimming pool that has at least two sets of parallel sides and and at least two sets of equal sides. Identify the figures shown above that appear to be like George's design?

Choose a STRATEGY

- Use Logical Reasoning
- Draw a Diagram or Picture
- Make a Model or Act It Out
- Make an Organized List
- Look for a Pattern
- Make a Table or Graph
- Guess and Check
- Work Backward
- Solve a Simpler Problem
- Write an Equation

Mixed Strategy Practice

4. Jack's aunt bought a new pool that was shaped like a diamond with two obtuse angles. Classify the shape of her pool in as many ways as possible.

USE DATA For 5, use the picture.

5. Jack and his sisters Rika and Daria combined their money to buy a snorkeling set to use in the new pool. The amounts they gave are shown in the picture. Jack gave more than Daria, and Rika gave more than Jack. How much did each person pay?

6. Rika threw 6 coins with a total value of $0.40 into the swimming pool. She had only two different kinds of coins. What coins did Rika throw into the pool?

7. *Swimmer* magazine costs $3 per issue at the newsstand. Daria will save $21 if she buys a 12-issue subscription. How much does a 12-issue subscription to the magazine cost?

8. **WRITE Math** Write down everything you know and everything you can find out about a rhombus and a square. **Compare** your two lists.

Extra Practice

Set A Name the geometric term that best represents the object. (pp. 258–259)

1. fishing pole **2.** the tip of a pen **3.** table top **4.** edge of ruler

Draw and label an example of each.

5. ray *AB* **6.** plane *CDE* **7.** line *NM* **8.** point *P*

9. Which geometric term is a straight path of points that continues without end in both directions with no endpoints?

Set B Classify each angle as *acute*, *right*, or *obtuse*. (pp. 260–261)

1.

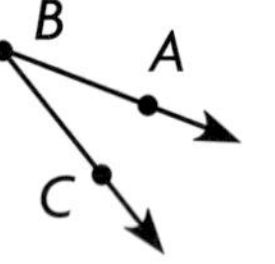

2. C D E

3.

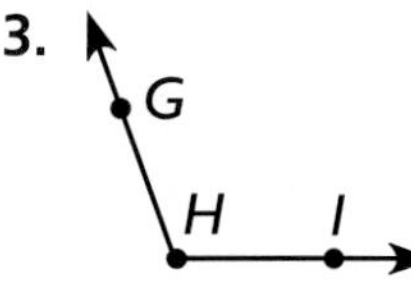

4. N M O

Draw and label an example of each.

5. right angle *HJW* **6.** obtuse angle *CMG* **7.** acute angle *RST* **8.** obtuse angle *XYZ*

Set C Name any line relationship you see in each figure. Write *intersecting*, *parallel*, or *perpendicular*. (pp. 262–263)

1.

2.

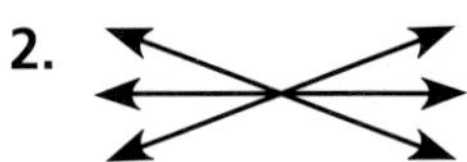

3.

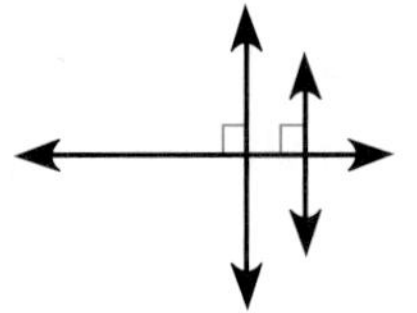

4.

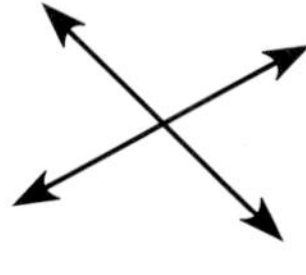

Set D Name the polygon. Tell if it appears to be *regular* or *not regular*. (pp. 264–267)

1.

2.

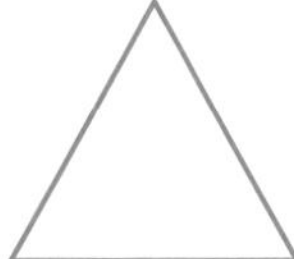

3.

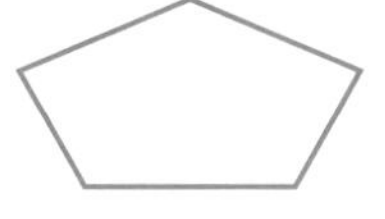

4.

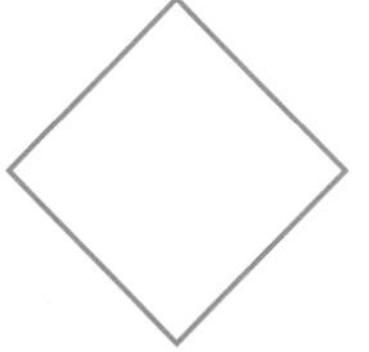

Tell if each figure is a polygon. Write *yes* or *no*. Explain.

5.

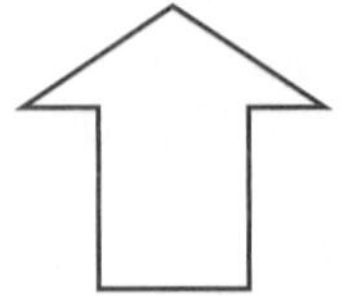

6.

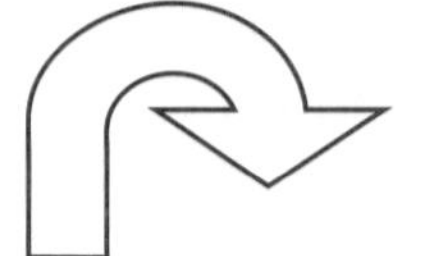

7.

8.

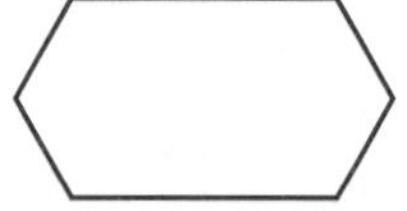

CD ROM **Technology**
Use Harcourt Mega Math, Ice Station Exploration, *Polar Planes,* Levels A, B, D, F, G.

Set E Classify each triangle. Write *isosceles*, *scalene*, or *equilateral*. Then write *right*, *acute*, or *obtuse*. (pp. 268–269)

1. 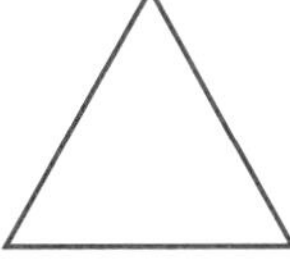
2. 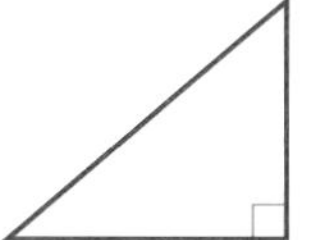
3. 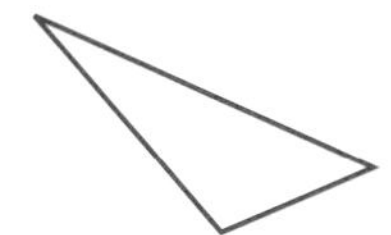
4. 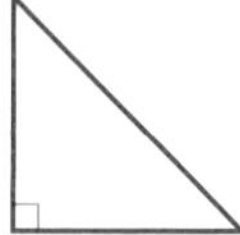

Classify each triangle by the lengths of its sides. Write *isosceles*, *scalene*, or *equilateral*.

5. 7 cm, 24 cm, 25 cm
6. 8 ft, 8 ft, 8 ft
7. 9 in., 9 in., 13 in.
8. 6 m, 8 m, 9 m

Set F Classify each figure in as many of the following ways as possible. Write *quadrilateral*, *parallelogram*, *rhombus*, *rectangle*, *square*, or *trapezoid*. (pp. 270–273)

1. 
2. 
3. 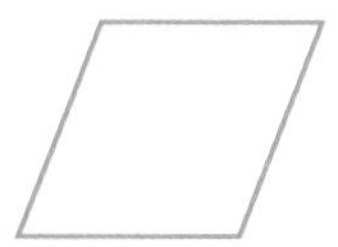
4. 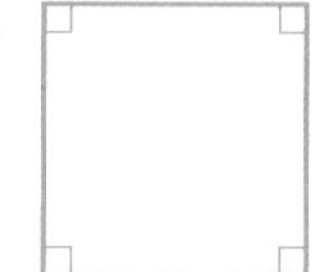

5. I have 4 sides and 4 angles. At least one of my angles is acute. What figures could I be?

Set G Use the drawing of circle Y and a centimeter ruler. Copy and complete the table. (pp. 274–275)

	Name	Part of circle	Length in cm
1.	$\overline{AB}$	?	■
2.	$\overline{YA}$	?	■
3.	$\overline{YE}$	?	■

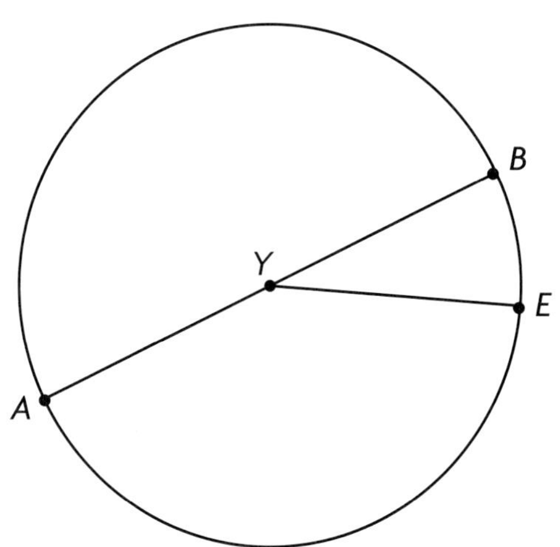

4. A carousel has a diameter of 50 feet. What is the length of the carousel's radius?

Chapter 10 Review/Test

Check Vocabulary and Concepts

Choose the best term from the box.

VOCABULARY
hexagon
octagon
two-dimensional

1. A(n) __?__ is a polygon with 8 sides. (TEKS 4.8C, p. 264)
2. __?__ is a line measure in two directions, such as length and width. (TEKS 4.8A, p. 258)

Check Skills

Classify each angle as *acute*, *right*, or *obtuse*. (TEKS 4.8A, pp. 260–261)

3. 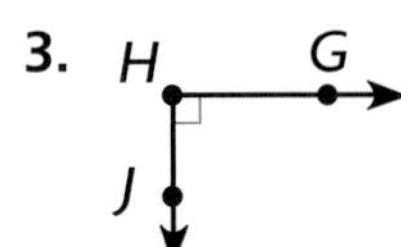

4. 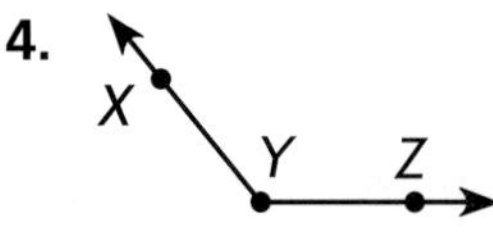

5. 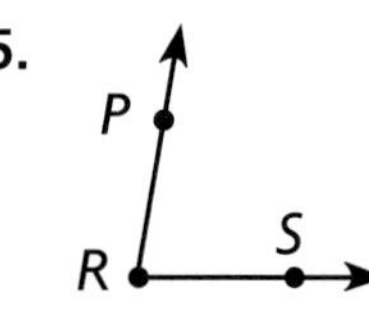

6. 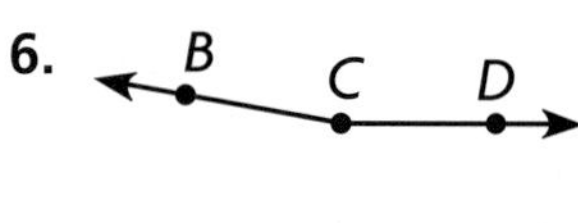

Name any relationship you see in each figure. Write *intersecting*, *parallel*, or *perpendicular*. (TEKS 4.8C, p. 262)

7. 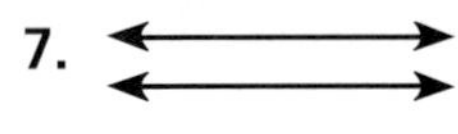

8. 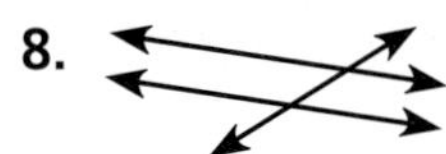

9. 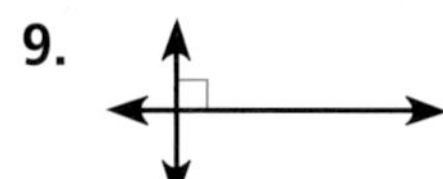

10. 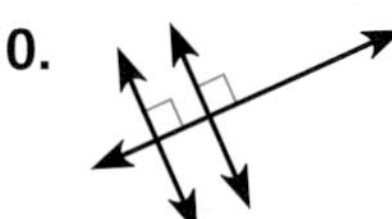

Classify each figure in as many ways as possible. (TEKS 4.8A, 4.8C pp. 268–269, 270–273)

11. 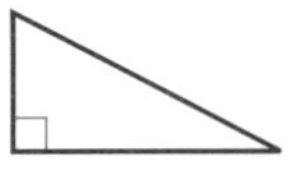

12. 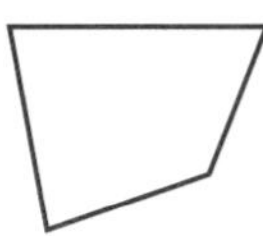

13. 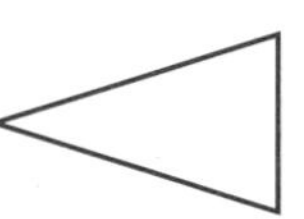

14. 

15. 

16. 

17. 

18. 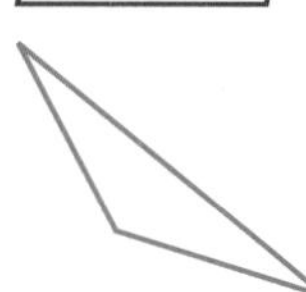

Check Problem Solving

Solve. (TEKS 4.14C, pp. 276–277)

19. Sort these figures into a Venn diagram showing *Polygons* and *Not A Polygon*.

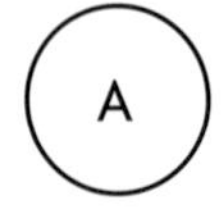

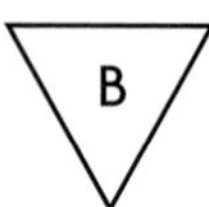

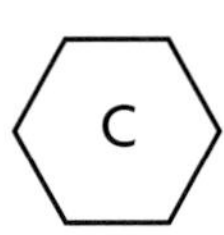

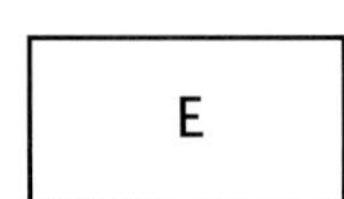

20. **WRITE Math** **Explain** how to draw a Venn diagram showing 6 types of quadrilaterals sorted into two groups, one with 2 *pairs of parallel sides* and one with *fewer than 2 pairs of parallel sides*.

GO ONLINE **Technology** Use *Online Assessment.*

Enrich • Use Visual Thinking

Look Closely

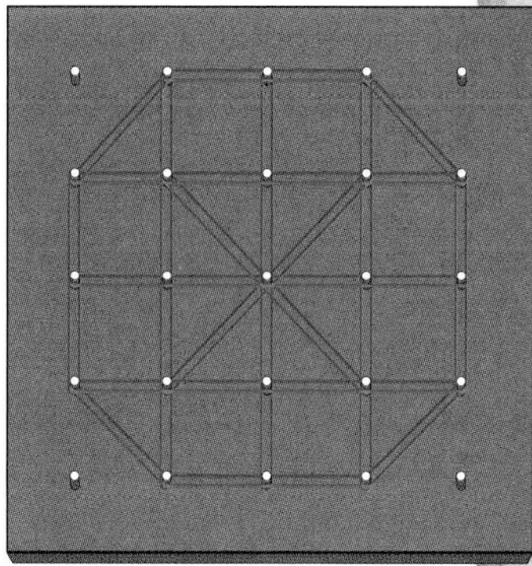

Kevin made this figure on his geoboard. How many triangles are in his figure?

To find the number of triangles in the figure, look for triangles that are made of one part, two parts, three parts, or four parts. Organize the information in a table to keep track of each type of triangle.

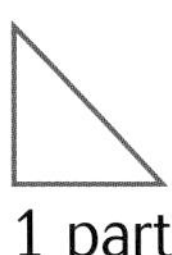

1 part

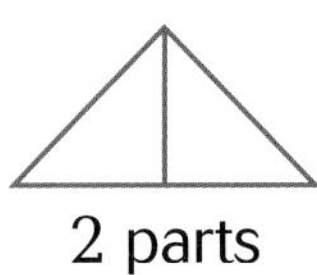

2 parts

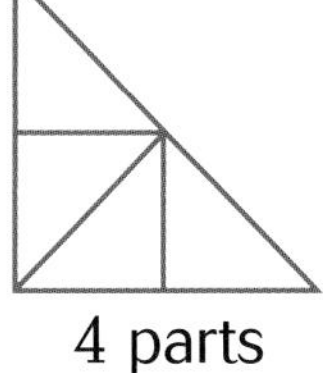

4 parts

Triangles	
Parts	**Number**
One Part	12
Two Parts	4
Three Parts	0
Four Parts	4

Number of triangles: $12 + 4 + 0 + 4 = 20$
So, the figure has 20 triangles.

Look Again!

What other polygons do you see in the figure? Do you see rectangles? trapezoids? pentagons? other polygons? You can find each of these polygons in the figure.

A How many squares are in the figure?

Think: Two triangles make a square.

Squares: $12 + 5 = 17$

Squares				
Parts	1	2	3	4
Number	12	0	0	5

B How many rectangles that are not squares are in the figure?

Rectangles: $16 + 8 + 4 + 4 + 2 = 34$

Rectangles that are not squares.							
Parts	2	3	4	5	6	7	8
Number	16	8	4	0	4	0	2

Go Figure!

Copy and complete the table. Find the number of polygons in each figure.

1.

Parts	1	2	3	4	5	6
Rectangles	■	■	■	■	■	■

2.

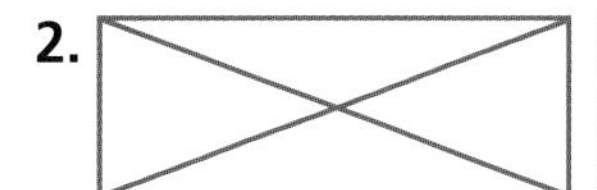

Parts	1	2	3
Triangles	■	■	■

WRITE Math ▸ **Explain** how a table can help you keep track of the number of polygons in a figure.

Getting Ready for the TAKS
Chapters 1–10

Number, Operation, and Quantitative Reasoning (TAKS Obj. 1)

1. The school district budgeted $678,500 for new classrooms. The contractor charged an additional $29,377 for the job. What was the total cost of the new classrooms?

   A $707,877

   B $704,177

   C $702,577

   D $699,377

2. The Arts Center has 28 rows of seats. There are 16 seats in each row. How many seats are in the Art Center?

   F 448 H 280

   G 160 J 44

3. The table shows the changes in the population of a city during 10 years.

City Population	
Year	**Population**
1995	11,692
2000	18,289
2005	22,966

   About how much did the population increase between 1995 and 2000?

   A 4,700 C 6,600

   B 5,300 D 11,300

4. WRITE Math Draw an array to represent one way to factor 24. **Explain** your thinking.

Patterns, Relationships, and Algebra Thinking (TAKS Obj. 2)

5. Which number sentence is in the same fact family as $56 \div 7 = ■$?

   F $7 + ■ = 56$

   G $56 \times 7 = ■$

   H $■ - 7 = 56$

   J $7 \times ■ = 56$

6. Kim's Caterers provides food for events. The table shows how many platters they need for different numbers of guests.

Kim's Caterers Platter Planning Chart				
Number of Guests	10	20	30	40
Number of Platters	2	4	6	■

   How many platters does Kim's Caterers need in order to provide food for 40 guests?

   A 4 C 10

   B 8 D 12

7. Which pair of numbers best completes the equation?

   $$■ \times 100 = ■$$

   F 43 and 430

   G 43 and 4,300

   H 43 and 43,000

   J 43 and 430,000

8. WRITE Math **Explain** how you could use a pattern to divide 20,000 by 5.

Geometry and Spatial Reasoning (TAKS Obj. 3)

9. What is the distance between Point *A* and Point *B*?

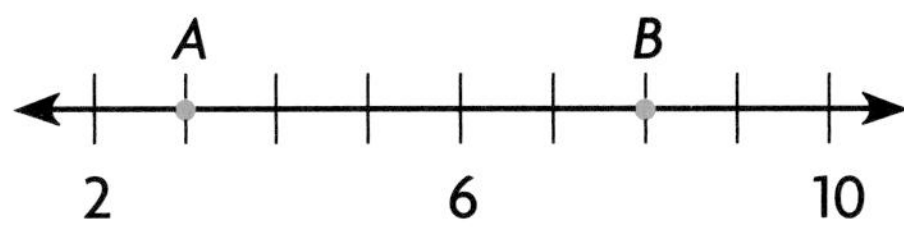

A 3 units
C 5 units
B 4 units
D 8 units

10. Classify this angle.

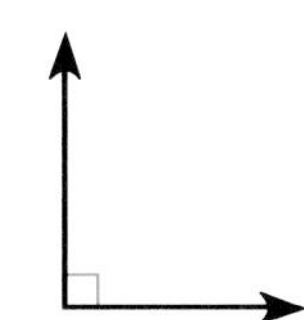

F Acute
G Right
H Obtuse
J Not here

11. Identify a radius of circle *T*.

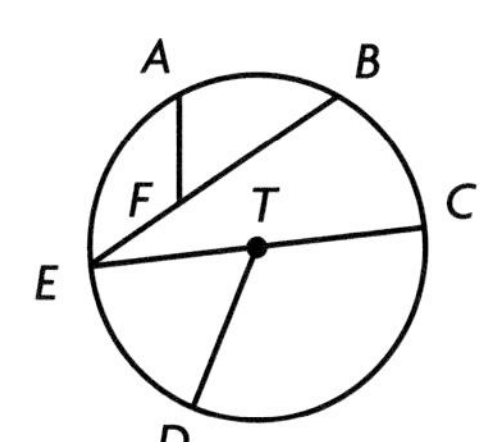

A $\overline{AF}$
C $\overline{CE}$
B $\overline{BE}$
D $\overline{DT}$

12. **WRITE Math** Look at this figure.

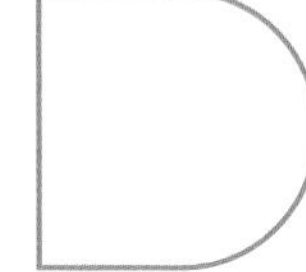

Is it a polygon? **Explain** how you know.

Probability and Statistics (TAKS Obj. 5)

Get the information you need.

See item 13. Look at the answer choices to see what information is needed from the graph. You need to know how many students prefer magazines and how many prefer fiction.

13. Leonardo surveyed 32 of his classmates to find what they preferred to read. The bar graph shows his findings.

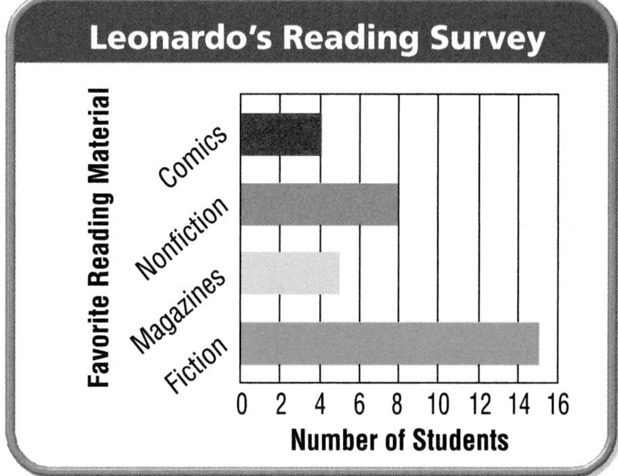

Which statement is true?

F 15 students prefer magazines.
G 8 students prefer magazines.
H 15 students prefer fiction.
J 8 students prefer fiction.

14. **WRITE Math** Is rolling a multiple of 3 on a number cube more likely than, less likely than, or equally likely as rolling an even number? **Explain** how you know.

11 Transformations, Symmetry, and Congruence

The Big Idea Two-dimensional figures can be classified according to their geometric properties.

Lady Bird Johnson got Texas to plant wildflowers along the state roadways. More than 33,000 pounds of seeds are spread each year. Each pound has about 170,000 seeds.

Investigate

The pink evening primroses, on the left, and the bearded grass-pink, on the right, have symmetry. Study and describe the symmetry in each flower. Draw a flower that has one line of symmetry and one that has more than one line of symmetry. Explain how your two flowers are alike and how they are different.

GO ONLINE **Technology** Student pages are available in the Student eBook.

Show What You Know

Check your understanding of important skills needed for success in Chapter 11.

Compare Figures

Tell whether the two figures appear to be the same size and shape. Write *yes* or *no*.

1. 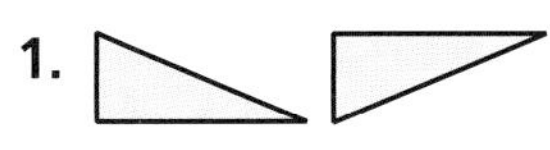
2. 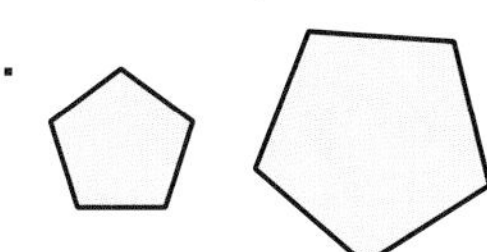
3. 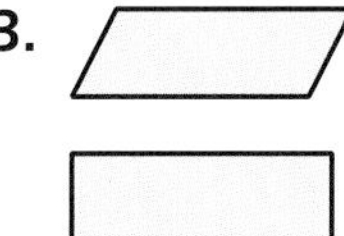
4. 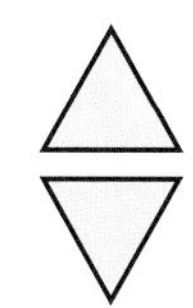

Identify Symmetric Figures

Tell whether the blue line appears to be a line of symmetry. Write *yes* or *no*.

5. 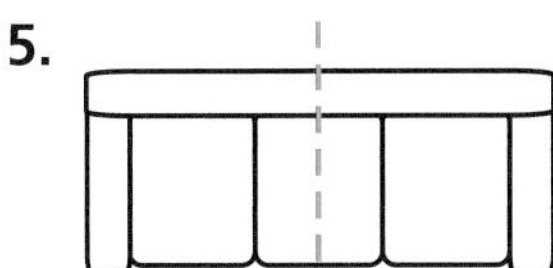
6. 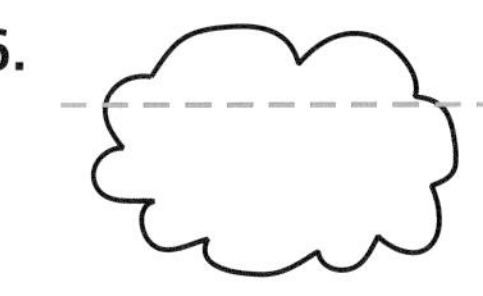
7. 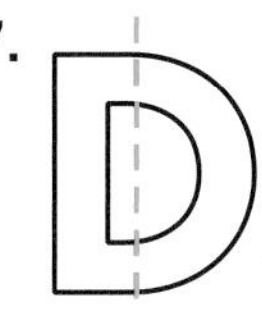
8. 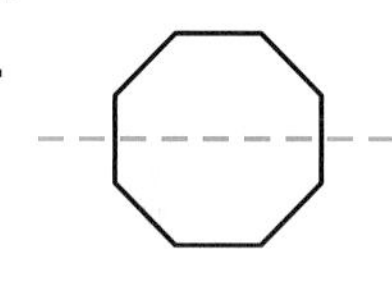

Parts of a Whole

Write a fraction for each shaded part.

9. 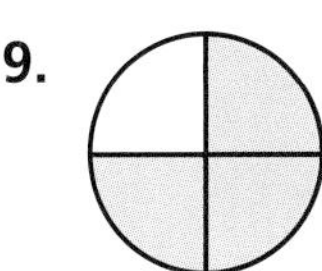
10. 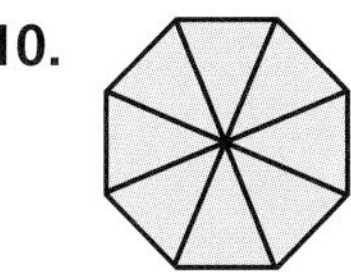
11. 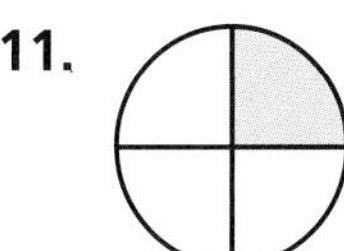
12. 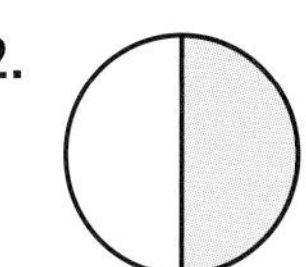

VOCABULARY POWER

CHAPTER VOCABULARY

clockwise
congruent
counterclockwise
line symmetry
pattern
pattern unit
reflection
rotation
tessellation
transformation
translation

WARM-UP WORDS

congruent having the same size and shape

transformation the movement of a figure by a translation, reflection, or rotation

translation A movement of a figure to a new position along a straight line

LESSON 1 Congruent Figures

OBJECTIVE: Identify congruent figures.

Quick Review

Identify the figure.

1. 
2. 
3. 
4. 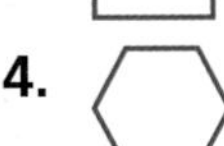
5. 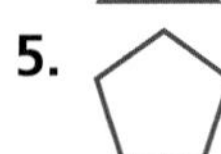

Vocabulary

congruent

Learn

PROBLEM **Congruent** figures have the same shape and size. Which pairs contain congruent figures?

  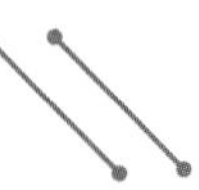 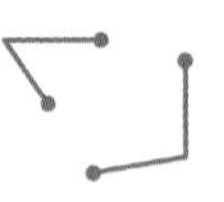 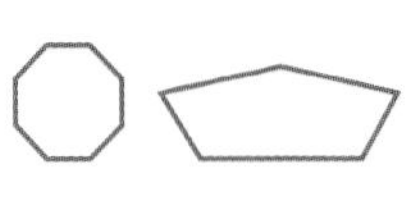

A B C D E

Pair	Shape	Size	Congruent?
A	Same	Same	Yes
B	Same	Different	No
C	Same	Same	Yes
D	Different	Different	No
E	Different	Different	No

So, pair A and pair C contain congruent figures.

- Are the two turtle designs congruent? Are the two train designs congruent? Explain your answers.

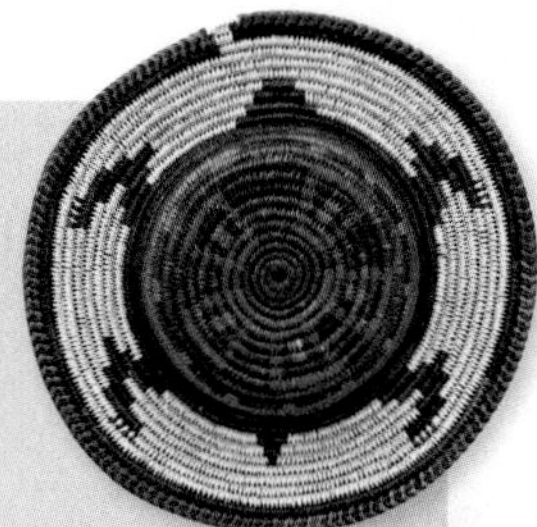

▲ Basket weaving designs:
Turtle
Train

Activity Explore congruent figures.

Materials ■ dot paper ■ scissors ■ ruler

Step 1

Copy the figures on dot paper.

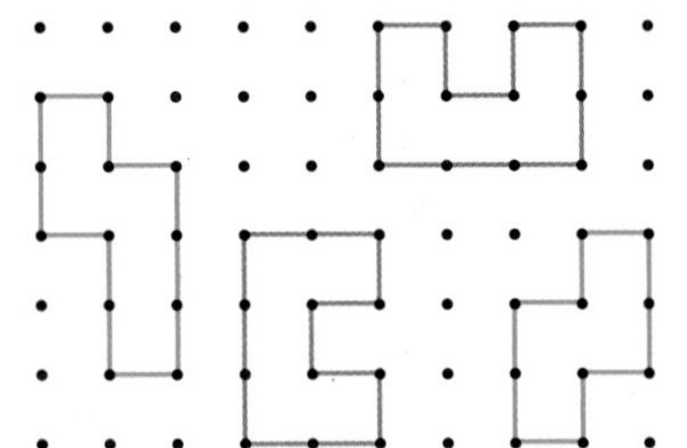

Step 2

Cut out one of each pair of figures and move it in any way to check for congruency.

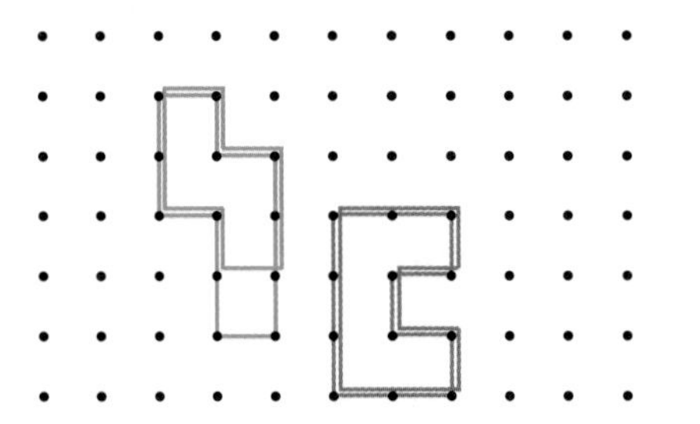

- Which pair of figures is congruent? Describe the movements you used to decide.

Figures that are the same size and shape but have a different position are still congruent.

TEKS 4.9B use translations, reflections, and rotations to verify that two shapes are congruent. *also* **4.9A, 4.14A, 4.14D, 4.15A, 4.15B, 4.16A**

Guided Practice

1. Do the figures have the same shape? Do they have the same size? Are they congruent?

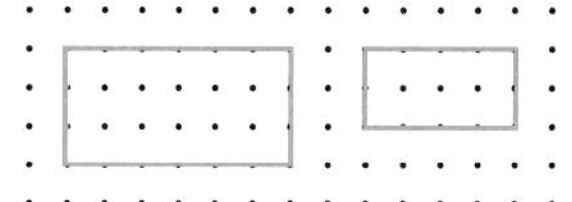

Tell whether the two figures appear to be *congruent* or *not congruent*.

2. 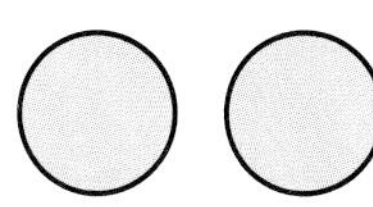

3. 

4. 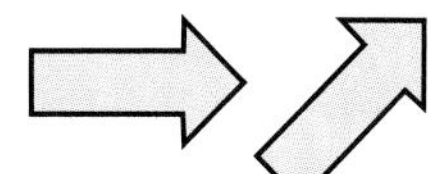

5. 

6. TALK Math Find two objects in your classroom that are congruent. **Explain** how you know they are congruent.

Independent Practice and Problem Solving

Tell whether the two figures appear to be *congruent* or *not congruent*.

7. 

8. 

9. 

10. 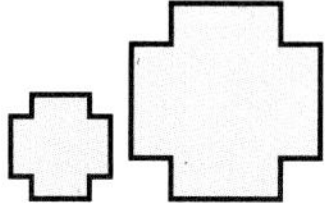

USE DATA For 11–13, use polygons A–E.

A B C D E

11. Which pairs of polygons are congruent?
12. Which pairs of trapezoids are not congruent?
13. On dot paper, draw a figure that is congruent to Figure D.
14. **Algebra** Two triangles are congruent. The sides of one are 3 feet, 4 feet, and 5 feet. Two sides of the other triangle are 3 feet and 5 feet. What is the measure of the third side?
15. **Reasoning** If you use two congruent figures to make a rectangle, what can the figures be? Draw an example.
16. WRITE Math **Sense or Nonsense** Amy says all circles are congruent. Use a compass and draw circles to show if Amy is correct.

Mixed Review and TAKS Prep

17. Matt lives 145 miles from Laredo. Mindy lives 154 miles from Laredo. Who lives farther away from Laredo? (TEKS 4.1A, p. 14)
18. What is the name of the triangle that has two congruent sides? (TEKS 4.8C, p. 268)
19. **TAKS Prep** Which figures appear to be congruent? (Obj. 3)

A 

C 

B  

D 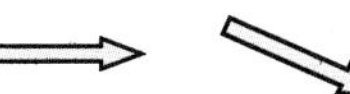

Extra Practice on page 306, Set A

LESSON 2 HANDS ON

Translations

OBJECTIVE: Identify, predict, and describe the results of translations.

Quick Review

Tell if the figures appear to be congruent. Write *yes* or *no*.

1. 
2. ◇ ♡
3. 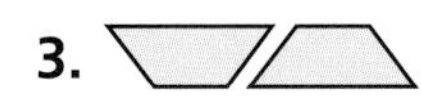
4. □ □
5. 

Vocabulary

transformation **translation**

Investigate

Materials ■ pattern blocks ■ dot paper ■ grid paper

Any movement of a figure is called a **transformation**. A **translation** moves a figure to a new position along a straight line. The figure may be moved up, down, left, right, or diagonally.

ERROR ALERT

When you translate the figure, be sure not to turn it or flip it.

You can use translations of pattern blocks to see if two figures are congruent.

A Choose a pattern block and trace it on dot paper. Label it *original*.

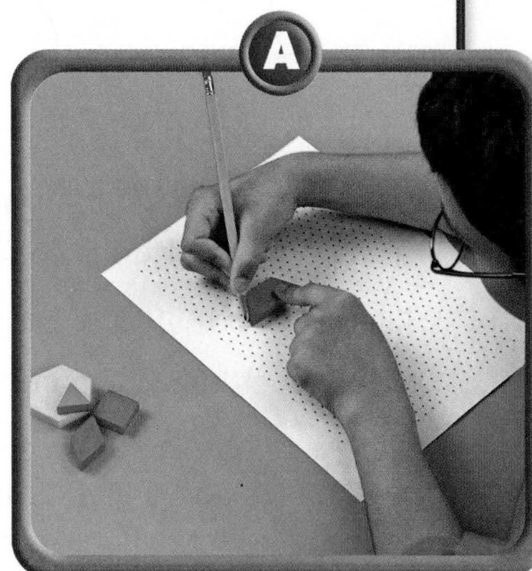

B Slide the pattern block up, down, left, or right. Trace and label the new position *translation*. Check to see if it is congruent to the original tracing.

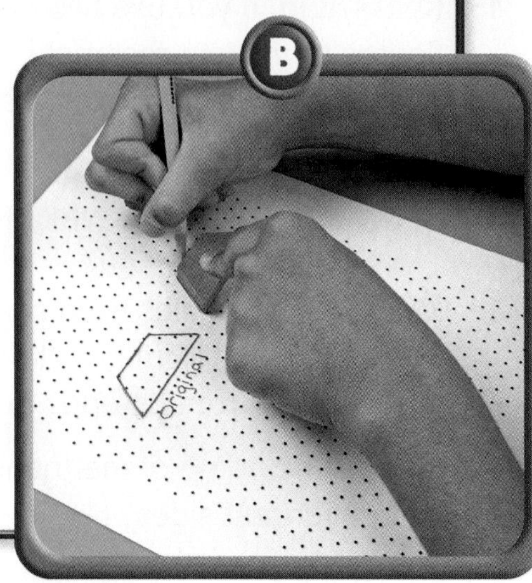

C Translate the pattern block into a new position, trace it, and label it *translation*. Check to see if it is congruent to the original tracing.

D Choose a different pattern block. Repeat the steps to draw translations of additional figures.

Draw Conclusions

Compare your translations with those of classmates.

1. Did the shapes of the figures you traced change when you translated them?
2. Did the sizes of the figures you traced change when you translated them?
3. **Analysis** Must a translated figure and its original always be congruent? **Explain** your answer.

TEKS 4.9B use translations, reflections, and rotations to verify that two shapes are congruent. *also* **4.9A, 4.14A, 4.14D, 4.15A, 4.15B, 4.16A**

Connect

You can see examples of translations in everyday experiences.

Examples

Moving checker pieces

Shooting a marble

Car going down a road

Marching along a line

TALK Math
What real-life examples of translations can you name?

Practice

Tell if only a translation was used to move the figure. Write *yes* or *no*.

1. 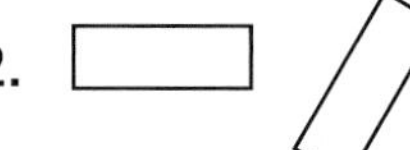
2. 
3. 
4. 

For 5–7, use the figures at the right. Write all the letters which make the statement true.

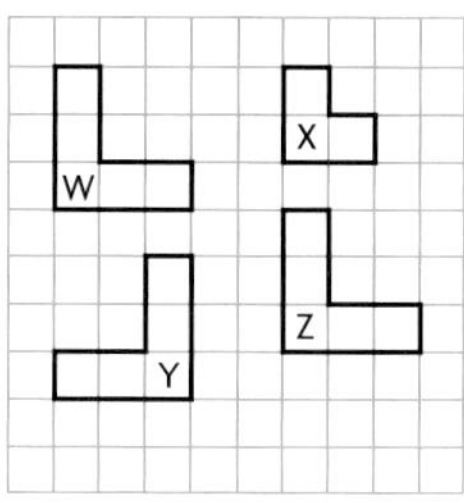

5. One figure is a translation of another figure.
6. The figures are congruent.
7. The figures are not congruent.

Copy each figure on dot paper. Then draw a figure to show a translation.

8. 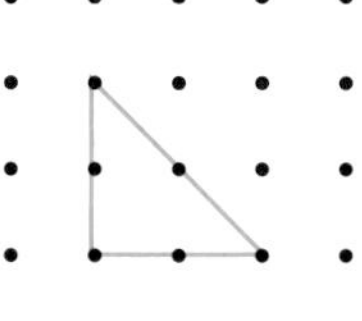
9. 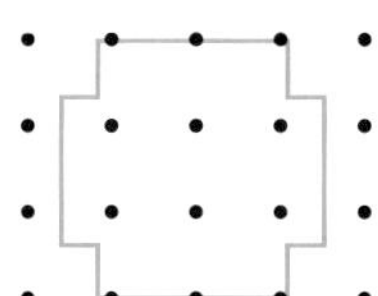
10. 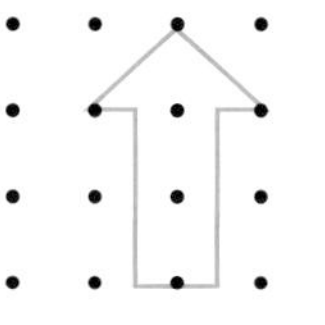
11. 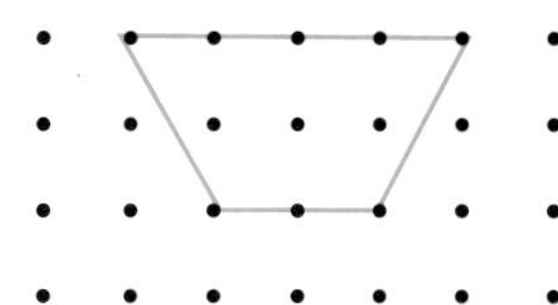

Tell whether each is an example of a translation. Write *yes* or *no*.

12. walking north to south
13. going around a curve
14. running east to west
15. **WRITE Math** Draw a figure on dot paper. Translate the figure at least 2 ways. **Explain** how the figure was translated.

LESSON 3

Rotations

OBJECTIVE: Identify, predict, and describe the results of translations and rotations.

Quick Review

Tad needs two congruent figures for a design. Which figures appear to be congruent?

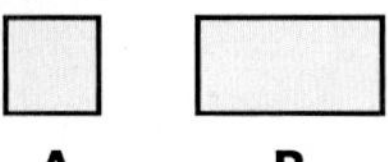

Vocabulary

rotation
clockwise
counterclockwise

Learn

The movement of a figure to a new position by turning the figure around a point is a **rotation**. A rotation that moves in the direction the clock hands move is **clockwise**. A rotation that moves in the direction opposite from the way the clock hands move is **counterclockwise**.

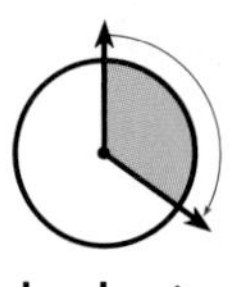
clockwise

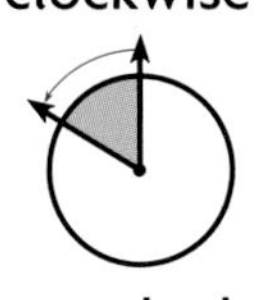
counterclockwise

Activity 1 Rotate a pattern block.

Materials ■ pattern blocks ■ dot paper ■ tracing paper

Step 1

Trace a pattern block. Label the drawing *original*. Move the original block clockwise $\frac{1}{4}$ turn around a point and trace it. Label the drawing $\frac{1}{4}$ rotation.

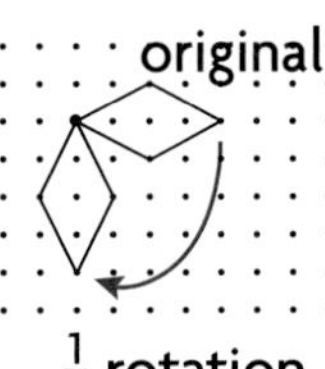

Step 2

Move the original block clockwise $\frac{1}{2}$ turn around the point, trace it, and label the drawing $\frac{1}{2}$ rotation.

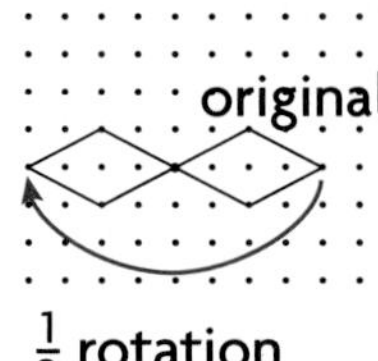

Step 3

Then move the original block clockwise $\frac{3}{4}$ turn around the point, trace it, and label the drawing $\frac{3}{4}$ rotation.

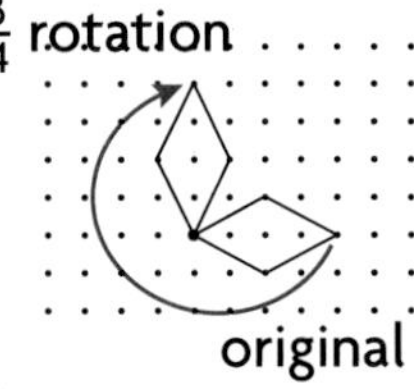

Step 4

Finally move the original block clockwise a full turn around the point, trace it, and label the drawing full rotation.

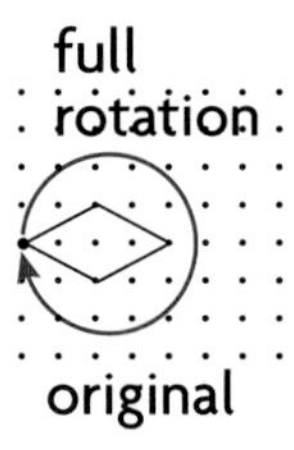

- What clockwise rotation looks like the result of a counterclockwise $\frac{1}{4}$ rotation? Explain.

▲ The space shuttle rotates $\frac{1}{2}$ turn shortly after liftoff and looks as if it is flying upside down. Then just before entering orbit, the space shuttle rolls again to a right-side-up position.

Activity 2 Check for congruence.

Materials ■ tracing paper

- Predict what transformations you will use to prove congruence. Trace the original figure. Test your prediction by transforming the tracing to match the next figure.

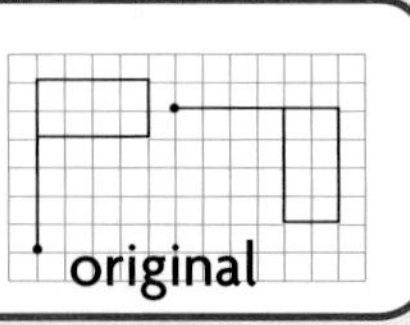

- How is the original figure alike and different from the transformed figure?

TEKS 4.9A demonstrate translations, reflections, and rotations using concrete models. *also* 4.9B, 4.14A, 4.14D, 4.15A, 4.15B, 4.16A

Guided Practice

1. Triangle B is a $\frac{1}{4}$ rotation of triangle A. Are the triangles congruent?

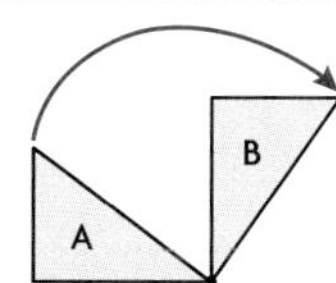

Tell how each figure was moved. Write *translation* or *rotation*.

2. 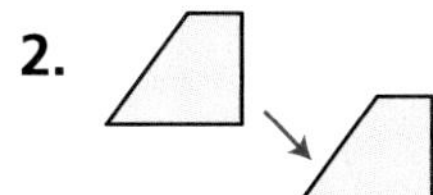

3. 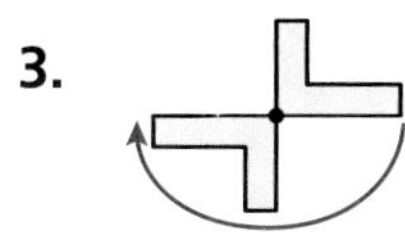

4. 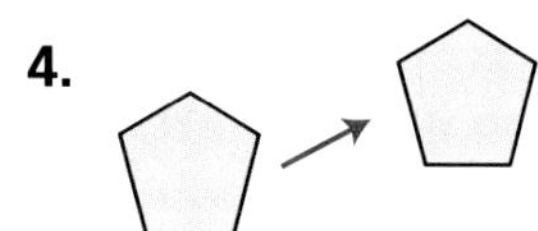

5. 

6. **TALK Math** **Explain** how you know that each pair of figures in Problems 3 and 4 are congruent.

Independent Practice and Problem Solving

Tell how each figure was moved. Write *translation* or *rotation*.

7. 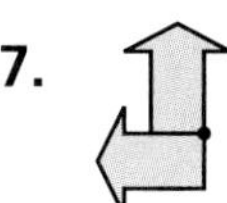

8. 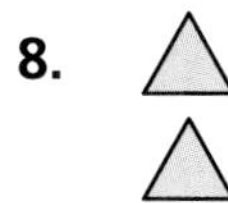

9. 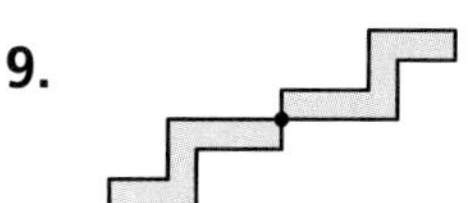

10. 

Copy each figure on dot paper. Then draw figures to show a translation and then a rotation of the original.

11.

12. 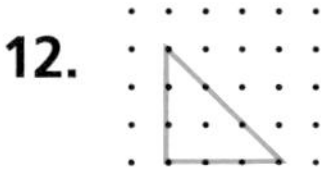

13. 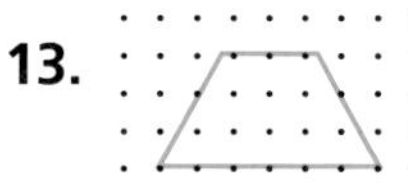

14. 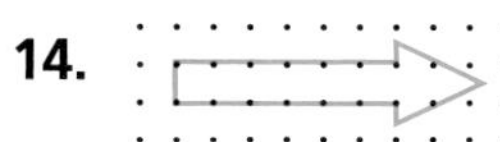

USE DATA **For 15–16, use the picture.**

15. Marta is putting together a puzzle. She turns the puzzle piece counterclockwise $\frac{1}{4}$ turn and then slides it along a straight line into the puzzle. How would you describe these movements?

16. Suppose Marta rotates the puzzle piece clockwise $\frac{1}{2}$ turn as she slides it forward. Then she rotates the puzzle piece again $\frac{1}{2}$ turn before placing it into the puzzle. Identify the movements.

17. **WRITE Math** **Explain** how to rotate the letter T back to its original position in two rotations and in four rotations.

Mixed Review and TAKS Prep

18. How many right angles does a rectangle have? (TEKS 4.8C, p. 270)

19. What is the length of the diameter of a circle with a radius of 7 in.? (TEKS 4.8C, p. 274)

20. **TAKS Prep** Which two figures do **NOT** appear to be congruent? (Obj. 3)

A Jſ

B MN

C HI

D ZN

Extra Practice on page 306, Set B

LESSON 4

Reflections

OBJECTIVE: Identify, predict, and describe the results of translations, rotations, and reflections.

Quick Review

Copy the figure. Then draw a translation and a rotation of the figure.

Vocabulary

reflection

Learn

Koko is looking at her reflection in the mirror. She sees a reflection of her face, including her eyes, nose, and mouth. A reflection creates a mirror image of a figure.

In geometry, a **reflection** is a movement of a figure to a new position by flipping the figure over a line.

▲ Koko, a female lowland gorilla, has been taught to use human sign language.

HANDS ON

Activity 1 Find reflections.

Materials ■ pattern blocks ■ dot paper or grid paper

Trace a pattern block on dot paper or grid paper. Label the drawing *original*.

Flip the block over the vertical line of reflection and trace it. Label the drawing *reflection*.

Then flip the block over the horizontal line of reflection and trace it. Label the drawing *reflection*.

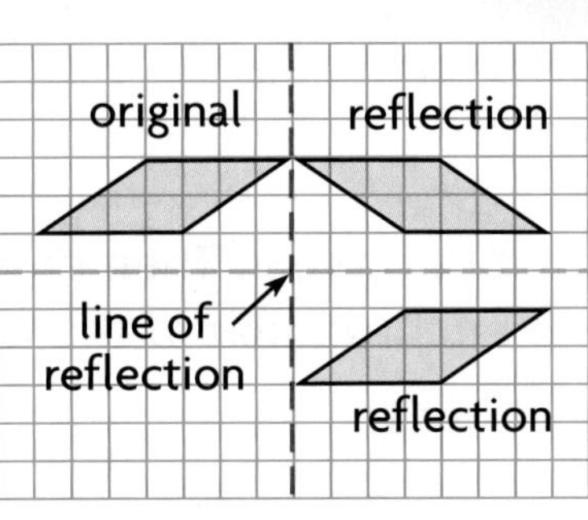

HANDS ON

Activity 2 Use translations, rotations, or reflections.

Materials ■ pattern blocks ■ scissors

Work with a partner. Fold a sheet of paper in half. Place a pattern block along the unfolded edge, and trace it. Then cut out the figure from both layers of the paper.

Lay out the two figures on the table randomly. Have a classmate predict, test, and describe whether translations, rotations, or reflections must be used to move one figure until it fits on top of the other figure.

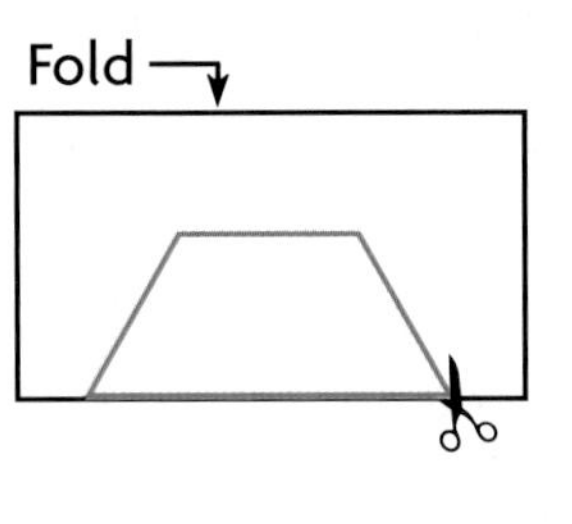

- Is there more than one way to move the first figure until it fits exactly on the other? Explain.
- Can you use the same transformations in a different order? Explain.

When you transform a figure and the size and shape stay the same, the original figure and the transformed figure are congruent.

TEKS 4.9A demonstrate translations, reflections, and rotations using concrete models. *also* **4.9B, 4.14A, 4.14D, 4.15A, 4.15B, 4.16A**

Guided Practice

1. Which shows a reflection of the original figure?

original a. b.

Tell how each figure was moved. Write *translation*, *rotation*, or *reflection*.

2. 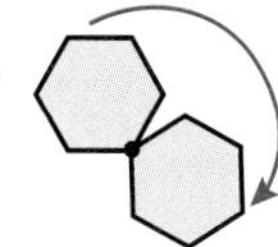

3. 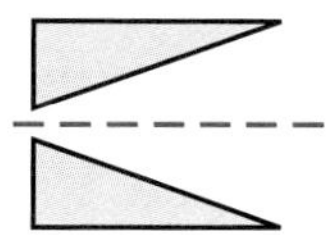

4. 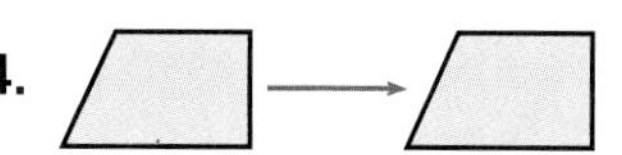

5. 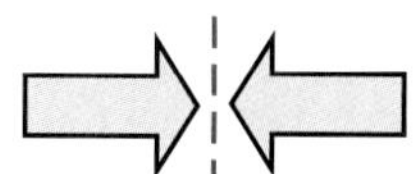

6. **TALK Math** **Explain** how a reflection and a rotation are similar and how they are different.

Independent Practice and Problem Solving

Tell how each figure was moved. Write *translation*, *rotation*, or *reflection*.

7. 

8. 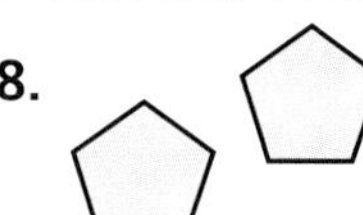

9. 

10. 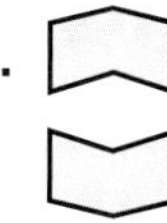

Copy the figure at the right on dot paper. Write the letter of the figure that shows how it will look after each move.

original

11. translation

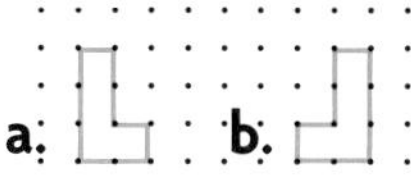

12. reflection

13. rotation

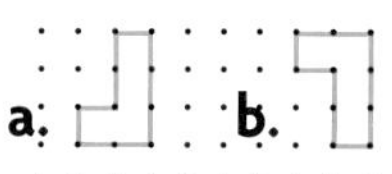

14. Draw a translation, a rotation, and a reflection of the letters in Koko's name. Which letter looks the same when you translate, rotate, and reflect it?

15. Koko knows American Sign Language. Koko can sign "LOVE." Make a design using one of the letters in "LOVE" in at least two different moves.

16. **Reasoning** Name a figure that looks the same after a translation, a rotation, or a reflection. Draw an example.

17. **WRITE Math** **Explain** how the reflection of the letter M across a vertical line differs from its reflection across a horizontal line.

Mixed Review and TAKS Prep

18. On a pictograph, each ▲ represents 3 trees. How many trees do ▲▲▲ represent? (Grade 3 TEKS 3.13A)

19. Draw the letter y and a rotation of the letter. Are the figures congruent? **Explain.** (TEKS 4.9B, p. 290)

20. **TAKS Prep** Which pair of figures shows a reflection? (Obj. 3)

A R R

B R R

C R ꓤ

D R Я

Extra Practice on page 306, Set C

LESSON 5

Symmetry

OBJECTIVE: Identify line symmetry in geometric figures, and use reflections to verify that a figure has symmetry.

Quick Review

Tell whether the two figures appear to be *congruent* or *not congruent*.

1. 2. 3. 4. 5.

Vocabulary

line symmetry

Learn

Symmetry can be found all around us in nature, art, architecture, and music. One type of symmetry found in geometric figures is line symmetry. How can you find line symmetry in geometric figures?

A figure has **line symmetry** if it can be folded on a line so that the two parts match exactly.

◀ The star in the Texas license plate has more than one line of symmetry.

Activity 1 Use reflections to explore line symmetry

Materials ■ dot paper ■ scissors ■ straightedge

Think of line symmetry as a line of reflection.

Step 1 Use pattern blocks or dot paper to make the letter *X*.

Step 2 Trace the *X*.

Step 3 Cut out the tracing.

Step 4 Fold the tracing vertically. Then open it and fold it horizontally.

Think: The fold line is actually a line of reflection.

So, the letter *X* has two lines of symmetry.

- Why is it important to use a line of reflection to check if a figure has symmetry?

Remember

You can fold horizontally, vertically, or diagonally as long as the sides match exactly.

Examples Describe the symmetry each figure appears to have.

A The Alamo has one line of symmetry.

B A Texas Purple has more than one line of symmetry.

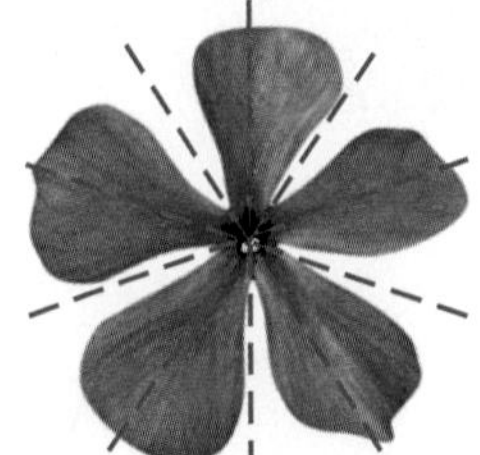

C The map of Texas has no lines of symmetry.

- How many lines of symmetry does a regular pentagon have?

TEKS 4.9C use reflections to verify that a shape has symmetry. *also* **4.9A, 4.9B, 4.14A, 4.14D, 4.15A, 4.15B, 4.16A**

Activity 2 Find lines of symmetry.

Materials ■ tracing paper ■ paper ■ pattern blocks ■ straightedge ■ scissors ■ tape

Step 1

Trace each type of pattern block.

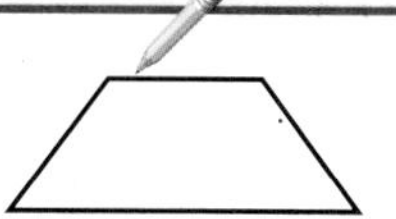

Step 2

Cut out each tracing. Fold each tracing in half so that one half matches the other exactly. Next, fold in other ways. Find all the lines of symmetry for each figure. Draw over the fold lines.

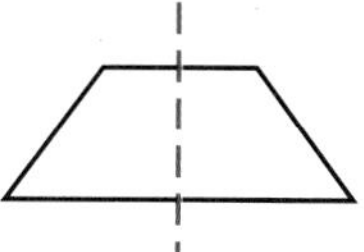

Step 3

Copy and complete the following table.

Pattern Block	Equilateral Triangle	Square	Parallelogram	Rhombus	Trapezoid	Hexagon
Number of Sides	■	■	■	■	4	■
Number of Lines of Symmetry	■	■	■	■	1	■

Step 4

Make a design, using more than one pattern block. Trace and cut out your design. Does your design have line symmetry? If it does, draw each line of symmetry. If not, make a design that does have line symmetry.

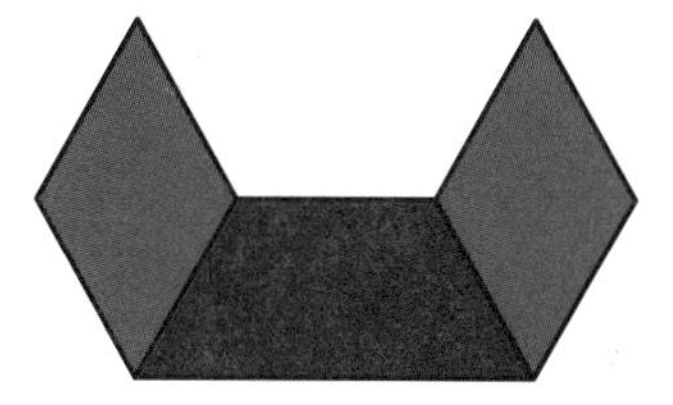

- What do you notice about the number of lines of symmetry of pattern blocks that are regular polygons?

Guided Practice

1. A line of symmetry is shown in the figure at the right. Trace the figure on dot paper and draw 3 other lines of symmetry.

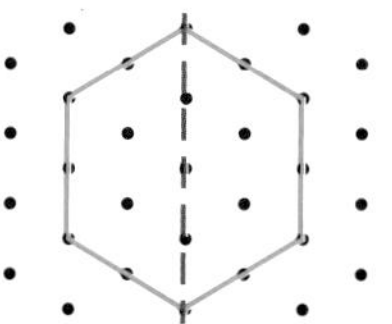

Tell whether the figure appears to have *no lines of symmetry*, *1 line of symmetry*, or *more than 1 line of symmetry*.

2. 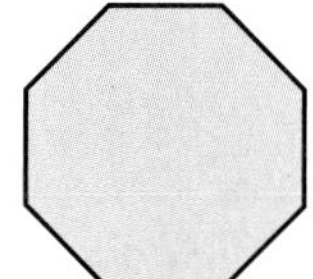

3. 

✓4. 

✓5. 

6. TALK Math **Explain** how to draw a figure with 2 lines of symmetry.

Independent Practice and Problem Solving

Tell whether the figure appears to have *no lines of symmetry*, *1 line of symmetry*, or *more than 1 line of symmetry*.

7. 

8. 

9. 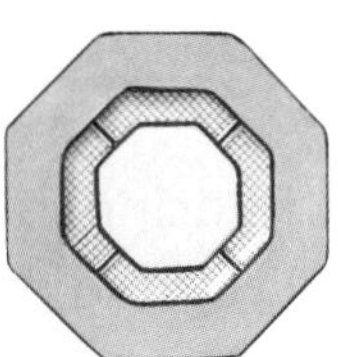

10. 

Trace each figure. Then draw the line or lines of symmetry.

11. 

12. 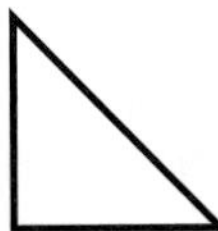

13. 

14. 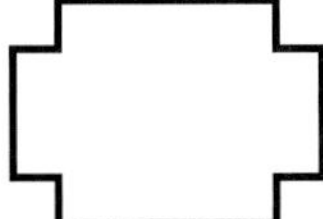

Draw a figure that has the following. For 16–17, also draw the line or lines of symmetry.

15. 0 lines of symmetry

16. 1 line of symmetry

17. 2 lines of symmetry

Copy each design on dot paper. Complete each design to show line symmetry.

18. 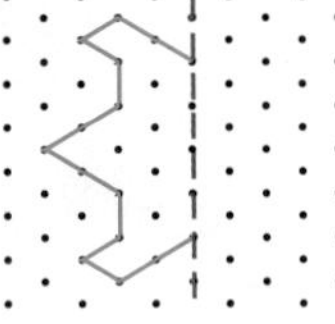

19. 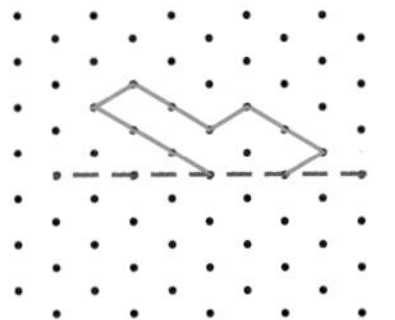

20. 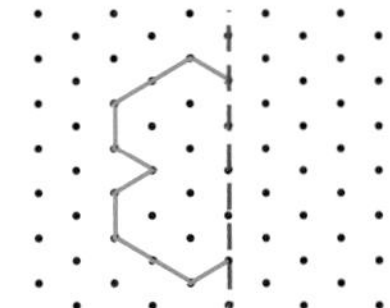

USE DATA For 21–23, copy and use the chart.

A	F	S
B	H	T
C	I	U
D	J	V
E	L	W

21. Which letters appear to have only one line of symmetry?

22. Which letters appear to have no lines of symmetry?

23. The letter E has horizontal symmetry. The letter A has vertical symmetry. Which letters appear to have both horizontal and vertical symmetry?

24. **Reasoning** Trace the figure. How could you finish this design so it would have at least one line of symmetry?

25. WRITE Math Draw a figure with two lines of symmetry. Then write instructions that **explain** how you found the lines of symmetry.

Technology
Use Harcourt Mega Math, Ice Station Exploration, *Polar Planes*, Level J.

 Extra Practice on page 306, Set D

Mixed Review and TAKS Prep

26. What is the next number in the pattern? (Grade 3 TEKS 3.6A)

    29, 26, 23, 20, 17, 14

27. **TAKS Prep** What letters and numbers in the license plate have lines of symmetry? (Obj. 3)

28. What single transformation is shown? (TEKS 4.9A, p. 292)

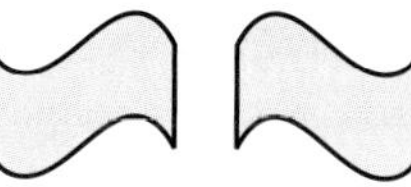

29. **TAKS Prep** How many lines of symmetry does a regular pentagon have? (Obj. 3)

    A 0

    B 1

    C 5

    D 10

Problem Solving connects to Art

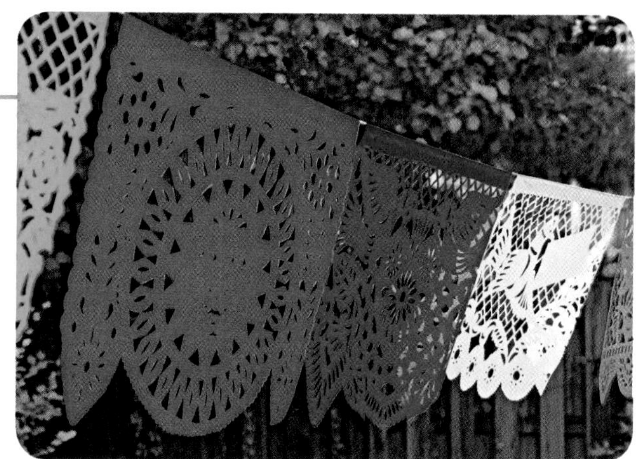

Papel Picado

Papel picado is the Mexican art of folding and cutting designs from tissue paper to make banners for festivals. The designs might be simple or very complicated. Sometimes the designs are hung on a wall or displayed across a table. These designs were made by folding paper several times both horizontally and vertically.

Materials ■ tissue paper ■ scissors

Fold a sheet of tissue paper in half and then in half again, edge to edge. Continue to fold both horizontally and vertically a total of four times. Cut out on the fold a variety of figures in whatever shapes you wish.

Use what you know about symmetry to predict what the design will look like. Then open the paper. Was your prediction correct?

Predict what the figure will look like when the paper is unfolded. Check by folding, cutting, and unfolding.

1. 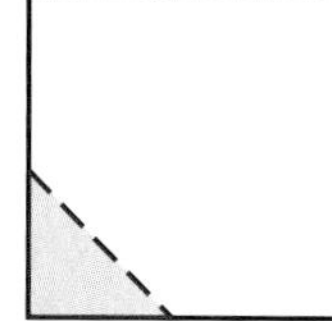

2. 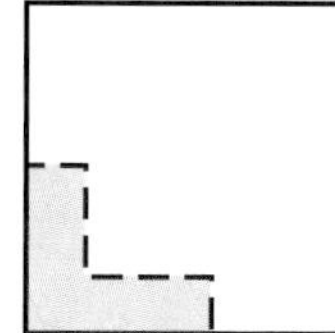

3. 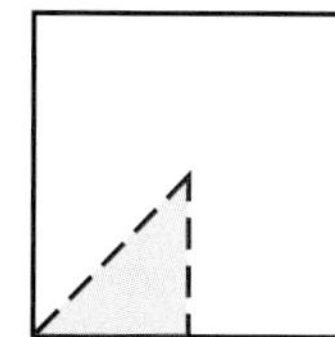

4. 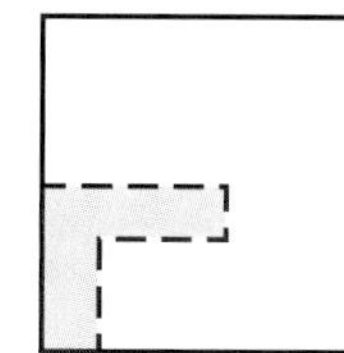

Problem Solving Workshop
Strategy: Act It Out

OBJECTIVE: Solve problems by using the strategy *act it out*.

Learn the Strategy

Acting out a problem can help you understand what it is about and find a reasonable solution. You can act it out by role-playing or using a model.

Act it out with your classmates.

Jim, Mark, and Hannah are finalists in a spelling bee. Before the last round starts, they will all shake hands once. How many handshakes are there in all?

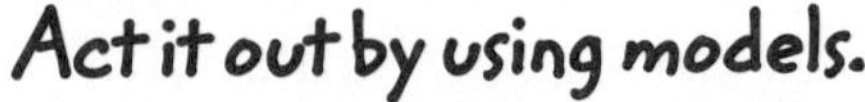

Act it out by using models.

A Betty bought a camping kit for \$96, lanterns for \$49, and a cabin tent for \$222. If Betty had \$500 to spend on her camping trip, how much does she have left after buying her camping supplies?

B Amy draws a parallelogram on dot paper. Her art teacher asks her to rotate the original figure clockwise $\frac{1}{4}$ turn, and then draw its vertical reflection in the last frame. What will Amy's geometric figure look like after she does this?

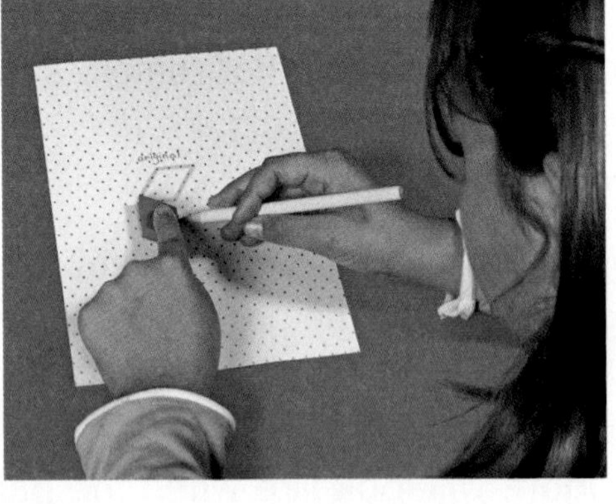

TALK Math

Explain how you decide which way to use the *act it out* strategy.

TEKS 4.14C select or develop an appropriate problem-solving plan or strategy, including drawing a picture, looking for a pattern, systematic guessing and checking, acting it out, making a table, working a simpler problem, or working backwards to solve a problem. *also* **4.9A, 4.9C, 4.14A, 4.14B, 4.14D, 4.15A, 4.15B, 4.16A, 4.16B**

Use the Strategy

PROBLEM Mein used pattern blocks to make a butterfly. How can you prove his design has line symmetry?

Read to Understand

- **Visualize what you are asked to find.**
- **What information is given?**

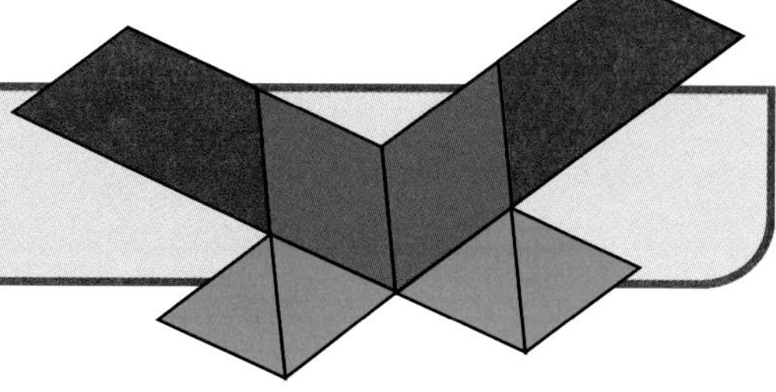

Plan

- **What strategy can you use to solve the problem?**
  You can act it out.

Solve

- **How can you use the strategy to solve the problem?**
  Copy the design, using pattern blocks. Use a mirror to act it out. Place the mirror where you think the line of symmetry is, and look into the mirror.

  Compare the reflection in the mirror to the side of the butterfly that is behind the mirror. If they are the same, the figure has line symmetry.

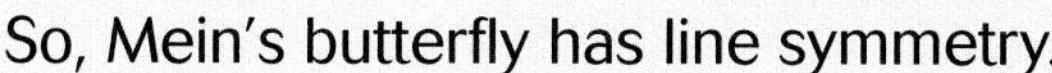

So, Mein's butterfly has line symmetry.

Check

- **What other strategies could you use to solve the problem?**
- **How can you check your results?**

Guided Problem Solving

1. Cassie made a butterfly, using different pattern blocks. Does her butterfly have line symmetry?

   First, act it out by using pattern blocks to make a butterfly design.

   Then, act it out by placing a mirror vertically and horizontally across the middle of your butterfly design to see if it has line symmetry.

2. **What if** Cassie wants to use the strategy act it out to determine whether her design has more than 1 line of symmetry? Does her butterfly have more than 1 line of symmetry? **Explain** how you know.

3. Buddy used pattern blocks to make the two rabbits shown at the right. Are the rabbits congruent? **Explain** how you know.

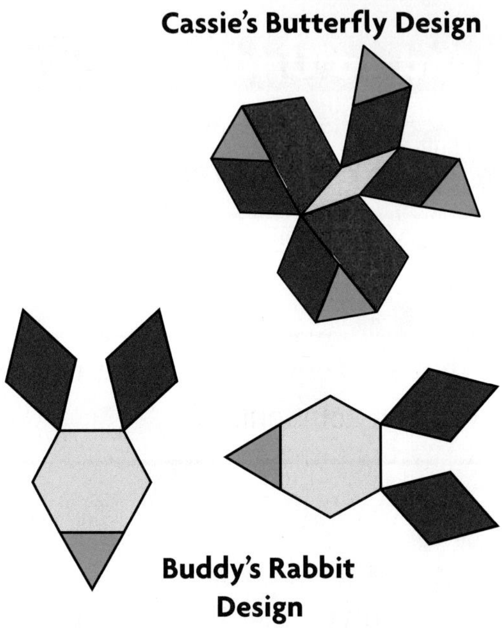

Problem Solving Strategy Practice

Act it out to solve.

4. Cody biked 2 miles north from the Lancaster Quilt & Textile Museum in Lancaster, Pennsylvania. Then he biked 6 miles east and 3 miles north. On the following day, he biked 4 miles east and then 5 miles south. How far is it directly back to the museum?

For 5–8, use the tangram puzzle pieces.

5. Trace and cut out all 7 tangram puzzle pieces shown in the grid on the right. Use some or all of the tangram puzzle pieces to design a figure that has line symmetry.

6. Make another figure using the tangram puzzle pieces. Then trace its reflection. Does the design have line symmetry?

7. WRITE Math Make a new design. Trace your design and label it *original*. Translate your design up, down, left, right or diagonally. Trace the design and label it *translation*. Are your two designs congruent? **Explain.**

8. Use your tangram puzzle pieces to make another design. Does your design have symmetry? If so, how many lines of symmetry does it have?

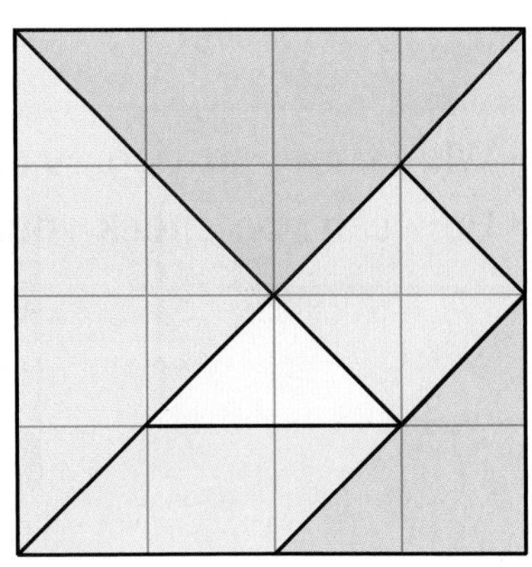

Mixed Strategy Practice

9. Missy uses one hexagonal, two rectangular, and four triangular pieces of fabric to make one bug design for a quilt. If she uses 70 pieces in all to make bug designs, how many of each shape does she use?

10. Grady is making a tablecloth by piecing together red, white, and blue fabric squares in a pattern. Colors in the first row are red, white, blue, red, and white. Colors in the second row are blue, red, white, blue, and red. These two rows repeat for a total of 8 rows. How many squares of each color does he use?

Choose a STRATEGY

- Draw a Diagram or Picture
- Make a Model or Act It Out
- Make an Organized List
- Look for a Pattern
- Make a Table or Graph
- Guess and Check
- Work Backward
- Solve a Simpler Problem
- Write an Equation
- Use Logical Reasoning

USE DATA For 11–14, use the toy quilt designs.

11. Lu is using each of the toy designs around the border of her quilt. The quilt is 20 squares wide and has 24 rows. How many of each design does she use?

12. Starting in the first square of her quilt, Lu lined up her toy designs in this order: plane, car, firetruck, helicopter, crane, and wagon. Using this pattern, which design will Lu place in the fifteenth square?

13. **Pose a Problem** Look back at Problem 11. Write a similar problem by changing the size of the quilt.

14. **Open-Ended** Lu plans a quilt that has 90 squares around the border. She uses at least two toy designs and the same number of each along the border. Name 4 ways she can do this? **Explain.**

CHALLENGE YOURSELF

A store sells quilt patterns for $8, squares for $9, $12, and $15, and designs for $6 each.

15. Hannah spends $92 at the store. She buys 1 pattern, 4 identical squares, and 6 designs. What is the cost of each square?

16. Lu buys a total of 6 squares for $69. She buys 3 for one price, 2 for a different price, and 1 for another different price. How many of each price of square does Lu buy?

LESSON 7 HANDS ON

Tessellations

OBJECTIVE: Identify and describe figures that tessellate and make tessellations.

Quick Review

Does the figure appear to be a regular polygon? Write *yes* or *no*.

1. 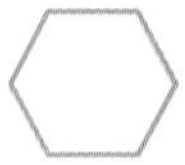

2. 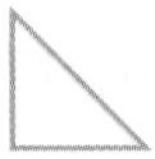

3. 

4. 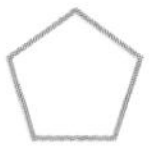

5. 

Vocabulary

tessellation

Investigate

Materials ■ tagboard ■ construction paper ■ ruler ■ scissors

A repeating pattern of closed figures that covers a surface with no gaps and no overlaps is called a **tessellation**.

Tessellations can be found in nature, art, and architecture patterns.

Test figures to see whether they tessellate.

A Using tagboard, draw and cut out a pattern for a triangle.

B Trace the triangle onto construction paper and cut out about 20 triangles.

C Use the triangles to design a tessellation.

D Repeat steps A through C, using a pentagon.

Draw Conclusions

1. Did your triangle tessellate? Explain how you know.
2. What transformations did you use to make your tessellation?
3. How many figures do you need to put together to prove that a figure will tessellate?
4. Did your pentagon tessellate? Explain how you know.
5. **Evaluation** Compare your classmates' pentagons. What is the difference between the figures that did tessellate and those that did not tessellate?

TEKS 4.9A demonstrate translations, reflections, and rotations using concrete models. *also* **4.14A, 4.14C, 4.14D, 4.15A, 4.15B, 4.16A**

Connect

You can make a design by tessellating more than one figure.

Materials ■ pattern blocks ■ colored pencils or markers

Step 1

Choose two pattern blocks that will tessellate.

Step 2

Trace several copies of each figure. Make a tessellation.

Step 3

Color it to make a pleasing design.

- Do the parallelogram and hexagon pattern blocks tessellate? Explain.
- What combinations of pattern blocks will not tessellate?
- Describe the figures in the tessellation by M. C. Escher. Other than shape, what does Escher use to complete the pattern?

Tessellation by M. C. Escher

TALK Math

Do circles tessellate? Explain your answer.

Practice

Trace and cut out several of each figure. Tell whether the figure will tessellate. Write *yes* or *no*.

1. 

2. 

3. 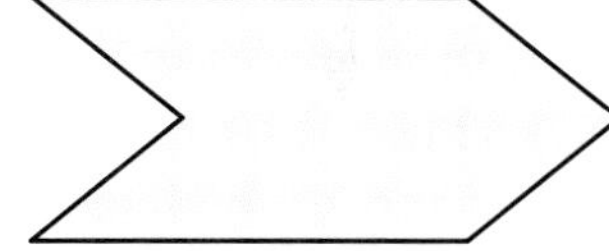

4. 

5. 

6. 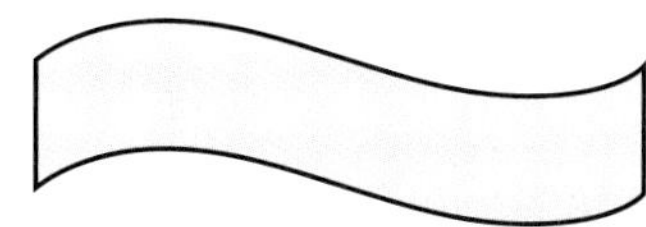

7. 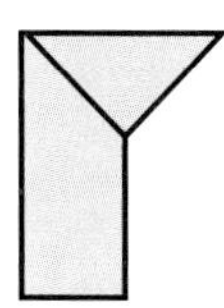

8. 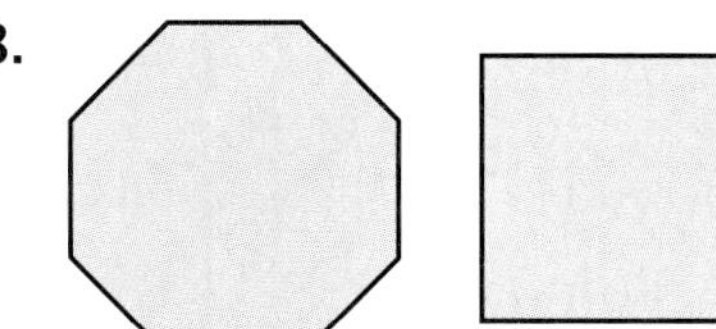

9. 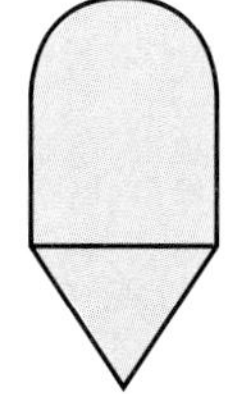

10. **WRITE Math** **Explain** how you know if a pattern of figures forms a tessellation.

LESSON 8

Geometric Patterns

OBJECTIVE: Identify, describe, extend, and make geometric patterns.

Quick Review

Write a rule for the pattern.

1. 2, 5, 8, 11
2. 2, 4, 8, 16
3. 30, 26, 22, 18
4. 80, 40, 20, 10
5. 7, 12, 9, 14, 11

Learn

PROBLEM Geometric patterns are often used as ornaments on buildings. They can be based on color, size, shape, position, and number of figures.

In geometric patterns, the pattern unit is repeated over and over. In this Victorian pattern, the unit is a leaf inside a border. The rule for this pattern is rotate $\frac{1}{2}$ turn, and then repeat.

Example Look for a possible pattern. Write a rule.

Color rule: yellow, orange, blue
Size rule: small, large

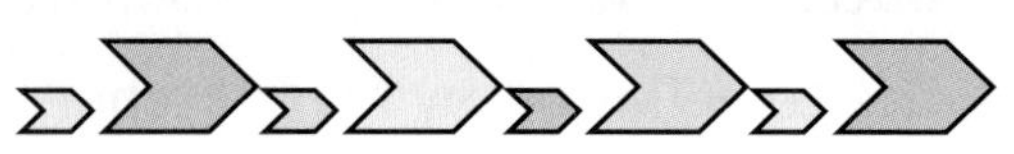

So, the color rule is yellow, orange, blue, and the size rule is small, large.

Activity **Materials** ■ 1-inch squares of tracing paper ■ colored pencils

Step 1

Draw the same simple design on five 1-inch squares of paper.

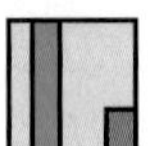

Step 2

Use transformations to form a repeating pattern with the squares.

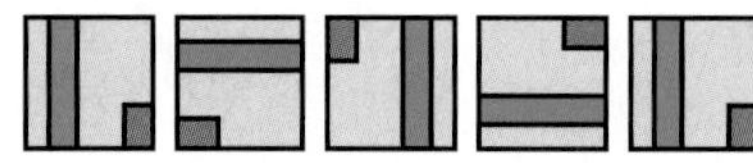

- What is the rule for this pattern?
- Where will the orange rectangle be in the eighth figure?

More Examples

A Write a rule for the pattern. Copy the pattern and draw the next figure.

▪▪ ▪▪▪ ▪▪▪▪

Rule: Increase the number of columns by 1.

So, the next figure is ▪▪▪▪▪.

B Write a rule for the pattern. Draw the missing figure.

⬡ ⬡ ⬡ ? ☐

Rule: Decrease the number of sides by 1.

So, the missing figure is ⬠.

- Describe the sixth figure of the pattern in Example A.

TEKS 4.16A make generalizations from patterns or sets of examples and nonexamples. *also* 4.7, 4.9A, 4.14A, 4.14C, 4.14D, 4.15A, 4.15B

Guided Practice

1. Use the rule repeat *orange square, rotate red trapezoid* $\frac{1}{4}$ *turn clockwise* to make a repeating pattern. Then trace each figure, and color the figures to match the pattern you made.

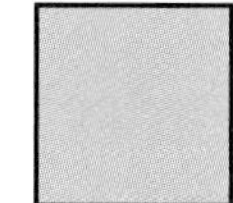
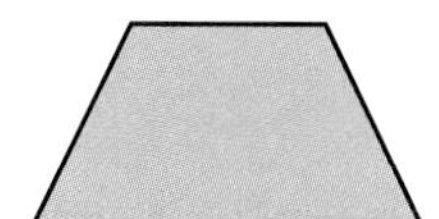

Find a possible pattern. Then copy and draw the next two figures in your pattern.

2.  3.  4.

5. TALK Math **Make** a pattern that uses a rectangle and a dot. Write a rule for your pattern.

Independent Practice and Problem Solving

Find a possible pattern. Then copy and draw the next two figures in your pattern.

6.   

7.

8.  

Find a possible pattern. Then draw the missing figure in your pattern.

9. ?

10. ?

11. ? ?

USE DATA For 12–13, use the quilt.

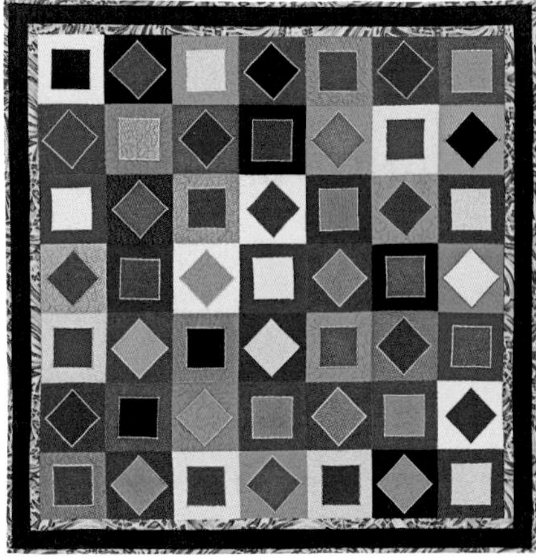

12. Does a rule for the pattern appear to include color? **Explain.**

13. Write a rule for the bottom two rows of the quilt. If another row is added to the quilt, what might it look like?

14. ***FAST FACT*** Frieze patterns repeat in one direction. Describe the slides, flips, or turns in this frieze pattern.

Frieze Pattern

15. WRITE Math Make your own pattern. **Explain** the rule you used to make your pattern.

Mixed Review and TAKS Prep

16. Make a bar graph showing Ari has 2 dogs, 3 cats, 5 birds, and 7 fish. (Grade 3 TEKS 3.13A)

17. Do equilateral triangles tessellate? **Explain.** (TEKS 4.16A, p. 302)

18. **TAKS Prep** Look at Problem 9. What will be the tenth figure in the pattern? (Obj. 2)

A

B

C

D

Extra Practice on page 306, Set E

Extra Practice

Set A **Tell whether the two figures appear to be *congruent* or *not congruent*.** (pp. 286–287)

1. 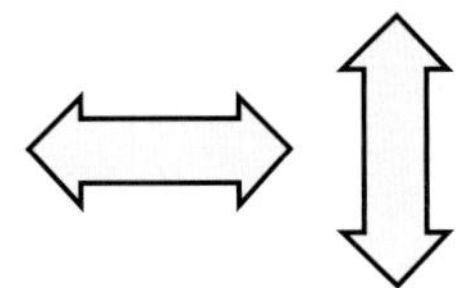
2. 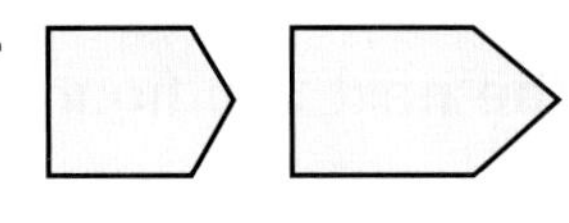
3. 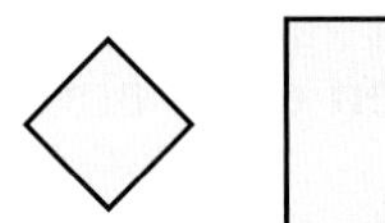
4.  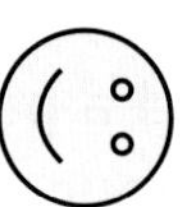
5. Draw a pair of congruent right triangles.

Set B **Copy each figure on dot paper. Then draw figures to show a translation and then a rotation of the original.** (pp. 290–291)

1. 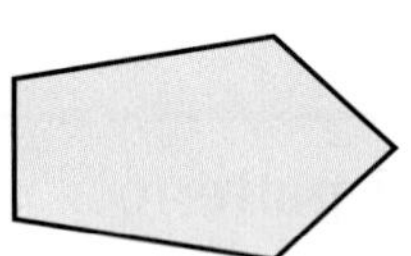
2. 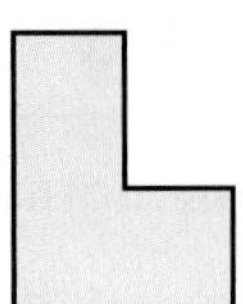
3. 
4. 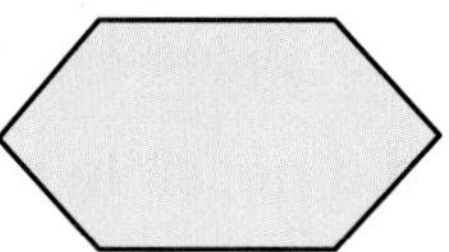

Set C **Tell how each figure was moved. Write *translation*, *rotation*, or *reflection*.** (pp. 292–293)

1. 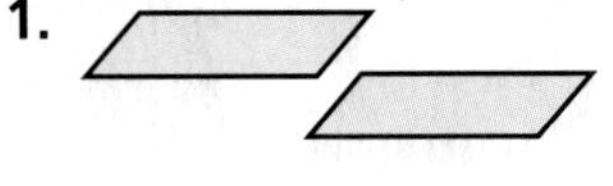
2. 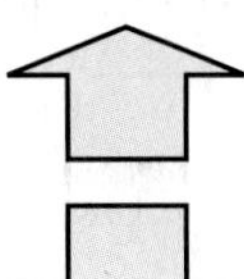
3. 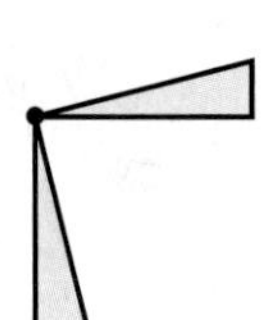
4. 

Set D **Trace each figure. Then draw the line or lines of symmetry.** (pp. 294–297)

1. 
2. 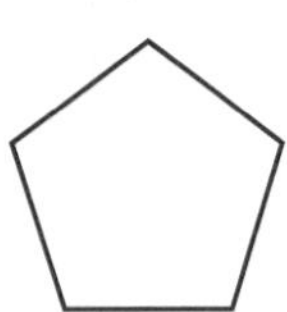
3. 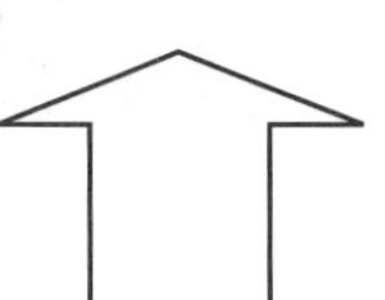
4. 
5. Draw a figure that has no lines of symmetry.

Set E **Find a possible pattern. Then draw the missing figures.** (pp. 304–305)

1. 
2. ?
3. ? 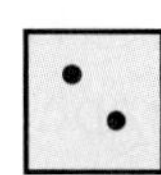  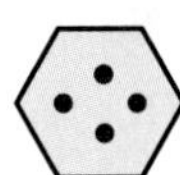

Technology
CD ROM Use Harcourt Mega Math, Ice Station Exploration, *Polar Planes,* Level H, I, J, L, N, O.

TECHNOLOGY CONNECTION

iTools: Geometry (TEKS 4.14D, 4.8C, 4.9A, 4.9B, 4.15A, 4.15B)

Geraldine wants to transform plane figures using translations, reflections, and rotations.

Step 1 Click on *Geometry*. Then select *Plane Figures* from the *Activities* menu. Next click on the third tab.	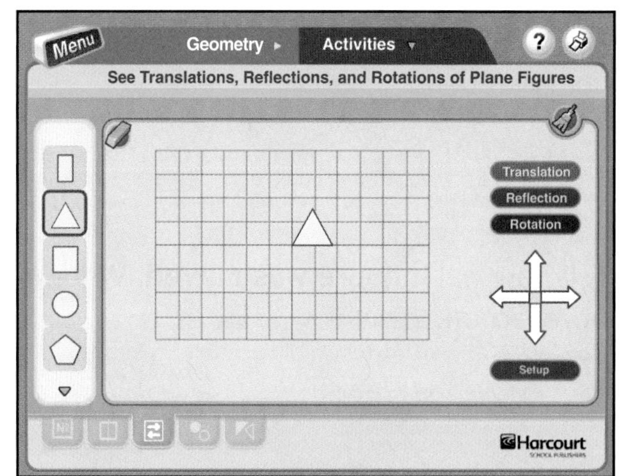
Step 2 Click on the triangle to the left of the workspace.	
Step 3 Click on an arrow to translate the triangle.	
Step 4 Click on *Reflection*. Click on an arrow to reflect the triangle.	
Step 5 Click on *Rotation*. Click and drag the red point of rotation to a vertex of the triangle. Click on an arrow to rotate the triangle.	

Click on the broom to clear the workspace.

Try It

Follow the same steps to transform other figures.

1. Show a translation, reflection, or rotation for a pentagon.
2. Show a translation, reflection, or rotation for a circle. How is a circle different from the other figures? **Explain.**
3. **Explore More** Can a translation to the right ever give the same figure as a reflection across a vertical line? **Explain.**

Technology
iTools are available online or on CD-ROM.

Chapter 11 Review/Test

Check Vocabulary and Concepts

Choose the best term from the box.

VOCABULARY
line symmetry
rotation
tessellation

1. A figure has __?__ if it can be folded on a line so that the two parts match exactly. (TEKS 4.9C, p. 294)
2. __?__ a repeating pattern of closed figures that covers a surface with no gaps and overlaps. (TEKS 4.9A, p. 302)

Check Skills

Tell whether the two figures appear to be *congruent* or *not congruent*. (TEKS 4.9B, pp. 286–287)

3. 
4. 
5. 
6. 

Tell how each figure was moved. Write *translation*, *rotation*, or *reflection*. (TEKS 4.9A, pp. 288–289, 290–291, 292–293)

7. 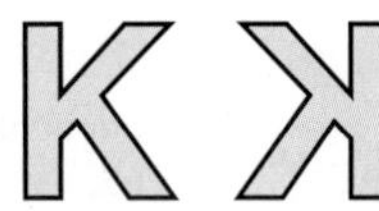
8. 
9. 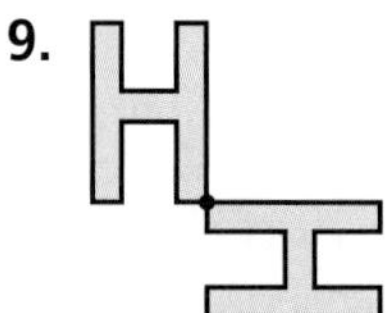
10. 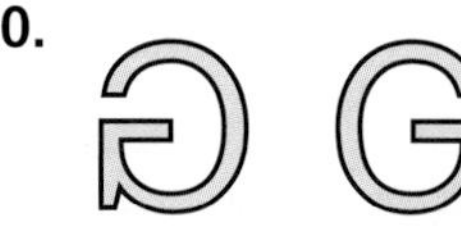

Find a possible pattern. Then copy and draw the next two figures in your pattern. (TEKS 4.16A, pp. 304–305)

11.
12. 
13. 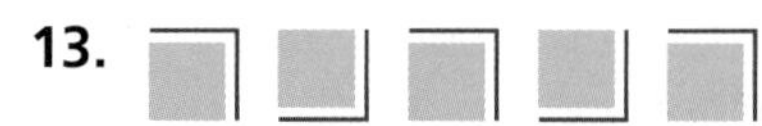

Check Problem Solving

Solve. (TEKS 4.14C, pp. 298–301)

14. Ed made this design using pattern blocks. Trace and cut out his design. How many lines of symmetry does Ed's design have?

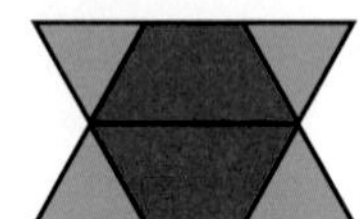

15. WRITE Math Draw the lines of symmetry for each regular polygon. Count the lines for each figure. **Explain** how to find the number of lines of symmetry in any regular polygon.

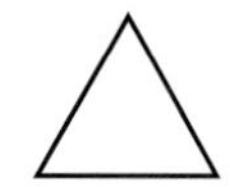   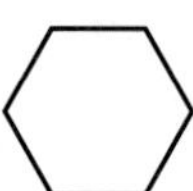

GO ONLINE **Technology** Use *Online Assessment.*

Enrich • Tangrams

Puzzle Pieces

Tangrams are originally from China and have been a popular puzzle for almost 200 years. You can make a tangram by following these steps.

Materials ■ large square sheet of unlined paper ■ scissors

Step 1 Use a large square sheet of unlined paper. Fold the paper on the diagonal. Cut along the fold to make two congruent isosceles right triangles.

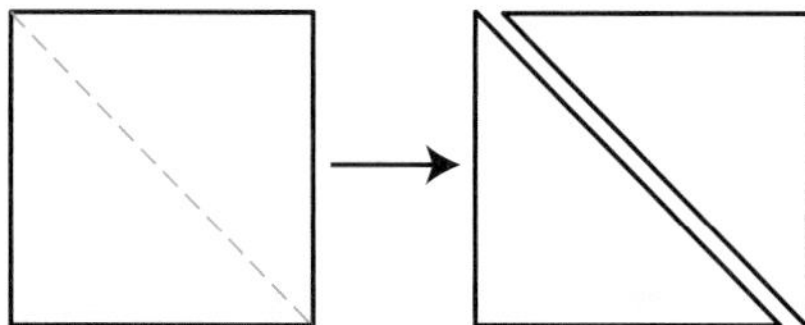

Step 2 Fold one triangle in half. Cut along the fold to make two congruent isosceles right triangles.

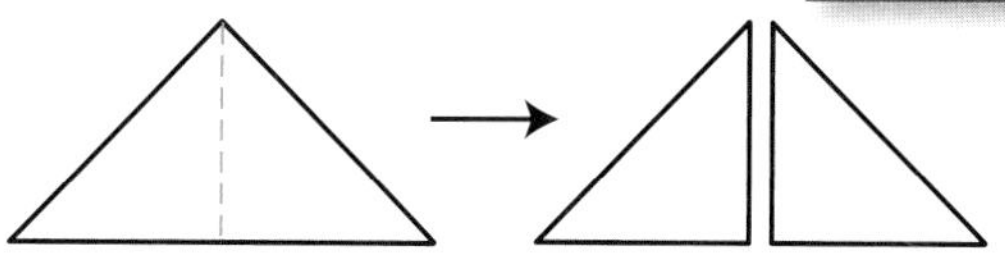

Step 3 Fold the other triangle from the vertex to the midpoint of the opposite side. Cut along the fold to make a triangle and a trapezoid.

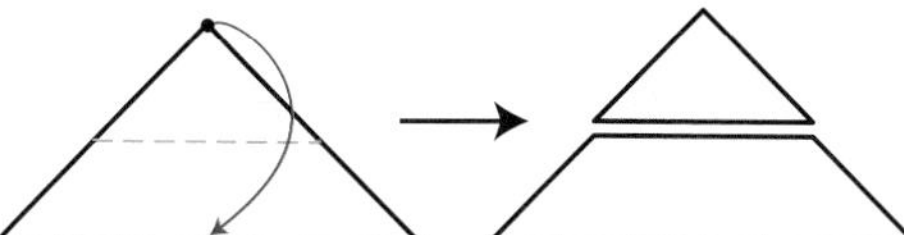

Step 4 Fold the trapezoid as shown. Cut along the fold to make a right triangle and a quadrilateral.

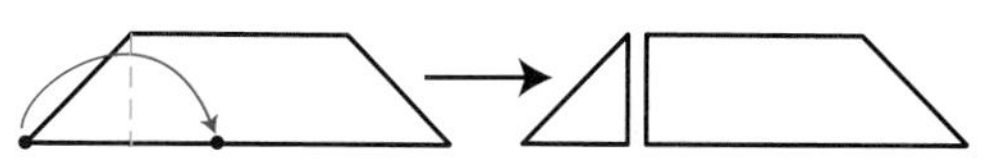

Step 5 Fold the quadrilateral as shown. Cut along the fold to make a square and a quadrilateral.

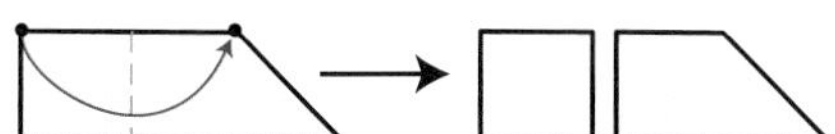

Step 6 Fold the quadrilateral as shown. Cut along the fold to make a right triangle and a parallelogram.

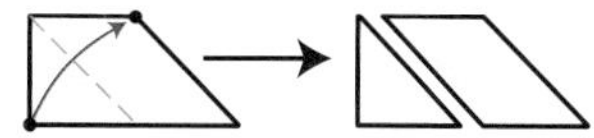

You will have seven tangram pieces with which to make figures.

Piece It Together

Use all of the tangram pieces to make each picture.

1. 

2. 

3. 

4. 

WRITE Math **Explain** in a set of instructions how to make a different figure or picture by using the tangram pieces. Use the terms *translate, reflect,* and *rotate*.

Getting Ready for the TAKS
Chapters 1–11

Number, Operation, and Quantitative Reasoning (TAKS Obj. 1)

1. There are 12 classrooms on the first floor of Davy Crockett Elementary School. If there are 6 erasers in each class, how many erasers are there in the first-floor classrooms?

   A 18

   B 36

   C 72

   D 144

2. The table shows the heights of some mountains.

Mountain Heights	
Mountain	**Height (in feet)**
Mount Everest	29,023
Mount Rainier	14,410
Pike's Peak	14,110

   Which is the best estimate of how much higher Mount Everest is than Pike's Peak?

   F 1,500 feet

   G 11,000 feet

   H 15,000 feet

   J 40,000 feet

3. **WRITE Math** The sheriff's office bought 95 bike helmets to hand out on Bike Safety Day. They paid $19 each. Estimate the total cost. **Explain** the strategy you used to estimate.

Measurement (TAKS Obj. 4)

Test Tip **Eliminate choices.**

See Item 4. Look at the small hand of the clock. It is pointing between the 3 and the 4. This means that the time is after 3:00 and before 4:00. So, answer choice A cannot be correct.

4. Tina's coach looked up at the clock and said, "Practice starts now."

   At what time did practice start?

   A 2:55 P.M.

   B 3:00 P.M.

   C 3:05 P.M.

   D 3:55 P.M.

5. Which measurement best describes the height of a classroom?

   F 9 inches

   G 9 feet

   H 9 yards

   J 9 miles

6. **WRITE Math** **Explain** how to find the perimeter of this regular pentagon.

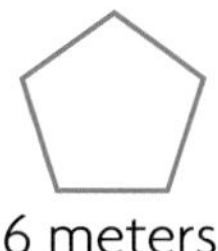

Patterns, Relationships, and Algebraic Thinking (TAKS Obj. 2)

7. Exactly 108 players signed up for basketball. There were 12 players on a team. Which number sentence is in the same fact family as $108 \div 12 = \blacksquare$?

   A $108 \times 12 = \blacksquare$

   B $9 \times \blacksquare = 108$

   C $\blacksquare \times 108 = 12$

   D $9 \times 108 = \blacksquare$

8. Ms. McGrail buys pencils for her class in packages of 12. If she buys 100 packages in a year, how many pencils does she buy?

   F 112

   G 120

   H 1,200

   J 12,000

9. WRITE Math The table below relates the number of triangular pyramids to the number of faces on those pyramids.

Triangular Pyramids	
Number of Triangular Pyramids	Number of Faces
3	12
6	24
9	36

Describe a rule that relates the number of pyramids to the number of faces. Use your rule to find the number of faces on 15 triangular pyramids.

Geometry and Spatial Reasoning (TAKS Obj. 3)

10. Which two figures appear to be congruent?

   A 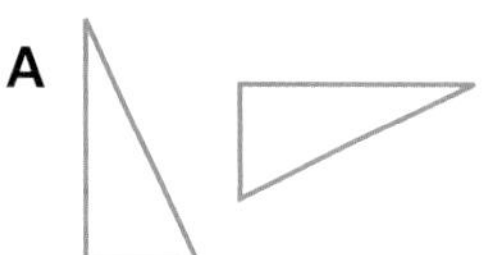

   B 

   C 

   D 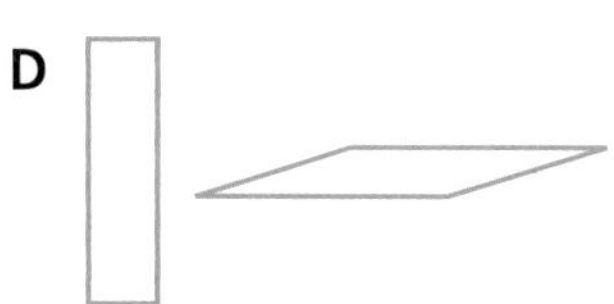

11. Which transformation is represented?

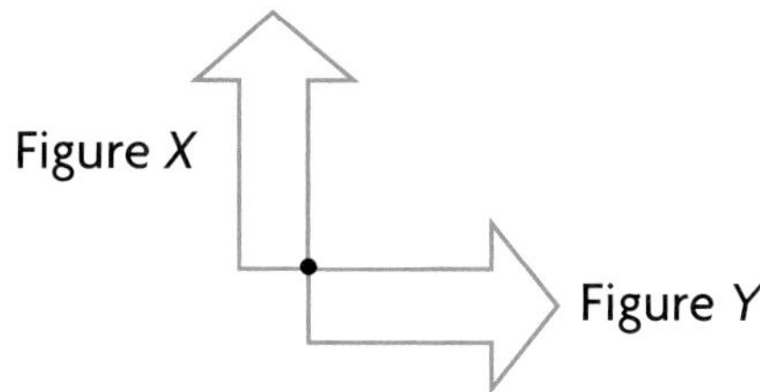

   F Rotation

   G Reflection

   H Translation

   J Not here

12. WRITE Math Gina draws the following triangles.

Explain two ways she can classify each triangle.

12 Three-Dimensional Geometric Figures

The Big Idea Three-dimensional figures can be classified according to their geometric properties.

TEXAS FAST FACT

The Bank of America Plaza building is the tallest skyscraper in Dallas. It is 921 feet tall and has 72 floors. At night, it is outlined by 2 miles of green light tubes.

Investigate

Design your own skyline. Choose different geometric solid figures for each building. Draw the front and side views of your skyline.

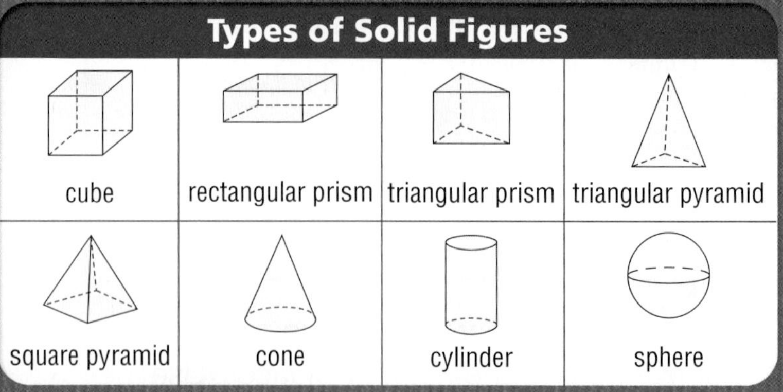

Types of Solid Figures

cube	rectangular prism	triangular prism	triangular pyramid
square pyramid	cone	cylinder	sphere

Technology
Student pages are available in the Student eBook.

Show What You Know

Check your understanding of important skills needed for success in Chapter 12.

▶ Identify Plane Figures

Name each plane figure.

1. 
2. 

3. 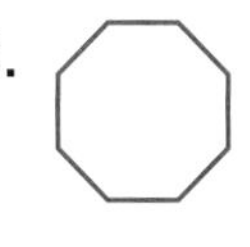
4. 
5. 
6. 
7. 
8. 

▶ Identify Solid Figures

Name each solid figure.

9. 

10. 
11. 

12. 
13. 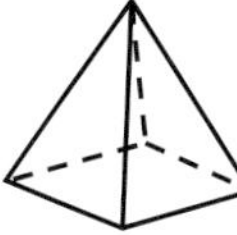
14. 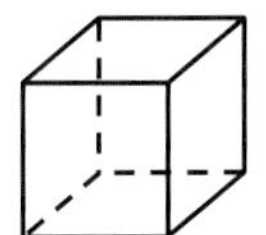
15. 
16. 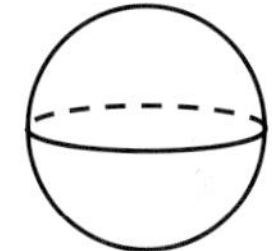

VOCABULARY POWER

CHAPTER VOCABULARY

base
cone
cube
cylinder
edge
face
net
rectangular prism
rectangular pyramid
sphere
square pyramid
three-dimensional
triangular prism
triangular pyramid
two-dimensional
vertex

WARM-UP WORDS

three-dimensional measured in three directions, such as length, width, and height

face a polygon that is a flat surface of a solid figure

edge the line segment where two faces of a solid figure meet

vertex the point where three or more edges meet in a solid figure; the top point of a cone

LESSON
1

Faces, Edges, and Vertices

OBJECTIVE: Identify, classify, describe, and make three-dimensional figures.

Quick Review

Identify the figure.

1. (pentagon) 2. (rectangle) 3. (triangle)

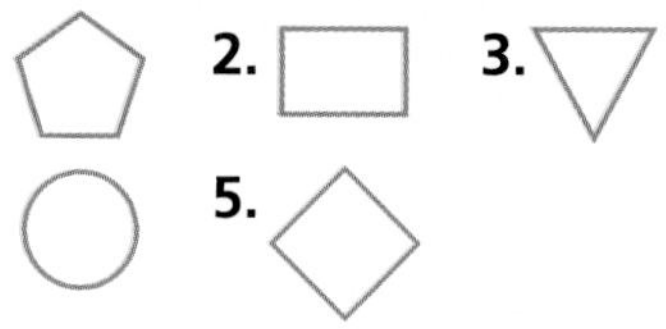

4. (circle) 5. (square turned on its side)

Vocabulary

edge	three-dimensional
face	triangular pyramid
vertex	rectangular pyramid
base	

Learn

Everywhere you look, you see solid figures—in buildings, in sculptures, and in everyday objects. Solid figures have length, width, and height, so they are **three-dimensional** figures.

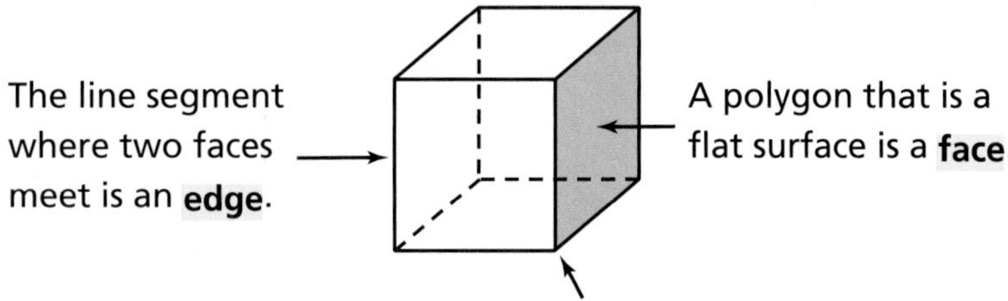
The line segment where two faces meet is an **edge**.
A polygon that is a flat surface is a **face**.
The point at which three or more edges meet is a **vertex**. The plural of *vertex* is *vertices*.

Math Idea

Three-dimensional figures can be classified by the shape and the number of their bases, faces, vertices, and edges.

Prisms and pyramids are named by the polygons that form their **bases**.

cube, square prism

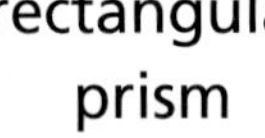

rectangular prism

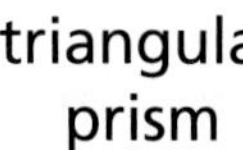

triangular prism

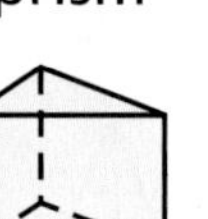

square pyramid

rectangular pyramid

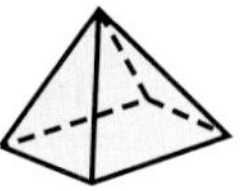

triangular pyramid

Prisms have two congruent and parallel bases.

Pyramids have one base.

• Look at the photograph on page 315. What solid figure do you see?

Look carefully at the faces of the rectangular pyramid below.

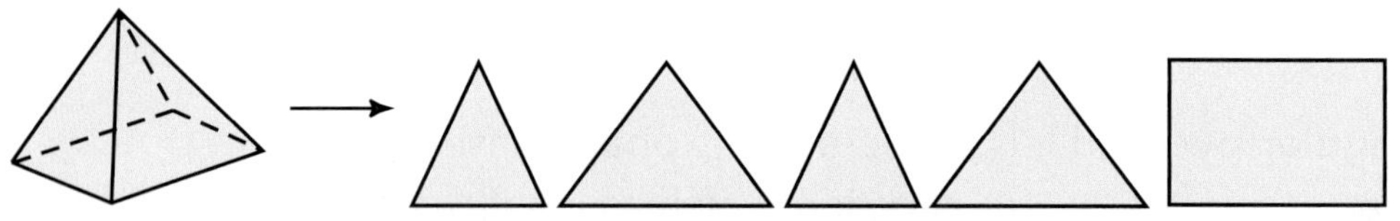

The faces are triangles and a rectangle. Name the plane figures found in the faces of the other solid figures above.

Some solid figures have curved surfaces. A cylinder has two circular bases. A cone has one circular base.

cylinder

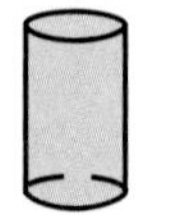

cone

sphere

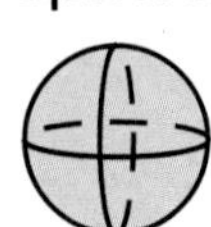

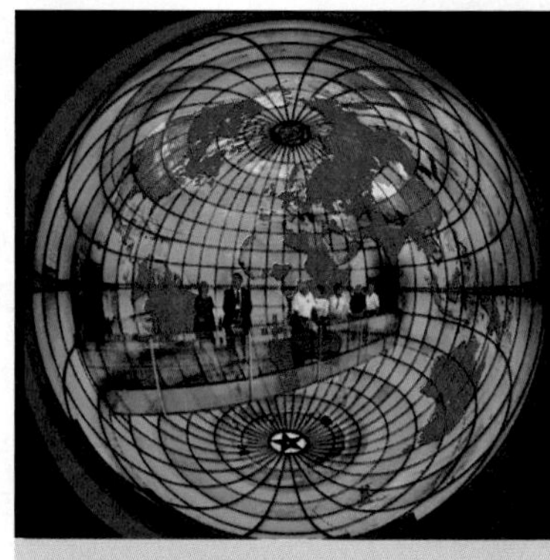

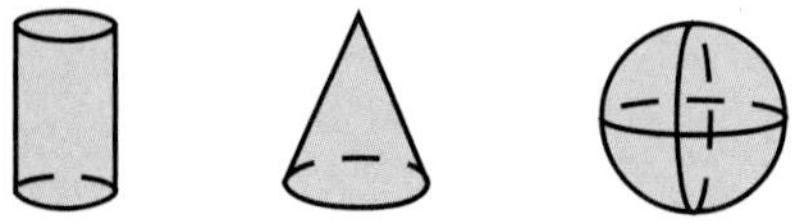

▲ The Mapparium, in Boston, Massachusetts, is a 3-story-tall stained-glass globe that has a diameter of 30 feet.

TEKS 4.8C use essential attributes to define two- and three-dimensional geometric figures. *also* **4.8B, 4.14A, 4.14D, 4.15A, 4.15B, 4.16A, 4.16B**

▶ Grande Louvre, Paris, France

Activity Make a cube.

Materials ■ straws ■ modeling clay or fastener material

Step 1

First, make a square.

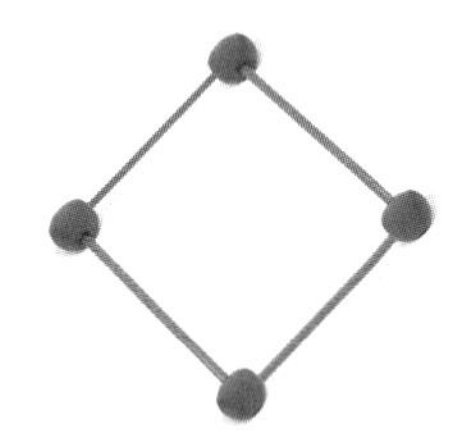

Step 2

Add a straw to each vertex so that it is perpendicular to the other straw. Add a lump of clay on the other end of each new straw.

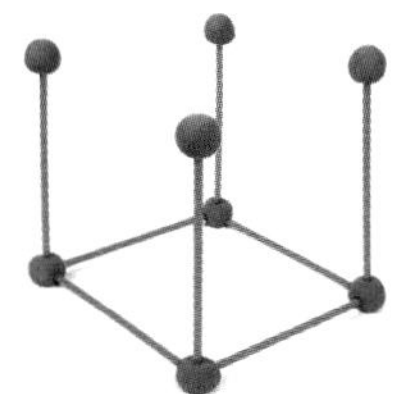

Step 3

To join the new straws, add 4 more straws to complete the cube.

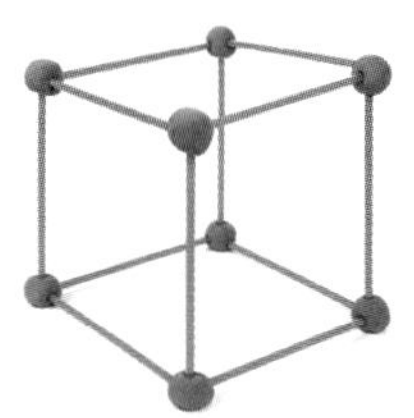

- How many straws did you use to make the cube? How many edges does a cube have? How many vertices? How many faces?
- **What if** you wanted to make a triangular pyramid? How many straws would you need? How many edges does a triangular pyramid have? How many vertices? How many faces?
- Look at the edges of the cube at the right. Trace and extend $\overline{AB}$ and $\overline{DC}$ to make lines. Trace and extend $\overline{EH}$ and $\overline{HG}$ to make lines. Which pairs of lines appear to be parallel? Which pairs of lines appear to be perpendicular?

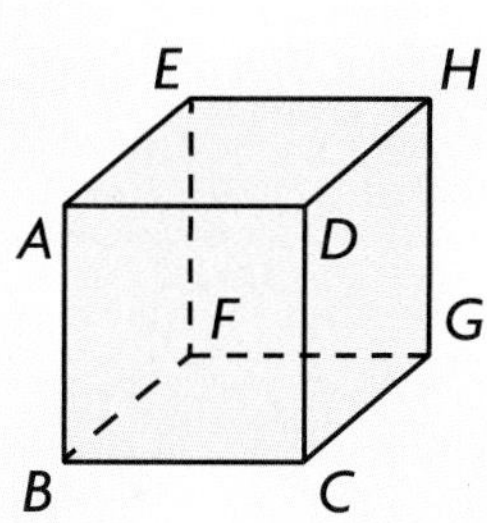

Guided Practice

1. What is the base of the solid figure at the right? Are the faces rectangles or triangles? Name the solid figure.

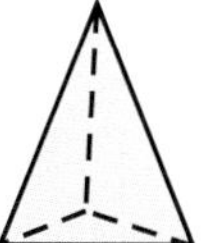

Name a solid figure that is described.

2. 12 edges
3. 4 vertices
4. fewer than 6 faces
5. 1 circular base

6. TALK Math **Explain** how cubes and rectangular prisms are alike. How are they different?

Technology
Use Harcourt Mega Math, Ice Station Exploration, *Frozen Solids,* Levels C, D, E.

Independent Practice and Problem Solving

Name a solid figure that is described.

7. 5 faces
8. all triangular faces
9. 2 circular bases
10. more than 5 vertices

Which solid figure or figures do you see in each?

11. 
12. 
13. 
14. 

For 15–17, copy and complete the table.

	Name	Name of Faces and Number of Each	Number of Faces	Number of Edges	Number of Vertices
15.	Rectangular Prism	■	■	■	■
16.	Triangular Prism	■	■	■	■
17.	Square Pyramid	■	■	■	■

For 18–19, look at the edges of the triangular prism.

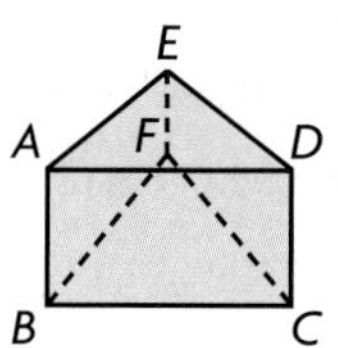

18. Name a pair of parallel line segments.
19. Name a pair of perpendicular line segments.
20. Which solid figure has more edges—a triangular prism or a triangular pyramid? How many more?
21. **Reasoning** If you remove a label from a soup can and look at the label, what plane figure do you see?
22. **Reasoning** Are all rectangular pyramids square pyramids? **Explain** your thinking.
23. **WRITE Math** **What's the Question?** The answer is 2 triangular faces and 3 rectangular faces.

Mixed Review and TAKS Prep

24. Use the table above. Make a pictograph that shows the number of faces for each solid figure. (Grade 3 TEKS 3.13A)
25. Which letter appears to have a line of symmetry?

    A N R S (TEKS 4.9C, p. 294)

26. **TAKS Prep** How many edges does a cube have? (Obj. 3)

    A 6 **C** 9
    B 8 **D** 12

 Extra Practice on page 326, Set A

Describe an Error

You must understand a math concept before you can identify an error. To correct an error, you must be able to describe the error and explain how to correct it.

Michelle keeps her photographs in a box that is the shape of a rectangular prism. She told her friend that the box has 8 edges. What error did Michelle make?

Alberto wrote this description of Michelle's error.

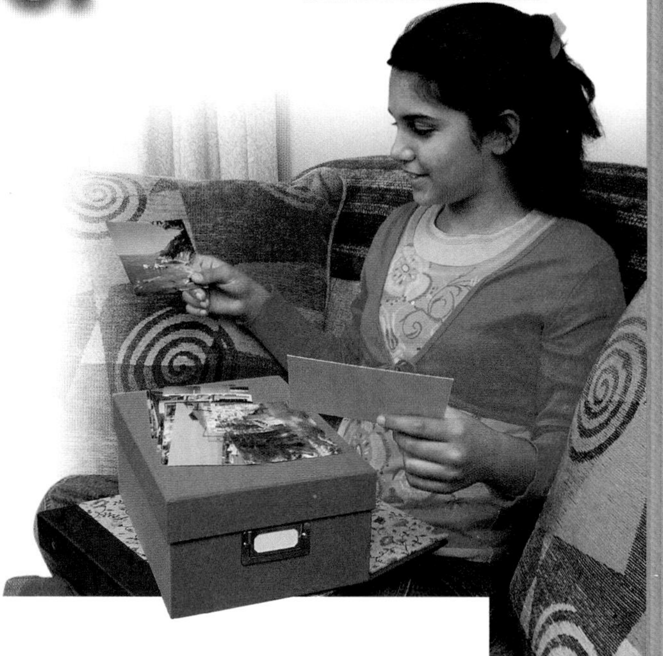

Michelle did not give the correct number of edges for a rectangular prism. There are 12 edges on a rectangular prism.

First, I reviewed the definition of an edge. An edge is the line segment where two or more faces of a solid figure meet.

Next, I counted the number of faces and vertices on the box to find the error she made. I know that a face is the flat surface of a solid figure and that it is a polygon. The box has 6 rectangular faces. I know that a vertex is a point in a solid figure at which three or more edges meet. I counted 8 vertices.

So, since her answer is the number of vertices, not the number of edges, I think Michelle confused the meanings of edge and vertex.

Tips

To describe an error:

- Tell what the error is and give the correct answer.
- Review definitions of math terms that might cause the error.
- Describe what you did to figure out what the error was.
- In the last sentence of your description, state how the error happened.

Problem Solving Describe each error.

1. Edward counted the faces of a triangular prism. He counted 3 faces that are triangles.
2. Hannah says that a square pyramid has 4 faces and 4 vertices.

LESSON

2 Draw Solid Figures

OBJECTIVE: Describe and draw three-dimensional figures.

Quick Review

Identify the solid figure.

1. 

2. 

3. 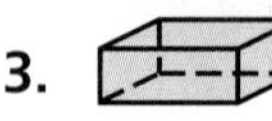

4.  

5. 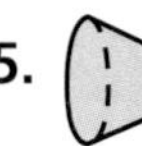

Learn

PROBLEM Thomas likes to record in his sketchbook each new object he builds with his toys. How can he use dot paper to draw a picture of a rectangular prism?

Activity 1 Draw a rectangular prism.

Materials ■ square dot paper ■ straightedge

Think: A rectangular prism has 6 faces, 12 edges, and 8 vertices.

Step 1 Draw a square with sides of 3 units. 3 units	**Step 2** Draw slanted line segments from 3 vertices, as shown.
Step 3 Connect the endpoints of the slanted line segments.	**Step 4** Draw dashed line segments to show the faces that are hidden. Then label the vertices. A B C D E F G H

- Identify two pairs of parallel and perpendicular line segments in the rectangular prism.

Activity 2 Draw a triangular pyramid.

Materials ■ isometric dot paper ■ straightedge

Think: A triangular pyramid has 4 faces, 6 edges, and 4 vertices.

Step 1 Draw a triangle, as shown.	**Step 2** Draw dashed line segments to show the faces that are hidden. Then label the vertices. A B C D

- Name the vertices, edges, and faces in the triangular pyramid.

TEKS 4.8C use essential attributes to define two- and three-dimensional geometric figures. *also* **4.8B, 4.14A, 4.14D, 4.15A, 4.15B**

Guided Practice

1. How many edges does a rectangular prism have? How many line segments are needed to draw a rectangular prism?

For 2–5, use the table.

Toy	Vertices	Edges	Faces
Number Cube	8	12	6 squares
Game Token	5	8	4 triangles 1 square

2. What solid figure does the number cube look like?
3. Use dot paper to draw the number cube.
4. What solid figure does the game token look like?
5. Use dot paper to draw the game token.
6. TALK Math **Explain** how to draw a square pyramid.

Independent Practice and Problem Solving

For 7–10, use the table.

Toy	Vertices	Edges	Faces
Video Game Player	8	12	6 rectangles
Model Tent	5	8	4 triangles 1 rectangle

7. What solid figure does the game player look like?
8. Use dot paper to draw the video game player.
9. What solid figure does the tent look like?
10. Use dot paper to draw the model tent.

For 11–12, use dot paper to draw each figure. Label the vertices. Identify any parallel and perpendicular line segments you see in each figure.

11. a rectangular prism that has at least one edge with a length of 4 units
12. a triangular pyramid whose base has one right angle
13. **Reasoning** A model railroad car is shaped like a rectangular prism. Its length is greater than its height and width. Is this model a cube? **Explain.**
14. WRITE Math **Explain** how to draw a cube in which each edge has a length of 4 units.

Mixed Review and TAKS Prep

15. How many faces, edges, and vertices does a triangular pyramid have?
(TEKS 4.8C, p. 314)
16. A school has 24 classrooms. Each room has 12 gray desks and 15 black desks. How many desks in all are there?
(TEKS 4.4D, p. 236)
17. **TAKS Prep** How many line segments do you need to draw a square pyramid?
(Obj. 3)

A 5 **C** 8
B 6 **D** 12

Patterns for Solid Figures

OBJECTIVE: Identify three-dimensional figures by their nets and make patterns to draw three-dimensional figures.

Quick Review

Tell the number of faces for each solid figure.

1. triangular pyramid
2. cube
3. rectangular prism
4. rectangular pyramid
5. triangular prism

Vocabulary

net

Learn

PROBLEM A **net** is a two-dimensional pattern that can be folded to make a three-dimensional figure. How can you make a net for the box shown?

You can cut apart a three-dimensional box to make a two-dimensional pattern.

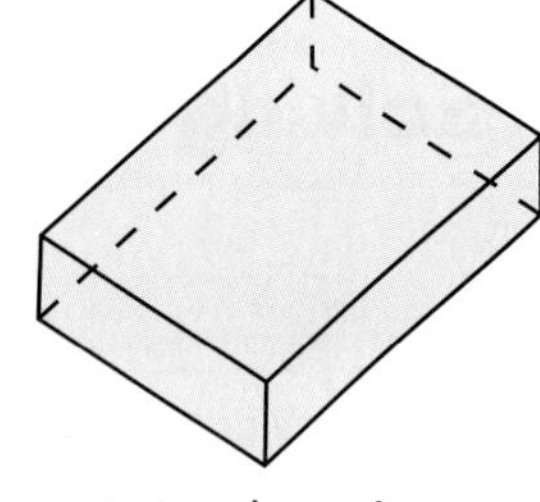
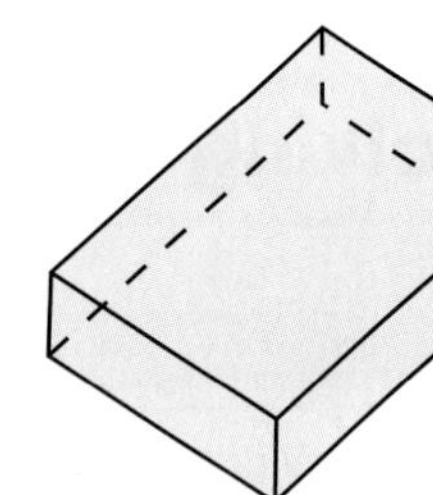

rectangular prism

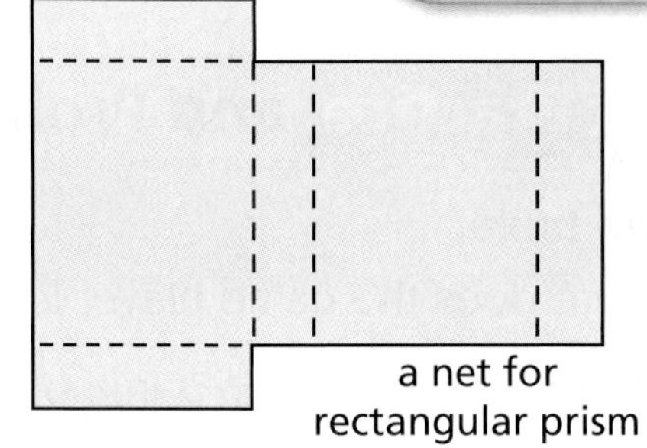

a net for rectangular prism

Activity Make a net.

Materials ■ empty container, such as a cereal box ■ scissors ■ tape

Step 1

Cut along some of the edges until the box is flat. Be sure that each face is connected to another face by at least one edge.

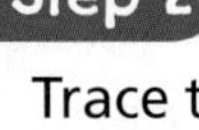

Step 2

Trace the flat shape on a sheet of paper. This shape is a net of the box.

Step 3

Cut out the net. Fold it into a three-dimensional box. Use tape to hold it together.

• Compare your net with those of your classmates. What can you conclude?

Guided Practice

1. What figures make up the net of a rectangular prism? How many of them are there?

TEKS 4.8C use essential attributes to define two- and three-dimensional geometric figures. *also* **4.8B, 4.14A, 4.14D, 4.15A, 4.15B, 4.16A**

Draw a net that can be cut to make a model of each solid figure.

2. 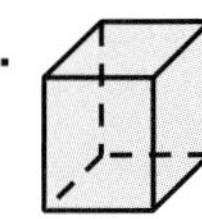
3. 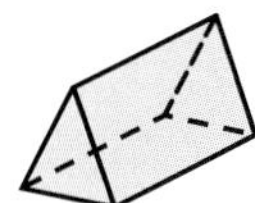
4. 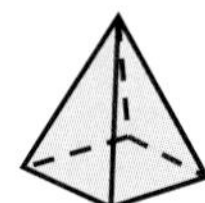
5. 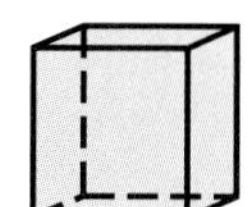

6. **TALK Math** **Explain** how the nets for a cube and a rectangular prism are alike. How they are different?

Independent Practice and Problem Solving

Draw a net that can be cut to make a model of each solid figure.

7. 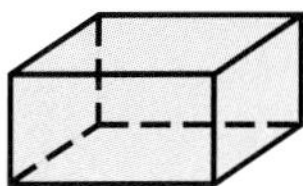
8. 
9. 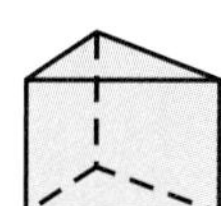
10. 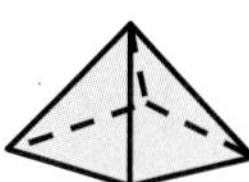

Would the net make a cube? Write *yes* or *no*.

11. 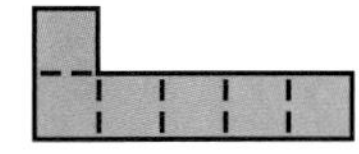
12. 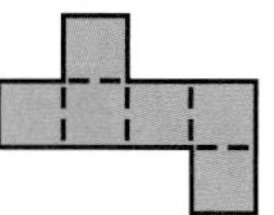
13. 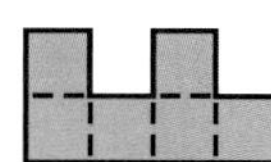
14. 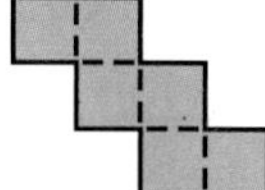

For 15–17, use the nets.

15. Which net can you use to make a triangular prism?
16. Identify the solid figure you can make with net B.
17. Which net can you use to make a triangular pyramid?

a. 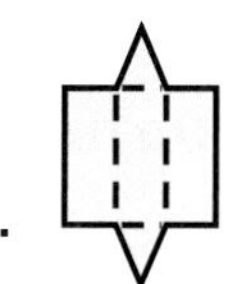
b. 
c. 

18. **Reasoning** Look at the net at the right. When the net is folded, which face will be parallel to face *A*? Which faces will be perpendicular to face *B*?

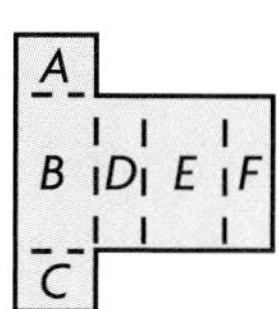

19. **WRITE Math** **What's the Error?** Eric said the net at the right can be folded to make a triangular pyramid. Describe Eric's mistake. Then draw a net he could use to make a triangular pyramid.

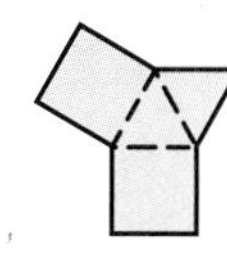

Mixed Review and TAKS Prep

20. Aiko drew this figure. How many lines of symmetry does this figure appear to have? (TEKS 4.9C, p. 294)

21. Bob and 3 of his friends rented some skates. They spent \$20. Write an equation to show the cost to rent 1 pair of skates.
(TEKS 4.15B, p. 162)

22. **TAKS Prep** What solid figure can you make from the net shown? (Obj. 3)

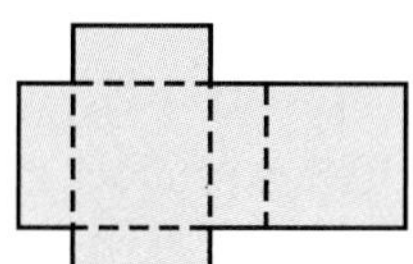

Extra Practice on page 326, Set C

Problem Solving Workshop
Strategy: Make a Model

OBJECTIVE: Solve problems by using the strategy *make a model.*

Learn the Strategy

It can be difficult to understand what is being described in a problem. Sometimes you can use a model to show the actions in a problem.

A model can show the actions in a problem.

Amy baked 16 brownies. She took half of them to school for the bake sale. She gave Jamie half of what was left. She wants to know how many brownies are left.

Action 1 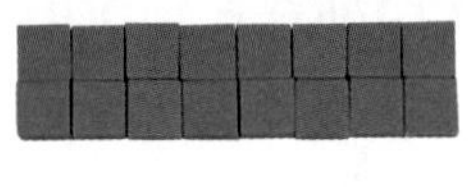 ← Amy baked 16 brownies.

Action 2  ← She took half to school.

Action 3  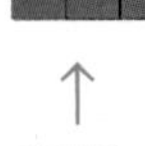

↑ She gave Jamie half of what was left.

↑ Brownies left.

A model can show a situation before and after a change.

Tyrell built a prism that was 3 cubes long, 3 cubes wide, and 3 cubes high. Then he removed 6 cubes. What might his model look like now?

Before

After

A model can show the relationships in a problem.

Susan wants to know how many cubes she will need to make the next cube in this pattern.

1

2

3

When making a model, reread the problem to make sure that your model shows each part of the problem.

TALK Math

How is the strategy *make a model* like the strategy *act it out*? How are they different?

TEKS 4.14C select or develop an appropriate problem-solving plan or strategy, including drawing a picture, looking for a pattern, systematic guessing and checking, acting it out, making a table, working a simpler problem, or working backwards to solve a problem. *also* **4.8C, 4.14A, 4.14B, 4.14D, 4.15A, 4.15B, 4.16B**

Use the Strategy

PROBLEM After John studied the buildings of architect Moshe Safdie, he used cubes to design a building. He drew a top view, a front view, and a side view of his building. How many cubes will John need to build his model?

top view | front view | side view

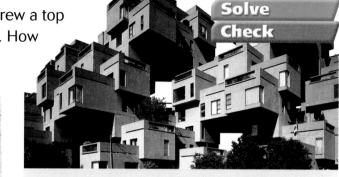

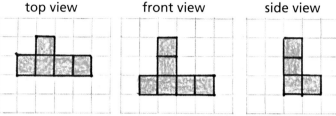

▲ **Moshe Safdie designed these buildings for Expo 67, the 1967 World's Fair in Montreal, Canada. They were made from 354 stacked cubes.**

Read to Understand | Plan | Solve | Check

Read to Understand

- **What are you asked to find?**
- **What information is given? Is there information you will not use? If so, what?**

Plan

- **What strategy can you use to solve the problem?**

You can make a model to help you visualize the details in the problem.

Solve

- **How can you use the strategy to solve the problem?**

You can use cubes to make a model of the building.

First, build the top view. The model shows 5 cubes.

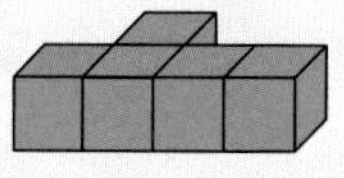

Next, stack cubes to match the front view. The model now shows 7 cubes.

Finally, decide whether the model matches the side view. If necessary, make any changes. Since the side view matches, no changes are needed.

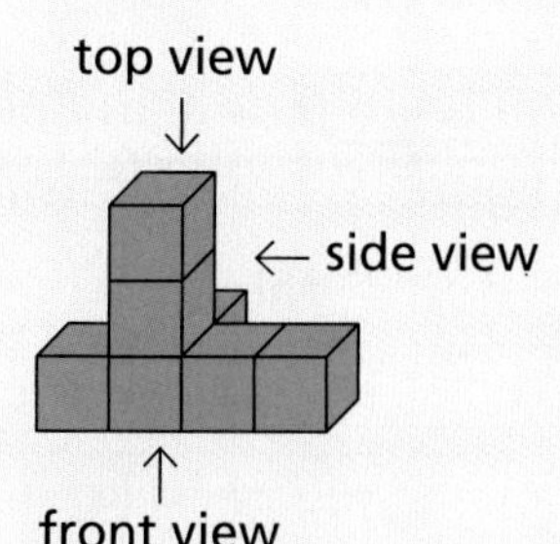

So, John will need 7 cubes to build his model.

Check

- **How can you check your model?**
- **What other strategy could you use to solve the problem?**

Guided Problem Solving

1. Antoine made the model shown at the right by using 9 cubes. Draw a top view, a front view, and a side view on grid paper.

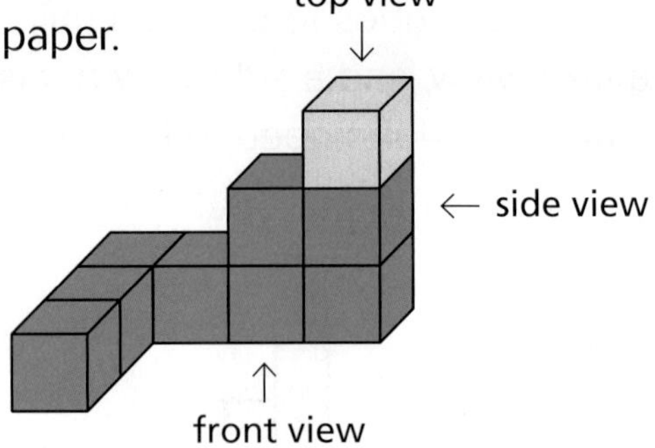

First, draw the top view.

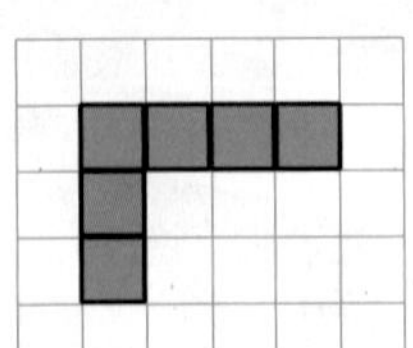

Next, look at the figure from the front, and draw what you see.

Finally, look at the figure from the side, and draw the side view.

2. **What if** the yellow cube was removed? Which of the three views would change? Draw each new view on grid paper, and label the view.

3. Alicia used the fewest possible cubes to make a building, whose views are shown at the right. How many cubes did she use?

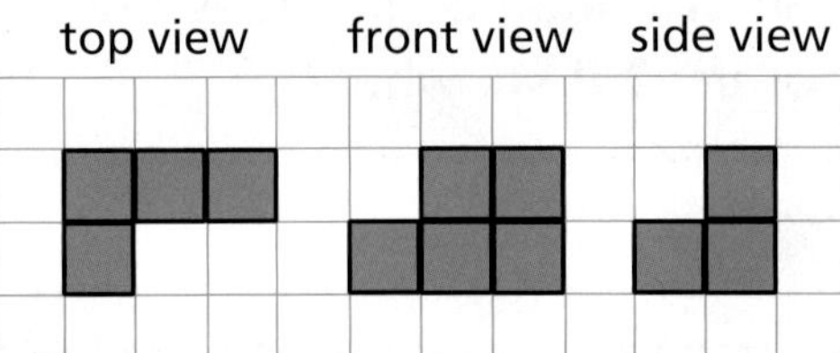

Problem Solving Strategy Practice

Make a model to solve.

4. Sandra has 40 cubes. She uses half of them to make a building. She gives Jeffrey half of what is not used so that he can make a building. If Jeffrey uses 8 cubes in his building, how many of the 40 cubes are still not used?

5. Riko has 60 cubes. She builds a staircase beginning with 1 cube, then 3, then 6, then 10, and so on. When she has made the largest possible staircase, how many cubes will she have left over?

6. WRITE Math Micah and Natalie each drew the front view of this figure. Whose drawing is correct? **Explain.**

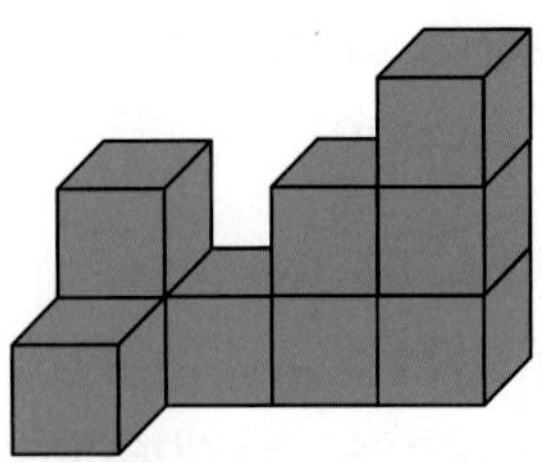

Micah

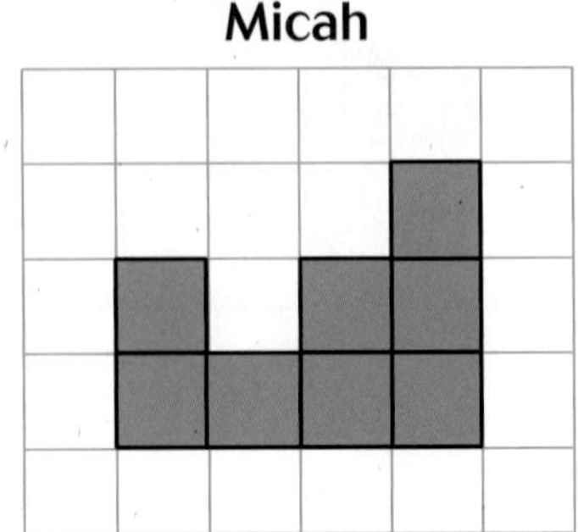

Natalie

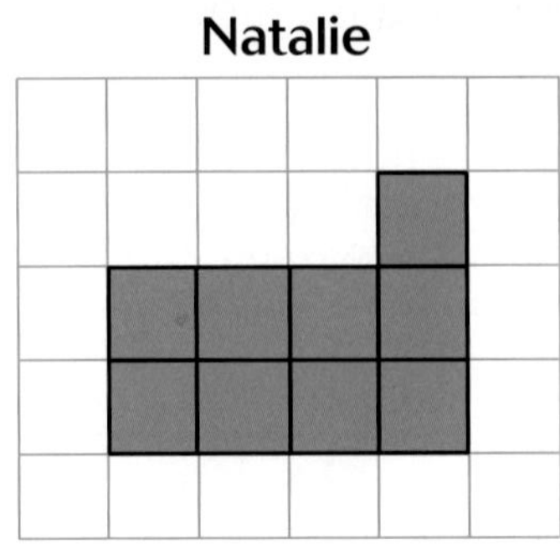

Mixed Strategy Practice

7. Ellie wants to sort the objects on the table according to their shapes. Make an organized list of how she can sort the objects.

Choose a STRATEGY

- Draw a Diagram or Picture
- Make a Model or Act It Out
- Make an Organized List
- Look for a Pattern
- Make a Table or Graph
- Guess and Check
- Work Backward
- Solve a Simpler Problem
- Write an Equation
- Use Logical Reasoning

USE DATA For 8–10, use the cube in the picture.

8. **What if** Rubik had designed a puzzle that was 6 cubes long, 6 cubes wide, and 6 cubes high, how many small squares would it have on one face?
9. The center of Rubik's puzzle is missing one small cube. How many small cubes make up the puzzle?
10. ***FAST FACT*** When Rubik was designing his puzzle, he first used colored paper squares to cover each small square on the outside of the big cube. How many small paper squares did he need?
11. **Pose a Problem** Write a problem about a model made with 10 cubes.
12. **Open-Ended** Suppose you have 40 cubes. How could you make a pattern with some or all of the cubes? Describe the pattern.

Erno Rubik invented one of the best-selling puzzles in history in 1974. The small cubes can be arranged in more than 43,000,000,000,000,000,000, or 43 quintillion, different ways. Only 1 of the ways is correct.

CHALLENGE YOURSELF

Use the figure at the right. There are no hidden cubes in the figure. Do not make a model to solve.

13. How many more cubes would be needed to change the model into a cube that has 16 small squares on each face? **Explain.**
14. Suppose you change the figure into a prism 2 cubes long, 2 cubes wide, and 2 cubes high. Would you need to add cubes or take cubes away? How many?

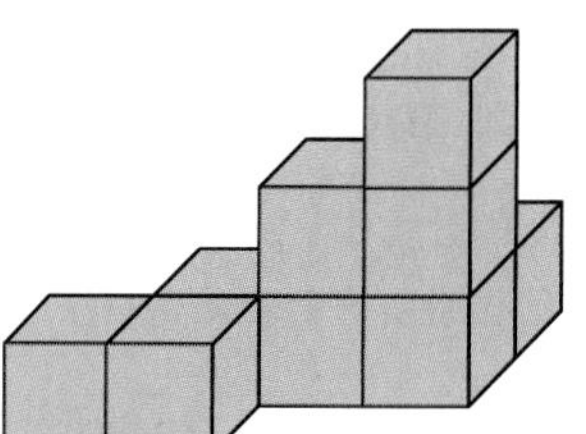

Extra Practice

Set A Name a solid figure that is described. (pp. 314–317)

1. 6 congruent faces
2. 4 triangular faces
3. 1 circular base
4. 12 edges

Which solid figure or figures do you see in each?

5. 
6. 
7. 
8. 

9. All of my faces are triangles. What solid figure am I?

Set B For 1–4, use the table. (pp. 318–319)

Item	Vertices	Edges	Faces
cake box	8	12	6 squares
paperweight	4	6	4 triangles

1. What solid figure does the cake box look like?
2. Use dot paper to draw the cake box.
3. What solid figure does the paperweight look like?
4. Use dot paper to draw the paperweight.
5. Use dot paper to draw a square pyramid with a base that measures 3 units on each side.

Set C Draw a net that can be cut to make a model of each solid figure. (pp. 320–321)

1. 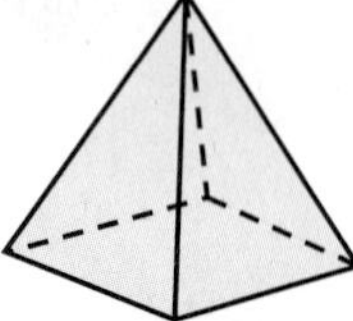
2. 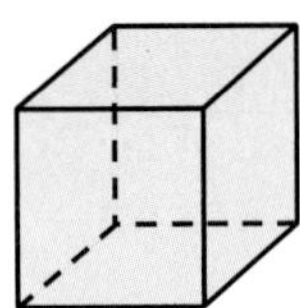
3. 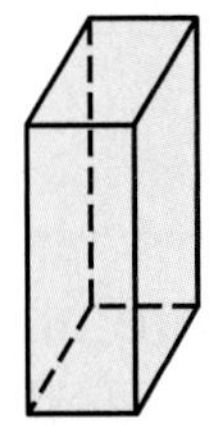
4. 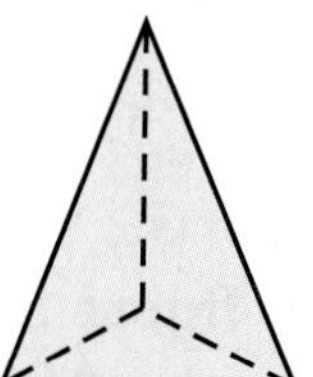

For 5–7, use the nets.

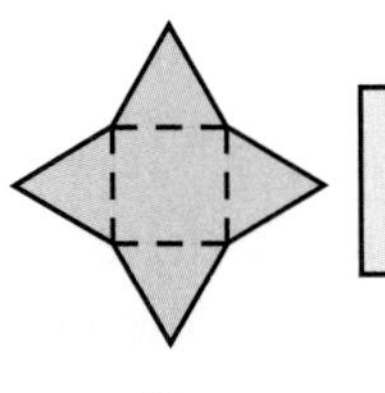

a.

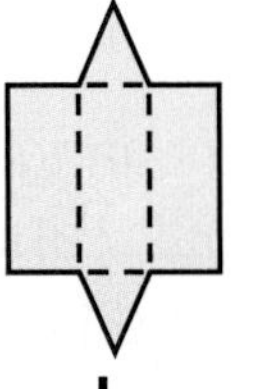

b.

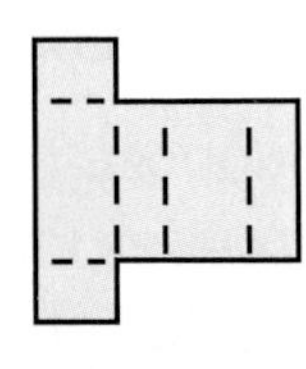

c.

5. Which net can you use to make a paperweight with a square base and 4 triangular faces.
6. Identify the solid figure you can make with net *C*.
7. Rosario folded net *A* into a model of a solid figure. How many faces, edges, and vertices did the model have?

Technology

Use Harcourt Mega Math, Ice Station Exploration, *Frozen Solids,* Levels A, B, C, D, E, F, G, H.

PRACTICE GAME

Build the View

Builders!

2 teams, at least 2 players on each team

Building Blocks!

- Index cards (15)
- Centimeter cubes (15 for each team)
- Two-color counters

START

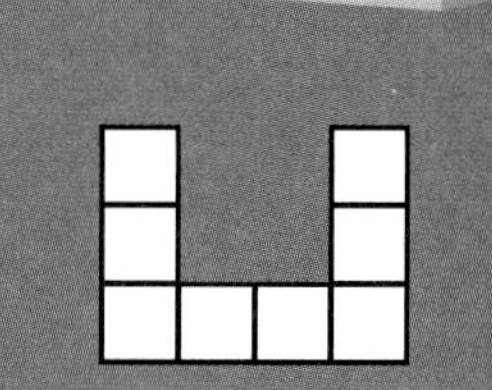

FINISH

Build!

- Shuffle the cards. Place them facedown in a stack.
- Begin with the space labeled START. Teams take turns drawing the top card. Teams use cubes to build a figure that has the view shown on the space and can be described by the view on the card.
- If both teams agree that the figure is correct, the team places a counter on that space. If the figure does not have that view, the other team draws the next view card and tries to build a figure. If neither team can build a figure with that view, the space is out of play.
- Move to the next space on the board. The team draws the top card and continues to play.
- Play ends with the space labeled FINISH. The team with the greater number of counters on the board wins.

Chapter 12 Review/Test

Check Vocabulary and Concepts

Choose the best term from the box.

VOCABULARY
rectangular pyramid
triangular prism
triangular pyramid

1. A __?__ has triangular bases and rectangular faces. (TEKS 4.8C, p. 314)
2. A __?__ has a rectangular base and triangular faces. (TEKS 4.8C, p. 314)

Check Skills

Name a solid figure that is described. (TEKS 4.8C, pp. 314–317)

3. curved surfaces
4. some or all rectangular faces
5. 5 faces, 9 edges, 6 vertices
6. 5 vertices

Which solid figure or figures do you see in each? (TEKS 4.8C, pp. 314–317)

7. 

8. 

9. 

10. 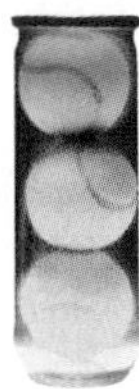

For 11–14, use the table. (TEKS 4.8C, pp. 318–319)

11. Use dot paper to draw the cereal box.
12. What solid figure does the cereal box look like?
13. Use dot paper to draw the light prism.
14. What solid figure does the light prism look like?

Item	Vertices	Edges	Faces
Cereal box	8	12	6 rectangles
Light prism	6	9	2 triangles 3 rectangles

Draw a net that can be cut to make a model of each solid figure. (TEKS 4.8C, pp. 320–321)

15. 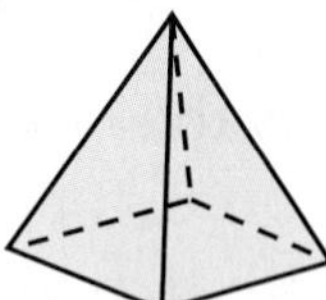

16. 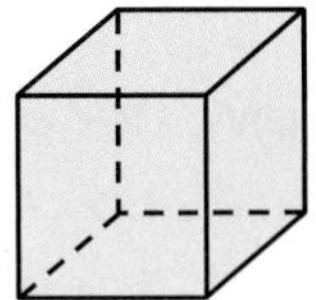

17. 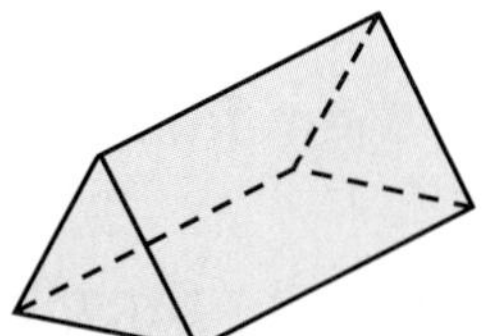

18. 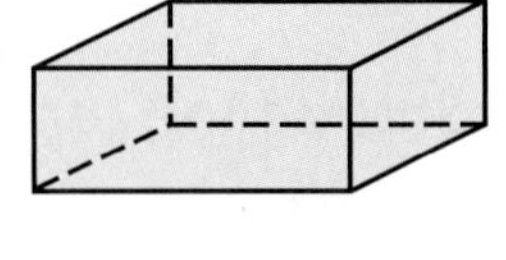

Check Problem Solving

For 19–20, use the picture to solve. (TEKS 4.14C, pp. 322–325)

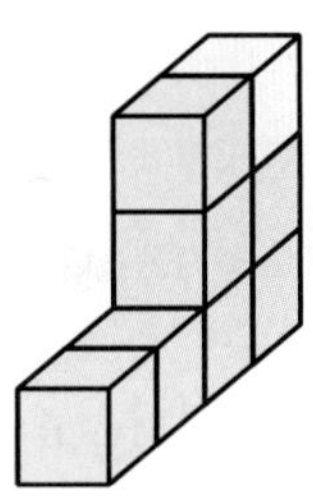

19. Melanie used 8 cubes to build this figure. Draw the top view, side view, and front view.
20. WRITE Math **Explain** how the views would change if the yellow cube were removed.

GO ONLINE **Technology** Use *Online Assessment.*

Enrich • Patterns in Prisms and Pyramids

Faces, Vertices, and Edges

▲ Leonhard Euler (1707–1783)

Leonhard Euler was a Swiss mathematician who lived in the 1700s. He discovered that the numbers of faces, vertices, and edges in prisms and in pyramids are related.

Prisms	Pyramids
sides = number of sides on the base	sides = number of sides on the base
sides + 2 = faces	sides + 1 = faces
sides × 2 = vertices	sides + 1 = vertices
sides × 3 = edges	sides × 2 = edges

Examples

A Find the number of faces, vertices, and edges of a cube.

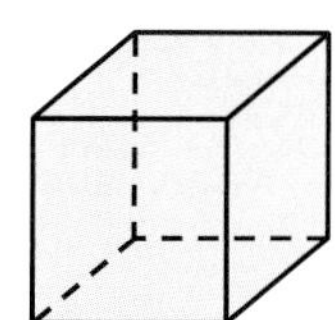

A cube has 4 sides on the base.

$4 + 2 = 6$ faces

$4 \times 2 = 8$ vertices

$4 \times 3 = 12$ edges

So, a cube has 6 faces, 8 vertices, and 12 edges.

B Find the number of faces, vertices, and edges of a square pyramid.

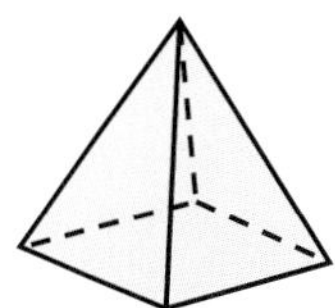

A square pyramid has 4 sides on the base.

$4 + 1 = 5$ faces

$4 + 1 = 5$ vertices

$4 \times 2 = 8$ edges

So, a square pyramid has 5 faces, 5 vertices, and 8 edges.

Try It

Tell how many faces, vertices, and edges each figure has.

1. rectangular pyramid
2. rectangular prism
3. triangular pyramid
4. triangular prism
5. **Challenge** If you read that a prism had 8 faces, 8 vertices, and 12 edges, how would you know that the information is incorrect?

WRITE Math **Explain** how to find the number of edges on any pyramid or prism if you know the number of sides on the base.

Unit Review/Test
Chapters 10–12

Multiple Choice

1. Which of the following appears to be an acute angle? (TAKS Obj. 3)

A 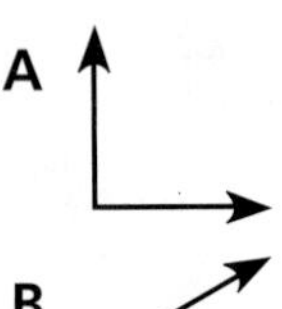

C 

B 

D 

2. The figure below is an example of what type of quadrilateral? (TAKS Obj. 3)

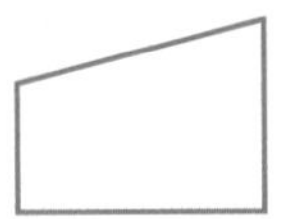

F Rectangle

G Square

H Parallelogram

J Trapezoid

3. Which pair of figures shows a translation? (TAKS Obj. 3)

A  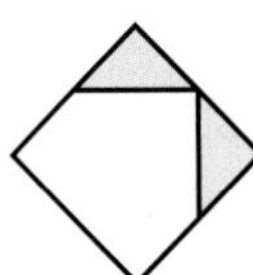

B 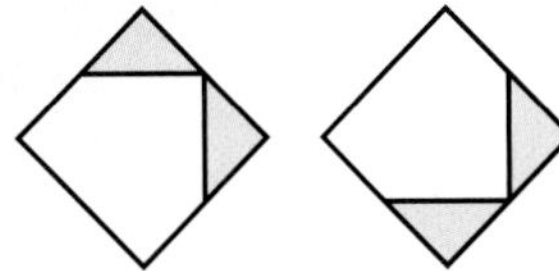

C 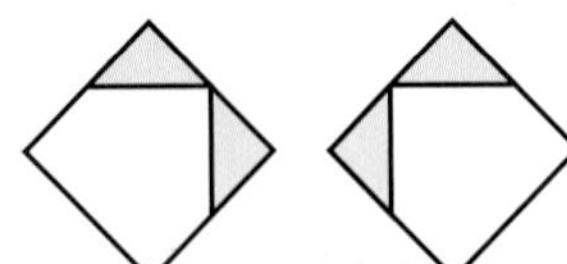

D 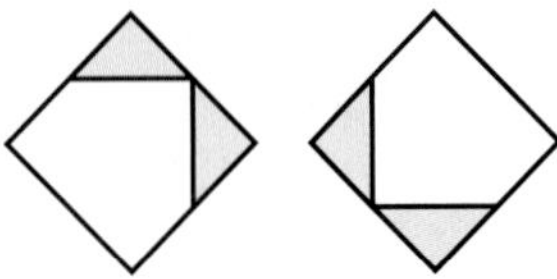

4. Which pair of lines appears to be perpendicular? (TAKS Obj. 3)

F

G 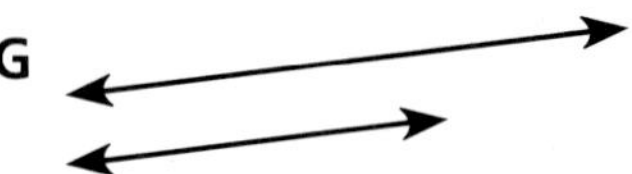

H 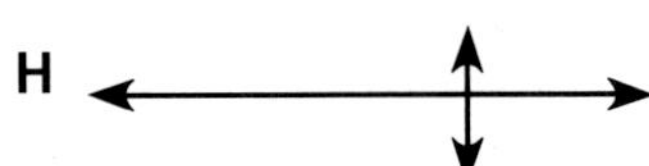

J 

5. How many lines of symmetry does the figure have? (TAKS Obj. 3)

A 1

B 2

C 3

D Not here

6. Carson drew this figure. (TAKS Obj. 3)

What is a good description of the figure Carson drew?

F A closed figure with 6 obtuse angles

G A closed figure with 4 obtuse angles and 2 acute angles

H A closed figure with 2 obtuse angles and 4 acute angles

J A closed figure with 6 acute angles

GO ONLINE Technology Use *Online Assessment.*

7. Which of the following triangles is an equilateral triangle? (TAKS Obj. 3)

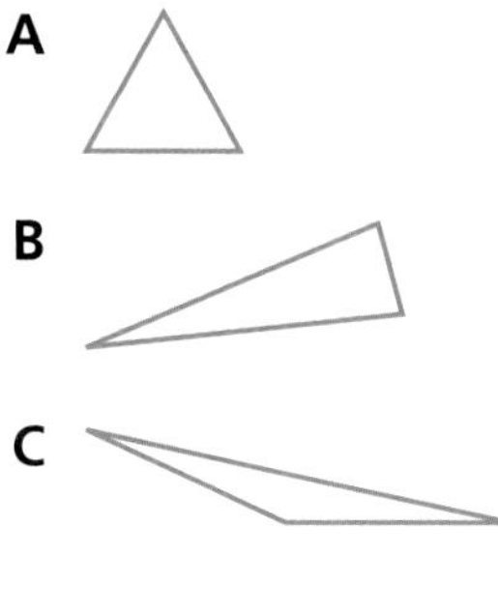

A

B

C

D

8. Elvis carved the model below from a bar of soap. How many edges does this figure have? (TAKS Obj. 3)

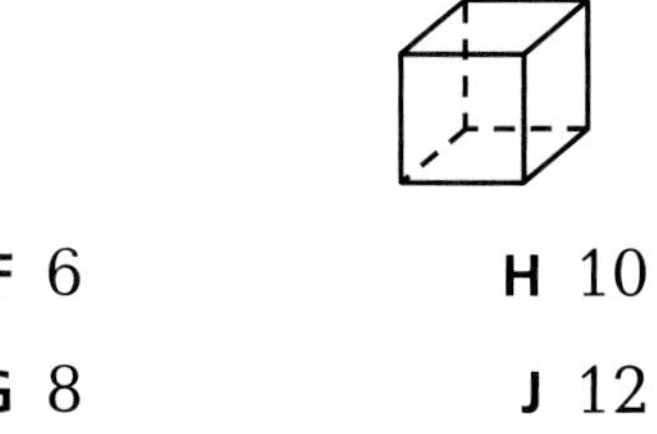

F 6

G 8

H 10

J 12

9. Jan drew a plane figure that is **NOT** a polygon. Which figure could she have drawn? (TAKS Obj. 3)

A Square

B Hexagon

C Cone

D Circle

10. What solid figure is represented below? (TAKS Obj. 3)

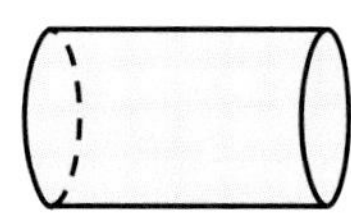

F Sphere

G Cylinder

H Cube

J Cone

Short Response

11. Classify this figure in as many ways as possible. (TAKS Obj. 3)

12. What single transformation is shown by these figures? (TAKS Obj. 3)

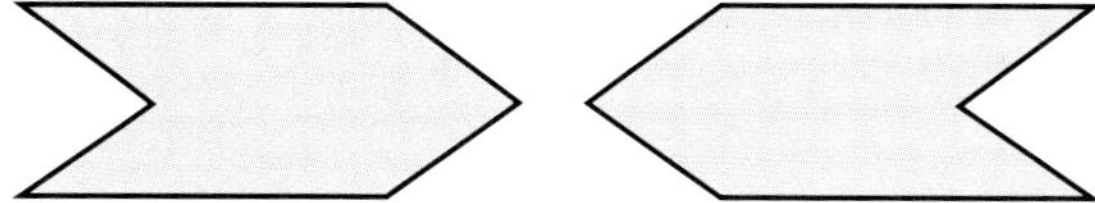

13. Draw a circle. Draw and label the diameter and the radius. (TAKS Obj. 3)

14. Look at the map. Which streets appear to be parallel to each other? (TAKS Obj. 3)

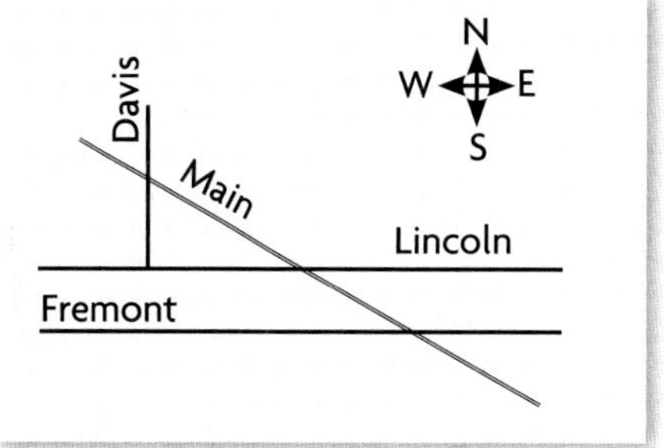

Extended Response WRITE Math

15. **Explain** why it is **NOT** possible to draw an equilateral scalene triangle. (TAKS Obj. 3)

16. **Explain** the differences between a triangular pyramid and a triangular prism. Draw an example of each. (TAKS Obj. 3)

17. Figure B shows a $\frac{1}{2}$ rotation of Figure A. Are the figures congruent? **Explain** how you know. (TAKS Obj. 3)

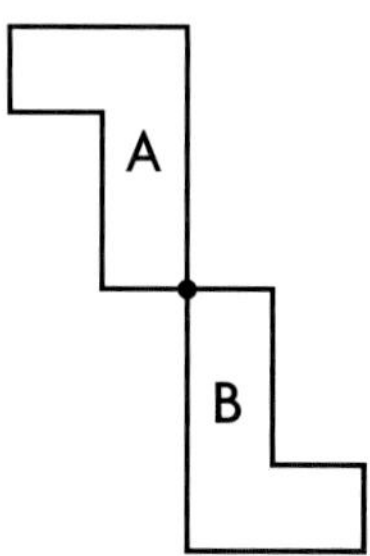

Looking at Toys

Symmetric Toys

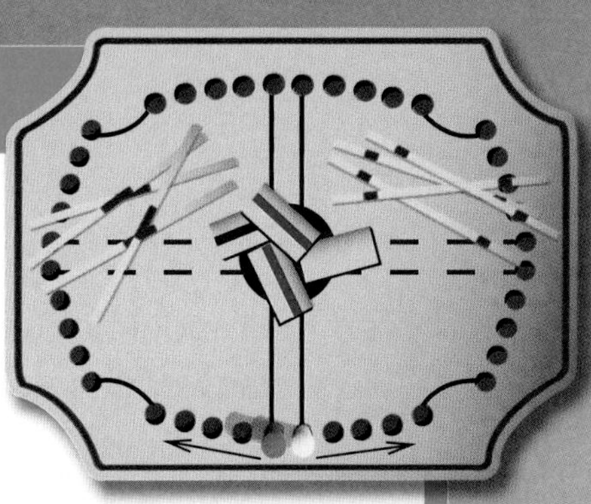

You can find board games about all kinds of topics, including Texas history. For example, there are games about the Texas Revolution, Texas cities such as Dallas, and about Texas oil. Many toys and games have symmetry. They may have one or more lines of symmetry or no lines of symmetry. How many lines of symmetry does the game board shown in the photograph have?

The game in the photograph is based on a game played by the Kiowa Indians, who once lived in Texas. The game uses a symmetric game board.

FACT · ACTIVITY

Tell whether each picture of a toy appears to have *no lines of symmetry*, *1 line of symmetry*, or *more than 1 line of symmetry*.

1. Game piece

2. Electronic game

3. Number cube

Each picture shows part of a toy. Copy and complete each picture to show line symmetry.

4. Robot

5. Football

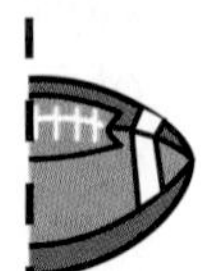

6. Guitar

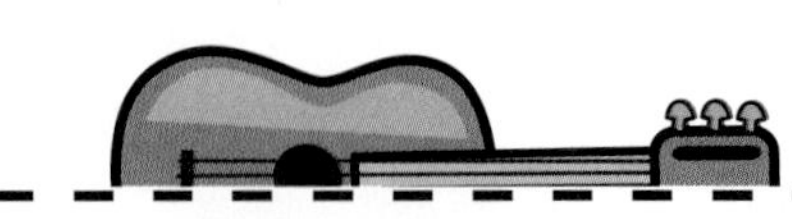

7. WRITE Math Describe a toy or game not pictured here that has symmetry. Explain how you know.

ALMANAC Fact

Kiowa Indians in Texas played a game similar to the one on the opposite page. Two players use four sticks to determine how many spaces their pegs can move.

Game Boards

Chess and backgammon are games that have been played all over the world for centuries. Backgammon is one of the oldest games in recorded history. Early versions were played in Mesopotamia thousands of years ago. Chess was developed in India in the sixth century. Both are games of strategy for two people. Plane figures and solid figures were used in the design of these board games.

FACT • ACTIVITY

Suppose a large toy company asks you to design a new board game.

1. Draw the game board. Decide what plane figures you want to use. Then color your design.
   - Name the plane figures you used.
   - Describe how you combined or transformed the plane figures to make your game board.
   - Does your design show a tessellating pattern? Explain.
   - Does your game board show symmetry? Explain.
2. Draw one of your game pieces. Show the front and top views.

UNIT

5 Divide by 1-Digit Divisors

Math on Location

with **Texas Chapter Projects**

1

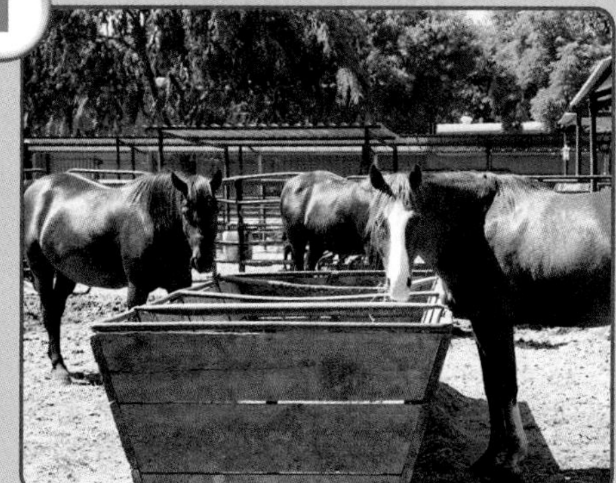

These actors live on a ranch near Hollywood. The fee paid to use them in movies pays for their hay.

2

The dirctor of the movie has a budget of $250 to rent a stagecoach for 3 days.

3

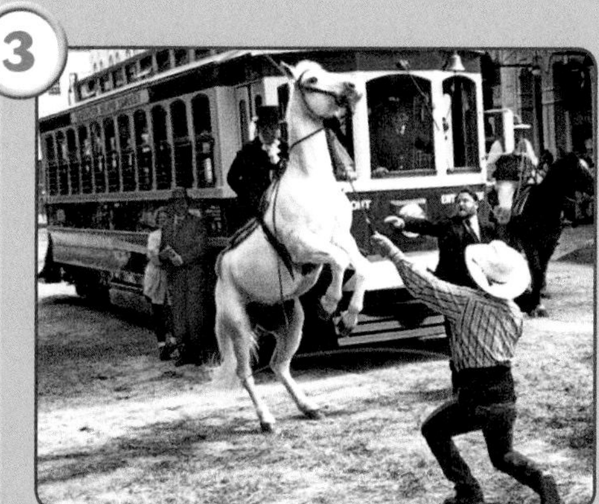

The actors, both human and animal, are ready for this scene. Lights, camera, action!

VOCABULARY POWER

TALK Math

Look at the **Math on Location** photographs. How can you find how much it costs the director to rent a stagecoach for one day?

READ Math

REVIEW VOCABULARY You learned the words below when you learned about division facts. How do these words relate to **Math on Location**?

divide to separate into equal groups; the opposite operation of multiplication

factor a number that is multiplied by another to find a product

quotient the number, not including the remainder, that results from dividing.

WRITE Math

Copy and complete the word knowledge chart below. Mark the division words you know now with a check mark. Use a star to show the new words you know at the end of the unit.

Word	I Know	Sounds Familiar	Don't Know
divisor	✔		
dividend		✔	
quotient			
remainder			
compatible numbers			

Technology
Multimedia Math Glossary link at
www.harcourtschool.com/hspmath

13 Understand Division

The Big Idea Division tells how many groups or how many in each group, is related to repeated subtraction, and is the inverse of multiplication.

TEXAS FAST FACT

Enchanted Rock is in Enchanted Rock State Natural Area, near Fredericksburg. This huge rock is 425 feet high, and it covers 640 acres, enough for 159 U.S. Capitol buildings.

Investigate

Visitors to Enchanted Rock State Natural Area can enjoy camping, hiking, climbing, bird watching, and stargazing. The table shows the number of people who were stargazing on four evenings. On each evening, how many equal-size groups of fewer than 10 people might have been stargazing? How could you use models to justify your answer?

Stargazers at Enchanted Rock

Night	Number of People
Monday	60
Tuesday	108
Wednesday	256
Thursday	240

Technology
Student pages are available in the Student eBook.

Show What You Know

Check your understanding of important skills needed for success in Chapter 13.

▶ 2-Digit Subtraction

Find the difference.

1. $\begin{array}{r} 47 \\ -26 \\ \hline \end{array}$ **2.** $\begin{array}{r} 23 \\ -14 \\ \hline \end{array}$ **3.** $\begin{array}{r} 76 \\ -34 \\ \hline \end{array}$ **4.** $\begin{array}{r} 83 \\ -31 \\ \hline \end{array}$ **5.** $\begin{array}{r} 54 \\ -39 \\ \hline \end{array}$

6. $63 - 26$ **7.** $39 - 17$ **8.** $96 - 29$ **9.** $31 - 20$ **10.** $73 - 52$

▶ Model Division

Write the division fact that each picture represents.

11.

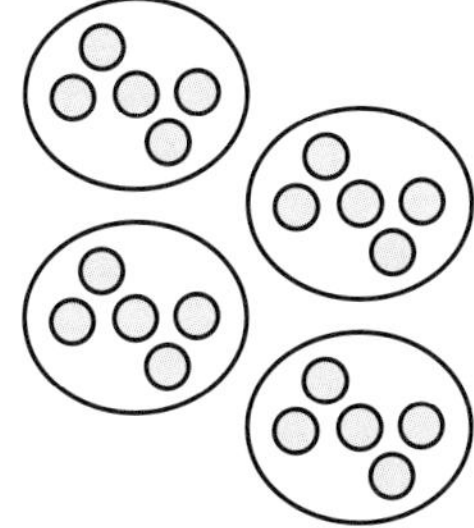

12.

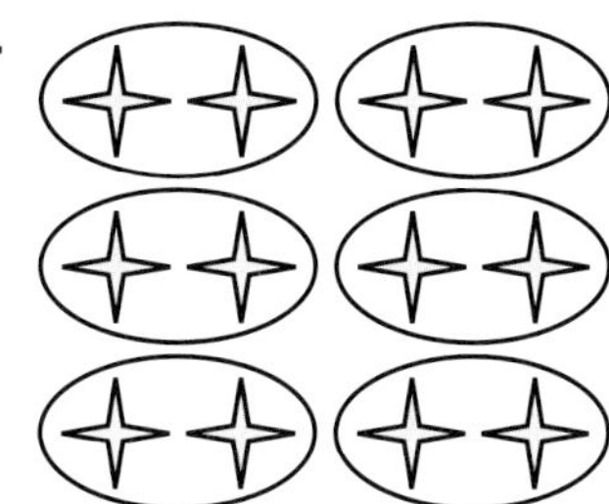

13.

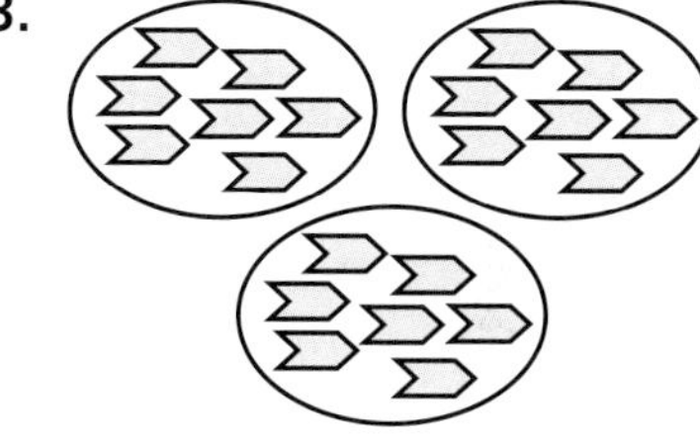

▶ Division Facts

Find the quotient.

14. $54 \div 6$ **15.** $8\overline{)72}$ **16.** $42 \div 6$ **17.** $24 \div 3$ **18.** $5\overline{)40}$

19. $6\overline{)18}$ **20.** $27 \div 9$ **21.** $8\overline{)32}$ **22.** $4\overline{)28}$ **23.** $63 \div 7$

VOCABULARY POWER

CHAPTER VOCABULARY

compatible numbers
dividend
divisor
estimate
mental math
quotient
remainder

WARM-UP WORDS

remainder the amount left over when a number cannot be divided equally

dividend the number that is to be divided in a division problem

divisor the number that divides the dividend

LESSON 1 HANDS ON

Divide with Remainders

OBJECTIVE: Divide whole numbers that do not divide evenly.

Quick Review

1. $27 \div 9$
2. 4×7
3. 3×8
4. $5\overline{)25}$
5. $3\overline{)12}$

Vocabulary

remainder

Investigate

Materials ■ counters

Chan and 2 friends are playing a game of dominoes. There are 28 dominoes in the set. He wants each player to receive the same number of dominoes. Can Chan divide them equally among the 3 players? Why or why not?

Remember

$42 \div 7 = 6$

↑ dividend ↑ divisor ↑ quotient

You can use division to find the number of dominoes each player will receive.

A Use 28 counters to represent the 28 dominoes. Then draw 3 circles to represent the 3 players.

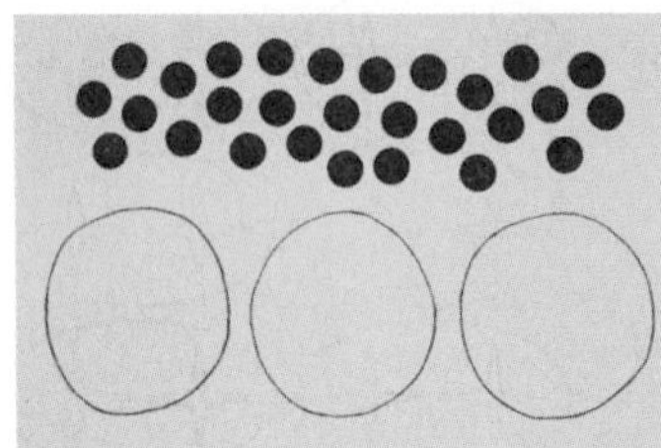

B Divide the 28 counters into 3 equal groups by putting them in the circles.

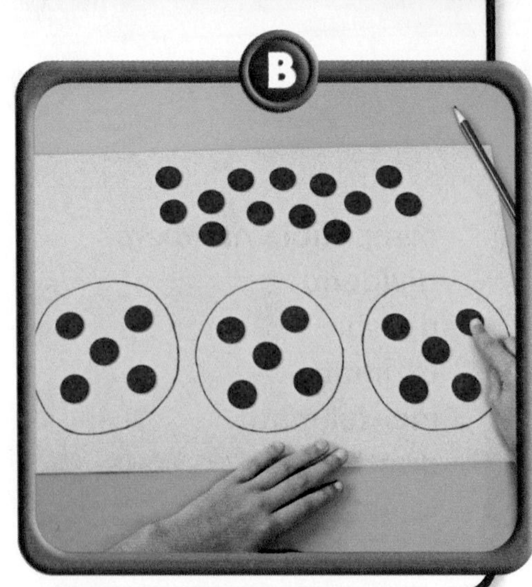

C Find the number of counters in each equal group and the number of counters left over. Record your answer.

Draw Conclusions

1. How many dominoes does each player receive? How many dominoes are left over?
2. How did the model help you find the number of dominoes each player receives? Why is 1 counter left outside the equal groups?
3. Use counters to find the number of dominoes each player will receive if there are 4 players using a set of 28 dominoes. Will there be any left over? Explain.
4. **Application** How can you use counters to divide 38 by 4?

TEKS 4.4B Represent multiplication and division situations in picture, word, and number form. *also* 4.4E, 4.14A, 4.14D, 4.15A, 4.15B

Connect

Sometimes a number cannot be divided evenly. The amount left over is called the **remainder**.

Use counters to divide 39 by 5.

Step 1

Use 39 counters.

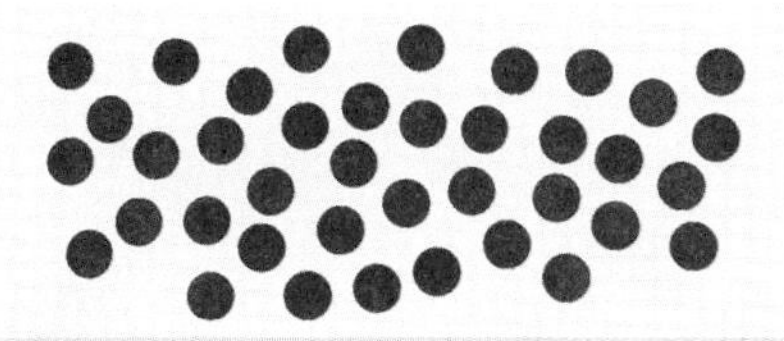

Step 2

Draw 5 circles. Divide the counters into 5 equal groups. The number of counters left over is the remainder.

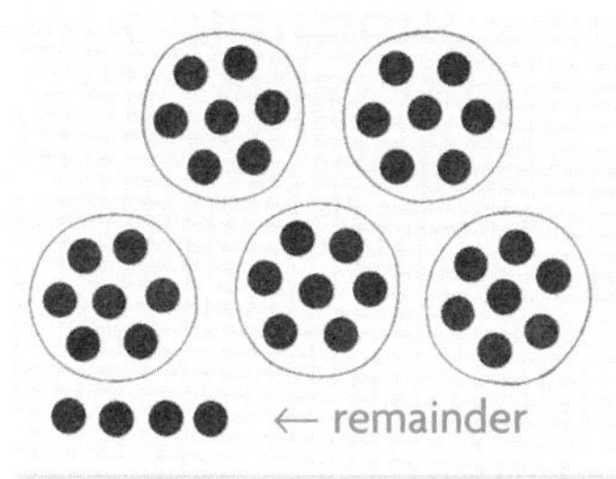

So, the quotient is 7 and the remainder is 4.

TALK Math

How do you know when there will be a remainder in a division problem?

Practice

Use counters to find the quotient and remainder.

1. $22 \div 3$
2. $28 \div 5$
3. $15 \div 6$
4. $11 \div 3$
5. $34 \div 5$
6. $6\overline{)58}$
7. $4\overline{)19}$
8. $4\overline{)38}$
9. $2\overline{)17}$
10. $9\overline{)26}$
11. $25 \div 3$
12. $7\overline{)20}$
13. $9\overline{)80}$
14. $10 \div 3$
15. $29 \div 4$

Divide. You may wish to use counters or draw a picture to help.

16. $5\overline{)47}$
17. $6\overline{)26}$
18. $4\overline{)35}$
19. $9\overline{)69}$
20. $7\overline{)66}$
21. $55 \div 9$
22. $63 \div 8$
23. $19 \div 3$
24. $58 \div 9$
25. $71 \div 8$
26. **WRITE Math** **What's the Error?** Frank says this model represents $4\overline{)13}$. What is his error? Draw a correct model.

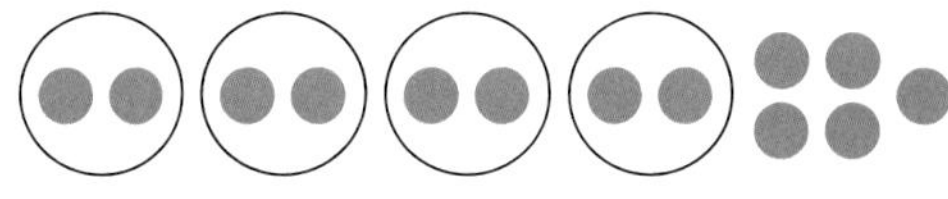

Technology
Use Harcourt Mega Math, The Number Games, *Up, Up, and Array,* Level L.

LESSON 2 HANDS ON

Model 2-Digit by 1-Digit Division

OBJECTIVE: Model division by using base-ten blocks.

Quick Review

1. 3×8
2. $12 \div 2$
3. 7×9
4. 6×8
5. $54 \div 6$

Investigate

Materials ■ base-ten blocks

The school lunchroom is serving 72 peaches on 3 trays. Each tray has the same number of peaches. How many peaches are on each tray?

You can use base-ten blocks to find the number of objects in equal groups.

A Use base-ten blocks to model the 72 peaches. Show 72 as 7 tens 2 ones. Draw three circles.

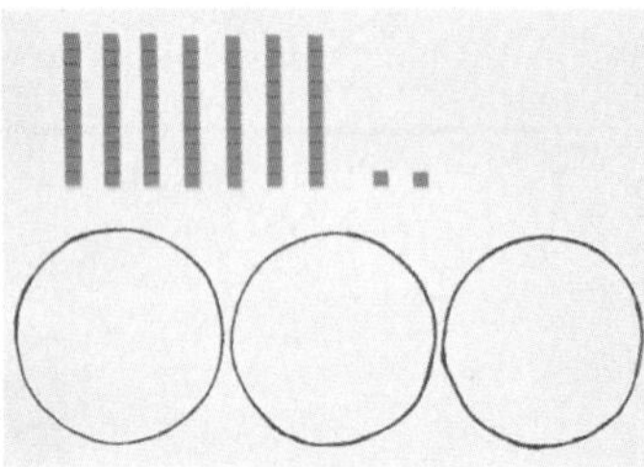

B Place an equal number of tens into each group.

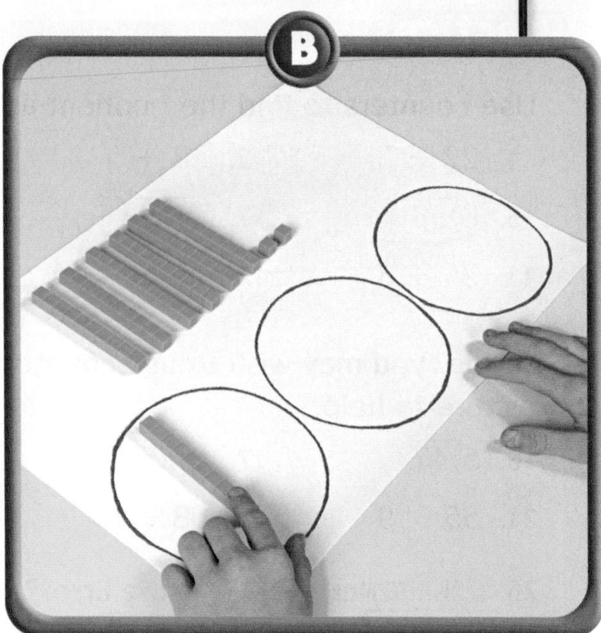

C If there are any tens left, regroup them as ones. Place an equal number of ones into each group.

D Count the number of tens and ones in each group to find the number of peaches on each tray. Record your answer.

Draw Conclusions

1. Why did you draw 3 circles in Step A?
2. Why do you need to regroup in Step C?
3. How many peaches are on each tray?
4. How can you check your answer?
5. **Synthesis** What if there are 96 peaches and 4 trays? How can you use base-ten blocks to find how many peaches will be on each tray?

TEKS 4.4B Represent multiplication and division situations in picture, word, and number form. *also* **4.4E, 4.14A, 4.14D, 4.15A, 4.15B**

Connect

You can use base-ten blocks to model division with remainders.

Miguel's robot kit has 46 mechanical parts. He can build 4 matching robots with the parts. How many parts does Miguel need for each robot? How many parts will be left over?

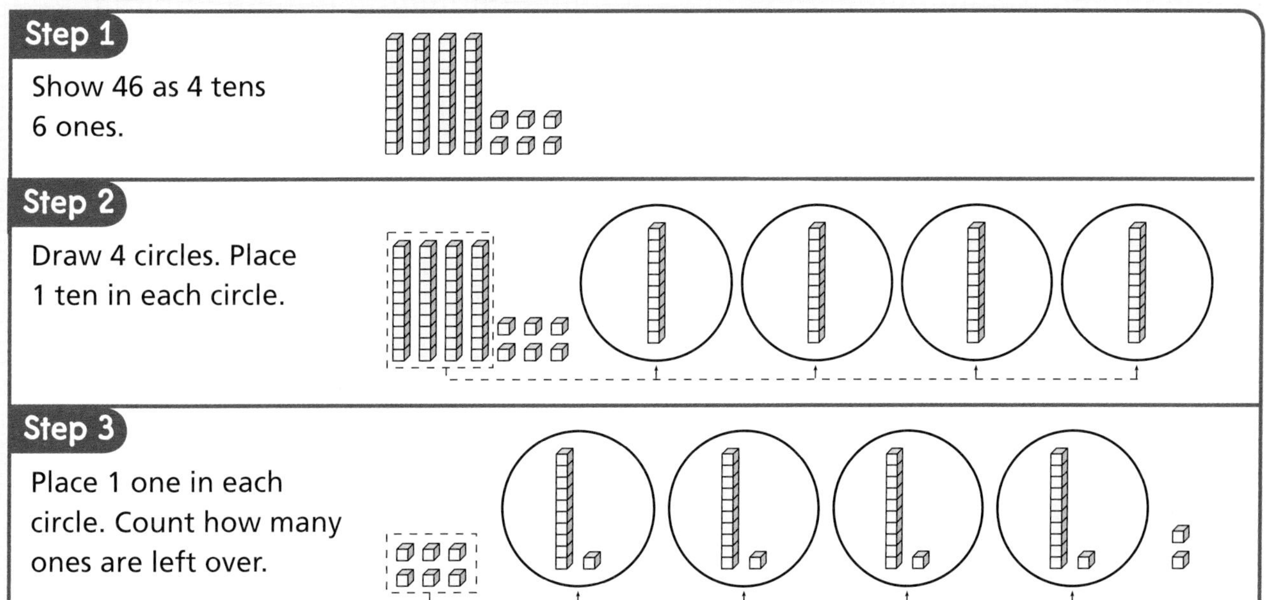

Step 1
Show 46 as 4 tens 6 ones.
Step 2
Draw 4 circles. Place 1 ten in each circle.
Step 3
Place 1 one in each circle. Count how many ones are left over.

So, each robot needs 11 parts. There will be 2 parts left over.

TALK Math

Explain the steps to model $48 \div 3$ using base-ten blocks.

Practice

Use base-ten blocks to find the quotient and remainder.

1. $2\overline{)84}$ **2.** $96 \div 6$ **3.** $99 \div 8$ **4.** $5\overline{)67}$ **5.** $84 \div 3$

6. $2\overline{)52}$ **7.** $26 \div 4$ **8.** $5\overline{)81}$ **9.** $44 \div 3$ ✓**10.** $7\overline{)84}$

Divide. You may wish to use base-ten blocks.

11. $52 \div 4$ **12.** $5\overline{)48}$ **13.** $87 \div 7$ **14.** $6\overline{)77}$ ✓**15.** $97 \div 6$

16. $3\overline{)22}$ **17.** $3\overline{)72}$ **18.** $40 \div 6$ **19.** $23 \div 9$ **20.** $5\overline{)88}$

21. **WRITE Math** **Explain** how to model the quotient for $73 \div 5$.

LESSON 3

Record 2-Digit by 1-Digit Division

OBJECTIVE: Divide 2-digit numbers by 1-digit numbers.

Quick Review

Write a division sentence that describes the model.

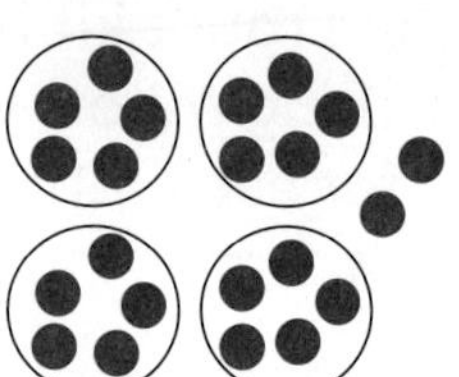

Learn

PROBLEM Raul, Jeremy, and Manuel have collected 53 baseball cards. They want to divide them equally. How many cards will each of the 3 boys get? How many cards will be left over?

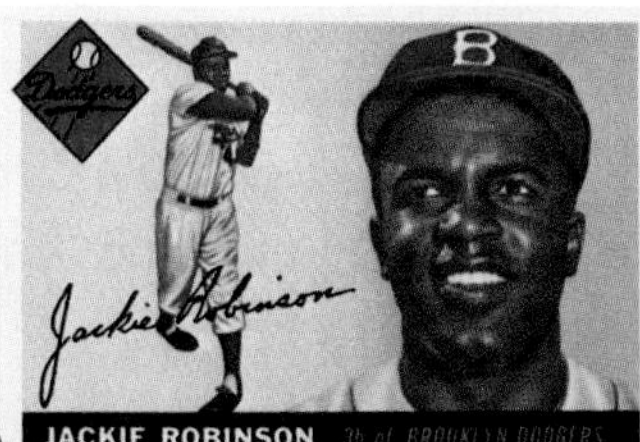

▲ In 1947 Jackie Robinson became the first African American to play on a major league baseball team.

ONE WAY **Use long division.**

Divide 53 by 3. Write 53 ÷ 3 or $3\overline{)53}$.

MODEL | **THINK** | **RECORD**

Step 1

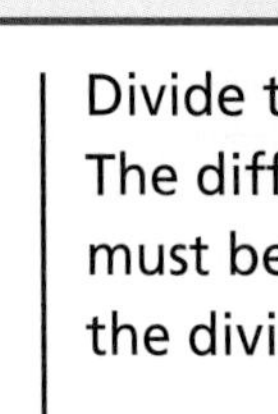

Divide the 5 tens. The difference, 2, must be less than the divisor.

$$\begin{array}{r} 1 \\ 3\overline{)53} \\ -3 \\ \hline 2 \end{array}$$

Divide. 5 ÷ 3
Multiply. 3 × 1
Subtract. 5 − 3
Compare. 2 < 3

Step 2

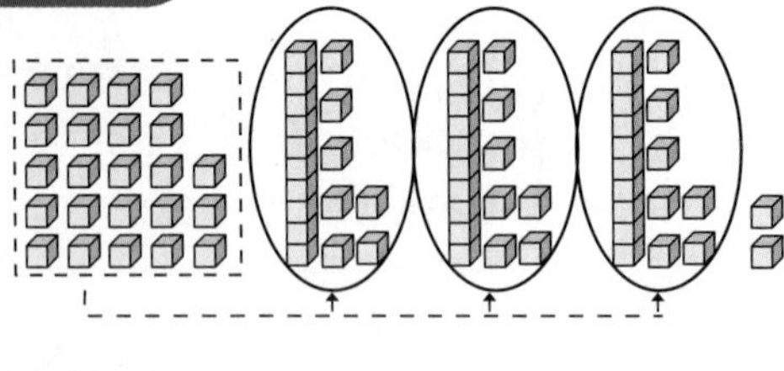

Bring down the 3 ones. Regroup 2 tens 3 ones as 23 ones. Then divide the 23 ones. Write the remainder next to the quotient.

$$\begin{array}{r} 17 \text{ r2} \\ 3\overline{)53} \\ -3\downarrow \\ \hline 23 \\ -21 \\ \hline 2 \end{array}$$

Divide. 23 ÷ 3
Multiply. 3 × 7
Subtract. 23 − 21
Compare. 2 < 3

Step 3

To check, multiply the quotient by the divisor. Then add the remainder.

$$\begin{array}{rl} 17 & \text{quotient} \\ \times\ 3 & \text{divisor} \\ \hline 51 & \\ +\ 2 & \text{remainder} \\ \hline 53 & \text{dividend} \end{array}$$

So, each boy gets 17 cards with 2 left over.

- **What if** the remainder is equal to or greater than the divisor? What should you do?
- What conclusion can you make if you compare the quotient to the dividend when you divide whole numbers?

Math Idea
The order of division is as follows:
Divide
Multiply
Subtract
Compare
Repeat this order until the division is complete.

TEKS 4.4E use division to solve problems (no more than one-digit divisors and three-digit dividends without technology). *also* **4.1A, 4.3A, 4.4B, 4.4C, 4.14A, 4.14D, 4.15A, 4.15B**

ANOTHER WAY **Use partial quotients.**

You can use partial quotients to divide.

Divide 53 by 3. Write $3\overline{)53}$.

Step 1

Make a list of multiples of 3.

$3 \times 2 = 6$
$3 \times 5 = 15$
$3 \times 10 = 30$
$3 \times 15 = 45$

Step 2

45 is close to 53, so use 15 as the first partial quotient. Subtract 53 − 45.

```
 3)53 |
 − 45 | 15 ← Record partial quotients in a column.
    8 |
```

Step 3

Repeat until the remainder is less than the divisor.

```
 3)53 |
 − 45 | 15
    8 |
  − 6 |  2 ← partial quotient
    2 |
```

Step 4

Add the partial quotients.

```
              3)53 |
              − 45 |  15
                 8 |
               − 6 | + 2
remainder →      2 |  17 ← quotient
```

So, 53 ÷ 3 = 17 r2.

- How can you use partial quotients to find 87 ÷ 5?

More Examples

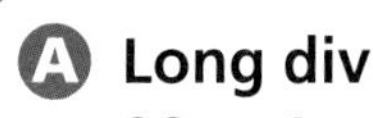

A Long division.

99 ÷ 4

```
  24 r3
 4)99
 − 8↓
   19
 − 16
    3
```

99 ÷ 4 = 24 r3

B Partial quotients.

65 ÷ 4

Try 4 × 10 = 40.

```
 4)65 |
 − 40 | ←  10  (4 × 10)
   25 |
 − 24 | ← + 6  (4 × 6)
    1 |    16
```

65 ÷ 4 = 16 r1

Guided Practice

1. What is 49 ÷ 3? Make a model to solve, and then record.

Choose a method. Then divide and record.

2. $4\overline{)59}$　3. $2\overline{)68}$　4. $3\overline{)76}$　✓ 5. $5\overline{)85}$　✓ 6. $8\overline{)93}$

7. **TALK Math** **Explain** how the long division and partial quotients methods are alike and how they are different.

Independent Practice and Problem Solving

Choose a method. Then divide and record.

8. $2\overline{)33}$　9. $7\overline{)91}$　10. $4\overline{)55}$　11. $9\overline{)94}$　12. $6\overline{)78}$

13. $93 \div 6$　14. $64 \div 4$　15. $77 \div 3$　16. $82 \div 8$　17. $90 \div 6$

18. $7\overline{)86}$　19. $59 \div 4$　20. $5\overline{)80}$　21. $96 \div 3$　22. $6\overline{)50}$

Algebra Copy and complete each table.

23.

Number of Feet	3	39	45	63	75
Number of Yards	1	13	■	■	■

24.

Number of Days	7	77	84	91	98
Number of Weeks	1	11	■	■	■

25. Fifty-six students signed up for baseball. The coach divided them into 4 equal teams. How many students are on each team?

26. Mr. Ro gave 81 golf tees to 7 golfers. Each golfer gets the same number of tees. How many did each get? How many are left over?

27. ***FAST FACT*** The highest scoring NFL game was November 27, 1966. The winning team scored 72 points! If touchdowns are worth 6 points, how many touchdowns could they have scored?

28. **WRITE Math** Write a set of directions to **explain** how to solve $47 \div 4$ using long division.

Mixed Review and TAKS Prep

29. If you make a bar graph of the number of days in each month of the year, which bars will be of equal height? (Grade 3 TEKS 3.13A)

30. Kara cut 35 cakes into 16 slices each and she cut 7 cakes into 10 slices each. How many slices did she cut in all? (TEKS 4.4D, p. 236)

31. **TAKS Prep** Jared and his two brothers divided a package of 75 building blocks equally. How many blocks did each receive? (Obj. 1)

A 23

B 25

C 72

D 78

 Extra Practice on page 354, Set A

Soccer Games

Draw Conclusions

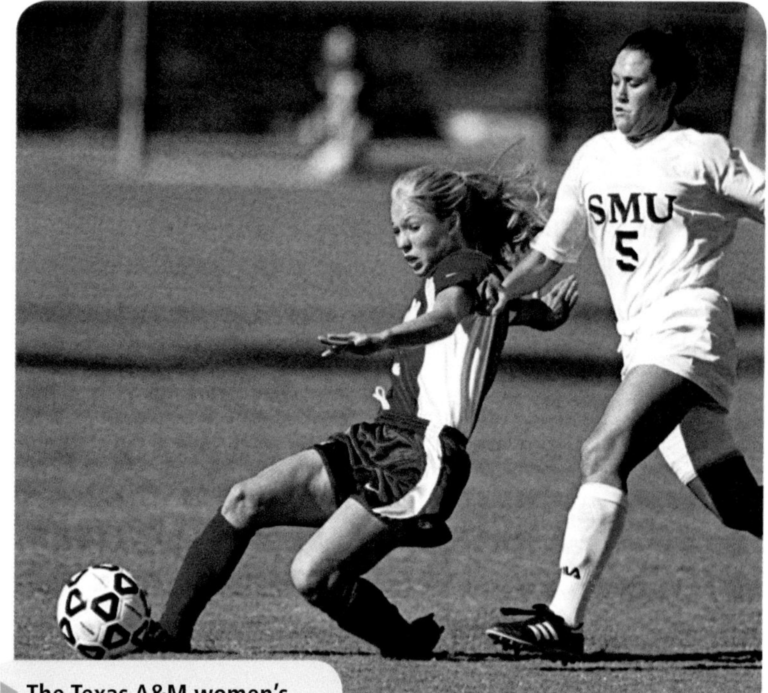

The Texas A&M women's soccer team won its second round game in the 2005 NCAA Soccer Tournament.

There are 64 teams playing in the Women's NCAA Division I Soccer Tournament. The teams that win each round advance to the next round. The rounds are: first round, second round, third round, quarterfinals, semifinals, and championship. How many games will be played in the tournament?

You can draw conclusions from the data in a problem to help you solve it.

What I know: Two teams play against each other in each game. For each game in each round, there can be only one winner.

Conclusion: So, dividing the total number of teams by 2 will give you the number of games in each round. Repeat until only one game remains.

Draw a diagram or make an organized list to keep track of the number of games played in each round. Add the total number of games in each round to find how many games are played in the Women's NCAA Division I Soccer Tournament.

Problem Solving Draw conclusions to solve the problem.

1. Solve the problem above.
2. If there were 32 teams playing in the tournament, how many games would be played in round 2?
3. **Explain** what conclusion you can draw about how many games the winning team will play to win the tournament.

Problem Solving Workshop
Strategy: Compare Strategies

OBJECTIVE: Compare different strategies to solve problems.

Read to Understand
Plan
Solve
Check

Use the Strategy

PROBLEM Evan's dog weighs 3 times as much as Oxana's dog. Together the dogs weigh 64 pounds. How much does Evan's dog weigh?

Read to Understand

- **Summarize what you are asked to find.**
- **What information is given?**

Plan

- **What strategy can you use to solve the problem?**
  You can draw a diagram or you can guess and check.

Solve

- **How can you use each strategy to solve the problem?**

Draw a Diagram

Draw a diagram that represents the relationship between the weights of the two dogs.

Evan's	■ lb	■ lb	■ lb	Total weight is 64 pounds.
Oxana's	■ lb			

Divide 64 by 4 to find the value of each equal part. $64 \div 4 = 16$

Each part is 16 pounds.

Add three parts to find the weight of Evan's dog. $16 + 16 + 16 = 48$

So, Evan's dog weighs 48 pounds.

Guess and Check

Predict and test to find the weight of each dog.

Oxana's dog weighs ■. Evan's dog weighs 3 × ■. So, ■ + (3 × ■) = 64.

Predict		Test	Does It Check?
Oxana's dog: ■	**Evan's dog: 3 × ■**	**Total Weight ■ + (3 × ■) = 64**	**Compare to 64**
13	39	$13 + (3 \times 13) = 52$	$52 < 64$ no
14	42	$14 + (3 \times 14) = 56$	$56 < 64$ no
15	45	$15 + (3 \times 15) = 60$	$60 < 64$ no
16	48	$16 + (3 \times 16) = 64$	$64 = 64$ yes ✔
17	51	$17 + (3 \times 17) = 68$	$68 > 64$ no

■ = 16 pounds. Multiply 3 by 16 to find the weight of Evan's dog.

$3 \times 16 = 48$

Check

- **Which strategy was more helpful? Explain.**

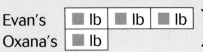

TEKS 4.14C Select or develop an appropriate problem-solving plan or strategy, including drawing a picture, looking for a pattern, systematic guessing and checking, acting it out, making a table, working a simpler problem, or working backwards to solve a problem. *also* **4.1A, 4.4D, 4.4E, 4.7, 4.14A, 4.14B, 4.14C, 4.15A, 4.15B, 4.16B**

Guided Problem Solving

1. Mia's dog weighs 4 times as much as her rabbit. Together the pets weigh 90 pounds. How much does Mia's dog weigh?

   First, decide whether to draw a diagram or work backward to find the dog's weight.

   Draw a Diagram

?	■ lb	■ lb	■ lb	■ lb	Total weight is 90 pounds.
?	■ lb				

   Find the value of each part. Add to find the dog's weight.

   Guess and Check

   ■ = weight of rabbit
   $(4 \times ■)$ = weight of dog
   $■ + (4 \times ■) = 90$

   Guess and check to find the value of ■. Then multiply 4 × ■ to find the weight of Mia's dog.

2. **What if** Mia's dog weighs 5 times as much as the rabbit. Together the pets weigh 60 pounds. How much does the dog weigh?

3. Ari runs a training school for pet actors. Last year he trained 3 times as many dogs as cats. If the total number of dogs and cats he trained last year is 84, how many cats did he train?

Mixed Strategy Practice

4. The Grant family paid $220 to attend a dog show for two days. Adult tickets were 3 times the cost of children's tickets. The Grants bought 3 adult tickets and 2 children's tickets. How much did they pay for each ticket?

USE DATA For 5–6, use the pictures.

5. Petra walked four of the dogs in the picture. The second dog is half as tall as the first. The third dog is 9 inches taller than the second. The last dog is 8 inches taller than the third. The last dog is the Irish setter. Which dog did Petra walk first?

6. WRITE Math A teacup poodle is 6 inches tall. **Explain** how to find how many teacup poodles you would have to stand on top of each other to reach the height of the Labrador retriever.

Choose a STRATEGY

- Draw a Diagram or Picture
- Make a Model or Act It Out
- Make an Organized List
- Look For a Pattern
- Make a Table or Graph
- Guess and Check
- Work Backward
- Solve a Simpler Problem
- Write an Equation
- Use Logical Reasoning

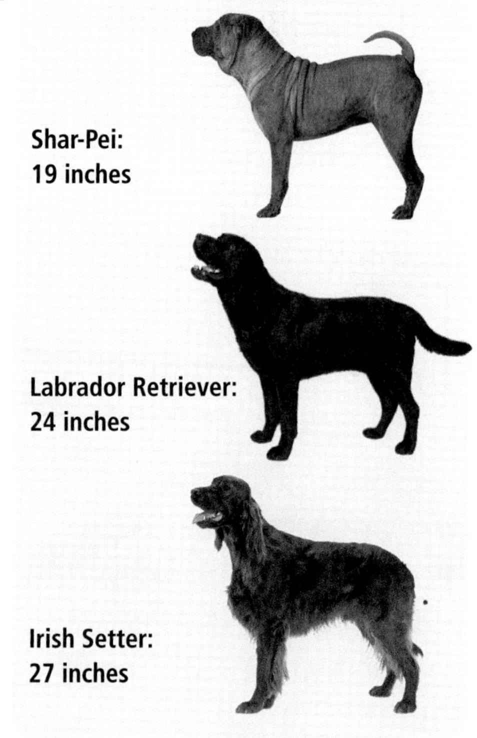

LESSON 5

MENTAL MATH
Division Patterns

OBJECTIVE: Use a basic fact and a pattern to divide mentally.

Quick Review

Jay ran a total of 40 miles in January. Each time that he ran, he ran 5 miles. How many times did Jay run?

Learn

If you know basic facts, you can use them to divide multiples of 10, 100, or 1,000 mentally.

PROBLEM Trams take people to the top of the Gateway Arch in St. Louis, Missouri. If a tram makes 6 trips, it can carry a total of 240 people. How many people fit in a tram?

▲ On a clear day, you can see 30 miles in any direction from the top of the arch.

Example Use a basic fact and a pattern.

Divide. 240 ÷ 6

Think: 24 divided by 6 is 4.

24 ÷ 6 = 4 ← basic fact

240 ÷ 6 = 40

2,400 ÷ 6 = 400

So, 40 people will fit in a tram.

Math Idea

As the number of zeros in the dividend increases, so does the number of zeros in the quotient.

More Examples

A Basic fact and a pattern

72 ÷ 9 = 8 ← basic fact
720 ÷ 9 = 80
7,200 ÷ 9 = 800
72,000 ÷ 9 = 8,000

B Basic fact with a zero and a pattern

30 ÷ 6 = 5 ← basic fact
300 ÷ 6 = 50
3,000 ÷ 6 = 500
30,000 ÷ 6 = 5,000

C Basic fact with a zero and a pattern

40 ÷ 10 = 4 ← basic fact
400 ÷ 10 = 40
4,000 ÷ 10 = 400
40,000 ÷ 10 = 4,000

Guided Practice

1. What basic division fact can you use to find 90 ÷ 3 and 9,000 ÷ 3? Find 90 ÷ 3 and 9,000 ÷ 3.

TEKS 4.4E use division to solve problems (no more than one-digit divisors and three-digit dividends without technology). *also* **4.4B, 4.4C, 4.6A, 4.14A, 4.15A, 4.15B, 4.16A**

Use mental math to complete the pattern.

2. $32 \div 8 = 4$
   $320 \div 8 = \blacksquare$
   $3{,}200 \div 8 = \blacksquare$

3. $28 \div 4 = \blacksquare$
   $280 \div 4 = \blacksquare$
   $2{,}800 \div 4 = \blacksquare$

4. $90 \div 9 = \blacksquare$
   $900 \div 9 = \blacksquare$
   $9{,}000 \div 9 = \blacksquare$

5. $64 \div 8 = \blacksquare$
   $640 \div 8 = \blacksquare$
   $6{,}400 \div 8 = \blacksquare$

6. **TALK Math** **Explain** how to use division facts you know to solve division problems with zeros at the end of the dividend.

Independent Practice and Problem Solving

Use mental math to complete the pattern.

7. $27 \div 9 = 3$
   $270 \div 9 = \blacksquare$
   $2{,}700 \div 9 = \blacksquare$
   $27{,}000 \div 9 = \blacksquare$

8. $20 \div 5 = \blacksquare$
   $200 \div 5 = \blacksquare$
   $2{,}000 \div 5 = \blacksquare$
   $20{,}000 \div 5 = \blacksquare$

9. $42 \div 7 = \blacksquare$
   $\blacksquare \div 7 = 60$
   $4{,}200 \div 7 = \blacksquare$
   $\blacksquare \div 7 = 6{,}000$

10. $\blacksquare \div 3 = 2$
    $60 \div 3 = \blacksquare$
    $\blacksquare \div 3 = 200$
    $6{,}000 \div 3 = \blacksquare$

Use mental math and patterns to find the quotient.

11. $120 \div 2$
12. $8{,}100 \div 9$
13. $400 \div 8$
14. $27{,}000 \div 3$

Algebra **Find the value of *n*.**

15. $360 \div 6 = n$
16. $6{,}300 \div n = 700$
17. $24{,}000 \div n = 3{,}000$
18. $n \div 7 = 1{,}000$

USE DATA **For 19–20, use the sign.**

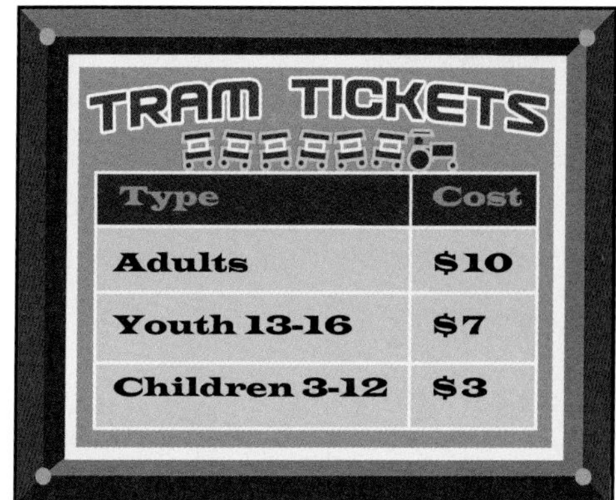

TRAM TICKETS
Type
Cost
Adults
$10
Youth 13-16
$7
Children 3-12
$3

19. A camp paid $5,600 for a group of 15-year-olds to ride the tram. How many tickets did the camp buy?

20. Fae paid $280 for youth tickets and $90 for children's tickets. How many of each kind of ticket did she buy?

21. **WRITE Math** **Explain** why there is one more zero in the dividend than in the quotient when you find $40{,}000 \div 5$.

Mixed Review and TAKS Prep

22. A theme park had 999 visitors on Saturday and 222 visitors on Sunday. How many visitors were there on both days? (TEKS 4.3A, p. 50)

23. A ball bounces half the height from which it is dropped. If the ball bounces 12 feet, from what height was it dropped? (TEKS 4.4B, p. 96)

24. **TAKS Prep** The zoo sold 210 train tickets. The train made 7 trips. If the train was full each trip, how many people rode on the train each trip? (Obj. 1)

    A 3
    B 7
    C 30
    D 70

Extra Practice on page 354, Set B

LESSON 6

MENTAL MATH

Estimate Quotients

OBJECTIVE: Estimate quotients by using rounding and compatible numbers, and then find the estimated quotient mentally.

Quick Review

1. 21,000 ÷ 3
2. 2,100 ÷ 3
3. 210 ÷ 3
4. 21 ÷ 3
5. 21,000 ÷ 7

Learn

PROBLEM A hummingbird beats its wings 6,240 times in 2 minutes. About how many times does it beat its wings in 1 minute?

Estimate. 6,240 ÷ 2

▲ **Hummingbirds visit more than 1,000 flowers a day!**

ONE WAY **Use rounding.**

Step 1	Step 2
Round the dividend to the nearest thousand. 6,240 ÷ 2 ↓ 6,000 ÷ 2	Use mental math. 6 ÷ 2 = 3 ⟵ basic fact 60 ÷ 2 = 30 600 ÷ 2 = 300 6,000 ÷ 2 = 3,000

So, a hummingbird beats its wings about 3,000 times in 1 minute.

ANOTHER WAY **Use compatible numbers.**

Step 1	Step 2
Find compatible numbers for 6,240 that can be divided evenly by 2. **Think:** 6 ÷ 2 = 3 and 8 ÷ 2 = 4 You can use 6,000 or 8,000 for 6,240.	Use mental math. 6,000 ÷ 2 = 3,000 8,000 ÷ 2 = 4,000

So, a hummingbird beats its wings between 3,000 and 4,000 times in 1 minute.

More Examples **Estimate the quotients.**

A Round to the nearest hundred.

5,363 ÷ 9

5,400 ÷ 9 = 600

B Use compatible numbers. 558 ÷ 6

Think: 54 ÷ 6 = 9 and 60 ÷ 6 = 10

You can use 540 or 600 for 558.

540 ÷ 6 = 90 and 600 ÷ 6 = 100

So, both 90 and 100 are reasonable estimates.

TEKS 4.5B use strategies including rounding and compatible number to estimate solutions to multiplication and division problems. *also* **4.1A, 4.4E, 4.5A, 4.14A, 4.15A, 4.15B, 4.16B**

Guided Practice

1. Round the dividend to the nearest 100. Use mental math to estimate the quotient. $263 \div 3$

Estimate the quotient.

2. $362 \div 4$
3. $798 \div 2$
4. $499 \div 7$
5. $147 \div 3$
6. $4,522 \div 9$
7. TALK Math **Explain** how you know whether your estimate is greater than or less than the exact quotient.

Independent Practice and Problem Solving

Estimate the quotient.

8. $498 \div 5$
9. $740 \div 7$
10. $5,402 \div 6$
11. $823 \div 9$
12. $3,337 \div 3$

Estimate to compare. Write <, >, or = for each ●.

13. $613 \div 3$ ● $581 \div 2$
14. $364 \div 4$ ● $117 \div 6$
15. $2,718 \div 8$ ● $963 \div 2$

USE DATA For 16–19, use the table.

16. About how many times do a damselfly's wings beat in 1 minute?
17. About how many times do a scorpion fly's wings beat in 2 minutes?
18. About how many more times do an Aeschnid dragonfly's wings beat in 1 minute than a large white butterfly's wings?
19. WRITE Math **What's the Question?** The answer is about 700 beats in 1 minute.

Insect Wing Beats in 3 Minutes

Insect	Number of Wing Beats
Aeschnid Dragonfly	6,840
Damselfly	2,880
Large White Butterfly	2,160
Scorpion Fly	5,040

Mixed Review and TAKS Prep

20. A teacher gave an equal number of pencils to 7 students. Write an expression to represent the situation. (TEKS 4.15B, p. 156)
21. In March, 18 schools signed up to do a bird count. Each school has 26 students counting birds. How many students are counting birds? (TEKS 4.4D, p. 236)
22. **TAKS Prep** A hummingbird's heart beats 3,782 times in 3 minutes. Which is the best estimate of the number of times its heart beats in 1 minute? (Obj. 1)

    A 600
    B 1,000
    C 2,000
    D 3,000

Extra Practice on page 354, Set C

LESSON 7 Place the First Digit

OBJECTIVE: Place the first digit in a quotient by estimating or using place value.

Quick Review

Yen put 791 caps in 9 boxes. He put about the same number in each box. About how many caps were in each box?

Learn

PROBLEM Tamiqua has a bunch of 8 black-eyed susans. In all, she counts 168 petals on her flowers. If all the flowers have the same number of petals, how many petals are on one flower?

ONE WAY **Use compatible numbers.** Divide 168 by 8.

Step 1

Use compatible numbers to estimate to place the first digit.

Think: $8\overline{)160}$ → 20 or $8\overline{)240}$ → 30

$8\overline{)168}$ So, the first digit is in the tens place.

Step 2

Divide the 16 tens.

```
   2
8)168
 -16
   0
```

Divide. $8\overline{)16}$
Multiply. 8×2
Subtract. $16 - 16$
Compare $0 < 8$

Step 3

Bring down the 8 ones. Divide the 8 ones.

```
   21
8)168
 -16↓
    8
   -8
    0
```

Divide. $8\overline{)8}$
Multiply. 8×1
Subtract. $8 - 8$
Compare. $0 < 8$

So, there are 21 petals on one flower.

ANOTHER WAY **Use place value.** Divide 423 by 5.

Step 1

Use place value to place the first digit. Look at the hundreds.

$5\overline{)423}$ $4 < 5$, so look at the tens.

$5\overline{)423}$ $42 > 5$, so use 42 tens. Place the first digit in the tens place.

Step 2

Divide 42 tens.

```
   8
5)423
 -40
   2
```

Divide. $5\overline{)42}$
Multiply. 5×8
Subtract. $42 - 40$
Compare. $2 < 5$

Step 3

Bring down 3 ones. Divide the 23 ones.

```
   84 r3
5)423
 -40↓
   23
  -20
    3
```

Divide. $5\overline{)23}$
Multiply. 5×4
Subtract. $23 - 20$
Compare. $3 < 8$

So, $423 \div 5 = 84$ r3.

ERROR ALERT

If you cannot divide the divisor into the first digit of the dividend, the quotient begins at the next place value to the right.

Guided Practice

1. Use place value to place the first digit. Where should you place the first digit? Divide. $4\overline{)459}$

TEKS 4.5B Use strategies including rounding and compatible numbers to estimate solutions to multiplication and division problems. *also* **4.1A, 4.4C, 4.4E, 4.14A, 4.15A, 4.15B, 4.16A, 4.16B**

Tell where to place the first digit. Then divide.

2. $7\overline{)228}$ **3.** $926 \div 4$ **4.** $777 \div 3$ ✓**5.** $6\overline{)126}$ ✓**6.** $889 \div 8$

7. TALK Math **Explain** why the first digit in the quotient $233 \div 3$ is in the tens place.

Independent Practice and Problem Solving

Tell where to place the first digit. Then divide.

8. $2\overline{)145}$ **9.** $455 \div 5$ **10.** $6\overline{)779}$ **11.** $132 \div 7$ **12.** $3\overline{)945}$

Divide.

13. $923 \div 8$ **14.** $2\overline{)184}$ **15.** $329 \div 5$ **16.** $4\overline{)696}$ **17.** $992 \div 6$

Algebra Find the missing digit.

18. $426 \div 6 = 7\blacksquare$ **19.** $647 \div 7 = 9\blacksquare$ r3 **20.** $667 \div 3 = \blacksquare22$ r1

USE DATA For 21, use the garden plan.

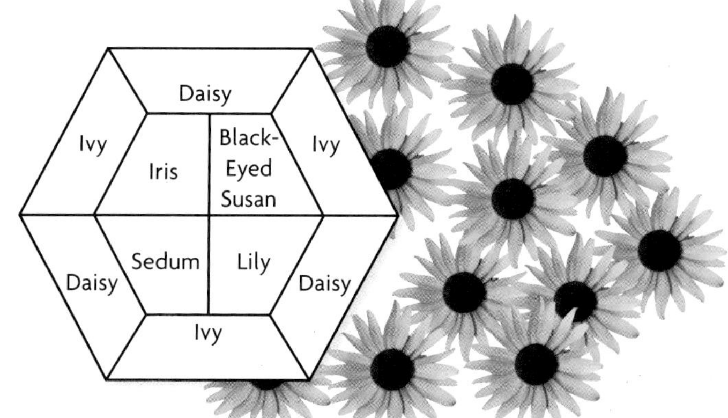

21. If Ty has 125 daisy plants, how many plants will be left if he plants an equal number in each daisy section?

22. Lillie has a total of 56 flowers. She has 14 irises. The rest are ivy and sedum. She has twice as many ivy as sedums. How many sedum plants does she have?

23. **Reasoning** If the dividend is 3 digits and you place the first digit in the tens place, what does that tell you about the divisor?

24. WRITE Math **Explain** how you can determine the number of digits in the quotient $726 \div 9$ without dividing.

Mixed Review and TAKS Prep

25. How many days are in 5 weeks? (TEKS 4.4C, p. 98)

26. A shop has 652 coins in 7 cases. Each case has about the same number of coins. To the nearest hundred, about how many coins are in each case? (TEKS 4.5B, p. 350)

27. **TAKS Prep** In which place is the first digit in the quotient $497 \div 2$? (Obj. 1)

A Thousands

B Hundreds

C Tens

D Ones

Extra Practice on page 354, Set D

Extra Practice

Set A Choose a method. Then divide and record. (pp. 342–345)

1. $88 \div 7$
2. $8\overline{)98}$
3. $65 \div 4$
4. $5\overline{)67}$
5. $79 \div 6$
6. $4\overline{)63}$
7. $57 \div 2$
8. $6\overline{)95}$
9. $76 \div 3$
10. $84 \div 5$
11. $46 \div 6$
12. $8\overline{)49}$
13. $78 \div 7$
14. $68 \div 3$
15. $6\overline{)99}$
16. Mr. Patel has 94 textbooks. He wants to divide them evenly on 7 shelves. How many books will he have left over?

Set B Use mental math and patterns to find the quotient. (pp. 348–349)

1. $150 \div 3$
2. $4{,}500 \div 5$
3. $64{,}000 \div 8$
4. $4{,}900 \div 7$
5. $3{,}600 \div 4$
6. $2{,}400 \div 3$
7. $36{,}000 \div 9$
8. $630 \div 7$
9. $2{,}800 \div 4$
10. $5{,}600 \div 7$
11. $7{,}200 \div 9$
12. $4{,}800 \div 6$
13. $2{,}100 \div 3$
14. $480 \div 8$
15. $3{,}500 \div 5$
16. Alan pays $320 for admission tickets to a theme park. If he buys 8 tickets, how much does he pay per ticket?

Set C Estimate the quotient. (pp. 350–351)

1. $299 \div 3$
2. $680 \div 5$
3. $5{,}402 \div 6$
4. $6{,}462 \div 8$
5. $4{,}211 \div 6$
6. $301 \div 5$
7. $549 \div 6$
8. $624 \div 7$
9. $333 \div 8$
10. $791 \div 8$
11. $635 \div 7$
12. $823 \div 5$
13. $325 \div 6$
14. $683 \div 4$
15. $303 \div 3$
16. Johanna collected 2,428 bottle caps, she divided them into 3 equal groups. About how many bottle caps were in each group?

Set D Tell where to place the first digit. Then divide. (pp. 352–353)

1. $3\overline{)358}$
2. $909 \div 6$
3. $325 \div 4$
4. $7\overline{)653}$
5. $525 \div 4$
6. $8\overline{)971}$
7. $457 \div 3$
8. $621 \div 7$
9. $5\overline{)491}$
10. $918 \div 7$
11. $537 \div 8$
12. $647 \div 5$
13. $7\overline{)481}$
14. $529 \div 6$
15. $5\overline{)396}$
16. Doria has 453 baseball cards. If she sorts them into 8 equal piles, how many cards will be left over?
17. Ivan is putting 387 pictures in a photo album. He plans to put 6 pictures on each page. How many pages will he fill?

CD ROM Technology
Use Harcourt Mega Math, The Number Games, *Up, Up, and Array,* Level L, M.

PRACTICE GAME

Divide All Five

Players

2 players

Materials

- 2-color counters
- Number cube labeled 1 to 6

35	27	64	81	90
76	50	28	41	52
49	43	39	56	4
18	82	70	60	12
65	32	26	24	80

How to Play

- The object is to cover 5 numbers in a row—across, down, or diagonally.
- Decide who will use yellow counters and who will use red counters.
- Players take turns. Toss the number cube. The player places his or her counter on the game board over any number that is divided evenly by the number tossed.
- If 1 is tossed, place a counter on any number still showing. If a number is tossed that does not divide evenly into one of the numbers still showing, the player loses his or her turn.
- The first player to cover five numbers in a row wins.

Chapter 13 Review/Test

Check Vocabulary and Concepts

VOCABULARY
quotient
remainder

Choose the best term from the box.

1. When a number cannot be divided evenly, the amount left over is called the __?__. (TEKS 4.4E, p. 338)

For 2–5, use counters to find the quotient and remainder. (TEKS 4.4E, pp 338–339)

2. $37 \div 6$
3. $44 \div 8$
4. $23 \div 5$
5. $38 \div 4$

Check Skills

Choose a method. Then divide and record. (TEKS 4.4E, pp. 342–345)

6. $72 \div 3$
7. $71 \div 5$
8. $4\overline{)72}$
9. $8\overline{)98}$

Use mental math and patterns to find the quotient. (TEKS 4.4E, pp. 348–349)

10. $3\overline{)150}$
11. $5{,}400 \div 9$
12. $6\overline{)360}$
13. $56{,}000 \div 8$
14. $7\overline{)4{,}900}$
15. $480 \div 6$
16. $7{,}200 \div 8$
17. $1{,}600 \div 4$

Estimate the quotient. (TEKS 4.5B, pp. 350–351)

18. $4{,}601 \div 9$
19. $3{,}999 \div 8$
20. $4{,}061 \div 5$
21. $349 \div 7$

Tell where to place the first digit. Then divide. (TEKS 4.4E, pp. 352–353)

22. $165 \div 4$
23. $342 \div 5$
24. $6\overline{)276}$
25. $736 \div 3$
26. $7\overline{)652}$
27. $8\overline{)672}$
28. $833 \div 7$
29. $260 \div 3$
30. $5\overline{)371}$
31. $851 \div 4$

Check Problem Solving

Solve. (TEKS 4.14C, pp. 346–347)

32. Pauline has 64 stuffed animals. She wants to put them on 3 shelves. If she puts the same number on each shelf, how many stuffed animals will be left over?

33. **WRITE Math** Sari weighs 8 times as much as her little brother. They weigh 108 pounds together. **Explain** how you can draw a diagram to find how much Sari weighs.

GO ONLINE **Technology** Use *Online Assessment.*

Enrich • Short Division
Maple Trees

▲ One sugar maple tree produces about 20 gallons of sap in the spring, which makes 2 quarts of maple syrup.

The state tree of Wisconsin is the sugar maple. Sugar maple trees produce sap that is used for maple syrup.

A farmer sold 582 pints of maple syrup to 3 stores. Each store bought the same number of pints. How many pints of maple syrup did each store buy?

You can use short division to find the quotient. Short division uses mental math to solve problems. You write only the quotients and the remainders.

Divide. $582 \div 3$ **Estimate.** $600 \div 3 = 200$

Step 1	Step 2	Step 3
Divide the hundreds.	Divide the tens.	Divide the ones.
$\begin{array}{r} 1 \\ 3\overline{)5} \\ -3 \\ \hline 2 \end{array}$ **Think:** 5 divided by 3 ones is 1 hundred with a remainder of 2 tens.	$\begin{array}{r} 9 \\ 3\overline{)28} \\ -27 \\ \hline 1 \end{array}$ **Think:** 28 tens divided by 3 ones is 9 tens with a remainder of 1 ten.	$\begin{array}{r} 4 \\ 3\overline{)12} \\ -12 \\ \hline 0 \end{array}$ **Think:** 12 tens divided by 3 ones is 4 tens.
Write 1 in the quotient. Write 2 in the tens place.	Write 9 in the quotient. Write 1 in the ones place.	Write 4 in the quotient.
$\begin{array}{r} 1 \\ 3\overline{)5^{2}82} \end{array}$	$\begin{array}{r} 19 \\ 3\overline{)5^{2}8^{1}2} \end{array}$	$\begin{array}{r} 194 \\ 3\overline{)5^{2}8^{1}2} \end{array}$

So, each store bought 194 pints of maple syrup. 194 is close to 200, so the answer is reasonable.

Golden Examples

A	B	C
$\begin{array}{r} 148 \\ 5\overline{)7^{2}4^{4}0} \end{array}$	$\begin{array}{r} 135 \\ 3\overline{)4^{1}0^{1}5} \end{array}$	$\begin{array}{r} 208 \\ 4\overline{)83^{3}2} \end{array}$

Sample It

Use short division to find the quotient.

1. $534 \div 2$ **2.** $784 \div 4$ **3.** $810 \div 6$ **4.** $816 \div 2$

5. $531 \div 3$ **6.** $903 \div 7$ **7.** $952 \div 4$ **8.** $746 \div 2$

Think About It

WRITE Math **Explain** how short division makes it easy to find $741 \div 3$.

Getting Ready for the TAKS
Chapters 1–13

Measurement TAKS Obj. 4

1. Oscar reads the temperature on the thermometer. It reads 58°F. Where could that thermometer be located?

   A In the backyard where Oscar is playing in the snow

   B Inside the oven where Oscar is baking muffins

   C In the backyard where Oscar is raking leaves

   D Inside the refrigerator

2. Mrs. Hitchcock was in the hardware store from 4:30 to 5:30. Which clock shows the time she left the store?

   F 

   H 

   G 

   J 

3. **WRITE Math** John wants to put a fence around his garden. **Explain** how he can find the number of feet of fencing to buy.

Garden	4 feet
9 feet	

Number, Operation, and Quantitative Reasoning TAKS Obj. 1

4. In 2005, the population of Dallas County, Texas was two million, three hundred five thousand, four hundred sixty-four. Which of the following is another way to write this number?

   A 23,005,464 **C** 2,350,464

   B 2,035,464 **D** 2,305,464

Test Tip **Check your work.**

See Item 5. If your answer does not match any of the choices, check your computation.

5. Jenny has 96 books. She wants to put them on 4 shelves. If she puts the same number of books on each shelf, how many books will be on each shelf?

   F 24 **H** 100

   G 92 **J** 384

6. Pedro bought 11 packages of pencils. Each package has 12 pencils in it. How many pencils did Pedro buy?

   A 132 **C** 111

   B 122 **D** 23

7. **WRITE Math** Cyril has 75 pictures for his album. If he can fit 8 on each page, how many pages will he need? **Explain** your answer.

Geometry and Spatial Reasoning

TAKS Obj. 3

8. Which angle appears to be acute?

F 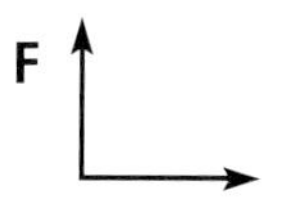

G 

H 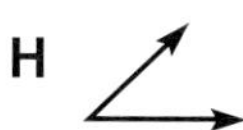

J 

9. Look at this picture.

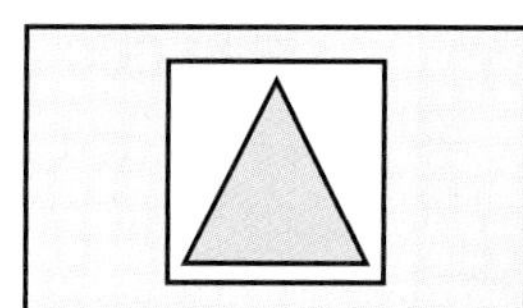

Which 2 figures appear to be congruent to the figures inside this rectangle?

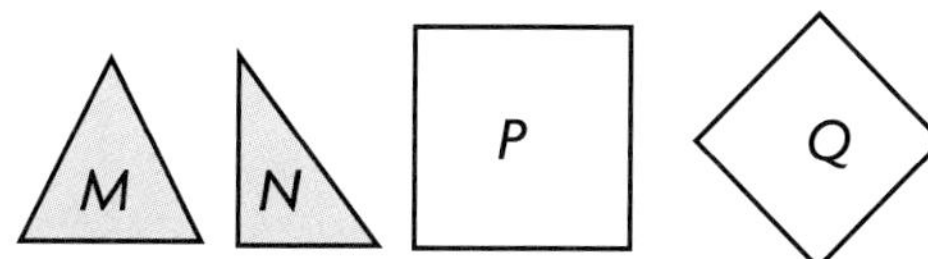

A *M* and *P*

B *N* and *P*

C *M* and *Q*

D *N* and *Q*

10. **WRITE Math** **Explain** the difference between perpendicular lines and parallel lines, and draw an example of each.

Patterns, Relationships, and Algebraic Thinking

TAKS Obj. 2

11. Which pair of numbers completes the equation?

$$■ \times 100 = ▲$$

F 12 and 120

G 8 and 800

H 5 and 50

J Not here

12. Saied used the strategy of doubles to help him remember some multiplication facts. Which fact could help him remember the product 8×9?

A 8×18

B 4×9

C 16×9

D 16×18

13. Mr. Rodriguez bought 25 boxes of tissues. Each box contains 100 tissues. How many tissues are there in all?

F 125

G 250

H 2,050

J 2,500

14. **WRITE Math** **Explain** how to find a rule for this pattern.

1, 3, 9, 27, 81

14 Practice Division

The Big Idea Fluency with basic division facts is based on using patterns and the inverse relationships to recall quotients.

TEXAS FAST FACT

One of the world's largest aquariums is at Moody Gardens in Galveston. It holds 1,500,000 gallons of water. It contains sea life from places around the world.

Investigate

An octopus can fill its body with water. Then it can move fast by shooting out the water like a jet. An octopus can also move by using its arms to walk very slowly. Pick a number of centimeters an octopus might walk. How can you find the time it would take each octopus in the graph to walk that distance?

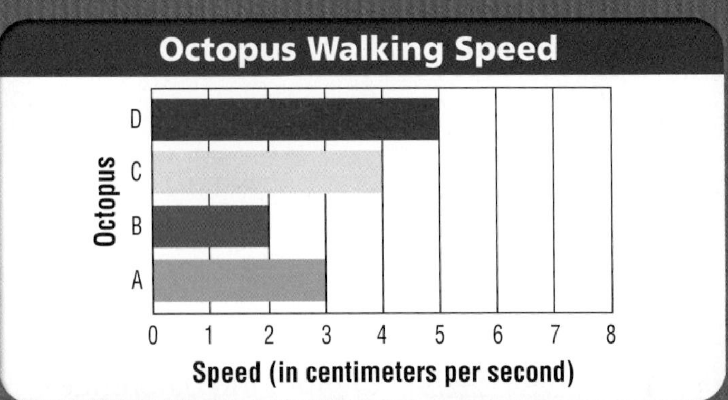

GO ONLINE
Technology
Student pages are available in the Student eBook.

Show What You Know

Check your understanding of important skills needed for success in Chapter 14.

▶ Estimate Quotients

Estimate the quotient.

1. 86 ÷ 3 **2.** 424 ÷ 7 **3.** 338 ÷ 8 **4.** 1,210 ÷ 4

5. 2,605 ÷ 5 **6.** 1,420 ÷ 2 **7.** 4,316 ÷ 2 **8.** 275 ÷ 6

▶ 2-Digit By 1-Digit Division

Use the model to find the quotient and remainder.

9. 25 ÷ 4 = ■

10.

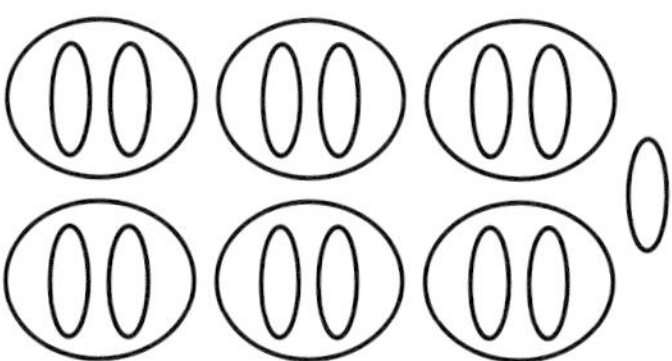

13 ÷ 6 = ■

11. 17 ÷ 5 = ■

12. 33 ÷ 6 = ■

▶ Place Value Through Thousands

Tell the value of the underlined digit.

13. 28,9$\underline{4}$3 **14.** 19,08$\underline{2}$ **15.** 96$\underline{1}$,354 **16.** 263,$\underline{8}$95

VOCABULARY POWER

CHAPTER VOCABULARY

average
dividend
divisor
quotient
remainder

WARM-UP WORDS

average a set of numbers found by dividing the sum of a set of numbers by the number of addends in a set

dividend the number that is to be divided in a division problem

divisor the number that divides the dividend

LESSON 1

Problem Solving Workshop
Skill: Interpret the Remainder

OBJECTIVE: Solve problems by using the skill *interpret the remainder.*

Read to Understand
Plan
Solve
Check

Use the Skill

PROBLEM There are 95 people with reservations for a guided raft trip on the Nenana River in Denali National Park in Alaska. Each raft holds 6 people. How many rafts are needed for the 95 people? How many rafts will be full? How many people will be in a raft that is not full?

When a division problem has a remainder, you interpret the remainder based on the situation and the question.

Divide. $95 \div 6$

$$\begin{array}{r} 15 \text{ r5} \\ 6\overline{)95} \\ -\ 6 \\ \hline 35 \\ -\ 30 \\ \hline 5 \end{array}$$

A Increase quotient by 1.

How many rafts are needed?
Think: Since 15 rafts only hold 90 people, one more raft is needed. So, drop the remainder, and increase the quotient by 1.
So, 16 rafts are needed.

B Quotient stays the same. Drop the remainder.

How many rafts will be full?
Think: A raft holds 6 people. Drop the remainder because 5 people do not fill a raft.

So, 15 rafts will be full.

C Use the remainder as the answer.

How many people will be in a raft that is not full?
Think: The remainder is the answer.

So, 5 people will be in a raft that is not full.

Think and Discuss

Solve the problem. Explain how you interpreted the remainder.

Another river guide company has rafts that hold 8 people. On Saturday, 99 people will take river trips.

a. How many rafts are needed to take them on river trips?

b. Will each raft be full? If not, how many people will be in the raft that is not full?

TEKS 4.4E Use division to solve problems (no more than one-digit divisors and three-digit dividends without technology). *also* **4.4C, 4.14A, 4.14B, 4.14C, 4.15A, 4.15B, 4.16B**

Guided Problem Solving

Read to Understand
Plan
Solve
Check

Solve. Write *a*, *b*, or *c*, to explain how to interpret the remainder.

a. Quotient stays the same. Drop the remainder.

b. Increase the quotient by 1.

c. Use the remainder as the answer.

1. A group of 57 people is camping in Denali National Park. Each tent holds 5 people. How many tents are needed for all of the campers?

First, divide.

Think: $57 \div 5$

Then, look back at the problem to see how to interpret the remainder.

2. **What if** you were asked how many tents will be full? How would your answer be different from your answer to Problem 1?

3. Guides lead groups of 7 people on biking tours in the park. There are 96 people who decided to go on the tours. How many people will be on a tour that is not full? Interpret the remainder.

Mixed Applications

USE DATA For 4–6, use the table. On float trips, the guides take 6 passengers in each raft.

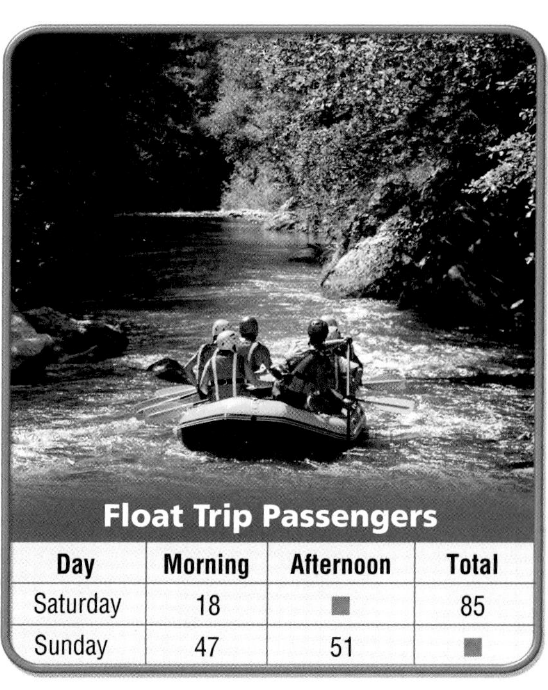

Float Trip Passengers

Day	Morning	Afternoon	Total
Saturday	18	■	85
Sunday	47	51	■

4. How many rafts are needed for the Saturday afternoon trips? Will all of the rafts on Saturday afternoon be full? **Explain.**

5. On which day were more trips taken? How many more trips were taken?

6. By the end of the week, the guides took 12 times as many people on float trips as were booked for the Sunday morning trips. How many people took float trips that week?

7. On Saturday morning, the temperature during the first trip was 63°F. The temperature during the first trip on Sunday was 7°F cooler. What was the temperature on Sunday?

8. **WRITE Math** A company signed 67 people up for float trips. If 8 people fit in a raft, how many rafts do they need? **Explain** whether you need an exact answer or estimate, and then solve.

LESSON 2

Divide 3-Digit Numbers

OBJECTIVE: Divide 3-digit numbers by 1-digit numbers.

Quick Review

1. 8×9
2. 6×7
3. 3×5
4. 1×4
5. 2×8

Learn

PROBLEM President Dwight D. Eisenhower liked vegetable soup so much that he created his own recipe. One recipe makes about 193 ounces of soup. How many 8-ounce bowls can be filled by using 193 ounces of soup?

Example 1 Divide 193 by 8. Write $8\overline{)193}$.

Step 1

Estimate by rounding.

Think: 193 is about 190, and 8 is about 10.

$190 \div 10 = 19$

$8\overline{)193}$ Place the first digit in the tens place.

Step 2

Divide the 19 tens.

$$\begin{array}{r} 2 \\ 8\overline{)193} \\ -16 \\ \hline 3 \end{array}$$

Divide. Multiply. Subtract. Compare.

Step 3

Bring down the 3 ones. Divide the 33 ones.

$$\begin{array}{r} 24 \text{ r1} \\ 8\overline{)193} \\ -16\downarrow \\ \hline 33 \\ -\ 32 \\ \hline 1 \end{array}$$

Divide. Multiply. Subtract. Compare.

Step 4

To check, multiply the quotient by the divisor and add the remainder.

$$\begin{array}{rl} 24 & \text{quotient} \\ \times\ 8 & \text{divisor} \\ \hline 192 & \\ +\ 1 & \text{remainder} \\ \hline 193 & \text{dividend} \end{array}$$

So, 24 8-ounce bowls can be filled using 193 ounces. There will be 1 ounce left over.

Example 2 Divide 756 by 6. Write $6\overline{)756}$.

Step 1

Use division facts for 6 to find compatible numbers for 756.

Think: $6\overline{)600}$ = 100 or $6\overline{)1,200}$ = 200

The quotient is between 100 and 200. So, place the first digit in the hundreds place.

Step 2

Divide the 7 hundreds.

$$\begin{array}{r} 1 \\ 6\overline{)756} \\ -6 \\ \hline \end{array}$$

Divide. Multiply. Subtract. Compare.

Step 3

Bring down the 5 tens. Divide the 15 tens.

$$\begin{array}{r} 12 \\ 6\overline{)756} \\ -6\downarrow \\ \hline 15 \\ -12 \\ \hline 3 \end{array}$$

Divide. Multiply. Subtract. Compare.

Step 4

Bring down the 6 ones. Divide the 36 ones.

$$\begin{array}{r} 126 \\ 6\overline{)756} \\ -6\downarrow \\ \hline 15 \\ -12\downarrow \\ \hline 36 \\ -\ 36 \\ \hline 0 \end{array}$$

Divide. Multiply. Subtract. Compare.

So, $756 \div 6 = 126$. Since 126 is between 100 and 200, the answer is reasonable.

TEKS 4.4E use division to solve problems (no more than one-digit divisors by three-digit dividends without technology). *also* **4.5B, 4.14A, 4.15A, 4.15B, 4.16A, 4.16B**

Divide Money

Divide money amounts as you divide whole numbers.

Example 3 Divide money.

Divide $645 by 5. Write $5\overline{)\$645}$.

Step 1	Step 2	Step 3	Step 4
Estimate by rounding. Think: $645 is about $600 and 5 is about 6. 600 ÷ 6 = 100 $6\overline{)600}$ Place the first digit in the hundreds place.	Divide the 6 hundreds. $\begin{array}{r} \$1 \\ 5\overline{)\$645} \\ -5 \\ \hline 1 \end{array}$ Divide. Multiply. Subtract. Compare. Write the dollar sign in the quotient.	Divide the 14 tens. $\begin{array}{r} \$12 \\ 5\overline{)\$645} \\ -5\downarrow \\ \hline 14 \\ -10 \\ \hline 4 \end{array}$ Divide. Multiply. Subtract. Compare.	Divide the 45 ones. $\begin{array}{r} \$129 \\ 5\overline{)\$645} \\ -5\downarrow \\ \hline 14 \\ -10\downarrow \\ \hline 45 \\ -45 \\ \hline 0 \end{array}$ Divide. Multiply. Subtract. Compare.

So, $645 ÷ 5 is $129.

- How do you know the answer is reasonable?

Example 4

Emilio owns a restaurant. He orders 3 new uniforms for the chefs that cost $258. What is the cost of one uniform?

Divide $258 ÷ 3. Write $3\overline{)\$258}$.

Step 1	Step 2	Step 3	Step 4
Use division facts for 3 to find compatible numbers for $258. Think: $3\overline{)240}$ = 80 or $3\overline{)270}$ = 90 $3\overline{)258}$ Place the first digit in the tens place.	Divide the 25 tens. $\begin{array}{r} \$\ 8 \\ 3\overline{)\$258} \\ -24 \\ \hline 1 \end{array}$ Divide. Multiply. Subtract. Compare. Write the dollar sign in the quotient.	Divide the 18 ones. $\begin{array}{r} \$\ 86 \\ 3\overline{)\$258} \\ -24\downarrow \\ \hline 18 \\ -18 \\ \hline 0 \end{array}$ Divide. Multiply. Subtract. Compare.	Multiply to check. $\begin{array}{r} \overset{1}{\$\ 86} \\ \times\ \ 3 \\ \hline \$258 \end{array}$ quotient divisor dividend

So, the cost of one uniform is $86.

Guided Practice

1. To find 456 ÷ 8, what two compatible numbers would you use for 456? Divide each compatible number by 8. In which place will you place the first digit of the quotient?

Divide and check.

2. $4\overline{)329}$ 3. $723 ÷ 3 4. $7\overline{)655}$ 5. 924 ÷ 8 6. $6\overline{)\$582}$

7. **TALK Math** **Explain** how to place the first digit in Problem 5.

Independent Practice and Problem Solving

Divide and check.

8. 188 ÷ 2 9. $5\overline{)\$723}$ 10. 854 ÷ 6 11. $3\overline{)112}$ 12. $768 ÷ 8

13. 621 ÷ 4 14. $9\overline{)\$459}$ 15. $679 ÷ 7 16. $6\overline{)468}$ 17. 172 ÷ 5

18. $4\overline{)296}$ 19. $2\overline{)\$223}$ 20. $9\overline{)189}$ 21. $125 ÷ 4 22. 292 ÷ 8

Algebra Find the missing digit.

23. 3■1 ÷ 7 = 45 r6 24. 688 ÷ ■ = 229 r1 25. 29■ ÷ 6 = 49 r5 26. 111 ÷ 8 = ■3 r7

USE DATA For 27–30 and 32, use the Farmer's Market price list.

27. Iris is at the Farmer's Market shopping for her restaurant. She buys 7 crates of cabbage to use for soup. How much does she pay for each crate?

28. How much would Iris pay for 4 crates of potatoes?

Farmer's Market Sales

Item	Amount
6 crates of carrots	$126
4 crates of lettuce	$156
3 crates of potatoes	$144
4 crates of cabbage	$92

29. How much would Iris pay for 3 crates of lettuce?

30. How much more per crate does the cabbage cost than the carrots?

32. **Pose a Problem** Look back at Problem 28. Exchange the known and unknown information. Then solve the problem.

31. **Reasoning** Which has the greater quotient, 654 ÷ 2 or 654 ÷ 3? **Explain** how you know.

33. **WRITE Math** **Sense or Nonsense?** Sari says the quotient of 526 ÷ 7 is 751. Does her answer make sense? **Explain.**

Mixed Review and TAKS Prep

34. Patty pulls a marble from a bag that has 3 green marbles, 6 blue marbles, and 3 red marbles, all of the same size. Is she likely, unlikely, or equally likely to pull a blue marble? (Grade 3 TEKS 3.13C)

35. How many lines of symmetry does a square have? (TEKS 4.9C, p. 294)

36. **TAKS Prep** James and Nani have 374 bars of soap for their fourth-grade art project. There are 4 fourth-grade classes. Each class will receive an equal number of bars of soap. **Explain** how to find how many bars of soap each class will receive. Are there any bars left over? (Obj. 1)

 Extra Practice on page 376, Set A

Pose a Problem

One way to pose, or write, a problem is to change the numbers in a problem you are given.

Sophia has a collection of 180 quarters. One out of every five quarters is a Washington quarter. It has the American bald eagle on its tails side. The rest of her quarters are State of Texas commemorative quarters. How many Texas quarters does Sophia have?

▲ The Texas quarter was released in 2004. The Washington quarter was first issued in 1932.

Wesley wrote this new problem by changing the numbers in the problem.

Sophia has a collection of 120 quarters. One out of every four quarters is a Washington quarter. The rest of the quarters are State of Texas commemorative quarters. How many Texas quarters does Sophia have?

Tips

Pose a Problem

- Change the numbers.
- Exchange the known and unknown information.
- Write your own problem about some given information.

When you pose a new problem by changing the numbers in the problem, you need to solve the new problem to make sure the answer is reasonable.

Problem Solving Use the problems about Sophia's quarters. Pose new problems. Solve.

1. Change the amount of coins in the collection. Hint: Choose a dividend that can be divided evenly by 4 or 5.
2. Exchange the known and unknown numbers to pose a new problem.

LESSON 3

Zeros in Division

OBJECTIVE: Divide 3-digit numbers by 1-digit numbers when there are zeros in the quotient.

Quick Review

Malcom has 23 quarts of spaghetti sauce. Each jar holds 2 quarts. How many jars does he need for the spaghetti sauce?

Learn

PROBLEM Mr. Bing collects 324 treasures for his backyard treasure hunt. He needs 3 treasures for each student who participates. How many students can participate?

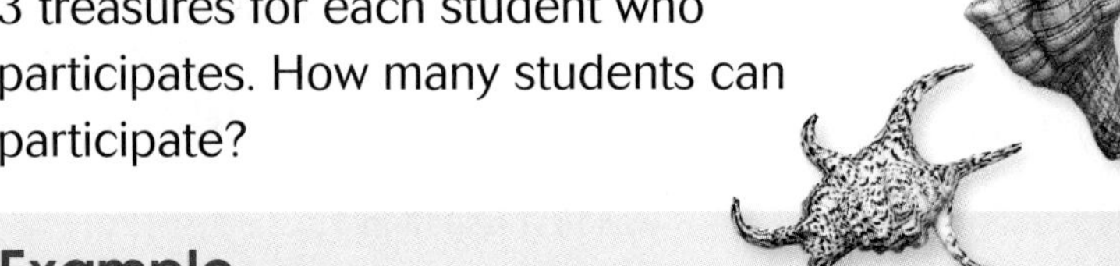

Example

Divide 324 by 3. Write $3\overline{)324}$

Step 1	Step 2	Step 3	Step 4
Estimate to place the first digit in the quotient. Think: $3\overline{)300}$ = 100 or $3\overline{)600}$ = 200 ■ $3\overline{)324}$ So, place the first digit in the hundreds place.	Divide the 3 hundreds. $$\begin{array}{r} 1 \\ 3\overline{)324} \\ -3 \\ \hline 0 \end{array}$$	Bring down the 2 tens. Divide the 2 tens. $$\begin{array}{r} 10 \\ 3\overline{)324} \\ -3\downarrow \\ \hline 02 \\ -\ 0 \\ \hline 2 \end{array}$$ The divisor 3 is greater than 2, so write a 0 in the quotient.	Bring down the 4 ones. Divide the 24 ones. $$\begin{array}{r} 108 \\ 3\overline{)324} \\ -3 \\ \hline 02 \\ -\ 0\downarrow \\ \hline 24 \\ -24 \\ \hline 0 \end{array}$$

So, 108 students can participate in the backyard treasure hunt.

- **What if** Mr. Bing had 420 treasures? How many students could participate?

More Examples

A Divide with Zeros

$$\begin{array}{r} 102 \text{ r1} \\ 4\overline{)409} \\ -4 \\ \hline 00 \\ -\ 0 \\ \hline 09 \\ -\ 8 \\ \hline 1 \end{array}$$

CHECK

$$\begin{array}{rl} 102 & \text{quotent} \\ \times\ \ 4 & \text{divisor} \\ \hline 408 & \\ +\ \ 1 & \text{remainder} \\ \hline 409 & \text{dividend} \end{array}$$

B Divide Money

$$\begin{array}{r} \$104 \\ 5\overline{)\$520} \\ -5 \\ \hline 02 \\ -\ 0 \\ \hline 20 \\ -20 \\ \hline 0 \end{array}$$

CHECK

$$\begin{array}{rl} \overset{2}{\$104} & \text{quotient} \\ \times\ \ 5 & \text{divisor} \\ \hline \$520 & \text{dividend} \end{array}$$

TEKS 4.4E use division to solve problems (no more than one-digit divisors and three-digit dividends without technology). *also* **4.1A, 4.5B, 4.14A, 4.15A, 4.15B, 4.16A, 4.16B**

Correcting Quotients

The fourth-grade science classes displayed their treasures on tables for nature night. They put the same number of treasures on each table. There were 480 animal treasures on 6 tables. How many treasures were on each table?

Look at Ethan's paper. Ethan divided 480 by 6.

Ethan

$$\begin{array}{r} 8 \\ 6\overline{)480} \\ -48 \\ \hline 0 \end{array}$$

- Describe Ethan's error. Find the correct number of treasures per table.
- Explain how basic facts and patterns could have helped Ethan find the correct answer.

Students who found plant and mineral treasures displayed 424 treasures on 4 tables. How many did they display on each table?

Look at Ava's paper. Ava divided 424 by 4.

Ava

$$\begin{array}{r} 16 \\ 4\overline{)424} \\ -4 \\ \hline 24 \\ -24 \\ \hline 0 \end{array}$$

- Describe Ava's error. Find the correct number of treasures per table.

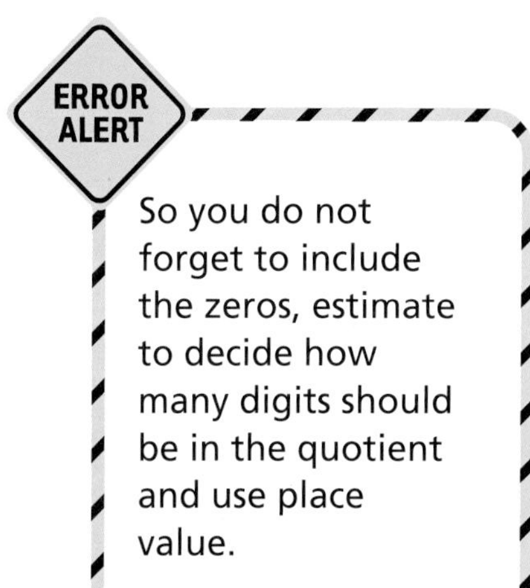

ERROR ALERT
So you do not forget to include the zeros, estimate to decide how many digits should be in the quotient and use place value.

Guided Practice

1. Copy the problem at the right. Estimate to place the first digit. Divide the hundreds. Divide the tens. Do you need to write a zero in the quotient? Then divide the ones. What is the quotient?

$2\overline{)210}$

Write the number of digits in each quotient.

2. $360 \div 4$ 3. $714 \div 7$ 4. $3\overline{)420}$ 5. $8\overline{)960}$ ✓6. $400 \div 5$

Divide and check.

7. $5\overline{)305}$ 8. $803 \div 4$ 9. $6\overline{)840}$ 10. $901 \div 2$ ✓11. $9\overline{)927}$

12. **TALK Math** Think about the problem $216 \div 2$. **Explain** how you know there will be a 0 in the quotient.

Independent Practice and Problem Solving

Write the number of digits in each quotient.

13. $7\overline{)560}$ 14. $282 \div 4$ 15. $3\overline{)510}$ 16. $7\overline{)805}$ 17. $540 \div 6$

Divide and check.

18. $5\overline{)601}$ 19. $860 \div 2$ 20. $8\overline{)704}$ 21. $609 \div 3$ 22. $9\overline{)919}$

23. $283 \div 4$ 24. $763 \div 7$ 25. $870 \div 3$ 26. $6\overline{)724}$ 27. $407 \div 5$

28. $4\overline{)700}$ 29. $3\overline{)325}$ 30. $417 \div 2$ 31. $462 \div 5$ 32. $306 \div 3$

Algebra Find the missing value.

33. $701 \div 2 = ■$ 34. $■ \div 5 = 106 \text{ r}2$ 35. $901 \div 3 = ■ \text{ r}■$ 36. $207 \div ■ = 51 \text{ r}3$

37. Anna is making papier-mâché rabbits for a nature celebration. It takes 240 strips of paper to make 8 rabbits. How many strips of paper does Anna need per rabbit?

38. **Reasoning** The Science Center wants to display 110 science projects. Each display area holds 45 projects. Will all of the projects fit in the 2 areas? **Explain.**

39. It takes 606 folds for Brian to make 6 praying mantis origami figures. It takes 540 folds to make 6 Gila lizard figures. How many more folds does Brian do to make one praying mantis than one Gila lizard?

40. Jeri is painting cherry blossoms. She plans to make 5 blossoms. If she spends the same amount of time on each blossom, she should finish in 100 minutes. How long will it take to paint one cherry blossom?

41. ***FAST FACT*** Japanese legend says that folding a thousand cranes brings good health or peace. Mai made 864 origami cranes in 8 months. If she made the same number of cranes each month, how many cranes did she make in one month?

42. **WRITE Math** **What's the Question?** Jolie's forest fun book tells about different beaver lodges and gives the amount of time it takes a beaver to build one. The answer is 103 hours for each beaver lodge.

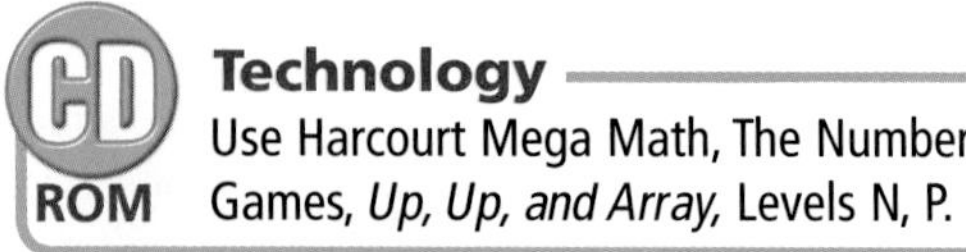

CD ROM
Technology
Use Harcourt Mega Math, The Number Games, *Up, Up, and Array,* Levels N, P.

 Extra Practice on page 376, Set B

Mixed Review and TAKS Prep

43. Manny drew a figure on the board. It has 6 equal sides. What figure did he draw? (TEKS 4.8C, p. 264)

44. **TAKS Prep** A total of 654 students will count turtle nests at 6 different sites. The same number of students will be at each site. How many students will be at one site? (Obj. 1)

A 19 **B** 109 **C** 119 **D** 190

45. Write an expression that shows twice the number of stuffed animals. Let *s* represent the number of stuffed animals. (TEKS 4.15B, p. 156)

46. **TAKS Prep** There are 525 cans of soup on 5 shelves at the grocery store. The number of cans is divided evenly among the 5 shelves. How do you find the number of cans per shelf? **Explain.** (Obj. 1)

Problem Solving and Reasoning

NUMBER SENSE When you estimate quotients, an underestimate gives you a quotient that is less than the actual quotient. An overestimate gives you a quotient that is more than the actual quotient.

Kari pays $105 for 3 DVDs on how to plant a garden. Estimate the cost of each DVD. Compare the estimate to the actual cost.

The actual cost of each DVD is $105 ÷ 3, or $35.

ONE WAY **Underestimate.**

Think: 90 is close to 105. 90 and 3 are compatible numbers since 9 ÷ 3 = 3.

90 ÷ 3 = 30 ← underestimate

So, the estimate of $30 is less than the actual cost of $35 since 90 is less than 105.

ANOTHER WAY **Overestimate.**

Think: 120 is close to 105. 120 and 3 are compatible numbers since 12 ÷ 3 = 4.

120 ÷ 3 = 40 ← overestimate

So, the estimate of $40 is greater than the actual cost of $35 since 120 is greater than 105.

Tell whether the estimate is an underestimate or an overestimate. Then compare the estimate to the actual quotient.

1. A community center has 120 volunteers in 8 animal rescue teams. Each team has the same number of volunteers.

Estimate: 160 ÷ 8 = 20 volunteers per team

2. Justin sells 330 pinecone bird feeders in 3 hours at the flea market. He sells the same number each hour.

Estimate: 300 ÷ 3 = 100 feeders per hour

LESSON 4 Choose a Method

OBJECTIVE: Choose a method to divide multidigit numbers.

Quick Review

1. 42 ÷ 6
2. 28 ÷ 7
3. 36 ÷ 4
4. 50 ÷ 5
5. 72 ÷ 9

Learn

PROBLEM There are about 2,580 different species of marine animals, birds, and fish in the Gulf of Maine. A photographic team took pictures of every species during a 6-month period. If they took the same number of pictures each month, about how many species did they photograph in 1 month?

Choose a method that works easily for the numbers given.

Example 1 Use paper and pencil.

Divide. 2,580 ÷ 6

Step 1

Estimate to place the first digit in the quotient.

Think:

$$6\overline{)2,400} = 400 \quad \text{or} \quad 6\overline{)3,000} = 500$$

$6\overline{)2,580}$ ■ So, place the first digit in the hundreds place.

Step 2

Divide the 25 hundreds.

```
     4
 6)2,580
  -24
     1
```

Step 3

Bring down the 8 tens. Divide the 18 tens.

```
     43
 6)2,580
  -24↓
     18
    -18
      0
```

Step 4

Bring down the 0 ones. Divide the 0 ones.

```
     430
 6)2,580
  -24
     18
    -18↓
      00
```

So, the team photographed about 430 species in 1 month.

Example 2 Use a calculator.

Divide. 7,635 ÷ 4.

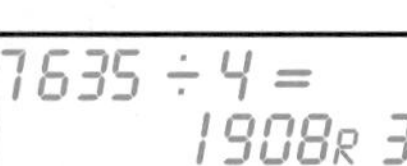

Estimate to check.
8,000 ÷ 4 = 2,000

So, 7,653 ÷ 4 = 1,908 r3.

Example 3 Use mental math.

Divide. 1,824 ÷ 6.

Think: 1,824 = 1,800 + 24

1,800 ÷ 6 = 300 24 ÷ 6 = 4 300 + 4 = 304

So, 1,824 ÷ 6 = 304.

Math Idea

You can divide by using paper and pencil, by using a calculator, or by using mental math. Choose the method that works best with the numbers in the problem.

TAKS 4.4E use division to solve problems (no more than one-digit divisors and three-digit dividends without technology). *also* **4.1A, 4.5B, 4.14A, 4.14D, 4.15A, 4.15B, 4.16A, 4.16B**

Guided Practice

1. Tell which problem would be easier to solve by using mental math. Then divide.
   a. $6,440 \div 8$ b. $2,758 \div 5$

Divide. Write the method you used.

2. $5\overline{)1,780}$
3. $840 \div 6$
4. $4\overline{)3,285}$
5. $8\overline{)2,608}$
6. $2,198 \div 3$
7. TALK Math **Explain** how you chose the method you used to divide in Problem 6.

Independent Practice and Problem Solving

Divide. Write the method you used.

8. $7\overline{)203}$
9. $5\overline{)2,411}$
10. $9\overline{)1,881}$
11. $5\overline{)2,822}$
12. $7\overline{)2,051}$
13. $4\overline{)4,963}$
14. $6\overline{)2,226}$
15. $4\overline{)3,238}$
16. $6\overline{)2,077}$
17. $8\overline{)2,496}$
18. $5,728 \div 3$
19. $2,450 \div 6$
20. $370 \div 5$
21. $4,876 \div 8$
22. $2,240 \div 7$

Algebra **Find the dividend.**

23. ■ $\div 4 = 392$
24. ■ $\div 7 = 506$
25. ■ $\div 6 = 416$ r1
26. ■ $\div 3 = 862$ r2

27. The same number of scientists from each of 9 nations worked to identify new fish. A total of 657 scientists worked on the project. How many scientists came from each nation? Which method did you use to solve the problem? Why?

29. WRITE Math Tell the method you would use to find the quotients of $4,248 \div 6$ and $4,526 \div 6$. **Explain** your choice.

28. Suppose 102 new fish species are found in one 6-month period and 126 new fish species are found in the next 6-month period. If the same number of fish species are found each month within each 6-month period, how many more new fish species are found in each month of the second 6-month period than in the first?

Mixed Review and TAKS Prep

30. Blair's team catalogs 850 fish. Bria's team catalogs 117 fewer fish. How many fish do they catalog in all? (TEKS 4.3A, p. 50)

31. Ron drives 618 miles in 3 days. He drives the same distance each day. How far does he drive each day? (TEKS 4.4C, p. 368)

32. **TAKS Prep** Mrs. Hansen donated $1,410 to charities over a period of 6 months. She donated the same amount each month. How much did she donate each month? (Obj. 1)

   A $225 **C** $236
   B $235 **D** $325

Extra Practice on page 376, Set C

LESSON 5

Find the Average

OBJECTIVE: Find the average of a set of numbers.

Quick Review

1. $3 + 8 + 5 + 4 + 9$
2. $6 + 21 + 15$
3. $23 + 38 + 19$
4. $96 + 73 + 65 + 47$
5. $324 + 126 + 207$

Vocabulary

average

Learn

PROBLEM Every year at the National Spelling Bee, students try to spell difficult, and sometimes long, words. Some words that have been used in the past are shown in the table. What is the average number of letters in these words?

The **average** of a set of numbers is found by dividing the sum of the set of numbers by the number of addends in the set.

Past Spelling Bee Words

Word	Number of Letters
abbreviation	12
abracadabra	11
brouhaha	8
dachshund	9
deciphered	10

▲ More than 200 students participate in the National Spelling Bee each year!

ONE WAY Use paper and pencil.

Step 1

Add the numbers.

$$\begin{array}{r} {}^{2}\\ 12 \\ 11 \\ 8 \\ 9 \\ +10 \\ \hline 50 \end{array}$$

5 addends; 50 ← sum

Step 2

Divide the sum by the number of addends.

$$\begin{array}{r} 10 \\ 5\overline{)50} \end{array}$$

10 ← average; number of addends → 5; 50 ← sum

So, the average number of letters in these words is 10 letters.

ANOTHER WAY Use a calculator.

Find the average of these numbers: 44, 48, 75, 39, 62, 57, 72, and 51.

4 4 + 4 8 + 7 5 + 3 9 + 6 2 + 5 7 + 7 2 + 5 1 Enter = → 448

4 4 8 ÷ 8 Enter = → 448 ÷ 8= 56

So, the average is 56.

- Can the average of a set of numbers be the same as one of the numbers in the set? Explain.

TEKS 4.4E use division to solve problems (no more than one-digit divisors and three-digit dividends without technology). *also* 4.3A, 4.14A, 4.14D, 4.15A, 4.15B, 4.16A

Guided Practice

1. Find the average of 13, 9, 16, and 18. First, add the numbers. Then, divide the sum by the number of addends.

Find the average.

2. 321, 238, 110, 207
3. 59, 67, 83, 74, 82, 79
4. 104, 128, 174, 152, 147
5. **TALK Math** **Explain** how to find the average of this set of data: 12, 16, 13, 25, 19.

Independent Practice and Problem Solving

Find the average.

6. 13, 16, 9, 6, 8, 14
7. 32, 45, 39, 46, 45, 32, 29, 36
8. 15, 19, 14, 19, 15, 17, 22, 14, 18

Algebra **Find the missing number.**

9. 5, 9, 10, ■ The average is 9.
10. 8, 14, 13, 18, ■ The average is 12.
11. 31, 15, 24, 14, ■ The average is 20.

USE DATA **For 12–13, use the table.**

12. What was the average number of spelling rounds from 2002 through 2005?
13. In 2006, 275 spellers participated in the spelling bee. How does this number compare to the average number of spellers from 2003 through 2005?
14. **WRITE Math** **Explain** whether the average of a set of numbers can be less than the least number or greater than the greatest number in the set.

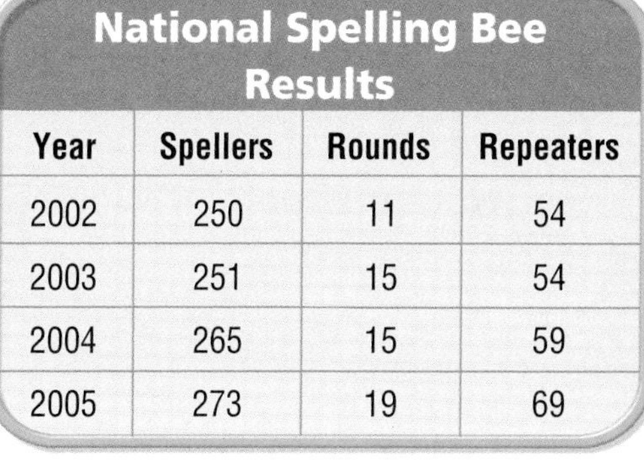

National Spelling Bee Results

Year	Spellers	Rounds	Repeaters
2002	250	11	54
2003	251	15	54
2004	265	15	59
2005	273	19	69

Mixed Review and TAKS Prep

15. Write the time shown on the clock in two different ways. (Grade 3 TEKS 3.12B)

16. There are 840 pens in 8 boxes. Each box has the same number of pens. How many pens are in each box? (TEKS 4.4E, p. 368)
17. **TAKS Prep** Use the spelling bee table above. What was the average number of repeaters who participated in the spelling bees from 2002 through 2005? (Obj. 1)

Extra Practice on page 376, Set D

Extra Practice

Set A Divide and check. (pp. 364–367)

1. $254 \div 3$ 2. $6\overline{)\$954}$ 3. $656 \div 8$ 4. $7\overline{)412}$ 5. $\$452 \div 4$
6. $\$548 \div 2$ 7. $3\overline{)893}$ 8. $284 \div 9$ 9. $4\overline{)\$756}$ 10. $2\overline{)\$654}$
11. $621 \div 5$ 12. $5\overline{)343}$ 13. $971 \div 4$ 14. $6\overline{)\$882}$ 15. $381 \div 7$

16. Chelsea bought 4 pieces of furniture for $596. If each piece is the same price, how much did each piece of furniture cost?

Set B Write the number of digits in each quotient. (pp. 368–371)

1. $6\overline{)480}$ 2. $682 \div 5$ 3. $7\overline{)892}$ 4. $3\overline{)245}$ 5. $960 \div 7$

Divide and check.

6. $4\overline{)240}$ 7. $918 \div 3$ 8. $5\overline{)650}$ 9. $609 \div 3$ 10. $4\overline{)356}$
11. $641 \div 8$ 12. $600 \div 4$ 13. $903 \div 5$ 14. $4\overline{)416}$ 15. $914 \div 7$

16. The fourth grade at Trails School took 9 buses on a field trip. If 360 people went on the field trip and each bus carried the same number of passengers, how many people rode on each bus?

Set C Divide. Write the method you used. (pp. 372–373)

1. $6\overline{)270}$ 2. $4\overline{)2,303}$ 3. $8\overline{)1,656}$ 4. $7\overline{)361}$ 5. $6\overline{)9,041}$
6. $3\overline{)4,952}$ 7. $9\overline{)1,837}$ 8. $5\overline{)4,517}$ 9. $6\overline{)3,485}$ 10. $9\overline{)8,632}$
11. $2,943 \div 4$ 12. $3,671 \div 2$ 13. $633 \div 9$ 14. $3,619 \div 6$ 15. $3,548 \div 9$

Set D Find the average. (pp. 374–375)

1. 15, 11, 11, 12, 14, 9 2. 131, 117, 130, 128, 119 3. 23, 24, 26, 12, 24, 28, 27, 20

4. Jana's math test average is 92 for 5 tests. The scores for her first 4 tests were 93, 96, 86, and 90. What was her score on the last test?

5. Chad and his friends played a board game. Their scores were 73, 25, 45, 19, and 38. What was the average score?

CD ROM **Technology**
Use Harcourt Mega Math, The Number Games, *Up, Up, and Array,* Levels N, O, P.

TECHNOLOGY CONNECTION

Calculator: Remainders (TEKS 4.14D, 4.4E, 4.15A, 4.15B)

A new shipment of books has arrived at a bookstore. There are 243 books. The manager wants to divide them equally among 5 sections. How many books will be in each section? How many will be left over?

On the Casio fx-55 calculator, you can find the remainder when numbers do not divide evenly.

Example

Find the quotient of 243 and 5 using the ÷ key.

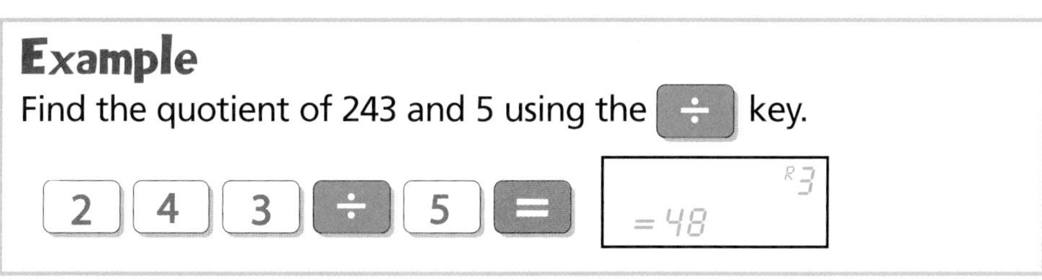

So, there will be 48 books in each section with 3 books left over.

Try It

Solve the problem. Explain how you interpreted the remainder.

1. There are 31 players who need a ride to a game. Each car holds 4 players. How many cars will be needed?
2. Shaun is packing 138 bike helmets into storage boxes. Each box holds 7 helmets. How many boxes will be full?
3. A vending machine holds 160 bottles of water. Bottles are delivered in 6-packs. How many 6-packs are needed to fill the machine for the first time?
4. There are 205 people at a party. Tables are set up to seat 8 people each. There is one table that is not full. How many people are at that table?
5. A toy company had 1,105 board games. It shipped the same number of games to each of 9 stores. How many games were left over at the toy company?
6. Kara has 2,125 photos. If she put 8 photos on a page, how many pages will she need for her photo album?

Chapter 14 Review/Test

Check Concepts

1. **Explain** how to find the number of digits in the quotient of a division problem. (TEKS 4.4E, p. 368)

2. **Explain** the error in this problem and find the correct quotient. (TEKS 4.4E, p. 364)

$$\begin{array}{r} 15 \\ 5\overline{)525} \\ -5 \\ \hline 025 \\ -\ 25 \\ \hline 0 \end{array}$$

Check Skills

Divide and check. (TEKS 4.4E, pp. 364–367, 368–371, 372–373)

3. $384 \div 4$
4. $6\overline{)252}$
5. $561 \div 6$
6. $801 \div 7$
7. $5\overline{)737}$
8. $246 \div 6$
9. $4\overline{)601}$
10. $920 \div 8$
11. $3\overline{)\$561}$
12. $367 \div 9$
13. $\$429 \div 3$
14. $3\overline{)928}$
15. $1{,}539 \div 5$
16. $5\overline{)\$645}$
17. $2\overline{)4{,}125}$
18. $6{,}305 \div 6$
19. $7\overline{)2{,}163}$
20. $7{,}261 \div 3$
21. $4\overline{)\$928}$
22. $9{,}104 \div 5$
23. $4{,}021 \div 7$
24. $9\overline{)\$270}$
25. $2{,}224 \div 2$
26. $420 \div 6$
27. $4\overline{)\$2{,}396}$

Find the average. (TEKS 4.4E, pp. 374–375)

28. 24, 28, 29, 29, 30, 32, 33, 35
29. 111, 113, 120, 130, 109, 119
30. 12, 16, 18, 15, 20, 21, 19, 17, 15

Check Problem Solving

Solve. (TEKS 4.14B, pp. 362–363)

31. Taylor has 686 stamps. He wants to put 6 on each page of an album. How many pages will he need for his stamps?

32. There are 123 fourth-grade students in the school. How many groups of 5 students can be formed?

33. WRITE Math **Explain** how you interpreted the remainder in Problems 31 and 32.

GO ONLINE **Technology** Use *Online Assessment.*

Enrich • Mental Math: Multiplication and Division

USE YOUR HEAD

You can use patterns and relationships to multiply and divide mentally.

If you know that $2 \times 7 = 14$, then you can find products using greater numbers.	If you know that $6 \div 3 = 2$, then you can find quotients using other dividends.
$2 \times 7 = 14$ $4 \times 7 = 28$ $8 \times 7 = 56$ $16 \times 7 = 112$ $32 \times 7 = 224$	$6 \div 3 = 2$ $12 \div 3 = 4$ $24 \div 3 = 8$ $48 \div 3 = 16$ $96 \div 3 = 32$
Look at the pattern for the first factor: 2, 4, 8, 16, 32. Each number is double the previous number. What happens to the product? Each product is doubled also.	The divisor stays the same, but the dividend changes. Look at the pattern for the dividend: 6, 12, 24, 48, 96. Each number is double the previous number. What happens to the quotient? Each quotient is doubled also.

You can use these patterns and the Distributive Property to find other products and quotients.

Examples

A Find the product 48×7 mentally.
Use the Distributive Property.

$$\begin{aligned} 48 \times 7 &= (32 + 16) \times 7 \\ &= (32 \times 7) + (16 \times 7) \\ &= 224 + 112 \\ &= 336 \end{aligned}$$

B Find the quotient $108 \div 3$ mentally.
Use the Distributive Property.

$$\begin{aligned} 108 \div 3 &= (96 + 12) \div 3 \\ &= (96 \div 3) + (12 \div 3) \\ &= 32 + 4 \\ &= 36 \end{aligned}$$

Try It

Complete.

1. $36 \times 7 = (■ + ■) \times 7 = (■ \times 7) + (■ \times 7) = ■ + ■ = ■$
2. $192 \div 3 = (■ + ■) \div 3 = (■ \div 3) + (■ \div 3) = ■ + ■ = ■$
3. $18 \times 5 = (■ + ■) \times 5 = (■ \times 5) + (■ \times 5) = ■ + ■ = ■$
4. $108 \div 3 = (■ + ■) \div 3 = (■ \div 3) + (■ \div 3) = ■ + ■ = ■$

WRITE Math **Explain** how you could find the product 402×9 mentally?

Unit Review/Test
Chapters 13–14

Multiple Choice

1. Jolie bought 5 pizzas for $85. How can she find the cost of 1 pizza? (TAKS Obj. 1)

   A multiply $85 by 5

   B add $85 5 times

   C subtract 5 from $85

   D divide $85 by 5

2. A pack of 54 cards is divided equally into 3 piles. How many cards are in each pile? (TAKS Obj. 1)

   F 18 **H** 23

   G 21 **J** 26

3. Find the average of this set of data. (TAKS Obj. 1)

   24, 18, 34, 25, 24

   A 125

   B 25

   C 24

   D 21

4. Heather is learning to type. She can type 108 words in 5 minutes. At this rate, about how many words can she type in 1 minute? (TAKS Obj. 1)

   F 10

   G 20

   H 103

   J 113

5. Max has 3 times as many quarters as his sister. If Max and his sister have 136 quarters altogether, how many quarters does Max have? (TAKS Obj. 1)

   A 34

   B 68

   C 102

   D 133

6. Which pair of numbers completes the equation? (TAKS Obj. 1)

   ▲ ÷ ■ = 16

   F 25 and 9

   G 9 and 128

   H 144 and 12

   J 128 and 8

7. Milltown School students are organized into groups of 5 to use a computer. How many computers are needed for the fourth grade? (TAKS Obj. 1)

Milltown School	
Grade	**Number of Students**
Third	280
Fourth	273
Fifth	295

   A 55

   B 54

   C 53

   D Not here

GO ONLINE **Technology** Use *Online Assessment.*

8. Steve spends $141 on 3 radios. If each radio costs the same amount, how much does each radio cost? (TAKS Obj. 1)

F $323

G $138

H $47

J $37

9. Tell where to place the first digit in this problem. (TAKS Obj. 1)

$$7\overline{)754}$$

A In the ones place

B In the tens place

C In the hundreds place

D In the thousands place

10. The average of this data set is 16. Which number is represented by ■? (TAKS Obj. 1)

19, 17, 14, 15, ■

F 15 H 17

G 16 J 19

11. Bryan has 97 cents. What is the greatest number of nickels he could have? (TAKS Obj. 1)

A 20 C 18

B 19 D 17

12. James has 3,015 magazines to store in 5 boxes. How many magazines can he store in each box? (TAKS Obj. 1)

F 630

G 603

H 601

J 63

Short Response

13. Lynn needs 3 tablespoons of chocolate powder to make 1 cup of chocolate milk. There are 54 tablespoons of chocolate powder left in the box. How many cups of chocolate milk can Lynn make? (TAKS Obj. 1)

14. Lillie has 22 charms. She plans to give each of her 4 friends the same number of charms. Draw a model to show how many charms each friend will receive and how many will be left over. (TAKS Obj. 1)

15. The table shows the number of students in the summer basketball league.

Summer Basketball League	
Grade	**Number of Students**
Third	124
Fourth	153
Fifth	135

Each team has 9 students. How many teams of fourth graders are there? (TAKS Obj. 1)

Extended Response WRITE Math

16. Mr. Sanchez spent $205 on train tickets for his family. Adult tickets cost $35 and children's tickets cost $25. How many of each type of ticket did he buy? **Explain** the strategy you used to solve the problem. (TAKS Obj. 1)

17. Corey has 141 CDs. His CD storage cases hold 8 CDs each. How many storage cases does Corey need for all of his CDs? **Explain** the meaning of the remainder. (TAKS Obj. 1)

Texas

Problem Solving

Amazing Collectibles

Collecting License Plates

Millions of people have hobbies that involve collectibles. Some people collect items from their state, such as signs or license plates. David Babcock from Texas had collected 120 old Texas license plates by the time he was 18 years old. Usually the oldest license plates are the most valuable.

Amazing Collections

Type of Collection	Number
Texas license plates	350
Colored vinyl records	1,180
Handmade walking canes	639
Model cars	3,711
Retired traffic signs	600

TEXAS-1933 TR 570

TEXAS 1939 TR 55·683

TEXAS-1933 F89·026

FACT·ACTIVITY

Use the Amazing Collections table to answer the questions.

1. If the walking-cane collector took 9 years to collect the canes and collected the same number each year, how many were collected each year?
2. If the Texas license plate collector displays the plates on the wall with 7 in each row, how many rows will there be?
3. If the collector of retired traffic signs collected 8 signs a year, how many years would it take to collect 600 signs?
4. A collector finds 4 colored vinyl records per month. Estimate how many years it would take to collect the number of records listed in the table.
5. **Pose a Problem** Write a division problem about the model car collection.

Almanac Fact

The U.S. Postal Service made a stamp that looks like an old postcard for each state. This Texas stamp shows things that remind people of Texas, such as a yellow rose.

What Do You Collect?

There is no limit to what you can collect! Many adult collectors began collecting when they were children. Kids all over the world collect objects that are interesting to them.

Bottle caps

Penguins

Stamps

Fact Activity

Think of something you would like to collect. Answer the questions about planning your collection.

- What do you want to collect? How many items would you like to have in your collection?
- Where will you keep the items? Will you arrange them in equal groups, such as 8 items per shelf? Will there be items left over?
- Write division sentences to show how your collection might be arranged in equal groups. Try a few different ways to arrange them.

UNIT 6

Fractions and Decimals

Math on Location

with **Texas Chapter Projects**

1

Customers choose the components of a skateboard by their size and color.

2

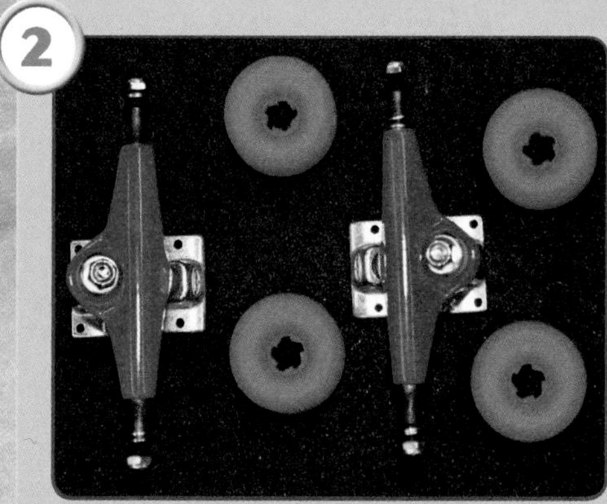

A skateboard is made up of a deck, grip tape, 2 trucks, 4 wheels, and 8 bearings.

3

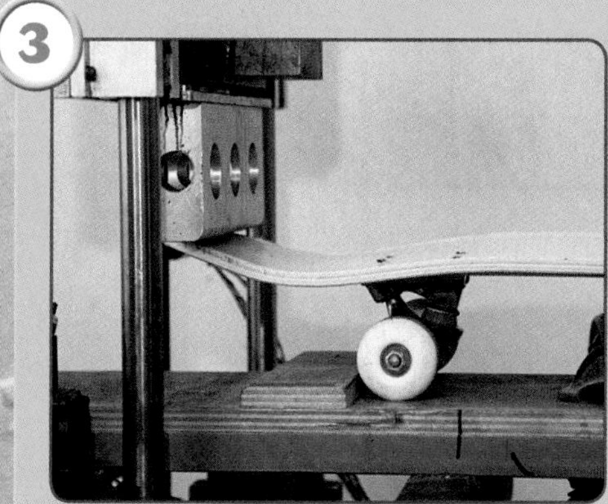

The deck is 7 layers of $\frac{1}{16}$-inch maple veneer. Its strengh is tested by measuring the amount of flex to a fraction of an inch.

VOCABULARY POWER

TALK Math

What math is used in making a skateboard? Look at the green, pink, red, clear, and white wheels in the **Math on Location** photographs. How could you represent what fraction of the wheels are each color?

READ Math

REVIEW VOCABULARY You learned the words below when you first learned about fractions. How do these words relate to **Math on Location**?

denominator the part of a fraction below the bar, that tells how many equal parts are in the whole or in the group

equivalent fractions two or more fractions that name the same amount

fraction a number that names part of a whole or part of a group

WRITE Math

Copy and complete the chart below, using what you know about fractions. Use your own words to write the definition. Write as many facts, examples, and nonexamples as you can think of.

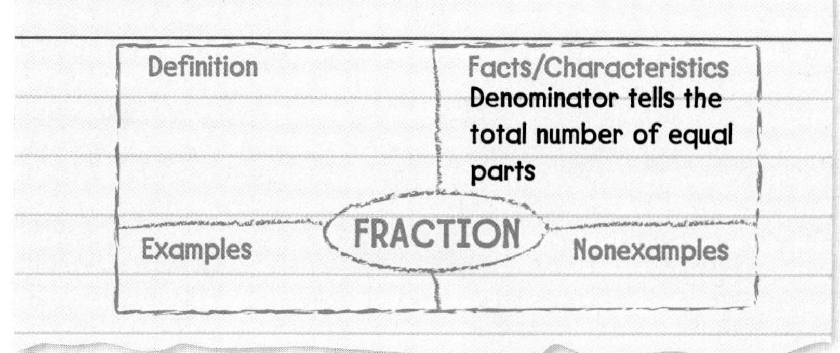

Definition
Facts/Characteristics
Denominator tells the total number of equal parts
FRACTION
Examples
Nonexamples

Technology
Multimedia Math Glossary link at www.harcourtschool.com/hspmath

15 Understand Fractions and Mixed Numbers

The Big Idea Fractions and mixed numbers can be expressed in equivalent forms and be compared and ordered.

TEXAS FAST FACT

This carousel, in the Memorial City Mall in Houston, is 29 feet tall and 36 feet wide. It has animals, 2 gondolas and 2 spinning tops that hold up to 48 people.

Investigate

Use the animals on the carousel. Using fractions compare the number of each animal to the number of each type. Then compare the number of each type of animal to the total number of animals on the carousel. Write as many fractions as you can.

Carousel at Memorial City Mall

Type of Animal	Jumping Cat	Jumping Horse	Jumping Ostrich	Jumping Rabbit	Jumping Tiger	Jumping Zebra	Rocking Horse	Standing Horse	Standing Lion
Number	1	12	1	1	1	1	13	1	1

Technology
Student pages are available in the Student eBook.

Show What You Know

Check your understanding of important skills needed for success in Chapter 15.

▶ Parts of a Whole

Write a fraction for each shaded part.

1. 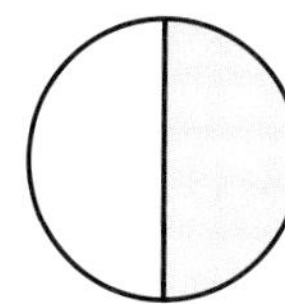

2. 

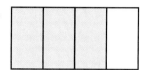

3. 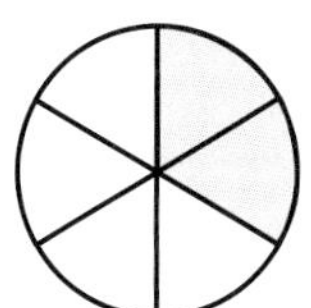

4. 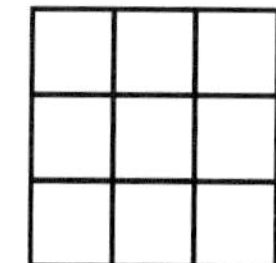

▶ Parts of a Group

Write a fraction for each shaded part.

5. 

6. 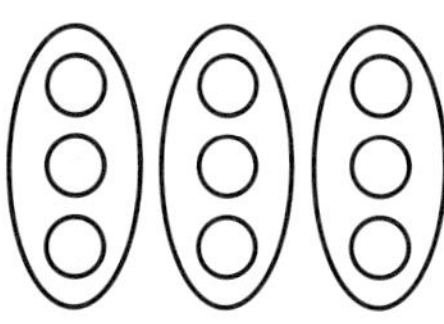

7. 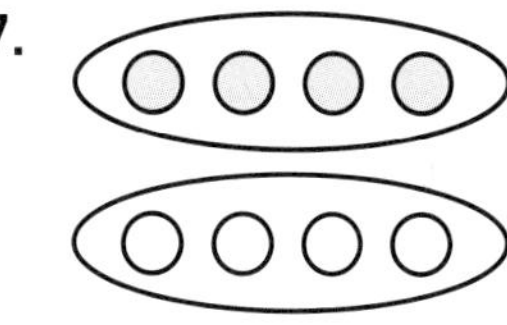

8. 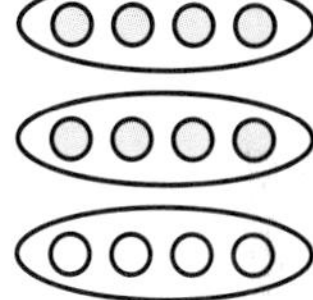

▶ Locate Numbers on a Number Line

Write the number that names the point.

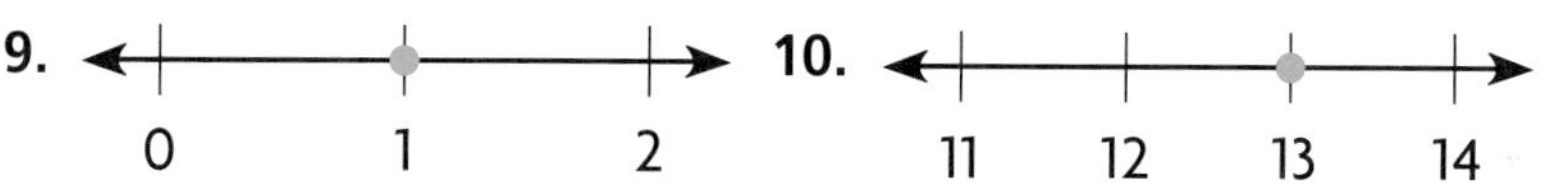

11. 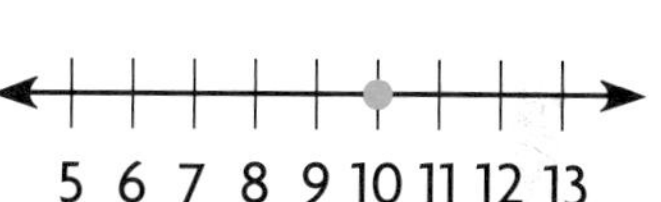

VOCABULARY POWER

CHAPTER VOCABULARY

denominator
equivalent fractions
fourths
fraction
group
halves
mixed number
numerator
simplest form
thirds
whole

WARM-UP WORDS

fraction a number that names part of a whole or part of a group

numerator the number above the bar in a fraction that tells how many parts of the whole or group are being considered

denominator the number below the bar in a fraction that tells how many equal parts are in the whole or in the group

LESSON 1

Read and Write Fractions

OBJECTIVE: Read and write fractions.

Quick Review

Name the number each letter represents.

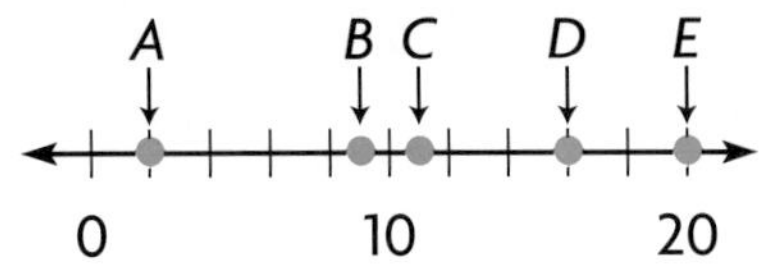

1. A 2. D 3. E
4. C 5. B

Vocabulary

fraction
denominator
numerator
unit fraction

Learn

PROBLEM For lunch Ben had an orange with 8 equal sections. He ate 2 of the sections. What fraction represents the amount of orange Ben ate?

A **fraction** is a number that names part of a whole or part of a group.

Example 1 Name part of a whole.

The number of sections Ben ate were part of the total number of sections in the orange.

number of parts Ben ate → $\frac{2}{8}$ ← numerator
total equal parts → ← denominator

Read: two eighths
two out of eight
two divided by eight

Write: $\frac{2}{8}$

So, Ben ate $\frac{2}{8}$ of the orange.

Example 2 Count equal parts of a whole.

You can count equal parts, such as eighths, to make one whole.

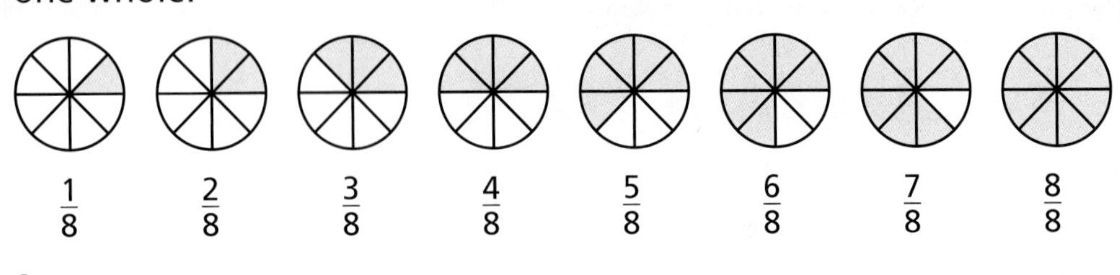

$\frac{1}{8}$ $\frac{2}{8}$ $\frac{3}{8}$ $\frac{4}{8}$ $\frac{5}{8}$ $\frac{6}{8}$ $\frac{7}{8}$ $\frac{8}{8}$

$\frac{8}{8}$ = one whole, or 1

Each equal part of the whole is $\frac{1}{8}$. The fraction $\frac{1}{8}$ is a unit fraction.

A **unit fraction** has a numerator of 1.

- In Example 1, how can you find the fraction of the orange that Ben did not eat by counting equal parts?

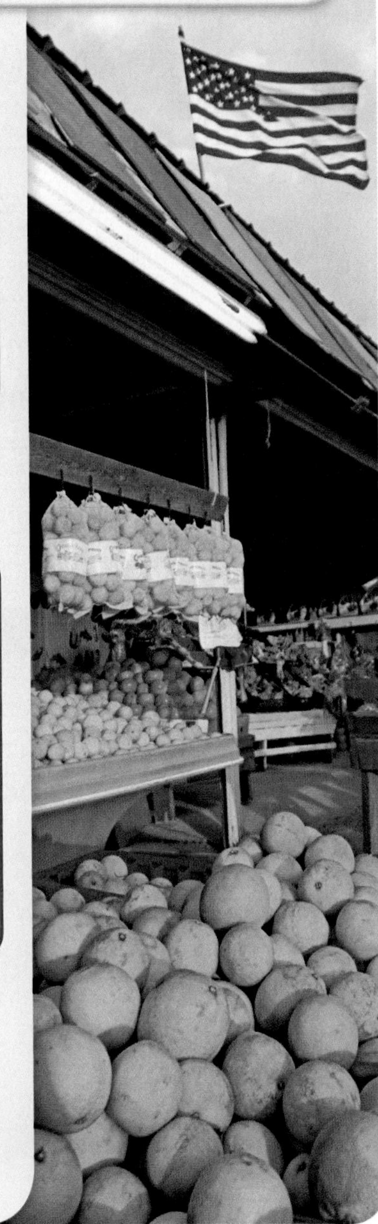

TEKS 4.2 The student describes and compares fractional parts of whole objects or sets of objects.
also **4.10, 4.14A, 4.14D, 4.15A, 4.15B**

Example 3 Show division.

ONE WAY **Use a model.**

Ben's 4 sisters share 3 waffles equally. How much waffle will each sister get?

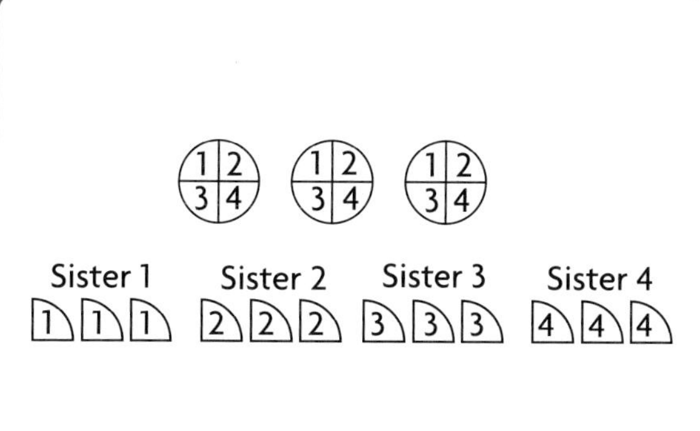

So, each sister will get $\frac{3}{4}$ of a waffle.

ANOTHER WAY **Use a number line.**

Emma's 3 brothers share a box of cereal equally. What fraction of the cereal will each brother get?

A number line can be used to represent one whole. The line can be divided into any number of equal parts.

This number line is divided into three equal parts, or thirds.

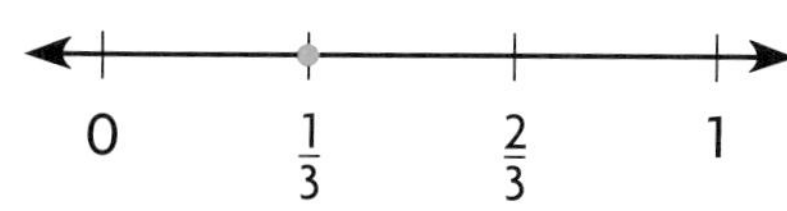

The point shows the location of $\frac{1}{3}$.

So, each brother will get $\frac{1}{3}$ of the box of cereal.

- In Example 3, what do the numerator and the denominator in $\frac{3}{4}$ represent?

Example 4 Name part of a group.

Kelly baked 12 muffins in one pan. She gave 5 of the muffins to her neighbor. What fraction of the muffins did Kelly give away?

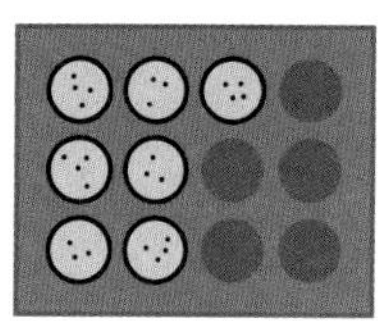

number given away → 5 ← numerator
total number in the group → 12 ← denominator

Read: five twelfths
five out of twelve
five divided by twelve

Write: $\frac{5}{12}$

So, $\frac{5}{12}$ of the muffins were given away.

Guided Practice

1. Sam drew a square with four equal parts. He shaded $\frac{3}{4}$ of the square. Which square could he have drawn?

A B C

Write a fraction for the shaded part. Write a fraction for the unshaded part.

2. 

3. 

✓4. 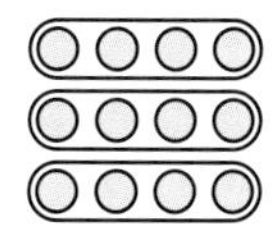

✓5. 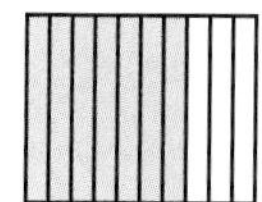

6. **TALK Math** **Explain** what a fraction can represent.

Independent Practice and Problem Solving

Write a fraction for the shaded part. Write a fraction for the unshaded part.

7. 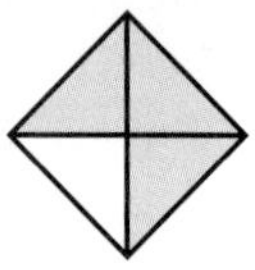

8. 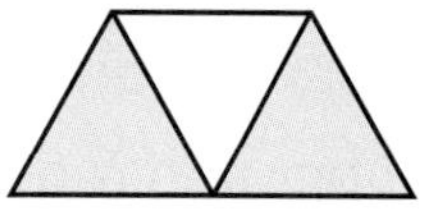

9. 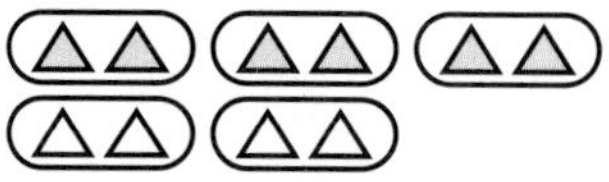

10. 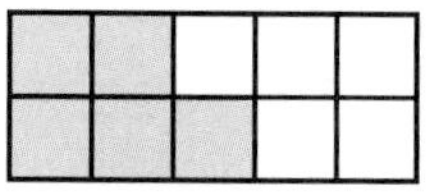

Draw a picture and shade part of it to show the fraction. Write a fraction for the unshaded part.

11. $\frac{7}{8}$

12. $\frac{5}{9}$

13. $\frac{12}{12}$

14. $\frac{8}{10}$

Write the fraction for each.

15. one seventh

16. six out of six

17. three divided by four

18. two thirds

Write the fraction that names the point.

19. 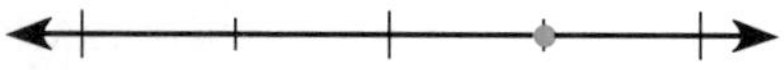
0 1

20. 
0 1

Algebra **Write the missing fraction.**

21. $\frac{1}{8}, \frac{2}{8}, \frac{■}{■}, \frac{4}{8}, \frac{5}{8}$

22. $\frac{5}{12}, \frac{6}{12}, \frac{7}{12}, \frac{8}{12}, \frac{■}{■}$

23. $\frac{7}{16}, \frac{6}{16}, \frac{5}{16}, \frac{■}{■}, \frac{3}{16}$

USE DATA For 24–26, use the picture.

24. What fraction of the items on the tray is fruit?

25. What fraction of the items on the tray is neither muffins nor apples?

26. Write the total number of items on the tray as a fraction.

27. Mike bought 15 apples, 5 bananas, and 10 pears for a party. What fraction of the fruit Mike bought is pears?

28. **WRITE Math** **Explain** how you can model the same fraction three different ways. Then give examples of your explanation.

 Extra Practice on page 410, Set A

Mixed Review and TAKS Prep

29. A meeting room needs 35 chairs set up in 7 equal rows. Write a division sentence to show how many chairs will be in each row. (TEKS 4.4B, p. 122)

30. Kim is buying candles to put on a cake. The candles come in boxes of 6. How many boxes does she need to buy in order to have 10 candles on the cake? (TEKS 4.3A, p. 56)

31. **TAKS Prep** Five friends share 3 small pizzas equally. What fraction of the pizzas will each friend get? (Obj. 1)

A $\frac{1}{5}$ **B** $\frac{1}{3}$ **C** $\frac{2}{5}$ **D** $\frac{3}{5}$

32. **TAKS Prep** Eli has 10 tiles. Of these tiles, $\frac{1}{10}$ are blue, $\frac{3}{10}$ are yellow, and the rest are green. What fraction of the tiles are green? **Explain.** (Obj. 1)

Problem Solving and Reasoning

NUMBER SENSE You can find a fraction of a group or a collection, even if the denominator of the fraction is not the same as the number in the group.

A Find $\frac{2}{3}$ of 6.

Draw 6 objects.

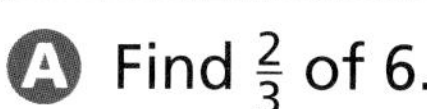

The denominator is 3. Make 3 equal groups.

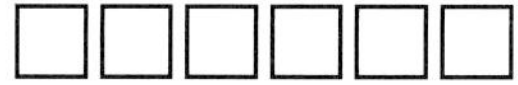

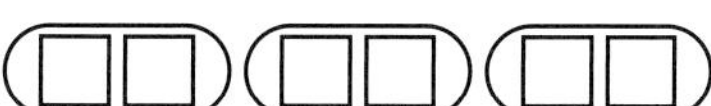

Then shade 2 groups. Count the total objects shaded.

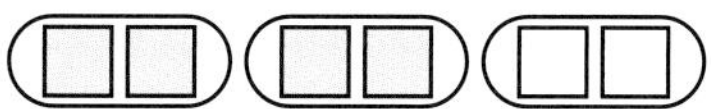

So, $\frac{2}{3}$ of 6 is 4.

B Find $\frac{3}{4}$ of 16.

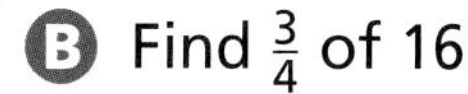

Draw 16 objects.

The denominator is 4. Make 4 equal groups.

Then shade 3 groups. Count the total objects shaded.

So, $\frac{3}{4}$ of 16 is 12.

Draw a picture to solve.

1. $\frac{1}{2}$ of 6 **2.** $\frac{1}{4}$ of 8 **3.** $\frac{2}{3}$ of 15 **4.** $\frac{5}{6}$ of 12 **5.** $\frac{3}{8}$ of 24

LESSON 2

Model Equivalent Fractions

OBJECTIVE: Model equivalent fractions.

Quick Review

Write the fraction.

1. one out of four
2. two thirds
3. three divided by five
4. five eighths
5. seven out of ten

Vocabulary

equivalent fractions

simplest form

Learn

PROBLEM As of 2005, there were 10 giant pandas in zoos in the United States and Mexico. The National Zoo, in Washington, D.C., had 2 of these pandas. What fraction of the pandas is this?

$\frac{2}{10}$ ← National Zoo pandas / ← total pandas

$\frac{1}{5}$ ← National Zoo pandas / ← total pandas

So, $\frac{2}{10}$, or $\frac{1}{5}$ of the giant pandas are at the National Zoo. $\frac{2}{10}$ and $\frac{1}{5}$ are **equivalent fractions** because they name the same amount.

Activity Find equivalent fractions for $\frac{2}{3}$.

Materials ■ fraction bars ■ number lines

ONE WAY Use fraction bars.

Step 1

Line up two $\frac{1}{3}$ bars for thirds with the bar for 1 to show $\frac{2}{3}$.

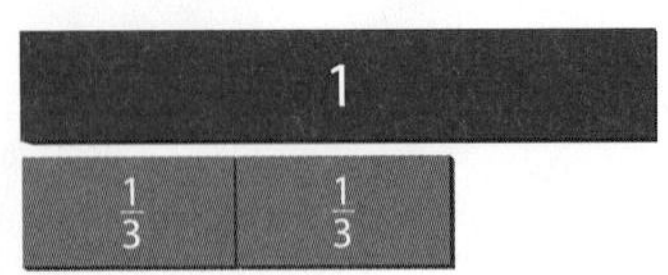

Step 2

Line up other bars of the same type to show the same amount as $\frac{2}{3}$.

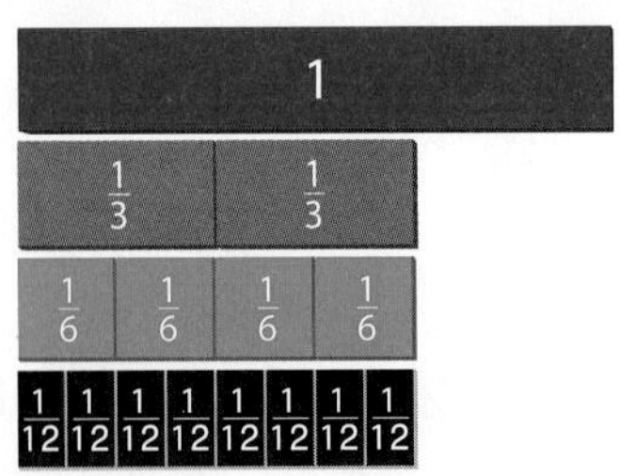

So, $\frac{4}{6}$ and $\frac{8}{12}$ are equivalent to $\frac{2}{3}$.

ANOTHER WAY Use number lines.

Fractions that line up with $\frac{2}{3}$ are equivalent to $\frac{2}{3}$.

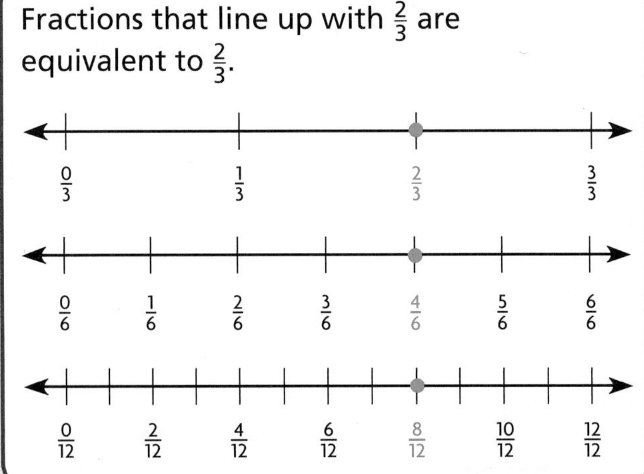

Remember

There are many ways to write 1 as a fraction. In every case, the numerator and denominator are the same.

TEKS 4.2A use concrete objects and pictorial models to generate equivalent fractions. *also* **4.10, 4.14A, 4.14D, 4.15A, 4.15B**

Multiply or Divide

You can multiply both the numerator and denominator of a fraction by any number except zero to find equivalent fractions.

If the numerator and denominator have a common factor, you can also divide both by that factor to find an equivalent fraction.

Find fractions that are equivalent to $\frac{4}{16}$.

ONE WAY **Multiply the numerator and the denominator by the same number.**

Try 2. $\frac{4}{16} = \frac{4 \times 2}{16 \times 2} = \frac{8}{32}$

So, $\frac{4}{16}$ is equivalent to $\frac{8}{32}$.

ANOTHER WAY **Divide the numerator and the denominator by the same number.**

Try 4. $\frac{4}{16} = \frac{4 \div 4}{16 \div 4} = \frac{1}{4}$

So, $\frac{4}{16}$ is equivalent to $\frac{1}{4}$.

You can also find equivalent fractions for whole numbers.

$1 = \frac{1}{1} = \frac{1 \times 10}{1 \times 10} = \frac{10}{10}$ $4 = \frac{4}{1} = \frac{4 \times 3}{1 \times 3} = \frac{12}{3}$

So, $\frac{10}{10}$ is equivalent to 1. So, $\frac{12}{3}$ is equivalent to 4.

A fraction is in **simplest form** when the only number that can be divided into the numerator and the denominator evenly is 1.

ONE WAY **Use a model.**

Find the simplest form of $\frac{8}{10}$.

Line up eight $\frac{1}{10}$ bars with the bar for 1 to show $\frac{8}{10}$.

1							
$\frac{1}{10}$	$\frac{1}{10}$	$\frac{1}{10}$	$\frac{1}{10}$	$\frac{1}{10}$	$\frac{1}{10}$	$\frac{1}{10}$	$\frac{1}{10}$

Then line up other bars of the same type with denominators smaller than 10 to show the same amount as $\frac{8}{10}$.

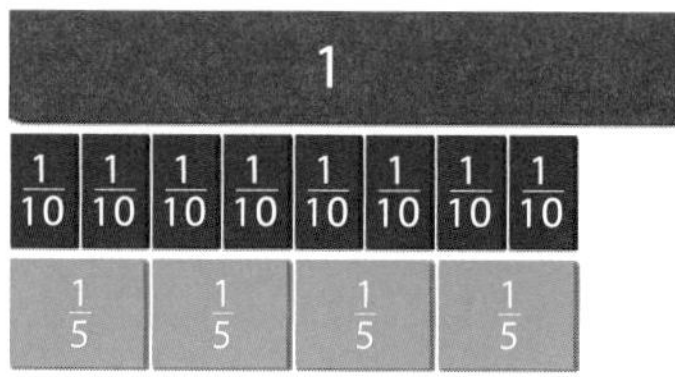

Fifths are the largest fraction pieces that are equal to tenths.

So, the simplest form of $\frac{8}{10}$ is $\frac{4}{5}$.

ANOTHER WAY **Divide.**

Find the simplest form of $\frac{36}{48}$.

Try 6. Divide the numerator and denominator by 6.

$\frac{36}{48} = \frac{36 \div 6}{48 \div 6} = \frac{6}{8}$

Next, try 2. Divide the numerator and denominator by 2.

$\frac{6}{8} = \frac{6 \div 2}{8 \div 2} = \frac{3}{4}$

Now the only number that can be divided into the numerator and denominator of $\frac{3}{4}$ is 1.

So, the simplest form of $\frac{36}{48}$ is $\frac{3}{4}$.

Guided Practice

1. What two equivalent fractions are shown by these models? Which fraction is in simplest form?

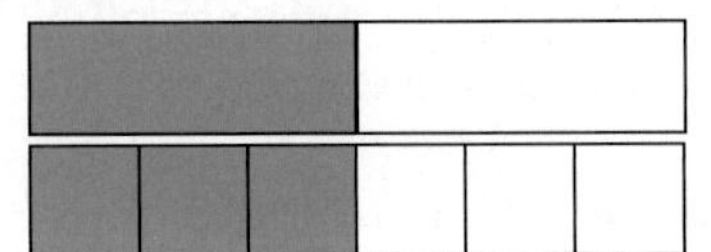

Write two equivalent fractions for each model.

2. 

3. $\frac{1}{4}$

4. 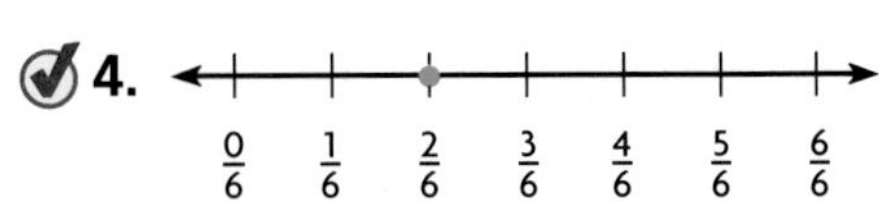

5. **TALK Math** **Explain** why equivalent fractions are equal. Use fraction bars.

Independent Practice and Problem Solving

Write two equivalent fractions for each model.

6. $\frac{0}{9}$ $\frac{1}{9}$ $\frac{2}{9}$ $\frac{3}{9}$ $\frac{4}{9}$ $\frac{5}{9}$ $\frac{6}{9}$ $\frac{7}{9}$ $\frac{8}{9}$ $\frac{9}{9}$

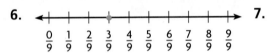

7. 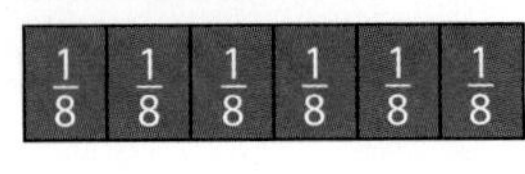

8. 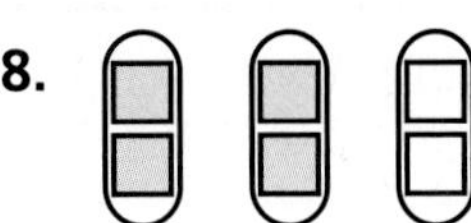

Write two equivalent fractions for each. You may use a model or drawing.

9. $\frac{1}{4}$
10. $\frac{12}{16}$
11. $\frac{3}{5}$
12. $\frac{7}{8}$
13. $\frac{4}{12}$
14. $\frac{9}{9}$

Tell whether the fractions are equivalent. Write *yes* or *no*. You may use a model or drawing.

15. $\frac{3}{4}, \frac{8}{10}$
16. $\frac{2}{18}, \frac{1}{9}$
17. $\frac{4}{12}, \frac{1}{3}$
18. $\frac{9}{12}, \frac{4}{6}$
19. $\frac{10}{25}, \frac{3}{5}$
20. $\frac{8}{16}, \frac{1}{2}$

Tell whether the fraction is in simplest form. If not, write it in simplest form. You may use a model or drawing.

21. $\frac{12}{18}$
22. $\frac{12}{20}$
23. $\frac{8}{15}$
24. $\frac{8}{8}$
25. $\frac{11}{12}$
26. $\frac{15}{25}$

Algebra Find the missing numerator or denominator.

27. $\frac{3}{5} = \frac{■}{15}$
28. $\frac{10}{16} = \frac{5}{■}$
29. $\frac{4}{4} = \frac{■}{8}$
30. $\frac{7}{14} = \frac{■}{2}$
31. $\frac{6}{9} = \frac{24}{■}$
32. $\frac{5}{6} = \frac{20}{■}$

33. **WRITE Math** **What's the Question?** If you multiply the numerator and denominator by 4, you get $\frac{12}{24}$.

34. **Reasoning** What is one way that you know that a fraction is in simplest form without dividing the numerator and denominator? **Explain.**

 Extra Practice on page 410, Set B

USE DATA For 35–37, use the graph.

35. What fraction of the cubs are cheetahs? Write the amount in simplest form.

36. What fraction of the cats are tigers? Write an equivalent fraction for the amount.

37. **Pose a Problem** Look back at Problem 36. Write a similar problem by changing the numbers.

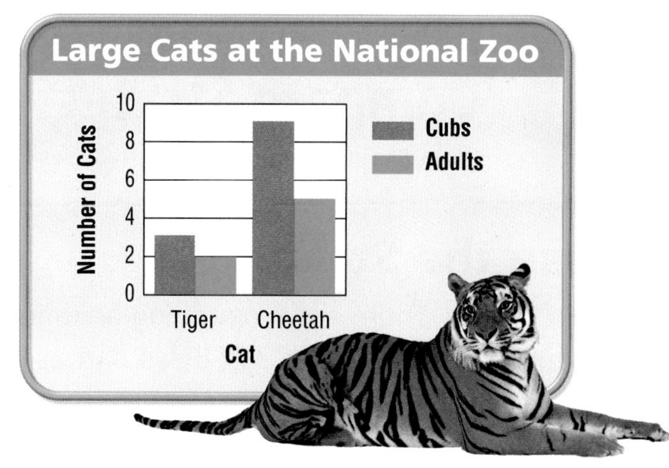

Mixed Review and TAKS Prep

38. Nina has 6 cousins. All but one of her cousins are boys. What fraction of her cousins are boys? (TEKS 4.2, p. 388)

39. The sum of 2 sides of a square is 12 centimeters. How long is each side? (Grade 3 TEKS 3.11A)

40. **TAKS Prep** Which fraction is equivalent to $\frac{4}{5}$? (Obj. 1)

A $\frac{8}{10}$ B $\frac{12}{16}$ C $\frac{16}{25}$ D $\frac{20}{35}$

41. **TAKS Prep** **Explain** why $\frac{6}{9}$ is not equivalent to $\frac{9}{12}$. (Obj. 1)

MATH POWER Problem Solving and Reasoning

VISUAL THINKING The charge to park a car at the National Zoo is $3 per car. You can use a ratio to compare the charge to the number of cars. A **ratio** compares two amounts.

A ratio can be shown as a picture.

Read: $3 per car

The ratio can be written three ways.

3:1 $\frac{3}{1}$ 3 to 1

Read: three to one

The ratio of the charge to park to the number of cars will be equivalent to 3:1 no matter the amount of money collected or number of cars parked.

Draw a picture and write a ratio to compare the cost to park and the number of cars.

1. 2 cars
2. $15
3. 6 cars
4. $24
5. 7 cars

Problem Solving Workshop
Compare Strategies

OBJECTIVE: Compare different strategies to solve problems.

Use the Strategy

PROBLEM There are 6 operating antique carousels in Texas. The Dentzel Company built 3 of these carousels. In simplest form, name the fraction of carousels built by the Dentzel Company.

Read to Understand

- **Identify the details to understand the problem.**
- **Are there details you will not use? If so, which ones?**

Plan

- **What strategy can you use to solve the problem?**

You can act it out with fraction bars or you can draw a picture.

Solve

- **How can you use each strategy to solve the problem?**

Act It Out

Start with the fraction bar for 1. Line up fraction bars to show $\frac{3}{6}$. Line up other fraction bars that represent the same amount as $\frac{3}{6}$.

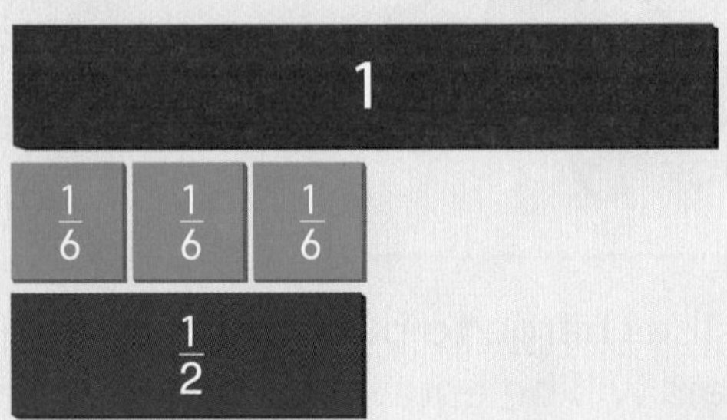

Draw a Picture

Draw a rectangle. Divide it into 6 equal parts. Shade 3 parts to show $\frac{3}{6}$.

$\frac{3}{6}$ ← Dentzel carousels / ← total carousels

Draw another rectangle of the same size and area shaded as the first, but with fewer equal parts.

$\frac{1}{2}$ ← Dentzel carousels / ← total carousels

So, $\frac{3}{6}$, or $\frac{1}{2}$ of the carousels were built by the Dentzel Company.

Check

- **Which strategy was more helpful, *act it out* or *draw a picture*? Explain.**

TEKS 4.2A use concrete objects and pictorial models to generate equivalent fractions. *also* 4.14A; 4.14B, 4.14C, 4.14D, 4.15A, 4.15B, 4.16B

Guided Problem Solving

1. Greg photographed $\frac{1}{4}$ of the jumping horses on the Firemen's Park Carousel in Brenham, Texas. What other fractions represent the same number of the jumping horses Greg photographed?

   Decide whether to act the problem out with fraction bars or draw a picture.

   Find equivalent fractions for $\frac{1}{4}$ to solve the problem.

   Act It Out

   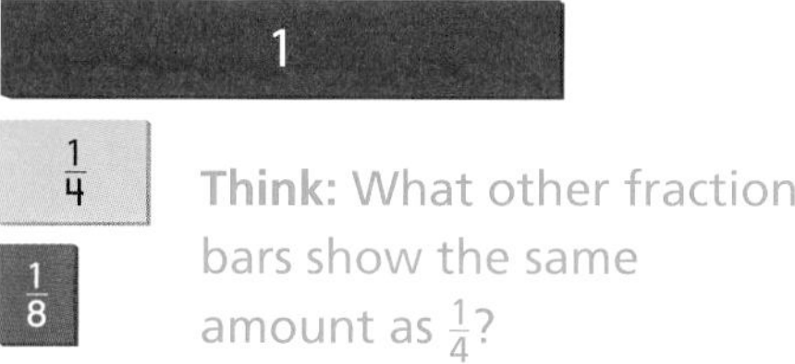

1
   1/4
   1/8
   Think: What other fraction bars show the same amount as 1/4?

2. **What if** you want to find an equivalent fraction for $\frac{1}{4}$ that has 16 as a denominator? Solve and explain the strategy you used.
3. What are two equivalent fractions that represent the fraction of jumping horses that Greg did not photograph?

Choose a STRATEGY

- Draw a Diagram or Picture
- Make a Model or Act It Out
- Make an Organized List
- Look for a Pattern
- Make a Table or a Graph
- Guess and Check
- Work Backward
- Solve a Simpler Problem
- Write an Equation
- Use Logical Reasoning

Mixed Strategy Practice

USE DATA For 4–5, use the table.

4. What are two equivalent fractions that represent what part of the carousels are in the same city? Draw a picture to show your answer.
5. What are two equivalent fractions that represent what part of the carousels were built after 1900? Draw a picture to show your answer.
6. A carousel has 24 horses in all. During one ride, 16 jumping horses and 4 standing horses had riders. In simplest form, what fraction of horses did not have riders?
7. Jorge rode a chariot, a jumping horse, and a standing horse on three carousel rides. He did not ride the jumping horse first. He rode the chariot after he rode the standing horse. In what order did Jorge ride the chariot and horses?

Selected Carousels of Texas

Carousel Location	City	Year built
Wonderland Park	Amarillo	1988
Sandy Lake Amus Park	Dallas	1950
Houston Zoo	Houston	2004
Fireman's Park	Brenham	1812
Fair Park	Dallas	1914

LESSON 4 HANDS ON

Compare Fractions

OBJECTIVE: Compare fractions with like and unlike denominators.

Quick Review

Find the missing number.

1. $\frac{1}{2} = \frac{4}{■}$
2. $\frac{6}{12} = \frac{■}{6}$
3. $\frac{1}{3} = \frac{■}{12}$
4. $\frac{4}{16} = \frac{2}{■}$
5. $\frac{6}{8} = \frac{3}{■}$

Investigate

Materials ■ counters ■ pattern blocks

You can use counters and pattern blocks to compare fractions.

A Use counters to compare sets that have the same number of counters. Compare $\frac{3}{4}$ and $\frac{1}{4}$. Use yellow counters to show the numerators.

$\frac{3}{4}$ ●●●● $\frac{1}{4}$ ●●●●  

B Which fraction has more yellow counters? Which fraction is greater? Complete by using <, >, or =. $\frac{3}{4}$ ● $\frac{1}{4}$

C Use pattern blocks to compare $\frac{1}{3}$ and $\frac{2}{6}$. Remember that if one yellow hexagon = 1, then one green triangle = $\frac{1}{6}$ and 1 blue rhombus = $\frac{1}{3}$.

Now use the green triangles to show $\frac{2}{6}$ on your model.

D How do $\frac{2}{6}$ and $\frac{1}{3}$ compare? Complete by using <, >, or =. $\frac{2}{6}$ ● $\frac{1}{3}$

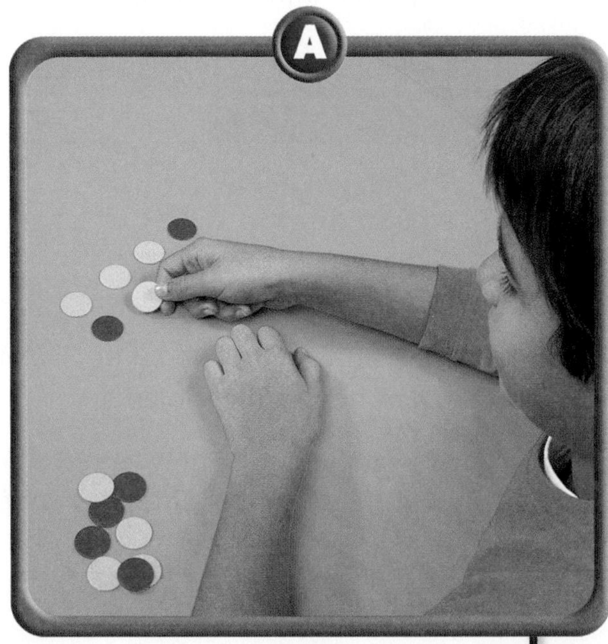

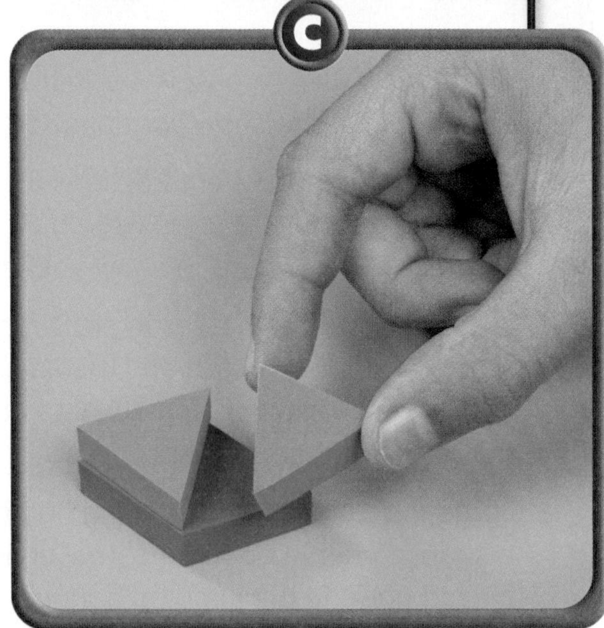

Draw Conclusions

1. How would you use counters to compare $\frac{2}{6}$ and $\frac{5}{6}$?
2. How would you use pattern blocks to compare $\frac{2}{3}$ and $\frac{4}{6}$?
3. **Synthesize** What conclusion can you draw about comparing fractions that have the same denominator?

Connect

You can also compare fractions by using number lines.

Activity Compare fractions using number lines.

A Like Denominators

Compare $\frac{2}{8}$ and $\frac{5}{8}$.
Use a number line divided into eighths. Locate $\frac{2}{8}$ and $\frac{5}{8}$ on a number line.

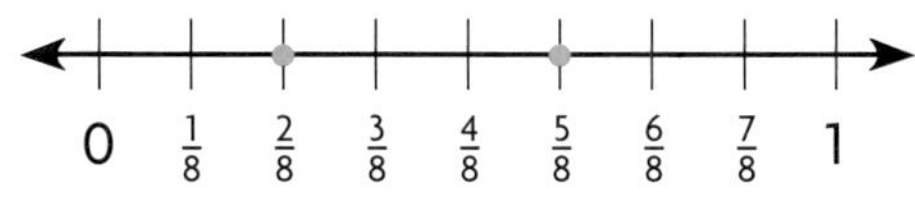

The fraction farther to the left is the lesser fraction.

So, $\frac{2}{8} < \frac{5}{8}$.

B Unlike Denominators

Compare $\frac{3}{4}$ and $\frac{5}{8}$.
Divide one number line into fourths and locate $\frac{3}{4}$ on it. Divide the other number into eighths and locate $\frac{5}{8}$.

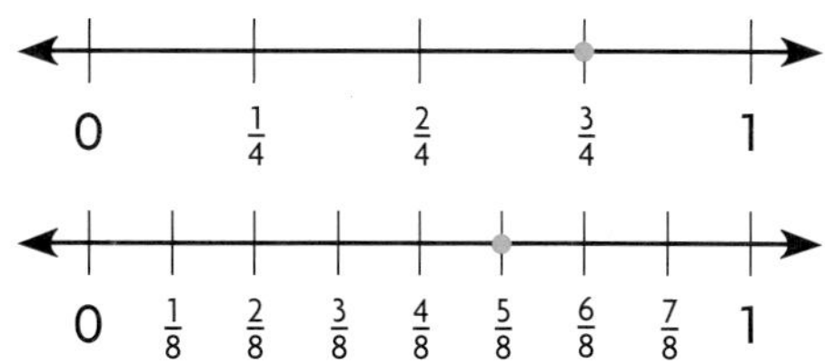

The fraction farther to the right is the greater fraction.

So, $\frac{3}{4} > \frac{5}{8}$.

When you compare fractions with like denominators, compare only the numerators. Use the symbols $<$, $>$, $=$, and $\neq$ to compare fractions.

TALK Math

How could you compare fractions by finding equivalent fractions?

Practice

Model each fraction to compare. Write $<$, $>$, or $=$ for each ●.

1. $\frac{1}{5}$ ● $\frac{4}{5}$
2. $\frac{2}{8}$ ● $\frac{4}{8}$
3. $\frac{1}{2}$ ● $\frac{2}{6}$
4. $\frac{4}{10}$ ● $\frac{1}{2}$
5. $\frac{2}{3}$ ● $\frac{7}{9}$
6. $\frac{3}{8}$ ● $\frac{5}{6}$

Use number lines to compare.

7. $\frac{4}{6}$ ● $\frac{5}{6}$
8. $\frac{1}{4}$ ● $\frac{1}{8}$
9. $\frac{1}{6}$ ● $\frac{1}{5}$
10. $\frac{5}{8}$ ● $\frac{1}{4}$
11. $\frac{3}{4}$ ● $\frac{6}{8}$
12. $\frac{9}{16}$ ● $\frac{2}{4}$
13. **WRITE Math** **Explain** the difference between comparing fractions with like denominators and comparing fractions with unlike denominators.

Technology
CD ROM
Use Harcourt Mega Math, Fraction Action, *Fraction Flare Up*, Level F.

LESSON 5 Order Fractions

OBJECTIVE: Order fractions.

Quick Review

Compare. Write <, >, or = for each ●.

1. $\frac{2}{6}$ ● $\frac{5}{6}$
2. $\frac{11}{18}$ ● $\frac{7}{18}$
3. $\frac{2}{3}$ ● $\frac{3}{5}$
4. $\frac{3}{4}$ ● $\frac{4}{12}$
5. $\frac{3}{8}$ ● $\frac{6}{16}$

Learn

PROBLEM Seth, Ryan, and Antonio each ride their bikes to school. Seth rides $\frac{1}{2}$ mile, Ryan rides $\frac{3}{10}$ mile, and Antonio rides $\frac{3}{5}$ mile. Which boy rides his bike the shortest distance to school?

Activity Use fraction bars.

Materials ■ fraction bars

Order $\frac{1}{2}$, $\frac{3}{10}$, and $\frac{3}{5}$ from greatest to least.

Step 1

Start with the bar for 1. Line up fraction bars for $\frac{1}{2}$, $\frac{3}{10}$, and $\frac{3}{5}$ below it.

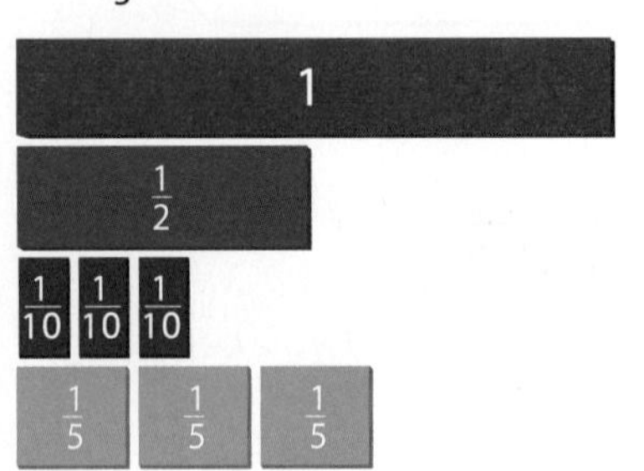

Compare the rows of fraction bars.

Step 2

Move the rows until you have them in order from longest to shortest.

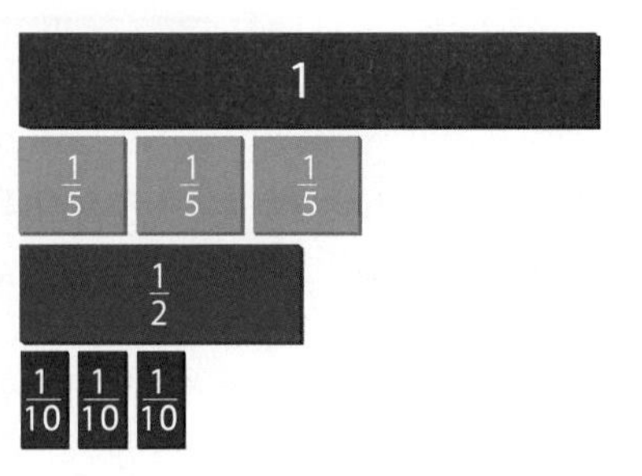

So, the order from greatest to least is $\frac{3}{5}$, $\frac{1}{2}$, $\frac{3}{10}$. Since $\frac{3}{10}$ is the least, Ryan rides his bicycle the shortest distance to school.

Example Use number lines.

Order $\frac{1}{2}$, $\frac{1}{8}$, and $\frac{1}{4}$ from least to greatest.

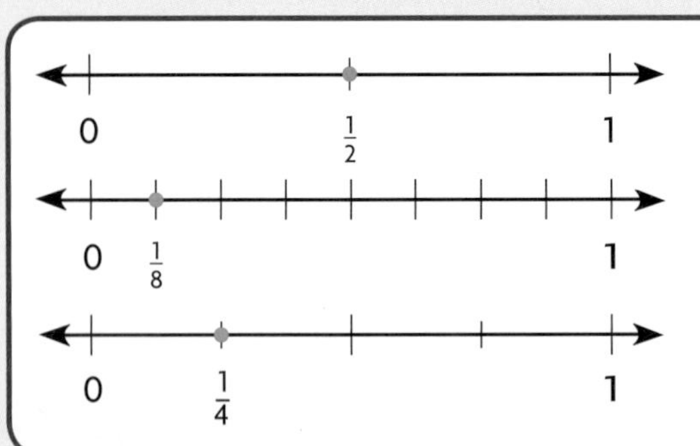

Locate $\frac{1}{2}$, $\frac{1}{8}$, and $\frac{1}{4}$ each on a number line.

The fraction farthest to the left is the least fraction.

So, the order from least to greatest is $\frac{1}{8}$, $\frac{1}{4}$, $\frac{1}{2}$.

TEKS 4.2C compare and order fractions using concrete objects and pictorial models. *also* **4.2A, 4.10, 4.14A, 4.14D, 4.15A, 4.15B**

Guided Practice

1. Use the fraction bars to order $\frac{2}{5}$, $\frac{3}{4}$, and $\frac{6}{10}$ from least to greatest.

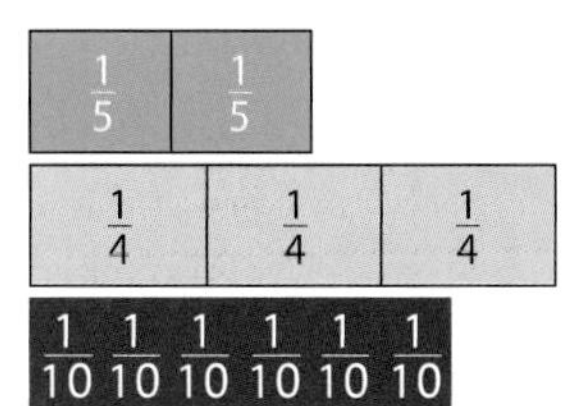

Order the fractions from greatest to least.

2. $\frac{1}{2}, \frac{7}{8}, \frac{4}{6}$

0 — $\frac{1}{2}$ — 1

0 — $\frac{7}{8}$ — 1

0 — $\frac{4}{6}$ — 1

3. $\frac{3}{8}, \frac{12}{12}, \frac{1}{6}$

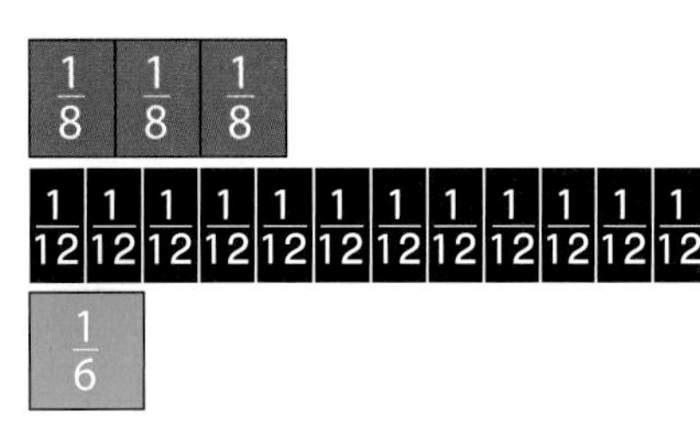

4. $\frac{4}{10}, \frac{1}{3}, \frac{3}{5}$

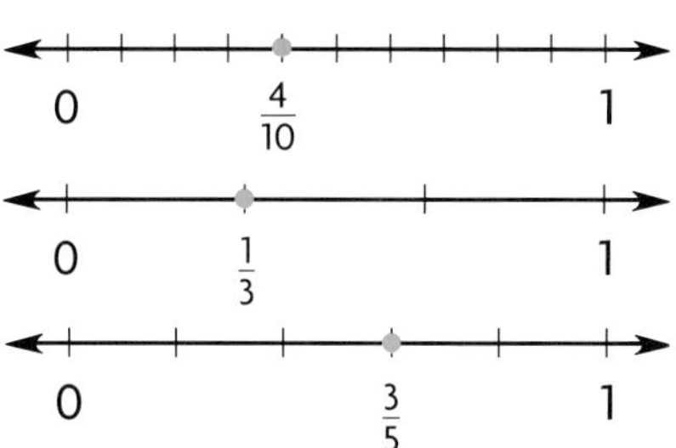

5. **TALK Math** **Explain** how you would use number lines to order $\frac{2}{3}$, $\frac{1}{2}$, and $\frac{4}{5}$ from least to greatest.

Independent Practice and Problem Solving

Order the fractions from least to greatest. You may use a model.

6. $\frac{1}{2}, \frac{1}{8}, \frac{1}{4}$
7. $\frac{8}{16}, \frac{1}{5}, \frac{3}{10}$
8. $\frac{5}{6}, \frac{2}{3}, \frac{1}{2}$
9. $\frac{3}{5}, \frac{2}{4}, \frac{8}{12}$

Order the fractions from greatest to least. You may use a model.

10. $\frac{2}{4}, \frac{8}{10}, \frac{3}{12}$
11. $\frac{1}{6}, \frac{1}{8}, \frac{1}{2}$
12. $\frac{2}{6}, \frac{9}{9}, \frac{1}{12}$
13. $\frac{2}{3}, \frac{2}{4}, \frac{2}{5}$

14. Lily used $\frac{3}{4}$ cup seeds, $\frac{5}{8}$ cup berries, and $\frac{3}{10}$ cup raisins to make trail mix. Order the ingredients from least to greatest.

15. **WRITE Math** **Explain** how you know which fraction is least or greatest using fraction bars.

Mixed Review and TAKS Prep

16. There are 4 red marbles and 2 green marbles in a bag. The marbles are all the same size. If you pull a marble without looking, is it *more likely* or *less likely* you will pull red? (Grade 3 TEKS 3.13C)

17. Draw and shade part of a figure to represent a fraction equivalent to $\frac{1}{3}$. (TEKS 4.2A, p. 392)

18. **TAKS Prep** Esteban jogged for $\frac{2}{3}$ hour, swam for $\frac{5}{6}$ hour, and biked for $\frac{1}{2}$ hour. Which activity took the longest? **Explain.** (Obj. 1)

Extra Practice on page 410, Set C

Read and Write Mixed Numbers

OBJECTIVE: Read and write mixed numbers and express fractions greater than one as mixed numbers.

Quick Review

Order from least to greatest.

1. $\frac{1}{4}, \frac{1}{2}, \frac{1}{8}$
2. $\frac{1}{8}, \frac{5}{8}, \frac{3}{8}$
3. $\frac{2}{3}, \frac{2}{10}, \frac{2}{5}$
4. $\frac{4}{6}, \frac{5}{6}, \frac{1}{6}$

Vocabulary

mixed number

Learn

PROBLEM Carlos made a large candle from one and two-thirds cups of wax. Write a mixed number for the number of cups of wax.

A **mixed number** is made up of a whole number and a fraction.

The picture shows one and two-thirds cups of wax.

Read: one and two thirds

Write: $1\frac{2}{3}$

HANDS ON

Activity 1 Use pattern blocks.

Materials ■ pattern blocks

A Model one and four sixths.

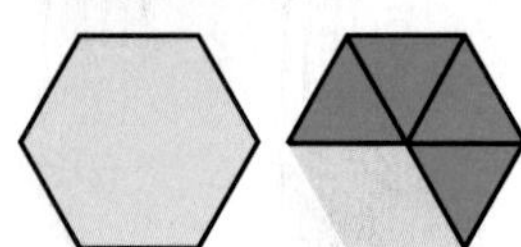

$1 + \frac{4}{6} = 1\frac{4}{6}$, or $1\frac{2}{3}$

B Model two and one half.

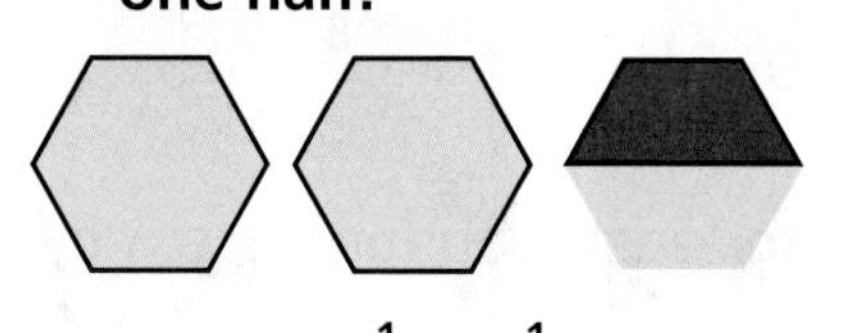

$2 + \frac{1}{2} = 2\frac{1}{2}$

C Model one and one third.

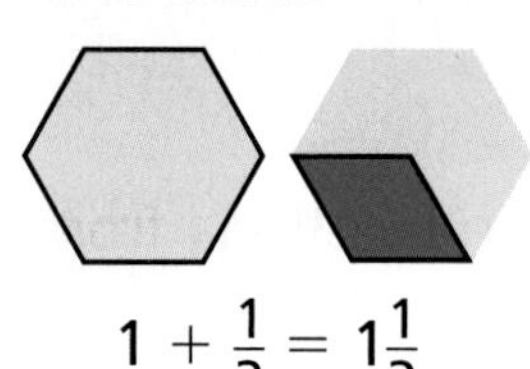

$1 + \frac{1}{3} = 1\frac{1}{3}$

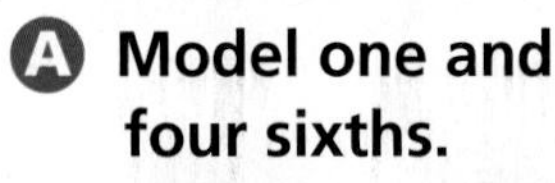

- Look at Example A. How many sixths make two wholes?

You can locate mixed numbers on a number line.

HANDS ON

Activity 2 Use a number line.

Draw a number line to locate $1\frac{4}{5}$ and $3\frac{2}{5}$.

First, divide the number line into four equal parts. Label the whole numbers.

Then, mark five equal parts between each whole number. Each part represents one fifth.

Locate and label $1\frac{4}{5}$ and $3\frac{2}{5}$.

TEKS 4.2B model fraction quantities greater than one using concrete objects and pictorial models. *also* **4.2A, 4.10, 4.14A, 4.14D, 4.15A, 4.15B**

Rename Fractions and Mixed Numbers

Sometimes the numerator of a fraction is greater than the denominator. These fractions have a value greater than 1. They can be renamed as mixed numbers.

ONE WAY **Use fraction bars.**

Rename $1\frac{3}{8}$ as a fraction.

Use fraction bars to rename the mixed number as a fraction. Model $1\frac{3}{8}$.

Place $\frac{1}{8}$ bars under the bars for $1\frac{3}{8}$.

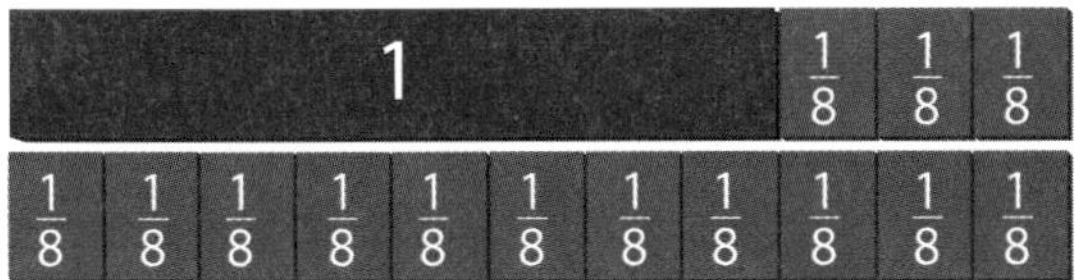

The total number of $\frac{1}{8}$ bars is the numerator of the fraction. The numerator of the fraction is 11.

So, $1\frac{3}{8}$ renamed as a fraction is $\frac{11}{8}$.

ANOTHER WAY **Use division.**

Rename $\frac{11}{3}$ as a mixed number.

Think: $\frac{3}{3} = 1$

Since $\frac{11}{3}$ means $11 \div 3$, you can use division to rename a fraction greater than 1 as a mixed number.

$$\begin{array}{r} 3\text{r}2 \\ 3\overline{)11} \\ -9 \\ \hline 2 \end{array}$$

denominator → 3; 11 ← numerator; 2 ← number of thirds left over

Write the quotient as the whole number part. Then write the remainder as the numerator and the divisor as the denominator.

So, $\frac{11}{3}$ renamed as a mixed number is $3\frac{2}{3}$.

A fraction greater than 1 is sometimes called an *improper fraction.*

So, $\frac{11}{8}$ and $\frac{7}{5}$ are examples of improper fractions.

- How can you use multiplication to rename a mixed number as a fraction?
- What does a mixed number represent?

Guided Practice

1. Copy and complete to name the mixed number shown by the picture. $1 + \frac{\blacksquare}{3} = \blacksquare$

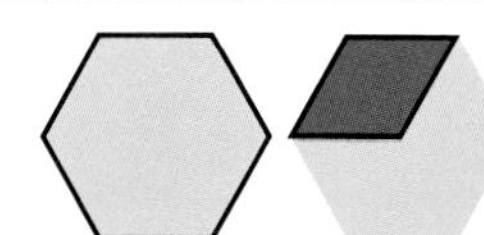

Write a mixed number for each picture.

2. 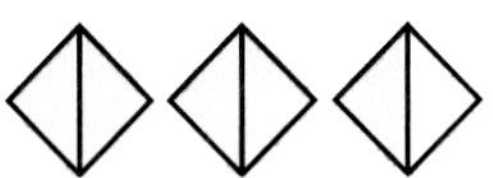

3. 

✓4. 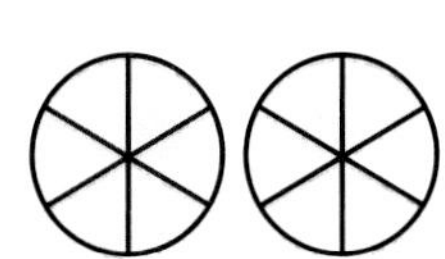

Rename each fraction as a mixed number and each mixed number as a fraction. You may wish to draw a picture.

5. $\frac{15}{2}$ **6.** $2\frac{3}{4}$ **7.** $\frac{12}{7}$ **8.** $9\frac{1}{3}$ **9.** $5\frac{5}{6}$ ✓**10.** $\frac{26}{8}$

11. TALK Math **Explain** how to model $3\frac{1}{6}$.

Independent Practice and Problem Solving

Write a mixed number for each picture.

12. 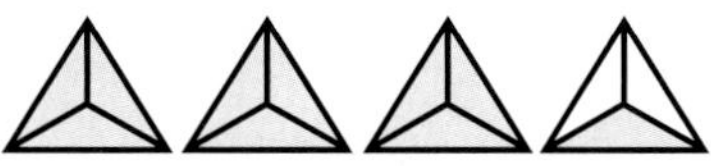

13. 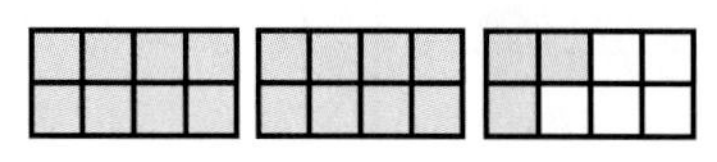

14. 

For 15–20, use the number line to write the letter each mixed number or fraction represents.

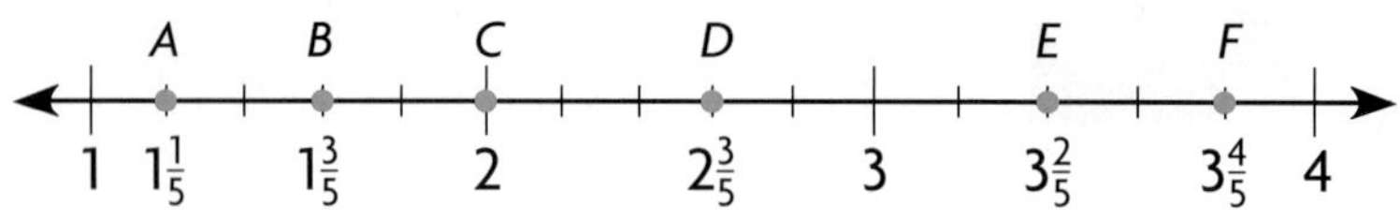

15. $\frac{6}{5}$ **16.** $2\frac{3}{5}$ **17.** $\frac{8}{5}$ **18.** $3\frac{2}{5}$ **19.** $\frac{19}{5}$ **20.** $\frac{10}{5}$

Rename each fraction as a mixed number and each mixed number as a fraction. You may wish to draw a picture.

21. $\frac{13}{5}$ **22.** $1\frac{1}{6}$ **23.** $\frac{21}{4}$ **24.** $2\frac{1}{2}$ **25.** $\frac{13}{6}$ **26.** $\frac{19}{3}$

27. $6\frac{2}{9}$ **28.** $\frac{17}{8}$ **29.** $7\frac{2}{7}$ **30.** $\frac{35}{6}$ **31.** $\frac{28}{12}$ **32.** $5\frac{3}{4}$

33. Jodi cut a piece of ribbon $3\frac{3}{8}$ inches long. Draw a number line and locate $3\frac{3}{8}$.

35. Miguel takes a craft class that lasts $2\frac{1}{2}$ hours. Draw a picture to represent the length of the class.

36. Madeleine buys six and a half dozen candles. Write the number of dozens she bought as a mixed number and a fraction.

34. **Reasoning** Adam needs 1 cup of wax to make a pear-shaped candle. Is this more than or less than $\frac{15}{8}$ cups, the amount of wax needed to make an apple-shaped candle? **Explain.**

37. WRITE Math **Sense or Nonsense** Jack thinks $4\frac{1}{3} = \frac{13}{3}$. Is he correct? You may use models or draw a picture. **Explain.**

 Extra Practice on page 410, Set D

CD ROM **Technology**
Use Harcourt Mega Math, Fraction Action, *Number Line Mine,* Levels F, H.

Mixed Review and TAKS Prep

38. Show tickets cost \$18 for adults and \$13 for children. What is the cost for 2 adults and 3 children? (TEKS 4.4D, p. 190)

39. **TAKS Prep** Stephanie made bread using $\frac{7}{4}$ cups of flour. Which shows $\frac{7}{4}$ as a mixed number? (Obj. 1)

A $1\frac{1}{4}$

B $1\frac{3}{4}$

C $1\frac{4}{7}$

D $4\frac{1}{3}$

40. Ahmed drank $\frac{1}{2}$ cup of milk for breakfast and $\frac{2}{3}$ cup of milk for lunch. Did he drink more milk for breakfast or for lunch? (TEKS 4.2C, p. 398)

41. **TAKS Prep** Drew's class ate $4\frac{5}{8}$ pizzas at their pizza party. Draw a picture to show the mixed number. **Explain** how you drew your picture. (Obj. 1)

Problem Solving and Reasoning

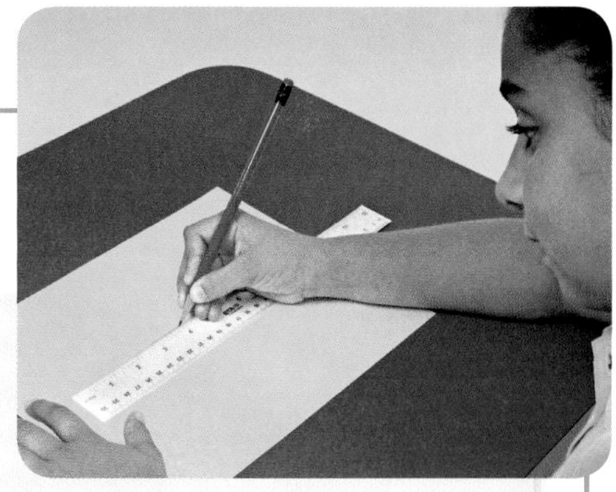

MEASUREMENT A ruler is a type of number line. You can locate mixed numbers on a ruler.

The longest marks on the rulers below show whole numbers. All the marks, including the shortest marks, show eighths. Notice that some marks are longer than others. These marks show quarters and halves.

Find $3\frac{7}{8}$ on the ruler.

Draw a line segment $3\frac{7}{8}$ inches long.

Start at the left edge of the ruler. Draw the line segment to reach $3\frac{7}{8}$ inches.

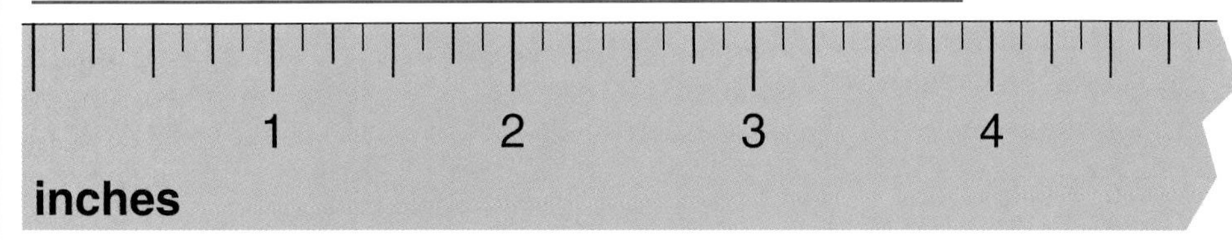

From 3, count seven $\frac{1}{8}$-inch marks to the right of the 3-inch mark to reach $3\frac{7}{8}$.

Use a ruler. Draw a line segment for each length.

1. $2\frac{3}{8}$ inches **2.** $4\frac{1}{8}$ inches **3.** $1\frac{3}{4}$ inches **4.** $3\frac{1}{2}$ inches **5.** $5\frac{1}{4}$ inches

Compare and Order Mixed Numbers

OBJECTIVE: Compare and order mixed numbers.

Compare. Use <, >, or =.

1. $\frac{2}{5}$ ● $\frac{4}{5}$
2. $\frac{6}{8}$ ● $\frac{6}{8}$
3. $\frac{5}{7}$ ● $\frac{5}{14}$
4. $\frac{2}{12}$ ● $\frac{3}{6}$
5. $\frac{8}{9}$ ● $\frac{2}{3}$

Learn

PROBLEM Amanda spent some of her time last week doing different after school activities. The table shows the amount of time she spent doing each activity. Did she spend more time working on her science project or at soccer practice?

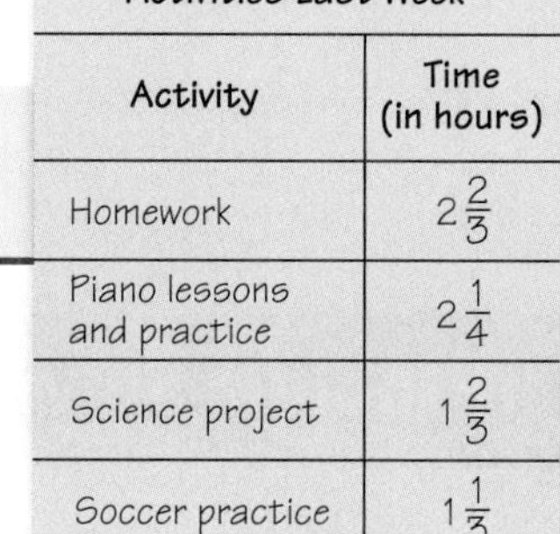

Amanda's After School Activities Last Week

Activity	Time (in hours)
Homework	$2\frac{2}{3}$
Piano lessons and practice	$2\frac{1}{4}$
Science project	$1\frac{2}{3}$
Soccer practice	$1\frac{1}{3}$

HANDS ON

Activity 1

Materials ■ fraction bars

A Compare mixed numbers with like denominators.

Compare $1\frac{2}{3}$ and $1\frac{1}{3}$ using fraction bars.

Model $1\frac{2}{3}$, then line up the bars for $1\frac{1}{3}$ below it.

1	$\frac{1}{3}$	$\frac{1}{3}$
1	$\frac{1}{3}$	

Compare the two rows of fraction bars. The longer row represents the greater mixed number.

$1\frac{2}{3} > 1\frac{1}{3}$, so Amanda spent more time on her science project than at soccer practice.

- When you compare $1\frac{2}{3}$ and $1\frac{1}{3}$, why do you have to compare only the fraction parts?

B Compare mixed numbers with unlike denominators.

Did Amanda spend less time doing homework or at piano lessons and practice?

Compare $2\frac{2}{3}$ and $2\frac{1}{4}$ using number lines.

Draw a number line, and divide it into thirds between each whole number. Locate $2\frac{2}{3}$.

Draw another number line, and divide it into fourths between each whole number. Locate $2\frac{1}{4}$.

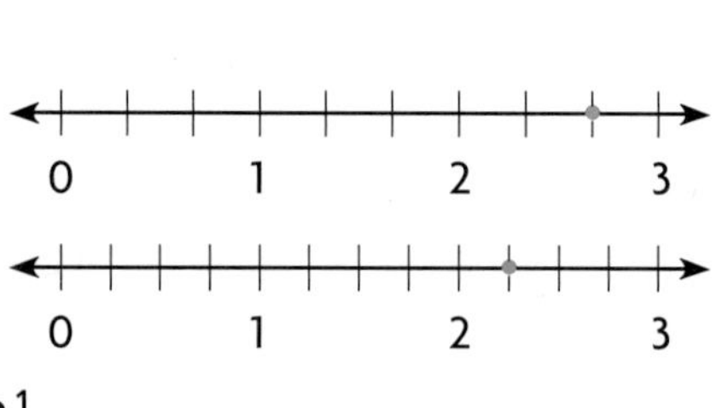

The mixed number farther to the right is the greater number.

$2\frac{2}{3} > 2\frac{1}{4}$, so Amanda spent less time at piano lessons and practice.

TEKS 4.2C compare and order fractions using concrete objects and pictorial models. *also* 4.2A, 4.2B, 4.10A, 4.14A, 4.14D, 4.15A, 4.15B, 4.16B

Activity 2 Compare and order mixed numbers.

ONE WAY **Use drawings.**

Compare and then order $2\frac{1}{2}$, $1\frac{1}{6}$, and $1\frac{3}{4}$ from greatest to least.

Draw pictures for $2\frac{1}{2}$, $1\frac{1}{6}$ and $1\frac{3}{4}$.

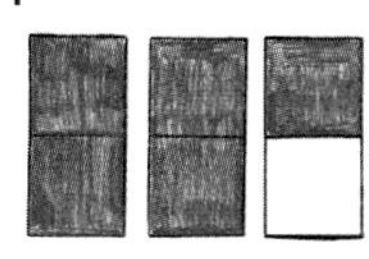

$2\frac{1}{2}$

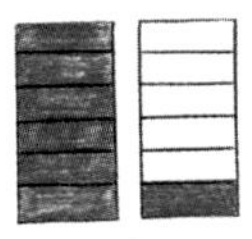

$1\frac{1}{6}$

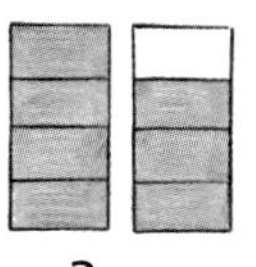

$1\frac{3}{4}$

First, compare the amount shaded to represent the whole numbers.
Since $2 > 1$, $2\frac{1}{2}$ is the greatest.

Then compare the other two fractions by finding equivalent fractions.

$1\frac{1}{6} = 1\frac{2}{12}$ $\quad$ $1\frac{3}{4} = 1\frac{9}{12}$

Since, $2 < 9$, $1\frac{3}{4}$ is greater than $1\frac{1}{6}$.

So, the order from greatest to least is $2\frac{1}{2}$, $1\frac{3}{4}$, $1\frac{1}{6}$.

Math Idea
To order mixed numbers, compare the whole number parts first. Then compare the fraction parts.

ANOTHER WAY **Use a number line.**

Order $\frac{5}{2}$, $2\frac{3}{4}$, and $2\frac{3}{8}$ from least to greatest using a number line.

Find equivalent fractions. $\frac{5}{2} = 2\frac{1}{2} = 2\frac{4}{8}$ $\quad$ $2\frac{3}{4} = 2\frac{6}{8}$

Draw a number line showing 2 and 3 with the distance between them divided into eighths.
Place each mixed number on the number line.

2 $\frac{1}{8}$ $\frac{2}{8}$ $\frac{3}{8}$ $\frac{4}{8}$ $\frac{5}{8}$ $\frac{6}{8}$ $\frac{7}{8}$ 3

The mixed number farthest to the right is the greatest number.
The mixed number farthest to the left is the least number.

So, the order from least to greatest is $2\frac{3}{8}$, $\frac{5}{2}$, $2\frac{3}{4}$.

Guided Practice

1. Use the number line. Is $3\frac{4}{5}$ greater than or less than $3\frac{2}{5}$?

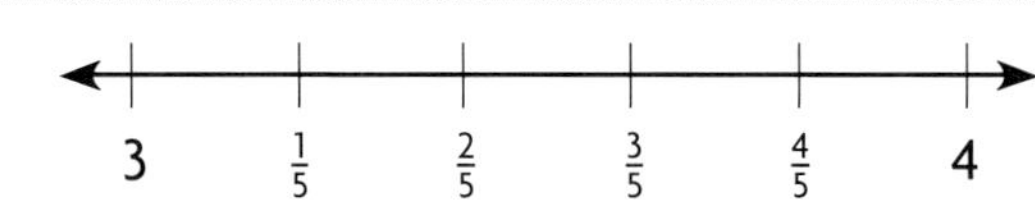

Compare the mixed numbers. Use <, >, or =.

2.

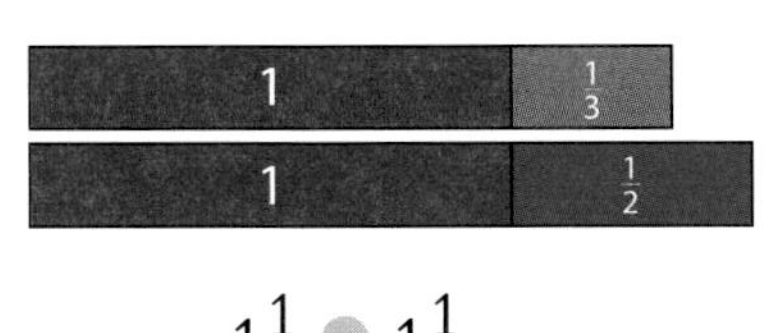

$1\frac{1}{3}$ ● $1\frac{1}{2}$

3.

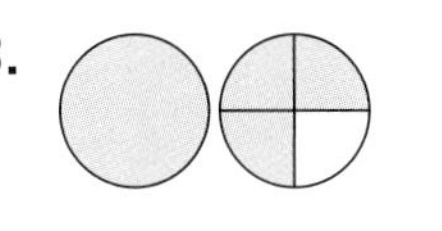

$1\frac{3}{4}$ ● $1\frac{3}{8}$

✔ 4.

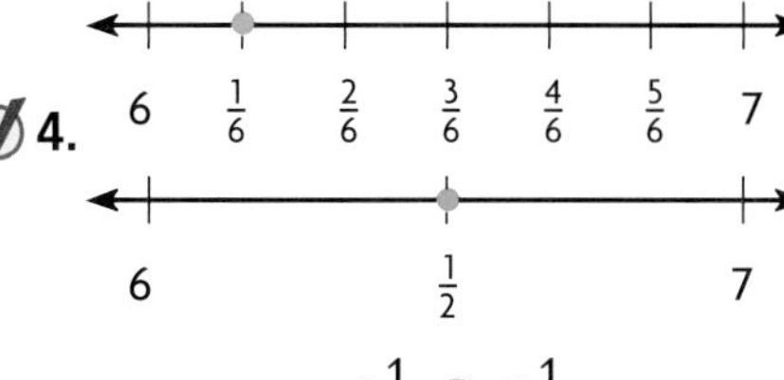

$6\frac{1}{6}$ ● $6\frac{1}{2}$

Order the mixed numbers from greatest to least. You may use a model.

5. $4\frac{1}{6}, 3\frac{2}{3}, 4\frac{3}{4}$ **6.** $5\frac{1}{4}, 6\frac{3}{8}, 5\frac{1}{12}$ **7.** $3\frac{3}{4}, 3\frac{2}{5}, 3\frac{1}{2}$ **8.** $1\frac{7}{9}, 1\frac{1}{2}, 1\frac{12}{18}$

9. TALK Math **Explain** how you would compare $4\frac{5}{12}$ and $2\frac{7}{8}$.

Independent Practice and Problem Solving

Compare the mixed numbers. Write <, >, or = for each ●.

10.

$1\frac{3}{4}$ ● $1\frac{2}{5}$

11.

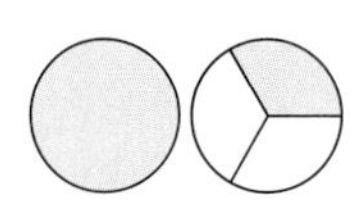

$1\frac{1}{8}$ ● $1\frac{1}{3}$

12.

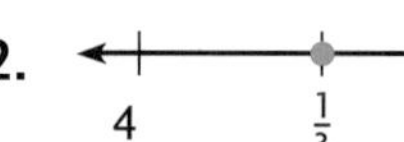

$4\frac{2}{3}$ ● $4\frac{1}{3}$

Order the mixed numbers from least to greatest. You may use a model.

13. $8\frac{3}{4}, 7\frac{3}{10}, 8\frac{1}{2}$ **14.** $3\frac{1}{2}, 3\frac{2}{3}, 2\frac{4}{16}$ **15.** $4\frac{2}{6}, 4\frac{2}{3}, 4\frac{2}{12}$ **16.** $5\frac{2}{5}, 5\frac{6}{10}, 5\frac{2}{7}$

Algebra **Find the missing number.**

17. $1\frac{1}{4} < 1\frac{1}{\blacksquare} < 1\frac{1}{2}$ **18.** $2\frac{5}{6} > 2\frac{\blacksquare}{5} > 2\frac{1}{3}$ **19.** $4\frac{\blacksquare}{6} < 4\frac{2}{5} < 4\frac{3}{4}$ **20.** $2\frac{1}{5} < 2\frac{3}{10} < 2\frac{\blacksquare}{2}$

USE DATA **For 21–23, use the table.**

How Amanda Spends Her Day

Activity	Free Time	Homework	Sleep
Time (in hours)	$2\frac{3}{4}$	$2\frac{2}{3}$	$9\frac{1}{4}$

21. Which activity takes Amanda the most time? the least time?

22. Which activity does Amanda spend $\frac{11}{4}$ hours doing? Which activity does she spend almost as much time doing?

23. **Pose a Problem** Use the information in the table to write a problem involving ordering mixed numbers. Have a classmate solve the problem.

24. WRITE Math **What's the Error?** Amy says that $3\frac{1}{2}$ is less than $\frac{13}{4}$ because a denominator of 2 is less than a denominator of 4. Describe her error.

Mixed Review and TAKS Prep

25. Find the missing numerator in the equivalent fraction. (TEKS 4.2A, p. 392)

$$\frac{\blacksquare}{3} = \frac{8}{12}$$

26. Julia hiked $\frac{14}{3}$ miles. Write $\frac{14}{3}$ as a mixed number. (TEKS 4.2B, p. 402)

27. **TAKS Prep** The lengths of four movies are shown. Which movie is the longest? (Obj. 1)

A $1\frac{7}{8}$ hours **B** $2\frac{2}{3}$ hours

C $2\frac{2}{5}$ hours **D** $2\frac{1}{2}$ hours

 Extra Practice on page 410, Set E

WRITE Math WORKSHOP

Write Number Riddles

Ms. Owens asked her students to write a riddle about fractions and mixed numbers. She told them to explain how they used what they knew about fractions and mixed numbers to write a riddle that had only one answer.

Elena's group wrote this riddle and explanation.

I am a mixed number between 1 and 2.

My fraction part is greater than $\frac{1}{2}$.

My denominator is 8 and my numerator is an even number.

What number am I?

First, we drew a number line and located a mixed number on it.

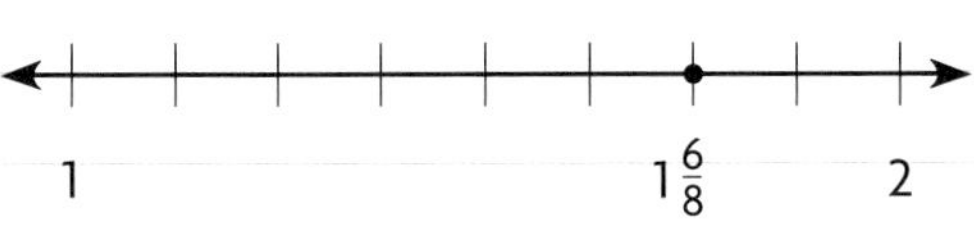

Our first clue tells about the whole number part of the answer to our riddle.

Next, we decided to give clues about the numerator and denominator in our riddle.

Finally, we checked our riddle.
$\frac{5}{8}, \frac{6}{8}, \frac{7}{8}$ are greater than $\frac{1}{2}$. 6 is the only even numerator. The answer is $1\frac{6}{8}$.

Tips

- Use a drawing or model to understand what is being asked.
- You may want to use comparisons in the riddle.
- Include clues about the numerator and the denominator of a fraction.
- Put the clues together to write the riddle.
- Solve your riddle to check that there are enough clues. Make sure the clues make sense and there is only one correct answer.

Problem Solving Write a number riddle for each answer given.

1. a fraction less than $\frac{1}{2}$
2. a fraction greater than $\frac{1}{2}$
3. a mixed number between 2 and 3
4. any fraction or mixed number written in simplest form

Extra Practice

Set A Write a fraction for the shaded part. Write a fraction for the unshaded part. (pp. 388–391)

1. 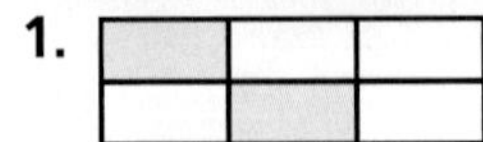
2. 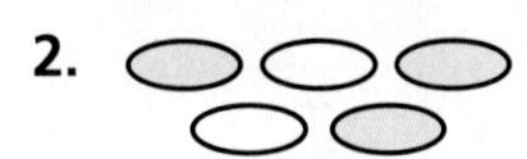
3.
4.

Set B Find two equivalent fractions for each. (pp. 392–395)

1. $\frac{3}{4}$ 2. $\frac{2}{10}$ 3. $\frac{8}{12}$ 4. $\frac{5}{8}$ 5. $\frac{3}{9}$ 6. $\frac{5}{5}$

7. Pam baked 20 cupcakes. She took 15 of them to school. Write the fraction of cupcakes she took to school in simplest form.

Set C Order the fractions from least to greatest. You may use a model (pp. 400–401)

1. $\frac{1}{3}, \frac{1}{8}, \frac{1}{6}$ 2. $\frac{3}{4}, \frac{6}{12}, \frac{2}{3}$ 3. $\frac{7}{8}, \frac{1}{2}, \frac{12}{12}$ 4. $\frac{3}{5}, \frac{9}{10}, \frac{1}{2}$

5. Haley jogged $\frac{7}{8}$ mile. Luke jogged $\frac{5}{6}$ mile. Rosa jogged $\frac{1}{4}$ mile. Who jogged farthest?

Set D Write a mixed number for each picture. (pp. 402-404)

1. 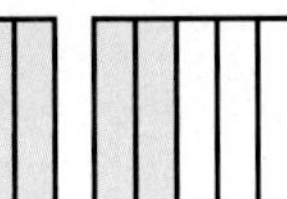
2. 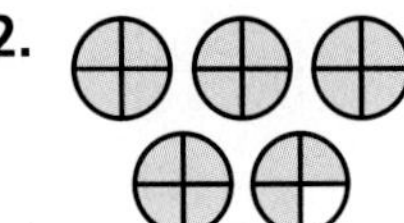
3. 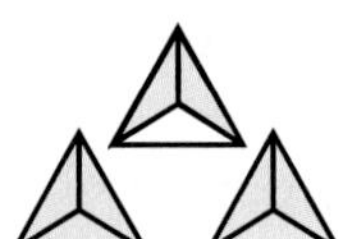
4. 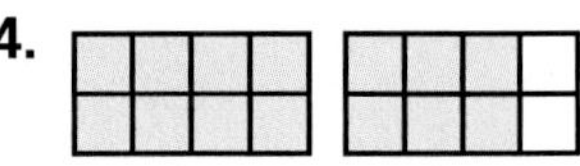

Rename each fraction as a mixed number and each mixed number as a fraction. You may use a model.

5. $\frac{9}{5}$ 6. $1\frac{2}{3}$ 7. $\frac{7}{3}$ 8. $3\frac{1}{4}$ 9. $\frac{12}{5}$ 10. $4\frac{1}{10}$

Set E Compare the mixed numbers. Use <, >, or = for each ●. (pp. 406-408)

1. 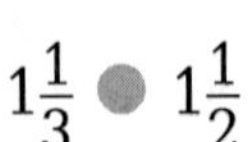

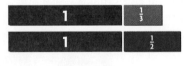

$1\frac{1}{3}$ ● $1\frac{1}{2}$

2. 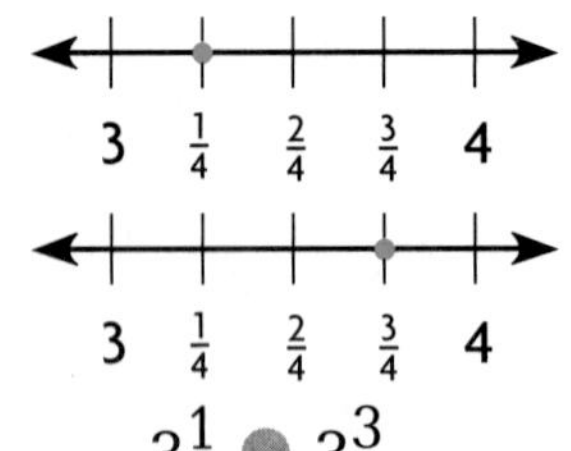

$3\frac{1}{4}$ ● $3\frac{3}{4}$

3. 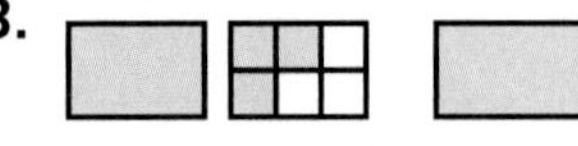

$1\frac{3}{6}$ ● $1\frac{5}{8}$

Order the mixed numbers from greatest to least. You may use a model.

4. $4\frac{5}{6}, 4\frac{3}{9}, 4\frac{2}{3}$ 5. $6\frac{3}{8}, 5\frac{3}{4}, 6\frac{1}{2}$ 6. $1\frac{2}{3}, 1\frac{5}{6}, 1\frac{5}{12}$ 7. $2\frac{1}{2}, 2\frac{7}{10}, 2\frac{3}{5}$

Technology
Use Harcourt Mega Math, Fraction Action, *Fraction Flare Up*, Levels B, C, D, E, F.

TECHNOLOGY CONNECTION

*i*Tools: Fractions (TEKS 4.14D, 4.2A, 4.2B, 4.2C, 4.14A, 4.15A, 4.15B)

Kelly's cookie recipe calls for $\frac{3}{4}$ cup brown sugar and $\frac{2}{3}$ cup powdered sugar. Does the recipe call for more brown sugar or more powdered sugar?

Step 1 Click on *Fractions*. Select *Compare* from the *Activities* menu.

Step 2 Click the fraction bar for $\frac{1}{4}$. Then click in the top workspace 3 times. Notice that $\frac{3}{4}$ appears at the bottom of the screen.

If you make a mistake, click on the eraser.

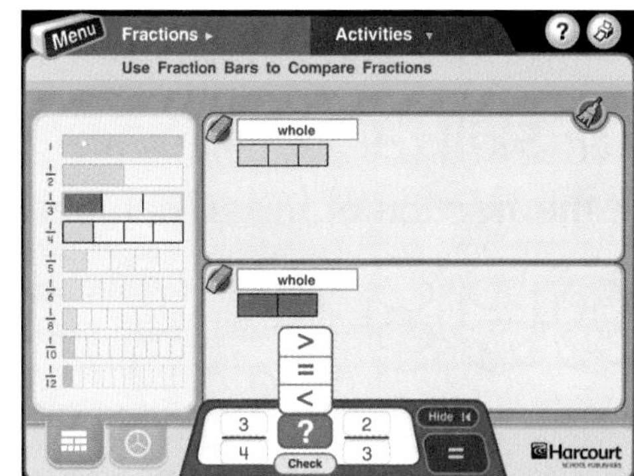

Step 3 Click the fraction bar for $\frac{1}{3}$. Then click in the bottom workspace 2 times. Notice that $\frac{2}{3}$ appears at the bottom of the screen.

Step 4 Click on the "?". Choose $>$, $=$, or $<$ to make a true comparison. Then click on *Check*.

$\frac{3}{4} > \frac{2}{3}$, so the recipe calls for more brown sugar than powdered sugar.

Try It

1. Click on the tab for Fraction Circles at the bottom of the left column. Do fraction circles make it easier to compare the fractions? **Explain.**

Click on the broom to clear the workspace.

Follow the same steps to compare fractions. Write $<$, $>$, or $=$ for each ●.

2. $\frac{3}{6}$ ● $\frac{4}{6}$
3. $\frac{4}{10}$ ● $\frac{1}{3}$
4. $\frac{3}{5}$ ● $\frac{5}{8}$
5. $\frac{4}{6}$ ● $\frac{8}{12}$
6. **Explore More Explain** how you decided whether to use $<$, $>$, or $=$ when comparing the fractions above.

GO ONLINE **Technology** *i*Tools are available online or on CD-ROM.

Chapter 15 Review/Test

Check Vocabulary and Concepts

Choose the best term from the box.

VOCABULARY
equivalent fractions
fraction
mixed number
simplest form

1. A ___?___ is made up of a whole number and a fraction. (TEKS 4.2B, p. 402)
2. Two or more fractions that name the same amount are ___?___. (TEKS 4.2A, p. 392)
3. A ___?___ is a number that names part of a whole or part of a set. (TEKS 4.2, p. 388)

Check Skills

Write the fraction or mixed number for the shaded part. (TEKS 4.2, pp. 388–391, TEKS 4.2B, pp. 402–405)

4. 
5. 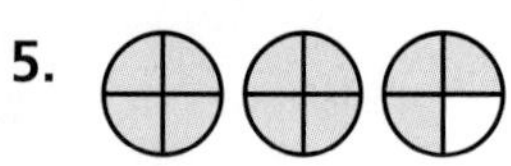
6. 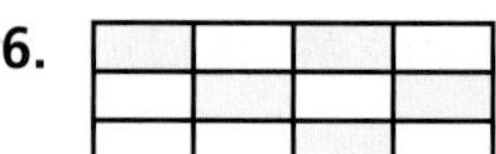
7. 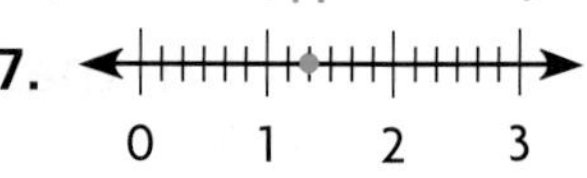

Write two equivalent fractions for each. You may use a model or drawing. (TEKS 4.2A, pp. 392–395)

8. $\frac{2}{12}$
9. $\frac{15}{20}$
10. $\frac{6}{9}$
11. $\frac{9}{16}$

Model to compare. Write <, >, or = for each ●. (TEKS 4.2C, pp. 398–399, 406–409)

12. $\frac{2}{3}$ ● $\frac{9}{12}$
13. $4\frac{1}{3}$ ● $4\frac{1}{4}$
14. $\frac{9}{10}$ ● $\frac{3}{5}$
15. $2\frac{2}{6}$ ● $2\frac{3}{9}$

Order the fractions or mixed numbers from greatest to least. (TEKS 4.2C, pp. 400–401, 406–409)

16. $\frac{1}{7}, \frac{1}{9}, \frac{1}{3}$
17. $2\frac{2}{3}, 2\frac{1}{6}, 2\frac{5}{12}$
18. $\frac{7}{8}, \frac{12}{12}, \frac{3}{4}$
19. $1\frac{2}{3}, 1\frac{3}{4}, 1\frac{5}{6}$

Rename each fraction as a mixed number and each mixed number as a fraction. (TEKS 4.2B, pp. 402–405)

20. $4\frac{1}{4}$
21. $\frac{17}{5}$
22. $2\frac{7}{8}$
23. $\frac{14}{9}$

Check Problem Solving

Solve. (TEKS 4.14C, pp. 396–397)

24. Reggie has a set of measuring cups. Three of the sizes are $\frac{1}{2}$, $\frac{1}{4}$ and $\frac{1}{3}$ cup. Which measuring cup holds the greatest amount?

25. WRITE Math Meg ran $3\frac{1}{2}$ laps, Jill ran $3\frac{3}{8}$ laps, and Randy ran $3\frac{1}{4}$ laps around a track. Explain how to use a number line to find who ran the greatest distance.

GO ONLINE **Technology** Use *Online Assessment.*

Enrich • Add and Subtract Like Fractions

PATTERN-BLOCK FRACTIONS

When two fractions have the same denominator, they are **like fractions**. You can use pattern blocks to add and subtract like fractions.

Use pattern blocks to represent fractions.

1

$\frac{1}{2}$

$\frac{1}{3}$

$\frac{1}{6}$

Sort It Out

A Add using pattern blocks.

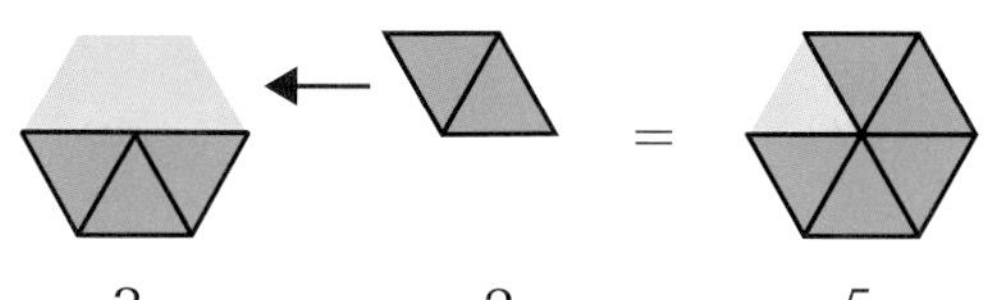

$\frac{3}{6} + \frac{2}{6} = \frac{5}{6}$

So, $\frac{3}{6} + \frac{2}{6} = \frac{5}{6}$.

B Subtract using pattern blocks.

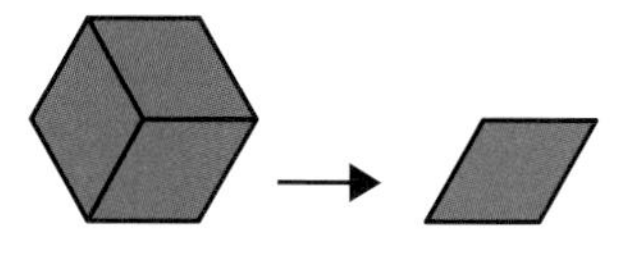

$\frac{3}{3} - \frac{1}{3} = \frac{2}{3}$

So, $\frac{3}{3} - \frac{1}{3} = \frac{2}{3}$.

Solve It

Find the sum or difference.

1. 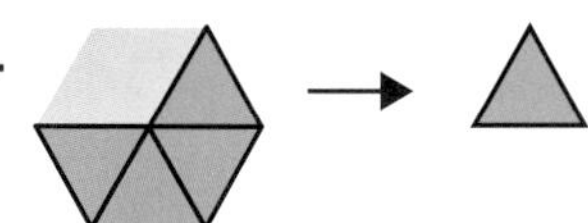

$\frac{4}{6} - \frac{1}{6}$

2. 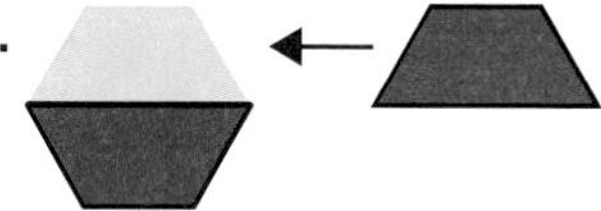

$\frac{1}{2} + \frac{1}{2}$

3.  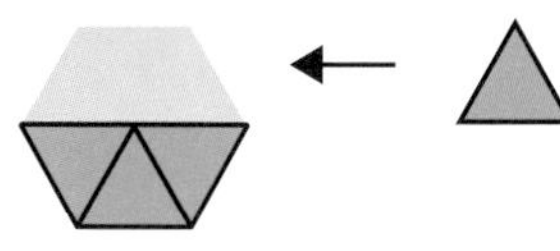

$\frac{3}{6} + \frac{1}{6}$

4. 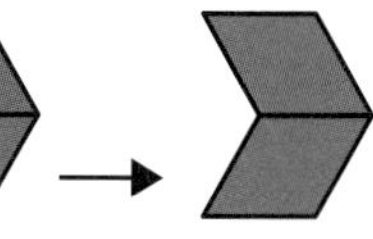

$\frac{3}{3} - \frac{2}{3}$

Piece It Together

WRITE Math **Explain** how else you could model addition or subtraction of like fractions.

Getting Ready for the TAKS
Chapters 1–15

Number, Operation, and Quantitative Reasoning TAKS Obj. 1

1. Amanda makes bead necklaces. She uses 25 beads in each necklace. How many beads does she need to make 36 necklaces?

   A 61   C 610

   B 90   D 900

Look for key words.

See Item 2. To find how many more people live in Lakeville in the summer, you need to find the difference.

2. The population of Lakeville is 2,124 in the winter and 6,903 in the summer. How many more people live in Lakeville in the summer than in the winter?

   F 9,027   H 4,879

   G 4,779   J 3,779

3. Which of the following is equivalent to the shaded part of the rectangle?

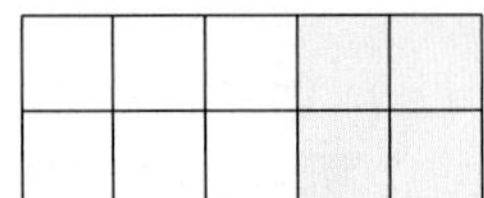

   A $\frac{1}{2}$ C $\frac{4}{6}$

   B $\frac{2}{5}$ D $\frac{2}{10}$

4. WRITE Math **Explain** how to find 12×26.

Geometry and Spatial Reasoning TAKS Obj. 3

5. Which line appears to be perpendicular to line *LQ*?

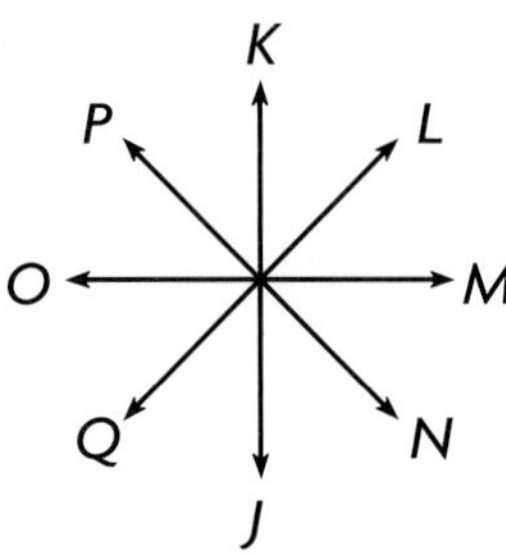

   F Line *KJ*

   G Line *MO*

   H Line *NP*

   J Not here

6. Jamie draws two triangles that appear to be congruent. Which of the following could be Jamie's triangles?

   A

   B

   C

   D

7. WRITE Math **Explain** the difference between an acute angle and an obtuse angle.

Patterns, Relationships, and Algebraic Thinking TAKS Obj. 2

8. The table shows how much Lana earns for mowing lawns.

Lawn Mowing				
Number of Lawns	1	2	3	4
Money Earned	\$5	\$10	\$15	\$20

How much will Lana earn if she mows 7 lawns?

F \$11

G \$24

H \$28

J \$35

9. In which number sentence does 7 make the equation true?

A $14 \div ■ = 7$

B $20 \div ■ = 3$

C $42 \div ■ = 7$

D $56 \div ■ = 8$

10. Tito's bookcase has 14 shelves. Each shelf holds 20 books. How many books does the bookcase hold in all?

F 28

G 142

H 280

J 2,800

11. WRITE Math **Explain** how to use patterns to multiply a number by 10.

Probability and Statistics TAKS Obj. 5

12. The graph below shows the number of medals won by the students in each fourth-grade class.

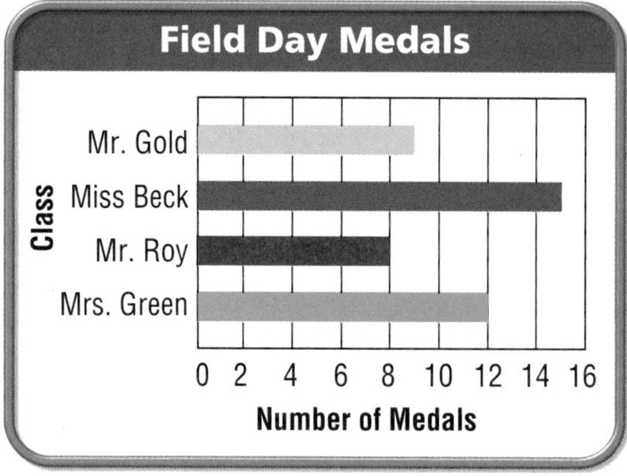

How many more medals were won by the students in Mr. Gold's class than by the students in Mr. Roy's class?

A 1

B 3

C 4

D 8

13. WRITE Math Randall takes a survey to find the number of pets owned by the students in his class. He finds that 4 students do not have pets, 8 students have 1 pet, 4 students have 2 pets, and 2 students have 3 or more pets. **Explain** why the pictograph does **NOT** represent Randall's data.

Number of Pets Owned	
Number of Pets	**Number of Students**
0	🯅🯅🯅🯅
1	🯅🯅🯅🯅
2	🯅🯅🯅🯅
3 or more	🯅🯅
Key: Each 🯅 = 2 students.	

16 Understand Decimals and Place Value

The Big Idea The place values to the right of the decimal point in the base-ten system name numbers less than one.

Investigate

The scoreboard shows some scores from the World Olympics Gymnastics Academy Classic in 2003. You are reporting the scores in the school newspaper. What can you write about the outcome of this competition?

Level 5 Girls 9 Years Old All-Around-Scores	
Name	Score
Danielle Blohm	27.25
Danielle Carty	30.35
Lauren Hulshouser	26.80
Sydney Johnson	33.20
Sarah Kinder	30.85
Karla London	32.90
Rachel Lusk	30.90
Caitlin Snell	31.05

Plano, Texas, is the home of the World Olympics Gymnastics Academy. More than 150 state, national, regional, and world champions have trained there.

Technology
Student pages are available in the Student eBook.

Show What You Know

Check your understanding of important skills needed for success in Chapter 16.

▶ Model Fractions and Mixed Numbers

Write the fraction or the mixed number for the shaded part.

1. 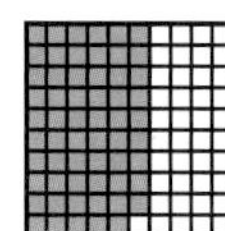

2. 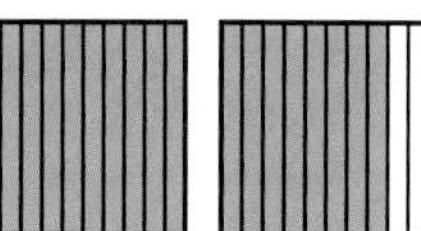

3. 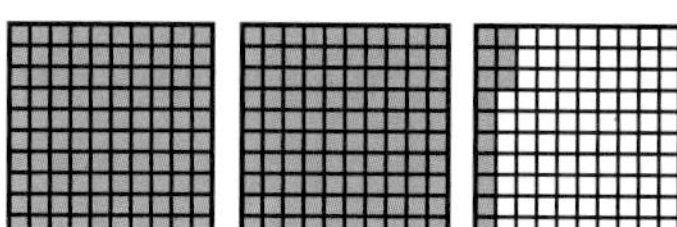

▶ Fractions with Denominators of 10 and 100

Write a fraction for each. You may wish to draw a picture.

4. six tenths

5. eight hundredths

6. thirty-three hundredths

Complete to show equivalent fractions. You may wish to draw a picture.

7. $\frac{1}{10} = \frac{■}{100}$

8. $\frac{4}{10} = \frac{■}{100}$

9. $\frac{8}{10} = \frac{■}{100}$

▶ Money Notation

Name the amount shown.

10.    

11.      

Write a decimal for the money amount.

12. five dollars and twenty-eight cents

13. twelve dollars and five cents

VOCABULARY POWER

CHAPTER VOCABULARY

decimal
decimal point
equal to (=)
fraction
hundredth
mixed number
not equal to (≠)
tenth

WARM-UP WORDS

decimal a number with the one or more digits to the right of the decimal point

decimal point a symbol used to separate dollars from cents in money amounts and to separate the ones and the tenths places in a decimal

Relate Fractions and Decimals

OBJECTIVE: Model, read, and write fractions as decimals.

Quick Review

Write in simplest form.

1. $\frac{5}{10}$
2. $\frac{8}{10}$
3. $\frac{25}{100}$
4. $\frac{60}{100}$
5. $\frac{75}{100}$

Vocabulary

decimal

decimal point

Learn

PROBLEM Ty is reading a 100-page book about metamorphic rocks. He has read $\frac{7}{10}$ of the book. Only 1 page has a picture. What decimal part of the book has Ty read? What decimal part has pictures?

A **decimal** is a number with one or more digits to the right of the **decimal point.**

Activity 1 Use models to read and write fractions as decimals.

Materials ■ decimal models

Shade the model to show 1.		Shade $\frac{7}{10}$ of the model.		Shade $\frac{1}{100}$ of the model.	
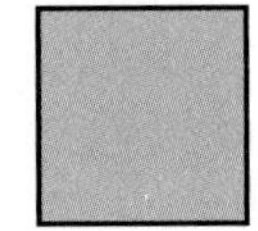		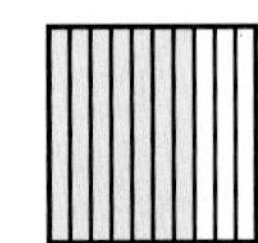		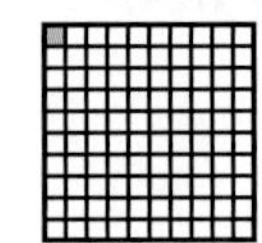	
Fraction	**Decimal**	**Fraction**	**Decimal**	**Fraction**	**Decimal**
Read: one	**Read:** one	**Read:** seven tenths	**Read:** seven tenths	**Read:** one hundredth	**Read:** one hundredth
Write: $\frac{1}{1}$	**Write:** 1.0	**Write:** $\frac{7}{10}$	**Write:** 0.7	**Write:** $\frac{1}{100}$	**Write:** 0.01

So, Ty has read 0.7 of the book, and $\frac{1}{100}$, or 0.01 of the book has pictures.

More Examples

A **Lea read $\frac{5}{10}$ of a book.**

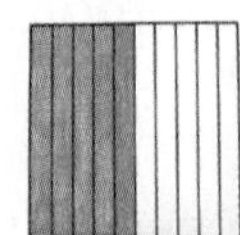

Fraction	**Decimal**
Read: five tenths	**Read:** five tenths
Write: $\frac{5}{10}$	**Write:** 0.5

B **$\frac{25}{100}$ of the book has illustrations.**

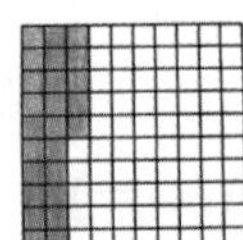

Fraction	**Decimal**
Read: twenty-five hundredths	**Read:** twenty-five hundredths
Write: $\frac{25}{100}$	**Write:** 0.25

TEKS 4.2D relate decimals to fractions that name tenths and hundredths using concrete objects and pictorial models. *also* **4.1B, 4.10, 4.14A, 4.14D, 4.15A, 4.15B, 4.16A**

Example 1 Use place value to read and write decimals.

Decimals, like whole numbers, can be written in standard form, word form, and expanded form.

Ones	.	Tenths	Hundredths
0	.	2	8
0×1	.	2×0.1	8×0.01
0	.	0.2	0.08

Standard Form	Word Form	Expanded Form
0.6	six tenths	0.6
0.28	twenty-eight hundredths	0.2 + 0.08
$0.14	fourteen cents	$0.10 + $0.04

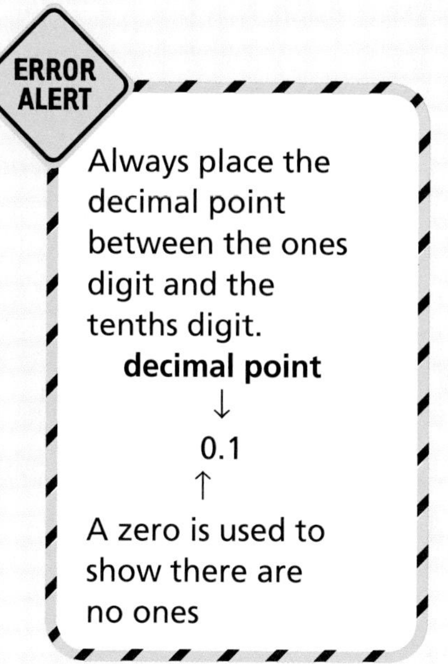

ERROR ALERT
Always place the decimal point between the ones digit and the tenths digit.
decimal point
0.1
A zero is used to show there are no ones

A number line divided into 100 equal parts can be used to model fractions and decimals.

Example 2 Use a number line to show the same amount.

Locate the point 0.75. What fraction names this point on the number line?

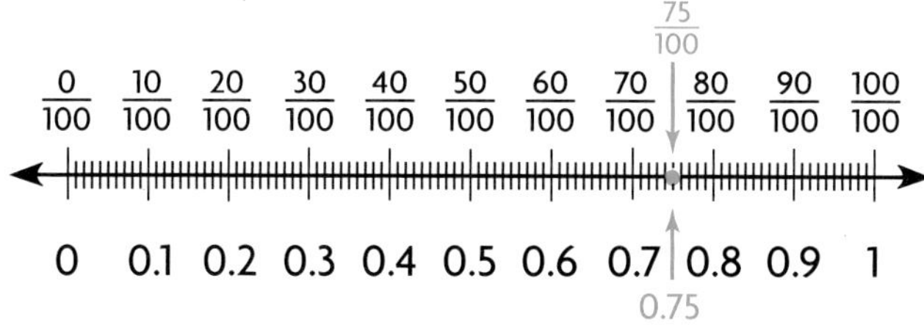

So, 0.75 names the same amount as $\frac{75}{100}$, or $\frac{3}{4}$.

- Label three other points on your number line. Write the decimal and fraction that names each point.

Guided Practice

1. Copy the model and shade to show $\frac{8}{10}$. Write the amount as a decimal.

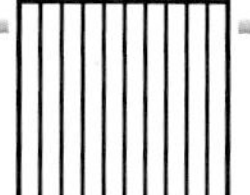

Write the fraction and decimal shown by each model.

2. 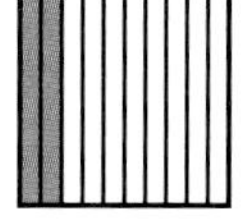

3. 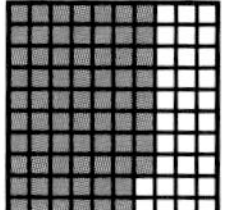

4. 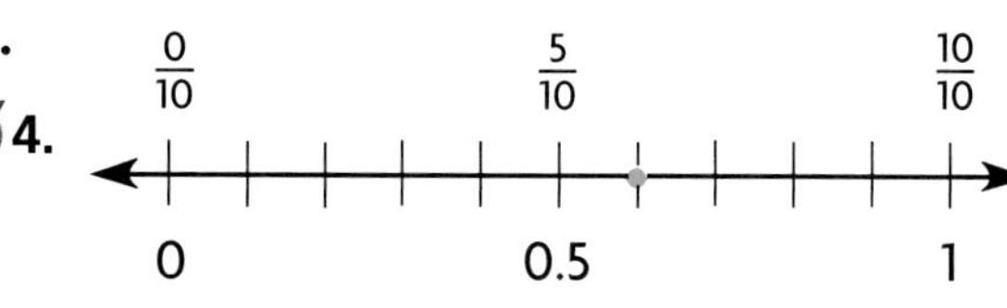

Write each fraction as a decimal. You may use a model or drawing.

5. $\frac{2}{10}$ **6.** $\frac{80}{100}$ **7.** $\frac{55}{100}$ **8.** $\frac{42}{100}$ ✓ **9.** $\frac{5}{100}$

10. **TALK Math** **Explain** what you notice about the size of the models that represent one whole, one tenth, and one hundredth. Tell how they are related.

Independent Practice and Problem Solving

Write the fraction and decimal shown by each model.

11. 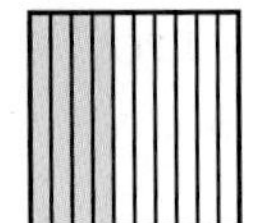

12.

13. 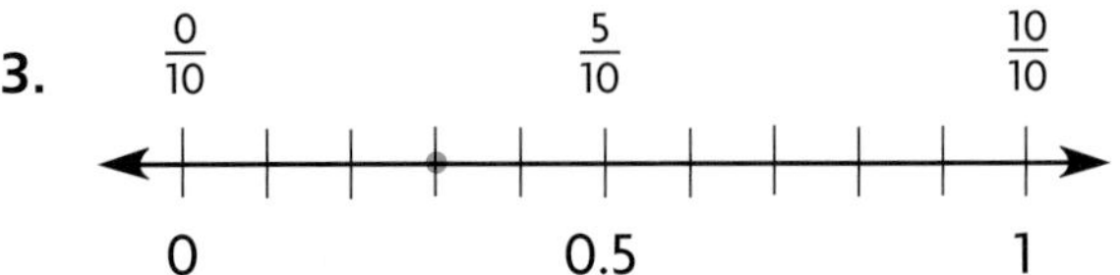

Write each fraction as a decimal. You may use a model or drawing.

14. $\frac{9}{10}$ **15.** $\frac{67}{100}$ **16.** $\frac{4}{10}$ **17.** $\frac{42}{100}$ **18.** $\frac{6}{10}$

Algebra **Find the missing number. You may use a model or drawing.**

19. 6 tenths + 2 hundredths = 0.■2

20. 0 tenths + ■ hundredths = 0.04

21. ■ tenths + 5 hundredths = 0.75

22. 4 tenths + 0 hundredths = 0.■

USE DATA **For 23–24, use the table.**

23. What part of the rocks listed in the table are igneous? Write your answer as a decimal.

24. Sedimentary rocks make of 0.3 of Ramon's collection. Write this decimal as a fraction and in word form.

25. Josh paid for three books with two $20 bills. He received $1 in change. Each book was the same price. How much did each book cost?

26. **WRITE Math** **Explain** how to use a model to write the fraction $\frac{12}{100}$ as a decimal.

Classifying Rocks

Name	Type
Basalt	Igneous
Rhyolite	Igneous
Granite	Igneous
Peridotite	Igneous
Shale	Sedimentary
Limestone	Sedimentary
Sandstone	Sedimentary
Gness	Metamorphic
Slate	Metamorphic
Scoria	Igneous

CD ROM **Technology**
Use Harcourt Mega Math, Fraction Action, *Fraction Flare Up*, Level N.

 Extra Practice on page 438, Set A

Mixed Review and TAKS Prep

27. Each student in the culture club bought tickets to 7 shows during the year. Each ticket cost $8. If there are 37 students in the club, how much in all did they spend on show tickets? (TEKS 4.4D, p. 242)

28. **TAKS Prep** Which decimal does the model represent? (Obj. 1)

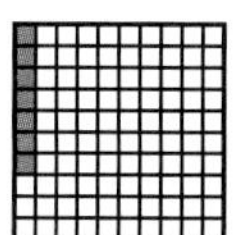

A 0.7 C 0.07

B 0.70 D 0.007

29. Bob used 7 eggs from a carton of 12. He used the expression $12 - n$ to find the number of eggs he had left. If n represents the number of eggs he used, how many eggs did Bob have left? (TEKS 4.15B, p. 68)

30. **TAKS Prep** Hal walks 0.5 mile to school. Anya walks $\frac{3}{10}$ mile to the same school. Hal says he has to walk farther than Anya. **Explain** how to use a number line to show if Hal is correct. (Obj. 1)

Problem Solving and Reasoning

TECHNOLOGY Ken says that 0.45 of the rocks in his collection are igneous rocks. What fraction of Ken's collection contains igneous rocks?

You can use a calculator to change a decimal to an equivalent fraction and a fraction to an equivalent decimal.

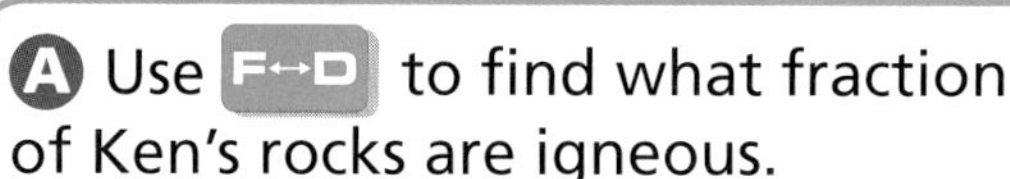

A Use F↔D to find what fraction of Ken's rocks are igneous.

Change 0.45 to a fraction.

So, Ken's collection contains $\frac{9}{20}$ igneous rocks.

B To change a fraction to an equivalent decimal, you can divide. Write the fraction as a division problem. Use the ÷ key.

Change $\frac{4}{5}$ to a decimal.

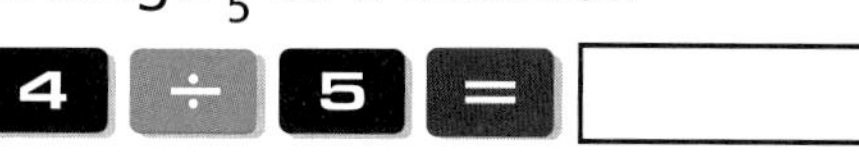

So, $\frac{4}{5}$ is equivalent to 0.8.

For each decimal, write an equivalent fraction. For each fraction, write an equivalent decimal. You may use a calculator.

1. 0.4
2. $\frac{4}{100}$
3. 0.65
4. $\frac{70}{100}$
5. $\frac{3}{8}$
6. 0.32
7. $\frac{2}{5}$
8. 0.78

LESSON 2 HANDS ON

Equivalent Decimals

OBJECTIVE: Find equivalent decimals.

Quick Review

Write each fraction as a decimal.

1. $\frac{4}{10}$
2. $\frac{40}{100}$
3. $\frac{4}{100}$
4. $\frac{60}{100}$
5. $\frac{6}{10}$

Vocabulary

equivalent decimals

Investigate

Materials ■ tenths and hundredths models

Equivalent decimals are decimals that name the same number.

Use shading and paper folding of tenths and hundredths models to find equivalent decimals.

Are 0.3 and 0.30 equivalent decimals?

A Shade 0.3 of the tenths model and 0.30 of the hundredths model.

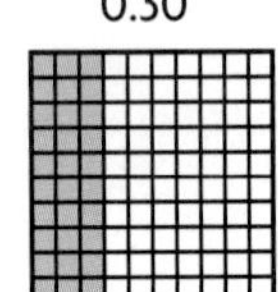

B Fold the tenths model to show 0.3 and the hundredths model to show 0.30.

C Compare the folded parts of the models for both decimals. What can you conclude?

D Repeat the steps to find whether 0.5 and 0.60 are equivalent. What can you conclude?

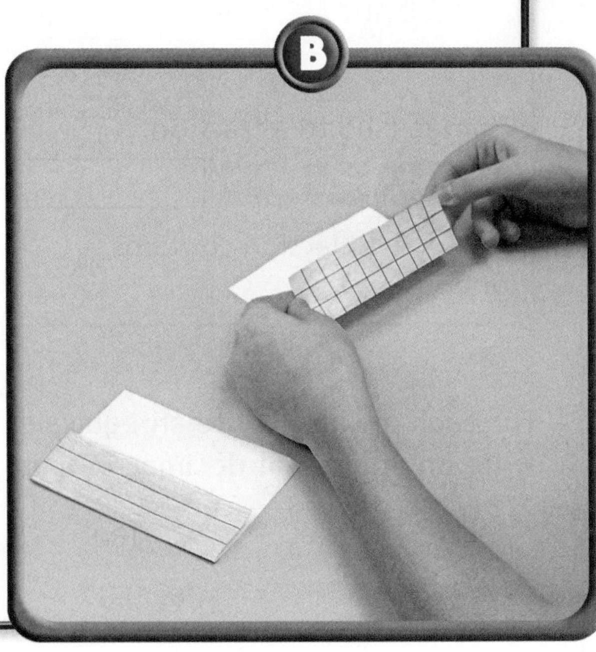

Draw Conclusions

1. How do you write 0.3 and 0.30 as fractions?
2. How much did you fold in each of the models?
3. How can you tell when a tenths decimal and a hundredths decimal are equivalent?
4. **Application** Is 0.03 equivalent to 0.3? Explain.

TEKS 4.1B use place value to read, write, compare, and order decimals involving tenths and hundredths, including money, using concrete objects and pictorial models. *also* **4.14A, 4.14D, 4.15A, 4.15B, 4.16A**

Connect

Three students drew the models shown below. You can use their models to find equivalent decimals.

Compare the models.

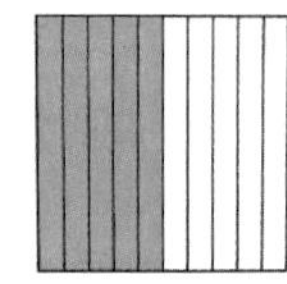

Jill's model

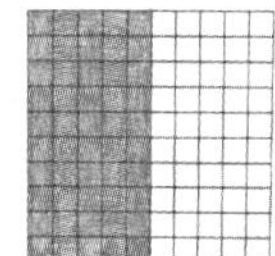

Omari's model

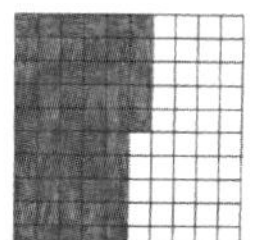

Carson's model

Step 1	Step 2	Step 3
Write the decimal each model represents. Jill's model represents 0.5. Omari's model represents 0.50. Carson's modelrepresents 0.55.	Compare the decimal models. You can see that the models for 0.5 and 0.50 are equivalent. The model for 0.55 is not equivalent to the others.	Write the decimals that are equivalent. So, 0.5 = 0.50. Jill's and Omari's models are equivalent

TALK Math

How do you know that 0.5 and 0.50 are equivalent?

Practice

Use a tenths model and a hundredths model. Are the two decimals equivalent? Write *equivalent* or *not equivalent*.

1. 0.4 and 0.44
2. 0.50 and 0.5
3. 0.71 and 0.17
4. 0.20 and 0.2
5. 0.60 and 0.06
6. 0.57 and 0.75

Write an equivalent decimal for each. You may use decimal models.

7. 0.4
8. 0.3
9. 0.70
10. 0.20
11. $\frac{1}{2}$
12. $\frac{1}{4}$
13. $\frac{3}{4}$
14. $1\frac{3}{4}$

Algebra **Write an equivalent decimal. Use the models to help.**

15. 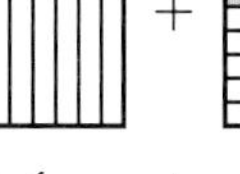 + 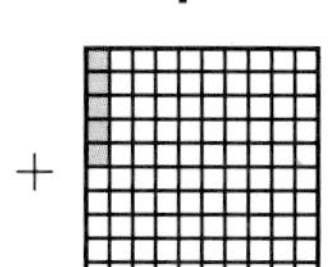 = 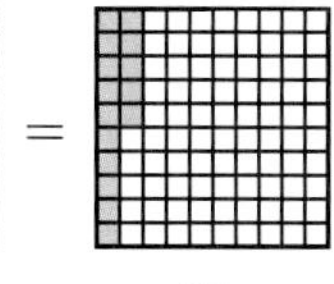

0.1 + 0.05 = 

16. 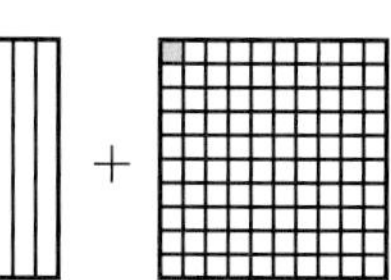 + 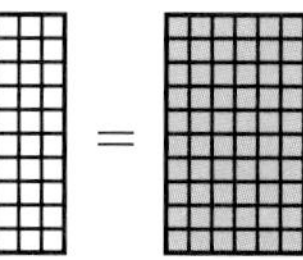 =

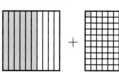

■ + ■ = 0.61

17. **WRITE Math** **Explain** why models can help you find if two decimals are equivalent.

LESSON 3 Relate Mixed Numbers and Decimals

OBJECTIVE: Model, read, and write mixed numbers as decimals.

Quick Review

Marni bought 1.7 pounds of cheese. Write a fraction for the amount of cheese that Marni bought.

Learn

PROBLEM Many pocket-sized toy cars are about two and six tenths inches long. How can you write this length as a mixed number and as a decimal?

HANDS ON

Activity 1 Use a model.

Materials ■ tenths models

Use models to write and read mixed numbers as decimals.

Shade the whole number and the fraction of the mixed number.

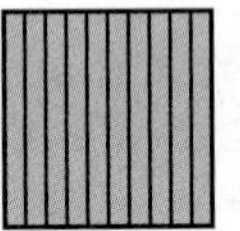 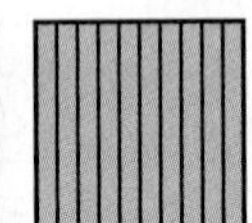 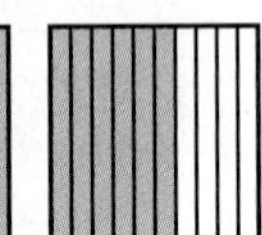

Mixed Number: $2\frac{6}{10}$

Decimal: 2.6

Read: two and six tenths

So, you can write the length as $2\frac{6}{10}$, or 2.6, inches.

Examples

A Write and read the value of the model as a mixed number and as a decimal.

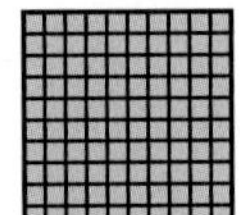 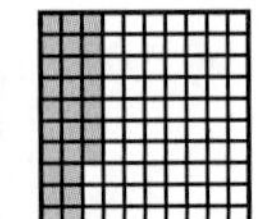

Mixed Number: $1\frac{27}{100}$

Decimal: 1.27

Read: one and twenty-seven hundredths

B Write and read the value of the model as a mixed number and as a decimal.

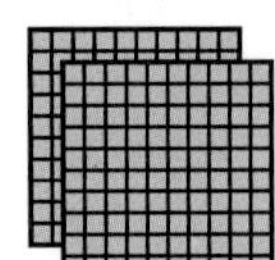 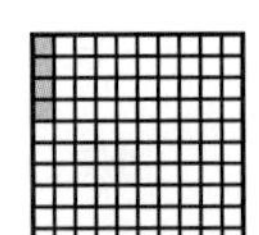

Mixed Number: $2\frac{4}{100}$

Decimal: 2.04

Read: two and four hundredths

- What model other than the one used in Activity 1 could you use to show 2.6?

TEKS 4.1B use place value to read, write, compare, and order decimals involving tenths and hundredths, including money, using concrete objects and pictorial models. *also* **4.2D, 4.2B, 4.10, 4.14A, 4.14D, 4.15A, 4.15B, 4.16A, 4.16B**

Activity 2 Use a number line.

Materials ■ number line

Find the decimal equivalent for $1\frac{25}{100}$.

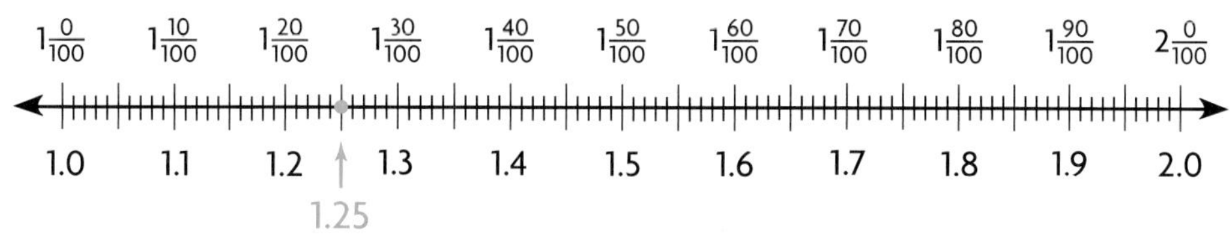

First, locate $1\frac{25}{100}$ on the number line.
Next, name the decimal that names this point.
Locate and label three other points on your number line.
Name the decimal and the mixed number that names each point.

Example 1 Use place value.

Decimals, like whole numbers, can be written in standard form, word form, and expanded form.

Ones	.	Tenths	Hundredths
2	.	7	
3	.	6	5

Standard Form	Word Form	Expanded Form
2.7	two and seven tenths	2 + 0.7
3.65	three and sixty-five hundreths	3 + 0.6 + 0.05

Example 2 Use models to show mixed numbers and decimals that are equivalent.

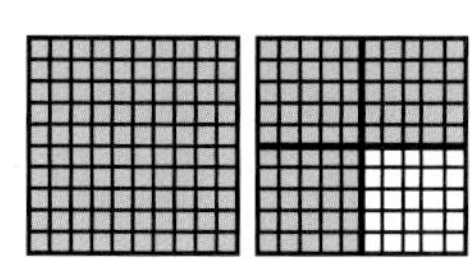

$1.75 = 1\frac{75}{100} = 1\frac{3}{4} = \frac{7}{4}$

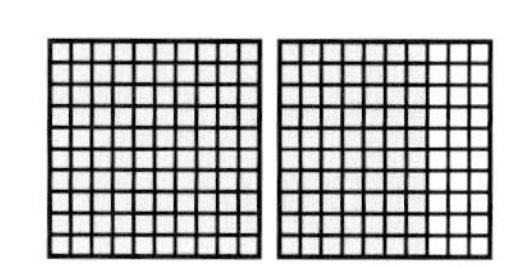

$1.70 = 1\frac{70}{100} = 1\frac{7}{10} = \frac{17}{10}$

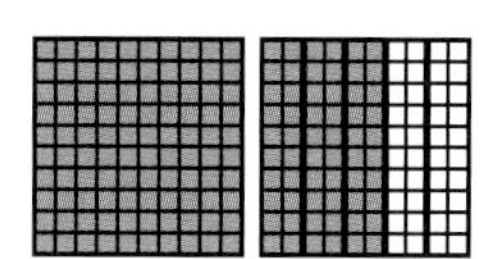

$1.60 = 1\frac{60}{100} = 1\frac{6}{10} = 1\frac{3}{5}$

Guided Practice

1. Look at the model at the right. What whole number part is modeled? What fraction is modeled? Write the mixed number as a decimal.

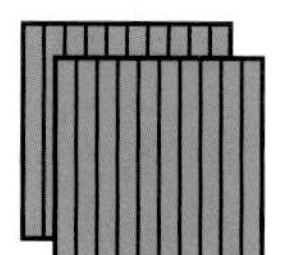
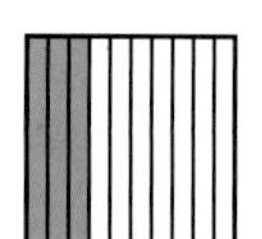

Write a mixed number and an equivalent decimal for each model.

2. 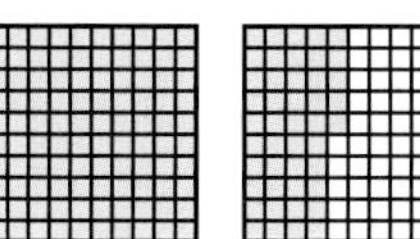

3. 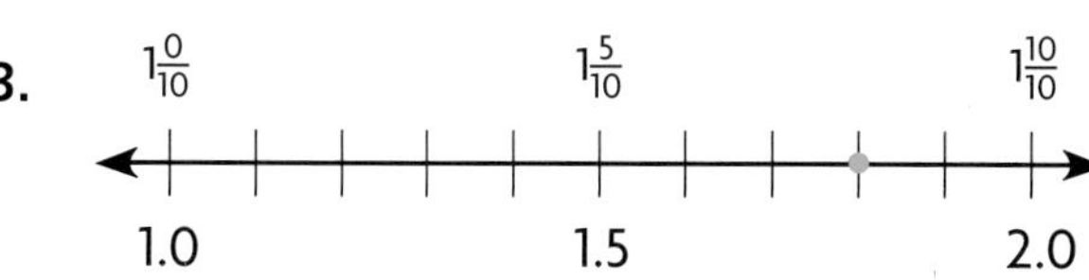

Write an equivalent mixed number and decimal for each. Then write the word form. You may use a model.

4. $1\frac{8}{10}$ 5. 3.1 6. $1\frac{57}{100}$ 7. 4.05 ✓8. $2\frac{3}{4}$

9. **TALK Math** **Explain** how a decimal equivalent for a mixed number is like a decimal equivalent for a fraction and how it is different.

Independent Practice and Problem Solving

Write a mixed number and an equivalent decimal for each model.

10. 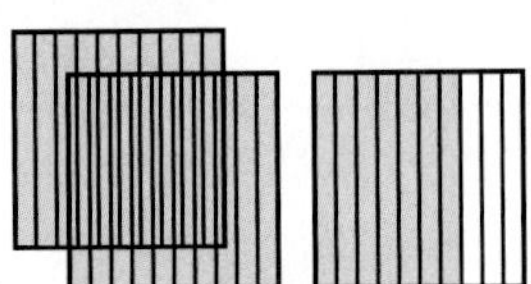

11. 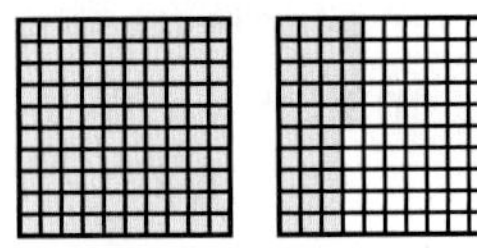

12. 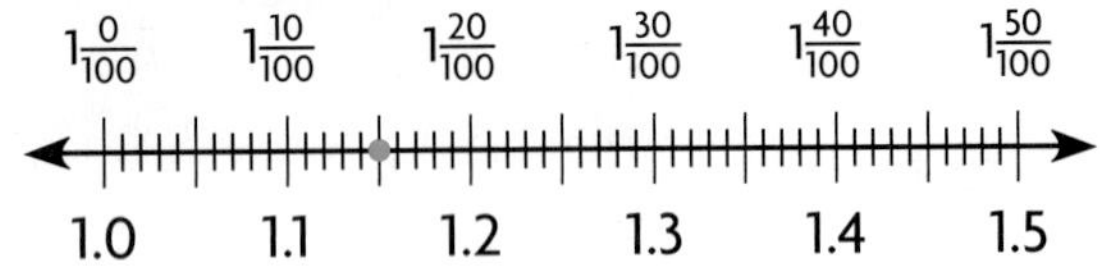

13. 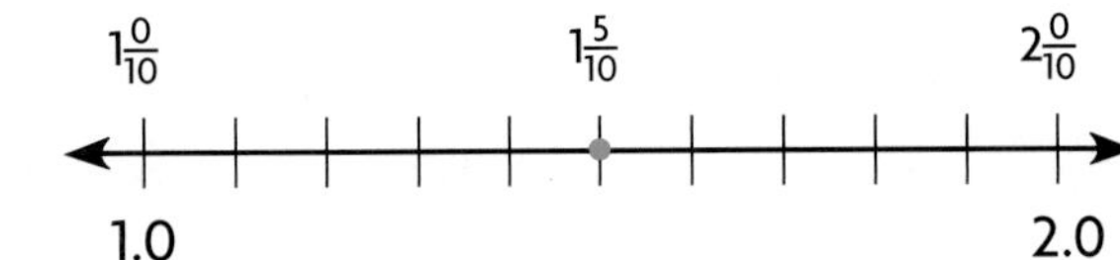

Write an equivalent mixed number and a decimal for each. Then write the word form. You may use a model.

14. 2.3 15. $7\frac{1}{2}$ 16. 3.45 17. $3\frac{3}{4}$ 18. 4.01

Algebra Write the missing number for each ■.

19. $7.16 = 7 + ■ + 0.06$ 20. $1.58 = 1 + 0.5 + ■$ 21. $4.02 = ■ + 0.02$

22. Nate is thinking of some decimals between 1 and 2. What might they be? Give at least 15 answers.

23. **Reasoning Sense or Nonsense** Tara said her temperature was 10.15 when she was sick. Does this make sense? **Explain.**

24. ***FAST FACT*** The smallest camera is only 1.65 centimeters thick. Write this measure as a mixed number.

25. **WRITE Math** **What's the Question?** The answer is one and six hundredths.

Mixed Review and TAKS Prep

26. Mark's bedroom is a square. If it is 12 feet long, what is the perimeter of the bedroom? **(Grade 3 TEKS 3.11B)**

27. In simplest form, what is an equivalent fraction for the decimal 0.50? **(TEKS 4.2D p. 418)**

28. **TAKS Prep** Which mixed number is equivalent to 2.05? **(Obj. 1)**

A $2\frac{1}{5}$

B $2\frac{5}{10}$

C $2\frac{5}{100}$

D $2\frac{1}{500}$

 Extra Practice on page 438, Set B

Tiny Trains

Reading Skill **Identify the Details**

In addition to its full size operating railroad, the Texas Transportation Museum has a model railroad display. It is in HO scale. Every 3.5 millimeters of train length in HO scale is 1 foot long in real life. What mixed number can you write for a length in HO scale that is 1 foot in real life?

In order to solve this problem, you must identify the details.

Then choose only the details you need to answer the question.

▲ The Texas Transportation Museum is located in San Antonio, Texas.

Make a list of the details you are given in the problem.	Has a full size operating railroad Has a layout in HO scale HO scale is 3.5 millimeters for every 1 foot in real life.
↓ Think about what you are asked to find.	Write a mixed number for the HO scale length for 1 foot.
↓ Choose the details you need to solve the problem.	Write a mixed number for 3.5 millimeters.

Problem Solving **Identify the details to understand the problem.**

1. Solve the problem above.
2. A railroad track's gauge is the distance between the edges of the rails. HO gauge rails are 16.5 millimeters apart. The train car is 11 inches long. What mixed number can you write for the track's gauge?

4 Fractions, Decimals, and Money

OBJECTIVE: Relate money amounts to fractions and decimals.

Quick Review

Write in decimal form.

1. $1\frac{7}{10}$
2. $2\frac{85}{100}$
3. $4\frac{15}{100}$
4. $3\frac{7}{100}$
5. $2\frac{3}{4}$

Learn

PROBLEM Caleb bought a new pencil and a ruler at the school store for twenty-five cents. Write this amount as a fraction of a dollar and as a decimal.

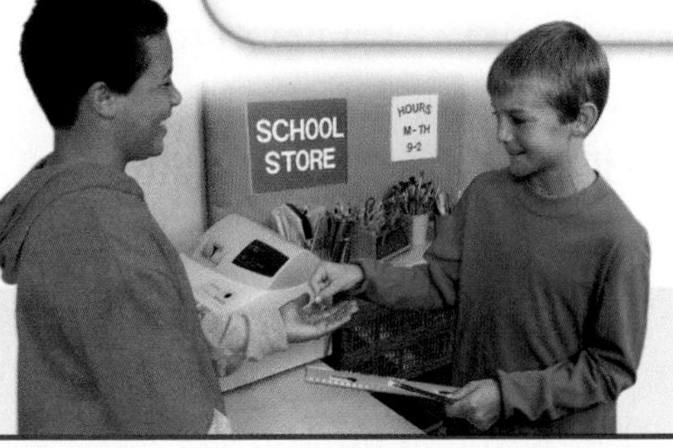

Activity 1

Materials ■ play money

A Find the fraction of a dollar equal to twenty-five cents.

Think: Twenty-five cents = 25¢, or \$0.25, or one quarter. How many quarters equal 1 dollar?

Use quarters to model one dollar. Draw a circle around the coin that represents twenty-five cents.

Write the value of twenty-five cents as a fraction of a dollar and as a decimal.

One quarter is equal to $\frac{25}{100}$, or $\frac{1}{4}$, of a dollar.

$\frac{1}{4}$ of a dollar is equal to \$0.25.

So, Caleb spent $\frac{1}{4}$ of a dollar.

B Model fifty cents. Write the total money amount. Then write the amount as a fraction of a dollar and as a decimal.

Write the total money amount: \$0.50.

Write as a fraction in simplest form: Fifty cents is equal to $\frac{1}{2}$ of a dollar, or 0.50 of a dollar.

So, \$0.50 is equal to $\frac{1}{2}$ of a dollar.

Examples Money can be used to model decimal numbers.

1 dollar
\$1.00

10 dimes = 1 dollar
1 dime = $\frac{1}{10}$ of a dollar, or
0.1 of a dollar
\$0.10

100 pennies = 1 dollar
1 penny = $\frac{1}{100}$ of a dollar, or
0.01 of a dollar
\$0.01

TEKS 4.1B use place value to read, write, compare, and order decimals involving tenths and hundredths, including money, using concrete objects and pictorial models. *also* **4.2D, 4.14A, 4.14D, 4.15A, 4.15B, 4.16A**

Activity 2 **Materials** ■ play money

Step 1

Use dimes to model $\frac{2}{10}$ of a dollar. Copy and complete the first row of the table.

Step 2

Model $0.04 in pennies. Copy and complete the second row of the table.

Step 3

Model twenty-three cents with as few coins as possible. Copy and complete the last row of the table.

Fractions, Decimals, and Money

Number and Type of Coin	Fraction of a Dollar	Decimal	Money Notation
■	$\frac{2}{10}$	■	■
■	■	■	$0.04
■	■	■	$0.23

You can think of dollars as ones, dimes as tenths, and pennies as hundredths.

$ Bills	.	Dimes	Pennies
0	.		56
0	.	5	6

56 pennies = $0.56 = 56 hundredths of a dollar

5 dimes 6 pennies = $0.56 = 5 tenths 6 hundredths of a dollar

Use the money amounts to understand place value of decimals.

Ones	.	Tenths	Hundredths
0	.	5	6

$0.56 = 56$ hundredths, or $0.56 = 5$ tenths 6 hundredths

- How can you use money amounts to understand place value of decimals?

Guided Practice

1. How many tenths of a dollar and hundredths of a dollar are there in the following set of coins?

Write the total money amount. Then write the amount as a fraction of a dollar and as a decimal.

2. 

✓3.

4. 5 dimes
5. 2 dimes, 8 pennies
6. 3 pennies
7. 1 dime, 16 pennies

Write the amount as a fraction of a dollar, as a decimal, and as a money amount.

8. 2 dimes **9.** 3 dimes 2 pennies **10.** 5 dimes 13 pennies ✓ **11.** 12 pennies

12. TALK Math **Explain** how to use money to model 0.46.

Independent Practice and Problem Solving

Write the total money amount. Then write the amount as a fraction of a dollar and as a decimal.

13.  

14. 

15. 8 dimes **16.** 1 dime 4 pennies **17.** 6 pennies **18.** 7 dimes 1 penny

Write the amount as a fraction of a dollar, as a decimal, and as a money amount.

19. 4 dimes **20.** 6 dimes 8 pennies **21.** 3 dimes 45 pennies **22.** 23 pennies

Algebra Find the missing number to tell the value of each digit.

23. $\$5.18 = ■$ dollars + ■ dimes + ■ pennies
$5.18 = ■$ ones + ■ tenths + ■ hundredths

24. $\$1.05 = ■$ dollars + ■ pennies
$1.05 = ■$ ones + ■ hundredths

USE DATA For 25–27, use the pictures.

25. **Reasoning** Andrea bought two items at the school store. She spent $\frac{3}{4}$ of a dollar in all. Which items did she buy? **Explain** how you know.

26. Mario has $\frac{1}{2}$ of a dollar. Which items in the school store are too expensive for Mario to buy?

27. **Pose a Problem** Use the pictures to write your own problem in which you relate fractions or decimals to money amounts.

28. **Open-Ended** Brynn bought a notebook for $0.70. She paid for it with exact change. What possible coins could she have used to pay for the notebook?

29. WRITE Math **Explain** how to write the fraction of a dollar that 6 dimes represents in simplest form.

 Extra Practice on page 438, Set C

Mixed Review and TAKS Prep

30. There are four children in the Howard family. Ann is 6 years old, Sara is 8, Warren is 13, and Josh is 3. Make a bar graph to show this data. (Grade 3 TEKS 3.13A)

31. TAKS Prep What decimal do the coins represent? (Obj. 1)

     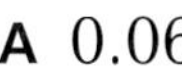

A 0.06 **C** 0.60

B 0.6 **D** 0.66

32. Write a decimal and a fraction for the model. (TEKS 4.2D, p. 428)

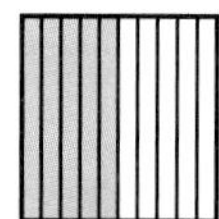

33. TAKS Prep What decimal do the coins represent? (Obj. 1)

Problem Solving and Reasoning

NUMBER SENSE Between 1875 and 1878, the United States made not only pennies, nickels, dimes, quarters, and half dollars, but also coins worth 20¢. Write the amount of money shown as a fraction of a dollar.

Write the money amount as a decimal: $0.70 = 0.70.

Write the decimal as a fraction in simplest form:

$0.70 = \frac{70}{100} = \frac{7}{10}$

So, the coins shown have the value of $\frac{7}{10}$ of a dollar.

U.S. Coins 1875-1878

Coin	Value
	1¢, or $0.01
	5¢, or $0.05
	10¢, or $0.10
	20¢, or $0.20
	25¢, or $0.25
	50¢, or $0.50

1. Which coins could you use to make $\frac{3}{4}$ of a dollar?
2. What fraction of a dollar is the 20¢ coin worth?
3. What different ways could you use the coins to equal the value of one dollar? Give three examples.

LESSON 5 HANDS ON

Compare Decimals

OBJECTIVE: Compare decimals.

Quick Review

Write an equivalent decimal for each.

1. 0.20
2. 0.4
3. 0.5
4. 0.10
5. 0.9

Investigate

Materials ■ hundredths models ■ number line

Which decimal is greater: 1.20 or 1.25?

A Shade decimal models.

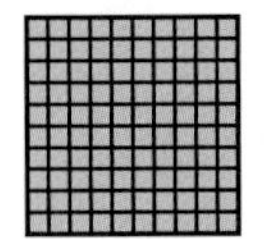 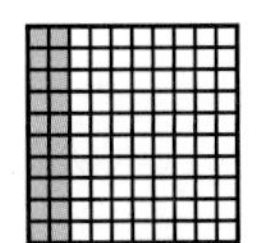

1.20

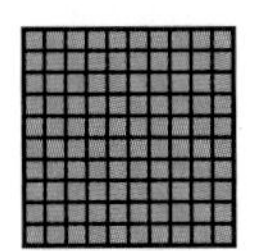 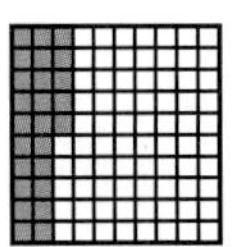

1.25

B Compare the models. What do you notice?

C Locate the points 1.20 and 1.25 on a number line to compare the decimals.

D Compare the location of the points on the number line. What do you notice?

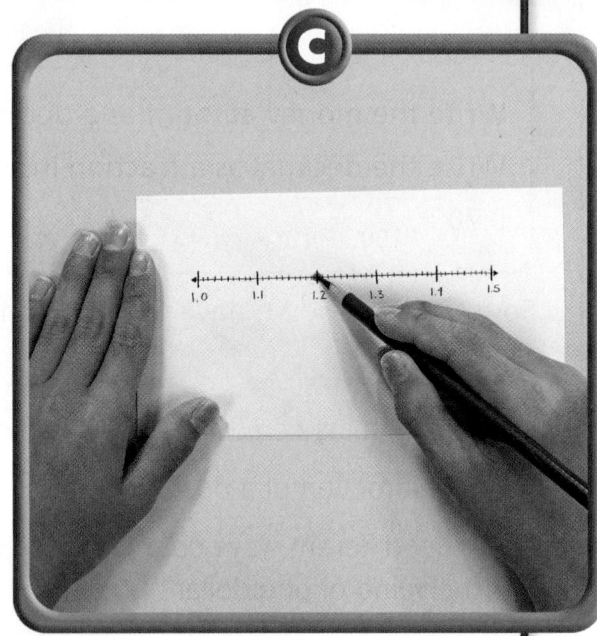

Draw Conclusions

1. How do decimal models help you compare decimals?
2. How does a number line help you compare decimals?
3. How are both methods alike? How are they different?
4. **Application** Explain which method you would use to compare 1.01 and 1.9. Tell why you would use that method.

TEKS 4.1B use place value to read, write, compare, and order decimals involving tenths and hundredths, including money, using concrete objects and pictorial models. *also* **4.2C, 4.10, 4.14A, 4.14D, 4.15A, 4.15B**

Connect

You can use a place-value chart to compare decimals.

Compare 2.89 and 2.8.

Ones	.	Tenths	Hundredths
2	.	8	9
2	.	8	0

Think: 2.8 and 2.80 are equivalent decimals.

2 = 2   8 = 8   9 > 0

Compare the digits beginning with the greatest place value.

Since 9 > 0, 2.89 > 2.8.

ERROR ALERT

Be sure to write a 0 in the hundredths place of the decimals with tenths only to help you correctly line up the decimal places.

TALK Math

How is using a place-value chart to compare decimals like using a model? How are the methods different?

Practice

Compare. Write <, >, or = for each ●.

1. 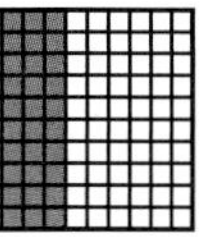 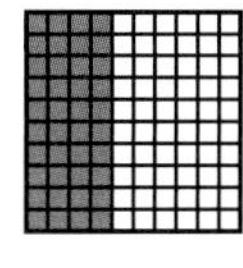

0.40 ● 0.4

2. 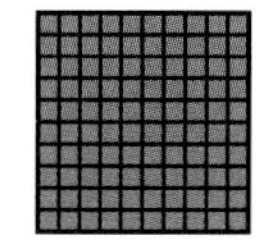 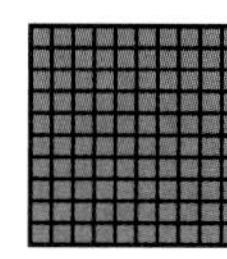

1.65 ● 1.56

3. 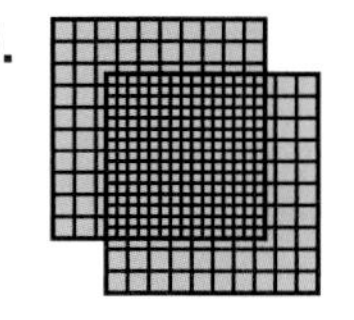 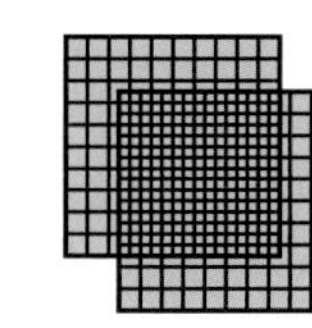

2.2 ● 2.15

4. 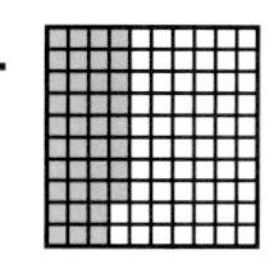 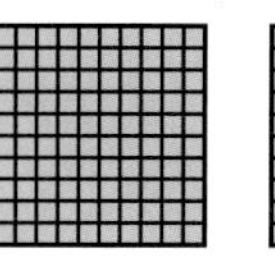

0.38 ● 1.27

Use the number line to determine whether the number sentences are *true* or *false*.

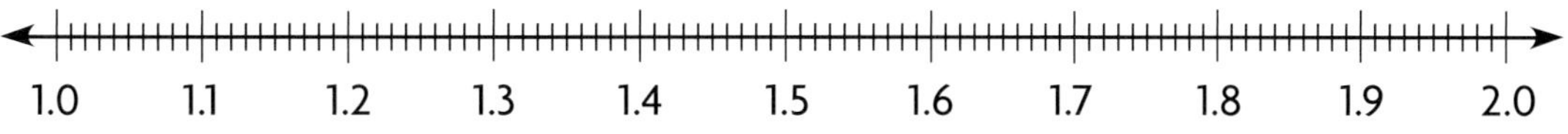

5. 1.07 > 1.70
6. 1.3 < 1.30
7. 1.54 > 1.45
8. 1.82 = 1.8
9. 1.65 > 1.6
10. 1.72 < 1.27
11. 1.18 < 1.20
12. 1.78 > 1.09
13. 1.9 < 1.90
14. 1.08 > 1.11

15. **WRITE Math** **What's the Error?** Erin says that 4.5 < 4.49 because the last digit in 4.5 is less than the last digit in 4.49. Describe and correct her error.

6 Order Decimals

OBJECTIVE: Order decimals.

Quick Review

Compare. Write <, >, or = for each ●.

1. 3.3 ● 3.30
2. 1.75 ● 1.7
3. 0.48 ● 0.84
4. 0.7 ● 0.70
5. 0.06 ● 0.11

Investigate

Materials ■ string ■ clothespins

Order 1.2, 1.9, 1.6 from least to greatest.

A Use your marker to mark the location of the points 1.0, 1.5, and 2.0 on your string.

B Use clothespins to label the points you marked.

C Now locate the points 1.2, 1.9, and 1.6 on your string by using labeled clothespins.

D Draw a picture of the number line you modeled.

E Compare your drawing and your model. What do you notice?

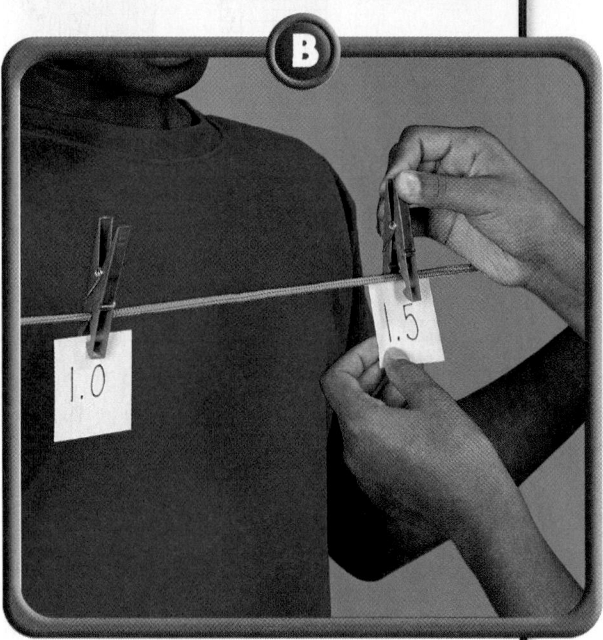

Draw Conclusions

1. What do you notice about the two number lines you made?
2. Use the drawing or model to order the decimals 1.4, 1.35, and 1.43 from least to greatest.
3. **Application** Explain how you can use a number line to compare and order decimals.

TEKS 4.1B use place value to read, write, compare, and order decimals involving tenths and hundredths, including money, using concrete objects and pictorial models. *also* **4.10, 4.14A, 4.14D, 4.15A, 4.15B**

Connect

You can also use place value to order decimals.

Order 1.52, 0.87, and 1.56 from least to greatest.

Step 1	Step 2	Step 3
Line up the decimal points. Think: Compare the digits in the greatest place. 1.52 ↓ $0 < 1$ 0.87 ↓ 1.56 Since $0 < 1$, 0.87 is the least.	Compare the tenths. 1.52 ↓ $5 = 5$ 1.56 0.87 There are the same number of tenths.	Compare the hundredths. 1.52 ↓ $2 < 6$ 1.56 0.87 So, the order from least to greatest is 0.87, 1.52, 1.56.

TALK Math

How is using place value to order decimals different from using a number line?

Practice

Use the number line to order the decimals from least to greatest.

1.0 1.1 1.2 1.3 1.4 1.5 1.6 1.7 1.8 1.9 2.0

1. 1.11, 1.2, 1.01, 1.1
2. 1.32, 1.23, 1.3, 1.2
3. 1.9, 1.09, 1.5, 1.55
4. 1.65, 1.56, 1.6, 2.0
5. 1.15, 1.1, 1.51, 1.3
6. 1.7, 1.75, 1.5, 1.05

Order the decimals from greatest to least.

7. \$1.41, \$0.14, \$1.14, \$1.40
8. 7.03, 7.3, 6.98, 6.89
9. \$2.15, \$1.89, \$1.09
10. 1.04, 0.96, 1.4, 0.9
11. 5.5, 5.55, 5.05, 5.15
12. \$0.95, \$0.80, \$1.00
13. 3.8, 3.06, 3.97, 3.61
14. \$1.35, \$3.15, \$1.53, \$3.51
15. 6.25, 7.2, 6.93, 7.11
16. **WRITE Math** **Explain** how a number line helps you order decimals.

Technology
Use Harcourt Mega Math Fraction Action, *Number Line Mine,* Levels P, Q.

Problem Solving Workshop
Skill: Draw Conclusions

OBJECTIVE: Solve problems by using the skill *draw conclusions.*

Use the Skill

PROBLEM The newspaper ads show the cost of basketball trading cards at three different sporting goods stores. Which store has the lowest price for a box of cards?

Sports Palace: The basketball players you want: 1 box of cards $6.59

Special bu

Best optns

Town Sports: Basketball trading cards $5.95 per box of cards

Accordian with

best offer

Angelo's Sports: Hottest new basketball stars: $6.95 per box of cards

Brand new

You can draw conclusions to help you solve the problem. To draw conclusions, combine the facts from the problem with what you know from your own experience.

Facts from the Problem	What You Know
Angelo's Sports: $6.95 per box Sports Palace: $6.59 per box Town Sports: $5.95 per box	• Bills and coins can be used to model decimals. • You can order decimals by comparing the place value of each digit, beginning with the greatest place value. • The best price is the lowest price.

To draw a conclusion about the lowest price, use models and place value to order the money amounts. Then choose the lowest price.

Materials ■ play money

Ones	.	Tenths	Hundredths
6	.	9	5
6	.	5	9
5	.	9	5

Order of prices from least to greatest: $5.95, $6.59, $6.95.
So, Town Sports has the lowest price for a box of cards.

Think and Discuss

Tell which facts from the problem and what information you know can be used to draw conclusions. Solve the problem.

a. Ted can run a mile in 7.25 minutes. Rick runs it in 7.05 minutes, and Leroy runs it in 7.5 minutes. Who can run the fastest mile?

b. At the store, Power Thirst costs $3.98. Sports Power sells for $3.89, and Zoom! costs $3.90. Which drink costs the most?

TEKS 4.1B use place value to read, write, compare, and order decimals involving tenths and hundredths, including money, using concrete objects and pictorial models. *also* **4.14A, 4.14C, 4.14D, 4.15A, 4.15B, 4.16B**

Guided Problem Solving

1. The ads to the right show the price of a new best-selling book at three different bookstores. Which bookstore has the best price for the book?

   Copy and complete the chart.

Facts from the Problem	What You Know
Bob's Bookstore: ■	• ? can be used to model decimals.
Books Are Us: ■	• You can order decimals by ?.
Books on Broadway: ■	• The best price is the ? price.

   How can you use the information in the chart to draw a conclusion?

2. **What if** Open Page Bookstore sells the same book for $9.80? Then which store has the best price?

3. Megan lives 2.4 miles from Bob's Bookstore. Josh lives 2.15 miles away, and Sam lives 2.09 miles away. Who lives closest to Bob's Bookstore?

Mixed Applications

USE DATA For 4–5, use the map.

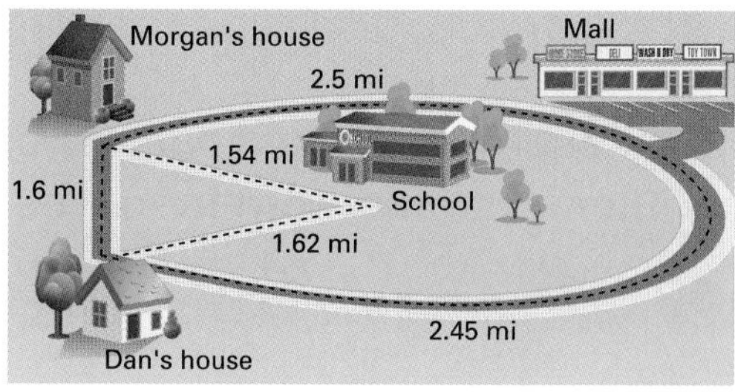

4. Who walks farther to school, Morgan or Dan? **Explain.**

5. Greg lives 2.8 miles from the mall. Warren lives 2.54 miles from the mall. Use the map and this information to list the four students in order from nearest to farthest distance from the mall.

6. A basketball jersey at a sporting goods store costs $45. Sharif paid for the jersey with three $20 bills. How much change did he get back? Do you need an estimate or an exact answer?

7. The school needs 150 boxes of juice to give to the students going to the baseball game. If the juice comes in packages of 4 boxes, how many packages must the school buy?

8. **WRITE Math** Ezra jogged 125 miles in 3 weeks of training. He jogged 32 miles during the first week and 39 miles during the second week. **Explain** how to choose the more reasonable answer for the number of miles he jogged during the third week: 54 miles or 34 miles.

9. Hannah ran the 50-yard dash in 8.23 seconds. Tarika ran the dash in 7.95 seconds, and Rita ran the dash in 8.2 seconds. Who ran the dash the fastest?

Extra Practice

Set A **Write the fraction and decimal shown by each model.** (pp. 418–421)

1. 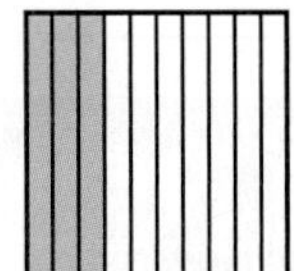

2. 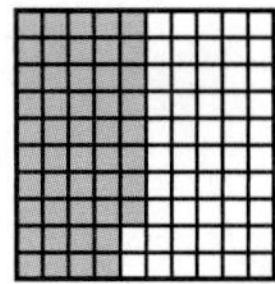

3. 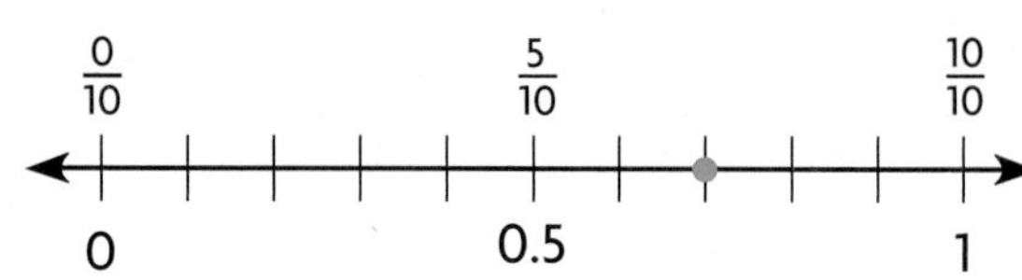

Write each fraction as a decimal. You may use a model or drawing.

4. $\frac{9}{10}$ 5. $\frac{17}{100}$ 6. $\frac{7}{10}$ 7. $\frac{5}{100}$ 8. $\frac{14}{100}$

9. Spencer has 10 math problems to do for homework. He has done 8 of the problems. What part of his math homework has Spencer done? Write the answer as a decimal and as a fraction.

Set B **Write a mixed number and an equivalent decimal for each model.** (pp. 424–427)

1. 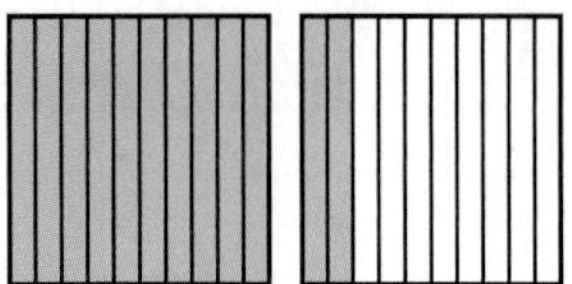

2. 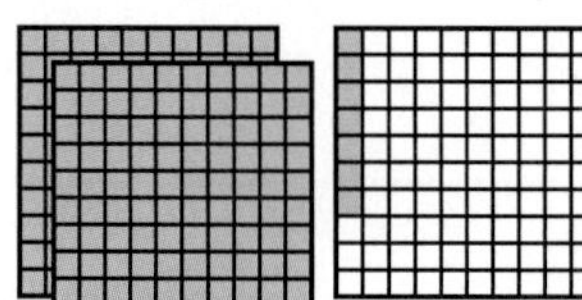

3. 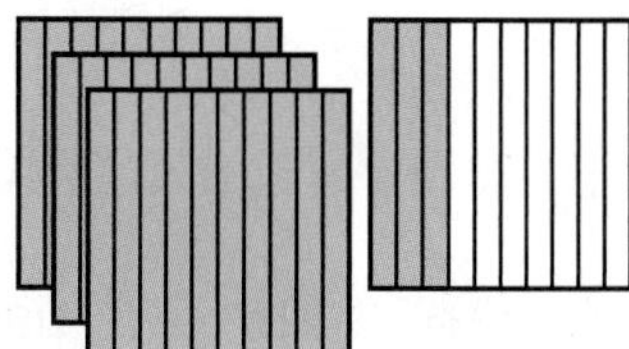

Write an equivalent mixed number or a decimal for each. Then write the word form. You may use a model.

3. 4.7 4. $3\frac{1}{4}$ 5. 5.08 6. $7\frac{3}{5}$ 7. 6.98

Set C **Write the total money amount. Then write the amount as a fraction of a dollar and as a decimal.** (pp. 428–431)

1.     

2.      

Write the amount as a fraction of a dollar, as a decimal, and as a money amount.

3. 6 dimes 4. 3 dimes, 7 pennies 5. 5 dimes

6. 17 pennies 7. 9 dimes, 9 pennies 8. 39 pennies

9. Dylan pulls out some coins from his pocket and sees that he has 7 dimes and 4 pennies. How much money does Dylan have?

CD ROM **Technology**
Use Harcourt Mega Math, Fraction Action, *Fraction Flare Up,* Levels M, N.

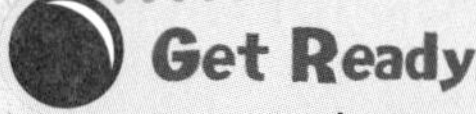

ORDER, PLEASE!

Get Ready!
2 or 3 players and a dealer

Get Set!
Set of index cards with these decimal numbers: 0.1–0.9, 0.15–0.25, 0.01–0.09

Play the Game!

- The object of the game is to have 5 decimal cards in order from least to greatest.
- The dealer shuffles the cards and places 5 cards faceup in front of each player and places the remaining cards facedown in a stack. The cards should remain in this order throughout the game.
- At each turn, a player chooses one card to replace, and places it in the discard stack. The dealer gives the player a new card from the top of the stack to be placed in the same spot as the card that was just given to the dealer.
- A player who thinks all 5 of his or her cards are in order from least to greatest calls out "Order!"
- If the cards are in order, that player wins.
- When all the cards in the stack have been used, the dealer shuffles the cards in the discard stack, places them facedown, and starts a new stack.
- Whoever wins becomes the dealer for the next round.

Chapter 16 Review/Test

Check Vocabulary and Concepts

Choose the best term from the box.

VOCABULARY
decimal
decimal point
equivalent decimals
hundredth

1. The __?__ separates the ones place and the tenths place. (TEKS 4.2D, p. 418)
2. One whole can be broken up into one hundred equal parts. Each equal part is called __?__. (TEKS 4.2D, p. 418)
3. __?__ are decimals that name the same number. (TEKS 4.1B, p. 422)

Check Skills

Write the decimal and fraction or mixed number shown by each model. (TEKS 4.2D, pp. 418–421, TEKS 4.1B, pp. 424–427)

4. 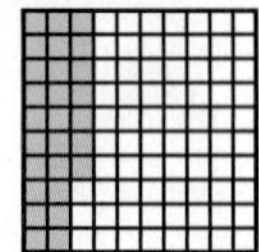

5. 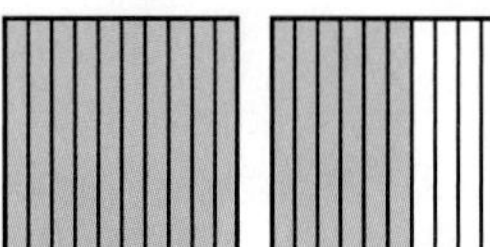

6. 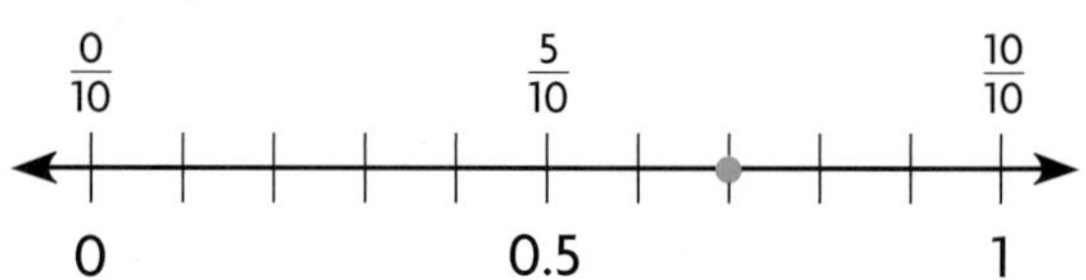

Write the total money amount. Then write the amount as a fraction of a dollar and as a decimal. (TEKS 4.1B, pp. 428–431)

7.     

8.     

Compare. Write $<$, $>$, or $=$ for each ●. (TEKS 4.1B, pp. 432–433)

9. 4.6 ● 4.06
10. \$3.70 ● \$4.00
11. 4.40 ● 4.4
12. 6.8 ● 6.08
13. 7.09 ● 7.18
14. 8.8 ● 8.80
15. \$5.50 ● \$5.25
16. 9.91 ● 9.19

Order the decimals from greatest to least. (TEKS 4.1B, pp. 434–435)

17. 8.06, 8.4, 7.89, 8.89
18. 1.35, 0.89, 1.05, 0.09

Check Problem Solving

Solve. (TEKS 4.1B, pp. 436–437)

19. Kate swam the 50-meter freestyle race in 30.05 seconds. Which of the girls listed in the table beat Kate in the race?
20. **WRITE Math** If Kate and the four girls listed in the table were the only ones in the race, who came in fourth place? **Explain.**

50-Meter Freestyle Results

Swimmer	Time (in seconds)
Larisa	31.02
Michelle	30.2
Sara	30.52
Rebecca	30.01

GO ONLINE **Technology** Use *Online Assessment.*

Enrich • Decimals to Thousandths

You do not say Michael Young's batting average as you would other decimals. You would say "three thirty-one," but it means 331 out of 1,000. How do you read his batting average as a decimal number?

▲ In 2005, Michael Young of the Texas Rangers had a batting average of .331.

Example 1 Use models.

Use the models below to read and write fractions as decimals through **thousandths**. If one hundredth is divided into ten equal parts, each part represents one thousandth.

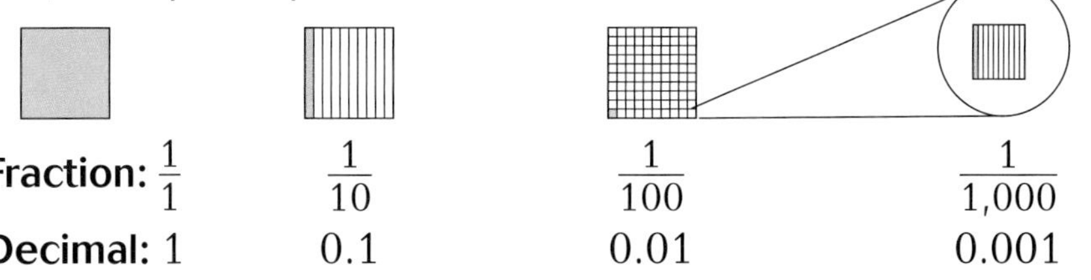

Fraction:	$\frac{1}{1}$	$\frac{1}{10}$	$\frac{1}{100}$	$\frac{1}{1,000}$
Decimal:	1	0.1	0.01	0.001
Read:	one	one tenth	one hundredth	one thousandth

0.331 has three decimal places.

So, as a decimal, 0.331 is read as three hundred thirty-one thousandths.

• What pattern do you see in the models for 0.1, 0.01, and 0.001?

Example 2 Use place value.

Ones	.	Tenths	Hundredths	Thousandths
0	.	5	2	4
0	.	0	3	5
0	.	0	0	6

You can show each decimal from the place-value chart in different forms.

Standard Form	Word Form	Expanded Form
0.524	five hundred twenty-four thousandths	0.5 + 0.02 + 0.004
0.035	thirty-five thousandths	0.03 + 0.005
0.006	six thousandths	0.006

Try It

Write each decimal as a fraction and each fraction as a decimal. Then write the decimal in word form and expanded form.

1. 0.621 **2.** $\frac{56}{1,000}$ **3.** 0.003 **4.** $\frac{707}{1,000}$ **5.** 0.895 **6.** $\frac{21}{1,000}$

WRITE Math ▸ **Explain** how to use a place-value chart to tell the value of the digit 7 in the decimal 0.467.

Getting Ready for the TAKS
Chapters 1–16

Number, Operation, and Quantitative Reasoning TAKS Obj. 1

1. Rachel drew this model to represent $\frac{3}{4}$.

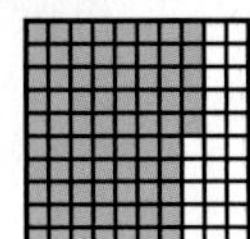

What decimal is also represented by this model?

A 0.5

B 0.65

C 0.7

D 0.75

2. What number on the number line does point *P* best represent?

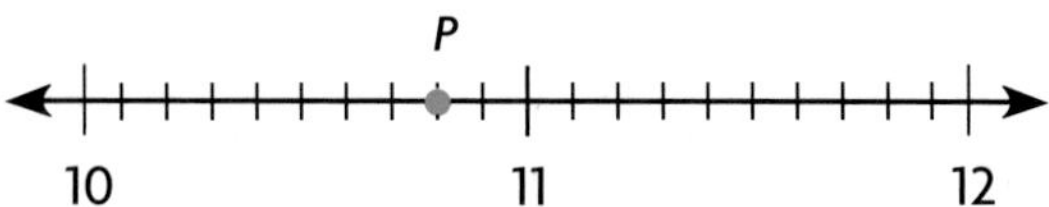

F $11\frac{8}{10}$

G $11\frac{2}{10}$

H $10\frac{8}{10}$

J $10\frac{2}{10}$

3. **WRITE Math** Neil bought 3 caps and 4 posters with his favorite team's logo.

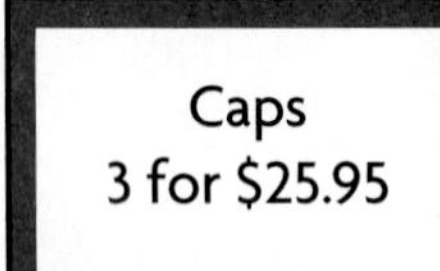

Caps 3 for $25.95	Team Posters 4 for $22.95

Estimate the cost of each cap and each poster. **Explain** the strategy you used.

Measurement TAKS Obj. 4

4. What is the perimeter of this swimming pool?

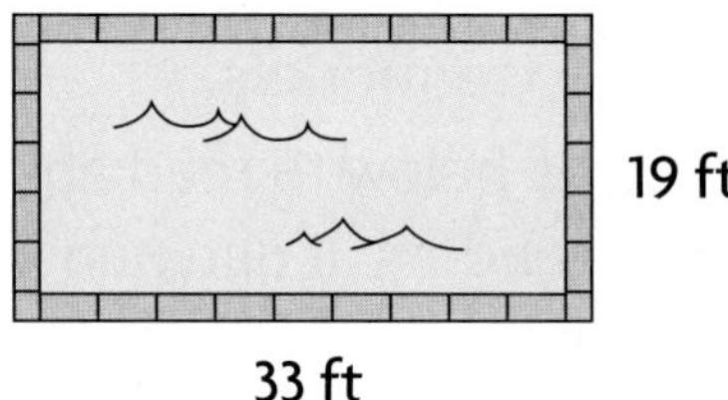

A 52 feet

B 104 feet

C 297 feet

D 627 feet

5. Sara's dance lesson begins at the time shown on the clock below.

At what time does Sara's dance lesson begin?

F 8:03

G 8:05

H 12:40

J 1:40

6. **WRITE Math** Janet wants to paint her room. What tool should she use to measure the length and height of the walls? **Explain** how you decided.

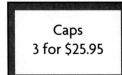

Patterns, Relationships, and Algebraic Thinking TAKS Obj. 2

7. What is the next number sentence in this pattern?

$$10 \times 7 = 70$$
$$10 \times 70 = 700$$
$$10 \times 700 = 7,000$$

A $10 \times 800 = 8,000$

B $10 \times 7,000 = 70,000$

C $100 \times 700 = 70,000$

D $100 \times 7,000 = 700,000$

8. Which pair of number sentences is part of a fact family?

F $2 \times 6 = 12$ and $3 \times 4 = 12$

G $2 \times 5 = 10$ and $2 \times 10 = 20$

H $3 \times 3 = 9$ and $9 \times 9 = 81$

J $5 \times 8 = 40$ and $8 \times 5 = 40$

Test Tip **Decide on a Plan**

See item 9. Look for a relationship between the input number and the output number. Think of a rule that matches this relationship.

9. **WRITE Math** Which numbers best complete this table? **Explain.**

Input	11	15	22	28	37	46	54
Output	18	22	29	35	44	■	■

Geometry and Spatial Reasoning TAKS Obj. 3

10. A basketball is the shape of which of these solid figures?

A Sphere

B Cylinder

C Cone

D Rectangular prism

11. Which figure is **NOT** a quadrilateral?

F 

H 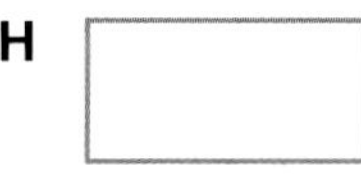

G 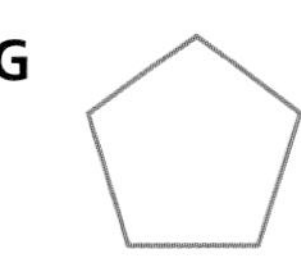

J 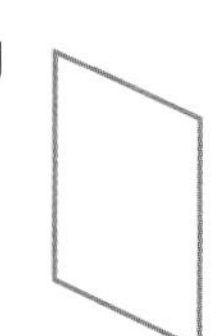

12. In which figure does the blue line appear to be a line of symmetry?

A 

C 

B 

D 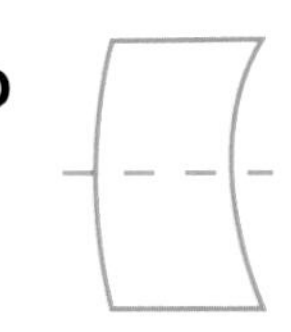

13. **WRITE Math** Mitch drew an obtuse triangle. **Describe** the angles of his triangle.

17 Add and Subtract Decimals and Money

The Big Idea Addition and subtraction of decimals is based on place value and addition and subtraction with whole numbers.

Investigate

Farmers' markets sell fresh fruits and vegetables that are locally grown. Suppose you have $10.00 to spend at the market. What foods could you buy without spending more than $10.00? How much money would you have left?

Tomatoes $1.99/pound
Carrots $1.29/pound
Okra 75¢/pint
Plums $2.29/pound
Watermelons $2.80 each
Fresh orange juice $1.75/pint
Prickly-pear Cactus $4.50/pound

TEXAS FAST FACT

Market Square is the largest Mexican market in San Antonio. You can buy many Mexican products such as piñatas, jewelry, and pottery.

GO ONLINE **Technology** Student pages are available in the Student eBook.

Show What You Know

Check your understanding of important skills needed for success in Chapter 17.

▶ Count Bills and Coins

Write the amount.

1. 

2. 

3. 

4. 

5. 

6. 

▶ Model Decimals

Write the decimal for the shaded part.

7. 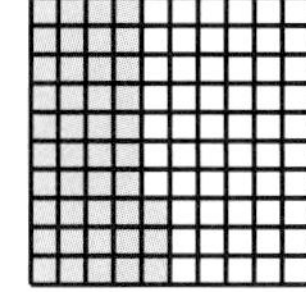

8. 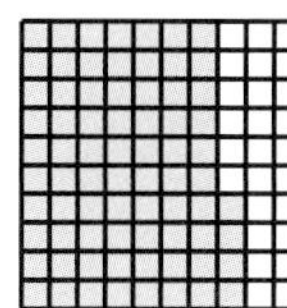

9. 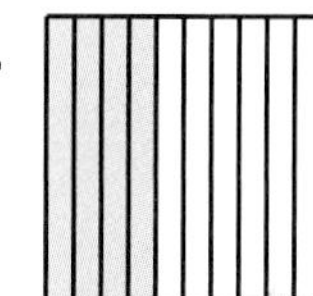

10. 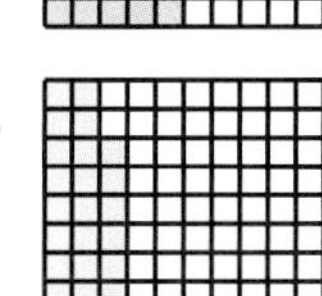

11. 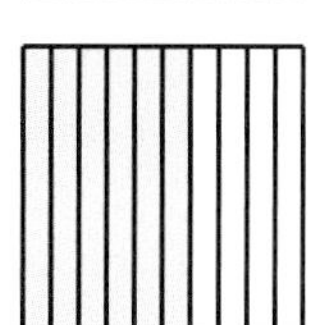

12. 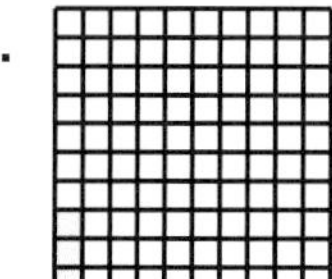

VOCABULARY POWER

CHAPTER VOCABULARY

decimal
decimal point
hundredth
tenth

WARM-UP WORDS

decimal a number with one or more digits to the right of the decimal point

decimal point a symbol used to separate dollars from cents in money amounts and to separate the ones and the tenths places in a decimal

hundredth one of one hundred equal parts

LESSON 1 HANDS ON

Model Addition

OBJECTIVE: Model addition of decimals.

Quick Review

1. 13 + 45
2. 48 + 123
3. 378 + 298
4. 32 + 47 + 89
5. 145 + 678 + 324

Investigate

Materials ■ decimal models ■ color pencils

Use decimal models to find 0.34 + 0.66.

A Shade 34 squares on a decimal model red to represent 0.34.

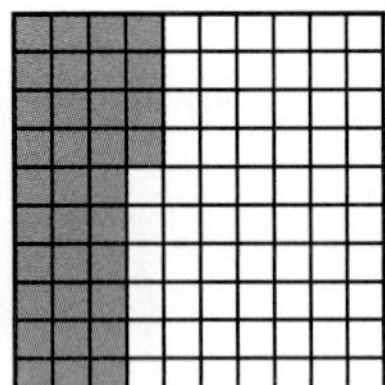

B Shade 66 squares on the same decimal model blue to represent 0.66.

C Make three more models with addends whose sum is 1.00.

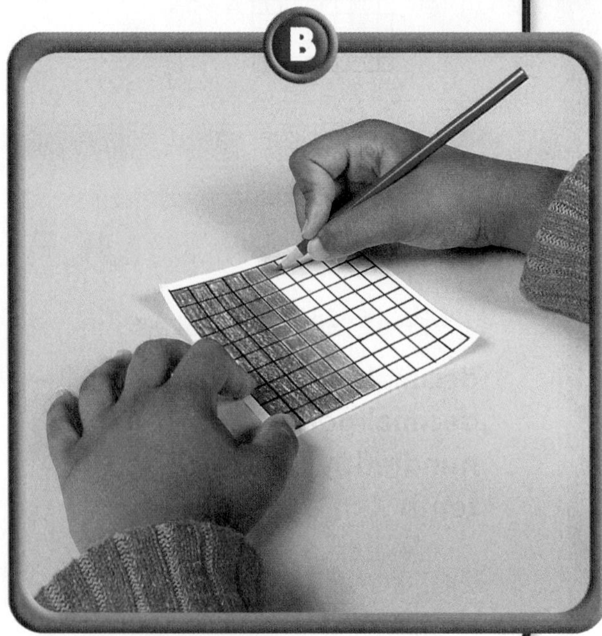

Draw Conclusions

1. What is the sum of 0.34 and 0.66?
2. How did the decimal models help you find the sum?
3. What are two decimals you could add by using tenths models?
4. **Synthesis** If you add two decimals that are both less than 0.5, will the sum be less than or greater than 1.0?

TEKS 4.3B add and subtract decimals to the hundredths place using concrete objects and pictorial models. *also* **AF 1.1, 4.14A, 4.14D, 4.15A, 4.15B, 4.16A**

Connect

You can draw a picture to help you add decimals.

Add. 0.5 + 0.8

Step 1

Shade 5 columns red.

Step 2

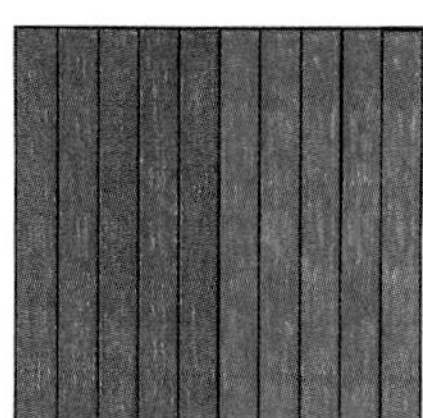

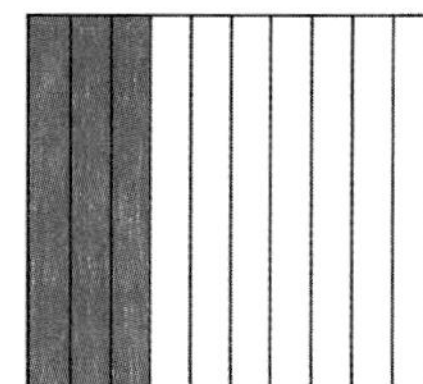

Shade 8 columns blue. Count the total number of columns shaded.

So, 0.5 + 0.8 = 1.3.

How would you model the sum of 1.42 and 0.36?

Practice

Use models to find the sum.

1. $\begin{array}{r} 0.45 \\ +0.89 \\ \hline \end{array}$
2. $\begin{array}{r} 0.9 \\ +0.7 \\ \hline \end{array}$
3. $\begin{array}{r} 0.92 \\ +0.47 \\ \hline \end{array}$
4. ✓ $\begin{array}{r} 1.6 \\ +1.0 \\ \hline \end{array}$
5. 3.71 + 0.54
6. 1.05 + 0.98
7. 2.75 + 0.84
8. ✓ 2.3 + 0.59

Algebra Use the models to find the missing addend.

9. 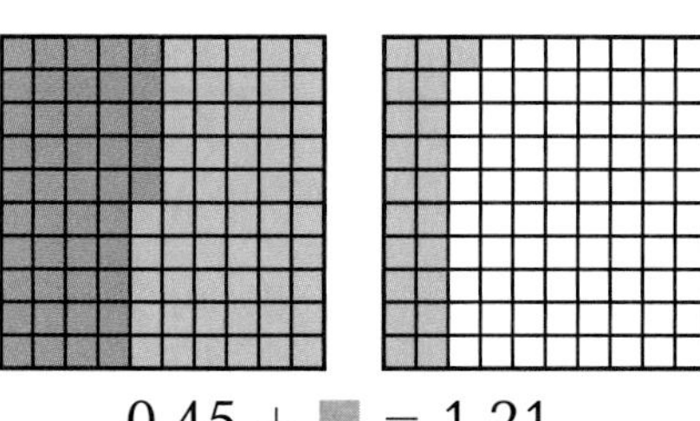

0.45 + ■ = 1.21

10. 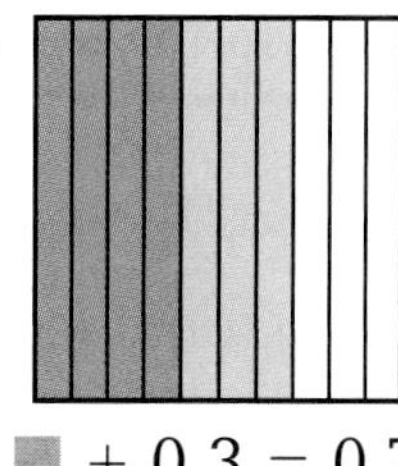

■ + 0.3 = 0.7

11. **WRITE Math** **Summarize** how you can use decimal models to find the sum of any two decimals.

CD ROM Technology
Use Harcourt Mega Math, Fraction Action, *Number Line Mine*, Levels P, Q.

LESSON 2 HANDS ON

Model Subtraction

OBJECTIVE: Model subtraction of decimals.

Quick Review

1. 67 − 25
2. 90 − 13
3. 313 − 210
4. 562 − 278
5. 400 − 164

Investigate

Materials ■ decimal models ■ color pencils

Use decimal models to find 0.8 − 0.5.

A Shade 8 columns on a decimal model red to represent 0.8.

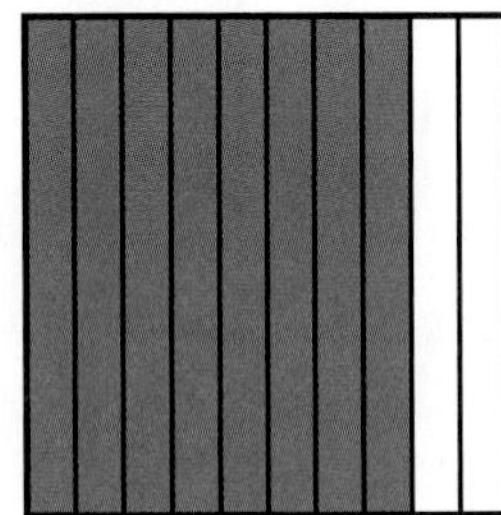

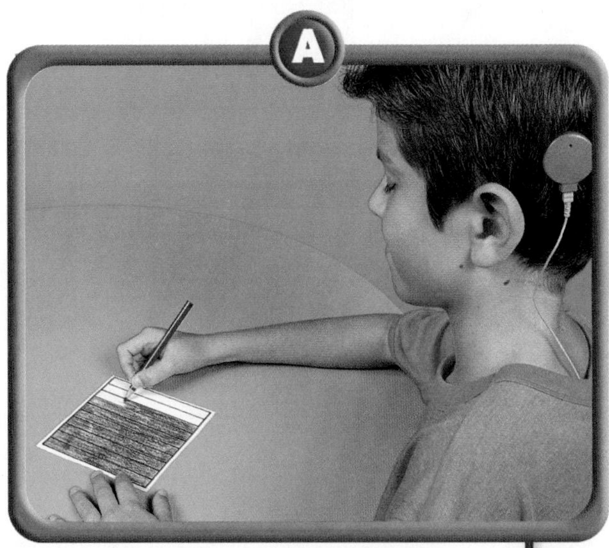

B Cut out 5 shaded columns from the shaded model.

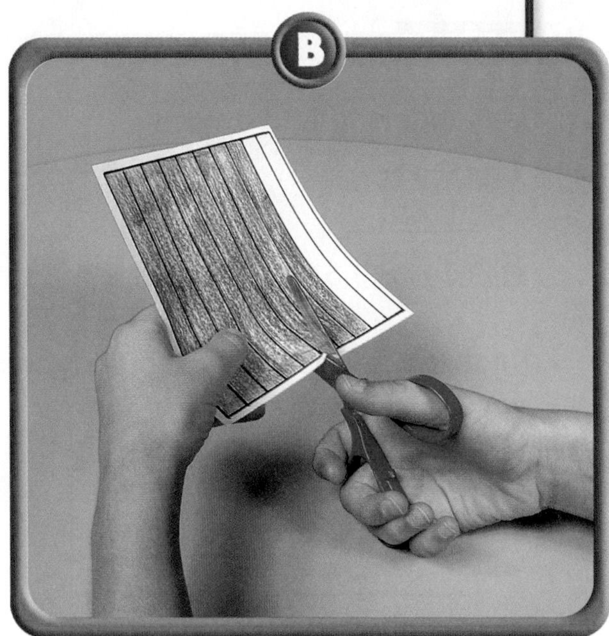

C Make three models to show subtracting a decimal from 1.0.

D Use decimal models to find 0.81 − 0.46.

Draw Conclusions

1. What is the difference between 0.8 and 0.5?
2. How did the decimal model help you find the difference?
3. What are two decimals you could find the difference between by using tenth models?
4. **Synthesis** If two decimals are both less than 1.0, what can you say about the difference between them?

TEKS 4.3B add and subtract decimals to the hundredths place using concrete objects and pictorial models. *also* **4.14A, 4.14D, 4.15A, 4.15B, 4.16A**

Connect

You can draw a picture to help you subtract decimals.

Subtract. 0.75 − 0.29

Step 1

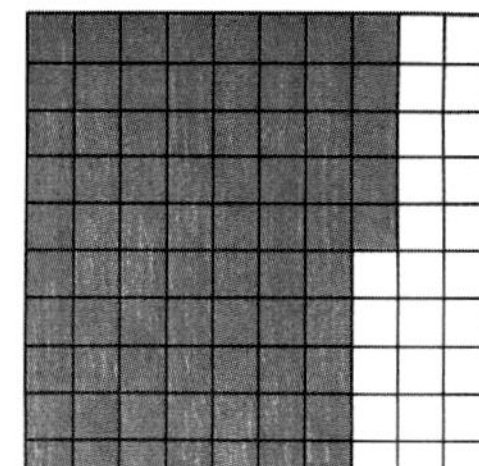

Shade 75 squares red.

Step 2

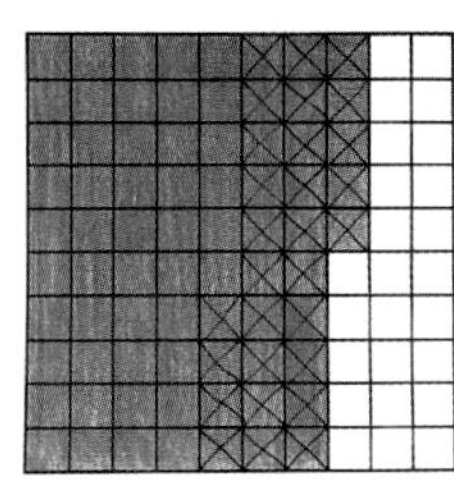

Draw Xs on 29 squares of the shaded part. Then, count the shaded squares that do not have Xs.

So, 0.75 − 0.29 = 0.46.

TALK Math

How would you use models to find the difference of any two decimals?

Practice

Use models to find the difference.

1. $\begin{array}{r} 0.56 \\ -\ 0.32 \\ \hline \end{array}$

2. $\begin{array}{r} 0.8 \\ -\ 0.2 \\ \hline \end{array}$

3. $\begin{array}{r} 0.72 \\ -\ 0.37 \\ \hline \end{array}$

✓ **4.** $\begin{array}{r} 1.1 \\ -\ 0.4 \\ \hline \end{array}$

5. $2.71 - 1.34$

6. $0.62 - 0.18$

7. $4.05 - 1.61$

✓ **8.** $1.3 - 0.52$

Algebra Use the models to find the missing number.

9.

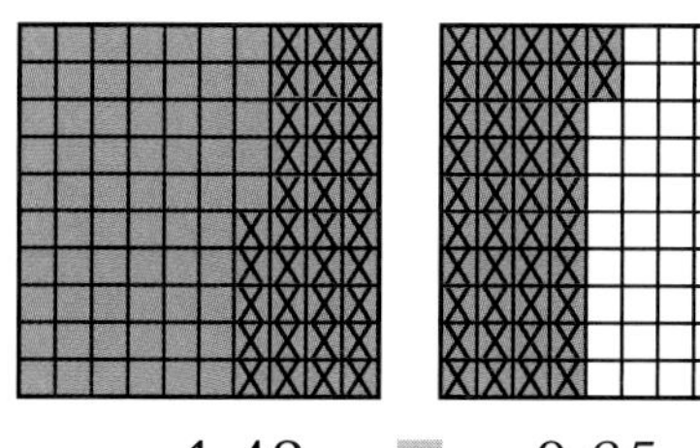

$1.42 - ■ = 0.65$

10.

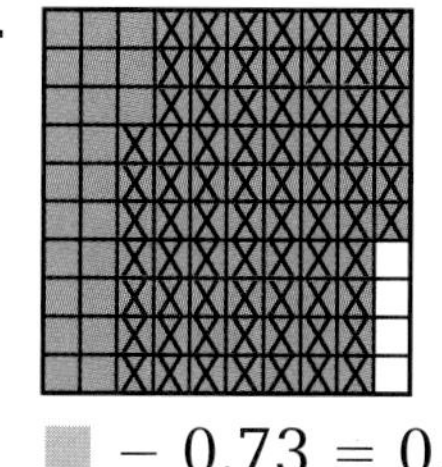

$■ - 0.73 = 0.23$

11. **WRITE Math** **Explain** how you can use models to find $0.6 - 0.45$.

Technology
CD ROM
Use Harcourt Mega Math, Fraction Action, *Number Line Mine*, Levels P, Q.

LESSON 3

Use Money

OBJECTIVE: Count, compare, order, and make change with decimal money amounts.

Quick Review

Compare. Use <, >, or =.

1. $0.75 ● $0.70
2. $2.55 ● $3.02
3. $1.17 ● $1.17
4. $4.21 ● $5.12
5. $0.08 ● $0.59

Learn

PROBLEM During her visit to Padre Island National Seashore, Mandy stopped to buy a frozen yogurt cone. A frozen yogurt cone costs $2.65. Mandy had two $1 bills, 2 quarters, 1 dime, and 1 nickel in her wallet. Did she have enough money to buy the cone?

Activity 1 Count money amounts.

Materials ■ play money

Use play money to find the total value of a given amount.

ONE WAY **Count the value of bills. Then count the value of coins.**

$1 → $2 → $2.25 → $2.50 → $2.60 → $2.65

ANOTHER WAY **Count the value of coins from greatest to least. Then count the value of bills.**

$0.25 → $0.50 → $0.60 → $0.65 → $1.65 → $2.65

So, Mandy had enough money to buy the cone.

Activity 2 Compare money amounts.

Materials ■ play money

Count each amount. Then compare to find the greater money amount.

$1.00 → $1.30 → $1.35 → $1.37

$1.00 → $1.75

Since $1.37 < $1.75, $1.75 is the greater amount.

TEKS 4.3B add and subtract decimals to the hundredths place using concrete objects and pictorial models. *also* **4.1B, 4.13A, 4.14A, 4.14D, 4.15A, 4.15B**

Activity 3 Use play money to make change.

Angel bought a sandwich. He paid with a $5 bill. How much change should he receive?

Count on from the amount owed to the amount paid.

BEACH SNACK BAR	
FOOD ITEM	PRICE
Salad	$1.75
Sandwich	$2.25
Frozen Yogurt Cone	$2.65
Fruit Cup	$1.45
Pizza by the slice	$1.25

Step 1 Use coins to count from $2.25 to the next dollar.

$2.25

$2.50 → $2.75 → $3.00

Step 2 Use bills to count to $5.

$4.00 → $5.00

Step 3 Count the coins and bills: 3 quarters and two $1 bills equal $2.75.

So, Angel receives $2.75 in change.

Here are some other possible ways that coins and bills equal $2.75.

$1 Bills	Quarters	Dimes	Nickels	Value
2	2	2	1	$2.75
1	7			$2.75
1	4	7	1	$2.75
1	4	5	5	$2.75

• What is another way coins and bills equal $2.75?

Guided Practice

1. Monique received $0.86 in change. What are the possible ways to represent the coins that are missing?

Compare. Write <, >, or =.

2. a.      

b.  

3. a.   

b.   

4. TALK Math **Explain** how you can order three different amounts of money from greatest to least.

Independent Practice and Problem Solving

Compare. Write <, >, or =.

5. a.  

b.   

6. a. 

b.   

Count the amounts of money and order from least to greatest.

7.      

8.      

Make change. List the bills and coins.

9. Cost: $12.49
Paid with: 

10. Cost: $6.57
Paid with: 

11. Cost: $3.34
Paid with: 

USE DATA For 12–13, use the pictures.

12. Juan bought a beach ball. He gave the cashier a $5 bill and received $1.11 in change. Did he get the correct change? **Explain** how you know.

13. Claire paid for one of the items with a $5 bill. She got back the following change. Which item did Claire buy?

14. Ty paid for 4 beach passes with two $20 bills. He received $4 change. How much did each beach pass cost?

 Extra Practice on page 462, Set A

15. **Reasoning** Erin buys a bottle of water for $\$0.55$. She pays with a $\$1$ bill. What is the least number of coins she can get back for change if none of the coins are quarters?

16. **WRITE Math** **What's The Error?** Nick has 3 dimes, 3 nickels, and 3 pennies. He says he has more money than Jose because Jose only has two quarters. Is he correct? **Explain.**

Mixed Review and TAKS Prep

17. Which number completes the pattern shown? (TEKS 4.6B, p. 224)

Meeting Room Space			
Rooms	16	18	20
Seats	1,600	1,800	■

18. Use the model to find $1.47 - 0.81$. (TEKS 4.3B, p. 448)

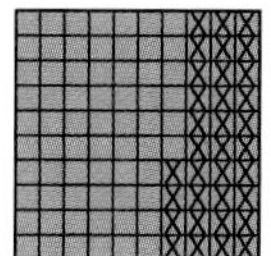 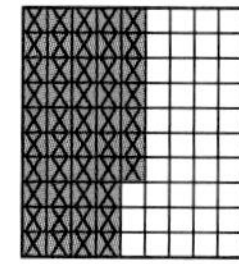

19. **TAKS Prep** Jamie has 2 quarters and a penny. Bill has 9 nickels, and Starr has 3 dimes and 5 nickels. Who has the most money? (Obj. 1)

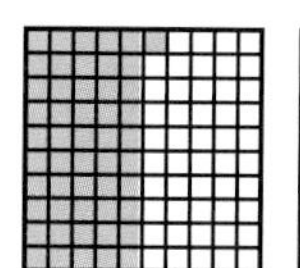 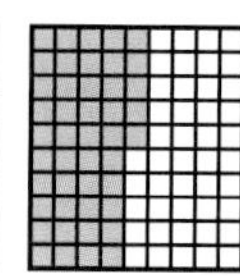 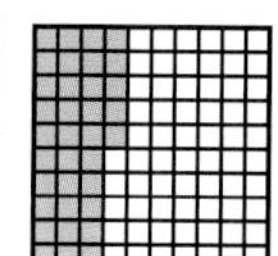

20. **TAKS Prep** Alton received $\$0.57$ in change. What coins are missing? (Obj. 1)

Problem Solving and Reasoning

1¢ 2¢ 20¢

NUMBER SENSE The greedy algorithm uses the least number of coins to make an amount. To use this method, begin with the coin of the greatest value and end with the least.

Example **Use the greedy algorithm and Australian coins.**

Make 35¢. Think about all of the possible coins available.

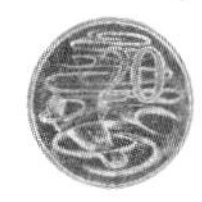 →  →  

20¢ 30¢ 35¢

So, 3 coins is the least number of coins needed to make 35¢.

Australian Money	
1¢ coin	20¢ coin
2¢ coin	50¢ coin
5¢ coin	$1 coin
10¢ coin	$2 coin
$5 banknote	

Use the greedy algorithm, the coins, and the banknote to find the change. List the coins.

1. a $\$1.35$ drink paid for with a $\$2$ coin
2. a $\$0.25$ pencil paid for with a $\$1$ coin
3. a $\$2.55$ toy paid for with a $\$5$ banknote
4. a $\$3.45$ ball paid for with a $\$5$ banknote

LESSON 4

Add and Subtract Decimals and Money

OBJECTIVE: Add and subtract decimal amounts and money.

Quick Review

Last year Henry traveled a total of 321.75 miles on his bicycle. What is this distance rounded to the nearest whole mile?

Learn

PROBLEM Each year, the average American eats about 3.36 pounds of peanut butter and about 2.21 pounds of fruit spread. How much peanut butter and fruit spread does each person eat per year?

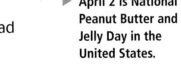

▶ April 2 is National Peanut Butter and Jelly Day in the United States.

Example 1 **Add.** 3.36 + 2.21

MODEL	THINK	RECORD
	Count the number of squares in the partially shaded models. Then count the number of models that are completely shaded.	$\begin{array}{r} 3.36 \\ +2.21 \\ \hline 5.57 \end{array}$

So, each person eats about 5.57 pounds of peanut butter and fruit spread per year.

Example 2

How much more peanut butter than fruit spread is eaten per person?

Subtract. 3.36 − 2.21

MODEL	THINK	RECORD
	Cross out 21 squares on the partially shaded model and 2 completely shaded models. Count the number of squares not crossed out to find what is left.	$\begin{array}{r} 3.36 \\ -2.21 \\ \hline 1.15 \end{array}$

So, each person eats 1.15 more pounds of peanut butter than fruit spread each year.

TEKS 4.3B add and subtract decimals to the hundredths place using concrete objects and pictorial models.
also **4.14A, 4.14D, 4.15A, 4.15B**

Add and Subtract Money Amounts

You can use models to help you record adding and subtracting money amounts.

A 16-ounce jar of peanut butter costs $4.25. An 8-ounce jar of jelly costs $2.85. How much do the jars of peanut butter and jelly cost in all?

Example 3 **Add.** $4.25 + $2.85

MODEL	THINK	RECORD
$1 $1 $1 $1 $1 $1 (25¢) (25¢) (25¢) (25¢) (10¢)	Count the value of the coins first. Then count the whole dollars.	1 1 $4.25 +$2.85 $7.10

So, the total cost for the jars of peanut butter and jelly is $7.10.

Math Idea

You can add decimals the same way you add whole numbers if you line up the decimal points first.

Example 4

How much more does the jar of peanut butter cost than the jar of jelly?

Subtract. $4.25 − $2.85

MODEL	THINK	RECORD
$1 $1 (25¢) $1 (25¢) (10¢) (25¢) (25¢) (10¢) (5¢)	Cross out $2.85 cents. Count the value of the coins and bills that are left.	3 12 $4.25 − $2.85 $1.40

So, the jar of peanut butter costs $1.40 more than the jar of jelly.

• How could you use decimal models to subtract money amounts?

Guided Practice

1. Look at the model at the right. Which of the choices below shows how to record what is shown in the model?

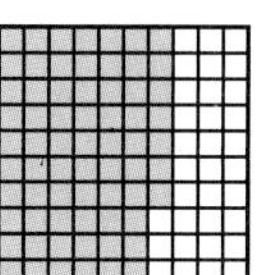

a. 1.00 − 0.67 **b.** 0.10 + 0.67 **c.** 1.00 + 0.67

Use models or pictures to find the sum or difference.
Record the answer.

2. $\begin{array}{r} 4.8 \\ +2.4 \\ \hline \end{array}$ **3.** $\begin{array}{r} 35.83 \\ -12.18 \\ \hline \end{array}$ **4.** $\begin{array}{r} \$23.44 \\ +\$19.85 \\ \hline \end{array}$ **✓5.** $\begin{array}{r} \$67.15 \\ -\ \$9.98 \\ \hline \end{array}$ **✓6.** $\begin{array}{r} 53.15 \\ +22.83 \\ \hline \end{array}$

7. **TALK Math** **Explain** how adding money amounts is like adding decimals and how it is different.

Independent Practice and Problem Solving

Use models or pictures to find the sum or difference.
Record the answer.

8. $\begin{array}{r} 6.5 \\ +3.9 \\ \hline \end{array}$ **9.** $\begin{array}{r} 71.82 \\ -52.39 \\ \hline \end{array}$ **10.** $\begin{array}{r} \$42.13 \\ +\$81.32 \\ \hline \end{array}$ **11.** $\begin{array}{r} \$31.56 \\ -\$19.17 \\ \hline \end{array}$

12. $2.03 + $27.89 **13.** 8.75 − 6.43 **14.** 3.5 + 42.32 **15.** 12.64 − 5

Compare. Write <, >, or = for each ●.

16. $19.54 + $63.29 ● $92.08 − $9.25 **17.** 3.46 + 32.75 ● 57.12 − 25.09

Algebra **Find the missing decimals. The sums are given at the end of each row and bottom of each column.**

18.	21.50	0.64	■	33.83
19.	■	17.16	65.20	85.34
20.	58.70	■	9.34	70.24
21.	83.18	20	86.23	■

22.	■	14.5	6.03	24.33
23.	7.56	■	74.68	99.89
24.	61.98	10.01	■	93.29
25.	73.34	42.16	102.01	■

USE DATA **For 26–29, use the table.**

26. The table shows the items on sale at a health food store. Tarika has $12.50. She is buying peanut butter, jelly, and lettuce. She has enough money left to buy one more item. What other item can she buy?

27. Draw pictures to show how much soy cheese and organic milk cost. Then use the pictures to find the difference in prices.

28. **Pose a Problem** Write a problem that uses the information in the table.

29. Colin gave the cashier a $5 bill. He got $1.81 in change. Write an equation that can be used to find out what item Colin bought. Use models or draw a picture to solve.

CD ROM
Technology
Use Harcourt Mega Math, The Number Games, *Buggy Bargains*, Levels F, G, I.

 Extra Practice on page 462, Set B

30. **FAST FACT** The world's largest peanut butter and jelly sandwich measured 2.44 meters long by 2.44 meters wide. It was made September 7, 2002, in Oklahoma City, OK. Do you need an estimate or an exact answer to determine whether the sandwich was longer than 2.03 meters? **Explain.**

▲ World's largest peanut butter and jelly sandwich.

31. **WRITE Math** **Explain** how adding and subtracting decimals is like adding and subtracting whole numbers. Then tell how it is different.

Mixed Review and TAKS Prep

32. What is the volume of the box? (Grade 3 TEKS 3.11F)

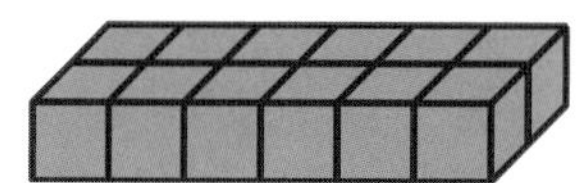

33. **TAKS Prep** Dale bought a pair of sneakers on sale for \$33.95. This was \$12.95 less than the original price. Use a model or draw a picture to find the original price of the sneakers. (Obj. 1)

A \$46.90 C \$22.00

B \$46.80 D \$21.00

34. Morgan jogs 0.75 miles each day. Jason jogs 0.50 miles each day. Who jogs farther? (TEKS 4.1B p. 432)

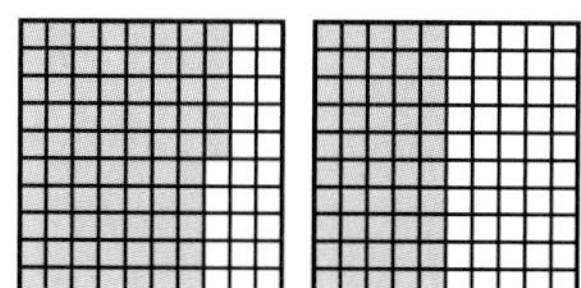

35. **TAKS Prep** Use the model to find 2.40 − 1.25. (Obj. 1)

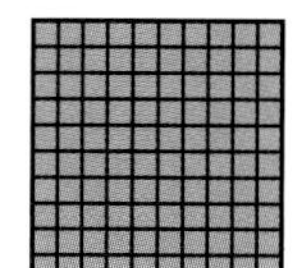 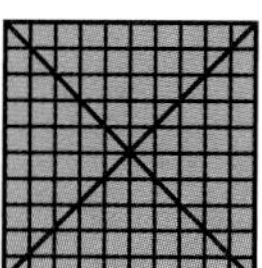 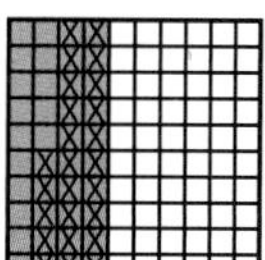

Problem Solving connects to Science

The recommended amount of protein for children ages 4 to 8 is 19 grams and for children ages 9 to 13 is 34 grams.

1. Gianna is 10 years old. She had a scrambled egg, an oat bran muffin, and a cup of low-fat milk for breakfast. How much more protein does she need to eat to reach the recommended level for a day?
2. Ming is 8 years old. His mom wants him to eat between 12 and 15 grams of his recommended amount of protein for breakfast. What items would make a good breakfast for Ming? How many grams of protein will he need to eat during the rest of the day?

Grams of Protein per Serving

Type of Food	Protein (in grams)
1 scrambled egg	6.76
1 cup shredded wheat cereal	5.56
1 oat bran muffin	3.99
1 cup low-fat milk	8.22

Problem Solving Workshop
Strategy: Make a Table

OBJECTIVE: Solve problems by using the strategy *make a table*.

Learn the Strategy

Making a table can help you organize the information in a problem to help you solve it. You can make tables for different types of problems.

Make a table to compare and order.

The community center snack cart sells granola bars for $1.25, peanuts for $1.15, yogurt for $0.95, and drinks for $1.29. Which item costs the most?

Snack Cart	
Snack	Price
Yogurt	$0.95
Peanuts	$1.15
Granola bar	$1.25
Drink	$1.29

Make a table to find different ways.

Hal has

He paid the cashier $2.80 for a new book binder. What are the different ways Hal could pay for the binder?

Coin Combinations			
Dollars	Quarters	Dimes	Nickels
2	3		1
2	2	3	
2	2	2	2

Make a table to show a relationship or pattern.

Bettina earns money walking her neighbors' dogs. She earns $8 for every two dog she walks. How much will she earn if she walks 8 dogs?

Dog Walking Earnings				
Number of dogs	2	4	6	8
Amount earned	$8	$16	$24	$32

To make a table, identify the information you need. Then organize the information based on the problem you are asked to solve.

TALK Math

What other questions could be answered by the information in each table?

TEKS 4.3B add and subtract decimals to the hundredths place using concrete objects and pictorial models. *also* **4.1B, 4.13A, 4.14A, 4.14B, 4.14C, 4.14D, 4.15A, 4.15B, 4.16B**

Use the Strategy

PROBLEM The vending machine at the Community Center takes exact change only, including bills and coins. Anthony wants to buy a bottle of water that costs $1.50. He has the following bills and coins.

What are the different ways Anthony can pay for the bottle of water?

Read to Understand

- **Classify and categorize the information by telling which coins and bills Anthony has.**
- **Is there information you will not use? If so, what?**

Plan

- **What strategy can you use to solve the problem?**
  You can make a table to record the different ways.

Solve

- **How can you use the strategy to solve the problem?**
  Make a table starting with the greatest values of bills and coins.

$1 Bills	Quarters	Dimes	Nickels
1	2		
1	1	2	1
1	1	1	3

So, Anthony can pay for the water in three different ways: one $1 bill and two quarters or one $1 bill, one quarter, two dimes, and one nickel or one $1 bill, one quarter, one dime, and three nickels.

Check

- **What other strategy could you have used to solve the problem? Explain.**

Guided Problem Solving

1. Sara wants to buy a can of apple juice from the vending machine. She needs exactly $2.30. She has the following bills and coins:

What are all the different ways Sara can pay for the juice? Make a table to show equivalent sets of money.

$1 Bills	Quarters	Dimes	Nickels	Value
2	1		1	$2.30
2		2	2	■
1	5		■	■
1	■	■	■	■

Complete your table to find all the different ways to make $2.30 with the dollars and coins available.

2. **What if** Sara wants to buy grape juice that costs $1.85? What are all the different ways she can make exactly $1.85 with the bills and coins she has? What coin must she use?

3. The vending machine has 10 drinks left. Some are juice and some are water. There are more cans of juice left than bottles of water. What possible combinations of water and juice could be left in the machine?

Guided Problem Solving Practice

USE DATA For 4–5, use the table.

4. The community center has a swimming pool. Henry paid the entrance fee with 8 coins. What coins did he use?

5. The community center pool has an entrance fee of $1.50 and sells bathing caps for $2.75 and towels for $5.55. Which item cost the least?

COMMUNITY CENTER POOL	
Item	Price
Entrance Fee	$1.50
Bathing Cap	$2.75

Mixed Strategy Practice

USE DATA For 6–9, use the poster.

6. Jana paid for herself and two friends for Open Skate Night. Jana had a membership card, but her friends did not. After paying, Jana received $6 change. How much money did Jana have before she paid for admission?

7. The Millers paid $6 more for skate rentals than the Johnsons. Together the two families paid $30. How many pairs of skates did the Millers rent?

8. **Pose a Problem** Look back at Problem 7. Write a similar problem by changing the amount the Millers paid and the sum of the amounts both families paid.

9. **Open-Ended** Ken and four of his friends are going to Open Skate Night. Ken does not have a membership card. Some of his friends do and some do not. What is the total amount that Ken and his friends might pay for admission?

10. Last Friday Pablo walked 5 blocks north, then 2 blocks east, to go to meet his friend Ralph. Both boys then walked back 2 blocks west and 3 blocks north to the Community Center. How many blocks does Pablo live from the Community Center?

Choose a STRATEGY

- Draw a Diagram or Picture
- Make a Model or Act It Out
- Make an Organized List
- Look for a Pattern
- Make a Table
- Guess and Check
- Work Backward
- Solve a Simpler Problem
- Write an Equation
- Use Logical Reasoning

Friday Night Open Skate
7 to 11 P.M. at The Arlington Community Center
Ages 9 and up
$5.00
admission
(without a
membership card)
$4.00
admission
(with a
membership card)
$3.00
skate rental

CHALLENGE YOURSELF

The concession stand will be open during Open Skate Night. It sells small drinks for $0.50, and large drinks for $1.00. Popcorn costs $0.85, and nachos cost $1.65. A small order of bread sticks costs $1.50, and a large order costs $2.00.

11. Ryan brought the amount shown above to the concession stand. He wants to buy a drink and something to eat. What snacks could Ryan buy if he buys a small drink?

12. Amanda bought a large drink, popcorn, and nachos at the concession stand. She gave the cashier a $5 bill and received 2 quarters in change. **Explain** how you can find whether Amanda received the correct change.

Extra Practice

Set A Compare. Write <, >, or =. (pp. 450–453)

1. a. 

   b.    

2. a. 

   b. 

3. a. 

   b.   

Count the amounts of money and order from least to greatest. (pp. 450–453)

4.      

5.      

6. Anita bought 3 books for $16.86. She gave the cashier a $20 bill. How much change should she receive?

Set B Use models or pictures to find the sum or difference. Record the answer. (pp. 454–457)

1. $\begin{array}{r} 5.8 \\ +\ 2.7 \\ \hline \end{array}$

2. $\begin{array}{r} 64.99 \\ -\ 37.53 \\ \hline \end{array}$

3. $\begin{array}{r} \$47.68 \\ +\ \ 24.09 \\ \hline \end{array}$

4. $\begin{array}{r} \$32.76 \\ -\ \ 18.96 \\ \hline \end{array}$

5. $1.91 + $13.77

6. 16.53 − 9.89

7. 7.3 + 55.67

8. 24.99 − 13

9. Rachel bought 2 packages of paper and a notebook. How much money did she receive in change if she gave the cashier a $20 bill?

10. Dylan bought a backpack and a 12-pack of pencils with three $5 bills. Does he have enough money to buy a pencil box? **Explain.**

School Supplies

Item	Price
Notebook	$5.57
Package of paper	$2.29
12-pack of pencils	$1.29
Backpack	$9.99
Pencil Box	$3.58

Technology
Use Harcourt Mega Math, The Number Games, *Buggy Bargains,* Levels D, F, G, H, I.

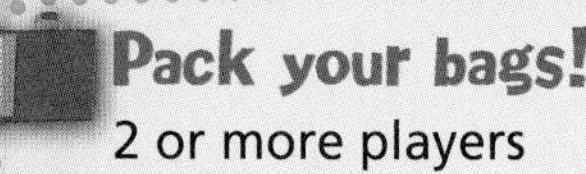

2 or more players

Buy your ticket!

Decimal cards

START

All aboard!

- Shuffle the decimal cards. Place them facedown in a stack. Players will take turns.
- The first player takes the top two decimal cards. Place one card on the engine and one card on the first car of the train. Find the sum of the two decimals. If the sum is correct, a player receives 1 point, and the cards stay on the train. If the sum is incorrect, the player receives no points, and the cards go to the bottom of the stack.

- After two cards are on the train, each player will choose one card from the stack and add it to the train. Each new decimal is added to the sum of all the previous decimals. Keep a running total. Do not forget to return a card to the stack if a sum is incorrect. Keep track of your scores, too.
- Repeat until the train is full of cards.
- The player with the most points wins.

FINISH

Chapter 17 Review/Test

Check Concepts

1. Explain how you can use hundredths models to find the sum of $0.15 + 0.81$. (TEKS 4.3B, pp. 446–447)

2. Summarize how you can draw a picture to help you subtract 0.63 and 0.36. (TEKS 4.3B, pp. 448–449)

Check Skills

Compare. Write <, >, or =. (TEKS 4.3B, pp. 450–453)

3. a.   

b.   

4. a.  

b.  

Count the amounts of money and order from least to greatest. (TEKS 4.3B, pp. 450–453)

5.     

6.      

Use models or pictures to find the sum or difference. Record the answer. (TEKS 4.3B, pp. 454–457)

7. $2.3 + 5.8$

8. $46.07 - 31.59$

9. $\$86.07 + \$53.57$

10. $\$39.64 - \$28.98$

Check Problem Solving

Solve. (TEKS 4.14C, pp. 458–461)

11. Devin wants to buy a movie ticket that costs \$6.50. He has one \$5 bill, one \$1 bill, 2 quarters, 3 dimes, and 2 nickels. What are all the different ways Devin can pay for the movie ticket?

12. Maria wants to buy a toy that costs \$2.45. She has two \$1 bills, 5 quarters, 2 dimes, and 2 nickels. What are all the different ways Maria can pay for the toy?

13. WRITE Math **Explain** how you can use a table to find all the different ways to make \$2.45 with the dollars and coins given in Exercise 12.

GO ONLINE Technology Use *Online Assessment.*

Enrich • Model Addition of Metric Measurements

Meletsticks and Decimals

Metric measures are based on the decimal system.
You can use a meterstick to model decimal numbers.

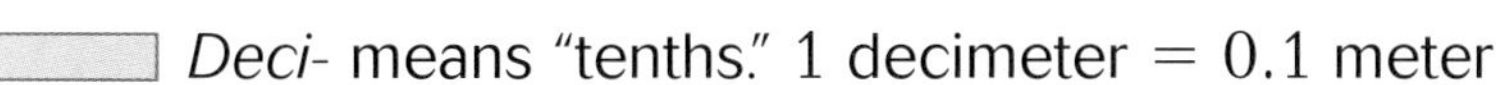 1.0 meter

Deci- means "tenths." 1 decimeter = 0.1 meter

Centi- means "hundredths." 1 centimeter = 0.01 meter

Write 2.73 meters as meters + decimeters + centimeters.

Think: 2.73 meters = 2 meters + 0.7 meters + 0.03 meters
0.7 meters = 7 decimeters
0.03 meters = 3 centimeters

So, 2.73 meters = 2 m + 7 dm + 3 cm.

▲ Some birds, such as orioles, nest in the mesquite tree. Their nests are an average of 2.73 meters above the ground.

Equivalent Measures

1 meter (m) = 10 dm
1 meter (m) = 100 cm
1 decimeter (dm) = 10 cm

Example

Write 4.59 meters as meters + decimeters + centimeters.

4.59 m = 4 m + 0.5 m + 0.09 m
So, 4.59 m = 4 m + 5 dm + 9 cm.

Try It

Complete. Draw models to show your work.

1. 1.38 m = 1 m + ■ dm + ■ cm
2. 2.41 m = 2 m + ■ dm + ■ cm
3. 4.91 m = ■ m + ■ dm + ■ cm
4. 0.43 m = ■ m + ■ dm + ■ cm
5. 3.1 m = ■ m + ■ dm + ■ cm
6. 2.07 m = ■ m + ■ dm + ■ cm

WRITE Math **Explain** how place value can help you write metric lengths as decimal numbers.

Unit Review/Test
Chapters 15–17

Multiple Choice

1. The model is shaded to represent $1\frac{4}{10}$.

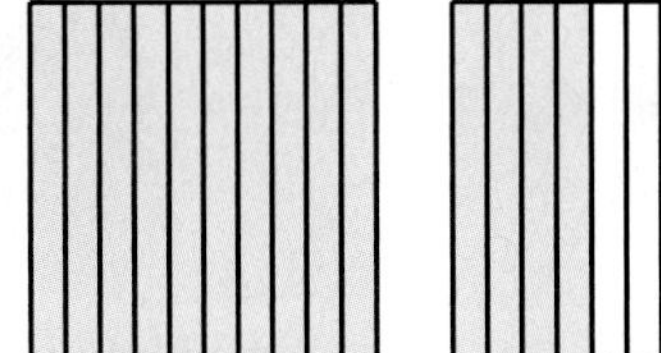

Which decimal does the model represent? (TAKS Obj. 1)

A 0.4

B 1.0

C 1.4

D 1.6

2. What number on the number line does point P best represent? (TAKS Obj. 1)

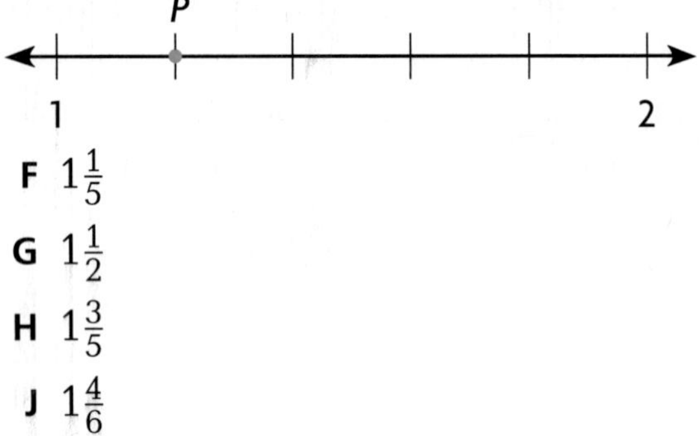

F $1\frac{1}{5}$

G $1\frac{1}{2}$

H $1\frac{3}{5}$

J $1\frac{4}{6}$

3. What decimal is represented by 2 dimes and 2 pennies? (TAKS Obj. 1)

A 0.22

B 0.24

C 0.4

D 0.44

4. Molly lives 0.97 mile from the library. Karen lives 0.83 mile from the library. How much farther from the library does Molly live? (TAKS Obj. 1)

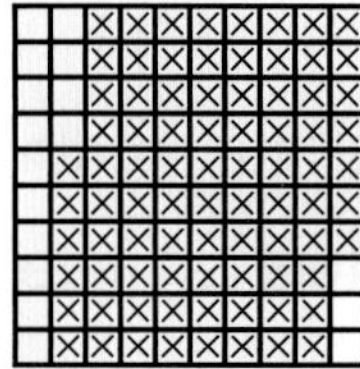

F 0.07 mile

G 0.14 mile

H 0.70 mile

J 1.4 miles

5. Hiro bought a set of notebooks for $\$3.79$. He paid with a $\$5.00$ bill. How much change did he receive? (TAKS Obj. 1)

A

B

C

D

GO ONLINE Technology Use *Online Assessment.*

6. Mindy baked a pizza. She put mushrooms on some of the slices.

Which of the following represents the portion of the pizza that has mushrooms? (TAKS Obj. 1)

F 0.6

G 0.4

H 0.2

J 0.1

7. Which of these expressions is **NOT** represented by the model? (TAKS Obj. 1)

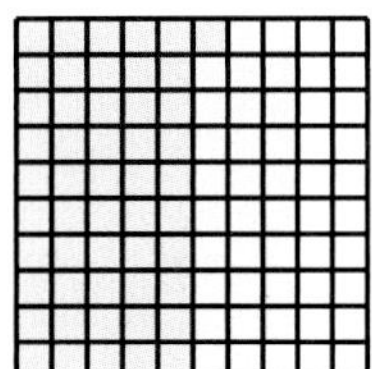

A $0.51 + 0.28$

B $0.28 + 0.79$

C $0.79 - 0.28$

D $0.79 - 0.51$

8. Look at the number line.

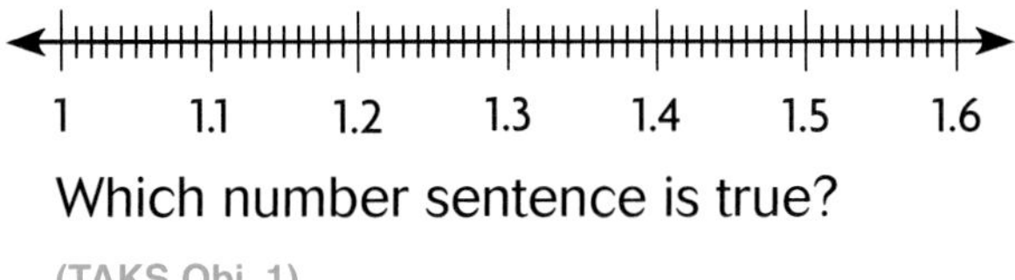

Which number sentence is true?
(TAKS Obj. 1)

F $1.54 < 1.5$

G $1.4 < 1.40$

H $1.29 < 1.19$

J $1.03 < 1.3$

Short Response

9. Nathan's soup recipe calls for $2\frac{1}{2}$ cups of tomato sauce. He has $2\frac{2}{3}$ cups of tomato sauce. Make a model to show whether Nathan has enough tomato sauce for the recipe. (TAKS Obj. 1)

10. Roeisha is 41 inches tall. There are 12 inches in a foot.

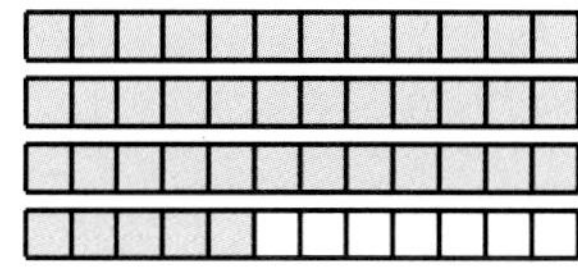

How many feet tall is she? Write your answer as a mixed number. (TAKS Obj. 1)

11. Write two fractions that are equivalent to $\frac{4}{8}$. (TAKS Obj. 1)

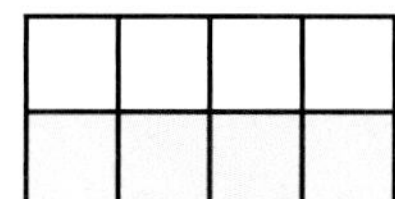

Extended Response WRITE Math

12. Look at the model.

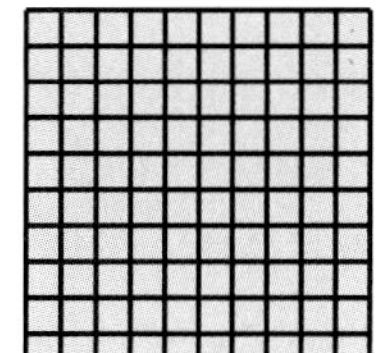

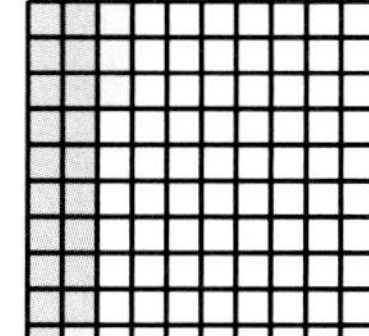

Matthew used the model to add 1.19 and 0.4. Is his model correct? **Explain.**
(TAKS Obj. 1)

13. Tonya says that 3.30 is greater than 3.3. Do you agree? Draw a model to **explain** why. (TAKS Obj. 1)

14. **Explain** how to use a model to find the missing number. (TAKS Obj. 1)

$$0.42 - \blacksquare = 0.29$$

Texas

Problem Solving

Cool Kites

KITES, NOT JUST FOR FLYING!

Think kites are just for flying? Kite sports are growing fast. Texas holds an annual kite buggy event in Galveston. At the event, a kite is attached to a three-wheeled vehicle to pull the "buggy" at speeds from 5 miles per hour to 100 miles per hour!

Kites can also be used in water sports. Kite boarding is surfing with a large kite attached to the board to help the surfer gain air. If the winds are good, the surfer can rise 30 feet in the air above the waves.

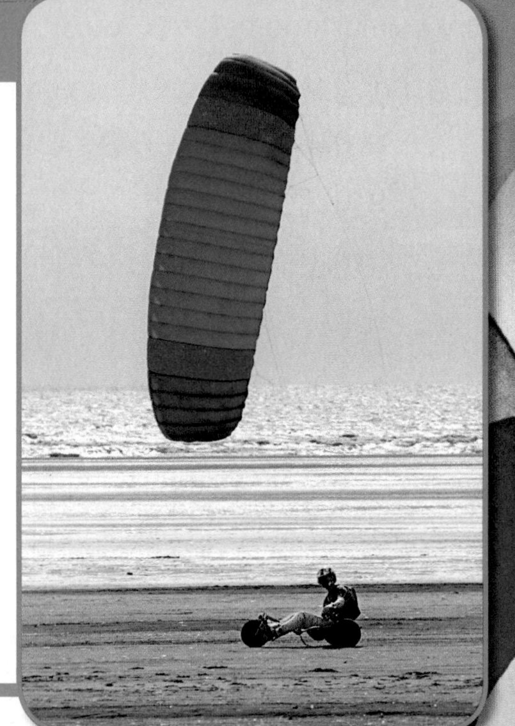

FACT·ACTIVITY

If you just like flying a kite, try a kite train. A kite train is two or more kites flown together in a line. Kite trains have been used to pull boats across water or go-carts across sand.

Use the kite train photos to answer the questions.

1. WRITE Math A student says that 3 kites in each kite train are red, so $\frac{3}{5} = \frac{3}{9}$. Is the student correct? **Explain** why or why not. Draw a diagram to support your answer.
2. What fraction of the 5-kite train is yellow? Draw and color a kite train with 10 kites that shows the equivalent fraction.

At the Zilker Kite Festival in Austin, Texas, people bring their homemade kites to compete in a variety of contests. Awards honoring contestants include the highest kite, the strongest kite, the steadiest kite, and the most unusual kite.

Design a Kite

The earliest known kites had simple flat shapes, like squares, rectangles, and diamonds, but kites can be made in other shapes. In the early 1900s, Orville and Wilbur Wright studied box-shaped kites to help them design the first airplane. Kites can even be made in fun shapes, like birds or dragons.

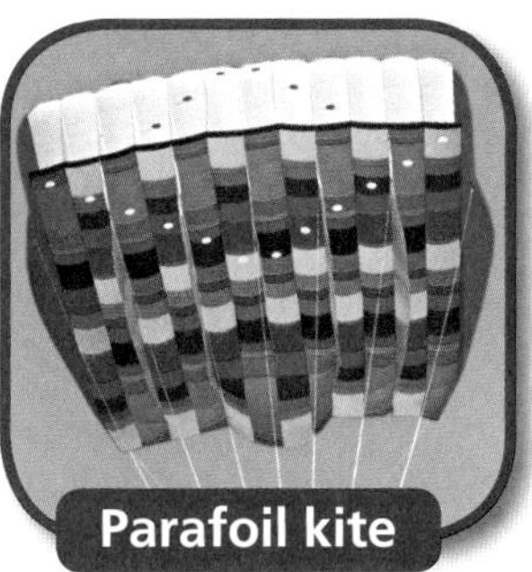
Parafoil kite

Box kite

Flat kite

FACT·ACTIVITY

Design your own flat kite.

- What shape will your kite be? What will its dimensions (length and width) be? Make at least one dimension a mixed number.
- Draw a diagram of your kite. Label its dimensions.
- Write a number sentence about the dimensions of your kite.
- Write a number sentence to compare the dimensions of your kite to those of a classmate's kite.
- WRITE Math Think about some different uses of kites. **Explain** how your kite alone or in a kite train might be useful. Then research and make a list of other ways kites can be useful.

UNIT 7

Time, Temperature, Data, and Combinations

Math on Location

with **Texas Chapter Projects**

1

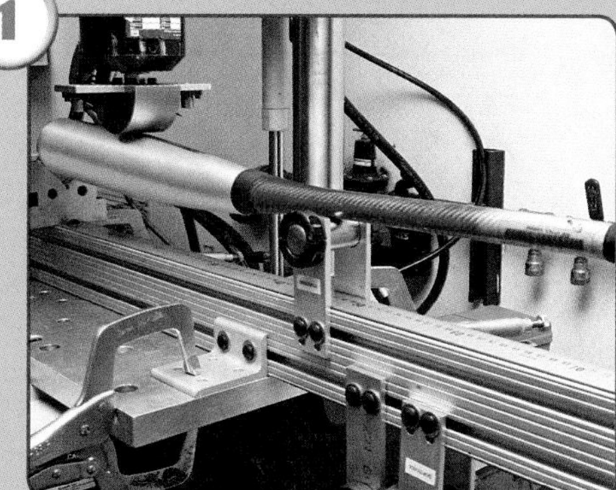

The data on how much of a bending load a bat takes is used to make a bar graph to compare bats.

2

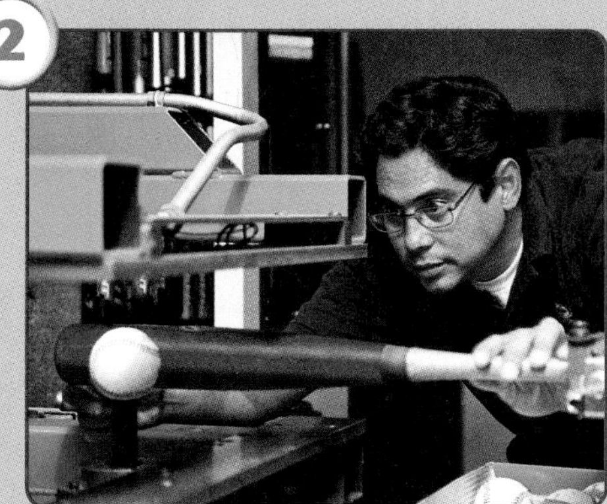

A test measures speed of the bat, speed of the ball, and turn of the bat.

3

A batter hits balls thrown from a pitching machine. A radar gun measures the speed of the balls hit.

VOCABULARY POWER

TALK Math

What math do you see in the **Math on Location** photographs? What type of graph would be used to compare the maximum speed of each ball hit from the pitching machine?

READ Math

REVIEW VOCABULARY You learned the words below when you learned how to organize and analyze data. How do these words relate to **Math on Location**?

bar graph a graph that uses bars to show data

data information collected about people or things

tally table a table that uses tally marks to record data

pictograph a graph that uses pictures to show and compare information

WRITE Math

Copy and complete a semantic map like the one below. Use **Math on Location** and what you know about organizing and analyzing data to complete the map.

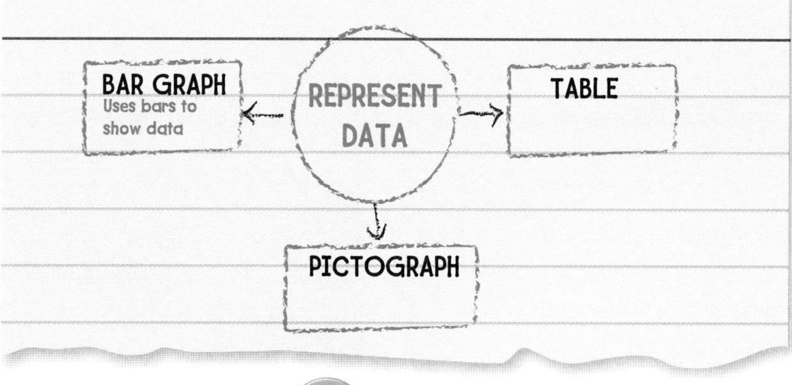

Technology
Multimedia Math Glossary link at
www.harcourtschool.com/hspmath

18 Time and Temperature

The Big Idea Time is the duration of an event; temperature is measured on a scale of positive and negative numbers.

Investigate

Temperatures usually rise from early morning lows to afternoon highs. Write a weather report. Use as many number sentences as you can to compare the change in temperature for each Texas city listed below. Tell which operation you used to find the changes in temperature.

Texas Temperatures, September 27, 2006 (°F)

City	High	Low
Abilene	91	68
Austin	93	63
Corpus Christi	86	65
Dallas	93	70
Houston	88	60
Waco	94	67

TEXAS FAST FACT

The highest recorded temperature in Texas is 120°F. It has been recorded in more than one city. It was first recorded in Seymour, Texas, on August 12, 1936.

GO ONLINE **Technology** Student pages are available in the Student eBook.

Show What You Know

Check your understanding of important skills needed for success in Chapter 18.

Use a Calendar

For 1–4, use the calendar.

March						
Sun	Mon	Tue	Wed	Thu	Fri	Sat
						1
2	3	4	5	6	7	8
9	10	11	12	13	14	15
16	17	18	19	20	21	22
23	24	25	26	27	28	29
30	31					

1. What is the date of the third Thursday in March?
2. What day of the week is March 22?
3. List the dates of all the Mondays in March.
4. What date is 2 weeks after March 12?

Tell Time

Write the time shown on the clock in numbers and words.

5. 

6. 

7. 

8. 

Measure Temperature

Use the thermometer to find the temperature.

9. 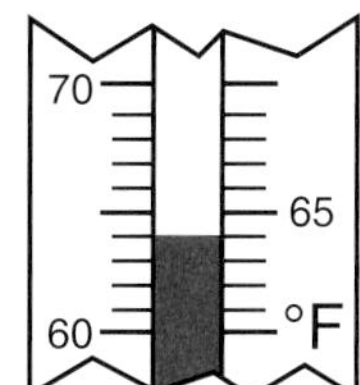

10. 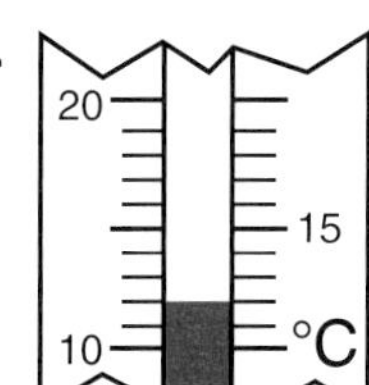

11. 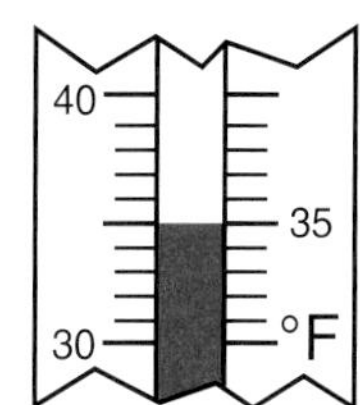

12. 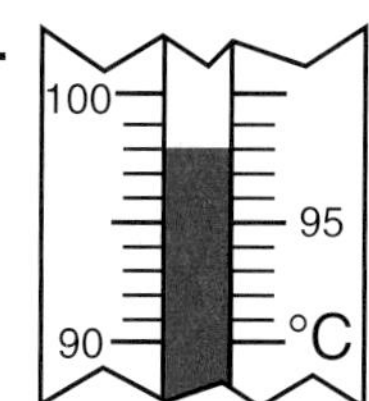

VOCABULARY POWER

CHAPTER VOCABULARY

A.M.
calendar
degree Celsius
degree Fahrenheit
elapsed time
half hour
minute
P.M.
quarter hour
schedule
second

WARM-UP WORDS

second a small unit of time

elapsed time the amount of time that passes from the start of an activity to the end of that activity

degree Fahrenheit a standard unit for measuring temperature

1 Measure Time

OBJECTIVE: Estimate and measure time to the nearest minute and second.

Quick Review

What is another way to write 30 minutes?

Vocabulary

second (sec)

Learn

PROBLEM Laci wants to see a movie. The movie starts at 2:10. The clock shows the time right now. Has the movie started yet?

Think: The time on the clock is 2:30, or 30 minutes after two. The movie started at 2:10, or 10 minutes after two.

So, the movie has already started.

The hour hand on a clock goes around the clockface twice each day to measure 24 hours. A.M. means "before noon" and P.M. means "after noon." Did the movie start in the morning or afternoon?

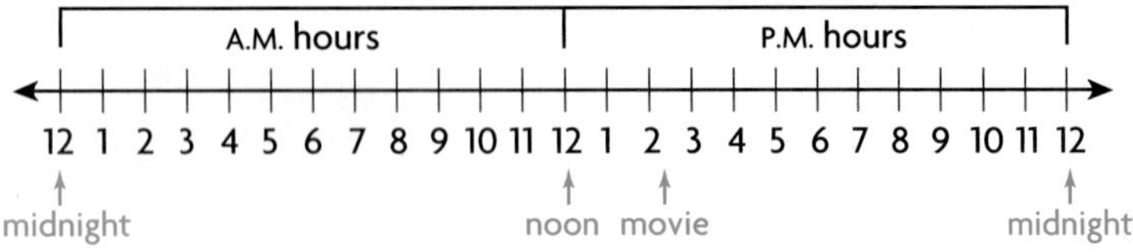

So, the movie started in the afternoon.

Units of Time
1 minute (min) = 60 seconds (sec)
1 quarter hour (hr) = 15 minutes
1 half hour = 30 minutes
1 hour = 60 minutes
1 day = 24 hours

Examples Estimate and measure time.

A To the nearest 5 minutes

Compare the location of the minute hand to the numbers on the clock.

Think: 1 is the 5-minute mark and 2 is the 10-minute mark.

3:07 is closer to 3:05 than 3:10.
So, it is about 3:05.

B Nearest minute

Write: 7:15 A.M.
Read: seven fifteen A.M.
15 minutes after seven in the morning, quarter after seven in the morning

C Nearest second

A **second** is a small unit of time.

Write: 5:10:12
Read: 5:10 and 12 seconds, 10 minutes and 12 seconds after five

- What unit of time would you use to measure the length of a school day?

Guided Practice

1. Copy and complete using the time shown. 46 __?__ and ■ seconds after ■

TEKS 4.12 The student applies measurement concepts. The student measures time and temperature (in degrees Fahrenheit and Celsius). *also* **4.14A, 4.14D, 4.15A, 4.15B**

Write the time as shown on a digital clock.

2. 32 minutes after six
3. 47 minutes after twelve
4. 20 minutes before four

5. TALK Math **Explain** how telling time to the nearest second is different from telling time to the nearest minute on an analog clock.

Independent Practice and Problem Solving

Write the time as shown on a digital clock.

6. 24 minutes after three
7. 18 minutes before ten
8. quarter to five

Write two ways to read the time. Then estimate to the nearest 5 minutes.

9. 

10. 

11. 

12. 

13. 

14. 

Tell whether to use seconds, minutes, hours, or days to measure the time.

15. to eat lunch
16. to run a 50-yd dash
17. to read a 400-page book

USE DATA For 18 and 20, use the watch.

18. The watch shows the time the movie ended. To the nearest 5 minutes, about what time was it? Include A.M. or P.M.
19. **FAST FACT** The silent movie *The Gold Rush* runs 96 minutes. To the nearest half hour, how long is that?
20. WRITE Math **What's the Error?** Alan's says his watch shows the movie ended at 2:48 P.M. **Explain** Alan's error.

Mixed Review and TAKS Prep

21. Write a rule for the pattern: 3, 9, 27, 81. (Grade 3 TEKS 3.16A)
22. Jason tosses a number cube labeled 1 to 6. Are his chances of tossing a 4 likely, less likely, or equally likely? (Grade 3 TEKS 3.13C)
23. **TAKS Prep** Marta says the time is eight minutes after two in the afternoon. Which time is it? (Obj. 4)

    A 2:08 A.M.
    B 2:08 P.M.
    C 8:02 A.M.
    D 8:02 P.M.

Extra Practice on page 488, Set A

LESSON 2

Elapsed Time

OBJECTIVE: Calculate elapsed time using clocks and stopwatches.

Quick Review

Write the time shown on the clock in two ways.

Vocabulary

elapsed time

Learn

PROBLEM From school, Darren and his dad are taking the bus to the mall to buy a new computer game. How long will the bus ride last?

The time that passes from the start of an activity to the end of that activity is **elapsed time**.

Bus Schedule

Bus Stop Location	Arrival Time
Avery School	3:00 P.M.
Post Office	3:15 P.M.
Library	4:05 P.M.
Central Mall	4:35 P.M.

Example 1 Use a clock to find elapsed time.

You can use a clock to count forward from the starting time to the ending time.

Think: From 3:00 P.M. to 4:00 P.M., 1 full hour has passed.

Think: From 4:00 P.M. to 4:35 P.M., 35 minutes have passed.

1 hour + 35 minutes = 1 hour 35 minutes

So, the bus ride will last 1 hour 35 minutes.

ERROR ALERT

When the hour hand moves from one number to the next, one hour has passed.

Example 2 Find the ending time.

Erin and her mother get on the bus at 4:35 P.M. Their ride home from Central Mall lasts 45 minutes. What time do they get home?

Count forward 5 minutes at a time.

So, Erin and her mother get home at 5:20 P.M.

TEKS 4.12B use tools such as a clock with gears or a stopwatch to solve problems involving elapsed time. *also* 4.14A, 4.14D, 4.15A, 4.15B, 4.16A

Example 3 **Find the starting time.**

Dora and her son hiked for 35 minutes.
They stopped for a snack at 4:15 P.M.
When did they start hiking?

Count backward 5 minutes at a time.

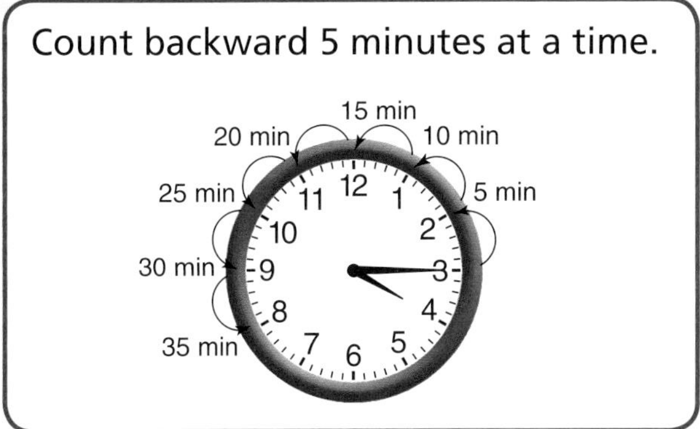

So, Dora and her son started hiking at 3:40 P.M.

READ Math

When you read time on most stopwatches, the first number names the minutes and the second number names the seconds. So, if the time shows 3:10, you read "three minutes, ten seconds."

Activity

Materials ■ stopwatch

Use a stopwatch to time and record everyday activities.

In pairs, you will time each other to find out how long it takes to do everyday activities.

- How long does it take to write your name ten times?

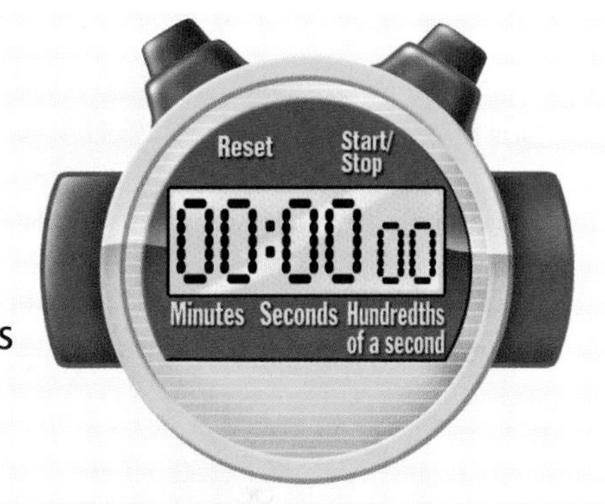

Copy and complete the table. Use a stopwatch. You run the stopwatch while your partner completes the activity.

Name	Activity	Elapsed Time
?	?	■

Step 1	Step 2	Step 3
You say, "GO!" Your partner begins writing. You push the Start/Stop button.	When finished, your partner says, "STOP!" You push the Start/Stop button.	You read the stopwatch readout and record the time on your table.

When you and your partner have completed the activity, compare your elapsed times.

- What are some other activities you could time with a stopwatch?

Guided Practice

1. A television cartoon show begins at 10:30 A.M. and ends at 11:00 A.M. Find the elapsed time.

Use a clock to find the elapsed time.

2. start: 8:10 A.M.
   end: 9:00 A.M.
3. start: 11:15 A.M.
   end: 12:45 P.M.
4. start: 6:15 P.M.
   end: 10:49 P.M.
5. start: 12:00 A.M.
   end: 3:07 P.M.

Use a clock to find the end time.

6. start: 12:00 P.M.
   elapsed time:
   5 hr 45 min
7. start: 1:37 P.M.
   elapsed time:
   40 min
8. start: 7:12 A.M.
   elapsed time:
   3 hr 15 min
9. start: 3:07 A.M.
   elapsed time:
   8 hr 55 min

10. **TALK Math** It is 3:47 P.M. The game began at 2:05 P.M. **Explain** how to find how much time has passed since the game began.

Independent Practice and Problem Solving

Use a clock to find the elapsed time.

11. start: 4:00 P.M.
    end: 11:30 P.M.
12. start: 9:15 P.M.
    end: 7:45 A.M.
13. start: 10:40 A.M.
    end: 2:10 P.M.
14. start: 7:30 P.M.
    end: 6:45 A.M.

Use a clock to find the start time.

15. end: 11:50 P.M.
    elapsed time:
    1 hr 10 min
16. end: 9:45 A.M.
    elapsed time:
    2 hr 20 min
17. end: 10:15 P.M.
    elapsed time:
    1 hr 45 min
18. end: 8:30 A.M.
    elapsed time:
    9 hr 30 min

Algebra **Copy and complete the tables.**

	Start Time	End Time	Elapsed Time
19.	3:13 P.M.	3:45 P.M.	■
20.	■	11:40 A.M.	4 hr 30 min

	Start Time	End Time	Elapsed Time
21.	4:45 A.M.	■	8 hr 5 min
22.	■	3:00 A.M.	3 hr 15 min

USE DATA For 23–24, use the table.

23. Vincent timed the wait at each stop with a stopwatch. At which stop did the bus spend the least time?

24. The bus arrived at the Avery School at 3:00 P.M. To the nearest second, what time did the bus leave the school?

Time Spent at Bus Stops

Stop	Elapsed Time (min:sec)
Avery School	2:05
Central Mall	3:15
Library	1:34
Post Office	1:12

Technology
Use Harcourt Mega Math, The Number Games, *Tiny's Think Tank*, Level D.

 Extra Practice on page 488, Set B

25. **Reasoning** **Explain** how you remember the difference between 12:00 P.M. and 12:00 A.M.

26. **WRITE Math** **What's the Question?** Ms. Morters takes dance class for 2 hours and music lessons for 1 hour 20 minutes. The answer is 3 hours 20 minutes.

Mixed Review and TAKS Prep

27. What is the missing number?
$8 + (7 - 4) = \blacksquare + 6$ (TEKS 4.3A, p. 32)

28. **TAKS Prep** The movie started at 6:52 P.M. and ended at 9:15 P.M. How long was the movie? (Obj. 4)

A 2 hours 23 minutes
B 2 hours 36 minutes
C 3 hours 27 minutes
D 3 hours 36 minutes

29. Estimate the time to the nearest 5 minutes: 4:07:28 P.M. (TEKS 4.12A, p. 474)

30. **TAKS Prep** It is 4:25 P.M. What time did Jo's party start, if 3 hours 10 minutes have passed? (Obj. 4)

F 2:40 P.M.
G 2:25 P.M.
H 1:35 P.M.
J 1:15 P.M.

Problem Solving and Reasoning

MEASUREMENT Seconds, minutes, and hours are used to describe short everyday activities. Days, weeks, months, and years are used to describe longer periods of time. Sometimes you may need to change units of time.

Multiply to find shorter units.

How many minutes are in 4 hours?

Think: 4 hours = ■ minutes

$$\begin{array}{rl} 60 & \text{minutes} \\ \times\ 4 & \text{hours} \\ \hline 240 & \text{minutes} \end{array}$$

So, 240 minutes are in 4 hours.

Divide to find longer units.

How many days are in 120 hours?

Think: 120 hours = ■ days

120 ÷ 24 = 5

So, 5 days are in 120 hours.

Use a calculator to solve.

1. How many minutes are in 180 seconds?
2. How many seconds are in 15 minutes?
3. How many minutes are in 7 hours?
4. How many days are in 96 hours?
5. How many months are in 3 years?
6. How many weeks are in 49 days?

Problem Solving Workshop
Skill: Sequence Information

OBJECTIVE: Solve problems by using the skill *sequence information.*

Use the Skill

PROBLEM Abigail made a bookmark, ate lunch, and ran the 3-legged race. She ate lunch at 12:00. She made a bookmark before lunch, but after she ran the race. What time did Abigail make the bookmark and run the 3-legged race?

▲ You can record a sequence by writing the information in a table.

Use the schedule to solve the problem.

Fun Fair

	3-Legged Race	Go Fish	Book Sale	Face Painting	Bookmarks	Lunch
10:00 A.M. - 10:30 A.M.						
10:30 A.M. - 11:00 A.M.						
11:00A.M. - 11:30 A.M.						
11:30 A.M - 12:00 P.M.						
12:00 P.M. - 12:30 P.M.						
12:30 P.M. - 1:00 P.M.						
1:00 P.M. - 1:30P.M.						
1:30 P.M. - 2:00 P.M.						
2:00 P.M. - 2:30 P.M.						
2:30 P.M. - 3:00 P.M.						

Since there is only one bookmark session before Abigail's lunch, she made a bookmark from 11:30 A.M. to 12:00 P.M. Since Abigail ran the race before she made the bookmark, she must have run the 3-legged race from 10:00 A.M. to 10:30 A.M.

So, Abigail made the bookmark at 11:30 A.M. and ran the race at 10:00 A.M.

TALK Math

Look at the activities on the poster. How can sequencing information help you solve problems about time?

Think and Discuss

Use the information in the poster to sequence the information to solve.

a. Linda arrives at the school fair at 10:00 A.M. and wants to play go fish, buy a book from the book sale, and have her face painted. She has to go home at 12:30 P.M. How can she sequence her activities?

b. **What if** Linda also wants to make a bookmark? How can she sequence her activities now?

c. Jim wants to do every activity at the school fair. He also volunteers at the lunch counter from 12:00 P.M. to 1:00 P.M. How can he sequence his activities so he has time for all of them?

TEKS 4.12B use tools such as a clock with gears or a stopwatch to solve problems involving elapsed time. *also* **4.14A, 4.14C, 4.14D, 4.15A, 4.15B, 4.16B**

Guided Problem Solving

1. Jobi is going to a children's museum. He will be there from 9:00 A.M. to 1:00 P.M. How can he schedule his time so he can visit each exhibit?

   Sequence the information to make a schedule.

Exhibit Schedule		
Exhibit	**Exhibit Times**	**Length**
Light Show	8:00 A.M., 8:30 A.M., 9:00 A.M., 9:30 A.M., 12:00 P.M., 12:30 P.M., 2:00 P.M.	30 minutes
Ecosystems	10:00 A.M., 1:30 P.M.	60 minutes
Claymation	9:00 A.M., 10:00 A.M., 11:30 A.M., 2:00 P.M.	45 minutes
Story Time	8:30 A.M., 9:30 A.M., 11:30 A.M., 3:30 P.M.	30 minutes
Lunch	11:00 A.M., 11:20 A.M., 12:00 P.M., 12:20 P.M., 12:40 P.M., 1:00 P.M.	20 minutes

2. **What if** Jobi wants to see the light show twice? How can he schedule his time now?

3. Plan a class trip to the children's museum. Make a schedule that includes 30 minutes of travel time both to and from the museum. Your trip should only last as long as your school day.

Mixed Applications

4. Jeniah saved $30 of her allowance. She bought a game for $10 and a box of popcorn for $1. Then Leila repaid the $16 she borrowed from Jeniah. How much money does Jeniah have now?

5. **WRITE Math** Sarah leaves home at 7:45 A.M. and arrives at school at 8:15 A.M. She leaves school at 3:00 P.M.. Her ride home is the same length as her ride to school. As soon as she gets home, her grandma takes her to ballet. They arrive at 4:15 P.M. How long does it take for Sarah and her grandma to get to ballet? **Explain.**

USE DATA For 6–7, use the sign.

6. The Corner Market sells T-shirts for $10 each. If you buy more than one, you pay less for each shirt. How can you buy 5 shirts and pay the least amount of money?

7. If 7 CDs and a T-shirt cost $59, how much do 2 CDs cost?

LESSON

4 Elapsed Time on a Calendar

OBJECTIVE: Find elapsed time on a calendar.

Quick Review

Marcy put a cake in the oven at 3:35 and took it out at 4:18. How long was the cake in the oven?

Learn

PROBLEM October 18, 1961, the New York Museum of Modern Art hung the painting *Le Bateau*, "The Sailboat," upside-down. The mistake was not noticed until December 4. About how many weeks did the painting hang upside-down?

You can use a calendar to find elapsed time.

▲ New York Museum of Modern Art

Example 1 Use a calendar to count.

To find the elapsed time, first count the weeks. Start with October 18, and count the weeks to November 29. Then count on the days to December 4.

October						
Sun	Mon	Tue	Wed	Thu	Fri	Sat
1	2	3	4	5	6	7
8	9	10	11	12	13	14
15	16	17	18	19	20	21
22	23	24	25	26	27	28
29	30	31				

November						
Sun	Mon	Tue	Wed	Thu	Fri	Sat
			1	2	3	4
5	6	7	8	9	10	11
12	13	14	15	16	17	18
19	20	21	22	23	24	25
26	27	28	29	30		

December						
Sun	Mon	Tue	Wed	Thu	Fri	Sat
					1	2
3	4	5	6	7	8	9
10	11	12	13	14	15	16
17	18	19	20	21	22	23
24	25	26	27	28	29	30
31						

Le Bateau hung upside-down for 6 weeks 5 days.

So, *Le Bateau* hung upside-down for about 7 weeks.

- Explain how to count the elapsed time by days.

Example 2 Use a calendar and change units.

Evan practiced the violin every day from April 18 through May 2. For how many weeks did he practice? How many days?

Calendar: Count the weeks from April 18 to May 2. There are 2 weeks.

Change Units: 2 weeks $\times$ 7 days in a week $=$ 14 days.

So, Evan practiced for 2 weeks, or 14 days.

April						
Sun	Mon	Tue	Wed	Thu	Fri	Sat
		1	2	3	4	5
6	7	8	9	10	11	12
13	14	15	16	17	18	19
20	21	22	23	24	25	26
27	28	29	30			

May						
Sun	Mon	Tue	Wed	Thu	Fri	Sat
				1	2	3
4	5	6	7	8	9	10
11	12	13	14	15	16	17
18	19	20	21	22	23	24
25	26	27	28	29	30	31

TEKS 4.12B use tools, such as a clock with gears or a stopwatch, to solve problems involving elapsed time.
also **4.14A, 4.14D, 4.15A, 4.15B, 4.16A**

Guided Practice

For 1–3, use the calendars.

January						
Sun	Mon	Tue	Wed	Thu	Fri	Sat
		1	2	3	4	5
6	7	8	9	10	11	12
13	14	15	16	17	18	19
20	21	22	23	24	25	26
27	28	29	30	31		

February						
Sun	Mon	Tue	Wed	Thu	Fri	Sat
					1	2
3	4	5	6	7	8	9
10	11	12	13	14	15	16
17	18	19	20	21	22	23
24	25	26	27	28	29	

1. Most months have 30 days. How many weeks is this? What is the remainder?
2. Li went to the dentist on January 15. If today is February 29, how many days is it since she saw the dentist?
3. Frank finished building a model ship on February 26. If he worked on it for 8 weeks, when did he start the ship?
4. TALK Math **Explain** how you use a calendar to find elapsed time.

Independent Practice and Problem Solving

For 5–6, use the calendars above.

5. A store is having a sale on paints starting on January 7 and ending on January 23. For how many days are paints on sale?
6. Presidents' Day was February 18. If Martin Luther King, Jr. Day was 4 weeks and 1 day earlier, what date was it?

Algebra Find the missing numbers.

7. 1 month 2 weeks 3 days = ■ days
8. 37 days = ■ weeks ■ days

For 9–11, use the table and the calendars above.

Art Gallery Winter Exhibits	
Type of Art	**Dates of Exhibit**
Paintings	Jan 4 through Jan 20
Drawings	Jan 24 through Feb 3
Pottery	Feb 5 through Feb 15

9. Which type of art will be shown for the greatest amount of time? Which will be shown for the least amount of time?
10. If the gallery doubles the number of days for its painting exhibit, what will be the last day of the exhibit?
11. How long is the period of winter exhibits, from the first day of the painting exhibit to the last day of the pottery exhibit?
12. WRITE Math **Explain** a pattern of the dates as you move down a calendar column for any day of the week.

Mixed Review and TAKS Prep

13. Allan paid $10.00 for lunch and got $4.39 change. How much was his lunch? Draw a picture to solve. (TEKS 4.3B, p. 454)
14. What kind of angles are in an obtuse triangle? (TEKS 4.8C, p. 268)
15. **TAKS Prep** Use the calenders above. If today is February 15, how many days have passed since January 2? (Obj. 4)

    A 22 days **C** 32 days
    B 26 days **D** 44 days

Extra Practice on page 488, Set C

Temperature: Fahrenheit

OBJECTIVE: Measure temperature and changes in temperature in degrees Fahrenheit.

Quick Review

Draw a number line to show the order of the numbers from least to greatest: 5, 1, 12, 21, and 15.

Vocabulary

degrees Fahrenheit (°F)

Learn

Degrees Fahrenheit (°F) are the customary units for measuring temperature. For example, the record high temperature in Amarillo, Texas, in December is 81°F. Read 81°F as "eighty-one degrees Fahrenheit."

Temperatures less than 0°F are negative temperatures. The record low temperature for Amarillo in December is ⁻8°F. Read ⁻8°F as "eight degrees below zero Fahrenheit."

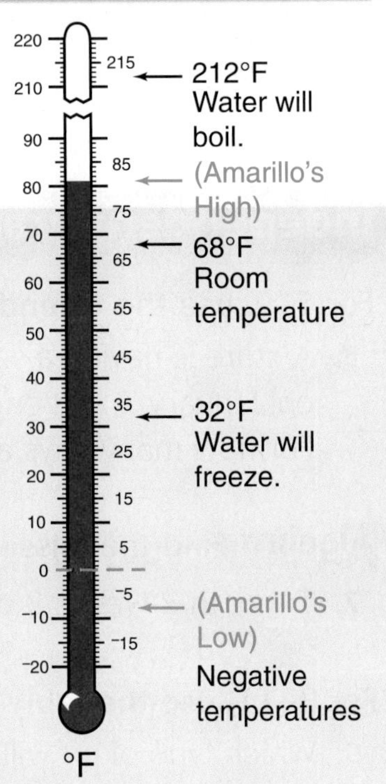

Example Find the change in temperature.

A Temperature rises.
⁻5°F to 12°F

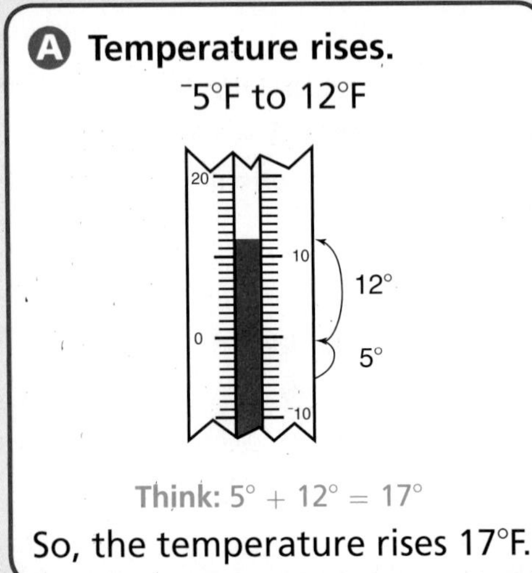

Think: 5° + 12° = 17°

So, the temperature rises 17°F.

B Temperature drops.
17°F to ⁻3°F

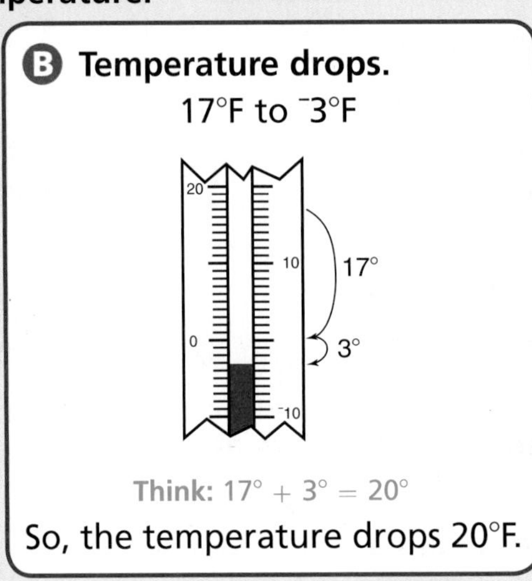

Think: 17° + 3° = 20°

So, the temperature drops 20°F.

Activity

Materials ■ Fahrenheit thermometers

- Use a Fahrenheit thermometer to measure the temperature outside your classroom in the morning. Copy the table and record the time and temperature.
- Measure the temperature outside your classroom again in the afternoon. Record the time and temperature in the table.
- Find the change in temperature. Did the temperature rise or drop during the day?

Temperature Outside The Classroom	
Time	Temperature (in °F)

TEKS 4.12A use a thermometer to measure temperature and changes in temperature. *also* **4.14A, 4.14D, 4.15A, 4.15B, 4.16A**

Guided Practice

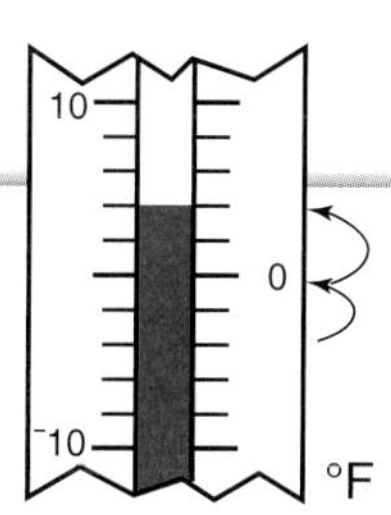

1. Count the degrees from ⁻4°F to 0°F and then from 0°F to 4°F. Add. Write the change in temperature.

Use the thermometer to find the temperature in °F.

2. 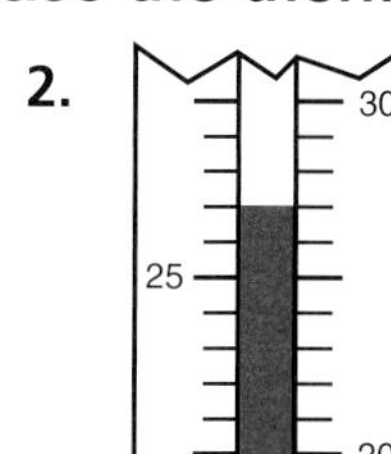

3. 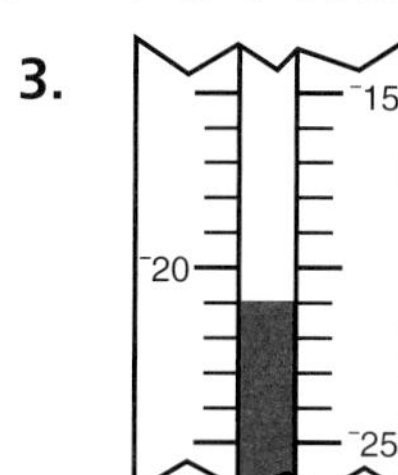

4. 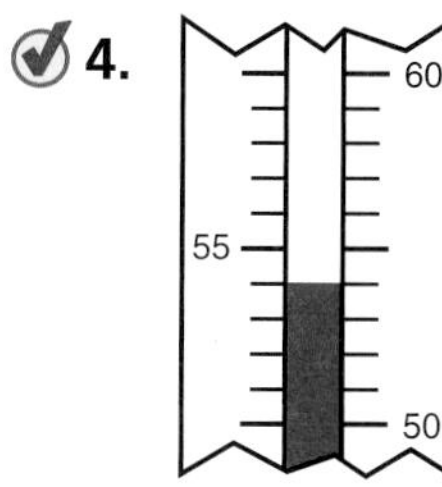

5. 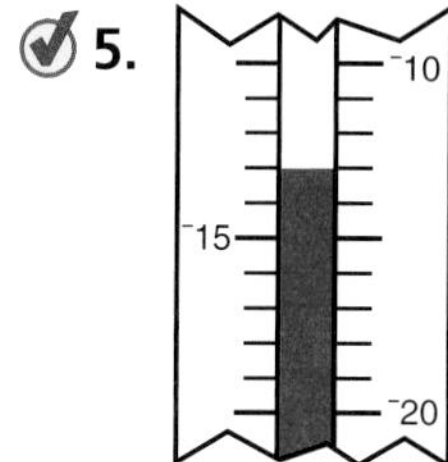

6. **TALK Math** **Explain** how to find a change in temperature on a Fahrenheit thermometer.

Independent Practice and Problem Solving

Use the thermometer to find the temperature in °F.

7. 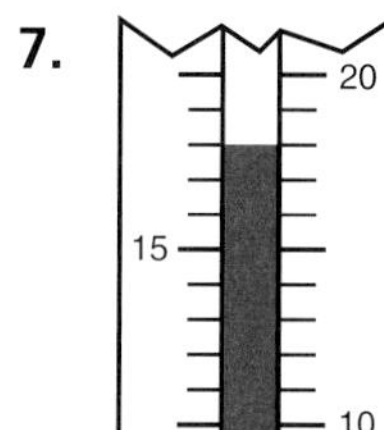

8. 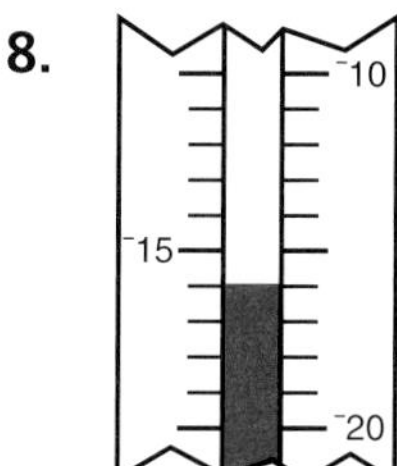

9. 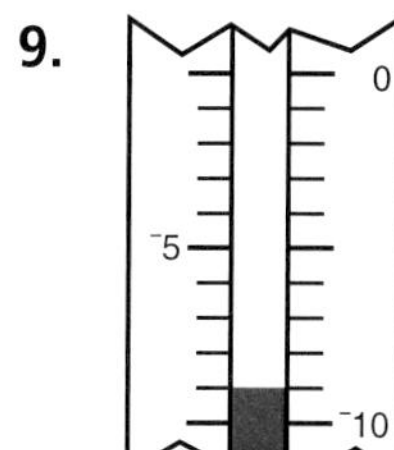

10. 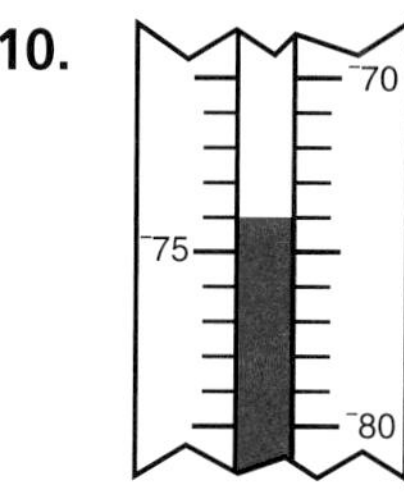

Algebra **Use a thermometer to find the change in temperature.**

11. 4°F to 17°F
12. ⁻8°F to 15°F
13. ⁻32°F to ⁻47°F
14. 19°F to ⁻4°F

USE DATA For 15–16, use the table.

15. Order the cities from the greatest to least change in temperature.
16. Which city has a greater difference between its January and July temperatures, Fairbanks or Madison?
17. **WRITE Math** **Explain** how to find rise in temperature on a Fahrenheit thermometer.

Average Temperatures

City	January (°F)	July (°F)
Detroit, MI	25	74
Fairbanks, AK	⁻10	62
Madison, WI	17	72

Mixed Review and TAKS Prep

18. If a right angle is divided into two smaller angles, what kind of angles are formed? (TEKS 4.8A, p. 260)

19. 65 days = ■ weeks ■ days (TEKS 4.12, p. 482)

20. **TAKS Prep** What is the change in temperature from 5°F to 12°F? (Obj. 4)

A 4°F
B 5°F
C 6°F
D 7°F

Extra Practice on page 488, Set D

Temperature: Celsius

OBJECTIVE: Measure temperature and changes in temperature in degrees Celsius.

Quick Review

What is the temperature?

30
25
20 °F

Vocabulary

degrees Celsius (°C)

Learn

Degrees Celsius (°C) are metric units for measuring temperature. Many countries use the Celsius scale. Water freezes at 0°C. Read 0°C as "zero degrees Celsius."

Temperatures less than 0°C are negative temperatures. For example, the temperature in Harbin, China, can reach $^{-}30$°C. Read $^{-}30$°C as "thirty degrees below zero Celsius."

Examples Find the change in temperature.

A Temperature rises.

$^{-}7$°C to 15°C

Think: 7° + 15° = 22°

So, the temperature rises 22°C.

20, 10, 0, $^{-}10$ °C — 15°, 7°

B Temperature drops.

36°C to 24°C

Think: 6° + 6° = 12°

So, the temperature drops 12°C.

40, 30, 20 °C — 6°, 6°

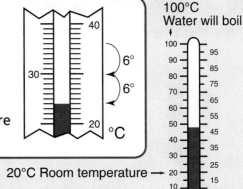

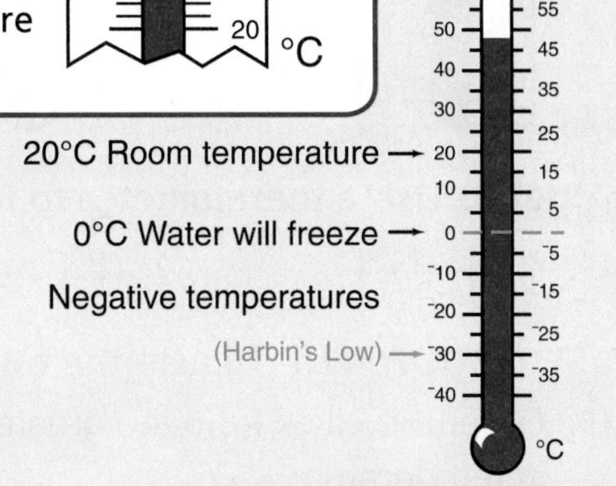

- Round to the nearest 5 degrees to estimate the temperatures in the examples. Which temperature is most like a spring day?

Activity **Materials** ■ Celsius thermometers

- Use a Celsius thermometer to measure the temperature outside your classroom in the morning. Copy the table.
- Measure the temperature outside your classroom again in the afternoon. Record the time and temperature in the table.
- Find the change in temperature. Did the temperature rise or drop during the day?

Temperature Outside The Classroom

Time	Temperature (in °C)

Guided Practice

1. Count the degrees from $^{-}4$°C to 0°C and then from 0°C to 4°C. Add. Write the change in temperature.

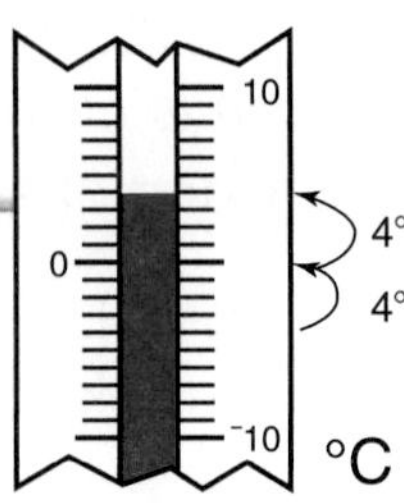

TEKS 4.12A use a thermometer to measure temperature and changes in temperature. *also* **4.14A, 4.14D, 4.15A, 4.15B, 4.16A**

Use the thermometer to find the temperature in °C.

2.
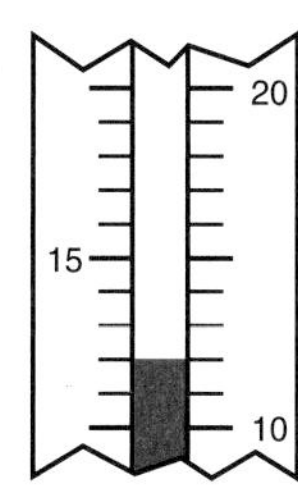

3.
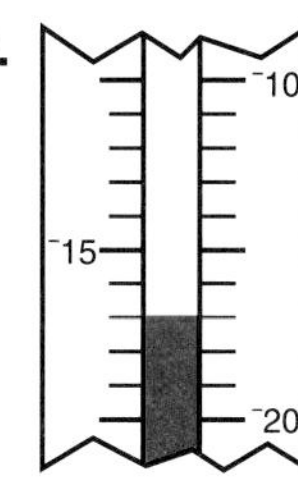

4.
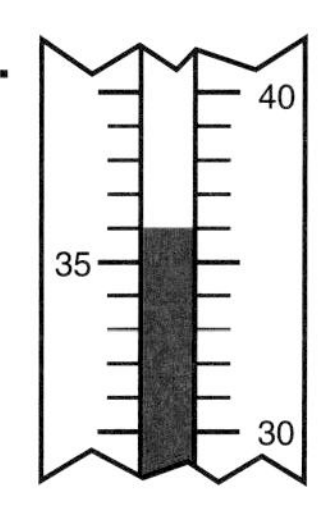

5.
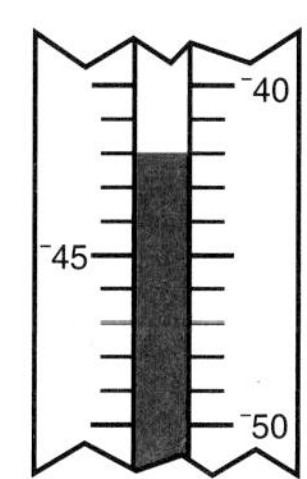

6. TALK Math **Explain** how you find the change in temperature from ⁻12°C to ⁻4°C. Is this a rise or drop in temperature?

Independent Practice and Problem Solving

Use the thermometer to find the temperature in °C.

7.
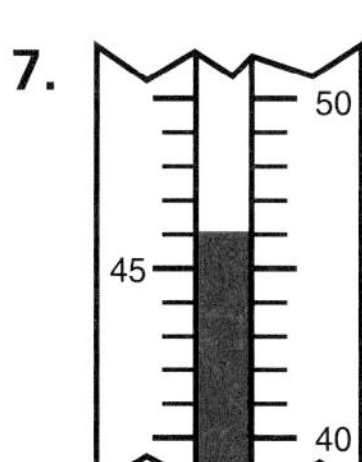

8.
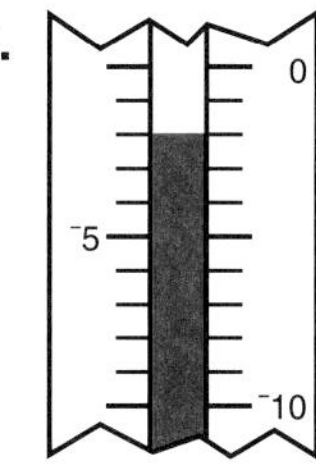

9.
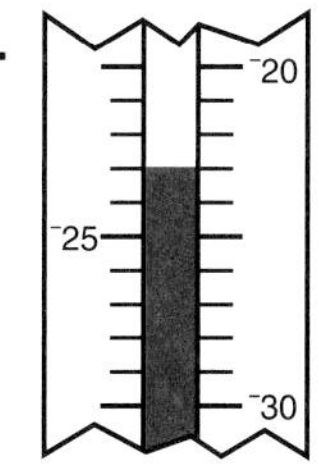

10.
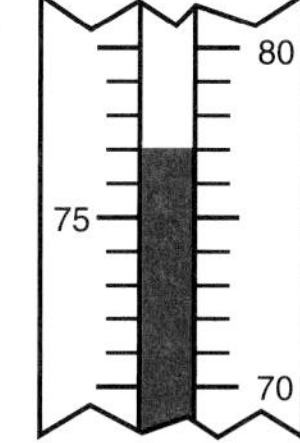

Algebra Use a thermometer to find the change in temperature.

11. 38°C falls ■ to 20°C.

12. ⁻2°C falls ■ to ⁻13°C.

13. ⁻12°C rises ■ to 5°C.

Write a reasonable temperature for each.

14. your classroom

15. a cold glass of water

16. a cup of hot cocoa

USE DATA For 17–18, use the table.

17. How much longer can whitefish be safely stored at ⁻29°C than herring at ⁻21°C?

18. What is the difference between the storage temperatures of herring for 6 months and whitefish for 1 month?

Seafood Safe Storage Times

Type of Fish	Temperature (in °C)		
	9°	⁻21°	⁻29°
Whitefish	1 month	4 months	8 months
Herring	1 month	3 months	6 months

19. **Reasoning Explain** whether the temperature of a warm car engine is about 50°C or about 50°F.

20. WRITE Math **Sense or Nonsense** Mari says you find the change in temperature on Fahrenheit and Celsius thermometers the same way. Is she correct? **Explain.**

Mixed Review and TAKS Prep

21. A pentagon has ■ sides. (TEKS 4.8C, p. 264)

22. How do you read ⁻3°F? (TEKS 4.12A, p. 484)

23. **TAKS Prep** A temperature of ⁻2°C rises 12°C. What is the new temperature? (Obj. 4)

Extra Practice on page 488, Set E

Extra Practice

Set A Write the time as shown on a digital clock (pp. 474–475)

1. 21 minutes after six
2. 8 minutes before nine
3. quarter after eleven
4. 18 minutes before two
5. quarter to one
6. 3 minutes to five

Set B Use a clock to find the elapsed time. (pp. 476–479)

1. Start: 2:00 P.M.
   End: 8:30 P.M.
2. Start: 6:15 P.M.
   End: 7:15 A.M.
3. Start: 11:00 P.M.
   End: 9:30 A.M.
4. Start: 7:30 P.M.
   End: 6:45 A.M.
5. Chris begins school at 9:15 A.M. He gets out at 3:45 P.M. How long is Chris at school?

Set C For 1–4, use the calendars. (pp. 482–483)

1. Melanie's birthday is 5 weeks and 2 days before June 30. On what day is Melanie's birthday?
2. Summer begins on June 21. How many days after May 29 is the first day of summer?
3. Flag Day is June 14. If today is May 17, how many weeks from today is Flag Day?
4. Sophie is planning a trip. She will leave on May 20 and return on June 4. What is the length of her trip in days?

May

Sun	Mon	Tue	Wed	Thu	Fri	Sat
	1	2	3	4	5	6
7	8	9	10	11	12	13
14	15	16	17	18	19	20
21	22	23	24	25	26	27
28	29	30	31			

June

Sun	Mon	Tue	Wed	Thu	Fri	Sat
				1	2	3
4	5	6	7	8	9	10
11	12	13	14	15	16	17
18	19	20	21	22	23	24
25	26	27	28	29	30	

Set D Use the thermometer to find the temperature in °F (pp. 484–485)

1. 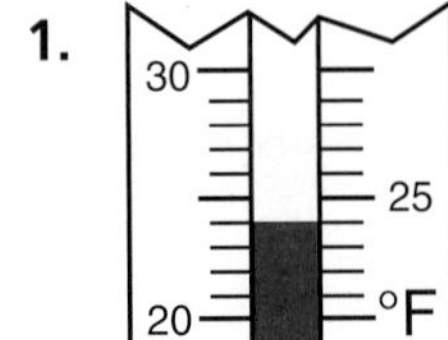

2. 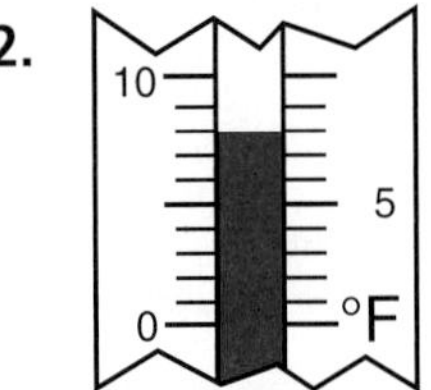

3. 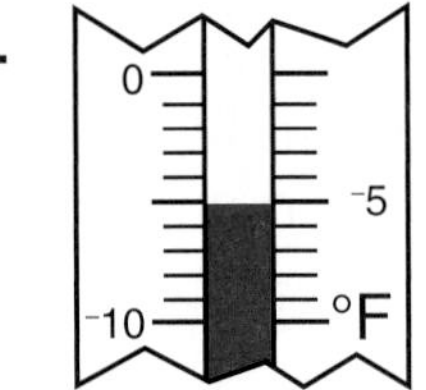

4. 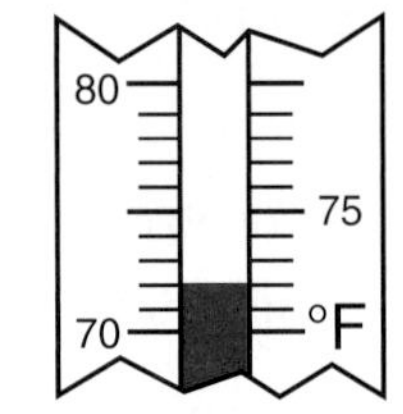

Set E Use the thermometer to find the temperature in °C (pp. 486–487)

1. 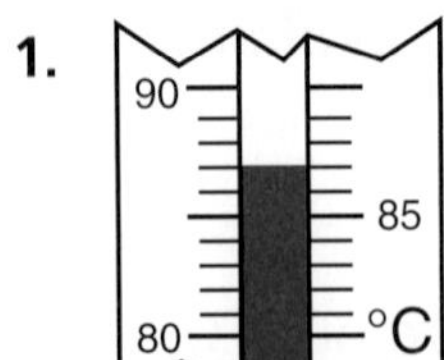

2. 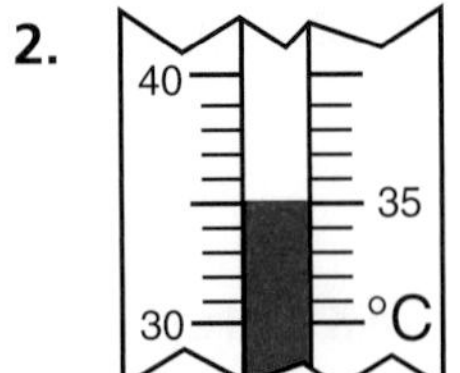

3. 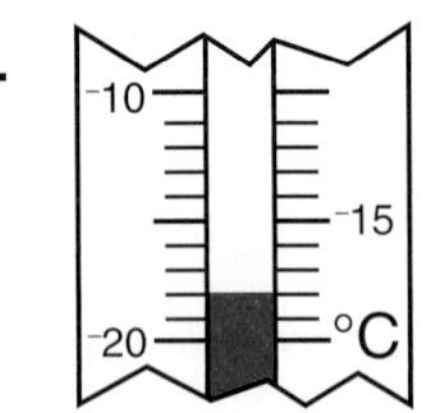

4. 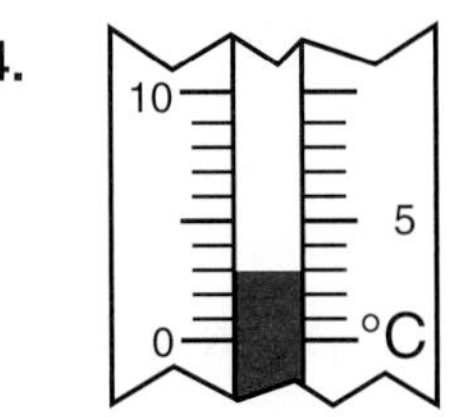

5. What is the change in temperature from $^{-}40$°F to $^{-}17$°F?

Technology
Use Harcourt Mega Math, The Number Games, *Tiny's Think Tank,* Levels D, E, P.

TECHNOLOGY CONNECTION

iTools: Measurement (TEKS 4.14D, 4.12B, 4.14A, 4.15A, 4.15B)

Sarah's softball game started at 2:45 P.M. and ended at 4:12 P.M. How long did Sarah's softball game last?

Step 1 Click on *Measurement*. Then select *Clocks* from the *Activities* menu. Next, click on the tab for Elapsed Time.	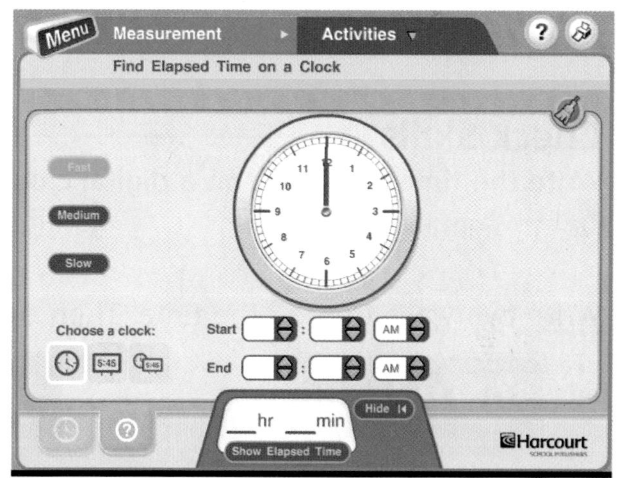
Step 2 Click on the arrows until the Start time is set for 2:45 P.M.	
Step 3 Click on the arrows until the End time is set for 4:12 P.M.	
Step 4 Click on *Show Elapsed Time* at the bottom of the screen.	

So, Sarah's softball game lasted for 1 hour 27 minutes.

To find the elapsed time for a new problem, enter the new *Start* and *End* times, and click on *Show Elapsed Time*.

Try It

Follow the same steps to find the elapsed time.

1. Start: 8:15 A.M
End: 10:55 A.M
2. Start: 9:45 P.M
End: 10:34 P.M
3. Start: 11:05 A.M
End: 2:42 P.M
4. Start: 10:22 P.M
End: 5:35 A.M
5. A movie started at 7:47 P.M. and ended at 9:42 P.M. How long did the movie last?
6. **Explore More** Suppose you were to switch the start time and end time when entering them into the computer. **Explain** how the incorrect elapsed time would relate to the correct elapsed time.

Technology
iTools are available online or on CD-ROM.

Chapter 18 Review/Test

Check Vocabulary and Concepts

Choose the best term from the box.

VOCABULARY
degrees Celsius
degrees Fahrenheit
elapsed time
second

1. The metric units for measuring temperature are __?__. (TEKS 4.12A, p. 486)
2. The customary units for measuring temperature are __?__. (TEKS 4.12A, p. 484)
3. The __?__ between 11:00 A.M. and 2:00 P.M. is 3 hours. (TEKS 4.12B, p. 476)

Check Skills

Write the time as shown on a digital clock. (TEKS 4.12, pp. 474–475)

4. 17 minutes after two
5. 26 minutes to twelve
6. quarter to nine

Write two ways to read the time. Then estimate to the nearest 5 minutes. (pp. 474–475)

7. 9:44 A.M.
8. 2:12 P.M.
9. 1:27 A.M.

Use a clock to find the elapsed time. (TEKS 4.12B, pp. 476–479)

10. Start: 10:20 P.M. End: 12:30 P.M.
11. Start: 8:15 A.M. End: 12:40 P.M.
12. Start: 7:35 A.M. End: 10:09 P.M.
13. Start: 12:11 A.M. End: 4:23 P.M.

Find the missing numbers. (TEKS 4.12B, pp. 476–479)

14. 3 weeks ■ days = 24 days
15. ■ weeks = 70 days
16. ■ weeks ■ days = 33 days
17. 1 month 4 weeks 1 day = ■ days

Use a thermometer to find the change in temperature. (TEKS 4.12A, pp. 484–485, 486–487)

18. 6°F rises ■ to 15°F
19. $^-2$°F rises ■ to 11°F
20. $^-6$°F falls ■ to $^-29$°F
21. 21°C falls ■ to 11°C
22. $^-4$°C falls ■ to $^-16$°C
23. $^-1$°C rises ■ to 17°C

Check Problem Solving

Solve. (TEKS 4.12B, pp. 480–481)

24. Leigh is visiting an International Fair. She will be here from 1:00 P.M. to 4:00 P.M. How can she schedule her time so she can visit each exhibit?
25. **WRITE Math** What if Leigh wants to see the Australia exhibit twice? Can she see the Australia exhibit twice? **Explain.**

Exhibit Schedule

Exhibit	Times	Length
Italy	1:00 P.M., 2:00 P.M.	15 minutes
Australia	1:00 P.M., 1:30 P.M., 2:00 P.M., 2:30 P.M., 3:00 P.M.	20 minutes
Japan	1:00 P.M., 2:15 P.M.	45 minutes

GO ONLINE **Technology** Use *Online Assessment.*

Enrich • 24-Hour Clock
Time Travel

There are different ways to tell time. The United States uses two 12-hour periods, A.M. and P.M., but many other countries use a system with one 24-hour period, called the 24-hour clock.

On a **24-hour clock**, the A.M. hours are from 0000 to 1200, and the P.M. hours are from 1200 to 2400 hours.

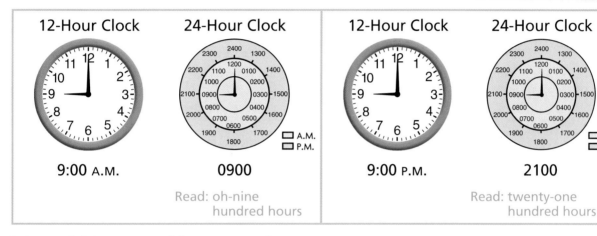

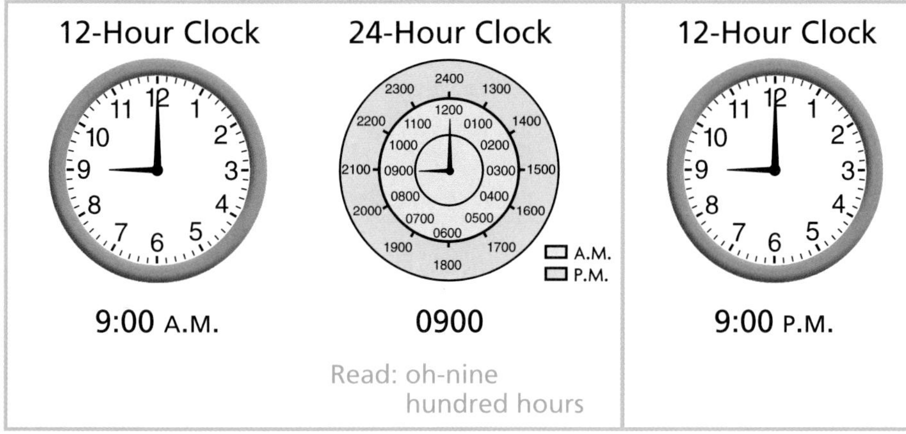

What is 3:00 P.M. on a 24-hour clock?

To change a P.M. hour to time on a 24-hour clock, add 12 hours.

$3{:}00 + 12{:}00 = 1500$ Read: fifteen hundred hours

So, 3:00 P.M. on a 24-hour clock is 1500.

Examples

A Find 0600 on a 12-hour clock.

0600 is A.M. on a 12-hour clock.

$0600 = 6{:}00$

So, 0600 on a 12-hour clock is 6:00 A.M.

B Find 2300 on a 12-hour clock.

Subtract 1200, or 12 hours.

$2300 - 1200 = 1100$

So, 2300 on a 12-hour clock is 11:00 P.M.

Try It

Write the time as shown on a 24-hour clock.

1. 1:00 P.M.
2. 1:00 A.M.
3. 8:00 P.M.
4. 11:00 A.M.

Write the time as shown on a 12-hour clock. Use A.M. or P.M.

5. 0900
6. 1800
7. 2200
8. 0500

9. WRITE Math **Explain** why A.M. and P.M. is not used on a 24-hour clock.

Getting Ready for the TAKS
Chapters 1–18

Number, Operation, and Quantitative Reasoning TAKS Obj. 1

1. Which mixed number does this model show?

   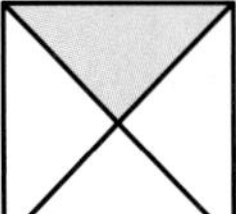

A $1\frac{3}{4}$

B $3\frac{1}{4}$

C $4\frac{1}{4}$

D $12\frac{1}{4}$

2. The table shows the prices of Elena's favorite books at BB's Bookstore.

BB's Bookstore	
Book	**Price**
The Schoolhouse Mystery	\$4
Jane's Adventure	\$5
Fun With Paper-Folding	\$7

Elena buys one copy of each book. She pays with \$20. How much change does she receive?

F \$4

G \$3

H \$2

J \$1

3. WRITE Math Each train car can hold 87 passengers. **Explain** how to estimate the total number of passengers in a train with 11 cars.

Patterns, Relationships, and Algebraic Thinking TAKS Obj. 2

4. If $12 \times 6 = 72$, what is 12×12?

A 144 **C** 112

B 132 **D** 78

5. Which number sentence is related to the multiplication fact $7 \times 8 = 56$?

F $56 + 7 = 63$

G $7 + 8 = 15$

H $15 - 7 = 8$

J $56 \div 7 = 8$

6. The table below shows how many tomatoes in each bag.

Bags of Tomatoes					
Bags	2	3	4	5	6
Tomatoes	8	12	16	20	■

Which expression shows how to find the number of tomatoes in 6 bags?

A 6×2

B 6×3

C 6×4

D 6×5

7. WRITE Math Find a rule for the pattern below.

5; 50; 500; 5,000; 50,000; ■

Explain how to use your rule to find the next number in the pattern.

Measurement TAKS Obj. 4

8. The thermometer below shows the high temperature for one day in June. The low temperature for that day was 18°F lower than the high temperature. What was the low temperature?

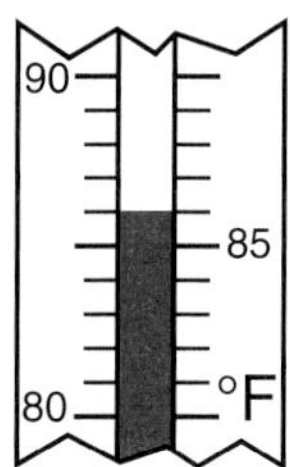

F 48°F　　H 68°F

G 66°F　　J 108°F

9. Diego buys a large bag of apples at the farm market. There are 18 apples in the bag. Estimate the weight of the apples.

A 10 ounces

B 1 pound

C 18 ounces

D 10 pounds

10. **WRITE Math** The clock below shows the time Jon's music and art lessons begin.

His lessons last 85 minutes altogether. At what time do his lessons end? **Explain** how you found your answer.

Geometry and Spatial Reasoning

TAKS Obj. 3

11. Which figure is a quadrilateral with congruent sides and angles?

F Triangle

G Square

H Pentagon

J Octagon

Understand the problem.

See Item 12. Hold your hand in the same position as the drawing. Move your hand in the same way the figure was moved. Look for the transformation that describes this motion.

12. What single transformation is represented from Figure A to Figure B?

Figure A

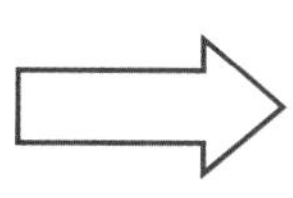

Figure B

A Translation

B Reflection

C Rotation

D Not here

13. **WRITE Math** **Explain** how a right angle is different from an obtuse angle. Draw an example of each.

19 Collect, Display, and Interpret Data

The Big Idea Data can be collected, analyzed, and displayed in various graphical formats.

Investigate

The Rio Grande is the longest river that flows through Texas. The table lists the lengths of some Texas rivers. How can you show the data another way? Show the data your way.

Rivers in Texas

Name	Length (in miles)
Blanco	87
Medina	116
Nueces	315
Pedernales	106
Rio Grande	1,896
San Antonio	180
San Marcos	75

TEXAS FAST FACT

The Rio Grande starts in Colorado and flows through New Mexico into Texas. It forms the entire border between Texas and Mexico. Its total length is 1,896 miles.

GO ONLINE **Technology** Student pages are available in the Student eBook.

Show What You Know

Check your understanding of important skills needed for success in Chapter 19.

Make and Use a Tally Table

Use the data.

1. Use the data to make a tally table.
2. Which grade has the most students on the bus?
3. What is the total number of first- and second-grade students on the bus?
4. How many more third-grade than fourth-grade students are on the bus?

The school bus from Tara's neighborhood carries 7 students who are in first grade, 12 students who are in second grade, 15 students who are in third grade, and 8 students who are in fourth grade.

Use Symbols in a Pictograph

Use the pictograph.

5. How many cats are on the Horton farm?
6. How many more dogs than rabbits are there?
7. How many Guinea pigs and rabbits are there altogether?
8. How many pets are on the Horton farm?

Horton Farm Pets	
Dogs	
Cats	
Guinea pigs	
Rabbits	
Key: Each = 2 animals.	

VOCABULARY POWER

CHAPTER VOCABULARY

- bar graph
- categorical data
- data
- double-bar graph
- frequency
- grid
- interval
- key
- numerical data
- ordered pair
- pictograph
- scale
- survey
- tally table
- Venn diagram

WARM-UP WORDS

survey a method of gathering information

categorical data data that can be sorted into different groups

frequency the number of times an event occurs

numerical data data that can be counted or measured

Collect and Organize Data

OBJECTIVE: Collect and organize data by conducting a survey and using a frequency table.

Quick Review

According to the tally table, who got the most votes?

Votes for Class President	
Student	**Tally**
Anna	卌 卌
Dan	卌 ||
Horatio	卌 |||

Vocabulary

survey

categorical data

frequency

numerical data

Learn

A **survey** is a method of gathering information.

Follow these rules to take a survey:

- Decide on a question about which you want to gather data.
- Ask each person the question only one time.
- Use a tally mark to record each person's response.

Max took a survey by asking his classmates the question "What is your favorite subject in school?" He recorded their responses in a tally table.

Favorite Subject Survey	
Subject	**Tally**
Reading	卌
Math	卌 ||
Science	卌
Social Studies	卌 ||

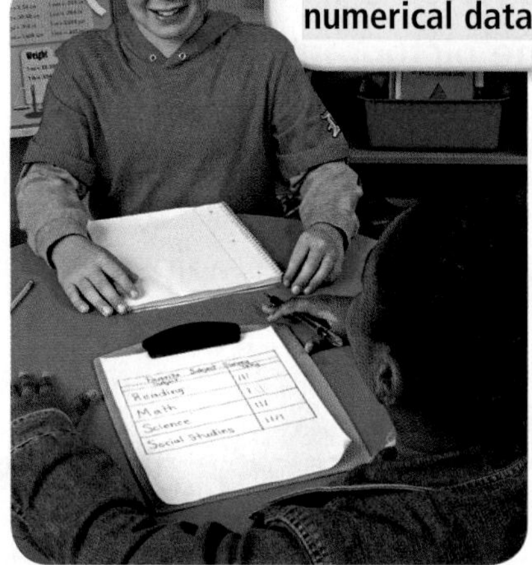

Since this set of data can be sorted into different groups, it is called **categorical data.** The groups in the table above are school subjects.

Activity Take a survey and record the results in a tally table.

Step 1

Write a question for your survey. Make the question clear and simple.

Decide on the response choices.

Organize your question and response choices in a table like the sample survey to the right.

Step 2

Survey your classmates.

- Be sure each classmate gives only one response.
- Use a tally mark to record each response.

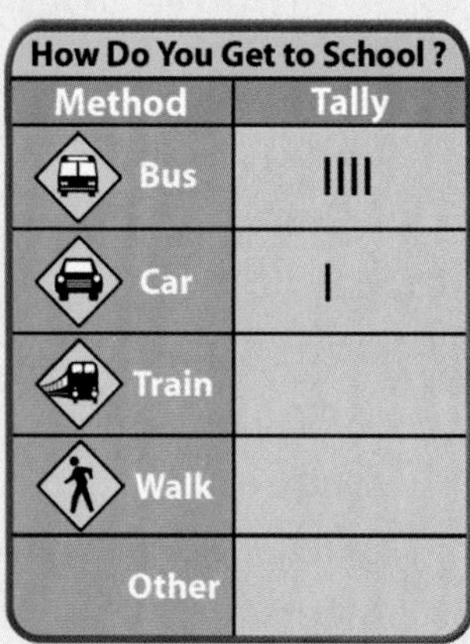

How Do You Get to School ?	
Method	**Tally**
Bus	||||
Car	|
Train	
Walk	
Other	

- Why do you ask each person the question only one time?

TEKS 4.13 The student solves problems by collecting, organizing, displaying, and interpreting sets of data. *also* **4.14A, 4.14D, 4.15A, 4.15B**

Frequency Tables

A frequency table helps you organize the data from a tally table. The **frequency** is the number of times a response occurs. In a frequency table, numbers are used instead of tally marks.

Favorite Drawing Tool	
Drawing Tool	Tally
Color Pencil	III
Crayon	~~IIII~~ III
Marker	~~IIII~~ II

Jenna asked her classmates to pick their favorite tool for drawing pictures. First, she made a tally table to show the results of her survey. Then Jenna showed the same data in a frequency table.

Favorite Drawing Tool	
Drawing Tool	Frequency
Color Pencil	3
Crayon	8
Marker	7

The table below shows numerical data. **Numerical data** are data that are counted or measured.

Time It Takes to Write Your Name	
Time (in seconds)	Frequency
3	7
6	3
7	7
8	2

• How are numerical data different from categorical data?

Guided Practice

1. Copy and complete the frequency table with the following data: eggs, toast, cereal, cereal, eggs, eggs, cereal, cereal, cereal.

Favorite Breakfast Food			
Food	Eggs	Cereal	Toast
Frequency			

For 2–3, use Jenna's data in the Favorite Drawing Tool table above. Tell whether each statement is true or false. Explain.

2. More students chose markers than crayons.
3. More students chose markers than color pencils.

For 4–6, use the School Population frequency table.

School Population (Washington Elementary)	
Grade	**Frequency (Number of Students)**
K	45
1	42
2	54
3	58
4	41
5	55
6	50

4. How many students are in fourth grade?
5. How many more students are in the grade with the greatest number of students than in the grade with the least number?
6. If 2 sixth graders move away and 5 fifth graders enroll, how many students will the fifth and sixth grades have in all?
7. **TALK Math** **Explain** how you can use a tally table to make a frequency table.

Independent Practice and Problem Solving

For 8–10, use the Favorite Type of TV Show frequency table. Tell whether each statement is true or false. Explain.

Students' Favorite Type of TV Show	
Type of Show	**Frequency (Votes)**
Comedy	8
Cartoons	9
Sports	7
Mysteries	6

8. More students chose comedies than mysteries as their favorite.
9. More students chose sports and comedy as their favorite than chose cartoons and mysteries.
10. Cartoons are the students' favorite choice to watch.

For 11–14, use the Lessons for Wind Instruments bar graph.

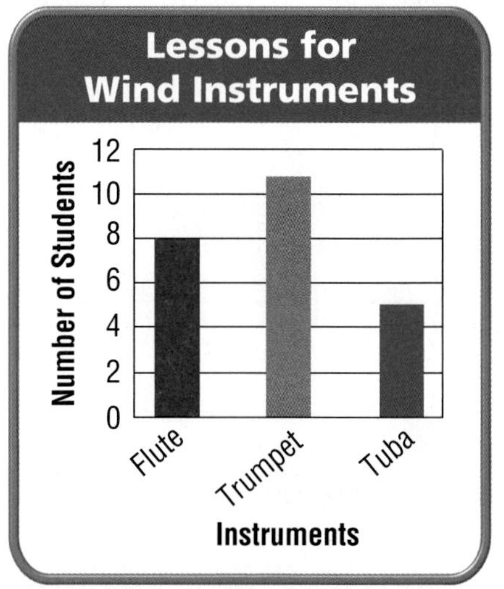

11. Describe the data set used to make this graph.
12. Which are the most popular lessons? the least popular?
13. How many more students take trumpet lessons than tuba lessons?
14. **Reasoning** Suppose 3 more students take flute lessons and 3 students stop taking tuba lessons. How will these data change the graph?

For 15–17, use the data in the Weights of Fruits table.

Weights of Fruits	
Fruit	**Weight (in ounces)**
Apple	6
Banana	10
Peach	5
Melon	20

15. How many fewer ounces did the banana weigh than the melon?
16. **Pose a Problem** Write a question that can be answered using the data. Then answer the question.
17. **WRITE Math** **What's the Error?** Sandra says the table shows that 6 students ate apples. **Explain** Sandra's mistake and how to correct it.

Mixed Review and TAKS Prep

18. Carl had 15 action figures to share. He divides them evenly between himself and two friends. How many action figures does each person get? (TEKS 4.4C, p.120)

19. School starts at 8:30 A.M. and ends at 2:45 P.M. Use a clock to find the length of the school day. (TEKS 4.12, p. 476)

20. **TAKS Prep** Use the Students' Favorite Type of TV Show frequency table above. How many people were surveyed? (Obj. 5)

A 17

B 19

C 20

D 30

Extra Practice on page 514, Set A

A Trip Through Time

Some sauropods, like the brachiosaurus, weighed up to 88 tons!

Compare and Contrast

Anita's class is taking a field trip to Dinosaur Valley State Park, in Glen Rose, Texas, to see dinosaur tracks. Dinosaurs called sauropods and theropods probably made the tracks in and near the riverbed of the Paluxy River. One sauropod, the brachiosaurus, was a plant-eating dinosaur that grew to about 80 feet long! It had a long neck and walked on 4 feet. It lived during the Jurassic period. The allosaurus, a theropod, was a meat-eater. It grew to about 40 feet long and walked on 2 feet. It lived during the Jurassic period as well.

Some theropods, like the allosaurus, had skulls measuring 3 feet long!

You can compare and contrast information in a table. When you compare and contrast, you find what is the same and what is different about the information. What is different about the two dinosaurs?

	Brachiosaurus	Allosaurus
Length	About 80 ft long	About 40 ft long
Diet	Plants	Meat
How It Walked	On 4 feet	On 2 feet
When It Lived	Jurassic period	Jurassic period

You can "walk in a dinosaur's shoes" at Dinosaur Valley State Park.

Problem Solving **Compare and contrast to solve.**

1. Solve the problem above.
2. *Brachiosaurus* means "arm lizard." It was named in 1903. Its fossils exist in North America and Africa. *Allosaurus* means "different lizard." It was named in 1877. Its fossils exist in Africa, Europe, and North America. What is the same about the two dinosaurs?

LESSON 2

Sort Data

OBJECTIVE: Interpret and construct Venn diagrams to sort and describe data.

Quick Review

Carl's scores on his math tests are 75, 80, 85, 97, 86, 99, 89, 79, 86, and 90. Sort and classify his scores by letter grades. Use A for 90 to 100, B for 80 to 89, and C for 70 to 79.

Learn

You can use Venn diagrams to sort information. A Venn diagram shows relationships among sets of things.

PROBLEM Every state has its own flag. Look at the state flags shown. What is one way these flags can be sorted?

Example Make a Venn diagram.

Step 1

Decide how you will sort the flags. Some of the flags have symbols of **animals**, some have symbols of **people**, and some have **both**.

Step 2

Draw two overlapping ovals. Label each section with the description of each set. The data inside the area where the sets overlap are described by both labels.

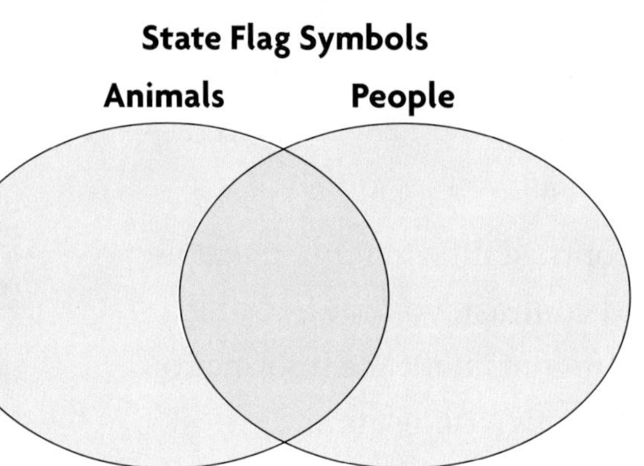

Step 3

Sort the state flag names.

State Flag Symbols

Animals **People**

Animals only: Pennsylvania, Illinois

Both: New York, New Jersey, Michigan

People only: Massachusetts

For the flags that have only animals, write the names in the diagram labeled Animals. For the flags that have only people, write the name in the diagram labeled People. Write the states that have both animals and people in the section where the sets overlap.

So, one way to sort these flags is by their symbols.

• How can you check that your answer is correct?

Pennsylvania

New York

Illinois

Massachusetts

New Jersey

Michigan

TEKS 4.13 The student solves problems by collecting, organizing, displaying, and interpreting sets of data. *also* **4.14A, 4.15A, 4.15B, 4.16A**

Guided Practice

Copy the Venn diagrams. Place the numbers where they belong.

1. 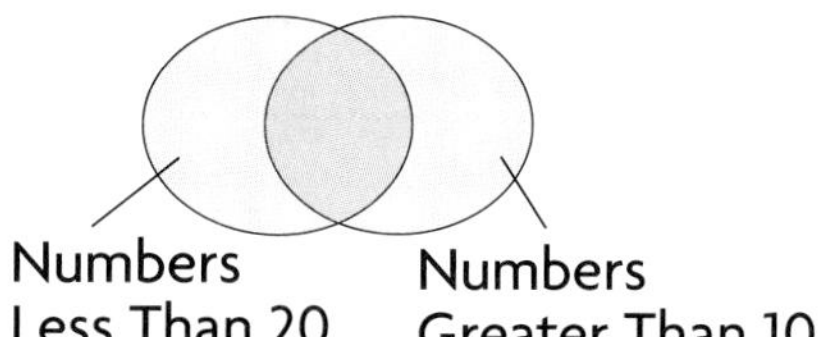

2, 14, 33, 19, 5, 79, 21, 50, 6

2. 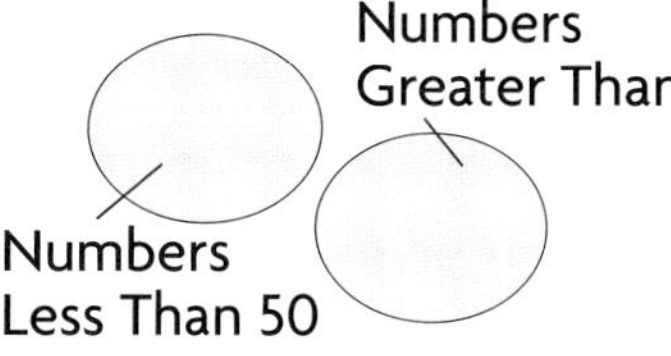

1, 22, 53, 89, 49, 13, 57, 4, 32

3. 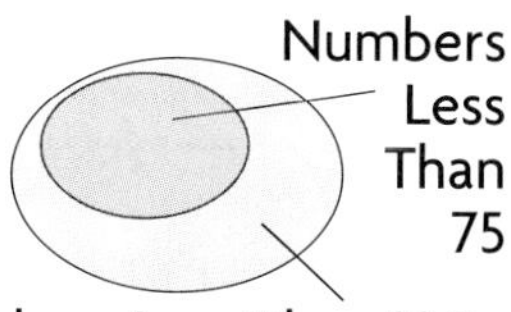

99, 24, 7, 63, 86, 24, 70, 12, 31

For 4–5, use the Venn diagram.

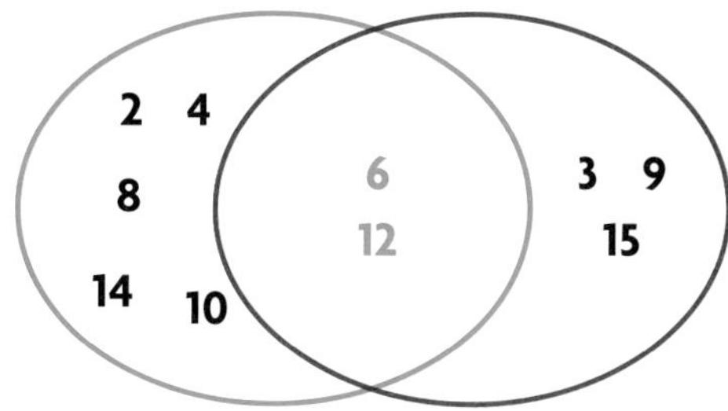

4. What label should you use for Section B?

5. Why are the numbers 6 and 12 sorted in the area where the sets overlap?

6. TALK Math **Explain** how a Venn diagram can help you understand relationships.

Independent Practice and Problem Solving

For 7–8, use the Venn diagram.

A Odd: 5 7 9

B ?: 4 12 18

7. What label can you use for Section B?

8. **Reasoning** Where would you sort the numbers 3, 175, and 2,001?

For 9–10, use the table.

9. Copy and complete the table by surveying 10 classmates. Show the results in a Venn diagram.

10. WRITE Math **Explain** whether to use a Venn diagram with 2 overlapping ovals or 2 separate ovals for the table.

Toppings Liked on Pizza

Topping	Names of Students
Pepperoni Only	?
Sausage Only	?
Pepperoni and Sausage	?

Mixed Review and TAKS Prep

11. Dena drew two lines that will never cross. What kind of lines did she draw? (TEKS 4.8B, p. 262)

12. At a football game, there were 64,856 fans. Round the number of fans to the nearest thousand. (TEKS 4.5A, p. 34)

13. **TAKS Prep** Look at the Venn diagram for Problems 7–8. Which number does **NOT** belong in Section A? (Obj. 5)

A 30 **C** 33

B 27 **D** 55

Extra Practice on page 514, Set B

LESSON 3

Make and Interpret Pictographs

OBJECTIVE: Make and interpret pictographs.

Quick Review

1. 2 × 8
2. 3 × 7
3. 3 × 3
4. 4 × 6
5. 5 × 9

Vocabulary

pictograph key

Learn

PROBLEM A class visited the Texas State Capitol Complex in Austin. They recorded which building they enjoyed visiting most. How do you show this in a pictograph?

A **pictograph** is a graph that uses pictures or symbols to show and compare information. The **key** shows what each symbol stands for.

SURVEY RESULTS
Favorite Building

Building	Votes
Capitol	8
Supreme Court	4
Library	5

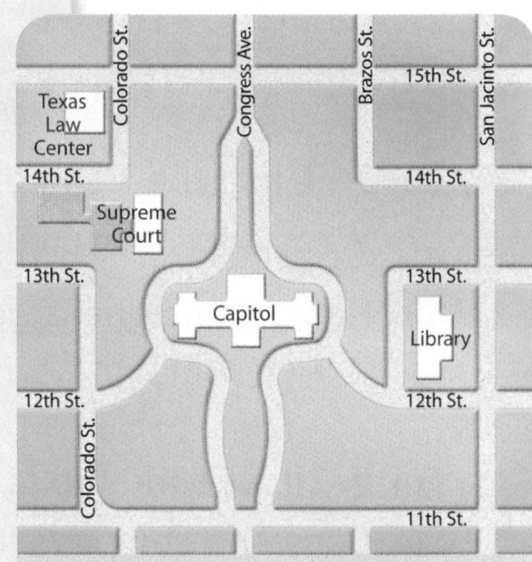

▲ Capitol Complex in Austin, Texas

Example Make a pictograph.

Step 1

Draw the pictograph. Write the title and a label for each row.

Favorite Building	
Capitol	
Supreme Court	
Library	

Step 2

Choose a symbol to stand for the data.

Let ★ stand for a number of votes.

Step 3

Make a key. Look at the data to decide what number each symbol should stand for.

The data are from 4 to 8 votes. Let ★ = 2 votes.

Step 4

Complete the pictograph. Decide how many symbols should be placed next to each building.

Favorite Building	
Capitol	★★★★
Supreme Court	★★
Library	★★½★

Key: Each ★ = 2 votes.

Guided Practice

1. If you were making a pictograph to show the following data, what symbol and key would you use?

Visiting Schools

Days	1	2	3
Number	4	12	8

TEKS 4.13 The student solves problems by collecting, organizing, displaying, and interpreting sets of data. *also* 4.14A, 4.15A, 4.15B

For 2–5, use the table.

2. Make a pictograph of the data in the table.
3. How many more students chose pizza than hamburgers?
4. How many students were surveyed in all?
5. **TALK Math** **Explain** how you can decide what each symbol should stand for in your key.

Field Trip Lunch

Lunch	Number of Students
Chicken	15
Hamburger	10
Pizza	20
Spaghetti	5

Independent Practice and Problem Solving

For 6–8, use the table.

6. The table shows how long each group spent touring the Capitol Complex. Make a pictograph to show the data.
7. How many hours did the group who visited the longest spend at the complex?
8. **Reasoning** If you used the symbol ☆ = 6 hours, how would you show how long Group 2 spent at the complex? **Explain.**

Time on Tour

Group	Number of Hours
1	6
2	3
3	9
4	6

USE DATA For 9–10, use the pictograph.

9. Which district has 2 counties?
10. ***FAST FACT*** District 44 has 3 counties. If you added District 44 to this pictograph, how many symbols would you use?
11. The sum of the counties in District 74 and District 68 is 29. The difference is 3. District 74 has fewer counties than District 68. How many counties are in each district?
12. **WRITE Math** **Explain** how a pictograph helps you compare information quickly.

Texas Counties

District 1	☆☆
District 2	☆☆
District 3	☆☆☆
District 4	☆

Key: Each ☆ = 2 counties.

Mixed Review and TAKS Prep

13. What question could you ask for a survey about tourist attractions? (TEKS 4.13, p. 496)
14. Mr. Lawrence drives a total of 29 miles per day to and from work. About how many miles does he drive in 5 days? (TEKS 4.5B, p. 228)
15. **TAKS Prep** Look at the pictograph for Problem 9. How many more counties are in District 3 than in District 4? (Obj. 5)

    A 1 **C** 3

    B 2 **D** 4

Extra Practice on page 514, Set C

Choose a Reasonable Scale

OBJECTIVE: Choose a reasonable scale and interval for a set of data.

Quick Review

Make a frequency table for the following survey results.

Question: What is your favorite pet?

Responses: dog, dog, dog, cat, bird, dog, cat, hamster, cat, dog, hamster, dog, bird

Vocabulary

scale **interval**

Learn

You can use different graphs to compare the same data.

A **scale** of a graph is a series of numbers placed at fixed, or equal, distances. The highest value on the scale should be greater than the greatest value of the data.

The **interval** of a graph is the difference between one number and the next on the scale of a graph.

Graph A

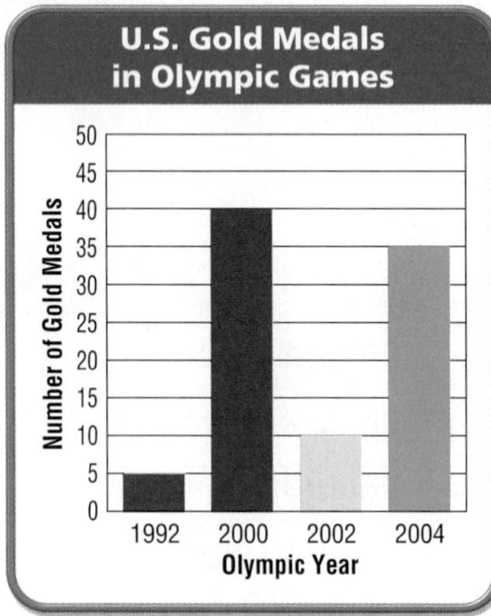

Graph B

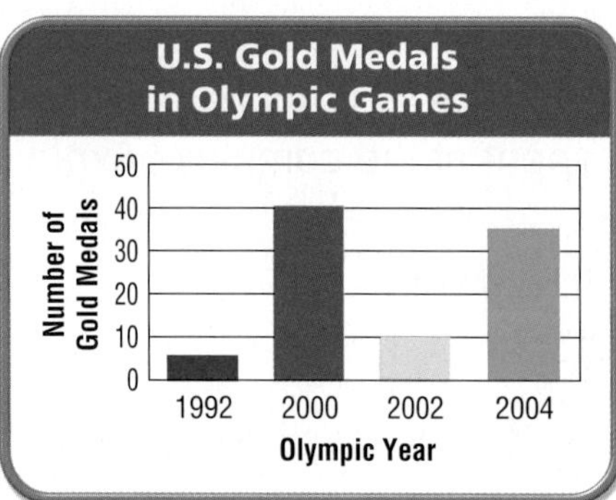

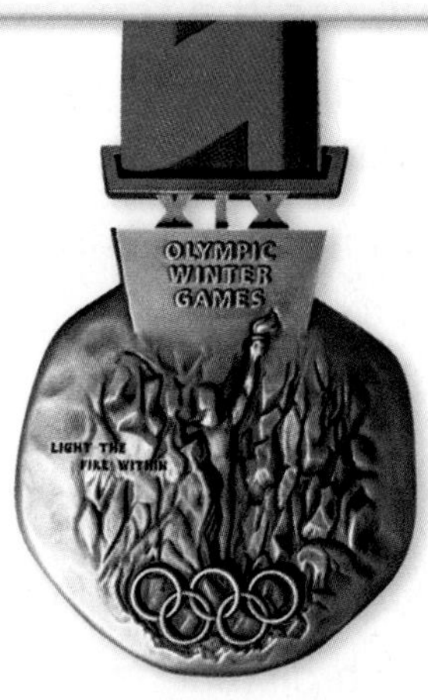

Math Idea

The interval should be small enough to show the data clearly, but large enough to fit all the data on the graph.

- Which graph makes it easier to compare the data? Why?

Guided Practice

1. Would you use an interval of 1 to show the data in Graph A? **Explain.**

For 2–4, choose 5, 10, or 100 as the most reasonable interval for each set of data. Explain your choice.

2. 25, 30, 20, 10, 15
3. 200, 350, 100, 250, 500
4. 25, 79, 50, 45, 90

5. **TALK Math** **Explain** how to decide which scale to use in graphs for the data in Problems 2, 3, and 4.

TEKS **4.13B** interpret bar graphs. *also* **4.13, 4.14A, 4.15A, 4.15B**

Independent Practice and Problem Solving

For 6–9, choose 5, 10, or 100 as the most reasonable interval for each set of data. Explain your choice.

6. 45, 79, 30, 80, 21
7. 4, 16, 6, 15, 30
8. 80, 490, 920, 550, 150
9. 92, 70, 12, 45, 60

For 10–11, use the Favorite Winter Olympic Event graph.

10. What is a better interval to use to show these data?
11. **Reasoning** Why wouldn't 1 and 100 be reasonable intervals to use for the data shown in the graph?

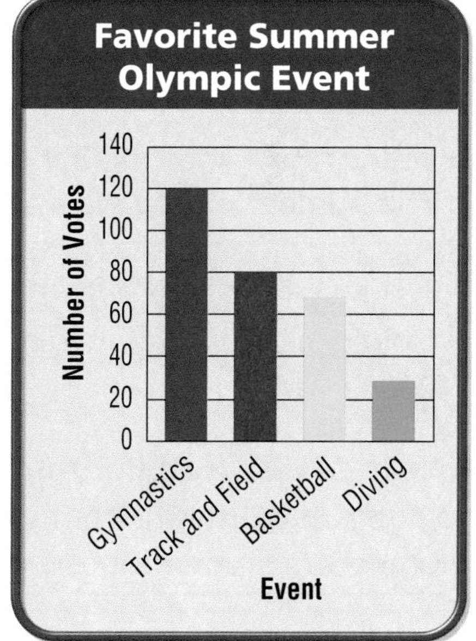

For 12–14, use the Favorite Summer Olympic Event graph.

12. What are the scale and interval used in the graph?
13. About how many more votes did gymnastics get than basketball and diving combined?
14. **Pose a Problem** Use the information in the graph to write a problem. Explain how to find the answer to your problem.
15. **FAST FACT** The Winter Olympic Games were held in Lake Placid, New York, in 1932. They were held in Lake Placid again in 1980. How many years later was this?
16. **WRITE Math** **What's the Question?** Haley made a graph for the data in a problem. The answer is 0–100.

Mixed Review and TAKS Prep

17. Last year there were 2,104 students in Wallace Elementary school. During the summer 120 students moved away and 85 new students enrolled in the school. How many students attend the school now? (TEKS 4.3A, p. 50)
18. Alan, Tim, and Tara are in the band. Grace and Paul are in the chorus. Sophie is in the band and the chorus. Draw a Venn diagram to show this information. (TEKS 4.13, p. 500)
19. **TAKS Prep** What is the scale for the graph below? (Obj. 5)

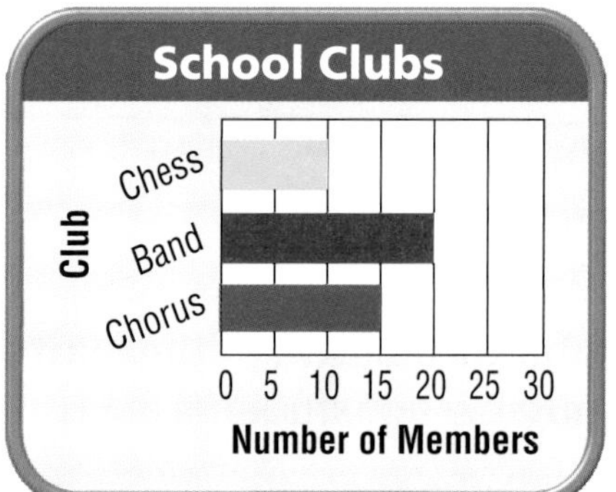

A 0–5 **C** 0–20

B 0–10 **D** 0–30

Extra Practice on page 514, Set D

LESSON 5

Interpret Bar Graphs

OBJECTIVE: Read and interpret bar graphs.

Quick Review

Compare. Write <, >, or = for each ●.

1. 45 ● 38
2. 190 ● 230
3. 98 ● 80
4. 590 ● 509
5. 378 ● 731

Vocabulary

bar graph

Learn

PROBLEM NASA has a school for astronauts. The bar graph shows how many students were in each class.

Use a **bar graph** to compare categorical data, or data about different groups. A bar graph can use vertical or horizontal bars to show data.

Example 1 Use a vertical bar graph.

How many students were in the 2004 class?

Find the bar for the year 2004.

Follow the top of the bar to the left to the scale. The number on the scale that matches the bar is 14.

So, the 2004 class had 14 students.

- How could you find how many students were in the 2000 class?

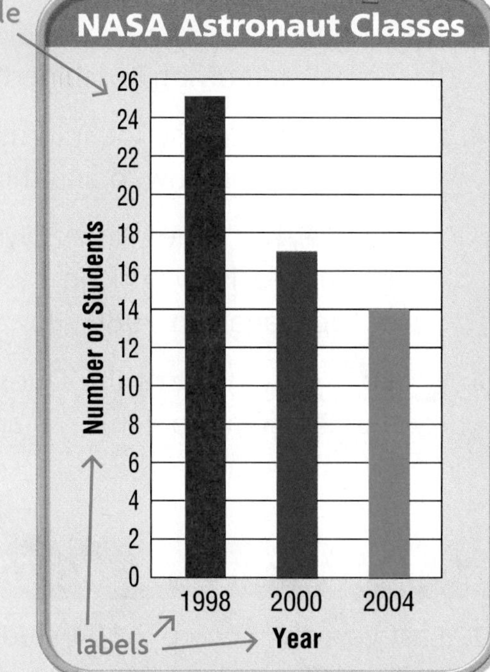

Example 2 Use a horizontal bar graph.

What is the difference between the least and greatest numbers of students in the classes?

Find the greatest bar. Follow the end of the bar down to the scale.

The greatest number of students is 25.

Find the least bar. Follow the end of the bar down to the scale.

The least number of students is 14.

25 − 14 = 11

So, the difference between the least and greatest numbers of students is 11.

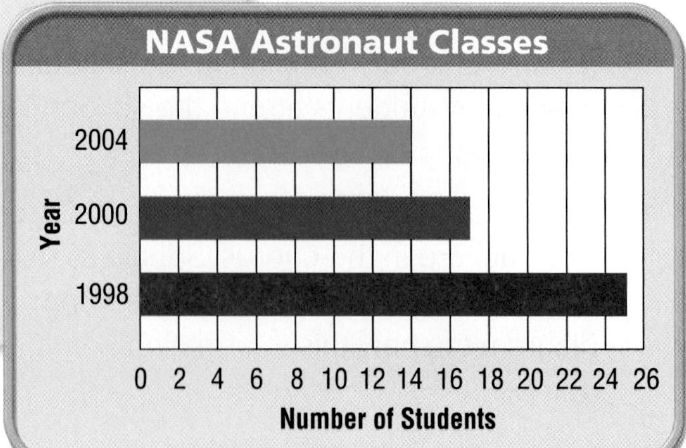

TEKS 4.13B interpret bar graphs. *also* 4.3A, 4.14A, 4.15A, 4.15B

Guided Practice

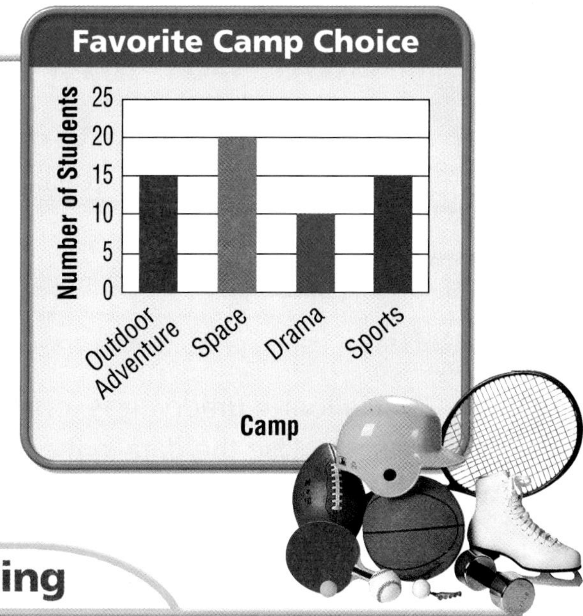

For 1–4, use the Favorite Camp Choice graph.

1. Which camp do most students prefer? Find the tallest bar. This bar has the greatest value. Follow the bar to the left to find the value.
2. Which camp was chosen by the fewest students?
3. How many students chose space camp?
4. TALK Math How many more students chose space camp than sports camp? **Explain.**

Independent Practice and Problem Solving

For 5–8, use the Favorite Camp Choice bar graph above.

5. What is the difference between the least and greatest number of votes for different camps?
6. Which two camps were chosen by the same number of students?
7. What interval is used on the scale?
8. Which camp was chosen by the most students?

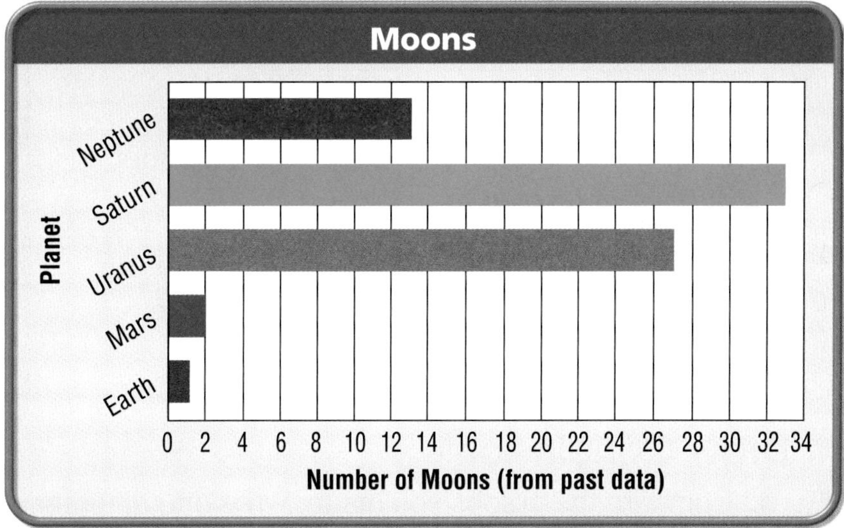

For 9–11, use the Moons graph.

9. Which planet has the fewest moons?
10. Which planet has more moons than Mars but fewer than Uranus?
11. WRITE Math **Sense or Nonsense** Jorge says that the interval for this bar graph is 34. Is Jorge correct? **Explain.**

Mixed Review and TAKS Prep

12. What is the length of the line segment to the nearest inch? (Grade 3 TEKS 3.11A)
13. Write the missing factor. (TEKS 4.6A, p. 160)

$$\blacksquare \times (4 \times 2) = 64$$

14. **TAKS Prep** Look at the Moons graph. Which planet has 1 more than 2 times as many moons as Neptune? (Obj. 5)

 A Uranus **C** Saturn

 B Mars **D** Earth

Extra Practice on page 514, Set E

Technology
Use Harcourt Mega Math, The Number Games, *ArachnaGraph*, Levels B, C.

LESSON HANDS ON

6 Make Bar and Double-Bar Graphs

OBJECTIVE: Make and interpret bar graphs and double-bar graphs.

Quick Review

How many more students have dogs than cats?

What Pet Do You Have?	
Animal	**Tally**
Dog	卌
Cat	||||
Bird	|
No pet	卌 |

Vocabulary

double-bar graph

Investigate

Materials ■ bar-graph patterns ■ crayons or markers

Mrs. Lyon's fourth grade class took a survey of their favorite sport. Use the data in the table to make two bar graphs.

A Make a bar graph of the boys' favorite sport to watch. Decide on a title, labels, and a scale for the graph.

Favorite Sport to Watch		
Sport	**Boys**	**Girls**
Football	17	5
Gymnastics	4	14
Ice Skating	6	12

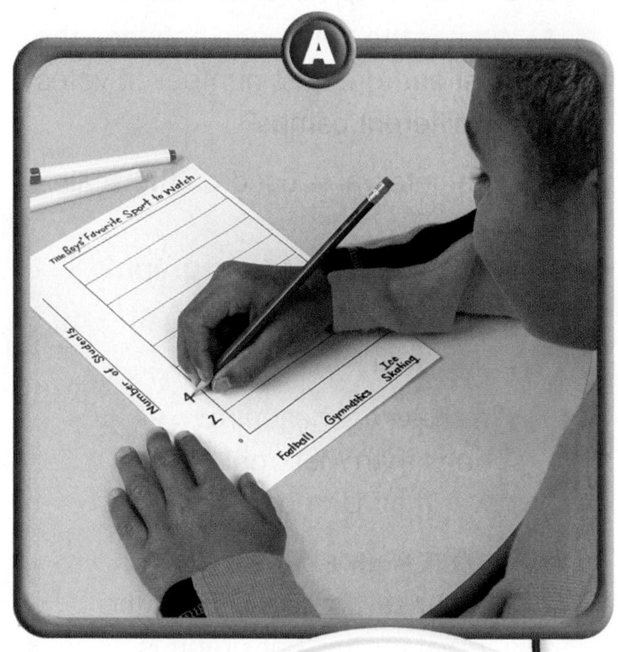

B Draw a bar for each sport. Graph the number of boys who voted for each sport.

C Repeat Steps A–B to make a bar graph for the girls' favorite sport to watch. Use the same scale and interval as on the first graph.

Draw Conclusions

1. Compare the graphs you made. Write one difference the graphs show between the girls' and boys' votes for their favorite sport.
2. **Evaluation** Suppose the scales and intervals of the two bar graphs were different from each other. Would it be more or less difficult to compare how many girls and boys voted for football? Explain.

Math Idea
You can use a bar graph to show categorical data.

TEKS 4.13 The student solves problems by collecting, organizing, displaying, and interpreting sets of data. *also* 4.13B, 4.14A, 4.14D, 4.15A, 4.15B

Connect

A **double-bar graph** is a graph used to compare similar types of data. This double-bar graph shows the same information as the two bar graphs you made on page 508.

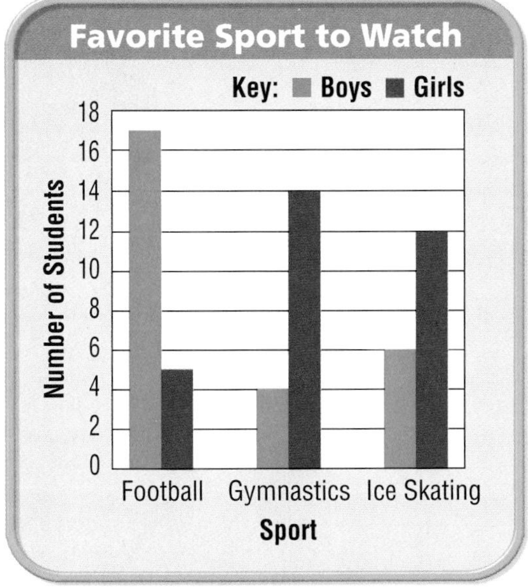

The key in the graph uses different colors to show the different data.

TALK Math

Which makes it easier to compare the data, the double-bar graph or the two single-bar graphs? Explain.

Practice

For 1–2, use the data in each table to make two bar graphs. Then make a double-bar graph.

1.

Average High Temperature (°F)			
City	**Jan**	**Feb**	**Mar**
Canton, Ohio	33	37	48
Detroit, Michigan	33	36	46

✓ 2.

Favorite Time of Day		
Time	**Boys**	**Girls**
Morning	6	8
Afternoon	20	17
Evening	33	31

For 3–6, use the double-bar graph.

✓ 3. Which city gets less rainfall from July through September?

4. Which city has a greater range of inches of rainfall during the three months? **Explain.**

5. How much more rain does Tampa get than Tucson in August?

6. **WRITE Math** Do you predict that Tucson or Tampa will have more rainfall in September next year? **Explain.**

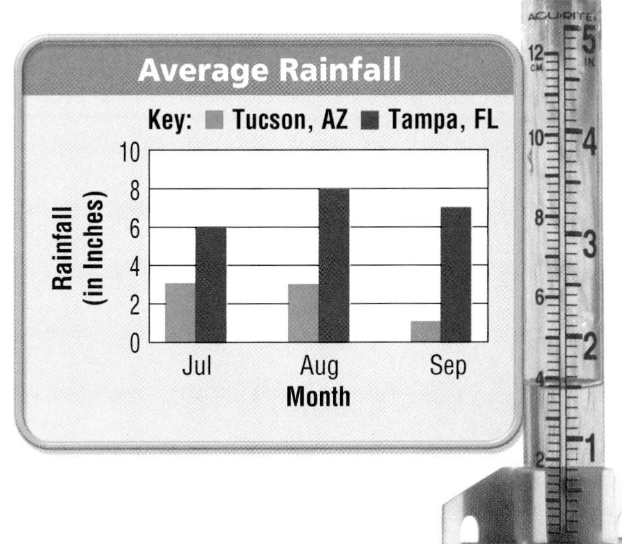

Problem Solving Workshop
Skill: Make Generalizations

OBJECTIVE: Solve problems by using the skill *make generalizations*.

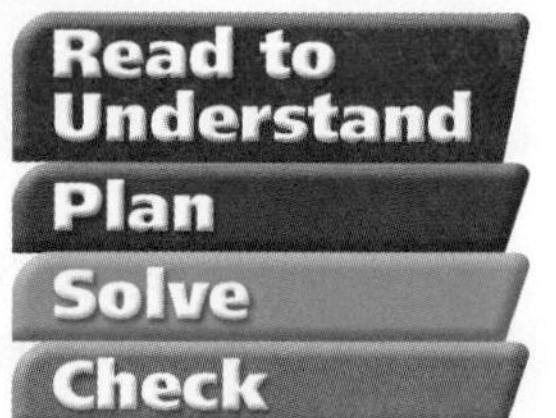

Use the Skill

PROBLEM A heart rate is the number of times the heart beats per minute. Grace has a resting heart rate of 85 beats per minute. Sara's resting heart rate is 77 beats per minute. Use the bar graph to find who is probably older, Grace or Sara.

A **generalization** is a conclusion based on given or known information. To help make a generalization, you can summarize data.

Identify the information in the bar graph.

Look at the graph. Write a paragraph identifying the known information.

> The heart rate at rest for newborns is about 140 beats per minute. For children, it is about 90 beats per minute. For adult females, it is about 80 beats per minute. For adult males, it is about 75 beats per minute. For adults over 65, it is about 65 beats per minute.

Look for patterns or connections in the information.

- The age groups go from younger to older.
- The beats per minute decrease, or go from faster to slower.

Make a generalization and use it to make a prediction or draw a conclusion.

You can make the generalization that, as people get older, their resting heart rate slows down. Since $77 < 85$, Sara's heart rate is slower than Grace's.

So, Sara is probably older than Grace.

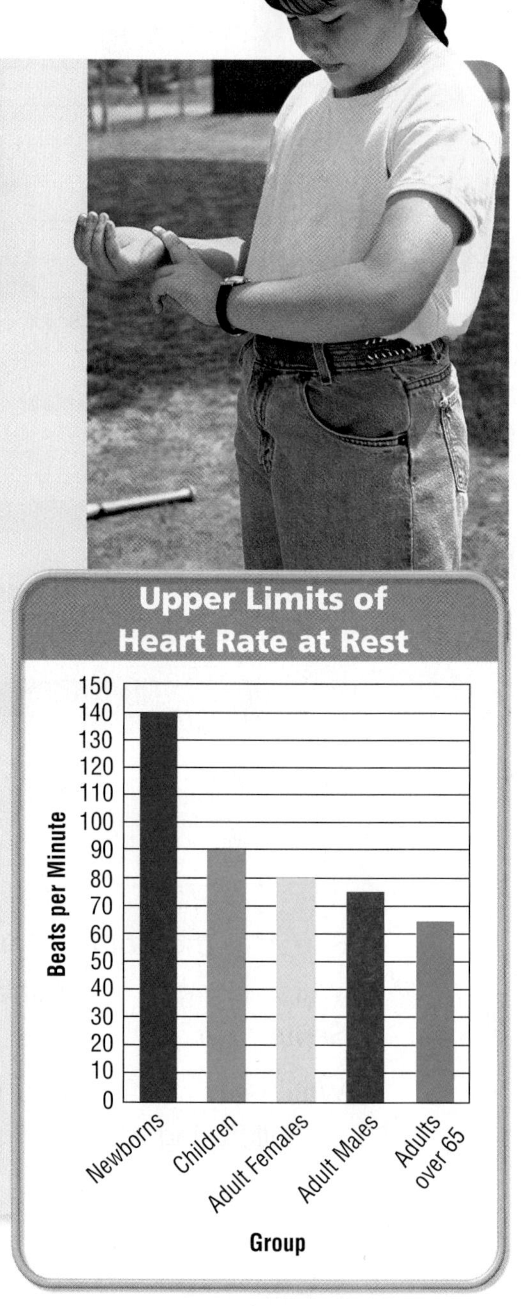

Think and Discuss

Make a generalization. Then solve the problem.

Jack and Mary are both 30 years old. Who probably has a faster heart rate, Jack or Mary?

TEKS 4.16A make generalizations from patterns or sets of examples and nonexamples. *also* **4.13B, 4.14A, 4.14C, 4.15A, 4.15B, 4.16B**

Guided Problem Solving

For 1–3, use the table. Make a generalization. Then solve the problem.

1. When you exercise, your heart beats faster. The table shows maximum target heart rates for different ages. Copy and complete the chart with the data from the graph.

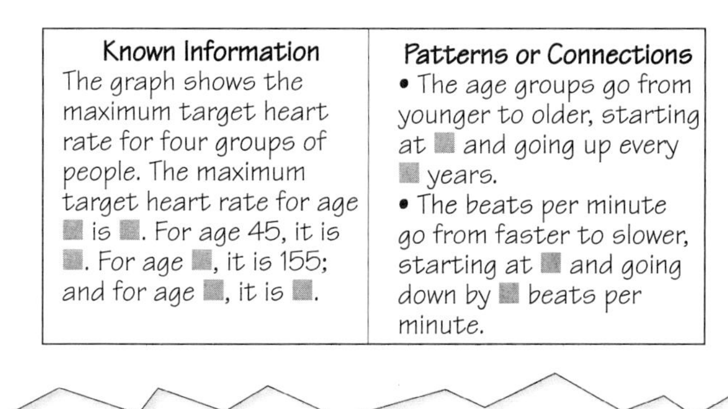

Known Information	Patterns or Connections
The graph shows the maximum target heart rate for four groups of people. The maximum target heart rate for age ■ is ■. For age 45, it is ■. For age ■, it is 155; and for age ■, it is ■.	• The age groups go from younger to older, starting at ■ and going up every ■ years. • The beats per minute go from faster to slower, starting at ■ and going down by ■ beats per minute.

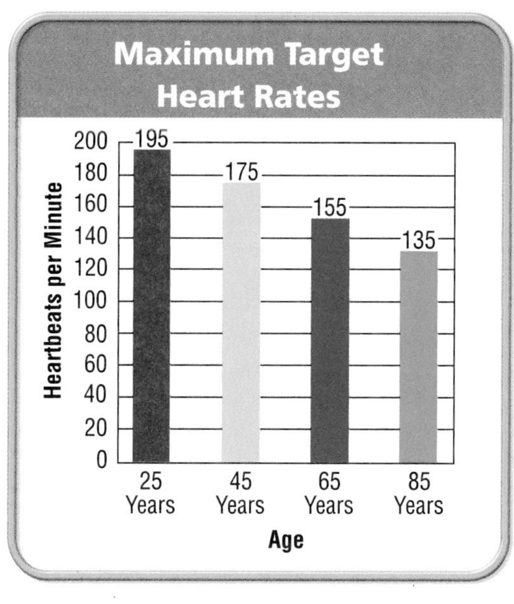

2. What might the target heart rate be for age 35?

3. Miyu is 25 years old. She does aerobics for a half hour and then measures her heart rate. If it is 180 beats per minute, should Miyu slow her exercise rate, or can she continue at the same rate? **Explain** your answer.

Mixed Applications

USE DATA For 4–6, use the table.

4. How many more calories does an 11-year-old male need than a 9-year-old female?

5. Beth and Travis are 12-year-old twins. Helena is 8 years old, and her sister Marta is 10 years old. List the names of the children in order from the one who needs the least calories to the one who needs the greatest calories. **Explain.**

6. Based on the data in the table, about how many calories might a 15-year-old male need?

7. **Algebra** Peter's dog weighs 24 pounds. His cat weighs n pounds. If his dog weighs 3 times as much as his cat, what is n?

8. **WRITE Math** On a hot, sunny day, bamboo can grow about an inch an hour. Ben's bamboo was 3 inches tall when he went to school. Now it is 11 inches tall. How can you use a generalization to decide about how long Ben was gone?

Calories Needed by Active Children

Age	Male	Female
8	2,000	1,800
9	2,000	1,800
10	2,200	2,000
11	2,200	2,000
12	2,400	2,200
13	2,400	2,200

LESSON **8**

ALGEBRA

Graph Ordered Pairs

OBJECTIVE: Describe the relationship between two sets of related data shown as ordered pairs.

Quick Review

Write the missing number.

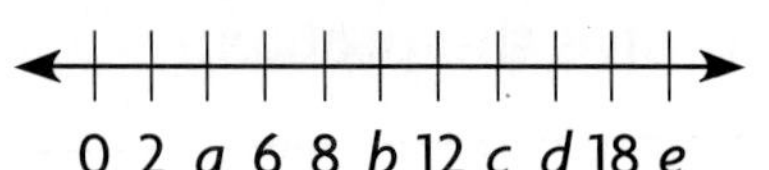

1. *a* **2.** *b* **3.** *c*
4. *d* **5.** *e*

Vocabulary

ordered pair

Learn

An **ordered pair** is a pair of numbers that names a point on a grid. The first number shows how many units to move horizontally. The second number shows how many units to move vertically.

(2,4)

move 2 units right — move 4 units up

ERROR ALERT

The first number shows how to move horizontally and the second number shows how to move vertically when graphing an ordered pair.

Example 1 Graph an ordered pair.

Graph (2,5).

- Start at 0.
- Count 2 units right.
- Count 5 units up.
- Graph a point.
- Label the point (2,5).

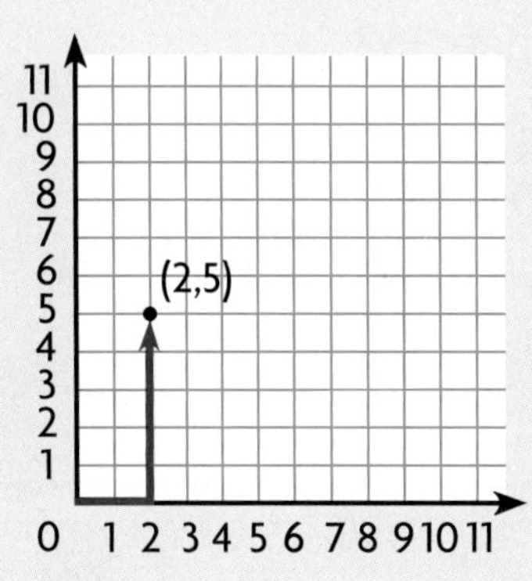

So, the point is located at (2,5).

You can also graph ordered pairs from a table to solve a problem.

Example 2 Graph ordered pairs from a table.

Pablo uses 4 slices of ham and 1 slice of cheese for each sandwich. How many cheese slices does he use if he uses 32 ham slices?

Slices of Ham	4	8	12	16	20	24	28	32
Slices of Cheese	1	2	3	4	5	6	7	8

Graph each ordered pair.

(4,1), (8,2), (12,3), (16,4), (20,5), (24,6), (28,7), (32,8)

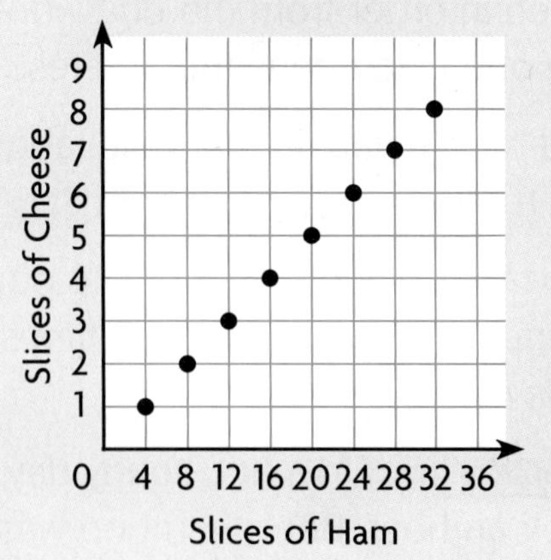

So, Pablo needs 8 slices of cheese.

TEKS 4.7 Describe the relationship between two sets of related data such as ordered pairs in a table. *also* 4.14A, 4.14C, 4.15A, 4.15B, 4.16A

Guided Practice

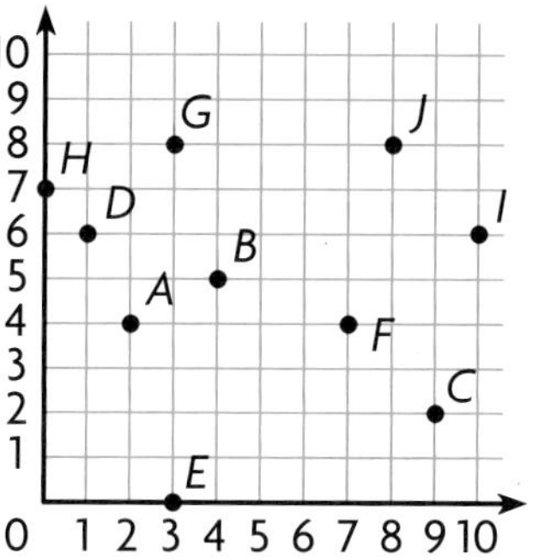

1. To graph the point (5,8), in which direction and how many units will you move first? What will you do next?

For 2–6, use the grid. Write the ordered pair for each point.

2. *A* 3. *B* ✓4. *C* ✓5. *D*

6. TALK Math **Explain** how to write ordered pairs from a table.

Independent Practice and Problem Solving

For 7–12 , use the grid above. Write the ordered pair for each point.

7. *E* 8. *F* 9. *G* 10. *H* 11. *I* 12. *J*

For 13–14, write ordered pairs for each table. Then use grid paper to graph the ordered pairs.

13.

Number of Pages	1	2	3	4
Number of Photos	4	8	12	16

14.

Miles Traveled	20	40	60	80
Gallons of Gas	1	2	3	4

For 15, complete the table to help solve. Then use grid paper to graph the ordered pairs.

15. Carter buys 32 slices of turkey. If he uses 8 slices of turkey for each sandwich, how many sandwiches can he make?

Number of Sandwiches	1	2		4
Number of Turkey Slices	8		24	

16. **Pose a Problem** Look at Problem 15. Write a similar problem by changing the number of slices of turkey.

17. WRITE Math **What's the Question?** You start at (0,0). You move 6 units right and then 2 units up.

Mixed Review and TAKS Prep

18. Jack made 3 rows of crackers with 3 in each row. He ate 2 crackers. How many are left? (TEKS 4.4C, p. 98)

19. Aaron has soccer practice from 3:45 P.M. to 5:00 P.M. How long is soccer practice? Use a clock to help. (TEKS 4.12B, p. 476)

20. **TAKS Prep** Avi uses 6 ounces of yogurt to make a smoothie. How many smoothies can he make from 42 ounces of yogurt? (Obj. 1)

A 48 **C** 7

B 36 **D** 6

Extra Practice on page 514, Set F

Extra Practice

Set A Use the Favorite Color frequency table. (pp. 496–499)

1. How many students said orange was their favorite color?
2. Which two colors were chosen by the same number of students?
3. How many more students chose blue than orange?
4. Which color was chosen most often?
5. How many students were surveyed?

Favorite Color	
Color	Frequency (Number of Students)
Blue	36
Green	28
Orange	11
Purple	41
Red	28

Set B Use the Venn diagram. (pp. 500–501)

1. List the fourth-grade students who are chorus members.
2. List the fourth-grade students who are band members.
3. Why are some of the students' names in the middle area where the sets overlap?

Fourth-Grade Musicians

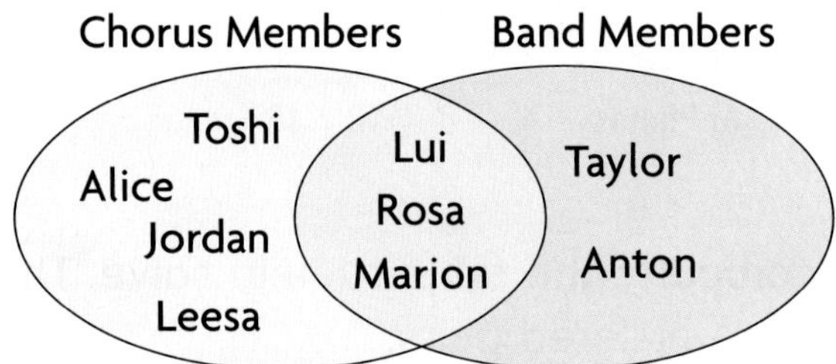

Set C Use the table. (pp. 502–503)

1. The table shows the numbers of students who speak foreign languages. Make a pictograph to show the data.
2. Which language is spoken by the most students?
3. Which languages are spoken by the same number of students?
4. Vera is making a pictograph and using a circle to represent 10 students. How should she show:

   a. the number of students who speak French?

   b. the number of students who speak Spanish?

Foreign Languages	
Language	Number of Students
Spanish	15
French	5
Russian	10
Mandarin	10

CD ROM **Technology** Use Harcourt Mega Math, The Number Games, *ArachnaGraph,* Levels A, B, C, D.

Set D Choose 5, 10, or 100 as the most reasonable interval for each set of data. Explain your choice. (pp. 504–505)

1. 201, 450, 550, 600, 799
2. 19, 25, 15, 31, 20
3. 51, 20, 28, 90, 60
4. 94, 25, 70, 49
5. 300, 199, 420, 690
6. 9, 14, 30, 15, 45

For 7–8, use the Library Books Borrowed graph. (pp. 504–505)

7. What are the scale and interval used to show these data?
8. About how many more books were borrowed on Friday than on Wednesday?

Set E Use the Favorite Type of Movie bar graph. (pp. 506–507)

1. How many more students chose comedies than cartoons?
2. What is the difference between the least favorite and the most favorite movie types?
3. Which types of movies were chosen by the same number of classmates?
4. What is the interval of the scale?

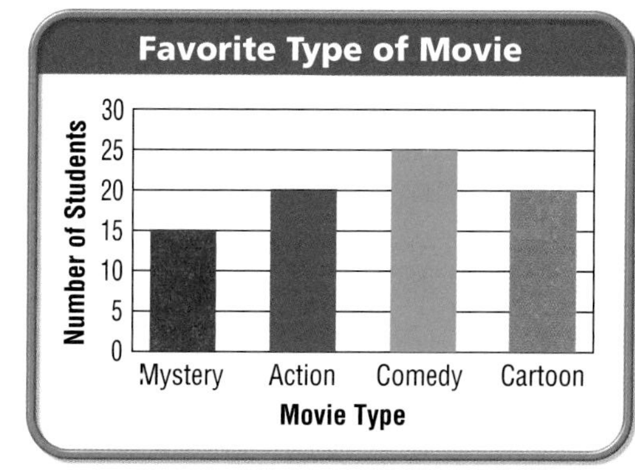

Set F Write ordered pairs for each table. Then use grid paper to graph the ordered pairs. (pp. 512–513)

1.

Number of Vases	Number of Flowers (per group)
1	2
2	4
3	6
4	8
5	10

2.

Number of Groups	Number of Campers (per group)
0	0
2	2
4	4
6	6
8	8

Chapter 19 Review/Test

Check Vocabulary and Concepts

Choose the best term from the box.

VOCABULARY
pictograph
bar graph
key

1. A ___?___ is a graph that uses pictures or symbols to show and compare information. (TEKS 4.13, p. 502)
2. The ___?___ shows what each symbol represents. (TEKS 4.13, p. 502)

Check Skills

For 3–4, use the Favorite Music frequency table. (TEKS 4.13, pp. 496–499, 508–509)

3. How many more students prefer rhythm and blues than classical music?
4. Use the data in the frequency table to make a bar graph.

Favorite Music	
Type of Music	Frequency (Number of Students)
Rock	23
Classical	7
Jazz	11
Hip-Hop	12
Rhythm and Blues	17

For 5–6, use the Venn diagram. (TEKS 4.13, pp. 500–501)

5. What labels should you use for section B?
6. Why are the numbers 12, 24, and 36 listed in the area where the sets overlap?

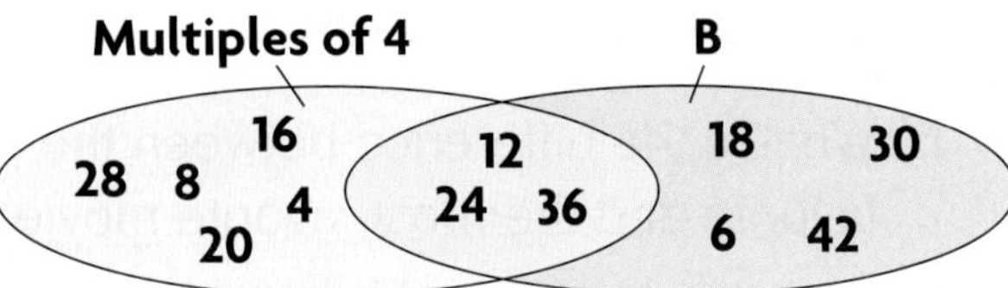

Choose 5, 10, or 100 as the most reasonable interval for each set of data. Explain your choice. (TEKS 4.13, pp. 504–505)

7. 28, 39, 40, 51, 80
8. 150, 225, 300, 401, 599

Check Problem Solving

Solve. (TEKS 4.13B, pp. 510–511)

9. The bar graph shows the number of hours James practiced piano each week in September. James started back to school one week in September. Which week did he probably start back?
10. WRITE Math **Explain** how you could estimate how long James will practice in all during 4 weeks in October.

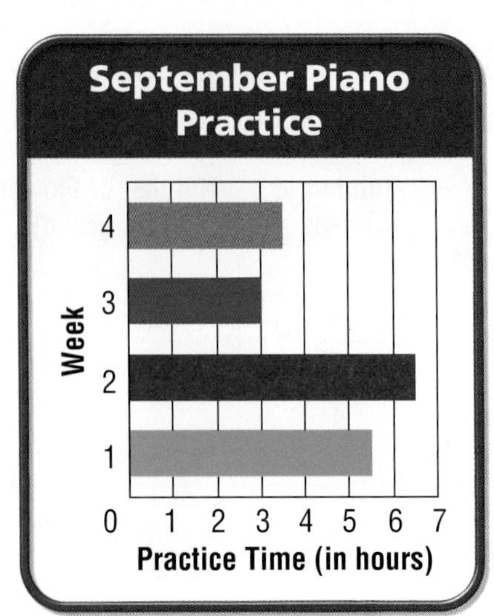

GO ONLINE **Technology** Use *Online Assessment.*

Enrich • Find Median, Mode, and Range

OLD FAITHFUL

Old Faithful Geyser, at Wyoming's Yellowstone National Park, got its name because of its frequent and regular eruptions.

Alan recorded the time between eruptions when he visited the park. The times are shown on the bar graph. Find the range, median, and mode of the set of data.

▲ Old Faithful's eruptions range in height from 90 to 184 feet high.

Materials ▪ index cards

Step 1 Find the range.

Write each number of minutes on an index card. Arrange the cards in a row from least to greatest. The **range** is the difference between the greatest and least numbers.

45 55 60 70 75 75 80

$80 - 45 = 35$

Step 2 Find the median.

Remove one card from each end of the row. Repeat until only one card remains. This number is the **median**, or middle number.

45 55 60 70 75 75 80

Step 3 Find the mode.

Sort the cards to find the number that occurs most often. This number is the **mode**.

45 55 60 70 75 75 80

So, the range is 35, the median is 70, and the mode is 75.

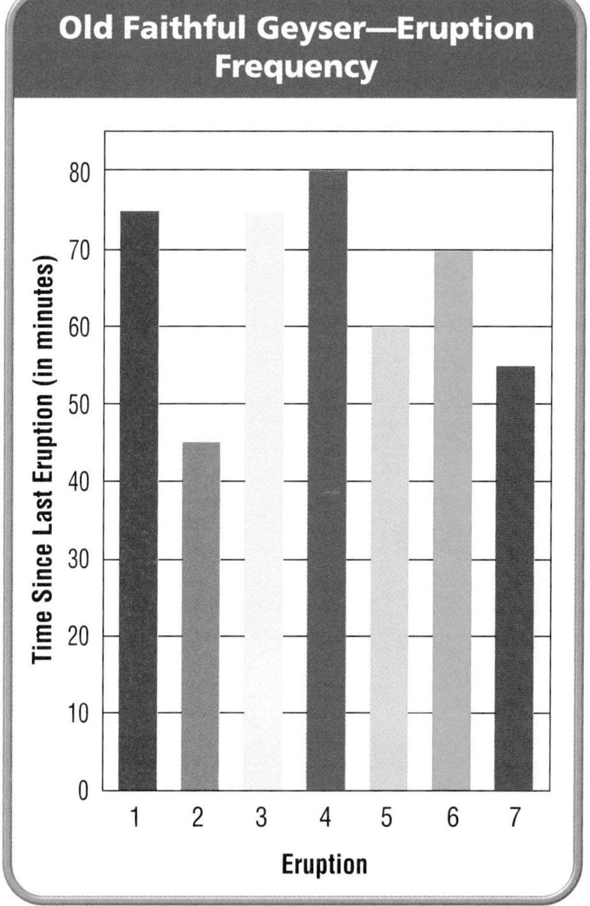

Try It

Find the range, median, and mode of each set of data.

1. 19, 18, 22, 18, 21
2. 120, 115, 126, 120, 120
3. 450, 600, 520, 350, 600
4. 17, 4, 11, 17, 9, 6, 12
5. 31, 52, 45, 38, 45, 51, 49
6. 71, 83, 66, 74, 66, 82, 66

WRITE Math **Explain** the difference between the range, median, and mode of a set of data.

Getting Ready for the TAKS
Chapters 1–19

Geometry and Spatial Reasoning TAKS Obj. 3

1. In the figure below, which two angles appear to be acute?

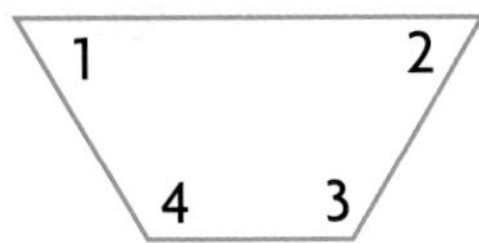

A Angles 1 and 3

B Angles 2 and 4

C Angles 3 and 4

D Angles 1 and 2

Look for important words.

See Item 2. The word *symmetry* is important. When you fold a shape over a line of symmetry, both sides match.

2. How many lines of symmetry does this shape have?

F 0

G 1

H 2

J Not here

3. WRITE Math Mr. Brock asked Leticia to identify the square that he had drawn on the board. She said it was a rectangle. **Explain** if Leticia and Mr. Brock are both correct.

Patterns, Relationships, and Algebraic Thinking TAKS Obj. 2

4. Which number sentence is part of the same fact family as $56 \div 8 = ■$?

A $8 + ■ = 56$

B $■ - 8 = 56$

C $8 \times ■ = 56$

D $56 \times 8 = ■$

5. Eddie collects nickels. He stores them in rolls of 40. If he has 100 rolls of nickels, how many nickels does Eddie have?

F 4

G 400

H 4,000

J 40,000

6. What number sentence can help you to remember that $96 \div 12 = 8$?

A $8 \times 12 = 96$

B $12 \times 4 = 48$

C $96 \div 3 = 32$

D $12 \div 3 = 4$

7. WRITE Math Sara has a sticker album. The table shows the numbers of stickers on 2, 5, and 7 pages.

Sara's Sticker Album				
Pages	2	5	7	8
Stickers	160	400	560	■

Explain how you can use the table to find the number of stickers Sara will have on 8 pages.

Probability and Statistics (Obj. 5)

8. The graph shows the grade levels of students involved in the after-school activity program.

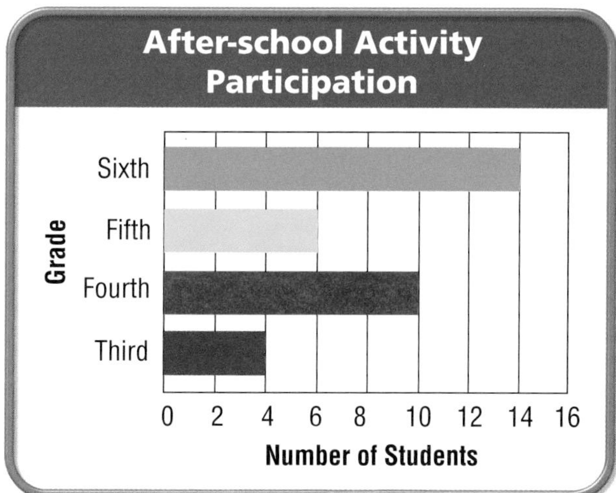

How many fifth-grade and sixth-grade students are participating in the program?

F 15 H 20

G 16 J 24

9. **WRITE Math** Amanda is teaching swimming at a summer camp. The campers are divided into 3 teams. The green team has 18 campers. How many symbols would you draw to complete the pictograph? **Explain** your thinking.

Lakeview Camp Swim Teams	
Red Team	◎◎◎◎◎
Blue Team	◎◎◎
Green Team	
Key: Each ◎ = 3 campers.	

Number, Operation, and Quantitative Reasoning (Obj. 1)

10. Tariq is planting tulip bulbs in his garden. He decides to plant 9 bulbs in each row with 12 rows. How many bulbs will he plant?

A 108

B 98

C 27

D Not here

11. Nicole used the treadmill for 38 minutes on Monday, 53 minutes on Tuesday, and 68 minutes on Wednesday. Estimate the time she used the treadmill during the three days.

F 100 minutes

G 160 minutes

H 200 minutes

J 260 minutes

12. Mr. Olsen bought 256 cases of dog food to sell in his pet stores. How many cases will each store get if there are 8 stores?

A 35 C 30

B 32 D 26

13. **WRITE Math** **Explain** how you can use the models to compare $\frac{11}{16}$ and $\frac{3}{4}$. Write a number sentence to show the relationship.

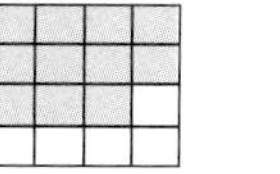 

20 Combinations

The Big Idea All possible combinations of a set of data can be shown using models and diagrams.

Investigate

At the Charro Days Youth Parade, children wear traditional Mexican costumes. Suppose you want to make a shirt to wear in the parade. You can choose a shirt color, a ribbon color, and a fringe color. How can you find the number of different combinations you can make? Find the number.

Shirt Choices

Shirt	Ribbon	Fringe
White	Yellow	Black
Red	Green	Purple
Blue	Orange	
	White	

TEXAS FAST FACT

Charro Days started about 70 years ago. People from Texas and Mexico wore traditional clothes to celebrate. Today, people from all over the world attend.

GO ONLINE **Technology** Student pages are available in the Student eBook.

Show What You Know

Check your understanding of important skills needed for success in Chapter 20.

▶ Make Equivalent Sets of Change

Matthew has 1 quarter, 3 dimes, 2 nickels, and 5 pennies. Copy and complete the table to find equivalent sets of coins he can use to make 30¢.

	Quarters	Dimes	Nickels	Pennies	Value
	1		1		30¢
1.	■			■	■
2.		■			■
3.		■	■		■
4.		■	■	■	■

▶ List All Possible Outcomes

List the possible outcomes for each experiment.

5. pulling a marble from this bag

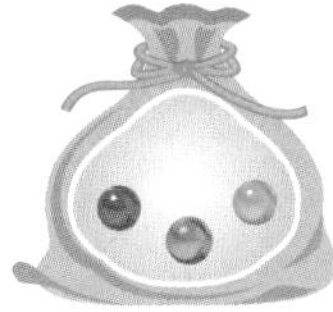

6. spinning the pointer of this spinner

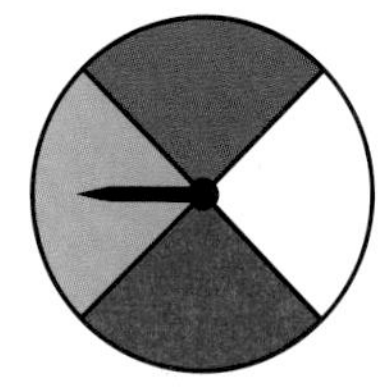

7. pulling a marble from this bag

8. spinning the pointer of this spinner

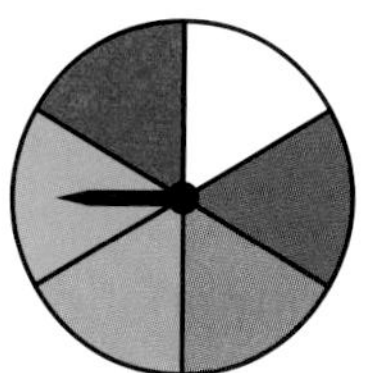

VOCABULARY POWER

CHAPTER VOCABULARY

combination
tree diagram

WARM-UP WORDS

combination a choice in which the order of items does not matter

tree diagram an organized list that shows all possible combinations

LESSON 1 HANDS ON

Model Combinations

OBJECTIVE: List all possible combinations of a set of data or objects.

Quick Review

Dave, Jenn, and Susie are standing in a line. List 3 different orders in which they can be standing.

Vocabulary

combination

Investigate

Materials ■ 3-inch by 8-inch strips of paper

Bill, Joe, Ruby, and Ina are at camp. Each activity takes 1, 2, 3, or 4 students at a time. The camp director needs to make groups of different combinations of students to attend each activity.

A **combination** is a choice in which the order of items does not matter. You can model combinations using strips of paper.

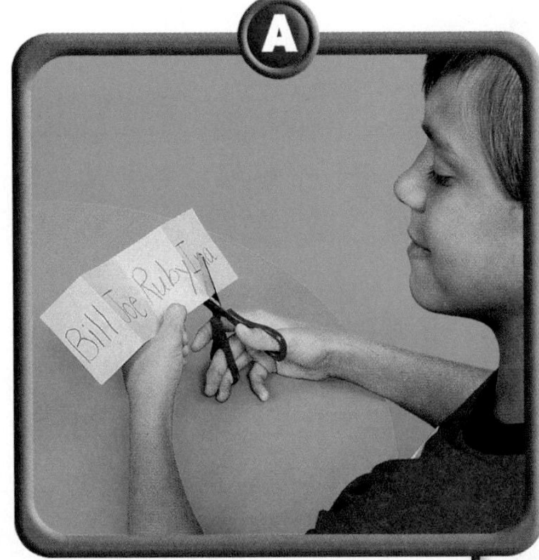

A Fold a strip of paper in half and then in half again. Unfold the paper. Write the names of the students so that one name is in each section of the paper. Cut the names apart on the folds.

B Use the names to form combinations of 4 students. List all possible combinations. Do not include combinations that list the same set of names. Bill, Joe, Ruby, Ina is the same as Ina, Bill, Joe, Ruby. Record the number of combinations and tell how many there are.

C Repeat the activity for groups of 3 students, 2 students, and 1 student. List all possible combinations. Record the number of combinations.

Draw Conclusions

1. Explain how you found the number of combinations of 3 students.
2. For which number of students was the most combinations possible? Why do you think this is?
3. **Synthesis** Suppose there were 5 students at camp instead of 4. How many combinations of 3 students are there? List all possible combinations.

TEKS 4.13A use concrete objects and pictures to make generalizations about determining all possible combinations of a given set of data or of objects in a problem situation. *also* **4.14A, 4.14D, 4.15A, 4.15B**

Connect

One way you can find all the combinations is to use a table to make an organized list.

Use a table to list all the combinations of 2 names.

Step 1

To organize the table, make columns for each name.

Combinations			
Bill	**Joe**	**Ruby**	**Ina**

Step 2

Use the first letter of each name to list all possible choices.

Combinations			
Bill	**Joe**	**Ruby**	**Ina**
B, J	J, B	R, B	I, B
B, R	J, R	R, J	I, J
B, I	J, I	R, I	I, R

Step 3

Cross off the pairs that reverse the ones already listed.

Think: B, J is the same as J, B because it uses the same names, so cross off J, B.

Combinations			
Bill	**Joe**	**Ruby**	**Ina**
B, J	~~J, B~~	~~R, B~~	~~I, B~~
B, R	J, R	~~R, J~~	~~I, J~~
B, I	J, I	R, I	~~I, R~~

So, there are 6 combinations of 2 students.

TALK Math

How does using a table help you find all possible combinations?

Practice

Write the letters of the word CHASE on a strip of paper with 5 sections. Use the paper to model all combinations of the given number of letters.

1. 3 letters **2.** 2 letters **3.** 1 letter **4.** 5 letters ✓**5.** 4 letters

Make a table to solve.

6. How many combinations of 2 letters can be made from the letters in the word ROCK?

✓**7.** How many combinations of 3 animals can be made from tiger, bear, horse, dolphin, and ostrich?

8. WRITE Math Which gives you a greater number of combinations, making combinations of 2 from a set of 3, or making combinations of 3 from a set of 4? **Explain.**

LESSON 2

Combinations

OBJECTIVE: Determine all possible combinations.

Quick Review

At Pottery Place, each piece of pottery is painted 2 colors. They have red, blue, green, and purple paint. How many combinations of two colors are there?

Learn

PROBLEM Joe's Pizza offers 3 sizes of pizzas, 3 types of crusts, and 3 types of toppings. How many different pizzas can Joe make?

You can make a flipbook to find all possible combinations.

Joe's Pizza menu

Sizes Small Medium Large

Crusts thin regular pan

Toppings onions mushrooms pepperoni

HANDS ON

Activity

Materials ■ 2 sheets of paper

Step 1

Stack two sheets of paper and fold them in half. Staple near the fold.

Step 2

Cut the first three pages into three strips each. Cut only as far as the staples.

Step 3

Write the size choices on the top third of each page. Write one size on each page. Use the middle third for crust choices. Use the bottom third for topping choices.

Step 4

Use one of each of the three choices to show the different pizzas. Record each combination in a list.

So, there are 27 pizza choices.

- **What if** Joe's Pizza offered 4 topping choices? How many different pizzas can he make?

TEKS 4.13A use concrete objects or pictures to make generalizations about determining all possible combinations of a given set of data or of objects in a problem situation. *also* **4.14A, 4.14D, 4.15A, 4.15B**

Example

Joe plans to offer a combo plate at dinner. You can choose a main dish and a side dish. The main dish choices are roasted chicken, meat loaf, and spaghetti. The side dish choices are carrots and a potato.

You can make a table to find the number of ways you can choose a main dish and a side dish.

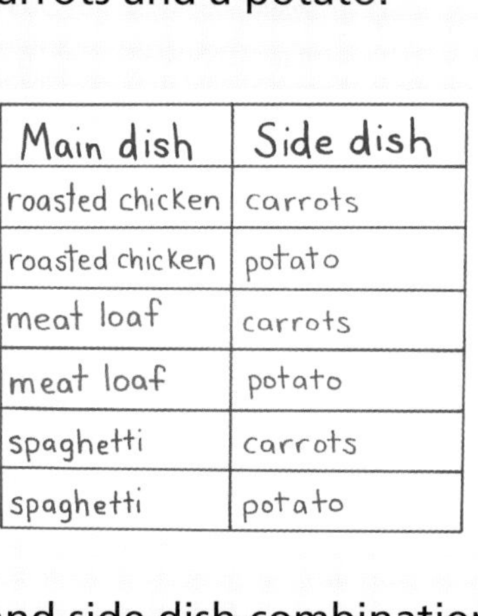

Main dish	Side dish
roasted chicken	carrots
roasted chicken	potato
meat loaf	carrots
meat loaf	potato
spaghetti	carrots
spaghetti	potato

So, there are 6 main dish and side dish combinations.

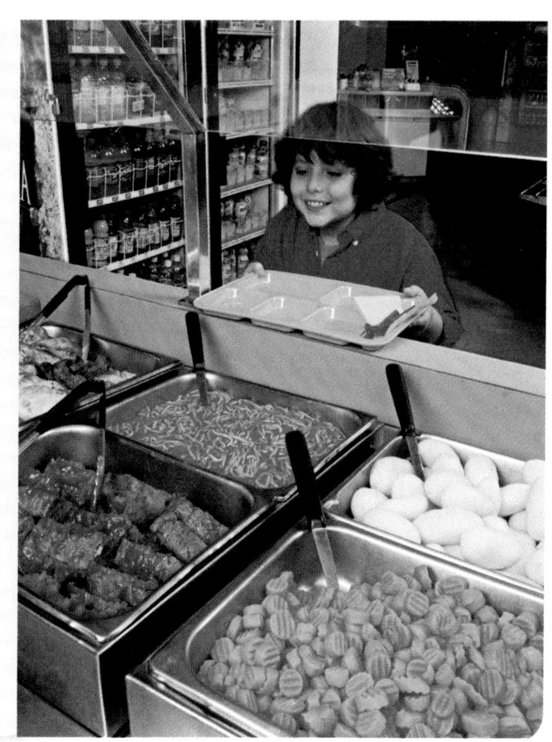

Guided Practice

1. Lalo is dancing or singing for talent night at his school. He can choose to use jazz or country music. Copy and complete the table to find all the possible combinations of talents and music Lalo can choose. How many combinations are possible?

Talent	Music
dancing	jazz
■	■

Make a model to find all the possible combinations.

2. Sandwich choices
meat: ham, turkey
cheese: American, cheddar

✓ 3. Ice cream sundae choices
ice cream flavor: vanilla, chocolate
sauce: caramel, hot fudge
topping: sprinkles, cherries

For 4–5, copy and complete the tables to show all possible combinations of each set of items.

4. Picture choices
photo: family, car, mountain
frame: gold, silver, wood

photo	frame
family	gold

✓ 5. Nametag choices
color: blue, red, yellow, green
border: dots, stars

color	border
blue	dots

6. **TALK Math** **Explain** how tables or models help you find all possible combinations.

Independent Practice and Problem Solving

Make a model to find all the possible combinations.

5. Doll choices
hair: blond, brown, black
eyes: green, blue, brown

6. Swim lesson choices
time: morning, afternoon
day: Monday, Tuesday, Wednesday
teacher: John, Maria

7. Dinner menu choices
meal: chicken, fish
vegetable: broccoli, beans
drink: milk, lemonade, water

8. Probability experiment
coin flip: heads, tails
cube toss: 1, 2, 3, 4, 5, 6

For 9–10, copy and complete the tables to show all possible combinations of each set of items.

9. Lunch choices
sandwich: cheese, ham
drink: water, tea, juice

sandwich	drink

10. Game piece choices
figure: square, circle, triangle
color: red, blue, green, yellow

figure	color

11. Rhonda has green pants and blue pants. She has a red shirt, a white shirt, and a striped shirt. How many different outfits of one pair of pants and one shirt can Rhonda choose from?

12. Adam can order a banana smoothie, a strawberry smoothie, or a blueberry smoothie. He can have a small, medium, or large size. How many different smoothies can Adam choose from?

USE DATA For 13–15, use the sign.

13. How many different activity combinations are possible? List them.

14. What is the most expensive combination?

15. How will the number of possible combinations change if the nature hike is cancelled?

WELCOME!
Here at Rudy's Ranch, choose a morning, afternoon, and evening activity for a day of outdoor excitement!
RUDY'S RANCH ACTIVITIES
Morning Activities
Afternoon Activities
Evening Activities
Horseback riding $7
Giant water slide $3
Campfire $6
Arts and crafts $4
Bird-watching $5
Stargazing $8
Nature hike $9

16. WRITE Math ▸ **What's the Error?** Justin has crunchy and smooth peanut butter. He has grape and strawberry jelly. He says there are 2 possible combinations of peanut butter and jelly. Describe Justin's error. Find the correct answer.

 Extra Practice on page 540, Set A

Mixed Review and TAKS Prep

17. Bob started a sign language class on Friday, April 14. The class ended on April 27. On what day of the week did the class end? (TEKS 4.12, p. 482)

April						
Sun	Mon	Tue	Wed	Thu	Fri	Sat
						1
2	3	4	5	6	7	8
9	10	11	12	13	14	15
16	17	18	19	20	21	22
23	24	25	26	27	28	29
30						

18. Robin rides a bike trail every weekend. The trail is 28 miles long. If she rode the trail once a week for 52 weeks, about how many miles did she ride in all?

(TEKS 4.4D, p. 236)

19. **TAKS Prep** The chart shows activity choices for summer campers.

Arts and Crafts	Sports
painting	soccer
woodworking	archery
ceramics	swimming

Each camper chooses one arts & crafts activity and one sports activity. How many different combinations are possible? (Obj. 5)

A 3 **B** 6 **C** 9 **D** 12

20. **TAKS Prep** Robert can buy a model car, truck, or airplane. He can paint it green or black. List all the possible combinations. (Obj. 5)

Problem Solving and Reasoning

Classify and Categorize

To *classify* information is to group information that is alike. To *categorize* information is to label the classified groups, or categories.

Julia is designing uniforms for the dance team. Students could wear white shirts or red shirts. They could wear blue jeans or black jeans. They could wear black shoes or white shoes.

Categorize ⟶ / Classify {

Shirts	Jeans	Shoes
white	?	?
?	?	?

Solve.

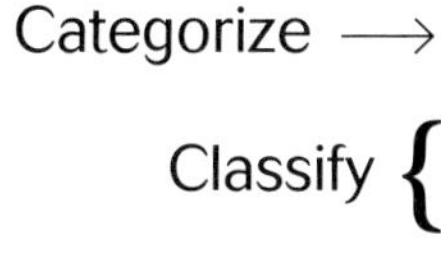

1. Copy and complete the table using the information above.
2. How many uniforms (1 shirt, 1 pair of jeans, 1 pair of shoes) can Julia design?
3. Julia is making a stage curtain. She has black, white, yellow, and blue fabric and gold ribbon for a trim. She buys green fabric and silver ribbon. How can you categorize and classify the information? How many kinds of curtains can Julia make if she can choose from one color fabric and one color trim?

LESSON 3

Tree Diagrams

OBJECTIVE: Use a tree diagram to determine all possible combinations.

Quick Review

Thomas put on a pair of jeans. He can choose a sweatshirt, t-shirt, or tank top. Name the combinations of pants and shirts Thomas can choose.

Vocabulary

tree diagram

Learn

PROBLEM Miranda wears a school uniform. She can choose from black or brown pants. She can choose from red, green, or yellow shirts. How many different combinations of shirts and pants can Miranda choose from?

A **tree diagram** is an organized list that shows all possible combinations. A tree diagram uses branches to connect the choices from each category.

HANDS ON

Activity

Materials ■ outfits pattern ■ scissors ■ red, green, yellow, black and brown crayons

Step 1

Color the shirts and pants Miranda can choose from. Then cut out the shirts and pants.

Step 2

Use the cutouts to make different combinations of shirts and pants.

Step 3

Record the combinations in a tree diagram.

Pants	Shirt		Combinations
black pants	red shirt	—	black pants, red shirt
	green shirt	—	black pants, ?
	yellow shirt	—	?
brown pants	?	—	?
	?	—	?
	?	—	?

So, Miranda can choose from 6 different combinations of shirts and pants.

Math Idea

You can use a tree diagram to list all the possible combinations and to find the total number of combinations.

TEKS 4.13A use concrete objects or pictures to make generalizations about determining all possible combinations of a given set of data or of objects in a problem situation. *also* **4.14A, 4.14D, 4.15A, 4.15B**

Example

Samuel is ordering a taco at a taco stand. How many different tacos can Samuel choose from if he chooses one item from each category?

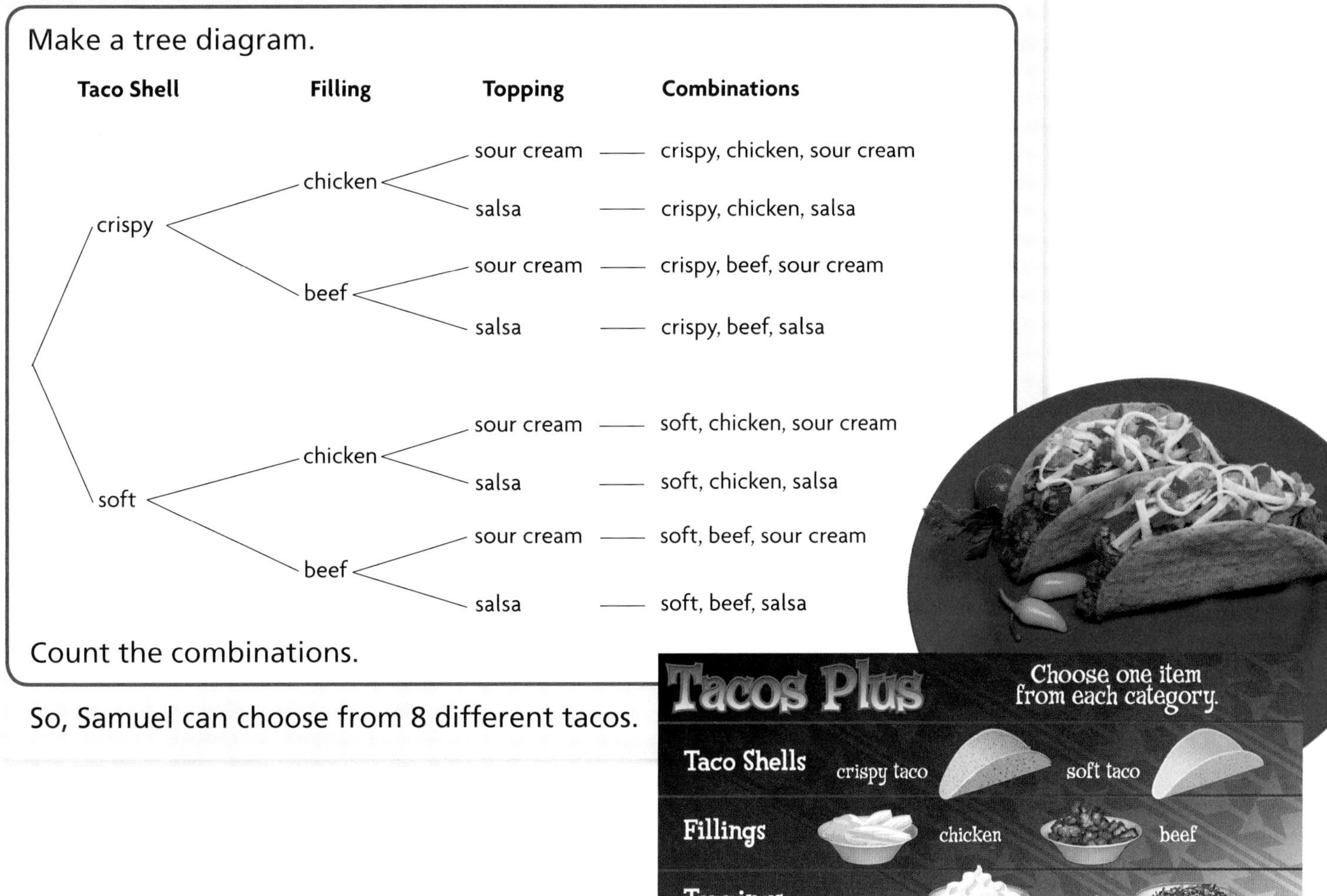

So, Samuel can choose from 8 different tacos.

Guided Practice

1. Copy and complete the tree diagram. List all possible combinations.

Pants	Shirt	Combinations
tan pants	?	tan pants, red shirt
	blue shirt	?
black pants	?	?
	?	?

Make a tree diagram to find the number of possible combinations.

2. Flower display choices
   flower: roses, daisies, lilies
   vase: white, blue

3. Ice cream choices
   flavor: strawberry, chocolate, vanilla
   topping: caramel, cherry, nuts

4. **TALK Math** **Explain** how drawing a tree diagram helps you find all possible combinations.

Independent Practice and Problem Solving

Make a tree diagram to find the number of possible combinations.

5. activity choices:
   activity: movie, shopping, zoo
   day: Saturday, Sunday, Monday

6. shirt choices:
   color: red, yellow, white
   style: short-sleeve, long-sleeve

7. report choices:
   state: Texas, Oklahoma, New Mexico, Arkansas, Louisiana
   topic: geography, natural resources, climate

8. backpack choices:
   design: striped, polka dots
   color: yellow, red, black, blue

9. breakfast choices:
   food: cereal, eggs, pancakes
   juice: orange, apple, pineapple, grapefruit

10. scarf choices:
    color: blue, black, gray, green, white
    trim: red, orange

Use the picture.

11. Belinda is getting ready for school. Draw a tree diagram to show the combinations of shirts and pants Belinda can choose from to wear to school.

USE DATA For 12–16, use the menu.

12. Billy wants a drink and a dessert. How many different combinations of a drink and dessert can Billy choose from?

13. Sarah wants a sandwich, a drink, and a dessert. She does not want to order milk. How many different combinations of a sandwich, a drink, and a dessert can Sarah choose from?

14. Addy paid for a turkey wrap, milk, and a dessert with a $10 bill. She got $4 in change. Which dessert did she order?

15. **Pose a Problem** Look back at Problem 12. Write a similar problem by changing the choices.

16. **WRITE Math** **What's the Question?** Ann wants lunch from the snack bar. The answer is 6.

Snack Bar Menu
Sandwich:
Turkey Wrap: $3
Hot Dog: $2
Grilled Cheese: $2
Drinks:
Lemonade: $1
Milk: $1
Fruit Punch: $1
Dessert:
Watermelon Slice: $2
Frozen Grapes: $1

Mixed Review and TAKS Prep

13. Shelly's grade has 124 students. There are 4 classes and each class has the same number of students in her grade. How many students are in each class? (TEKS 4.4E, p.364)

14. **TAKS Prep** Brad is making a cookie. He can choose a star or diamond cookie cutter. He can choose yellow or blue frosting. How many different combinations are possible? (Obj. 5)

A 2 **C** 6

B 4 **D** 8

15. List the ways Karen can choose 2 letters from the word PICK. (TEKS 4.13A, p. 522)

16. **TAKS Prep** Jorge is making a scrapbook page. He can choose blue or green paper. He can decorate the page with stickers, stamps, or ribbon. How many combinations do not use green paper or stickers? **Explain.** (Obj. 5)

Problem Solving and Reasoning

NUMBER SENSE Charley is going to buy a music player and case. How many different combinations are possible?

You can multiply to find the number of combinations.

6 choices for player		3 choices for case		18 possible combinations
6	×	3	=	18

So, there are 18 possible combinations.

What number sentence can you use to find the number of possible combinations?

1. sandwich choices:
bread: white, whole wheat, rye
filling: tuna fish, peanut butter, turkey, chicken salad

2. decorating choices:
paint: yellow, tan, blue, white
trim: white, gray

3. poster choices:
poster board: white, yellow, light blue
paint: black, blue, green, red, purple, silver, gold

4. car choices:
style: sedan, van, convertible, SUV, sports car
color: black, silver, white, red, green

Problem Solving Workshop
Strategy: Make an Organized List

OBJECTIVE: Solve problems by using the strategy *make an organized list.*

Learn the Strategy

Making an organized list is a good way to keep track of information. You can use different types of organized lists for different types of problems.

Make a list to sequence information.

Mr. Wong puts the daily schedule for his class on the board.

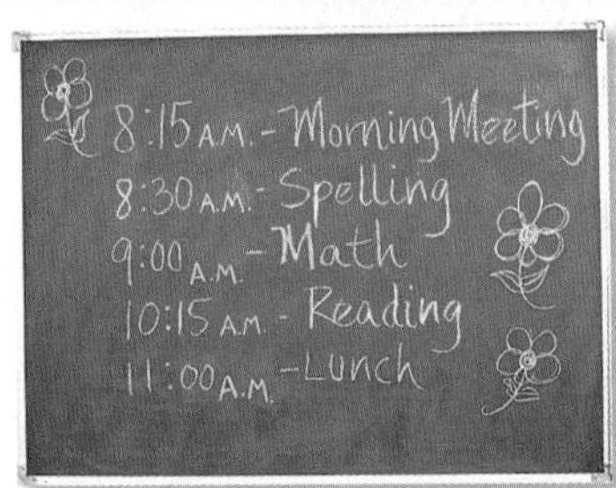

Make a list to organize information.

Each night, Kelly writes her homework assignments in a notebook. She organizes her homework by subject.

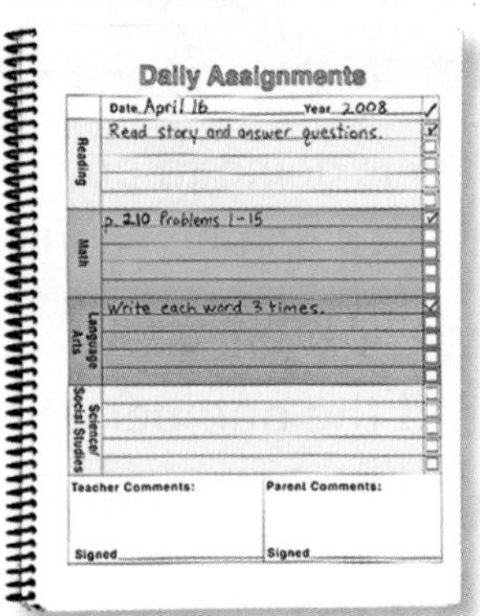

Make a list to find combinations.

A bakery offers 3 different flavors and 2 different fillings for their layer cakes.

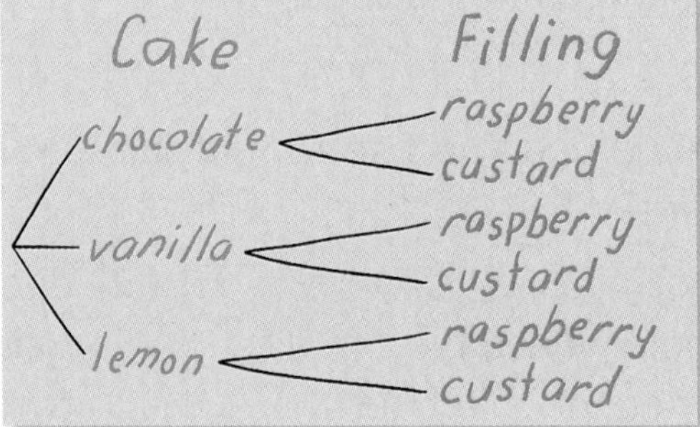

TALK Math

Explain how using a list can help to represent information.

When you make a list, organizing the list into categories or parts can help you make sure you don't forget anything.

TEKS 4.13A use concrete objects or pictures to make generalizations about determining all possible combinations of a given set of data or of objects in a problem situation. *also* **4.14A, 4.14B, 4.14C, 4.14D, 4.15A, 4.15B, 4.16B**

Use the Strategy

Read to Understand
Plan
Solve
Check

PROBLEM Molly is playing a game at the state fair. Without looking, she reaches into a bag and pulls out a marble. Then, she reaches into a different bag and pulls out another marble. All the marbles are the same size. If the marbles have the same color, Molly wins a prize. List and count the possible combinations. Then, name the way Molly can win a prize.

Read to Understand

- **Summarize what you are asked to find.**
- **What information will you use?**

Plan

- **What strategy can you use to solve the problem?**
  You can make an organized list.

Solve

- **How can you use the strategy to solve the problem?**
  Make a list of all the possible combinations. Organize your list by writing the combinations that could result if the first marble is green. Then, list the combinations that could result if the first marble is another color.

green, black	red, black	yellow, black
green, purple	red, purple	yellow, purple
green, green	red, green	yellow, green

There is one combination in which the two marbles have the same color: *green, green.*

So, of the nine combinations there is one in which Molly can win a prize with the combination *green, green.*

Check

- **In what other ways could you solve the problem?**

Guided Problem Solving

Read to Understand
Plan
Solve
Check

1. Marianne is playing a game that uses the two spinners shown. Each spinner has equal sections. She spins both pointers and adds the numbers. If the total is less than 4, she wins a prize. List the possible combinations. Name the ways Marianne can win a prize.

First, use a table to make an organized list.

Then, find the total for two spins.

Finally, find the totals that are less than 4.

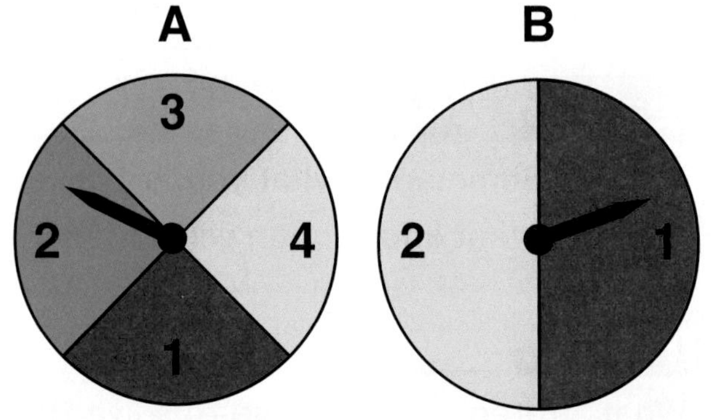

Spinner A	Spinner B	Total
1	1	2
1	2	3
2	1	3
2	■	■

2. **What if** Spinner A had two equal sections labeled 1 and 2? How would the number of possible combinations change?

3. Yuri is playing a game using a coin and Spinner A. He tosses the coin and spins the pointer. List all the possible combinations.

Problem Solving Strategy Practice

Make an organized list to solve.

4. Lorrie is making tickets for the fair. Each type of ticket will be a different color. There will be adult, child, and senior tickets. There will be one-day and two-day tickets. How many ticket colors will there be?

USE DATA For 5–6, use the information in the pictures.

5. Robin plays a game in which she spins the pointer and pulls one duck from the bag. How many possible combinations are there?

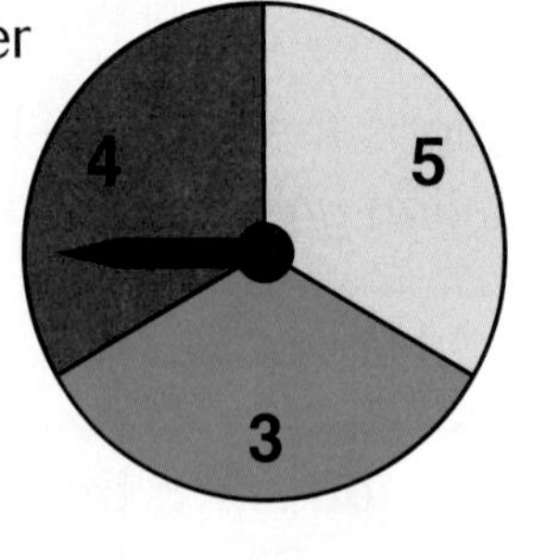

6. For George to win a prize, the pointer must stop on a number that is greater than 3 and he must pull the green duck. Name the ways George can win.

7. WRITE Math Shelly wants to find the total number of possible combinations of spinning a pointer and tossing a coin. **Explain** how Shelly can organize a list of the possible combinations.

Mixed Strategy Practice

USE DATA For 8–12, use the pictures.

8. ***FAST FACT*** The Kentucky State Fair was started in 1902. Which state fair was started 61 years before that?

9. The Illinois State Fair was started after the Michigan and Indiana State Fairs, but before the California State Fair. In what year was the Illinois State Fair started?

10. **Pose a Problem** The Texas State Fair was started in 1886. Use this information and the years in which other state fairs were started to write a problem.

11. **Open-Ended** Make a table that shows the number of state fairs started during each decade from the 1840s to the 1880s. Name one fact your table shows.

12. My year is even. The sum of the first two digits is less than the sum of the last two. The number formed by the sum of the last two digits is 2 more than the number formed by the sum of the first two digits. What state fair am I?

Choose a STRATEGY

- Draw a Diagram or Picture
- Make a Model or Act It Out
- Make an Organized List
- Look for a Pattern
- Make a Table or Graph
- Guess and Check
- Work Backward
- Solve a Simpler Problem
- Write an Equation
- Use Logical Reasoning

Michigan
Started: 1849

New York
Started: 1841

Nevada State Fair
Started: 1874

California
Started: 1854

West Virginia
Started: 1854

Arizona
Started: 1884

Indiana
Started: 1852

CHALLENGE YOURSELF

General admission to the Texas State Fair is $13. Admission is $9 for children less than 48 inches tall. Discounts are offered for groups of 20 or more people.

13. A group of 14 people paid $162 for admission to the fair. How many of the people were children less than 48 inches tall? **Explain** how you found your answer.

14. Altogether, a group of 22 adults saved $66 off regular prices by using the group discount. What was the price of each adult admission?

LESSON 5

More About Combinations

OBJECTIVE: Find all possible combinations of a given set of data.

Quick Review

Omar has 3 books to read. One is non-fiction, one is fiction, and one is a biography. List the orders in which he can read the 3 books.

Learn

PROBLEM Roger has a banana, an apple, a pear, and an orange. He wants to choose 2 pieces of fruit to pack for lunch. How many combinations are possible?

Example 1

The order is not important, so do not include pairs that are the reverse of pairs already shown.

So, 6 combinations are possible.

Example 2

Molly has a banana, an apple, a pear, and an orange. She wants to eat one piece of fruit now and pack one in her lunch. In how many different ways could she choose the fruit?

The order is important, so include every pair listed.

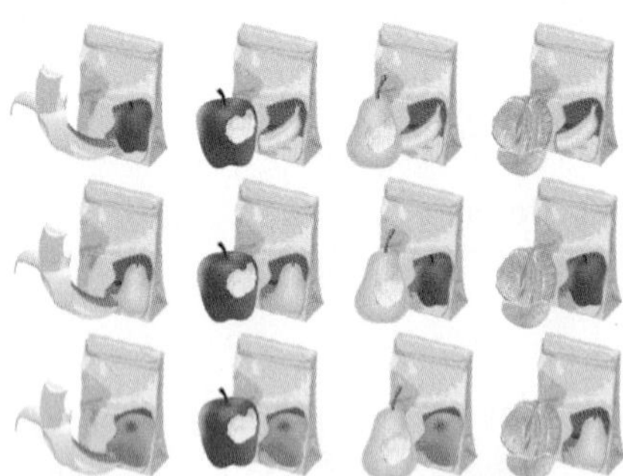

So, there are 12 ways in which Molly could choose the fruit.

- **What if** Molly had 5 pieces of fruit? In how many different ways could she choose the fruit?

TEKS 4.13A use concrete objects or pictures to make generalizations about determining all possible combinations of a given set of data or of objects in a problem situation. *also* **4.14A, 4.14D, 4.15A, 4.15B**

Ways to Find All Possible Combinations

Josh is making an animal poster for Zoo Night. He has 3 pictures—of an elephant, a tiger, and a zebra. He wants to put them in a row. In how many different ways can Josh arrange the pictures?

The order of the pictures is important, so include every possible way.

ONE WAY **Make a tree diagram.**

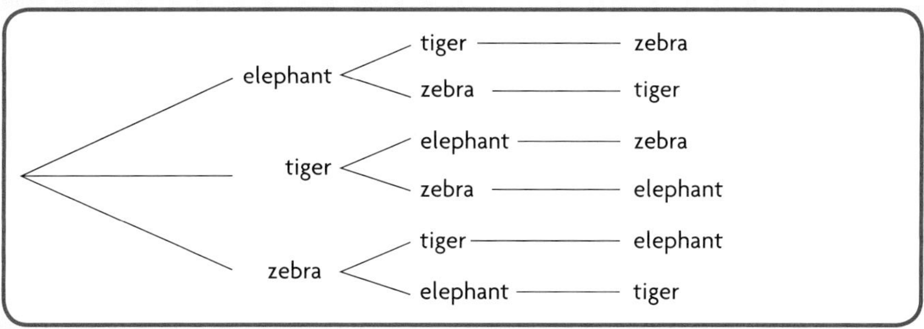

OTHER WAYS

 **Multiply.**

Multiply to find how many different ways Josh can arrange the pictures.

Think: What choices are available for each of the three positions?

first position	second position	third position
3	× 2	× 1 = 6

B Make a table.

Make a table to find how many different ways Josh can arrange the pictures.

first position	second position	third position
E	T	Z
E	Z	T
T	E	Z
T	Z	E
Z	T	E
Z	E	T

So, there are 6 possible ways Josh can arrange the pictures.

Guided Practice

1. Look at the tree diagram. In how many different ways can the students line up?

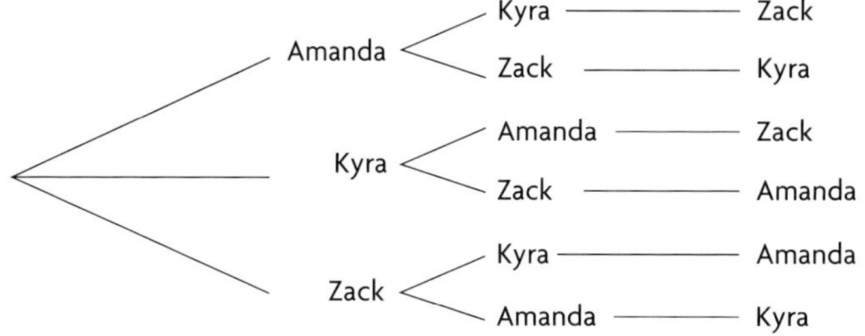

Carlos has the snacks shown. He wants to eat one snack after school and the other after football practice. In how many different ways can he choose the snacks?

2.

3.

How many different groups of 3 students can there be?

4. Luke, Sarah, Ken, Tanya

5. Helene, George, Edward, Lara, Mike, Rima

6. **TALK Math** **Explain** how multiplication helps you find all the different ways 4 planes can line up for take-off.

Independent Practice and Problem Solving

How many different pairs of students can there be if each pair must have 1 boy and 1 girl?

7. **Girls:** Karen, Briana, Patti
   Boys: Emmanuel, Jerry, Tyrone, Louis

8. **Girls:** Nancy, Carly, Heather, Mary, Dena
   Boys: Sid, Bill, David, Kareem, Jeff

USE DATA For 9–10, use the picture.

9. List the different ways the animals can be arranged on a shelf.

10. Every stuffed animal comes with a red or a blue case. How many combinations of animals and cases are there?

11. **WRITE Math** **Explain** how a tree diagram helps you find all the possible 4-digit numbers you can make with the digits 2, 4, 6, and 8.

Mixed Review and TAKS Prep

12. Bob started a marathon at 9:15 A.M. He crossed the finish line at 1:10 P.M. How long did it take Bob to run the race? (TEKS 4.12B, p. 476)

13. Joelle and Eleora collect teacups. Joelle has 19 teacups. Eleora has 3 times as many as Joelle. How many teacups does Eleora have? (TEKS 4.4D, p. 206)

14. **TAKS Prep** Grace has three beads.

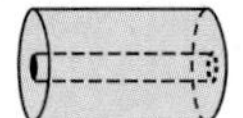

In how many different ways can she string the three beads? (Obj. 5)

A 1 **C** 6

B 3 **D** 9

 Extra Practice on page 540, Set C

Draw to Explain

WRITE Math
WORKSHOP

One way to explain an answer is to draw a picture. A picture helps you visualize the solution to a problem.

Drawing a picture to solve a math problem is different from drawing a picture for an art class. Math drawings should be simple and clear. They should be labeled. They must clearly represent the information given in the problem. The explanation should include a sentence that tells how your drawing shows the solution.

Vanessa has a frame that holds 3 photos in a row. She has photos of flowers, a house, and a boat. What are the different ways Vanessa can put the photos in the frame?

Vanessa drew these pictures to show 6 different combinations. Then she wrote a sentence to answer the question given in the problem.

The pictures show that there are 6 different ways I can put the photos of flowers, a house, and a boat in a frame that holds 3 photos.

Problem Solving **Draw a picture to explain your answer.**

1. Kylie is visiting a museum. The museum has exhibits on birds, zebras, and fish. She has time to visit only 2 exhibits. How many combinations of 2 exhibits can she choose?

2. Oscar wants to read a book, watch TV, play soccer, and use the computer. He has time to do only 3 of these activities. How many combinations of 3 activities can he choose?

Extra Practice

Set A Make a model to find all the possible combinations. (pp. 524–527)

1. Wall decorating choices
   paint color: yellow, blue, green, white
   border: shapes, airplanes, clouds

2. Sport choices
   sport: soccer, basketball, football
   days: Friday, Saturday, Sunday

3. Gardening choices
   vegetable: radishes
   location: front of house, back of house
   season: fall, spring, summer

4. Study choices
   subject: reading, math
   day: Monday, Wednesday
   time: 15 minutes, 25 minutes

5. Tatiana can choose to swim, have a snack, or watch a movie. She can do the activity in the morning, afternoon, or evening. How many different combinations of activities and times are there?

6. Alicia has salami, turkey, and ham. She has wheat bread, white bread, potato bread, and rye bread. How many different sandwiches can she make with one type of meat and one type of bread?

Set B Make a tree diagram to find the number of possible combinations. (pp. 528–531)

1. Pant choices:
   style: corduroy, slacks, jeans
   color: blue, black, beige, white

2. Snack choices
   cookie: chocolate chip, oatmeal
   drink: water, fruit punch, lemonade

Use the picture.

3. James is getting ready to go to the movies. How many different combinations of a shirt and pants can James choose?

Set C For 1–2, Joey can do the activities shown. He wants to do one activity now and one after supper. In how many different ways can he choose the activities? (pp. 536–539)

1. puzzle, computer game, tag, paint

2. soccer, origami, read a book

For 3–4, how many different pairs of students can there be if each pair must have one boy and one girl?

3. **Boys:** Jean, Owen, Randy
   Girls: Amelia, Shayna, Ellie

2. **Boys:** Tyrese, Frank, Ronnie, Chen
   Girls: Molly, Pam

Fashion Show

Models!

2–3 players

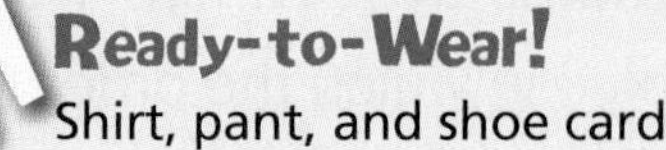

Ready-to-Wear!

Shirt, pant, and shoe cards

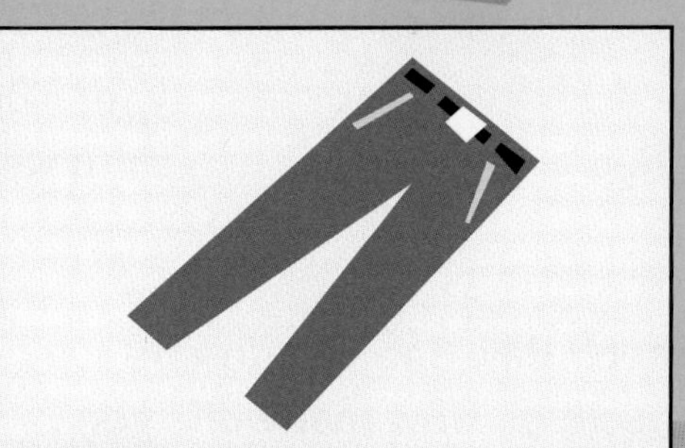

Walk the Runway!

- Players shuffle each set of shirt, pant, and shoe cards and place them facedown in three stacks.
- A player turns one card from each stack faceup and finds the total number of outfit combinations. The other players check his or her answer.
- If the player finds the correct answer, he or she keeps the cards. If not, the cards are placed in the discard pile.
- Players take turns until all cards have been used.
- The player with the most cards wins.

Chapter 20 Review/Test

Check Vocabulary and Concepts

VOCABULARY
combination
outcome
tree diagram

For 1–2, choose the best term from the box.

1. A choice in which the order of items does not matter is called a __?__. (TEKS 4.13A, p. 522)
2. An organized list that shows all possible combinations of a set of data or group of objects is called a __?__. (TEKS 4.13A, p. 528)
3. **Explain** how to use a table to find the number of combinations of 2 that can be made from a set of 3. (TEKS 4.13A, pp. 522–523)

Check Skills

Make a model or table to find all the possible combinations. (TEKS 4.13A, pp. 524–527)

4. Dinner choices
   meal: pizza, salad, tacos
   drink: water, lemonade, fruit punch
5. Sport choices
   sport: hockey, tennis
   day: Monday, Wednesday, Friday, Sunday

Make a tree diagram to find the number of possible combinations. (TEKS 4.13A, pp. 528–531)

6. Dog choices
   gender: female, male
   breed: Poodle, Labrador Retriever, German Shepherd, Terrier
7. Cake choices
   type: white, yellow, chocolate, sponge
   icing: vanilla, chocolate, strawberry

Mikki has to do her chores each day. She will do one before school and one after school. How many different ways can she choose to do her chores? (TEKS 4.13A, pp. 536–539)

8. clean bedroom, vacuum, dishes, dust
9. walk dog, feed fish, take out garbage

Check Problem Solving

Solve. (TEKS 4.13A, pp. 532–535)

10. WRITE Math Amir wants to find the total number of possible outcomes of tossing two number cubes labeled 1 to 6. **Explain** how Amir can organize a list of all the possible combinations.

GO ONLINE **Technology** Use *Online Assessment.*

Enrich • List All Possible Outcomes

Pet Possibilities

Bobtail

Wirehair

Shorthair

Amy is getting a cat! She needs to decide what breed of cat she wants and to choose a name. She made equal-size cards listing some possible choices for cat breeds and names. She will choose the breed and name that she pulls the most times.

You can make a table to record all the possible outcomes for an event. **Outcomes** are the results of an experiment. An **event** can be one outcome or a set of outcomes.

Cat Decisions

Materials ■ index cards ■ brown paper bags

Step 1 Make the table to show all 6 possible outcomes. Write the cat breed and name choices on cards. Each breed or name should be on a separate card.

Step 2 Put the cat breed cards in a bag and the name cards in a different bag. Label each bag.

Step 3 Pull 1 cat breed card and 1 name card. Record your results in the table. Repeat this until you have pulled the cards 20 times.

Experiment Results			
	American Cat Breed		
Name	Bobtail	Wirehair	Shorthair
Taffy			I
Garf			

- Which cat breed and name was chosen the most times?

Choosing Dogs

Use dog breed and name cards.

1. Make cards for each breed and name choice from the cards below. Put your cards into two different bags. Label each bag. Choose 1 card from each bag 10 times, and record your results.

Experiment Results		
	Dog Breed	
Name		

Name Cards				
	Tiger	Champ	Lucky	Duke

Dog Breed Cards	
Pug	Poodle
Beagle	Bulldog

Decision Time

WRITE Math How many possible outcomes are there for choosing 4 dog breeds and 4 names? **Explain** how you know.

Unit Review/Test
Chapters 18–20

Multiple Choice

1. Johnny is making a bar graph of the money he earned on his paper route. The least number in his data is $11. The greatest number is $56. Which would be a reasonable scale for the bar graph? (TAKS Obj. 5)

A 0–5

B 0–10

C 0–60

D 0–600

2. Joan started gymnastics class at 4:45 P.M. The class ended at 6:15 P.M. How long did the class last? (TAKS Obj. 4)

F 30 minutes

G 45 minutes

H 1 hour 15 minutes

J Not here

3. Which collector collected more stamps than coins? (TAKS Obj. 5)

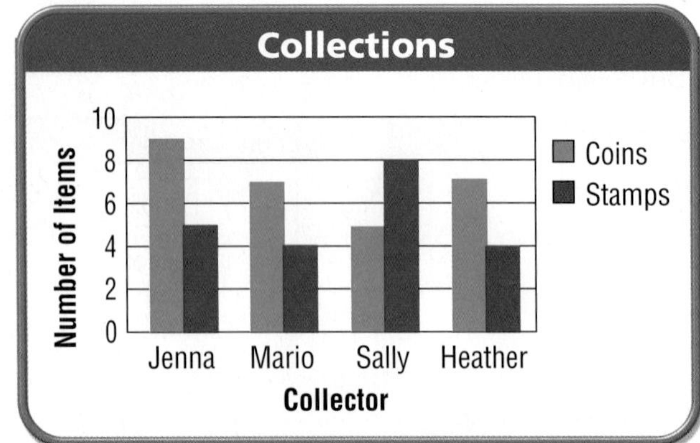

A Mario **C** Jenna

B Sally **D** Heather

4. The menu shows the choices for sandwiches, drinks, and desserts. How many different combinations of a sandwich, drink and dessert are there? (TAKS Obj. 5)

Menu		
Sandwich	**Drink**	**Dessert**
Turkey	Soda	Cookie
Ham	Milk	Apple
Tuna Salad	Juice	

F 8

G 9

H 18

J 27

5. Which temperature is shown on the thermometer? (TAKS Obj. 4)

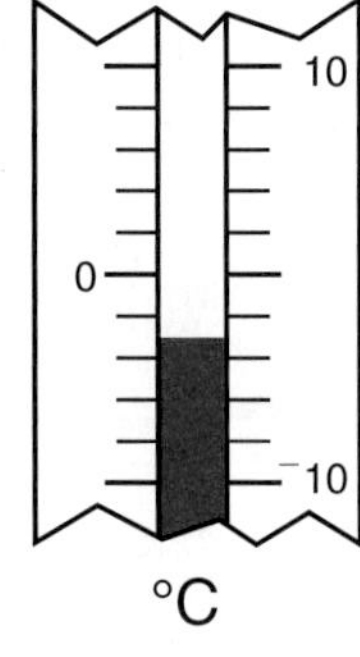

A $^{-}10$°C

B $^{-}7$°C

C $^{-}3$C

D 3°C

6. The key on a pictograph reads = 3 miles. How many symbols would be used to show 36 miles? (TAKS Obj. 5)

F 108

G 36

H 18

J 12

7. Michelle's school day starts at 8:00 A.M. It ends at 2:45 P.M. How long is Michelle's school day? (TAKS Obj. 4)

A 5 hours 15 minutes

B 6 hours 15 minutes

C 6 hours 45 minutes

D 10 hours 15 minutes

8. The graph shows the results of pulling a marble from a bag. How many times was a marble pulled? (TAKS Obj. 5)

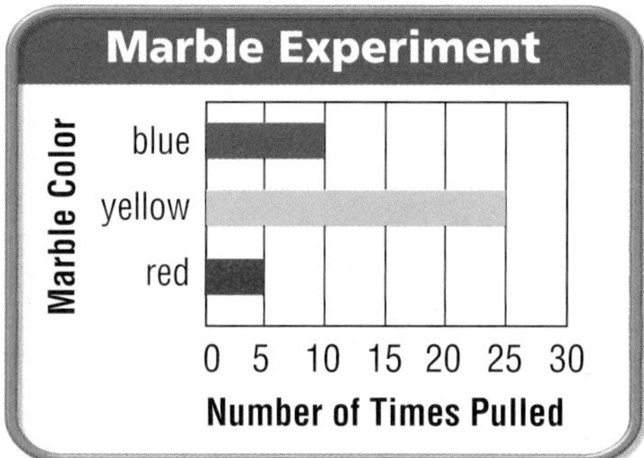

F 10

G 35

H 40

J 45

9. The thermometer shows the morning temperature April 9. The afternoon temperature was 12°F colder. What was the afternoon temperature? (TAKS Obj. 4)

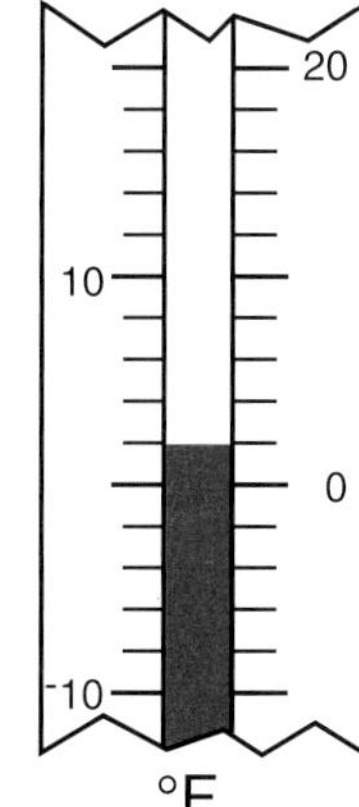

A 12°F

B $^-4$°F

C $^-5$°F

D $^-10$°F

Short Response

10. Mike is choosing two flowers to put in his flowerbed. He has a choice of roses, carnations, daisies, and lilies. How many different combinations of two flowers can Mike choose? (TAKS Obj. 5)

11. Kenny has a car, a truck, an SUV, and a convertible to wash. He will wash one in the morning and one in the afternoon. How many different ways can he choose to wash the cars? (TAKS Obj. 5)

12. The deli special is a choice of tuna fish, grilled cheese, or peanut butter and jelly sandwich, with either lemonade or fruit punch. How many different choices of a sandwich and drink are there? (TAKS Obj. 5)

Extended Response WRITE Math

13. Sierra made a bar graph to show the eye colors of people in her family. The bars for blue and hazel were the same height. **Explain** what this means. (TAKS Obj. 5)

14. Ben has a stuffed bear, a game, and a puzzle in his room. **Explain** how to use a tree diagram to find the orders in which he can play with them. (TAKS Obj. 5)

15. Marla measured the temperature outside her house in the morning as 68°F. When she got home from school, the temperature was 92°F. **Explain** how to find the change in temperature from the morning until Marla got home from school. (TAKS Obj. 4)

Problem Solving

Record High Temperatures

Hot Enough to Fry an Egg?

Although people joke about temperatures being hot enough to fry an egg on the sidewalk, it is really hard to do. Egg white begins to cook at 144°F, and yolk begins to cook at 149°F. Do you think a person could have fried an egg on the sidewalk on the date of the highest recorded temperature in Texas?

Use the table to answer the questions.

1. If the temperature data were in a bar graph, which states' bars would be the same length or same height? **Explain.**
2. Is a bar graph with a scale from 0 to 200 with intervals of 100 a good way to display this data? **Explain.**
3. Make a bar graph to display the temperature data in the table. **Explain** why you chose that kind of display.
4. What do you notice about the dates of the record temperatures?

Top 10 Record High State Temperatures

State	Temperature (in °F)	Date
Arizona	128	June 29, 1994
Arkansas	120	August 19, 1936
California	134	July 10, 1913
Kansas	121	July 24, 1936
Nevada	125	June 29, 1994
New Mexico	122	June 27, 1994
North Dakota	121	July 6, 1936
Oklahoma	120	June 27, 1994
South Dakota	120	July 5, 1936
Texas	120	June 28, 1994

ALMANAC **Fact**

One of the country's worst heat waves was during the summer of 1980. Dallas, TX had temperatures higher than 100°F for 69 days. On June 26th and 27th, the temperature in Dallas reached an all-time high of 113°F!

Heat Waves

Record temperatures of 100°F or higher can occur in all of the United States, but they are rare. More often, you will hear about heat waves. A heat wave means that the high temperature for the day, measured in the shade, is 90°F or greater at least three days in a row.

Temperature (in °F) August, 2005

Date	Dallas, TX	Amarillo, TX	Laredo, TX
June 10	100°	97°	101°
June 11	97°	97°	104°
June 12	98°	95°	104°
June 13	95°	92°	104°

FACT·ACTIVITY

Use the data on these two pages to answer the questions.

1. Can you tell whether each Texas city above had a heat wave? Explain.
2. Which Texas city's temperature varied the least between June 10 and June 13?
3. WRITE Math Explain how you could show the temperatures of Dallas and Amarillo for the same four days on the same graph.

You are a science reporter in a Texas city that has had a 7-day heat wave. Write a report to share with your class.

- Tell your audience about heat waves. Include a graph showing the temperature changes for the 7-day heat wave.
- Include some history and another display of data showing the highest recorded temperatures in some Texas cities.
- Find and include real data about the highest recorded temperature in your city.

UNIT 8 Measurement

Different woods are cut to exact lengths, widths, and depths and glued together to form the guitar's body.

Custom guitars have different shapes. Each surface has a different length and width or area.

Choices of shape, wood, finish, number of strings and electronics result in many different guitars.

VOCABULARY POWER

TALK Math

What math is used in the **Math on Location** photographs? How could you find the length of each string on a guitar? What units would you use to measure the length? Why?

READ Math

REVIEW VOCABULARY You learned the words below when you learned about measurement. How do these words relate to **Math on Location**?

centimeter a metric unit for measuring length or distance; 100 centimeters = 1 meter

foot a customary unit used for measuring length or distance; 1 foot = 12 inches

perimeter the distance around a figure

WRITE Math

Copy and complete the word association tree below. Use what you know about measurement to complete the tree.

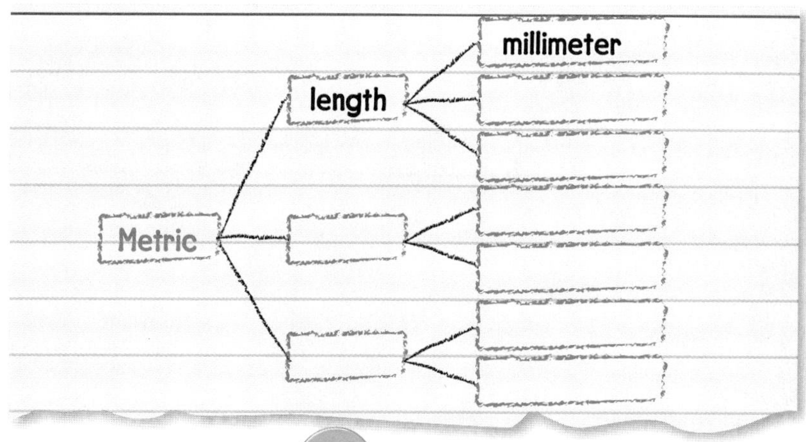

Technology
Multimedia Math Glossary link at www.harcourtschool.com/hspmath

21 Customary Measurement

The Big Idea Measurement involves a comparison of an attribute of an object or situation with a unit that has the same attribute.

TEXAS FAST FACT

The Austin Zoo is a rescue zoo for all types of animals with nowhere else to live. It has about 100 different types of animals and about 300 animals in all.

Investigate

When a rescued wild animal arrives at a shelter, it is usually underweight. The table shows the weights of some rescued animals. How could you compare the weights of the animals when rescued and when released?

Wildlife Shelter Rescues

Animal	Bobcat	Baby raccoon	Gray fox	Armadillo	White-tailed jackrabbit	Kemp's ridley turtle
Weight When Rescued	10 pounds	32 ounces	64 ounces	5 pounds	48 ounces	8 pounds
Weight When Released	240 ounces	10 pounds	7 pounds	144 ounces	7 pounds	384 ounces

GO ONLINE **Technology** Student pages are available in the Student eBook.

Show What You Know

Check your understanding of important skills needed for success in Chapter 21.

▶ Measure Length to the Nearest Inch and Half Inch

Measure the length of each to the nearest inch.

1. 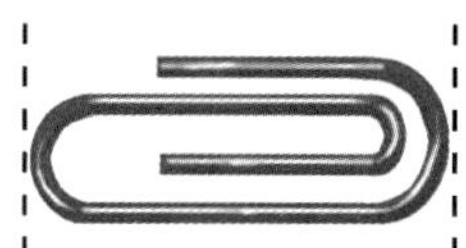

2. 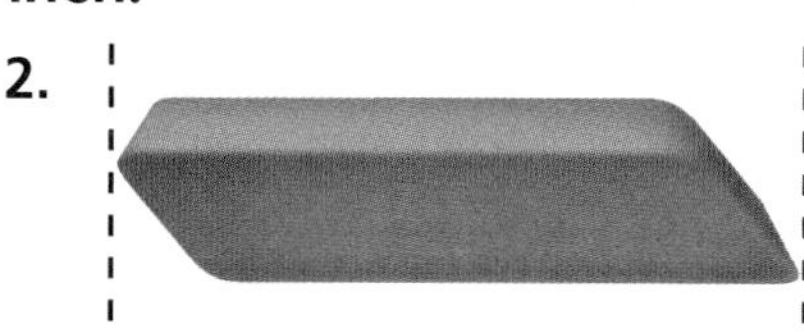

Measure the length of each to the nearest $\frac{1}{2}$ inch.

3. 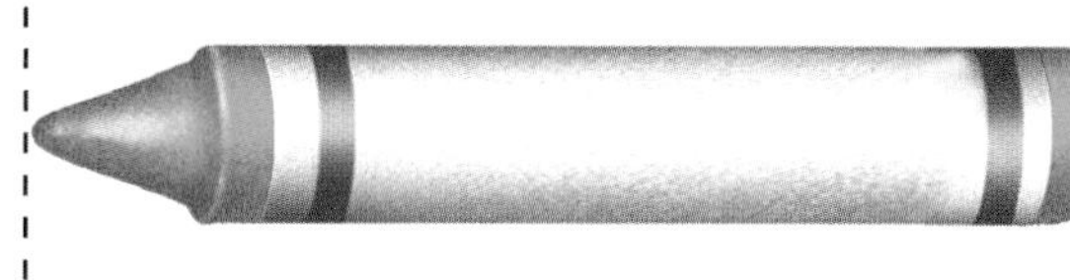

4. 

▶ Multiply

Find the product.

5. 24×2 **6.** 35×3 **7.** 12×4 **8.** 16×5

9. 16×2 **10.** 12×12 **11.** 45×3 **12.** 18×3

▶ Divide

Find the quotient.

13. $16 \div 2$ **14.** $21 \div 3$ **15.** $32 \div 4$ **16.** $36 \div 12$

17. $42 \div 3$ **18.** $40 \div 4$ **19.** $72 \div 12$ **20.** $536 \div 4$

VOCABULARY POWER

CHAPTER VOCABULARY

capacity
cup (c)
fluid ounce (fl oz)
foot (ft)
gallon (gal)
inch (in.)
length
linear units
mile (mi)
ounce (oz)
pint (pt)
pound (lb)
quart (qt)
ton (T)
weight
yard (yd)

WARM-UP WORDS

linear units units that measure length, width, height, or distance

inch (in.) a customary unit used for measuring length or distance

foot (ft) a customary unit used for measuring length or distance
1 foot = 12 inches

Measure Fractional Parts

OBJECTIVE: Estimate and measure length to the nearest whole, $\frac{1}{2}$, $\frac{1}{4}$, and $\frac{1}{8}$ inch.

Quick Review

Compare. Write >, <, or =.

1. $\frac{1}{2}$ ● $\frac{2}{4}$
2. $\frac{3}{4}$ ● $\frac{7}{8}$
3. $3\frac{4}{8}$ ● $3\frac{2}{4}$
4. $5\frac{1}{8}$ ● $4\frac{3}{4}$
5. $2\frac{1}{2}$ ● $2\frac{3}{8}$

Vocabulary

linear units
yard (yd)
inch (in.)
mile (mi)
foot (ft)

Learn

Units of measure used to measure length, width, height, or distance are called **linear units**. The customary units of length include **inch (in.)**, **foot (ft)**, **yard (yd)**, and **mile (mi)**.

You can use a common object or event to help you visualize the size of each unit.

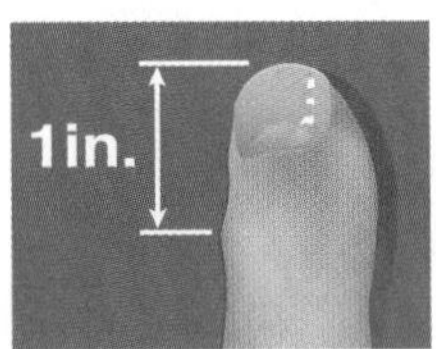

The length of your thumb from the tip to the knuckle is about 1 inch.

The length of a license plate is about 1 foot.

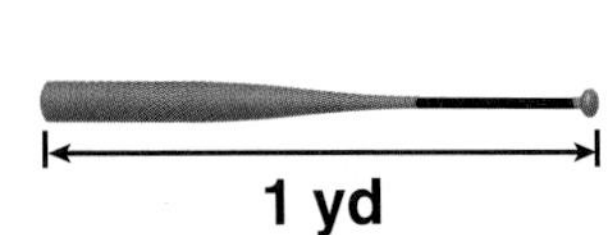

The length of a baseball bat is about 1 yard.

The distance you can walk in 20 minutes is about 1 mile.

- What unit would you use to measure the length of a driveway? Explain.

You can use an inch ruler to measure to the nearest inch.

Activity 1

Materials ■ paper clips ■ inch ruler ■ desk

Length				
	Paper Clips		Inches	
Object	Estimate	Actual	Estimate	Actual
desk	■	■	■	■

Step 1

Look at the length of a paper clip. Use that length to estimate the width of your desk in paper clips. Record your estimate in a table like the one shown.

Step 2

Measure your desk. Use a paper clip as your unit. Count the number of paper clips you used. Record the measurement to the nearest paper clip in the table.

Step 3

A paper clip measures about 1 inch long. Use the paper clip to estimate the length of your desk in inches. Then measure the length of your desk to the nearest inch with the inch ruler. Record your measurement in the table.

- How does your estimate compare to the actual measurement you found by using the ruler?

TEKS 4.11A estimate and use measurement tools to determine length (including perimeter), area, capacity and weight/mass using standard units SI (metric) and customary. *also* **4.2C, 4.14A, 4.14D, 4.15A, 4.15B**

Fractions in Measurements

Sometimes the length of an object is not a whole unit. For example, the length of a paper clip is more than 1 inch but less than 2 inches.

You can use an inch ruler to measure objects to the nearest $\frac{1}{2}$, $\frac{1}{4}$, and $\frac{1}{8}$ inch. Measuring to the nearest fractional unit is like rounding a number.

Remember

A ruler is like a number line.

0 $\frac{1}{8}$ $\frac{1}{4}$ $\frac{1}{2}$ 1

inches 1

Example 1 **Measure to the nearest $\frac{1}{2}$ inch.**

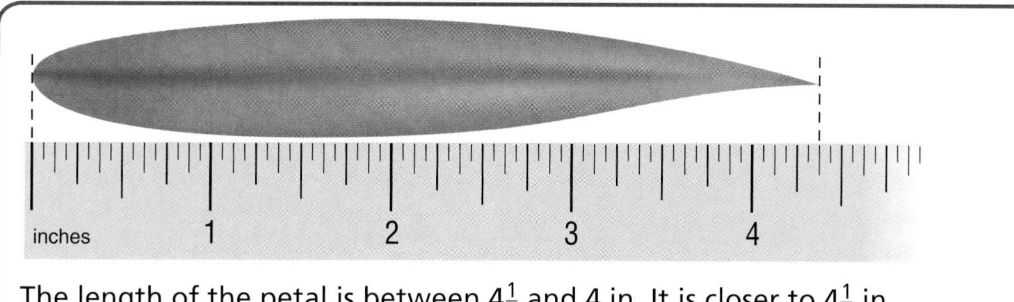

The length of the petal is between $4\frac{1}{2}$ and 4 in. It is closer to $4\frac{1}{2}$ in.

So, to the nearest $\frac{1}{2}$ inch, the petal's length is about $4\frac{1}{2}$ in.

Example 2

Measure to the nearest $\frac{1}{4}$ inch.

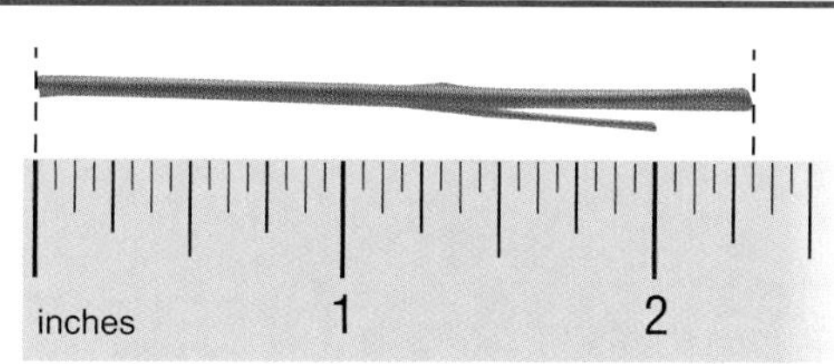

The length of the twig is closer to $2\frac{1}{4}$ in. than $2\frac{2}{4}$ in. So, to the nearest $\frac{1}{4}$ in., the twig's length is about $2\frac{1}{4}$ in.

Example 3

Measure to the nearest $\frac{1}{8}$ inch.

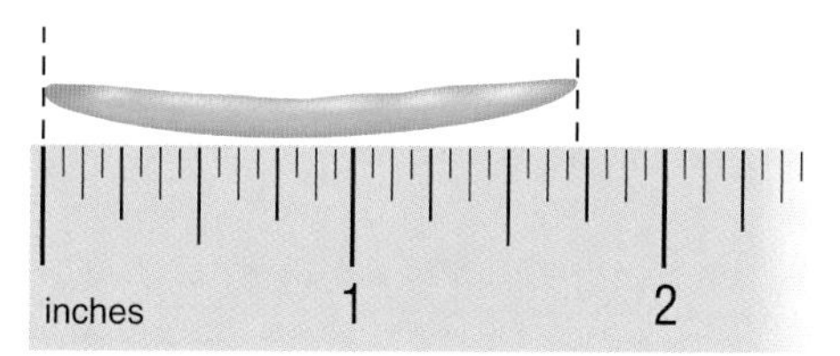

The length of the peapod is closer to $1\frac{6}{8}$ in. than $1\frac{5}{8}$ in. So, to the nearest $\frac{1}{8}$ in., the peapod's length is about $1\frac{6}{8}$ in., or $1\frac{3}{4}$ in.

Activity 2

Materials ■ 5 classroom objects ■ inch ruler ■ yardstick

Step 1

Make a table like the one shown. Estimate the length of 5 classroom objects to the nearest inch. Record your estimates in the table.

Step 2

Use a ruler to measure the length of each object to the nearest $\frac{1}{2}$, $\frac{1}{4}$, and $\frac{1}{8}$ inch. Record your measurements.

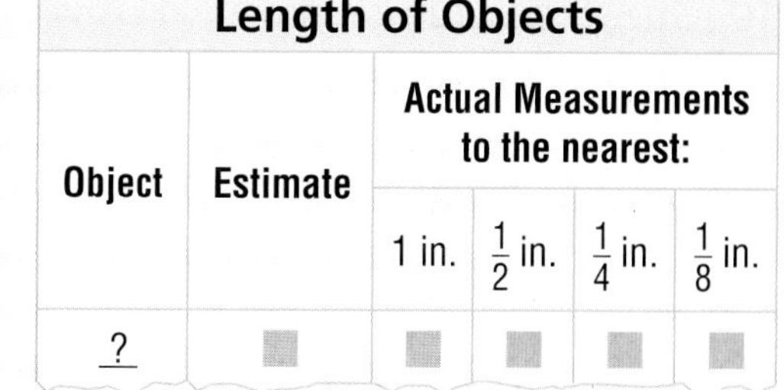
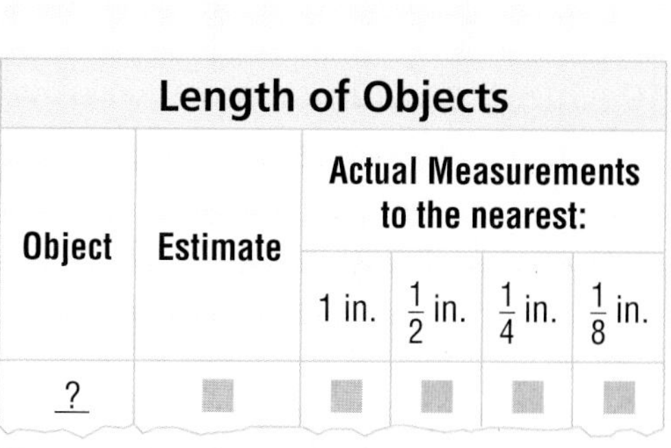

Length of Objects

Object	Estimate	Actual Measurements to the nearest:			
		1 in.	$\frac{1}{2}$ in.	$\frac{1}{4}$ in.	$\frac{1}{8}$ in.
?	■	■	■	■	■

- What is the order of the objects from shortest to longest?
- Is a measurement ever exact? Explain.

Guided Practice

1. What is the length of the leaf to the nearest $\frac{1}{4}$ inch?

Estimate to the nearest inch. Then measure to the nearest $\frac{1}{2}$ inch.

2.

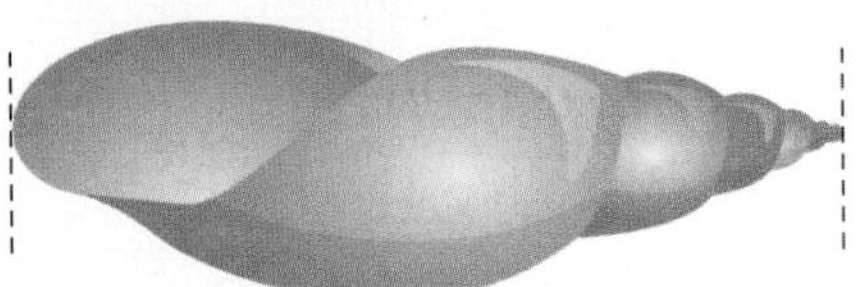

3.

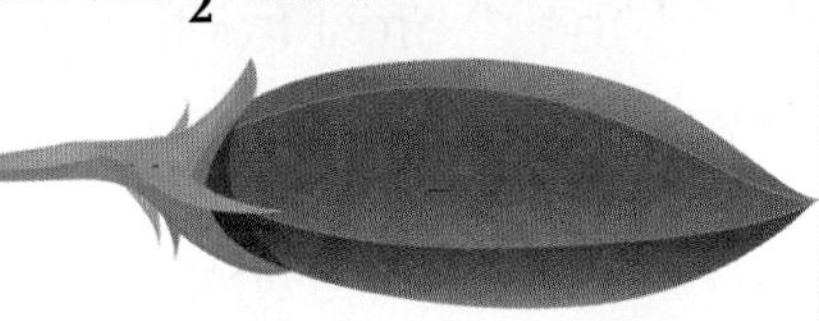

4. **TALK Math** How can you order $5\frac{1}{2}$ inches, $4\frac{3}{4}$ inches, 5 inches, and $5\frac{1}{4}$ inches from least to greatest? **Explain.**

Independent Practice and Problem Solving

Estimate to the nearest $\frac{1}{2}$ inch. Then measure to the nearest $\frac{1}{8}$ inch.

5.

6.

USE DATA For 7–9, use the graph.

7. **Reasoning** Lydia measured each plant in inches. Which measurements are more accurate, Lydia's or the measurement given? **Explain.**

8. For which plant would it be most reasonable to measure the height in yards? **Explain.**

9. **WRITE Math** **Sense or Nonsense** Thomas has a plant that is about the height of 6 license plates placed end to end. He thinks his plant is the same size as the cosmo plant. Is he right? **Explain.**

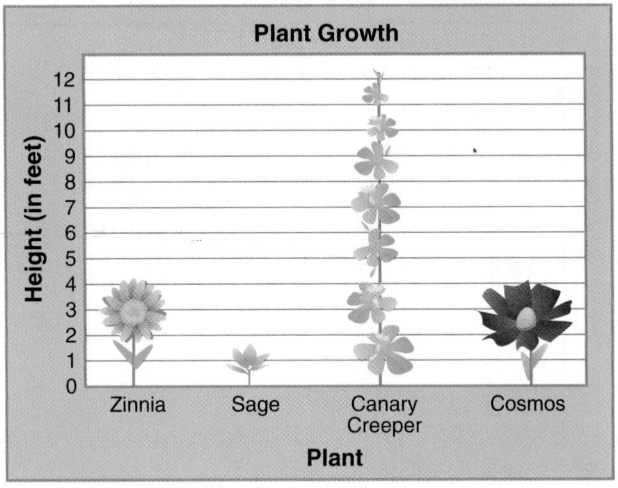

Mixed Review and TAKS Prep

10. Judy can choose a brown or white stuffed bear. Her bear can have a red, blue, or yellow ribbon. How many different choices of bears does Judy have? (TEKS 4.13A, p. 524)

11. Myra spends $14.66 on soil and $12.75 on plants. She pays with $40. How much change does she get? (TEKS 4.3B, p. 454)

12. **TAKS Prep** What is the length of the ribbon to the nearest $\frac{1}{8}$ inch? (Obj. 4)

A 2 inches
B $2\frac{1}{2}$ inches
C $2\frac{1}{4}$ inches
D $2\frac{1}{8}$ inches

 Extra Practice on page 566, Set A

Technology
CD ROM Use Harcourt Mega Math Ice Station Explortation, *Linear Lab*, Level D, F.

Put Your Body to Work!

Reading Skill **Generalize**

Width: about 7 big steps
Length: about 10 big steps

When people first started measuring, they didn't have rulers, so they used parts of their bodies as guides. For example, a foot was the length of a human adult foot.

Gardeners often use hand spans, big steps, and other nonstandard measures to plant and measure. They can use what they know about body measurements to make generalizations about unknown lengths or distances.

Matt is helping his father put a fence around their vegetable garden. How can they find about how many yards of fencing they will need?

Matt's father knows that he can take a big step that is about the same length as 1 yard.

When he walks around the garden, he takes 7 big steps along the width and 10 steps along the length.

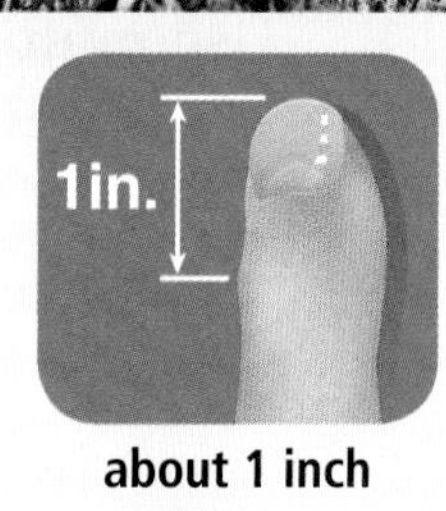

about 1 inch

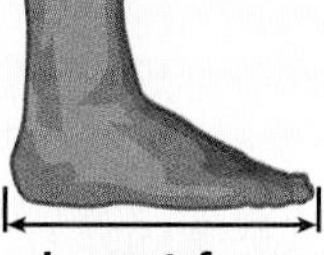
about 1 foot

about 1 yard

Problem Solving Generalize to understand the problem.

1. Solve the problem above.
2. Heads of lettuce should be spaced 6 thumb-lengths apart. About how many inches of space does Matt need to plant a row of 4 heads of lettuce?

LESSON 2

ALGEBRA

Change Customary Linear Units

OBJECTIVE: Change linear units by multiplying or dividing.

Quick Review

1. 3×12
2. 9×3
3. $84 \div 12$
4. 10×3
5. $24 \div 3$

Learn

PROBLEM Myra needs 3 feet of fabric to make a hat for her costume. She has 40 inches of fabric. Does Myra have enough material to make the hat?

You can use multiplication and division to change from one customary unit of measure to another.

Example 1 Use multiplication.

3 feet = ■ inches

Think: 1 foot = 12 inches, so multiply the number of feet by 12.

feet		inches in 1 foot		total inches
↓		↓		↓
3	×	12	=	36

36 inches is less than 40 inches.

So, Myra has enough fabric to make the hat.

Customary Units of Length
1 foot (ft) = 12 inches (in.)
1 yard (yd) = 3 feet, or 36 inches
1 mile (mi) = 5,280 feet, or 1,760 yards

Math Idea

To change from a larger unit to a smaller unit, you need more of them, so multiply.
To change from a smaller unit to a larger unit, you need fewer of them, so divide.

Example 2 Use division.

11,379 feet = ■ yards

Think: 1 yard = 3 feet, so divide the number of feet by 3.

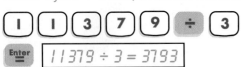

1 1 3 7 9 ÷ 3

Enter = 11379 ÷ 3 = 3793

So, 11,379 feet equal 3,793 yards.

Example 3 Use an equation.

Use the rule divide *f* by 3 to find the value of *y*. Complete the table.

Feet, *f*	Yards, *y*
27	■
33	■
36	■

Divide *f* by 3.

$27 \div 3 = 9$

$33 \div 3 = 11$

$36 \div 3 = 12$

Feet, *f*	Yards, *y*
27	9
33	11
36	12

TEKS 4.11B perform simple conversions between different units of length, between different units of capacity, and between different units of weight within the customary measurement system. *also* **4.1A, 4.7, 4.4C, 4.4D, 4.4E, 4.14A, 4.15A, 4.15B, 4.14D**

Guided Practice

1. Use the rule multiply *f* by 12. Copy and complete the table to find the number of inches in 5, 7, and 9 feet.

Feet, *f*	5	7	9
Inches, *i*	■	■	■

Complete. Tell whether you *multiply* or *divide*.

2. 15,840 ft = ■ mi 3. 7 yd = ■ in. ✓4. 12 ft = ■ in. ✓5. 48 ft = ■ yd

6. **TALK Math** **Explain** how you know whether to multiply or divide to change from one unit to another.

Independent Practice and Problem Solving

Complete. Tell whether you *multiply* or *divide*.

7. 34 ft = ■ in. 8. 132 in. = ■ ft 9. 23 yd = ■ ft

Compare. Write <, >, or = for each ●.

10. 30 in. ● 4 ft 11. 72 ft ● 24 yd 12. 200 in. ● 5 yd

Algebra **Write a rule you can use to complete each table. Copy and complete each table.**

13.

Yards, *y*	4	5	6	7	8
Feet, *f*	12	15	■	■	■

14.

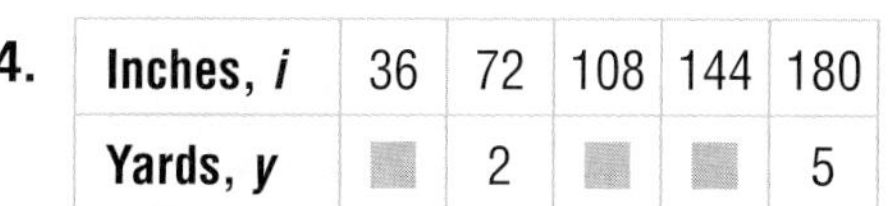

Inches, *i*	36	72	108	144	180
Yards, *y*	■	2	■	■	5

USE DATA For 15–17, use the pictures.

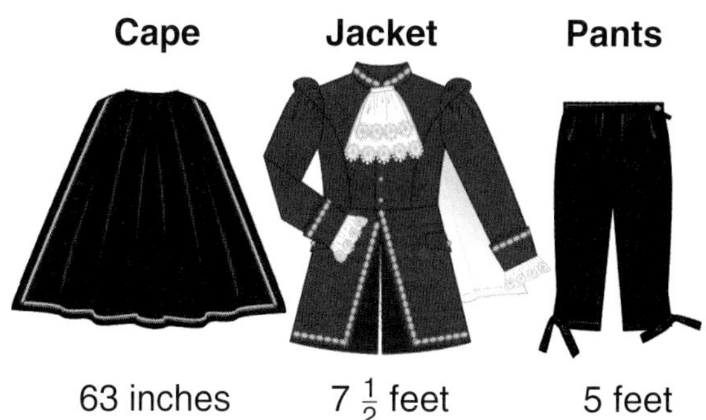

15. Kenny has 11 feet of fabric to make the cape. Does he have enough fabric to make two capes? **Explain.**
16. The jacket is made from red velvet. How many inches of red velvet are needed?
17. **WRITE Math** **What's the Error?** Zanta has 6 yards of pants fabric. She thinks she has enough fabric to make 4 pairs of pants. Is she correct? **Explain.**

Mixed Review and TAKS Prep

18. Jake wants to make a bar graph using this data: green–20, red–12, blue–8. Which color will have the longest bar? (TEKS 4.13, p. 508)

19. How long is the ribbon to the nearest $\frac{1}{8}$ inch? (TEKS 4.11A, p. 552)

20. **TAKS Prep** Stephen is 48 inches tall. How many feet tall is he? (Obj. 4)

Extra Practice on page 566, Set B

LESSON 3

Weight

OBJECTIVE: Estimate and measure the weights of objects and change units of weight.

Quick Review

1. 5×16
2. 16×9
3. $6 \times 2,000$
4. $1,000 \times 30$
5. $12 \times 2,000$

Vocabulary

ounce (oz)

pound (lb)

ton (T)

Learn

Weight is how heavy an object is. Customary units of weight include **ounce (oz)**, **pound (lb)**, and **ton (T)**.

Common objects can be used as benchmarks for customary units of weight.

5 new pencils weigh about 1 ounce.

4 sticks of butter weigh about 1 pound.

A car weighs about 1 ton.

Activity 1

Materials ■ spring scale ■ classroom objects

- Make a table like the one at the right. Estimate the weight of 5 classroom objects in ounces or pounds. Record your estimates in the table.
- Now weigh each object using the spring scale. Record the actual weight in the table.

Weight			
Object	**Unit (oz/lb)**	**Estimate**	**Actual**
dictionary	lb	3 lb	■
?	■	■	■

- Are your estimates reasonable? Explain how you know.
- Compare one of the objects you weighed to the weight of 5 new pencils. What can you conclude?

Customary Units of Weight
1 pound (lb) = 16 ounces (oz)
1 ton (T) = 2,000 pounds (lb)

You can use multiplication and division to change units of weight.

Example 1 Use multiplication.

How many ounces equal 6 pounds?

6 pounds = ■ ounces

pounds		ounces in 1 pound		ounces
↓		↓		↓
6	×	16	=	96

So, 6 pounds equal 96 ounces.

Example 2 Use division.

How many tons equal 8,000 pounds?

8,000 pounds = ■ tons

8 0 0 0 ÷ 2 0 0 0 Enter

8,000 ÷ 2,000 = 4

So, 8,000 pounds equal 4 tons.

TEKS 4.11A estimate and use measurement tools to determine length (including perimeter), area, capacity and weight/mass using standard units SI (metric) and customary. *also* **4.11B, 4.11E, 4.7, 4.14A, 4.14D, 4.15A, 4.15B**

Guided Practice

1. An adult elephant weighs about 17,500 pounds. Does this baby elephant weigh about 200 ounces, 200 pounds, or 200 tons?

Complete. Tell whether you *multiply* or *divide*.

2. ■ lb = 56 T
3. 128 oz = ■ lb
4. 7 lb = ■ oz

5. **TALK Math** Which number of units is greater, the weight of a baby giraffe in ounces or the weight of the giraffe in pounds? **Explain.**

Independent Practice and Problem Solving

Choose the more reasonable measurement.

6. 
9 oz or 9 lb

7. 
2 lb or 2 T

8. 
6 oz or 6 lb

Complete. Tell whether you *multiply* or *divide*.

9. 5 lb = ■ oz
10. ■ lb = 192 oz
11. 6,000 lb = ■ T
12. 11 T = ■ lb
13. 4 lb = ■ oz
14. ■ lb = 160 oz

USE DATA **For 15–18, use the table.**

15. How many pounds of monkey biscuits are used by the zoo each year?
16. Order the amounts in the table from least to greatest.

Food Used Each Year at the St. Louis Zoo

Food Type	Amount
Apples	21 T
Earthworms	120 lb
Monkey Biscuits	6 T

17. ***FAST FACT*** An Australian Gippsland Earthworm can weigh up to 24 ounces. About how many of these earthworms could the zoo use per year?
18. **WRITE Math** The weight of three apples is about 1 pound. About how many apples does the zoo use per year? **Explain.**

Mixed Review and TAKS Prep

19. Sean's dog is 36 inches tall. How many feet tall is the dog? (TEKS 4.11B, p. 556)
20. Diane packs 9 books in each of 8 boxes. How many books did she pack in all? (TEKS 4.4C, p. 100)
21. **TAKS Prep** Jeff buys 25 pounds of dog food. How many ounces is that? (Obj. 4)
    - **A** 300 ounces
    - **B** 400 ounces
    - **C** 850 ounces
    - **D** 50,000 ounces

Extra Practice on page 566, Set C

Customary Capacity

OBJECTIVE: Estimate and measure the capacity of containers and change units of capacity.

Quick Review

Divide each number by 4.

1. 40 **2.** 48 **3.** 36 **4.** 16 **5.** 20

Vocabulary

capacity	pint (pt)
teaspoon (tsp)	quart (qt)
tablespoon (tbsp)	gallon (gal)
fluid ounce (fl oz)	cup (c)

Learn

Capacity is the amount a container can hold when filled. Customary units of capacity include **teaspoon (tsp)**, **tablespoon (tbsp)**, **cup (c)**, **pint (pt)**, **quart (qt)**, **gallon (gal)**, and **fluid ounce (fl oz)**.

Commonly used containers can be used as benchmarks for customary units of capacity.

1 teaspoon (tsp)

1 tablespoon (tbsp)

1 cup = 8 fluid ounces

1 pint

1 quart

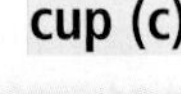

1 gallon

Activity 1

Materials ■ 1-cup, 1-pint, 1-quart, and 1-gallon containers ■ water

- A coffee cup holds about 1 cup. Estimate the number of cups in a pint, a quart, and a gallon. Record your estimates in the table.
- Use the 1-cup measure to fill each container. Record the actual number of cups in the table.
- Compare your estimates with the actual measurements. Are your estimates reasonable? Explain.

Capacity		
Container	**Estimate (cups)**	**Actual (cups)**
Pint	■	■
Quart	■	■
Gallon	■	■

Customary Units for Measuring Liquids
1 tablespoon (tbsp) = 3 teaspoons (tsp)
1 cup (c) = 8 fluid ounces (fl oz)
1 pint (pt) = 2 cups (c)
1 quart (qt) = 2 pints
1 gallon (gal) = 4 quarts

You can use multiplication and division to change units of capacity.

Example 1 Use multiplication.

How many cups equal 5 pints?

5 pints = ■ cups

pints		cups in 1 pint		cups
↓		↓		↓
5	×	2	=	10

So, 5 pints equal 10 cups.

Example 2 Use division.

How many gallons equal 16 quarts?

16 quarts = ■ gallons

quarts		quarts in 1 gallon		gallons
↓		↓		↓
16	÷	4	=	4

So, 16 quarts equal 4 gallons.

- What if you wanted to fill a bathtub with water? Which would be better to use, a bucket or a paper cup? Explain.

TEKS 4.11A estimate and use measurement tools to determine length (including perimeter), area, capacity and weight/mass using standard units SI (metric) and customary. *also* **4.1A, 4.4C, 4.4D, 4.4E, 4.7, 4.11B, 4.14A, 4.14D, 4.15A, 4.15B**

Guided Practice

1. Does this pitcher of iced tea hold 3 gallons, 3 quarts, 3 pints, or 3 cups?

Copy and complete each table. Change the units.

2.

Teaspoon, t	9	12	36
Tablespoon, s	■	■	■

✓3.

Gallons, g	5	■	8
Pints, p	■	56	■

✓4.

Cups, c	28	40	■
Quarts, q	■	■	16

5. **TALK Math** Which is greater, the number of cups or the number of quarts needed to fill a pitcher? **Explain.**

Independent Practice and Problem Solving

Choose the more reasonable unit of capacity.

6. 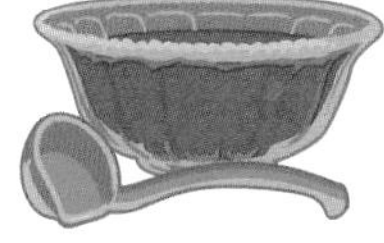
gallon or cup

7. 
quart or cup

8. 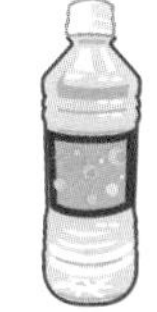
pint or tablespoon

Copy and complete each table. Change the units.

9.

Cups, c	10	16	20
Pints, p	■	■	■

10.

Gallons, g	■	9	■
Quarts, q	20	■	48

11.

Cups, c	48	■	■
Gallons, g	■	4	9

USE DATA For 13–15, use the recipe.

APRICOT ORANGE TEA

$2\frac{1}{2}$ cups apricot nectar
1 cup orange juice
1 cup water
1 tablespoon sugar
4 lemon slices
12 whole cloves
2 teaspoons instant tea
1 teaspoon ground cinnamon sugar

Makes four 1-cup servings

12. How many total fluid ounces of orange juice and water are used in the recipe?

13. Leah doubles the recipe. Does she need more or less than 1 quart of apricot nectar? **Explain.**

14. **Reasoning** Could 2 different containers have the same capacity? **Explain.**

15. **WRITE Math** **What's the Question?** Vinny makes 4 times the recipe. The answer is 1 gallon.

Mixed Review and TAKS Prep

16. Mr. Jansen bought 16 packs of tea. Each pack has 10 bags. How much tea does he have? (TEKS 4.6B, p. 226)

17. Linda baked 2 pounds of scones. How many ounces of scones did Linda bake? (TEKS 4.11B, p. 558)

18. **TAKS Prep** Abigail makes 3 gallons of lemonade. How many pints of lemonade does she make? **Explain.** (Obj. 4)

Extra Practice on page 566, Set D

LESSON 5

ALGEBRA

Change Units

OBJECTIVE: Change units of customary weight and capacity.

Quick Review

1. 5×14
2. $96 \div 8$
3. 4×9
4. 8×9
5. 16×7

Learn

You can use multiplication and division to change units.

PROBLEM Kenny has 5 pounds of sand. He needs 75 ounces of sand to make pillars for his sand castle. Does he have enough sand for the pillars?

Customary Units of Weight
1 pound (lb) = 16 ounces (oz)
1 ton (T) = 2,000 pounds (lb)

Customary Units of Capacity
1 pint (pt) = 2 cups (c)
1 quart (qt) = 2 pints
1 gallon (gal) = 4 quarts

Example 1 Use multiplication.

5 lb = ■ oz

Think: 1 lb = 16 oz

$5 \text{ lb} = 5 \times 16 = 80 \text{ oz}$

So, 5 pounds equal 80 ounces.

Since 75 < 80, Kenny has enough sand for the pillars.

Example 2 Use division.

64,000 lb = ■ T

Think: 1 T = 2,000 lb

64,000 ÷ 2000 = 32

So, 64,000 pounds equal 32 tons.

Example 3 Use multiplication.

4 pt = ■ c

Think: 1 pt = 2 c

$4 \text{ pt} = 4 \times 2 = 8 \text{ c}$

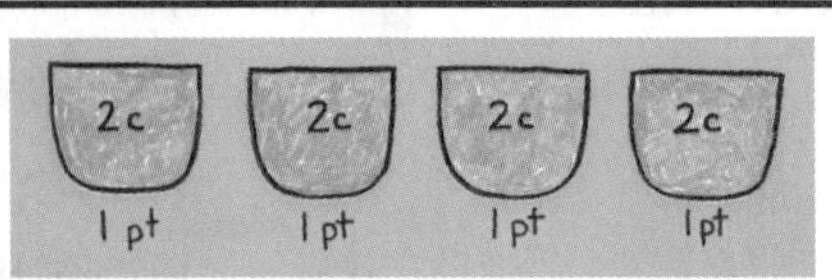

So, 4 pints equal 8 cups.

Example 4 Use division.

16 pt = ■ gal

Think: 1 qt = 2 pt

$16 \text{ pt} \div 2 = 8 \text{ qt}$

Think: 1 gal = 4 qt

$8 \text{ qt} \div 4 = 2 \text{ gal}$

So, 16 pints equal 2 gallons.

ERROR ALERT

Multiply when changing larger units to smaller units, because you need more units. Divide when changing smaller units to larger units, because you need fewer units.

▶ Every June there is a sand castle competition in Galveston, TX. There are about 2,000 competitors every year

TEKS 4.11B perform simple conversions between different units of length, between different units of capacity, and between different units of weight within the customary measurement system. *also* **4.1A, 4.4C, 4.4D, 4.4E, 4.7, 4.14A, 4.14D, 4.15A, 4.15B**

Guided Practice

1. How can you use a calculator to divide to find the number of gallons in 9,203 quarts?

Complete. Tell whether you *multiply* or *divide*.

2. 16 pt = ■ qt.
3. 12 ft = ■ in.
4. 3 lb = ■ oz

5. **TALK Math** **Explain** how you know whether to multiply or divide to change cups to gallons.

Independent Practice and Problem Solving

Complete. Tell whether you *multiply* or *divide*.

6. 7 T = ■ lb
7. ■ oz = 6 lb
8. ■ qt = 100 c
9. 12 gal = ■ pt
10. ■ yd = 288 in.
11. 10 c = ■ pt

Compare. Write >, <, or = for each ●.

12. 8 pt ● 1 gal
13. 72 oz ● 5 lb
14. 200 in. ● 4 yd

Algebra Copy and complete each table. Change the units.

15.

Pints, p	■	■	24
Quarts, q	15	9	■

16.

Pounds, p	2,000	6,000	■
Tons, t	■	■	144

17.

Gallons, g	6	■	4
Cups, c	■	16	■

18. **FAST FACT** The best sand for making sand castles has 8 parts sand to 1 part water. If Ned uses 8 gallons of sand to make a sandcastle, how many cups of water does he need? **Explain.**

19. **WRITE Math** There are 2 gallons of water in Jen's bucket. She wants to fill 15 jars that each hold 1 pint. Is there enough water in her bucket? **Explain.**

Mixed Review and TAKS Prep

20. How long is the shell to the nearest $\frac{1}{4}$ in.? (TEKS 4.11A, p. 552)

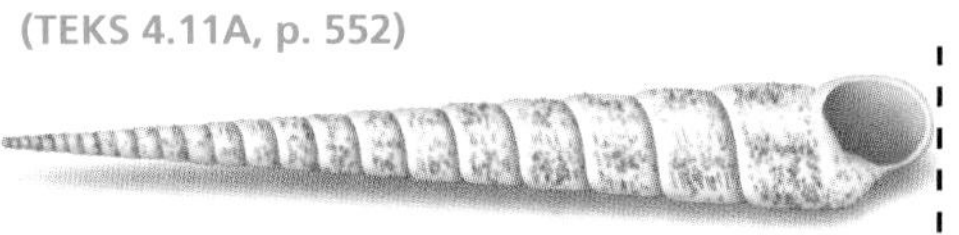

21. What transformation shows that these shells are congruent? (TEKS 4.9B, p. 292)

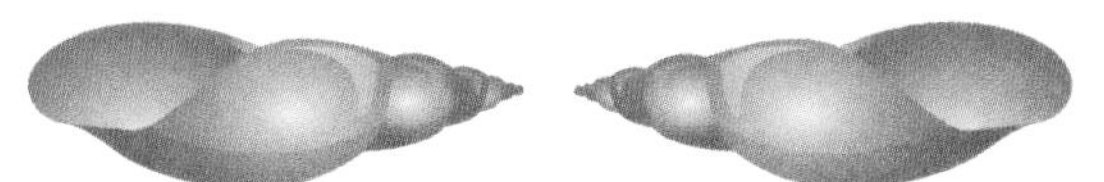

22. **TAKS Prep** Jason uses 5 quarts of orange juice and 3 pints of pineapple juice to make punch. How many pints of juice does he use in all? (Obj. 4)

Extra Practice on page 566, Set E

Problem Solving Workshop
Strategy: Compare Strategies

OBJECTIVE: Compare different strategies to solve problems.

Read to Understand
Plan
Solve
Check

Use the Strategy

PROBLEM Rosanna has a fishbowl that holds 4 quarts of water. She plans to use a pint container to fill the bowl. How many pints of water will Rosanna need to fill her fishbowl?

Read to Understand

- **Identify the details.**
- **What are you asked to find?**

Plan

- **What strategy can you use to solve the problem?**

  Sometimes you can use more than one strategy to solve a problem. You can *draw a diagram* or *make a table* to help you solve this problem.

Solve

- **How can you use the strategies to solve the problem?**

Draw a Diagram

Show how to find the total number of pints.

4 quarts = ■ pints

Think: 1 quart = 2 pints

$4 \times 2 = 8$

Make a Table

Show the relationship between quarts and pints.

Use this information to complete the table.

Think: 1 quart = 2 pints

Quart, *q*	1	2	3	4
Pint, *p*	2	4	6	8

So, Rosanna needs 8 pints of water.

Check

- **How can you check your answer?**
- **What other ways could you solve the problem?**

TEKS 4.14C select or develop an appropriate problem-solving plan or strategy, including drawing a picture, looking for a pattern, systematic guessing and checking, acting it out, making a table, working a simpler problem, or working backwards to solve a problem. *also* **4.4C, 4.4D, 4.4E, 4.7, 4.11B, 4.14A, 4.14B, 4.14D, 4.15A, 4.15B, 4.16B**

Guided Problem Solving

Choose a strategy to solve. Explain your choice.

1. Tim has a fish tank that is 3 feet long. How many inches long is the tank?

   First, decide if you should draw a diagram or make a table.

   Think: 1 foot = 12 inches

   Then, make a table.

Feet, f	1	2	3
Inches, i	12	■	■

   Finally, use the table to show many inches are in 3 feet.

2. **What if** Tim had a tank that was 5 feet long? How many inches long would the tank be?

3. **FAST FACT** The longest catfish caught and released in fresh water by a Texas angler was about 48 inches long. About how many feet long was the fish?

Choose a STRATEGY

- Draw a Diagram or Picture
- Make a Model or Act It Out
- Make an Organized List
- Look for a Pattern
- Make a Table or Graph
- Guess and Check
- Work Backward
- Solve a Simpler Problem
- Write an Equation
- Use Logical Reasoning

Mixed Strategy Practice

USE DATA For 4–6 and 8, use the picture.

4. How many ounces does the white bass weigh?

5. **Pose a Problem** Use the information in the table to write a problem changing inches to feet.

6. How much longer is the catfish than the walleye?

7. Ian is going fishing with his dad. He can fish in either the ocean or a lake. He can use shrimp, worms, or minnows for bait. How many different fishing choices does Ian have? **Explain.**

8. **WRITE Math** Lilly's favorite fish is shown in the picture. She catches a different fish that weighs 3 more pounds than half the weight of her favorite fish. The fish she caught weighs 11 pounds. Which fish is Lilly's favorite? **Explain.**

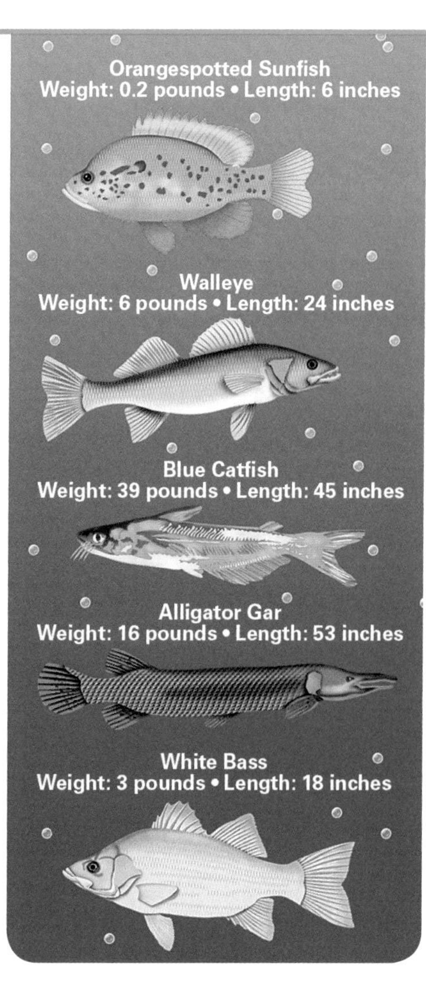

Extra Practice

Set A **Estimate to the nearest $\frac{1}{2}$ inch. Then measure to the nearest $\frac{1}{8}$ inch.** (pp. 552–555)

1. 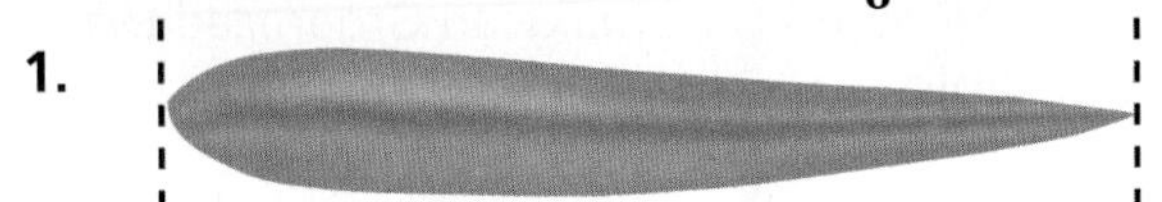

2. 

3. Sally cut 3 ribbons to decorate gifts. They measured $8\frac{1}{2}$ inches, $7\frac{5}{8}$ inches, and $8\frac{1}{4}$ inches long. How long is the longest piece Sally cut?

Set B **Complete. Tell whether you *multiply* or *divide*.** (pp. 556–557)

1. 3 mi = ■ yd
2. 2 yd = ■ in.
3. ■ yd = 372 ft

Compare. Write <, >, or = for each ●.

4. 14 yd ● 40 ft
5. 22 ft ● 270 in.
6. 6 yd ● 216 in.

Set C **Choose the more reasonable measurement.** (pp. 558–559)

1. 6 T or 6 lb
2. 8 lb or 8 oz
3. 10 oz or 10 lb

Complete. Tell whether you *multiply* or *divide*.

4. ■ lb = 48 oz
5. 6 T = ■ lb
6. ■ lb = 80 oz

Set D **Copy and complete each table. Change the units.** (pp. 560–561)

1.

Pints, p	16	■	56
Gallons, g	■	5	■

2.

Tablespoons, s	■	■	12
Teaspoons, t	18	27	■

3.

Quarts, q	5	■	■
Cups, c	■	32	40

4. A recipe for 8 quarts of punch calls for juice and 20 cups of ginger ale. How much juice is needed?

Set E **Complete. Tell whether you *multiply* or *divide*.** (pp. 562–563)

1. ■ pt = 4 gal
2. ■ T = 6,000 lb
3. 432 in. = ■ yd

Compare. Write <, >, or = for each ●.

4. 2 gal ● 8 qt
5. 150 yd ● 500 ft
6. 160 oz ● 9 lb

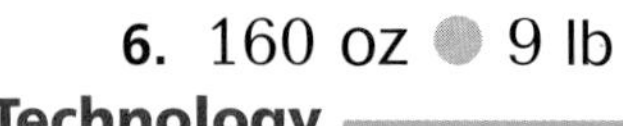

Technology

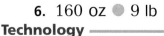

Use Harcourt Mega Math, The Number Games, *Tiny's Think Tank*, Levels M, N, O, Q.

TECHNOLOGY CONNECTION

(TEKS 4.14D, 4.4C, 4.4D, 4.4E, 4.7, 4.11B, 4.14A, 4.15A, 4.15B)

Calculator: Change Customary Measures

You can use the TI-15 calculator to change units of measure.

Example 1

Decide which operation to use.

To change from a larger unit to a smaller unit, multiply.

You can use the Op1 key to change from yards (larger unit) to feet (smaller unit).

6 yd = ■ ft

So, 6 yards is the same as 18 feet.

Example 2

To change from a smaller unit to a larger one, divide.

16 fl oz = ■ c

8 Op1 1

So, 16 fluid ounces is the same as 2 cups.

Tips

Before entering a new problem, clear the stored operations.

Try It

Use the TI-15 Op1 key to complete each table.

1.

Yards	14	25	37	58
Feet	■	■	■	■

2.

Fluid Ounces	32	128	152	192
Cups	■	■	■	■

3.

Feet	3	9	14	26
Inches	■	■	■	■

4.

Ounces	48	112	176	256
Pounds	■	■	■	■

5.

Gallons	5	9	13	28
Quarts	■	■	■	■

6.

Inches	108	288	468	792
Yards	■	■	■	■

7. **Explore More Explain** how you know what factor or divisor to use when you change customary units of measure.

Chapter 21 Review/Test

Check Vocabulary and Concepts

Choose the best term from the box.

VOCABULARY
centimeter
yard
linear unit
capacity

1. A __?__ is a unit of measure used to measure length, width, and height. (TEKS 4.11A, p. 552)
2. A __?__ is a customary unit equal to 3 feet. (TEKS 4.11B, p. 556)
3. __?__ is the amount of liquid a container can hold. (TEKS 4.11A, p. 560)

Check Skills

Choose the more reasonable measurement. (TEKS 4.11A, pp. 558–559)

4. 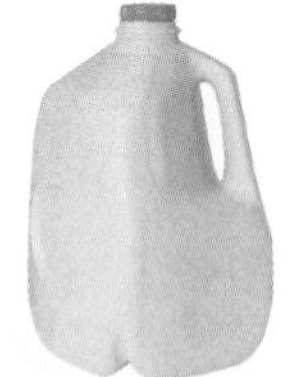

8 T or 8 lb

5. 

2 lb or 2 T

6. 

70 oz or 70 lb

Estimate to the nearest $\frac{1}{2}$ inch. Then measure to the nearest $\frac{1}{8}$ inch. (TEKS 4.11A, pp. 552–553)

7. 

8. 

9. 

Complete. Tell whether you *multiply* or *divide*. (TEKS 4.11B, pp. 556–557, 558–559, 562–563)

10. ■ yd = 180 in.
11. ■ mi = 5,280 yd
12. 23 ft = ■ in.
13. ■ lb = 112 oz
14. 6,000 lb = ■ T
15. ■ T = 10,000 lb
16. ■ oz = 6 lb
17. 4 T = ■ lb
18. 12 lb = ■ oz

Check Problem Solving

Solve. (TEKS 4.14C, pp. 564–565)

19. For a science experiment, Marla has to divide 2 pounds of salt into containers that hold 3 ounces each. How many containers can Marla fill?

20. **WRITE Math** Michael drew a line 75 inches long. Susan's line was 7 feet long, and Ed's was 2 yards long. **Explain** how you can order the lengths from least to greatest.

GO ONLINE **Technology** Use *Online Assessment.*

Enrich • Add and Subtract Customary Measurements

Crafty Measures

Marcia needs 5 feet 8 inches of yellow fabric and 3 feet 6 inches of red fabric to make a blanket. How much fabric does she need?

To add measurements, you may need to change units.

Example 1

Step 1	Step 2	Step 3
Add each kind of unit. 5 ft 8 in. + 3 ft 6 in. 8 ft 14 in.	Think: 12 in. = 1 ft Since 14 in. is more than 1 ft, rename 14 in. as 1 ft + 2 in. 8 ft 14 in. = 8 ft + (1 ft + 2 in.)	Combine like units. 8 ft + (1 ft + 2 in.) = (8 ft + 1 ft) + 2 in. = 9 ft 2 in.

So, Marcia needs 9 feet 2 inches of fabric.

Jon needs 2 feet of string for his kite. Kyle needs 17 inches of string for his kite. How much more string does Jon need than Kyle?

To subtract measurements, you may need to change units.

Example 2

Step 1	Step 2
Think: 1 ft = 12 in. Use 24 in. for 2 ft. 24 in. − 17 in.	Subtract. 1 14 ~~2~~~~4~~ in. − 17 in. 7 in.

So, Jon needs 7 inches more string than Kyle.

Try It

1. Rachael needs 3 feet 4 inches of ribbon for the edge of her pillow. Cheryl needs 3 feet 8 inches of ribbon. How much ribbon do both girls need?

2. Scott needs 6 feet 6 inches of white cloth to make a sign. He only has 4 feet 2 inches of cloth. How much more cloth does Scott need?

WRITE Math Grace needs 4 feet 9 inches of wood to make a table. How much wood does she need to make two tables? **Explain** how you know.

Getting Ready for the TAKS
Chapters 1–21

Number, Operation, and Quantitative Reasoning TAKS Obj. 1

1. Janet has read $\frac{3}{4}$ of a book. Which fraction is equivalent to $\frac{3}{4}$?

$\frac{1}{4}$	$\frac{1}{4}$	$\frac{1}{4}$

$\frac{1}{8}$	$\frac{1}{8}$	$\frac{1}{8}$	$\frac{1}{8}$	$\frac{1}{8}$	$\frac{1}{8}$

A $\frac{2}{8}$

B $\frac{5}{8}$

C $\frac{6}{8}$

D $\frac{7}{8}$

Eliminate choices.

See Item 2. The ones place is the same for all answer choices, so check your subtraction of the tens and hundreds places.

2. There were 3,548 visitors at the science museum in 2006. In 2007, there were 3,397 visitors. How many more people visited the science museum in 2006?

F 141

J 251

H 241

G 151

3. **WRITE Math** Leo planted 40 flower seeds. He planted the same number of seeds for 5 different types of flowers. How many seeds were there for each type of flower? **Explain** how you know.

Patterns, Relationships, and Algebraic Thinking TAKS Obj. 2

4. Each number of inches is related in the same way to the number of feet.

Inches, *i*	12	24	36	48
Feet, *f*	1	2	3	4

When given a number of inches, what is one way to find its related number of feet?

A Multiply i by 12.

B Add 12 to i.

C Divide i by 12.

D Subtract 12 from i.

5. What multiplication fact can be used to solve the division problem below?

$$36 \div 4 = \blacksquare$$

F 6×6

G 3×7

H 4×9

J 7×2

6. For which number sentence is $m = 5$ the answer?

A $35 \div m = 7$

B $35 \times 7 = m$

C $m \div 35 = 7$

D $m \times 5 = 35$

7. **WRITE Math** How can you use multiplication to check that $36 \div 6 = 6$? **Explain** how you know.

Measurement TAKS Obj. 4

8. Order the lengths from least to greatest.

3 inches, $1\frac{3}{4}$ inches, $2\frac{1}{2}$ inches, $3\frac{1}{8}$ inches

F 3 in., $3\frac{1}{8}$ in., $2\frac{1}{2}$ in., $1\frac{3}{4}$ in.

G $3\frac{1}{8}$ in., 3 in., $1\frac{3}{4}$ in., $2\frac{1}{2}$ in.

H $2\frac{1}{2}$ in., $1\frac{3}{4}$ in., $3\frac{1}{8}$ in., 3 in.

J $1\frac{3}{4}$ in., $2\frac{1}{2}$ in., 3 in., $3\frac{1}{8}$ in.

9. A lemonade recipe calls for 2 cups of water. Linda wants to double the recipe. How many pints of water will Linda need?

A 1 pint

B 2 pints

C 3 pints

D Not here

10. Marco is 5 feet 4 inches tall. Alonzo is 72 inches tall. How much taller is Alonzo than Marco?

F 6 inches

G 7 inches

H 8 inches

J 9 inches

11. WRITE Math Jeannie's mother bought 5 pounds of fruit at the store. How many ounces is 5 pounds? **Explain** how you know.

Probability and Statistics TAKS Obj. 5

12. Stacey has 6 pairs of pants and 5 shirts. How many combinations of pants and shirts can she wear?

A 30

B 32

C 34

D 36

13. Al can buy a model train, car, or truck. He can paint it red or blue. How many combinations are possible?

F 3

G 5

H 6

J 9

14. Beatrice received the following scores on her math tests this year. For a bar graph, which is the most reasonable interval for this data?

88, 94, 100, 89, 91, 98, 77

A 1

B 10

C 20

D 100

15. WRITE Math The book club is having an ice cream party. The ice cream choices are strawberry and vanilla. The topping choices are hot fudge and caramel. How many combinations are possible? **Explain.**

22 Metric Measurement

The Big Idea Measurement involves a comparison of an attribute of an object or situation with a unit that has the same attribute.

Investigate

This statue of Sam Houston is just over 20 meters tall. The base is about 3 meters more. Suppose you wanted to add the data on the statue of Sam Houston to the graph. How would you decide how high to draw the bar? Describe one relationship you would see in the new graph.

American Monuments

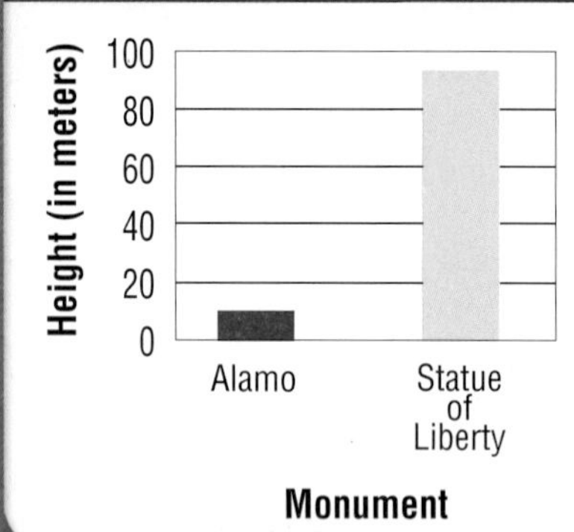

TEXAS FAST FACT

This statue of General Sam Houston is in Huntsville, Texas. It is the world's tallest statue of an American hero. You can still see "Big Sam" from 10.5 kilometers away.

SAM HOUSTON
1793 – 1863

GO ONLINE **Technology** Student pages are available in the Student eBook.

Show What You Know

Check your understanding of important skills needed for success in Chapter 22.

▶ Measure Length to the Nearest Centimeter

Measure the length of each to the nearest centimeter.

1. 

2. 

3. 

▶ Choose the Appropriate Tool and Unit

Choose the tool and unit to measure each.

Tools

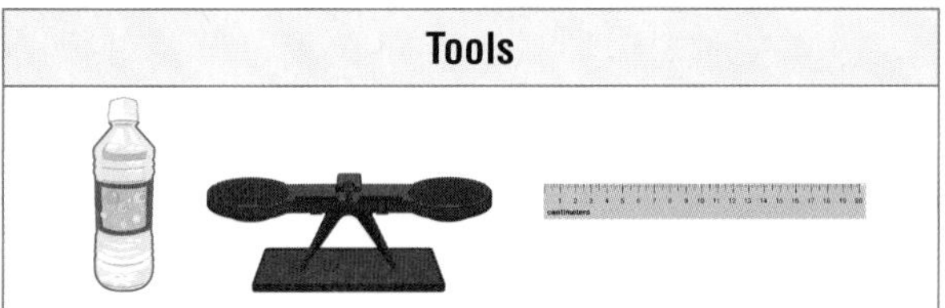

Units	
centimeter	gram
kilogram	milliliter
liter	meter

4. capacity of a bucket
5. length of a sticker
6. mass of a strawberry
7. capacity of a coffee mug
8. length of a marker
9. capacity of a glass
10. mass of an eraser
11. length of a paper clip

VOCABULARY POWER

CHAPTER VOCABULARY

centimeter (cm)
decimeter (dm)
kilometer (km)
liter (L)
mass
meter (m)
milliliter (mL)
millimeter (mm)

WARM-UP WORDS

millimeter (mm) a metric unit for measuring length or distance
1 centimeter = 10 millimeters

meter (m) a metric unit for measuring length or distance
1 meter = 100 centimeters

liter (L) a metric unit for measuring capacity
1 liter = 1,000 milliliters

LESSON 1

Metric Length

OBJECTIVE: Estimate and measure metric length.

Quick Review

Round to the nearest whole number.

1. 5.7
2. 10.9
3. 0.7
4. 8.3
5. 3.4

Vocabulary

millimeter (mm)
meter (m)
centimeter (cm)
kilometer (km)
decimeter (dm)

Learn

PROBLEM Is the wingspan of a dragonfly about 10 millimeters, 10 centimeters, or 10 meters?

Length can be measured using SI, or metric, units of measure. The metric units of length include **millimeter (mm)**, **centimeter (cm)**, **decimeter (dm)**, **meter (m)**, and **kilometer (km)**.

Common objects can be used as benchmarks for metric units of length.

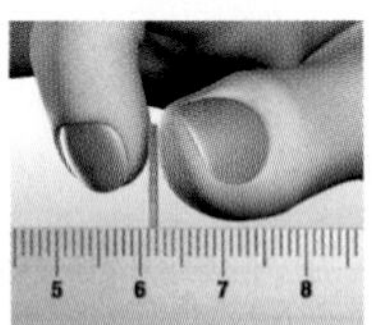

The thickness of a dime is about 1 millimeter.

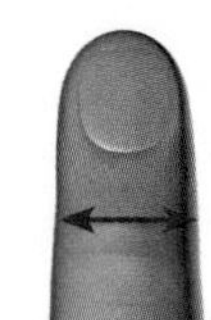
The width of your index finger is about 1 centimeter.

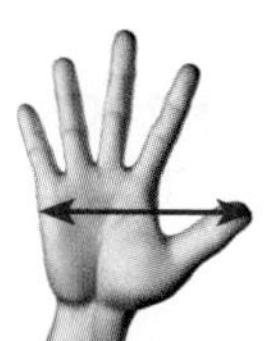
The width of an adult's hand is about 1 decimeter.

The width of a door is about 1 meter.

It takes about 10 minutes to walk 1 kilometer.

So, the wingspan of a dragonfly is about 10 centimeters.

- Which metric unit of length would you use to measure your driveway? Explain.

Activity 1

Materials ■ 5 classroom objects ■ centimeter ruler ■ meterstick

Step 1

Estimate the lengths of 5 objects in your classroom. Record your work in a table like the one shown.

Step 2

Choose the unit you would use to measure each object. Write *mm*, *cm*, *dm*, or *m* in the table. Then measure each object to the nearest millimeter, centimeter, decimeter, or meter.

Length			
Objects	Unit	Estimate	Actual Measurement
desk	dm	■	■
?	■	■	■

- Order the objects in the table from shortest to longest.

TEKS 4.11A estimate and use measurement tools to determine length (including perimeter), area, capacity and weight/mass using standard units SI (metric) and customary. *also* **4.14A, 4.14D, 4.15A, 4.15B**

Measure Longer Lengths with Different Units

You can also measure longer lengths.

Activity 2 **Materials** ■ centimeter ruler ■ meterstick

• Estimate the length of your classroom.Decide which tool and which unit you should use. Measure the length of your classroom.	• Compare your results with a classmate. Are the measurements of your classroom the same? If not, why not?

Using different metric units to measure the length of an object can help you understand how the units are related.

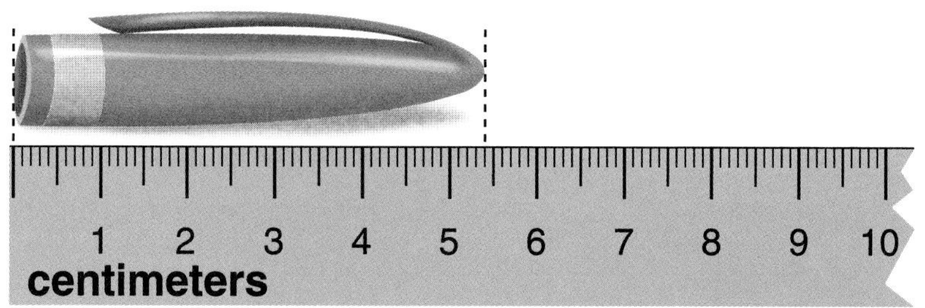

Math Idea

In the metric system, fractional widths are usually written by using decimals.

$6\frac{1}{2}$ cm = 6.5 cm

The right edge of the pen cap is closest to the 54 millimeter mark. So, the pen cap is 54 millimeters long to the nearest millimeter.

The right edge of the pen cap is closest to the 5.5 centimeter mark. So, the pen cap is 5.5 centimeters long to the nearest half centimeter.

The right edge of the pen cap is closest to the 1 decimeter mark. So, the pen cap is 1 decimeter long to the nearest decimeter.

Guided Practice

1. What is the length of this yarn to the nearest half centimeter and to the nearest millimeter?

1 2 3 4 5 6 7
centimeters

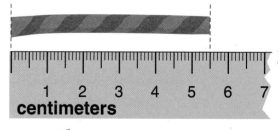

Choose the most reasonable unit of measure. Write ***mm, cm, dm, m,*** **or** ***km.***

2. 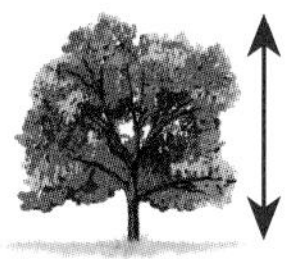

3. 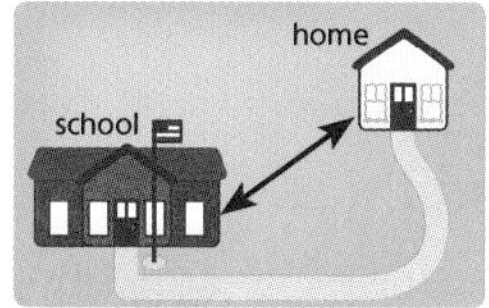

4. 

5. TALK Math Linda measured the length of her insect house to the nearest half centimeter. Charlie measured the length of his insect house to the nearest millimeter. Whose measurement is more exact? **Explain.**

Independent Practice and Problem Solving

Choose the most reasonable unit of measure. Write *mm*, *cm*, *dm*, *m*, or *km*.

6. 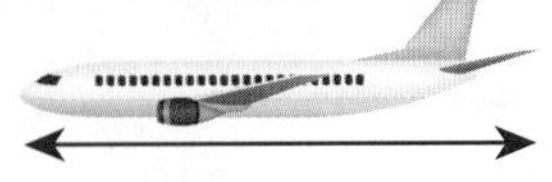

7. 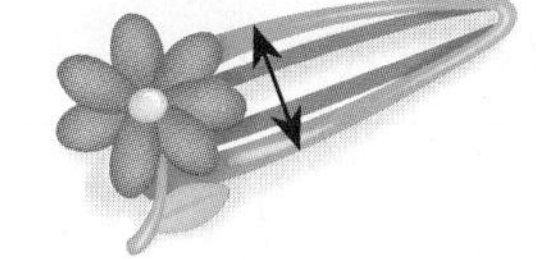

8. 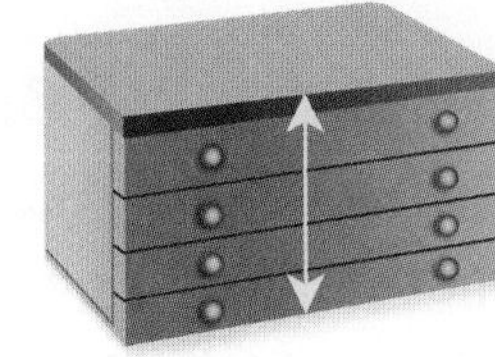

Estimate the nearest centimeter. Then measure to the nearest half centimeter. Write your answer as a decimal.

9. 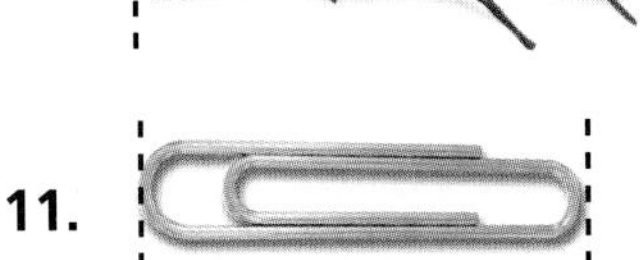

10. 

11.

12.

Estimate to the nearest half centimeter. Then measure to the nearest millimeter.

13.

14. 

15. 

16. 

Compare. Write <, >, or = for each ●.

17. 4 m ● 4 cm

18. 10 km ● 10 m

19. 25 cm ● 25 dm

Use a metric ruler. Draw a line for each length.

20. 7 cm

21. 25 cm

22. 16 cm

23. 56 cm

USE DATA For 24–26, use the graph.

24. About how big is the ladybug? Write the length in centimeters.

25. **Reasoning** How many millimeters longer is the checkerspot butterfly than the honeybee? **Explain.**

26. **WRITE Math** For which insect can the length be written as a whole number using three different units? Write each of the measurements. **Explain.**

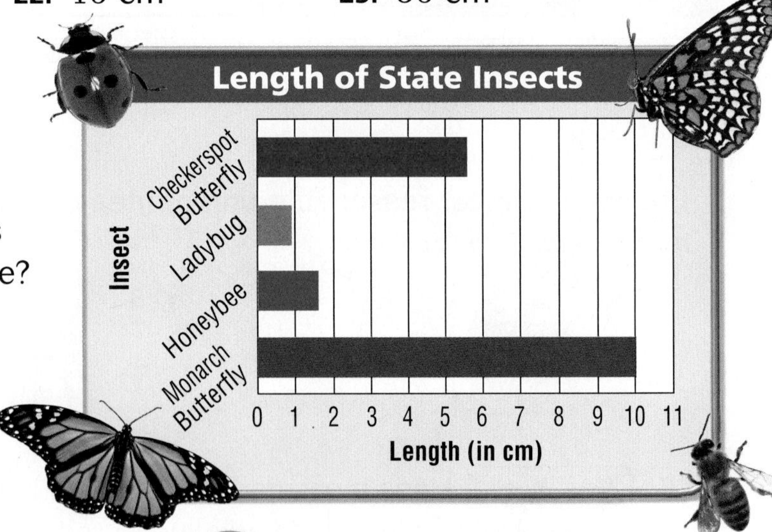

Technology Use Harcourt Mega Math, Ice Station Exploration, *Linear Lab*, Level I.

 Extra Practice on page 592, Set A

Mixed Review and TAKS Prep

27. A monarch butterfly can migrate more than 2,500 miles. How many yards is that? (TEKS 4.11B, p. 556)

28. **TAKS Prep** What is the length of the inchworm to the nearest half centimeter?

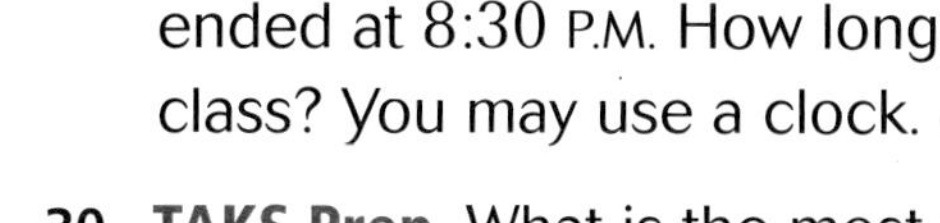

A 2 centimeters

B 2.5 centimeters

C 3 centimeters

D 3.5 centimeters

29. Joan's art class started at 5:45 P.M. and ended at 8:30 P.M. How long was the class? You may use a clock. (TEKS 4.12, p. 476)

30. **TAKS Prep** What is the most reasonable unit of measure that can be used to measure the length of a pen? (Obj. 4)

A Millimeter

B Centimeter

C Meter

D Kilometer

Problem Solving and Reasoning

MEASUREMENT A map gives information about a place. A map scale shows how distances on a map compare to actual distances. Maps use scales to show distance. Scales represent the actual distances between places on the map.

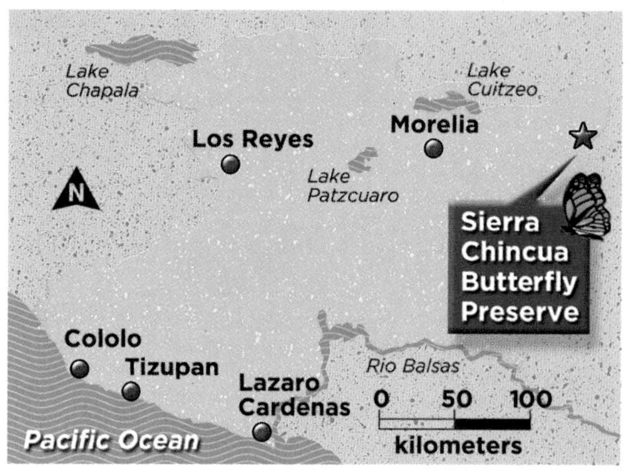

The map at the right shows Michoacán, Mexico, where the famous Sierra Chincua Butterfly Preserve is located. More than 100 million monarch butterflies migrate to the preserve every fall from up to 4,800 kilometers away.

The scale on this map is 1 centimeter = 50 kilometers. This means that every 1 centimeter shown on the map represents 50 kilometers of actual distance.

On the map, the distance from Morelia to the Butterfly Preserve is about 2 centimeters. $2 \times 50 = 100$. So, the actual distance is about 100 kilometers.

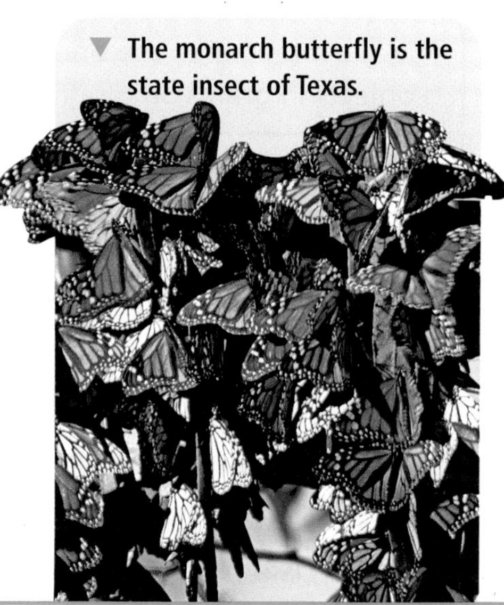
▼ The monarch butterfly is the state insect of Texas.

Use your ruler and the scale to find each actual distance.

1. Lazaro Cardenas to Butterfly Preserve

2. Butterfly Preserve to Cololo

3. Morelia to Los Reyes

4. Tizupan to Morelia

LESSON 2

Mass

OBJECTIVE: Estimate and measure the mass of objects.

Quick Review

Compare. Write $>$, $<$ or $=$ for each ●.

1. 10 ● 16
2. 60 ● 53
3. 3,456 ● 3,456
4. 713 ● 731
5. 890 ● 809

Vocabulary

mass

gram (g)

kilogram (kg)

Learn

PROBLEM Lincoln plays ice hockey. Is the mass of Lincoln's hockey stick about 500 grams or 500 kilograms?

Matter is what all objects are made of. **Mass** is the amount of matter an object contains. It is measured with a balance. Metric units of mass include **gram (g)** and **kilogram (kg)**.

Mass and weight are not the same thing. Weight is a measure of the gravitational force acting on an object. It is measured with a scale.

Common objects can be used as benchmarks for metric units of mass.

The mass of a dollar bill is about 1 gram.
1 kg = 1,000 g

The mass of a baseball bat is about 1 kilogram.

So, the mass of Lincoln's hockey stick is about 500 grams.

You can use a balance to find the mass of objects.

HANDS ON

Activity 1 **Materials** ■ balance ■ gram and kilogram masses ■ objects

- Make a table like the one shown. Estimate the masses of 5 objects in grams or kilograms. Record your estimates in the table.
- Find the mass of each object by using the balance and gram and kilogram masses. Record the actual mass in the table.

Mass			
Object	**Unit (g/kg)**	**Estimate**	**Actual**
scissors	g	50 g	■
?	■	■	■

- Are your estimates reasonable? **Explain** how you know.
- List the objects in your table in order from least mass to greatest mass.

Guided Practice

1. Which is a more reasonable measurement for the cereal box, 200 grams or 20 kilograms?

TEKS 4.11A estimate and use measurement tools to determine length (including perimeter), area, capacity and weight/mass using standard units SI (metric) and customary. *also* **4.11E, 4.14A, 4.14D, 4.15A, 4.15B**

Choose the more reasonable measurement.

2. 
500 g or 50 kg

3. 
200 g or 200 kg

4. 
3 g or 300 g

5. **TALK Math** **Explain** the difference between weight and mass.

Independent Practice and Problem Solving

Choose the more reasonable measurement.

6. 

14 g or 14 kg

7. 

5,000 kg or 500 g

8. 
1 kg or 10 g

Compare the mass of each object to a kilogram. Write *about 1 kilogram*, *less than 1 kilogram*, or *more than 1 kilogram*.

9. 

10. 

11. 

USE DATA For 12–15, use the pictures.

12. What is the order of the sports balls from greatest mass to least mass?

13. A baseball's mass is about 145 grams. Kelly has 2 basketballs and 5 baseballs in her gym bag. Which is greater, the mass of the basketballs or the mass of the baseballs? **Explain.**

14. **WRITE Math** How would you find the total mass of the basketball, table tennis ball, and tennis ball? **Explain.**

Mass of Sports Balls

Basketball
616 grams

Bowling ball
6 kilograms

Table tennis ball
2.5 grams

Tennis ball
57 grams

Mixed Review and TAKS Prep

15. Bowling shoes cost $39 a pair. How much do 4 pairs of bowling shoes cost? (TEKS 4.4D, p. 206)

16. Which metric unit of length would you use to measure the distance around a basketball? (TEKS 4.11A, p. 574)

17. **TAKS Prep** Al is measuring an object's mass in kilograms. Which of the following is he most likely measuring? (Obj. 4)

A Sheet of paper **B** Paperback book

C Pencil **D** Bookshelf

Extra Practice on page 592, Set B

LESSON 3

Capacity

OBJECTIVE: Estimate and measure capacity of containers.

Quick Review

Compare. Write >, <, or = for each ●.

1. 21 ● 12
2. 55 ● 101
3. 7,899 ● 7,899
4. 608 ● 680
5. 1,011 ● 999

Vocabulary

liter (L)

milliliter (mL)

Learn

Joanne's dad is putting gas in their minivan. Will it take 88 liters or 88 milliliters to fill the gas tank?

Metric units of capacity include **liter (L)** and **milliliter (mL)**.

Commonly used containers can be used as benchmarks for metric units of capacity.

A dropper holds about 1 milliliter

This water bottle holds 1 liter.
1 liter (L) = 1,000 milliliters (mL)

So, it will take 88 liters to fill the gas tank.

- What unit would you use to measure the amount of juice in a lemon?

HANDS ON

Activity **Materials** ■ 1-liter container ■ metric measuring cup ■ dropper ■ large and small containers

Step 1

Make a table like the one shown. Estimate the capacities of 5 containers in milliliters or liters. Record your work in the table.

Step 2

Now select the 1-liter container, metric measuring cup, or dropper and find the capacity of each container. Record the actual capacity in the table.

Capacity

Object	Unit (mL/L)	Estimate	Actual
spoon	mL	5	■
?	■	■	■

- Are your estimates reasonable? **Explain** how you know.
- Order the containers in your table from least capacity to greatest capacity.

Guided Practice

1. Does this bottle of maple syrup hold about 250 mL or 250 L?

TEKS 4.11A estimate and use measurement tools to determine length (including perimeter), area, capacity and weight/mass using standard units SI (metric) and customary. *also* **4.1A, 4.14A, 4.14D, 4.15A, 4.15B**

Choose the most reasonable measurement. Write *a*, *b*, or *c*.

2. 
a. 2 L
b. 20 mL
c. 5 mL

3. 
a. 5 mL
b. 15 mL
c. 10 mL

4. 

a. 1 mL
b. 100 mL
c. 100 L

5. **TALK Math** Which number of units is greater, the capacity of a container given in liters or milliliters? **Explain.**

Independent Practice and Problem Solving

Choose the most reasonable measurement. Write *a*, *b*, or *c*.

6. 
a. 20 mL
b. 20 L
c. 250 mL

7. 
a. 10 mL
b. 10 L
c. 100 mL

8. 
a. 5 L
b. 500 mL
c. 5 mL

Estimate and tell whether each object has a capacity of *about a liter*, *less than a liter*, or *more than a liter*.

9. 

10. 

11. 

Compare. Write <, >, or = for each ●.

12. 650 mL ● 605 mL

13. 13 L ● 31 L

14. 7,000 mL ● 7 L

USE DATA For 15–18, use the table.

Fuel Usage	
Vehicle	**Amount Used (per 100 km)**
Traditional Car	9,000 mL
Smart Car	4 L
Bus	64 L

15. You can save money by driving vehicles that use less fuel per 100 kilometers. Which car helps you save the most money? **Explain.**

16. Write the vehicles in order from most fuel used to least fuel used.

17. **Reasoning** Kim drives 300 kilometers in a smart car. Does she use more or less than 10 liters of fuel? **Explain.**

18. **WRITE Math** Jerry's minivan uses 12 liters of fuel for every 100 kilometers of driving. Which vehicle costs more than Jerry's minivan to use? **Explain.**

Mixed Review and TAKS Prep

19. Find a rule. Then find the next number in the pattern. (TEKS 4.7, p. 144)
21, 18, 15, 12, ■

20. Is the mass of a large car about 3,000 kilograms or 3,000 grams? (TEKS 4.11A, p. 578)

21. **TAKS Prep** Bev is measuring a container's capacity in liters. Which of the following objects is she most likely measuring? (Obj. 4)
A Bucket
B Tea cup
C Drinking glass
D Shampoo bottle

Extra Practice on page 592, Set C

Problem Solving Workshop
Strategy: Make a Table

OBJECTIVE: Solve problems by using the strategy *make a table*.

Read to Understand
Plan
Solve
Check

Use the Strategy

PROBLEM Connor is buying a hat. He needs to know the distance around his head to buy the right size. He knows that he is 135 centimeters tall. How can he use this information to find his hat size?

Read to Understand

- What information is given?
- What are you asked to find?

Plan

- What strategy can you use to solve the problem?

You can *make a table* to help you solve this problem.

Solve

- How can you use the strategy to solve the problem?

Materials ■ string ■ centimeter ruler or metric tape measure

Estimate, then measure your height and the distance around your head in centimeters. Then estimate and measure the head size and height of three other classmates. Record your measurements in the table.

Measurements (in cm)				
Head size	■	■	■	■
Height	■	■	■	■

Generalize.
Look for a pattern in each classmate's head size and height.

Think: Each person's height is about 3 times their head size.

Connor's height is 135 centimeters and $135 \div 3$ is 45.
So, Connor's hat size is about 45 centimeters.

Check

- How can you check your answer?

TEKS 4.14C select or develop an appropriate problem–solving plan or strategy, including drawing a picture, looking for a pattern, systematic guessing and checking, acting it out, making a table, working a simpler problem, or working backwards to solve a problem. *also* **4.7, 4.11A, 4.14A, 4.14B, 4.14D, 4.15A, 4.15B, 4.16B**

Guided Problem Solving

1. Mia knows the length of her foot is 21 centimeters. How can she use this measurement to find the length of her forearm?

   First, measure the length of your forearm and foot and the forearm and foot of at least three other classmates.

   Then, record the measurements in a table.

   Finally, look for patterns between the length of each person's foot and the length of their forearm.

2. **What if** Katie's forearm is 2 decimeters long. How many decimeters long is her foot?

3. Juan is making keychains to sell at a craft fair. He plans to sell them for $4 each. How much money will he make if he sells 14 keychains?

Choose a STRATEGY

- Draw a Diagram or Picture
- Make a Model or Act It Out
- Make an Organized List
- Look for a Pattern
- Make a Table or Graph
- Guess and Check
- Work Backward
- Solve a Simpler Problem
- Write an Equation
- Use Logical Reasoning

Mixed Strategy Practice

4. **FAST FACT** The length of a person's arm span is about the same as the height of the person. Perry is 60 inches tall. How many feet long is his arm span?

5. **Pose a Problem** Look back at Problem 4. Write a similar problem by changing the units.

6. The 42-ton mechanical elephant in the picture was part of a French theater group's performance in London, England, in 2006. How many pounds did the elephant weigh?

7. A 18-foot tall girl marionette was also part the French theater group's performance. About how many times taller is the girl marionette than a 6-foot tall person?

8. It costs Elizabeth 12 cents a minute to make a call on her cell phone. How much will a 10-minute call cost?

9. **WRITE Math** Bea is buying a sandwich for lunch. She can choose from two types of bread, white or wheat. She can choose turkey, ham, or roast beef. How many different sandwich choices does Bea have? **Explain.**

LESSON 5

Choose the Appropriate Tool and Unit

OBJECTIVE: Choose the appropriate tool and unit to measure.

Quick Review

Which is the more reasonable estimate of the weight of a calculator, 5 ounces or 5 pounds?

Learn

When measuring an object, it is important to know which tool and unit of measure to use.

Customary or metric units can be used to measure objects.

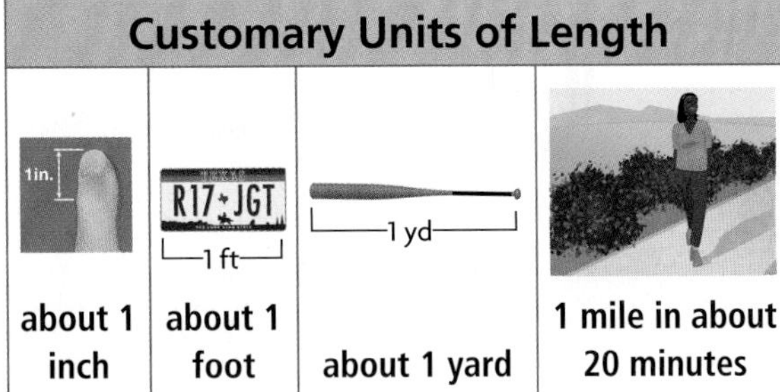

Customary Units of Length
1in.
R17·JGT
1 ft
1 yd
about 1 inch
about 1 foot
about 1 yard
1 mile in about 20 minutes

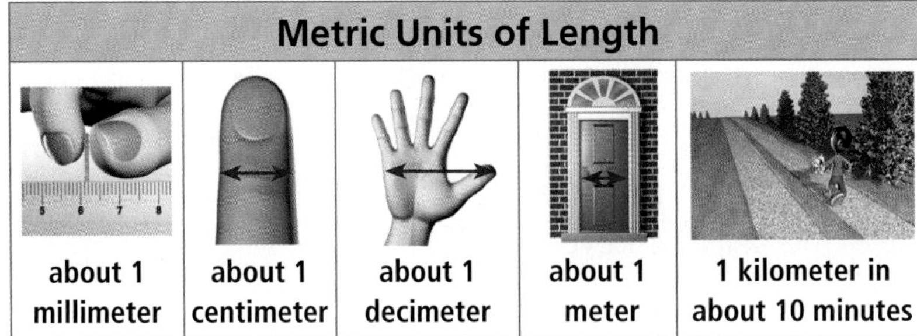

Metric Units of Length
about 1 millimeter
about 1 centimeter
about 1 decimeter
about 1 meter
1 kilometer in about 10 minutes

Activity 1

Materials ■ centimeter ruler ■ inch ruler ■ yardstick ■ meterstick ■ classroom objects or distances

Step 1

Choose 5 objects or distances. Choose the customary unit and the metric unit you will use to measure each length or distance. Estimate each length or distance using the units. Record your estimates in a table like the one shown.

Length				
	Customary Units		Metric Units	
Object/Distance	Estimate	Actual	Estimate	Actual
Length of Room	■	■	■	■
?	■	■	■	■

Step 2

Choose the tool you will use to measure each length or distance. Then measure using customary and metric units. Record your measurements in the table.

- How did you decide which units to use to measure the lengths or distances?
- How did you decide which tools to use to measure the lengths or distances?
- How close were your estimates to the actual measurements?

TEKS 4.11A estimate and use measurement tools to determine length (including perimeter), area, capacity and weight/mass using standard units SI (metric) and customary. *also* **4.1B, 4.14A, 4.14D, 4.15A, 4.15B**

Customary Units of Weight		
about 1 ounce	about 1 pound	about 1 ton

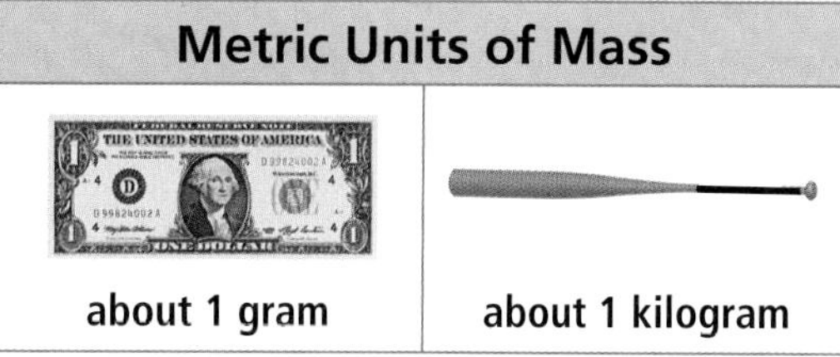

Metric Units of Mass	
about 1 gram	about 1 kilogram

Activity 2 **Materials** ■ spring scale ■ balance ■ kilogram and gram masses ■ classroom objects

- Choose 5 classroom objects. Choose the customary unit and the metric unit you will use to measure the weight or mass of each object. Estimate the weight and mass of each object using the units. Record your estimates in a table like the one shown.
- Choose the tool you will use to measure mass and weight of each object. Then measure the weight and mass of each object using customary and metric units. Record your measurements in the table.

Weight and Mass				
	Customary Units		Metric Units	
Object	Estimate	Actual	Estimate	Actual
dictionary	■	■	■	■
?	■	■	■	■

- How did you decide which units to use to measure the objects?
- How did you decide which tools to use to measure the objects?

Customary Units of Capacity				
1 teaspoon 1 tablespoon	1 cup = 8 fluid ounces	1 pint	1 quart	1 gallon

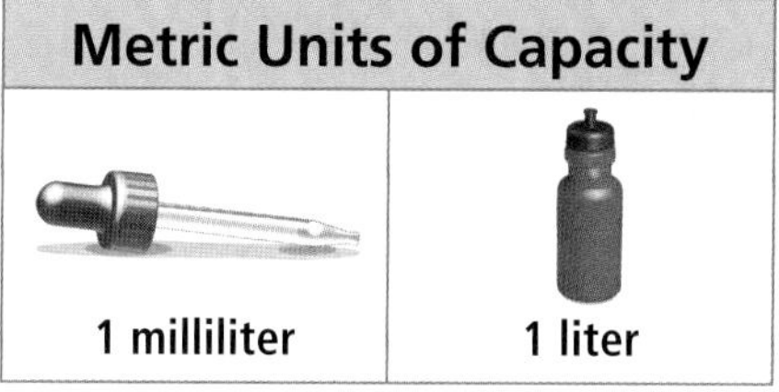

Metric Units of Capacity	
1 milliliter	1 liter

Activity 3 **Materials** ■ 1-cup, 1-pint, 1-quart, 1-gallon containers ■ dropper ■ metric measuring cup ■ 1-liter container ■ containers ■ water

- Choose 5 containers. Choose the customary unit and the metric unit you will use to measure the capacity of each container. Estimate the capacity of each container. Record your estimate in a table like the one shown.
- Choose the tool you will use to measure the capacity of each container. Then measure the capacity. Record your measurements in the table.

Capacity				
	Customary Units		Metric Units	
Object	Estimate	Actual	Estimate	Actual
spoon	■	■	■	■
?	■	■	■	■

- How did you decide which unit to use to measure each capacity?
- How did you decide which tool to use to measure each capacity?

Guided Practice

1. Which customary unit would you use to measure the height of a building? Which metric unit?

Choose the tool and unit to measure each.

Tools	Units	
ruler	lb	g
measuring cup	in.	c
balance	mm	kg
spring scale	gal	km
yard		
meterstick		
odometer		

2. mass of a strawberry
3. capacity of a coffeepot
4. length of a cell phone
5. weight of a puppy
6. mass of a large pumpkin
7. distance traveled on vacation
8. **TALK Math** Natalie has a box and a textbook that are the same size. Do the objects also have the same mass? **Explain.**

Independent Practice and Problem Solving

Choose the tool and unit to measure each.

Tools	Units	
ruler	mi	gal
measuring cup	mL	T
balance	mm	kg
spring scale	lb	cm
dropper		
odometer		

9. capacity of a medicine bottle
10. weight of a table
11. distance between states
12. height of a vase
13. mass of a cat
14. capacity of a pitcher

Write the best unit of measure.

15. length of a football field
16. capacity of a swimming pool
17. weight of a baby

USE DATA For 18–21, use the table.

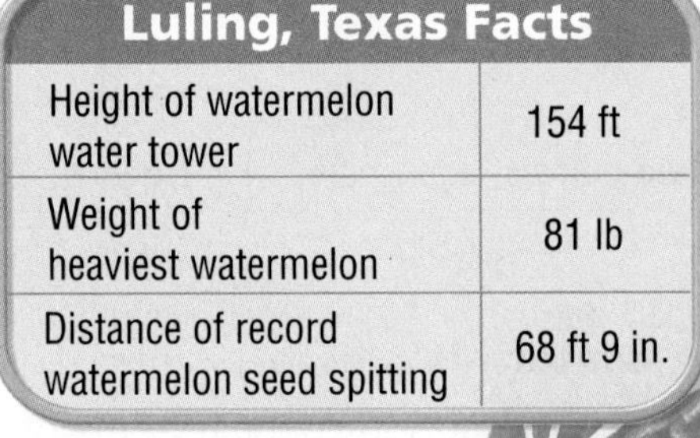

Luling, Texas Facts	
Height of watermelon water tower	154 ft
Weight of heaviest watermelon	81 lb
Distance of record watermelon seed spitting	68 ft 9 in.

18. **Reasoning** Are millimeters a reasonable unit to use to measure the watermelon seed spitting distance? **Explain.**
19. Which metric unit and customary unit would most likely be used to measure the capacity of the water tower?
20. **FAST FACT** Ashburn, Georgia, is the location of the tallest peanut statue in the world. The statue is about 3 meters tall. Which is taller, the peanut statue or the watermelon tower? **Explain.**
21. **WRITE Math** **What's the Question?** Look at the information for the heaviest watermelon. The answer is kilograms.

The 56 foot diameter storage tank and a little green and yellow paint work together to make this huge watermelon water tower in Luling, Texas. Luling is most famous for its "Watermelon Thump," an annual watermelon festival.

 Extra Practice on page 592, Set D

Mixed Review and TAKS Prep

23. Look at the graph below. How many more students chose blue than yellow? (TEKS 4.13B, p. 506)

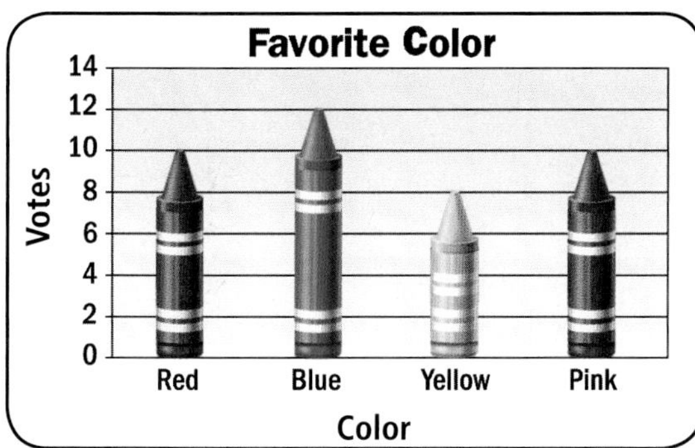

25. TAKS Prep Which customary and metric unit would you use to measure the length of a football field? (Obj. 4)

24. What is the length of the fish to the nearest half centimeter and the nearest millimeter? (TEKS 4.11A, p. 574)

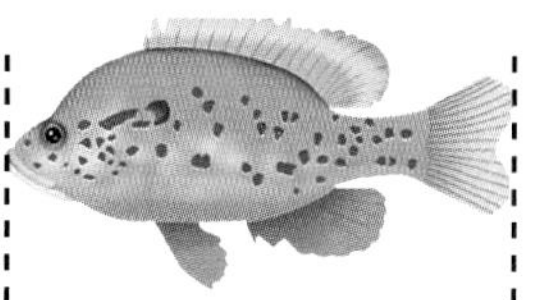

26. TAKS Prep What tool would you use to measure the capacity of a coffee mug? (Obj. 4)

A Meterstick

B Spring scale

C Measuring cup

D Not here

Problem Solving and Reasoning

MEASUREMENT You can use benchmark measurements to relate metric and customary units of length to each other. This relationship can be expressed with the symbol, ≈, which means "is approximately equal to."

Table of Conversions
1 inch is about $2\frac{1}{2}$ centimeters.
1 meter is a little longer than 1 yard.
1 kilometer is a little longer than $\frac{1}{2}$ mile.
1 mile is about 1,600 meters.
1 mile is a little longer than $1\frac{1}{2}$ kilometers.

Example 1

4 in. ≈ ■ cm

Think: 1 in. is about $2\frac{1}{2}$ cm.

$2\frac{1}{2}$ cm	$2\frac{1}{2}$ cm	$2\frac{1}{2}$ cm	$2\frac{1}{2}$ cm
1 in.	1 in.	1 in.	1 in.

$2\frac{1}{2} + 2\frac{1}{2} + 2\frac{1}{2} + 2\frac{1}{2} = 10$ cm

So, 4 in. is about 10 cm.

Example 2

14 m ≈ ■ yd

Think: 1 m is a little longer than 1 yd.

So, 14 m is a little longer than or about equal to 14 yd.

Example 3

3 mi ≈ ■ m

Think: 1 mi is about 1,600 m.

$3 \times 1,600 = 4,800$

So, 3 mi is about 4,800 m.

Estimate the conversion.

1. 9 km ≈ ■ mi

2. 15 cm ≈ ■ in.

3. 123 m ≈ ■ yd

4. 10 mi ≈ ■ m

5. 12 mi ≈ ■ km

6. 7 in. ≈ ■ cm

LESSON 6

Reasonable Estimates

OBJECTIVE: Make reasonable estimates for metric measurements.

Quick Review

1. 28×4
2. 32×6
3. $65 \div 5$
4. 72×3
5. $84 \div 2$

Learn

If you know how metric and customary units of measure are related, you can estimate measurements in metric units.

Customary and Metric Units of Length			
1 in. is about 2.5 cm.	1 m is a little longer than 1 yd.	Walk 1 km in about 10 minutes	Walk 1 mi in about 20 minutes
		1 km is a little longer than $\frac{1}{2}$ mi.	

Activity 1

Materials ■ centimeter ruler ■ inch ruler ■ yardstick ■ meterstick

Antonio wants to know how wide the hallway outside his classroom is. He asks his classmates what they think. Here are the responses he receives:

2 kilometers   2 inches   2 centimeters   2 yards

How can Antonio know which is the most reasonable estimate?

- How can you decide which units are too small?
- How can you decide which estimate is too large?
- How can you decide which estimate is most reasonable and why?

Now, measure to check your estimates.

- How close were your estimates to the actual measurements? Explain.
- **What if** a hiking trail is 3 kilometers, will it take about 30 minutes or 3 hours to hike the trail? Explain.

TEKS 4.11A estimate and use measurement tools to determine length (including perimeter), area, capacity and weight/mass using standard units SI (metric) and customary. *also* **4.1B, 4.14A, 4.14D, 4.15A, 4.15B, 4.16A, 4.16B**

Customary and Metric Units of Weight and Mass

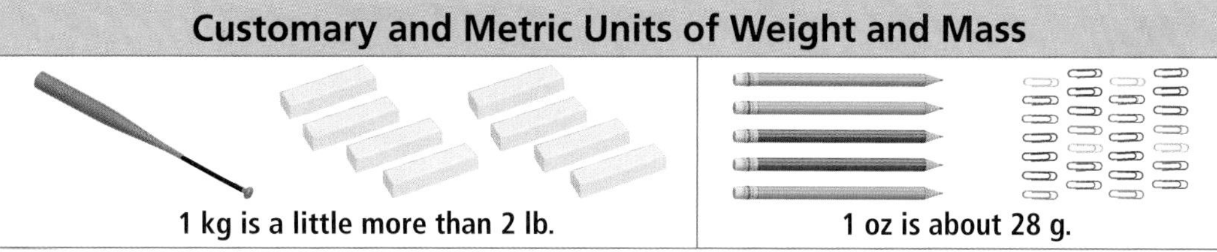

1 kg is a little more than 2 lb.	1 oz is about 28 g.

Activity 2 **Materials** ■ spring scale ■ balance ■ kilogram and gram masses ■ oranges

Jacob and Sophie are buying some fruit at the store. They need to know the weight/mass of 6 oranges. They make a list of what they think.

3 kilograms   3 pounds   3 ounces   3 grams

How can Jacob and Sophie know which is the most reasonable estimate?

- How can you decide which units are too small?
- How can you decide which estimate is too large?
- How can you decide which estimate is most reasonable and why?

Now, measure to check your estimates.

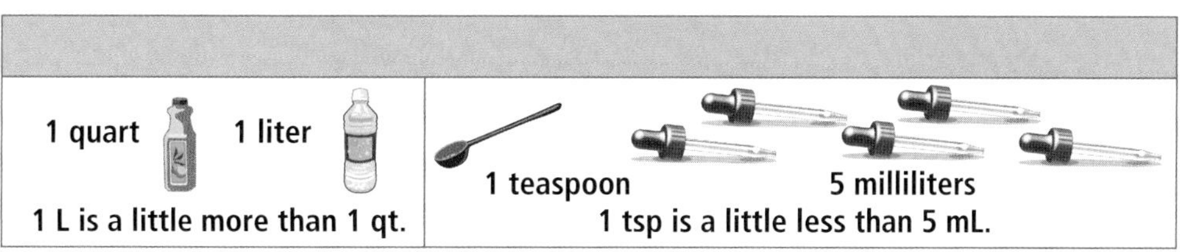

1 L is a little more than 1 qt.	1 tsp is a little less than 5 mL.

Activity 3 **Materials** ■ 1-cup ■ 1-gallon containers ■ dropper ■ 1-liter container ■ water

Olivia's family is planning a picnic. There will be about 50 people at the picnic. Olivia asked her brother and sister how much iced tea is needed for the picnic. Here are the answers she receives:

40 cups   40 liters   40 milliliters   40 gallons

How can Olivia know which is the most reasonable estimate?

- How can you decide which units are too small?
- How can you decide which estimate is too large?
- How can you decide which estimate is most reasonable and why?

Now, measure to check your estimates.

Guided Practice

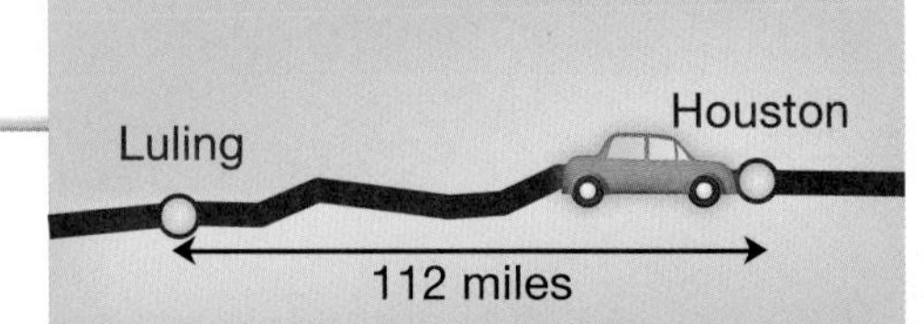

1. Mark traveled 112 miles. About how many kilometers did Mark travel?

Choose the more reasonable estimate.

2. 

1 in. or $\frac{1}{2}$ in.

3. 

10 g or 10 kg

4. 

250 mL or 25 L

5. **TALK Math** Marilyn bought 2 liters of orange juice. Stephen bought 2 quarts of apple juice. Who bought more juice? **Explain.**

Independent Practice and Problem Solving

Choose the more reasonable estimate.

6. 

2,500 km or 2,500 m

7. 

8 c or 1 gal

8. 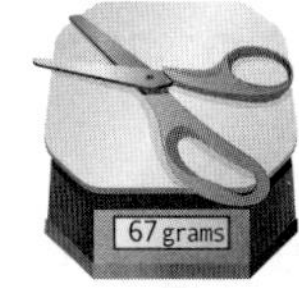

2 oz or 30 oz

USE DATA For 9–12, use the journal entry.

9. What metric unit would you use to measure the distance from El Paso to Hueco Tanks historical site?

10. **Reasoning** Is Guadalupe Peak more than 1 mile tall? **Explain.**

11. About how many gallons of water does the pool in Monahans Sandhills State Park hold?

12. **WRITE Math** **What's the Error?** Milan thinks that the best metric unit to measure the mass of the horse is grams. Is she correct? **Explain.**

My West Texas Outdoor Adventure Tour

Day 1- Today we drove 32 miles from El Paso to Hueco Tanks. Historical site where we climbed HUGE rocks. I think 1 rock weighed 100 pounds!

Day 3- Today we are at Guateloupe National Park. This is the home of the tallest mountain in Texas. Guadalupe Peak is 2,667 meters tall.

Day 5- Today we went sand boarding in Monahans Sandhills State Park. Wow, it was really hot. We went swimming in a big pool. The pool held MORE than 64,000 liters of water! That sure cooled us off.

Day 7- Today was great! We went mountain biking at Fort Davis. There were 75 miles of trails to explore. I rode my new mountain bike. It is light, only 13 kilograms. Tommorrow we are going horseback riding at Big Bend National Park. My dad said the horse I will ride is 800 pounds. This is the best vacation ever!

 Extra Practice on page 592, Set E

Mixed Review and TAKS Prep

13. Which transformation is shown? (TEKS 4.9A, p. 290)

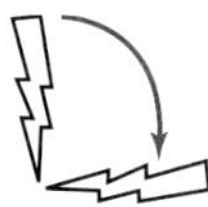

14. Stanley drank 1 liter of water on Monday. He drank 750 milliliters of water on Tuesday. How many milliliters of water did Stanley drink in all? (TEKS 4.11A, p. 580)

15. TAKS Prep Celia bought lunch meat to make sandwiches for her classmates. Which of the following is the most reasonable estimate for the amount of lunch meat she bought? (Obj. 4)

A 2 grams **C** 20 grams

B 2 kilograms **D** 20 kilograms

16. TAKS Prep Joseph hiked the Good Water Trail in Texas. Which is a better estimate of how far he hiked, 16 miles or 1,600 miles? (Obj. 4)

Problem Solving and Reasoning

MEASUREMENT Sometimes an accurate measurement is needed to solve a problem. Sometimes just an estimate is enough. You choose to estimate or measure based on the situation.

Example 1

Julie and her dad need about 3 pounds of fruit to make fruit salad.

estimate

Example 2

The veterinarian needs Casey's weight so he knows how much medicine to give.

accurate measurement

Example 3

Bob needs to cut boards to make a fence around his backyard.

accurate measurement

Decide if you need an *estimate* or an *accurate measurement*.

1. water needed to fill a baby pool

2. medicine a mother gives her sick child

3. orange juice needed for a recipe

4. mass of a packed suitcase

5. distance from home to school

6. length of "cut to fit" silver necklace

Extra Practice

Set A Choose the most reasonable unit of measure. Write *mm*, *cm*, *dm*, *m*, or *km*. (pp. 574–576)

1. 
2. 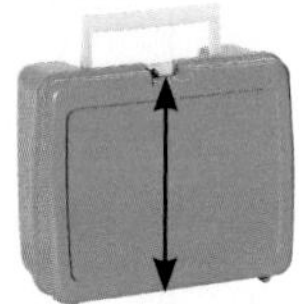
3. 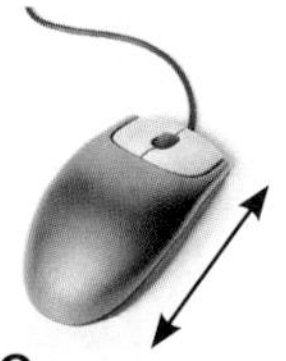

Estimate the length to the nearest centimeter. Then measure to the nearest half centimeter. Write your answer as a decimal.

4. 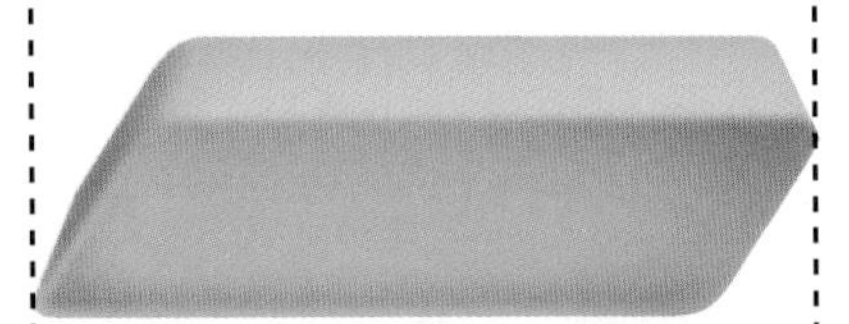
5. 

Set B Choose the more reasonable measurement. (pp. 578–579)

1. 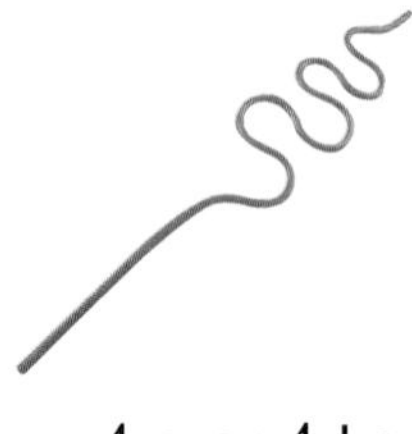
4 g or 4 kg
2. 

36 kg or 36 g
3. 
5 kg or 50 kg

Set C Choose the most reasonable measurement. Write *a*, *b*, or *c*. (pp. 580–581)

1. 
   a. 20 L
   b. 200 L
   c. 200 mL
2. 
   a. 120 mL
   b. 12 L
   c. 12 mL
3. 
   a. 40 mL
   b. 40 L
   c. 4 L

Set D Choose the tool and unit to measure each. (pp. 584–586)

1. weight of a book
2. distance to the next state
3. height of a doll
4. mass of a bag of flour

Tool	Unit	
ruler	mi	gal
measuring cup	mL	T
balance	mm	kg
spring scale	lb	cm
odometer		

Set E Choose the more reasonable estimate. (pp. 588–590)

1. 

2 L or 2 mL
2. 
330 g or 330 kg
3. 
1 m or 1 km

Technology
Use Harcourt Mega Math, Ice Station Exploration, *Linear Lab*, Level I.

PRACTICE GAME Centimeter Swim

Swimmers!

2–4 players

Get Set!

- Construction paper
- Scissors
- Centimeter rulers
- Measurement cards
- 4 different coins

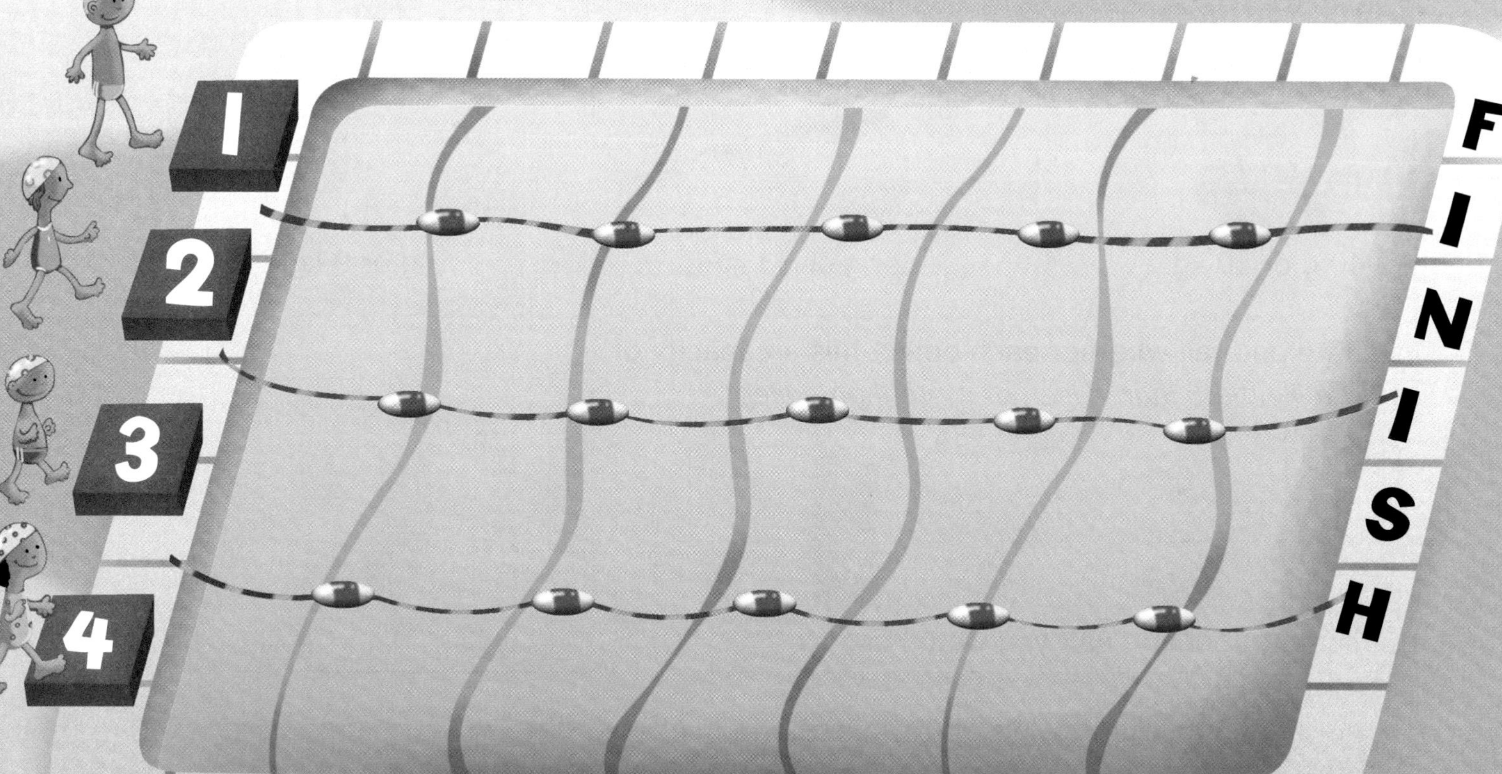

Swim!

- Each player selects a different coin and places the coin on one of starting blocks.
- Players shuffle the cards and place them facedown in a stack. The top card is turned face up for the starting measurement.
- Each player cuts a strip of paper he or she estimates to be equal to the measurement shown on the card.
- Players use rulers to measure his or her strip. The player closest to the exact measurement moves his or her marker one space.
- Players take turns turning the top card face up and repeat the activity.
- The first player to reach the end of the pool wins.

Chapter 22 Review/Test

Check Vocabulary and Concepts

Choose the best term from the box.

VOCABULARY
centimeter
liter
mass
meter

1. A metric unit that is about the width of your finger is a _?_. (TEKS 4.11A, p. 574)
2. The amount of matter an object contains is called _?_. (TEKS 4.11A, p. 578)
3. A _?_ is a metric unit of capacity. (TEKS 4.11A, p. 580)

Check Skills

Choose the more reasonable measurement. (TEKS 4.11A, pp. 578–579)

4. 

40 g or 40 kg

5. 

23 g or 23 kg

6. 

9 g or 9 kg

Estimate and tell whether each object has a capacity of *about a liter, less than a liter,* or *more than a liter.* (TEKS 4.11A, pp. 576–577)

7. 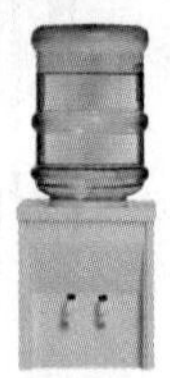

8. 

9. 

Choose the tool and unit you would use to measure each. (TEKS 4.11A, pp. 580–583)

10. height of a door
11. weight of a bag of apples
12. capacity of a mug
13. distance to Michigan

Tools	Units	
ruler	km	gal
measuring cup	mL	T
balance	in.	kg
spring scale	lb	m
dropper		
odometer		

Check Problem Solving

Solve. (TEKS 4.14C, pp. 582–583)

14. Angie waters the 2 plants in her room once each week. One plant gets 200 milliliters of water, and the other gets 300 milliliters. How much water, in liters, does Angie give her plants in 6 weeks?

15. **WRITE Math** Michael is making batches of pizza dough. He needs 6 cups of flour for 2 batches and 15 cups for 5 batches. **Explain** how Michael can find how much flour he needs for 8 batches of dough.

Technology Use *Online Assessment.*

Enrich • Change SI (Metric) Units

All About Armadillos

The official mammal of Texas is the nine-banded armadillo. An adult nine-banded armadillo weighs about 7 kilograms. How many grams does a nine-banded armadillo weigh?

To change from a larger unit to a smaller unit, you need more of them, so multiply. To change from a smaller unit to a larger unit, you need fewer of them, so divide.

Equivalent Measures

1 centimeter (cm)	=	10 millimeters (mm)
1 decimeter (dm)	=	10 centimeters (cm)
1 meter (m)	=	1,000 millimeters (mm)
1 kilometer (km)	=	1,000 meters (m)
1 liter (L)	=	1,000 milliliters (mL)
1 kilogram (kg)	=	1,000 grams (g)

Example 1 Use multiplication.

7 kg = ■ g

Think: 1kg = 1,000 g, so multiply the number of kg by 1,000.

1 kg = 1,000 g
7 × 1,000 = 7,000
7 kg = 7,000 g

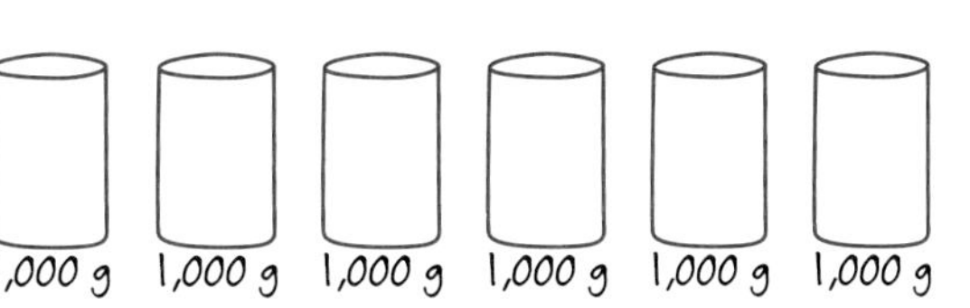

So, a nine-banded armadillo weighs about 7,000 grams.

A nine-banded armadillo digs a burrow that is about 20 centimeters wide. How many decimeters wide is the burrow?

Example 2 Use division.

20 cm = ■ dm

Think: 10 cm = 1 dm, so divide the number of cm by 10.

1 dm = 10 cm
20 ÷ 10 = 2
20 cm = 2 dm

10 cm	10 cm
1 dm	1 dm

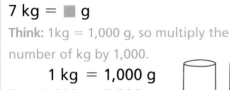

You can divide 20 by 10 with a calculator.

2 0 ÷ 1 0 Enter = 20 ÷ 10 = 2

So, the burrow is about 2 decimeters wide.

Try It

Complete. Tell whether to *multiply* or *divide*.

1. An armadillo drank 3,000 milliliters of water. How many liters did the armadillo drink?

2. An armadillo's tail is about 40 centimeters long. How many millimeters long is an armadillo's tail?

WRITE Math A nine-banded armadillo's body is about 40 centimeters long. What is the length in decimeters of two Nine-Banded Armadillos? **Explain.**

Getting Ready for the TAKS
Chapters 1–22

Number, Operation, and Quantitative Reasoning TAKS Obj. 1

1. There are 586 students in the fourth grade at Eugene's school. Which shows the number 586 rounded to the nearest hundred?

   A 500

   B 550

   C 600

   D 650

Understand the problem.

See item 2. Read the problem carefully. What operation should you use to find how many people are invited to the recital?

2. There are 7 students in Gina's piano class. Each student invites 5 people to a recital. How many people are invited to the recital in all?

   F 35

   G 30

   H 25

   J 20

3. **WRITE Math** There are 6 people in Mitchell's family. Each person read 10 books. How many books did Mitchell's family read altogether? **Explain** how you know.

Patterns, Relationships, and Algebraic Thinking TAKS Obj. 2

4. Paul wrote the division sentence shown below on the board.

   $$24 \div 6 = \blacksquare$$

   Which number sentence is in the same fact family?

   A $4 \times 6 = 24$

   B $5 \times 5 = 25$

   C $6 \times 3 = 18$

   D $6 \times 6 = 36$

5. Which rule can be used to show the relationship in the ordered pairs below?

Input, x	1	2	3	4
Output, y	4	5	6	7

   F Add 1 to x.

   G Add 2 to x.

   H Add 3 to x.

   J Add 4 to x.

6. **WRITE Math** A saltwater crocodile is about 17 feet long. Alex says he can add the products of the multiplication sentences 17×10 and 17×2 to find how long a saltwater crocodile is in inches. Is he correct? **Explain.**

Measurement TAKS Obj. 4

7. An adult cat weighs about 5 kilograms. How many grams does an adult cat weigh?

A 50 grams

B 500 grams

C 5,000 grams

D Not here

8. Centimeters are the most reasonable measurement unit for which object below?

F 

H 

G 

J 

9. WRITE Math Which tool would you use to measure the length of a hallway, a ruler or a yard stick? **Explain** how you know.

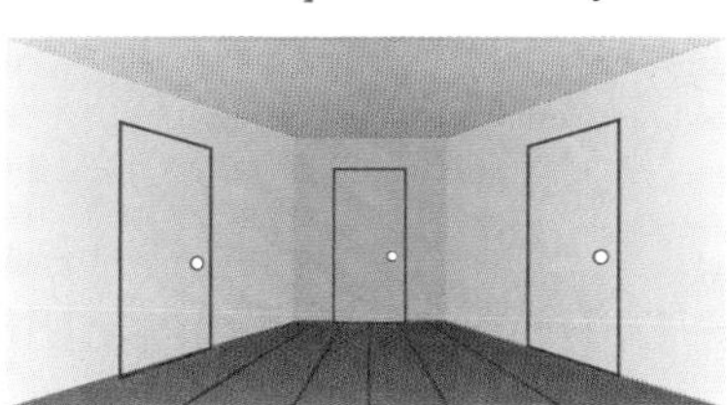

Probability and Statistics TAKS Obj. 5

10. Brian is making a flower display. He can choose lilies, roses, or daisies, and a red, yellow, or blue vase. How many combinations are possible?

A 3

B 6

C 9

D 12

11. The graph below shows the results of a survey of favorite colors.

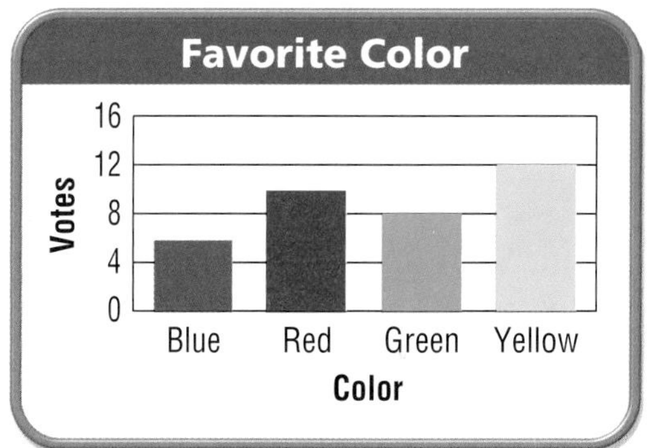

Which color received 10 votes?

F Blue

G Red

H Green

J Yellow

12. WRITE Math Bree is making a scrapbook page. She can choose pink or green paper. She can decorate the page with stickers or stamps. How many combinations are possible? **Explain.**

23 Perimeter and Area

The Big Idea Attributes of two- and three-dimensional figures can be measured.

Investigate

Archaeologists divide a dig area into smaller work sites. Suppose you are working on an archaeological dig. Your job is to lay out rectangular work sites with the areas shown in the table. Use models. In how many different ways could you set up each site?

Archaeological Dig Sites

Work Site	Area (in square feet)
A	20
B	24
C	30
D	36

TEXAS FAST FACT

Caddoan Mounds State Historic Site is a park near Alto, Texas. The Caddoan people lived here from about A.D. 800 to 1300. At the park, you can visit one of their villages.

GO ONLINE **Technology** Student pages are available in the Student eBook.

Show What You Know

Check your understanding of important skills needed for success in Chapter 23.

▶ Add Whole Numbers

Find the sum.

1. $5 + 6 + 8 = \blacksquare$ **2.** $9 + 4 + 2 + 7 = \blacksquare$ **3.** $2 + 6 + 9 + 1 + 5 = \blacksquare$

4. $11 + 27 + 18 = \blacksquare$ **5.** $5 + 46 + 28 + 31 = \blacksquare$ **6.** $53 + 21 + 66 + 34 = \blacksquare$

▶ Multiplication Facts

Find the product.

7. $8 \times 3 = \blacksquare$ **8.** $9 \times 8 = \blacksquare$ **9.** $12 \times 5 = \blacksquare$ **10.** $5 \times 6 = \blacksquare$

11. $6 \times 6 = \blacksquare$ **12.** $9 \times 7 = \blacksquare$ **13.** $8 \times 5 = \blacksquare$ **14.** $7 \times 4 = \blacksquare$

▶ Expressions and Variables

Find the value of the expression.

15. $a \times 3$ if $a = 9$

16. $7 + f + 18$ if $f = 13$

17. $7 \times c$ if $c = 5$

18. $s + 13 + 46$ if $s = 8$

19. $26 + 34 + r + 78$ if $r = 23$

20. $6 \times g$ if $g = 12$

21. $38 + h + 51$ if $h = 10$

22. $y \times 8$ if $y = 8$

VOCABULARY POWER

CHAPTER VOCABULARY

area
formula
perimeter
square unit (sq un)

WARM-UP WORDS

perimeter the distance around a figure

formula a set of symbols that expresses a mathematical rule

area the number of square units needed to cover a surface

LESSON 1 HANDS ON

Estimate and Measure Perimeter

OBJECTIVE: Estimate and measure perimeter.

Quick Review

What is the length of the pen cap to the nearest centimeter?

Vocabulary

perimeter

Investigate

Materials ■ string ■ scissors ■ centimeter ruler ■ meterstick ■ 3 classroom objects

You can use string and a ruler to help you estimate and measure the perimeter of an object or a figure. **Perimeter** is the distance around a figure.

A Make a table to record the names, units, estimates, and actual measurements of 3 classroom objects.

Perimeter of Classroom Objects			
Object	Unit	Estimate	Actual Measurement
?	■	■	■
?	■	■	■

B Choose the unit you would use to measure the perimeter of each object. Then estimate and record the estimated perimeter of each object.

C Now use string to measure the perimeter of each object. Place string around the outside of the object. Cut or mark the string to show the perimeter. Then measure and record the length of the string in the units you used to estimate.

Draw Conclusions

1. How did you estimate the perimeter of the objects?
2. How did you choose which unit to use to measure the perimeter of each object?
3. How do your measurements compare to your estimates? Were your estimates reasonable? Explain.
4. **APPLICATION** What unit would you use to meaure the perimeter of your classroom? Explain.

TEKS 4.11A estimate and use measurement tools to determine length (including perimeter), area, capacity and weight/mass using standard units SI (metric) and customary. *also* **4.3A, 4.14A, 4.14D, 4.15A, 4.15B**

Connect

You can find the perimeter of a rectangle on a geoboard or dot paper by counting the number of units on each side.

This rectangle is 2 units wide and 4 units long. So, the perimeter of the rectangle is 4 units + 2 units + 4 units + 2 units, or 12 units.

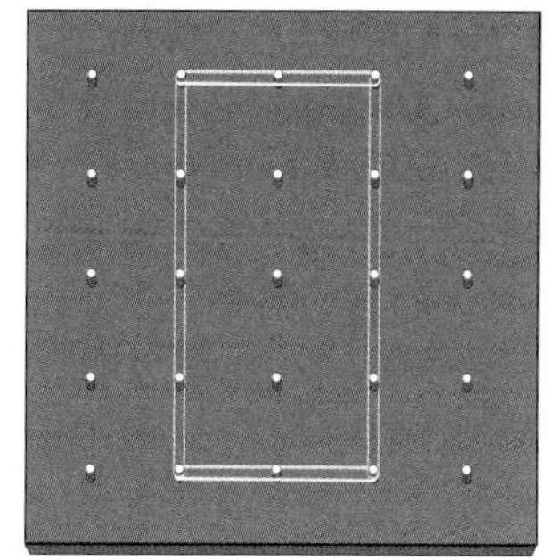

TALK Math

Explain how to find the perimeter of a square with sides 5 units long.

Practice

Use string to estimate and measure the perimeter of each object.

1. a sheet of notebook paper
2. an index card
3. a chalkboard eraser
4. your desk

Find the perimeter of each figure.

5. 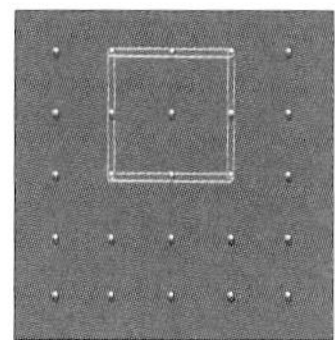
6. 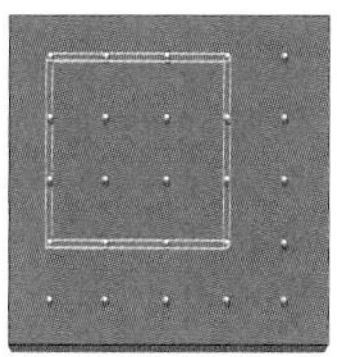
7. 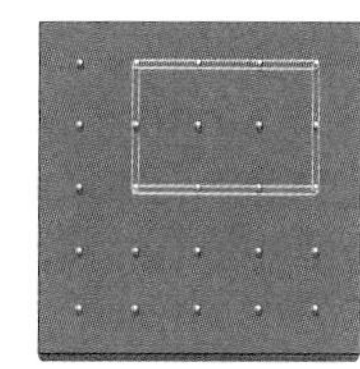
8. 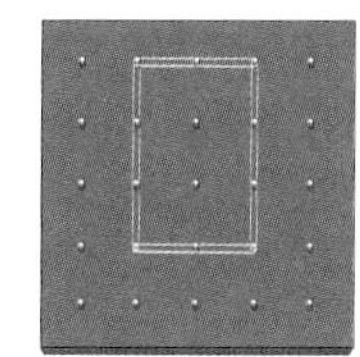
9. 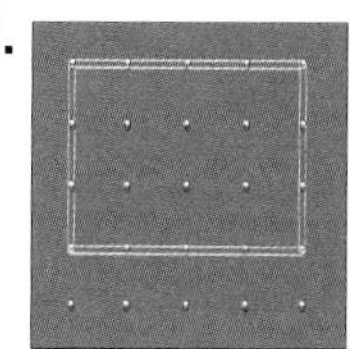

Use dot paper or grid paper to draw a rectangle with the given perimeter. Then record the lengths of the sides.

10. 10 units
11. 20 units
12. 14 units
13. 12 units
14. 24 units
15. 16 units
16. 18 units
17. 26 units

Zach is helping his dad build a rectangular sandbox that has a perimeter of 24 feet.

18. On dot paper or grid paper, draw the different rectangular sandboxes that Zach and his dad could build. Label the length of each side.
19. **WRITE Math** Zach and his dad decide to make a sandbox that is square. What dimensions could they use? **Explain.**

LESSON 2

Perimeter

OBJECTIVE: Estimate and measure perimeter.

1. 115 ÷ 3
2. 96 ÷ 12
3. 20 + 4 + 20 + 4
4. 48 + 5 + 6 + 23
5. 89 × 36

Learn

PROBLEM Kurt's father is putting a fence around his pool and deck. The space is a rectangle 60 feet long and 30 feet wide. Fencing is sold by the yard. How many yards of fencing does Kurt's father need?

You can use grid paper to find the perimeter of a figure by counting the number of grid squares on each side of the figure.

Activity 1 **Materials** ■ grid paper

- Draw a rectangle 3 units long and 6 units wide on grid paper to represent the pool and deck. Estimate the perimeter.
- Count the number of units on each side to find the perimeter. The perimeter of the pool and deck is 18 units. Since each unit stands for 10 feet, the perimeter is 18 × 10 = 180 feet.
  To change feet to yards, divide by 3. 180 ÷ 3 = 60 yards

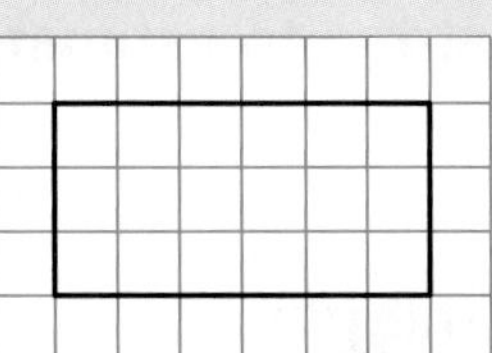

Side of 1 grid square = 10 feet

So, Kurt's father needs 60 yards of fencing.

You can also estimate and measure the perimeter of some objects using string and a ruler or grid paper.

Activity 2 **Materials** ■ string ■ ruler ■ 3 classroom objects

- Trace the outline of 3 classroom objects on grid paper. Estimate the perimeter of each object. Record.
- Now place the string around the outline of each object. Cut or mark the string to show the perimeter of each object. Then record the actual perimeter of each object.

Perimeter of Classroom Objects

Object	Unit	Estimate	Actual Measurement
stapler	■	■	■
?	■	■	■

Guided Practice

1. Count the units. What is the perimeter of this figure?

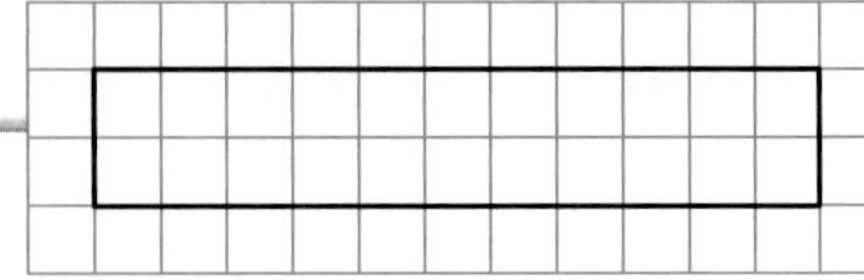

TEKS 4.11A estimate and use measurement tools to determine length (including perimeter), area, capacity and weight/mass using standard units SI (metric) and customary. *also* **4.3A, 4.11B, 4.14A, 4.14D, 4.15A, 4.15B**

Find the perimeter.

2. 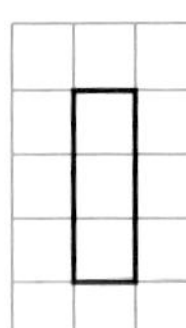

3. 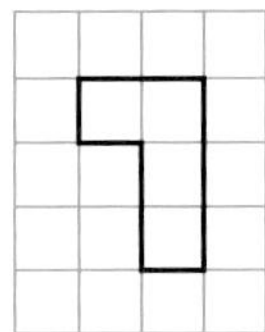

4. 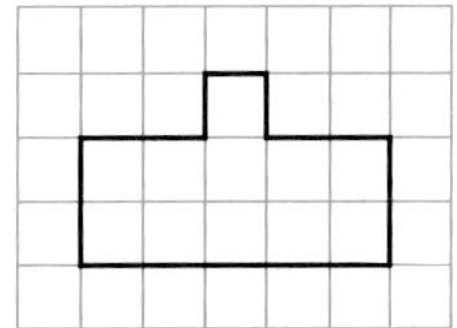

5. 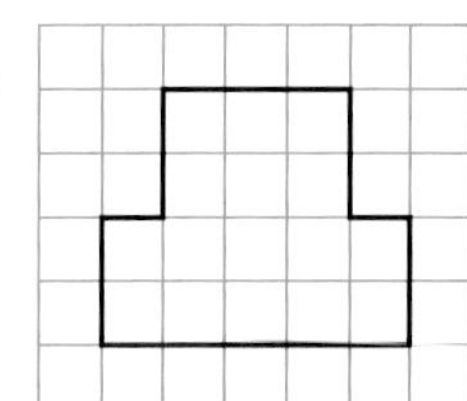

6. **TALK Math** Andrew drew a square on grid paper. **Explain** how he can use multiplication to find the perimeter of the square.

Independent Practice and Problem Solving

Find the perimeter.

7. 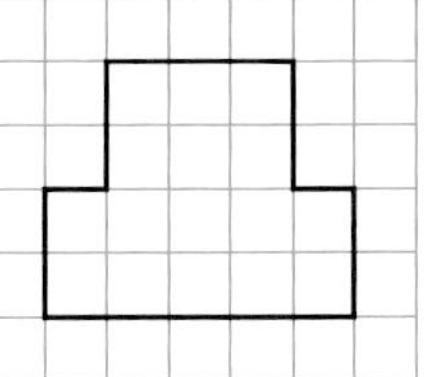

8. 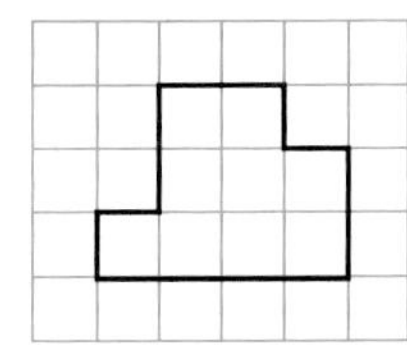

9. 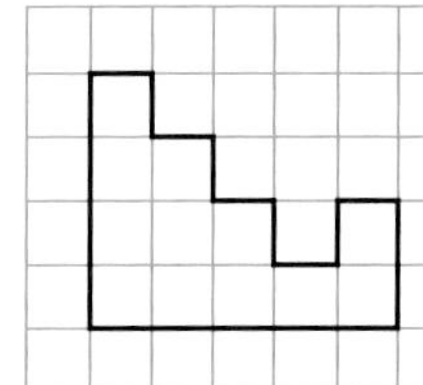

10. 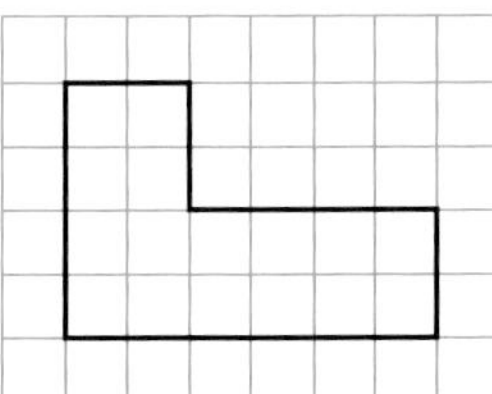

11. 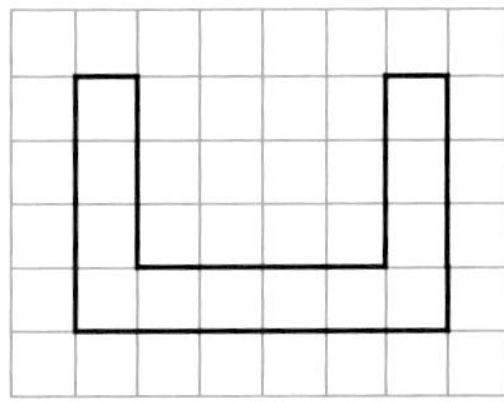

12. 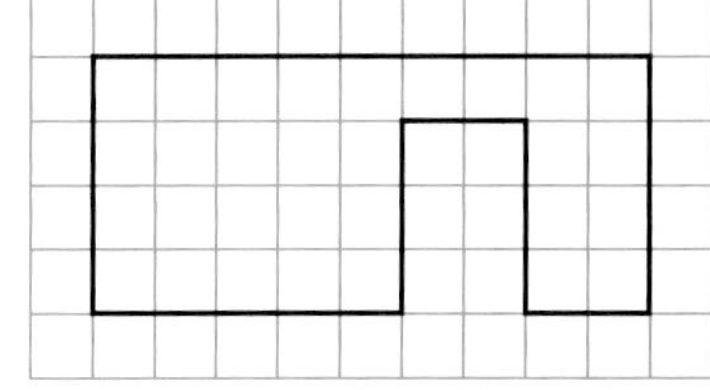

USE DATA For 13–15, use the map.

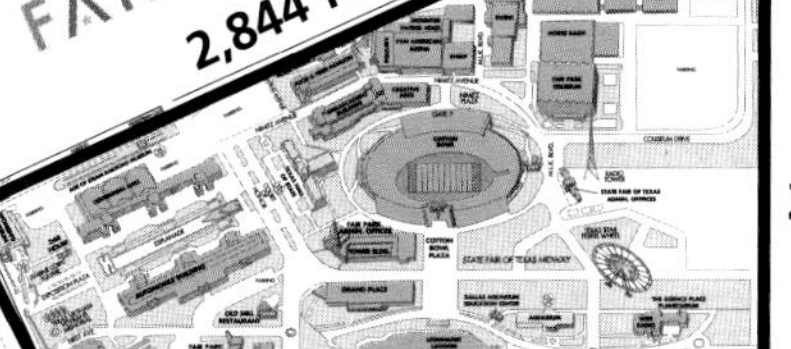

13. ***FAST FACT*** The Texas State Fair has been held at Fair Park since 1886. Estimate the perimeter of Fair Park.

14. **Reasoning** There is a parking lot at the park that is shaped like a square. The parking lot is about 660 feet wide. What is the perimeter of the parking lot in yards? **Explain.**

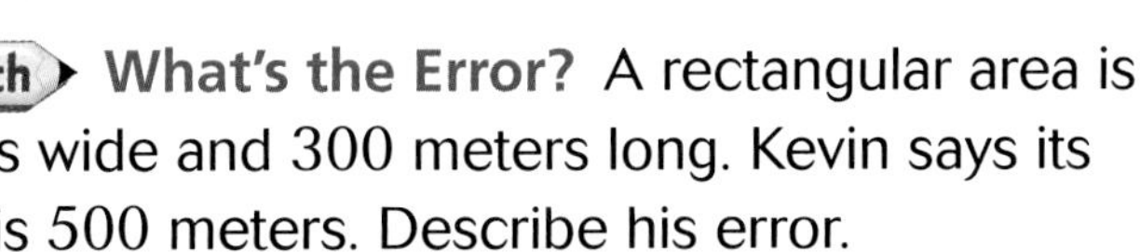

15. **WRITE Math** **What's the Error?** A rectangular area is 200 meters wide and 300 meters long. Kevin says its perimeter is 500 meters. Describe his error.

Mixed Review and TAKS Prep

16. Tom drank 2 glasses of lemonade. Did he drink about 500 milliliters or 5 liters? (TEKS 4.11A, p. 580)

17. Write the fact family for $5 \times 6 = 30$. (TEKS 4.6A, p. 118)

18. **TAKS Prep** What is the perimeter of this figure? (Obj. 4)

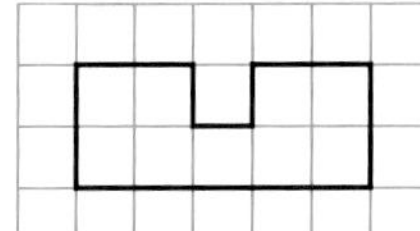

Extra Practice on page 624, Set A

LESSON 3

ALGEBRA

Find Perimeter

OBJECTIVE: Use a formula to find perimeter.

Quick Review

1. 16 + 19 + 21
2. (2 × 4) + (2 × 10)
3. 55 + 31 + 65 + 29
4. (2 × 12) + (2 × 11)
5. 9 + 13 + 8 + 17 + 22

Vocabulary

formula

Learn

PROBLEM Julio is putting a stone border around his garden. How many feet long is the border of Julio's garden?

To find how many feet of stones Julio needs, find the perimeter of the garden.

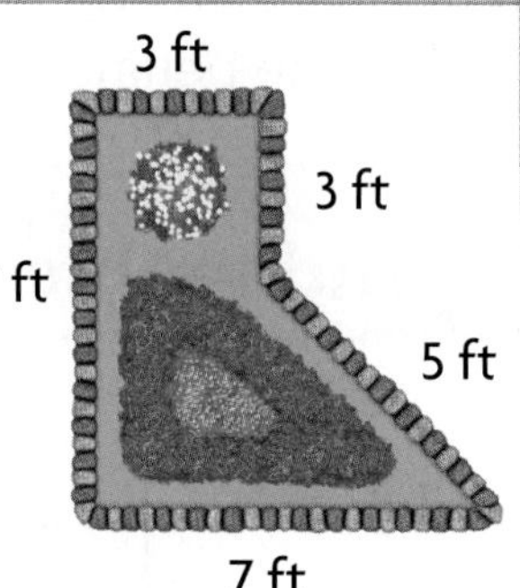

Example **Add the lengths of the sides.**

3 ft + 3 ft + 5 ft + 7 ft + 7 ft = 25 ft

So, Julio needs 25 feet of stones.

More Examples **Find the perimeter.**

A **Figure A**

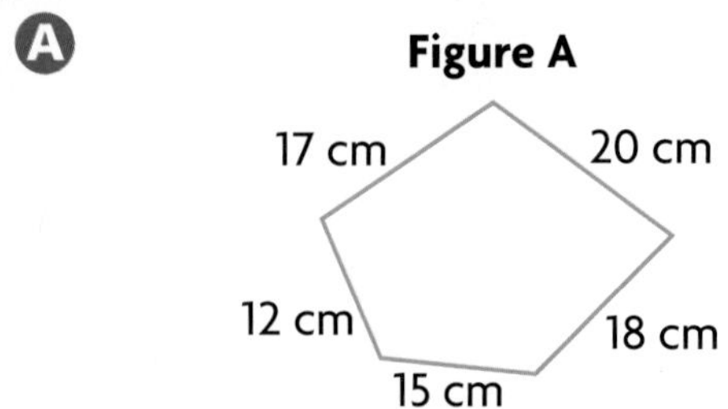

P = sum of the lengths of the sides

$P = 20 + 17 + 12 + 15 + 18$

$P = 82$

So, the perimeter of Figure A is 82 cm.

B **Figure B**

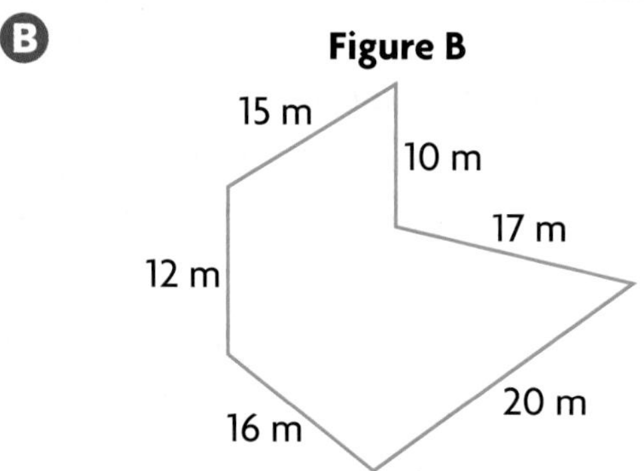

P = sum of the lengths of the sides

$P = 15 + 12 + 16 + 20 + 17 + 10$

$P = 90$

So, the perimeter of Figure B is 90 m.

- Describe some situations in which you might need to find perimeter.
- What do you notice about the number of sides in each figure and the number of addends?

TEKS **4.11A** estimate and use measurement tools to determine length (including perimeter), area, capacity and weight/mass using standard units SI (metric) and customary. *also* **4.3A, 4.3B, 4.14A, 4.14D, 4.15A, 4.15B, 4.16A**

Perimeter of Rectangles and Squares

A **formula**, or mathematical rule, can also be used to find perimeter.

You can use special formulas to find the perimeter of a rectangle and a square.

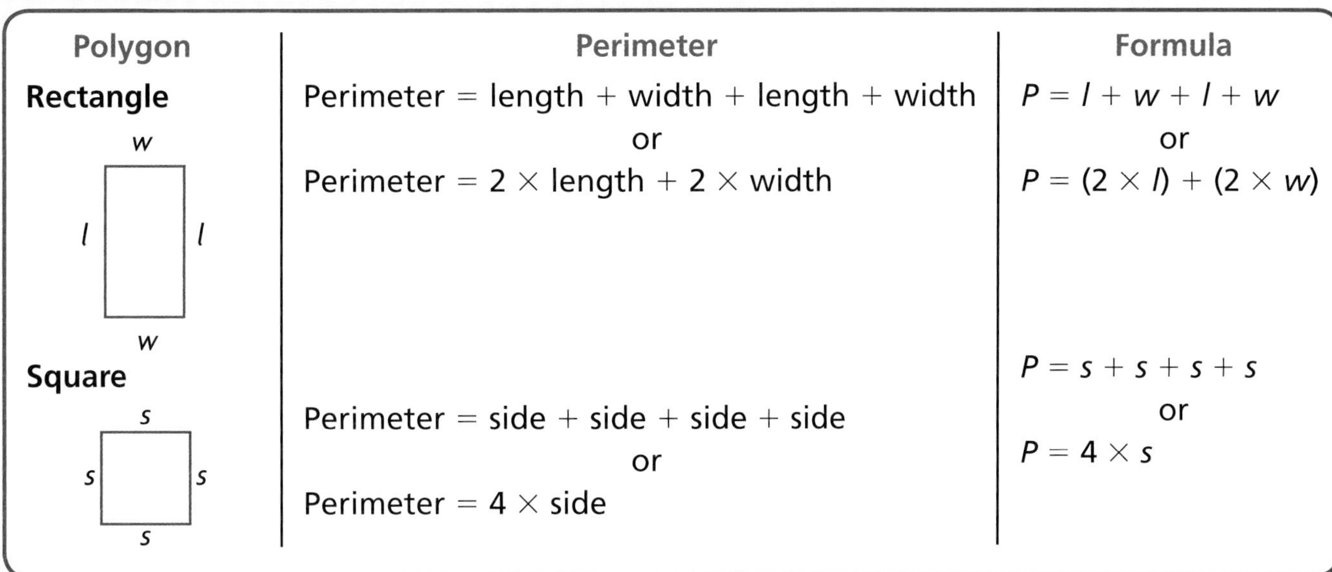

Polygon	Perimeter	Formula
Rectangle (sides w, l, l, w)	Perimeter = length + width + length + width or Perimeter = 2 × length + 2 × width	$P = l + w + l + w$ or $P = (2 \times l) + (2 \times w)$
Square (sides s, s, s, s)	Perimeter = side + side + side + side or Perimeter = 4 × side	$P = s + s + s + s$ or $P = 4 \times s$

Examples **Use a formula.**

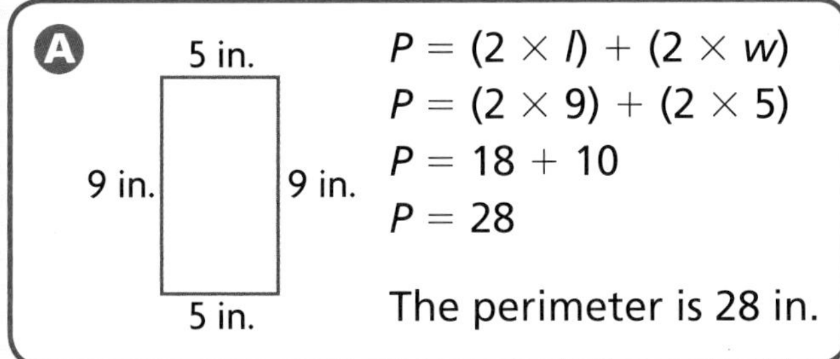

$P = (2 \times l) + (2 \times w)$
$P = (2 \times 9) + (2 \times 5)$
$P = 18 + 10$
$P = 28$

The perimeter is 28 in.

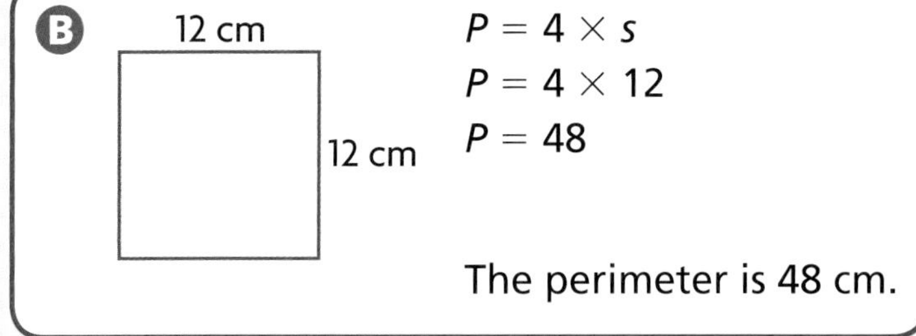

$P = 4 \times s$
$P = 4 \times 12$
$P = 48$

The perimeter is 48 cm.

- If you know the perimeter of a square, how can you find the length of each side?

Guided Practice

1. Add the lengths of the sides. What is the perimeter of this figure?

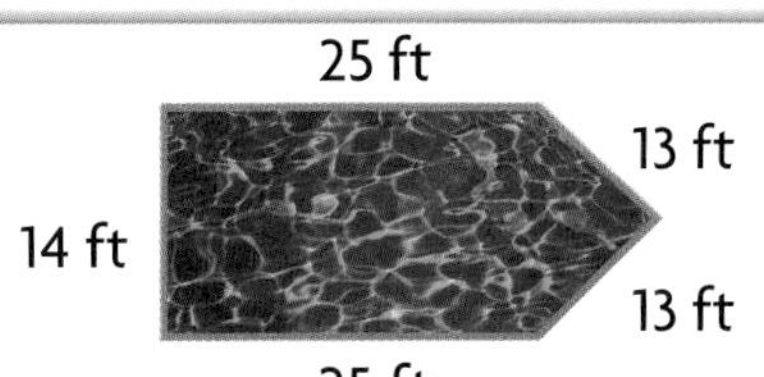

Find the perimeter.

2.

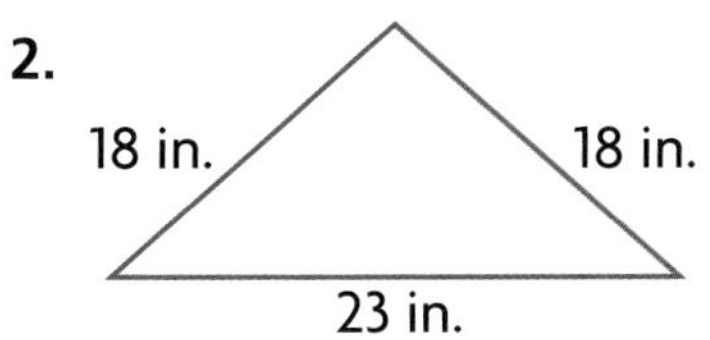

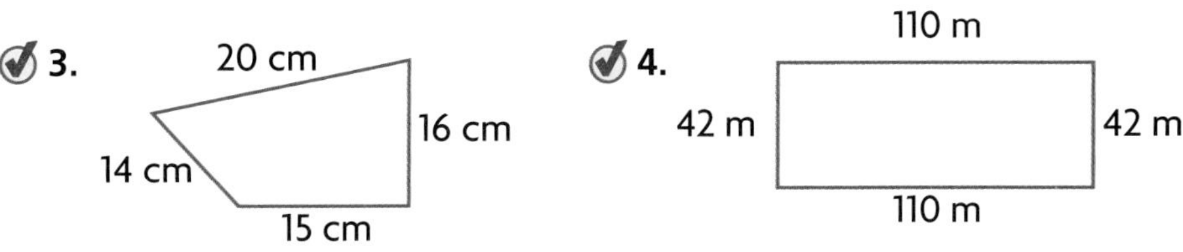

5. **TALK Math** All the sides of a pentagon are 6 decimeters long. **Explain** how you can use multiplication to find the perimeter.

Independent Practice and Problem Solving

Find the perimeter.

6. 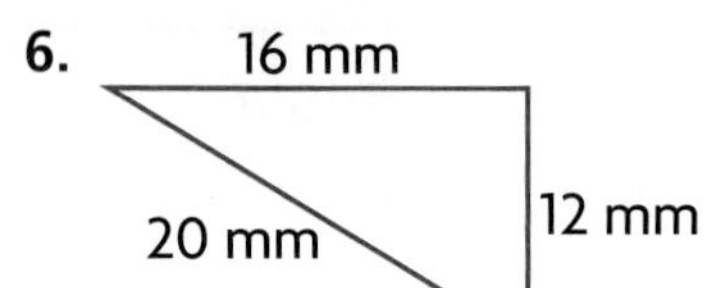

7. 26 in.
26 in.

8. 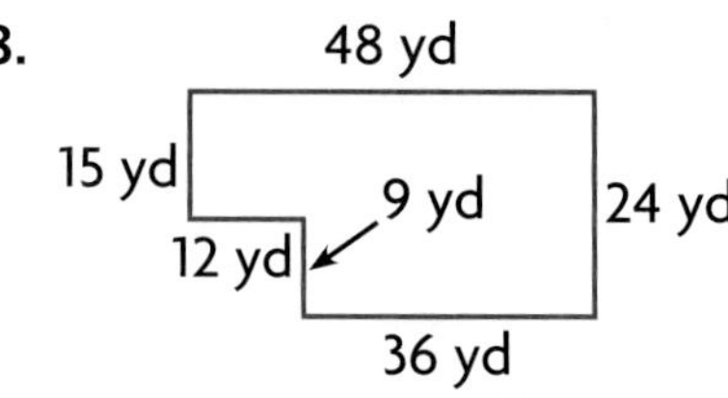

9. 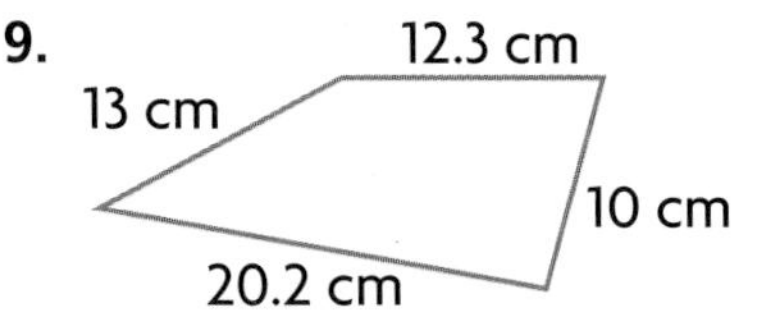

10. 9 ft 9 ft
13 ft 13 ft
9 ft 9 ft

11. 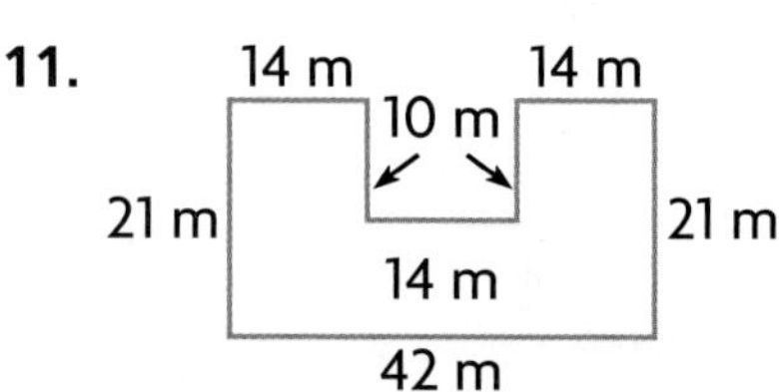

Use a formula to find the perimeter.

12. 116 ft
116 ft

13. 11 dm
33 dm

14. 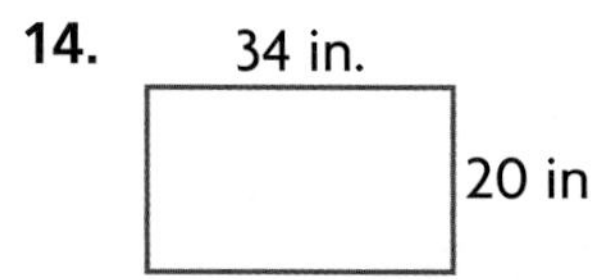

Measure with a centimeter ruler to find each perimeter.

15. 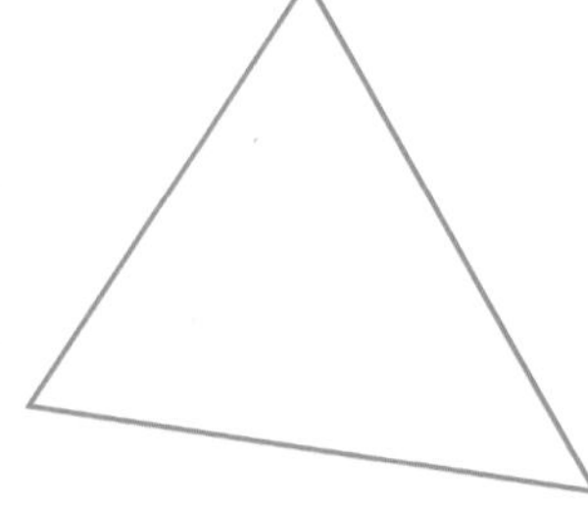

16. 

17. 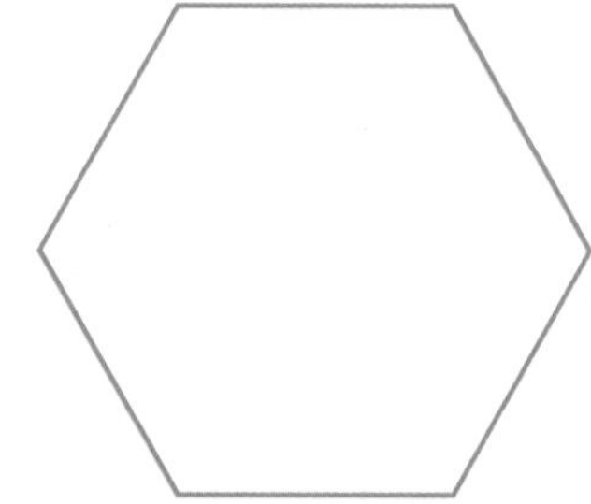

18. **Reasoning** A square and an equilateral triangle both have a perimeter of 36 centimeters. Draw and label the figures.

19. **Reasoning** The perimeter of a rectangle is 30 inches. The width of the rectangle is 5 inches. What is the length?

20. Mary is putting a brick edge around her patio. Her patio is shaped like a hexagon. Each side of the patio is 4 yards long. The bricks she is using are 12 inches long. How many bricks does Mary need? **Explain.**

21. **WRITE Math** **Sense or Nonsense** Tim wants to frame a square painting. One side of the painting is 4 feet long. He says 5 yards of frame is enough for the painting. Does this make sense? **Explain.**

Technology
CD ROM Use Harcourt Mega Math, Ice Station Exploration, *Polar Planes*, Level P.

 Extra Practice on page 624, Set B

Mixed Review and TAKS Prep

22. Lynn is selecting outfits from the shirts and pants shown. She can select 1 shirt and 1 pair of pants. List all the different outfits Lynn can make. (TEKS 4.13A, p. 524)

23. Jimmy cut 4 pieces of ribbon that were each 36 inches long. Does he have more or less than 3 yards of ribbon cut? (TEKS 4.11B, p. 574)

24. TAKS Prep What is the perimeter of this figure? (Obj. 4)

40 in.

13 in.

A 53 inches

B 66 inches

C 106 inches

D 520 inches

25. TAKS Prep What is the perimeter of a square with sides 16 centimeters long? **Explain.** (Obj. 4)

Problem Solving and Reasoning

ALGEBRA A **regular polygon** is a polygon that has all sides equal in length and all angles equal in measure. You can use a formula to find the perimeter.

Since all sides of a regular polygon are the same length, use the formula $P = n \times s$, in which n is the number of sides in the polygon and s is the length of each side.

Examples Find the perimeter.

A pentagon

$P = n \times s$

$P = 5 \times 12$ ← There are 5 sides in a pentagon so replace n with 5. The sides are each 12 inches long, so replace s with 12.

$P = 60$ in.

The perimeter is 60 inches.

B octagon

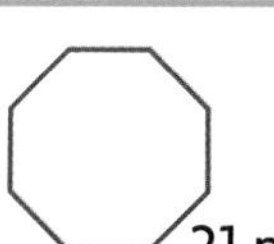

$P = n \times s$

$P = 8 \times 21$ ← There are 8 sides in an octagon so replace n with 8. The sides are each 21 meters long, so replace s with 21.

$P = 168$ m

The perimeter is 168 meters.

Write a formula and use it to find the perimeter.

1. 35 mm

2. 16 ft

3. 25 yd

4. 19 km

Problem Solving Workshop
Strategy: Compare Strategies

OBJECTIVE: Compare different strategies to solve problems.

Use the Strategy

PROBLEM Alicia is sewing fringe on a triangular scarf. She has one more side left to sew. The perimeter of the scarf is 96 inches. How many inches of fringe does she need to finish the scarf?

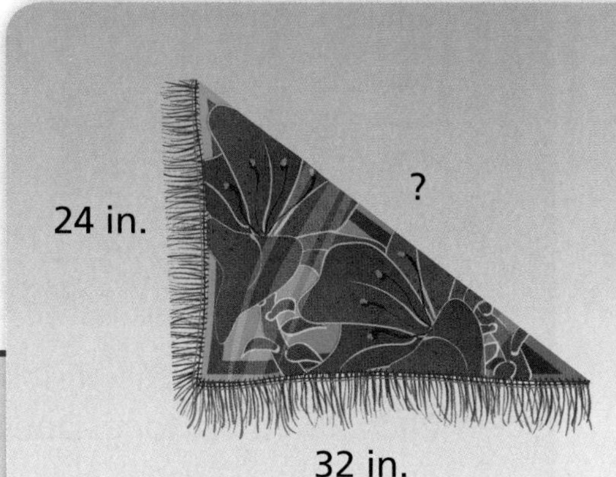

Read to Understand

- **Read the graphic aid.**
- **What information is given?**

Plan

- **What strategy can you use to solve the problem?**

  Sometimes you can use more than one strategy to solve a problem. You can *work backward* or *write an equation* to help you solve this problem.

Solve

- **How can you use the strategies to solve the problem?**

Work backward

Work backward by subtracting the given side lengths from the perimeter.

perimeter ↓ side 1 ↓

$96 - 24 = 72$

side 2 ↓ side 3 ↓

$72 - 32 = 40$

So, Alicia needs 40 inches of fringe.

Write an equation

The perimeter of a figure is the sum of the lengths of its sides. Write an equation to find the length of the unknown side.

$96 = 24 + 32 + c$ Let c represent the length of the unknown side.

$96 = 56 + c$ Add.

$96 - 56 = c$ Subtracting 56 is the inverse operation to adding 56.

$40 = c$

Check

- **How can you check your answer?**

TEKS 4.14C select or develop an appropriate problem-solving strategy, including drawing a picture, looking for a pattern, systematic guessing and checking, acting it out, making a table, working a simpler problem, or working backwards to solve a problem. *also* **4.3A, 4.11A, 4.14A, 4.14B, 4.14D, 4.15A, 4.15B, 4.16B**

Guided Problem Solving

1. Emanuel is sewing a satin border around a square blanket. The perimeter of the blanket is 16 feet. What is the length of each side?

   First, decide if you should work backward or write an equation. Write an equation by using the formula for the perimeter of a square: $P = 4 \times s$.

   Then, replace P with the value given in the problem.

   Finally, use inverse operations to solve for s.

2. **What if** the blanket was a pentagon with the same perimeter, but one side was 28 inches, one side was 42 inches, one side was 38 inches, and one side was 2 feet long? What would be the length of the fifth side?

3. The triangular park shown at the right has a perimeter of 1,190 feet. What is the length of the third side?

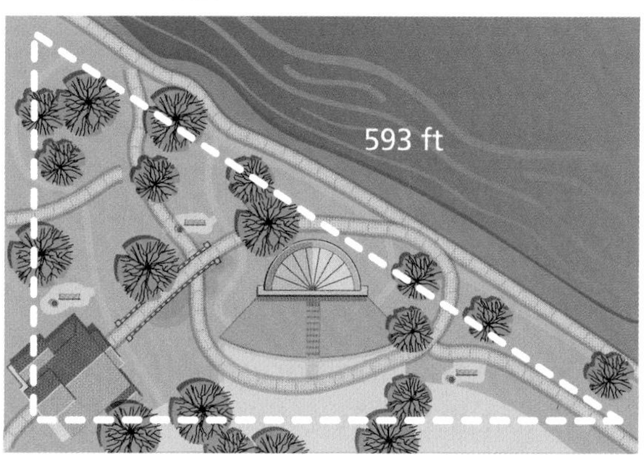

Choose a STRATEGY

- Draw a Diagram or Picture
- Make a Model or Act It Out
- Make an Organized List
- Look for a Pattern
- Make a Table or Graph
- Guess and Check
- Work Backward
- Solve a Simpler Problem
- Write an Equation
- Use Logical Reasoning

Mixed Strategy Practice

Choose a strategy to solve. Explain your choice.

4. The perimeter of a pentagon is 105 meters. The sides all have the same length. What is the length of each side?

5. **Pose a Problem** Write a problem similar to problem 4, but change the number and length of the sides of the polygon.

6. There are 4 cars in a line. The red car and the yellow car are not next to the blue car. The blue car is first. The red car is not last. One of the cars is black. In what order are the cars?

7. Sid's father gave him $10 more than he already had. Then Sid spent half of his money. He found $5 more in his piggy bank. Now he has $25. How much money did Sid have to start?

8. Gerri is knitting a scarf. She knits 8 inches of the scarf the first day. She knits 5 inches more each day after that. How long is her scarf after 5 days?

9. **WRITE Math** A rectangle has a length that is 4 inches longer than its width. The perimeter of the rectangle is 20 inches. What are the length and width of the rectangle? **Explain.**

LESSON 5

Estimate Area

OBJECTIVE: Estimate area.

Quick Review

1. 15 + 5 + 6
2. 8 ÷ 2
3. 9 + 5
4. 13 + 12 + 8
5. 10 ÷ 2

Vocabulary

area

square unit (sq un)

Learn

PROBLEM Jordan's dad is buying carpet for his bedroom. He used grid paper to make a diagram of his room to estimate the area. How can Jordan's dad use the grid to estimate the area of his bedroom?

Area is the number of square units needed to cover a surface. A **square unit (sq un)** is a square that is 1 unit long and 1 unit wide.

You can use grid paper to estimate the area of a figure.

Activity 1

Materials ■ grid paper ■ 2 different color pencils

- Copy the diagram of Jordan's room on grid paper. Shade the full squares one color and count them.
  There are about 67 full squares.
- Shade the number of half-full squares a second color and count them. Two half-full squares equal one full square.
  There are about 10 half-full squares. 10 ÷ 2 = 5 full squares
- Find the sum of the squares you counted.
  67 + 5 = 72 squares

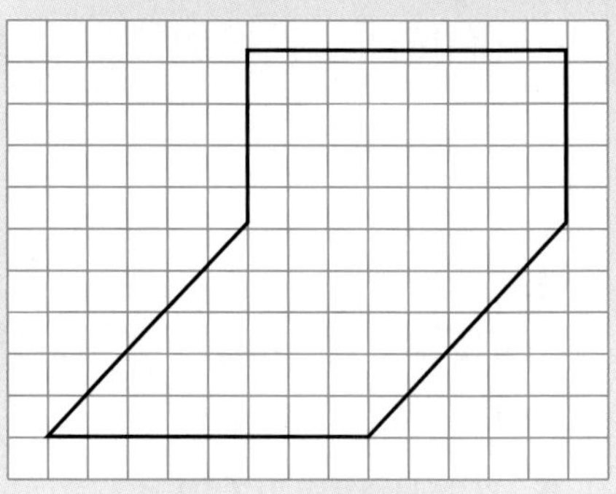

1 square = 1 square yard

So, Jordan's dad will need about 72 square yards of carpet.

Sometimes a figure on a grid has units that are almost full or less than half-full. To estimate the area, you will need to estimate the number of squares that are full, almost full, and half-full.

Example Estimate the area.

The green squares are full. There are 12 full squares.

The orange square is almost full. There is 1 almost-full square.

The yellow squares are half-full or almost half-full.
There are 4 half-full or about half-full squares. 4 ÷ 2 = 2 full squares

Find the sum of the squares. 12 + 1 + 2 = 15

Figure A

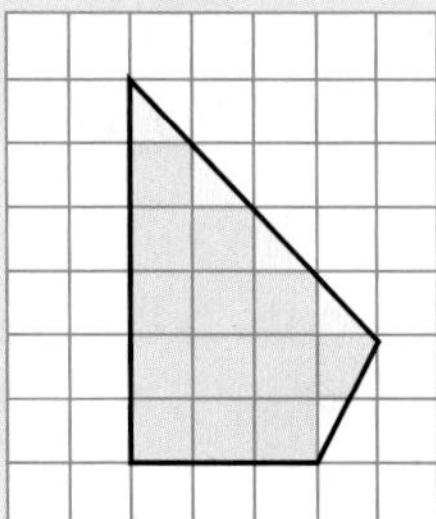

1 square = 1 square centimeter

So, the area of Figure A is about 15 square centimeters.

TEKS 4.11A estimate and use measurement tools to determine length (including perimeter), area, capacity and weight/mass using standard units SI (metric) and customary. *also* **4.3A, 4.14A, 4.14D, 4.15A, 4.15B**

Activity 2 **Materials** ■ grid paper ■ 3 different color pencils

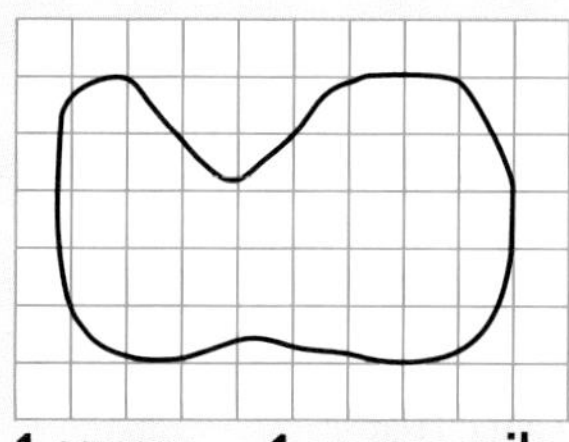

1 square = 1 square mile

- Copy the figure on grid paper. Shade all the full squares in one color. Then shade the almost-full squares in another color. There are 18 full squares and 10 almost-full squares.
- Now shade the half-full and almost half-full squares in a third color. Divide the sum of the squares by 2 to estimate the number of full squares. There are 10 half-full or almost half-full squares. 10 ÷ 2 = 5 full squares
- Find the sum of the squares. 18 + 10 + 5 = 33 squares

So, the area is about 33 square miles.

- Why is your answer an estimate, rather than an exact answer? Explain.

More Examples **Estimate the area.**

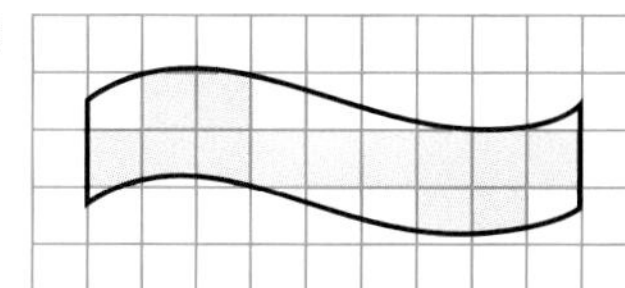

1 square = 1 square foot

The green squares are full.

There are 3 full squares.

The orange squares are almost full.

There are 10 almost-full squares.

The yellow squares are half-full or almost half-full. There are 6 half-full or almost half-full squares. 6 ÷ 2 = 3 full squares

Find the sum of the squares.

3 + 10 + 3 = 16 squares

So, the area is about 16 square feet.

B

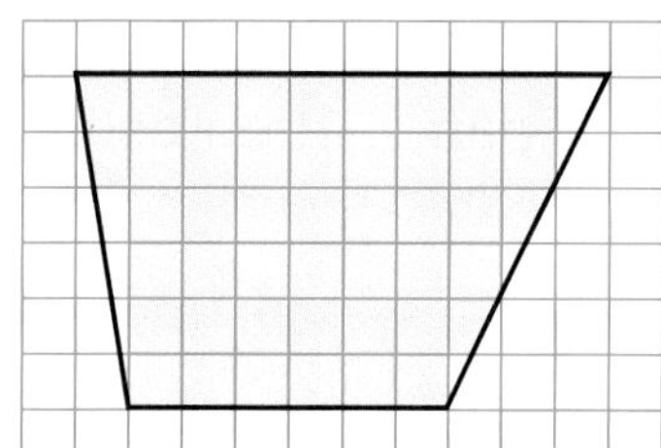

1 square = 1 square meter

The green squares are full or almost full. There are 42 full squares and 4 almost full squares.

The yellow squares are half-full or almost half-full. There are 2 half-full or almost half-full squares. 2 ÷ 2 = 1 full squares.

Find the sum of the squares counted.

42 + 4 + 1 = 47 squares

So, the area is about 47 square meters.

Guided Practice

1. Find the area of the figure.

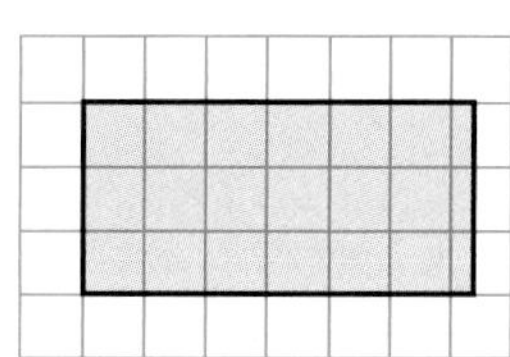

Estimate the area of each figure. Each unit represents 1 sq cm.

2. 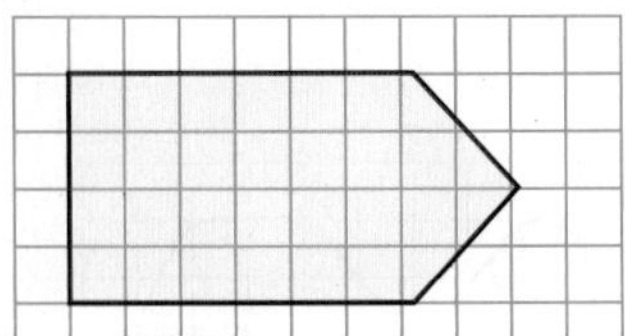

3. 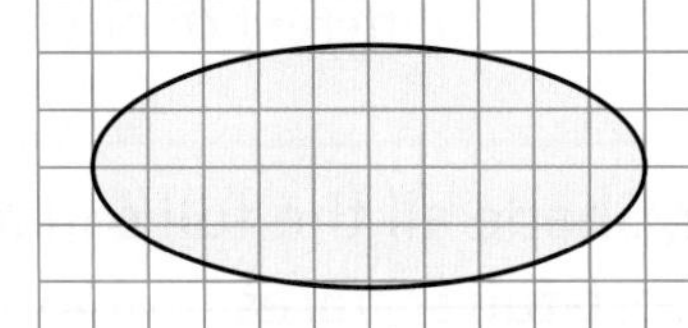

4. 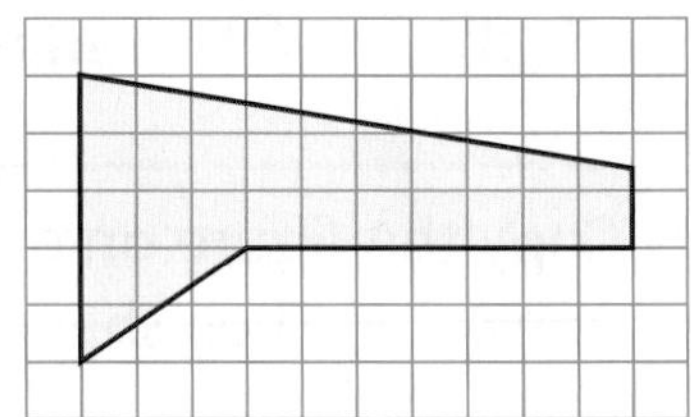

5. **TALK Math** Tommy drew a circle on grid paper and estimated the number of squares to find the area. Is the area he found an exact measurement or an estimate? **Explain.**

Independent Practice and Problem Solving

Estimate the area of each figure. Each unit represents 1 sq ft.

6. 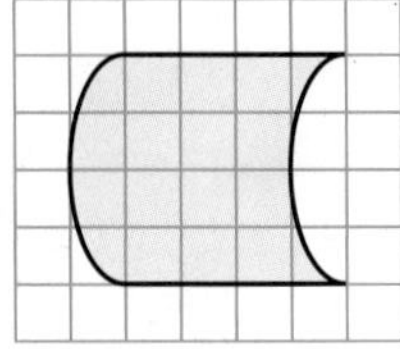

7. 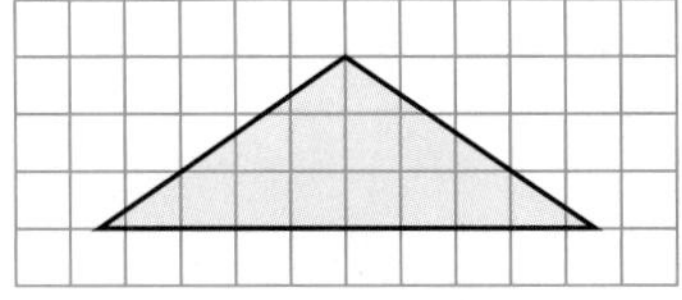

8. 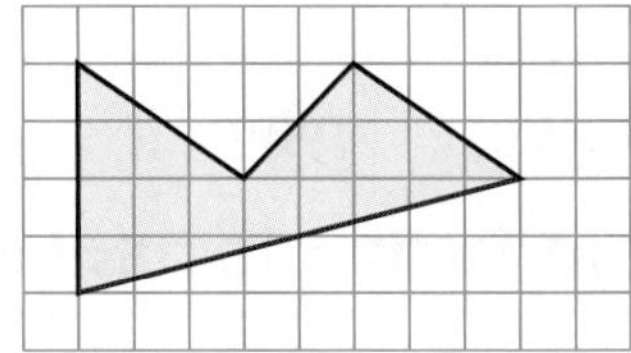

Draw each figure on grid paper. Then estimate its area in square units.

9. circle

10. triangle

11. parallelogram

USE DATA For 12–14, use the diagram.

12. Rosa drew a floor plan of part of her house. About how many square yards is the area of the closet?

13. Which is greater, the area of the family room or the area of the living room? **Explain.**

14. **WRITE Math** Is the total area of Rosa's floor plan greater or less than 96 square yards? **Explain.**

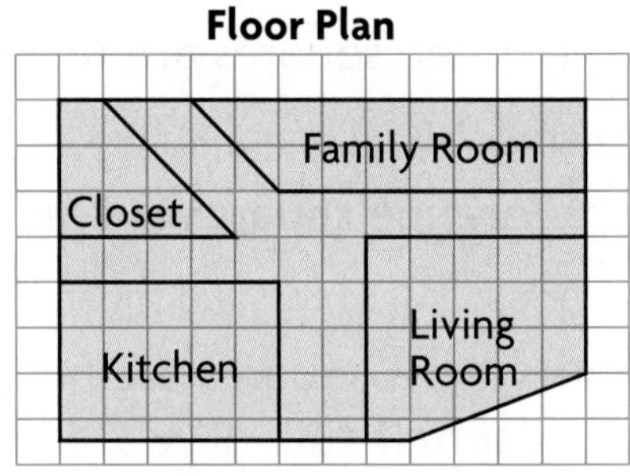

1 square = 1 square yard

Mixed Review and TAKS Prep

15. A rectangle has a length of 27 inches and a width of 10 inches. What is the perimeter of the rectangle? (TEKS 4.11A, p. 602)

16. Mr. Wallace can put 78 packs of staples in one box. He fills 52 boxes. How many packs of staples does he put in the boxes in all? (TEKS 4.4D, p. 236)

17. **TAKS Prep** In the figure below, each square stands for 1 square kilometer. What is the best estimate of the area of the figure? (Obj. 4)

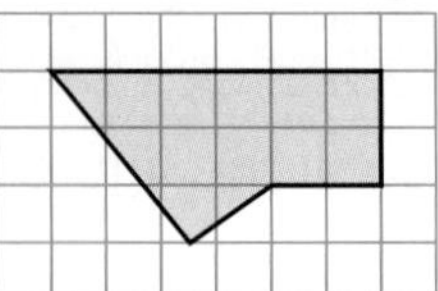

 Extra Practice on page 624, Set C

Describe an Error

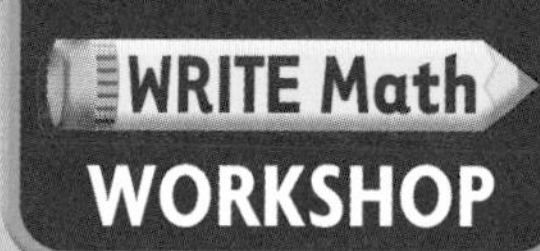

When you find and describe an error, it helps you avoid making errors in similar types of problems.

To describe an error, you need to
- Identify the error and the reason for it.
- Know how to do the math correctly.
- Show how to correct the error.
- Explain the steps you took to find the correct answer.

Our Room

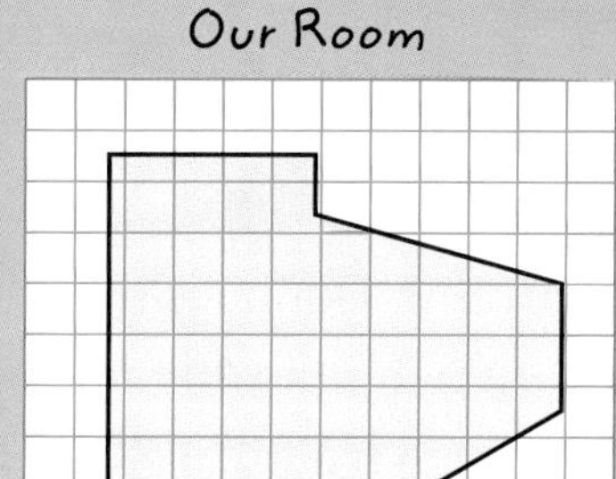

Each square is 1 square foot.

Tommy's brother sketched their room on grid paper. His brother recorded this estimate of the area.

Read Tommy's description of the error and his explanation of how to find the correct area.

Area of Our Room
The area is about 65 full squares.
The area is about 65 square feet.

My brother did not understand how to count the half-full and almost half-full squares. He included them in his estimate of full squares. So, his estimate of 65 squares is too high.

To estimate correctly:
- estimate the full and almost-full squares
  There are about 45 full or almost-full squares.
- estimate the number of half-full or almost-half-full squares.
  There are about 18 half-full or almost half-full squares.
  $18 \div 2 = 9$ full squares

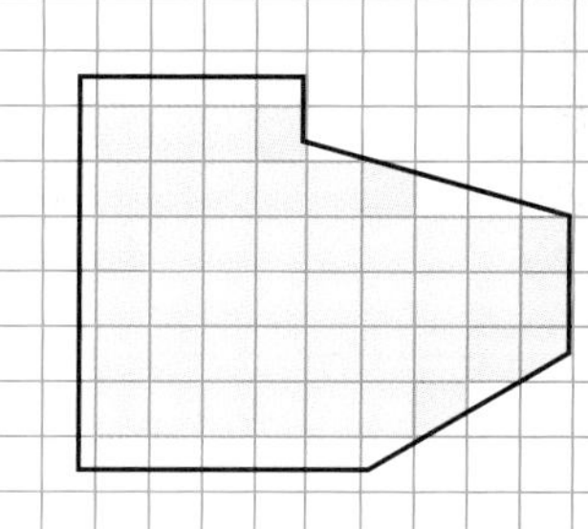

The area is about $45 + 9 = 54$ square feet.

Problem Solving **Describe each error and explain how to correct it. Give the correct area.**

1. 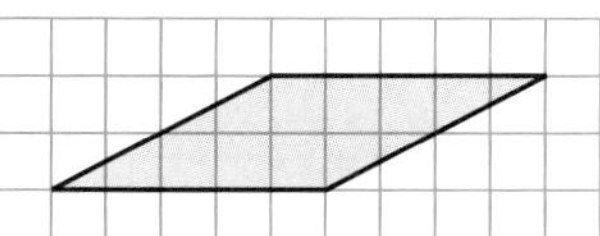

Area: about 14 square meters

2. 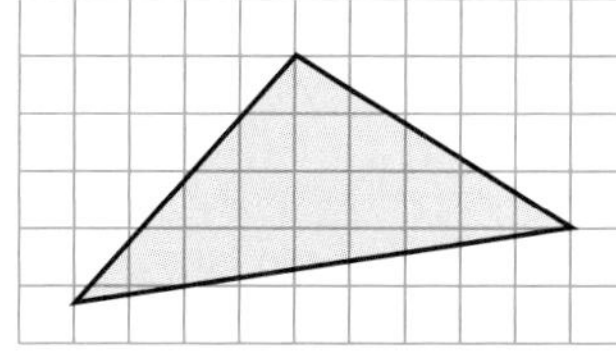

Area: about 10 square meters

3. 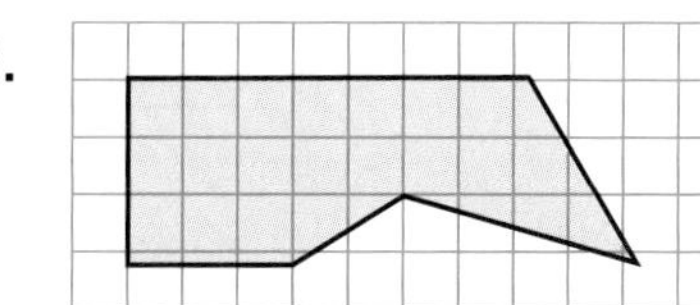

Area: about 30 square meters

ALGEBRA

Find Area

OBJECTIVE: Measure and find area by counting, multiplying, and using a formula.

Quick Review

1. 16×10
2. 12×21
3. 44×23
4. 8×13
5. 23×11

Learn

PROBLEM Danny is tiling the floor in his kitchen. The floor is a rectangle 8 feet wide and 14 feet long. How many square feet of tile does Danny need?

To find how many square feet of tile Danny needs, find the area of the floor. There are different ways to find the area of a rectangle.

ONE WAY **Count square units.**

Step 1

To represent the floor, draw a rectangle 14 feet long and 8 feet wide on grid paper. Let each square represent 1 square foot.

Step 2

Estimate the number of squares inside the rectangle. Then count the squares. There are 112 squares, so the area of the floor is 112 feet.

So, Danny needs 112 square feet of tile.

- **What if** the rectangle was 12 feet long by 7 feet wide? How could you use grid paper to find the area?

OTHER WAYS

A Use multiplication.

To find the area of a rectangle, multiply the number of rows by the number of units in each row.

number of rows		number in each row		area
↓		↓		↓
3	×	5	=	15 square units

3 rows of 5

So, the area is 15 square units.

B Use a formula.

The formula for the area of a rectangle is Area = length × width, or $A = l \times w$.

Use the formula to find the area of the rectangle.

5 yd, 3 yd, 3 yd, 5 yd

$A = l \times w$

$A = 3 \times 5$

$A = 15$

So, the area of the rectangle is 15 square yards.

4.11A estimate and use measurement tools to determine length (including perimeter), area, capacity and weight/mass using standard units, SI (Metric) and customary. *also* **4.4A, 4.4B, 4.4C, 4.4D, 4.14A, 4.14D, 4.15A, 4.15B**

Area of Rectangles and Squares

You can use special formulas to find the area of a rectangle and a square.

Polygon	Area	Formula
Rectangle 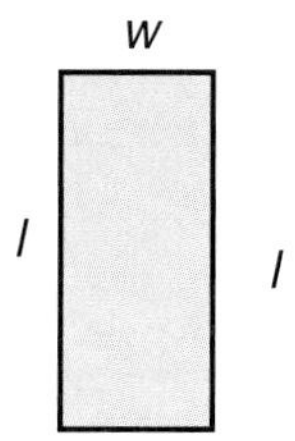	Area = length × width	$A = l \times w$
Square 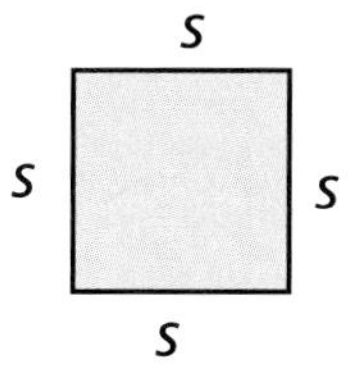	Area = length × width or A = side × side	$A = l \times w$ or $A = s \times s$

Examples Use the formula.

A

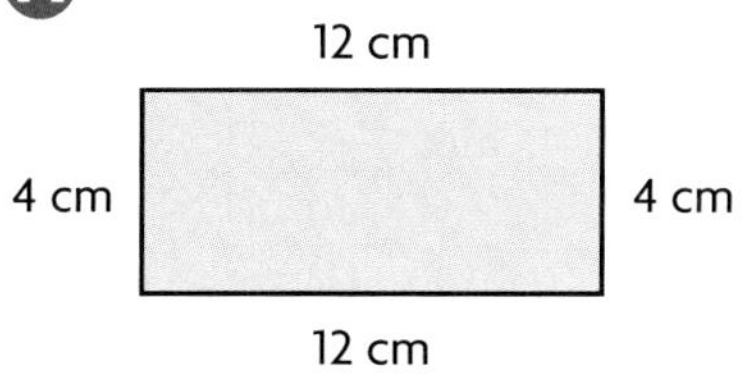

$A = l \times w$
$A = 12 \times 4$
$A = 48$

The area is 48 sq cm.

B

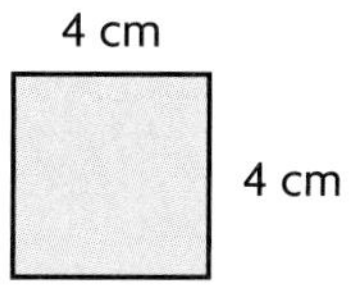

$A = l \times w$
$A = 4 \times 4$
$A = 16$

The area is 16 sq cm.

Guided Practice

1. Use a formula to find the area of this square.

$A = ■ \times ■$

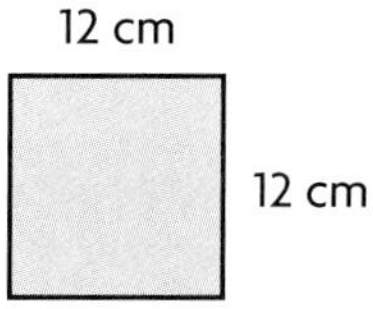

Find the area.

2. 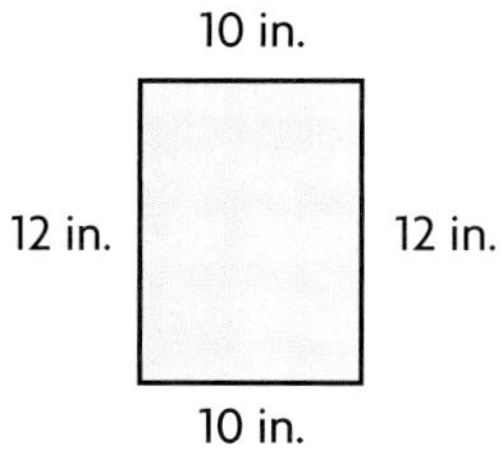

✓3. 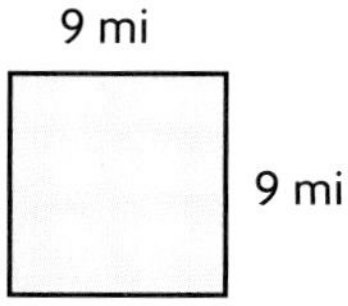

✓4. 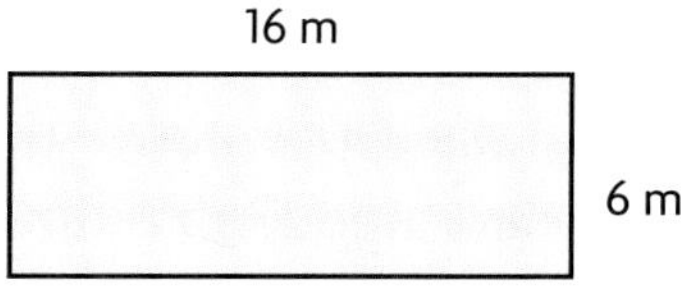

5. **TALK Math** **Explain** how can you find the area of a rectangle without counting each individual square unit.

Independent Practice and Problem Solving

Find the area.

6. 6 km

6 km | 6 km

6 km

7. 13 ft

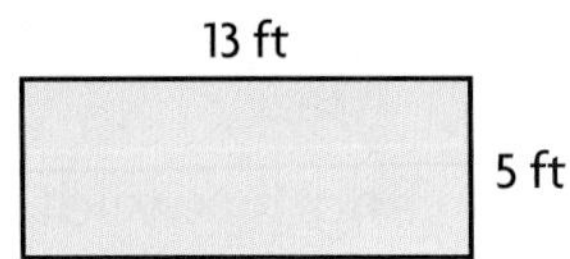

5 ft

8. 20 cm

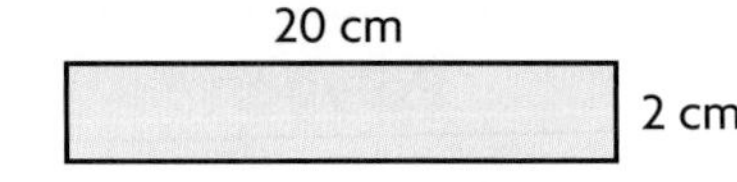

2 cm

Use a centimeter ruler to measure each figure. Find the area and perimeter.

9.

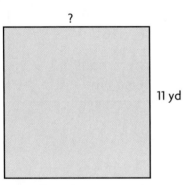

10.

11.

Algebra **Find the unknown length.**

12. ?

11 yd

Area = 121 sq yd

13. ?

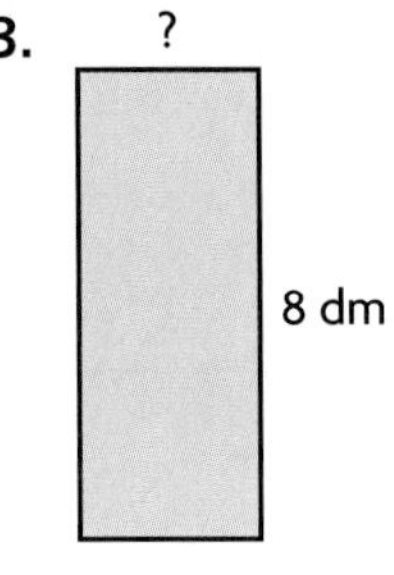

8 dm

Area = 24 sq dm

14. 16 mm

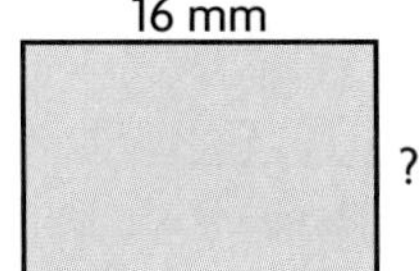

?

Area = 80 sq mm

USE DATA **For 15–17, use the diagram.**

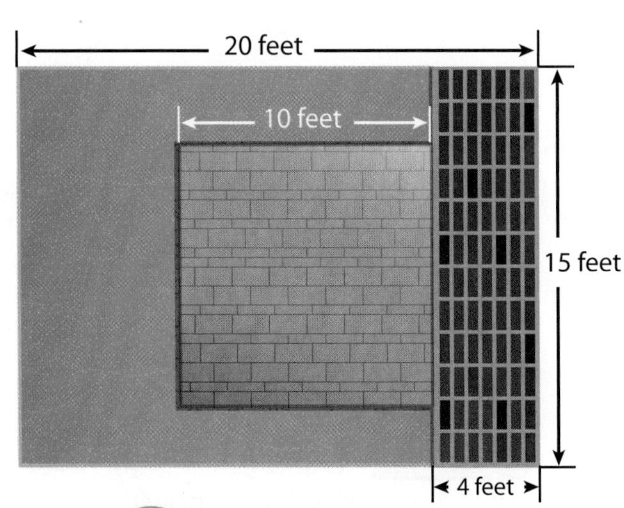

15. The gray brick area is a square. How many square feet of gray bricks does Mark need for that area?

16. **Reasoning** The area surrounding the patio is grass. How many square feet of grass does Mark need? **Explain.**

17. **WRITE Math** **What's the Question?** Mark compared the number of square feet of gray bricks to the number of square feet of red bricks needed for the patio. The answer is red bricks.

CD ROM **Technology**
Use Harcourt Mega Math, Ice Station Exploration, *Polar Planes*, Level Q.

 Extra Practice on page 624, Set D

Mixed Review and TAKS Prep

18. Find a rule. Then find the next number in the pattern. (TEKS 4.7, p. 144)

16, 20, 24, 28, ■

19. **TAKS Prep** What is the area of this figure? (Obj. 4)

A 20 square centimeters

B 40 square centimeters

C 60 square centimeters

D 96 square centimeters

20. Kenny is framing a picture 12 inches long and 14 inches wide. How many inches of framing material does Kenny need? (TEKS 4.11A, p. 604)

21. **TAKS Prep** Use a formula to find the area of a square with sides 7 feet in length. **Explain.** (Obj. 4)

MATH POWER

Problem Solving and Reasoning

MEASUREMENT You can use fractions to help you find the area of figures.

Think of Figure A as $\frac{1}{2}$ of a whole figure. You can use what you know about fractions and area to draw what the whole figure might look like and find its area.

- Find the area of Figure A.
  There are about 28 full squares.
  There are about 8 half full squares. $8 \div 2 = 4$ full squares
  The area is about $28 + 4 = 32$ square units.

- Find the area of the whole figure.
  The whole figure is twice the size of Figure A.
  So, the area of the whole figure is about $32 \times 2 = 64$ square units.
  Draw the other half of the figure so the total area is 64 square units.

Figure A

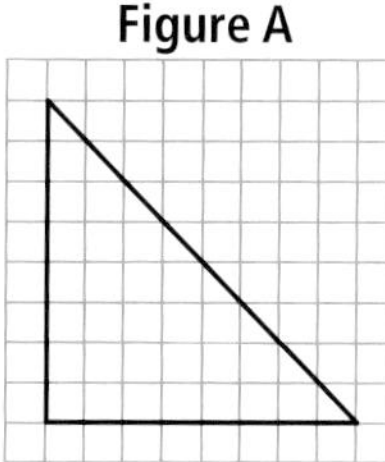

$\frac{1}{2}$ whole figure

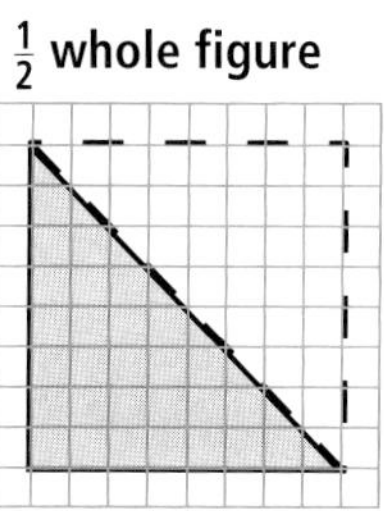

Draw the whole figure given each part. Find the area of the whole figure.

1.

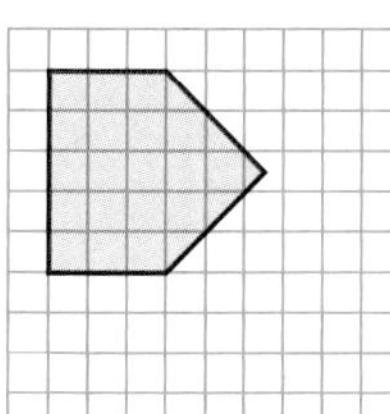

$\frac{1}{2}$ of the whole figure

2.

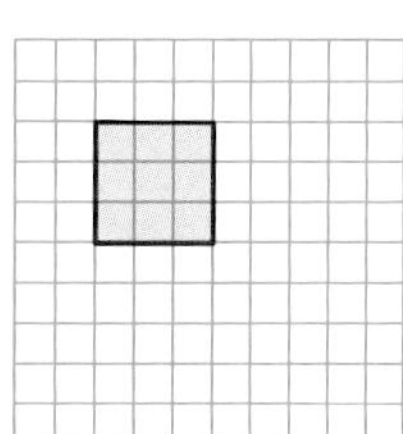

$\frac{1}{4}$ of the whole figure

3.

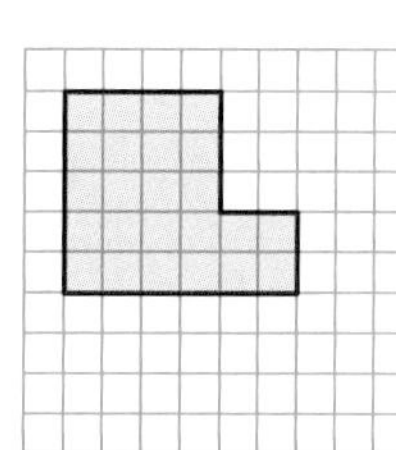

$\frac{2}{3}$ of the whole figure

LESSON 7

Perimeter and Area of Complex Figures

OBJECTIVE: Find the perimeter and area of complex figures.

Quick Review

1. 12×13
2. $88 + 65 + 24$
3. $14 + 12 + 6 + 9 + 12$
4. 19×5
5. 21×10

Learn

PROBLEM Johanna is visiting a botanical garden with her family. The diagram shows 2 sections of the garden. How much fencing would be needed to enclose both sections? What is the total area of the two sections?

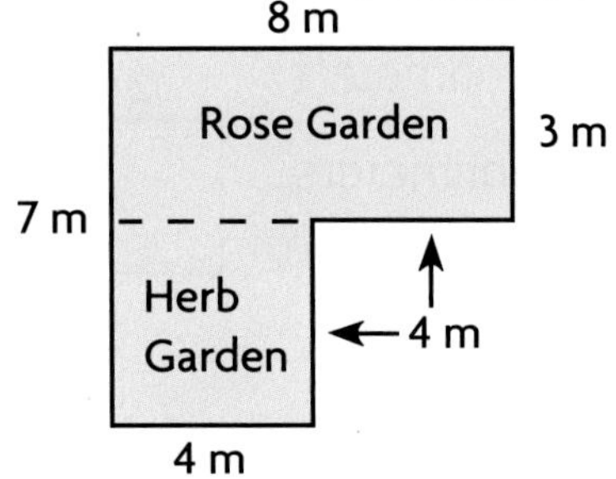

There are different ways to find the perimeter and area of complex figures.

ONE WAY Use grid paper.

- Draw the garden on grid paper.
- Find the perimeter of each section by counting the squares around the outside of the figure.

Rose Garden and Herb Garden
$P = 30$ meters

- Find the area of each section by counting squares inside the figure.

Rose Garden
$A = 24$ square meters

Herb Garden
$A = 16$ square meters

Then find the sum of the areas. $24 + 16 = 40$ square meters.

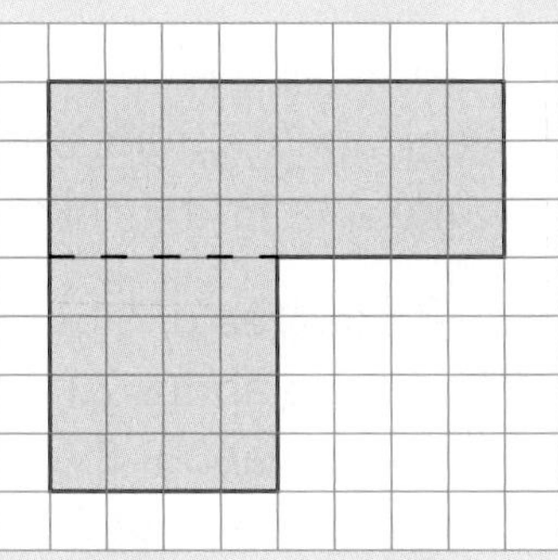

Side of each grid square = 1 meter

So, it would take 30 meters of fencing to enclose both sections, and the total area of the sections is 40 square meters.

ANOTHER WAY Use paper and pencil.

Perimeter of Both Sections

The perimeter of a figure is the sum of the lengths of its sides.

$P = 3 + 4 + 4 + 4 + 7 + 8 = 30$

$P = 30$ m

Area of Each Section

Rose Garden
$A = l \times w$
$A = 8 \times 3$
$A = 24$ sq m

Herb Garden
$A = l \times w$
$A = 4 \times 4$
$A = 16$ sq m

Sum of the areas: $24 + 16 = 40$ sq m

So, the total perimeter is 30 meters. So, the total area is 40 square meters.

- Is there another way you could divide the figure to find the total area?

TEKS 4.11A estimate and use measurement tools to determine length (including perimeter), area, capacity and weight/mass using standard units SI (metric) and customary. *also* **4.3A, 4.4C, 4.4D, 4.14A, 4.14C, 4.14D, 4.15A, 4.15B, 4.16A**

Guided Practice

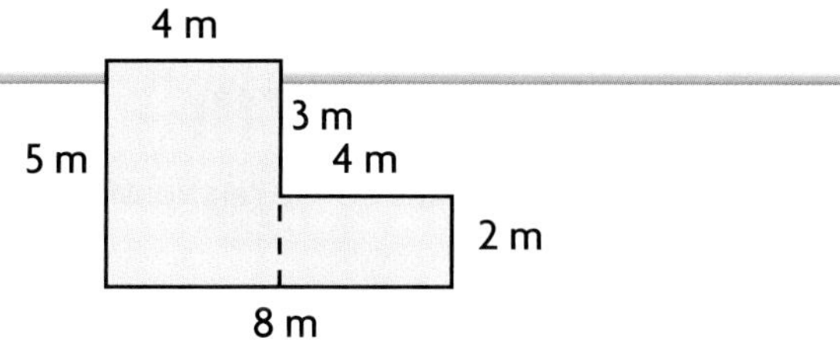

1. How much fencing would be needed to enclose both sections of the yard shown at the right?

Find the perimeter and area of each figure.

2. 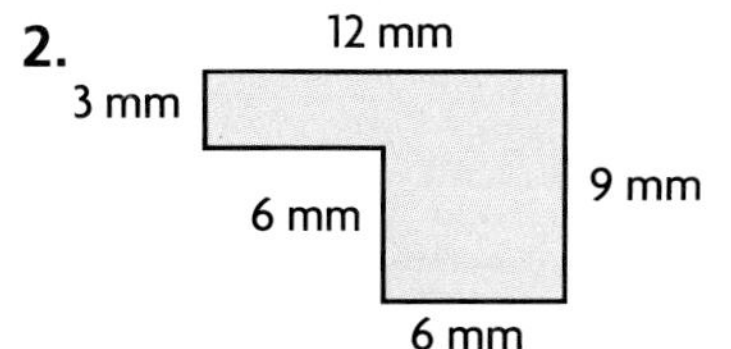

3. 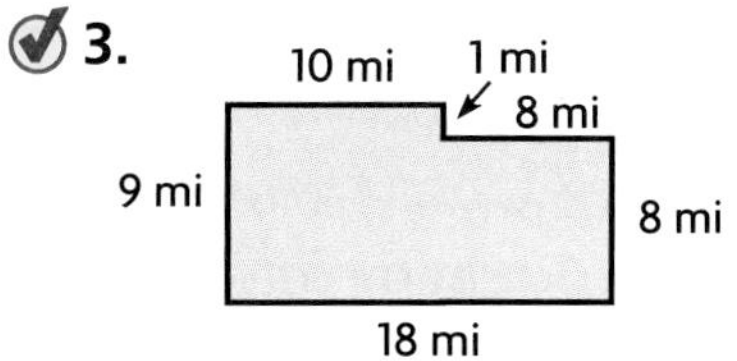

4. 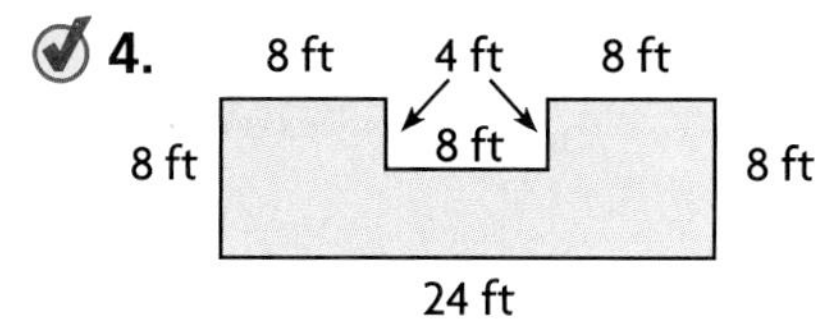

5. **TALK Math** **Explain** how you could use grid paper to find the total area of the figure in problem 2.

Independent Practice and Problem Solving

Find the perimeter and area of each figure.

6. 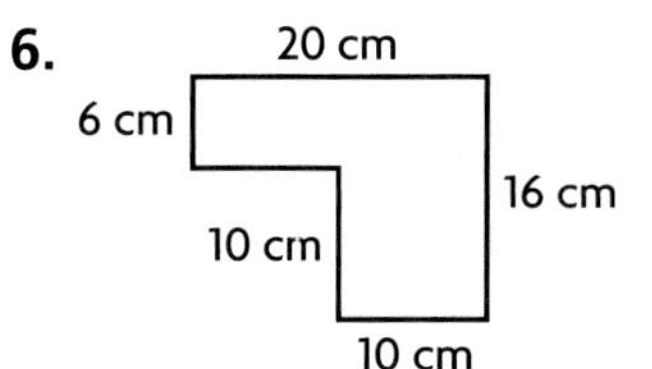

7. 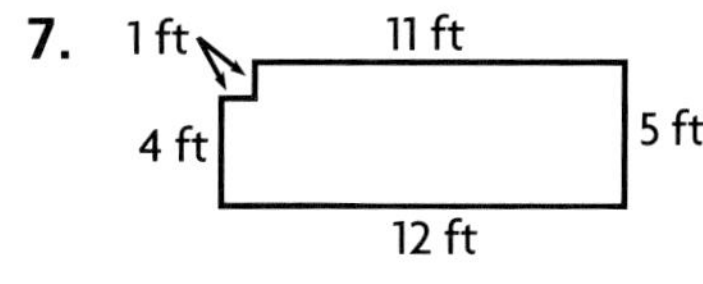

8. 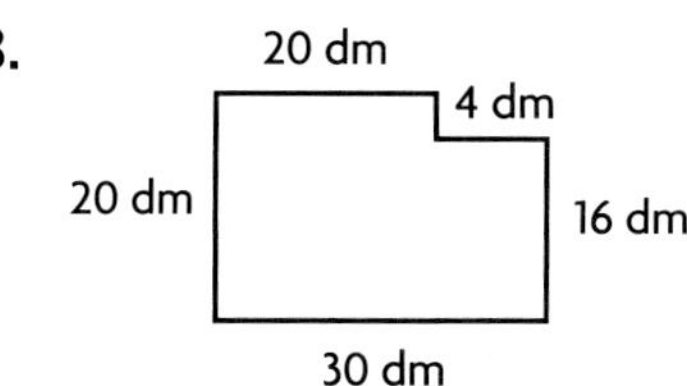

USE DATA For 9–11, use the diagram.

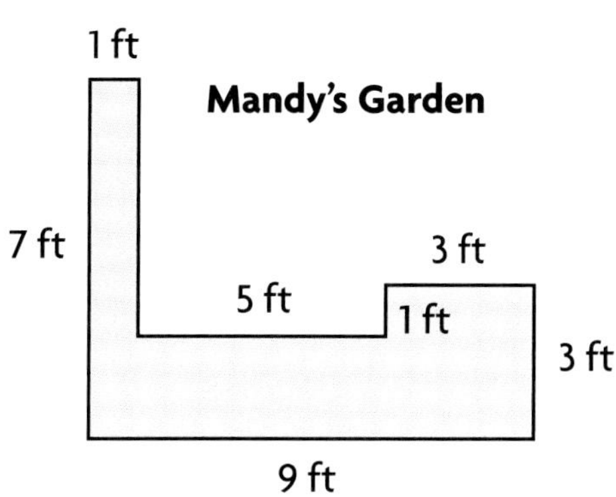

9. The diagram shows the layout of Mandy's garden. What is the area of the entire garden?
10. Mandy digs a trench to drain water around the outside of her garden. What is the total length of the trench?
11. **WRITE Math** Mandy is going to line the outside of her garden with bricks. Each brick is 8 inches long. How many bricks does Mandy need? **Explain.**

Mixed Review and TAKS Prep

12. Sierra drinks $2\frac{1}{2}$ glasses of milk. Johnny drinks $2\frac{1}{3}$ glasses. Who drinks more milk? (TEKS 4.2C, p. 406)
13. One side of a square is 7 inches. What is the perimeter of the square? (TEKS 4.11A, p. 604)
14. **TAKS Prep** What is the total area of this figure? (Obj. 4)

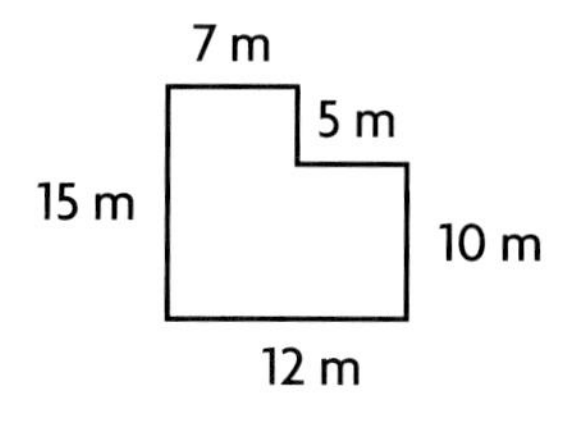

A 35 square meters

B 120 square meters

C 49 square meters

D 155 square meters

Extra Practice on page 624, Set E

Relate Perimeter and Area

OBJECTIVE: Explore the relationship between perimeter and area.

1. $(2 \times 6) + (2 \times 10)$
2. 9×11
3. $14 + 16 + 14 + 16$
4. $(2 \times 10) + (2 \times 12)$
5. 8×19

Learn

PROBLEM Mr. Foster is framing three pictures. Does he need the same amount of framing for each picture? Does he need the same number of square inches of glass for each picture?

7 in.

3 in.

To find how much framing Mr. Foster needs, find the perimeter of each picture. To find how much glass he needs, find the area of each picture.

6 in.

4 in.

5 in.

5 in.

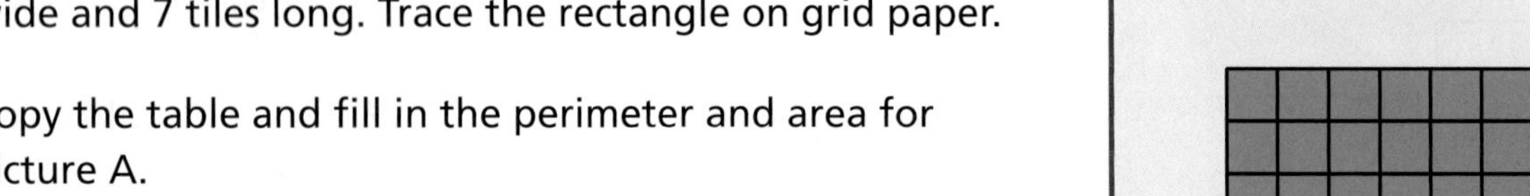

Activity 1 Materials ■ square tiles ■ grid paper

- Use square tiles to model Picture A. Make a rectangle 3 tiles wide and 7 tiles long. Trace the rectangle on grid paper.
- Copy the table and fill in the perimeter and area for Picture A.
- Repeat Steps 1 and 2 for the other pictures. Record your work in the table.

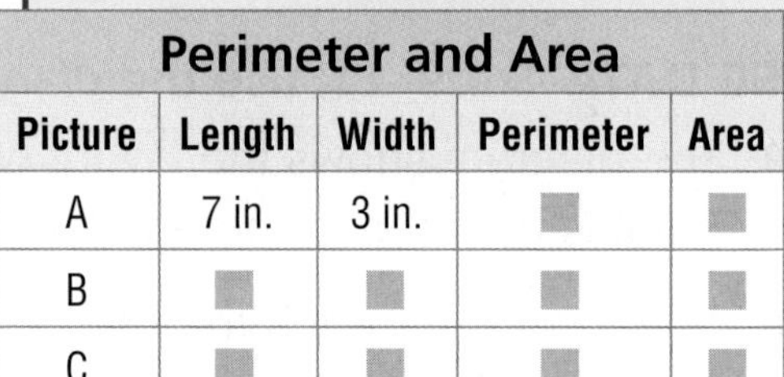

Perimeter and Area

Picture	Length	Width	Perimeter	Area
A	7 in.	3 in.	■	■
B	■	■	■	■
C	■	■	■	■

So, for each picture, Mr. Foster needs the same amount of framing but a different number of square inches of glass.

Activity 2 Materials ■ 24 square tiles ■ grid paper

- Use 24 square tiles to make a rectangle. Trace the rectangle onto grid paper. Copy the table and record the length and width. Find the perimeter and area, and record them in the table.
- Use the 24 tiles to make as many different rectangles as you can. Trace each rectangle and find the perimeter and area. Record each length, width, perimeter, and area in the table.

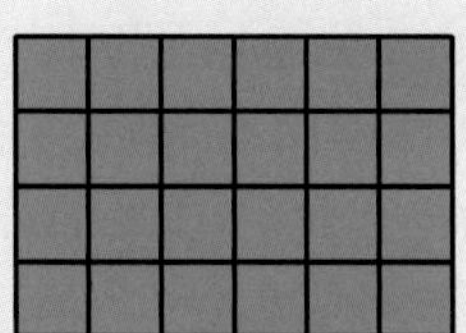

Perimeter and Area

Rectangle	Length	Width	Perimeter	Area
1	6 un	4 un	20 un	24 sq un
2	■	■	■	■
3	■	■	■	■

4.11A estimate and use measurement tools to determine length (including perimeter), area, capacity and weight/mass using standard units, SI (metric) and customary. *also* **4.3A, 4.4A, 4.4B, 4.4C, 4.4D, 4.14A, 4.14D, 4.15A, 4.15B, 4.16A**

Activity 3 **Materials** ■ square tiles ■ grid paper

- Use square tiles to make a rectangle 12 tiles long and 1 tile wide. Trace the rectangle on grid paper.
- Find the perimeter and area. Copy and complete the table.
- Continue to make rectangles with 12 tiles by decreasing the length and increasing the width. Make as many rectangles as you can. Trace each rectangle, find the perimeter and area, and record your work in the table.

Perimeter and Area				
Rectangle	**Length**	**Width**	**Perimeter**	**Area**
1	12 un	1 un	■ un	■ sq un
2	■	2	■	■
3	■	3	■	■

- What is the difference between area and perimeter? Explain.

Math Idea
Two figures can have the same area but different perimeters or different areas but the same perimeter.

Guided Practice

1. How can you change this rectangle so that it has the same perimeter, but a greater area? Model and then record your answer.

6 cm
2 cm

Find the area and perimeter of each figure. Then draw another figure that has the same perimeter but a different area.

2. 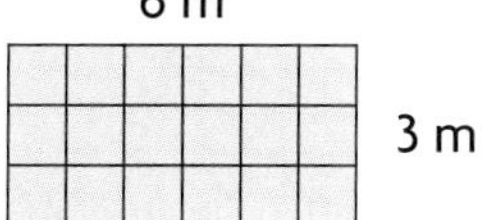

3. 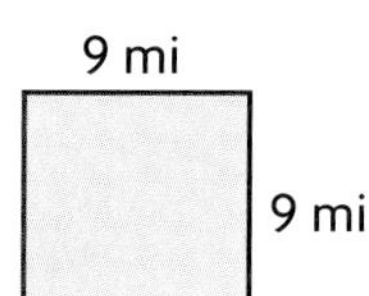

4. 

Find the area and perimeter of each figure. Then draw another figure that has the same area but a different perimeter.

5. 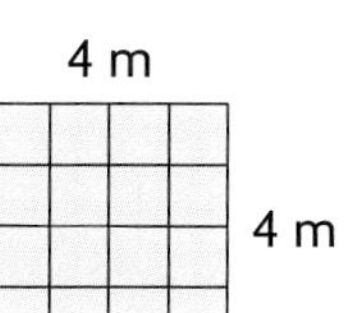

6. 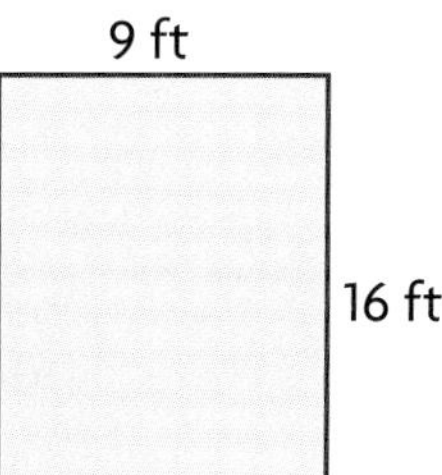

7. 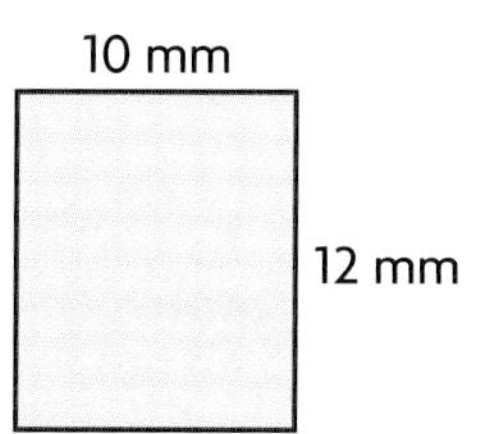

8. **TALK Math** **Explain** how knowing the factors of a number can help you find all the rectangles with an area of that number.

Independent Practice and Problem Solving

Find the area and perimeter of each figure. Then draw another figure that has the same perimeter but a different area.

9. 5 in.

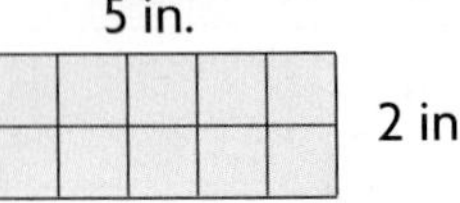

2 in.

10. 16 yd

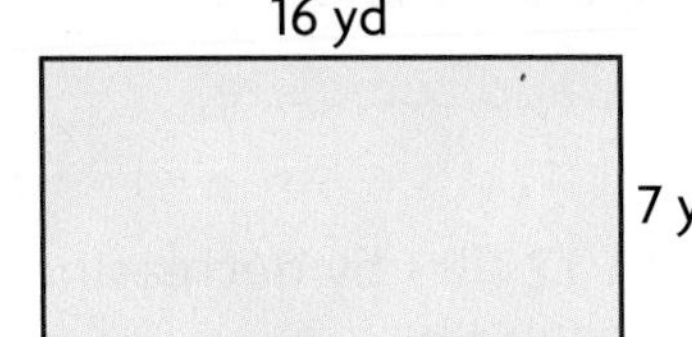

7 yd

11. 12 cm

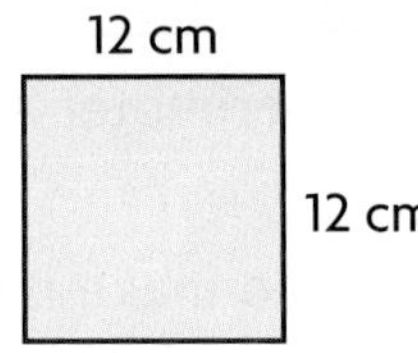

12 cm

12. 9 ft

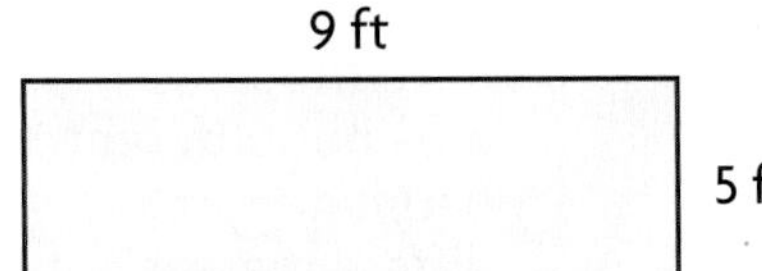

5 ft

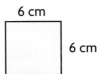

13. 6 cm

6 cm

14. 10 m

4 m

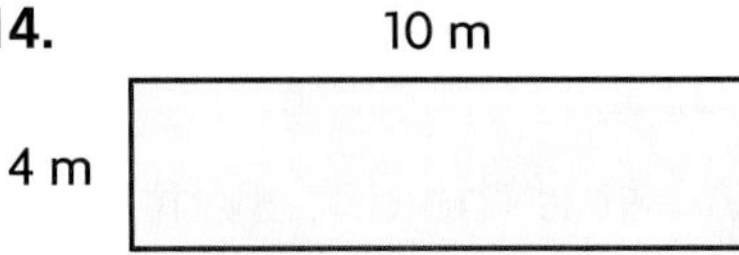

Find the area and perimeter of each figure. Then draw another figure that has the same area but a different perimeter.

15. 7 m

2 m

16. 6 mi

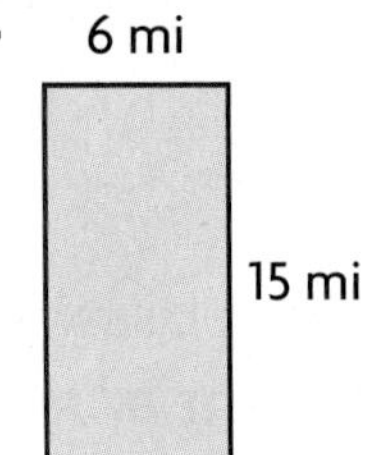

15 mi

17. 20 ft

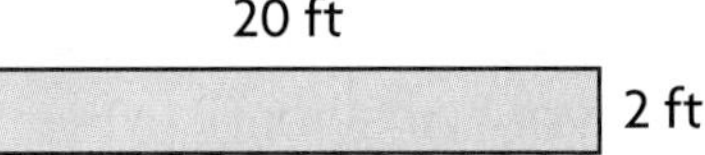

2 ft

For 18–19, use figures a–d.

18. Which figures have the same area but different perimeters?

19. Which figures have the same perimeter but different areas?

a.

b.

c.

d.

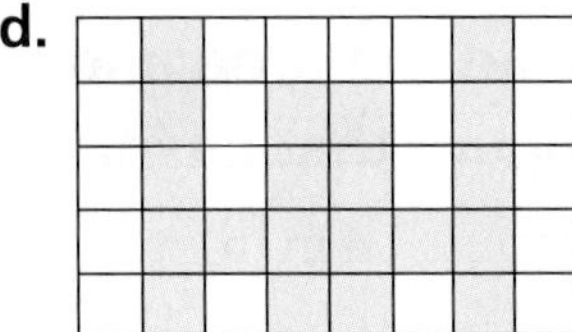

20. The area of Seth's painting is 80 square inches. Give 3 possible perimeters for his painting.

21. Len's drawing has an area of 36 square inches and a perimeter of 26 inches. What are the length and the width of his drawing?

22. Corynn paints a picture that has a perimeter of 22 centimeters. What are 3 possible areas for her picture?

23. WRITE Math Mia has two pictures, both with an area of 36 square inches. One is a rectangle, and one is a square. Which has the greater perimeter? **Explain.**

 Extra Practice on page 624, Set F

Mixed Review and TAKS Prep

24. Susie draws a circle. The diameter of the circle is 16 millimeters. What is the radius of the circle? (TEKS 4.8C, p. 274)

25. The length of a rectangle is 14 meters and the width is 11 meters. What is the area of the rectangle? (TEKS 4.11A, p. 614)

26. **TAKS Prep** The rectangles below have the same perimeter. Which has the greatest area? (Obj. 4)

A

C 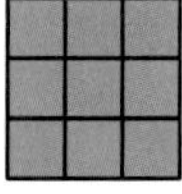

 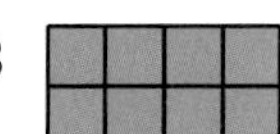

D 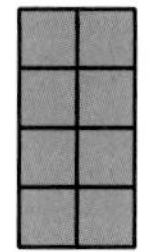

Problem Solving and Reasoning

MEASUREMENT You can use grid paper to show how the perimeter and area of a rectangle change when its length and width are halved or doubled.

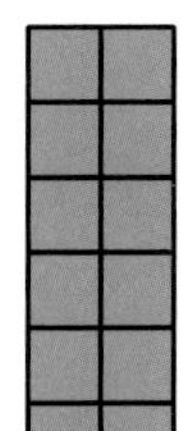

Rectangle 1

Perimeter and Area				
	Length	Width	Perimeter	Area
Rectangle 1	6 un	2 un	16 un	12 sq un
Rectangle 2	12 un	4 un		
Rectangle 3				
Rectangle 4				

Step 1

Multiply the length and width of a rectangle by 2. Record these new dimensions for rectangle 2 in a table.

Step 2

Find the perimeter and area of rectangle 2. Record your work.

Step 3

Multiply the length and width of rectangle 2 by 2. Record these new dimensions in the table for rectangle 3. Then find the perimeter and area of rectangle 3. Record your work.

Step 4

Now divide the length and width of rectangle 1 by 2. Record these new dimensions in the table for rectangle 4. Then find the perimeter and area of rectangle 4. Record your work.

For 1–2 use the table above.

1. Compare the areas of rectangle 1, rectangle 2, and rectangle 3. What happened to the area when the length and width were doubled?

2. Compare the perimeter and area of rectangle 1 and rectangle 4. What happened to the perimeter and area when the length and width were halved?

Extra Practice

Set A Find the perimeter. (pp. 602–603)

1. 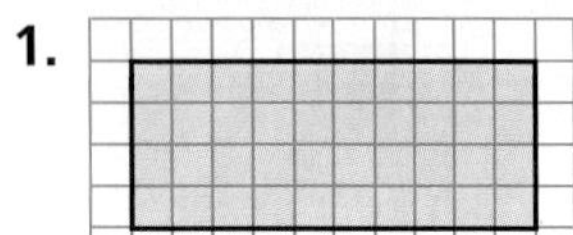

2. 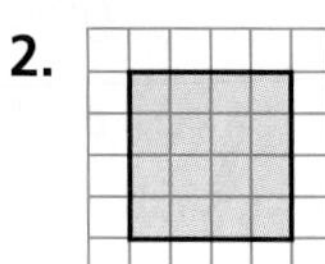

3. 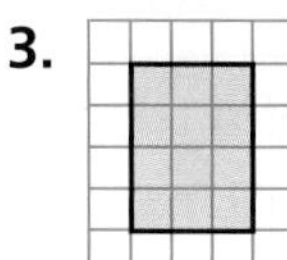

Set B Find the perimeter. (pp. 604–607)

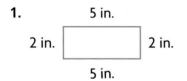

1. 5 in.
2 in. 2 in.
5 in.

2. 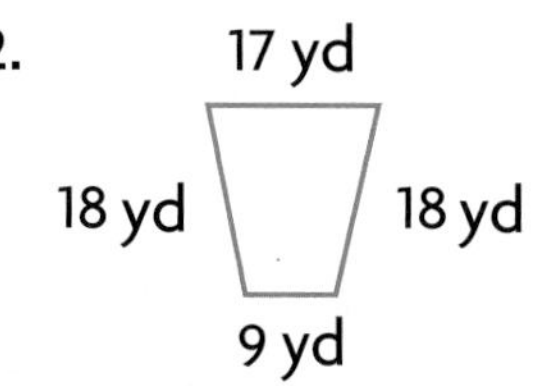

3. 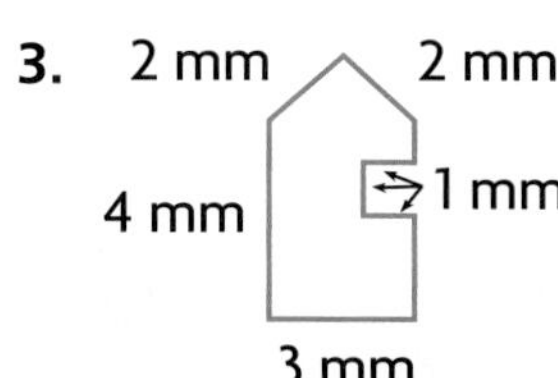

Set C Estimate the area of each figure. Each unit represents 1 sq ft. (pp. 610–613)

1.

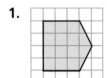

2. 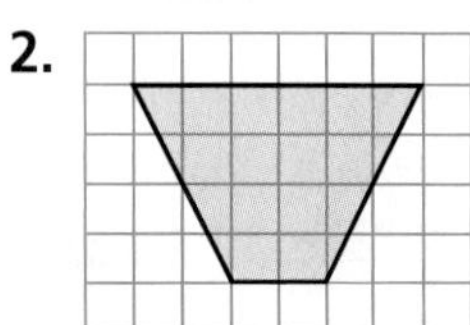

3. 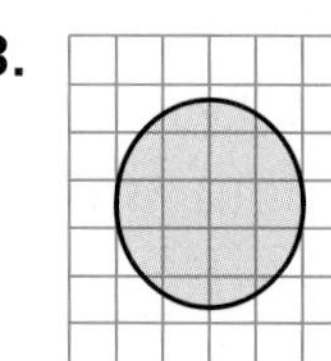

Set D Find the area. (pp. 614–617)

1. 11 in.
2 in.

2. 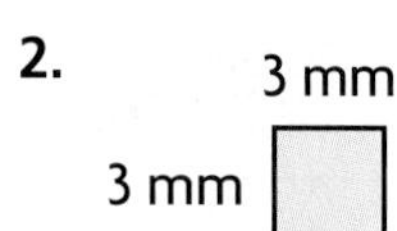

3. 

Set E Find the perimeter and area of each figure. (pp. 618–619)

1. 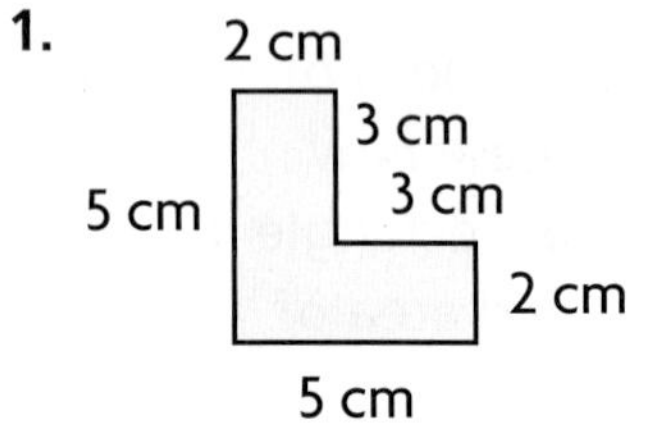

2. 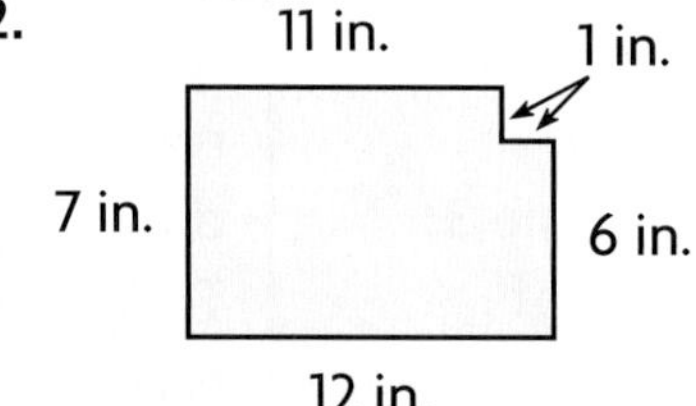

3. 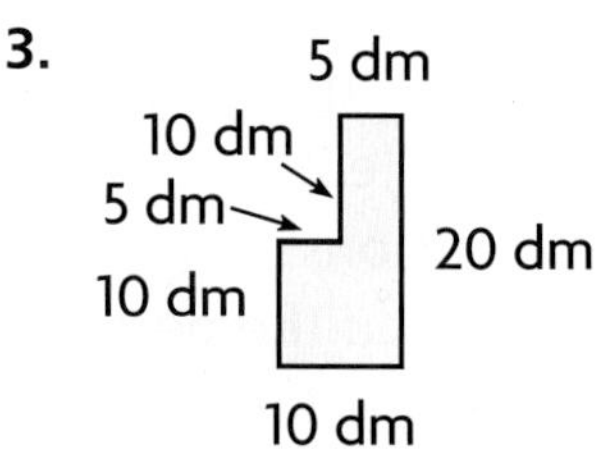

Set F Find the area and perimeter of each figure. Then draw another figure that has the same perimeter but a different area. (pp. 620–623)

1.

2. 13 mi
4 mi

3. 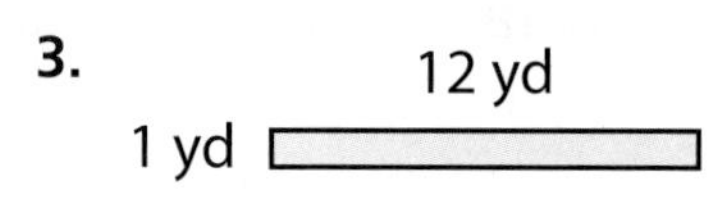

CD ROM Technology
Use Harcourt Mega Math, Ice Station Exploration, *Polar Planes*, Levels P, Q, R, S.

3 Steps Forward, 2 Steps Back

The Band!
2–4 players

Instruments!
- 2–4 different coins
- Number cube labeled 1 to 6

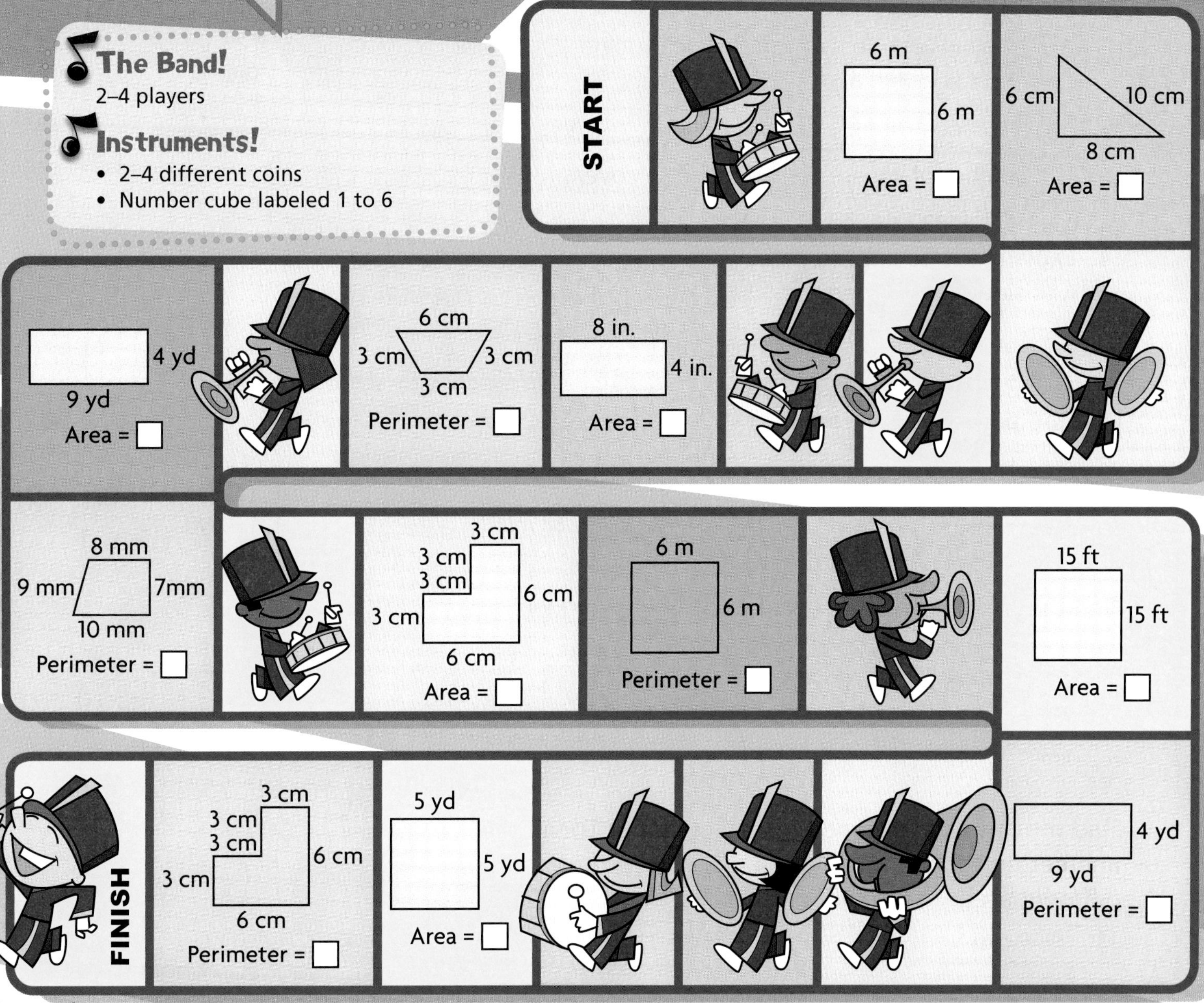

START

6 m, 6 m — Area = ☐

6 cm, 10 cm, 8 cm — Area = ☐

4 yd, 9 yd — Area = ☐

6 cm, 3 cm, 3 cm, 3 cm — Perimeter = ☐

8 in., 4 in. — Area = ☐

8 mm, 9 mm, 7mm, 10 mm — Perimeter = ☐

3 cm, 3 cm, 3 cm, 6 cm, 3 cm, 6 cm — Area = ☐

6 m, 6 m — Perimeter = ☐

15 ft, 15 ft — Area = ☐

3 cm, 3 cm, 3 cm, 6 cm, 3 cm, 6 cm — Perimeter = ☐

5 yd, 5 yd — Area = ☐

4 yd, 9 yd — Perimeter = ☐

FINISH

March!

- Each player selects a different coin and places the coin on START. Players toss the cube to determine who goes first.
- If the player lands on a space with a problem, he or she solves that problem. All the other players check his or her answer.
- If the answer is correct, the player moves his or her marker 3 spaces forward. If the answer is incorrect, the player moves his or her marker 2 spaces back.
- If a player lands on an empty space, he or she loses the turn.
- The first player to reach FINISH, wins.

Chapter 23 Review/Test

Check Vocabulary and Concepts

For 1–3, choose the best term from the box.

VOCABULARY
area
formula
perimeter
square unit

1. A mathematical rule that can be used to find perimeter is called a __?__. (TEKS 4.11A, p. 605)
2. The distance around a figure is called __?__. (TEKS 4.11A, p. 600)
3. The number of square units needed to cover a surface is called __?__. (TEKS 4.11A, p. 610)
4. **Explain** how to find the perimeter of a square with sides 2 units long. (TEKS 4.11A, pp. 600–601)

Check Skills

Find the perimeter and area. (TEKS 4.11A, pp. 600–601, 602–603, 604–607, 614–617)

5. 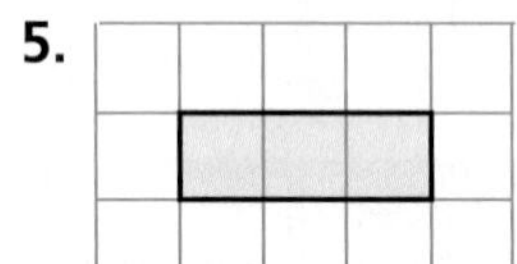

6. 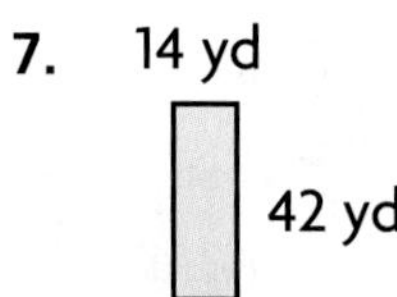

7. 14 yd, 42 yd

Find the perimeter and area of each figure. (TEKS 4.11A, pp. 618–619)

8. 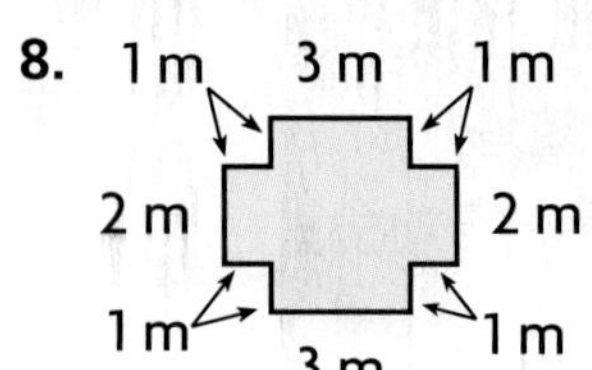

9. 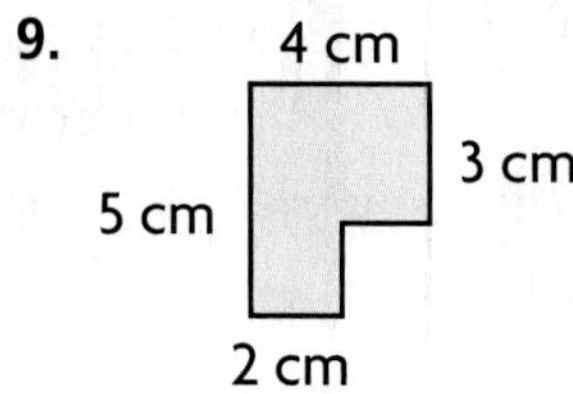

10. 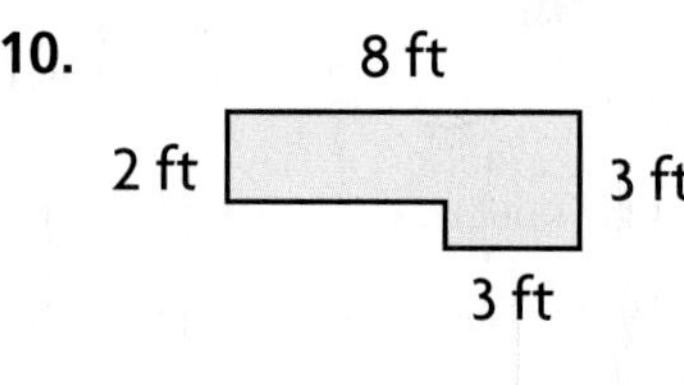

Find the area and perimeter of each figure. Then draw another figure that has the same perimeter but a different area. (TEKS 4.11A, pp. 620–623)

11. 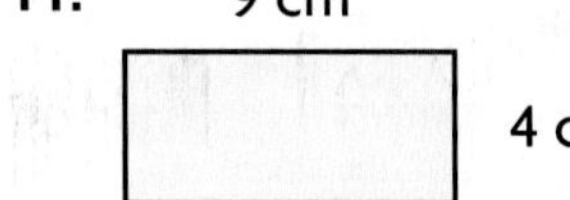

12. 12 yd, 5 yd

13. 18 ft, 3 ft

Check Problem Solving

Solve. (TEKS 4.14C, pp. 608-609)

14. Danielle is building a fence around a square dog run. The perimeter of the dog run is 36 feet. What is the length of each side?

15. WRITE Math **Explain** how you can write an equation to find the perimeter of a rectangle measuring 10 inches long by 5 inches wide.

GO ONLINE **Technology** Use *Online Assessment.*

Enrich • Perimeter of a Circle

All the Way Around

The **circumference** of a circle is the distance around a circle. The distance around other plane figures is called the perimeter, so circumference is also known as the perimeter of a circle.

To find the perimeter of a square or a triangle, you can use a ruler to measure each side. You can use a string to measure the circumference of a circle.

Activity

Materials ■ string ■ circular lids ■ ruler ■ scissors

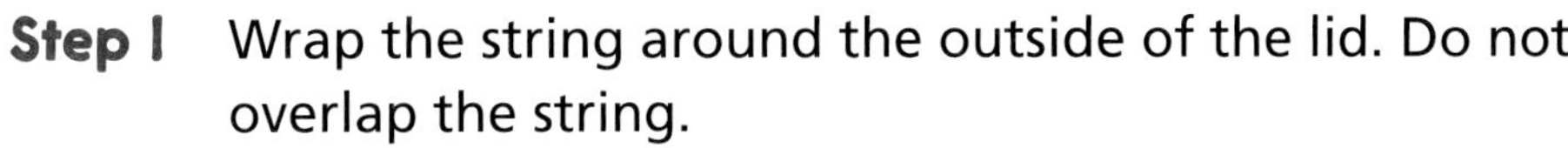

Step 1	Wrap the string around the outside of the lid. Do not overlap the string.
Step 2	Mark the string where it meets the other end of the string. Cut it to show the distance around the lid.
Step 3	Measure the string with a centimeter ruler. The length of the string is the circumference of the circle.

Try It

Copy and complete the table. Choose three circular lids to measure. Measure and record each circumference, using string and a centimeter ruler.

	Type of Circle	Measurement (in cm)
1.		
2.		
3.		

4. Compare the three circumferences. What is the difference between the largest circumference and the smallest circumference?

WRITE Math Julie's dinner plate is twice the circumference of her salad plate. The circumference of the salad plate is 15 centimeters. What is the circumference of the dinner plate? **Explain.**

Getting Ready for the TAKS
Chapters 1–23

Number, Operation, and Quantitative Reasoning TAKS Obj. 1

1. There are 192 students in the fourth grade. They are divided equally among 8 classes. How many students are in each class?

   A 18

   B 20

   C 24

   D Not here

Eliminate Choices.

See Item 2. You need to multiply two whole numbers to find the answer. You can eliminate any answer choices that are less than the numbers in the problem.

2. Sarah bought 6 packs of erasers. There were 12 erasers in each pack. How many erasers did Sarah buy?

   F 2

   G 4

   H 62

   J 72

3. Nate had 312 baseball cards. He gave 148 to his brother. Which shows how many baseball cards Nate has left?

   A 164 C 236

   B 260 D 460

4. WRITE Math Which is greater, 5.82 or 5.19? **Explain** how you found your answer.

Patterns, Relationships, and Algebraic Thinking TAKS Obj. 2

5. Which number sentence is in the same fact family as $6 \times 9 = 54$?

   F $6 \div 6 = 1$

   G $9 \div 3 = 3$

   H $54 \div 6 = 9$

   J $54 \div 3 = 18$

6. Which correctly describes the relationship between the number of dogs and the number of tags in the table?

Dogs	6	7	8	9
Tags	12	14	16	18

   A The number of tags is twice the number of dogs.

   B The number of tags is 6 more than the number of dogs.

   C The number of dogs is twice the number of tags.

   D The number of tags is one–half the number of dogs.

7. What is the value of the expression?

$$4 \times (3 + 7)$$

   F 11 H 19

   G 14 J 40

8. WRITE Math Emily wants to find the product 4×500. **Explain** how she can use the basic fact $4 \times 5 = 20$ to help her.

Geometry and Spatial Reasoning TAKS Obj. 3

9. What kind of angle is shown?

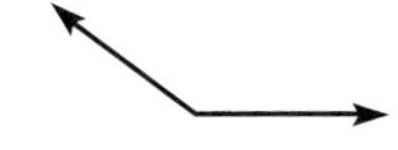

A Obtuse

B Right

C Acute

D Left

10. Hanna stores her CDs in a case like the one shown below. How many edges does the case have?

F 6

G 8

H 12

J 16

11. WRITE Math Rolando moved the arrow shape as shown below. What two transformations could Rolando have used to move the figure? **Explain** your answer.

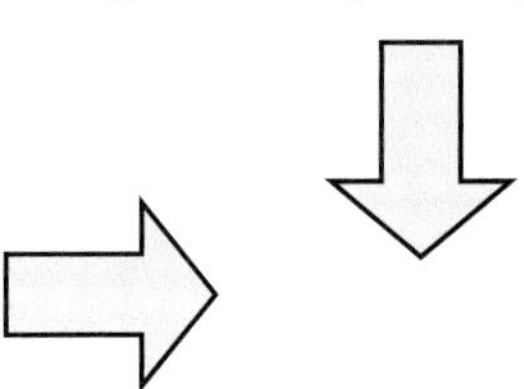

Probability and Statistics TAKS Obj. 5

12. The graph shows the number of coins students collected.

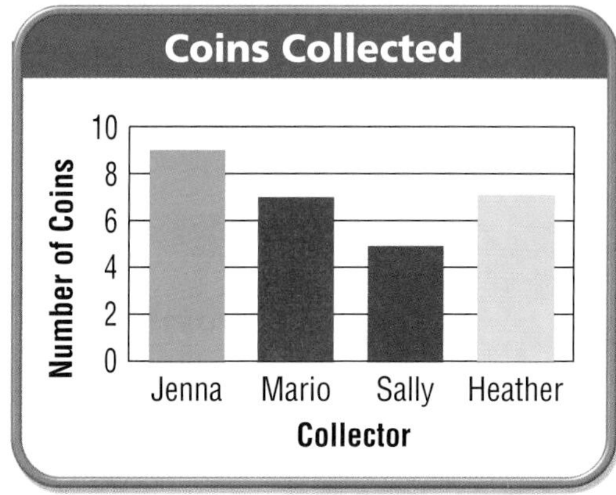

According to the graph, how many more coins did Jenna collect than Sally?

A 14

B 9

C 4

D 3

13. Stephanie has the shirts and pants shown below. How many different combinations of outfits can she make?

F 3

G 6

H 9

J 12

14. WRITE Math Jennifer took a survey of her classmates' favorite subjects. She made a bar graph showing the data she collected. The bars for Math and Reading were the same height. **Explain** what this means.

CHAPTER

24 Volume

The Big Idea Attributes of three-dimensional figures can be measured.

TEXAS FAST FACT

The Dallas World Aquarium in Dallas, holds more than 85,000 gallons of salt seawater. It has life from around the world. You can walk through a clear tunnel to see the life on a reef.

Investigate

Suppose you design an aquarium to hold 20 gallons of water. Each gallon takes up about 250 cubic inches. What different dimensions could the aquarium be? Choose the dimensions that you think are best. Explain your choice.

GO ONLINE **Technology** Student pages are available in the Student eBook.

Show What You Know

Check your understanding of important skills needed for success in Chapter 24.

▶ Length, Width, and Height

Find the length, width, and height of each.

1. 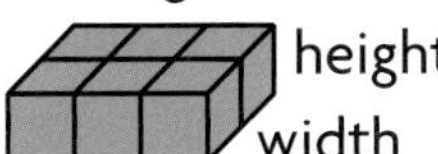

2. 

3. 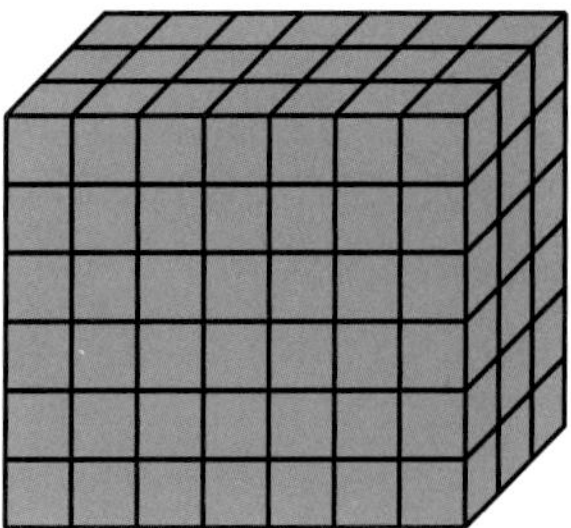

4. 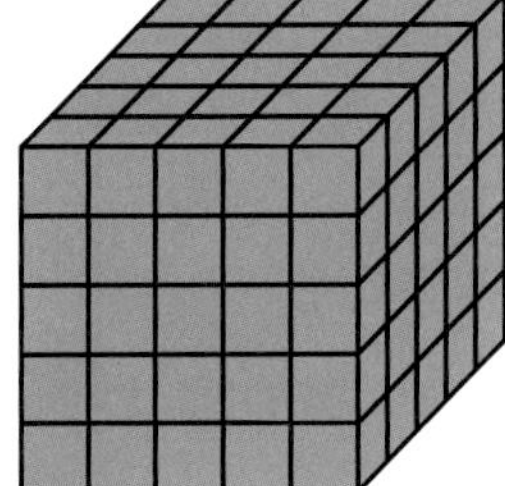

5. 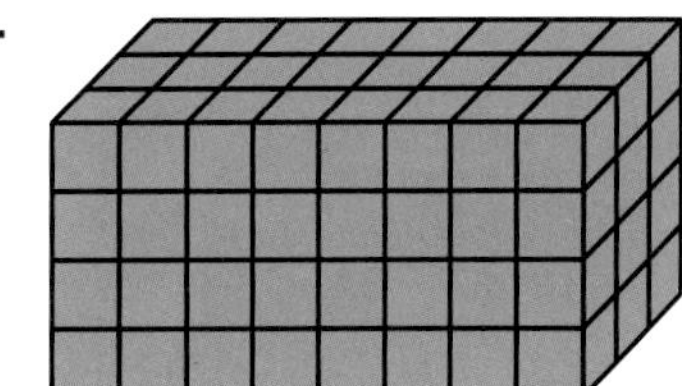

6. 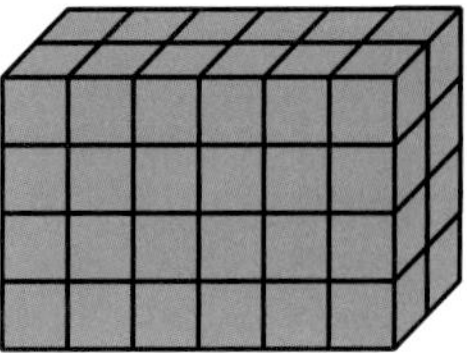

▶ Multiply Three Factors

Show two ways to group using parentheses. Find the product.

7. $2 \times 2 \times 3 = \blacksquare$

8. $3 \times 4 \times 5 = \blacksquare$

9. $6 \times 4 \times 3 = \blacksquare$

10. $7 \times 6 \times 1 = \blacksquare$

11. $5 \times 2 \times 7 = \blacksquare$

12. $8 \times 5 \times 5 = \blacksquare$

VOCABULARY POWER

CHAPTER VOCABULARY

capacity
cubic unit
volume

WARM-UP WORDS

volume the amount of space a solid figure occupies

cubic unit a unit of volume with dimensions of $1 \text{ unit} \times 1 \text{ unit} \times 1 \text{ unit}$

capacity the amount a container can hold when filled

1 Estimate and Measure Volume of Prisms

OBJECTIVE: Estimate and measure the volume of rectangular prisms.

Quick Review

1. $2 \times 3 \times 5$
2. $4 \times 1 \times 2$
3. $8 \times 3 \times 4$
4. $6 \times 7 \times 2$
5. $3 \times 4 \times 6$

Vocabulary

volume

cubic unit

Learn

Volume is the amount of space a solid figure occupies. Volume is measured using **cubic units**. Volume can be measured in units such as cubic centimeters, cubic inches, or cubic feet.

1 unit 1 unit
1 unit

Activity Estimate volume.

Materials ■ prism net ■ scissors ■ tape ■ centimeter cubes

Step 1

Cut out the net. Fold along the lines, and tape the sides to make an open box.

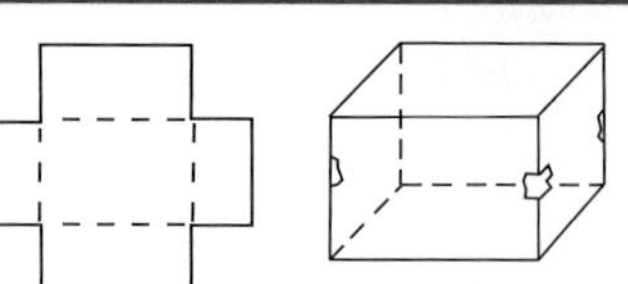

Step 2

Estimate how many cubes will fill the box. Record your estimate.

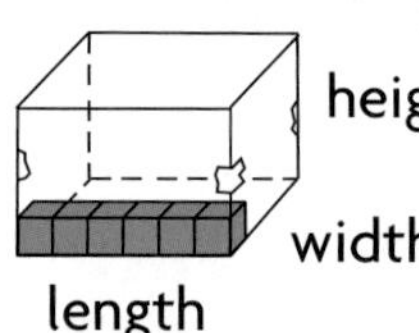

Step 3

Place as many cubes as you can in the box. Count the cubes you used. Record the number.

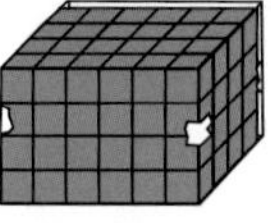

- Is your estimate greater than or less than the actual number of cubes in the box? Explain.

Math Idea
To help estimate the volume of a prism, you can visualize the number of cubes that will fit along the length, width, and height of a prism.

Example Estimate volume.

Estimate the number of cubes that will fit along the length, width, and height of the prism.

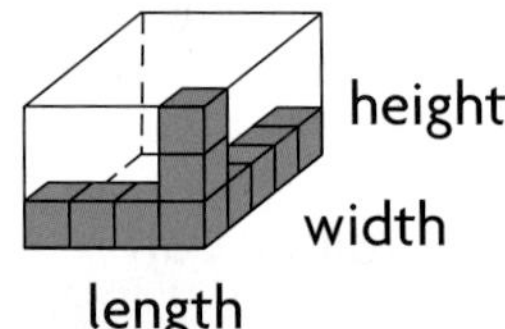

Think: About 4 cubes fit along the length, about 5 cubes fit along the width. So, the bottom layer has about 4×5, or 20 cubes. There are about 3 layers of 20 cubes each.

20 cubes + 20 cubes + 20 cubes = 60 cubes

So, the volume is about 60 cubic units.

TEKS 4.11D estimate volume in cubic units. **4.11C** use concrete models of standard cubic units to measure volume. *also* **4.11A, 4.14D, 4.15A, 4.15B**

Measure Volume

You can measure volume in more than one way.

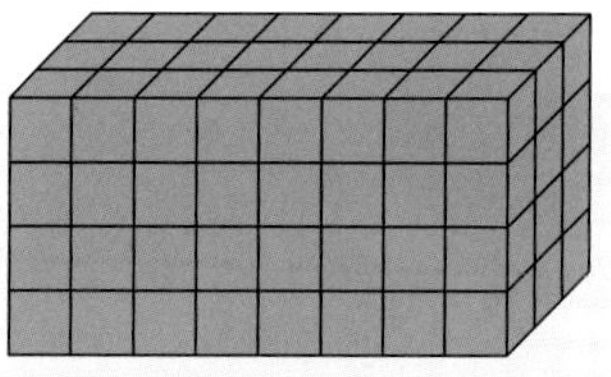

Example 1 **Build a rectangular prism.**

Count the number of cubic units as you build a rectangular prism with a volume of 96 cubic units.

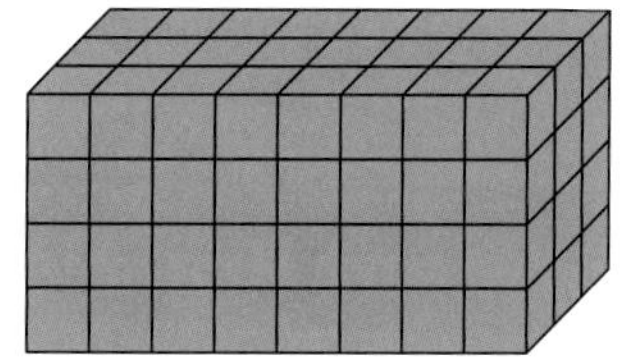

You can find the total number of cubic units in a rectangular prism by counting the number of units in each layer.

Example 2 **Count the number of cubic units in each layer. Then add.**

Step 1

Count the number of cubic units in the layer.

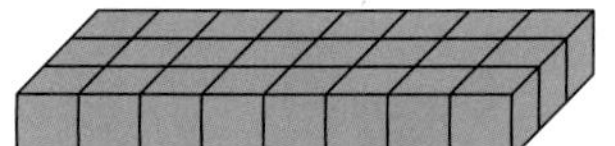

There are 24 cubic units.

Step 2

Count the number of cubic units in the layer.

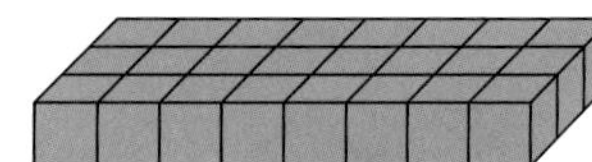

There are 24 cubic units.

Step 3

Count the number of cubic units in the layer.

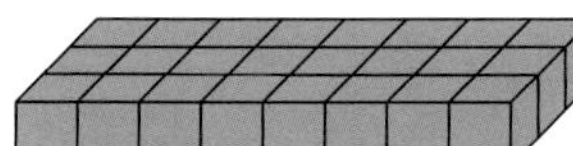

There are 24 cubic units.

Step 4

Count the number of cubic units in the layer.

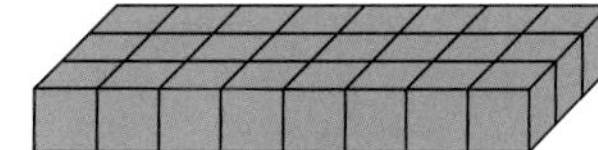

There are 24 cubic units.

Step 5

Add the total number of cubes in each layer.

$24 + 24 + 24 + 24 = 96$

So, the volume of the prism is 96 cubic units.

Guided Practice

1. How many cubes make up the bottom layer of the rectangular prism shown at right? What is the volume?

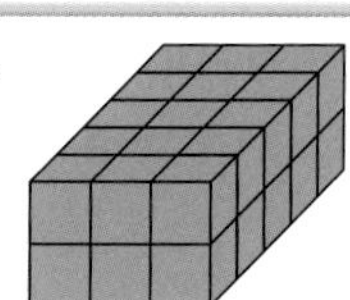

Estimate. Then count to find the volume.

2. 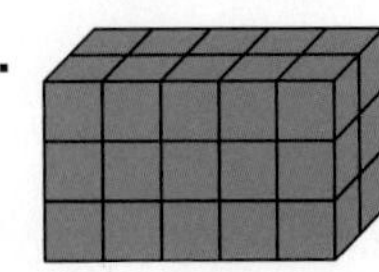

✓3. 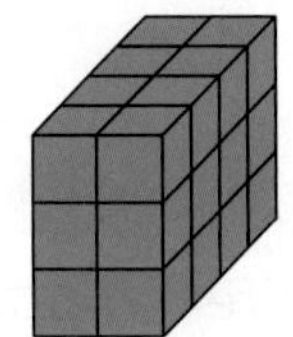

✓4. 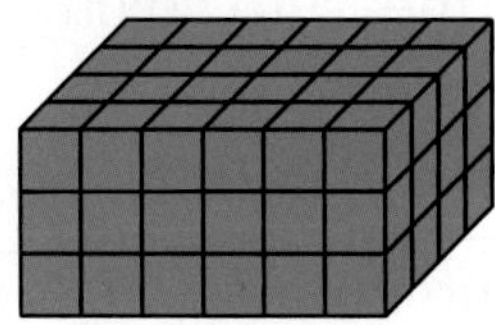

5. **TALK Math** **Explain** why you can add the number of cubes in each layer to find the volume of a rectangular prism.

Independent Practice and Problem Solving

Estimate. Then count to find the volume.

6. 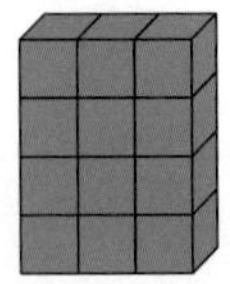

7. 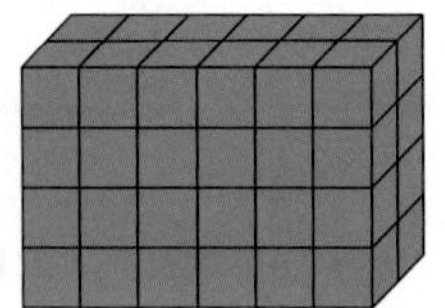

8. 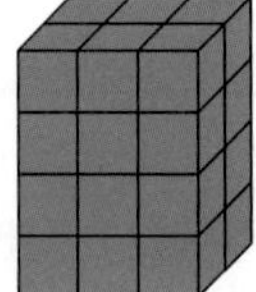

9.

10. 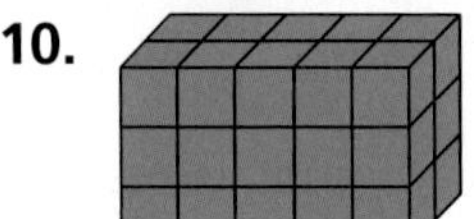

11. 

12. 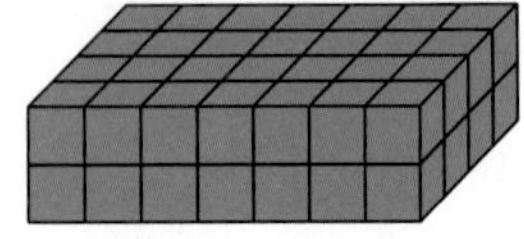

13. 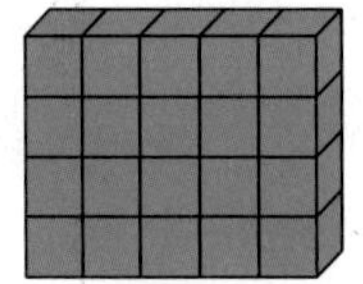

14. 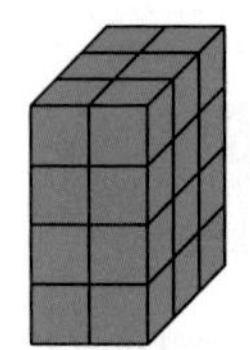

15. **Reasoning** What is the difference between a foot, a square foot, and a cubic foot? Name something you might measure with each unit and then draw a picture of each.

16. **Reasoning** Karla has 24 centimeter cubes. Name 3 different ways Karla can use all the cubes to build a rectangular prism.

17. Hayden's sand box is 6 feet long, 5 feet wide, and 1 foot deep. What is the volume of his sandbox? Make a model to solve.

18. **WRITE Math** **Explain** how to estimate the number of centimeter cubes needed to fill a tissue box.

Technology
Use Harcourt Mega Math, Ice Station Exploration, *Frozen Solids*, Level J.

 Extra Practice on page 642, Set A

Mixed Review and TAKS Prep

19. An index card measures 3 inches by 5 inches. What is the area of an index card? (TEKS 4.11A, p. 614)

20. A pizza parlor offers cheese, mushrooms, pepperoni, and vegetables as toppings. If Alice chooses 2 different toppings, how many combinations are possible? (TEKS 4.13A, p. 524)

21. **TAKS Prep** The volume of a rectangular prism is 96 square inches. The height is 8 inches. What could the length and width of the rectangular prism be? **Explain** how you know. (Obj. 4)

22. **TAKS Prep** Sam built the figure below using centimeter cubes. What is the volume of the figure? (Obj. 4)

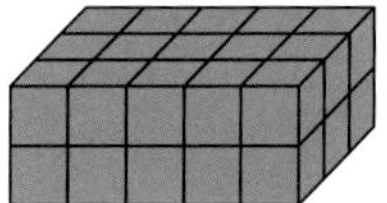

A 10 cubic centimeters

C 15 cubic centimeters

B 18 cubic centimeters

D 30 cubic centimeters

Problem Solving and Reasoning

MEASUREMENT Wanda and Marianne found the volume of a box of crackers. Wanda used cubic centimeters. Marianne used cubic inches.

Each layer of the prism has 60 cubic centimeters. There are 10 layers. The volume of the box is 600 cubic centimeters. Is the volume of the box greater than or less than 600 cubic inches?

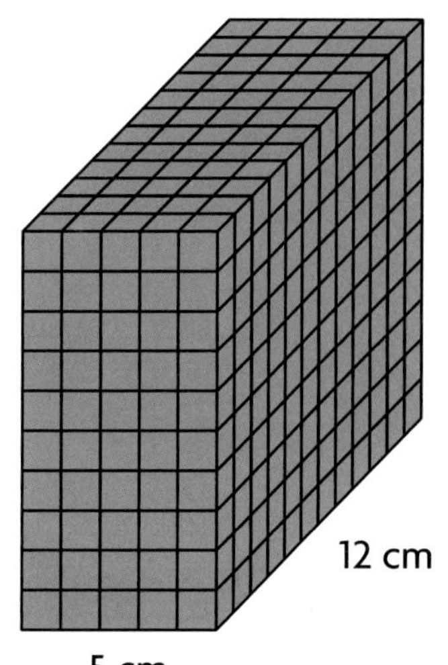

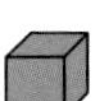
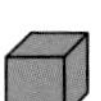

cubic centimeter

cubic inch

Since a cubic inch is larger than a cubic centimeter, fewer cubic inches will fit inside the box of crackers.

So, the volume of the box of crackers is less than 600 cubic inches.

Choose the greater volume.

1. 15 cubic centimeters
15 cubic feet

2. 11 cubic yards
11 cubic inches

3. 23 cubic inches
23 cubic feet

4. 8 cubic centimeters
8 cubic meters

Problem Solving Workshop
Skill: Too Much/Too Little Information

Read to Understand
Plan
Solve
Check

OBJECTIVE: Solve problems by using the skill *too much/too little information.*

Use the Skill

PROBLEM Leo is packing his suitcase to go on a trip to visit his cousins. His suitcase is 28 inches by 19 inches by 10 inches. His flight leaves at 1:30 P.M. and is 2 hours long. What is the volume of his suitcase?

Sometimes a problem has extra information that is not needed to solve the problem. Sometimes a problem does not have enough information to be solved.

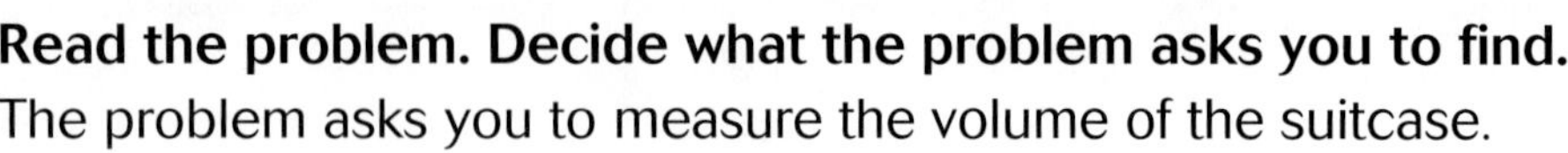

Read the problem. Decide what the problem asks you to find.
The problem asks you to measure the volume of the suitcase.

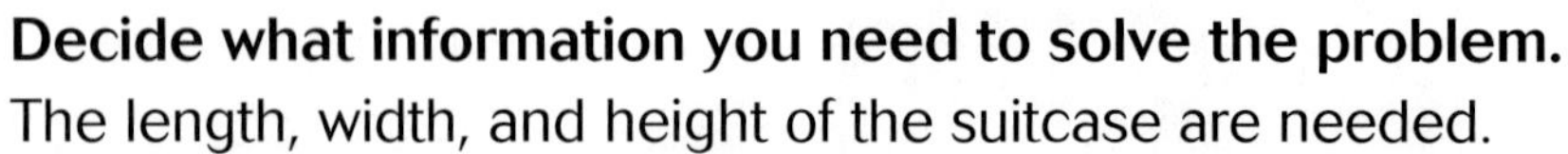

Decide what information you need to solve the problem.
The length, width, and height of the suitcase are needed.

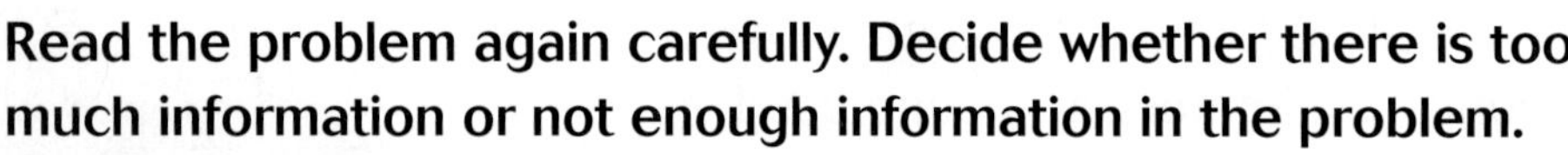

Read the problem again carefully. Decide whether there is too much information or not enough information in the problem.
There is too much information. The time the flight leaves and the length of the flight are not needed.

Solve the problem, if possible.
Find the volume.
Each layer has 28×19, or 532 cubes.
volume $= 532 + 532 + 532 + 532 + 532 + 532 + 532 + 532 + 532 + 532$, or 532×10
volume $= 5{,}320$

So, the volume of the suitcase is 5,320 cubic inches.

TALK Math
What if the height of the suitcase was not given in the problem? Would you have too much or too little information to solve the problem?

Think and Discuss

Decide whether the problem has too much or too little information. Then solve, if possible.

a. Riley wrapped a gift box that is 4 inches long and 8 inches high. What is the volume of Riley's gift box?

b. Holly has a shoe box that is 3 inches long, 2 inches wide, and 6 inches high. Roger has a shoe box with a greater volume. What is the volume of Holly's shoe box?

TEKS 4.14C select or develop an appropriate problem-solving plan or strategy, including drawing a picture, looking for a pattern, systematic guessing and checking, acting it out, making a table, working a simpler problem, or working backwards to solve a problem. *also* **4.4B, 4.4C, 4.4D, 4.11C, 4.11D, 4.14D, 4.15A, 4.15B, 4.16B**

Guided Problem Solving

Decide if the problem has too much or too little information. Then solve, if possible.

1. The volume of the clubhouse in Mason's backyard is 80 cubic feet. The perimeter of the floor of the clubhouse is 18 feet. The clubhouse is 4 feet long and 5 feet wide. What is the height of the clubhouse?

   What information do you need? Was it given?

   What information is not needed?

   Solve the problem.

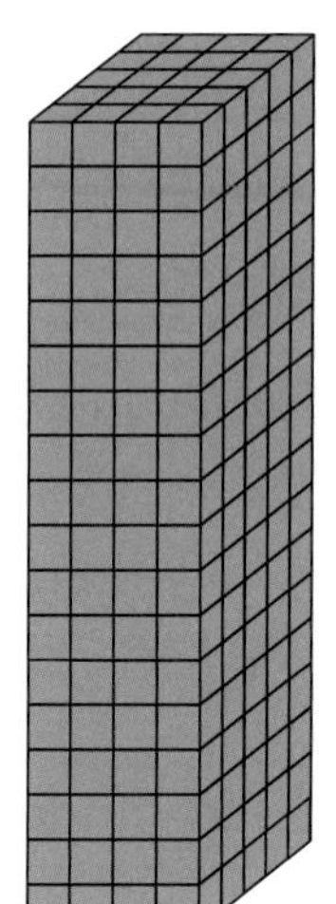

2. **What if** the clubhouse had a volume of 100 cubic feet? What would the height be?

3. Two students are building rectangular prisms in math class. Tim's rectangular prism uses 100 centimeter cubes. Rachel's rectangular prism uses more centimeter cubes than Tim's. Rachel's figure is 9 centimeters long and 6 centimeters high. How many centimeter cubes did Rachel use to build her prism?

Mixed Applications

4. Carolyn needs 28 wood screws to build a birdhouse. There are 8 screws in each pack. Each pack costs $3.49. How many packs does Carolyn need to buy?

5. A roller coaster has 6 cars with 9 rows in each car. There are 3 seats in each row. How many people can ride the roller coaster at once?

USE DATA For 6–9, use the table.

6. How many more centimeter cubes did Henry use than Emily?

7. Whose rectangular prism used the most centimeter cubes? How many?

8. **Reasoning** Suppose Patty took her rectangular prism apart, then used all the centimeter cubes to build a different rectangular prism. What could its length, width, and height be? **Explain** your answer.

9. **WRITE Math** **What's the Question?** Patty compared the number of centimeter cubes she used to build her rectangular prism to the numbers used by the others. The answer is three times as many.

Rectangular Prism Game

Student	Number of Cubes		
	Length	Width	Height
Patty	2	3	4
Emily	1	2	4
Justin	5	2	5
Henry	6	1	2

LESSON 3

Compare Volume of Prisms

OBJECTIVE: Compare volume of prisms.

Quick Review

Compare. Write <, >, or =.

1. 420 ● 402
2. 2,320 ● 2,023
3. 5×15 ● 4×20
4. $3 \times 4 \times 5$ ● $2 \times 5 \times 4$
5. $5 \times 2 \times 8$ ● $3 \times 9 \times 4$

Learn

PROBLEM Rosario's mailbox is 5 inches by 15 inches by 6 inches. She was sent a package that measures 3 inches by 12 inches by 5 inches. Which has the greater volume, the mailbox or the package?

Example 1 Build models to compare.

Estimate. Then build a model of the mailbox to measure the volume. Count the cubic units.

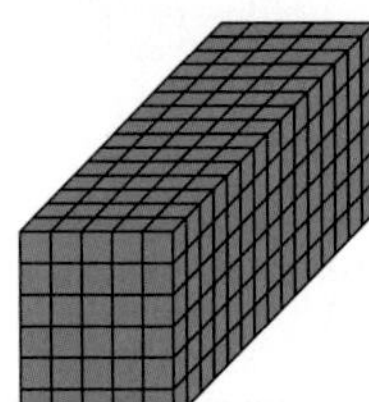

$75 + 75 + 75 + 75 + 75 + 75 = 450$

The volume is equal to 450 cubic units, or 450 cubic inches.

Estimate. Then build a model of the package to measure the volume. Count the cubic units.

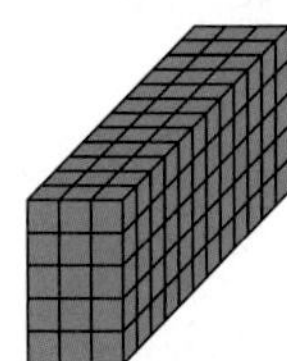

$36 + 36 + 36 + 36 + 36 = 180$

The volume is equal to 180 cubic units, or 180 cubic inches.

Since $450 > 180$, the mailbox has the greater volume.

Example 2 Compare figures with equal volume.

Estimate. Then count the cubic units.

volume $= 12 + 12 + 12 + 12$
$= 48$ cubic units

Estimate. Then count the cubic units.

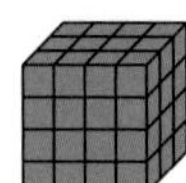

volume $= 12 + 12 + 12 + 12$
$= 48$ cubic units

So, both rectangular prisms have a volume of 48 cubic units.

Guided Practice

1. One prism is made using 48 cubes. Another is made using 46 cubes. Which prism has greater volume? **Explain.**

TEKS 4.11C use concrete models of standard cubic units to measure volume. *also* **4.1A, 4.4B, 4.4C, 4.4D, 4.14A, 4.14D, 4.15A, 4.15B**

Compare the volumes of the prisms. Write <, >, or = for each ●.

2.  ● 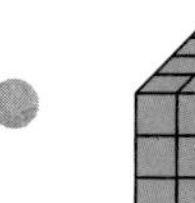

3. 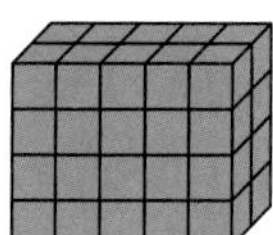 ● 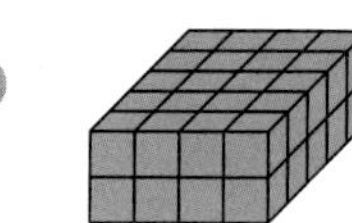

4. TALK Math **Explain** how you can decide which of two prisms has the greater volume.

Independent Practice and Problem Solving

Compare the volumes of the figures. Write <, >, or = for each ●.

5. 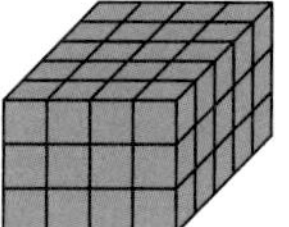 ● 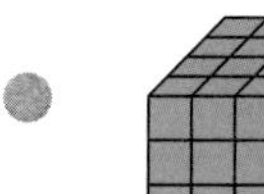

6. 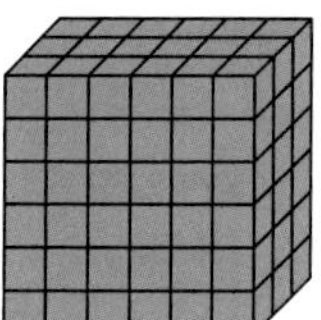 ● 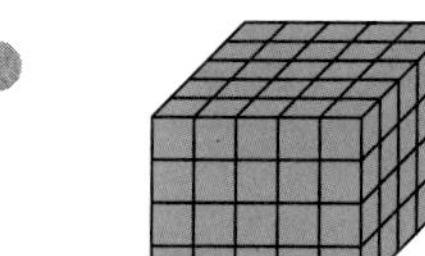

Use cubes to build each prism. Then compare the volumes.

7. Prism A
length: 8 centimeters
width: 7 centimeters
height: 4 centimeters

Prism B
length: 6 centimeters
width: 9 centimeters
height: 9 centimeters

8. Prism A
length: 10 centimeters
width: 12 centimeters
height: 3 centimeters

Prism B
length: 9 centimeters
width: 4 centimeters
height: 10 centimeters

9. Which has greater volume, a prism 2 units long, 3 units wide, and 4 units high or a cube with a length, width, and height of 3 units?

10. Two prisms have the same volume. One is 9 units long, 3 units wide, and 4 units high. The other is 2 units long, 18 units wide, and n units high. What is the value of n?

11. **Reasoning** Is every rectangular prism with volume 27 cubic units a cube? **Explain** how you know.

12. WRITE Math **Explain** how two prisms that are different shapes can have the same volume.

Mixed Review and TAKS Prep

13. How many vertices does a rectangular prism have? How many edges? (TEKS 4.8C, p. 314)

14. Walt measured a board eight and seven-eighths inches long. Write the length as a mixed number. (TEKS 4.2B, p. 402)

15. **TAKS Prep** Sheryl has a box shaped like a rectangular prism. The volume of the box is 36 cubic feet. What could be the length, width, and height of the box? (Obj. 4)

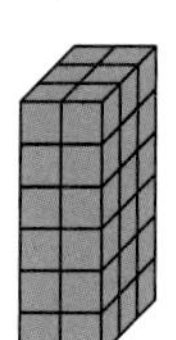

Extra Practice on page 642, Set B

Relate Volume and Capacity

OBJECTIVE: Relate volume and capacity of rectangular prisms.

Quick Review

Measure the volume.

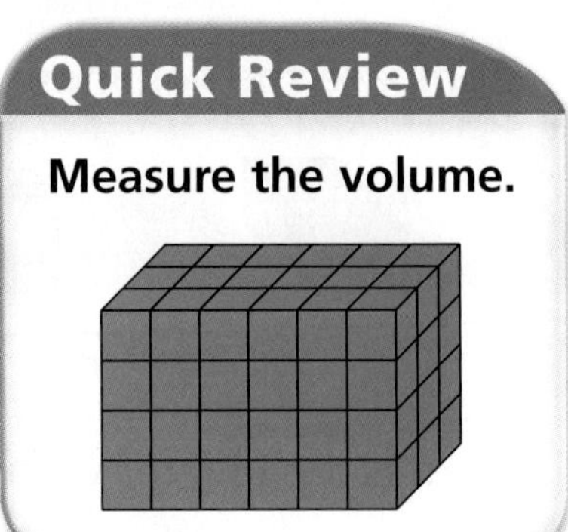

Learn

There are different ways to measure the space inside an object. Volume uses cubic units to measure the space an object takes up. Capacity measures how much an object can hold when filled.

Activity Measure the volume and capacity of a cereal box.

Materials ■ empty cereal box ■ centimeter cubes ■ 1-cup measuring cup ■ rice

Step 1

Estimate. Then, measure the volume. Use centimeter cubes to fill the box.

Step 2

Estimate. Then, measure the capacity. Use cups of rice to fill the box.

ERROR ALERT

In Step 1, be sure to place the cubes in layers.

In the metric system, measures of volume and capacity are related. A container with a volume of 1 cubic centimeter (cc) can hold 1 milliliter (mL) of water.

Equivalent Measures

Volume of Container (in cc)	Capacity (in mL)
1	1
10	10
100	100

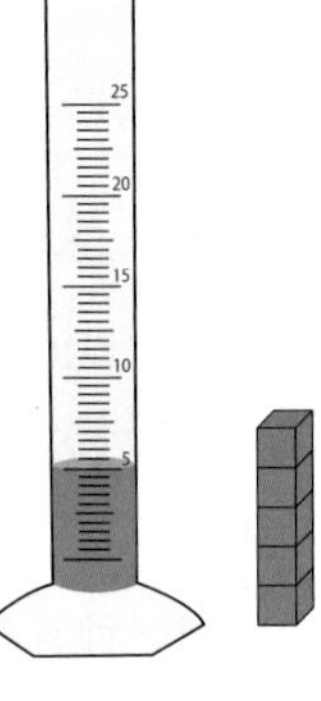

5 mL = 5 cubic centimeters

Guided Practice

1. Name two units used to measure volume. Name two units used to measure capacity.

Tell whether you would measure the capacity or the volume.

2. the amount of water in a bucket
3. the amount of space a brick takes up
4. **TALK Math** **Explain** how you could use measuring cups and water to find the capacity of a pitcher.

Independent Practice and Problem Solving

Tell whether you would measure the *capacity* or the *volume*.

5. the amount of space an ice cube takes up
6. the amount of space inside a toy box
7. the amount of water in a swimming pool
8. the amount of soup in a pot
9. the amount of cake mix in a box
10. the amount of space inside a closet

USE DATA For 11–13, use the table.

Object	Capacity	Volume
Eye dropper	2 milliliters	2 cubic centimeters
Gas tank	15 gallons	2 cubic feet
Milk carton	1 cup	14 cubic inches

11. A medicine cup holds 10 milliliters of medicine. What is the volume of the medicine cup?
12. **Reasoning** There are 16 tablespoons in 1 cup. Is the volume of a tablespoon greater than or less than 1 cubic inch? **Explain.**
13. How many gallons of gas can be held in a tank with volume of 2 cubic yards? (Hint: 1 cubic yard = 9 cubic feet)
14. ***FAST FACT*** The capacity of a healthy adult's lungs is about 5,000 milliliters. What is the volume of a healthy adult's lungs in cubic centimeters?
15. **WRITE Math** **What's the Error?** Sean says that his sports bottle has a volume of 1 liter. Is he correct? **Explain.**

Mixed Review and TAKS Prep

16. In the table below, when given an input, *x*, what is a way to find its related output, *y*? (TEKS 4.7, p. 170)

Input, *x*	4	5	6	7
Output, *y*	16	20	24	28

17. Which of these units would best measure the capacity of a coffee cup, ounces or gallons? (TEKS 4.11A, p. 580)
18. **TAKS Prep** Alan wants to know how much water he needs to fill his new fish tank. Which measurement should Alan find? (Obj. 4)

 A Capacity

 B Length

 C Mass

 D Perimeter

Extra Practice on page 642, Set C

Extra Practice

Set A Estimate. Then count to find the volume. (p. 632–635)

1. 

2. 

3. 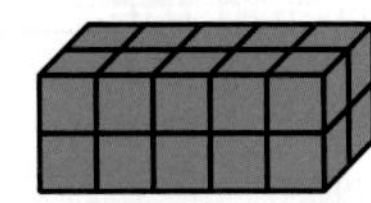

4. 

5. 

6. 

10. Parker's toy box is 5 feet long, 4 feet wide, and 2 feet deep. What is the volume of his toy box?

Set B Compare the volumes of the figures. Write <, >, or = for each ●. (p. 638–639)

1. 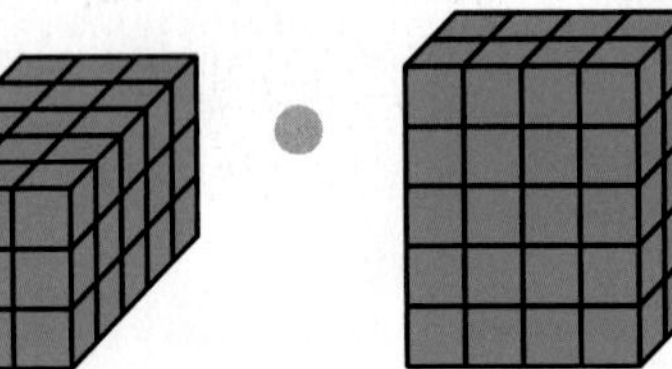

2. 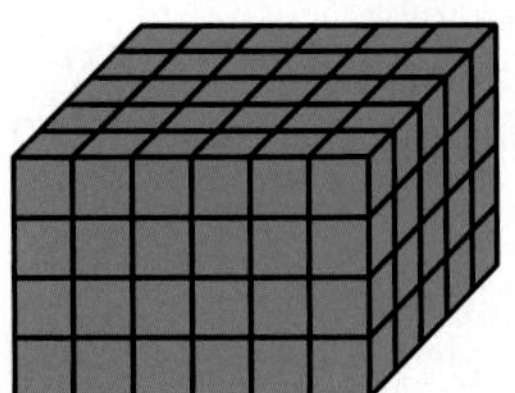  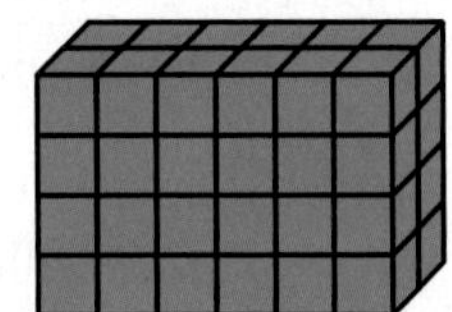

Use cubes to build each prism. Then, compare the volumes.

3. **Prism A**
   length: 8 cm
   width: 6 cm
   height: 5 cm

   Prism B
   length: 9 cm
   width: 5 cm
   height: 6 cm

4. **Prism A**
   length: 2 cm
   width: 10 cm
   height: 6 cm

   Prism B
   length: 6 cm
   width: 5 cm
   height: 7 cm

5. Which has the greater volume, a prism 3 units long, 5 units wide, and 6 units high or a cube with a length, width, and height of 5 units?

Set C Tell whether you would measure the *capacity* or *volume*. (p. 640–641)

1. the amount of lemonade in a pitcher
2. the amount of space inside a suitcase
3. the amount of soup in a bowl
4. the amount of space in a cereal box
5. the amount of space in a bag of sugar
6. the amount of water in a lake

Technology
CD ROM Use Harcourt Mega Math, Ice Station Exploration, *Frozen Solids*, Level J.

Shipping Yo-Yos

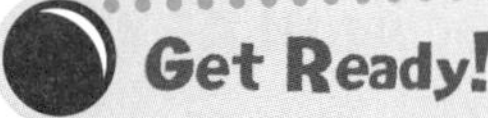

Get Ready!
2 players

Pack!
10 scenario cards

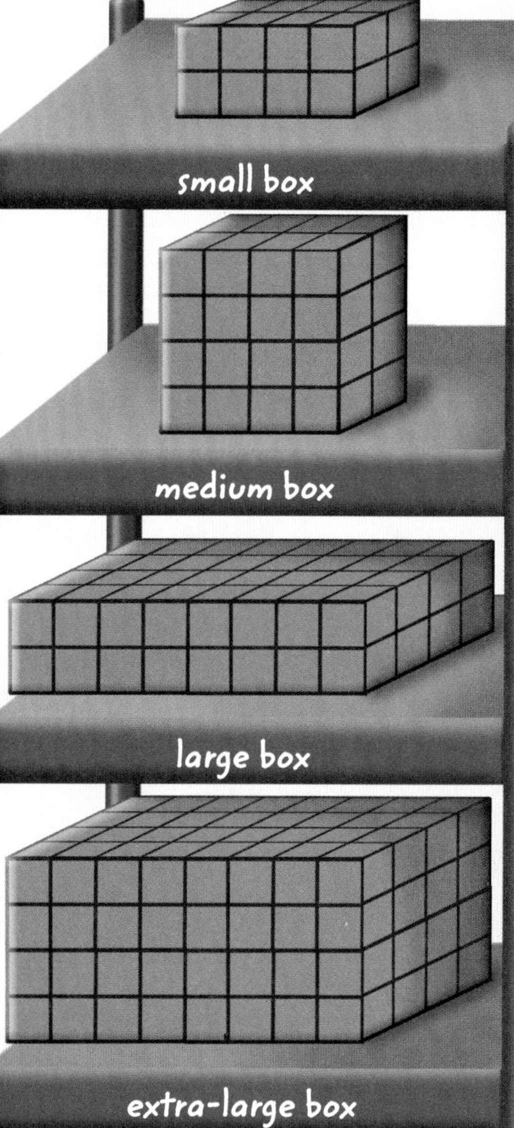

Ship!

Joe's Toy Company is shipping yo-yos to 10 different places. Each yo-yo is packaged individually before being placed in a shipping box. Help Joe decide which size box should be used.

- A player shuffles the scenario cards.
- Player 1 chooses a card and reads the scenario out loud.
- Player 1 decides which box should be used in the scenario and announces the answer.
- Player 2 checks the answer. If correct, Player 1 keeps the card.
- Player 2 chooses a card and repeats the steps.
- Players take turns until all cards have been attempted. The player with more cards is the winner.

Chapter 24 Review/Test

Check Vocabulary and Concepts

VOCABULARY
cubic unit
volume

Choose the best term from the box.

1. The amount of space a solid figure occupies is its __?__. (TEKS 4.11D, 4.11C, p. 632)
2. Would you measure the capacity or the volume of the amount of milk in a carton? (TEKS 4.11C, p. 640)
3. Which has a greater volume, a prism that is 3 units long, 3 units wide, and 6 units high, or a prism that is 4 units long, 5 units wide, and 6 units high? (TEKS 4.11C, p. 638)

Check Skills

Estimate. Then count to find the volume. (TEKS 4.11D, 4.11C, pp. 632–635)

4. 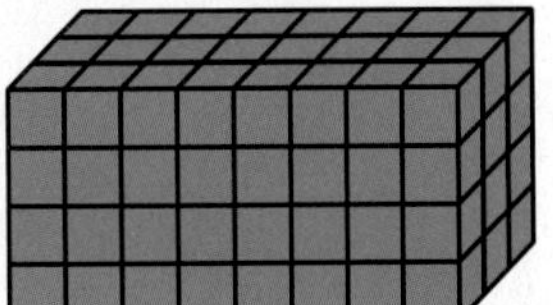

5. 

6. 

Use cubes to build each prism. Then, compare the volumes. (TEKS 4.11C, pp. 638–639)

7. **Prism A**
length: 7 cm
width: 4 cm
height: 6 cm

Prism B
length: 5 cm
width: 6 cm
height: 4 cm

8. **Prism A**
length: 3 cm
width: 8 cm
height: 3 cm

Prism B
length: 2 cm
width: 6 cm
height: 9 cm

Check Problem Solving

Decide if the problem has too much or too little information. Then solve, if possible. You may use a model. (TEKS 4.14C, pp. 636–637)

9. Darryl has a box of crayons that is 6 inches long and 5 inches high. The box holds 64 crayons. What is the volume of Darryl's box of crayons?
10. **WRITE Math** Kyle is packing a box of toys to send to his cousins. The box is 32 inches by 15 inches by 5 inches. What is the volume of the box? **Explain** how you know.

GO ONLINE **Technology** Use *Online Assessment.*

Enrich • Use a Formula

Various Volumes

There are several ways to find the volume of a rectangular prism. One way is to count all of the cubes. Another way is to use a formula.

The formula for volume is Volume = length × width × height,

or

$$V = l \times w \times h.$$

The Texas Historical Commission's traveling art exhibit in Austin is made of cubes that feature photos of treasures from Texas history.

What is the volume of this rectangular prism?

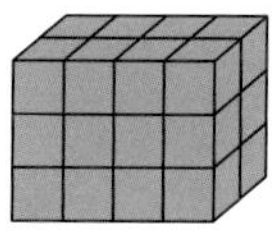

Example **Use a formula.**

Find the length, width, and height of the rectangular prism.

Step 1	**Step 2**
Find the length. Count the number of cubes in one row. 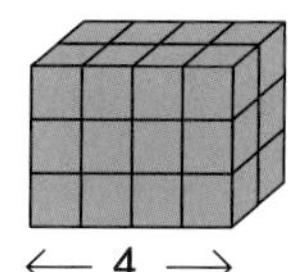 The length is 4 cubes.	Find the width. Count the number of rows in one layer. 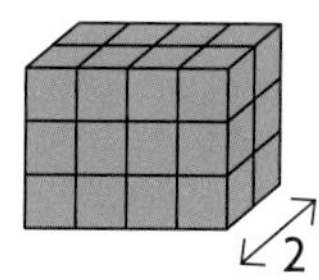 The width is 2 cubes.
Step 3	**Step 4**
Find the height. Count the number of layers in the rectangular prism. 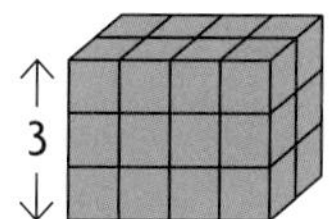 The height is 3 cubes.	Multiply length × width × height to find the volume. $V = l \times w \times h$ $V = 4 \times 2 \times 3$ V = 24 cubic units

So, the volume of the rectangular prism is 24 cubic units.

Try It

Use the formula to find the volume.

1. 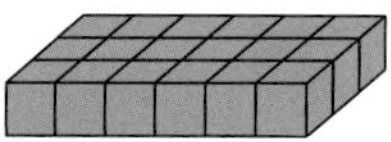

2. 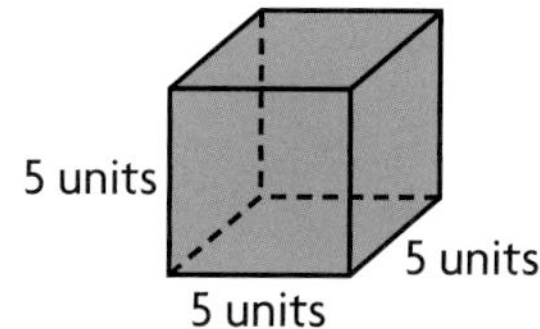

3. 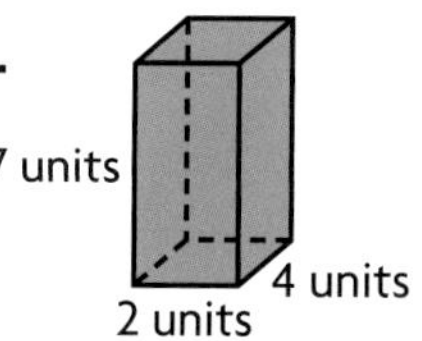

WRITE Math The volume of a rectangular prism is 32 cubic units. The length is 4 and the height is 4. What is the width? Use the formula $V = l \times w \times h$ to help. **Explain.**

Unit Review/Test
Chapters 21–24

Multiple Choice

1. What is the volume of this prism?
(TAKS Obj. 4)

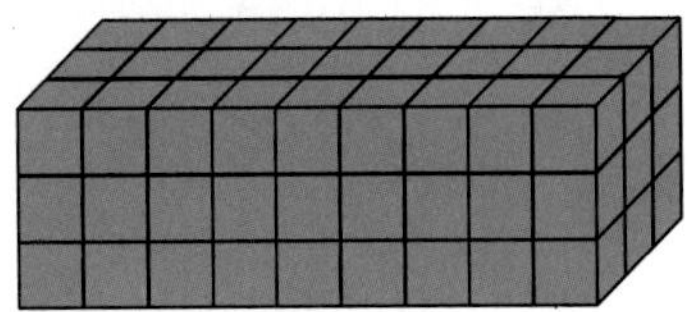

A 27 cubic units

B 54 cubic units

C 81 cubic units

D 108 cubic units

2. Find the perimeter of the rectangle.
(TAKS Obj. 4)

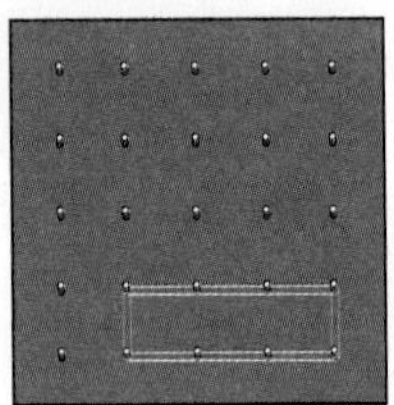

F 8 units

G 12 units

H 20 units

J 24 units

3. Which object has a mass of about 200 grams? (TAKS Obj. 4)

A 

B 

C 

D 

4. This is a diagram of Melissa's backyard.

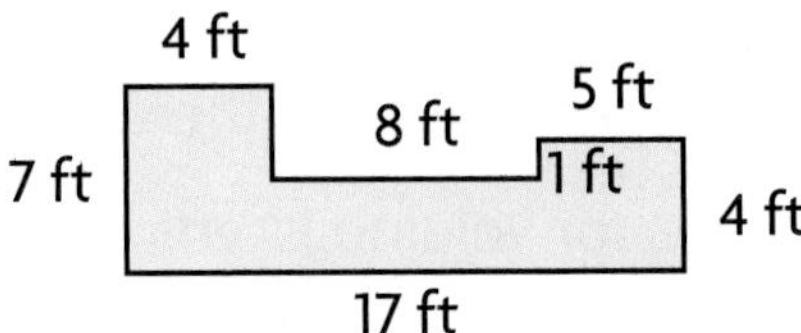

What is the area of the entire backyard?
(TAKS Obj. 4)

F 40 square feet

G 46 square feet

H 52 square feet

J 72 square feet

5. Which object is the most likely to be measured in inches? (TAKS Obj. 4)

A 

B 

C 

D 

6. The length of Mark's bedroom is 180 inches. How many yards is that?
(TAKS Obj. 4)

F 5 yards

G 7 yards

H 11 yards

J 13 yards

7. Find the perimeter of the tennis court. (TAKS Obj. 4)

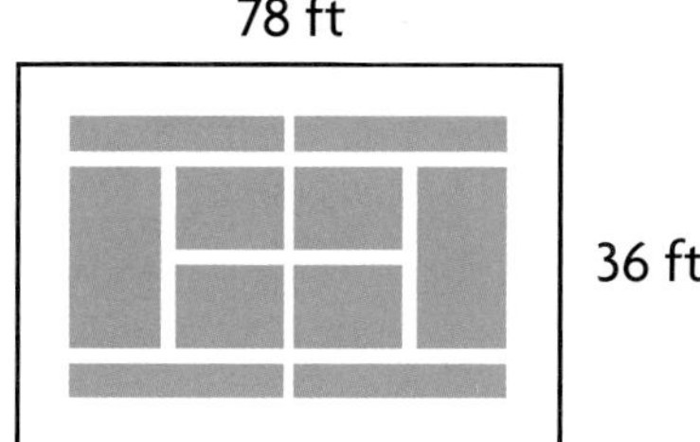

A 192 feet

B 212 feet

C 224 feet

D 228 feet

8. Choose the situation where volume is being measured. (TAKS Obj. 4)

F Amount of milk in a glass

G Amount of space in a bag

H Amount of water in a birdbath

J Amount of soap in a bottle

9. Which shows the correct order of the measurements from least to greatest. (TAKS Obj. 4)

A 1 inch, $2\frac{1}{2}$ inches, $1\frac{1}{4}$ inches

B 3 inches, $2\frac{1}{2}$ inches, 1 inch

C $2\frac{1}{2}$ inches, $1\frac{1}{4}$ inches, 1 inch

D 1 inch, $1\frac{1}{4}$ inches, $2\frac{1}{2}$ inches

10. Find the area. (TAKS Obj. 4)

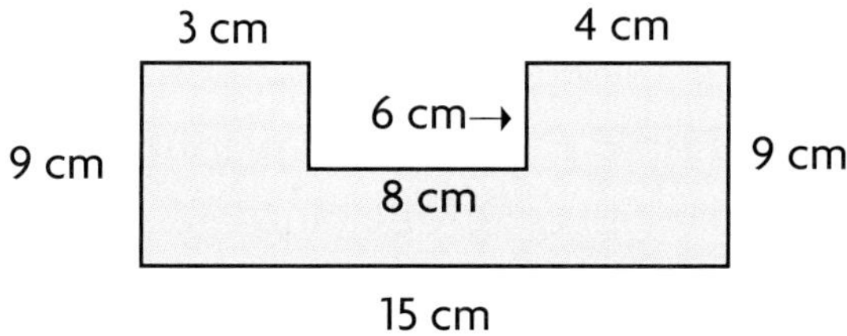

F 87 square centimeters

G 61 square centimeters

H 60 square centimeters

J 43 square centimeters

Short Response

11. What is the best measurement for the bowl: 2 liters, 20 milliliters, or 5 milliliters? (TAKS Obj. 4)

12. Rachele doubled this brownie recipe. Does she need more than or less than 1 pint of sugar? (TAKS Obj. 4)

Brownie Recipe

4 ounces chocolate	1 teaspoon vanilla
$1\frac{1}{2}$ sticks butter	$\frac{1}{2}$ teaspoon baking soda
2 cups sugar	salt
3 large eggs	1 cup canned walnuts

13. Jen framed a photo that has an area of 32 centimeters. What are 2 possible perimeters for her photo? (TAKS Obj. 4)

Extended Response WRITE Math

14. What is the better estimate for the pitcher, 1 cup or 1 gallon? **Explain.** (TAKS Obj. 4)

15. How can you estimate the number of centimeter cubes needed to fill this shoe box? **Explain.** (TAKS Obj. 4)

Texas

Problem Solving

Wildlife Habitats

Backyard Habitats

Texas Wildscapes is a program of the Texas Parks and Wildlife Department that encourages people to set up wildlife habitats in Texas. These habitats provide places for animals to eat, drink, raise their young, and hide from predators. You might see a fox, a porcupine, a tiny frog, and colorful birds in a Texas backyard habitat.

A successful Wildlife Habitat

FACT·ACTIVITY

Blanchard's cricket frog
$1\frac{1}{4}$ inches long
1 inch tall

Porcupine
24 inches long
$12\frac{3}{8}$ inches tall

Swift fox
30 inches long
$10\frac{1}{2}$ inches tall

Use the data on this page.

1. How many feet long is a porcupine?
2. A porcupine can weigh 12 pounds. How many ounces is this?
3. You see two cricket frogs, one on each side of a pond 6 yards long. How many feet apart are the two frogs?
4. **WRITE Math** Is a swift fox longer or shorter than 3 feet long? **Explain.**
5. Make a mural. Measure and draw full size pictures of the fox, the porcupine, and the frog. Draw and color a backyard habitat on poster paper. Cut out and paste your pictures in the scene. Label each animal.

There are 133 million acres of wildlife habitat in Texas.

Habitats approved by Texas Wildscapes will have a sign like this one.

Building a Habitat

People build wildlife habitats in their backyards, in schoolyards, in parks, or in empty lots. First, they decide what wildlife they want to attract. Then they research what the habitat might need to attract those animals. For example, water, shade, and different kinds of plants.

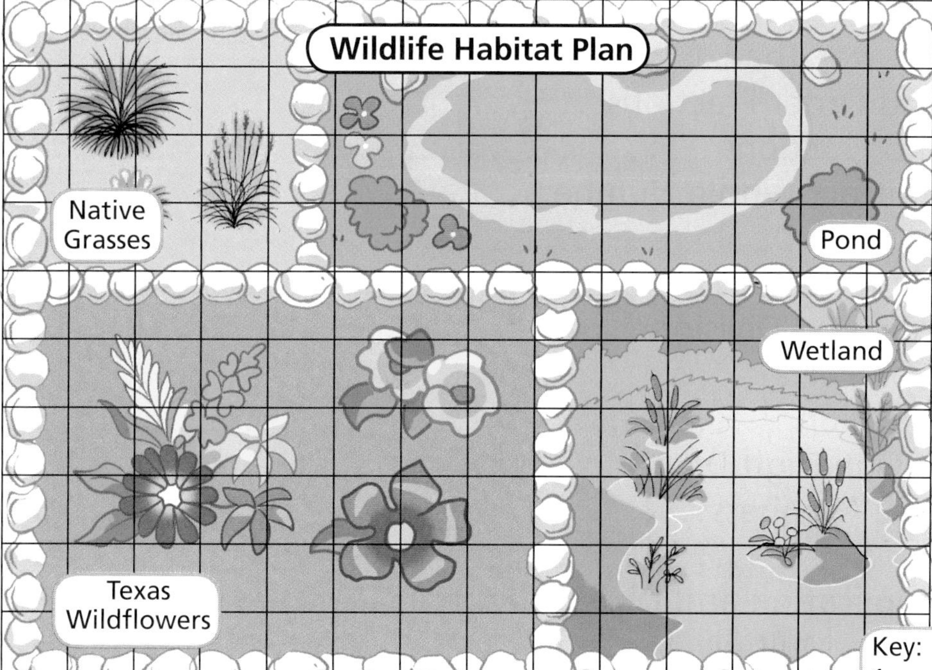

FACT·ACTIVITY

For 1–2, use the Wildlife Habitat Plan located above.

1. How can you find the perimeter of the Texas Wildflowers section? **Explain.**
2. What is the area of the habitat?

Design a habitat.

3. Make a plan for a habitat that has a perimeter of 44 feet. What animals do you want to attract? Use a drawing like the one above. Label your habitat's length and width.
4. Find the area of your habitat. Then find the perimeter and area of each section.

Student Handbook

Review the TEKS

These pages provide review of every state standard for your grade. They also help you avoid errors students often make.

Whole Number Place Value H2
Equivalent Fractions H3
Fractions Greater Than 1 .... H4
Compare and Order Fractions H5
Decimals and Fractions H6
Add and Subtract Whole Numbers H7
Add and Subtract Decimals H8
Factors and Products H9
Multiplication and Division H10
Multiplication Facts H11
Use Multiplication H12
Divide by a One-Digit Divisor H13
Round Whole Numbers H14
Estimation H15
Relate Multiplication and Division Facts H16
Use Patterns to Multiply H17
Describe Relationships H18
Identify Angles H19
Identify Lines H20
Two-Dimensional Figures H21
Three-Dimensional Figures H22
Congruent Figures H23
Symmetry H24
Fractions and Decimals on a Number LIne H25
Customary Measurement H26
Combinations H27
Bar Graphs H28
Problem Solving H29

TAKS Test-Taking Strategies H32
Review these strategies before the TAKS test to improve your test-taking skills. There are tips for reading and understanding a test item and understanding and answering the question.

Basic Facts Review H40
These pages will help you improve your memory of basic facts. Review addition, subtraction, multiplication, and division facts by using these sets of exercises throughout the year.

Table of Measures H44
This table will help you remember the relationship of important measures you have learned.

Texas Essential Knowledge and Skills. H46
The standards on these pages describe what you will learn and do in mathematics this year.

Glossary H49
The mathematics vocabulary words and phrases you will learn and use are defined in this glossary. Following each entry is the Spanish translation.

Index. H62
When you want to review a topic look in the index for a list of the pages where the topic is taught.

Review the TEKS

Whole Number Place Value

TEKS 4.1A use place value to read, write, compare, and order whole numbers through 999,999,999.

You can use place value to compare and order whole numbers with the same number of digits. If two whole numbers have different numbers of digits, the number with more digits is greater.

MILLIONS			THOUSANDS			ONES		
Hundreds	Tens	Ones	Hundreds	Tens	Ones	Hundreds	Tens	Ones
6	2	5,	7	2	3,	5	4	6
$6 \times 100{,}000{,}000$	$2 \times 10{,}000{,}000$	$5 \times 1{,}000{,}000$	$7 \times 100{,}000$	$2 \times 10{,}000$	$3 \times 1{,}000$	5×100	4×10	6×1
600,000,000	20,000,000	5,000,000	700,000	20,000	3,000	500	40	6

Examples

A Compare 845,027 and 8,453,027.

845,027 ← 6 digits

8,453,027 ← 7 digits

So, 845,027 $<$ 8,453,027.

B Write these numbers in order from least to greatest: 531, 476, 479.

Hundreds	Tens	Ones
5	3	1
4	7	6
4	7	9
$5 > 4$ 531 is the greatest.	$7 = 7$ Same number of tens.	$6 < 9$ 476 is the least.

ERROR ALERT

Always start at the left and compare digits in the same place-value position to compare and order.

Try It

Compare. Write $<$, $>$, or $=$ for each ●.

1. 468,809 ● 46,809
2. 532,634 ● 532,346
3. 2,298,759 ● 20,307,213

Order the numbers from least to greatest.

4. 40,326,058; 4,365,925; 400,684,244
5. 16,548,848; 16,485,922; 16,854,033

6. Read the problem below. **Explain** why B cannot be the correct answer choice. Then choose the correct answer.

COMMON ERROR

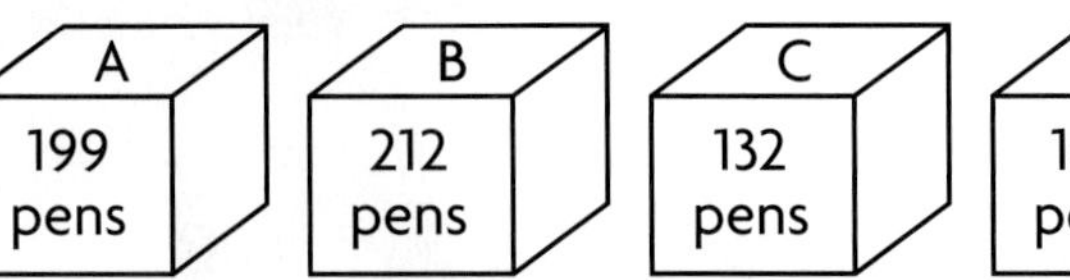

Which box has the least number of pens?

A Box A

B Box B

C Box C

D Box D

Review the TEKS

Equivalent Fractions

TEKS 4.2A use concrete objects and pictorial models to generate equivalent fractions.

A fraction names a part of a whole. The denominator tells how many equal parts are in the whole. The numerator tells how many parts are being considered.

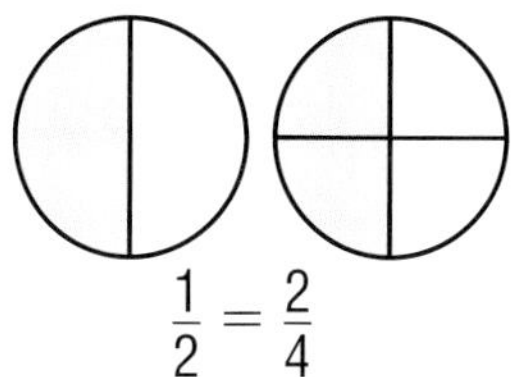

$\frac{1}{2} = \frac{2}{4}$

Fractions that name the same amount are called equivalent fractions. You can use models to find equivalent fractions.

Examples

A Write a fraction equivalent to $\frac{1}{3}$.

Use number lines. A fraction that lines up with $\frac{1}{3}$ is equivalent to $\frac{1}{3}$.

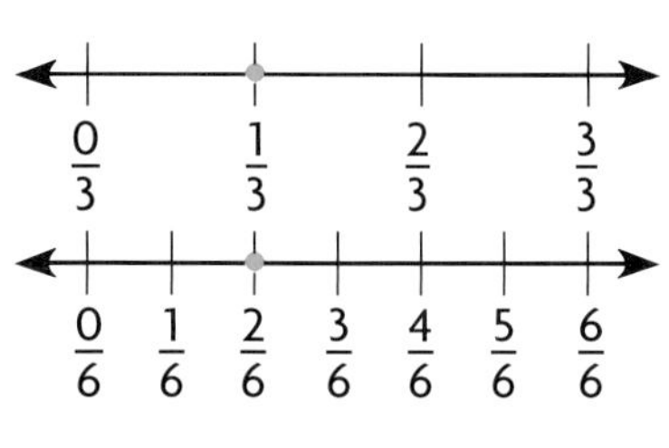

So, $\frac{2}{6}$ is equivalent to $\frac{1}{3}$.

B Write three fractions that are equivalent to $\frac{3}{4}$.

Use fraction bars. Line up fraction bars of the same type to show the same amounts.

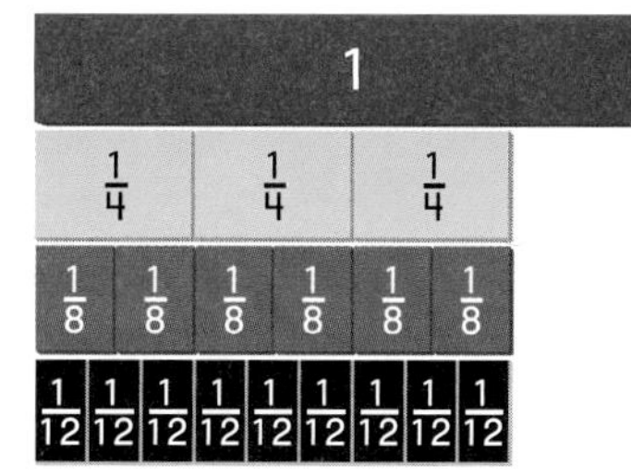

So, $\frac{3}{4}$, $\frac{6}{8}$, and $\frac{9}{12}$ are equivalent.

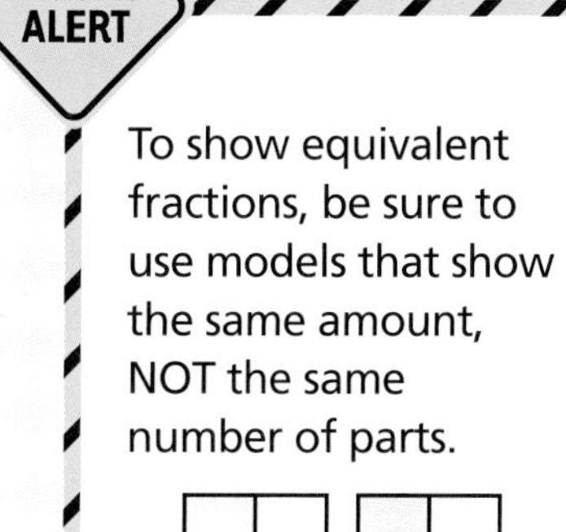

To show equivalent fractions, be sure to use models that show the same amount, NOT the same number of parts.

$\frac{1}{4}$ does not equal $\frac{1}{2}$.

Try It

Write two equivalent fractions for each model.

1. 

2. 

3. 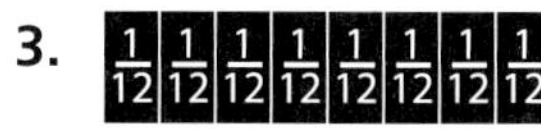

4. 

5. Read the problem below. **Explain** why C cannot be the correct answer choice. Then choose the correct answer.

COMMON ERROR

This model represents a fraction.

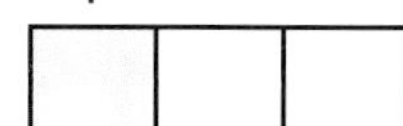

Which model shows an equivalent fraction?

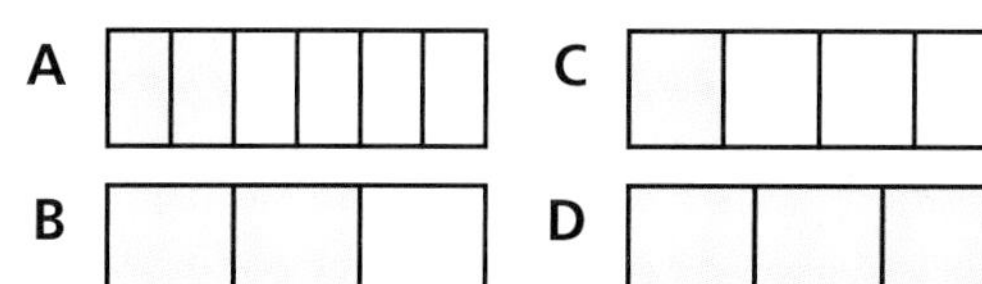

Review the TEKS

Fractions Greater Than One

TEKS 4.2B model fraction quantities greater than one using concrete objects and pictorial models.

A mixed number is made up of a whole number and a fraction. A mixed number has a value greater than 1. You can locate mixed numbers on a number line.

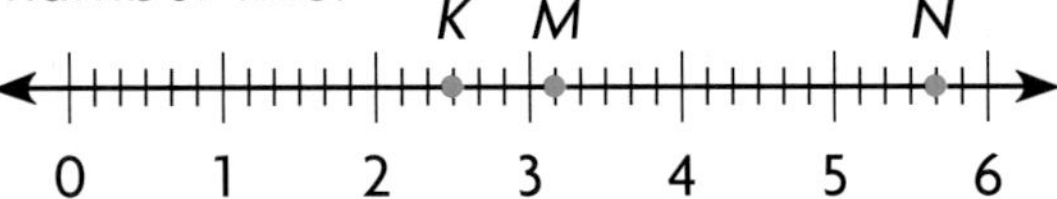

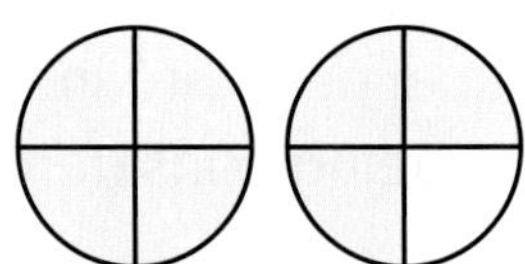

Read: one and three fourths

Write: $1\frac{3}{4}$

There are 6 equal parts marked between each whole number. That means there are 6 equal parts in one whole.

So, point *K* is located at $2\frac{3}{6}$, point *M* at $3\frac{1}{6}$, and point *N* at $5\frac{4}{6}$.

Examples

A Draw a model to show $2\frac{2}{8}$.

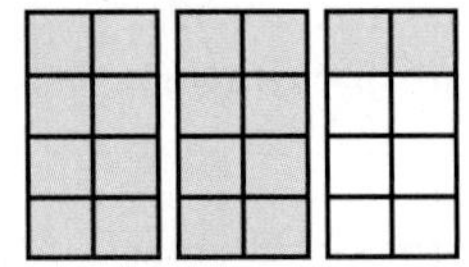

$2 + \frac{2}{8} = 2\frac{2}{8}$, or $2\frac{1}{4}$

B What mixed number on the number line does point *A* best represent?

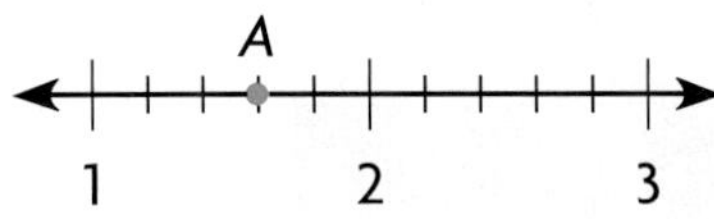

The number line shows fifths.

So, point *A* represents $1\frac{3}{5}$.

ERROR ALERT

Be sure to write the correct numbers for the numerator and denominator of the fractional part.

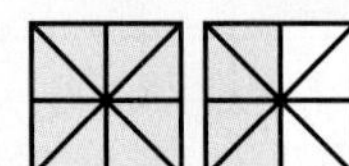

This model does not show $1\frac{12}{8}$. It shows $1\frac{4}{8}$, or $1\frac{1}{2}$.

Try It

Draw a model for each mixed number.

1. $2\frac{2}{3}$
2. $1\frac{1}{2}$
3. $3\frac{1}{4}$
4. $3\frac{3}{5}$

For 5–8, use the number line to write the letter each mixed number represents.

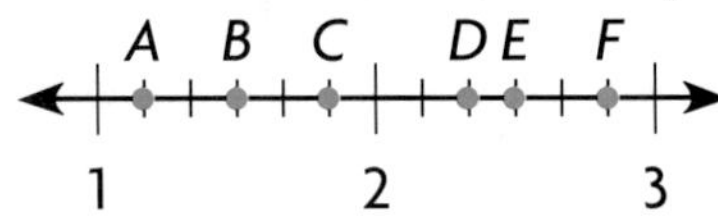

5. $2\frac{3}{6}$
6. $1\frac{1}{6}$
7. $2\frac{2}{6}$
8. $1\frac{5}{6}$

9. Read the problem below. **Explain** why A cannot be the correct answer choice.Then choose the correct answer.

COMMON ERROR

Which mixed number does the model represent?

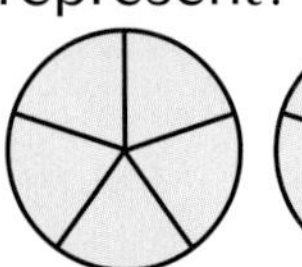
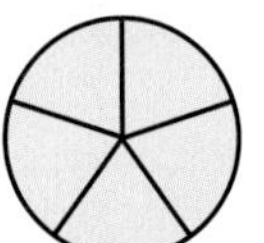

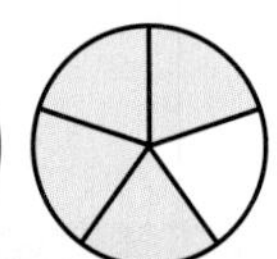

A $3\frac{5}{4}$

B $3\frac{19}{5}$

C $3\frac{1}{5}$

D Not here

Review the TEKS

Compare and Order Fractions

TEKS 4.2C compare and order fractions using concrete objects and pictorial models.

To compare two fractions, decide which fraction is greater or which is less. To order fractions, write them from least to greatest or greatest to least.

You can use pictures, number lines, or fraction bars to compare and order fractions. On a number line, the numbers on the right are greater than the numbers on the left.

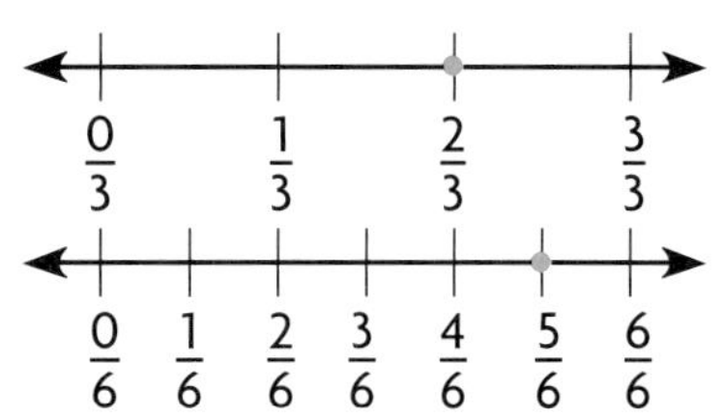

Examples

A Compare $\frac{2}{5}$ and $\frac{3}{5}$.

Use pictures. Compare the number of shaded circles. 2 < 3

When you compare fractions with like denominators, compare only the numerators.

So, $\frac{2}{5} < \frac{3}{5}$.

B Order $\frac{1}{2}$, $\frac{3}{4}$, and $\frac{5}{8}$ from least to greatest.

Use fraction bars. Line up the fraction bars and compare them.

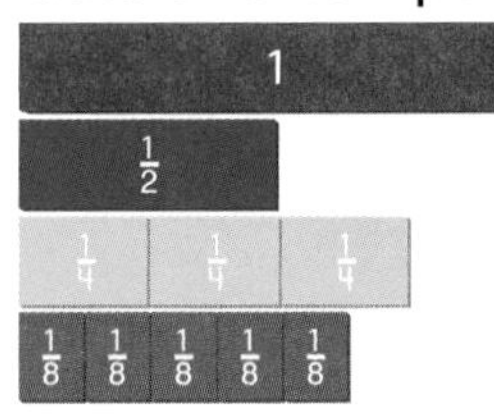

The shortest row represents the least fraction. So, the order from least to greatest is $\frac{1}{2}$, $\frac{5}{8}$, $\frac{3}{4}$.

ERROR ALERT

Be sure to use the signs < and > correctly.

< means "less than."

> means "greater than."

Incorrect: $\frac{3}{5} < \frac{2}{5}$

Correct: $\frac{3}{5} > \frac{2}{5}$

Try It

Compare. Write <, >, or = for each ●. You may use a model or picture.

1. $\frac{3}{8}$ ● $\frac{7}{8}$
2. $\frac{5}{6}$ ● $\frac{3}{6}$
3. $\frac{3}{5}$ ● $\frac{7}{10}$
4. $\frac{5}{8}$ ● $\frac{10}{16}$
5. $\frac{2}{3}$ ● $\frac{5}{6}$
6. $\frac{1}{4}$ ● $\frac{1}{5}$

Order the fractions from least to greatest. You may use a model or picture.

7. $\frac{1}{2}, \frac{1}{4}, \frac{5}{8}$
8. $\frac{2}{3}, \frac{1}{6}, \frac{5}{6}$
9. $\frac{3}{4}, \frac{1}{2}, \frac{7}{8}$
10. $\frac{3}{4}, \frac{9}{16}, \frac{5}{8}$

11. Read the problem below. **Explain** why B cannot be the correct answer choice. Then choose the correct answer. **COMMON ERROR**

The pizzas show how much is left over.

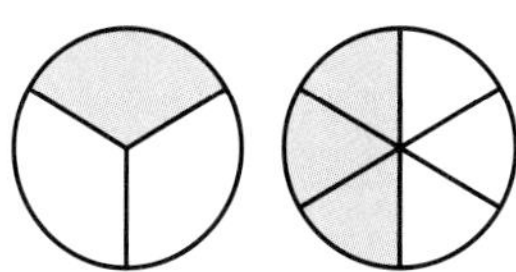

Which compares the leftover pizza?

A $\frac{1}{3} < \frac{3}{6}$ **C** $\frac{1}{2} > \frac{3}{6}$

B $\frac{1}{3} > \frac{3}{6}$ **D** $\frac{3}{6} > \frac{1}{2}$

Review the TEKS

Decimals and Fractions

TEKS 4.2D relate decimals to fractions that name tenths and hundredths using concrete objects and pictorial models.

You can draw a picture to relate fractions with denominators of 10 or 100 to decimals with tenths or hundredths. A decimal is a number with one or more digits to the right of the decimal point.

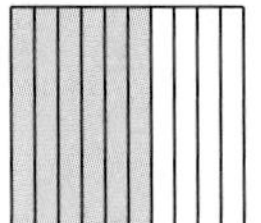

Fraction	**Decimal**
Read: six tenths	Read: six tenths
Write: $\frac{6}{10}$	Write: 0.6

Ones	.	Tenths	Hundredths
0	.	5	
0	.	7	8

Read: five tenths **Write:** 0.5

Read: seventy-eight hundredths **Write:** 0.78

Examples

A Write the decimal and fraction shown by the model.

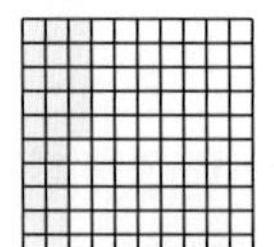

Write the shaded part of the whole as a decimal: 0.25. Then write the shaded part of the whole as a fraction: $\frac{25}{100}$.

B Write the fraction $\frac{9}{10}$ as a decimal. Draw a picture to show $\frac{9}{10}$.

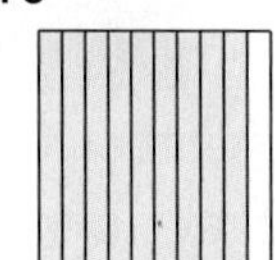

Then write the shaded part of the whole as a decimal: 0.9.

ERROR ALERT

Be sure to write digits in the decimal in the correct place-value position. $\frac{9}{10}$ does **not** equal 0.09.

Try It

Write the decimal and fraction shown by each model.

1. 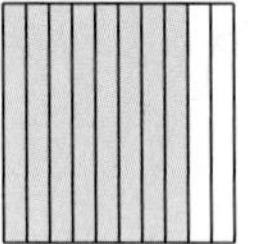

2. 

Write the fraction as a decimal. You may use a model or drawing.

3. $\frac{4}{10}$

4. $\frac{1}{10}$

5. $\frac{85}{100}$

6. $\frac{5}{100}$

7. Read the problem below. **Explain** why D cannot be the correct answer choice. Then choose the correct answer.

COMMON ERROR

Which number shows $\frac{3}{100}$ as a decimal?

A 1.3

B 0.13

C 0.03

D 0.3

Review the TEKS

Add and Subtract Whole Numbers

TEKS 4.3A use addition and subtraction to solve problems involving whole numbers.

Use place value to add and subtract numbers. Line up the digits by place value. Remember to regroup when necessary.

Examples

A The museum had 1,756 visitors on Monday and 1,425 visitors on Tuesday. How many total people visited the museum on the two days?

Step 1	Step 2	Step 3	Step 4
Add the ones. Regroup.	Add the tens.	Add the hundreds. Regroup.	Add the thousands.
1,756 + 1,425 = 1	1,756 + 1,425 = 81	1,756 + 1,425 = 181	1,756 + 1,425 = 3,181

ERROR ALERT

Do not subtract the top number from the bottom.

INCORRECT:

$$\begin{array}{r} 52 \\ -25 \\ \hline 33 \end{array}$$

B Joe had 2,252 hockey cards. He sold 1,246 at a garage sale. How many hockey cards does Joe now have?

Step 1	Step 2	Step 3
Subtract the ones. Regroup.	Subtract the tens.	Subtract the hundreds and thousands.
2,252 − 1,246 = 6	2,252 − 1,246 = 06	2,252 − 1,246 = 1,006

Try It

1. In 2000, the population of Orange Grove, Texas was 1,288. The population of Palmhurst, Texas was 4,872. What was the total population of Orange Grove and Palmhurst?

2. The Williamsburg Bridge in New York is 7,308 feet long. The Manhattan Bridge is 453 feet shorter. How long is the Manhattan Bridge?

3. Read the problem below. **Explain** why B cannot be the correct answer choice. Then choose the correct answer. **COMMON ERROR**

   There are 711 children at the game. If 423 are boys, how many are girls?

   A 1,134 **C** 308

   B 312 **D** 288

Review the TEKS

Add and Subtract Decimals

TEKS 4.3B add and subtract decimals to the hundredths place using concrete objects and pictorial models.

Make models to add and subtract decimal numbers. To add, shade the model to show the first decimal. Then shade the model to show the second decimal. Count the total number of shaded parts to find the sum.

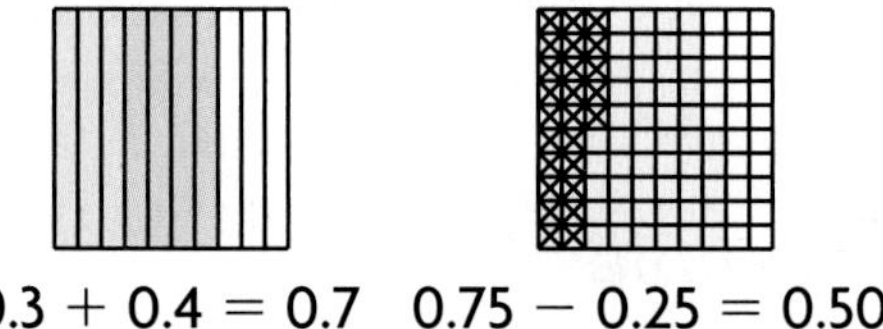

$0.3 + 0.4 = 0.7$ $0.75 - 0.25 = 0.50$

To subtract, shade the model to show the decimal. Then cross out the amount being subtracted. Count the number of shaded parts not crossed out to find the difference.

Examples

A Add. 0.29 + 0.56

Shade 29 squares orange and 56 squares blue.

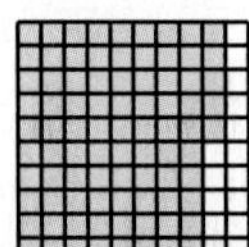

Then count the total number of shaded squares, 85.

So, 0.29 + 0.56 = 0.85.

B Subtract. 0.9 − 0.5

Shade 9 columns purple. Cross off 5 columns.

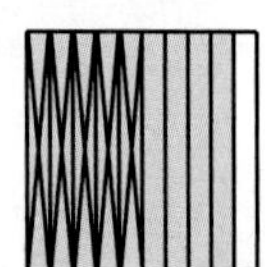

Then count the shaded columns that are left, 4.

So, 0.9 – 0.5 = 0.4.

ERROR ALERT

Write the correct decimal for the picture you make.

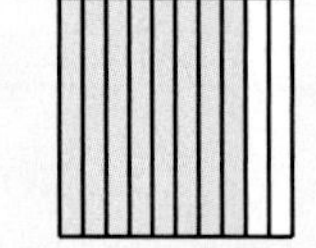

0.6 + 0.2 does **NOT** equal 0.08, but equals 0.8.

Try It

Use models to find the sum.

1. 0.2 + 0.4
2. 0.7 + 0.3
3. 0.5 + 0.2
4. 0.33 + 0.09
5. 0.17 + 0.82
6. 0.47 + 0.02

Use models to find the difference.

7. 0.8 − 0.4
8. 0.5 − 0.2
9. 0.6 − 0.2
10. 0.45 − 0.08
11. 0.83 − 0.56
12. 0.70 − 0.05

COMMON ERROR

13. Read the problem below. **Explain** why D cannot be the correct answer choice. Then choose the correct answer.

The model shows 0.3 + 0.6.

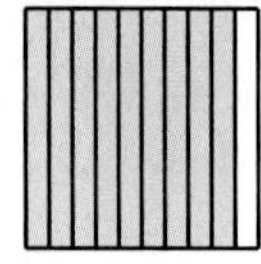

Which sum does the model show?

A 0.9 **C** 0.1

B 0.6 **D** 0.09

Review the TEKS

Factors and Products

TEKS 4.4A model factors and products using arrays and area models.

An array is an arrangement of objects in rows and columns.

Use arrays to show multiplication. Each side of the array should model one of the factors. The array shows the product.

Use arrays to show division. Use tiles or counters to show the dividend. Put the tiles in rows. The number of tiles in each row should equal the divisor. The number of rows is the quotient.

Examples

A Multiply. 6×7

Draw an array. Make it 7 units wide and 6 units high.

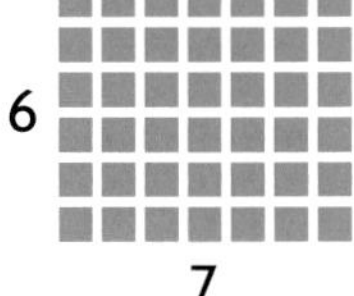

So, $6 \times 7 = 42$.

B Divide. $30 \div 5$

Use 30 square tiles to build an array. Put them in 5 equal rows.

So, $30 \div 5 = 6$.

ERROR ALERT

Draw equal rows and columns to match each factor when you draw an array.

3×4

4
3 ○○○○
○○○○
○○○○

Try It

Find the product or quotient.

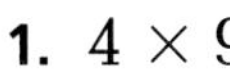
1. 4×9

2. $35 \div 5$

Write the factors and product shown in each array.

3. △△△△△△△△
△△△△△△△△

4.

5. Read the problem below. **Explain** why B cannot be the correct answer choice. Then choose the correct answer.

Which is an array for the number 48?

A

C

B

D

Review the TEKS

Multiplication and Division

TEKS 4.4B represent multiplication and division situations in picture, word, and number form.

Draw a model to solve a multiplication or division problem. Make an array, use a number line, or draw equal-size groups.

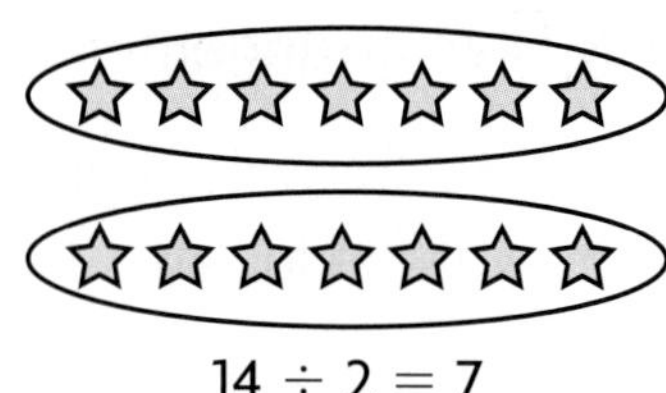

Evelyn gives 2 bracelets to each of 7 friends. How many total bracelets does Evelyn give to her friends?

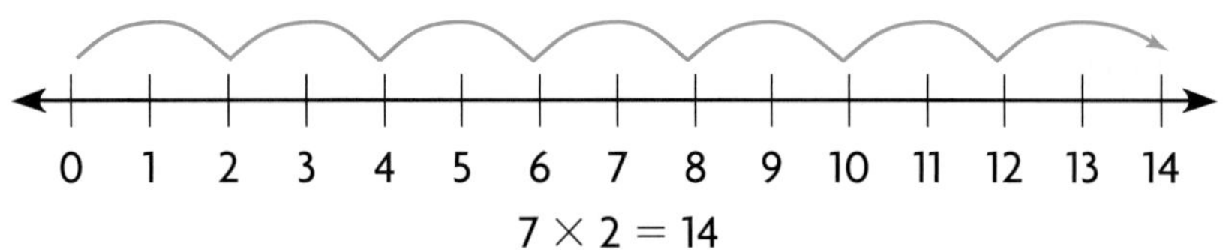

Examples

A How many books are there if there are 3 shelves with 8 books on each shelf?

Make an array.

So, $3 \times 8 = 24$.

B Tim shares 18 cookies equally among his 6 cousins. How many cookies does each receive?

Draw a number line.

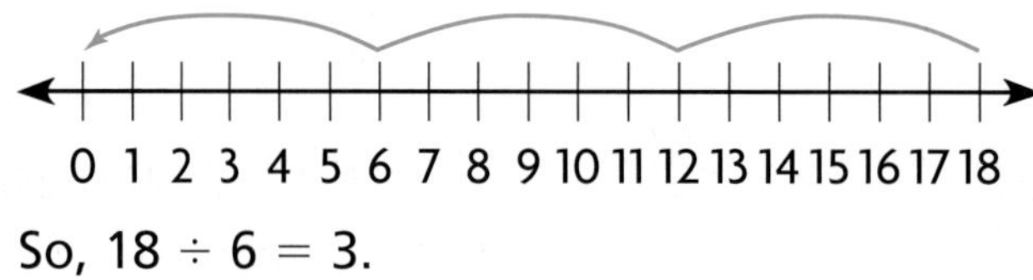

So, $18 \div 6 = 3$.

ERROR ALERT

Choose the correct operation to represent a situation:

9 students, each with 5 textbooks. How many textbooks in all?

INCORRECT: $9 \div 5$

CORRECT: 9×5

Try It

Find the product.

1. 5×5
2. 8×4
3. 4×6
4. 6×7
5. 7×8
6. 9×3

Find the quotient.

7. $64 \div 8$
8. $81 \div 9$
9. $42 \div 6$
10. $40 \div 5$
11. $35 \div 7$
12. $36 \div 4$

13. Read the problem below. **Explain** why C cannot be the correct answer choice. Then choose the correct answer. **COMMON ERROR**

Michael has to pack 72 books in boxes. Each box holds 9 books. Which would be the best way to find out how many boxes are needed?

A Add 9 to 72.

B Subtract 9 from 72.

C Multiply 72 by 9.

D Divide 72 by 9.

Review the TEKS

Multiplication Facts

TEKS 4.4C recall and apply multiplication facts through 12×12.

When you multiply, you put equal groups together. The answer to a multiplication fact is the product. The numbers you multiply are the factors. You can also skip-count to find a product.

You can use multiplication facts to divide.

Examples

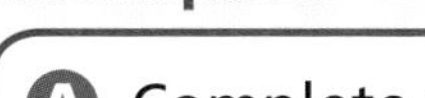

A Complete the table.

Nickels	Pennies
1	5
4	■
8	■
12	■

Recall multiplication facts for 5.

$4 \times 5 = 20$
$8 \times 5 = 40$
$12 \times 5 = 60$

So, the missing numbers are 20, 40, and 60.

B Use a multiplication fact to divide.

$24 \div 6$

Think: $6 \times ■ = 24$

Use multiplication facts for 6:

$6 \times 1 = 6$
$6 \times 2 = 12$
$6 \times 3 = 18$
$6 \times 4 = 24$

So, $24 \div 6 = 4$.

ERROR ALERT

Use the correct facts to solve a problem.

$24 \div 6$ does **NOT** equal 3 because

6×3 does **NOT** equal 24.

Try It

Find the missing numbers.

1.

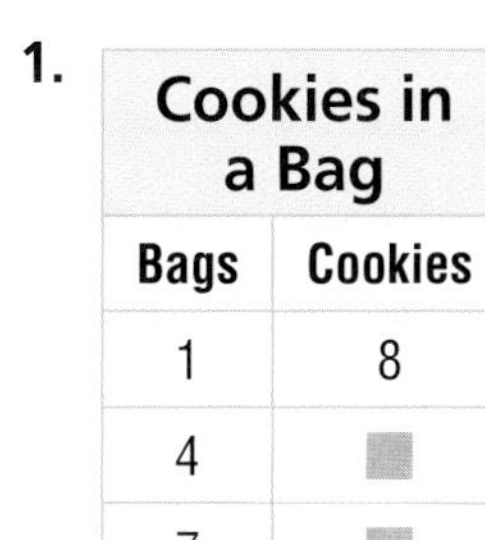

Cookies in a Bag	
Bags	Cookies
1	8
4	■
7	■

2.

Eggs in a Carton	
Cartons	Eggs
4	48
8	■
10	■

Use a multiplication fact to find the quotient.

3. $81 \div 9$
4. $56 \div 7$
5. $63 \div 7$
6. $48 \div 8$

7. Read the problem below. **Explain** why D cannot be the correct answer choice. Then choose the correct answer. **COMMON ERROR**

Tomas made 4 equal stacks of pennies. There are 36 pennies in all. Which number sentence shows how to find the number of pennies in each stack?

A $36 + 4 = 40$
B $36 - 4 = 32$
C $36 \div 4 = 9$
D $32 \div 4 = 8$

Review the TEKS

Use Multiplication

TEKS 4.4D use multiplication to solve problems (no more than two digits times two digits without technology).

Use partial products or place value to multiply numbers.

Examples

A There are 24 hours in a day. How many hours are there in 5 days?

Use partial products.

Step 1

Multiply ones by ones.

$$\begin{array}{r} 24 \\ \times\ 5 \\ \hline 20 \end{array}$$

5 × 4 ones = 20 ones

Step 2

Multiply tens by ones.

$$\begin{array}{r} 24 \\ \times\ 5 \\ \hline 20 \\ 100 \\ \hline \end{array}$$

5 × 2 tens = 10 tens

Step 3

Add the partial products.

20 + 100 = 120

So, 24 × 5 = 120.

B Luis worked 35 hours each week for the last 46 weeks. How many total hours did Luis work?

Use place value. Regroup when necessary.

Step 1

Multiply by 6 ones.

$$\begin{array}{r} \overset{3}{3}5 \\ \times\ \ 46 \\ \hline 210 \end{array}$$

6 × 35

Step 2

Multiply by 4 tens.

$$\begin{array}{r} \overset{\overset{2}{3}}{3}5 \\ \times\ \ 46 \\ \hline 210 \\ 1\,400 \end{array}$$

40 × 35

Step 3

Add the partial products.

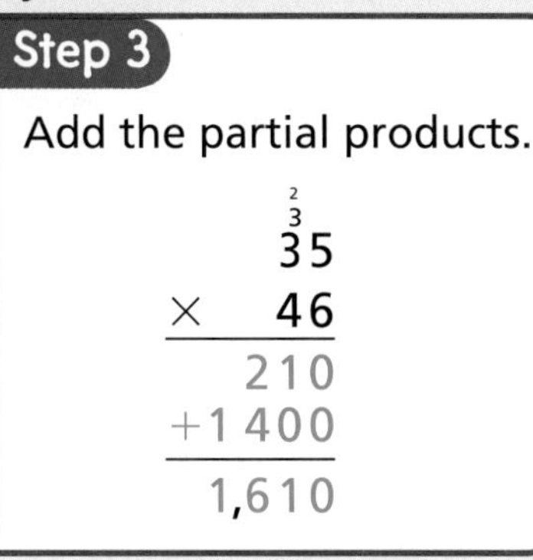

$$\begin{array}{r} \overset{\overset{2}{3}}{3}5 \\ \times\ \ 46 \\ \hline 210 \\ +1\,400 \\ \hline 1{,}610 \end{array}$$

ERROR ALERT

Remember to add the regrouped number.

INCORRECT:

$$\begin{array}{r} \overset{3}{3}5 \\ \times\ 6 \\ \hline 180 \end{array}$$

Try It

Use partial products to multiply.

1. 47 × 8
2. 32 × 4
3. 56 × 12
4. 67 × 23

Use place value to multiply.

5. 18 × 9
6. 28 × 7
7. 34 × 87
8. 73 × 95

9. Read the problem below. **Explain** why B cannot be the correct answer choice. Then choose the correct answer. **COMMON ERROR**

There are 54 stickers in each of 6 albums. How many stickers are there in all?

A 324 **B** 304 **C** 60 **D** 9

Review the TEKS

Divide by a One-Digit Divisor

TEKS 4.4E use division to solve problems (no more than one-digit divisors and three-digit dividends without technology).

Use long division to divide a multi-digit number by a one-digit divisor. Use compatible numbers to determine where to place the first digit.

Example

A baker has 87 donuts to put on 7 racks. How many donuts can he put on each rack and how many will be leftover?

Step 1	Step 2	Step 3
Divide the tens.	Then bring down the 7 ones. Divide the 17 ones.	To check, multiply the quotient by the divisor. Then add the remainder.
$\begin{array}{r} 1 \\ 7\overline{)87} \\ -7 \\ \hline 1 \end{array}$ Divide. 8 ÷ 7 Multiply. 7 × 1 Subtract. 8 − 7 Compare. 1 < 7	$\begin{array}{r} 12 \text{ r3} \\ 7\overline{)87} \\ -7\downarrow \\ \hline 17 \\ -14 \\ \hline 3 \end{array}$ Divide. 17 ÷ 7 Multiply. 7 × 2 Subtract. 17 − 14 Compare. 3 < 7	$\begin{array}{r} 12 \\ \times\ 7 \\ \hline 84 \\ +\ 3 \\ \hline 87 \end{array}$ 12 quotient 7 divisor 3 remainder 87 dividend

So, 87 ÷ 7 = 12 r3.

ERROR ALERT

Place the first digit in the correct place.

INCORRECT:

$$\begin{array}{r} 360 \text{ r1} \\ 4\overline{)145} \\ -12\downarrow \\ \hline 25 \\ -24 \\ \hline 1 \end{array}$$

Try It

Divide.

1. $43 \div 8$
2. $37 \div 4$
3. $9\overline{)56}$
4. $67 \div 3$
5. $329 \div 9$
6. $4\overline{)217}$
7. $837 \div 5$
8. $722 \div 3$
9. $7\overline{)585}$
10. $825 \div 6$
11. $158 \div 5$
12. $3\overline{)463}$

13. Read the problem below. **Explain** why C cannot be the correct answer choice. Then choose the correct answer. **COMMON ERROR**

The team manager divided 126 baseball bats equally among 6 boxes. How many bats are in each box?

A 21

B 120

C 210

D 756

Review the TEKS

Round Whole Numbers

TEKS 4.5A round whole numbers to the nearest ten, hundred, or thousand to approximate reasonable results in problem situations.

Not all problems need an exact answer. When a number is rounded, replace it with a number that tells about how many or how much.

Round 34,825 to the nearest

ten	→	34,830
hundred	→	34,800
thousand	→	35,000

Examples

Jennifer's teacher asked her to write 5,265,563 and round it to the nearest thousand. What is the number Jennifer wrote?

Step 1

Find the place value to which you want to round.

Place to be rounded to–thousands

↓

5,265,563

Step 2

Look at the digit to the right. If the digit is less than 5, the digit in the rounding place remains the same. If the digit is 5 or greater, the digit in the rounding place increases by 1.

5,265,563

The digit in the hundreds place is 5. Since 5 = 5, the digit 5 increases by 1.

Step 3

Change all the digits to the right of the rounding place to zero.

5,265,563 → 5,266,000

ERROR ALERT

If there is a 5 to the right of the place you want to round, you must increase the digit in the rounding place by 1.

So, Jennifer wrote 5,266,000.

Try It

Round each number to the nearest thousand.

1. 628,532
2. 896,341
3. 154,420
4. 505,757
5. 2,637,137
6. 4,650,005
7. 23,488,988
8. 33,495,228

Round each number to the place value of the underlined digit.

9. 8,<u>4</u>58
10. 9<u>6</u>,301
11. 125,0<u>5</u>1
12. 42<u>8</u>,916
13. 14,609,3<u>3</u>5
14. 81,254,<u>0</u>39

15. Read the problem below. **Explain** why C cannot be the correct answer choice. Then choose the correct answer. **COMMON ERROR**

Emma flew 21,597 miles last year. Su-Lin flew 17,238 miles. About how many more miles did Emma fly?

A About 2,000 miles

B About 3,000 miles

C About 4,000 miles

D About 5,000 miles

Review the TEKS

Estimation

TEKS 4.5B use strategies including rounding and compatible numbers to estimate solutions to multiplication and division problems.

Estimation is used to give a quick idea of the size of the product or quotient. Use rounding or compatible numbers to estimate products or quotients.

Examples

A Estimate. 44×315

Use rounding and mental math.

44×315
↓ ↓
$40 \times 300 = 12{,}000$

Use compatible numbers and mental math.

44×315
↓ ↓
$50 \times 300 = 15{,}000$

B Estimate. $731 \div 8$

Use rounding and mental math.

$731 \div 8$
↓ ↓
$700 \div 10 = 70$

Use compatible numbers and mental math.

Think: $72 \div 8 = 9$ and $80 \div 8 = 10$

You can use 720 or 800 for 731.

$720 \div 8 = 90$

$800 \div 8 = 100$

So, both 90 and 100 are reasonable estimates.

ERROR ALERT

Be sure that your estimate makes sense.

44×315
↓ ↓
40×300

40×300 does **NOT** equal 1,200.

Try It

Estimate the product or quotient.

1. 18×32
2. $\$27 \times 31$
3. $259 \div 3$
4. 55×29
5. $605 \div 8$
6. 47×189
7. $1{,}319 \div 4$
8. $792 \div 9$
9. 68×429
10. $2{,}337 \div 4$
11. $504 \div 6$
12. 226×83
13. $\$71 \times 51$
14. $1{,}308 \div 3$

15. Read the problem below. **Explain** why A cannot be the correct answer choice. Then choose the correct answer.

COMMON ERROR

Choose the best estimate for the product.

519×42

A 2,000 **C** 15,000

B 10,000 **D** 20,000

Review the TEKS

Relate Multiplication and Division Facts

TEKS 4.6A use patterns and relationships to develop strategies to remember basic multiplication and division facts (such as the patterns in related multiplication and division number sentences (fact families) such as $9 \times 9 = 81$ and $81 \div 9 = 9$).

Multiplication and division are related. The relationship can help you remember multiplication and division facts.

Examples

A Write the fact family for the numbers 7, 8, and 56.

Write a related multiplication sentence.

factor × factor = product

$$7 \times 8 = 56$$

Use that fact to write another related multiplication sentence.

$$8 \times 7 = 56$$

Write the two related division sentences for the family.

dividend ÷ divisor = quotient

$$56 \div 7 = 8$$

$$56 \div 8 = 7$$

B Write the fact family for the numbers 9, 9, and 81.

Write a related multiplication sentence.

factor × factor = product

$$9 \times 9 = 81$$

There is only one multiplication sentence.

Write the related division sentence using the product, 81, as the dividend.

dividend ÷ divisor = quotient

$$81 \div 9 = 9$$

ERROR ALERT

Be sure to write a related division sentence using the correct number as the dividend.

Correct:
$7 \times 8 = 56$
$56 \div 8 = 7$

Incorrect:
$7 \times 8 = 56$
$7 \div 8 = 56$

Try It

Write the fact family for the set of numbers.

1. 2, 7, 14
2. 5, 1, 5
3. 9, 3, 27
4. 6, 4, 24

Find the value of the variable. Then write a related sentence.

5. $4 \times w = 20$
6. $32 \div 8 = h$
7. $7 \times 6 = x$
8. $27 \div 3 = r$

9. Read the problem below. **Explain** why D cannot be the correct answer choice. Then choose the correct answer. **COMMON ERROR**

Which set of numbers forms a multiplication and division fact family?

A 3, 6, 15

B 2, 9, 11

C 1, 3, 3

D 3, 7, 10

Review the TEKS

Use Patterns to Multiply

TEKS 4.6B use patterns to multiply by 10 and 100.

Use basic facts to multiply by 10 and 100.

Once a basic multiplication fact is known, multiply by placing the correct number of zeros in the product.

Examples

A Find the product 9×500.

Use a basic fact and a multiplication pattern to find the product.

$9 \times 5 = 45$ ← basic fact

$9 \times 50 = 450$

$9 \times 500 = 4{,}500$

The number of zeros in the product is equal to the sum of the zeros in the factors.

So, $9 \times 500 = 4{,}500$.

B Find the product 50×600.

Use a basic fact and a multiplication pattern to find the product.

$5 \times 6 = 30$ ← basic fact

$50 \times 60 = 3{,}000$

$50 \times 600 = 30{,}000$

The number of zeros in the product is one greater than the sum of the zeros in the factors because the basic fact ends in zero.

So, $50 \times 600 = 30{,}000$.

ERROR ALERT

Remember to recall the basic facts that end in zero.

$2 \times 50 = 100$

$20 \times 5 = 100$

$20 \times 50 = 1{,}000$

Try It

Use a basic fact and a pattern to find the product.

1. 5×30
2. 9×200
3. 10×110
4. 40×600
5. 50×90
6. 80×600
7. 70×70
8. 30×300
9. 800×30
10. 12×200
11. 11×300
12. 90×20
13. 500×40
14. 80×50

15. Read the problem below. **Explain** why D cannot be the correct answer choice. Then choose the correct answer. **COMMON ERROR**

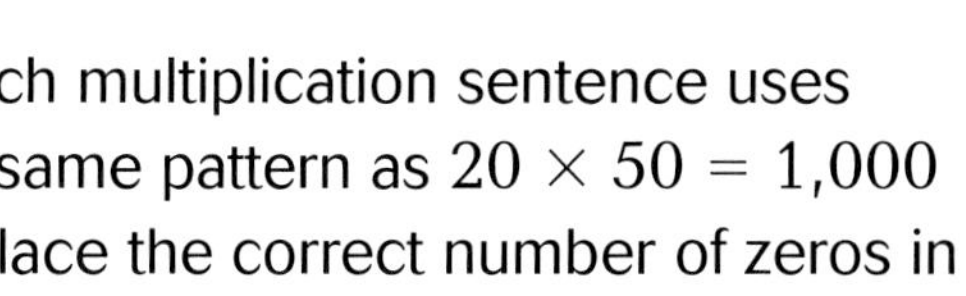

Which multiplication sentence uses the same pattern as $20 \times 50 = 1{,}000$ to place the correct number of zeros in the product?

A $8 \times 30 = 240$

B $7 \times 400 = 2{,}800$

C $80 \times 50 = 4{,}000$

D $90 \times 70 = 6{,}300$

Review the TEKS

Describe Relationships

TEKS 4.7 The student is expected to describe the relationship between two sets of related data such as ordered pairs in a table.

You can describe a pattern in an input/output table using a rule. Then use the rule to continue your pattern.

Each input and its output in the table make up an ordered pair.

Input, *x*	8	13	18	23	28
Output, *y*	12	17	22	27	32

Each output y is 4 more than the input x. So, the rule is *add 4 to x*.

Examples

A Find a rule. The rule for the table below is *subtract 8 from the input*. What is the next output number?

Input	12	15	18	21	24
Output	4	7	10	13	■

Each output is found by subtracting 8 from the input. So, the next number is 24 − 8, or 16.

B Find a rule. Use your rule to complete the table.

Input, *x*	5	9	13	17	24
Output, *y*	12	16	20	24	■

Each output is 7 more than the input. So, the rule is *add 7 to x*. The last number is 24 + 7, or 31.

ERROR ALERT

Be sure that the rule works for each ordered pair in the table.

Try It

Find a rule for the table. Use your rule to extend the pattern.

1.

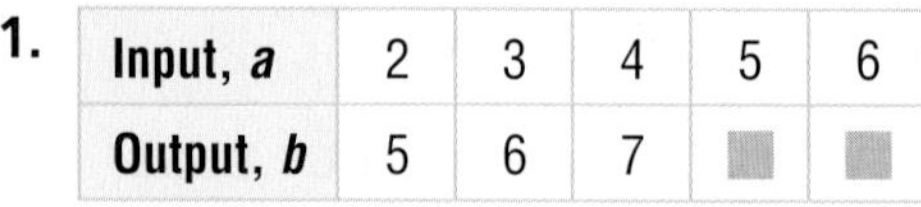

Input, *a*	2	3	4	5	6
Output, *b*	5	6	7	■	■

2.

Input, *b*	10	14	18	22	26
Output, *c*	7	11	15	■	■

3. Read the problem below. **Explain** why A cannot be the correct answer choice. Then choose the correct answer.

Which rule describes the relationship in the table?

Input, *w*	3	5	7	9	11
Output, *z*	6	8	10	12	14

A Subtract 3 from *w*.
B Subtract 6 from *w*.
C Add 6 to *w*.
D Add 3 to *w*.

Review the TEKS

Identify Angles

TEKS 4.8A identify and describe right, acute, and obtuse angles.

Angles can be compared to a right angle. A right angle forms a square corner. If an angle's measure is less than a right angle, it is acute. If an angle's measure is greater than a right angle, it is obtuse.

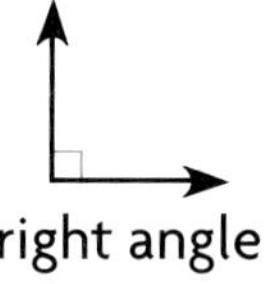

right angle

Examples

A Is the angle right, acute, or obtuse?

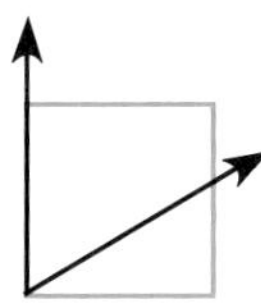

The angle's measure is less than a square corner. The angle's measure is smaller than a right angle.

So, it is an acute angle.

B Identify the angle as right, acute, or obtuse.

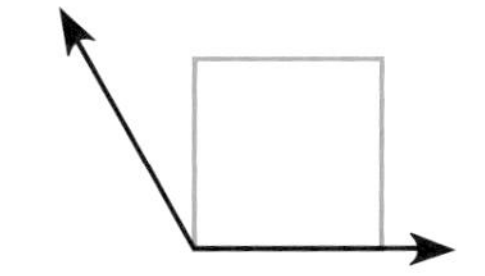

The angle's measure is greater than a square corner and less than a straight line.

So, it is an obtuse angle.

ERROR ALERT

Be sure to line up one side of the square corner with one ray of the angle to see whether the angle can hold the square corner.

Try It

Use a square corner. Classify each angle. Write *acute*, *right*, or *obtuse*.

1. 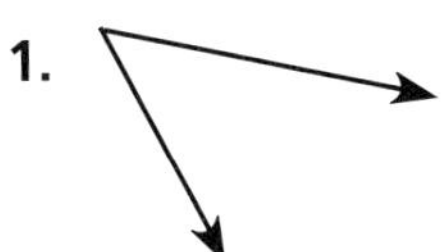

2. 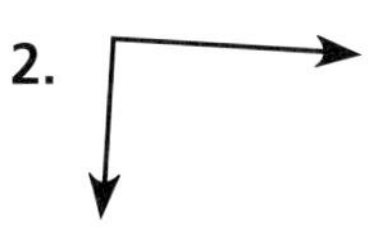

3. 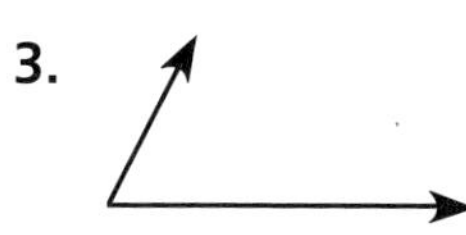

4. 

5. 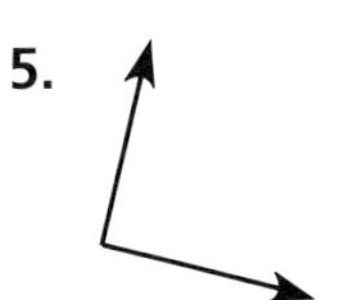

6. 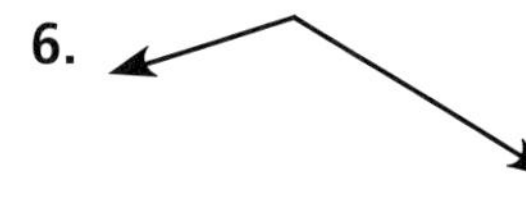

7. Read the problem below. **Explain** why C cannot be the correct answer choice. Then choose the correct answer. **COMMON ERROR**

   Which angle has a greater measure than angle *R*?

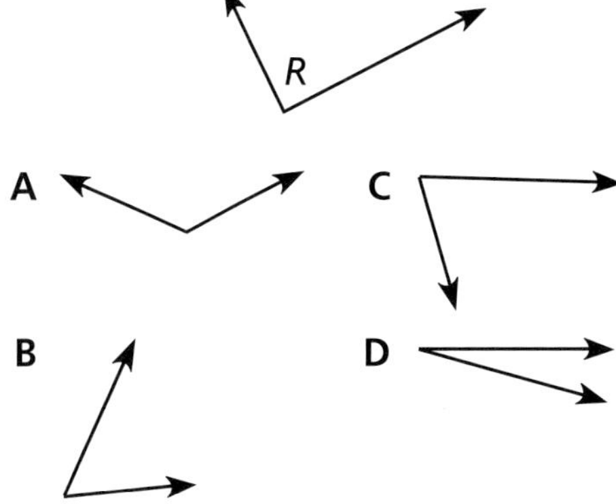

Review the TEKS

Identify Lines

TEKS 4.8B identify and describe parallel and intersecting (including perpendicular) lines using concrete objects and pictorial models.

If you place two straws on your desk, they will be in the same plane. If they are in the same plane, they will be either parallel or intersecting. If they intersect, they could be perpendicular.

Examples

A

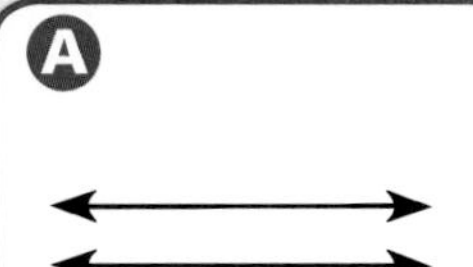

These lines will never cross one another.

So, they are parallel.

B

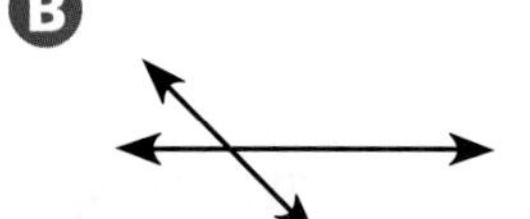

These lines cross one another but do not form right angles.

So, they are intersecting.

C

These lines cross one another and form right angles.

So, they are perpendicular.

ERROR ALERT

Be sure that when you identify intersecting lines as perpendicular, they form four right angles.

These lines intersect but are not perpendicular.

Try It

Name any line relationship you see in the pair of lines. Write *intersecting*, *parallel*, or *perpendicular*.

1. 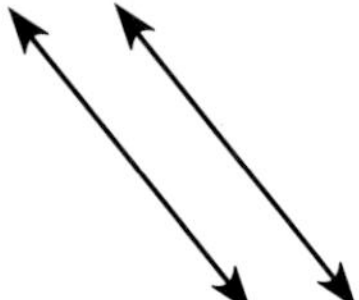

2. 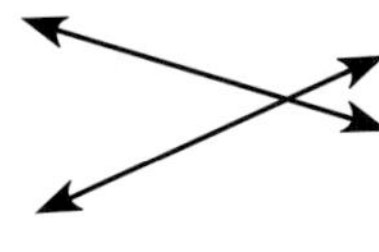

3. 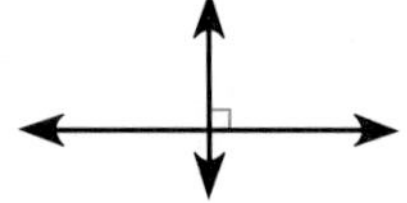

4. 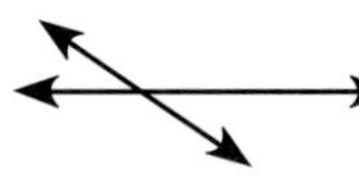

5. 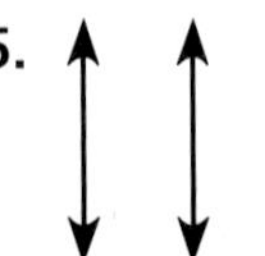

6. 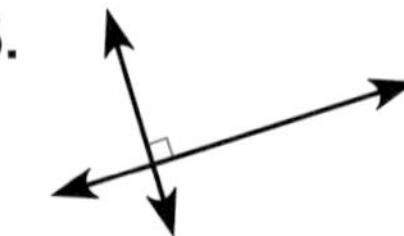

7. Read the problem below. **Explain** why A cannot be the correct answer choice. Then choose the correct answer. **COMMON ERROR**

   Which two lines both intersect and are perpendicular?

   A 

   B 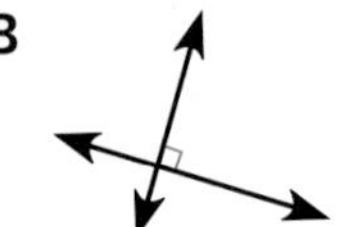

   C 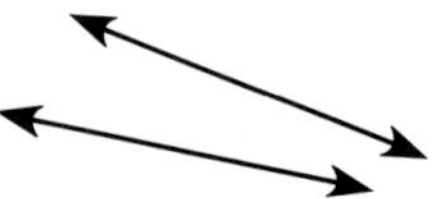

   D

Review the TEKS

Two-Dimensional Figures

TEKS 4.8C use essential attributes to define two- and three-dimensional geometric figures.

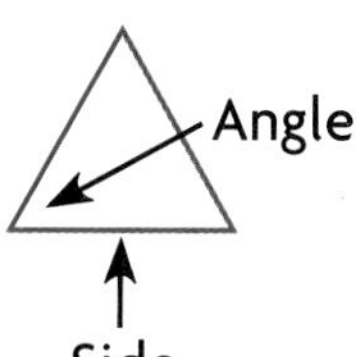

Polygons are closed plane figures with straight sides and each side is a line segment.

Triangles can be named by their sides.

Scalene | Isosceles | Equilateral

0 equal sides | 2 equal sides | 3 equal sides

Triangles can be named by their angles.

Acute | Right | Obtuse

3 acute angles | 1 right angle | 1 obtuse angle

Quadrilaterals can be named by the pairs of parallel sides they have.

Parallelograms: 2 pairs of parallel sides

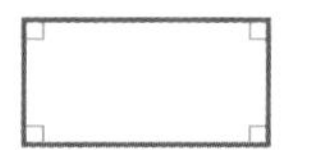
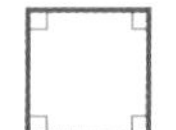

parallelogram | rhombus | rectangle | square

Trapezoids: exactly 1 pair of parallel sides

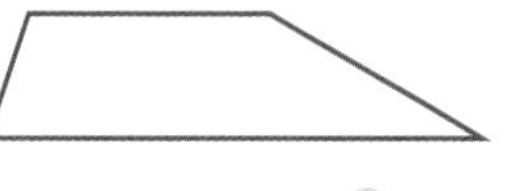

Examples

A Which quadrilaterals have more than 1 pair of parallel sides?

A parallelogram, rhombus, rectangle, and square have more than 1 pair of parallel sides.

B What type of triangle can be equilateral?

Only an acute triangle can be equilateral.

ERROR ALERT

Parallelograms have 1 pair of parallel sides, but they also have a second pair of parallel sides. So parallelograms are not trapezoids.

Try It

Classify each figure in as many ways as possible. Write *quadrilateral*, *parallelogram*, *rhombus*, *rectangle*, *square*, or *trapezoid*.

1.  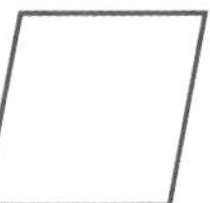

2. 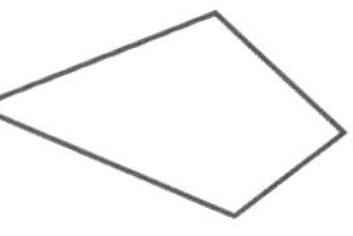

3. 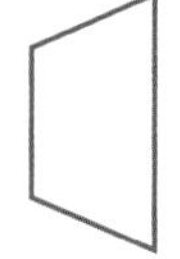

4. 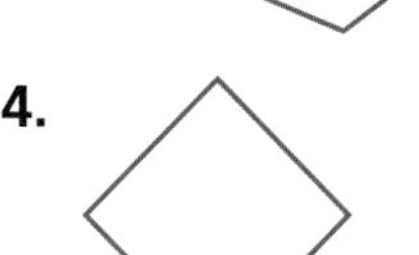

5. Read the problem below. **Explain** why D cannot be the correct answer choice. Then choose the correct answer.

COMMON ERROR

Which figure below is **NOT** a parallelogram?

A 

B

C 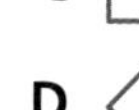

D 

Review the TEKS

Three-Dimensional Figures

TEKS 4.8C use essential attributes to define two- and three-dimensional geometric figures.

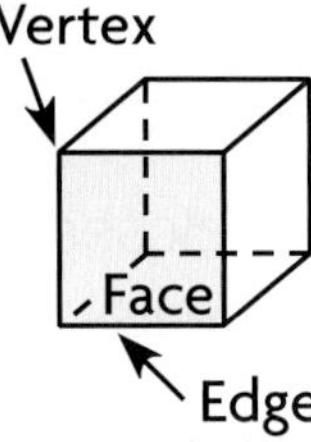

Prisms and pyramids are named by the polygons that form their bases. Some solid figures have curved surfaces. A cylinder has two circular bases, and a cone has one circular base.

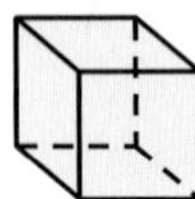
cube

rectangular prism

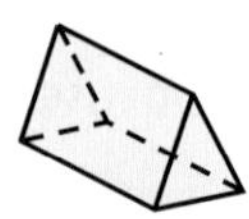
triangular prism

triangular pyramid

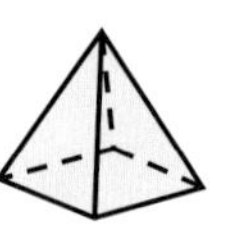
square pyramid

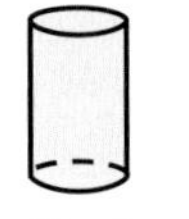
cylinder

cone

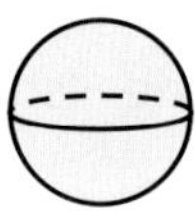
sphere

Examples

A How many more edges than faces does a pentagonal prism have?

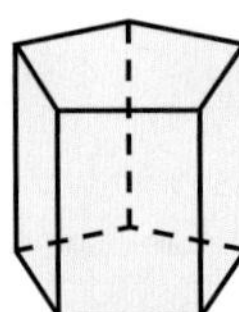

The pentagonal prism has 15 edges and 7 faces. So, it has 15 − 7, or 8 more edges than faces.

B These three-dimensional figures have square bases. What shapes are the faces?

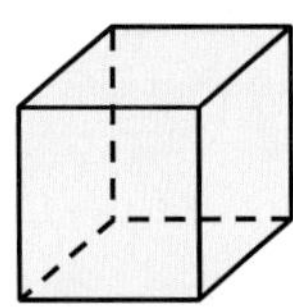

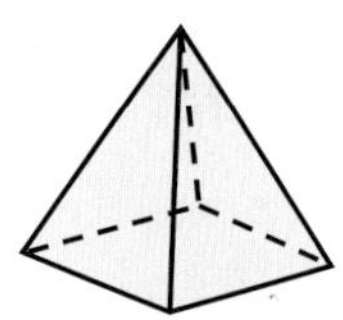

A cube and a square pyramid have square bases. A cube has 6 square faces. A square pyramid has 1 square face and 4 faces that are triangles.

ERROR ALERT

Remember to include hidden faces, edges, or vertices when you count.

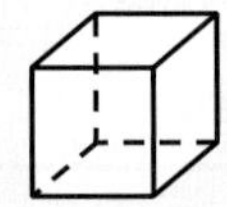

A cube does **NOT** have 3 faces, 7 vertices, and 9 edges.

Try It

Name each figure.

1. 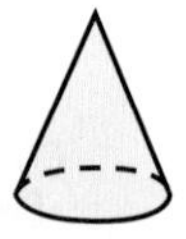

2. 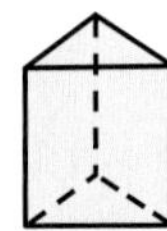

3. 

4. 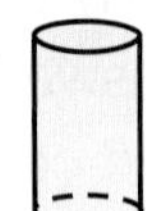

5. Read the problem below. **Explain** why A cannot be the correct answer choice. Then choose the correct answer. **COMMON ERROR**

The difference between the number of faces and number of vertices of a figure is 1. What is the figure?

A Square pyramid
B Cube
C Hexagonal pyramid
D Triangular prism

Review the TEKS

Congruent Figures

TEKS 4.9B use translations, reflections, and rotations to verify that two shapes are congruent.

Figures are congruent if they have the same size and same shape. They **do not** need to be in the same position to be congruent.

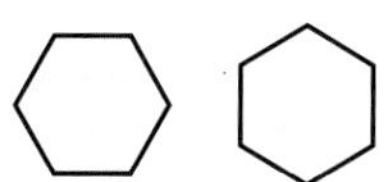

These hexagons appear to be congruent.

If you can move one figure to exactly cover another one, the two figures are congruent. Transformations can be used to move one figure onto another. You can make two identical pattern block cutouts exactly cover one another using transformations.

Examples

A Are the figures congruent?

Use a translation (slide).

Slide one triangle in the direction shown until it exactly covers the other. The two triangles are congruent.

B Are the figures congruent?

Use a reflection (flip).

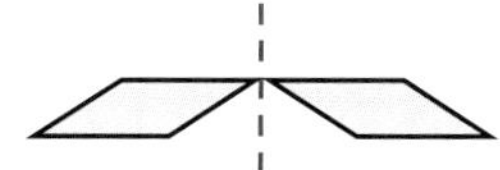

Flip one figure across the line so that it covers the other. The two figures are congruent.

C Are the figures congruent?

Use a rotation (turn).

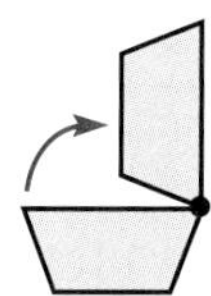

Turn one figure around the point until it covers the other. The two figures are congruent.

ERROR ALERT

Be sure a figure *exactly* covers another to show they are congruent.

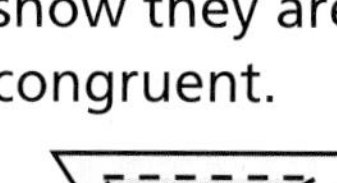

These triangles are **NOT** congruent.

Try It

Tell which transformation was used. Write *translation*, *rotation*, or *reflection*. Then write why the two figures appear to be congruent.

1. 

2.  

3. 

4. 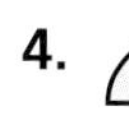 

5. 

6. 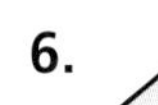

COMMON ERROR

7. Read the problem below. **Explain** why C cannot be the correct answer choice. Then choose the correct answer.

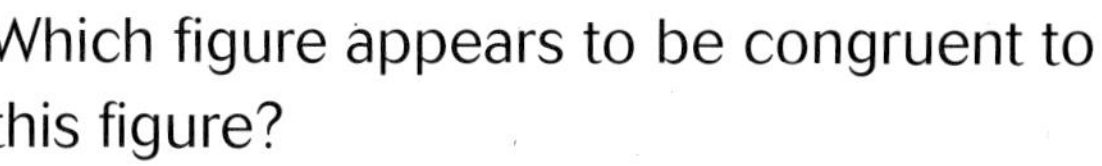

Which figure appears to be congruent to this figure?

A 

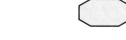

C 

B 

D 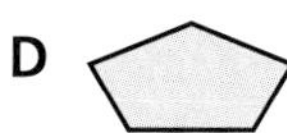

Review the TEKS

Symmetry

TEKS 4.9C use reflections to verify that a shape has symmetry.

A figure has line symmetry if it can be folded so that the two halves match exactly.

When a figure is folded across a line of symmetry, a reflection is made.

Examples

A How many lines of symmetry does the figure have?

If the figure is folded across the line, each half will exactly match the other half. There is one line of symmetry.

B How many lines of symmetry does the figure have?

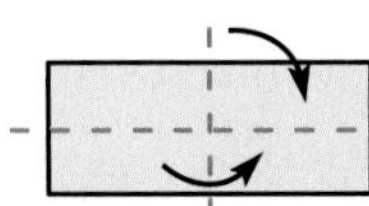

A rectangle that is not a square has two lines of symmetry.

C How many lines of symmetry does the figure have?

The figure cannot be folded so that the two halves match. It has no line of symmetry.

ERROR ALERT

Be sure that a figure has line symmetry.

Copy and test a parallelogram that is not a rhombus or a rectangle. It cannot be folded so that the two halves match.

Try It

Tell whether the figure appears to have *no lines of symmetry*, *one line of symmetry*, or *more than one line of symmetry*.

1. 

2.   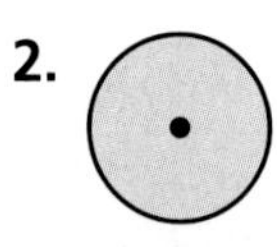

3. 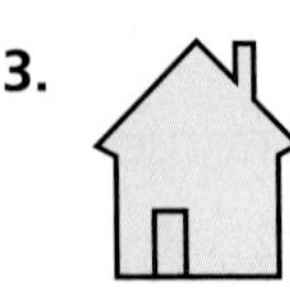

4. 

5. 

6. 

7. Read the problem below. **Explain** why A cannot be the correct answer choice. Then choose the correct answer. **COMMON ERROR**

   Which figure appears to have more than one line of symmetry?

   A 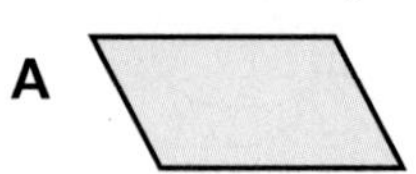

   C 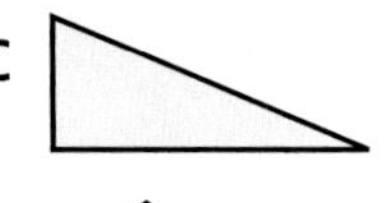

   B 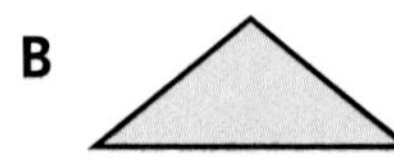

   D 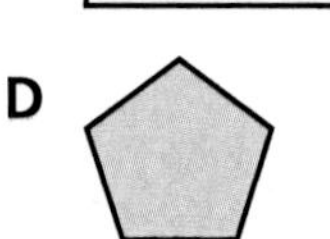

Review the TEKS

Fractions and Decimals on a Number Line

TEKS 4.10 The student is expected to locate and name points on a number line using whole numbers, fractions such as halves and fourths, and decimals such as tenths.

Use number lines to place fractions and decimals. When a fraction and a decimal are located at the same point on a number line, they are equivalent.

Examples

Use the number line.

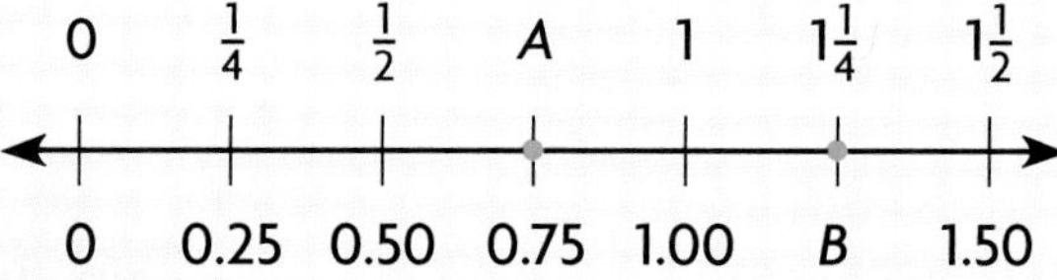

A fraction and a decimal at the same point are equivalent. For example, $\frac{1}{4} = 0.25$, $\frac{3}{4} = 0.75$, and $1\frac{1}{4} = 1.25$.

A What fraction does point *A* name?

Each section on the number line represents $\frac{1}{4}$.

Locate point *A*.

So, $\frac{3}{4}$ names point *A*.

B What decimal does point *B* name?

Each section on the number line also represents 0.25.

Locate Point *B*.

So, 1.25 names point *B*.

ERROR ALERT

Be sure that a fraction and decimal on the same number line are equivalent.

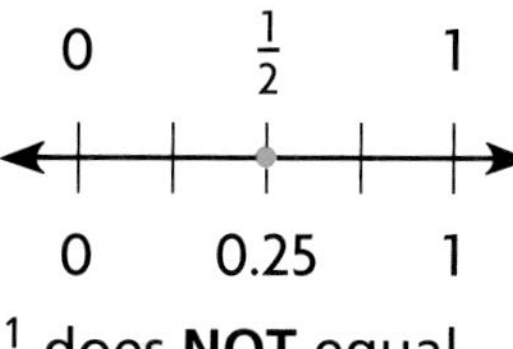

$\frac{1}{2}$ does **NOT** equal 0.25.

Try It

Write the value of each letter shown on the number line.

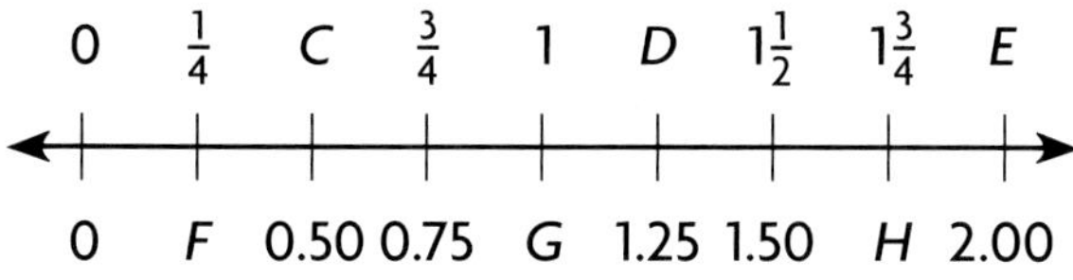

1. $C = \blacksquare$
2. $D = \blacksquare$
3. $E = \blacksquare$
4. $F = \blacksquare$
5. $G = \blacksquare$
6. $H = \blacksquare$

7. Read the problem below. **Explain** why B cannot be the correct answer choice. Then choose the correct answer. **COMMON ERROR**

What decimal does point *M* name?

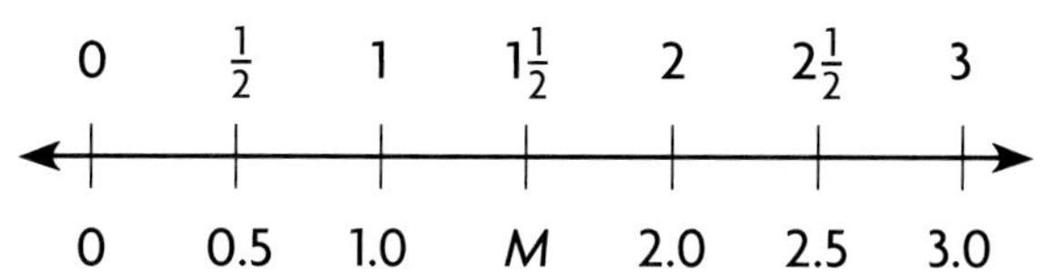

A 0.5
B 1.0
C 1.5
D 2.5

Review the TEKS

Customary Measurement

TEKS 4.11B perform simple conversions between different units of length, between different units of capacity, and between different units of weight within the customary measurement system.

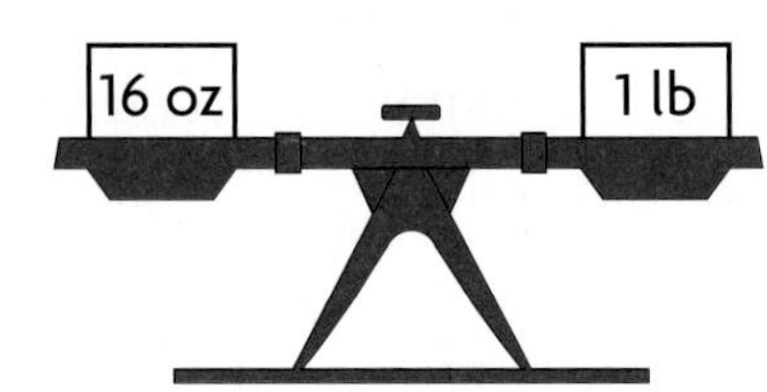

To convert between units of measure, you need to know the relationship between the units.

Length	Capacity	Weight
1 ft = 12 in. 1 yd = 3 ft = 36 in. 1 mi = 5,280 ft 1 mi = 1,760 yd	1 cup = 8 fl oz 1 pt = 2 c 1 qt = 2 pt 1 gal = 4 qt = 128 fl oz	1 lb = 16 oz 1 ton = 2,000 lb

To change from a smaller unit to a larger unit, divide.
To change from a larger unit to a smaller unit, multiply.

Examples

A Complete.

204 in. = ■ ft

Divide to change from a smaller unit to a larger unit.

1 ft = 12 in.

204 in. ÷ 12 = 17 ft

B Complete.

8 gal = ■ qt

Multiply to change from a larger unit to a smaller unit.

1 gal = 4 qt

8 gal × 4 = 32 qt

B Complete.

9 lb = ■ oz

Multiply to change from a larger unit to a smaller unit.

1 lb = 16 oz

9 lb × 16 = 144 oz

ERROR ALERT

Choose the correct operation—multiplication or division—to change units.

24 ft ÷ 12 is **NOT** 2 in.

6 ft × 3 is **NOT** 18 yd.

Try It

Complete. Tell whether you *multiply* or *divide*.

1. 8 yd = ■ ft
2. 3 tons = ■ lb
3. 16 pt = ■ qt
4. 3 yd = ■ in.
5. 24 c = ■ pt
6. 240 oz = ■ lb
7. 35 ft = ■ in.
8. 6,000 lb = ■ tons
9. 72 fl oz = ■ c
10. 8,800 yd = ■ mi
11. 12 gal = ■ qt
12. 7 lb = ■ oz
13. 2 mi = ■ ft
14. 32 qt = ■ gal

15. Read the problem below. **Explain** why A cannot be the correct answer choice. Then choose the correct answer.

Mia measured 57 yards of material to make costumes. How many feet of material did she measure?

A 19 feet
B 60 feet
C 171 feet
D 684 feet

Review the TEKS

Combinations

TEKS 4.13A use concrete objects or pictures to make generalizations about determining all possible combinations of a given set of data or of objects in a problem situation.

A combination is a choice in which the order of the items does not matter. Make an organized list, make a tree diagram, or write a number sentence to find possible combinations.

8 possible outfits
$4 \times 2 = 8$

Examples

Megan is going to the city. She can go during the week or on the weekend. She can go by train or bus, or she can drive. How many choices does Megan have?

A You can make an organized list to show the combinations.

When	How
Weekday	Train
Weekday	Bus
Weekday	Drive
Weekend	Train
Weekend	Bus
Weekend	Drive

So, Megan has 6 choices.

B You can make a tree diagram to show the combinations.

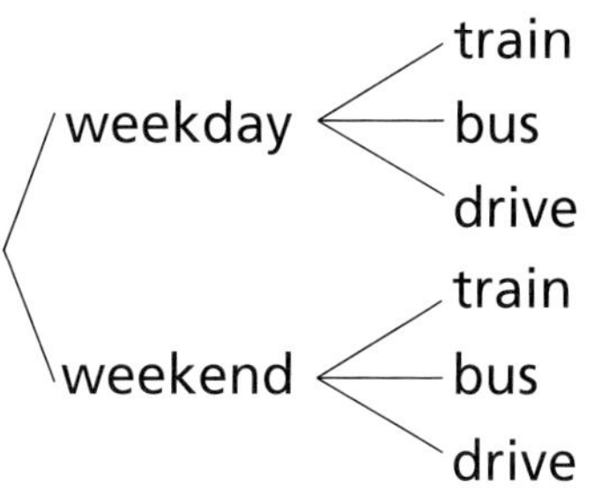

So, Megan has 6 choices.

ERROR ALERT

Be sure to count all the possible combinations in your list or diagram.

Try It

Find the number of possible combinations.

1. Sandwich choices
   bread: wheat, rye, white, marble
   fillings: cheese, tuna, peanut butter, turkey

2. After school activity choices
   activity: baseball, soccer, volleyball, tennis
   place: gym, schoolyard, park

3. Read the problem below. **Explain** why C cannot be the correct answer choice. Then choose the correct answer. **COMMON ERROR**

   For her art project, Kiana can use paints, crayons, pastels, or markers. She can draw trees, flowers, people, dogs, cats, or birds. How many choices does Kiana have?

   A 4   **C** 10
   B 6   **D** 24

Review the TEKS

Bar Graphs

TEKS 4.13B interpret bar graphs.

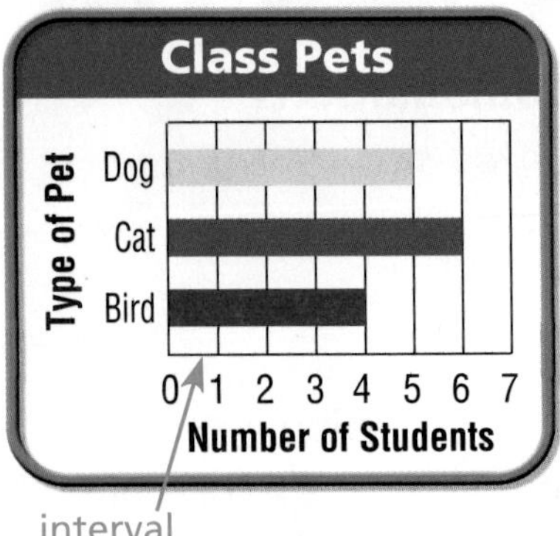

Bar graphs are useful for comparing data about different groups. A bar graph can use vertical or horizontal bars to show data. At least one set of data will be numbers. The other data set might be numbers or categories.

Example

What information can you get from this graph?

- The interval on the vertical scale is 50 feet.
- The longest playing area shown on the graph is hockey, 200 feet.
- The shortest playing area shown on the graph is bowling, 60 feet.

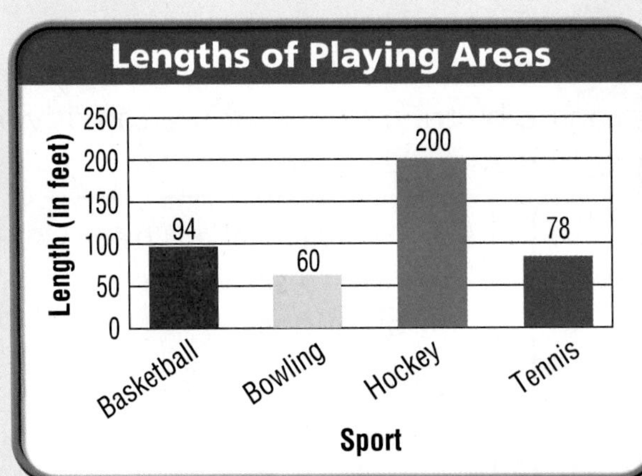

ERROR ALERT

Remember to trace a line from the top of a bar to the scale.

The length of a bowling alley is greater than 50 feet.

Try It

For 1–3, use the Lengths of Playing Areas graph.

1. The center ice line on a hockey rink is exactly in the middle of the rink. How many feet from the end is the center ice line?
2. What is the difference between the longest and shortest playing areas?
3. Which playing area appears to be about 75 ft?

4. Read the problem below. **Explain** why D cannot be the correct answer choice. Then choose the correct answer. **COMMON ERROR**

   Use the Lengths of Playing Areas graph in the Example above. Some sports have playing areas that are divided in half. For which sport is each half of the playing area 47 feet long?

   A Basketball **C** Hockey

   B Bowling **D** Tennis

Review the TEKS

Problem Solving

TEKS 4.14 The student applies Grade 4 mathematics to solve problems connected to everyday experiences and activities in and outside of school.
TEKS 4.15 The student communicates about Grade 4 mathematics using informal language.
TEKS 4.16 The student uses logical reasoning.

When you use **logical reasoning** in mathematics, you

- Solve problems in a step-by-step manner, or
- Look for a pattern.

Sample

Which pair of figures does not belong with the others? See whether you can find more than one answer that makes sense. Explain your reasoning.

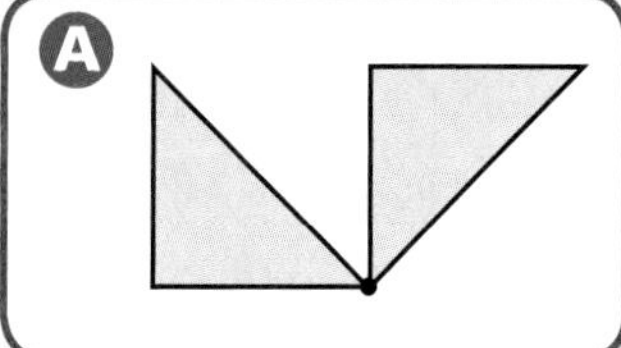

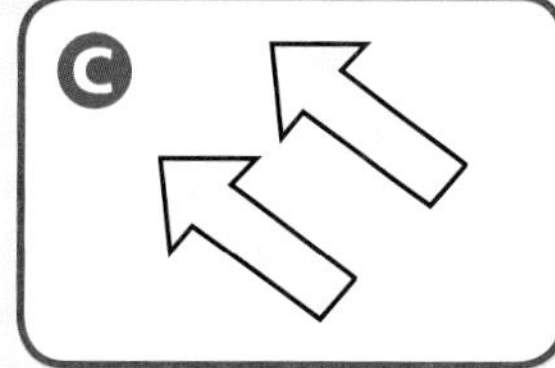

Use logical reasoning. Look for a pattern.

- The two figures in each pair are congruent. They have the same size and shape. So, the size and shape of the figures does not determine which pair does not belong.
- The two figures in B are the only ones that are not made of line segments. So, a possible answer is that the figures in B do not belong. Another reason that the figures in B might not belong is that they are the only ones with anything drawn inside them.
- The figures in B, C, and D all represent translations. The figures in A represent a rotation. So, another possible answer is that A does not belong because it represents a different transformation from the others.
- The figures in C are the only ones that could represent a reflection. So, it also would be correct to say that C does not belong with the others because the others do not represent reflections.

An important part of problem solving is learning to use mathematical language and symbols to represent everyday situations.

Sample

The Crafts Club needs 40 yards of fabric for a quilt project. Ten students each bring 3 yards of fabric. Five students each bring 3 feet of fabric. Is there enough fabric? If not, how much more is needed? Is there too much? If so, how much extra is there?

This is a long problem. It can be turned into several short, simple mathematical operations. You can write word equations to represent the problem. Then match the words to write an equation.

Begin with what students bring to the class.

Ten students	each bring	three yards.	
10	×	3	= 30 yards
Five students	each bring	three feet.	
5	×	3	= 15 feet

Be sure that both amounts use the same unit.

There are 3 feet in 1 yard.

Number of feet		divided by the number of feet in a yard.		
15	÷	3	=	5 yards

Finally, find out whether there is enough.

Amount needed	−	Amount brought	=	Difference
40	−	(30 + 5)	=	5 yards

So, 5 more yards of fabric are needed.

Test Tip A two-column table helps organize the information in the problem.

What I Know	What I Need to Find
• Need 40 yd • 10 students bring 3 yd • 5 students bring 3 ft	• Is there enough? • How much extra is there? or • How much more is needed?

Try It

1. Barry is 9 years older than Joe. Joe is 6 years younger than Asia. If Asia is 12 years old, how old is Barry?

2. Billie rides his bike $\frac{1}{2}$ mile each day. How many miles does Billie ride in 3 days?

3. Alicia is on page 79 of her library book. If she reads 25 pages each day for another 7 days, she will finish the book. How many pages does the book have?

4. Jermaine has 20 math homework problems. He does $\frac{1}{10}$ of them after school and another $\frac{5}{10}$ before dinner. What fraction of his homework does he do before dinner?

Solve the problem.

5. Each car on a train can carry 66 people. If the car starts out full, how many people are still in it after the first 3 stops if 15, 11, and 9 people leave?

6. Ernesto walks to and from school. The total trip is 3 miles. If he walks on 19 days in March, 21 days in April, and 18 days in May, how many miles does he walk in all?

7. Mrs. Pearl put 9 gallons of gasoline in her car. She is able to drive 243 miles using the 9 gallons. How many miles is she able to drive on each gallon?

8. A factory packs 24 bottles of juice in each shipping carton. If they ship 8 cartons, how many bottles of juice do they pack?

9. May-Li pays $3.50 per hour to rent skates and buys knee pads for $14. Which number sentence tells the amount she pays if she rents the skates for 5 hours?

   A $5 + 3.50 + 14 = 22.50$

   B $5 \times 14 + 3.50 = 73.50$

   C $5 \times 3.50 + 14 = 31.50$

   D $14 \times 3.50 + 5 = 54$

10. Which pair of numbers best completes the equation?

    ■ × 100 = ▲

    F 32 and 3,020

    G 19 and 190

    H 43 and 4,030

    J 27 and 2,700

11. Which two sides appear to be parallel in the figure?

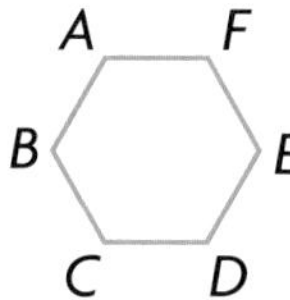

    A *AB* and *CD*

    B *AF* and *BC*

    C *DE* and *CD*

    D Not here

12. The area of the square is 36 square feet. What is the perimeter?

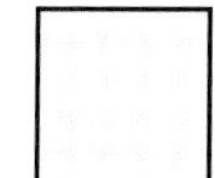

    F 6 feet

    G 9 feet

    H 24 feet

    J 36 feet

13. At Ed's Diner, the lunch special offers 3 soups, 2 sandwiches, and 2 desserts. At Rosa's Café, the lunch special offers 2 soups, 5 sandwiches, and 1 dessert. If a lunch is soup, a sandwich, and a dessert, which is true?

    A Ed's offers more choices.

    B Rosa's offers more choices.

    C They offer the same number of choices.

    D You cannot tell.

14. Carlo has a yellow shirt and a blue shirt. He has 2 pairs of jeans and 3 sweaters. If he picks the yellow shirt, how many different shirt-jeans-sweater outfits can he make?

    F 4

    G 5

    H 6

    J 8

TAKS Test-Taking Strategies

Being a good test taker is like being a good problem solver. When you solve problems, it is good to know strategies for solving problems. These strategies will help you become a good test taker.

Reading the Problem

- Watch for special terms (*about, least, most, second*).
- Pay attention to words that are in **boldface**, *italics*, or CAPITALS.
- Decide what information to use and what information not to use.

Sample Problem 1

The table shows the number of rectangular prisms and the number of faces on these rectangular prisms.

Faces on Rectangular Prisms				
Number of Rectangular Prisms	3	6	9	12
Number of Faces	18	36	54	72

Which correctly describes the relationship in the table?

A Number of rectangular prisms $+$ 15 $=$ Number of faces

B Number of rectangular prisms $+$ 30 $=$ Number of faces

C Number of rectangular prisms $\times$ 6 $=$ Number of faces

D Number of faces $-$ 15 $=$ Number of rectangular prisms

Deciding What Information to Use

- When you first see a problem, read it several times before trying to solve it. Problems often have information that you do not need. If you understand what you are given and what you are being asked, it will be easier to decide which information is important.
- You might not need information that you do not understand. For example, if you do not recognize the term *rectangular prism*, you can still solve the problem by looking at the information in the table.
- When information is in a table, the information often shows a pattern. So, it is important to read the entire table.
- Look at the sample problem. If you look only at the first column of the table, you will see that answer choice A describes the relationship. But if you look at each column of the table, you will see that choice A does not describe the relationship shown in the other columns.

Sample Problem 2

Alexis is thinking about buying a new car. She visits four car dealerships and is given these prices for the car she wants to buy.

New Car Prices	
Car Dealership	**Price**
A	$18,245
B	$21,088
C	$19,659
D	$20,355

Which is about the difference between the highest price and the lowest price Alexis is given?

F $1,000

G $2,000

H $3,000

J $4,000

Special Terms

- The term *about* lets you know that you do not need an exact answer. The problem is asking for an estimate.
- When you see special terms, such as *about*, ask yourself, "How does this affect the way I solve the problem?"

Sample Problem 3

Cleavon tossed a number cube labeled 1 to 6 twice. Which of these is **NOT** a possible combination?

A 1, 6

B 4, 4

C 2, 7

D 6, 6

Words Printed Differently

- Pay special attention to words that are **bold**, in CAPITALS, or in *italics*.
- The term **NOT** tells you that all choices except one are possible. You could read the problem without the term **NOT** and decide which outcomes are possible. Then the only one left will be the solution.

TAKS Test-Taking Strategies

Understanding the Problem

If the problem has a graph, table, or chart, be sure you understand what information is in it.

- Restate the problem by using simpler words, by drawing a picture, or by using simpler numbers.
- Put the information in a number sentence.
- Be sure you solve all steps of the problem.
- Is there information missing?

Sample Problem 1

Look at the 2 sets of numbers below.

Set A
1234
7654
3456
9876

Set B
1357
9753
2468
7531

Which number belongs in Set A?

A 8642

B 6543

C 3579

D 5791

Understand Information, Restate the Problem

- Often, you can help yourself understand information by putting it into your own words. You might want to ask yourself:

  "What is the same about all of the numbers in Set A?"

  "What is the same about all of the numbers in Set B?"

  "How could I complete this sentence: 'All of the numbers in Set A are __________?'"

  "How could I complete this sentence: 'All of the numbers in Set B are __________?'"

  "How are the numbers in Set A different from the numbers in Set B?"

Sample Problem 2

Carla is on a 30-mile hike. She has already walked 6 miles and has 3 days left to complete the trip. How can Carla find the number of miles she should walk each day to finish the hike on time?

F Subtract 3 from 30, and then divide by 6.

G Multiply 6 by 3.

H Divide 30 by 3.

J Subtract 6 from 30, and then divide by 3.

Use a Number Sentence

- You can write word sentences for the information in the problem.

Total distance	−	Distance already walked	=	Distance left to walk
30 miles	−	6 miles	=	24 miles
Distance left to walk	÷	Number of days left	=	Distance each day
24 miles	÷	3 days	=	8 miles each day

- You can change word sentences in the answer choices into number sentences and then solve. For choice F, you could write $(30 - 3) \div 6$; for choice G, 6×3; for choice H, $30 \div 3$; and for choice J, $(30 - 6) \div 3$.

Sample Problem 3

Derrick needs to plant 40 bushes in 7 hours. He plants 4 in the first hour. How many should he plant each hour if he plants the same number each hour?

A 36 bushes

B 33 bushes

C 28 bushes

D 6 bushes

Solve All Steps of the Problem

When you think you have solved the problem, you need to ask yourself "Have I answered the question?"

- There is a difference between doing the operations correctly and answering the question correctly. For example, here the solution is 6 bushes each hour. If you had stopped when you found how many bushes he had left, you would have done the subtraction correctly, but you would not have had the correct answer.
- You might want to underline the question and then see whether you have answered it.

TAKS Test-Taking Strategies

Understanding the Question

- What unit is used in the question?
- Is the question asking for a number?
- Is the question asking about the steps used to find the answer?
- Is the question asking what information is missing?

Sample Problem

What information is needed to find the total distance Seth drives during his 5-day work week? He drives to work every morning and drives home for lunch. He drives back to work after lunch and drives home in the evening.

A Where Seth lives

B The type of job Seth has

C The length of Seth's car

D The distance Seth lives from his job

Types of Information

- A good strategy for all problems is to find the question and read it several times. Remember that the question is not always at the end of the problem. In the Sample Problem, the question is asked before most of the information is given.
- Questions do not always ask you to find a number as an answer. In many problems, you do not have to do any arithmetic. In the Sample Problem, no arithmetic is needed. You are asked to use reasoning skills to decide which piece of information you need.

Missing Information

To decide which piece of information is needed, you might want to make up information for each answer choice to see whether that helps you. Which of these are helpful?

- For answer choice A: Suppose Seth lives in Dallas.
- For answer choice B: Suppose Seth is a fourth-grade teacher.
- For answer choice C: Suppose Seth's car is 16 feet long.
- For answer choice D: Suppose Seth lives 3 miles from his job.

Answering the Question

- Estimate the answer.
- Draw a picture to see what information you are asked to find.
- Make no stray marks on the answer sheet.

Sample Problem

A football team needs coaches. Each coach will supervise 6 players. What should the team's manager do to find the number of coaches that will be needed for the season?

A Multiply the total number of players by 6

B Add 6 to the total number of players

C Subtract 6 from the total number of players

D Divide the total number of players by 6

Estimate the Answer

- Many problems contain hints about the size of the solution. Problems often let you know whether the solution will be less than or greater than the numbers given in the problem.

  In the Sample Problem, you know that there are more players than coaches from the sentence "Each coach supervises 6 players." So, whatever the manager needs to do, it will not be an answer that is greater than the number of players.

- In the Sample Problem, you are not told how many players there are. So, you cannot just add, subtract, multiply, or divide two numbers.

Draw a Picture

- In order to understand the problem more clearly, it may help to draw a picture of the information.
- You are not told how many players there are, so you might want to try drawing some number that is a multiple of 6.

  Try 24. Then match 1 coach to each 6 players.

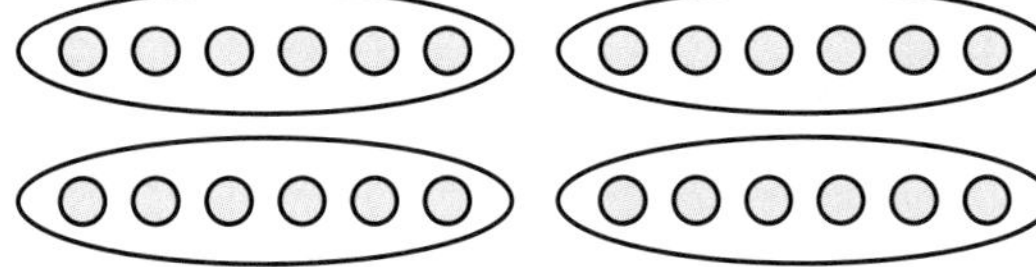

- With 1 coach for each 6 players, there will be 4 coaches needed. Now you know the information you need to find. Go through the answer choices to find the operation that will give 4 coaches as the solution if you had 24 players.

TAKS Test-Taking Strategies

Multiple Choice

- Look at the answers one at a time.
- Eliminate choices.
- Try each answer in the problem to see whether it works.
- If the answer isn't there—
  Check the numbers you used.
  Check your arithmetic.
  Look for an equivalent number.

Sample Problem 1

Some arrays for the number 12 are shown.

Which shows another array for the number 12?

A

B

C

D

Try Each Answer, Eliminate Choices

- Many multiple-choice problems can be solved by examining each answer choice in order to see whether it answers the question. In the Sample Problem, you know that you need to find an array for 12. If an answer choice does not contain 12 squares, it cannot be correct. Look at the answer choices one at a time until you find the correct one.

Sample Problem 2

Bettina's room is in the shape of a rectangle that is 9 feet wide and 11 feet long. What is the area of her room?

F 20 square feet

G 40 square feet

H 90 square feet

J Not here

When to Use "Not here"

- Solve the problem, and compare your solution to the answer choices. If no answer choice matches your answer, choose "Not here."

Griddable Responses

- Write the response at the top of the grid.
- Write only one digit in each column.
- Write the digits in the correct order.

Sample Problem 1

A bus trip takes 4 hours more than 3 times the time needed to make the same trip by plane. The plane trip takes 2 hours. How many hours does the bus trip take?

	1	0
0	0	●
1	●	1
2	2	2
3	3	3
4	4	4
5	5	5
6	6	6
7	7	7
8	8	8
9	9	9

Write Only One Digit in Each Column, Use the Correct Order

- Solve the problem before you look at the grid.
  $(3 \times 2) + 4 = 10$ hours by bus

  The grid is not part of the solution. It is just a way to record the answer.

- When you are ready to enter your answer:

  All digits of this answer will be entered to the left of the decimal point.

  Then use place value.

  Write the ones digit (0) in the column to the left of the decimal point. Write the tens digit (1) in the column to the left of the ones digit.

  (If there were a hundreds digit, you would write it in the column to the left of the tens digit. If there were no hundreds digit, you would leave the column blank—**do not write a zero**.)

- Fill in the circle that corresponds to the digit at the top of each column. Fill only one circle in each column. Fill the circle completely.

Sample Problem 2

Diego has 170 bottle caps. He arranges them in 5 equal groups. How many bottle caps are in each group?

	3	4
0	0	0
1	1	1
2	2	2
3	●	3
4	4	●
5	5	5
6	6	6
7	7	7
8	8	8
9	9	9

Fill Only One Circle, Fill it Completely

- When you see a problem with a grid, look to see if there are answer columns to the right of the decimal point. If there are answer columns to the right, then the answer most likely will contain a decimal. If not, then the answer will most likely be a whole number.

Addition Facts

	K	L	M	N	O	P	Q	R
A	6 + 7	9 + 6	3 + 5	8 + 9	0 + 7	2 + 8	6 + 4	7 + 7
B	1 + 6	8 + 4	5 + 1	2 + 7	3 + 3	8 + 2	4 + 5	2 + 6
C	6 + 6	3 + 7	7 + 8	4 + 6	9 + 0	4 + 2	10 + 4	3 + 8
D	6 + 1	5 + 9	10 + 6	5 + 7	3 + 9	9 + 8	8 + 7	8 + 1
E	7 + 6	7 + 1	6 + 9	4 + 3	5 + 5	8 + 0	9 + 5	2 + 9
F	9 + 1	8 + 5	7 + 0	8 + 3	7 + 2	4 + 7	10 + 5	4 + 8
G	5 + 3	9 + 9	3 + 6	7 + 4	0 + 8	4 + 4	7 + 10	6 + 8
H	8 + 6	10 + 7	0 + 9	7 + 9	5 + 6	8 + 10	6 + 5	9 + 4
I	9 + 7	8 + 8	1 + 9	5 + 8	10 + 9	6 + 3	6 + 2	9 + 10
J	9 + 2	7 + 5	6 + 0	10 + 8	5 + 4	4 + 9	9 + 3	10 + 10

Subtraction Facts

	K	L	M	N	O	P	Q	R
A	13 − 4	7 − 1	9 − 7	9 − 9	11 − 5	6 − 3	12 − 7	8 − 5
B	8 − 8	16 − 8	15 − 6	10 − 2	6 − 5	8 − 7	14 − 4	11 − 9
C	9 − 5	12 − 8	15 − 8	11 − 7	14 − 8	18 − 9	15 − 5	8 − 1
D	10 − 4	16 − 10	13 − 9	9 − 1	7 − 2	7 − 0	13 − 8	6 − 4
E	10 − 9	9 − 6	17 − 9	7 − 3	6 − 0	11 − 8	8 − 6	9 − 4
F	8 − 4	13 − 6	11 − 2	15 − 7	19 − 10	12 − 3	17 − 8	7 − 5
G	9 − 8	13 − 7	7 − 4	15 − 9	8 − 2	10 − 6	14 − 7	12 − 5
H	10 − 7	6 − 6	8 − 0	12 − 4	14 − 6	11 − 4	6 − 2	17 − 7
I	13 − 5	12 − 9	16 − 7	7 − 6	10 − 5	11 − 3	12 − 6	14 − 9
J	10 − 8	11 − 6	14 − 5	16 − 9	9 − 3	5 − 4	18 − 10	20 − 10

Multiplication Facts

	K	L	M	N	O	P	Q	R
A	5×6	5×9	7×7	9×10	7×5	12×2	10×6	6×7
B	6×6	0×6	2×7	12×8	9×2	3×5	5×8	8×3
C	7×0	5×1	4×5	9×9	6×8	8×11	11×7	10×5
D	1×7	9×4	0×7	2×5	9×7	10×9	3×3	12×7
E	5×7	1×9	4×3	7×6	11×3	3×8	4×2	10×10
F	10×12	5×5	6×4	9×8	0×8	9×6	11×2	12×6
G	5×3	4×6	6×3	7×9	12×5	0×9	5×4	12×11
H	7×1	6×9	1×6	4×4	3×7	11×11	4×8	12×9
I	7×4	2×4	8×6	3×4	11×5	2×9	8×9	7×8
J	8×0	3×9	12×12	8×5	4×7	6×2	9×5	8×8

Division Facts

	K	L	M	N	O	P	Q	R
A	$7\overline{)56}$	$5\overline{)40}$	$6\overline{)24}$	$6\overline{)30}$	$6\overline{)18}$	$7\overline{)42}$	$8\overline{)16}$	$9\overline{)45}$
B	$3\overline{)9}$	$10\overline{)90}$	$1\overline{)1}$	$1\overline{)6}$	$10\overline{)100}$	$3\overline{)12}$	$10\overline{)70}$	$8\overline{)56}$
C	$6\overline{)48}$	$12\overline{)60}$	$4\overline{)32}$	$6\overline{)54}$	$7\overline{)0}$	$3\overline{)18}$	$9\overline{)90}$	$11\overline{)55}$
D	$2\overline{)16}$	$3\overline{)21}$	$5\overline{)30}$	$3\overline{)15}$	$11\overline{)110}$	$9\overline{)9}$	$8\overline{)64}$	$9\overline{)63}$
E	$4\overline{)28}$	$2\overline{)10}$	$9\overline{)18}$	$1\overline{)5}$	$7\overline{)63}$	$8\overline{)32}$	$2\overline{)8}$	$9\overline{)108}$
F	$8\overline{)24}$	$4\overline{)4}$	$2\overline{)14}$	$11\overline{)66}$	$8\overline{)72}$	$4\overline{)12}$	$7\overline{)21}$	$6\overline{)36}$
G	$12\overline{)36}$	$5\overline{)20}$	$7\overline{)28}$	$7\overline{)14}$	$4\overline{)24}$	$11\overline{)121}$	$9\overline{)36}$	$11\overline{)132}$
H	$9\overline{)27}$	$3\overline{)27}$	$7\overline{)49}$	$4\overline{)20}$	$9\overline{)72}$	$5\overline{)60}$	$8\overline{)88}$	$10\overline{)80}$
I	$4\overline{)44}$	$8\overline{)48}$	$5\overline{)35}$	$8\overline{)40}$	$5\overline{)10}$	$2\overline{)12}$	$10\overline{)60}$	$9\overline{)54}$
J	$10\overline{)120}$	$12\overline{)72}$	$9\overline{)81}$	$4\overline{)16}$	$1\overline{)7}$	$12\overline{)60}$	$12\overline{)96}$	$12\overline{)144}$

Table of Measures

SI (Metric)		Customary	
Length			
1 centimeter (cm)	= 10 millimeters (mm)	1 foot (ft)	= 12 inches (in.)
1 decimeter (dm)	= 10 centimeters	1 yard (yd)	= 3 feet, or 36 inches
1 meter (m)	= 10 decimeters, or 100 centimeters	1 mile (mi)	= 1,760 yards, or 5,280 feet
1 kilometer (km)	= 1,000 meters		
Capacity			
1 liter (L)	= 1,000 milliliters (mL)	1 tablespoon (tbsp)	= 3 teaspoons (tsp)
1 metric cup	= 250 milliliters	1 cup (c)	= 8 fluid ounces (fl oz)
		1 pint (pt)	= 2 cups
		1 quart (qt)	= 2 pints
		1 gallon (gal)	= 4 quarts, or 128 fluid ounces
Mass/Weight			
1 gram (g)	= 1,000 milligrams (mg)	1 pound (lb)	= 16 ounces (oz)
1 kilogram (kg)	= 1,000 grams	1 ton (T)	= 2,000 pounds

Time	
1 minute (min)	= 60 seconds (sec)
1 quarter hour (hr)	= 15 minutes
1 half hour (hr)	= 30 minutes
1 hour (hr)	= 60 minutes
1 day	= 24 hours
1 week (wk)	= 7 days
1 year (yr)	= 12 months (mo), or about 52 weeks
1 year	= 365 days
1 leap year	= 366 days

Money	
1 penny	= 1¢ or \$0.01
1 nickel	= 5¢ or \$0.05
1 dime	= 10¢ or \$0.10
1 quarter	= 25¢ or \$0.25
1 half dollar	= 50¢ or \$0.50
1 dollar	= 100¢ or \$1.00

Symbols

$\perp$	is perpendicular to	$<$	is less than	°	degree
$\parallel$	is parallel to	$>$	is greater than	°F	degrees Fahrenheit
$\overleftrightarrow{AB}$	line *AB*	$\leq$	is less than or equal to	°C	degrees Celsius
$\overrightarrow{AB}$	ray *AB*	$\geq$	is greater than or equal to	$^{+}8$	positive 8
$\overline{AB}$	line segment *AB*	$\approx$	is approximately equal to	$^{-}8$	negative 8
$\angle ABC$	angle *ABC*	$=$	is equal to	¢	cent
(2,3)	ordered pair (x,y)	$\neq$	is not equal to	$	dollar

Formulas

Perimeter of polygon = sum of length of sides

Perimeter of rectangle $P = (2 \times l) + (2 \times w)$, $P = 2l + 2w$, or $P = 2(l + w)$

Perimeter of square $P = 4 \times s$, $P = 4s$

Area of rectangle $A = l \times w$, $A = lw$. or $A = bh$

Volume of rectangular prism $V = l \times w \times h$

Texas Essential Knowledge and Skills

TEKS
Number, Operation, and Quantitative Reasoning
(4.1) The student uses place value to represent whole numbers and decimals. The student is expected to:
(A) use place value to read, write, compare, and order whole numbers through 999,999,999; and
(B) use place value to read, write, compare, and order decimals involving tenths and hundredths, including money, using concrete objects and pictorial models.
(4.2) The student describes and compares fractional parts of whole objects or sets of objects. The student is expected to:
(A) use concrete objects and pictorial models to generate equivalent fractions;
(B) model fraction quantities greater than one using concrete objects and pictorial models;
(C) compare and order fractions using concrete objects and pictorial models; and
(D) relate decimals to fractions that name tenths and hundredths using concrete objects and pictorial models.
(4.3) The student adds and subtracts to solve meaningful problems involving whole numbers and decimals. The student is expected to:
(A) use addition and subtraction to solve problems involving whole numbers; and
(B) add and subtract decimals to the hundredths place using concrete objects and pictorial models.
(4.4) The student multiplies and divides to solve meaningful problems involving whole numbers. The student is expected to:
(A) model factors and products using arrays and area models;
(B) represent multiplication and division situations in picture, word, and number form;
(C) recall and apply multiplication facts through 12×12;
(D) use multiplication to solve problems (no more than two digits times two digits without technology); and
(E) use division to solve problems (no more than one-digit divisors and three-digit dividends without technology).
(4.5) The student estimates to determine reasonable results. The student is expected to:
(A) round whole numbers to the nearest ten, hundred, or thousand to approximate reasonable results in problem situations; and
(B) use strategies including rounding and compatible numbers to estimate solutions to multiplication and division problems.

TEKS
Patterns, Relationships, and Algebraic Thinking
(4.6) The student uses patterns in multiplication and division. The student is expected to:
(A) use patterns and relationships to develop strategies to remember basic multiplication and division facts (such as the patterns in related multiplication and division number sentences (fact families) such as $9 \times 9 = 81$ and $81 \div 9 = 9$); and
(B) use patterns to multiply by 10 and 100.
(4.7) The student uses organizational structures to analyze and describe patterns and relationships.
The student is expected to describe the relationship between two sets of related data such as ordered pairs in a table.
Geometry and Spatial Reasoning
(4.8) The student identifies and describes attributes of geometric figures using formal geometric language. The student is expected to:
(A) identify and describe right, acute, and obtuse angles;
(B) identify and describe parallel and intersecting (including perpendicular) lines using concrete objects and pictorial models; and
(C) use essential attributes to define two- and three-dimensional geometric figures.
(4.9) The student connects transformations to congruence and symmetry. The student is expected to:
(A) demonstrate translations, reflections, and rotations using concrete models;
(B) use translations, reflections, and rotations to verify that two shapes are congruent; and
(C) use reflections to verify that a shape has symmetry.
(4.10) The student recognizes the connection between numbers and their properties and points on a line.
The student is expected to locate and name points on a number line using whole numbers, fractions such as halves and fourths, and decimals such as tenths.
Measurement
(4.11) The student applies measurement concepts. The student is expected to estimate and measure to solve problems involving length (including perimeter) and area. The student uses measurement tools to measure capacity/volume and weight/mass. The student is expected to:
(A) estimate and use measurement tools to determine length (including perimeter), area, capacity and weight/mass using standard units SI (metric) and customary;

TEKS Continued

TEKS
(B) perform simple conversions between different units of length, between different units of capacity, and between different units of weight within the customary measurement system;
(C) use concrete models of standard cubic units to measure volume;
(D) estimate volume in cubic units; and
(E) explain the difference between weight and mass.
(4.12) The student applies measurement concepts. The student measures time and temperature (in degrees Fahrenheit and Celsius). The student is expected to:
(A) use a thermometer to measure temperature and changes in temperature; and
(B) use tools such as a clock with gears or a stopwatch to solve problems involving elapsed time.
Probability and Statistics
(4.13) The student solves problems by collecting, organizing, displaying, and interpreting sets of data. The student is expected to:
(A) use concrete objects or pictures to make generalizations about determining all possible combinations of a given set of data or of objects in a problem situation; and
(B) interpret bar graphs.
Underlying Processes and Mathematical Tools
(4.14) The student applies Grade 4 mathematics to solve problems connected to everyday experiences and activities in and outside of school. The student is expected to:
(A) identify the mathematics in everyday situations;
(B) solve problems that incorporate understanding the problem, making a plan, carrying out the plan, and evaluating the solution for reasonableness;
(C) select or develop an appropriate problem-solving plan or strategy, including drawing a picture, looking for a pattern, systematic guessing and checking, acting it out, making a table, working a simpler problem, or working backwards to solve a problem; and
(D) use tools such as real objects, manipulatives, and technology to solve problems.
(4.15) The student communicates about Grade 4 mathematics using informal language. The student is expected to:
(A) explain and record observations using objects, words, pictures, numbers, and technology; and
(B) relate informal language to mathematical language and symbols.
(4.16) The student uses logical reasoning. The student is expected to:
(A) make generalizations from patterns or sets of examples and nonexamples; and
(B) justify why an answer is reasonable and explain the solution process.

Glossary

Pronunciation Key

a	**a**dd, m**a**p	f	**f**it, hal**f**	n	**n**ice, ti**n**	p	**p**it, sto**p**	yōō	**fu**se, **few**
ā	**a**ce, r**a**te	g	**g**o, lo**g**	ng	ri**ng**, so**ng**	r	**r**un, poo**r**	v	**v**ain, e**v**e
â(r)	c**a**re, **a**ir	h	**h**ope, **h**ate	o	**o**dd, h**o**t	s	**s**ee, pa**ss**	w	**w**in, a**w**ay
ä	p**a**lm, f**a**ther	i	**i**t, g**i**ve	ō	**o**pen, s**o**	sh	**s**ure, ru**sh**	y	**y**et, **y**earn
b	**b**at, ru**b**	ī	**i**ce, wr**i**te	ô	**o**rder, j**aw**	t	**t**alk, si**t**	z	**z**est, mu**s**e
ch	**ch**eck, cat**ch**	j	**j**oy, le**dg**e	oi	**oi**l, b**oy**	th	**th**in, bo**th**	zh	vi**s**ion, plea**s**ure
d	**d**og, ro**d**	k	**c**ool, ta**k**e	ou	p**ou**t, n**ow**	t͟h	**th**is, ba**th**e		
e	**e**nd, p**e**t	l	**l**ook, ru**l**e	o͝o	t**oo**k, f**u**ll	u	**u**p, d**o**ne		
ē	**e**qual, tr**ee**	m	**m**ove, see**m**	ōō	p**oo**l, f**oo**d	û(r)	b**ur**n, t**er**m		

ə the schwa, an unstressed vowel representing the sound spelled *a* in **a**bove, *e* in sick**e**n, *i* in poss**i**ble, *o* in mel**o**n, *u* in circ**u**s

Other symbols:
- • separates words into syllables
- ′ indicates stress on a syllable

A.M. [ā•em′] **a.m.** The time between midnight and noon (p. 474)

acute angle [ə•kyōōt′ ang′əl] **ángulo agudo** An angle that measures less than a right angle (greater than 0° and less than 90°) (p. 260)
Example:

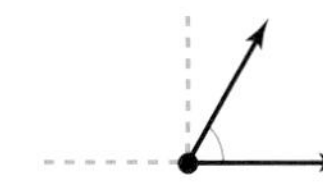

acute triangle [ə•kyōōt′ trī′ang•əl] **triángulo acutángulo** A triangle with three acute angles (p. 268)
Example:

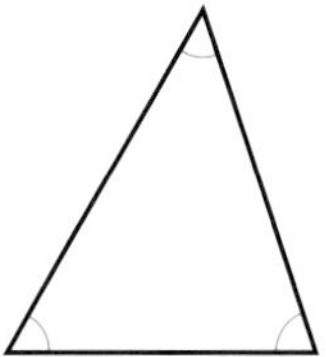

addend [a′dend] **sumando** A number that is added to another in an addition problem
Example: 2 + 4 = 6;
2 and 4 are addends.

addition [ə•di′shən] **suma** The process of finding the total number of items when two or more groups of items are joined; the opposite operation of subtraction

analog clock [a′nəl•ôg kläk] **reloj analógico** A device for measuring time by moving hands around a circle for showing hours, minutes, and sometimes seconds (p. 474)
Example:

angle [ang′əl] **ángulo** A figure formed by two line segments or rays that share the same endpoint (p. 260)
Example:

area [âr′ē•ə] **área** The number of square units needed to cover a surface (p. 610)
Example:

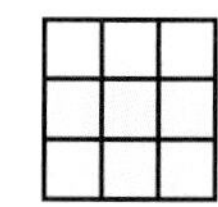

area = 9 square units

array [ə•rā′] **matriz** An arrangement of objects in rows and columns (p. 96)
Example:

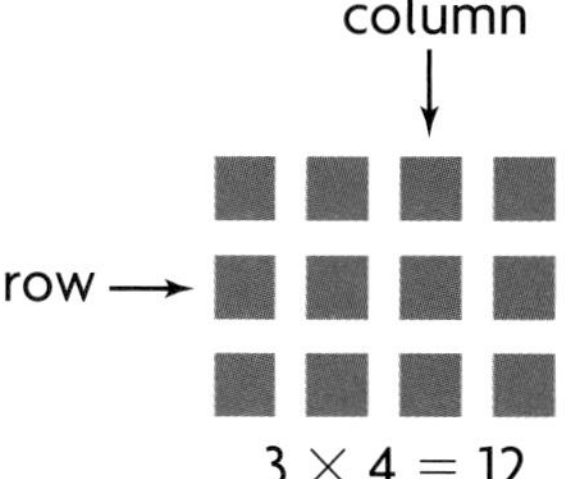

Associative Property of Addition [ə•sō′shē•ə•tiv prä′pər•tē əv ə•di′shən] **propiedad asociativa de la suma** The property that states you can group addends in different ways and still get the same sum (p. 68)
Example: 3 + (8 + 5) = (3 + 8) + 5

Associative Property of Multiplication [ə•sō′shē•ə•tiv prä′pər•tē əv mul•tə•plə•kā′shən] **propiedad asociativa de la multiplicación** The property that states you can group factors in different ways and still get the same product (p. 152)
Example: 3 × (4 × 2) = (3 × 4) × 2

average [av′rij] **promedio** The number found by dividing the sum of the set of numbers by the number of addends (p. 374)

B

bar graph [bär graf] **gráfica de barras** A graph that uses bars to show data (p. 506)
Example:

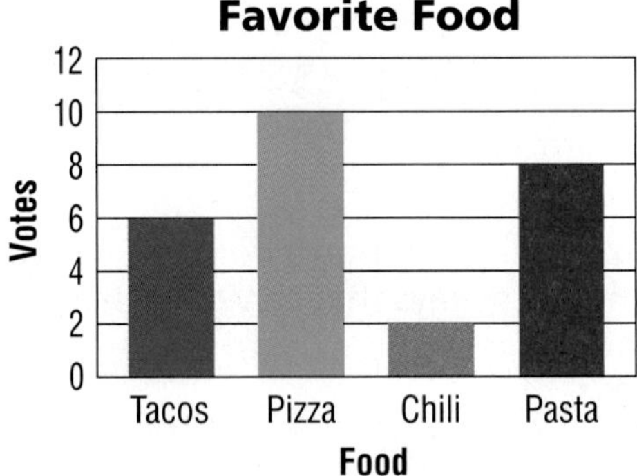

base [bās] **base** A polygon's side or a solid figure's face by which the figure is measured or named (p. 314)
Examples:

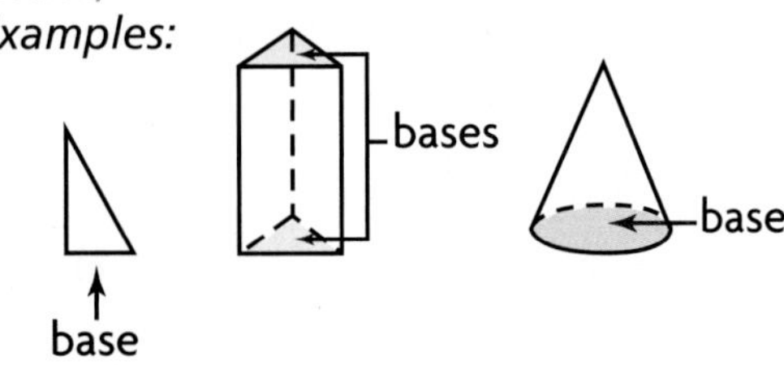

benchmark [bench′märk] **punto de referencia** A known number of things that helps you understand the size or amount of a different number of things (p. 15)

C

calendar [ka′lən•dər] **calendario** A table that shows the days, weeks, and months of a year (p. 482)

capacity [kə•pa′sə•tē] **capacidad** The amount a container can hold when filled (p. 560)

categorical data [ka•tə•gôr′i•kəl dā′tə] **datos categóricos** Data that can be sorted into different groups (p. 496)

center [sen′tər] **centro** The point inside a circle that is the same distance from each point on the circle (p. 274)
Example:

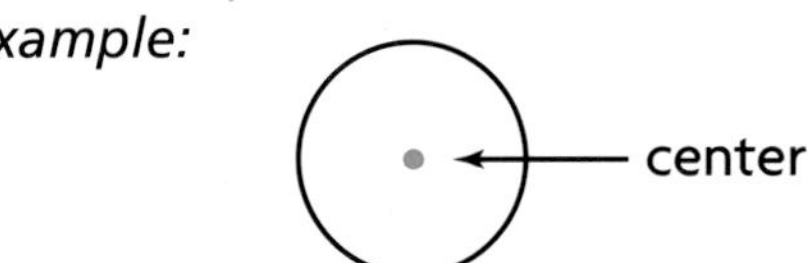

Word History

The word *center* comes from a Greek root, *kentrus*, meaning "spur, or sharp, pointed object." A sharp point was made at a center point to fix the spot and a duller object was dragged around the center to form the circle.

centimeter (cm) [sen′tə•mē•tər] **centímetro (cm)** A metric unit for measuring length or distance (p. 574)
100 centimeters = 1 meter
Example:

1 centimeter

circle [sûr′kəl] **círculo** A closed figure made up of points that are the same distance from the center (p. 274)
Example:

circumference [sər•kum′fər•əns] **circunferencia** The distance around a circle (p. 627)

clockwise [klok′wīz′] **en el sentido de las manecillas del reloj** In the same direction in which the hands of a clock move (p. 290)

closed figure [klōzd fi′gyər] **figura cerrada** A figure that begins and ends at the same point
Example:

combination [kam•bə•nā′•shən] **combinación** A choice in which the order of items does not matter (p. 522)

common factor [kä′mən fak′tər] **factor común** A number that is a factor of two or more numbers (p. 137)

Commutative Property of Addition [kə•myo͞o′tə•tiv prä′pər•tē əv ədi′shən] **propiedad conmutativa de la suma** The property that states that when the order of two addends is changed, the sum is the same (p. 68)
Example: 4 + 5 = 5 + 4

Commutative Property of Multiplication [kə•myo͞o′tə•tiv prä′pər•tē əv mul•tə•plə•kā′shən] **propiedad conmutativa de la multiplicación** The property that states that when the order of two factors is changed, the product is the same (p. 152)
Example: 4 × 5 = 5 × 4

compare [kəm•pâr′] **comparar** To describe whether numbers are equal to, less than, or greater than each other (p. 12)

compass [kəm′pəs] **compás** A tool used to construct circles (p. 274)

compatible numbers [kəm•pa′tə•bəl num′bərz] **números compatibles** Numbers that are easy to compute mentally (p. 40)

cone [kōn] **cono** A solid, pointed figure that has a flat, round base (p. 314)
Example:

congruent [kən•gro͞o′ənt] **congruente** Having the same size and shape (p. 286)
Example:

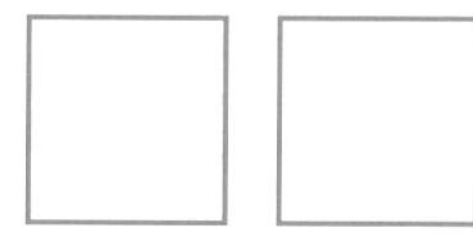

corner [kôr′nər] **esquina** See *vertex*.

counterclockwise [koun′tər•klok′wīz′] **en sentido contrario a las manecillas del reloj** In the opposite direction in which the hands of a clock move (p. 290)

cube [kyo͞ob] **cubo** A solid figure with six congruent square faces (p. 314)
Example:

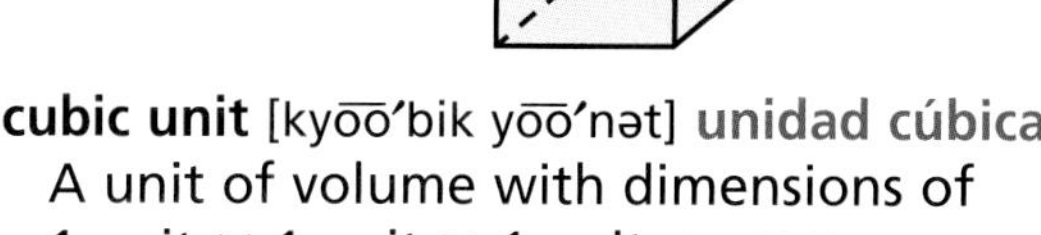

cubic unit [kyo͞o′bik yo͞o′nət] **unidad cúbica** A unit of volume with dimensions of 1 unit × 1 unit × 1 unit (p. 632)

cup (c) [kup] **taza (t)** A customary unit used to measure capacity (p. 560) 8 fluid ounces = 1 cup

cylinder [si′lən•dər] **cilindro** A solid figure that is shaped like a can (p. 314)
Example:

D

data [dā′tə] **datos** Information collected about people or things (p. 496)

decagon [de′kə•gän] **decágono** A polygon with ten sides and ten angles (p. 264)

decimal [de′sə•məl] **decimal** A number with one or more digits to the right of the decimal point (p. 418)

decimal point [de′sə•məl point] **punto decimal** A symbol used to separate dollars from cents in money amounts and to separate the ones and the tenths places in a decimal (p. 418)
Example: 6.4
↑ decimal point

decimeter (dm) [de′sə•mē•tər] **decímetro (dm)** A metric unit for measuring length or distance (p. 574) 10 decimeters = 1 meter

degree (°) [di•grē′] **grado (°)** The unit used for measuring angles and temperatures (pp. 260, 484)

degree Celsius (°C) [di•grē′ sel′sē•əs] **grado Celsius (°C)** A metric unit for measuring temperature (p. 486)

degree Fahrenheit (°F) [di•grē′ fâr′ən•hīt] **grado Fahrenheit (°F)** A standard unit for measuring temperature (p. 484)

denominator [di•nä′mə•nā•tər] **denominador** The number below the bar in a fraction that tells how many equal parts are in the whole (p. 388)
Example: $\frac{3}{4}$ ← denominator

diagonal [dī•a′gə•nəl] **diagonal** A line segment that connects two vertices of a polygon that are not next to each other (p. 309)

diameter [dī•am′ə•tər] **diámetro** A line segment that passes through the center of a circle and has endpoints on the circle (p. 274)
Example:
diameter

difference [di′fər•əns] **diferencia** The answer to a subtraction problem

digit [di′jət] **dígito** Any one of the ten symbols 0, 1, 2, 3, 4, 5, 6, 7, 8, or 9 used to write numbers (p. 5)

digital clock [di′jə•təl kläk] **reloj digital** A clock that shows time to the minute using digits (p. 474)
Example:

dimension [də•men′shən] **dimensión** A measure in one direction (p. 258)

Distributive Property [di•stri′byə•tiv prä′pər•tē] **propiedad distributiva** The property that states that multiplying a sum by a number is the same as multiplying each addend by the number and then adding the products (p. 153)
Example: $5 \times (10 + 6) = (5 \times 10) + (5 \times 6)$

divide [di•vīd′] **dividir** to separate into equal groups; the opposite operation of multiplication

dividend [di′və•dend] **dividendo** The number that is to be divided in a division problem (p. 118)
Example: 36 ÷ 6; $6\overline{)36}$; the dividend is 36.

division [də•vi′zhən] **división** The process of sharing a number of items to find how many groups can be made or how many items will be in each group; the opposite operation of multiplication

divisor [də•vī′zər] **divisor** The number that divides the dividend (p. 118)
Example: 15 ÷ 3; $3\overline{)15}$; the divisor is 3.

double-bar graph [du′bəl bär graf] **gráfica de doble barra** A graph used to compare similar kinds of data (p. 509)
Example:

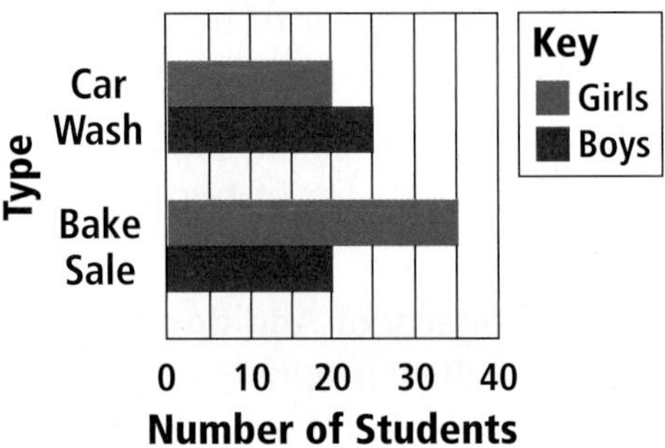

doubles [du′bəlz] **dobles** Two addends that are the same number

edge [ej] **arista** The line segment where two faces of a solid figure meet (p. 314)
Example:

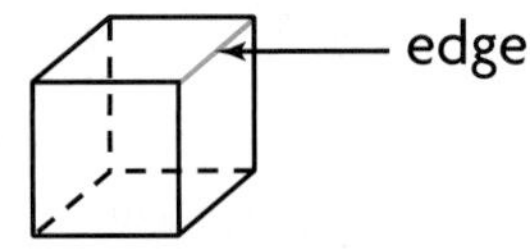

elapsed time [i•lapst′ tīm] **tiempo transcurrido** The time that passes from the start of an activity to the end of that activity (p. 476)

endpoint [end pôint] **extremo** The point at either end of a line segment or the starting point of a ray (p. 258)

equal to (=) [ē′kwəl to͞o] **igual a** Having the same value
Example: 4 + 4 is equal to 3 + 5.

equally likely [ē′kwə•lē lī′klē] **igualmente probable** Having the same chance of happening

equation [i•kwā′zhən] **ecuación** A number sentence which shows that two quantities are equal (p. 74)
Example: 4 + 5 = 9

equilateral triangle [ē•kwə•la′tə•rəl trī′ang•əl] **triángulo equilátero** A triangle with three equal, or congruent, sides (p. 268)
Example:

6 cm 6 cm

6 cm

equivalent [ē•kwiv′ə•lənt] **equivalente** Having the same value or naming the same amount

equivalent decimals [ē•kwiv′ə•lənt de′sə•məlz] **decimales equivalentes** Two or more decimals that name the same amount (p. 422)

equivalent fractions [ē•kwiv′ə•lənt frak′shənz] **fracciones equivalentes** Two or more fractions that name the same amount (p. 392)
Example: $\frac{3}{4}$ and $\frac{6}{8}$ name the same amount.

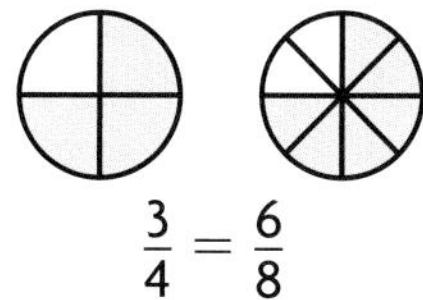

$\frac{3}{4} = \frac{6}{8}$

estimate [es′tə•māt] **estimar** *verb* To find an answer that is close to the exact amount

estimate [es′tə•mət] **estimación** *noun* A number close to an exact amount (p. 40)

even [ē′vən] **par** A whole number that has a 0, 2, 4, 6, or 8 in the ones place

event [i•vent′] **suceso** One outcome or a combination of outcomes in an experiment

expanded form [ik•span′dəd fôrm] **forma desarrollada** A way to write numbers by showing the value of each digit (p. 5)
Example: 253 = 200 + 50 + 3

expression [ik•spre′shən] **expresión** A part of a number sentence that has numbers and operation signs but does not have an equal sign (p. 70)

F

face [fās] **cara** A polygon that is a flat surface of a solid figure (p. 314)
Example:

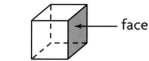

face

fact family [fakt fam′ə•lē] **familia de operaciones** A set of related multiplication and division, or addition and subtraction, equations (pp. 32, 118)
Example: $7 \times 8 = 56$; $8 \times 7 = 56$;
$56 \div 7 = 8$; $56 \div 8 = 7$

factor [fak′tər] **factor** A number that is multiplied by another number to find a product (p. 98)

flip [flip] **inversión** See *reflection*.

fluid ounce (fl oz) [flü′ed aûn(t)s] **onza fluida** A customary unit used to measure liquid capacity (p. 560) 1 cup = 8 fluid ounces

foot (ft) [fo͝ot] **pie** A customary unit used for measuring length or distance (p. 552)
1 foot = 12 inches

formula [fôr′myə•lə] **fórmula** A set of symbols that expresses a mathematical rule (p. 605)
Example: $A = l \times w$

fraction [frak′shən] **fracción** A number that names a part of a whole or part of a group (p. 388)
Example:

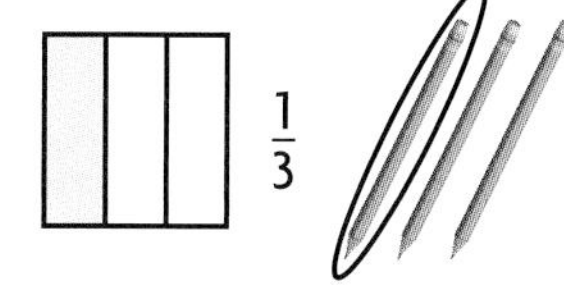

$\frac{1}{3}$

frequency [frē′kwen•sē] **frecuencia** The number of times an event occurs (p. 497)

frequency table [frē′kwen•sē tā′bəl] **tabla de frecuencia** A table that uses numbers to record data about how often something happens (p. 497)
Example:

Favorite Color	
Color	**Number**
blue	10
red	7
green	8
yellow	4

G

gallon (gal) [ga′lən] **galón (gal)** A customary unit for measuring capacity (p. 560)
4 quarts = 1 gallon

gram (g) [gram] **gramo (g)** A unit for measuring mass (p. 578) 1,000 grams = 1 kilogram

greater than (>) [grā′tər t͟han] **mayor que** A symbol used to compare two quantities, with the greater quantity given first (p. 12)
Example: $6 > 4$

greater than or equal to (≥) [grā′tər t͟han ôr ē•kwəl to͞o] **mayor que o igual a** A symbol used to compare two quantities when the first is greater than or equal to the second
Example: $4 + 5 \geq 7$

grid [grid] **cuadrícula** Evenly divided and equally spaced squares on a figure or flat surface

Grouping Property of Addition [gro͞o′ping prä′pər•tē əv ə•di′shən] **propiedad de agrupación de la suma** See *Associative Property of Addition.*

Grouping Property of Multiplication [gro͞o′ping prä′pər•tē əv mul•tə•plə•kā′shən] **propiedad de agrupación de la multiplicación** See *Associative Property of Multiplication.*

half hour [haf our] **media hora** 30 minutes (p. 474)
Example: Between 4:00 and 4:30 is one half hour.

hexagon [hek′sə•gän] **hexágono** A polygon with six sides and six angles (p. 264)
Example:

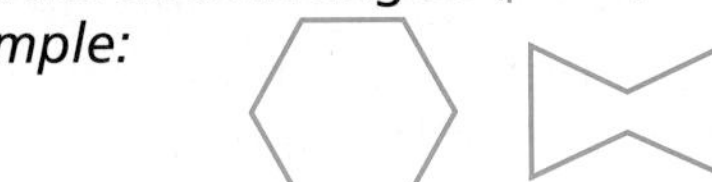

hour (hr) [our] **hora (hr)** A unit used to measure time (p. 474) 60 minutes = 1 hour

hour hand [our hand] **horario** The short hand on an analog clock (p. 474)

hundredth [hun′drədth] **centésimo** One of one hundred equal parts (p. 418)
Example:

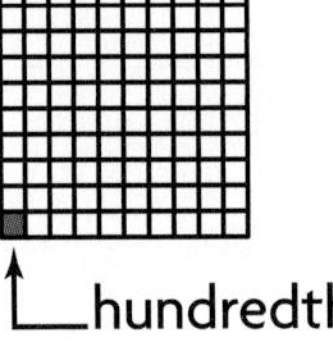

Identity Property of Addition [ī•den′tə•tē prä′pər•tē əv ə•di′shən] **propiedad de identidad de la suma** The property that states that when you add zero to any number, the sum is that number (p. 68)
Example: $16 + 0 = 16$

Identity Property of Multiplication [ī•den′tə•tē prä′pər•tē əv mul•tə•plə•kā′shən] **propiedad de identidad de la multiplicación** The property that states that the product of any number and 1 is that number (p. 152)
Example: $9 \times 1 = 9$

improper fraction [im•prä′pər frak′shən] **fracción impropia** A fraction greater than 1 (p. 403)

inch (in.) [inch] **pulgada (pulg)** A customary unit used for measuring length or distance (p. 552)
Example:

1 inch

inequality [in•i•kwol′ə•tē] **desigualdad** A mathematical sentence that shows two expressions do not represent the same quantity
Example: $4 < 9 - 3$

intersecting lines [in•tər•sek′ting līnz] **líneas secantes** Lines that cross each other at exactly one point (p. 262)
Example:

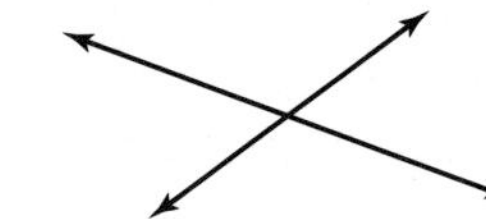

interval [in′tər•vəl] **intervalo** The distance between one number and the next on the scale of a graph (p. 504)

inverse operations [in′vərs ä•pə•rā′shənz] **operaciones inversas** Operations that undo each other. Addition and subtraction are inverse operations. Multiplication and division are inverse operations. (pp. 32, 118)
Example: $6 \times 8 = 48$ and $48 \div 6 = 8$

is approximately equal to (≈) [iz ə•präk′sə•mət•lē ē•kwəl to͞o] **es aproximadamente igual a** A symbol that indicates one amount, size, or value is about the same as another
Example: 1 kg ≈ 2 lb (p. 587)

isosceles triangle [ī•sä′sə•lēz trī′ang•əl] **triángulo isósceles** A triangle with two equal, or congruent, sides (p. 268)
Example:

10 in. 10 in.
7 in.

Word History

When you look at the sides on an *isosceles* triangle, you see that the two sides are equal in length. The Greek root *iso-* means "same or equal," and *skelos* means "legs."

key [kē] **clave** The part of a map or graph that explains the symbols (p. 502)

kilogram (kg) [ki′lə•gram] **kilogramo (kg)** A metric unit for measuring mass (p. 578)
1 kilogram = 1,000 grams

kilometer (km) [kə•lä′mə•tər] **kilómetro (km)** A metric unit for measuring length or distance (p. 574) 1,000 meters = 1 kilometer

less than (<) [les *th*an] **menor que** A symbol used to compare two numbers, with the lesser number given first (p. 12)
Example: $3 < 7$

less than or equal to (≤) [les *th*an ôr ē′kwəl to͞o] **menor que o igual a** A symbol used to compare quantities, when the first is less than or equal to the second *Example:* $8 \leq 14 - 5$

like fractions [līk frak′shənz] **fracciones semejantes** Fractions with the same denominator (p. 413)

likely [līk′lē] **probable** Having a greater than even chance of happening

line [līn] **línea** A straight path of points in a plane that continues without end in both directions with no endpoints (p. 258)
Example:

S T

line segment [līn seg′mənt] **segmento** A part of a line that includes two points called endpoints and all the points between them (p. 258)
Example:

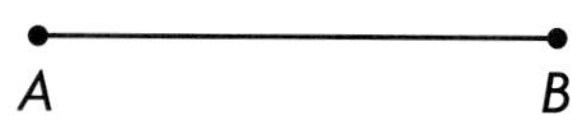

line symmetry [līn si′mə•trē] **simetría axial** What a figure has if it can be folded about a line so that its two parts match exactly (p. 294)
Example:

line of symmetry

linear units [li′nē•ər yo͞o′nəts] **unidades lineales** Units that measure length, width, height, or distance (p. 552)

liter (L) [lē′tər] **litro (L)** A metric unit for measuring capacity (p. 580)
1 liter = 1,000 milliliters

mass [mas] **masa** The amount of matter in an object (p. 578)

median [mē′dē•ən] **mediana** The middle number in an ordered set of data (p. 517)

meter (m) [mē′tər] **metro (m)** A metric unit for measuring length or distance (p. 574)
100 centimeters = 1 meter

mile (mi) [mīl] **milla (mi)** A customary unit for measuring length or distance (p. 552)
5,280 feet = 1 mile

milliliter (mL) [mi′lə•lē•tər] **mililitro (mL)** A metric unit for measuring capacity (p. 580)
1,000 milliliters = 1 liter

millimeter (mm) [mi′lə•mē•tər] **milímetro (mm)** A metric unit for measuring length or distance (p. 574) 1 centimeter = 10 millimeters

millions [mil′yənz] **millones** The period after thousands (p. 9)

minute (min) [mi′nət] **minuto (min)** A unit to measure short amounts of time (p. 474)
60 seconds = 1 minute

minute hand [mi′nət hand] **minutero** The long hand on an analog clock (p. 474)

mixed number [mikst num′bər] **número mixto** An amount given as a whole number and a fraction (p. 402)

mode [mōd] **moda** The number(s) or item(s) that occur most often in a set of data (p. 517)

multiple [mul′tə•pəl] **múltiplo** The product of two counting numbers is called a multiple of each of those numbers (p. 105)

multiplication [mul•tə•plə•kā′shən] **multiplicación** A process to find the total number of items in equal-sized groups, or to find the total number of items in a given number of groups when each group contains the same number of items; multiplication is the inverse of division

multiply [mul′tə•plī] **multiplicar** When you combine equal groups, you can multiply to find how many in all; the opposite operation of division (p. 96)

multistep problem [mul′ti•step prä′bləm] **problema de varios pasos** A problem requiring more than one step to solve (p. 244)

net [net] **plantilla** A two-dimensional pattern that can be folded to make a three-dimensional figure (p. 320)
Example:

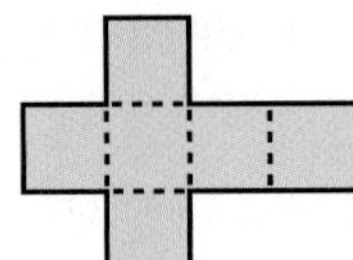

not equal to (≠) [nät ē′kwəl to͞o] **no igual a** A symbol that indicates one quantity is not equal to another (p. 13)
Example: $12 \times 3 \neq 38$

number line [num′bər līn] **recta numérica** A line on which numbers can be located
Example:

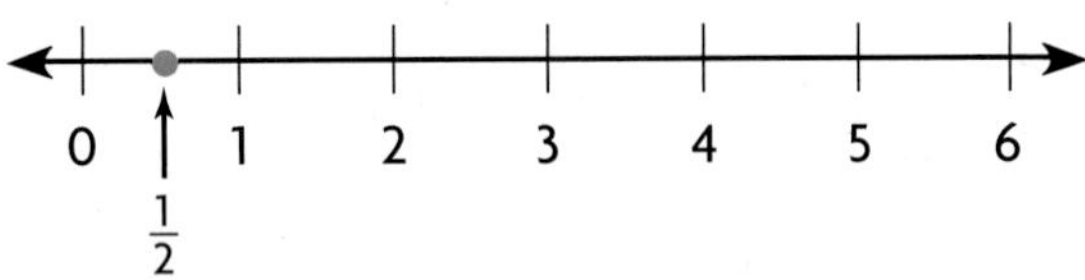

numerator [no͞o′mə•rā•tər] **numerador** The number above the bar in a fraction that tells how many parts of the whole or group are being considered (p. 388)

Example: $\frac{2}{3}$ ← numerator

numericial data [no͞o•mer′i•kəl dā′tə] **datos numéricos** Data that can be counted or measured (p. 497)

obtuse angle [äb•to͞os′ ang′əl] **ángulo obtuso** An angle that measures greater than a right angle (greater than 90° and less than 180°) (p. 260)
Example:

Word History

The Latin prefix *ob-* means "against." When combined with *-tuse*, meaning "to beat," the word *obtuse* means "to beat against." This makes sense when you look at an obtuse angle because the angle is not sharp or acute. The angle has been beaten against and become blunt and rounded.

obtuse triangle [äb•to͞os′ trī′ang•əl] **triángulo obtusángulo** A triangle with one obtuse angle (p. 268)
Example:

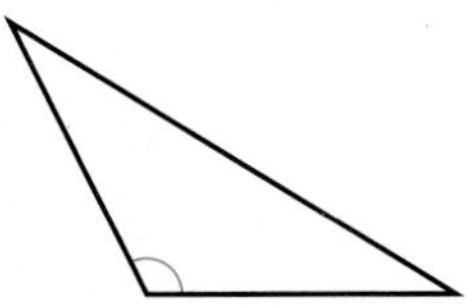

octagon [äk′tə•gän] **octágono** A polygon with eight sides and eight angles (p. 264)
Examples:

odd [od] **impar** A whole number that has a 1, 3, 5, 7 or 9 in the ones place

one-dimensional [wən′ də•men(t)′shə•nəl] **unidimensional** A measure in only one direction, such as length (p. 258)
Examples:

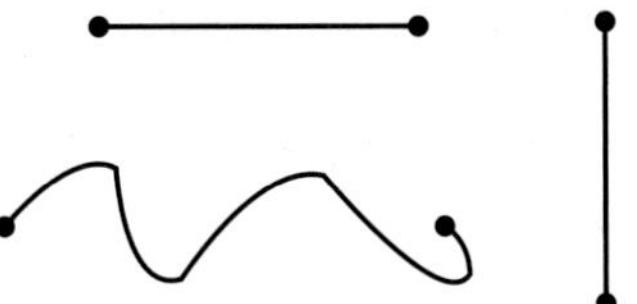

open figure [ō′pən fi′gyər] **figura abierta** A figure that does not begin and end at the same point
Examples:

order [ôr′dər] **orden** A particular arrangement or placement of things one after the other (p. 16)

Order Property of Addition [ôr′dər prä′pər•tē əv ə•di′shən] **propiedad de orden de la suma** See *Commutative Property of Addition.*

Order Property of Multiplication [ôr′dər prä′pər•tē əv mul•tə•plə•kā′shən] **propiedad de orden de la multiplicación** See *Commutative Property of Multiplication.*

ordered pair [ôr′dərd pâr] **par ordenado** A related or matched pair of numbers always arranged the same way—the first number followed by the second number (p. 82)

ordered pair [ôr′dərd pâr] **par ordenado** A pair of numbers used to locate a point on a coordinate grid. The first number tells how far to move horizontally, and the second number tells how far to move vertically. (p. 512)

ounce (oz) [ouns] **onza** A customary unit for measuring weight (p. 558) 16 ounces = 1 pound

P.M. [pē•em′] **p.m.** The time between noon and midnight (p. 474)

parallel lines [par′ə•lel līnz] **líneas paralelas** Lines in the same plane that never intersect and are always the same distance apart (p. 262)
Example:

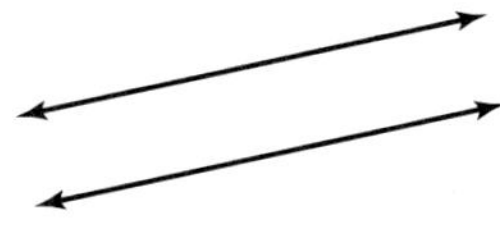

Word History

Euclid, an early Greek mathematician, was one of the first to explore the idea of parallel lines. The prefix *para-* means "beside or alongside." This prefix helps you understand the meaning of the word *parallel*.

parallelogram [par•ə•lel′ə•gram] **paralelogramo** A quadrilateral whose opposite sides are parallel and equal, or congruent (p. 271)
Example:

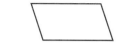

parentheses [pə•ren′thə•sēz] **paréntesis** The symbols used to show which operation or operations in an expression should be done first (p. 68)

partial product [pär′shəl prä′dəkt] **producto parcial** A method of multiplying in which the ones, tens, hundreds, and so on are multiplied separately and then the products are added together (p. 189)

pattern [pat′ərn] **patrón** An ordered set of numbers or objects; the order helps you predict what will come next (p. 144)
Example: 2, 4, 6, 8, 10

pattern unit [pat′ərn yo͞o′nət] **unidad de patrón** The part of a pattern that repeats (p. 304)
Example:

pentagon [pen′tə•gän] **pentágono** A polygon with five sides and five angles (p. 264)
Examples:

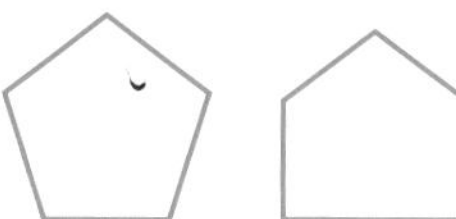

perimeter [pə•ri′mə•tər] **perímetro** The distance around a figure (p. 600)

period [pir′ē•əd] **período** Each group of three digits separated by commas in a multidigit number (p. 5)
Example: 85,643,900 has three periods.

perpendicular lines [pər•pən•di′kyə•lər līnz] **líneas perpendiculares** Two lines that intersect to form four right angles (p. 262)
Example:

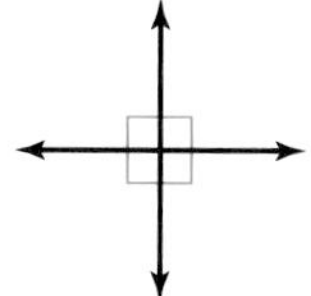

pictograph [pik′tə•graf] **pictografía** A graph that uses symbols to show and compare information (p. 502)
Example:

How We Get To School

Walk	✳ ✳ ✳
Ride a Bike	✳ ✳ ✳ ✳
Ride a Bus	✳ ✳ ✳ ✳ ✳ ✳
Ride in a Car	✳ ✳

Key: Each ✳ = 10 students.

pint (pt) [pīnt] **pinta (pt)** A customary unit for measuring capacity (p. 560) 2 cups = 1 pint

place value [plās val′yo͞o] **valor posicional** Place value determines the value of a digit in a number, based on the location of the digit (p. 5)

plane [plān] **plano** A flat surface that extends without end in all directions (p. 258)
Example:

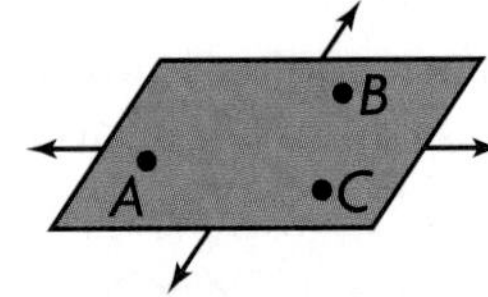

plane figure [plān fi′gyər] **figura plana** A figure in a plane that is formed by lines that are curved, straight, or both

point [point] **punto** An exact location in space (p. 258)

polygon [pä′lē•gän] **polígono** A closed plane figure formed by three or more straight sides that are connected line segments. (p. 264)
Examples:

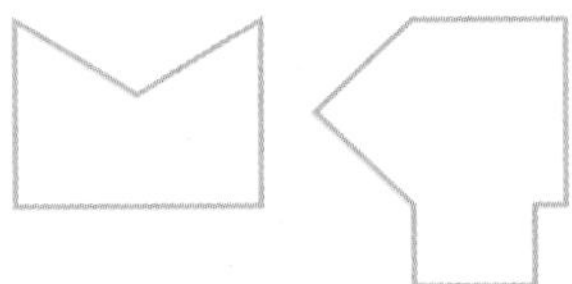

Polygons

Not Polygons

pound (lb) [pound] **libra (lb)** A customary unit for measuring weight (p. 558) 16 ounces = 1 pound

product [prä′dəkt] **producto** The answer to a multiplication problem (p. 98)

pyramid [pir′ə•mid] **pirámide** A solid figure with a polygon base and triangular sides that meet at a single point
Example:

quadrilateral [kwä•drə•la′tə•rəl] **cuadrilátero** A polygon with four sides and four angles (p. 264)

quart (qt) [kwôrt] **cuarto (ct)** A customary unit for measuring capacity (p. 560) 2 pints = 1 quart

quarter hour [kwôr•tər our] **cuarto de hora** 15 minutes (p. 474)
Example: Between 4:00 and 4:15 is one quarter hour

quotient [kwō′shənt] **cociente** The number, not including the remainder, that results from dividing (p. 118)
Example: $8 \div 4 = 2$; 2 is the quotient.

radius [rā′dē•əs] **radio** A line segment with one endpoint at the center of a circle and the other endpoint on the circle (p. 274)
Example:

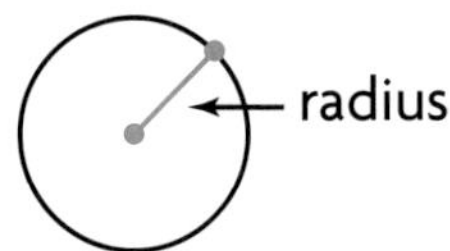

range [rānj] **rango** The difference between the greatest and the least number in a set of data (p. 517)

ratio [rā′shē•ō] **razón** The comparison of two numbers by division (p. 395)

ray [rā] **rayo** A part of a line; it has one endpoint and continues without end in one direction (p. 258)
Example:

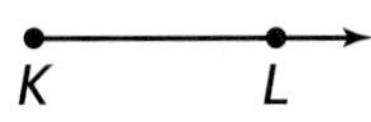

rectangle [rek′tang•gəl] **rectángulo** A parallelogram with opposite sides that are equal, or congruent, and with four right angles (p. 271)
Example:

rectangular prism [rek•tang′gyə•lər pri′zəm] **prisma rectangular** A solid figure in which all six faces are rectangles (p. 314)
Example:

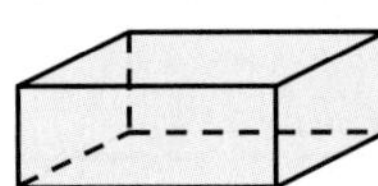

rectangular pyramid [rek•tang′gyə•lər pir′ə•mid] **pirámide rectangular** A pyramid with a rectangular base and with four triangular faces (p. 314)
Example:

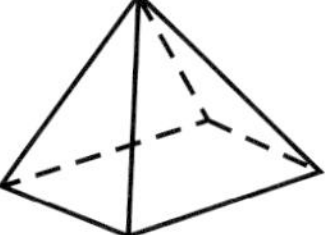

reflection (flip) [rē•flek′shən] **reflexión (inversión)** A movement of a figure to a new position by flipping the figure over a line (p. 292)
Example:

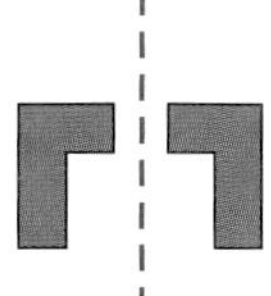

regroup [rē•grōōp′] **reagrupar** To exchange amounts of equal value to rename a number
Example: 5 + 8 = 13 ones or 1 ten 3 ones

regular polygon [reg′yə•lər pä′lē•gän] **polígono regular** A polygon that has all sides that are equal in length and all angles equal in measure (p. 265) *Examples:*

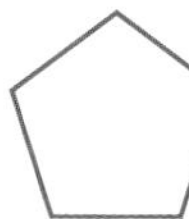

remainder [ri•mān′dər] **residuo** The amount left over when a number cannot be divided equally (p. 339)

rhombus [räm′bəs] **rombo** A parallelogram with four equal, or congruent, sides (p. 271)
Example:

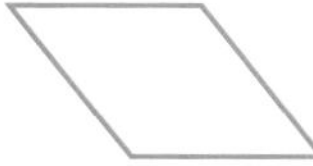

right angle [rīt ang′əl] **ángulo recto** An angle that forms a square corner and has a measure of 90° (p. 260)
Example:

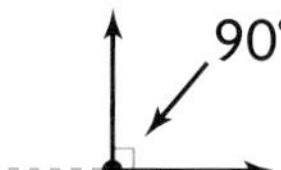

right triangle [rīt trī′ang•əl] **triángulo rectángulo** A triangle with one right angle (p. 268)
Example:

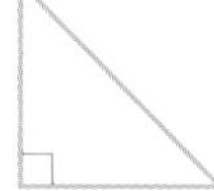

rotation (turn) [rō•tā′shən] **rotación (giro)** A movement of a figure to a new position by rotating the figure around a point (p. 290)
Example:

point of rotation

round [round] **redondear** To replace a number with another number that tells about how many or how much (p. 34)

S

scale [skāl] **escala** A series of numbers placed at fixed distances on a graph to help label the graph (p. 504)

scalene triangle [skā′lēn trī′ang•əl] **triángulo escaleno** A triangle with no equal, or congruent, sides (p. 268)
Example:

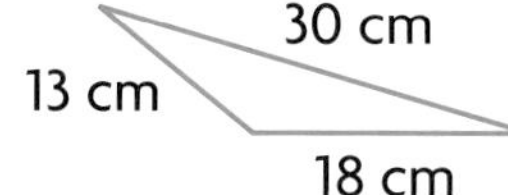

schedule [ske′jōōl] **horario** A table that lists activities or events and the times they happen (p. 480)

second (sec) [se′kənd] **segundo (seg)** A small unit of time (p. 474) 60 seconds = 1 minute

simplest form [sim′pləst fôrm] **mínima expresión** A fraction is in simplest form when 1 is the only number that can divide evenly into the numerator and the denominator (p. 393)

slide [slīd] **traslación** See *translation*.

solid figure [so′ləd fi′gyər] **cuerpo geométrico** A three-dimensional figure

sphere [sfēr] **esfera** A round object whose curved surface is the same distance from the center to all its points (p. 314)
Example:

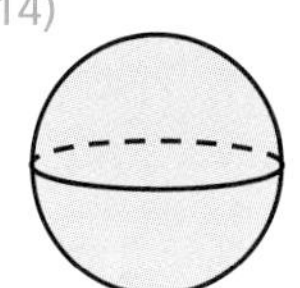

square [skwâr] **cuadrado** A parallelogram with four equal, or congruent, sides and four right angles (p. 271)
Example:

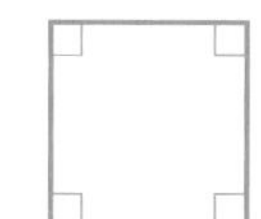

square number [skwâr num′bər] **número cuadrado** The product of a number and itself (p. 142)
Example: 2 × 2 = 4, so 4 is a square number.

square pyramid [skwâr pir′ə•mid] **pirámide cuadrada** A pyramid with a square base and with four triangular faces (p. 314)
Example:

square unit (sq un) [skwâr yo͞o′nət] **unidad cuadrada** A unit of area with dimensions of 1 unit × 1 unit (p. 610)

standard form [stan′dərd fôrm] **forma normal** A way to write numbers by using digits (p. 5)
Example: 3,540 ← standard form

subtraction [səb•trak′shən] **resta** The process of finding how many are left when a number of items are taken away from a group of items; the process of finding the difference when two groups are compared; the opposite operation of addition

sum [sum] **suma o total** The answer to an addition problem (p. 38)

survey [sûr′vā] **encuesta** A method of gathering information (p. 496)

tablespoon (tbsp) [tā′bəl•spo͞on] **cucharada (cda)** A customary unit used for measuring capacity (p. 560) 3 teaspoons = 1 tablespoon

tally table [ta′lē tā′bəl] **tabla de conteo** A table that uses tally marks to record data (p. 496)

Word History

Some people keep score in card games by making marks on paper (IIII). These marks are known as tally marks. The word *tally* is related to *tailor*, from the Latin *talea*, meaning "one who cuts." In early times, a method of keeping count was by cutting marks into a piece of wood or bone.

teaspoon (tsp) [tē′spo͞on] **cucharadita (cdta)** A customary unit used for measuring capacity (p. 560) 1 tablespoon = 3 teaspoons

tenth [tenth] **décimo** One of ten equal parts (p. 418)
Example:

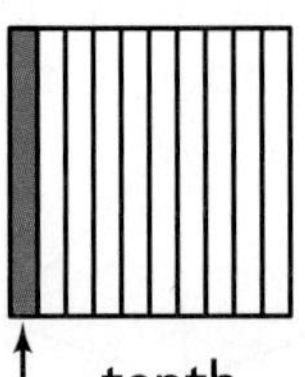

tessellation [tes•ə•lā′shən] **teselación** A repeating pattern of closed figures that covers a surface with no gaps and no overlaps (p. 302)
Example:

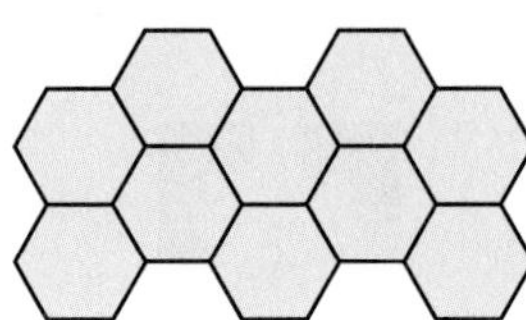

thousandth [thou′zəndth] **milésimo** One of one thousand equal parts (p. 441)

three-dimensional [thrē•də•men′shən•əl] **tridimensional** Measured in three directions, such as length, width, and height (p. 314)
Example:

time line [tīm līn] **línea cronológica** A schedule of events or an ordered list of historic moments

ton (T) [tun] **tonelada (T)** A customary unit for measuring weight (p. 558) 2,000 pounds = 1 ton

transformation [trans•fər•mā′shən] **transformación** The movement of a figure by a translation, reflection, or rotation (p. 288)

translation [trans•lā′shən] **traslación** A movement of a figure to a new position along a straight line (p. 288)
Example:

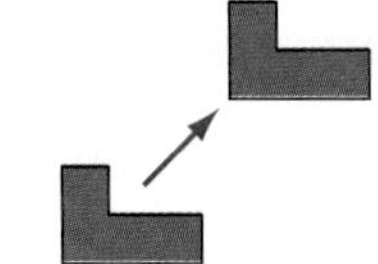

trapezoid [tra′pə•zoid] **trapecio** A quadrilateral with exactly one pair of parallel sides (p. 271)
Examples:

tree diagram [trē dī′ə•gram] **diagrama de árbol** An organized list that shows all possible combinations (p. 528)
Example:

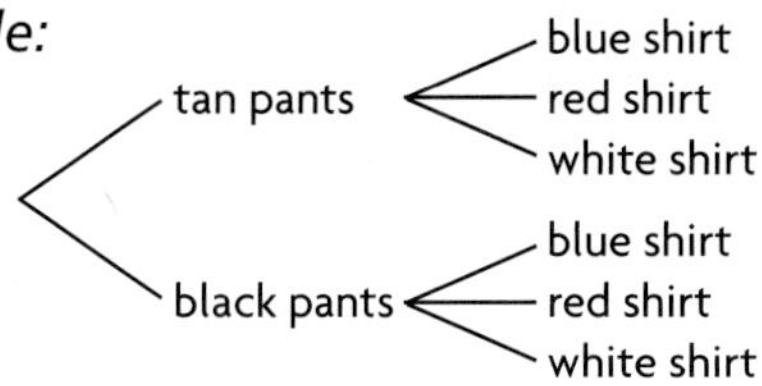

triangle [trī′ang•gəl] **triángulo** A polygon with three sides and three angles (p. 264)
Examples:

triangular prism [trī•ang′gyə•lər pri′zəm] **prisma triangular** A solid figure that has two triangular bases and three rectangular faces (p. 314)
Example:

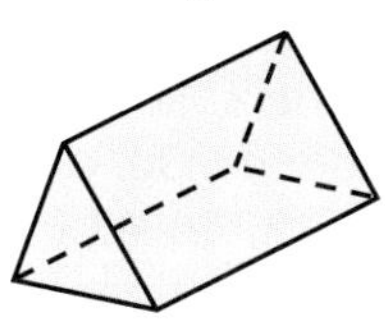

triangular pyramid [trī•ang′gyə•lər pir′ə•mid] **pirámide triangular** A pyramid that has a triangular base and three triangular faces (p. 314)
Example:

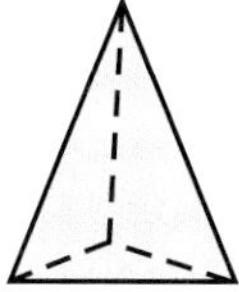

turn [tûrn] **giro** See *rotation*.

two-dimensional [to͞o•də•men′shən•əl] **bidimensional** Measured in two directions, such as length and width (p. 258)
Example:

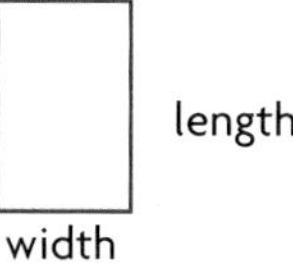

unit fraction [yo͞o′nit frak′shən] **fracción unitaria** A fraction that has a numerator of one (p. 388)

unlikely [un•lī′klē] **poco probable** Having a less than even chance of happening

variable [vâr′ē•ə•bəl] **variable** A letter or symbol that stands for a number or numbers (p. 71)

Venn diagram [ven dī′ə•gram] **diagrama de Venn** A diagram that shows relationships among sets of things (p. 276)
Example:

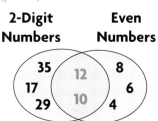

2-Digit Numbers **Even Numbers**

35 17 29 | 12 10 | 8 6 4

vertex [vûr′teks] **vértice** The point at which two rays of an angle meet or two (or more) line segments meet in a plane figure, or where three or more edges meet in a solid figure; the top point of a cone (pp. 260, 314)
Examples:

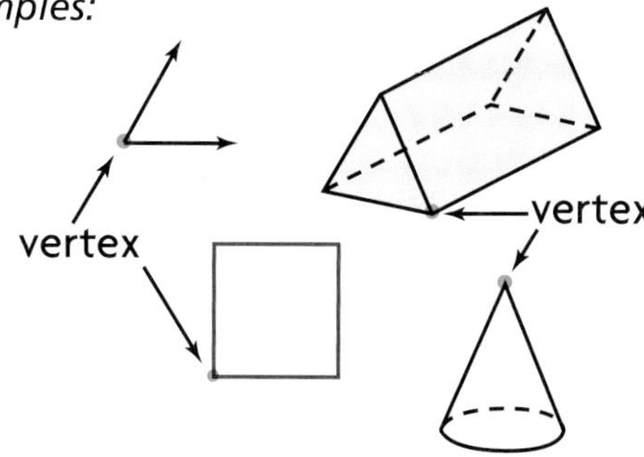

volume [väl′yo͞om] **volumen** The measure of the amount of space a solid figure occupies (p. 632)

weight [wāt] **peso** How heavy an object is (p. 556)

whole number [hōl num′bər] **número entero** One of the numbers 0, 1, 2, 3, 4 . . . ; the set of whole numbers goes on without end

word form [wûrd fôrm] **en palabras** A way to write numbers by using words (p. 5)
Example: Sixty-two million, four hundred fifty-three thousand, two hundred twelve

yard (yd) [yärd] **yarda (yd)** A customary unit for measuring length or distance (p. 552)
3 feet = 1 yard

Zero Property of Multiplication [zē′rō prä′pər•tē əv mul•tə•plə•kā′shən] **propiedad del cero de la multiplicación** The property that states that the product of 0 and any number is 0 (p. 152)
Example: $0 \times 8 = 0$

Index

Act It Out strategy, 298–301, 396–397
Activities
Hands On, 4, 8–9, 82, 100, 104–105, 122, 130, 142, 153, 234, 260, 262, 265, 270, 274, 286, 288–289, 290, 292, 294–295, 304–305, 315, 318, 320, 392, 399, 400, 402, 406–407, 418, 424–425, 428–429, 450–451, 477, 484, 486, 496, 524, 528, 552, 553, 558, 560, 574, 575, 578, 580, 584–585, 588–591, 602, 610–611, 620–621, 632, 640
Puzzles and games, 25, 59, 111, 135, 217, 281, 309, 327, 355, 439, 463, 541, 593, 625, 643
See also Hands On lessons
Acute angles, 260–261
Acute triangles, 268–269
Addition
Associative Property, 40, 68–69
basic facts, 32–33, 38–39
with a calculator, 56–59
choose a method, 56–59
column, 50
Commutative Property, 40, 68–69
of customary measurements, 569
of decimals, 446–447, 454–457
concrete objects, 446
pictorial models, 447, 465
equations, 66, 74–77
estimation and, 40–43, 50
expressions, 70–73
fact families and, 32–33
of four-digit numbers, 50–53
of greater numbers, 56–59
Identity Property, 68–69
of like fractions, 413
mental math, 38–39, 40–43, 44–47, 56
of metric measurements, 465
modeling, 96–97, 446–447, 454–457
with money, 454–457, 458–461
patterns, 38–39
practice with, 39, 42, 46, 52, 58, 60–61, 69, 72–73, 76, 84, 87, 447, 456
properties of, 68–69
recording, 50, 454–457
related to addition, 96–97
related to subtraction, 32–33
repeated, 96–97, 118, 184, 224
review, H7, H8
strategies, 44–47
sums, 40–43, 50–53, 56–59, 446–447, 454–457
symbol for, 96
of three-digit numbers, 50–53
three or more addends, 30, 47, 48, 68–69
of two-digit numbers, 44–47
Addition properties, 68–69
Algebra and algebraic thinking, 32–33, 96–97, 118–119, 142–143, 144–147, 148–151, 152–155, 156–159, 160–161, 162–165, 166–167, 170–171, 512–513, 556–557, 562–563, 604–607, 614–617
balancing equations, 165
equations, 66, 74–77, 140, 162–165, 166–169, 557, 608–609
expressions, 70–74, 140, 156–159
finding a rule, 82–83, 144–147, 170–171, 175, 192
formulas, using, 605, 607, 615, 645
graph ordered pairs, 512–513
inequalities, 12–15, 16–19, 563
input/output tables, 82–83, 85, 102, 105, 170–171, 175, 192, 225, 344, 478, 567
inverse operations, 32–33, 118–119
missing numbers, 14, 18, 52, 58, 121, 123, 124, 126, 127, 132, 144–147, 152, 160–161, 209, 213, 225, 227, 241, 243, 353, 366, 370, 373, 375, 390, 394, 408, 420, 426, 430, 447, 449, 456, 483
patterns and functions, 82–83, 170–171, 175
problem solving, 78–81, 87, 148–151, 155, 287, 511
solving for *n* as an unknown, 71, 99, 160–161, 162–165, 166–169, 185, 349, 511
variables, 66, 70–73, 74–77, 78–81, 87, 140, 156–159, 162–165, 166–169
Algebraic expressions, 71
Analyze data, *See* Data
Analyzing information, 47, 77, 155, 317, 345, 367, 539, 613
Angles, 260–261
acute, defined, 260
classifying and identifying, 260
concrete models, 260
and line relationships, 262–263
obtuse, defined, 260
pictorial models, 260–261
in polygons, 264–265
in quadrilaterals, 264, 270–273
review, H19
right, defined, 260
in triangles, 264, 268–269
vertex of, 260

Arabic numerals, 27
Area
of complex figures, 618–619
defined, 610
equal, 598
estimating, 610–613
finding, 153, 614–617, 618–619, 620–623
modeling, 153, 610–611, 614, 617, 618, 620–621, 623
of plane figures, 614–617
practice with, 612, 616–617, 619, 622, 624, 625
relating to perimeter, 620–623
square units, 153, 610–612
Arrays
division, 120, 336
multiplication, 96–97, 98–99, 100–101, 130–131, 142, 153, 188–189, 190, 195, 234–235, 236
in patterns, 148
relating addition and multiplication, 96–97
Assessment
Chapter Review/Test, 26, 62, 86, 112, 136, 174, 200, 218, 248, 280, 308, 328, 356, 378, 412, 440, 464, 490, 516, 542, 568, 594, 626, 644
Getting Ready for the TAKS, 28–29, 64–65, 114–115, 138–139, 202–203, 220–221, 282–283, 310–311, 358–359, 414–415, 442–443, 492–493, 518–519, 570–571, 596–597, 628–629
Show What You Know, 3, 31, 67, 95, 117, 141, 183, 205, 223, 257, 285, 313, 337, 361, 387, 417, 445, 473, 495, 521, 551, 573, 599, 631
Unit Review/Test, 88–89, 176–177, 250–251, 330–331, 380–381, 466–467, 544–545
Associative Property, 40, 68–69, 152–155, 249
Average, 374–375

B

Bar graphs
double, 508–509
interpret, 506–507
review, H28
Base-ten blocks. *See* Manipulatives and visual aids
Basic Facts Review, H40–H43
Benchmarks
for conversions in measurement, 587
for customary units, 558, 560
in estimation, 15
for metric units, 574, 578, 580
numbers, 15
Big Idea, 2, 30, 66, 94, 116, 140, 182, 204, 222, 256, 284, 312, 336, 360, 386, 416, 444, 472, 494, 520, 550, 572, 598, 630
Break Apart strategy, 44, 100, 104, 122, 188–189, 230–231

C

Calculators
adding and subtracting with, 56–59
changing decimals to fractions with, 421
changing fractions to decimals with, 421
changing units of measure using, 556, 558, 562–563, 567
division using, 372, 374, 377, 479
evaluate expressions with, 173
finding averages with, 374
multiplication using, 212
See also Choose a Method *and* Technology Connections
Calendars, 482–483
Capacity. *See* Measurement
Categorizing, 273, 527
Celsius temperature, 486–487
Centimeter ruler, 574–577, 584–587, 588–591
Centimeters, 574
Challenge Yourself, 23, 81, 109, 151, 169, 197, 233, 301, 325, 461, 535
Chapter Review/Test. *See* Assessment
Choose a Method, 56–59, 212–213, 242–243, 372–373
Choose the Operation, 128–129
Choose a Strategy, 23, 81, 109, 151, 169, 197, 233, 277, 301, 347, 397, 461, 535, 565, 583, 609
Circles
center of, 274
circumference of, 627
constructing, 274–275
defined, 274
diameter of, 274
parts of, 274
practice with, 275
radius of, 274
Circumference, 627
Classifying
angles, 260–261
polygons, 264–265
quadrilaterals, 270–273
triangles, 268–269
Clocks
analog, 474–475, 476–479
digital, 474–475
24-hour, 491
Closed figures, 264–265
Combinations, 522–523, 524–527, 528–531, 532–535, 536–538, 541
concrete objects, 522, 524, 528, 536
make generalizations, 522–523
modeling, 522–523, 524–525, 528–531, 532–535, 536–539
pictures, 525, 528–529, 534
review, H27

Common factors, 137, 393
Common multiples, 133
Communications. *See* Hands On lessons, Talk Math, *and* Write Math
Commutative Property, 40, 68–69, 101, 152–155, 249
Compare Strategies, 346–347, 396–397, 564–565, 608–609
Comparing
angles, 260
customary and metric units, 584–587, 588–591
data, 499, 502–503, 504–505, 506–507, 508–509
decimals, 432–433, 439
fractions, 398–399, H5
on a number line, 12–15, 399, 432–433
and ordering, 16–19, 400–401, 434–435
sorting and, 500–501
weights, 550
whole numbers, 12–15
Compass, 274
Compatible numbers, 40–41, 186–187, 214, 228–229, 350–351
Complex figures, area of. *See* Area
Computer software. *See* Technology *and* Technology Connection
Computer use
Base-Ten Blocks, multiply with, 199
Compare Fractions, 411
Spreadsheet, using, 85
Transformations, show, 307
Cones, 314
Congruence, 286–287
Congruent figures, 286–287, H23
Coordinate grid, 512–513
Counters. *See* Manipulatives *and* visual aids
Counting, skip, 101, 131
Critical thinking
analyze, 8, 288
apply, 104, 338, 422, 432, 434, 600
comprehend, 77, 103, 193, 273, 345, 427, 499, 555
draw conclusions, 8, 104, 188, 288, 302, 338, 340, 345, 398, 422, 432, 434, 436–437, 446, 448, 508, 522, 600
evaluate, 188, 508
synthesize, 340, 398, 446, 448, 522
See also Read Math, Talk Math, *and* Write Math
Cross-curricular connections
art, 159, 267, 297
reading, 527
science, 457
technology, 85, 173, 199, 307, 377, 411, 467, 489
Cube (geometric figure), 314–315
Cubic units, 632–635
Cumulative Review. *See* Getting Ready for the TAKS
Cups, 560
Customary system
adding measurements in, 569
benchmarks for, 558, 560
capacity, 560–561, 640–641
changing units in, 479, 556–557, 558–559, 560–561, 562–563, 567, 569
with a calculator, 556, 558, 562–563, 567
comparing units of, 584–587, 588–591
equivalent measures in, 556, 558, 560
estimating in, 552–554, 558–559, 560–561, 574–577, 588–591
length, 552–554
metric units compared to, 584–587, 588–591
practice with, 488, 554, 557, 559, 561, 563, 565, 566, 567, 569, 586, 590, 592, 593
relating metric and customary units, 587
review, H26
subtracting measurements in, 569
temperature, 484–485
weight, 550, 558–559
Cylinder, 314

Data
analyzing, 193, 239, 273, 374–375, 427, 494, 499, 500–501, 502–503, 504–505, 506–507, 508–509, 510–511, 517
average of, 374–375
bar graphs, 39, 49, 81, 187, 209, 238, 395, 504–505, 506–507, 517, 554, 576, H28
categorical, 496
collect, 496–498
compare, 499, 502–503, 504–505, 506–507, 508–509
diagrams, 194–197, 346–347, 396–397, 564–565
display, 494, 496–498, 500–501, 502–503, 506–507, 508–509
double-bar graphs, 509
frequency tables, 497
intervals and, 504–505
make decisions, 502–503, 504–505, 508–509
make generalizations, 510–511, 555
make predictions, 510–511
interpret, 494, 500–501, 502–503, 506–507, 508–509
median of, 517
mode of, 517
numerical, 497
organize, 496–499
in organized lists, 532–535
outcomes, 543
pictographs, 33, 119, 502–503
range of, 517
scale and, 504–505
sort, 500–501
surveys, 496

tables, 21, 46, 55, 69, 83, 85, 90–91, 106–109, 124, 161, 164, 185, 193, 207, 225, 227, 245, 273, 281, 295, 319, 349, 351, 366, 375, 382, 397, 408, 420, 431, 458–459, 487, 496–499, 501, 503, 526, 546, 559, 564–565, 581, 582–583, 586, 623, 627, 637, 641
tally tables, 496–499
tree diagrams, 528–531, 537, H27
Venn diagrams, 132, 137, 276–277, 500–501
See also Statistics
Data labels, on graphs, 506
Days, 474
Decagons, 264
Decimal models. *See* Manipulatives and visual aids
Decimal points, 418–419
Decimals
adding, 446–447, 450–453, 454–457, 458–461, 465
calculators and, 421
comparing, 432–433, 436–437, 439
compose and decompose, 419, 425
concept of, 418–421
concrete objects, 418, 422, 424, 428–431, 432, 434
equivalent, 422–423, 458–461, 463
expanded form of, 419, 425, 441
hundredths, 418–421, 422–423, 424–427, 428–431, 432–433, 434–435, 439, 446–447, 448–449, 450–453, 454–457, 458–461, 463
metric measures and, 465
modeling, 418–421, 422–423, 424–426, 428–431, 432–433, 434–435, 436–437, 441, 446–447, 448–449, 450–453, 458–461, 454–455
money and, 428–431, 450–453, 455, 458–461
ordering, 434–435, 436–437, 439
pictorial models, 418–421, 423, 424–427, 428–431, 447, 449, 450–453, 454–457, 458–461, 465
place value in, 419, 425, 429, 433, 435, 441
point, 418–419
reading and writing, 418–421, 424–427
relate fractions and, 418–421, H6
relate mixed numbers to, 424–427
review, H6, H8, H25
standard form of, 419, 425, 441
subtracting, 448–449, 450–453, 454–457
tenths, 418–421, 422–423, 424–427, 428–431, 432–433, 434–435, 439, 446–447, 448–449, 450–453, 454–457, 458–461, 463
thousandths, 441
See also Money
Decimeters, 574
Degrees Celsius, 486
Degrees Fahrenheit, 472, 484
Denominator
defined, 388
like, 399
unlike, 399
Diagrams
drawing, 194–197, 346–347, 396–397, 564–565
using, 11, 121, 275, 291, 353, 501, 612, 616, 619
tree, 528–531, 537
Venn, 132, 137, 276–277, 500–501
See also Data
Diameter, 274
Differences. *See* Subtraction
Digits, value of, 5, 9, 10. *See also* Place value
Dimension, defined, 258
Distance, 53, 577
Distributive Property, 153, 219
Dividends
defined, 118
three-digit, 352–353, 364–366
two-digit, 340–341, 342–344
Division
applying, 336, 345, 346–347, 360, 362–363, 367, 369, 374–375
averages and, 374–375
basic facts, 118–119, 120–121, 122–125, 126–127, 128–129, 135, 348–349
with a calculator, 372–373, 374–375, 377, 479, 562–563, 567
choose a method, 372–373
concept of, 118
correcting quotients, 369
counting back in, 123
dividends, 118, 338, 342
divisors, 118, 338, 342
equations, 162–165
estimation in, 350–351
expressions, 156–159
fact families and, 118–119, 123
and fractions, 125, 389
interpreting remainders, 362–363, 377
as inverse of multiplication, 118–119
long, 342–345, 364–367, 368–371, 372–373
mental math, 348–349, 350–351, 372–373, 379
modeling, 120, 122, 125, 336, 338–339, 340–341, 342, 348, 389
with money, 365, 368
on multiplication tables, 123, 126–127
by one-digit divisors, 338–339, 340–341, 342–344, 346–347, 348–349, 350–351, 352–353, 355, 362–363, 364–367, 368–371, 372–373, H13
patterns in, 348–349, 379
placing first digit in quotient, 352–353
practice with, 121, 124, 127, 129, 134, 344, 347, 349, 351, 353, 354, 355, 363, 366, 367, 370, 371, 373, 375, 376, 377, 379, 382–383
problems requiring, 118–119, 120–121, 122–125, 126–127, 128–129, 338–339, 340–341, 342–345, 346–347, 348–349, 350–351, 352–353, 362–363, 364–367, 368–371, 372–373, 374–375
procedures in, 342–344, 364–365, 368, 369
properties of, 155
quotients, 118, 338, 342
recording, 342–345, 352–353, 364–367, 368–371, 372–373

related to multiplication, 118–119, 123, 126, 342, 346–347
remainders in, 338–339, 340–341, 342–345, 352–353, 362–363, 364–367, 368–371, 372–373, 377
repeated subtraction and, 348
review, H10, H13, H16
short, 357
strategies, 122–125
of three-digit dividends, 350–351, 352–353, 364–367, 368–371
of two-digit dividends, 338–339, 340–341, 342–345
using multiplication to check, 126, 342
zeros in, 368–371
Divisors. *See* Division
Draw conclusions, 8, 104, 188, 288, 302, 338, 340, 345, 398, 422, 432, 434, 436–437, 446, 448, 508, 522, 600
Draw a Diagram strategy, 194–197, 346–347, 564–565
Draw a Picture strategy, 396– 397

E

eBook, 2, 30, 66, 94, 116, 140, 182, 204, 222, 256, 284, 312, 336, 360, 386, 416, 444, 472, 494, 520, 550, 572, 598, 630
Edges, 314–316, 329
Egyptian numerals, 27
Elapsed time, 476–479, 482–483
Endpoints, 258–259
Enrich, 27, 63, 87, 113, 137, 175, 201, 219, 249, 281, 309, 329, 357, 379, 413, 441, 465, 491, 517, 543, 569, 595, 627, 645
Equations
balancing, 165
defined, 74
modeling, 75, 163, 165, 166
with parentheses, 68
solving, 74–77, 78–81, 162–165, 166–169, 608–609
with variables, 66, 74–77, 78–81
writing, 66, 74–77, 78–80, 140, 166–169, 557, 608–609
Equilateral triangles, 268–269
Equivalent
decimals, 422–423, 463
fractions, 392–395, H3
fractions and decimals, 421
measures in the customary system, 556, 558, 560
measures in the metric system, 465, 595
Error Alert, 5, 35, 54, 70, 96, 130, 170, 210, 212, 288, 352, 369, 407, 419, 433, 476, 512, 640
Error analysis. *See* What's the Error? *and* Write Math Workshop
Estimation
of area, 610–613
benchmarks, 15
to check reasonableness of answer, 190, 364–365
compatible numbers and, 40–41, 186–187, 214, 228–229, 350–351
of differences, 41–43, 48–49
or exact answer, 48–49
of measurements, 552–554, 558–559, 560–561, 574–577, 578–579, 580–581, 588–591, 593
overestimate, 43, 371
of perimeters, 600–601
of products, 186–187
of quotients, 350–351, 352–353
review, H14, H15
rounding, 34–37, 40–43, 186–187, 228–229, 350–351
of sums, 40–43, 48–49
underestimate, 43, 371
of volume, 632–635
Evaluate reasonableness, 214–215
Even numbers, 111, 142–143
Events, 543
Examples, *provided in every lesson;* nonexamples, 265
Expanded form, 5, 10, 419, 425
Expressions
defined, 70
evaluating, 70–74, 99, 156–159
with a calculator, 173
modeling, 71, 73, 156–157
with variables, 71, 140, 156–159
writing, 70–73, 156–159
Extra Practice, 24, 60–61, 84, 110, 134, 170–171, 198, 216, 246–247, 278–279, 306, 326, 354, 376, 410, 438, 462, 488, 514–515, 540, 566, 592, 624, 642

F

Faces, 314–316, 329
Fact families
addition and subtraction, 32–33
multiplication and division, 118–119
Factors
common, 137, 393
missing, 123, 126, 152, 160–161
model
area model, 196, 614–615, 618–619
array, 96–97, 98–99, 100–101, 130–131, 142, 153, 188–189, 190, 195, 234–235, 236, H9
multiplying three, 152–155, 249
review, H9
Fahrenheit temperature, 484–485
Fast Fact, 2, 6, 30, 36, 52, 66, 80, 94, 99, 116, 119, 127, 140, 158, 182, 192, 204, 207, 222, 229, 235, 256, 269, 275, 284, 305, 312, 325, 336, 344, 360, 370, 386, 416, 426, 444, 457, 472, 475, 494, 503, 505, 520, 535, 550, 559, 563, 565, 572, 583, 586, 598, 603, 630, 641

Feet, 552–554
Fibonacci pattern, 147
Figures. *See* Geometry
Find a rule, 82–83, 144–147, 148–151, 170–171, 175, 192, 304–305, H18
Formulas, 605, 607, 615, 645
Fraction bars. *See* Manipulatives and visual aids
Fractions
adding like, 413
calculator and, 421
comparing, 398–399, 400–401, 406–409, 411, H5
concepts of, 388–391, 402–405
concrete objects, 392–395, 396–397, 398, 400–401, 402–405, 406–409
denominators, defined, 388
and division, 125, 389
equivalent, 392–395, H3
generate, 386, 392–395, 396–397
of a group, 391
like, 413
in measurements, 405, 552–554
in mixed numbers, 402–405, 406–409, H4
modeling
compare fractions, 398–399
with fraction bars, 392–393, 396–397, 400–401, 403, 406, 411
with fraction circles, 388, 411
fractions greater than one, 402–405, 406–408, H4
with pattern blocks, 398, 402–403, 413
on a number line, 389, 392, 399, 400–401, 402, 406–409
parts of a group, 389, 391, 392
parts of a whole, 388, 392
numerators, defined, 388
ordering, 400–401, H5
pictorial models, 388–391, 395, 402–405, 407
practice with, 390, 394, 399, 401, 404, 408, 410
read and write, 388–391, 402–405
relate decimals to, 418–421, 424–427, H6
review, H3–H6, H25
on a ruler, 405, 553
simplest form of, 393
subtracting like, 413
unit, 388
See also Mixed numbers
Frequency table, 497
Function tables. *See* Input/output tables

G

Gallons, 560–561
Generalizations, make, 510–511, 555, 582
combinations, 522–523
patterns, 304–305
sets of examples and nonexamples, 265
Geoboard, 270
Geometry
angles
classifying and identifying, 260–261
and line relationships, 262–263
in triangles, 264, 268–269
in quadrilaterals, 264, 270–273
review, H19
area, 610–613, 614–617, 618–619, 620–623, 625
circles, 274–275
classifying
angles, 260–261
figures by number of dimensions, 258, 314
polygons, 264–267, 281
quadrilaterals, 270–273
solids, 314–317
triangles, 264, 268–269
closed figures, 264–267
cones, 314
congruent figures, 286–287, H23
coordinate grids, 512–513
cubes, 314–315
cylinders, 314
dimensions (number of) in figures
defined, 258
one-dimensional figures, 258
three-dimensional figures, 314, 327
two-dimensional figures, 258
edges of solids, 314–316, 329
faces of solids, 314–316, 329
figures, 258–259, 260–261, 262–263, 264–267, 268–269, 270–273, 274–275, 276–277, 286–287, 288–289, 290–291, 292–293, 294–297, 298–301, 302–303, 304–305, 314–317, 318–319, 320–321
hexagons, 264
line symmetry, 284, 294–297, H24
lines, 258–259, 262–263
angle relationships and, 262
endpoints of, 258
intersecting, defined 262
parallel, defined 262
perpendicular, defined 262
ray, defined, 258
review, H20
segment, defined, 258
motion
reflections, 292–293
rotations, 290–291
tessellations and, 302–303
transformations, defined, 288
translations, 288–289
octagons, 264
one-dimensional figures, 258
parallelograms, 271
patterns, 82, 85, 302–303, 304–305
pentagons, 264
perimeter, 600–601, 602–603, 604–607, 608–609, 620–623, 625

plane, defined, 258
plane figures, 264–267, 268–269, 270–273, 274–275
point, defined, 258
polygons
classifying, 264–265, 270–273, 276–277
identifying, 264–265, 281
not regular, 265
regular, 265, 607
prisms, 314–315, 318, 320
pyramids, 314–315, 318
quadrilaterals, 264–265
classifying and identifying, 270–273
special, 271
rectangles, 271
rectangular prism, 314
reflections, 292–293
review, H19–H24
rhombuses, 271
rotations, 290–291
solid figures, 314–317, 318–319, 320–321, 322–325, 327
spheres, 314
squares, 271
symmetry, 281, 294–297, H24
tangram puzzle, 300, 309
tessellations, 302–303
three-dimensional figures, 314–317, 318–319, 320–321, 322–325, 327
transformations, 288–289, 290–291, 292–293
translations, 288–289
trapezoids, 271
triangles, 264
classifying and identifying, 268–269
triangular prism, 314
two-dimensional figures, 258, 264–267, 268–269, 270–273, 274–275, 276–277, 286–287, 288–289, 290–291, 292–293, 294–297, 302–303, 304–305
vertices of solids, 314–316, 329
views of solid figures, 322–325, 327
Getting Ready for the TAKS, 28–29, 64–65, 114–115, 138–139, 202–203, 220–221, 282–283, 310–311, 358–359, 414–415, 442–443, 492–493, 518–519, 570–571, 596–597, 628–629
Glossary, H49–H61
Grams, 578–579
Graphic organizers, 1, 93, 181, 255, 335, 385, 471, 549
Graphs
analyzing, 502–503, 504–505, 506–507, 508–509, 510–511, 517
bar, 39, 49, 81, 116, 187, 196, 204, 209, 238, 336, 360, 395, 498, 504–505, 506–507, 517, 554, 572, 576
comparing, 504–505
data labels, 506
double-bar, 508–509
identifying parts of, 502, 506
interpreting, 502–503, 504–505, 506–507, 508–509
intervals and, 504–505
key of, 502
making, 502–503, 506–507, 508–509
pictographs, 33, 119, 502–503
practice with, 503, 505, 507, 509, 511, 514–515, 517
scale of, 504–505
Greedy algorithm, 453
Grid paper. *See* Manipulatives and visual aids
Guess and Check strategy, 106–109

Hands On activities, 4, 82, 100, 122, 130, 142, 153, 234, 260, 262, 265, 270, 274, 286, 290, 292, 294–295, 304–305, 315, 318, 320, 392, 399, 400, 402, 406–407, 418, 424–425, 428–429, 450–451, 477, 484, 486, 496, 524, 528, 552, 553, 558, 560, 574, 575, 578, 580, 584–585, 588–589, 588–591, 602, 610–611, 620–621, 632, 640
Hands On lessons, 8–9, 104–105, 188–189, 288–289, 302–303, 338–339, 340–341, 398–399, 422–423, 432–433, 434–435, 446–447, 448–449, 508–509, 522–523, 600–601
Harcourt Mega Math, 36, 52, 105, 124, 146, 164, 213, 237, 266, 296, 315, 339, 399, 404, 420, 435, 447, 449, 456, 478, 507, 554, 576, 606, 616, 634
Hexagons, 264
Hour, 474
Hundred thousands, 4–7
Hundreds
multiples, 224–225
place value, 4–7
rounding to, 34–37, 40–43
Hundredths, 416, 418–421

Identity Property, 68–69, 104, 152–155
Inches, 552–554
Inequalities, 12–15, 16–19, 398–399, 406–408, 563
Input/output tables, 82–83, 85, 102, 105, 170–171, 175, 192, 225, 344, 478, 567, H18
Interpret the remainder, 362–363, 377
Intersecting lines, 262–263
concrete objects, 262
pictorial models, 263
Intervals, 504–505
Inverse operations, 33, 118

Investigate, 2, 8, 30, 66, 94, 104, 116, 140, 182, 188, 204, 222, 256, 284, 288, 302, 312, 336, 338, 340, 360, 386, 398, 416, 422, 432, 434, 444, 446, 448, 472, 494, 508, 520, 522, 550, 572, 598, 630
"Is approximately equal to" symbol (≈), 587
Isosceles triangle, 268–269
iTools, 199, 307, 411, 489

K

Key, of graph, 502
Kilograms, 578–579
Kilometers, 574–577
Klee, Paul, 264

L

Lattice multiplication, 201
Length. *See* Linear units
Like fractions, 413
Line segments, 258–259
Line symmetry, 284, 294–297
Linear units
changing, 556–557, 587
customary units, 552–554
defined, 552
estimating, 593
fractions with, 552–554
meters, 465
metric, 574–577
practice with, 554, 557, 565, 576, 583
See also Measurement *and* Perimeter
Lines
defined, 258
intersecting, 258–259
modeling, 262
parallel, 258–259
perpendicular, 258–259
relationships between, 262–263
List, organized, 532–535
Liters, 580–581
Logical reasoning, 20–24, 133. *See also* Reasoning
Look for a Pattern strategy, 148–151

M

Make a Model strategy, 322–325
Make an Organized List strategy, 532–535
Make a Table strategy, 458–459, 564–565, 582–583
Manipulatives and visual aids
area models, 100, 122, 153, 188, 190, 195–196, 234–235, 236, 614–617, 618–619
arrays
division, 120, 336
multiplication, 96–97, 98–99, 100–101, 130–131, 142, 153, 188–189, 190, 195, 234–235, 236
in patterns, 148
relating addition and multiplication, 96–97
balances, 75, 163, 165, 578, 589
base-ten blocks
comparing numbers, 12–15
division, 340–341, 342
multiplication, 189, 191, 199, 234–235
ordering numbers, 16–17
place value, 4
calendar, 482–483
centimeter cubes, 322–325, 632–635, 636–637, 638–639, 640
clocks, 474–475, 476–477
compasses, 274
counters
division, 122, 338–339
equations, 166
fractions, 398
multiples, 131
multiplication, 152, 160
decimal models, 418–421, 422–423, 424–426, 432–433, 434–435, 446–447, 448–449, 454–455
dot paper
congruence, 286–287, 292
polygons, 265, 270
geometric solids, 318
symmetry, 295
transformations, 288
fraction bars, 392–393, 396–397, 400–401, 403, 406, 411
fraction circles, 389, 411
geoboards, 270
gram and kilogram masses, 578
grid paper
area, 618, 620–621, 623
division, 120
multiplication, 100–101, 130, 188–189, 234–235, 236
perimeter, 602–603, 623
place value, 8
symmetry, 294
transformations, 288
measuring cups, 560, 580, 585
meterstick, 574–576, 584, 588
multiplication tables, 101, 104–105, 123, 126–127, 142–143
number lines
addition on, 51, 53, 96–97
common multiples on, 133
comparing on, 12–14, 399, 432–433
decimals on, 419–420, 425–426, 432–433, 434–435
division on, 120, 348, 389
evaluating expressions on, 73

fractions on, 389, 392, 399, 400–401, 402, 406–409
mixed numbers on, 402–405, 406–409
multiplying on, 96–97, 98–99, 184, 224
ordering on, 16–18, 434–435
for problem solving, 53
repeated addition on, 96, 184, 224
rounding on, 34–35
ruler as, 405, 553
subtracting on, 45, 51, 53
whole numbers on, 12, 14, 16, 18
pattern blocks, 71, 82, 85, 156–157, 288, 290, 292, 294–295, 299, 300, 303, 398, 402–403, 413
play money, 298, 428–431, 436, 450–451, 453, 455
rulers, 265, 274, 286, 405, 552–555, 574–577, 584, 588
spinners, 534
spring scale, 558, 585, 589
stopwatch, 477
thermometers, 484–485, 486–487
tiles, 130, 148, 153, 620–621
yardstick, 553, 584, 588
Maps
reading, 18, 193, 263, 437, 577, 603
scale, 577
Mass, 578–589. *See also* Measurement, of weight/mass
Math Idea, 10, 13, 17, 32, 38, 56, 64, 101, 123, 131, 145, 184, 190, 224, 226, 240, 268, 292, 342, 348, 372, 407, 454, 504, 508, 528, 556, 575, 621, 632
Math on Location, 1, 92– 93, 180–181, 254–255, 334–335, 384–385, 470–471, 548–549
Math Power, 7, 15, 19, 37, 43, 53, 59, 73, 125, 133, 147, 165, 371, 391, 395, 405, 421, 431, 453, 479, 531, 577, 587, 591, 607, 617, 623, 635
Mathematical symbols. *See* Symbols
Mean, 517
Measurement
of area, 153, 610–613, 614–617, 618–619, 620–623, 625
area/perimeter relationship, 620–623
benchmarks, 552, 558, 560, 574, 578, 580, 584–587, 588–591
of capacity, 560–561, 580–581
Celsius degrees, 486–487
centimeters, 574–577
changing units of, 465, 479, 556–557, 558–559, 560–561, 562–563, 564–565, 567, 569, 595
choosing the appropriate unit of, 584–587
circumference, 627
comparing units of, 584–587, 588–591
converting between customary and metric, 587
cubic units, 632–635
cups, 560–561
customary system of, 552–555, 556–557, 558–559, 560–561, 562–563, 564–565, 567, 569, 584–587, 588–591, H26
days, 474
decimeters, 574–577
of distance, 574–577
estimating, 552–554, 558–559, 560–561, 574–577, 578–579, 580–581, 588–591, 593
exact or estimate, 48–49, 591
Fahrenheit degrees, 484–485
feet, 552–554
fluid ounces, 560–561
fractions in, 405, 552–554
gallons, 560–561
grams, 578–579
hours, 474
inches, 552–554
kilograms, 578–579
kilometers, 574–577
of length, 552–555, 574–577
liters, 580–581
meters, 465, 572, 574–577, 584, 588
meterstick, 574–577, 584–587, 588–591
metric system of, 574–577, 578–579, 580–581, 582–583, 584–587, 588–591, 593, 595
miles, 552–554
milliliters, 580–581
millimeters, 574–577
minutes, 474
months, 483
nonstandard units, 555
ounces, 558–559
of perimeters, 600–601, 602–603, 604–607, 608–609, 625
pints, 560–561
pounds, 558–559
prefixes for metric units, 465
quarts, 560–561
relating metric and customary units, 584–587
review, H26
seconds, 474
square units, 153, 610–612
Table of Measures, H44–H45
tablespoon, 560–561
teaspoon, 560–561
of temperature, 484–485, 486–487
of three-dimensional figures, 632–635
of time, 474–475, 476–479, 480–481, 482–483, 491
tons, 558–559
of two-dimensional figures, 600–601, 614–617
using rulers, 265, 274, 286, 405, 552–554, 574–577, 584–587, 588–591
of volume, 632–635, 636–637, 638–639, 643, 645
volume/capacity relationship, 640–641
of weight/mass, 558–559, 578–579
difference between, 578
yards, 552–554
Median, 517
Mental math
addition, 38–39, 40–43, 44–47, 56
compatible numbers and, 40–41, 186–187, 228–229

division, 348–349, 350–351, 379
multiplication, 184–185, 186–187, 212, 242–225, 226, 242–243, 379
patterns and, 38–39, 184–185, 379
properties and, 40, 153
rounding, 186–187, 228–229
solving equations with, 75
strategies, 44–47
subtraction, 38–39, 40–43, 44–47, 57
Meters, 574–577
Metric (or SI) system
adding measurements in, 465
benchmarks for, 574, 578, 580, 584–587, 588–591
capacity, 580–581
changing units in, 595
customary units compared to, 584–587, 588–591, 595
decimals and, 465
equivalent measures in, 465, 575, 578, 580, 595
estimating in, 574–577, 578–579, 580–581, 588–591
length, 574–577
mass, 578–579
practice with, 576–577, 579, 581, 583, 586, 590, 593, 595
relating metric and customary units, 587
relating units in, 574–577, 578–579, 580–581
temperature, 486–487
Miles, 552–555
Milliliters, 580–581
Millimeters, 574–577
Millions, 8–9, 10–11, 13, 17
Minutes, 474
Mixed Applications, 49, 129, 215, 245, 363, 437, 481, 511, 637
Mixed numbers
defined, 402
modeling, 402–405, 406–408
practice with, 404, 408, 409
read and write, 402–405
relate decimals and, 424–427
review, H4
Mixed Review. *See* TAKS Prep
Mixed Strategy Practice, 23, 81, 109, 151, 169, 197, 233, 277, 301, 325, 397, 461, 535, 565, 583, 609
Mode, 517
Modeling
addition
with arrays, 96–97
with decimal models, 446–447, 454
on a number line, 96–97
angles, 260–261
area, 96, 100, 130, 153, 188, 610–611, 614–615, 617, 618, 620–621, 623
capacity, 560, 564, 580
combinations, 522–523, 524–525, 536
comparing numbers, 12–13, 16–17, 398–399, 406–407, 432–434
congruent figures, 286–287, 288
decimals
using decimal models, 418–419, 422–423, 424–426, 428–429, 432–433, 434–435, 446–447, 448–449, 454–455
using number lines, 419–420, 425, 432–433, 434–435
using play money, 428–431
division
using an area model, 122
using arrays, 120, 336
using base-ten blocks, 340–341, 342
using counters, 122, 166, 338–339
using number lines, 120, 348, 389
equations, 75, 78–79, 163, 165, 166
expressions, 71, 73, 156–157
factors, 96–97, 98–99, 122, 130–131, 142, 160, 195
fractions
comparing, 398–399, 406–407
equivalency of decimals and, 418–419
equivalent, 392–395
fraction bars, 392–393, 396–397, 400–401, 403, 406, 411
on a number line, 389, 392, 399, 400–401, 402, 406–409
parts of a group, 389, 391, 392
parts of a whole, 388, 392
simplest form of, 393
geometric solids, 315, 318, 320, 322–323, 327
length, 574–575
line relationships, 262
line symmetry, 284, 294–297
mass/weight, using a scale, 558, 578
millions, 8
mixed numbers, 402–405, 406–407, 424–425
money amounts, 428–431, 436, 450–451, 453, 455
multiples, 131, 133
multiplication
using area models, 96, 100, 130, 153, 188, 236
using arrays, 96–97, 98–99, 100–101, 130–131, 142, 153, 188–189, 190, 195, 234–235, 236
using base-ten blocks, 189, 191, 199, 234
using counters, 152, 160, 166
using grid paper, 100–101, 130, 188–189, 234
using number lines, 96–97, 98–99, 224
numbers, whole
using grid paper, 8
using number lines, 12, 14, 16, 18, 73
ordered pairs, 82
ordering numbers, 16, 18, 434–435
patterns, 82, 85, 148, 302–303
perimeter, 600–601, 602–603, 623
place value, 4, 8, 12
polygons, 265, 270, 273
in problem solving, 322–323
subtraction
using decimal models, 448–449, 454
using number lines, 45, 51, 53
using play money, 455

symmetry, 294–297
temperature change, 484, 486
tessellations, 302–303
three-dimensional figures, 315, 320, 322–323, 327
transformations, 288, 290, 292, 307
two-dimensional figures, 260, 270, 273
volume, 632–633, 638, 640
See also Data; Manipulatives and visual aids; *and* Problem solving strategies, make a model

Money
adding with, 454–457, 458–461
count, 450, 453
dividing with, 365, 368, 371, 395
make change, 428–429, 436–437, 450–451, 453, 455
relate fractions and decimals to, 428–427
subtracting with, 451, 454–457

Motion geometry. *See* Geometry, motion

Multimedia Math Glossary, 1, 93, 181, 255, 335, 385, 471, 549

Multiples
common, 133
defined, 105
estimating products with, 186–187
finding, 131–133
of hundred, 224–225
modeling, 131, 133
multiplying by, 224–225, 226–227
patterns with, 8–9, 142–143
of ten, 8–9, 226–227
of thousand, 224–225

Multiplication
applying, 103, 113, 137, 166–168, 193, 204, 214–215, 230–232, 239, 244–245
Associative Property, 152–155, 249
basic facts, 98–99, 100–103, 104–105, 113, 135, H11, H16
with a calculator, 212, 242
choose a method, 212–213, 242–243
common multiples, 133
Commutative Property, 101, 152–155, 249
concept of, 96–97, 118–119
Distributive Property, 153, 219, 230–233
equations, 162–165
estimating products, 186–187, 228–229
expressions, 156–159
fact families and, 118–119
factors in, 98, 118, 130–134, 137, 160–161
Identity Property, 104, 152–155
as inverse of division, 118
lattice, 201
mental math and, 153, 186–187, 212, 224–225, 226, 242–243, 228–229, 379
modeling, 96–97, 98–99, 100–101, 130–131, 142, 152–153, 160, 188–189, 190–192, 194–195, 199, 224–225, 234–235, 236
with money, 210–211
multiples, 130–133, 184–185, 224–225, 226–227
by multiples of ten, 226–227
one-digit by three-digit, 208–209, 214–215, 217
one-digit by two-digit, 188–189, 190–193, 206–207, 217
partial products of, 189, 190, 206, 236–239, 240–241
patterns in, 104–105, 184–185, 224–225, 379, H17
practice with, 99, 102, 103, 105, 110, 143, 154, 155, 158–159, 161, 164, 168, 171, 185, 187, 192, 196, 199, 207, 209, 211, 213, 215, 217, 225, 227, 229, 232, 235, 238, 239, 240–241, 243, 246
problems requiring, 106–109, 128–129, 166–169, 194–197, 206–207, 208–209, 210–211, 212–213, 214–215, 219, 224–225, 226–227, 228–229, 230–233, 234–235, 236–239, 240–241, 242–243, 244–245
products of, 98, 106–109, 113, 118, 186–187, 188–189, 190–193, 194–197, 199
properties of, 152–155, 219, 249
recording, 98, 190–193, 206–207, 208–209, 210–211, 212–213, 226–227, 236–239, 240–241
related to addition, 96–97, 184–185, 224–225
related to division, 118–119, 123
and repeated addition, 96–97, 118, 224–225
review, H10–H12, H16, H17
skip-counting in, 101, 131, 184–185, 224–225
strategies, 100–103, 104–105, 194–197, 230–233
symbol for, 96
table, using a, 101, 104–105, 106–109, 123, 126–127, 142–143
of three factors, 152–155, 249
two-digit by two-digit, 226–227, 228–229, 230–233, 234–235, 236–239, 240–241, 242–243
using related facts, 118–119, 123
Zero Property, 104, 152–155
with zeros, 210–211
See also Measurement, changing units of

Multiplication properties, 152–155, 219, 249

Multiplication table, 101, 104–105
division on, 123, 126–127
patterns on, 142–143

Nets, 320–321

Nonstandard units, 555

"Not equal to" symbol (≠), 12

Number lines
addition on, 51, 53, 96–97
common multiples on, 133
comparing on, 12–15, 432–433
decimals on, 419–420, 425–426, 432–433, 434–435, H25
distances on, 53
division on, 120, 348, 389
evaluating expressions on, 73

fractions on, 389, 392, 399, 400–401, 402, 406–409, H25
measure time, 474
mixed numbers on, 402–405, 406–409
multiplying on, 96–97, 98–99, 184, 224
ordering on, 16–19, 434–435
for problem solving, 53
repeated addition on, 96, 184, 224
rounding on, 34–35
ruler as, 405, 553, 575
subtracting on, 45, 51, 53
whole numbers on, 12–15, 16–19
Number patterns, 142–143, 144–147, 148–151, 175, 379
Number sense, 7, 19, 37, 43, 59, 125, 371, 391, 431, 453, 531
Number sentence, 32–33, 38
Numbers
average of, 374–375
benchmark, 15
comparing, 12–15
even, 111
expanded form of, 5, 10
factoring, 137
millions, 8–9, 10–11, 13, 17
mixed, 402–405, 406–409
odd, 111
ordered pairs of, 82–83, 170–171, 512–513
ordering, 16–19, 25
patterns, 142–143, 144–147, 148–151, 175, 379
place value of, 4–5, 9, 10–11
reading and writing, 5, 10
sorting, 132, 501
square, 142
standard form of, 5, 10
thousands, 4–5
using, 19
word form of, 5, 10
See also Decimals *and* Fractions
Numeration systems, 27
Numerator, defined, 388

O

Obtuse angles, 260–261
Obtuse triangles, 268–269
Octagons, 264
Odd numbers, 111, 142–143
One-dimensional figures, 258
Ones, 4–5
Open-ended, 23, 81, 109, 151, 169, 197, 233, 301, 430, 461, 535
Operations, choosing, 128–129, 567. *See also* Addition, Division, Multiplication, *and* Subtraction
Ordered pairs, 82–83, 170–171, 512–513
Ordering
of decimals, 434–435, 439
of fractions, 400–401, 406–409, H5
on number line, 16–19, 434–435, 439
practice with, 18–19, 24, 401, 408, 410, 435, 439
whole numbers, 16–19
Organization of data, 496–499, 528–530, 532–535
Organized lists, 532–535
Ounces, 558–559
Outcomes, 543
Overestimate, 43, 371

P

Palindromes, 59
Parallel lines, 262–263
concrete objects, 262
pictorial models, 263
Parallelograms, 271
Parentheses, 68
Partial products, 189, 190, 206, 236–237
Pattern blocks, 71, 82, 85, 156–157, 288, 290, 292, 295, 299, 398, 402–403, 413
Patterns
in addition and subtraction, 38–39
analyze, 82–83, 144–147
describe, 82–83, 144–147
in division, 348–349, 379
extending, 144–147
Fibonacci, 147
finding, 145
finding with a calculator, 145
functions, 82–83, 170–171, 175
generalize, 304–305
geometric, 85, 148, 302–303, 304–305
identifying, 144–147
looking for, 82–83, 148–151
making, 145, 302–303
modeling, 82, 85, 148, 302–303
with multiples, 8–9, 142–143, 224–225
in multiplication, 142–143, 224–225, 379
number, 142–143, 144–147, 148–151, 175
predict, 175
repeating, 302–303, 304–305
rules for, 82–83, 144–147, 170–171, 304–305
for solid figures, 320–321
visual, 148–151, 175, 302–303, 304–305
of zeros, 38–39, 224–225
Pei, I. M., 267
Pentagons, 264
Perimeter
defined, 600
estimating, 600–601
finding, 600–601, 602–603, 604–607
formula for, 605
modeling, 600–601, 602–603, 623

of plane figures, 604–607
practice with, 603, 606, 622, 624, 625
relating to area, 620–623
units of measurement for, 604–607
Periods, 5, 9, 10
Perpendicular lines, 262–263
concrete objects, 262
pictorial models, 263
Picasso, Pablo, 266
Pictograph, 33, 119, 502–503
Pints, 560–561
Place value
compare, 12, 432
concrete objects, 12, 432
pictorial models, 12, 432
decimal, 419, 425, 429
digits, value of, 5, 9, 10
hundred millions, 9, 10–11
hundred thousands, 4–7
hundreds, 4–7
hundredths, 418–421
millions, 9, 10–11
modeling, 4, 8
in money figures, 429
numeration systems and, 27
ones, 4–7
order, 16, 434
concrete objects, 16, 434
pictorial models, 16, 434
periods, 5, 9, 10
placing first digit in quotient, 352–353
practice with, 6–7, 9, 11, 14–15, 18–19, 22–23, 24, 25, 420, 423, 426
read, 5–7, 9, 10–11
review, H2
tens, 4–7
tenths, 418–421
thousands, 4–7
thousandths, 441
whole numbers, 4–7, 9, 10–11, 12–15, 16–19, H2
write, 5–7, 9, 10–11
Plane figures. *See* Two-dimensional geometric figures
Planes, 258
Play money, 428–431, 436, 450–451, 453, 455
Points, 258–259
Polygons, 264–267, 281
decagons, 264
hexagons, 264
modeling, 265, 270, 273
not regular, 265
octagons, 264
pentagons, 264
quadrilaterals, 264–265, 270–273
rectangles, 271
regular, 265, 607
squares, 271
triangle, 264, 268–269
vertices of, 260
Pose a Problem, 14, 23, 39, 52, 58, 76, 81, 109, 121, 129, 146, 151, 154, 161, 169, 187, 197, 209, 227, 233, 272, 301, 325, 366, 395, 407, 408, 430, 456, 461, 498, 505, 513, 530, 535, 565, 583, 609
Possible outcomes, 534, 543
Pounds, 558–559
Practice Game, 25, 111, 135, 217, 327, 355, 439, 463, 541, 593, 625, 643
Predictions, make, 510–511
Prefixes, in metric units, 465
Prisms
classifying, 314
comparing, 638–639
rectangular, 314, 318, 320
square (cube), 314–315
triangular, 314
volume of, 632–635, 636–637, 638–639
Probability
events, 543
possible outcomes, 534, 543
Problem solving
analysis, 8, 288
applications, *provided in every lesson*
check skills in, 49, 129, 215, 245, 363, 437, 481, 511, 637
choose a method (paper/pencil, calculator, mental math), 56–59, 212–213, 242–243, 372–373
choose the operation, 128–129
choose a strategy, 23, 81, 109, 151, 169, 197, 233, 277, 301, 347, 397, 461, 535, 565, 583, 609
open-ended, 23, 81, 109, 151, 169, 197, 233, 301, 430, 461, 535
review, H29–H31
Problem solving applications
algebra, 165, 287, 511, 607
art, 159, 267, 297
data, use, 6, 11, 14, 18, 23, 36, 39, 49, 52, 55, 58, 69, 72, 76, 80, 83, 99, 102, 108, 119, 121, 124, 129, 132, 143, 161, 164, 168, 169, 171, 185, 187, 196, 207, 209, 211, 225, 227, 233, 238, 241, 245, 259, 263, 266, 269, 272, 275, 277, 287, 291, 296, 301, 305, 325, 347, 349, 351, 353, 363, 366, 375, 390, 395, 397, 408, 420, 430, 437, 452, 456, 460, 461, 478, 481, 483, 485, 487, 498, 503, 505, 511, 526, 530, 534, 535, 538, 554, 557, 559, 561, 563, 565, 576, 579, 581, 583, 586, 590, 603, 612, 616, 619, 637, 641
diagrams, use, 11, 121, 275, 291, 353, 501, 612, 616, 619
estimation, 37, 43, 371, 591
geometry, 259, 261, 263, 266, 267, 269, 272, 275, 277, 291, 293, 296, 297, 301, 305, 316, 319, 321, 325
graph, using a, 33, 39, 49, 81, 119, 187, 196, 204, 209, 238, 336, 360, 395, 498, 503, 505, 507, 554, 572, 576
hands on, 104, 338, 422, 432, 434, 600

journals, use, 590
logical reasoning, 22, 133, 277
maps, use, 18, 193, 263, 437, 577, 603
measurement, 14, 18, 49, 554, 557, 559, 561, 563, 565, 576, 577, 579, 581, 583, 586, 590, 591, 603, 606, 612, 616, 617, 619, 622, 623, 634, 637, 639, 641
mental math, 46
money, 349, 431, 444, 452, 456, 481
number sense, 7, 19, 37, 43, 59, 125
patterns, 127, 143, 146
pictures, use, 102, 151, 164, 211, 233, 241, 259, 266, 269, 272, 277, 301, 347, 430, 452, 534, 538, 557, 565, 579
reading, 527
reasoning, 6, 7, 15, 18, 36, 52, 76, 97, 124, 143, 146, 159, 161, 164, 211, 213, 225, 229, 238, 259, 272, 287, 293, 296, 316, 319, 321, 353, 366, 370, 394, 404, 430, 453, 479, 487, 498, 503, 505, 554, 561, 563, 576, 581, 590, 603, 606, 616, 634, 637, 639, 641
science, 11, 39, 52, 55, 58, 80, 124, 168, 169, 171, 187, 192, 197, 209, 225, 233, 351, 420, 457, 576, 641
social studies, 6, 36, 158, 229, 235, 503, 505, 535, 586
tables and charts, use, 6, 14, 35, 36, 42, 46, 48, 52, 55, 58, 69, 72, 76, 80, 83, 99, 109, 124, 161, 168, 169, 171, 185, 193, 207, 225, 227, 296, 319, 349, 351, 363, 366, 375, 397, 408, 420, 456, 460, 478, 481, 483, 485, 487, 498, 503, 511, 526, 530, 559, 561, 581, 586, 637, 641
time, 475, 478, 483, 485, 487
visual thinking, 15, 53, 73, 395

Problem Solving connects
to art, 159, 267, 297
to reading, 527
to science, 457

Problem solving skills
choose the operation, 128–129
draw conclusions, 436–437
estimate or exact answer, 48–49
evaluate reasonableness, 214–215
interpret the remainder, 362–363
make generalizations, 510–511
multistep problems, 244–245
sequence information, 480–481
too much/too little information, 636–637

Problem solving strategies
act it out, 298–301, 396–397
compare strategies, 346–347, 396–397, 564–565, 608–609
draw a diagram, 194–197, 346–347, 564–565
draw a picture, 396–397
guess and check, 75, 106–109, 163, 346–347
look for a pattern, 148–151
make a model, 322–325
make an organized list, 532–535
make a table, 458–459, 564–565, 582–583
practice, 23, 81, 109, 151, 169, 197, 233, 277, 301, 325, 397, 461, 535, 565, 583, 609
solve a simpler problem, 230–231
use logical reasoning, 20–24, 276–277
work backward, 78–79, 163, 608–609
write an equation, 166–169, 608–609

Products
concept of, 98
estimating, 186–187, 214–215
model
area, 196, 614–615, 618–619
array, 96–97, 98–99, 100–101, 130–131, 142, 153, 188–189, 190, 195, 234–235, 236
partial, 189, 190, 206, 236–237
review, H9

Properties
Associative, 40, 68–69, 152–155, 249
Commutative, 40, 68–69, 152–155, 249
Distributive, 153, 219
Identity, 68–69, 152–155
Zero, 152–155

Puzzles, 281, 309

Pyramids
classifying, 314
square, 314
triangular, 314, 318

Q

Quadrilaterals
building models of, 273
classifying and identifying, 270–273
defined, 264
drawing, 265, 270
not regular, 265
parallelograms, 271
rectangles, 271
regular, 265
rhombuses, 271
special, 271
squares, 271
trapezoids, 271

Quantitative reasoning, 63, 113, 137, 379, 491, 595, H18

Quarts, 560–561

Quotients
correcting, 369
defined, 118
estimating, 350–351
placing the first digit in, 352–353
three-digit, 364–366, 368–371, 372–373
zeros in, 368–371

R

Radius, 274
Range, 517
Ratio, 395
Ray, 258–259
Read Math, xx–xxi, 1, 51, 93, 157, 181, 191, 255, 335, 385, 471, 477, 549
Read Math Workshop, 77, 103, 193, 273, 345, 427, 499, 555
Reading Skills
  cause and effect, 77
  classify and categorize, 273, 276–277, 459, 527
  compare and contrast, 499
  draw conclusions, 345
  generalize, 555, 582
  identify the details, 107, 396, 427, 564
  sequence of events, 79
  summarize, 195, 346, 533
  use graphic aids, 21, 149, 193, 231, 608
  visualize, 103, 167, 299, 323
Reasoning, 6, 7, 15, 19, 36, 37, 43, 52, 53, 59, 73, 76, 97, 105, 123, 124, 125, 133, 143, 146, 159, 161, 164, 211, 213, 225, 229, 238, 259, 272, 287, 293, 296, 316, 319, 321, 353, 366, 370, 371, 391, 394, 395, 404, 405, 421, 426, 430, 431, 453, 479, 487, 498, 501, 503, 505, 531, 561, 576, 577, 581, 586, 587, 590, 591, 603, 606, 607, 616, 617, 623, 634, 635, 637, 639, 641. *See also* Critical thinking *and* Write Math
Recording division, 342–344
Recording multiplication, 98, 190–192, 206, 208, 236–238
Rectangles
  area of, 615
  as face of solid figure, 314
  identifying, 271
  perimeter of, 605
  relationship between area and perimeter in, 620–623
Rectangular prism, 314
Reflections, 292–293
  concrete objects, 292
  verify congruence, 294
  verify symmetry with, 294–295
Regular polygons, 265, 607
Related facts, 123
Remainders, in division, 338–339, 362–363, 377
Repeated addition, 96–97, 118, 224
Repeated subtraction, 348
Review the TEKS, H2–H31
Rhombuses, 271
Right angles, 260–261
Right triangles, 268–269
Roman numerals, 27
Rotations, 290–291
  concrete objects, 290
  verify congruence, 290–291
Rounding, 34–37, 40–43, H14
Rulers, 265, 274, 286, 405, 552–555, 574–577, 584–587, 588–591

Scalene triangles, 268–269
Scales, on graphs, 504–505
Schedules, 480–481
Seconds, 474
Sense or Nonsense, 108, 164, 209, 287, 366, 426, 487, 507, 554, 606
Sequence information, 480–481
Short division, 357
Show What You Know. *See* Assessment
Simplest form of a fraction, 393
SI (or Metric) system. *See Metric (or SI) system*
Skip-counting and multiplication, 101, 131
Smith, Leon Polk, 256
Solid figures. *See* Geometry *and* Three-dimensional geometric figures
Solve a Simpler Problem strategy, 230–231
Sorting
  numbers, 132, 501
  two-dimensional figures, 276–277
Spatial reasoning, 194–197, 262–263, 286–287, 288–289, 290–291, 292–293, 298–300, 314–317, 318–319, 320–321, 322–325, 632–635, 638–639
Special quadrilaterals, 271
Sphere, 314
Spinners, 534
Spreadsheets, 85
Square numbers, 142
Square pyramids, 314
Square units, 153, 610–612
Squares, 271
  area of, 615
  perimeter of, 605
Standard form, 5, 10, 419, 425
Standardized Test Prep. *See* Getting Ready for the TAKS
Statistics
  averages, 374–375
  bar graphs, 39, 49, 81, 116, 187, 196, 204, 209, 238, 336, 360, 498, 506–507, 572, 576
  frequency tables, 497
  interpreting data, 494, 500–501, 502–503, 506–507, 508–509
  median, 517
  mode, 517
  pictographs, 33, 119, 502–503

range, 517
taking surveys, 496
See also Data
Stopwatch, 477
Strategies
addition, 44–47
break apart, 44, 100, 104, 122, 188–189, 230–231
division, 122–125
mental math, 44–47, 379
multiplication, 100–103, 104–105
subtraction, 44–47
See also Problem solving strategies
Subtraction
with a calculator, 57
basic facts, 32–33, 38–39
choose a method, 56–59
of customary measurements, 569
of decimals, 448–449, 454–457
concrete objects, 448, 454
pictorial models, 449, 455
differences, 40–43, 50–53, 54–55, 56–59, 448–449, 454–457
equations, 74–77
estimation and, 40–43, 51
expressions, 70–73
fact families and, 32–33
of four-digit numbers, 50–53
of greater numbers, 56–59
of like fractions, 413
mental math, 38–39, 40–43, 44–47, 57
modeling, 45, 51, 53, 448–449, 454–457
money, 454–457
on a number line, 45, 51, 53
patterns, 38–39
practice with, 39, 42, 46, 52, 55, 58, 60–61, 72–73, 76, 84
recording, 50–53, 54–55, 454–455
related to addition, 32–33
repeated, 348
review, H7, H8
strategies, 44–47
of three-digit numbers, 50–53
of two-digit numbers, 44–47
across zeros, 54–55
Sums. *See* Addition
Surveys, 496
Symbols. *See also* Table of Measures
for addition, 96
for angles, 260
for degrees, 260
for "is approximately equal to," 587
line relationships, 262
lines, 258
for multiplication, 96
for "not equal to," 12
rays, 258
Symmetry
line, 284, 294–297
review, H24
verify, 294–295

T

Table of Measures, H44–H45
Tables and charts
frequency, 497
looking for patterns in, 82–83, 142–143, 170–171
making, 21, 458–459, 564–565, 582–583
multiplication, 101, 104–105, 123, 126–127, 142–143
ordered pairs in, 82–83, 170–171, 512–513
organizing data in, 20–22
practice with, 22, 83, 143, 171, 460, 498, 513, 565, 583
tally, 496
using, 6, 14, 35, 36, 42, 46, 48, 52, 55, 58, 69, 72, 76, 80, 83, 99, 109, 124, 161, 168, 169, 171, 185, 193, 207, 225, 227, 296, 319, 349, 351, 363, 366, 375, 397, 408, 420, 456, 460, 478, 481, 483, 485, 487, 498, 503, 511, 526, 530, 559, 561, 581, 586, 637, 641
Tablespoons, 560–561
TAKS Prep, 7, 11, 15, 19, 33, 37, 39, 43, 46, 52, 55, 59, 69, 73, 76, 83, 97, 99, 102, 119, 121, 125, 127, 133, 143, 147, 154, 159, 161, 165, 171, 185, 187, 192, 207, 209, 211, 213, 225, 227, 229, 235, 238, 241, 243, 259, 261, 263, 267, 269, 272, 275, 287, 291, 293, 297, 305, 316, 319, 321, 344, 349, 351, 353, 366, 371, 373, 375, 391, 395, 401, 405, 408, 421, 426, 431, 453, 457, 475, 479, 485, 487, 498, 501, 503, 505, 507, 512, 527, 531, 538, 554, 559, 561, 563, 577, 579, 581, 587, 591, 603, 607, 612, 617, 619, 623, 635, 639, 641
TAKS Test-Taking Skills, H32–H39
Talk Math, xx–xxi, 1, 6, 11, 14, 18, 20, 33, 36, 38, 42, 45, 52, 55, 58, 69, 72, 76, 78, 83, 93, 97, 99, 102, 105, 106, 119, 121, 124, 127, 132, 143, 146, 148, 154, 158, 161, 164, 166, 171, 181, 185, 187, 189, 192, 194, 207, 209, 211, 213, 214, 225, 227, 229, 230, 235, 237, 241, 243, 255, 259, 261, 263, 266, 269, 271, 275, 287, 289, 291, 293, 296, 298, 303, 305, 315, 319, 321, 322, 335, 339, 341, 344, 349, 351, 353, 366, 370, 373, 375, 385, 390, 394, 399, 401, 404, 407, 408, 420, 423, 426, 430, 433, 435, 447, 449, 452, 456, 458, 471, 475, 478, 480, 483, 485, 487, 501, 503, 504, 507, 508, 513, 523, 525, 529, 532, 538, 549, 554, 557, 559, 561, 563, 575, 579, 581, 586, 590, 601, 603, 606, 612, 615, 619, 621, 634, 636, 639, 641
Tally table, 496–498

Tangram puzzle, 300, 309
Teaspoons, 560–561
Technology
calculator, 56–59, 173, 212, 372, 374, 377, 421, 479, 556, 558, 562–563, 567
eBook, 2, 30, 66, 94, 116, 140, 182, 204, 222, 256, 284, 312, 336, 360, 386, 416, 444, 472, 494, 520, 550, 572, 598, 630
Harcourt Mega Math, 6, 18, 24, 36, 52, 60, 72, 84, 105, 110, 124, 134, 146, 164, 172, 198, 213, 237, 246, 266, 278, 296, 306, 315, 326, 339, 344, 354, 376, 399, 404, 410, 420, 435, 438, 447, 449, 456, 462, 478, 488, 507, 514, 554, 555, 566, 576, 606, 616, 624, 634, 642
iTools, 199, 307, 411, 489
lessons, 85, 173, 199, 307, 377, 411, 489, 567
Multimedia Math Glossary, 1, 93, 181, 255, 335, 385, 471, 549
spreadsheets, 85
Technology Connection
calculators, 173, 377, 567
iTools, 199, 307, 411, 489
spreadsheets, 85
Temperature
Celsius, 486–487
Fahrenheit, 484–485
measure changes in, 484–485, 486–487
Tens
multiples of, 8–9
place value, 4–7
rounding to, 34–37, 40–43
Tenths, 418–421
Tessellations, 302–303
Test Prep. *See* Getting Ready for the TAKS *and* TAKS Prep
Texas State Standards, H46–H48
Thermometers, 484–485, 486–487
Thousands
place value, 4–7
rounding to, 34–37, 40–43
Thousandths, 441
Three-digit numbers
adding, 50–53
dividing, 352–353, 364–366, 368–371
multiplying by one-digit numbers, 208–209, 214–215, 217
quotients, 364–366, 368–371, 372–373
subtracting, 50–53
Three-dimensional geometric figures
attributes of, 314
classify, 314–317
compare, 314, 318–319, 638–639
drawing, 318–319
identify, 314
modeling, 315, 320, 322–325, 327
nets of, 320–321
review, H22
views of, 322–325
See also Geometry
Time, 474–475, 476–479
A.M., 474
calendars, 482–483
change units of, 479, 482–483
clocks, 474, 476
days, 482–483
elapsed, 476–479, 482–483
hours, 474
minutes, 474
months, 482–483
noon, 474
P.M., 474
practice with, 478–479, 480–481, 483
schedules, 480–481
seconds, 474
stopwatch, 477
units of, 474
weeks, 482
years, 482
Tons, 558–559
Too Much/Too Little Information, 558–559
Tools
manipulatives, 8–9, 82–83, 288–289, 292–293, 294–295, 302–303, 338–339, 340–341, 398–399, 422–423, 432–433, 534–535, 446–447, 448–449, 450–453, 508–509, 522–523, 528–531, 618–619, 620–623
real objects, 262–263, 318–319, 552–555, 558–559, 560–561, 574–577, 578–579, 580–581, 584–587, 588–591, 600–601, 610–613, 632–635, 640–641
technology, 85, 173, 199, 307, 377, 411, 489, 467
Transformations, 288–289, 290–291, 292–293, 302–303, 307
Translations, 288–289
concrete objects, 288
pictorial models, 289
verify congruence, 288
Trapezoids, 271
Tree diagrams, 528–531, 537
Triangles
acute, 268–269
classifying and identifying, 268–269
congruent, 287
defined, 264
equilateral, 268–269
as faces of solid figure, 314
isosceles, 268–269
obtuse, 268–269
pictorial models, 268–269
right, 268–269
scalene, 268–269
Triangular prism, 314
Triangular pyramid, 314

24-hour clocks, 491
Two-digit numbers
adding, 44–47
dividing, 340–341, 342–344
multiplying by, 234–235, 236–239, 240–241
subtracting, 44–47
Two-dimensional geometric figures
attributes of, 264–265
classify, 264–265, 268, 270–271, 274
compare, 264–265
describe, 258, 264–265
drawing, 265, 270, 274
identify, 264
modeling, 260, 270, 273
sort, 276–277
review, H21
transforming, 288–289, 290–291, 292–293
See also Geometry

Underestimate, 43, 371
Unit Review/Test, *See* Assessment
Units of measurement. *See* Measurement
Use Logical Reasoning strategy, 20–24, 276–277

Variables
defined, 71
equations with, 66, 74–77, 78–80, 132, 162–165, 166–169
expressions with, 71–73, 140, 156–159
Venn diagram, 20, 132, 137, 276–277, 500–501
Vertex, 260–261, 314–315, 318–319, 329
Visual Thinking, 15, 53, 73, 395
Visualizing, 103, 167, 281, 299, 329, 323. *See also* Manipulatives and visual aids *and* Modeling
Vocabulary Power, 1, 3, 31, 67, 93, 95, 117, 141, 181, 183, 205, 223, 255, 257, 285, 313, 335, 337, 361, 385, 387, 417, 445, 471, 473, 495, 521, 549, 551, 573, 599, 631
Volume
comparing, 635, 638–639
concrete models and, 632–635, 636–637, 638–639, 640–641
cubic units, 632–635
defined, 632
equal, 630
estimating, 632–635, 643
formula for, 645
modeling, 632–633, 636–637, 638–639, 640–641
relating to capacity, 640–641

Weeks, 482
Weight, 558–559, 578
What If? 22, 49, 74, 80, 100, 108, 119, 129, 131, 150, 164, 165, 168, 170, 196, 209, 215, 225, 232, 234, 245, 264, 265, 300, 315, 324, 342, 347, 363, 397, 437, 460, 476, 480, 481, 524, 534, 536, 565, 583, 588, 609, 637
What's the Error?, 15, 19, 33, 39, 55, 73, 97, 119, 124, 159, 187, 213, 227, 241, 243, 261, 263, 321, 339, 453, 475, 498, 526, 557, 590, 603, 641
What's the Question?, 19, 83, 99, 121, 132, 154, 211, 229, 266, 316, 351, 370, 394, 426, 479, 505, 513, 530, 561, 586, 616, 637
Whole numbers
average of, 374–375
comparing, 12–15
compose and decompose, 4–7, 10–11
expanded form of, 5, 10
median of, 517
mode of, 517
ordering, 16–19
place value of, 4–7, 9, 10–11, H2
range of, 517
reading and writing, 4–7, 8–9, 10–11
review, H2, H7, H14
rounding, 34–37, H14
standard form of, 5, 10
word form of, 5, 10
See also Addition, Division, Multiplication, *and* Subtraction
Word form, 5, 10, 419, 425
Work Backward strategy, 78–79, 608–609
World Almanac for Kids, 90–91, 178–179, 252–253, 332–333, 382–383, 468–469, 544–545, 648–649
Write an Equation strategy, 166–169, 608–609
Write Math, xx–xxi, 1, 9, 11, 15, 19, 27, 33, 36, 39, 42, 46, 47, 49, 52, 55, 58, 63, 69, 73, 76, 80, 83, 87, 93, 97, 99, 102, 105, 108, 113, 119, 121, 124, 127, 129, 132, 137, 155, 143, 146, 151, 154, 159, 161, 164, 168, 171, 175, 181, 185, 187, 189, 192, 193, 196, 201, 207, 209, 211, 213, 215, 219, 225, 227, 229, 232, 235, 238, 241, 243, 245, 249, 255, 259, 261, 263, 266, 269, 272, 275, 281, 287, 289, 291, 293, 296, 300, 303, 305, 309, 316, 319, 321, 324, 329, 335, 339, 341, 344, 347, 349, 351, 353, 357, 363, 370, 373, 375, 379, 385, 390, 394, 399, 401, 404, 413, 420, 423, 426, 430, 433, 435, 437, 441, 447, 449, 453, 457, 465, 471, 475, 479, 481, 483, 485, 487, 491, 498, 501, 503, 505, 507, 508, 511, 513, 517, 523, 526, 530, 534, 538, 543, 549, 554, 557, 559, 561, 563, 565, 569, 576, 579, 581, 583, 586, 590, 595, 601, 603, 606, 609, 612, 616, 619, 622, 627, 634, 637, 639, 641, 645
See also Pose a Problem, What's the Error?, *and* What's the Question?

Write Math Workshop
Describe an Error, 317, 613
Draw to Explain, 539
Pose a Problem, 367
Write to Explain, 47, 239
Write Number Riddles, 409
Write to Prove or Disprove, 155

Yards, 552–554
Years, 482

Zero Property, 104, 152–155
Zeros
in division, 368–371
in multiplication, 210–211
patterns of, 38–39, 224–225
subtracting across, 54–55

Photo Credits

KEY: (t) top, (b) bottom, (l) left, (r) right, (c) center, (bg) background, (fg) foreground

Front Cover: (l) Frank Krahmer/Masterfile; (r) Bill Heinsohn/Getty Images.
Back Cover: (l) Bill Heinsohn/Getty Images; (r) Jeremy Woodhouse/Masterfile.

Front Endsheets: Page 1 & 2 Bruce Fritz/Agricultural Research Unit/USDA; Page 3 Kaz Chiba/Photodisc Red/Getty Images.
Back Endsheets: Page 1 DC Productions/Photodisc/Getty Images; Page 2 & 3 Dennis Flaherty/Photodisc/Getty Images.

Title Page: (l) Frank Krahmer/Masterfile; (r) Bill Heinsohn/Getty Images.
Copyright Page: Jeremy Woodhouse/Masterfile.

Table of Contents: iv (l) John Lund/Getty Images; vi (l) Mihovil Photography; viii (l) AP Photo/Kathy Willens; x (l) Darrell Gulin/Corbis; xii (l) Bob Daemmrich/THE IMAGE WORKS; xiv (l) Becky Phillips; xvi (l) Laurence Parent Photography; xviii (l) Index Stock Imagery.

Unit 1: 1 (tl) The Futures Channel, Inc; 1 (cl) The Futures Channel; 1 (bl) The Futures Channel; 2 John Lund/Getty Images; 4 Peter Titmuss/Alamy; 5 Medioimages/Alamy; 6 (t) Stockdisc Classic/Alamy; 6 (tc) GK Hart/Vikki Hart/ Getty Images (Royalty-free); 6 (bc) Juniors Bildarchiv/Alamy; 6 (b) Dave King/ Dorling Kindersley; 12 Gibson Stock Photography; 13 Garry Black/Masterfile; 16 Julie Mowbray/Alamy; 21 Jeff Gentner/Icon SMI/Corbis; 23 (tl) Kit Kittle/Corbis; 23 (bg) Getty Images/Harcourt; 27 Corbis/Harcourt ; 30 Ron Niebrugge/Alamy; 32 Unicorn Stock Photos L.L.C.; 34 JIM WATSON/AFP/Getty Images; 36 Getty Images/Harcourt; 37 Nancy Kaszerman/NewsCom; 39 Getty Images/Harcourt; 40 El Paso Zoo; 41 El Paso Zoo; 43 Bob Daemmric /The Image Works; 44 Syracuse Newspapers/Dick Blume/The Image Works; 47 Alamy; 48 Tim Heneghan/Index Stock imagery; 49 Lonely Planet Images/Photo 20-20; 50 DALTON, STEPHEN/Animals Animals - Earth Scenes; 54 Gabriel M Covian/Getty Images; 55 CORBIS; 56 NASA; 57 NASA; 62 Gabriel M Covian/Getty Images; 63 CORBIS; 66 Photo by Jason Clarke/IRELAND OUT; 66 (inset) Patti McConville/Getty Images; 68 (tr) Photo Network/Alamy; 68 (br) Getty Images/Harcourt; 69 Getty Images/Harcourt; 71 Tony Freeman/PhotoEdit; 74 Courtesy of Canine Companions for Independence; 75 Stella Davis/Associated Press; 76 Getty Images/Harcourt; 77 Jeff Greenberg/Photo Edit; 79 Jupiter Images; 80 (tr) Tannen Maury/Associated Press; 80 (br) ABPL/HAAGNER, CLEM/Animals Animals - Earth Scenes; 81 Galen Rowell/Corbis; 85 Court Mast/Taxi/Getty Images; 90 Jose Luis Pelaez/Corbis; 91 Sheila Terry/Photo Researchers.

Unit 2: 93 (t) The Futures Channel; 93 (c) The Futures Channel; 93 (b) The Futures Channel; 94 Bob Daemmrich/The Image Works; 94 Mihovil Photography; 96 Jennifer Crites Photography; 98 Image Works, Inc., The; 100 PhotoSpin, Inc/Alamy; 103 AP Photo/Edis Jurcys; 109 The Maize; 113 (bg) Royalty-Free/Corbis; 116 Jim Olive/ Stockyard.com; 121 Andre Jenny/Alamy; 122 Fort Worth Zoo/Patty Ryan; 124 Joe McDonald/Animals Animals -Earth Scenes; 126 Blue Lemon Productions/Getty Images; 127 Henryk T. Kaiser/Index Stock Imagery; 140 (t) Cathy & Gordon Illg/Animals Animals - Earth Scenes; 144 John Birdsall/age fotostock; 147 (r) Scott Camazine/Photo Researchers, Inc.; 147 (l) Getty Images/Harcourt; 149 Dynamic Graphics/Jupiterimages; 150 (t) Corbis; 150 (b) ShutterStock.com; 156 (tr) The Granger Collection, New York; 158 Randall K. Roberts; 159 Lauren Victoria Burke/AP Photo; 167 Harold W. Hoffman/Photo Researchers, Inc.; 168 (t) Larry Ditto/Bruce Coleman, Inc.; 168 (tc) Darren Bennett/Animals Animals -Earth Scenes; 168 (c) Corbis/Harcourt; 168 (bc) Russell C. Hansen; 168 (b) Estate of Perry D. Slocum/Animals Animals - Earth Scenes; 169 Larry Ditto/Bruce Coleman USA; 170 (tr) Holly Kuper/AGStockUSA; 170 (b) Robert Warren/Getty Images; 173 (bg) Court Mast/Taxi/Getty

Images; 178 (tr) Gerald C. Kelley/Photo Researchers; 178 (c) Michael & Patricia Fogden/Corbis; 178 (cr) Steve Maslowski/Photo Researchers; 178-179 (bg) Peter Arnold, Inc./Alamy; 179 Millard H. Sharp/Photo Researchers.

Unit 3: 181 (t) The Futures Channel; 181 (c) The Futures Channel; 181 (b) The Futures Channel; 182 Corbis; 186 Robert Winslow/Animals Animals - Earth Scenes; 179 Photodisc Green/Getty Images; 190 (tr) Victoria McCormick/Animals Animals - Earth Scenes; 190 (b) Corbis; 193 Tom Bean/Corbis; 195 Kelley Mooney Photography/Corbis; 196 Steve Bloom/Getty Images; 199 Brand X/SuperStock; 199 Getty Images; 201 (tr) Photo courtesy of the San Antonio Botanical Society; 204 Wally Eberhart/Botanica; 206 Courtesy Texas Sports Hall of Fame; 207 John Williamson /MLB Photos via Getty Images; 208 Gala/SuperStock; 211 Bill Heinsohn/Alamy; 212 NASA/Corbis; 214 Masterfile; 215 Jason Kirk/Online USA, Inc./NewsCom; 219 (tr) White Cross Productions/The Image Bank/Getty Images; 222 Jerry Alexander/Getty Images; 224 Kim Taylor/Dorling Kindersley; 225 James King-Holmes/Science Photo Library; 231 BIOS Ferry Eric & Oertel Bruno/Peter Arnold, Inc.; 232 Warren Stone/Bruce Coleman USA; 233 (tl) Arco Images/ Alamy; 233 (tr) Joe McDonald/Corbis; 233 (c) Rod Planck/Dembinsky Photo Associates; 233 (b) Alan G. Nelson/Dembinsky Photo Associates; 233 (bg) Getty Images/Harcourt; 234 (tr) Jerry and Marcy Monkman/EcoPhotography.com/Alamy; 234 (b) Dennis MacDonald/PhotoEdit; 236 Kevin Dodge/Masterfile; 238 Holger Wulschlaeger/iStockPhoto; 240 Hulton-Deutsch Collection/ Corbis; 242 The Photolibrary Wales/Alamy; 244 (t), (b) Gail Mooney/Masterfile; 249 Benjamin Rondel/Corbis; 252 (t) Bettmann/Corbis; 252 (cl) NASA/SCIENCE PHOTO LIBRARY; 252 (cr) CBS Photo Archive/Getty Images; 252-253 Bettmann/Corbis.

Unit 4: 255 (t) The Futures Channel; 255 (c) Ford Motor Company; 255 (b) Ford Motor Company; 256 (t) David Woo; 256 (br) Leon Polk Smith, "Homage to Victory Boogie Woogie No. 2," 1946-47, oil on wood. © Leon Polk Smith Foundation/Licensed by VAGA, New York, NY; 258 (t) Royalty-Free/Corbis; 258 (tc) Steve Gorton and Karl Shone/ Dorling Kindersley; 258 (c) Wesley Hitt/Alamy; 258 (bc) Kevin Britland/Alamy; 258 (b) Stockdisc/Getty Images; 259 Juptier Images; 260 Another Off The Wall Production, Inc.; 263 (tl) iStockphoto; 263 (tcl) Jon Shireman/Getty Images; 263 (tcr) Jupiter Images; 263 (tr) Age Fotostock; 264 Bildarchiv Preussischer Kulturbesitz/Art Resource, NY; 266 Picasso, Pablo (1881-1973) Mandolin and Guitar. Oil and sand on canvas, 1924. © 2007 Estate of Pablo Picasso/Artists Rights Society (ARS), New York. The Granger Collection, NY.; 267 (cr) ERIC FEFERBERG/AFP/Getty Images; 267 (bc) TerraServer; 267 (br) Jim Pickerell/Alamy; 268 Neil Fletcher and Matthew Ward/DK Images; 269 ImageState/Alamy; 270 Jeffrey Greenberg/Photo Researchers, Inc.; 271 Kactus Foto/ SuperStock; 272 Spencer Grant/PhotoEdit; 273 (l) Kevin Taylor/IPNStock; 273 (r) New Hights Photography/fred hights/photographersdirect; 284 (t) Darrell Gulin/Corbis; 284 (bc) Chad Weckler/Corbis; 284 (br) Caroline R. Dean; 286 (cl) Agnes Gray/Twin Rocks Trading post; 286 (cr) 2006 Twin Rocks Trading Post; 286 (bl) Elsie Holiday/Twin Rocks Trading Post; 286 (br) 2006 Twin Rocks Trading Post; 289 (tl) Blend Images/ SuperStock; 289 (tcl) Cameron/Corbis; 289 (tcr) Getty Images; 289 (tr) PhotoStockFile/Alamy; 290 NASA; 292 Gorilla Foundation; 294 (bl) Jim Cummins/Getty Images; 294 (bc) Bob Richardson/ Alamy; 295 (bcr) age fotostock/ SuperStock; 295 (br) Stockbyte /Gettty Images; 296 (tl) Siede Preis/Getty Images; 296 (tcl) Colin Young-Wolff/ PhotoEdit; 296 (tr) Leroy Simon/Visuals Unlimited; 297 Alejandro Rivera Photography; 301 Cindy England/iStockphoto; 303 M.C. Escher's "Sun and Moon" © 2007 The M.C. Escher Company-Holland. www.mcesher.com/Art Resource, NY; 304 Tyrrell-Lewis Associates; 305 "98 Bright Dancing Squares" (40" x 40") by Debby Kratovil. Published in Bold, Black & Beautiful Quilts (American Quilter's Society 2004). Photo by Charles R. Lynch.; 307 Court Mast/Taxi/Getty Images; 312 Laurence Parent Photography; 314 The Christian Science Monitor/Getty Images; 315 Stephen Johnson/Getty Images; 316 (tl) Bruce Chashin/Jupiter Images; 316 (tcl) Andrew Woodley/Alamy; 316 (tcr) Artefaqs Corporation; 316 (tr) Index Stock; 323 SuperStock; 325 (tc) Klaus Hackenberg/zefa/Corbis; 325 (bcr) Stefano Bianchetti/Corbis; 326 (tl) Dynamic Graphics Group/Creatas/Alamy; 326 (tcl) Elvele Images/Alamy; 326 (tcr) Alex Bramwell/iStockPhoto; 326 (tr) P. Narayan/age fotostock; 328 (tl) Carolyn Ross/Jupiter Images; 328 (tcl) Corel Stock Photo Library - royalty free; 328 (tcr) Christopher O Driscoll; 328 (tr) SuperStock/Alamy; 329 (tr) HIP/ Art Resource, NY; 329 (bg) Comstock Images/Alamy; 332 (cl) Alamy; 332 (c) Handout/NewsCom; 332 (cr) Steve Gorton/Getty Images; 332-333 (bg) World Almanac Books; 333 (tr) Getty Images/ Harcourt; 333 (c) Getty Images/Harcourt; 333 (cr) Glenn Mitsui/Photodisc/Getty Images.

Unit 5: 334 Karen Whylie/Masterfile; 335 (t) The Futures Channel; 335 (c) The Futures Channel; 335 (b) Movin' On Livestock; 336 Bob Daemmrich/THE IMAGE WORKS; 342 The Granger Collection, New York; 343 Photo File/MLB Photos via Getty Images; 345 AP Photo/Bryan-College Station Eagle, Dave McDermand; 346 ML Harris/Getty Images; 347 (t) Yann Arthus-Bertrand/Corbis; 347 (tr) Imagebroker/Alamy; 347 (c) Vario Images GmbH & Co.KG/Alamy; 347 (b) DK Limited/Corbis; 347 (br) Yann Arthus-Bertrand/Corbis; 348 Kelly-Mooney Photography/Corbis; 350 Michael & Patrica Fogden/Minden Pictures; 351 (tc) Michael Durham/Minden Pictures; 351 (c) Stephen Dalton/Minden Pictures; 351 (c) Tim Oram/Alamy; 351 (bc) Arco Images/Alamy; 352 Philip Krejcarek/JupiterImages; 353 Philip Krejcarek/JupiterImages; 357 (tr) Richard Hamilton Smith/Corbis; 357 (bg) Danita Delimont/Alamy; 357 (tr), (t) PhotoDisc/Getty Images/Harcourt; 360 NHPA/Daniel Heuclin; 362 Richard T. Nowitz/Corbis; 363 Sandro Vannini/Corbis; 364 Bettmann/Corbis; 366 Chuck Eckert/Alamy; 368 (tc) Getty Images/Harcourt; 368 (tc) Getty Images/Harcourt; 369 (br) Getty Images/Harcourt; 369 (tr) Jack Cox - Travel Pics Pro/Alamy; 369 (tc) Brand X Pictures/Alamy; 371 AM Corporation/Alamy; 372 Florian Graner/Nature Picture Library; 374 Stefan Zaklin/epa/Corbis; 375 Reuters/Corbis; 377 (bg) Court Mast/Taxi/Getty Images; 382 (tl) Alamy; 382 (tr) francesco survara/Alamy; 382 (cr) Texas Department of Transportation; 382 (cl), (br) Corbis; 382-383 (bg) ImageState/Alamy; 383 (tc) Tom Massung/Photographers Direct; 383 (cl) Anthony Nex/Jupiterimages; 383 (c) iStockphoto; 383 (c) Jupiterimages; 383 (cr) Bill Ross/Corbis; 383 (br) Robertstock.

Unit 6: 385 (t) The Futures Channel; 385 (c) The Futures Channel; 385 (b) The Futures Channel; 386 Becky Phillips; 388 (r) Bob Daemmrich/PhotoEdit; 391 iStockphoto; 392 Taylor S. Kennedy/National Geographic/Getty Images; 393 AP Images/Jessie Cohen, National Zoo; 395 AP Images/Evan Vucci; 396 Davis McCown; 400 Alamy; 402 Lisa Belleman courtesy of Ramsey House Plantation, Knoxville Tennessee; 411 (bg) Court Mast/Taxi/Getty Images; 416 Don Johnson/jsgrey.com; 420 (tr) Scientifica/Visuals Unlimited; 420 (cr) Joyce Photographics/Photo Researchers, Inc.; 420 (bl) Andrew J. Martinez/Photo Researchers; 420 (bc) Scientifica/Visuals Unlimited; 420 (br) Stephen J. Krasemann/Photo Researchers; 421 Alamy; 427 (t) Courtesy of the Texas Transportation Museum; 427 (b) Courtesy Texas Transportation Museum; 431 (bl), (br) Douglas Plasencia/Courtesy of Stack's Rarities; 441 (tr) Ron Vesely/MLB Photos via Getty Images; 441 (bg) Rick Chapman/Corbis Outline; 444 Guillen Photography/ Alamy; 453 Spectrum Photofile; 455 (tr) Howard Shooter/Dorling Kindersley; 457 Ken Bidel/Oklahoma Peanut Commission; 465 (tr) Rolf Nussbaumer/Nature Picture Library; 465 (bg) Royalty-Free/Corbis; 468 (t)StockShot/Alamy; 468 (c) Sal Maimone/SuperStock; 468 (b) Robert Llewellyn/SuperStock; 468-469 (bg) age fotostock/SuperStock; 469 (cl) Chris Luneski/Alamy; 469 (c) Chris Luneski/Alamy; 469 (cr) photodisc/PunchStock.

Unit 7: 471 (t) The Futures Channel; 471 (c) The Futures Channel; 471 (b) The Futures Channel; 472 (c) Laurence Parent Photography; 476 Tony Freeman/Photo Edit; 477 Getty Images; 481 Ed Lallo/NewsCom; 482 Ambient Images; 489 (bg) Court Mast/Taxi/Getty Images; 491 (tr) Lourens Smak/Alamy; 491 (bg) José Fuste Raga/zefa/Corbis; 494 Airphoto/Jim Wark; 499 Frank Staub/IndexStock; 504 Chris Trotman/Duomo/Corbis ; 506 NASA ; 507 Masterfile ; 509 (t) Jules Frazier/Getty Images; 509 (b) Tony Freeman/PhotoEdit; 510 Michael Newman/Photo Edit; 517 (tr) PhotoDisc/Getty Images/Harcourt; 520 Brad Doherty/Photo.net; 529 Burke/Triolo Productions/JupiterImages; 530 (tl) Siede Preis/Getty Images ; 530 (bl) Lois & Bob Schlowsky/Getty Images; 530 (br) C Squared Studios/Getty Images ; 535 (t) Michigan State Fair & Expo Center; 535 (tl) Nevada State Fair; 535 (tr) New York State Fair; 535 (cl) California Exposition & State Fair; 535 (cr) Corbis; 535 (bl) Arizona State Fair; 535 (br) Indiana State Fairgrounds; 546-547 Masterfile; 547 (tr) Michael Newman/PhotoEdit; 547 (br) Jupiter Images.

Unit 8: 549 (t) The Futures Channel; 549 (c) The Futures Channel; 549 (b) The Futures Channel; 555 Peter Anderson/Getty Images; 559 age fotostock/SuperStock; 561 Judd Pilossof/JupiterImages; 562 F.CARTER SMITH/Corbis SYGMA; 564 Lee Hacker/Alamy; 566 (cl) David Fleetham/Getty Images; 566 (c) Getty Images; 567 (bg) Court Mast/Taxi/Getty Images; 568 (tl) Bruce Chashin/Jupiter Images; 568 (tcl) Andrew Woodley/Alamy; 568 (tc) Car Culture/Getty Images; 568 (tcr) Artefaqs Corporation; 568 (br) Index Stock; 569 (tr) Index Stock/Alamy; 569 (bg) PhotoLink/Getty Images; 572 Index Stock Imagery; 574 Steve Hamblin/Alamy; 576 (c) WoodyStock/Alamy; 576 (cr) Rick & Nora Bowers/Alamy; 576 (bc) JIM BRANDENBURG/Minden

Pictures; 576 (br) Don Farrall/Getty Images; 577 Gordon & Cathy Illg/ AnimalsAnimals; 578 (r) Dan Lim/Masterfile; 579 (tr) iStockphoto; 579 (cl) Getty Images/Photodisc/Harcourt Index; 579 (br) Getty Images/PhotoDisc /Harcourt Index; 580 Blend Images/Alamy; 583 David Reed/ Alamy; 586 New Hights Photography/PhotographersDirect; 590 (bl) Andrzej Gorkowski/ PhotographersDirect; 590 (bc) Danny Lehman/Corbis; 590 (bc) Stephen Saks Photography/ Alamy; 590 (br) Texas Parks and Wildlife Department; 592 (tl) Corbis/Harcourt; 592 (tr) Luis Carlos Torres/iStockPhoto; 592 (cl) Craig Veltri/iStockPhoto; 592 (c) Thomas Northcut/Getty Images (Royalty-free); 592 (bl) Masterfile Royalty Free; 592 (bc) David Bishop/JupiterImages; 592 (br) DK Limited/Corbis; 594 (tl) Corbis; 594 (tr) Masterfile; 594 (bl) Masterfile; 594 (br) Corbis; 595 (tr) Tom Brakefield/Photodisc Green/Getty Images; 595 (bg) David Muench/Corbis; 597 (tl) roberto della vite/age fotostock; 597 (c) EuroStyle Graphics/Alamy; 597 (bl) Zap Art/ Getty Images; 597 (bc) GoodShoot/age fotostock; 598 Courtesy Texas Archeological Research Laboratory, The University of Texas at Austin. Ulrich Kleinschmidt, photographer, 6 November 1978; catalog # 41CE19-C6218; 601 imagebroker/Alamy; 602 Benjamin Rondel Photography/ JupiterImages; 603 Dallas Fair Park; 610 Manor Photography/Alamy; 620 (tr) 'Thomas Henderson ABEL/Getty Images; 620 (cl) Mike Powell/Getty Images; 620 (cr) Alberto Biscaro/ Masterfile; 629 (cl) iStockphoto; 630 (t) Thinkstock Royalty Free Photograph; 645 (tr) Courtesy of the Texas Historical Commission; 646 (tl) Corbis/Harcourt; 646 (tr) Getty Images/Harcourt; 646 (cl) Getty Images/Harcourt; 646 (cr) Andrew Paterson/Alamy; 646 (cr) Stockdisc/Getty Images (Royalty-free); 646 (br) Brian Drake/Time Life Pictures/Getty Images; 647 (cr) Douglas Johns/Getty Images; 648 (tl) Larry L. Miller/Photo Researchers, Inc.; 648 (tr) Kelly Bender/Texas Parks and Wildlife Department; 648 (c) Daryl Benson/Masterfile; 648 (bl) Erwin & Peggy Bauer/ Animals Animals-Earth Scenes; 648-649 (bg) William Luther/San Antonio Expre/Newscom; 649 (tr) Photo by Texas Parks and Wildlife Department/Glen Mills;

Student Handbook: page H Jim Brandenburg/Minden Pictures; H1 GK Hart/Vikki Hart/ Getty Images (Royalty-free).

All other photos © Harcourt School Publishers. Harcourt photographers; Weronica Ankarorn, Eric Camden, Don, Couch, Doug Dukane, Ken Kinzie, April Riehm, and Steve Williams.

Construction of the Alamo began in 1744.

The famous battle at the Alamo took place in 1836.

About **1,500**
Mexican troops fought